CW00970006

Fodor's Road Guide USA

Illinois
Iowa
Missouri
Wisconsin

First Edition

Fodor's Travel Publications
New York Toronto London Sydney Auckland
www.fodors.com

Fodor's Road Guide USA: Illinois, Iowa, Missouri, Wisconsin

Fodor's Travel Publications
President: Bonnie Ammer
Publisher: Kris Kliemann
Executive Managing Editor: Denise DeGennaro
Editorial Director: Karen Cure
Director of Marketing Development: Jeanne Kramer
Associate Managing Editor: Linda Schmidt
Senior Editor: Constance Jones
Director of Production and Manufacturing: Chuck Bloodgood
Creative Director: Fabrizio La Rocca

Contributors
Editor: Anne Davies
Editorial Production: Tom Holton
Additional Editing: JoAnn Milivojevic (Wisconsin), Beth Schlau (Illinois), Donna Cornachio, Holly Hammond, Lynn Harris, Amy Hegarty, Shannon Kelly, Lisa Leventer, Emmanuelle Morgen, Amy O'Neil, Eric Reymond, and Karen Weller-Watson
Writing: Joanne Kempinger Demski (Wisconsin), Sarah Hoban (Illinois), and Diana Lambdin Meyer (Iowa and Missouri), with Michele Bloom, Sally Van Doren, Hannah Fons, William Fox, Steve Knopper, Victor Ledezma, Brandon Leong, LaKeisha Light, Kate Lorenz, JoAnn Milivojevic, Eric Reymond, Betsy Rubiner, Peggy Ammerman Sailors, Michael Schiller, and Kirsten Weisenberger
Research: Toure Carpette, Robin Hicks, Peter Jhon, Kristina Klurman, Becky Peterson, Darnell Roberts, Amanda Robinson, Nathan Semler, and Brendan Walsh
Black-and-White Maps: Rebecca Baer, Robert Blake, David Lindroth, Todd Pasini
Production/Manufacturing: Robert B. Shields
Cover Photos: Gary Irving/Stone (background photo), Bart Nagel (photo, illustration)
Interior Photos: Corbis (Iowa), Photodisc (Illinois), "Permission granted by the Missouri Division of Tourism" (Missouri), Wisconsin Department of Tourism (Wisconsin)

Copyright
Copyright © 2001 by Fodors LLC

Color-map atlas copyright © 2001 by Maps.com and Fodor's LLC. All other maps copyright © 2001 by Fodors LLC.

Fodor's is a registered trademark of Random House, Inc.

All rights reserved under International and Pan-American Copyright Conventions. Published in the United States by Fodor's Travel Publications, a unit of Fodors LLC, a subsidiary of Random House, Inc., New York, and simultaneously in Canada by Random House of Canada Limited, Toronto. Distributed by Random House, Inc., New York.

No maps, illustrations, or other portions of this book may be reproduced in any form without written permission from the publisher.

First Edition
ISBN 0–679–00497–1
ISSN 1528–1493

Special Sales
Fodor's Travel Publications are available at special discounts for bulk purchases for sales promotions or premiums. Special editions, including personalized covers, excerpts of existing guides, and corporate imprints, can be created in large quantities for special needs. For more information, contact your local bookseller or write to Special Markets, Fodor's Travel Publications, 280 Park Ave., New York, NY 10017. Inquiries from Canada should be directed to your local Canadian bookseller or sent to Random House of Canada, Ltd., Marketing Department, 2775 Matheson Boulevard East, Mississauga, Ontario L4W 4P7. Inquiries from the United Kingdom should be sent to Fodor's Travel Publications, 20 Vauxhall Bridge Road, London SW1V 2SA, England.

PRINTED IN THE UNITED STATES OF AMERICA
10 9 8 7 6 5 4 3 2 1

CONTENTS

Great Road Trips

Of all the things that went wrong with Clark Griswold's vacation, one stands out: The theme park he had driven across the country to visit was closed when he got there. Clark, the suburban bumbler played by Chevy Chase in 1983's hilarious *National Lampoon's Vacation,* is fictional, of course. But his story is poignantly true. Although most Americans get only two precious weeks of vacation a year, many set off on their journeys with surprisingly little guidance. Many travelers find out about their destination from friends and family or wait to get travel information until they arrive in their hotel, where racks of brochures dispense the "facts," along with free city magazines. But it's hard to distinguish the truth from hype in these sources. And it makes no sense to spend priceless vacation time in a hotel room reading about a place when you could be out seeing it up close and personal.

Congratulate yourself on picking up this guide. Studying it—before you leave home—is the best possible first step toward making sure your vacation fulfills your every dream.

Inside you'll find all the tools you need to plan a perfect road trip. In the hundreds of towns we describe, you'll find thousands of places to explore. So you'll always know what's around the next bend. And with the practical information we provide, you can easily call to confirm the details that matter and study up on what you'll want to see and do, before you leave home.

By all means, when you plan your trip, allow yourself time to make a few detours. Because as wonderful as it is to visit sights you've read about, it's the serendipitous experiences that often prove the most memorable: the hole-in-the-wall diner that serves a transcendent tomato soup, the historical society gallery stuffed with dusty local curiosities of days gone by. As you whiz down the highway, use the book to find out more about the towns announced by roadside signs. Consider turning off at the next exit. And always remember: In this great country of ours, there's an adventure around every corner.

HOW TO USE THIS BOOK

Alphabetical organization should make it a snap to navigate through this book. Still, in putting it together, we've made certain decisions and used certain terms you need to know about.

LOCATIONS AND CATEGORIZATIONS

Color map coordinates are given for every town in the guide.

Attractions, restaurants, and lodging places are listed under the nearest town covered in the guide.

Parks and forests are sometimes listed under the main access point.

Exact street addresses are provided whenever possible; when they were not available or applicable, directions and/or cross-streets are indicated.

CITIES

For state capitals and larger cities, attractions are alphabetized by category. Shopping sections focus on good shopping areas where you'll find a concentration of interesting shops. We include malls only if they're unusual in some way and individual stores only when they're community institutions. Restaurants and hotels are grouped by price category then arranged alphabetically.

RESTAURANTS

All are air-conditioned unless otherwise noted, and all permit smoking unless they're identified as "no-smoking."

Dress: Assume that no jackets or ties are required for men unless otherwise noted.

Family-style service: Restaurants characterized this way serve food communally, out of serving dishes as you might at home.

Meals and hours: Assume that restaurants are open for lunch and dinner unless otherwise noted. We always specify days closed and meals not available.

Prices: The price ranges listed are for dinner entrées (or lunch entrées if no dinner is served).

Reservations: They are always a good idea. We don't mention them unless they're essential or are not accepted.

Fodor's Choice: Stars denote restaurants that are Fodor's Choices—our editors' picks of the state's very best in a given price category.

LODGINGS

All are air-conditioned unless otherwise noted, and all permit smoking unless they're identified as "no-smoking."

AP: This designation means that a hostelry operates on the American Plan (AP)—-that is, rates include all meals. AP may be an option or it may be the only meal plan available; be sure to find out.

Baths: You'll find private bathrooms with bathtubs unless noted otherwise.

Business services: If we tell you they're there, you can expect a variety on the premises.

Exercising: We note if there's "exercise equipment" even when there's no designated area; if you want a dedicated facility, look for "gym."

Facilities: We list what's available but don't note charges to use them. When pricing accommodations, always ask what's included.

Hot tub: This term denotes hot tubs, Jacuzzis, and whirlpools.

MAP: Rates at these properties include two meals.

No smoking: Properties with this designation prohibit smoking.

Opening and closing: Assume that hostelries are open year-round unless otherwise noted.

Pets: We note whether or not they're welcome and whether there's a charge.

Pools: Assume they're outdoors with fresh water; indoor pools are noted.

Prices: The price ranges listed are for a high-season double room for two, excluding tax and service charge.

Telephone and TV: Assume that you'll find them unless otherwise noted.

Fodor's Choice: Stars denote hostelries that are Fodor's Choices—our editors' picks of the state's very best in a given price category.

NATIONAL PARKS

National parks protect and preserve the treasures of America's heritage, and they're always worth visiting whenever you're in the area. Many are worth a long detour. If you will travel to many national parks, consider purchasing the National Parks Pass ($50), which gets you and your companions free admission to all parks for one year. (Camping and parking are extra.) A percentage of the proceeds from sales of the pass helps to fund important projects in the parks. Both the Golden Age Passport ($10), for those 62 and older, and the Golden Access Passport (free), for travelers with disabilities, entitle holders to free entry to all national parks, plus 50% off fees for the use of many park facilities and services. You must show proof of age and of U.S. citizenship or permanent residency (such as a U.S. passport, driver's license, or birth certificate) and, if requesting Golden Access, proof of your disability. You must get your Golden Access or Golden Age passport in person; the former is available at all federal recreation areas, the latter at federal recreation areas that charge fees. You may purchase the National Parks Pass by mail or through the Internet. For information, contact the National Park Service (Department of the Interior, 1849 C St. NW, Washington, DC 20240-0001, 202/208—4747, *www.nps.gov*). To buy the National Parks Pass, write to 27540 Ave. Mentry, Valencia, CA 91355, call 888/GO—PARKS, or visit www.national-parks.org.

IMPORTANT TIP

Although all prices, opening times, and other details in this book are based on information supplied to us at press time, changes occur all the time in the travel world, and Fodor's cannot accept responsibility for facts that become outdated or for inadvertent errors or omissions. So always confirm information when it matters, especially if you're making a detour to visit a specific place.

Let Us Hear from You

Keeping a travel guide fresh and up-to-date is a big job, and we welcome any and all comments. We'd love to have your thoughts on places we've listed, and we're interested in hearing about your own special finds, even the ones in your own back yard. Our guides are thoroughly updated for each new edition, and we're always adding new information, so your feedback is vital. Contact us via e-mail in care of roadnotes@fodors.com (specifying the name of the book on the subject line) or via snail mail in care of Road Guides at Fodor's, 280 Park Avenue, New York, NY 10017. We look forward to hearing from you. And in the meantime, have a wonderful road trip.

THE EDITORS

Important Numbers and On-Line Info

LODGINGS

Adam's Mark	800/444—2326	www.adamsmark.com
Baymont Inns	800/428—3438	www.baymontinns.com
Best Western	800/528—1234	www.bestwestern.com
	TDD 800/528—2222	
Budget Host	800/283—4678	www.budgethost.com
Clarion	800/252—7466	www.clarioninn.com
Comfort	800/228—5150	www.comfortinn.com
Courtyard by Marriott	800/321—2211	www.courtyard.com
Days Inn	800/325—2525	www.daysinn.com
Doubletree	800/222—8733	www.doubletreehotels.com
Drury Inns	800/325—8300	www.druryinn.com
Econo Lodge	800/555—2666	www.hotelchoice.com
Embassy Suites	800/362—2779	www.embassysuites.com
Exel Inns of America	800/356—8013	www.exelinns.com
Fairfield Inn by Marriott	800/228—2800	www.fairfieldinn.com
Fairmont Hotels	800/527—4727	www.fairmont.com
Forte	800/225—5843	www.forte-hotels.com
Four Seasons	800/332—3442	www.fourseasons.com
Friendship Inns	800/453—4511	www.hotelchoice.com
Hampton Inn	800/426—7866	www.hampton-inn.com
Hilton	800/445—8667	www.hilton.com
	TDD 800/368—1133	
Holiday Inn	800/465—4329	www.holiday-inn.com
	TDD 800/238—5544	
Howard Johnson	800/446—4656	www.hojo.com
	TDD 800/654—8442	
Hyatt & Resorts	800/233—1234	www.hyatt.com
Inns of America	800/826—0778	www.innsofamerica.com
Inter-Continental	800/327—0200	www.interconti.com
La Quinta	800/531—5900	www.laquinta.com
	TDD 800/426—3101	
Loews	800/235—6397	www.loewshotels.com
Marriott	800/228—9290	www.marriott.com
Master Hosts Inns	800/251—1962	www.reservahost.com
Le Meridien	800/225—5843	www.lemeridien.com
Motel 6	800/466—8356	www.motel6.com
Omni	800/843—6664	www.omnihotels.com
Quality Inn	800/228—5151	www.qualityinn.com
Radisson	800/333—3333	www.radisson.com
Ramada	800/228—2828	www.ramada.com
	TDD 800/533—6634	
Red Carpet/Scottish Inns	800/251—1962	www.reservahost.com
Red Lion	800/547—8010	www.redlion.com
Red Roof Inn	800/843—7663	www.redroof.com
Renaissance	800/468—3571	www.renaissancehotels.com
Residence Inn by Marriott	800/331—3131	www.residenceinn.com
Ritz-Carlton	800/241—3333	www.ritzcarlton.com
Rodeway	800/228—2000	www.rodeway.com

Sheraton	800/325—3535	www.sheraton.com
Shilo Inn	800/222—2244	www.shiloinns.com
Signature Inns	800/822—5252	www.signature-inns.com
Sleep Inn	800/221—2222	www.sleepinn.com
Super 8	800/848—8888	www.super8.com
Susse Chalet	800/258—1980	www.sussechalet.com
Travelodge/Viscount	800/255—3050	www.travelodge.com
Vagabond	800/522—1555	www.vagabondinns.com
Westin Hotels & Resorts	800/937—8461	www.westin.com
Wyndham Hotels & Resorts	800/996—3426	www.wyndham.com

AIRLINES

Air Canada	888/247—2262	www.aircanada.ca
Alaska	800/426—0333	www.alaska-air.com
American	800/433—7300	www.aa.com
America West	800/235—9292	www.americawest.com
British Airways	800/247—9297	www.british-airways.com
Canadian	800/426—7000	www.cdnair.ca
Continental Airlines	800/525—0280	www.continental.com
Delta	800/221—1212	www.delta.com
Midway Airlines	800/446—4392	www.midwayair.com
Northwest	800/225—2525	www.nwa.com
SkyWest	800/453—9417	www.delta.com
Southwest	800/435—9792	www.southwest.com
TWA	800/221—2000	www.twa.com
United	800/241—6522	www.ual.com
USAir	800/428—4322	www.usair.com

BUSES AND TRAINS

Amtrak	800/872—7245	www.amtrak.com
Greyhound	800/231—2222	www.greyhound.com
Trailways	800/343—9999	www.trailways.com

CAR RENTALS

Advantage	800/777—5500	www.arac.com
Alamo	800/327—9633	www.goalamo.com
Allstate	800/634—6186	www.bnm.com/as.htm
Avis	800/331—1212	www.avis.com
Budget	800/527—0700	www.budget.com
Dollar	800/800—4000	www.dollar.com
Enterprise	800/325—8007	www.pickenterprise.com
Hertz	800/654—3131	www.hertz.com
National	800/328—4567	www.nationalcar.com
Payless	800/237—2804	www.paylesscarrental.com
Rent-A-Wreck	800/535—1391	www.rent-a-wreck.com
Thrifty	800/367—2277	www.thrifty.com

Note: Area codes are changing all over the United States as this book goes to press. For the latest updates, check www.areacode-info.com.

Fodor's Road Guide USA

Illinois
Iowa
Missouri
Wisconsin

Illinois

Illinois' official state nickname, the Prairie State, conjures up some warm, homespun images: wide-open spaces, plain-talking folks, and acre after acre after acre of corn.

It's all true, of course, as many Illinoisans will tell you—and as the plethora of autumn sweet corn festivals in the state certainly prove. The prairie originally attracted pioneer farmers eager to dig into its vast holdings, and eventually turned Illinois into an agricultural powerhouse. But while the prairie helped define a slice of Illinois' destiny, it's not the state's only characteristic—topographically or culturally. And to see that, a traveler has only to stand on the rocky Mississippi River bluffs near Alton or drive through the gently rolling hills of northwestern Illinois or stroll down State Street in Chicago. Illinois stretches 385 mi from its northernmost to its southernmost points, and the scenery, the food, and the accents that you experience in Rockford, for example, are going to be quite a bit different from what you'll get in Cairo.

It's this variety that attracts millions of visitors to Illinois every year, and that keeps its residents happily seeking out the state's treasures as well. Those craving the adrenaline boost that a world-class metropolis provides head for Chicago. The city admittedly casts a giant shadow over the rest of the state, both politically and culturally, but it is well-earned. The diversity of the city's museums, music, nightlife, shops, restaurants, and activities is hard to match.

But the rest of the state does a good job of holding travelers' interest. If you want to track down history you can follow the path of French explorers, tour buildings left by Utopian communities, immerse yourself in the life of Abraham Lincoln—all without ever going anywhere near the Big City. And those seeking an antidote to urban living can find solace on quiet waterways, in peaceful forests, and in those wide-open spaces.

Illinois' official slogan, the "Land of Lincoln," is also accurate if a bit limiting. It is hard to go many places in the state without running into Honest Abe—whether it's a life-sized statue in a Freeport park or a Lincoln-tagged motor hotel somewhere in the state's center. But while Abe still holds favored-son status, many other names and

CAPITAL: SPRINGFIELD	POPULATION: 11,431,000	AREA: 57,918 SQUARE MI
BORDERS: WI, IN, IA, MO, KY, LAKE MICHIGAN	TIME ZONE: CENTRAL	POSTAL ABBREVIATION: IL
WEB SITE: WWW.ENJOYILLINOIS.COM		

personalities did their part in shaping and personifying the state: Carl Sandburg, John Deere, Clarence Darrow, Jane Addams, Ernest Hemingway, Adlai Stevenson, Ronald Reagan, and many other luminaries all give Illinois pieces of its heritage and character.

History

Among Illinois' earliest settlers were several groups of Indians who left burial mounds, both in the Illinois River Valley (Dickson Mounds, near Lewiston, is one of the best-known examples) and near present-day Collinsville. By the 1500s, a group of about 12 Native American tribes called the Illiniwek, meaning "the men," or "the people," settled in the region. They fished in well-stocked rivers, hunted on the prairie, and farmed the soil.

The French were the first Europeans to arrive in Illinois; they began to colonize the southern part of the state in the early 18th century and built forts and trading posts. They gave the region its name as well, frenchifying the word "Illini" to "Illinois." The British won the lands in 1763, and then lost them during the Revolutionary War. During the next 100 years, pioneers streamed out from the East, eager to work the rich soil, and to build towns, railroads, and canals. Lead mining in the northwest corner of the state and coal mining in the south brought thousands of immigrants to work the mines.

After the Civil War, industry began to compete with agriculture as the state's main pastime. Chicago, which had already become a thriving city, rose from the ashes of its 1871 fire and grew at an incredible pace to become not only a major force in the state but in the country as well. Illinois factories turned out railroad cars and farm implements and packed meat; banks and the Midwest Stock Exchange joined the financial markets. Illinois' geographic position, as well as its well-developed transportation system, ensured a thriving success, which continues today.

Regions

1. CHICAGO METROPOLITAN AREA

The metropolitan area is getting bigger every year, and it's not unusual to think of towns some 60 mi outside of the city as still being commuter towns. (This is helped by Chicago's commuter rail system, which fans out from the city.) The Wisconsin border, some 50 mi from Chicago, makes for a natural northern border, but the broad expanses of farmland to the west and south make it tempting to push the boundaries ever farther.

Chicago, naturally, is the major player of the region. Its sheer size and number of attractions make it a prime destination, and millions flock to it every year, visiting its museums, going to sporting events, and shopping in its stores.

But the suburbs offer their own attractions. Residents no longer have to travel downtown to see a play, a symphony, or a ballet. Larger suburbs are establishing their own cultural and performing arts

IL Timeline

500 BC–AD 500	AD 900–1400	ca. 1500	Mid-1500s
The early American Hopewell culture thrives in Illinois.	Native Americans build city on the site of Cahokia Mounds.	Cahokia site abandoned.	The Illiniwek begin to settle in the region.

centers that nurture hometown talent and attract national names. Restaurants and shopping venues have become increasingly sophisticated, particularly as suburbs' populations become more diverse. And although Chicago has a beautiful lakefront and neighborhood parks, the suburbs can probably win that particular round. The six-county region surrounding the city—the "collar counties"—offer expansive forest preserves and nature areas for boaters, birders, and hikers.

Towns listed: Antioch, Arlington Heights, Aurora, Barrington, Brookfield, Chicago, Chicago O'Hare Airport Area, Crystal Lake, Des Plaines, Downers Grove, Dundee, Elgin, Elmhurst, Evanston, Geneva, Glen Ellyn, Glenview, Gurnee, Highland Park, Highwood, Hinsdale, Homewood, Itasca, Joliet, La Grange, Lake Forest, Libertyville, Lisle, Lockport, McHenry, Naperville, Northbrook, Oak Brook, Oak Lawn, Oak Park, Richmond, St. Charles, Schaumburg, Skokie, Vernon Hills, Wauconda, Waukegan, Wheaton, Wheeling, Wilmette, Woodstock.

2. NORTHWEST ILLINOIS

In rough terms, this covers everything outside of the Chicago metro area, north of I–80, and east of the Mississippi. The landscape includes the vast acres of flat farmland that spread out west of Chicago as well as the rolling hills and dramatic cliffs that mark land closer to the Mississippi River. It also includes a couple of urban areas—Rockford, about 90 mi northwest of Chicago, and the Quad Cities, which sit on the Mississippi.

The rivers that cut through this region—the Rock, the Illinois, and the Mississippi—have created popular visitor areas as well. The far northwest corner, by Galena, particularly emphasizes its historical attractions, but important sites in Illinois' history are spread throughout the region.

Towns listed: De Kalb, Dixon, Freeport, Galena, Grand Detour, Moline, Oregon, Princeton, Rockford, Rock Island, Union.

3. CENTRAL ILLINOIS

Here's where the Prairie State label really kicks in. Lots of central Illinois is just plain flat, and no matter how much you appreciate American agriculture, a ride on the interstate through the state's midsection can seem—well, hypnotizing. Lots of corn, lots of soybeans, big barns, broad sight lines. But destinations in central Illinois are generally worth the trip. You have big state universities, charming small towns, and lots of history, thanks to those pioneers who were busy breaking the prairie sod. And you've got Springfield—the state capital and treasure trove of Lincoln shrines.

And it's not all prairie, anyway. The Mississippi continues its run down the western edge of the state, and the Illinois River Valley—which includes Peoria—livens up the scenery, as does Lake Shelbyville on the east side of the state.

Towns listed: Arcola, Bement, Bishop Hill, Bloomington and Normal, Champaign and Urbana, Charleston, Clinton, Danville, Decatur, Effingham, Galesburg, Havana, Jacksonville, Kankakee, Kewanee, Lincoln, Macomb, Marshall, Mattoon, Monmouth, Monticello, Morris, Nauvoo, Ottawa, Peoria, Peru, Petersburg, Quincy, Rantoul, Shelbyville, Springfield, Utica.

INTRODUCTION
HISTORY
REGIONS
WHEN TO VISIT
STATE'S GREATS
RULES OF THE ROAD
DRIVING TOURS

1673	**1681**	**Early 1700s**	**1763**	**1778**
Louis Jolliet and Fr. Jacques Marquette explore the Mississippi and Illinois rivers.	Robert Cavelier, sieur de LaSalle, hoping to claim land for France, builds several forts along the Illinois River.	French settlements, among them Kaskaskia and Prairie du Rocher, are established in southern Illinois.	Treaty of Paris, at the end of the French and Indian War, awards France's North American possessions—including Illinois—to Great Britain.	Revolutionary soldiers, led by George Rogers Clark, capture Kaskaskia from the British.

4. SOUTHERN ILLINOIS

The scenery shifts as you move into southern Illinois, generally regarded as everything south of Vandalia. Prairies give way to the Shawnee Hills—also known as the Illinois Ozarks—as well as thick forests toward the southern end of the state. The very southern tip, though, is flat, part of the Gulf Coastal Plain.

It's here where Illinois was first settled, so historical remnants are easy to find, particularly old French settlements along the Mississippi. The region is also rich in coal, which attracted many to the area to work in the mines.

Towns listed: Alton, Belleville, Benton, Cahokia, Cairo, Carbondale, Centralia, Chester, Collinsville, Du Quoin, Edwardsville, Grafton, Greenville, Marion, Metropolis, Mt. Vernon, Olney, Prairie du Rocher, Salem, Vandalia.

When to Visit

Illinois weather can be unpredictable, since the state's flat topography leaves it vulnerable to warm or cold winds blowing in from elsewhere. In Chicago, it can snow in April or be balmy in December.

Some generalities, though: The northern part of the state has colder winters and somewhat cooler summers. (Although in 1995, a week-long July heat wave descended in Chicago, with temperatures reaching an all-time high of 106°F. More than 500 people died.) Southern Illinois, on the other hand, has warmer, more humid summers and milder winters. January temperatures average 25°F up north and 36°F in the south. Average July temperature is 75°F in the north and 79°F down south.

It's also wise to prepare for seasonal precipitation. Although the south gets more of it, spring and summer rainstorms can be fierce anywhere in the state. Tornadoes are a less-common but still-possible phenomenon, particularly in rural areas. Snow can also be tricky to generalize about: in the Chicago area, it can be reasonably mild one day and blizzarding the next. One pretty safe bet: Autumn can be a very pleasant season in which to travel. Most of the state enjoys moderate temperatures that can stretch well into November.

CLIMATE CHART

Average High/Low Temperatures (°F) and Monthly Precipitation (in inches)

	JAN.	FEB.	MAR.	APR.	MAY	JUNE
CARBONDALE	40/19	44/22	56/22	68/44	77/53	85/62
	2.5	2.9	4.6	4.0	4.6	4.1

	JULY	AUG.	SEPT.	OCT.	NOV.	DEC.
	89/66	87/63	81/55	70/43	57/34	44/24
	3.8	2.9	4.0	3.0	4.0	3.8

1779	1812	1818	1832	1833
Jean Baptiste Point du Sable establishes a trading post on the site of Chicago.	Fort Dearborn, built in 1803 near du Sable's trading post, is attacked as its occupants attempt evacuation. Some 44 of the settlers are killed, and the fort is burned to the ground.	Illinois becomes the 21st state in the Union.	Black Hawk War, the last battle between Native Americans and white settlers in Illinois, takes place.	Chicago is incorporated as a city.

INTRODUCTION
HISTORY
REGIONS
WHEN TO VISIT
STATE'S GREATS
RULES OF THE ROAD
DRIVING TOURS

CHICAGO

	JAN.	FEB.	MAR.	APR.	MAY	JUNE
	29/13	33/12	46/28	58/38	70/47	79/57
	1.5	3.6	1.3	2.7	3.3	3.8
	JULY	AUG.	SEPT.	OCT.	NOV.	DEC.
	83/62	82/61	75/54	63/42	48/31	34/19
	3.6	3.8	4.2	2.4	2.9	2.4

PEORIA

	JAN.	FEB.	MAR.	APR.	MAY	JUNE
	30/13	35/17	48/29	62/41	72/51	82/60
	1.5	1.4	2.9	3.7	3.7	4.0
	JULY	AUG.	SEPT.	OCT.	NOV.	DEC.
	85.7/65	83/63	77/55	64/43	50/32	34/19
	4.2	3.1	3.8	2.6	2.7	2.4

ROCKFORD

	JAN.	FEB.	MAR.	APR.	MAY	JUNE
	26/91	31/14	44/26	58/37	70/47	80/57
	.28	1.1	2.4	3.6	3.6	4.52
	JULY	AUG.	SEPT.	OCT.	NOV.	DEC.
	83/62	81/60	74/52	62/40	46/29	32/16
	2.9	2.5	4.1	4.1	3.8	2.0

SPRINGFIELD

	JAN.	FEB.	MAR.	APR.	MAY	JUNE
	32/16	37/20	50/31	64/42	75/52	3.6
	84/62	1.5	1.8	3.2	3.7	3.4
	JULY	AUG.	SEPT.	OCT.	NOV.	DEC.
	87/66	84/62	78/56	67/44	51/34	37/22
	3.5	3.2	3.3	2.6	2.5	2.7

FESTIVALS AND SEASONAL EVENTS

WINTER

mid-Nov.–Jan.: **Victorian Splendor Light Festival.** Shelbyville has a fantastically elaborate holiday lighting display, accompanied by a live Nativity scene, a gingerbread house contest, and other holiday festivities. | 217/774–2244.

Dec.: **Geneva Christmas Walk.** Geneva rolls out the Christmas season with a tree lighting, carolers, carriage rides, and house tours. Shops stay open late and serve refreshments to Christmas shoppers. | 630/232–6060.

Jan.: **Illinois Snow Sculpting Competition.** You won't see just your average snowpeople at this festival in Rockford. Snow sculptors compete and give demonstrations of their craft in Sinnissippi Park. | 815/987–8841.

1839
State capital moves from Vandalia to Springfield.

1830s–50s
Illinois and Michigan Canal and railroads are built.

1858
Lincoln-Douglas debates mark campaign for U.S. senator. Douglas wins.

1860
Lincoln is elected president.

1865
Lincoln is assassinated; he is buried in Springfield.

SPRING

Mar.:	**The Chicago Flower and Garden Show at Navy Pier** is a welcome harbinger of spring. Elaborate displays, plant information, and vendors greet gardeners tired of the cold.	800/226–6632.
Mar.–Apr.:	**The American Passion Play,** in Bloomington, is the nation's oldest continuously performed Passion play. Many area residents take part in the show, including some whose families have worked on it since its inception in the 1920s.	800/354–9640.

SUMMER

June–Sept.:	The **Ravinia Festival** is held all summer long on the Ravinia grounds in Chicago's north suburban Highland Park. A range of musical acts, from classical (it's the summer home of the Chicago Symphony) to jazz to pop is presented. Concertgoers can sit under an open-air pavilion or bring a picnic and sit on the lawn.	847/266–5000.
Aug.:	The **Illinois State Fair** is just what you think a state fair should be: lots of rides, livestock, and produce judging, pig races, and corn dogs, and lemonade stands everywhere you look. It all takes place in Springfield.	217/782–6661.
Aug.:	Can't get by without mentioning at least one corn festival; **Urbana's Sweet Corn Festival** has plenty of hot buttered ears along with vendors, kids' activities, live music, and arts and crafts.	217/384–6304.

AUTUMN

Sept.:	Don't try to pronounce it—just enjoy Bishop Hill's **Jordbruksdagarna.** The festival, on the last weekend of September, celebrates Swedish harvest traditions at the Utopian colony; demonstrations of pioneer crafts, and tastings of pioneer food abound.	309/927–3345.
Oct.:	Autumn is a fine time to see the **Spoon River Valley** in central Illinois. To give you a hand, local communities have assembled the Spoon River Valley Scenic Drive, a circular tour through the area. You can stop along the way for local festivities and food.

State's Greats

Beaches, Forests, and Parks

It's generally pretty easy to get into the great outdoors in Illinois—the state has plenty of parks, forests, and other natural areas to enjoy. Even in Chicago, for instance, **Lincoln**

1871	1880s–90s	1893	1920s	1942
The Chicago Fire destroys a sizable portion of the city.	Labor strife in Chicago, marked by the Haymarket Square bombing in 1886 and Pullman strike in 1894.	Columbian Exposition held in Chicago.	Prohibition brings gang warfare to Chicago, led by such names as Al Capone and Bugs Moran.	Atomic Age begins when University of Chicago scientists produce the first manmade nuclear chain reaction.

INTRODUCTION
HISTORY
REGIONS
WHEN TO VISIT
STATE'S GREATS
RULES OF THE ROAD
DRIVING TOURS

Park gives city dwellers a whole range of outdoor activities, from beaches lining the Lake Michigan shore, to bike paths, to a zoo and conservatory, to softball and soccer fields. The **Chicago Botanic Garden,** in Glencoe, near Highland Park, is a treasure for plant lovers or anyone who enjoys a walk in lovely gardens. **The Grove,** in Glenview, is a National Historic Landmark, with a hiking trail, an interpretive center, and peaceful grounds.

Three state parks clustered near Utica—**Starved Rock State Park, Matthiessen State Park,** and **Buffalo Rock State Park**—have hiking trails that cut through cool rocky canyons; they also offer other activities like boating, cross-country skiing, and biking. Illinois' largest state park, **Pere Marquette,** near Grafton, has hiking, horseback riding, boating, and other activities, as well as a rustic lodge. **Wayne Fitzgerrell State Park,** in Whittington (near Benton), holds the 18,000-acre **Rend Lake** for water activities of all kinds.

Culture, History, and the Arts

Lincoln slept here, Sandburg wrote here, Grant Wood hangs here. Illinois' historical and cultural treasures reflect the rich diversity of its people as well as their deep pride in its history. Nothing, for example, shows off the state's Lincoln pride better than the collection of **Lincoln sites in the Springfield area.** Those on the trail of the 16th president can walk through his home, see where he practiced law, visit the train depot where he left for Washington, and pay tribute at his tomb, all within a few square miles. A little farther out of town, you can even see where he got started in his adult life at New Salem, a reconstruction of the village where Lincoln spent six years as a young man. Carl Sandburg—who wrote a biography of Lincoln as well as poems, stories, and essays—also gets his due at the **Carl Sandburg State Historic Site** in Galesburg. There, visitors can see the tiny cottage where the poet was born and where his ashes are buried.

Some of the state's most important cultural sites are in Chicago, where museums celebrate everything from holography to Mexican folk art. Several, of course, are must-sees—the **Art Institute,** the **Field Museum,** the **Museum of Science and Industry,** the **Chicago Historical Society,** and the **John G. Shedd Aquarium.** The city is also famous for its thriving theater scene, where you can attend storefront performances or lavish Broadway musicals. Some of the better-known venues are the **Goodman Theater,** the **Chicago Theatre, Second City,** and **Steppenwolf.**

The diversity of beliefs in Illinois' citizens has made its mark on its historical sites. The Mormons built **Nauvoo,** a thriving town on the Mississippi, before they left for Salt Lake City. Today, it's possible to see how they lived and where they worked. Swedish Utopians founded the tiny colony of **Bishop Hill,** where their buildings still stand, educating visitors on the settlers' heritage. In Wilmette, the grand and ornate **Baha'i House of Worship** welcomes visitors with the serenity of its surroundings. Those who helped build Illinois receive recognition as well. Restored buildings and museums in **Lockport,** southwest of Chicago, pay tribute to the town's roots as a pivotal player on the Illinois & Michigan Canal, which helped to link up the waterways of Illinois to the Mississippi.

1955	1970	1973	1993	1998
Richard J. Daley is elected mayor of Chicago; he serves four terms in office until 1976.	New state constitution is ratified by voters.	Sears Tower, one of the world's tallest buildings, is completed.	Illinois towns along the Mississippi are damaged during heavy summer floods.	Michael Jordan announces his retirement from basketball after having led the Chicago Bulls to six NBA championships.

Sports

Whether your idea of sport is plummeting through the air or just serenely gazing through binoculars, there are places in Illinois where you can pursue your passion. The ski runs at **Chestnut Mountain Resort,** near Galena, take you right down to the banks of the Mississippi River. For a little flatter snow experience, **Moraine Hills State Park,** near McHenry, has trails that take cross-country skiers through peaceful woods. The **Chain O'Lakes area,** near Antioch, buzzes with boaters during the warm-weather months. **Skydive Chicago,** near Ottawa, takes advantage of that nice, flat Illinois terrain, as hardy parachutists take the leap into wide-open cornfields.

For some quieter outdoor fun, **Rend Lake State Fish and Wildlife Area** invites anglers who want to reel in crappie or bass. **Crab Orchard National Wildlife Refuge,** near Marion, is a haven for birders who can see, among other things, the thousands of Canada geese who overwinter there every year. Birdwatchers can also see a vast concentration of waterfowl at the **Illinois River National Wildlife and Fish Refuges** near Havana. For many people, sports are just fine from the spectator point of view. Chicago's teams—the **Cubs, White Sox, Bulls, Bears,** and **Blackhawks**—pull in fans who get a vigorous workout just cheering. Minor league baseball's **Kane County Cougars,** who play near Geneva, attract families and fans who can get closer to the action. Something a little more genteel? There are **polo matches** in Oakbrook on Sundays.

Rules of the Road

License Requirements: Drivers must have a valid driver's license from their state of residence.

Right Turn on Red: Right turn on red is permitted everywhere in the state except where posted.

Seatbelt and Helmet Laws: Seat belts must be worn by all drivers and front-seat passengers six years of age and over even if the vehicle has air bags. Illinois does not have motorcycle-helmet laws, although riders are required to wear protective eyewear.

Speed Limit: The maximum speed limit in Illinois is 65 mph on rural interstate highways where posted. The maximum speed limit on most other highways is 55 mph.

For More Information: Contact the driver's services department at the office of the Illinois Secretary of State at 800/252–8980. Or visit the Secretary of State's motorist services web page at www.sos.state.il.us/depts/drivers/mot_info.html

Illinois' Northwest Corner
FROM THE ROCK RIVER VALLEY TO THE MISSISSIPPI

Distance: 110 mi   Time: 2 days

Breaks: Stay overnight at White Pines State Park. Not only will you be able to explore the park itself, but you'll stay in its cozy, rustic cabins, and you can eat in the lodge's woodsy dining room.

Sammy Sosa of the Chicago Cubs becomes the first major league baseball player to hit 60 home runs in 2 different seasons.

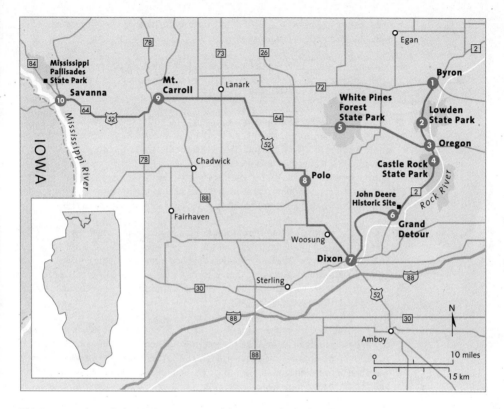

This tour runs through the northwest corner of the state and provides some gorgeous natural sightseeing as well as opportunities to stop and learn about history, take in a play, or even eat some chocolate. The trip is particularly lovely in autumn; both the Rock River and Mississippi River valleys offer fine fall color. But late spring and summer work fine, too. Winter could be trickier; often parts of Mississippi Palisades Park get treacherous in snow and are closed off.

❶ Start your tour at Route 2 in Byron. The road south from here is tree-lined and occasionally runs right next to the river. The Rock River has retained much of its natural beauty because it was never deep enough for commercial navigation and so avoided a lot of development that sprang up along larger waterways.

❷ The road into Oregon provides a stunning view of the 50-ft Loredo Taft sculpture of a Native American chief that's in **Lowden State Park** on a bluff across the river. To get an up-close look, go through town and across the river to the park itself. The park provides some great views of the river; it also has a camping area and hiking trails.

❸ **Oregon** is a pleasant river town with some interesting old houses and a small downtown area. Sitting right on the river is **Conover Square,** a converted piano factory that houses some shops, coffeehouses, and a pottery studio. The **Ogle County Courthouse,** right in town, is a fine, old brick courthouse; on its front lawn is the Soldier's and Sailor's Monument, also designed by Taft.

❹ Just south of town is **Castle Rock State Park,** which also skirts the river. There's a boat ramp and some hiking trails in the park, but the prime feature is Castle Rock itself— a tall sandstone overlook that affords a panoramic view of the river. Wooden stairs lead to the top, where, on a clear fall day you can watch hawks circling overhead while speedboaters circle in the river below.

❺ Still another state park, **White Pines Forest State Park** is about 5 mi west of Oregon. It offers woods and trails to explore, and the park's lodge offers a dinner theater series from May through December.

❻ Route 2 leads farther south into the tiny hamlet of **Grand Detour.** It was here that black-smith John Deere forged the first steel plow that allowed farmers to more easily till the rich prairie soil. Today, the **John Deere Historic Site** traces the story of Deere's work as well as how it affected the future of farming. Deere's company is now based in Moline and has restored the site. The original blacksmith shop has been excavated and an inter-pretive exhibition building has been constructed around it; elsewhere on the site are a re-created, working blacksmith's shop as well as Deere's refurbished home.

❼ A few miles south of Grand Detour, Route 2 leads into **Dixon,** where historical sites honor two presidents. Ronald Reagan lived on Hennepin Avenue for three years as a child, and you can visit the **Ronald Reagan Boyhood Home.** The home is furnished with 1920s-era furnishings and guided tours are available. Abraham Lincoln is memorial-ized by a statue in a riverside park downtown; the statue commemorates Lincoln's service at Fort Dixon during the Black Hawk War.

❽ At Dixon, the tour leaves the river, cuts north on U.S. 52, and heads into Polo. The little town (whose football team is the Marcos, making them the Polo Marcos) has some nice turn-of-the-century storefront buildings; it's also the home of the **Blackhawk Water-ways and Convention Bureau.** The bureau has put together the Blackhawk Chocolate Trail, which leads chocolate lovers through a four-county area. Stop by the bureau's office at 201 North Franklin and pick up a guide.

❾ U.S. 52 continues northwest through farmland that starts to become hillier. The little town of Mt. Carroll, about 20 mi from Polo, is a fine place to stop for a look around. The town has a historic district, lined with homes from the 19th and early 20th centuries, and significant houses are marked with plaques. The downtown area is set around the Carroll County courthouse and is a good stroll as well.

❿ Ten more miles takes you to Savanna, a long, narrow town that sits on the Mississippi. Just north of town along Route 84 is **Mississippi Palisades State Park,** whose steep cliffs rise abruptly from the road. Once you drive into the park, you can get an eye-popping view of the Mississippi from a platform perched at the top of one bluff. The park has many hiking trails, some of them quite rugged and not for the faint of foot.

To return to Oregon, pick up Route 64 in Savanna and drive east for approximately 45 mi.

A Tour of Southern Illinois History
FROM COLLINSVILLE TO CARBONDALE

Distance: 200–250 mi   Time: 3–4 days
Breaks: The first night you could stop at either Chester or ferry across the river to the French colonial town of Ste. Genevieve, Missouri. The second—and third, if necessary—nights, try the cabins or lodge at Giant City Lodge, in Giant City State Park. Both the park and the lodge are listed on the National Register of Historic Places.

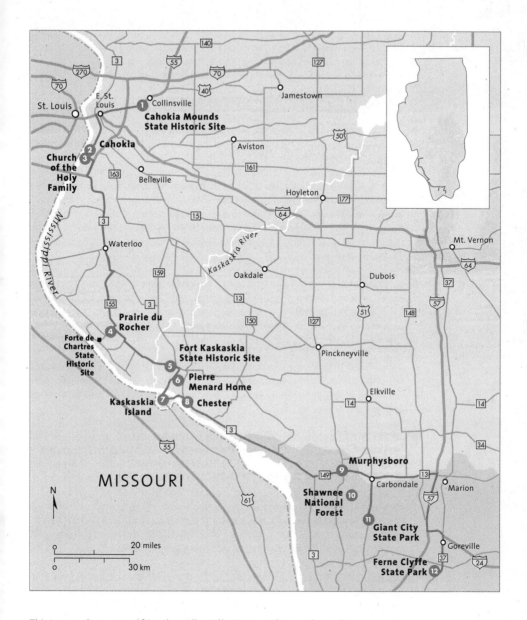

This tour explores more of Southern Illinois' heritage and spans the era between early Indian settlers and early 19th-century Americans. Southern Illinois, particularly along the Mississippi, is noted for its fall color. Be forewarned—the area's summers can be hot and sticky.

❶ The tour starts outside of Collinsville, at **Cahokia Mounds State Historic Site.** There, between AD 900 and 1400, Native Americans built an enormous city covering 6 square mi with a population of more than 20,000; it was the largest city north of Mexico. One of their ceremonial mounds—Monks Mound—is the largest prehistoric earthwork in North America, and today it's part of the site. There are roughly 60 other mounds, as well as a museum and interpretive center.

❷ To get to the town of **Cahokia,** take I–55 down through East St. Louis and switch to Route 3. The town is the oldest community in Illinois, founded in 1699 by French-Canadian missionaries. The **Cahokia Courthouse State Historic Site** was built in 1737 and first used as a residence by French colonists; later, when the area came under U.S. rule, it became a courthouse and was used as one until 1814. It's the oldest building in Illinois. You can visit both the courthouse and its visitors' center.

❸ Also in Cahokia is the stone-and-wood **Church of the Holy Family,** the oldest church in Illinois, built in 1799. You can drop in only in the summer, but you can make an appointment other times of the year.

❹ Forty miles south of Cahokia is the small town of **Prairie du Rocher,** site of **Fort de Chartres State Historic Site.** The French built the fort in the 1750s and surrendered to the British in 1765. Only one original structure—the powder magazine—still stands; the rest of the garrison has been reconstructed. Exhibits at the visitors' center, though, include fort artifacts found in the area. Every June, French-era fort life is re-created at the Fort de Chartres Rendezvous.

❺ Your next stop is the fort and park at **Fort Kaskaskia State Historic Site.** The French built it on a bluff overlooking the Mississippi during the French and Indian War, but it burned in 1766. Garrison Hill Cemetery, on the site, contains the graves of some 3,000 early settlers to the region; the graves were moved from their original location to protect them from Mississippi flood waters.

❻ At the foot of the hill where the fort stood, the first lieutenant governor of Illinois built "the Mount Vernon of the West." The French Colonial **Pierre Menard Home** overlooks the river and was built in 1802. Here you can see the mansion's original furnishings and artifacts.

❼ Just south of the home is the broad, flat Kaskaskia Island—the only part of Illinois that lies west of the Mississippi. The original Kaskaskia settlement was the first capital of Illinois, but the capital moved to Vandalia not long after statehood was granted. The town struggled continuously against Mississippi flooding, but was eventually washed away in a terrible flood in 1881. During the same flood, the river cut a new channel to the east of the town, creating the island. In the middle of the island, in a little pavilion, is the **Kaskaskia Bell State Memorial.** Although it was a gift to French settlers by Louis XV of France, American residents rechristened it the Liberty Bell of the West. It was fished from the river after the 1881 flood and set in its current location.

❽ You can take a break from the historic and venture into a more fanciful realm in **Chester,** just to the east of Kaskaskia on Route 3. The statue that overlooks the mighty Mississippi in Chester's downtown Segar Park is *Popeye.* The Sailor Man's creator, Elzie Segar, was born in Chester, and the statue and park salute him.

❾ Route 3 intersects with Route 149, which will take you into Murphysburo, where you can meet up with Route 13, which leads to Carbondale. This could be a good place to stop before you enter the Shawnee National Forest. Neighboring Carbondale is the home of Southern Illinois University.

❿ The **Shawnee National Forest** sprawls across the southern tip of the state from the Mississippi to the Ohio River. It contains numerous state parks, lakes, and natural areas, and a drive through it could take you hours or days, depending on your stamina and your curiosity. The Little Grand Canyon off of Route 149 near Murphysburo, for example, has stunningly steep canyon walls and a 3½-mi hiking trail that cuts through them.

⓫ If you'd rather stick closer to Carbondale, **Giant City State Park** is only 12 mi south. The park's unusual blocky stone formations gave it its name; they made the area look like a "giant city." The park also has a comfortable lodge and cabins.

⓬ To venture farther into the Shawnee National Forest, you can go east from Carbondale on Route 13, get onto I–57, and travel south to I–24. Take I–24 south to I–37, where you'll go through Goreville; beyond that lies **Ferne Clyffe State Park.** This park, too, has trails that lead through beautiful rock formations; there's also camping and fishing. Fern Clyffe's proximity to the interstate can put you back onto I–57, which cuts back up through the middle of the state and connects with other main arteries.

For a quick—although less-scenic—route back to Collinsville, take I–57 north to Mt. Vernon; there you can pick up I–64 and take that west to Collinsville.

ALTON

(Nearby towns also listed: Belleville, Cahokia, Collinsville, Edwardsville, Grafton)

Settled at the juncture of the Mississippi and Missouri rivers, Alton is an industrial town with a historic past. The last Lincoln-Douglas debate was held here in 1858; it was also where Elijah Lovejoy, an Abolitionist preacher and editor, was murdered by a mob in 1837. Today visitors come for the river scenery, which includes winter bald eagle-watching. Alton has 32,905 residents.

Information: Greater Alton/Twin Rivers Convention and Visitors Bureau | 200 Piasa St., 62002 | 618/465–6676 or 800/258–6645 | www.visitalton.com.

Attractions
Confederate Soldiers' Cemetery. Confederate prisoners of war who were jailed at Alton Prison are buried here. | Rozier St. 2 blocks west of State St. | 800/258–6645 | Free | Daily.

Piasa Bird Painting Reproduction. This modern rendering of a monster (its name means "a bird devouring men") from local Native American legend is painted on the bluffs above Alton 1 mi west of town on Rte. 100. | Rte. 100 | Free | Daily.

Village of Elsah. Eleven miles west of Alton is this late 19th-century river village which is on the National Register of Historic Places. You can tour the town and see how today's residents have preserved Elsah's history. | Great River Rd. | 618/374–1568 | fax 618/374–1522 | Free | Daily.

ON THE CALENDAR
OCT.: *Alton Area Landmarks Association House Tour.* By self-guided tour the first Sunday of the month, you can explore 10 different buildings selected for their historical significance throughout town each fall here. | 618/463–5761.
OCT.: *Alton Cultural Festival.* This is a celebration of the diverse cultures that settled and continue to influence this part of the country. | 618/463–0961.
NOV.: *Great River Road Run.* Don your shorts and running shoes and join this annual 10-mi run or one of the 2-mi "fun runs" on the last week of the month. | 800/258–6645.

Dining
Midtown Restaurant and Lounge. American/Casual. This restaurant, decorated with antiques, birdhouses, and wildlife prints, serves homecooked pasta, pizza, sandwiches, and chili and is known for its impromptu piano sing-a-longs. | 1026 E. 7th St. | 618/465–1321 | No lunch Sat. | $13–$26 | AE, D, DC, MC, V.

Tony's. Italian. Family-owned and operated since 1954, this restaurant, made up of six dining rooms, serves pasta, steak, and seafood dishes. Kids' menu. | 312 Piasa St. | 618/462–8384 | No lunch | $15–$30 | AE, D, DC, MC, V.

Lodging

Days Inn. This standard motel has a "fundome," with an indoor pool, sauna, jacuzzi, putting green, and video games, to help you loosen up; and it's just 5 mi from the Alton Belle Casino, where you can try your luck. Restaurant, bar, complimentary Continental breakfast. Cable TV. Indoor pool. Video games. Pets allowed (fee). | 1900 Homer Adams Pkwy. | 618/463–0800 | fax 618/463–4397 | www.daysinn.com | 115 rooms | $59–$75 | AE, DC, D, MC, V.

Holiday Inn. Thirty minutes from downtown St. Louis, this motel has a Holidome indoor recreation center, where you can relax in the sauna, play video games, or use the tanning beds. Restaurant, bar with entertainment, room service. In-room data ports, cable TV, in-room VCRs (and movies). Indoor pool. Hot tub. Exercise equipment. Video games. Business services, airport shuttle. Pets allowed. | 3800 Homer Adams Pkwy. | 618/462–1220 | fax 618/462–0906 | www.basshotels.com | 137 rooms | $75–$100 | AE, D, DC, MC, V.

Homeridge Bed and Breakfast. You can get a taste of the past in Jerseyville, 12 mi north of Alton, at this Italianate inn dating from the Civil War, complete with period furnishings. Complimentary breakfast. No room phones, no TV. Pool. No smoking. | 1470 N. State St., Jerseyville | 618/498–3442 | fax 618/498–5662 | 5 rooms | $85–$95 | AE, MC, V.

ANTIOCH

MAP 6, G1

(Nearby towns also listed: Gurnee, McHenry, Richmond, Waukegan)

Just south of the Wisconsin state line, Antioch is the northern anchor of the Chain O'Lakes region. Potawatomi Indians were the original residents of the area; they began to leave after the Black Hawk War in the 1830s. As white settlers moved in, they farmed the area, but by the turn of the century, the lakes in the area had made it a popular tourism area. It remains so to this day, but it's also begun to attract suburbanites moving farther out from Chicago.

Information: Antioch Chamber of Commerce | 882 Main St., 60002 | 847/395–2233 | www.lake-online.com/antioch.

Attractions

Chain O'Lakes State Park. You have 10 lakes to choose among for your boating and fishing in this 6,000-acre park a few miles southwest of Antioch. | 8916 Wilmot Rd., Spring Grove | 847/587–5512 | Free | Summer, daily 6 AM–sunset; winter, daily 8–6.

Hiram Butrick Sawmill. This replica of the 1839 sawmill that Hiram Butrick built making Antioch a center of commerce, was constructed in 1976 on the banks of Sequot Creek. | 790 Cunningham Dr. | 847/395–2160 | Free | Daily dawn–dusk.

Lodging

Best Western Regency Inn. Only a half mile from downtown where you can shop and dine, this inn overlooks Lake Antioch. Bar, complimentary Continental breakfast. In-room data ports, some refrigerators, some minibars, cable TV, in-room VCRs. Indoor pool. Hot tub. Business services. Some pets (fee). | 350 Rte. 173 | 847/395–3606 | 68 rooms, 24 suites | $71–$114 | AE, D, DC, MC, V.

ARCOLA

(Nearby towns also listed: Bement, Champaign and Urbana, Charleston, Decatur, Mattoon, Monticello)

The fertile Central Illinois farms surrounding Arcola are home to many of the state's Amish residents. The city became well-known for manufacturing brooms from broom corn grown in the area. Today it has a population of 3,000.

Information: **Arcola Chamber of Commerce** | 135 N. Oak St., 61910 | 217/268–4530 or 800/336–5456 | www.arcola-il.org.

Attractions

Rockome Gardens. You can wander these beautiful gardens and unusual rockworks 4 mi west of Arcola or take an old-fashioned buggy or train ride here. | 125 N. Hwy. 425 E | 217/268–4106 | www.rockome.com | $8.50 | Daily 9–5:30.

ON THE CALENDAR

SEPT.–OCT.: *Horse Farming Days Festival.* Held in Rockome Gardens, this festival celebrates real old-fashioned farming, including demonstrations and contests in horse- and steam-powered threshing, disking, and silage cutting. | 800/549–ROCK.
OCT.: *Art Show.* Paintings of all types are displayed, judged, and offered for sale at this fall art show in Rockome Gardens. | 800/549–ROCK.

Dining

Dutch Kitchen. American. Here's a homey place where you can sample old-fashioned Amish dishes, including shoofly pie, which has a molasses and brown sugar filling. Salad bar and kids' menu. | 127 E. Main St. | 217/268–3518 | Breakfast also available | $2–$8 | No credit cards.

Rockome Family Style. American. At Rockome Gardens, just west of Arcola, you can choose fried chicken and all the fixin's, Dutch shoofly pie, or other dishes made from Amish recipes. | 125 N. Hwy. 425 E | 217/268–4106 | $9–$11 | D, MC, V.

Lodging

Comfort Inn. In Amish country, this standard motel is 20 mi north of the Lincoln Log Cabin Historical Site, 15 mi north of Eastern Illinois University, and less than 10 mi from a big out-

PLAIN AND SIMPLE

They're not tourist attractions—they're simply enclaves of farmers who have chosen a simpler way of life. But in spite of that, Amish communities in central Illinois are still a draw to curious visitors passing through the state's midsection. Towns like Arthur and Arcola still have sizable Amish populations living in farms around them, and the familiar black buggies can be seen making their way down area roads. Local stores sell Amish handiwork—wooden furniture, quilts, and baked goods—and restaurants serve up hearty Pennsylvania Dutch–style cooking—roast chicken, potatoes, and apple butter.

© Corbis

let mall. Complimentary Continental breakfast. Cable TV. Business services. | 610 E. Springfield St. | 217/268–4000 | fax 217/268–4001 | www.comfortinn.com | 40 rooms | $46–$70 | AE, D, DC, MC, V.

ARLINGTON HEIGHTS

MAP 6, H2

(Nearby towns also listed: Barrington, Chicago and O'Hare Airport, Des Plaines, Northbrook, Schaumburg, Wheeling)

Like many of Chicago's thriving northwest suburbs, Arlington Heights boasts a sprucedup downtown clustered around the Metra Union Pacific tracks. The community was settled in the mid-19th-century and today has a population of more than 75,000.

Information: Arlington Heights Chamber of Commerce | 180 N. Arlington Heights Rd., 60004 | 847/253–1703 | www.arlingtonhtschamber.com.

Attractions

Arlington Park. This six-story grandstand provides the ultimate setting to watch thoroughbred racing, including the Arlington Million, a turf race with a purse of a million dollars. | 2200 W. Euclid Ave. | 847/255–4300 | www.arlingtonpark.com | $5 | May–Sept., Wed.–Sun., 11AM–10PM.

Historical Museum. You can get a glimpse of this region's past in the complex of 18th- and 19th-century buildings here, including a reconstructed log cabin. | 500 N. Vail Ave. | 847/255–1225 | $2 | Fri.–Sun. 1–5.

ON THE CALENDAR
OCT.: *Fall Antique Show.* This three-day antiques show held on the grounds of Arlington Park, at Euclid Avenue and Wilke Road, includes more than 200 dealers from around the country. | 847/255–4300.

Dining
Le Titi De Paris. French. At this somewhat formal restaurant, you can choose from among fresh seasonal offerings such as potato-encrusted halibut with saffron sauce and boneless quail with mushroom mousse and calvados infusion. | 1015 W. Dundee Rd. | 847/506–0222 | Jacket required | No lunch. Closed Sun. and Mon. | $26–$29 | AE, D, DC, MC, V.

Palm Court. Continental. Here specialties such as veal Oscar and Dover sole are served in an art deco dining room, where a pianist plays every night but Sunday. | 1912 N. Arlington Heights Rd. | 847/870–7770 | No lunch Sat. | $12–$22 | AE, D, DC, MC, V.

Retro Bistro. French. The menu changes seasonally so you get the freshest ingredients at this turn-of-the-century–style bistro in Mt. Prospect, 3 mi southeast of Arlington Heights, but one selection you can always try is the steak frites; it's a favorite. | 1746 W. Golf Rd., Mt. Prospect | 847/439–2424 | No lunch Sat. Closed Sun. | $10.50–$17 | AE, D, DC, MC, V.

Lodging
Amerisuites. This six-story all-suites hotel is in the business district, 1 mi off I–90, 10 mi from the Chicago O'Hare airport, and 1½ mi from Woodfield Mall. Complimentary Continental breakfast. Refrigerators, cable TV. Hot tub. Exercise equipment. Business services, free parking. Some pets. | 2111 S. Arlington Heights Rd. | 847/956–1400 | fax 847/956–0804 | www.amerisuites.com | 114 suites | $69–$129 | AE, D, DC, MC, V.

Arlington Park Sheraton Conference Center. Best-known for its conference facilities, this large hotel is 16 mi from Chicago O'Hare, within 5 mi of I–290, I–294, and I–90, and 2 mi from Woodfield Mall. Restaurant, bar. In-room data ports, cable TV. Indoor pool. Hot tub, massage. Tennis. Gym. Business services. Some pets. | 3400 W. Euclid Ave. | 847/394–2000 | fax 847/394–2095 | www.sheraton.com | 428 rooms | $69–$209 | AE, D, DC, MC, V.

Courtyard by Marriott. On the corner of two main thoroughfares in the midst of many restaurants and theaters, this three-story motel is 3 mi from Woodfield Mall. Restaurant. In-room data ports, refrigerators, some microwaves, cable TV, in-room VCRs. Indoor pool. Hot tub. Exercise equipment. Laundry facilities. Business services, free parking. | 100 W. Algonquin Rd. | 847/437–3344 | fax 847/437–3367 | www.courtyard.com | 135 rooms, 12 suites | $129; $154 suites | AE, D, DC, MC, V.

Holiday Inn Express. Eight mi from the Chicago O'Hare Airport, this standard motel is just 2 mi from Woodfield Mall. Complimentary Continental breakfast. In-room data ports, some refrigerators, cable TV. Business services, free parking. | 2120 S. Arlington Heights Rd. | 847/593–9400 | fax 847/593–3632 | www.holiday-inn.com | 125 rooms | $79–$129 | AE, D, DC, MC, V.

La Quinta. This four-story motel is 4 mi north of downtown, 2 mi from the Arlington Park Race Track and 15 mi from the Chicago O'Hare airport. It is right off of I–290, on the Dundee Rd Exit. Complimentary Continental breakfast. In-room data ports, cable TV, in-room VCRs. Pool. Business services. Some pets. | 1415 W. Dundee Rd. | 847/253–8777 | fax 847/818–9167 | www.laquinta.com | 123 rooms | $59–$89 | AE, D, DC, MC, V.

Radisson. You can lounge on the sundeck at this six-story hotel 2 mi from downtown Arlington Heights and 8½ mi from Chicago O'Hare. Restaurant, bar with entertainment. In-room data ports, some refrigerators, cable TV. Indoor pool. Hot tub. Exercise equipment. Busi-

USEFUL EXTRAS YOU MAY WANT TO PACK

- ☐ Adapters, converter
- ☐ Alarm clock
- ☐ Batteries
- ☐ Binoculars
- ☐ Blankets, pillows, sleeping bags
- ☐ Books and magazines
- ☐ Bottled water, soda
- ☐ Calculator
- ☐ Camera, lenses, film
- ☐ Can/bottle opener
- ☐ Cassette tapes, CDs, and players
- ☐ Cell phone
- ☐ Change purse with $10 in quarters, dimes, and nickels for tollbooths and parking meters
- ☐ Citronella candle
- ☐ Compass
- ☐ Earplugs
- ☐ Flashlight
- ☐ Folding chairs
- ☐ Guidebooks
- ☐ Luggage tags and locks
- ☐ Maps
- ☐ Matches
- ☐ Money belt
- ☐ Pens, pencils
- ☐ Plastic trash bags
- ☐ Portable TV
- ☐ Radio
- ☐ Self-seal plastic bags
- ☐ Snack foods
- ☐ Spare set of keys, not carried by driver
- ☐ Travel iron
- ☐ Travel journal
- ☐ Video recorder, blank tapes
- ☐ Water bottle
- ☐ Water-purification tablets

*Excerpted from *Fodor's: How to Pack: Experts Share Their Secrets*
© 1997, by Fodor's Travel Publications

ness services, airport shuttle. Some pets. | 75 W. Algonquin Rd. | 847/364–7600 | fax 847/364–7665 | www.radisson.com | 201 rooms, 10 suites | $79–$169, $175–$210 suites | AE, D, DC, MC, V.

Wyndham Garden Hotel. This hotel with a garden courtyard is in Buffalo Grove, a half mile east of Arlington Heights and 5 mi from the village of Long Grove. Restaurant, bar. In-room data ports, cable TV. Indoor pool. Hot tub. Exercise equipment. Laundry facilities. Business services, airport shuttle. | 900 W. Lake Cook Rd., Buffalo Grove | 847/215–8883 | fax 847/215–9304 | www.wyndham.com | 155 rooms | $89–$129 | AE, D, DC, MC, V.

AURORA

MAP 6, G2

(Nearby towns also listed: Elgin, Geneva, Joliet, Naperville, St. Charles)

First settled in the 1830s, Aurora has become one of the fastest-growing cities in Illinois; in 1999 it became third in population in the state with 123,000 residents. The downtown, built around the Fox River, has seen a revitalization in the last 15 years, thanks to a renovated movie palace and the arrival of a casino riverboat.

Information: Aurora Area Convention and Tourism Council | 44 W. Downer Pl., 60506 | 630/897–5581 or 800/477–4369 | fax 630/897–5589 | marketing@enjoyaurora.com | www.enjoyaurora.com.

Attractions

Aurora Art and History Center. Home of the Aurora Historical Society and the Aurora Public Art Commission, this three-story center has changing exhibits hightlighting local history, photography, and public art. | 20 E. Downer Pl. | 630/906–0650 | $3 | Wed.–Sun. noon–4.

Blackberry Farm's Pioneer Village. At this 60-acre living-history park off I–88, you can see exhibits of everything from the Victorian era. You can also ride on a train, twirl on a carousel, and trot on a horse or other farm animal. | 100 S. Barnes Rd., I–88, exit Orchard Rd. | 630/892–1550 | $7.50; special rates for Fox Valley residents, senior citizens, and kids | end Apr.–Labor Day, daily 10–4:30; after Labor Day–Oct., Fri.–Sun. 10–4:30.

Fermi National Accelerator Laboratory. You can see and learn about the world's highest-energy particle accelerator, watch the video program in the observation area, and take self-guided tours at this lab in Batavia, 2 mi north of Aurora. | Kirk Rd., Batavia | 630/840–3351 | www.fnal.gov | Free | Daily 8:30–5.

Paramount Arts Center. In this restored 1920s art deco movie palace, you can see musicals, plays, dance performances, concerts, and stand-up comedy. | 23 E. Galena Blvd. | 630/896–6666 | Prices vary by show | Weekdays 9–5, Sat. 9–1.

Schingoethe Center for Native American Cultures. A collection of art and artifacts from many native cultures in North America can be viewed at this museum. | 347 S. Gladstone Ave. | 630/844–5402 | Free | Feb.–Dec., Tues.–Fri. 10–4, Sun. 1–4.

SciTech–Science and Technology Interactive Center. You can learn how to make slime, for example, at this hands-on science museum in downtown Aurora. There are more than 200 exhibits on astronomy, physics, and mathematics. | 18 W. Benton St. | 630/859–3434 | $5; special rates for senior citizens, kids, and families | Tues.–Fri. noon–8, Sat. 10–5, Sun. noon–5.

ON THE CALENDAR

MAY: *Annual Native American Pow Wow.* The many ceremonies and activities of a pow wow, including Native American singing and drumming, hoop dancing, and basket and pottery making are held for three days at the end of the month at the Schingoethe Center for Native American Cultures. You can also sample wares from a variety of vendors at this spring gathering. | 630/844–5402.

DEC.: *Holiday Celebrations in Many Lands.* Trees beautifully decorated in the traditions of 20 different cultures are on display throughout the month at the Aurora Art and History Center at 20 East Downer Place during this event sponsored by the Aurora Public Library. | 630/264–4100.

DEC.: *Polar Express and Yuletide.* A steam locomotive takes you on a night tour of Christmas lights and yuletide festivities one weekend in mid-month through Blackberry Farm's Pioneer Village in Fox Valley. | 630/892–1550.

Dining

America's Brewpub at Walter Payton's Roundhouse Complex. Contemporary. In a converted railroad roundhouse festooned with memorabilia of the late Walter Payton, including his trophies and lots of photos, you can enjoy music in the courtyard and sample homemade brews from the on-site microbrewery. Known for its simply prepared steaks, seafood, chicken, and pasta, Payton's also serves New Orleans spicy jambalaya. | 205 N. Broadway | 630/264–2739 | www.walterpaytonsroundhouse.com | $11–$27 | AE, D, DC, MC, V.

Lodging

Best Western Fox Valley Inn. This motel is 3 mi from Fox River and the Riverboat Casino and just 2 mi from the Fermi National Accelerator Laboratory. Restaurant, bar with entertainment. Cable TV. Pool. Exercise equipment. Business services. | 2450 N. Farnsworth St. | 630/851–2000 | fax 630/851–8885 | www.bestwestern.com | 112 rooms | $57–$85 | AE, D, DC, MC, V.

Comfort Inn. When you stay at this motel, you are across the street from the Fox Valley Mall, 3 mi from the Paramount Arts Center, and 3 mi from Fox River. Complimentary Continental breakfast. Cable TV. Business services. | 4005 Gabrielle La. | 630/820–3400 | fax 630/820–7081 | www.comfortinn.com | 51 rooms | $76–$89 | AE, D, DC, MC, V.

Comfort Suites. This all-suites motel is 2 blocks from Paramount Arts Center, within walking distance to the Hollywood Casino and 3 mi from the Fox Valley Mall. Complimentary Continental breakfast. In-room data ports, refrigerators, cable TV, VCRs, and movies. Indoor pool. Hot tub. Exercise equipment. Video games. Laundry facilities. Business services. | 111 N. Broadway | 630/896–2800 | fax 630/896–2887 | www.comfortinn.com | 82 suites | $79–$229 | AE, D, DC, MC, V.

BARRINGTON

MAP 6, G2

(Nearby towns also listed: Arlington Heights, Crystal Lake, Dundee, Elgin, Schaumburg, Wauconda, Wheeling)

Barrington, established by early settlers from New England in the 1840s, still respects its rural roots. Shops and restaurants nestle in the center of this residential village of 9,538, along with a homey 1920s movie theater. Surrounding the village are forest preserves and nature areas, including Bakers Lake, home to a heron rookery. The city is only 50 minutes by train from downtown Chicago.

Information: **Barrington Area Chamber of Commerce** | 325 N. Hough St., 60010 | 847/381–2525 | www.barringtonchamber.com.

Attractions

Health World. Here you can learn how to stay well, from more than 200 interactive hands-on exhibits on health, the environment, and safety. | 1301 S. Grove Ave. | 847/842–9100 | www.jfkhealthworld.com | $5; special rates for kids | Mon.–Thurs. 10–3, Fri. 10–8, weekends 10–5.

JUNE: *Art Show.* Dozens of regional and national artists of all types display and sell their work at this annual art show held at Cook and Station Streets. | 847/382–5626.

Dining

The Barn of Barrington. Continental. This country inn in a renovated barn is known for its Mediterranean chicken breast and its crab cakes. | 1415 S. Barrington Rd. | 847/381–8585 | www.thebarnofbarrington.com | $15–$37 | AE, D, DC, MC, V.

Barrington Country Bistro. French. Pork tenderloin, steak au poivre, and salmon are the favorites at this bistro, which has an enticing mural of Provence on its wall. | 700 W. Northwest Hwy. | 847/842–1300 | Reservations essential | Daily, 11:30–8:30 | No lunch Sun. | $23–$25 | AE, DC, MC, V.

The Greenery. Contemporary. Specialties served in the intimate dining rooms of this 1880s schoolhouse are beef medallions, blackened prawns, sea bass, and for dessert, bread pudding. | 117 North Ave. | 847/381–9000 | No lunch. Closed Sun. | www.thegreenery.com | $16–$26 | AE, D, DC, MC, V.

Millrose Restaurant and Brewing Company. American. Antler chandeliers and other hunting memorabilia decorate this tri-level dining complex on 14 acres in South Barrington, where favorites are baby-back ribs, big bison burgers, and chops, with a beer from the on-site brewery. Kids' menu. Sunday brunch. | 45 S. Barrington Rd., South Barrington | 847/382–7673 | $16–$30 | AE, D, DC, MC, V.

Lodging

Days Inn. This inn is right next to Lageschulte Park and its pool, golf, tennis, and playground facilities, which you can appreciate whether you are visiting on business or for pleasure. Restaurant, bar. Kitchenettes, some refrigerators, cable TV. Gym. Laundry facilities. Business services. Pets (fee). | 405 W. Northwest Hwy. | 847/381–2640 | fax 847–381–6208 | www.daysinn.com | 57 rooms | $69–$74 | AE, D, DC, MC, V.

BELLEVILLE

MAP 6, E9

(Nearby towns also listed: Alton, Cahokia, Collinsville, Edwardsville)

Only 20 minutes from downtown St. Louis, Belleville is the seat of St. Clair County. German miners helped settle this southern Illinois coal-mining town in the 19th century, and it boasts 700 homes and buildings on the National Register of Historic Places. Because of its proximity to St. Louis, Belleville (population 42,785) attracts commuters, but it's also still possible to pick your own fruit from the apple and peach orchards around the town.

Information: **Belleville Tourism Inc.** | 216 E. A St., 62220 | 618/233–6769 or 800/677–9255 | www.beti.org.

Attractions

Emma Kunz Museum. This restored Greek Revival house is itself a museum of the structure's era, complete with 1830s furnishings. | 602 Fulton St. | 618/234–0600 | $2; special rates for kids | Daily by appointment.

National Shrine of Our Lady of the Snows. This outdoor shrine for Our Lady of the Snows covers more than 200 acres and has devotional areas where you can attend a mass or take a guided tour. | 442 S. DeMazenod Dr. | 618/397–6700 | www.sitc.org/natshrn.html | Free | Daily.

SEPT.: *World Youth Day Weekend.* Mass, a keynote speaker, a dinner, a dance, and a closing commissioning ceremony in honor of young people are all held the last weekend of September on the acreage at the National Shrine of Our Lady of the Snows, off of South DeMazenod Drive, for this celebration. | 618/397–6700.

NOV.: *Woodcarvers Show.* Both local and national woodcarvers display their work and provide exhibitions of their talents at the Belle Clair Fairgrounds during this fall event that takes place the first weekend of the month. | 618/233–0052.

NOV.–DEC.: *Secret Lives of Teddy Bears.* Teddy bears from around the nation can be viewed at the Emma Kunz Museum on Fulton Street. | 618/234–0600.

Dining

Fischer's. American. There are linen cloths on the tables at this contemporary restaurant, where the specialties are prime rib and fried chicken. Kids' menu. | 2100 W. Main St. | 618/233–1131 | fax 618/233–1135 | Breakfast also available | $8.95–$35 | AE, D, DC, MC, V.

Lodging

Days Inn. This motel is just 5 mi from Our Lady of the Snows shrine. Restaurant, bar, complimentary Continental breakfast. In-room data ports, microwaves, refrigerators, cable TV. Pool. | 2120 W. Main St. | 618/234–9400 | fax 618/234–6142 | www.daysinn.com | 74 rooms, 6 suites | $56–$69; $80–$100 suites | AE, D, DC, MC, V.

Swans Court Bed and Breakfast. This small B&B, on a quiet street in the historic district, was built in 1883. Photos of the family that owned the house for 86 years adorn the entrance way, parlor, and dining room. The antique-filled rooms have floor to ceiling closets, walnut furniture, and canopied beds, and the swan motif is reflected throughout with carved decoys in all rooms. Some baths shared. Complimentary breakfast. In-room data ports, TV in common area. No smoking. | 421 Court St. | 618/233–0779 | www.bbonline.com/il/swanscourt | 4 rooms | $65–$90 | AE, D, MC, V.

BEMENT

MAP 6, G6

(Nearby towns also listed: Arcola, Champaign and Urbana, Clinton, Decatur, Mattoon, Monticello)

The small central Illinois town of Bement (population 1,668) has its roots in railroading; it's now a trade center for the area. Its most famous event happened in July 1858 when Abraham Lincoln and Stephen Douglas met to map out a schedule for their series of debates later that year.

Information: Bement Area Chamber of Commerce | Box 111, 61813 | 217/678–4171 | chamber@bement.com | www.bement.com.

Attractions

Bryant Cottage State Historical Site. You can view this four-room cottage, built in 1856, where it is thought that Lincoln and Douglas met in July of 1858 to discuss the format for their debates. The cottage has period furnishings, and special events are held here periodically. | 146 E. Wilson St. | 217/678–8184 | Free | Mar.–Oct., daily 9–5; Nov.–Feb., daily 9–4.

BENTON

MAP 6, G10

(Nearby towns also listed: Du Quoin, Marion, Mt. Vernon)

The seat of Franklin County (population 7,344) is named for the statesman Thomas Hart Benton. Outdoor recreation activities make the area a popular spot.

Information: **Benton Area Chamber of Commerce** | 211 N. Main St., 62812 | 618/438–2121 | www.bentonwestcity.com.

Attractions

Rend Lake. Five miles north of Benton, on Route 37, you can boat and fish on this 19,000-acre lake, alongside which there are two beaches, four campgrounds, and two lodges. | Rte. 37 | 618/724–2493 | Free | Lake open year-round; campgrounds open Apr.–Oct.

Southern Illinois Artisan Shop and Visitors Center. In Whittington, 6 mi from Benton, you can learn about the state's many artisans whose works are displayed and sold here. Go north on I–57 to exit 77, then head west on Route 154. | 14967 Gun Creek Tr., Whittington | 618/629–2220 | Free | Daily 9–5.

Wayne Fitzgerrell State Park. Just 6 mi north of Benton via I–57 and Route 154, you can boat, fish, and swim in the lake in this 3,300-acre state park, where you can also camp and hike. | 11094 Ranger Rd., Whittington | 618/629–2320 | Free | Daily.

ON THE CALENDAR

MAY: *Rend Lake Water Festival.* This spring festival takes place for three days mid-month. It includes a car show, as well as many food vendors. | 618/438–2121 or 800/661–9998.

Lodging

Days Inn. This standard motel is just 5 mi from Rend Lake. Just off I-57. Restaurant, bar with entertainment. Cable TV. Business services. Pets allowed. | 711 W. Main St. | 618/439–3183 | www.daysinn.com | 113 rooms | $55 | AE, D, DC, MC, V.

Rend Lake Resort and Conference Center. You can rent a room or a cottage with views of Rend Lake, a fireplace, or a sleeping loft at this conference center and resort in Whittington, 5 mi north of Benton. Restaurant. Some refrigerators, cable TV. Pool, wading pool. Playground. Business services. | 11712 E. Windy La., Whittington | 618/629–2211 or 800/633–3341 | fax 618/629–2584 | www.dnr.state.il.us/parks/parkinfo/rendlake.htm | 68 rooms, 22 cottages | $78; $83 cottages | AE, D, DC, MC, V.

BISHOP HILL

MAP 6, E3

(Nearby towns also listed: Galesburg, Kewanee, Moline, Princeton, Rock Island)

This tiny settlement was founded in the 1840s as a Swedish religious colony. Today, the town's buildings house displays and art illustrating colony life; shops and restaurants offer period crafts and Swedish cuisine. Seasonal festivals celebrate the town's agricultural heritage.

Information: **Bishop Hill Arts Council** | 110 W. Bjorkland St., 61419 | 309/927–3885.

Attractions

Bishop Hill Heritage Association. The association conducts guided tours of this 1840s settlement and operates several buildings in Bishop Hill including a blacksmith shop, a colony store, and the Steeple Building, which houses a museum. | 103 N. Bishop Hill Rd. | 309/927–3899 | Free | Early Mar.–late Dec., Mon.–Sat. 10–5, Sun. noon–5.

Bishop Hill State Historic Site. Three of the buildings in this 1840s settlement make up this historic site: the colony church, an old hotel, and an art museum, all of which you can explore by self-guided tours. 2 miles north of US 34. | 309/927–3345 | $2 | Mar.–Oct., daily 9–5; Nov.–Feb., daily 9–4.

JUNE: *Concert Series.* Every Sunday during the month, you can enjoy outdoor performances of traditional and folk music in Bishop Hill Park. | 309/927–3345.

SEPT.: *Bishop Hill Jordbruksdagarna.* This harvest festival on the last weekend of the month celebrates the foods and crafts of the Swedish pioneers who settled this area. | 309/927–3345.

NOV.–DEC.: *Julmarknad.* You can purchase Swedish crafts, foods, and other treats at Bishop Hill's Christmas market during the last weekend of November and the first weekend of December. | 309/927–3345.

DEC.: *Lucia Nights.* During this festival of lights commemorating Swedish St. Lucia, carolers stroll the streets of the village, and a "Lucia" in each shop serves cider and cookies. A single candle in every window sets the whole town aglow. | 309/927–3345.

Lodging

Colony Hospital Bed and Breakfast. This small B&B is housed in the original hospital of the Bishop Hill Colony, which was built in 1855. Complimentary Continental breakfast. Refrigerators, microwaves, cable TV, some in-room VCRs. Playground. Business services. No smoking. | 110 N. Olson St. | 309/927–3506 | www.inn-dex.net/colonyhospital | 4 rooms | $65–$135 | MC, V.

BLOOMINGTON AND
NORMAL

INTRO
ATTRACTIONS
DINING
LODGING

BLOOMINGTON AND NORMAL

MAP 6, F5

(Nearby towns also listed: Clinton, Lincoln, Peoria)

Illinois State University gave Normal its name (the school was originally a normal college for teachers). Bloomington is the older and larger of the two towns (population 57,707); it's also the site of Illinois Wesleyan University. The twins are also home to several national headquarters for insurance companies, as well as to a healthy agribusiness community. Normal has 42,000 residents.

Information: **Bloomington–Normal Area Convention and Visitors Bureau** | 210 S. East St. (Box 1586), Bloomington 61702 | 309/829–1641 | www.visitbloomingtonnormal.org.

Attractions

Funk Prairie Home. In a restored 1864 home with much of its original furniture and some of the first electric appliances, this museum is just south of Bloomington, in Shirley, and includes a gem and mineral museum with specimens from all over the world. | RR 1, Box 75A, Shirley | 309/827–6792 | Free | Mar.–Dec, Tues.–Sat. 9–4.

Illinois State University. Founded in 1847, ISU is the first state college to be established in Illinois, where today more than 20,000 students seek their higher education and you are welcome to visit. The University is at the intersection of I-74, I-55, and I-39. | Office of Admissions, 201 Hovey Hall, Normal | 309/438–2181 | www.ilstu.edu | Free | Daily.

Illinois Wesleyan University. Approximately 2,000 students attend this small private liberal arts college in Bloomington. | 1312 N. Park St., Bloomington | 309/556–1000 | fax 309/556–3411 | www.iwu.edu | Free | Daily.

The **Evelyn Chapel,** built in 1984, is known both for its extraordinary design and its pipe organ, which has an incredible 1,650 pipes. | 1301 N. Park St., Bloomington | 309/556–3161 | Free | Sept.–May, Mon.–Thurs. 8 AM–9 PM, Fri. 8–5, weekends 10–5.

The **Sheean Library,** in the central quad of the IWU campus, includes both print and nonprint collections. The three-story building also houses the University archives and a repository for the papers of former U.S. Congressman Leslie C. Arends. Each fall, the library hosts the Great Illinois Book Fair with opportunities to trade and buy rare books. | Beecher St.

at East St. | 309/556–3407 | www.iwu.edu/library | Free | Mon.–Thurs. 7:45 AM–1:30 AM, Fri. 7:45 AM–10 PM, Sat. 10–10, Sun. 11:30 AM–1:30 AM.

Miller Park Zoo. You can admire Sumatran tigers and wander through an indoor tropical rain forest, two of the many exhibits at this 11-acre zoo. | 1020 Morris Ave., Bloomington | 309/434–2250 | $3; special rates for senior citizens and kids | Summer, daily 10–5; fall–spring, daily 10–4:30.

Old Courthouse Museum. Explore the history of McLean County chronicled through the exhibits at this museum in the 100-year-old courthouse on Main Street. | 200 N. Main St., Bloomington | 309/827–0428 | fax 309/827–0100 | www.mchistory.org | $2; special rates for kids | Mon. and Wed.–Sat. 10–5; Tues. 10–9.

ON THE CALENDAR

MAR.–APR.: *The American Passion Play.* This Passion play, which has been performed each year since 1924, can be seen at the Scottish Rite Temple on Mulberry Street in Bloomington. | 309/829–3903 or 800/354–9640.
JULY–AUG.: *Illinois Shakespeare Festival.* These summer stagings of William Shakespeare's works, which include madrigal performances, are held in the Ewing Manor at Emerson and Towanda Streets in Bloomington. | 309/438–2535.

Dining

Central Station Café. Contemporary. House specialties are prime ribs, pasta, and seafood at this renovated turn-of-the-century fire station, which has exposed brick walls in its interior and a copper canopy over its complete bar, where you can hear live music Thursday through Saturday. | 220 E. Front St., Bloomington | 309/828–2323 | Closed Sun. and Mon. | $10–$20 | AE, DC, MC, V.

Jim's Steak House. Steak. Dry-aged steaks are Jim's specialty, but other favorites here are lobster and pork chops. A pianist plays Thursday through Saturday nights. | 2307 E. Washington St., Bloomington | 309/663–4142 | No lunch weekends | $12–$35 | AE, D, DC, MC, V.

Lodging

Best Inns of America. This motel is 2 mi from the Illinois Wesleyan campus and 5 mi from Illinois State University. Complimentary Continental breakfast. In-room data ports, cable TV. Pool. Business services. Pets allowed. | 1905 W. Market St., Bloomington | 309/827–5333 | fax 309/827–5333 | www.bestinn.com | 106 rooms | $46–$66 | AE, D, DC, MC, V.

Best Western University Inn. It's a one-mile walk from this motel to Illinois State University, and the Amtrak station is only 2 mi, but the motel provides free parking in this rather busy section of town. Complimentary Continental breakfast. Cable TV. Pool. Sauna. Business services, airport shuttle, free parking. | 6 Traders Cir., Normal | 309/454–4070 | fax 309/888–4505 | www.bestwestern.com | 102 rooms | $65 | AE, D, DC, MC, V.

Eastland Suites Hotel and Conference Center. This hotel and conference center is 1 mi from the Bloomington-Normal airport. Some suites have fireplaces, lofts, or balconies. Cable TV. Indoor pool. Exercise equipment. Laundry facilities. Business services, airport shuttle. | 1801 Eastland Dr., Bloomington | 309/662–0000 | fax 309/663–6668 | www.eastland-suites.com | 88 suites | $99–$129 | AE, D, DC, MC, V.

Fairfield Inn by Marriott. Three miles from downtown Normal, this standard motel is also just 2 mi from Illinois State University. Complimentary Continental breakfast, cable TV. Pool. Business services. | 202 N. Landmark Dr., Normal | 309/454–6600 | fax 309/454–6600 | www.fairfieldinn.com | 128 rooms | $59–$69 | AE, D, DC, MC, V.

Hampton Inn. You can walk the quarter mile to Eastland Mall from this motel and find many restaurants in the neighborhood as well. Complimentary Continental breakfast. In-room data ports, cable TV. Pool. Business services, airport shuttle. | 604½ Iaa Dr., Bloomington | 309/662–2800 | fax 309/662–2811 | www.hamptoninn.com | 108 rooms | $75–$79 | AE, D, DC, MC, V.

Holiday Inn. This motel and its approximately 14,000 square ft of conference space are one mile from downtown Bloomington and Illinois State University. Restaurant, bar, room service. Cable TV, in-room VCRs (and movies). Indoor pool. Hot tub. Exercise equipment. Video games. Business services, airport shuttle, free parking. Pets allowed. | 8 Traders Cir., Normal | 309/452–8300 | fax 309/454–6722 | www.holiday-inn.com | 160 rooms | $81 | AE, D, DC, MC, V.

Jumer's Chateau. This five-story Old World–style hotel has an opulent lobby and is furnished with antiques. Restaurant, bar with entertainment. Refrigerators, some in-room minibars, cable TV. Indoor pool. Hot tub, sauna. Exercise equipment. Business services, airport shuttle. Pets allowed. | 1601 Jumer Dr., Bloomington | 309/662–2020 or 800/285–8637 | fax 309/662–2020, ext. 617 | www.jumers.com | 180 rooms, 26 suites | $98–$158; $135–$175 suites | AE, D, DC, MC, V.

Ramada Empire Inn. This motel is known for its indoor recreation center, which is the largest in the area. Restaurant, bar, room service. Cable TV. Indoor pool. Hot tub. Miniature golf. Exercise equipment. Video games. Laundry facilities. Business services, airport shuttle. Pets allowed. | 1219 Holiday Dr., Bloomington | 309/662–5311 | fax 309/663–1732 | www.empire.com | 209 rooms | $59 | AE, D, DC, MC, V.

BROOKFIELD

MAP 8, D6

(Nearby towns also listed: Elmhurst, Hinsdale, La Grange, Oak Park, Riverside)

With its tree-lined streets and quiet pace, Brookfield (population 18,876) looks like any other pleasant western Chicago suburb—even when you consider that it does have a world-renowned zoo in its backyard.

Information: **Brookfield Chamber of Commerce** | 3724 Grand Blvd., 60513 | 708/485–1434.

Attractions
Brookfield Zoo. This was the first zoo in the country to put animals in natural habitats. You can see Tropic World, Fragile Kingdom, Seven Seas Panorama, and Habitat Africa in this world-class zoo. | 1st Ave. at 31st St. | 708/485–0263 | www.brookfieldzoo.org | $7; special rates for senior citizens and kids; parking $4 | Daily 10–5.

CAHOKIA

MAP 6, D9

(Nearby towns also listed: Alton, Belleville, Collinsville, Edwardsville)

Cahokia is the oldest town in Illinois; it was settled by French-Canadian missionaries in 1699. Today this community of 16,149 is primarily residential.

Information: **Cahokia Area Chamber of Commerce** | 905 Falling Springs Rd., 62206 | 618/332–1900 | fax 618/332–6690.

Attractions
Cahokia Courthouse State Historic Site. This 1740s courthouse is the oldest building in Illinois. Here you can learn about the state's history through interactive exhibits. | 107 Elm St. | 618/332–1782 | fax 618/332–1737 | Free | Tues.–Sat. 9–5.

The Church of the Holy Family. In summer you can go through this log church, which was built in 1799, making it the oldest church in Illinois. | 116 Church St. | 618/337–4548 | fax 618/332–1699 | Free | June–Aug., daily.

Lodging

Holiday Inn Express. Used primarily by business travelers, this motel is 7 mi from the St. Louis Gateway Arch and approximately 20 mi from shopping and restaurants. Complimentary Continental breakfast. In-room data ports, some microwaves, refrigerators, cable TV. Indoor pool. Business services. | 1607 Pontiac Dr. | 618/332–2000 | fax 618/332–3660 | www.basshotels.com | 65 rooms, 6 suites | $69; $89 suites | AE, D, DC, MC, V.

CAIRO

MAP 6, F12

(Nearby town also listed: Metropolis)

The Ohio and Mississippi rivers join here at the southernmost city in Illinois (population 4,643). Early settlers from the St. Louis area named it for its assumed resemblance to Egypt; Illinoisans today say CARE-o.

Information: **Cairo Chamber of Commerce** | 220 8th St., 62914 | 618/734–2737 | www.southernmostillinois.com.

Attractions

Custom House Museum. The exhibits in this 1860s building include items of historic significance from the Cairo area and the Civil War. | 1400 Washington Ave. | 618/734–1019 | Free | Weekends 10–3.

Fort Defiance Park. You get a great view of the juncture of the Ohio and Mississippi rivers from this park 2 mi south of Cairo, where there is also a monument dedicated to those who lost their lives on the river. | Off Rte. 51 | 618/734–2737 | Free | Daily.

Horseshoe Lake State Conservation Area. Fifteen miles from Cairo on Route 3, this 645-acre preserve has large stands of tupelo and cottonwood trees, and a shallow lake that covers about 24 acres, where bird lovers come to observe Canada geese and bald eagles. | Rte. 3, Miller City | 618/776–5689 | Free | Daily.

Magnolia Manor. Built in 1869, this 14-room Italianate brick mansion houses much of the original furniture among its many treasures. | 2700 Washington Ave. | 618/734–0201 | $5; special rates for kids | Mon.–Sat 9–5, Sun. 1–5.

ON THE CALENDAR

OCT.: *Riverboat Days.* Held the first weekend of the month, this festival includes ballgames, a parade, and many crafts and food vendors. | 618/734–2737 or 800/248–4373.
DEC.: *Christmas Luminary Stroll.* Lights, decorations, and carolers are on the agenda at this twilight walk through Cairo's decorated historic district one evening in the beginning of the month. | 618/734–2737.

Lodging

Days Inn. On Rural Route 1 near downtown Cairo, this motel is 3 mi from the Custom House Museum, 5 mi from the Mississippi and Ohio rivers and 7 mi from Fort Defiance. Rooms with wheelchair access available. Restaurant, complimentary Continental breakfast. Cable TV. Pool. Pets allowed. | RR 1, 62914 | 618/734–0215 | fax 618/734–1754 | www.daysinn.com | 38 rooms | $32–$60 | AE, D, DC, MC, V.

CARBONDALE

(Nearby towns also listed: Benton, Chester, Du Quoin, Marion, Prairie du Rocher)

Carbondale was the site of the first coal-mining operation in the state of Illinois, opened in 1810. Today the city is known more for being the home of Southern Illinois University. The lush Shawnee National Forest begins not far from town.

Information: Carbondale Convention and Tourism Bureau | 111 S. Illinois Ave., 62901 | 618/529–4451 or 800/526–1500 | www.cctb.org.

Attractions

Alto Vineyards and Winery. This vineyard on Route 127 off Alto Pass produces nationally recognized estate wines. Tours are available on Saturday. | Rte. 127, Alto Pass | 618/893–4898 | Free | Sun.–Fri. 1–5; Sat. 10–5.

Bald Knob. This 111-ft steel and white porcelain cross tops one of the highest hills in Southern Illinois. You can get the best view from Alto Pass, west of Route 127. | 618/893–2344 | Free | Daily.

Giant City State Park. Ten miles south of Carbondale, unusual rock formations looking like the streets of a giant city inspired this state park's name. Here there are horse trails, a nature preserve, and a lodge. | 235 Giant City Rd., Makanda | 618/457–4836 | Free | Daily.

Pomona Winery. This wine-making establishment in the hills of Shawnee National Forest, specializes in dry apple wines, which you can sample in its tasting room. | 2865 Hickory Ridge Rd., Pomona | 618/893–2623 | Free | Mon.–Sat. 10–5, Sun. noon–5.

Shawnee National Forest. You can hike and backpack among five ecological zones in this lush 277,000-acre wilderness, which is 40 mi east of Carbondale, outside of Harrisburg. | 50 Rte. 145 S, Harrisburg | 618/253–7114 or 800/699–6637 | Free | Daily.

Southern Illinois University. With its 22,000 students, SIU, in the southwest side of Carbondale, is the second-largest university in Illinois. Founded in 1869, it now has more than 100 academic programs. | Rt. 51 at Grand Avenue, Carbondale | 618/453–2121 | fax 618/453–3250 | www.siu.edu | Free | Daily.

CHATEAU ILLINOIS

Illinois' wine industry has been growing at a healthy rate in the last 10 years; in fact, the state has formed a grape wine council to encourage production and sale of Illinois vintages.

The state's oldest winery, **Baxter's Vineyard** (217/453–2528), is in Nauvoo, but other wineries have sprung up in various areas of the state. **Lynfred Winery** (630/529–WINE) is in Roselle, about 25 mi west of Chicago, and housed in an opulent Victorian home. **Galena Cellars** (815/777–3330) operates a store in Galena, and the **Seminary Winery** (309/343–2512) has a shop in Galesburg.

But Illinois' true wine country is in southern Illinois where the soil best lends itself to wine grapes. Vineyards such as **Alto Vineyards** (618/893–4898) in Carbondale, **Chateau Ra-Ha Winery** (618/786–3335) in Grafton, and **Pomona Winery** (618/893–2623) in Carbondale, have been producing wines that have won awards and fans from around the state—and around the country.

© Corbis

The **University Museum** is an arts and sciences museum exhibiting fine and decorative arts, geology collections, and world cultural artifacts. | 2469 Faner Hall | 618/453–5388 | www.museum.siu.edu | Free | When school is in session, Tues.–Sat. 9–3, Sun. 1:30–4:30.

ON THE CALENDAR

FEB.: *Orchids, Planes, Trains, and Stamps Show.* The predominant exhibits in this show held the second weekend of the month in the University Mall are of orchids and stamps, but model trains, planes, and cityscapes are also displayed. | 800/526–1500.

Dining

Booby's. Delicatessen. Five blocks from the Southern Illinois University campus, you can get subs and other deli dishes, and order a brew in the beer garden outdoors. | 406 S. Illinois Ave. | 618/549–3366 | $3–$6 | D, MC, V.

Mary Lou's Grill. American. This homey family-owned diner has counter service and a good-size dining room, where you can order midwestern home cooking, such as biscuits and gravy, or try a blue-plate special and a piece of freshly baked pie. | 114 S. Illinois Ave. | 618/457–5084 | Breakfast also available | $5–$7 | MC, V.

Tres Hombres. Mexican. Bright south-of-the-border art in this restaurant adds visual spice to the fajitas, burritos, tacos, and enchiladas, which you can enjoy with one of the many beers from around the world offered here. Entertainment Thursdays. | 119 N. Washington St. | 618/457–3308 | $6–$10 | AE, D, MC, V.

Lodging

Best Inn. This standard motel is close to Giant City State Park and Crab Orchard National Wildlife Refuge and only 3 mi from Southern Illinois University. Complimentary Continental breakfast, cable TV. Pool. Pets allowed. | 1345 E. Main St. | 618/529–4801 | fax 618/529–7212 | www.bestinn.com | 86 rooms | $50–$60 | AE, D, DC, MC, V.

Giant City Lodge. Part of Shawnee National Forest (12 mi south of Carbondale), the sandstone and white timber cottages that make up this lodge, sit on the highest point in the park. The lodge, which is on the National Register of Historic Places, has many of the original oak furnishings in the guest rooms and brass chandeliers in the dining room. Restaurant, bar. Some refrigerators, cable TV. Pool. | 460 Giant City Lodge Rd., Makanda | 618/457–4921 | 34 cottages (4 with suites) | $54–$66; $99 suites | AE, DC, MC, V | Closed mid-Dec.–Jan.

Holiday Inn. You are 2 mi from the Southern Illinois University campus, 3 mi from Crab Lake, and 5 mi from Shawnee National Forest at this motel. Restaurant, complimentary Continental breakfast, room service. In-room data ports, refrigerators, some in-room VCRs, cable TV. Indoor pool. Video games. Laundry facilities, laundry service. Business services, airport shuttle. Some pets. | 800 E. Main St. | 618/529–1100 | fax 618/457–0292 | www.basshotels.com | 95 rooms, 1 suite | $74; $135 suite | AE, D, DC, MC, V.

Super 8. This motel offers standard accommodations just across the way from University Mall and 3 mi from Crab Orchard Lake. Complimentary Continental breakfast. Cable TV. Pets allowed. | 1180 E. Main St. | 618/457–8822 | fax 618/457–4186 | www.super8.com | 63 rooms | $46–$51 | AE, D, DC, MC, V.

CENTRALIA

MAP 6, F9

(Nearby towns also listed: Mt. Vernon, Salem, Vandalia)

The Illinois Central Gulf Railroad gave Centralia its name in the 1850s; the town was a pivotal transportation center after train service started here in 1853. Today its main industries include manufacturing and agriculture. Centralia's population is 18,000.

Information: Greater Centralia Chamber of Commerce and Economic Development | 130 S. Locust St., 62801 | 618/532–6789 | fax 618/533–7305 | www.centraliail.com.

Attractions

Centralia Carillon. You can catch three performances a week of this 65-bell carillon on North Elm at Noleman Street. Tours of the premises are also available. | 114 N. Elm St. | 618/533–4381 | http://members.accessus.net/~carlo | Free | Concerts Wed. and Fri. noon, Sun. 2; tours available.

Fairview Park. This city park has a pool, lighted tennis courts, a softball field, basketball courts, and several picnic areas. There is a 225-ton old steam engine on display in the playground. | W. Broadway at S. Brookdale Ave., Fairview Park Plaza | 618/533–7623 | Free | Daily.

Raccoon Lake. You can enjoy boating and fishing on this 950-acre lake. From the center of town, head east on I-161 East to Country Club Road. Then head north, until you see the boat docks. | Country Club Rd. N | Free | Apr.–Oct., daily.

Dining

Centralia House. Cajun. You can dress casually for rather elegant dining in this 1854 building. Two of the favorites here are the Cajun shrimp and the pepper steak. | 111 N. Oak St. | 618/532–9754 | Closed Sun. | $19–$38 | AE, D, DC, MC, V.

CHAMPAIGN AND
URBANA

INTRO
ATTRACTIONS
DINING
LODGING

CHAMPAIGN AND URBANA

MAP 6, G6

(Nearby towns also listed: Arcola, Bement, Clinton, Danville, Monticello, Rantoul)

The University of Illinois sprawls across these central Illinois twin cities (you cross a street to get from one to the other). While the campus provides plenty of interest in terms of cultural and athletic activities, both cities' downtowns are worth a visit as well. The cities, because of the work done at the university, have also become home to a number of high-tech and computer-based industries. Urbana is the older of the two; it was settled in 1822. Champaign began its existence as West Urbana, but when Urbana tried to annex the town, voters turned down the plan and incorporated as Champaign in 1860.

Information: Champaign-Urbana Convention and Visitors Bureau | 1817 S. Neil St., Suite 201, Champaign 61820 | 217/351–4133 or 800/369–6151 | www.ccchamber.org.

Attractions

Lake of the Woods County Park. This park near Mahomet, 10 mi west of Champaign, encompasses 900 acres. You can wander the sand-bottomed lake in a paddle-boat, lounge on the beach, golf, hike, and visit the Early American museum here. | I-74, exit 174 | 217/586–3360 (park), 217/586–2612 (museum), 217/586–2183 (golf course) | www.ccfpd.org | Free | Daily.

University of Illinois. The 1,400-acre campus of the university spreads into both Champaign and Urbana. Its 36,000-student body makes it the state's largest university, and the school's library houses an impressive 8 million volumes. | 115 Illini Union, 1401 W. Green St., Urbana | 217/333–1000 or 217/333–INFO | www.uiuc.edu | Free | Daily.

   On the Champaign side, the **Krannert Art Museum** exhibits European and Asian art, photography, ceramics, and glassware. | 500 E. Peabody Dr., Champaign | 217/333–1861 | www.art.uiuc.edu/kam | Free | Tues. and Thurs.–Sat. 10–5, Wed. 10–8, Sun. 2–5.

William M. Staerkel Planetarium. Educational astronomy shows are presented at this planetarium. There's also a matinee showing during the summer in addition to regular hours. | 2400 W. Bradley Ave., Champaign | 217/351–2200 | www.parkland.cc.il.us/coned/pla/ | $3 | Fri.–Sat., 7 PM–9:30.

ON THE CALENDAR

JUNE: *Taste of Champaign–Urbana.* Samplings of food served by local restaurants are offered in the West Side Park on Church Street in Champaign at this summer food fair, where arts and crafts are sold as well. | 217/398–2550.

AUG.: *Sweet Corn Festival.* At this summer festival, you can wander Urbana's Main Street, sampling hot buttered sweet corn and other treats from food vendors, while listening to live music. There's also a sidewalk sale of arts and crafts. | 217/384–6304.

Dining

The Great Impasta. Italian. Among the pasta dishes of northern Italy here, lasagna is a favorite, but this eatery is also known for its homemade soups and breads. | 114 W. Church St., Champaign | 217/359–7377 | $10–$15 | AE, D, DC, MC, V.

Kennedy's. Contemporary. Best known for its fresh seafood and game, Kennedy's also serves steak and pasta. Early-bird suppers. | 2560 S. Stone Creek Blvd., Urbana | 217/384–8111 | No lunch Sun. | $17–$33 | AE, D, DC, MC, V.

Ned Kelly's. Contemporary. This informal place serves steak, rotisserie chicken, prime rib, and pasta, and there's a kids' menu. | 1601 N. Cunningham Ave., Urbana | 217/344–8201 | $12–$18 | AE, D, DC, MC, V.

Timpone's. Italian. The pasta, pizza, fish, and game dishes here are Tuscan, and the ornate floors and arches are like those you might see in Florence. | 710 S. Goodwin Ave., Urbana | 217/344–7619 | Closed Sun. No lunch Sat. | $17–$30 | MC, V.

Lodging

Best Western Lincoln Lodge. This small motel in central Urbana is 1 mi from the University of Illinois and 1 block from Crystal Lake Park. Cable TV. Pool. Business services. | 403 W. University Ave., Urbana | 217/367–1111 | fax 217/367–8233 | www.bestwestern.com | 31 rooms | $49–$55 | AE, D, DC, MC, V.

Best Western Paradise Inn. Five miles south of Urbana in Savoy, this motel is 2 mi from Willard Airport. Complimentary breakfast. In-room data ports, cable TV. Pool, wading pool. Playground. Laundry facilities. Business services, airport shuttle. Some pets. | 1001 N. Dunlap Ave., Savoy | 217/356–1824 | www.bestwestern.com | 62 rooms | $44–$70 | AE, D, DC, MC, V.

Clarion Hotel. The property of this large seven-story hotel in Champaign includes a 20,000-square-ft convention center. Restaurant, bar, complimentary Continental breakfast. In-room data ports, some microwaves, cable TV. 2 pools, wading pool. Hot tub. Exercise equipment. Business services, airport shuttle. Pets allowed. | 1501 S. Neil St., Champaign | 217/352–7891 | fax 217/352–8108 | www.clarion.com | 224 rooms | $49–$99 | AE, D, DC, MC, V.

Comfort Inn. These standard accommodations are 3 mi north of the University of Illinois campus. Complimentary Continental breakfast. Some microwaves, some refrigerators, cable TV. Indoor pool. Hot tub. Business services. Some pets allowed. | 305 W. Marketview Dr., Champaign | 217/352–4055, ext. 329 | fax 217/352–4055 | www.hotelchoicece.com | 66 rooms | $59–$79 | AE, D, DC, MC, V.

Courtyard by Marriott. Off of I–74 at the Neil St. North exit, this hotel is 1 mi from shopping and 4 mi from the University of Illinois. Restaurant, bar. In-room data ports, some microwaves, refrigerators, some in-room VCRs, cable TV. Indoor pool. Hot tub. Gym. Laundry facilities, laundry service. Business services. | 1811 Moreland Blvd. | 217/355–0411 | fax 217/355–0411 | 75 rooms, 3 suites | $79–84; $120 suites | AE, D, DC, MC, V.

Eastland Suites. This hostelry in Urbana is a 10-minute drive from the University of Illinois and serves a complimentary breakfast buffet during the week. Bar, complimentary Continental breakfast. Some refrigerators, microwaves, some in-room VCRs, cable TV. Indoor pool. Exercise equipment. Business services, airport shuttle. Pets allowed. | 1907 N. Cunningham Ave., Urbana | 217/367–8331 | fax 217/384–3370 | www.eastlandsuitesurbana.com | 105 rooms, 48 suites | $59–$150; $95–$130 suites | AE, D, DC, MC, V.

Jumer's Castle Lodge. This restored 1924 hotel in downtown Urbana, a mile south of I–74, recalls Old World Bavaria with its German decor, many antiques, and woodwork of cherry and oak. Restaurant, bar, room service. In-room data ports, cable TV. Indoor pool. Hot tub, sauna. Shops. Business services, airport shuttle. Some pets (fee). | 209 S. Broadway, Urbana | 217/384–8800 or 800/285–8637 | fax 217/384–9001 | www.jumers.com | 127 rooms | $82–$143 | AE, D, DC, MC, V.

La Quinta. Across the street from the Market Place mall, which has a food court in the shopping area, this motel is also within 2 mi of more than 20 restaurants and 6 mi from Willard Airport. Complimentary Continental breakfast. In-room data ports, cable TV. Pool. Laundry facilities. Free parking. Some pets allowed. | 1900 Center Dr., Champaign | 217/356–4000 | fax 217/352–7783 | www.laquinta.com | 122 rooms | $59–$62 | AE, D, MC, V.

Hawthorn Suites. This all-suites hotel is near both downtown and the University of Illinois, and 1 block west of the city park. Complimentary Continental breakfast. In-room data ports, microwaves, some refrigerators, some in-room VCRs, cable TV. Indoor pool. Hot tub. Exercise equipment. Laundry facilities. Business services, airport shuttle. | 101 Trade Center Dr., Champaign | 217/398–3400 | fax 217/398–6147 | www.hawthorn.com | 199 suites | $89–$125 | AE, D, DC, MC, V.

Red Roof Inn. Just a mile north of downtown Champaign, this motel is 3 mi from the University of Illinois, and within 2 mi of more than 20 restaurants. Cable TV. Business services. Pets allowed. | 212 W. Anthony Dr., Champaign | 217/352–0101 | fax 217/352–1891 | www.redroof.com | 112 rooms | $29–$51 | AE, D, DC, MC, V.

Quality Hotel. This circular 21-story hotel in the heart of the University of Illinois campus is the area's tallest building. Restaurant, bar, complimentary Continental breakfast. Some refrigerators, cable TV. Hot tub. Airport shuttle. | 302 E. John St., Champaign | 217/384–2100 or 800/322–8282 | fax 217/384–2298 | www.stadiumview.com | 202 rooms | $99 | AE, D, DC, MC, V.

CHARLESTON

MAP 6, H7

(Nearby towns also listed: Arcola, Effingham, Mattoon, Shelbyville)

Abraham Lincoln's father and stepmother lived in the area, and Lincoln practiced law here in the 1840s when he was riding the circuit. Today, the town (population 20,398) is home to Eastern Illinois University and the seat of Coles County.

Information: **Charleston Area Chamber of Commerce** | 501 Jackson Ave. (Box 77), 61920 | 217/345–7041.

Attractions

Coles County Courthouse. Abraham Lincoln practiced law in this courthouse, which dates from 1898, and still functions as the county seat today. | 6th and Monroe Sts. | 217/348–0501 | Free | Daily.

Eastern Illinois University. Eleven thousand students attend EIU, where liberal arts, sciences, and preparation for teaching careers are emphasized. | 600 Lincoln Ave. | 217/581–5000 | www.eiu.edu | Free | Daily.

Fox Ridge State Park. In this park on the Embarras River, 8 mi south of Charleston, you can hike or ride a horse along the 4 miles of trails. There are also cabins to rent on park property. | 18175 State Park Rd. | 217/345–6416 | Free | Daily.

Lincoln Log Cabin State Historic Site. The cabin where Abe Lincoln's father and stepmother lived is in this 86-acre site 7 mi south of Charleston. Costumed interpreters portray life as it was here in 1845, in this site's presentations from Memorial Day through Labor Day. | 400 S. Lincoln Hwy Rd. | 217/345–6489 | www.lincolnlogcabin.org | Free | Daily 8:30–dusk.

Moore Home State Historic Site. This restored 19th-century frame house dates from the mid-1800s, when Abraham Lincoln's family lived in the area. 1 mi north of the Lincoln Log Cabin State Historic Site. | 217/345–6489 | Free | Memorial Day–Labor Day, 9–5.

ON THE CALENDAR
APR.: *Celebration: A Festival of the Arts.* All manner of fine arts can be viewed during this annual spring exhibit held on the Eastern Illinois University campus. | 217/581–7650.
JULY–AUG.: *Coles County Fair.* In summer at the Coles County Fairgrounds you can enjoy agricultural exhibitions at the oldest continuous fair in Illinois. | 217/345–2656.
OCT.: *Harvest Frolic and Trades Fair.* At the Lincoln Log Cabin Historic Site, this harvest festival includes 1845-era crafts and music, a hayride, a barn dance, and all-you-can-eat fried chicken. | 217/345–1845.

Dining
Tapestries. Contemporary. This restaurant in the Best Western Worthington Inn is known for its taco salad, classic burgers, and roast chicken. The restaurant has a kids' menu, and serves Sunday brunch. | 920 W. Lincoln Hwy. | 217/348–8161 | No dinner | $5–$12 | AE, D, DC, MC, V.

Lodging
Best Western Worthington Inn. Convenient to Eastern Illinois University, this motel is also close to Town Square and 8 mi from the Lincoln Log Cabin. Restaurant. Some microwaves, refrigerators, cable TV. Pool. Business services, airport shuttle. Some pets. | 920 W. Lincoln Hwy. | 217/348–8161 | fax 217/348–8165 | www.bestwestern.com | 67 rooms | $56–$116 | AE, D, DC, MC, V.

Days Inn. Just 1½ mi from Eastern Illinois University, this motel is also not far from the Lincoln Log Cabin. Complimentary Continental breakfast. Microwaves, some refrigerators, cable TV. Business services. | 810 W. Lincoln Hwy. | 217/345–7689 | fax 217/345–7697 | www.daysinn.com | 52 rooms | $42–$85 | AE, D, DC, MC, V.

CHESTER

MAP 6, E10

(Nearby towns also listed: Carbondale, Du Quoin, Marion, Prairie du Rocher)

Chester was settled in the 1830s, and one of its first industries was castor oil production. Today, this quiet Mississippi River town of 8,194 is centrally located for river tourism, and boasts a statue of Popeye in a downtown park. Chester is also the burial place of Shadrach Bond, first governor of Illinois.

Information: **Chester Chamber of Commerce** | 217 E. Buena Vista, 62233 | 618/826–2721.

Attractions
Fort Kaskaskia State Historic Site. You can explore the remains of Fort Kaskaskia, built by the French in 1733, as you wander in this 275-acre park, which also has excellent views of the Mississippi River. | 4372 Park Rd., Ellis Grove | 618/859–3741 | Free | Daily.

Pierre Menard Home State Historic Site. Built around 1802, this French Colonial house overlooking the Mississippi River was the home of the first lieutenant governor of Illinois. It is in Ellis Grove north of Chester. | 4230 Kaskaskia Rd., Ellis Grove | 618/859–3031 | Free | Mar.–Oct., daily 9–5; Nov.–Feb., daily 9–4.

Popeye Statue. Next to Chester Bridge in Segar Memorial Park, this statue of Popeye is a monument to Chester native Elzie Segar, who created the famous cartoon character. | 618/826–4567 | Free | Daily.

ON THE CALENDAR
SEPT.: *Popeye Picnic.* This community picnic and carnival, held on Swanick Street, includes an antique-car show, a parade, dancing, and fireworks. | 618/826–2326.

Lodging
Best Western Reids Inn. This standard motel is on partially wooded grounds on Route 150 1 mi from downtown Chester, 2 mi from the Popeye Statue, 2½ mi from the Mississippi river, and 10 mi from Fort Kaskaskia. Complimentary Continental breakfast. In-room data ports, cable TV, some VCRs. Gym. Laundry facilities. Business services. | 2150 State St. | 618/826–3034 | fax 618/826–3034 | www.bestwestern.com | 46 rooms | $49–$80 | AE, D, DC, D, V.

CHICAGO

MAP 6, H2

(Suburbs also listed: Arlington Heights, Brookfield, Downers Grove, Elmhurst, Evanston, Geneva, Glen Ellyn, Glenview, Gurnee, Highland Park, Highwood, Hinsdale, Homewood, Itasca, La Grange, Naperville, Northbrook, Oak Brook, Oak Lawn, Oak Park, St. Charles, Schaumburg, Skokie, Wheaton, Wheeling, Wilmette)

Many images come to mind at the mention of this great city's name. Mrs. O'Leary's cow. The Stockyards. The Second City. The Windy City. The City That Works. The Sears Tower. Al Capone. The Loop. Michael Jordan. Oprah. Some of these images, it's true, have become outdated. The Stockyards are long gone. The Second City title was lost to L.A. in the 1990 census. Historians now seem to be pretty sure that the O'Leary cow didn't knock over any lantern; the Great Fire was likely started by a neighbor. And Michael Jordan—well, Chicagoans have their memories.

But the wide variety of these images illustrates the diversity of Chicago's past as well as its present. It's a city where the stone lions in front of one of the nation's finest art museums wear giant football helmets to celebrate an important Bears victory. And it's a city where knowing a good hot dog stand is as important as reservations at a four-star restaurant.

The French explorers Jolliet and Marquette were the first Europeans to explore the area in 1673. The first permanent settlement wasn't established until 1779, however, when Jean Baptiste Point du Sable started a trading post. Local traders, as well as Native Americans, built a village and named it for checagou, the Native American word for the wild onions that grew along the lakeshore.

The city's fortunes grew in the 1830s and 1840s as railroads and canals connected Lake Michigan with the rest of the state and points east. After the Civil War, the city was booming, thanks to industries like meat-packing, lumber, and shipping. But the city suffered a tremendous loss when, in October 1871, the Great Chicago Fire swept across the city, killing 300 people and destroying 18,000 buildings. Chicagoans took it in stride, quickly rebuilding and improving as they went. The city that rose out of the ashes is known today for its distinctive and innovative architecture, strong business backbone, and cultural institutions (including a world-class symphony, top-flight museums, and an impressive literary heritage). Chicago's lakefront is a big-city wonder—a vast expanse of water fringed with parks and beaches.

Information: **Chicago Convention and Tourism Bureau** | 2301 S. Lake Shore Dr., McCormick Place on the Lake | 312/567–8500 | fax 312/567–8533 | www.chicago.il.org.

NEIGHBORHOODS

The Loop. The city's central business district is so named for the loop of elevated tracks that encircle it. Chicago's financial district is here, as is State Street, the city's original downtown shopping area. A thriving theater district is also becoming established, and the area is experiencing an influx of residential development aimed at professionals who work downtown.

North Michigan Avenue. North Michigan Avenue represents the city's new major shopping area. North of the river is a dizzying choice of upscale national chains, themed entertainment stores, and sophisticated high-rise malls. Michigan Avenue ends at a curve in Lake Shore Drive; above there, the Gold Coast and Near North neighborhoods are filled with exclusive boutiques and upscale restaurants.

Lincoln Park. In addition to being the park that runs along the lakefront, Lincoln Park is also the neighborhood next to it. Long known as a haven for up-and-coming young professionals, it's got tree-lined streets with beautifully restored brownstones as well as bustling commercial strips of trendy shops, eateries, and theaters.

Hyde Park. Five miles south of the Loop, this neighborhood is Chicago's intellectual center, reflecting the proximity of the University of Chicago. The place is an interesting mix: the University's grand Gothic structures and modern research facilities, and the neighborhood's lively commercial areas, and gracious old apartment buildings. The Museum of Science and Industry is on one side of the area, the DuSable Museum of African-American History is on the other.

TRANSPORTATION

Airports: O'Hare International Airport, covering 7,700 acres, has four terminals with 162 aircraft gates and more than 50 airlines that provide domestic and international passenger and cargo services. It's 30 minutes from downtown. | I–190 West | 773/686–2200 | www.ohare.com.

Midway Airport, 10 mi southwest of downtown, has been a port for air traffic since 1923. | 5700 South Cicero St. | 773/838–0600 | www.ohare.com/midway.

Public Transit: The Chicago Transit Authority operates buses, subways, and rapid-transit trains. Fares are $1.50; prepaid transit cards are available at train stations, currency exchanges, selected merchants, and on the Internet. The CTA also offers visitor passes for one, two, three, and five days, available at O'Hare airport, Chicago's visitor information centers, and on the Internet. | CTA Main Offices, Merchandise Mart Plaza, 7th Floor, Box 3555 | 312/664–7200 | www.yourcta.com/.

Metra is the commuter rail system that services the six counties in the Chicago area. | Passenger Services, 312/322–6777; TTY 312/322–6774, evenings and weekends; 312/836–7000, TTY 312/836–4949 | www.metrarail.com.

Rail Passenger Service: Amtrak | Chicago Union Station, 210 S. Canal | 800/USA–RAIL | www.amtrak.com.

WALKING TOURS

The Waterfront (2 mi, about 2 hours)

Chicago's best-known waterfront is the park-lined lakefront; a stroll down the banks of the Chicago River, on the other hand, reveals myriad city structures and landmarks.

Begin on the curving street at the main entrance to ① **Navy Pier.** Bear left, and follow the sidewalk south and west. The area on the left is a sculpture park; beyond that is Ogden Slip—a narrow inlet from the lake. On the right, look straight up at the sinuous lines of Lake Point Tower, the 70-story glass cloverleaf-shaped apartment building. The sidewalk goes to Illinois Street, where you'll cross lower Lake Shore Drive.

Once you've crossed, take a left and walk to the stairs that lead to a walkway next to Ogden Slip. Walk west along North Pier Terminal. This old structure, once a shipping warehouse, is now the shop-filled River East Plaza. At McClurg Court, turn left and head toward the bank of the river, about a block away.

There you'll see the ② **Centennial Fountain and Water Arc.** The fountain is interesting enough; the big surprise is the giant arc of water that shoots up from it across the river. You can watch this for 10 minutes on the hour from May through September.

Walk next to the Sheraton Hotel as you continue west; across the river are the towers of Illinois Center, the hotel and office complex. As you pass under the Columbus Street bridge, turn and note the sculpture on the west side of the bridge; it's ③ **"Chicago Rising From the Lake,"** which once graced a postwar parking garage in the Loop. (When the garage was torn down, the sculpture disappeared; years later, it was found, rescued, and installed on the bridge.)

You'll pass the art deco NBC Tower as well as the University of Chicago's Gleacher Center, the school's downtown business school. A selection of stairways goes up to Michigan Avenue, leading to ④ **Pioneer Court.**

The plaza, between ⑤ **Chicago Tribune Tower** and the Equitable Building, was the original site of the trading post of Jean Baptiste Point du Sable, one of the original settlers of the city. Pause to peer into the broadcast booth of WGN radio on the ground floor of the Tribune Tower, or circle the building to see the collection of stones embedded in the facade.

Head south on the Michigan Avenue bridge; on the opposite side, embedded in the sidewalk, are the outlines of the site of Fort Dearborn. Cross Michigan and follow Wacker along the river to take in a highly eclectic collection of architecture. On the north bank is the white terra-cotta facade of the ⑥ **Wrigley Building,** the Chicago Sun-Times building, the IBM building, and the twin circular towers of ⑦ **Marina City**. On the south side are older skyscrapers such as 333 North Michigan Avenue and 360 North Michigan Avenue, as well as newer structures such as the Leo Burnett and R. R. Donnelley buildings.

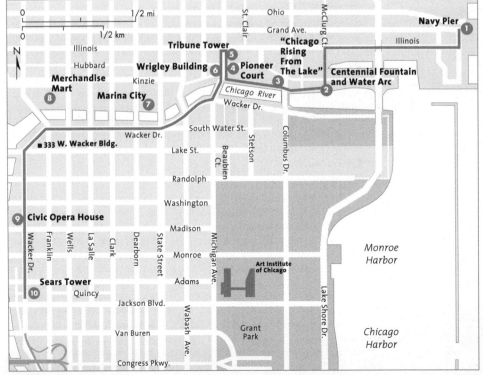

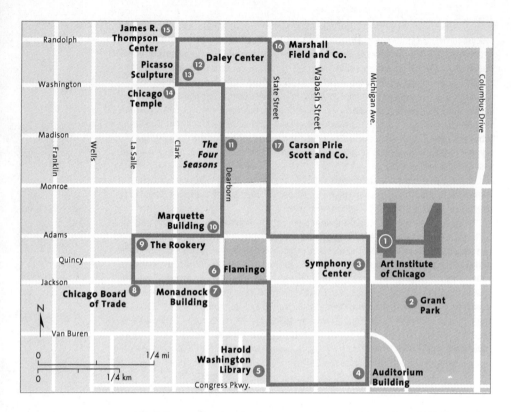

At LaSalle, pause and read a plaque commemorating the sinking of the Eastland—the worst marine disaster in Chicago's history. You can also stop at any time at any of a number of river cafés that line the lower bank of Wacker; just watch for the signs and the stairs.

At the curve of the river is the 333 West Wacker Building, whose form imitates the river's direction; on the opposite bank is the massive ⑧ **Merchandise Mart.** Before heading south on Wacker, look out over the river's wide Turning Basin, where the north and south branches of the river meet.

As you proceed south on Wacker, you'll pass by the ⑨ **Civic Opera House,** before finishing up the last few blocks of the walk where you'll find yourself at the base of the ⑩ **Sears Tower.**

Loop the Loop (3–4 hours)

Start at the ① **Art Institute** at Michigan and Adams. Take a left and walk south; on the left is ② **Grant Park;** on the right is ③ **Symphony Center,** home of the Chicago Symphony Orchestra. Farther along on Michigan is the ④ **Auditorium Building,** a National Historic Landmark. A turn right on Congress leads down to the ⑤ **Harold Washington Library,** the city's main library named for the former mayor. Turn north at State past two former department stores—the old Sears Roebuck flagship at 401 South State and the Goldblatt's store at 333 South State—which have been turned into retail, office, and educational facilities. At Jackson, go left and walk down a block to Dearborn. Just to the north on Dearborn is Federal Center Plaza, in which stands ⑥ **Flamingo,** Alexander Calder's bright red stabile. On the south side of Jackson is the ⑦ **Monadnock Building,** a famous 1891 skyscraper.

Farther west on Jackson, at the foot of LaSalle, is the ⑧ **Chicago Board of Trade,** interesting from close up, but even more impressive, in a big-picture way, from a vantage point farther down LaSalle—perhaps from in front of the ⑨ **Rookery,** another landmark skyscraper. The lobby, designed by Frank Lloyd Wright, is especially worth a stop. Turn right onto Adams; down two blocks at Dearborn is the ⑩ **Marquette Building,** another 19th-century skyscraper, whose mezzanine balcony is graced with Tiffany mosaics. A left turn onto Dearborn leads to First National Bank Plaza, two blocks up; in the southeast corner of the plaza is Marc Chagall's mosaic sculpture ⑪ ***The Four Seasons.*** Proceed another block up Dearborn to Madison and take a left. Up one block is the ⑫ **Daley Center,** with the enigmatic untitled ⑬ **Picasso sculpture** in the plaza out front, and the 21-story ⑭ **Chicago Temple** at 77 West Washington. Continue north on Clark past the County Building and City Hall to the gigantic glass ⑮ **James R. Thompson Center,** the Helmut Jahn–designed glass cylinder also known as the State of Illinois Center.

On the next block east on Randolph, at the corner of Dearborn, the Goodman Theater is developing a new complex, incorporating the facades of two old movie theaters on Dearborn. Farther east on West Randolph, at No. 36, is the Delaware Building, the oldest building in the Loop, built just after the Chicago Fire in 1871. Also in that block is the **Ford Center for the Performing Arts,** once the Oriental movie theater. On the south side of Randolph is Block 37, a rare piece of undeveloped Loop property that's used as a skating rink in winter and as Gallery 37—an arts training center for youth—in summer. Look a block north on State to see the facade of the venerable **Chicago Theatre.**

A right turn onto State leads you past two giants of Chicago commerce. The distinction of the streetfront of ⑯ **Marshall Field's** is its famous clock, on the corner of State and Randolph. The facade of ⑰ **Carson Pirie Scott and Co.,** an amazing Louis Sullivan building, is wonderfully rich and intricate. Proceed another block to Adams, past the Palmer House Hotel, and go east—under the elevated tracks at Wabash—back to the Art Institute.

Attractions

ART AND ARCHITECTURE

Amoco Building. Originally clad in marble from the same quarry Michelangelo used, this shaftlike 80-story building had to be re-clad in its pale granite because the thin slabs of marble, unable to withstand Chicago's harsh climate, warped and fell off soon after the building's completion. | 200 E. Randolph St. | 312/856–6111 | Free | Daily.

Untitled Sounding Sculpture. This steel alloy sculpture in the plaza outside of the Amoco Building, was created by Harry Bertoia to create musical sounds when touched or brushed by the wind. | 200 E. Randolph St. | Free | Daily.

Auditorium Building. The former home of the Chicago Symphony Orchestra, this landmark designed by the firm of Sullivan and Adler in 1887, reflects the "form over function" ideals of the "Chicago School" of architecture. The theater has been dark for a while, but you can still view the beautifully mosaiced interior. | 430 S. Michigan Ave. | 312/341–3500 | Free | Daily.

Batcolumn. This 100-ft-tall welded-steel baseball bat by sculptor Claes Oldenburg is outside the Harold Washington Social Security Administration Building plaza, in the Loop. | 600 W. Madison St. | 312/744–7487 | Free | Daily.

Biograph Theatre. This theater on the National Register of Historic Places is where gangster John Dillinger met his end at the hands of the FBI in July, 1934. It is now a multiplex that shows first-run films. Its history, however, is still flaunted by such things as the female mannequin in 1930s-style dress sitting in the ticket booth with a copy of the edition of the Chicago Daily News that bears the headline: "Girl Tricks Dillinger," and reminders of the film playing when it happened, *Manhattan Melodrama.* | 2433 N. Lincoln Ave. | 773/348–4123.

Chicago Board of Trade. Watch the traders in action from viewing galleries overlooking the trading floor. On Jackson Boulevard at LaSalle Street in the Loop, the art-deco tower is as interesting on the outside as it is inside. There's a center for visitors, as well as self-guided tours and information on this and the other exchanges. | 141 W. Jackson Blvd. | 312/435–3590 | Free | Weekdays 8–2.

Chicago Cultural Center. This former home of the Chicago Public Library, with Tiffany glass domes and mosaics, now houses a visitor information center and offers over 600 free concerts, performances and art exhibits a year. | 78 E. Washington St. | 312/744–6630; 312/FINE ART (performances) | www.cityofchicago.org/culturalaffairs/ | Free | Mon.–Wed. 10–7, Thurs. 10–9, Fri. 10–6, Sat. 10–5, Sun. 11–5.

Museum of Broadcast Communications. Home of the Radio Hall of Fame, this museum also contains television and radio archives as well as vintage radios and TVs. | 312/629–6000 | www.mbcnet.org | Free | Mon.–Sat. 10–4:30, Sun. noon–5.

Chicago Mercantile Exchange. You can observe the financial futures exchange from the visitors' galleries overlooking the action here. | 30 S. Wacker Dr. | 312/930–8249 | Free | Weekdays 7:15–2 upper gallery, 8–3:15 lower gallery 8–3:15; group tours arranged in advance.

Chicago Public Library–Harold Washington Library Center. The city's main public library has 10 floors in a total of 756,000 sq ft. It has over 70 mi of shelving, an auditorium, and classrooms. The library also houses a special collection detailing the life and accomplishments of Harold Washington and hosts changing exhibits and cultural programs. | 400 S. State St. | 312/747–4300 | Free | Sun. 1–5, Mon. 9–7; Tues., Thurs. 11–7; Wed., Fri., Sat. 9–5.

***Chicago Tribune* Tower.** This elaborate 36-story Gothic tower on North Michigan is home to the *Chicago Tribune* as well as WGN radio; you can view live broadcasts through a window on the southwest corner. The building's design is a result of an international competition held in 1922 by Tribune co-editors Robert McCormick and Joseph Patterson. McCormick had builders include stones at street level from historical structures around the world, including the Taj Mahal, Westminster Abbey, the Great Wall of China, the Parthenon, and the Alamo. | 435 N. Michigan Ave. | 312/222–3994 | www.tribune.com | Free | Daily.

Fine Arts Building. Built in 1895 to house showrooms for carriages made by the Studebaker Company, this structure later became working studios and offices for publishers, painters, and sculptors, and is today occupied principally by professional musicians and those who cater to musicians' needs. Carved in the marble of the building's ornate lobby is the motto "All Passes–Art alone endures," and the ground floor, converted in 1982 to a four-screen cinema but retaining much of the original ornamentation, now houses the Fine Arts Theatre, which presents avante-garde and foreign films, and works by independent directors. | 410 S. Michigan Ave. | 312/ 939–3380 | Free | Daily.

Flamingo. This 53-foot tall red-colored steel stabile sculpture by Alexander Calder is on Federal Center Plaza. | Adams and Dearborn Sts. | Free | Daily.

The Four Seasons. Designed by forerunner of surrealism Marc Chagall, this 3,000-square-ft, 5-sided mosaic composed of thousands of tiles, depicts the changing seasons in Chicago. It was installed in the southeast corner of First National Plaza in 1974. | Monroe and Dearborn Sts. | Free | Daily.

Jane Addams' Hull House. This home, a center for social reform in the first half of the 20th century, established by Nobel Peace Prize–winning social worker Jane Addams to serve the neighborhood poor, is on the west side of the University of Illinois at Chicago campus, where you can see much of the house's original furnishings and learn its history. | 800 S. Halsted St. | 312/413–5353 | www.uic.edu/jaddams/hull/hullhouse.html | Free | Weekdays 10–4, Sun. noon–5.

Louis Sullivan Row Houses. These houses, designed by this famous architect and built in 1885, have in them elements of the geometric ornamentation for which Sullivan would eventually become known, particularly the terra-cotta cornices and decorative window tops. | 1826–1834 N. Lincoln Park W | 312/744–2400 | Free | Daily.

Marina City. Referred to locally as the "corn cobs," these two round futuristic-looking towers, designed by Bertram Goldberg and completed in 1967, house condominiums and restaurants. | 300 N. State St. | 312/661–0046 | Free | Daily.

Miró's *Chicago*. In the plaza outside of the Brunswick Building, you can see surrealist Joan Miró's 39-foot-tall steel, wire mesh, bronze, and ceramic-tile sculpture, installed in 1981. | 69 W. Washington St. | Free | Daily.

Monadnock Building. This building designed by Daniel Burnham and John Root and completed in 1891, is considered a sterling example of the Chicago school of architecture, and arguably the nation's first skyscraper. | 53 W. Jackson Blvd. | 312/922–1890 | Free | Daily.

Nuclear Energy. Said to represent both a human skull and an atomic mushroom cloud, this 12-ft bronze sculpture by Henry Moore marks the spot where Enrico Fermi and other physicists set off the first controlled nuclear chain reaction on December 2, 1942, under the bleachers of what was then Stagg Field. | East side of Ellis Ave. between 56th and 57th streets | Free | Daily.

Richard J. Daley Center and Plaza. City and county courts and administrative offices are housed in this bustling plaza at Randolph and Clark streets. | Randolph and Clark Sts. | 312/443–5500 | Free | Daily.

Untitled. You can marvel over Pablo Picasso's mysterious, nameless 50-ft steel sculpture in the court in front of the Richard J. Daley Plaza. | Washington and Dearborn Sts. | 312/443–5500 | Free | Daily.

Robie House. You can tour this famous Frank Lloyd Wright–designed house, considered to be one of the finest examples of Prairie School architecture. | 5757 S. Woodlawn Ave. | 773/834–1847 | www.robiehouse.com | $8; special rates for students, senior citizens, and kids | House tours weekdays 11, 1, 3; weekends every half hour 11–3:30. Bookstore daily 10–5.

The Rookery. Designed by Daniel Burnham and John Root, and built in 1886, the oldest steel-skeleton skyscraper in the world also boasts a lobby court designed by Frank Lloyd Wright. | 209 S. LaSalle St. | 312/553–6150 | Free | Daily.

Union Station. This grand train station, completed in 1925, is graced with gilded statues and Corinthian columns and a 10-story waiting room crowned by skylights. The steep steps leading into it from Canal Street were the scene for a runaway baby-carriage caught in a shoot-out in director Brian De Palma's 1987 film, *The Untouchables*. | 210 S. Canal St. | 312/655–2231 | Free | Daily.

Water Tower. Fortunately, the devastating Chicago fire of 1871 did not destroy this Gothic Revival structure, which now houses the Chicago Office of Tourism Visitor Information Center, in Near North Side. | 806 N. Michigan Ave. | 312/744–2400 | Free | Daily 7:30–7.

Wrigley Building. This white terra-cotta tower in Near North Side, was modeled on the Giralda of the Cathedral in Seville, Spain. It is particularly dramatic at night, when it is brightly illuminated for the effect. | 400 N. Michigan Ave. | 312/644–2121 | Free | Daily.

CULTURE, EDUCATION, AND HISTORY

The Apollo Theater. This Lincoln Park theater presents prestigious productions of plays by such authors and performers as David Mamet and the Steppenwolf Theatre Company | 2540 N. Lincoln Ave. | 773/935–6100 | www.apollochicago.com | Mon.–Tues. 10–6, Wed.–Sat. 10–8:15, Sun. noon–7:15.

Arie Crown Theater. This enormous theater seats 4,249, and stretches along McCormick Place from East 23rd Street to South Lake Shore Drive. It hosts everything from pop concerts to large-scale lectures and presentations. | 2301 S. Lake Shore Dr. | 312/791–6000 | www.mccormickplace.com/arie.html | Mon.–Sat. 10–6, call for Sun. hours.

Auditorium Theater. An 1889 landmark, this theater is the crowning achievement of famed architects Louis Sullivan and Dankmar Adler, and has exquisite acoustics making it an especially popular stage for musicals and ballet. | 50 E. Congress Pkwy. | 312/902–1500 | fax 312/431–2360 | www.auditoriumtheatre.org | Call for showtimes and prices.

Briar Street Theatre. You can see plays and revues at this North Side theater. | 3133 N. Halsted St. | 773/348–4000.

Chicago Theatre. This Beaux-Arts 1921 movie theater was renovated in 1986 and now hosts musicals and concerts. | 175 N. State St. | 312/443–1130 | www.artswire.org/~studio/chicago/.

Civic Opera House. The Lyric Opera of Chicago performs at this cavernous opera house, which is a blend of art deco and art nouveau styles. The space is dominated by gilt cornices, Austrian crystal chandeliers, and elaborately stenciled ceilings. | 20 N. Wacker Dr. | 312/372–7800; performance schedules 312/332–2244 | Prices vary with shows | Daily 7–7.

Court Theatre. Designed in 1981 by Harry Weese and Associates, there are unobstructed views of the stage from every seat in the house at this intimate theater, and its own theater company is considered one of the city's finest. | 5535 S. Ellis Ave. | 773/753–4472 | www.courttheatre.org | $24–$38 | Sept.–June; call for performance schedule.

DePaul University. Two urban campuses, one in Near North Side and one in the Loop, offer some 130 degree programs to 18,000 students. | 1 E. Jackson Blvd. | 312/362–8300 | www.depaul.edu | Free | Daily.

The Ford Center for the Performing Arts. Formerly a movie theater, this is now one of the newest theaters on the Loop's performing arts scene with big name musicals and plays. | 24 W. Randolph St. | 312/855–9400.

The Goodman Theater. One of Chicago's theatrical institutions, tucked behind the Art Institute, this space includes a main stage and studio theaters. | 200 S. Columbus Dr. | 312/443–3800 | www.goodman-theatre.org.

Illinois Institute of Technology. IIT is known particularly for its engineering and architecture programs and its renowned Institute of Design. The main campus was designed by Ludwig Mies van der Rohe. | 3300 S. Federal St. | 312/567–3000 | www.iit.edu | Free | Daily.

Loyola University Chicago. Two city campuses—Water Tower in Near North Side and Lake Shore in Rogers Park—provide 144 programs including liberal arts, law, business, criminal justice, and social work to 13,359 students. | 820 N. Michigan Ave. (Water Tower campus); 6525 N. Sheridan Rd. (Lake Shore campus) | 312/915–6000 | www.luc.edu | Free | Daily.

The Mayfair. This venue is home to the hilarious audience-participation whodunit *Shear Madness*, which has been running since 1982. | 636 S. Michigan Ave. | 312/786–9120.

Music Box Theater. The ceiling in this restored 1920s movie house is painted to resemble the sky, bearing lights that twinkle like stars; and the lavish interior is a tribute to a grand era for film, now past—you can even catch a pipe organ performance before the features on weekends, which are now primarily art and revival films. Definitely a movie-going experience not easily forgotten. | 3733 N. Southport Ave. | 773/871–6604 | $8 | Daily.

The Newberry Library. Named for Walter Loomis Newberry, a businessman and prominent citizen, who had been an active book collector, and president of the Chicago Historical Society before his death in 1868, this library's extensive scholarly collection includes an especially impressive history division. | 60 W. Walton St. | 312/255–3510 | www.newberry.org | Free | Tues.–Thurs. 10–6, Fri.–Sat. 9–5.

Northwestern University Chicago Campus. While the main campus of NUC is in Evanston, the university's medical and law school campuses are here in Chicago's Near North Side. | Lake Shore Dr. and Chicago Ave. | 312/503–8649, Chicago campus; 847/491–3741, Evanston campus | www.nwu.edu | Free | Daily.

Petrillo Music Shell. This band shell in Grant Park was commissioned in 1931 by Mayor A.J. Cermak to lift the spirits of Chicagoans in the wake of the Great Depression. Free summer concerts draw big-name talent and large crowds (the shell can accommodate 3,800). | E. Jackson Blvd. and S. Columbus Dr. | 312/294–2420 | Free.

Prairie Avenue Historic District. In this South Side neighborhood on Prairie Avenue, you can tour two of Chicago's earliest residences: the Clarke House, which is Chicago's oldest, and the Richardson Romanesque Glessner House. | 1800 S. Prairie Ave. | 312/326–1480 | www.glessnerhouse.org | $11 (both houses), $7 (one house) | Wed.–Sun.; tours at noon, 1, 2, 3.

Roosevelt University. In the Auditorium Building, Roosevelt offers degree programs in arts and sciences, music, and business administration. | 430 S. Michigan Ave. | 312/341–3500 | www.roosevelt.edu | Free | Daily.

The Royal George. Musicals and traveling shows are often on the bill at this Near North theater. | 1641 N. Halsted Ave. | 312/988–9000.

The Second City. Home to Chicago's famed improvisational troupe, Second City also houses the smaller Second City Etc. theater. | 1616 N. Wells St. | 312/337–3992 | www.secondcity.com.

The Shubert. This Loop performance space typically hosts touring plays and musicals. | 22 W. Monroe St. | 312/902–1500.

Steppenwolf. Chicago's acclaimed theater company of the same name, whose members have made waves on the national theater scene, as well as in television and movies, performs here. | 1650 N. Halsted St. | 312/335–1650 | www.steppenwolf.org.

Symphony Center. The home of the Chicago Symphony Orchestra boasts a refurbished Orchestra Hall as well as a restaurant, an atrium, and a new performance/rehearsal space. | 220 S. Michigan Ave. | 312/294–3333 | fax 312/294–3329 | www.cso.org | Prices vary with shows | Mon.–Sat. 10–6, Sun. 11–4.

Theatre Building. This North Side venue hosts productions by a number of the city's smaller companies. | 1225 W. Belmont Ave. | 773/327–5252.

The Victory Gardens. Dramatic and new works are performed at this North Side theater. | 2257 N. Lincoln Ave. | 773/871–3000.

University of Chicago. The Gothic structures of this 203-acre South Side campus, cluster around Midway Plaisance, a parkway created for the 1893 Columbian Exposition. Founded by John D. Rockefeller, the university is known for its academic excellence and faculty Nobel laureates, serving a student body of 12,300. | 5801 S. Ellis Ave. | 773/702–1234; 773/702–9739 (visitors center) | www.uchicago.edu | Free | Daily.

University of Illinois at Chicago. The modern campus of U of I's urban branch includes the 9,500-seat UIC Pavilion, used for athletic and entertainment events. | Taylor St. and Ashland Ave. | 312/996–7000 | www.uic.edu | Free | Daily.

MUSEUMS

★ **The Art Institute of Chicago.** This world-class art museum includes among its holdings an impressionist collection, contemporary paintings, and Asian art. | 111 S. Michigan Ave. | 312/443–3600 | www.artic.edu | $8 | Mon., Wed.–Fri. 10:30–4:30, Tues. 10:30–8, weekends 10–5.

Balzekas Museum of Lithuanian Culture. Exhibits of textiles and costumes, photo archives, and genealogy resources here represent Lithuanian culture. | 6500 S. Pulaski Rd. | 773/582–6500 | fax 773/582–5133 | $4; special rates for students, senior citizens, and kids | Daily 10–4.

Chicago Children's Museum. Hands-on exhibits encourage exploration and education at this interactive museum for kids. | Navy Pier, 700 E. Grand Ave. | 312/527–1000 | www.chichildrensmuseum.org | $6.50; special rates for senior citizens and kids | Tues.–Sun. 10–5, Thurs. 5 PM–8 PM.

Chicago Historical Society. The city's development is chronicled through dioramas and other exhibits here. | 1601 N. Clark St. | 312/642–4600 | www.chicagohistory.org | $5; special rates for senior citizens and kids | Mon.–Sat 9:30–4:30, Sun. noon–5.

David and Alfred Smart Museum of Art. Founded in 1974 through a gift from the Smart Family Foundation, whose members David and Alfred started *Esquire* magazine, this is the

University of Chicago's fine-arts museum, in which the diverse 8,000-piece permanent collection includes works by old masters; photographs by Walker Evans; furniture by Frank Lloyd Wright; sculptures by Degas, Matisse, Rodin, and Henry Moore; ancient Chinese bronzes; and modern Japanese ceramics. A sculpture garden is adjacent. | 5550 Greenwood Ave. | 773/702–0200 | Free | Tues., Wed., Fri. 10–4; Thurs 10–9; weekends noon–6.

DuSable Museum of African-American History. African and African–American history, art, and artifacts are exhibited at the DuSable. | 740 E. 56th Pl. | 773/947–0600 | www.dusable-museum.org | $3; special rates for senior citizens and students | Mon.–Sat. 10–5, Sun. noon–5.

Field Museum. This natural-history museum has an extensive collection, including Sue, the largest and most complete Tyrannosaurus rex skeleton on exhibit. | 1400 Lake Shore Dr. | 312/922–9410 | www.fmnh.org | $8; special rates for students, senior citizens, and kids; free Wed. | Daily 9–5.

Mexican Fine Arts Center Museum. Paintings, folk art, and contemporary art representing the culture of Mexico are displayed here; workshops are offered, as well. | 1852 W. 19th St. | 312/738–1503 | www.mfacmchicago.org | Free | Tues.–Sun. 10–5.

Museum of Contemporary Art. In addition to its revolving exhibits of the works of contemporary painters, sculptors, and other visual artists, this museum offers films, lectures, and performing arts. | 220 E. Chicago Ave. | 312/280–2660 or 312/280–5161 | www.mcachicago.org | $8; special rates for students, senior citizens, and kids; free Tues. | Tues. 10–8, Wed.–Sun. 10–5.

Museum of Holography/Chicago. Among the more than 200 depictions included in the still and animated holograms here are scenes from medicine and sports. | 1134 W. Washington Blvd. | 312/226–1007 | $3; special rates for kids | Wed.–Sun. 12:30–5.

Museum of Science and Industry. This is the largest science museum in a single building in the Western hemisphere, and it includes a coal mine replica, an Omnimax theater, and a submarine tour. | 57th St. at Lake Shore Dr. | 773/684–1414; 800/IGOTOMSI; TDD 773/684–3323 | www.msichicago.org | $7; special rates for senior citizens and kids; additional fee for the theater | Weekdays 9:30–4, weekends 9:30–5:30.

Oriental Institute Museum. This museum's holdings include archaeological materials from the ancient Near East and Egypt. | 1155 E. 58th St. | 773/702–9514 | Free | Call for hours.

Peace Museum. Exhibits here focus on peace and the people who work for it throughout the world. | 314 W. Institute Pl. | 312/440–1860 | $3.50; special rates for senior citizens, students, and kids | Tues.–Sat. 11–5.

Peggy Notebaert Nature Museum. This structure's great expanses of glass and many open-air terraces bring into its spaces the natural landscape of the surrounding park and nearby pond. Inside are exhibits where you can walk among hundreds of Midwest species of butterflies, explore environmental forces in the wilderness, uncover critters that inhabit all urban homes, and educate yourself about the impact of rivers and lakes on your daily life. The Children's Gallery focuses on teaching three- to eight-year-olds about the environment. | 2060 N. Clark St. | 773/871–2668 | $6, free Tues. | Thurs.–Tues. 10–5, Wed. 10–8.

Polish Museum of America. These galleries exhibit folk costumes, artifacts, and military memorabilia from Poland, and there's also a library and archives. | 984 N. Milwaukee Ave. | 773/384–3352 | $3 (suggested); special rates for senior citizens and kids | Daily 11–4; call for library and archive hours.

Spertus Museum. An extensive collection of Jewish art and cultural artifacts is housed here, as well as a library devoted to Jewish history. | 618 S. Michigan Ave. | 312/922–9012 or TTY 312/922–4950 | fax 312/922–6406 | www.spertus.edu | $5; special rates for students, senior citizens, and families; free Fri. | Sun.–Wed. 10–5, Thurs. 10–8, Fri. 10–3.

Swedish American Museum Center. This museum has movingly intimate permanent exhibits of such things as the personal items—trunks and clothing and toiletries—that Swedish immigrants brought to Chicago, as well as rotating exhibits representing the art and culture of Sweden. | 5211 N. Clark St. | 773/728–8111 | $4 | Tues.–Fri. 10–4, Weekends 10–3.

Terra Museum of American Art. American art of the 18th through 20th centuries is exhibited here. | 664 N. Michigan Ave. | 312/664–3939 | $7 (suggested); special rates for senior citizens and children; free Tues. | Tues. 10–8, Wed.–Sat. 10–6; Sun. noon–5.

Ukrainian National Museum. The culture and artistry of the people from the Ukraine are represented here in exhibits of such things as intricately painted Easter eggs, elaborate wood carvings, and other traditional folk objects. | 721 N. Oakley St. | 312/421–8020 | $2 | Thurs.–Sun. 11–4.

PARKS, NATURAL AREAS, AND OUTDOOR RECREATION
Garfield Park and Conservatory. These outdoor gardens, in Chicago's West Side, showcase plants from different parts of the world, grouped by type. The Conservatory hosts five flower shows a year. | 300 N. Central Park Blvd. | 312/746–5100 | Free | Daily 9–5.

Graceland Cemetery. The more than 100 acres of landscaped lawn here is the final resting place for many famous entrepreneurs, such as Marshall Field, George Pullman, and Potter Palmer, as well as greats in architecture, such as Louis Sullivan, John Wellborn Root, Daniel Burnham, and Ludwig Mies van der Rohe. One of the most outstanding of the cemetery's diverse monuments is the Getty Tomb, designed by Louis Sullivan in 1890. Maps available at the entrance. | 4001 N. Clark St. | 773/525–1105 | Free | Daily 8–4:30.

Grant Park. This lakefront downtown park is where many of the city's major festivals are held, including Taste of Chicago, the city's 4th of July celebration, and music events such as the blues, the jazz, and the gospel festivals. It's also home to the Petrillo Music Shell, where concerts of both classical and popular music are performed, and the Buckingham Fountain. The park is a favorite spot for biking, skating, and strolling, while taking in a spectacular view of the lake. | 331 E. Randolph St. | Free | 312/747–6820 | Daily.
Buckingham Fountain. Designed and built in 1926 by Bennett, Parsons, and Frost of Chicago and Jacques Lambert of Paris, it is modeled after a fountain at Versailles. Evening light shows from May to October draw Chicagoans and visitors alike. | Free | Daily.

★ **Lincoln Park.** This is where Chicago comes to play: volleyball on North Avenue Beach, golf on the Waveland course, and soccer with a neighborhood league off Wilson Avenue. The park stretches along Chicago's North Side lakefront, where you can stroll, bicycle, jog, and picnic. | 2400 N. Stockton Dr. | 312/742–7726 | Free | Daily.
Lincoln Park Conservatory. In the four display buildings here, you can see hundreds of plant species, from Indonesian banana trees to Mexican ficus, and reflective pools fed by trickling fountains. The Conservatory also has seasonal exhibits such as the fall Chrysanthemum Show, the poinsettia-rich Winter Show, and the February Azalea Show. | Fullerton Ave. and Stockton Dr. | 312/742–7736 | Free | Daily 9–5.

★ **Lincoln Park Zoological Gardens.** You can see more than a thousand rare, exotic, and familiar animals here in such exhibits as the great-ape house, the penguin enclosure, and the "farm in the zoo." | 2200 N. Cannon Dr. | 312/742–2000 | Free; parking $7 | Open weekdays 8–6, weekends and holidays 8–7.

Shakespeare Garden. A bronze statue of the great playwright, cast by William Ordway Partridge in 1894, is installed in this garden in the northeast quadrant of Northwestern University, where species of flowers and other plants mentioned in the famous bard's works are cultivated and you are welcome to wander. | Belden Ave. at Lincoln Park W | Free | Daily.

RELIGION AND SPIRITUALITY
Chicago Loop Synagogue. An outstanding feature in this synagogue is its expansive wallful of modern stained-glass windows. | 16 S. Clark St. | 312/346–7370 | Free | Mon.–Thurs. 9–4:30, Fri. 9–2.

Chicago Temple. Built in 1923, this 21-story Methodist church is 550 ft high and has an eight-story spire. | 77 W. Washington St. | 312/236–4548 | Free | Sanctuary 7–6; sky chapel tours Mon.–Sat. 2, Sun. following services.

Fourth Presbyterian Church. Its Gothic architecture and stained-glass windows are this 1912 church's highlights, and you can stroll in its peaceful courtyard just off Michigan Avenue. | 126 E. Chestnut St. | 312/787–4570 | Free | Daily 9–5.

Holy Name Cathedral. This cathedral built in 1875 for the Archdiocese of Chicago has retained its Gothic appearance despite several renovations. Note the massive 1,200-pound bronze doors. | 735 N. State St. | 312/787–8040 | www.holynamecathedral.org | Free | Daily.

Old St. Patrick's Church. Chicago's oldest church, started in 1852 and completed in 1856, survived the devastating fire of 1871. Its two towers—one Romanesque and one Byzantine, symbolizing the West and the East—and the church's statue of Jesus can be seen from Kennedy Expressway, if you don't drive by too quickly. Exit at Monroe Street, head east one block, and turn right onto Des Plains Street. | 700 W. Adams St. | 312/648–1021 | Free | Daily.

Our Lady of Sorrows Basilica. Built in 1874, this church's interior and exterior are beautifully detailed, including its windows, altars, and paintings. Tours by arrangement. | 3121 W. Jackson Blvd. | 773/638–5800 | Free | Daily.

Rockefeller Memorial Chapel. Its Gothic design and 72-bell carillon make this chapel a standout. | 5850 S. Woodlawn Ave. | 773/702–8374 | Free | Daily 8–4.

SHOPPING

Carson Pirie Scott. This popular Loop department store sports a Louis Sullivan–designed facade. | State and Madison Sts. | 312/641–4000 | Free | Mon.–Sat; sometimes Sun.

Marshall Field's. Folks often visit this major downtown department store solely for its famously yummy Frango mints, at the 1st floor and lower level candy counters. | 111 N. State St. | 312/781–4882 | Free | Daily.

Merchandise Mart. In the largest commercial building in the world, you can lose yourself in the many shops and restaurants on the public floors. | Wells St. | 312/527–7600 | Free | Daily.

Michigan Avenue. Michigan Avenue, including its northernmost stretch called the Magnificent Mile, is one of the most famous shopping streets in America, full of upscale shops and chain department stores, such as Neiman Marcus, Marshall Field's, and Saks Fifth Avenue, where at Christmastime the store windows rival those of their New York City cousins.
900 N. Michigan Shops. This upscale mall has not only shops but many restaurants and theaters. | 900 N. Michigan Ave. | 312/915–3916 | Free | Daily.
Chicago Place. In this high-rise shopping mall, there is a food court and grocery stores. | 700 N. Michigan Ave. | 312/642–4811 | Free | Daily.
Neiman Marcus. Prices are high at this Dallas-headquartered chain, but there'a huge selection of designer clothing and a gourmet food section with lots of difficult-to-find goodies. | 737 N. Michigan Ave. | 312/642–5900 | Free | Daily.
Nike Town. You can compare running shoes to cross-trainers, watch sports videos, and ogle the athletic memorabilia at this popular tourist attraction disguised as a store. | 669 N. Michigan Ave. | 312/642–6363 | Free | Daily.

Water Tower Place. This eight-story shopping mall includes restaurants and theaters, a Saks Fifth Avenue and a Marshall Field's. | 835 N. Michigan Ave. | 312/440–3165 | Free | Daily.

Oak Street. This few-block stretch of upscale boutiques may have expensive merchandise, but there's plenty of activity here, including heavy tourist traffic. | Oak St. and N. Michigan Ave. | Free | Daily.

State Street. A massive late-20th-century overhaul of the streets and sidewalks in this neighborhood makes for pleasant trekking among the theaters, specialty shops, and bargain stores, including famous Filene's Basement (312/553–1055). | State Street in the Loop | 312/35–STATE | Free | Daily.

SPECTATOR SPORTS

Balmoral Park Race Track. You can try your luck on harness racing at this track, 25 mi south of Chicago. | 26435 S. Dixie Hwy. | 708/672–7544 | www.balmoralpark.com | $2 | Sun.-Wed., 11–11; Thurs. 11AM–12AM; Fri.-Sat., 11AM–1AM.

Hawthorn Race Course. In Stickney, 9 mi west of Chicago, you can bet on thoroughbreds. | 35th St. (at Laramie Ave.), Stickney | 708/780–3700 | www.hawthornracecourse.com | $3 | Oct.–Dec., Wed.–Sun. 1–5:30.

Maywood Park Race Track. Harness racing is the specialty at this track in the town of Maywood, 12.4 mi west of Chicago. | 8600 W. North Ave., Maywood | 708/343–4800 | $2 | Mon., Wed., Fri. 7:40 PM.

Sportsman's Park Race Track. Six miles west of Chicago, Cicero has thoroughbred racing and an autotrack, offering championship team auto-racing events. | 3301 S. Laramie Ave., Cicero | 708/652–2812 | Grandstand free; clubhouse $3.50 | Feb.–May, daily 7 AM–11 PM.

Chicago Bears. This NFL team is still the most popular sports draw in Chicago, and there's always a full house at Soldier Field, near South Side, whenever the beloved team is in town. | Lake Shore and E. McFetridge Drs. | 847/615–2327.

Chicago Blackhawks. The United Center is where this NHL team heats up the ice from October through April. | 1901 W. Madison St. | 312/559–1212 (Ticketmaster) | www.chicagoblackhawks.com.

Chicago Bulls. Michael Jordan won't be forgotten in the United Center stadium, where he led the team to so many NBA championships and you can still pull for the Bulls. | 1901 W. Madison St. | 312/455–4000 | www.nba.com/bulls.

Chicago Cubs. The Cubbies (of baseball's National League) are found each summer in their classic ivy-covered Wrigley Field stadium on Chicago's North Side. | 1060 W. Addison St. | 773/404–2827 | www.cubs.com.

Chicago White Sox. You can join the fans who flock to the South Side concrete-and-metal Comiskey Park to watch their favorite baseball team fight for the American League pennant. | 333 W. 35th St. | 312/674–1000 | www.whitesox.com.

SIGHTSEEING TOURS/TOUR COMPANIES

American Sightseeing Tours/Gray Line. This line's tours cover either the North or the South Side or a combination of both, and one tour includes admission to the Sears Tower. | 55 E. Monroe St. | 312/251–3100 | Priced by the tour | Daily 9:30, 11:30, 1:30, 3:30.

Architectural Tours by the Chicago Architecture Foundation. Chicago's architectural treasures can be viewed by boat, bus, and on foot in the 65 different tours offered by the foundation. | 312/922–3432 or 312/922–TOUR (recording) | www.architecture.org | Prices vary with tours.

Friends of the Chicago River. Thanks to this association, you can take informative tours of the Chicago River by canoe, a riverboat cruise, or on foot along its banks. | 407 S. Dearborn St. | 312/939–0490 | $20–$40; walking tours free | Weekdays 9–5.

Mercury Cruise Lines. A number of river and lake cruises are offered throughout the day and into the evening by this cruise lines. | Wacker Dr. and Michigan Ave. | 312/332–1353 | Priced by the cruise | Call for schedule.

Shoreline Sightseeing Co. This tour company provides architectural, lake shoreline, and evening cruises as well as a water-taxi service. | Navy Pier and Buckingham Fountain | 312/222–9328 | Priced by the cruise | Call for schedule.

Spirit of Chicago. You can dine, dance, and enjoy a floor show aboard this luxury sightseeing ship. | Navy Pier | 312/836–7899 | www.spiritcruises.com | $38.95–$99.95 | Call for schedule.

Untouchables Tours. On these two-hour bus tours that trace the Prohibition-era hot spots, costumed guides retell gangland exploits, incorporating other tidbits of Chicago's history. This theater on wheels departs from in front of the Rock 'n' Roll McDonald's at Clark and Ohio streets. | Clark and Ohio Sts. | 773/881–1195 | $22, special rates for kids | Daily.

Walking Tours of Pullman Historic District. Tours take place on the first Sunday of each month and include an introductory video, guided walk through the Pullman Historic District, and a visit to the Greenstone Church and the Hotel Florence. | 11141 S. Cottage Grove Ave. | 773/785–8181 | $4 | May–Oct., 12:30 and 1:30.

Wendella. Both river and lake cruises as well as a commuter boat running from the Loop to Michigan Avenue and a water bus are at your service through this company on North Michigan at the Wrigley Building. | 400 N. Michigan Ave. | 312/337–1446 | www.wendellaboats.com | Priced by the service | Call for schedule.

OTHER POINTS OF INTEREST

★ **Adler Planetarium.** In addition to the astronomy and space exhibits and the sky shows in the theater at this museum, there are live telescope viewings on Friday evenings. | 1300 S. Lake Shore Dr. | 312/922--STAR (recorded schedule) or 312/322–0304; TDD/TT 312/322–0995 | www.adlerplanetarium.org | $5; special rates for senior citizens and kids; $5 sky show; free Tues. | Mon.–Thurs. 9–5, Fri. 9–9, weekends 9–6.

John G. Shedd Aquarium. Your head will swim with all the sharks, eels, and penguins here as well as whales and dolphins in the oceanarium. | 1200 S. Lake Shore Dr. | 312/939–2438 | www.sheddaquarium.org | $15; special rates for senior citizens and kids | Daily 9–6.

John Hancock Center. From this observatory on the 94th-floor of the building, you have spectacular views of the city and the lake, and for an additional $3 you can get a personal "sky tour" of the land below. | 875 N. Michigan Ave. | 312/751--3681 | www.hancock-observatory.com | $8.75; special rates for senior citizens and kids | Daily 9 AM–midnight.

McCormick Place Convention Complex. This center includes large convention exhibition halls and the Arie Crown Theater. | 2301 S. Lake Shore Dr. | 312/791–7000 | fax 312/791–6543 | www.mccormickplace.com | Priced per exhibition and performance | Daily.

★ **Navy Pier.** This restored pier built in 1916 is now home to shops, restaurants, an IMAX theater, a Ferris wheel, and the Skyline Stage. | 600 E. Grand Ave. | 312/595–PIER | www.navypier.com | Free | Daily; call for performance schedules.

River East Plaza. You can stroll, shop, and launch your dreams from this pier, which is made up of promenades, a gift shop, and tour-boat docks. | 435 E. Illinois St. | 312/836–4300 | Free | Daily.

★ **Sears Tower.** The world's second-tallest building, this business tower has an observation deck, where on clear days you have a 40- to 50-mi view. | 233 S. Wacker Dr. | 312/875–9696; sky–deck information 312/875–9447 | www.the-skydeck.com | $9.50; special rates for senior citizens, kids, and families | Daily 9AM–11PM; last ticket sold at 10:30PM.

ON THE CALENDAR

FEB.: *Chicago Auto Show.* You get a preview of the year's models of sensible family cars to hot new prototypes at this show in the McCormick Place Convention Center. | 312/949–8800.

MAR.: *Chicago Flower and Garden Show.* Held on the Navy Pier, this botanical show includes an array of floral and other plant displays and vendors. | 312/567–8500.

MAR.: *St. Patrick's Day Parade.* This celebratory event includes politicians, bands, and theme floats parading in the Loop, not far from where the Chicago River is annually dyed green for the day. | 312/744–3315.

JUNE: *Gay and Lesbian Pride Celebration.* In conjunction with this national celebration, floats parade along Halsted Street in recognition of the Gay and Lesbian community. | 773/348–8243.

JUNE–JULY: *Taste of Chicago.* Many of the city's restaurants dish up their specialties during this 10-day foodfest in Grant Park starting on June 30th, where there's live entertainment as well. | 312/744–3315.

JUNE–SEPT.: *Grant Park Concerts.* Free summer concerts—classical, opera, pop, and blues—are performed at the James C. Petrillo Music Shell on Wednesday, Friday, and Saturday nights. | 312/742–7638.

JULY: *Chicago to Mackinac Races.* You can join or cheer the sailors who race the length of Lake Michigan, departing from Belmont Harbor. | 312/861–7777.

JULY: *Grant Park July 3 Concert.* On the evening before Independence Day, you can hear the Chicago Symphony and see fireworks at the Petrillo Music Shell in Grant Park. | 312/744–3315.

JULY: *Venetian Night.* In the Monroe Street Harbor on the 31st, this night-time decorated-boat parade and fireworks program can dazzle you with its brilliance. | 312/744–3315.

AUG.: *Air and Water Show.* From along North Avenue Beach, you can see thrilling aircraft stunts and demonstrations both on and over Lake Michigan in this show. | 312/744–3315.

AUG.–SEPT.: *Jazz Festival.* In Grant Park, you can get in the musical groove during the outdoor performances by nationally known jazz artists. | 312/744–3315.

OCT.: *Chicago International Film Festival.* Several theaters participate in the showings of new American and foreign films for you to enjoy during this fall festival. | 312/644–3400 or 312/644–3456 (24-hour hotline).

Dining

INEXPENSIVE

Angelia Ristorante. Italian. Locals flock to this Old World–style trattoria, where you dine beneath chandeliers but sense no pretentiousness; dishes to try are the calamari, rock shrimp,

CHICAGO

INTRO
ATTRACTIONS
DINING
LODGING

CHI FOOD

Chicago has its share of restaurants serving wonderful food made with local ingredients and imaginatively prepared.

But you'll know true Chicagoans by the more, ah, casual food that they consume.

Chicago deep-dish pizza, for instance, is the source of much intracity squabbling—whose was first, whose is best? It's substantial food, whichever you pick: extra-thick, saucy slabs, oozing with cheese. Some have tried variations; one version is "stuffed" on the more-is-more theory; others put in vegetables like spinach and broccoli.

And then there's the Chicago hot dog, a colorful version of the American favorite. No chili or sauerkraut or cheese for these dogs. Instead you need mustard, tomatoes, onions, relish (the brighter green, the better), a shake of celery salt, and for the brave, a couple of sport peppers that'll give your lips a sting. Coney Island, indeed.

© Corbis

or linguine in a spicy sauce. Sunday brunch here is popular, too. | 3561 N. Broadway | 773/935–5933 | Reservations essential | $10–$17 | AE, V | No lunch.

Ann Sather. Swedish. Known for its cinnamon rolls and feather-light Scandinavian pancakes—both of which are served all day, along with the full gamut of breakfast fare—this is the original Ann Sather, just a few blocks south of Wrigley Field. | 929 W. Belmont Ave. | 773/348–2378 | www.annsather.com | $8–$12 | AE, MC, V | Breakfast also available.

Ann Sather. Swedish. This Andersonville branch of the Belmont Avenue original offers up the same ultra-thin pancakes, meatballs, and other fare that made the original famous. Early-bird supper weekends. | 5207 N. Clark St. | 773/271–6677 | Daily, 7AM–3PM | $8–$12 | AE, MC, V.

Big Bowl Café. Asian. This casual place serves several different noodles, satay, and stir-fry dishes, even on Sundays, when it is open from 4 to 9. | 159½ W. Erie St. | 312/787–8297 | www.big-bowl.com | $8–$11 | AE, D, DC, MC, V.

Café Iberico. Spanish. Authentic tapas and sangria are served at this bustling restaurant, which is splashed with murals of musicians and bullfights. You can indulge in the *pulpo a la plancha* (grilled octopus) or the *queso de cabra* (goat cheese), either in the main dining area or in *la bodega* (the cellar) with its fireplace and service bar. | 739 N. LaSalle St. | 312/573–1510 | Reservations accepted only Sun.–Thurs. for parties of six or more | $9–$13 | AE, D, DC, MC, V.

Dellwood Pickle. American/casual. While you wait for your meal, or even as you dine, indulge your artistic side and draw with the crayons on your butcher-paper-covered table, and if your masterpiece is good enough, it could end up on the "art wall." Try vegetable lasagna, pot roast, or any one of the sandwiches or salads here. Sunday breakfast. | 1475 W. Balmoral Ave. | 773/271–7728 | No reservations accepted | $6.50–$14 | AE, D, DC, MC, V | No lunch.

Emilio's Tapas. Spanish. Window boxes in this peppy place in Lincoln Park make it seem you're in a garden, where you can order unusual tapas, such as cracked-pepper beef brochette with caramelized onions, and chicken-stuffed red peppers. | 444 W. Fullerton St. | 773/327–5100 | $12–$16 | AE, DC, MC, V | No lunch Mon.–Thurs.

La Creperie. French. In this intimate restaurant, which also has tables outdoors in a garden, you can savor dinner crepes filled with chicken curry, with seafood, or with beef bourguignonne. The dessert crepes include one made of chocolate and another made of crème anglaise (custard sauce and fresh berries). | 2845 N. Clark St. | 773/528–9050 | $3.50–$9 | AE, D, DC, MC, V | Closed Mon.

Manny's Coffee Shop and Deli. Delicatessen. This no-frills cafeteria-style delicatessen has been a Chicago landmark since the '40s because the food, served with a dollop of Borscht-

© Corbis

YOU CAN'T MOVE MOUNTAINS, BUT . . .

. . . In Chicago engineers changed the course of the river. If you expect the Chicago River to run into Lake Michigan, you're in for a surprise.

In the late 1800s, sewage was routinely dumped into the Chicago River, and excessive rainfall caused the river to spew large quantities of contaminated water into the lake. So engineers built the Chicago Sanitary and Ship Canal, which linked the river to the Des Plaines River and carried the waste away from the city. Today, boats must go through locks to pass to or from the lake.

Belt humor, has the reputation of being first-rate, such as Manny's chicken soup, latkes, corned beef, and braised short ribs with horseradish. Cafeteria service. | 1141 S. Jefferson St. | 312/939–2855 | $10–$15 | No credit cards | No dinner.

N. N. Smokehouse. Southern. This barbecue joint with its murals and blues music touts some of the best down-home cooking this side of Memphis. Specials include the pulled pork, the fried catfish, or the spare ribs; if you have room left, top it off with a slice of sweet potato or pecan pie. Kids' menu. | 1465 W. Irving Park Rd. | 773/868–4700 | $10–$20 | D, DC, MC, V | No lunch Mon.–Thurs.

The Parthenon. Greek. Simple preparations of fish, lamb, and other Greek favorites, such as spinach pie and stuffed grape leaves, are served in either of two muraled Greektown dining rooms here. Kids' menu. | 314 S. Halsted St. | 312/726–2407 | www.theparthenon.com | $7–$11 | AE, D, DC, MC, V.

★ **Pizzeria Uno.** Pizza. Deep-dish pizza is the draw here, as this is the popular and therefore buzzing home of that style of the Italian pie. | 29 E. Ohio St. | 312/321–1000 | www.pizzeri-auno.com | Reservations not accepted | $10–$20 | AE, D, DC, MC, V.

Pockets. Italian. This very casual neighborhood restaurant-and-pizzeria is named for its "pockets"—pita bread stuffed with salad, with a choice of dressing on the side. The Original Pocket is filled with lettuce, tomatoes, green peppers, shredded carrots, mushrooms, and mozzarella cheese. You can also get calzones filled with everything from jalapeños to broccoli. | 2618 N. Clark St. | 773/404–7587 | $5–$6 | AE, MC, V.

Redfish. Cajun/Creole. Mardi Gras decorations and displays of voodoo dolls and masks set the scene in this Louisiana-style River North restaurant, where you can enjoy regional dishes like jambalaya with dirty rice and listen to live blues Thursday through Saturday. Kids' menu. | 400 N. State St. | 312/467–1600 | www.redfishamerica.com | $6.95–$18.95 | AE, D, DC, MC, V.

Wishbone. Southern. Just down the street from the studio where Oprah's show is filmed, you might catch a glimpse of a star as you enjoy broiled chicken, blackened catfish, crab cakes, or sautéed spinach and the corn bread here. | 1001 Washington Blvd. | 312/850–2663 | $4–$14 | AE, D, DC, MC, V | Breakfast also available; brunch weekends. No dinner Mon.

MODERATE

Arun's. Thai. Exquisitely fiery Southeast Asian cuisine, such as three-combination curry and grilled, and the famous golden baskets, in which bite-sized flower baskets made of golden-brown pastry are filled with diced bits of shrimp, chicken, corn and shiitake mushrooms, are served with finesse in the stylish two-level dining room filled with art indigenous to Thailand in this restaurant on the northwest side of the city. | 4156 N. Kedzie Ave. | 773/539–1909 | $18–$25 | AE, D, DC, MC, V | No lunch. Closed Mon.

Berghoff. German. This bustling Loop landmark, where it seems some of the waiters are permanent fixtures, has dark paneling, crisp linens, and locally renowned sauerbraten and schnitzels. Kids' menu. | 17 W. Adams St. | 312/427–3170 | www.berghoff.com | $11.95–$19.95 | AE, MC, V | Closed Sun.

Bice Ristorante. Italian. Traditional dishes from northern Italy such as tagliatelle with clams, shrimp, scallops, and calamari; al dente porcini risotto; and stuffed chicken breast with ham, spinach, mushrooms, and fontina are served in the stylish dining room with art deco accents or at tables with umbrellas on the sidewalk patio here. | 158 E. Ontario St. | 312/664–1474 | Mon.–Thu., Sun. 11:30 AM–10:30 PM; Fri.–Sat. 11:30 AM–11:00 PM | $13–$27 | AE, D, DC, MC, V.

Biggs. Continental. An early innovator of the 1970s burgeoning culinary scene in Chicago, this restaurant is housed in an elegant Gold Coast landmark mansion. Beef Wellington, buttery escargot, and the Dover sole are some favorites. | 1150 N. Dearborn St. | 312/787–0900 | $15–$39 | AE, D, DC, MC, V | No lunch.

Blackbird. Contemporary. In his neo-modern dining room, Chef Paul Kahan serves a mid-'60s menu with millennium-era twists, such as grilled sturgeon on braised celery root.

CHICAGO

INTRO
ATTRACTIONS
DINING
LODGING

Try the crepes stuffed with chocolate mascarpone for desert. | 619 W. Randolph St. | 312/715–0708 | www.blackbirdrestaurant.com | $18–$26 | AE, D, DC, MC, V.

Blackhawk Lodge. Contemporary. You may be north of the Loop in the city but the setting here is straight out of the woods, and you can order dishes made with wild game in season, and seafood such as halibut and jumbo lump-crab cakes anytime. There's a screened porch where you can dine when the weather suits. Sunday brunch. Kids' menu. | 41 E. Superior St. | 312/280–4080 | www.blackhawklodge.com | $15–$30 | AE, D, DC, MC, V.

★ **Brasserie Jo.** French. Here you can eat your chicken, steak frites, or onion tart inside the stylish brasserie or outdoors under umbrellas at tables set up like those in a sidewalk café in Paris. | 59 W. Hubbard St. | 312/595–0800 | www.brasseriejo.com | $13.95–$23.95 | AE, D, DC, MC, V | No lunch weekends.

Celebrity Café. Contemporary. You have good views of the Chicago River from this spacious dining room where the menu changes seasonally, including such dishes as sea bass, grilled salmon, and vegetable lasagna. Kids' menu and Sunday brunch offered. | 320 N. Dearborn St. | 312/744–1900, ext. 35 | $15–$25 | AE, D, DC, MC, V | Breakfast also available.

Chicago Chop House. Steak. This is a prime place in River North for steak lovers, where you can also enjoy live entertainment from a piano player who performs nightly in the first-level room. | 60 W. Ontario St. | 312/787–7100 | www.chicagochophouse.com | $23–$45 | AE, D, DC, MC, V | No lunch weekends.

Club Lucky. Italian. This restaurant is reminiscent of 1940s supper clubs, with its red Naugahyde booths and chrome fixtures, and the bar/lounge was refurbished to look exactly as it did in 1938. Specialties here include chicken Vesuvio and capellini Siciliana. Late-night hours in the lounge. | 1824 W. Wabansia | 773/227–2300 | $7–$25 | AE, D, DC, MC, V | No lunch weekends.

Coco Pazzo. Italian. Wood-roasted meats, pizzas, and Tuscan dishes make up the menu in this contemporary River North loft space, softened with blue velvet curtains. You can also dine out on the simple patio along Franklin Street. | 300 W. Hubbard St. | 312/836–0900 | www.tribads.com/cocopazzo | $13–$30 | AE, DC, MC, V | No lunch weekends.

Como Inn. Italian. Veal and pasta dishes from northern Italy are among the traditional favorites in this quiet but popular spot. Kids' menu. | 546 N. Milwaukee Ave. | 312/421–5222 | $14–$30 | AE, D, DC, MC, V.

Crofton on Wells. Contemporary. Chef-owner Suzy Crofton adds Gallic accents to her basically American menu in this sophisticated dining room, where favorites are the barbecued shrimp, the grilled beef tenderloin, and the white-truffle-scented sturgeon with chanterelles and pears. Up to 12 people can be seated outdoors at tables with white linen, surrounded by metallic flower boxes and cascading ivy. | 535 N. Wells St. | 312/755–1790 | www.croftononwells.com | $16–$29 | AE, DC, MC, V | No lunch weekends.

Cuisines. Mediterranean. This lovely restaurant on the 2nd floor of the Chicago Renaissance Hotel serves such dishes as veal medallions with wild mushrooms, crabmeat and shiitakes in phyllo with smoked tomato coulis, and seared snapper with artichokes. Wine cellar. | 1 W. Wacker Dr. | 312/372–4459 | $15–$30 | AE, D, DC, MC, V.

Ed Debevic's. American. This 1950s-style diner in River North has hip, wisecracking waitstaff who serve the chili, hamburgers, meat loaf, and salads here with a side of ribbing. | 640 N. Wells St. | 312/664–1707 | $16–$20 | AE, DC, V.

Erwin. American. Everything in this lakeview eatery is made from scratch on the premises using heartland produce, down to the multigrain bread and the pickles that top the hand-ground burgers. Wood-grilled pork chops are a specialty of the house. Sun. brunch. | 2925 N. Halsted St. | 773/528–7200 | www.erwincafe.com | $10–$26 | AE, D, DC, MC, V | No lunch.

★ **Frontera Grill.** Mexican. The casual sister of Topolobampo, the Frontera is filled with bright Mexican folk art and serves renowned chef Rick Bayless's regional Mexican fare, which you can also enjoy on the patio right on the sidewalk among flower boxes and hanging plants. Saturday brunch. | 445 N. Clark St. | 312/661–1434 | $12–$24 | AE, D, DC, MC, V | Closed Sun. and Mon.

Genesee Depot. American. At this restaurant, which has been serving dinners since 1973, the favorites are beef brisket, stuffed chicken, duck, and prime rib. | 3736 N. Broadway Ave. | 773/528–6990 | $12–$20 | AE, CB, D, DC, MC, V | No lunch. Closed Mon.

Greek Islands. Greek. This taverna harkens back to the Old World, where you can enjoy such Southern European fare as lamb with artichokes. | 200 S. Halsted St. | 312/782–9855 | $14–$20 | AE, D, DC, MC, V.

Hard Rock Café. American. Lots of electric guitars and rock music memorabilia fill this busy, cavernous Chicago branch of the international chain known for its hamburgers. | 63 W. Ontario St. | 312/943–2252 | www.hardrock.com | $15–$18 | AE, DC, MC, V.

Harry Caray's. American. Baseball mementos fill this River North restaurant named for the Chicago Cubs' late announcer and known for its steaks and chops. | 33 W. Kinzie St. | 312/828–0966 | $15–$40 | AE, D, DC, MC, V | No lunch Sun.

Hudson Club. Contemporary. A vintner's storage machine the size of a stretch limo keeps approximately 100 bottles of wine at just the right temperature and humidity at this club, where there's a huge selection of both wines and cuisines from many regions of the world. Try the lobster-mashed potato martini, an innovative appetizer served in a cocktail glass. | 504 N. Wells St. | 312/467–1947 | www.thehudsonclub.com | $15–$26 | AE, D, DC, MC, V.

Iron Mike's Grille. American. Known for its jumbo pork chops, this restaurant filled with football memorabilia saluting former Chicago Bears coach Mike Ditka is in a posh neighborhood off Michigan Avenue, has a pianist playing Thursday through Saturday, and serves brunch on the weekend. | 100 E. Chestnut St. | 312/587–8989 | $13–$30 | AE, D, DC, MC, V.

Klay Oven. Indian. Many of the richly spiced northern Indian dishes, such as meat and vegetable curries, are prepared tableside here, where you dine among an appealing collection of modern Indian art. | 414 N. Orleans St. | 312/527–3999 | www.klayoven.com | $15–$18 | AE, DC, MC, V.

Le Bouchon. French. Favorites in this authentic bistro north of the Loop are the roasted duck for two and the monkfish Provençale, which you can accompany with wine from Le Bouchon's regional selections. | 1958 N. Damen Ave. | 773/862–6600 | $12.50–$22.95 | AE, D, DC, MC, V | Closed Sun. No lunch.

Maggiano's Little Italy. Italian. This small busy restaurant in River North has a World War II–era old-neighborhood look made homey with checked tablecloths and the smell of its fresh-baked bread. You can also eat at the tables on the sidewalk-patio overlooking the street. | 516 N. Clark St. | 312/644–7700 | $12–$23 | AE, D, DC, MC, V.

Marché. French. Spit-roasted rabbit, braised lamb shank, and steak frites are the specialties in this colorful, noisy dining room in the West Loop market district, frequented by celebrities. | 833 W. Randolph St. | 312/226–8399 | $12–$18 | AE, DC, MC, V | No lunch weekends.

Mia Francesca. Italian. You can enjoy authentic southern Italian cooking in this simple Wrigleyville storefront trattoria with butcher-papered tables indoors and a patio with six tables in the garden. | 3311 N. Clark St. | 773/281–3310 | Reservations not accepted | $10.95–$24.95 | AE, MC, V | No lunch weekends.

Mon Ami Gabi. French. At Chef Gabino Sotelino's casual Lincoln Park cousin to the more-formal Ambria, the dishes to try are the boeuf bourguignonne and the steak frites topped with profiteroles. The oak-paneled dining room is trimmed with copper cooking pots, mirrors, and black-and-white photos. | 2300 Lincoln Park W | 773/348–8886 | $17–$26 | AE, D, DC, MC, V | No lunch.

Nacional 27. Eclectic. The menu at this lively River North restaurant covers culinary high points of 27 Caribbean and Central and South American nations, including crab fritters, pork adobado, Argentinian steak, and South American seafood dishes. Dancing after 10:30 on Friday and Saturday evenings. | 325 W. Huron St. | 312/664–2727 | $14–$24 | AE, D, DC, MC, V | No lunch.

Papagus. Greek. The dining room in this River North restaurant in the Embassy Suites Hotel is similar to a rural island taverna, where you can try grilled octopus with a selection from the all-Greek wine list, followed by dried-cherry baklava. | 620 N. State St. | 312/642–8450 | www.leye.com | $18–$30 | AE, D, DC, MC, V.

Russian Tea Time. Russian. Sitting in burgundy leather booths beneath brass chandeliers, you can enjoy caviar, borscht, shashlik, and wild game dishes in this Loop restaurant. You can also admire the display of beautiful Russian dolls here. | 77 E. Adams St. | 312/360–0000 | www.russianteatime.com | Reservations essential | $15–$28 | AE, D, DC, MC, V.

Santorini. Greek. You can enjoy seafood dishes from the coast of Greece in this authentic country-style taverna in the heart of Chicago's Greektown. | 800 W. Adams St. | 312/829–8820 | www.santoriniseafood.com | $15–$25 | AE, D, DC, MC, V.

Sayat Nova. Middle Eastern. Stuffed grape leaves, baba ghannouj or red lentil soup are good starters at this North of the Loop spot. Entrees include kebabs (lamb, chicken, beef, shrimp or vegetable); couscous with lamb, chicken or vegetables; spicy lamb meatballs; and sauteed scallops with rice pilaf. | 157 E. Ohio St. | 312/644–9159 | $12–$17 | AE, D, DC, MC, V.

Scoozi! Italian. The dining room in this River North restaurant is open and noisy, especially on the weekends when you may wait a long time for a table. The friendly waitstaff, whimsical decor ("sculptures" made up of wine bottles or tomatoes, Italian words on the walls), and the country-style seafood and pasta dishes, make it worth the wait. | 410 W. Huron St. | 312/943–5900 | $9–$25 | AE, D, DC, MC, V | No lunch weekends.

Su Casa. Mexican. At this north-of-the-loop restaurant, you can enjoy such south-of-the-border representations as enchiladas and frijoles either in the dining room filled with Mexican artifacts or on the patio in the garden. | 49 E. Ontario St. | 312/943–4041 | $15–$25 | AE, D, DC, MC, V.

Szechuan Restaurant. Chinese. Smoked duck, General Tso's chicken, and the sizzling lamb are favorites in this restaurant north of the Loop, which is particularly popular for lunch. | 625 N. Michigan Ave. | 312/329–9494 | $15–$25 | AE, D, DC, MC, V.

Szechwan East. Chinese. This opulent Asian favorite north of the Loop is dominated by an immense gilded Buddha, serves drinks from an outdoor bar, and offers Sunday brunch. | 340 E. Ohio St. | 312/255–9200 | $15–$25 | AE, D, DC, MC, V.

Topolobampo. Mexican. Owners Rick and Deann Bayless offer elegant Mexican cuisine in this River North favorite, where you can try huitlacoche crepes, grilled elk and other wild game—all unique dishes with complex sauces—in this colorful dining room filled with Mexican artifacts. | 445 N. Clark St. | 312/661–1434 | $19–$26 | AE, D, DC, MC, V | No lunch Sat. Closed Sun. and Mon.

Trattoria Parma. Italian. Ossobuco (veal shank served with whipped potatoes and other vegetables) is a favorite in this North River restaurant, where the walls are covered with paintings of Venice and you can also dine at tables on the sidewalk in front. | 400 N. Clark St. | 312/245–9933 | $12–$20 | AE, DC, MC, V | No lunch weekends.

Tucci Benucch. Italian. Though you are on the fifth floor of the building in this restaurant north of Lake Michigan, you could almost swear you're in a villa in northern Italy, especially when you dig in to the roasted chicken and veal piccata specialities here. Kids' menu. | 900 N. Michigan Ave. | 312/266–2500 | $18–$26 | AE, D, DC, MC, V.

Vinci. Italian. The lace curtains and columns draped with ivy give this restaurant, a short walk from the George and Steppenwolf theaters, a warm and rustic feel. Specialties include grilled polenta with portobello and cremini mushrooms; rosemary skewered shrimp with artichokes and whipped potatoes; and grilled duck breast with balsamic vinegar sauce. | 1732 N. Halsted St. | 312/266–1199 | Reservations essential (for pre-theater seating) | $18–$33 | AE, DC, MC, V | No lunch.

Vivere. Italian. In this Loop restaurant, the cone-shaped fixtures in the ceiling and the gilded scrolls provide an elegant glow in the dining room where you can choose dishes from northern Italy, such as medallions of veal and fish. | 71 W. Monroe St. | 312/332–4040 | www.italianvillage-chicago.com | $15–$30 | AE, D, DC, MC, V | Closed Sun. No lunch Sat.

Zinfandel. Contemporary. Folk art brightens this informal and airy restaurant, where Chef Susan Goss prepares her monthly menu of regional recipes, such as pecan-encrusted Pacific mahimahi. Saturday brunch. | 59 W. Grand Ave. | 312/527–1818 | www.zinfandel-restaurant.com | $18–$24 | AE, D, MC, V | Closed Sun.

EXPENSIVE

Ambria. French. In the contemporary dining room of an old Lincoln Park hotel, the Ambria has been a star for years in the Chicago culinary scene owing to its ever changing menu of exquisite French cuisine. | 2300 Lincoln Park W | 773/472–5959 | $28–$35 | AE, D, DC, MC, V | No lunch. Closed Sun.

Ben Pao. Chinese. In this contemporary black-and-red environment, you can order from an exotic selection of Asian fare, such as Ben Pao's spicy eggplant dish. | 52 W. Illinois St. | 312/222–1888 | www.leye.com | $20–$30 | AE, D, DC, MC, V | No lunch weekends.

The Big Downtown. American. In this vintage diner with its tiny Chicago El model and jazz artifacts on the walls, there's a late-night menu for night owls, and you can try the roast chicken, or the crabmeat pepper linguine if you don't feel like having steak. You can also dine on the patio, which has tables with umbrellas. Kids' menu. | 124 S. Wabash Ave. | 312/917–7399 | $26–$42 | AE, D, DC, MC, V.

Bistro 110. French. Opt for one of the intimate, mirrored booths in this bustling bistro, where a Sunday jazz brunch is also served. Specialties include braised lamb shank, smoked salmon, and oven-roasted chicken. | 110 E. Pearson St. | 312/266–3110 | $25–$35 | AE, D, DC, MC, V.

GRAVE SUBJECTS

They're kind of like house tours except, of course, that the occupants aren't living anymore. Chicago's larger cemeteries are the final resting places for many of the city's better-known citizens, and the graveyards have become popular touring grounds for those interested in the city's history. There's even a Web site devoted to the subject: www.graveyards.com.

Graceland, on the North Side, is probably best known, and in fact, the Chicago Architecture Foundation offers tours through it. Among those buried there are department store founder Marshall Field, railroad baron George Pullman, architect Ludwig Mies van der Rohe, and early settler John Kinzie.

Also on the North Side is the city's largest cemetery, Rosehill; here lie Montgomery Ward, former vice president Charles Gate Dawes, and weiner baron Oscar Mayer.

The South Side's Oak Woods Cemetery has a number of famous occupants—among them Chicago Mayor Harold Washington, Olympic runner Jesse Owens, and nuclear scientist Enrico Fermi—along with the graves of some 6,000 Confederate soldiers who died while imprisoned at nearby Camp Douglas during the Civil War.

© Artville

Buckingham's. Steak. This steak house has lavish marble and polished wood in its dining room, where you can enjoy chops and seafood as well as the steaks for which the establishment is known. Sunday brunch. | 720 S. Michigan Ave. | 312/294–6600 | $28–$36 | AE, D, DC, MC, V.

Café Ba Ba Reeba. Spanish. This busy tapas bar has both indoor and outdoor dining, where the menu has traditional dishes from the coast of Spain such as grilled squid with lemon, garlic, and olive oil. | 2024 N. Halsted St. | 773/935–5000 | $20–$25 | AE, D, DC, MC, V.

Cape Cod Room. Seafood. Seated at tables with linen cloths and candles in this fish house in the Drake Hotel, you can feast on traditional sea fare, such as the popular crabcakes, and on the expansive views of Lake Michigan. | 140 E. Walton St. | 312/787–2200 | www.thedrakehotel.com | $21–$43 | AE, D, DC, MC, V.

Centro. Italian. Chicken Vesuvio, calamari fritti, and baked cavatelli are among the characteristic dishes you can try seated amid black-and-white photos of celebrities in the dark-wood paneled dining room, or on Centro's front patio. | 710 N. Wells St. | 312/988–7775 | www.rosebudrestaurants.com | $25–$30 | AE, D, DC, MC, V | No lunch Sun.

Cielo. Italian. You can watch the action along Michigan Avenue from the tables in this bistro, where wood-fired pizza, seafood, steaks, and pasta are served. Sunday brunch. | 676 N. Michigan Ave. | 312/944–7676 | $24–$36 | AE, D, DC, MC, V | Breakfast also available.

Eli's the Place for Steak. Steak. This dark, clubby longtime favorite north of the Loop has leather chairs, and art by local talents hanging on the walls, as well as a piano bar. | 215 E. Chicago Ave. | 312/642–1393 | www.eliplaceforsteak.com | $28–$35 | AE, D, DC, MC, V | No lunch weekends.

Emperor's Choice. Chinese. This Chinatown storefront filled with Chinese art and artifacts serves Cantonese dishes, such as fried soft-shell crabs, and spicy Hunan shrimp, and lobster seven ways. | 2238 S. Wentworth Ave. | 312/225–8800 | $20–$35 | AE, D, MC, V.

Geja's Café. Fondue. Private, softly lit alcoves make this a Valentine's Day favorite, where you can enjoy practically any kind of fondue imaginable and a live Flamenco and classical guitarist nightly. | 340 W. Armitage Ave. | 773/281–9101 | $25–$40 | AE, D, DC, MC, V | No lunch.

Gene and Georgetti. Steak. In a century-old River North building under the El, where paneling and murals cover the walls, you can get generous servings of steak and baked potatoes, a perfect martini, and shrimp de Jonghe, which is a '30s Chicago dish of breaded shrimp sautéed in a lot of garlic. | 500 N. Franklin St. | 312/527–3718 | $26–$38 | AE, DC, MC, V | Closed Sun. and first week in July.

Gibsons Steakhouse. Steak. Lovers of large well-prepared cuts of beef pack this art deco Gold Coast dining room, where a pianist plays, and you can drink martinis and smoke fat cigars, which are sold here. | 1028 N. Rush St. | 312/266–8999 | Reservations essential | $22–$35 | AE, D, DC, MC, V | No lunch.

Hatsuhana. Japanese. Devoted fans of Japanese cuisine claim some of the best can be found at this serene Streeteville offshoot of the New York Sushi star, where you can also dine and be entertained at its popular sushi bar. | 160 E. Ontario St. | 312/280–8808 | $25–$35 | AE, DC, MC, V | No lunch Sat. Closed Sun.

Kiki's Bistro. French. Brick walls and thick wood beams give this River North bistro the look of a French country inn, where a must-try is the baked Alaskan halibut. | 900 N. Franklin St. | 312/335–5454 | $20–$25 | AE, D, DC, MC, V | Closed Sun. No lunch Sat.

La Strada. Italian. Just a few steps from Michigan Avenue, opposite Grant Park in the Loop, you can find peace and quiet and such northern Italian dishes as zuppe de pesce, red snapper, and veal scallopini in this serene and somewhat darkened setting. | 155 N. Michigan Ave. | 312/565–2200 | $28–$35 | AE, D, DC, MC, V | Closed Sun.

Lawry's the Prime Rib. American. This elegant turn-of-the-century former home of the McCormick family, just off Michigan Avenue north of the Loop, is now home to this restaurant known for its prime rib. | 100 E. Ontario St. | 312/787–5000 | $20–$35 | AE, D, DC, MC, V | No dinner Mon.–Fri.

Lutz Continental Café and Pastry Shop. German. You can dine either at tables with umbrellas in the garden or indoors at this Old World café in a bustling neighborhood bakery in Lincoln Square, a place not to be missed if you have a sweet tooth. | 2458 W. Montrose Ave. | $20–$24 | MC, V | Closed Mon.

Morton's of Chicago. Steak. Huge slabs of prime-cut beef are served with softball-size potatoes and giant tomatoes at this locals' favorite Gold Coast steakhouse, where servers are enthusiastic and a must-try is the prime dry-aged porterhouse steak. Wine cellar. | 1050 N. State St. | 312/266–4820 | www.mortons.com | $20–$33 | AE, D, DC, MC, V | No lunch.

Prairie. Contemporary. Architectural photographs and drawings hang throughout this Prairie School–inspired dining room, where seasonal specialties include pheasant, sturgeon, venison, and buffalo. Sunday brunch. | 500 S. Dearborn St. | 312/663–1143 | $20–$35 | AE, D, DC, MC, V.

Printer's Row. Contemporary. Chef Michael Foley's unique and elegant cuisine is served in a wood-paneled dining room in this 1897 building that originally housed a printing press. Touted to serve the best veal in the nation, this is also the place to try pheasant. | 550 S. Dearborn St. | 312/461–0780 | $30–$40 | AE, D, DC, MC, V | No lunch Sat. Closed Sun.

Pump Room. Contemporary. This legendary dining room in the Gold Coast Omni Ambassador East Hotel is as integral a part of Chicago as the Stockyards, Studs Turkel, and Carl Sandburg. First-rate chef Martial Noguier offers a menu of such unique dishes as hamachi carpaccio with marinated seaweed, and rare duck-breast with figs. Pianist and Sunday brunch. | 1301 N. State Pkwy. | 312/266–0360 | www.omnihotels.com | Jacket required (after 4:30) | $22–$34 | AE, D, DC, MC, V | Breakfast also available.

Riva. Seafood. Floor-to-ceiling windows in this second-story Navy Pier restaurant north of the Loop provide sweeping views of Lake Michigan and the Chicago skyline. Riva is made up of an elegant, white-tablecloth dining room on the upper floor and a less formal café and bar on the lower level. Try the Chilean sea bass, the herb-crusted halibut, or the Dover sole | 700 E. Grand Ave. | 312/644–7482 | $18–$30 | AE, D, DC, MC, V.

The Saloon. Steak. The Kansas City strip, a New York steak with the bone left in, is the specialty at this popular Gold Coast steak house along with its porterhouse, double pork chops, and seafood dishes. | 200 E. Chestnut St. | 312/280–5454 | $25–$40 | AE, D, DC, MC, V.

Salpicón! Mexican. Chef-owner Priscila Satkoff creates sophisticated Mexican food in this relaxed but elegant restaurant with original Mexican art on its walls, where dishes to try are quail and the jalapeños rellenos (spicy stuffed peppers). You can also eat at one of the six tables on the sidewalk, surrounded by flowers. Sunday brunch. | 1252 N. Wells St. | 312/988–7811 | www.salpiconrestaurant.com | $30–$45 | AE, D, DC, MC, V | No lunch.

Shaw's Crab House and Blue Crab Lounge. Seafood. This 1940s-style River North fish house is a lively seafood emporium that includes a more formal wood-paneled dining room, where you can enjoy classic fish dishes such as grilled yellow fin tuna, soft shell crabs, grilled scallops, and Maine lobster. The small informal oyster bar is always hopping. Entertainment Sunday, Tuesday, and Thursday. | 21 E. Hubbard St. | 312/527–2722 | $30–$40 | AE, D, DC, MC, V | No lunch weekends.

Signature Room at the 95th. Contemporary. On the 95th-floor of the John Hancock building, this restaurant's dining room is known for its unparalleled panorama of the city and lake as well as for its polished service of elegantly prepared food. Live music, salad bar, buffet lunch, and Sunday brunch. | 875 N. Michigan Ave. | 312/787–9596 | www.signatureroom.com | $25–$35 | AE, D, DC, MC, V.

CHICAGO

INTRO
ATTRACTIONS
DINING
LODGING

Soul Kitchen. Southern. This ultra-hip Wicker Park restaurant serves a melange of Caribbean-spiced Southern cuisine, such as the Herbsaint-infused shrimp and grits and the country-fried quail with molasses-baked peaches. Raw bar. | 1576 N. Milwaukee Ave. | 773/342–9742 | Reservations not accepted | $20–$35 | AE, MC, V | No lunch.

Spago. Contemporary. Chef Wolfgang Puck's creative cuisine stars here in both the formal dining room and a more casual grill area in this River North complex with large windows and a collection of contemporary art. Prices slightly lower in the grill. | 520 N. Dearborn St. | 312/527–3700 | Reservations essential weekends | $25–$40 | AE, D, DC, MC, V | No lunch Sat. Closed Sun.

★ **Spiaggia.** Italian. In this modern and somewhat luxurious dining room with huge windows providing views of Lake Michigan, dine on pan-roasted rabbit loin, prawns, squab, and quail from the seasonal menu. There's a pianist at dinner, and valet parking in the building's garage. | 980 N. Michigan Ave. | 312/280–2750 | www.levyrestaurants.com | Reservations essential | Jacket required at dinner | $16–$25 | AE, D, DC, MC, V | No lunch Sun. and Mon.

Spruce. Contemporary. There's a surprisingly open feel to this subterranean dining room with brick walls, wood beams, and sidewalk-level windows, where you can try such favorites as the poached lobster and the roasted rabbit. | 238 E. Ontario St. | 312/642–3757 | www.sprucerestaurant.com | $20–$26 | AE, D, DC, MC, V | No lunch. Closed Sun. and Mon.

Streeterville Grille and Bar. American. Satisfy a craving for steak at this dining room on the ground floor of the Sheraton. | 301 E. North Water St. | 312/670–0788 | $22–$30 | AE, D, DC, MC, V.

Tuscany on Taylor. Italian. South of the Loop, this casual storefront restaurant's dining room has large windows looking out on the street and is known for its homemade pasta, gourmet pizzas baked in a woodburning oven, and tender grilled veal. | 1014 W. Taylor St. | 312/829–1990 | $22–$35 | Mon.-Thurs., 11:00 AM–11:00 PM, Fri.-Sat., 11 AM–midnight, Sun. 2–9:30 | AE, D, DC, MC, V.

Vivo. Italian. Grilled pepper tuna and Black Angus sirloin are two of the contemporary dishes you can choose among in addition to the more traditional southern Italian fare that draws folks to this restaurant with its dining room of redbrick and metalwork. You can also eat on the patio surrounded by flowers. | 838 W. Randolph St. | 312/733–3379 | $25–$30 | AE, DC, MC, V | No lunch weekends.

VERY EXPENSIVE

★ **Charlie Trotter's.** Contemporary. This celebrated Lincoln Park restaurant's chef Charlie Trotter is famous for his seven- to twelve-course degustation menus filled with small, complex dishes such as squab laid over crispy polenta, and slowly grilled lamb loin paired with caramelized bits of julienned rutabaga and braised legumes. The menu changes nightly in this sophisticated place. | 816 W. Armitage Ave. | 773/248–6228 | Reservations essential | Jacket required | $90–$110 for 6– to 8–course prix fixe dinner | AE, DC, MC, V | No lunch. Closed Sun. and Mon.

The Dining Room. French. In this classy dining room in the Ritz-Carlton on the Magnificent Mile, Chef Sarah Stegner uses infused oils and vegetable reductions to create a full-flavored signature cuisine with a relatively low fat content. The innovative menu changes daily. Pianist and Sunday brunch. | 160 E. Pearson St. | 312/573–5223 | Reservations essential | Jacket and tie | $32–$36; prix fixe $60–$97 | AE, D, DC, MC, V | No lunch.

★ **Everest.** French. Alsatian-born chef Jean Joho serves up rich French dishes made with premium American ingredients, including quail, sea bass, and shellfish, in this 40th-floor Loop dining room with art deco accents and views of the city that can't be beat. He also serves select wines from Alsace. | 440 S. LaSalle St. | 312/663–8920 | Reservations essential | Jacket required | $40–$60; 6–course tasting menu $79 | AE, D, DC, MC, V | No lunch. Closed Sun. and Mon.

Les Nomades. French. At this sophisticated upscale contemporary restaurant, try the lamb shank, roasted monkfish, or the Jonah crab cakes. | 222 E. Ontario St. | 312/649–9010 | www.lesnomades.com | Reservations essential | Jacket required | $70 4–course prix fixe | AE, DC, MC, V | No lunch. Closed Sun. and Mon.

Nick's Fishmarket. Seafood. Curvy loveseats and booths with individual light dimmers makes Nick's a great spot for a romantic dinner for two, but the main dining room with bar and cabaret space makes it a great setting for groups also. Nick's serves seafood with Asian accents. Specialties include Abalone, seared pepper salmon, and black and blue ahi. | 2 S. Dearborn St. | 312/621–1118 | www.harman-nickolas.com | $35–$50 | AE, D, DC, MC, V | No lunch Sat. Closed Sun.

One Sixtyblue. Contemporary. Michael Jordan is a silent partner in this modern West Loop restaurant where the basketball-court-size dining room is clean-lined with high ceilings and subtle lighting and the food is complex and sculpted. Try the grilled salmon, the grilled lamb, the peekytoe crab sandwiches, and the chocolate souffle. | 160 N. Loomis St. | 312/850–0303 | $35–$45 | AE, DC, MC, V | No lunch. Closed Sun.

The Palm. Steak. In the Loop, this restaurant has good views of Lake Michigan and Navy Pier from its wood-trimmed dining room with high-backed booths, where you can enjoy the high-class steak-house menu among caricatures of the regulars, both famous and not. You can also dine at one of the eight tables on the patio, which also has a lake view. Get the New York strip steak or the fresh whole Nova Scotia lobster. | 323 E. Wacker Dr. | 312/616–3717 | www.thepalm.com | Reservations essential | Daily, 11:30–11 | $35–$45 | AE, DC, MC, V.

Park Avenue Café. Contemporary. In the Gold Coast Doubletree Guest Suites, this casual, contemporary, folk-art-strewn restaurant is known for its swordfish chop, salmon cured pastrami-style, and brioche-crusted cod with wild mushrooms. Sunday brunch. | 199 E. Walton Pl. | 312/944–4414 | $35–$60 | AE, D, DC, MC, V | No lunch.

Seasons and the Café. Contemporary. Chef Mark Baker presides over two dining rooms in the Four Seasons Hotel on the Magnificent Mile: the elegant Seasons and the smaller and more casual Café. In both, the menus change seasonally and are likely to feature fresh fish, such as Parma-roasted salmon, with unique side dishes, and sinful desserts. Pianist, jazz trio Saturday, brunch Sunday, and a kids' menu. | 120 E. Delaware Pl. | 312/649–2349 | www.fourseasons.com | Reservations essential | Jacket required at dinner, ties optional | $30–$44 | AE, D, DC, MC, V.

Lodging

INEXPENSIVE

Cass Hotel. This hotel was built in 1927 and has small but functional rooms just a short walk from shopping on Michigan Avenue and the River North night life. Restaurant, bar. In-room data ports, some refrigerators, cable TV. Laundry facilities. Parking (fee). | 640 N. Wabash Ave. | 312/787–4030 or 800/227–7850 | fax 312/787–8544 | www.casshotel.com | 150 rooms | $69–$99 | AE, D, DC, MC, V.

Comfort Inn. You are only a mile from Wrigley Field at this Lincoln Park motel and also within walking distance of the Sears Tower, the Art Institute of Chicago, and Chinatown. Complimentary Continental breakfast. Some in-room hot tubs, cable TV. Business services. | 601 W. Diversey Pkwy. | 773/348–2810 | fax 773/348–1912 | www.comfortinn.com | 74 rooms | $80–$250 | AE, D, DC, MC, V.

Days Inn. This boutique-like hotel is in Chicago's Lincoln Park neighborhood just barely a mile away from Wrigley Field. Complimentary Continental breakfast. Some in-room data ports, refrigerators, microwaves, cable TV. Laundry facilities. Business services. | 644 W. Diversey Pkwy. | 773/525–7010 | fax 773/525–6998 | www.daysinn.com | 129 room, 3 suites | $89–$145; $220 suites | AE, D, DC, MC, V.

Days Inn Lake Shore Drive. You can get stunning views of Lake Michigan from rooms in this hotel, and you can walk to Navy Pier when you stay here. Restaurant, bar. In-room data ports, cable TV. Pool. Exercise equipment. Laundry facilities. Business services, airport shuttle. | 644 N. Lake Shore Dr. | 312/943–9200 | fax 312/255–4411 | www.daysinn.com | 578 rooms | $79–$189; $175–$700 suites | AE, D, DC, MC, V.

Hampton Inn. Just two blocks from the Midway Airport, this Bedford Park motel also provides shuttle service to McCormick Place when you stay here. Complimentary Continental breakfast, room service. In-room data ports, cable TV. Exercise equipment. Business services, airport shuttle, free parking. | 6540 S. Cicero Ave. | 708/496–1900 | fax 708/496–1997 | www.hamptoninn.com | 167 rooms | $99–$129 | AE, D, DC, MC, V.

HoJo Inn. This well-maintained classic L-shaped motor lodge on a main boulevard downtown is representative of Chicago in the 1950s. Restaurant. Some refrigerators, cable TV. Free parking. | 720 N. Lasalle St. | 312/664–8100 or 800/446–4656 | fax 312/664–2365 | www.hojo.com | 67 rooms, 4 suites | $103–$125 | AE, D, DC, MC, V.

Holiday Inn–Midway Airport. Two miles south of Midway Airport, this Holiday Inn is 12 mi from downtown Chicago. Restaurant, bar, room service. Cable TV. Pool. Exercise equipment. Business services, airport shuttle. | 7353 S. Cicero Ave. | 773/581–5300 | fax 773/581–8421 | www.basshotels.com | 161 rooms | $104–$114 | AE, D, DC, MC, V.

Hostelling International–Chicago Hostel. In Printer's Row, a neighborhood of artist's live/work loft spaces just south of the Loop, this large hostel, in the George F. Kimball building built in 1886 in the Queen Anne style, includes 24-hour access and security, linen rental, and free walking tours. Early June through early September, when the half used as a dorm by Columbia College students during school sessions is vacated, the hostel offers 500 beds, and during September through June, it offers 250 beds. There is a café and meeting rooms on the premises. TV in common area. Video games. Laundry facilities. No smoking. | 24 E. Congress | 312/360–0300 or 800/909–4776 | fax 312/360–0313 | www.hichicago.org | 500 dorm-style beds, 8 private rooms | $22–$79 | MC, V.

Motel 6. This inexpensive motel is dressier than most in the chain as it's in a tall, old-fashioned building with a marbled lobby that features a crystal chandelier. It's only 1/2 mi from Michigan Avenue and 4 mi to Wrigley Field. Restaurant. Cable TV. Business services. | 162 E. Ontario St. | 312/787–3580 | fax 312/787–1299 | www.motel6.com | 191 rooms | $91–$101 | AE, D, DC, MC, V.

Ramada Inn Lake Shore. From this inexpensive Hyde Park hostelry's rooms you can have views of Lake Michigan and the Chicago skyline. It's 3 mi from Soldier Field and 5 mi from Navy Pier and the Sears Tower. Restaurant, bar, room service. Pool. Business services, free parking. | 4900 S. Lake Shore Dr. | 773/288–5800 | fax 773/288–5745 | www.ramada.com | 184 rooms | $125 | AE, D, DC, MC, V.

© Artville

RIGHT OVER THE PLATE

Other cities may have stickball or Little League or other variations on America's Favorite Pastime. Chicago's got its own too: 16-inch softball. The differences: The ball is bigger, the field is smaller, the pitches are high and arching, and gloves are absent. The city claims to be the birthplace of the game, and come summer, you can see its presence everywhere, from lakefront Lincoln Park to small fields in far-flung pockets of the city where neighborhood teams take each other on. Numerous high schools around the city have even been sanctioned to field teams.

Sleep Inn. In Beford Park, adjacent to the Midway Airport and near the rapid transit line to downtown, this motel is 7 mi from downtown Chicago and Chinatown, 9 mi from Soldier Field, and 10 mi from the Magnificent Mile. Complimentary Continental breakfast. In-room data ports, cable TV. Hot tub. Exercise equipment. Business services, airport shuttle. | 6650 S. Cicero Ave. | 708/594–0001 | fax 708/594–0058 | www.sleepinn.com | 120 rooms (118 with shower only) | $69–$119 | AE, D, DC, MC, V.

MODERATE

Ambassador West–Wyndham Grand Heritage. Built in 1924, this hotel often hosted movie stars and celebrities during the 1930s and '40s; it has been restored to its original elegance, with chandeliers and tapestries in the lobby. It's within a block of the Magnificent Mile, the John Hancock Center, and an extensive collection of restaurants and bars. Restaurant, bar, room service. Some in-room VCRs, cable TV. Barbershop, beauty salon. Exercise equipment. Business services. | 1300 N. State Pkwy. | 312/787–3700 | fax 312/640–2967 | www.wyndham.com | 218 rooms | $109–$249 | AE, D, DC, MC, V.

Belden–Stratford. Many rooms in this elegant 1920s building overlook Lincoln Park, Lake Michigan, and the city. The lobby is three stories high with a gold and alabaster chandelier and a dazzling hand-painted sky motif ceiling. Guest rooms have 9-ft ceilings, crown moldings, and plush carpeting. 2 restaurants, bar. In-room data ports, microwaves, cable TV. Barbershop, beauty salon. Exercise equipment. Laundry facilities. Business services. | 2300 Lincoln Park W | 773/281–2900 or 800/800–8301 | fax 773/880–2039 | www.belden-stratford.com | 30 rooms | $139–$269 | AE, D, DC, MC, V.

Best Western–Hawthorne Terrace. In the heart of the Lakeview neighborhood, this hotel is easily overlooked, but the American Colonial lobby, the cozy rooms, and the street-level outdoor terrace make it a real find. Continental breakfast. In-room data ports, some microwaves, some refrigerators, some in-room hot tubs, cable TV. Gym. Business services, parking (fee). | 3434 N. Broadway | 773/244–3434 or 888/675–BEST | fax 773/244–3535 | www.hawthorneterrace.com | 48 rooms, 11 suites | $119–$159 | AE, D, DC, MC, V.

Best Western Inn. There is a sundeck on the top floor of this motor inn, where you can get great city views. There are many shops and restaurants in the area. Restaurant, bar. Cable TV. Laundry facilities. Parking (fee). | 162 E. Ohio St. | 312/787–3100 | fax 312/573–3136 | www.bestwestern.com | 357 rooms | $129–$169 | AE, D, DC, MC, V.

Best Western River North. This hotel is in the heart of the Near North restaurant and entertainment district. The hotel was converted from a warehouse, so the rooms are spacious. It is also steps away from the many restaurants on Ontario Street, and to the historic courtyard district. Restaurant, bar, room service. In-room data ports, some refrigerators, cable TV. Indoor pool. Exercise equipment. Business services. | 125 W. Ohio St. | 312/467–0800 | fax 312/467–1665 | www.bestwestern.com | 150 rooms | $165 | AE, D, DC, MC, V.

City Suites Hotel. Built in the 1920s, this former transient dive once housed vaudeville performers and is now a cozy Lakeview neighborhood hotel. Blues bars, nightclubs, and restaurants abound in the neighborhood and room service is available from the Swedish diner Ann Sather, a neighborhood institution. Complimentary Continental breakfast. Some microwaves, some refrigerators, some in-room VCRs, cable TV. Laundry facilities. | 933 W. Belmont Ave. | 773/404–3400 or 800/248–9108 | fax 773/404–3405 | www.cityinns.com | 17 rooms, 31 suites | $129–$149; $169–$199 suites | AE, D, DC, MC, V.

Courtyard by Marriott. Conveniently located north of the Loop, two blocks from Michigan Avenue, this motel is popular with business travelers. Restaurant, bar. In-room data ports, some microwaves, refrigerators, cable TV. Indoor pool. Hot tub. Exercise equipment. Laundry facilities. Business services. | 30 E. Hubbard St. | 312/329–2500 | fax 312/329–0293 | www.courtyard.com | 334 rooms | $139–$289 | AE, D, DC, MC, V.

Gold Coast Guest House. This small pension in an 1873 Gold Coast rowhouse has a living room with an 18 ft window wall overlooking a private garden. Complimentary Continental break-

fast. Cable TV, in-room VCRs. Business services. | 113 W. Elm St. | 312/337–0361 | fax 312/337–0362 | www.bbchicago.com | 4 rooms (2 with shower only) | $129–$199 | AE, D, MC, V.

Holiday Inn–City Centre. You can walk to the shopping and restaurants on both Navy Pier and North Michigan Avenue when you stay at this large Holiday Inn. Restaurant, bar. In-room data ports, some in-room VCRs, cable TV. Pool. Some hot tubs, massage, some saunas. Gym. Laundry facilities. Business services. | 300 E. Ohio St. | 312/787–6100 | fax 312/787–6238 | www.basshotels.com | 500 rooms | $139–$205 | AE, D, DC, MC, V.

Hotel Burnham. In the landmark 1895 Reliance Building, this fully restored hotel has Carrara marble wainscoting and ceilings, terrazzo tile floors, and mahogany trim, just a few examples of the detailing in the more-than-$25-million renovation, during which the guest rooms were lavishly decorated in shades of regal gold and navy. Restaurant, bar, room service. In-room data ports, minibars, cable TV. Gym. Business services. | 1 W. Washington St. | 312/782–1111 or 877/294–9712 | fax 312/782–0899 | 103 rooms, 19 suites | $125–$260 | AE, D, DC, MC, V.

Hyatt at University Village. This hotel is within the University of Illinois' environs and provides access to the university pool for a small fee ($5 per person) and complimentary transportation to all of the university's facilities. Restaurant, bar. Some microwaves, some refrigerators, some in-room VCRs, cable TV. Exercise equipment. Business services, parking (fee). | 625 S. Ashland Ave. | 312/243–7200 | fax 312/243–1289 | www.hyatt.com | 114 rooms | $109–$255 | AE, D, DC, MC, V.

Hyatt Regency. This large, popular convention hotel has views of Lake Michigan and a lush multi-level atrium lobby filled with trees. The hotel also has Big, the longest freestanding bar in the country. Restaurant, bar, room service. In-room data ports, minibars, some refrigerators, some in-room VCRs (and movies), cable TV. Barbershop, beauty salon, hot tubs. Shops. Business services. | 151 E. Wacker Dr. | 312/565–1234 | fax 312/565–2966 | www.hyatt.com | 2,019 rooms | $145–$160 | AE, D, DC, MC, V.

Midland Hotel. In the Loop, this large hotel is in the center of the business district at the south end of the Loop. The small lobby area has a modest turn-of-the-century feel to it, while the mezzanine offers a dazzling ceiling mosaic with silver and gold patterns. Rooms are named after famous architects. Restaurant, bar. Some refrigerators, cable TV. Exercise equipment. Business services. | 172 W. Adams St. | 312/332–1200 or 800/621–2360 | fax 312/ 332–5909 | www.midlandhotelchicago.com | 390 rooms | $119–$235 | AE, D, DC, MC, V.

Park Brompton Inn. Across from Lake Michigan and Lincoln Park, this hotel has the look of an English inn with poster beds, lace curtains, and butler's pantries. Complimentary Continental breakfast. Some kitchenettes, some minibars, microwaves, refrigerators, cable TV. Laundry facilities. | 528 W. Brompton Pl. | 773/404–3499 or 800/727–5108 | fax 773/404–3495 | www.cityinns.com | 52 rooms, 21 suites | $129–$149, $149–$189 suites | AE, D, DC, MC, V.

Omni Chicago Hotel. An opulent downtown hotel, north of the Loop, on the lower floors of an office tower. The lobby has large domed chandeliers, marble floors, and beautiful flower arrangements. All the rooms are suites decorated in deep greens and burgundies with french doors separating the bedroom from the living room. Restaurant, bar with entertainment, room service. In-room data ports, minibars, some microwaves, some in-room VCRs, cable TV. Indoor pool. Hot tub. Exercise equipment. Business services. | 676 N. Michigan Ave. | 312/944–6664 or 800/THE–OMNI | fax 312/266–3015 | www.omnihotels.com | 347 rooms | $179–$349 | AE, D, DC, MC, V.

Raphael Hotel. This medium-size hotel off Michigan Avenue is just two blocks from the lake north of the Loop. Restaurant, bar with entertainment, room service. Minibars, cable TV. | 201 E. Delaware Pl. | 312/943–5000 | fax 312/943–9483 | 100 rooms, 72 suites | $130–$225; $179–$239 suites | AE, D, DC, MC, V.

The Willows Hotel. This small Lincoln Park hotel has a 19th-century French countryside feeling that borders on being overdone, complete with large, frilly sitting rooms adorned with chandeliers and columns. Complimentary Continental breakfast, room service. In-room data ports, cable TV. Pets allowed (fee). | 555 W. Surf St. 60657 | 773/528–8400 or 800/787–3108 | fax 773/528–8483 | www.cityinns.com | 55 rooms | $109–$200 | AE, D, DC, MC, V.

EXPENSIVE

Chicago Hilton and Towers. Facing Grant Park and Lake Michigan, this enormous 1920s hotel has been renovated to reflect its original furnishings. Four restaurants, bar with entertainment, room service. Minibars, cable TV. Indoor pool. Barbershop, beauty salon, hot tubs, massage. Gym. Shops. Business services, parking (fee). | 720 S. Michigan Ave. | 312/922–4400 | fax 312/922–5240 | www.hilton.com | 1,543 rooms | $139–$289 | AE, D, DC, MC, V.

Claridge. Limousines are available every morning to take you wherever you want to go within a 2-mi radius when you stay at this quiet, elegant hotel on the Gold Coast. Restaurant, bar, complimentary Continental breakfast. Minibars, cable TV. Business services. Some pets allowed. | 1244 N. Dearborn Pkwy. | 312/787–4980 or 800/245–1258 | fax 312/266–0978 | www.claridge.com | 162 rooms | $139–$250 | AE, D, DC, MC, V.

Clarion Hotel Executive Plaza. When you stay at this large hotel overlooking the Chicago River and close to Michigan Avenue, you are two blocks to Lake Michigan, and one block to Michigan Ave. Restaurant, bar. Some minibars, cable TV. Exercise equipment. Business services. | 71 E. Wacker Dr. | 312/346–7100 | fax 312/346–1721 | www.clarionhotel.com | 421 rooms, 60 suites | $189–$250; $300–$400 suites | AE, D, DC, MC, V.

Doubletree Guest Suites. This all-suites hotel is just off Michigan Avenue, and is a half-mile from Oak Street Beach. Restaurants, bar, room service. In-room data ports, minibars, microwaves, refrigerators, some in-room VCRs, cable TV. Indoor pool. Hot tub. Exercise equipment. Laundry facilities. Business services. | 198 E. Delaware Pl. | 312/664–1100 | fax 312/664–9881 | www.doubletreehotels.com | 345 suites | $189–$325 | AE, D, DC, MC, V.

Embassy Suites. In this business-oriented all-suites hotel three blocks east of Magnificent Mile, you can sip a cocktail in the impressive 11-story lobby atrium before riding up to your room in a glass elevator. Restaurant, bar, complimentary breakfast. In-room data ports, minibars, microwaves, refrigerators, cable TV. Indoor pool. Hot tub. Exercise equipment. Business services. | 600 N. State St. | 312/943–3800 | fax 312/943–7629 | www.embassy-suites.com | 358 suites | $189–$269 | AE, D, DC, MC, V.

Holiday Inn–Mart Plaza. This full-facilities hotel is on the 16th through 23rd floors of the Apparel Center, next to the Merchandise Mart, where you could easily spend your entire visit to Chicago. Restaurant, bar. In-room data ports. Some refrigerators, cable TV. Indoor pool. Exercise equipment. Shops. Laundry facilities. Some pets. | 350 N. Orleans St. | 312/836–5000 | fax 312/222–9508 | www.basshotels.com | 526 rooms | $179–$225 | AE, D, DC, MC, V.

Hotel Allegro. This downtown hotel is in the heart of Chicago's theater district, should the performing arts be a draw to the city for you. It has suites named after famous plays, like "Rent." Enjoy the funky surroundings at a nightly cocktail hour. Restaurant, bar, room service. In-room data ports, minibars, cable TV, some VCRs. Pool. Laundry service. Business services, parking (fee). | 171 W. Randolph St. | 312/236–0123 | fax 312/236–3440 | 453 rooms, 30 suites | $165–$215; $275–$375 suites | AE, D, DC, MC, V.

Hotel Monaco. You are offered free pet goldfish to keep you company during your stay at this downtown hotel, overlooking the Chicago River that's a block from Michigan Avenue. Restaurant, bar, room service. In-room data ports, minibars, cable TV, some VCRs. Gym. Video games. Laundry service. Business services. Parking (fee). Pets allowed. | 225 N. Wabash Ave. | 312/960–8500 | fax 312/960–1883 | 170 rooms, 22 suites | $185–$230; $325–$425 suites | AE, D, DC, MC, V.

Hyatt on Printers Row. Located 1½ mi from Michigan Avenue's shops, this hotel has retained its boutique setting with replications of turn-of-the century antiques. The ceilings are high, and the rooms airy. Restaurant, bar. Minibars, some in-room VCRs, cable TV. Exercise equipment. Business services, airport shuttle. | 500 S. Dearborn St. | 312/986–1234 | fax 312/939–2468 | www.hyatt.com | 161 rooms | $165–$250 | AE, D, DC, MC, V.

Lenox Suites. Just a block off of Michigan Avenue, this all-suites motel is a block west of Magnificent Mile and close to shopping, restaurants, movie theaters, and entertainment complexes. Three restaurants, bar, room service. Complimentary Continental breakfast. In-room data ports, kitchenettes, microwaves, cable TV. Exercise equipment. Laundry facilities. Business services. | 616 N. Rush St. | 312/337–1000 or 800/445–3669 | fax 312/337–7217 | www.lenoxsuites.com | 324 suites | $179–$279 | AE, D, DC, MC, V.

Regal Knickerbocker. This refurbished 1920s hotel with a European feel is close to North Michigan Avenue shopping and restaurants. Restaurant, bar, room service. In-room data ports, minibars, some refrigerators, cable TV. Exercise equipment. Business services. | 163 E. Walton Pl. | 312/751–8100 or 800/621–8140 | fax 312/751–9205 | www.regalhotel.com | 305 rooms | $165–$275 | AE, D, DC, MC, V.

★ **Renaissance.** You can ask for a room with a view of the Chicago River at this hotel with a lavish lobby, complete with high ceilings, a marble floor, and chandeliers. The rooms are simple and classic. 2 restaurants, bar, room service. In-room data ports, minibars, cable TV. Indoor pool. Hot tub, massage. Gym. Shops. Business services. Some pets. | 1 W. Wacker Dr. | 312/372–7200 | fax 312/372–0093 | www.renaissancehotels.com | 553 rooms | $179–$350 | AE, D, DC, MC, V.

Residence Inn by Marriott. This 19-story hostelry is 2 blocks away from Oak Street Beach, north of the Loop, and provides complimentary evening refreshments—salad, buffalo wings, and other appetizers. Complimentary Continental breakfast. In-room data ports, kitchenettes, microwaves, cable TV. Exercise equipment. Business services. Some pets (fee). | 201 E. Walton Pl. | 312/943–9800 | fax 312/943–8579 | www.marriott.com | 221 rooms | $169–$315 | AE, D, DC, MC, V.

The Seneca. Part hotel and part apartment building, where you can rent by the night or by the month, the Seneca is just down the street from the John Hancock Center and two blocks from Lake Michigan. Dramatic touches include high arched doorways, chandeliers, and mahogany furnishings. 2 restaurants, bar. Refrigerators, cable TV, some VCRs. Beauty salon. Exercise equipment. Laundry facilities. Business services. Parking (fee). | 200 E. Chestnut St. | 312/787–8900 or 800/800–6261 | fax 312/988–4438 | www.senecahotel.com | 120 rooms; 150 apartments | $149–$269; $1,875–3,000 per month apartments | AE, D, DC, MC, V.

Sheraton Chicago Hotel and Towers. This large 1992 convention-style hotel is right along the Chicago River, near Navy Pier, and has good views of both the lake and the city. Restaurant, bar, room service. In-room data ports, minibars, some in-room VCRs, cable TV. Indoor pool. Massage. Exercise equipment. Business services. | 301 E. North Water St. | 312/464–1000 | fax 312/464–9140 | www.sheraton.com | 1,152 rooms, 52 suites | $119–$369; $350–$1,500 suites | AE, D, DC, MC, V.

Summerfield Suites. This all-suites hotel is a half block from Michigan Avenue. Restaurant, bar, complimentary breakfast. In-room data ports, some kitchenettes, microwaves, refrigerators, some in-room VCRs (and movies), cable TV. Pool. Barbershop. Exercise equipment. Laundry facilities. Business services. | 166 E. Superior St. | 312/787–6000 | fax 312/787–4331 or 312/787–6133 | www.summerfieldsuites.com | 120 suites | $149–$219 | AE, D, DC, MC, V.

Sutton Place Hotel. This hotel is in a prime shopping location—just one block east of Magnificent Mile. Restaurant, bar, room service. In-room data ports, minibars, cable TV, in-room VCRs (and movies). Exercise equipment. Business services, airport shuttle. Some pets (fee). | 21 E. Bellevue Pl. | 312/266–2100 or 800/606–8188 | fax 312/266–2103 | 206 rooms, 40 suites | $199–$240; $240–$360 suites | AE, D, DC, MC, V.

Swissôtel. This 54-story tower has glorious panoramas of Lake Michigan, the Chicago skyline, Grant Park, and the Navy Pier. 2 restaurants, bar. In-room data ports, minibars, room service, cable TV, in-room VCRs available. Indoor pool. Hot tub. Massage. Gym. Business services. | 323 E. Wacker Dr. | 312/565–0565 or 800/654–7263 | fax 312/565–0540 | www.swissotel.com | 632 rooms | $159–$399 | AE, D, DC, MC, V.

Talbott. Just off the Magnificent Mile, this hotel was once apartments, so many of the rooms and all of the suites have a kitchen and dining area, and the lobby's twin parlors' hunt-club appeal promotes hanging out among the guests. The hotel bar, Basil's, offers light fare. Restaurant, bar, room service. In-room data ports, in-room safes, some kitchenettes, mini-bars, some refrigerators, cable TV. Laundry service. Parking (fee). | 20 E. Delaware Pl. | 312/944–4970 or 800/TALBOTT | fax 312/944–7241 | www.talbotthotel.com | 116 rooms, 32 suites | $150–$499 | AE, D, DC, MC, V.

Tremont. Underneath the high ceilings and chandeliers of this impressive lobby, you can relax with live piano music at this hotel one block from Michigan Avenue, in the shadow of the John Hancock Center. Restaurant, bar, room service. In-room data ports, minibars, some microwaves, cable TV, in-room VCRs (and movies). Business services. | 100 E. Chestnut St. | 312/751–1900 or 800/621–8133 | fax 312/751–8691 | 130 rooms | $179–$330 | AE, D, DC, MC, V.

Westin. Across the street from the John Hancock Center, this hotel is just a block from the Water Tower Place shopping mall. Restaurant, bar, room service. In-room data ports, mini-bars, some microwaves, cable TV. Massage. Exercise equipment. Business services. Some pets. | 909 N. Michigan Ave. | 312/943–7200 | fax 312/397–5580 | www.westin.com | 751 rooms | $189–$214 | AE, D, DC, MC, V.

Whitehall. Just off of Michigan Avenue, this small hotel is across from the 900 North Michigan shopping mall. Restaurant, bar, room service. In-room data ports, minibars. Exercise equipment. Business services. Cable TV. | 105 E. Delaware Pl. | 312/944–6300 or 800/948–4255 | fax 312/944–8552 | www.whitehall-chicago.com | 221 rooms | $169–$350 | AE, D, DC, MC, V.

VERY EXPENSIVE

Chicago Marriott. Rooms in this 46-story Michigan Avenue motel right on the Magnificent Mile have views of Lake Michigan. Restaurant, bar. In-room data ports, some microwaves, some in-room VCRs, cable TV. Indoor pool. Barbershop, beauty salon, hot tub, massage. Basketball, gym. Shops, video games. Business services. Pets allowed. | 540 N. Michigan Ave. | 312/836–0100 | fax 312/836–6139 | www.marriott.com | 1,172 rooms | $189–$449 | AE, D, DC, MC, V.

Crowne Plaza–Allerton. This 1923 Italian Renaissance landmark hotel just off Michigan Avenue was completely refurbished in 1999 to reflect the original furnishings. Al Capone used to stay here. Rooms reflect 18th-century Renaissance style, with period antique replicas and many look out on Michigan Avenue. Restaurant, bar, room service. In-room data ports, in-room safes, minibars, some refrigerators, some in-room VCRs, cable TV. Sauna, gym. Laundry facilities, laundry service. Business services. | 701 N. Michigan Ave. | 312/440–1500 | fax 312/440–1819 | www.allertoncrowneplaza.com | 386 rooms, 57 suites | $209; $309 suites | AE, D, DC, MC, V.

Crowne Plaza–The Silversmith. This 1896 hotel in a refurbished building is in Chicago's jewelry district in the heart of the Loop. You can warm yourself by the antique fireplace in the lobby while someone brings you a cocktail. It's two blocks from Michigan Avenue. Restaurant, bar, room service. In-room data ports, in-room safes, refrigerators, some microwaves, cable TV, VCRs. Video games. Laundry service. Business services, parking (fee). | 10 S. Wabash Ave. | 312/372–7696 | fax 312/372–7320 | www.crowneplaza.com | 80 rooms, 63 suites | $249; $289–$319 suites | AE, D, DC, MC, V.

★ **The Drake Hotel.** You can enjoy tea or a cocktail in the opulent lobby of this 1920 hotel, as well as grand vistas of the lake from a porch here, at the north end of Michigan Avenue north of the Loop. Restaurant, bar, room service. In-room data ports, some minibars, some microwaves, some in-room VCRs, cable TV. Barbershop. Exercise equipment. Shops. Business services, parking (fee). | 140 E. Walton Pl. | 312/787–2200 or 800/553–7253 | fax 312/787–1431 | www.hilton.com | 482 rooms, 55 suites | $275–$355; $395–$795 suites | AE, D, DC, MC, V.

Fairmont. This 42-story tower is filled with fine art depicting old Chicago. Pool privileges are available at the Lake Shore Athletic Club; an indoor walkway takes you directly there

from the hotel. 3 restaurants, 3 bars with entertainment, room service. In-room data ports, minibars, some in-room VCRs, cable TV. Business services. | 200 N. Columbus Dr. | 312/565–8000 or 800/527–4727 | fax 312/856–1032 | www.fairmont.com | 692 rooms | $260–$325 | AE, D, DC, MC, V.

★ **Four Seasons Hotel.** This hotel is on floors 30–46 in the the Nine-Hundred Building, which also houses Bloomingdale's and other upscale shops and restaurants. It's across the street from Water Tower Place and the John Hancock Center, and three blocks from Lake Michigan. The lobby has Italian marble floors and reception desks, chandeliers, and large assortments of fresh flowers, all of which can make you feel like royalty. Restaurant, bar with entertainment, room service. In-room data ports, minibars, some in-room VCRs (and movies), cable TV. Indoor pool. Barbershop, beauty salon, hot tub, massage. Gym. Shops. Business services, parking (fee). Pets allowed. | 120 E. Delaware Pl. | 312/280–8800 | fax 312/280–1748 | www.fourseasons.com | 186 rooms, 157 suites | $380–$425; $535–$3,000 suites | AE, D, DC, MC, V.

House of Blues Hotel. The spacious rooms of this hotel have CD players and Southern folk art in them, and throughout the place there are unique artifacts and artwork, such as a 125-year-old carved-wood Burmese Buddha rubbed with goldleaf and the blue-glass panels behind the bar, which are from an ancient meditation temple in East India. You can relax in the lobby's tented seating area for tarot-card readings on Friday evening and live music on Saturday night. Restaurant, bar. In-room data ports, minibars, cable TV, in-room VCRs. Sauna, steam room. Bowling, health club. Laundry services. Business services, parking (fee). | 333 N. Dearborn St. | 312/245–0333 or 800/23–LOWES | fax 312/245–0504 | www.loewshotels.com | 345 rooms, 22 suites | $219–$325 rooms, $325–$1,500 suites | AE, D, DC, MC, V.

Inter-Continental. The first of the two towers of this historic structure on Michigan Avenue was built in 1929 as the Medinah Athletic Club. Rooms have maple furniture with plush patterned carpet and some accommodations are available with views of the city and Lake Michigan. Restaurants, bar with entertainment, room service. In-room data ports, minibars, some in-room VCRs, cable TV. Indoor pool. Massage. Gym. Business services. | 505 N. Michigan Ave. | 312/944–4100 or 800/327–0200 | fax 312/944–1320 | www.chicago.interconti.com | 844 rooms, 42 suites | $149–$359; $399–$800 suites | AE, D, DC, MC, V.

Omni Ambassador East. This quiet 1920s hostelry on the Gold Coast is one of only three Chicago hotels to be listed on the Historic Hotels of America. It houses the popular Pump Room restaurant which served movie stars such as Clark Gable, Frank Sinatra, and Doris Day. The lobby has high ceilings with crystal chandeliers, marble, fresh flowers, and mirrors. Restaurant, bar. Minibars, microwaves available, room service, cable TV. Barbershop, beauty salon. Business services. | 1301 N. State Pkwy. | 312/787–7200 | fax 312/787–4760 | www.omnihotels.com | 289 rooms | $269 | AE, D, DC, MC, V.

Palmer House Hilton. In the heart of the Loop, this grand old hotel has lavish lobbies and public areas. Three restaurants, 3 bars with entertainment. In-room data ports, minibars, some refrigerators, cable TV. Indoor pool. Barbershop, beauty salon, hot tub, massage. Gym. Shops. Business services, parking (fee). Some pets. | 17 E. Monroe St. | 312/726–7500 | fax 312/917–1707 | www.hilton.com | 1,640 rooms | $159–$479 | AE, D, DC, MC, V.

Radisson Hotel and Suites. Just off Michigan Avenue and one block east of the Northwestern University medical complex and law school, this large hotel is just two blocks from such stores as Bloomingdale's, Tiffany's, Hammacher Schlemmer, Godiva, and Water Tower Place. Restaurant, bar, room service. In-room data ports, minibars, some microwaves, some refrigerators, some in-room VCRs, cable TV. Pool. Barbershop. Exercise equipment. Business services. Some pets. | 160 E. Huron St. | 312/787–2900 | fax 312/787–5158 | www.radisson.com | 350 rooms, 100 suites | $239; $279 suites | AE, D, DC, MC, V.

The Ritz-Carlton. The lobby of this hotel is two-stories high and made comfortable by its intimate groupings of wicker chairs, potted palms, and grand floral arrangements. Guest rooms are richly decorated in deep colors like burgundy, navy blue, and dark green. The hotel is within two blocks of the Magnificent Mile's most popular stores. Pet kennels are available. Restaurant, bar, room service. In-room data ports, minibars, some refrigerators, some in-room VCRs, cable TV. Hot tub, massage. Gym. Business services. Pets allowed. | 160 E. Pearson St. | 312/266–1000 or 800/621–6906 (except IL) | fax 312/266–1194 | www.fourseasons.com | 347 rooms, 88 suites | $400–$475; $435–$1,050 suites | AE, D, DC, MC, V.

Westin River North Chicago. The gleaming black lacquer, mahogany, and granite in this 20-story River North tower create clean, contemporary lines and surfaces in common areas of this hotel, where the guest rooms are either traditional or contemporary in design. Restaurant, bar, room service. In-room data ports, minibars, cable TV. Massage. Gym. Business services. Some pets. | 320 N. Dearborn St. | 312/744–1900 | fax 312/527–2650 | www.westinrivernorth.com | 424 rooms | $399 | AE, D, DC, MC, V.

Wyndham Chicago. Completed in 1999, this hotel is connected a block east of Michigan Avenue. Restaurant, room service. In-room data ports, minibars, some in-room VCRs, cable TV. Indoor pool. Health club. Laundry service. Business services, airport shuttle, parking (fee). | 633 N. St. Clair St. | 312/573–0300 | fax 312/346–0974 | www.wyndham.com | 368 rooms, 49 suites | $318; $418 suites | AE, D, DC, MC, V.

CHICAGO O'HARE AIRPORT AREA

MAP 8, C5

CHICAGO O'HARE
AIRPORT AREA

INTRO
ATTRACTIONS
DINING
LODGING

(Nearby towns also listed: Arlington Heights, Des Plaines, Elmhurst, Itasca, Oak Brook, Schaumburg)

The O'Hare area is home to dozens of hotels and restaurants catering to busy travelers' needs, as well as a large number of malls and outlets ranging from outrageously expensive designers to J. Crew and Nike. The landscape is dominated by busy highways such as the Kennedy Expressway (1–90).

Information: Des Plaines Chamber of Commerce | 1401 Oakton St., 60018 | 847/824–4200 | www.dpchamber.com.

Attractions

Allstate Arena. This sports arena's seating capacity is 18,500, and it hosts not only the Chicago Wolves hockey team and other sports events but circuses, concerts, and civic affairs. | 6920 N. Mannheim Rd., Rosemont | 847/635–6600 (recording) | www.rosemont.com/horizon.html | Priced per event | Call for schedule.

CAR RENTAL TIPS

- ❑ Review auto insurance policy to find out what it covers when you're away from home.
- ❑ Know the local traffic laws.
- ❑ Jot down make, model, color, and license plate number of rental car and carry the information with you.
- ❑ Locate gas tank—make sure gas cap is on and can be opened.
- ❑ Check trunk for spare and jack.
- ❑ Test the ignition—make sure you know how to remove the key.
- ❑ Test the horn, headlights, blinkers, and windshield wipers.

*Excerpted from *Fodor's: How to Pack: Experts Share Their Secrets*
© 1997, by Fodor's Travel Publications

Cernan Earth and Space Center. Laser light shows, telescope viewing, and astronomy shows geared to kids are among the offerings at this center. | 2000 N. 5th Ave., River Grove | 708/583–3100 | $5; special rates for kids | Fri.–Sat. evenings; matinees weekends.

Donald E. Stephens Convention Center. One of the nation's largest convention facilities, this center has 600,000 square ft of exhibition space. | 5555 N. River Rd., Rosemont | 847/692–2220 | www.rosemont.com | Priced per event | Daily 8–5.

Dining

Carlucci in Riverway. Italian. Vaulted ceilings and colorful frescoes are the draw at this upscale trattoria just 2 mi from Chicago O'Hare Airport. Specialties include arcobaleno di vegetali (fresh seasonal vegetables with a fine basil and mint sauce, served on thinly sliced bread); pizza con aragosta (with fresh Maine lobster, fresh mozzarella, tomato sauce, and parsley); and lombata di vitello (grilled veal chop served with a Chianti sauce and broccoli. | 6111 N. River Rd., Rosemont | 847/518–0990 | www.carluccirestaurant.com | $12.95–$30 | AE, D, DC, MC, V | No lunch weekends.

Nick's Fishmarket. Seafood. Offshoot of a popular fish house in the Loop, Nick's has saltwater aquariums and private booths, both of which make for soothing dining on the wide array of fresh fish here. | 10275 W. Higgins Rd., Rosemont | 847/298–8200 | $30–$50 | AE, D, DC, MC, V | No lunch.

Rosewood. Continental. The wood of the beautiful flooring in this restaurant is what gives the place its name, where the favorites are the rack of lamb, roasted-potato-encrusted sea bass, and crab cakes, and you can enjoy a pianist Wednesday through Saturday. | 9421 W. Higgins Rd., Rosemont | 847/696–9494 | www.rosewoodrestaurant.com | $21.95–$32.95 | AE, D, DC, MC, V | No lunch weekends.

Walter's of Park Ridge. American. Known for its grilled seafood, rack of lamb, and steak, Walter's also offers seasonal dishes in its New Orleans-style courtyard and dining room in Park Ridge, 3½ mi from Chicago O'Hare Airport and just over a mi from I–90. | 28 Main St., Park Ridge | 847/825–2240 | $6.95–$24.95 | AE, D, DC, MC, V | Closed Sun.

Lodging

Best Western Midway. Two miles off of I–90, in Elk Grove, you can enjoy the glassed-in atrium pool area at this chain motel with its otherwise typical Best Western accommodations. Restaurant, bar, complimentary Continental breakfast, room service. In-room data ports, some refrigerators, cable TV. Pool. Hot tub, sauna. Business services, airport shuttle. | 1600 Oakton St., Elk Grove Village | 847/981–0010 | fax 847/364–7365 | www.bestwestern.com | 165 rooms | $119–$200 | AE, D, DC, MC, V.

Hampton Inn. You will find these reasonably priced accommodations 8 mi from Chicago O'Hare, in Elk Grove Village, amid a number of corporate office parks. Complimentary Continental breakfast. Cable TV. Business services, airport shuttle. | 100 Busse Rd., Elk Grove Village | 847/593–8600 | fax 847/593–8607 | www.hamptoninn.com | 125 rooms | $94–$99 | AE, D, DC, MC, V.

Holiday Inn O'Hare International. Extensive meeting space, which will accommodate up to 3,000 people, distinguishes this Holiday Inn in Rosemont, just 1½ mi from Chicago O'Hare. Restaurant, bar with entertainment. In-room data ports, minibars, some refrigerators, cable TV. Indoor Pool. Hot tub. Exercise equipment. Video games. Laundry facilities. Business services, airport shuttle. | 5440 N. River Rd., Rosemont | 847/671–6350 | fax 847/671–5406 | www.basshotels.com | 505 rooms | $119–$129 | AE, D, DC, MC, V.

Holiday Inn O'Hare Kennedy. Just 3 mi east of the airport at this Holiday Inn, which has a complimentary shuttle to take you to the nearby business district's corporate offices, you are only 11 mi from downtown Chicago by Blueline train. Restaurant, bar. Cable TV. Pool. Exercise equipment. Business services. Airport shuttle. | 8201 W. Higgins Rd., Chicago | 773/693–2323 | fax 773/693–3771 | www.basshotels.com | 122 rooms | $190 | AE, D, DC, MC, V.

Hotel Sofitel. Although this is a 10-story high rise, the lobby and guest rooms have details and furnishings reminiscent of France, just 2½ mi from Chicago O'Hare, in Rosemont. Two restaurants, bar, room service. In-room data ports, minibars, some refrigerators, cable TV. Indoor pool. Exercise equipment. Business services, airport shuttle. Some pets. | 5550 N. River Rd., Rosemont | 847/678–4488 | fax 847/678–4244 | www.sofitel.com | 300 rooms | $235 | AE, D, DC, MC, V.

Hyatt Regency. This immense 10-story Hyatt on the Kennedy Expressway is connected by a "skywalk" to the Rosemont Convention Center. Restaurant, bar, room service. In-room data ports, some minibars, cable TV. Indoor pool. Massage. Exercise equipment. Business services, airport shuttle, parking (fee). | 9300 W. Bryn Mawr Ave., Rosemont | 847/696–1234 | fax 847/698–0139 | www.hyatt.com | 1,099 rooms | $199 | AE, D, DC, MC, V.

La Quinta. This representative La Quinta's standard accommodations are 8 mi from Chicago O'Hare and 4 mi from the Allstate Arena. Complimentary Continental breakfast. In-room data ports, some refrigerators, cable TV. Pool. Business services, airport shuttle, free parking. Some pets. | 1900 Oakton St., Elk Grove Village | 847/439–6767 | fax 847/439–5464 | www.laquinta.com | 142 rooms | $109–$135 | AE, D, DC, MC, V.

Marriott. You take the Cumberland Avenue exit from the Kennedy Expressway, 3 mi east of Chicago O'Hare, to reach this 12-story Marriott, where you are only 11 mi from downtown Chicago. Two restaurants, bars, room service. In-room data ports, some refrigerators, cable TV. Indoor pool, outdoor pool, wading pool. Hot tub. Exercise equipment. Laundry facilities. Business services, airport shuttle. | 8535 W. Higgins Rd., Chicago | 773/693–4444 | fax 773/714–4297 | www.marriott.com | 681 rooms | $189–$219 | AE, D, DC, MC, V.

Marriott Suites. In Rosemont, a five-minute drive from the Chicago O'Hare airport, this all-suites hotel also has meeting spaces. Restaurant, bar. In-room data ports, some microwaves, some refrigerators, some in-room VCRs, cable TV. Indoor pool. Hot tub. Exercise equipment. Business services, airport shuttle. Pets allowed. | 6155 N. River Rd., Rosemont | 847/696–4400 | fax 847/696–2122 | www.marriott.com | 256 suites | $234–$389 | AE, D, DC, MC, V.

Ramada Plaza Hotel O'Hare. This convention complex in Rosemont includes a penthouse ballroom among its many facilities. Two restaurants, 2 bars. In-room data ports, some refrigerators, cable TV. Indoor-outdoor pool. Hot tub. Nine-hole par-3 golf course, putting green, tennis. Exercise equipment. Video games. Business services, airport shuttle. | 6600 N. Mannheim Rd., Rosemont | 847/827–5131 | fax 847/827–5659 | www.ramada.com | 723 rooms | $99–$157 | AE, D, DC, MC, V.

Residence Inn by Marriott. This all-suites hotel is in Schiller Park, a five-minute shuttle ride to O'Hare. Restaurant, picnic area, complimentary Continental breakfast. In-room data ports, kitchenettes, microwaves, refrigerators, cable TV. Pool. Laundry facilities. Business services, airport shuttle, free parking. Pets allowed (fee). | 9450 W. Lawrence Ave., Schiller Park | 847/725–2210 | fax 847/725–2211 | www.residenceinn.com | 171 suites | $129–$350 | AE, D, DC, MC, V.

Rosemont Suites O'Hare. This all-suites hotel is two blocks south of I-90 across from the Rosemont Convention Center, which is 2 mi from the airport, and 12 mi from Chicago. Restaurant, bar, complimentary breakfast, room service. In-room data ports, minibars, microwaves, refrigerators, cable TV. Indoor pool. Hot tub. Exercise equipment. Business services, airport shuttle. | 5500 N. River Rd., Rosemont | 847/678–4000 or 888/476–7366 | fax 847/928–7659 | www.rosemontsuites.com | 296 suites | $99–$239 | AE, D, DC, MC, V.

Sheraton Gateway Suites. Just a mile from the Expo Center, home to craft and dog shows and charity balls, this all-suites hotel is about the same distance from O'Hare. Restaurant, bar, room service. In-room data ports, some microwaves, refrigerators, some in-room VCRs, cable TV. Indoor pool. Hot tub. Exercise equipment. Business services, airport shuttle. | 6501 N. Mannheim Rd., Rosemont | 847/699–6300 | fax 847/699–0391 | www.sheraton.com | 297 suites | $199–$274 | AE, D, DC, MC, V.

CHICAGO O'HARE
AIRPORT AREA

INTRO
ATTRACTIONS
DINING
LODGING

Sheraton Suites. This all-suites hotel is in Elk Grove Village, 8 mi from Chicago O'Hare and 3 mi to Woodfield Mall. Restaurant, bar. In-room data ports, some microwaves, refrigerators, some in-room VCRs, cable TV. Outdoor pool, indoor pool. Hot tub. Exercise equipment. Laundry facilities. Business services. Some pets allowed (fee). | 121 Northwest Point Blvd., Elk Grove Village | 847/290–1600 | fax 847/290–1129 | www.sheraton.com | 253 suites | $79–$219 | AE, D, DC, MC, V.

The Westin–O'Hare. Just a five-minute drive from Chicago O'Hare, this motel is in the business district of Rosemont. Restaurant, bar, room service. Minibars, cable TV. Indoor pool. Hot tub, sauna. Gym. Business services, airport shuttle. | 6100 River Rd., Rosemont | 847/698–6000 | fax 847/698–3522 | www.westin.com | 525 rooms | $199–$279 | AE, D, DC, MC, V.

CLINTON

MAP 6, F6

(Nearby towns also listed: Bloomington-Normal, Champaign-Urbana, Decatur, Lincoln, Monticello)

A statue of Abraham Lincoln on Clinton's courthouse lawn commemorates his 1858 speech delivered here, in which he said, "You can fool some of the people all of the time, and all of the people some of the time, but you cannot fool all of the people all of the time." Lincoln had a law office here in the 1840s, when the town was still new (it had been settled about a decade earlier.) Today it's the base for two recreational areas—Clinton Lake and Weldon Springs State Recreational Area; it's also the home of Revere Copper and Brass.

Information: **Clinton Chamber of Commerce** | 100 S. Center St., 61727 | 217/935–3364.

ON THE CALENDAR
SEPT.: *Apple and Pork Festival.* Primarily a large flea market held the last full weekend in September, this two-day event, attended by around 80,000 people, includes more than 300 crafts and antiques dealers, a tractor show, music, and food vendors dressed in pilgrim's garb. | 217/935–8722.

Dining

Monical's Restaurant. Pizza. This place on the south edge of town sports prints of old-fashioned ads on its walls and touts the house specialty, Monical's Delight, which is loaded with sausage and pepperoni, while another favorite is the hot Sicilian sandwich, with pepperoni and ham. But you can also get a plain cheese pizza, pasta, or salad for lighter fare here. | Rte. 10 East | 217/935–2919 | $4–$15 | D, MC, V.

Lodging

Days Inn. You are just 7 mi from Clinton Lake at this motel, where you can picnic, barbecue, and play basketball on the motel's grounds. Complimentary Continental breakfast, picnic area. Some microwaves, some refrigerators, some in-room hot tubs, some in-room VCRs, cable TV. Gym, basketball. Video games. Playground. Laundry facilities. Business services. Some pets. | U.S. 51 Bypass and Kleeman Dr. | 217/935–4140 or 800/544–8313 | fax 217/935–4140 | www.daysinn.com | 46 rooms, 4 suites | $38–$68; $80–$130 suites | AE, D, DC, MC, V.

Wye Motel. This practical motel is a mile from the town square. There is a Subway sandwich shop next to the motel, but other than that you have to go into town for food. Some kitchenettes, microwaves, refrigerators, some in-room hot tubs, cable TV. No pets. | 721 E. Rte. 54 | 217/935–3373 | fax 217/935–6589 | 26 rooms | $40 | AE, D, MC, V.

COLLINSVILLE

(Nearby towns also listed: Alton, Belleville, Cahokia, Edwardsville)

This St. Louis suburb was settled in the 1830s and 1840s; coal mining began here in the 1870s. However, by the mid-20th century, most of the mines closed and today Collinsville (population 20,289) leads a quiet suburban existence. A healthy portion of the world's horseradish supply comes from this area, and the town has a festival to celebrate the pungent root every spring.

Information: Collinsville Convention and Visitors Bureau | 1 Gateway Dr., 62234 | 618/345–4999 or 800/289–2388.

Attractions

Cahokia Mounds State Historic Site. This site of a 1,000-year-old Native American community includes 55 burial mounds, a museum, and an interpretive center. | 30 Ramey St. | 618/346–5160 | www.cahokiamounds.com | Free | Daily 9–5.

Horse Racing at Fairmount Park. In the city limits of Collinsville at the intersection of I–55 and I–255, this track is open for simulcast racing every day and holds live thoroughbred racing seasonally. | 9301 Collinsville Rd. | 618/345–4300 | www.fairmountpark.com | Live racing $2 | Daily 11 AM simulcast; call for live racing schedule.

ON THE CALENDAR

SEPT.: *Italian Fest.* This fall festival, held the third weekend of the month, celebrates the Italian heritage of this area, with food booths, a wine garden, and a crafts fair downtown on Main Street. Activities include a parade and a moonlight bike ride. | 618/344–4999.
SEPT.: *Rediscover Cahokia.* Formerly called Prehistoric Lifeways, this fall celebration at Cahokia Mounds one September weekend includes traditional dancing by the Choctaw and other Native American groups, demonstrations of flint knapping, basket and pottery making, and gourd decorating. | 618/346–5160.

Dining

Horseshoe Lounge. American. Known as a meat-lovers' paradise, this modest eatery with checked tablecloths and sports memorabilia has rib-eye steaks and Italian beef burgers, but you can also order a whole channel catfish and other nonbeef fare. | 410 St. Louis Rd. | 618/345–9350 | $3–$19 | D, MC, V | No lunch Sun.

Old Peking. Chinese. Despite the formal Chinese statuary here, this restaurant is made homey by an abundance of photographs of the owners' family. Favorite dishes are the emperor's chicken and the triple crown, which includes shrimp, steak, and chicken. | 604 W. Main St. | 618/345–0804 | $7–$9 | AE, D, DC, MC, V | Closed Mon.

Porter's Steakhouse. Steak. Grilled peppercorn steak and pork chops with apple chutney sauce are two of the more creative twists on the meat dishes you can choose from in this marble-floor establishment with marble-top tables, a working fireplace, and low lighting. | 1000 Eastport Plaza | 618/345–2400 | $19–$50 | AE, D, DC, MC, V | Breakfast also available.

Ramon's Eldorado Restaurant. Mexican. In this restaurant with tile floors and Aztec motifs the most popular dishes are the shrimp Valentino and the flautas plates. | 1711 Collinsville Rd. | 618/344–6435 | $7–$14 | AE, MC, V.

Top of the Turf. Steak. This restaurant is on the grounds of the Fairmont Park racetrack, and you won't have to miss a second of the action while enjoying filet mignon or boneless strip steak, because all the tables have monitors, and individual sky boxes are available. You can even place bets here while waiting for your meal. | 9301 Collinsville Rd. | 618/345-4300 | Reservations essential | $9-$16 | AE, D, MC, V.

Lodging

Best Western Heritage Inn. This motel has blended for 30 years with the residential neighborhood it is in, 11 mi east of downtown St. Louis and near I-55 and I-70, just across the street from a small four-plex movie theater. Complimentary Continental breakfast. Microwaves, some refrigerators, cable TV, in-room VCRs (and movies). Indoor pool. Hot tub. Exercise equipment. Laundry facilities. Business services. | 2003 Mall Rd. | 618/345-5660 or 800/228-5150 | fax 618/345-8135 | www.bestwestern.com | 80 rooms | $45-$74 | AE, D, DC, MC, V.

Days Inn. You can see St. Louis and the Mississippi River valley from rooms in this motel, which is convenient to downtown Collinsville. Restaurant, bar with entertainment. Complimentary Continental breakfast. Some in-room data ports, microwaves, refrigerators, cable TV. Pool. Laundry services. Business services. Some pets allowed. | 1803 Ramada Blvd. | 618/345-8100 or 800/544-8313 | fax 618/345-8110 | www.daysinn.com | 57 rooms, 2 suites | $40-$75; $100-$150 suites | AE, D, DC, MC, V.

Drury Inn. This redbrick motel, 12 mi east of downtown St. Louis and 25 mi east of the Lambert airport, sits on a hill in a business district in Collinsville that has several chain restaurants. Complimentary Continental breakfast. In-room data ports, cable TV. Indoor pool. Exercise equipment. Business services. | 602 N. Bluff Rd. | 618/345-7700 or 800/378-7946 | www.druryinn.com | 123 rooms | $72-$82 | AE, D, DC, MC, V.

Econo Lodge. This motel in Marysville is 3 mi northeast of Collinsville, 15 mi east of downtown St. Louis, and 8 mi south of Southern Illinois University. Complimentary Continental breakfast. In-room data ports, cable TV. Pool. Business services. No pets. | 2701 Maryville Rd., Maryville | 618/345-5720 or 800/55-ECONO | fax 618/345-5721 | www.econolodge.com | 40 rooms | $52-$70 | AE, D, DC, MC, V.

Fairfield Inn. The contemporary floral bedding and paintings in this standard motel brighten the rooms. Complimentary Continental breakfast. Cable TV. Indoor pool. Laundry service. Business services. No pets. | 4 Gateway Dr. | 618/346-0607 or 800/228-2800 | fax 618/346-0607 | www.fairfieldinn.com/stlc | 56 rooms, 8 suites | $69-$85 | AE, D, DC, MC, V.

Holiday Inn. Adjacent to the Gateway Convention Center, this large motel has an immense amount of meeting space and is just 12 minutes from downtown St. Louis. Restaurant, bar. In-room data ports, some microwaves, cable TV. Indoor pool. Hot tub, sauna. Exercise equipment. Video games. Laundry facilities, laundry service. Business services. | 1000 Eastport Plaza Dr. | 618/345-2800 or 800/HOLIDAY | fax 618/345-9804 | www.basshotels.com | 229 rooms | $89-$129 | AE, D, DC, MC, V.

Howard Johnson Express Inn. Just one block from exit 11 off I-70, this modest motel with its standard accommodations is two blocks from the Gateway Convention Center. Restaurant, bar. Cable TV. Pool, wading pool. Laundry facilities. Business services. Some pets allowed. | 301 N. Bluff Rd. | 618/345-1530 or 800/406-1411 | fax 618/345-1321 | www.hojo.com | 88 rooms | $30-$70 | AE, D, DC, MC, V.

Maggie's Bed and Breakfast. On two rural landscaped acres 1 mi north of Collinsville, this house, built around 1900, is filled with period furnishings. Complimentary breakfast. Cable TV, in-room VCRs (and movies). Hot tub. Some pets allowed. No smoking. | 2102 N. Keebler Rd. | 618/344-8283 | 5 rooms | $55-$100 | No credit cards.

Ramada Limited. The rooms in this motel are spacious and painted in bright colors. Complimentary Continental breakfast. In-room data ports, some microwaves, some refrigerators, some in-room hot tubs, cable TV. Indoor pool. Business services. No pets. | 12 Commerce Dr. | 618/345-2000 | fax 618/345-2626 | www.ramadastlil.com | 56 rooms | $59-$125 | AE, D, DC, MC, V.

CRYSTAL LAKE

(Nearby towns also listed: Barrington, Dundee, Elgin, McHenry, Woodstock)

In the early part of the twentieth century, Crystal Lake was a popular resort; today residential and retail development have made it one of the fastest-growing towns (population 34,000) in Chicago's northwest suburbs.

Information: Crystal Lake Chamber of Commerce | 427 Virginia St. | 815/459–1300 | fax 815/459–0243 | www.clchamber.com.

Attractions

Wingate Prairie. As you wander these 39 acres of prairie land, you can encounter endangered species with vivid names like Purple Flowering Raspberries and Silver Blue Butterflies. Apart from this small preserve, there are only 20 known acres of this rare topography. | 300 N. Main St. | 815/459–0680 | www.crystallakeparks.org | Free | Daily 9–dusk.

ON THE CALENDAR
JULY: *Taste of Crystal Lake and Lakeside Festival.* This summer festival at Lakeside Center, held the first week of the month, includes a parade, a run-walk, a teen dance, and numerous events for younger kids, as well as assorted live entertainment for all ages. | 815/459–1300.
AUG.: *CABA World Series.* This international series for 15-year-old baseball players draws participants and spectators from around the world. | 815/459–0243.

Dining

1776. Continental. Wild game, pork chops, risotto, and fish dishes can be accompanied by a selection from the more than 500 wines on the list—which has won many national restaurant-wine awards—offered in this softly lit eatery on Route 14. | 397 Virginia St. | 815/356–1776 | www.1776andy.com | $12–$26 | AE, D, DC, MC, V | No lunch Sat. Closed most Sun.

Port Edward. Seafood. In Algonquin, 5 mi south of Crystal Lake, you can dine on seafood and steaks in the nautical environment of this dining room overlooking the Fox River. There's an international seafood buffet on Friday night and brunch on Sundays. | 20 W. Algonquin Rd., Algonquin | 847/658–5441 | www.portedwardrestaurant.com | $16–$35 | AE, D, DC, MC, V | No lunch Sat.

Lodging

Holiday Inn and Conference Center. This large hotel and conference center has a Holidome recreation center on its grounds. Restaurant, bar, room service. In-room data ports, some refrigerators, cable TV. Indoor pool. Hot tub. Exercise equipment. | 800 S. Rte. 31 | 815/477–7000 or 800/Holiday | fax 815/477–7027 | www.basshotels.com | 196 rooms | $129 | AE, D, DC, MC, V.

Super 8 Motel–Crystal Lake. This motel is 1½ mi from downtown Crystal Lake in a business area. Complimentary Continental breakfast. In-room data ports, microwaves, some refrigerators, some in-room VCRs, cable TV. Laundry facilities. Business services. Pets allowed (fee). | 577 Crystal Point Dr. | 815/455–2388 or 800/800–8000 | fax 815/455–2388 | www.super8.com | 54 rooms, 5 suites | $41–$59; $76–$96 suites | AE, D, DC, MC, V.

Victorian Rose Garden Bed & Breakfast. Six miles south of Crystal Lake, in nearby Algonquin, this bed-and-breakfast is in a residential neighborhood on a quiet street and has a small yard that somehow manages to boast 100 rosebushes. Rooms here have either ornate floral wallpaper or stencils of flowers, and the antiques and decorative touches reflect the home's Victorian heritage, which dates from 1886. Complimentary breakfast. No room phones, TV in common area. No pets. No kids under 12. No smoking. | 314 Washington St., Algonquin | 847/854–9667 or 888/854–9667 | www.7comm.com/rosegarden | 5 rooms | $70–$140 | MC, V.

DANVILLE

MAP 6, H6

(Nearby towns also listed: Champaign and Urbana, Rantoul)

The area around Danville was ceded to the U.S. government by the Kickapoo Indians in 1819. Salt mines helped bring manufacturers and traders to the area, and the town was established—and named for settler Dan Beckwith—in 1827. Today, Danville (population 40,000) is the seat of Vermilion County, and its central location and proximity to interstates give its industrial base a boost. Danville and its surrounding area also contain thousands of acres of parks.

Information: Danville Area Convention and Visitors Bureau | 100 West Main, Suite 146, Box 992, 61832 | 217/442–2096 or 800/383–4386 | fax 217/442–2137 | www.danvillecvb.com.

Attractions

The Depot Museum. In Rossville, 18 mi north of Danville on Route 1, this restored 1902 brick station houses a collection of railway artifacts for you to enjoy. The centerpiece of this collection is the 1948 Wabash Caboose. | Benton St. at CSX Railway | 217/748–6615 | Free | Memorial Day–Labor Day, weekends 1–4.

Forest Glen Preserve. You can picnic and camp in this 1,800-acre forest preserve in Westville, 15 mi southeast of Danville, where there are also a 72-ft observation tower, an aboretum, and a homestead cabin for you to explore. | 20301 E. 900 North Rd., Westville | 217/662–2142 | www.vccd.org | Free | Daily Mar.–Dec. 8–8, Dec.–Mar. 8–4:30.

Kickapoo State Park. In Oakwood, 5 mi west of Danville, you can boat, fish, scuba dive, and hike in this 2,500-acre state park. | 10906 Kickapoo Park Rd., Oakwood | 217/442–4915 | Free | Daily.

Vermilion County Museum. You can learn all about the history of the Vermilion area from the many exhibits at this museum. | 116 N. Gilbert St. | 217/442–2922 | $2; special rates for kids | Tues.–Sat 10–5; Sun 1–5.

ON THE CALENDAR

JUNE: *Oldsmobile Balloon Classic Illinois.* Held at the Vermilion County Airport the first or second weekend of the month, this is the largest hot-air balloon race in Illinois. | 217/442–2096.

SEPT.: *National Sweet Corn Festival.* In Hoopeston, 25 mi north of Danville, you can eat a tiny portion of the 29 tons of roasted sweet corn given away during this four-day Labor Day weekend celebration. | 217/283–7873.

Dining

Cahill's Family Restaurant. American. You can always get breakfast here—from the crack of dawn until close—including omelets, Belgian waffles with fruit toppings, and biscuits and gravy, in addition to the complete lunch and dinner fare. Wreaths of dried and silk flowers on the walls add cheer to the dining area. | 334 N. Gilbert St. | 217/442–3992 | $1.50–$7 | AE, D, MC, V | Breakfast also available. No dinner Sun. and Mon.

Deluxe Restaurant. Greek. Gyros, pork chops, and grilled halibut are some of the favorites in this booming restaurant in which the dining room is made somewhat exotic by its photos of Greece on the walls, and the booths and tables seat over 200. | 21 W. North St. | 217/442–0685 | $7–$13 | AE, D, DC, MC, V | Breakfast also available. Closed Sun.

Sirloin Stockade. Steak. Most everyone goes for the giant buffet. Many kinds of steaks are available, from sirloins to rib-eyes to T-bones. With such an abundance of food, the plain interior is hardly noticed. | 3215 N. Vermilion St. | 217/446–1237 | $5–$10 | MC, V.

Lodging

Comfort Inn. Maroon and blue accents in the rooms at this motel 3 mi from the center of the town are picked up in the floral bedding and curtains. The suites include couches that convert into queen-size beds. Complimentary Continental breakfast. Some microwaves, some refrigerators, cable TV. Indoor pool. Hot tub. Business services. Pets allowed. | 383 Lynch Dr. | 217/443–8004 or 800/228–5150 | fax 217/443–8004 | 42 rooms, 14 suites | $65–$75 | AE, D, DC, MC, V.

Days Inn. Only two blocks from the civic center, this motel is right near the downtown shopping area, which includes a number of popular eateries. Restaurant, bar with entertainment. Some microwaves, some refrigerators, cable TV. Pool. Exercise equipment. Laundry services. | 77 N. Gilbert St. | 217/443–6600 or 800/325–2525 | fax 217/443–2345 | www.daysinn.com | 95 rooms | $55–$79, $129–$149 suites | AE, D, DC, MC, V.

Fairfield Inn by Marriott. Four miles to the east of downtown Danville and the civic center, this motel is in a corporate business district. Complimentary Continental breakfast. Cable TV. Indoor pool. Hot tub. Laundry services. Business services. | 389 Lynch Rd. | 217/443–3388 or 800/228–2800 | www.fairfieldinn.com | 55 rooms, 8 suites | $64–$68 | AE, D, DC, MC, V.

Ramada Inn. Just off exit 220 of I–74, in the farm country along the highway, this motel has wide-screen TVs in its lounge so that you can catch the afternoon and evening off-track betting broadcasts. Restaurant, bar. Some minibars, cable TV. Pool. Exercise equipment. Laundry facilities. Business services, airport shuttle. Some pets allowed. | 388 Eastgate Dr. | 217/446–2400 or 888/298–2054 | fax 217/446–3878 | www.ramada.com | 131 rooms | $55–$76 | AE, D, DC, MC, V.

Regency Inn. This motel is 5 mi east of downtown Danville, and right next to Big Boy Restaurant. In-room data ports, microwaves, refrigerators, cable TV. Indoor pool. Hot tub. Exercise equipment. Pets allowed (fee). | 360 Eastgate Dr. | 217/446–2111 | fax 217/446–2444 | 36 rooms, 6 suites | $62–$68; $95–$115 suites | AE, D, MC, V.

DECATUR

MAP 6, F6

(Nearby towns also listed: Champaign and Urbana, Clinton, Lincoln, Mattoon)

Eighty acres of Decatur's buildings are listed on the National Register of Historic Places; the buildings range in style from Italianate and Second Empire to art deco. The town, settled in 1829, is also home to a variety of agriculture-related businesses, particularly those centering on soybeans. Its population is 83,000.

Information: Decatur Area Convention and Visitors Bureau | 202 E. North St., 62523 | 217/423–7000 or 800/331–4479 | fax 217/423–7455 | www.decaturcvb.com.

Attractions

Birks Museum. You can admire the large collection of porcelain, glassware, and china housed in this museum in Gorin Hall on the Millikin University campus. | 1184 W. Main St. | 217/424–6337 | Free | Daily 1–4.

Children's Museum of Illinois. This interactive museum has hands-on exhibits. | 55 S. Country Club Rd. | 217/423–KIDS | $3.50; special rates for senior citizens and kids | Tues.–Sun.; call for hours.

Fairview Park. You can ride the bike trails, swim in the pool, and observe the ducks in the pond in this recreational park. | U.S. 36 at Rte. 48 | 217/422–5911 | Free | Daily.

Friends Creek Regional Park. Twelve miles northeast of town, you can camp, fish, and hike the trails at Friends Creek. | 217/795–4421 | Free | Open Tues.–Sun.

Lake Decatur. The Sangamon River flows into this lake in town, where you can boat, fish, and enjoy a lakeside picnic. | Nelson Park Blvd. | 217/424–2837 | Free; $5 permits for boaters | Daily.

Macon County Historical Society Museum. In addition to the exhibits gallery in this living-history museum, there are a Lincoln library, a log courthouse, and a town hall you can go through. | 5580 North Fork Rd. | 217/422–4919 | $2 (suggested) | Tues.–Sun. 1–4.

Mari-Mann Herb Farm. You'll find formal and theme gardens, such as heirloom roses and a "fairy garden," on this 20-acre property, where you can also purchase the farm's own herb jellies and teas, and take classes in cooking, decorative arts, and homeopathy. | 1405 Marimann La. | 217/429–1404 | www.marimann.com | Free | Mon.–Sat. 9–5, Sun. noon–5.

Millikin Place. In a cul-de-sac one block north of West Main Street, you can tour this 1909 housing development laid out by an architect from Canberra, Australia, in which Frank Lloyd Wright is credited with the design of several homes. Maps and walking-tour information available through the Decatur Visitors Bureau. | Millikin Pl. | 800/331–4479 or 217/423–7000 | Free | Daily.

Rock Springs Center for Environmental Discovery. Covering over 1,300 acres, this nature center includes hiking and biking trails, where you can view birds and other wildlife, and learn about the environment through the exhibits in the living-history museum and visitors center. | 1495 Brozio La. | 217/423–4913 | Free | Weekdays 9–4, weekends 10–4.

Scovill Park and Zoo. You can admire animals from many parts of the world at this 10-acre zoo and park. | 71 S. Country Club Rd. | 217/421–7435 | $2.75; special rates for kids; free Thurs. | Apr.–Oct., daily 10–8.

ON THE CALENDAR

JULY: *Pride of the Prairie Country Western Dance Festival.* This festival, held the 4th of July weekend, includes exhibits and workshops in which you can learn about country and western dance styles and then put your knowledge to work at the many parties revolving around this summer festival celebrating the art. | 217/243–3159.
AUG.: *Decatur Celebration.* You can join all of Decatur downtown for this free family street festival the first full weekend of the month. Twenty-two blocks are closed off for this outdoor extravaganza that includes 13 stages featuring headline bands, arts and crafts, commercial and food vendors, and a carnival. There's a televised parade on Saturday. | 217/423–4222.

Dining

The Blue Mill. American. This popular restaurant is known for its steaks, prime rib, and seafood, served in a bright dining room with antique walnut furnishings. Early-bird suppers. | 1099 W. Wood St. | 217/423–7717 | $14–$25 | AE, D, DC, MC, V | No lunch Sat. Closed Mon.

Central Park West Restaurant and Bar. American. Beef Blackstone and chicken cordon bleu are two of the most requested dishes on the menu in this restaurant, which is in the old Post Building, formerly a bank, then a jewelry store. Exposed brick, mahogany woodwork, and stained glass retain the turn-of-the-century feel. | 170 Merchant St. | 217/429–0669 | $7–$23 | AE, D, DC, MC, V | No lunch Sat. Closed Sun.

Marcia's Waterfront Restaurant. Continental. Fine linens and china dress up such specialties as crab-stuffed shrimp and salmon au poivre in this popular lakeside restaurant, where you can choose indoor-dining among paintings by a local artist or outdoor-dining on the deck, overlooking Lake Decatur. | 2301 E. Lake Shore Dr. | 217/422–7202 | $10–$30 | AE, D, MC, V | No lunch Sat.

Mongolian Gardens. Chinese. You can make the possibly familiar choice of Peking duck, or take the more exotic route and order the steaming Mongolian barbecue in this restaurant full of Pan-Asian accents. | 351 W. 1st Dr. | 217/428–4100 | $9–$11 | MC, V.

Lodging

Baymont Inn. You are just 6 mi north of the civic center and Millikin University's campus when you stay at this motel. Complimentary Continental breakfast. In-room data ports, microwaves, some refrigerators, cable TV. Business services. Pets allowed. | 5100 Hickory Point Frontage Rd. | 217/875–5800 | fax 217/875–7537 | www.baymontinns.com | 105 rooms | $49–$69 | AE, D, DC, MC, V.

Days Inn. Convenient to U.S. Route 36, this motel is also close to area restaurants. Complimentary Continental breakfast. Cable TV. Pets allowed. | 333 N. Wyckles Rd. | 217/422–5900 or 800/325–2525 | www.daysinn.com | 62 rooms, 4 suites | $38–$62 | AE, D, DC, MC, V.

Fairfield Inn by Marriott. In Forsyth, 6 mi north of Decatur, this inn is close to a shopping mall and a golf course and near several chain restaurants. Complimentary Continental breakfast. Some microwaves, refrigerators, cable TV. Indoor pool. Hot tub. Laundry services. Business services. | 1417 Hickory Point Dr., Forsyth | 217/875–3337 or 800/228–2800 | www.fairfieldinn.com | 62 rooms, 4 suites | $70–$90 | AE, D, DC, MC, V.

Holiday Inn Select Conference Hotel. Two miles west of Millikin University's campus and just a few blocks from the Scovill Golf Course, this six-story business-class hotel has a Holidome recreation center. Three restaurants, bar with entertainment, room service. In-room data ports, cable TV. Indoor pool. Hot tub. Exercise equipment. Video games. Laundry service. Business services, airport shuttle. Pets allowed. | U.S. 36 and Wyckles Rd. | 217/422–8800 or 800/HOLIDAY | fax 217/422–9690 | www.basshotels.com | 383 rooms | $65–$120 | AE, D, DC, MC, V.

Red Carpet Inn. There are a number of restaurants close to these standard accommodations. In-room dataports, cable TV. Business services. No pets. | 3035 N. Water St. | 217/877–3380 | 43 rooms, 2 suites | $49–$69 | AE, D, DC, MC, V.

Shelton Motor Inn. This motel is 5 mi from downtown. Restaurant, bar. Some in-room data ports, some microwaves, some refrigerators, some in-room hot tubs, cable TV. Outdoor pool. No pets. | 450 E. Pershing Dr. | 217/877–7255 | fax 217/875–4085 | 125 rooms, 5 suites | $52–$89 | AE, D, DC, MC, V.

DEKALB

MAP 6, G2

(Nearby towns also listed: Dixon, Rockford)

Joseph Glidden invented barbed wire here in 1874, leading to the town's nickname of "Barb City." Today, Northern Illinois University is the town's most prominent feature, although DeKalb Genetics, the well-known developer of agricultural seeds, also makes its home here. Its population is 37,264.

Information: DeKalb Chamber of Commerce | 122 N. 1st St., 60115 | 815/756–6306 | fax 815/756–5164 | www.dekalb.org.

Attractions

DeKalb Public Library. This grand art deco building was constructed in 1931 from funds donated by barbed wire magnate Jacob Haish. The facade is Indiana Bedford limestone, and interior detailings include art deco marble, carvings, and mouldings. | 309 Oak St. | 815/756–9568 | www.dkpl.org | Free | Mon.–Thurs. 9–9, Fri. 9–6, Sat. 9–5; Sept.–May, Sun. 1–4.

Ellwood House Museum. This dwelling, built in 1879, now houses exhibits of much of its original furnishings along with other period artifacts and information about the history of the area. | 509 N. 1st St. | 815/756–4609 | www.bios.niu.edu/ellwood | $4; special rates for kids | By appointment.

Northern Illinois University. DeKalb's institution is the main campus of this university and includes seven degree-granting colleges and a law school, in which combined there are 22,000 students. | 1425 W. Lincoln Hwy. | 815/753–1000 | www.niu.edu | Free | Daily; tours available Mon.–Sat.

ON THE CALENDAR

JUNE OR JULY: *Baron DeKalb Day.* To celebrate this German-American Revolutionary War hero, this day's events throughout town include museum tours, Revolutionary War reenactments, and a vintage bathing-suit show. The "Baron" himself makes surprise appearances. | 815/748–7788.

JUNE–SEPT.: *StageCoach Players Community Theater.* The community stages a variety of performances throughout the summer, including musicals, in the theater at 1516 Barber Green Road. | 815/758–1940.

AUG.: *Corn Fest.* You can indulge in the shopping, eating, and drinking offered by the many vendors and local businesses. There's also a carnival, music, and other live entertainment. It all takes place downtown during three days the last weekend of the month. | 815/748–2676.

Dining

Hillside Restaurant. American. This homey dining room filled with antiques has a seasonally changing menu but regularly offers a Bohemian night on Wednesday, an Italian night on Thursday and Sunday, brunch on Sunday, and a kids' menu. | 121 N. 2nd St. | 815/756–4749 | $9–$15 | AE, D, MC, V.

Rosita's. Mexican. Pottery and Aztec imagery create an old-Mexico environment here, where in addition to the customary burritos and tacos, you can choose less common fare such as Mexican steak grilled with green peppers, and fried Mexican sausage with scrambled eggs. There's a kids' menu, too. | 642 E. Lincoln Hwy. | 815/756–1201 | $8–$12 | AE, D, MC, V.

Thai Pavilion. Thai. Dishes to try in this ethnic eatery near the Northern Illinois University campus are the pad Thai, fried red snapper, and hot and sour soup. | 131 E. Lincoln Hwy. | 815/756–6445 | $7–$22 | MC, V | Closed Sun.

Lodging

Best Western DeKalb Inn and Suites. When you stay at this motel, you are 3 mi from downtown DeKalb and right next to NIU's stadium, which means all campus facilities are just down the road. Complimentary Continental breakfast. Some kitchenettes, cable TV. Pool. Exercise equipment. Laundry facilities, laundry services. Business services. Free parking. Some pets allowed. | 1212 W. Lincoln Hwy. | 815/758–8661 or 800/528–1234 | fax 815/758–0001 | www.bestwestern.com | 95 rooms | $69–$130 | AE, D, DC, MC, V.

Comfort Inn. At the junction of Routes 251 and 38, these typical chain accommodations are 16 mi west of DeKalb, in Rochelle. Restaurant, bar. Complimentary Continental breakfast. Indoor-outdoor pool. Hot tub. Health club. In-room data ports, refrigerators, some microwaves, cable TV. Laundry facilities, laundry service. Business services. | 1133 N. 7th St., Rochelle | 815/562–5551 or 800/228–5150 | fax 815/562–3911 | www.comfortinn.com | 77 rooms, 18 suites | $69–$150; $75–$175 suites | AE, D, DC, MC, V.

Harbor Inn. No frills in this motel keeps the prices down, and you are 3 mi from downtown. Some refrigerators, cable TV. Outdoor pool. No pets. | 2675 Sycamore Rd. | 815/756–3552 | fax 815/756–8257 | 46 rooms, 3 suites | $59–$69 | AE, D, DC, MC, V.

Howard Johnson Express Inn. These standard accommodations are only ½ mi west of the Northern Illinois University campus. Complimentary Continental breakfast. Cable TV. Business services. | 1321 W. Lincoln Hwy. | 815/756–1451 or 800/446–4656 | fax 815/756–7260 | 59 rooms | $39–$56 | AE, D, DC, MC, V.

Super 8. Just off of I–88, this motel is near the NIU campus and downtown DeKalb. Complimentary Continental breakfast. Some microwaves, cable TV. Indoor pool. Hot tub. Laundry facilities. Business services. | 800 W. Fairview Dr. | 815/748–4688 or 800/800–8000 | fax 815/748–4688 | www.super8.com | 44 rooms | $43–$64, $89 suites | AE, D, DC, MC, V.

DES PLAINES

(Nearby towns also listed: Arlington Heights, Chicago, Chicago O'Hare Airport, Itasca)

This northwest Chicago suburb (population 54,000) next to O'Hare Airport was home to the first McDonald's franchise restaurant, opened by Ray Kroc in 1955.

Information: Des Plaines Chamber of Commerce | 1401 Oakton St., 60018 | 847/824–4200 | fax 847/824–7932 | www.dpchamber.com.

Attractions

Des Plaines Historical Museum. This mansion, built during the late 1800s and early 1900s, now houses rotating exhibits with seasonal themes. | 789 Pearson St. | 847/391–5399 | Free | Mon.–Sat. 9–4, Sun. 1–4; call for special events schedule.

McDonald's #1 Store Museum. There are exhibits and memorabilia representing the development of this fast-food chain, including a replica of the first McDonald's, which opened in 1955. | 400 N. Lee St. | 847/297–5022 | Free | Call for open months, Thurs.–Sat. 10:30–2:30.

ON THE CALENDAR

AUG.: *Sister Fest.* Sponsored by the Sisters of the Holy Family of Nazareth, this festival includes an antique car show, raffles, bake sales, food booths, and live music. Kids can romp with the animals at a petting zoo and run around on an obstacle course. | 847/298–6760.

Dining

Black Ram. American. Steaks and chops are the favorites in the Ram's forest green dining room with oak detailing, a mile north of I–90, off the River Road exit. Live entertainment Fridays and Saturdays. | 1414 Oakton St. | 847/824–1227 | $16–$32 | AE, D, DC, MC, V.

Café La Cave. French. A mile north of Chicago O'Hare, this restaurant has two dining rooms, one with classic French decor and the other a more romantic, dimly lit room, both of which claim the steak au poivre and the beef stroganoff as top sellers on the menu. | 2777 Mannheim Rd. | 847/827–7818 | $21–$45 | AE, D, DC, MC, V | No lunch weekends.

David's Bistro. French. The decidedly creative approach to cooking here includes such dishes as grilled venison with chile sauce, and encrusted tilapia with mango saffron sauce. The bistro's interior focal point is its 18th-century handcarved oak mantelpiece. | 623 N. Wolf Rd. | 847/803–3233 | $12–$19 | AE, D, DC, MC, V | Closed Mon. Sun. brunch only.

Lodging

Comfort Inn. Near the Allstate Arena and the Expo Center, this motel is 2 mi northeast of the Chicago O'Hare. Restaurant, bar, complimentary Continental breakfast. Cable TV. Hot tub. Exercise equipment. Laundry facilities, laundry service. Airport shuttle, free parking. | 2175 E. Touhy Ave. | 847/635–1300 or 800/228–5150 | fax 847/635–7572 | www.comfortinn-ohare.com | 148 rooms | $99–$120 | AE, D, DC, MC, V.

Courtyard by Marriott. These standard Marriott accommodations are 2½ mi northeast of Chicago O'Hare. Restaurant, bar, room service. In-room data ports, some refrigerators, cable TV. Indoor pool. Hot tub. Exercise equipment. Laundry facilities, laundry service. Business services, airport shuttle, free parking. | 2950 S. River Rd. | 847/824–7000 or 800/228–9290 | fax 847/824–4574 | www.courtyard.com | 180 rooms | $99–$189 | AE, D, DC, MC, V.

Doubletree Club. A gold-and-maroon color scheme, oversize work desks with ergonomic chairs, and Sony Playstations in the rooms, as well as an array of services here make these accommodations appropriate for pleasure and business trips alike. Restaurant, bar, complimentary Continental breakfast. In-room data ports, cable TV. Outdoor pool. Exercise equipment. Business services. No pets. | 1450 E. Touhy Ave. | 847/296–8866 | fax 847/296–8268 | www.doubletree.com | 246 rooms | $149 | AE, D, DC, MC, V.

DIXON

MAP 6, E2

(Nearby towns also listed: DeKalb, Oregon, Princeton)

Dixon is most famous these days as the boyhood home of Ronald Reagan, who lived here for three years in his youth. (He was born in nearby Tampico.) The town also pays tribute to its 19th-century pioneer heritage with a statue of Abraham Lincoln, who served here during the Black Hawk War. Rock River flows through this town with a current population of about 19,500.

Information: **Dixon Area Chamber of Commerce** | 74 S. Galena Ave. | 815/284–3361.

Attractions

Blackhawk Chocolate Trail. Through the Blackhawk Waterways Convention and Visitors Bureau in Polo, you can obtain self-guided tours for the four-county region—Carroll, Ogle, Lee, and White Side counties—focusing on restaurants and stores where you'll find special chocolate treats—fudge, sundaes, and variations on something called Death by Chocolate. | 201 N. Franklin St., Polo | 800/678–2108 | Free | Daily.

Lincoln Statue Park. A statue of Lincoln, who served in the 1832 Black Hawk War, is the focal point of this park which also has the Old Settlers' Memorial Log Cabin. | 115 Lincoln Statue Dr., 61021 | 815/ 288–7204 | Free | Daily.

Ronald Reagan's Boyhood Home. During the 1920s, the boy who when he grew up became the 40th president of the United States lived for three years in this house in the 1920s. | 816 S. Hennepin St. | 815/288–3404 | Free | Sat. 10–4, Sun. 1–4.

ON THE CALENDAR

JULY: *Petunia Festival.* You can enjoy the games and rides of the carnival and the live entertainment, including a midwestern drum-and-bugle competition, at this festival held around the 4th of July. | 815/284–3361.

SEPT.: *Scarecrow Festival.* These mid-September festivities scattered throughout town include a pig roast and music along the Rock River on Friday and Saturday nights, and daytime activities for kids, such as pumpkin painting, a pet parade, and a soapbox derby. Saturday's highlight for everyone is the scarecrow-decorating competition. | 815/ 288–2308.

Dining

Rivers Edge Inn. American. Chicken strips and ribs are the favorites in this dining room surrounded by large windows, through which you have a smashing view of the Rock River. | 2303 W. 1st St. | 815/288–7396 | $8–$14 | AE, MC, V | No lunch.

Lodging

Best Western Brandywine Lodge. Five state parks, including White Pines Forest, Castle Rock, and Lowden, where you can hike and bike the trails, are within 30 mi of this redbrick lodge in the rural Rock River Valley. Restaurant, bar, room service. In-room data ports, some in-room VCRs (and movies), cable TV. Pool. Hot tub. Exercise equipment. Business services. Pets allowed (fee). | 443 Rte. 2 | 815/284–1890 or 800/528–1234 | fax 815/284–1174 | www.best-western.com | 91 rooms | $59–$80 | AE, D, DC, MC, V.

Comfort Inn. Though surrounded by cornfields, this motel and its rooms are thoroughly modern, and for those with interest in the former actor and president Ronald Reagan, a suite with his name is offered here. In-room data ports, some microwaves, some refrigerators, some in-room hot tubs, cable TV. Indoor pool. Exercise equipment. Business services. No pets. | 136 Plaza Dr. | 815/284–0500 | fax 815/284–0509 | www.comfortsuites.com | 41 rooms, 7 suites | $71–$104 | AE, D, DC, MC, V.

Hillendale Bed and Breakfast. You can choose among theme rooms, such as the Aloha and the Australian Outback, in this 1890s Tudor mansion in Morrison, about 25 mi west of Dixon, which are furnished with antiques and mementos from the owners' world travels. Some rooms have fireplaces, and some, Jacuzzis, and there's a billiards room for your pleasure. Complimentary breakfast. Some in-room VCRs, cable TV. Exercise equipment. Cross-country skiing. No smoking. | 600 W. Lincolnway, Morrison | 815/772–3454 | fax 815/772–7023 | 10 rooms | $60–$160 | AE, D, DC, MC, V.

DOWNERS GROVE

MAP 8, C7

(Nearby towns also listed: Glen Ellyn, Lisle, Naperville, Oak Brook, Wheaton)

Downers Grove was originally settled as a small farming community by pioneers from New York state and incorporated in 1873. Today, it's a quiet Chicago suburb (population 47,883) on Metra's Burlington Northern railroad line.

Information: **Downers Grove Visitors Bureau** | 1015 Curtiss St., 60515 | 630/968–4050 | fax 630/968–8368 | www.downersgrove.org.

Attractions

Downers Grove Golf Course. Established in 1892 by golf legend Charles Blair Macdonald, this is the oldest course west of the Alleghenies. Price structures vary depending on your age, residency status, and the time of day, but you can expect to pay about $15 for a day. | 2420 Haddow Ave. | 630/963–1306 | Call for prices | Mar.–Nov., weekdays 6 AM–dusk, weekends 5:30 AM–dusk.

Historical Museum. Artifacts from local history fill this 1890s home, where you are free to wander. | 831 Maple Ave. | 630/963–1309 | Free | Sun.–Fri. 1–3.

ON THE CALENDAR
JUNE: *Downers Grove Heritage Festival.* Half a million people throng this four-day festival held over the last weekend in June, when you can ride a tilt-a-whirl or Ferris wheel, down a cool brew at the beer garden, purchase unique arts and crafts, and enjoy a prominent oldies band. In years past, such artists as The Turtles and Herman's Hermits have performed. | 630/434–5555.

Dining
Bohemian Garden. Czech. Actually more pan-European than simply Czech, this place festooned with Old Europe plaques serves dishes from eastern and northern European countries. Try sauerbrauten, stuffed cabbage, and pickled beef, and also sample the Czech Pilsner. | 980 W. 75th St. | 630/960–0078 | $8.50–$17 | AE, D, DC, MC, V | Closed Mon.

Founders Hill Brew Company. American. The original tin ceilings and limestone floor have been retained in this refurbished warehouse dating from 1932, which also served as a dance hall at one time. Now the focus here is Scarlett's grilled chicken breast and the beer-braised pot roast, and the ales and stouts you can order to accompany your meal. | 5200 Main St. | 630/963–2739 | $12–$22 | AE, D, DC, MC, V.

Golden Duck. Continental. You can enjoy large portions of traditional Old World recipes such as chicken cordon bleu and sauerbraten as well as breaded pork loin and seafood dishes in this Bohemian-style restaurant. Salad bar and kids' menu. | 500 W. Ogden Ave. | 630/968–8887 | $10–$15 | AE, MC, V | Closed Mon.

K.C. Masterpiece. Barbecue. Photos of local scenes from before World War II cover the walls in this restaurant, where baby-back ribs and steak are favorites. | 1400 Butterfield Rd. | 630/889–1999 | $9–$22 | AE, D, DC, MC, V.

Xander's Café. American. Locals consider this place a hidden treasure, as it is "buried" in a strip mall but is devoted to preparing gemlike dishes, including chargrilled whitefish with artichokes, and succulent sautéed pork chops. | 2241 Maple Grove Ave. | 630/435–9520 | Reservations not accepted | $5–$13 | AE, MC, V | Closed Sun.

Lodging

Amerisuites. Surrounded by malls, movie theaters, and restaurants, this hotel offers high-speed Internet access and Nintendo in its rooms. Complimentary Continental breakfast. In-room data ports, microwaves, refrigerators, cable TV, in-room VCRs. Indoor pool. Exercise equipment. Business services. Some pets. | 2340 Fountain Square Dr. | 630/932–6501 | fax 630/932–6502 | 151 suites | $49–$152 | AE, D, DC, MC, V.

Comfort Inn. When you stay in these chain lodgings you are 2 mi east of Morton Arboretum (see Lisle) and have shopping and restaurants nearby. Complimentary Continental breakfast. In-room data ports, cable TV. Pool. Exercise equipment. Laundry services. Business services, free parking. | 3010 Finley Rd. | 630/515–1500 or 800/228–5150 | fax 630/515–1595 | www.comfortinn.com | 121 rooms | $79–$89 | AE, D, DC, MC, V.

Comfort Inn. This three-story motel offers lots of amenities. Complimentary Continental breakfast. In-room data ports, microwaves, refrigerators, some in-room hot tubs, cable TV. Indoor pool. Spa. Exercise equipment. Business services. No pets. | 225 W. South Frontage Rd. | 630/226–0000 | fax 630/226–1111 | 99 rooms, 12 suites | $85–$110 | AE, D, DC, MC, V.

Doubletree Guest Suites. Adjacent to Corporate Towers, this all-suites hotel offers complimentary passes to a full-service health club and a shuttle service to the local shopping and business districts. The hotel also has an impressive seven-story atrium lobby. Restaurant, bar, complimentary breakfast. In-room data ports, refrigerators, some in-room VCRs, cable TV. Indoor pool. Hot tub. Gym. Business services. | 2111 Butterfield Rd. | 630/971–2000 or 800/222–8733 | fax 630/971–1168 | www.doubletreehotels.com | 247 suites | $99–$249 | AE, D, DC, MC, V.

Embassy Suites. In Lombard, 4 mi north of Downers Grove, this 10-floor suites hotel is close to corporate centers and across from a shopping mall. Restaurant, bar. In-room data ports, microwaves, refrigerators, cable TV. Indoor pool. Hot tub. Exercise equipment. Laundry services. Business services. | 707 E. Butterfield Rd., Lombard | 630/969–7500 or 800/362–2779 | fax 630/969–8776 | www.embassy-suites.com | 262 suites | $109–$189 | AE, D, DC, MC, V.

Holiday Inn Express. Close to the Morton Arboretum and shopping. Complimentary Continental breakfast. In-room data ports, cable TV. Laundry service. Business services. | 3031 Finley Rd. | 630/810–9500 or 800/HOLIDAY | fax 630/810–0059 | www.basshotels.com | 123 rooms | $89–$119 | AE, D, DC, MC, V.

Marriott Suites. This all-suites hotel is about 35 mi from downtown Chicago. Restaurants are within 2 miles. Restaurant, bar, complimentary Continental breakfast. In-room data ports, refrigerators, cable TV. Indoor-outdoor pool. Hot tub. Exercise equipment. Business services. | 1500 Opus Pl. | 630/852–1500 or 800/228–9290 | fax 630/852–6527 | www.marriott.com | 254 suites | $69–$169 | AE, D, DC, MC, V.

Red Roof Inn. This standard motel is close to Good Samaritan Hospital and College of DuPage. In-room data ports, cable TV. Business services. Pets allowed. | 1113 Butterfield Rd. | 630/963–4205 or 800/843–7663 | fax 630/963–4425 | www.redroof.com | 135 rooms | $42–$79 | AE, D, DC, MC, V.

DU QUOIN

(Nearby towns also listed: Benton, Carbondale, Mt. Vernon)

The town is named for Kaskaskia Indian chief Jean Baptiste Ducoigne, who served in the Revolutionary army under Lafayette. Du Quoin and its surrounding area is known both for mining and for agriculture.

Information: **Du Quoin Chamber of Commerce** | 20 N. Chestnut St., 62832 | 800/455–9570 | www.duquoin.org.

Attractions

Harvey Pitt's Waterfowl Museum. Run by a biologist with meticulous taxidermy skills, the museum's displays include more than 100 species of waterfowl (mounted) and 740 antique duck decoys, some dating back to 1875. Admission fees are used by the biologist's wife to bake delectables for the guests, such as gooey buttercake. | 522 Orchard La. | 618/542–3562 | $1.25 | By appointment only.

ON THE CALENDAR
APR.: *Bradford Pear Tree Festival.* Where else can you find frog-jumping and baby-picture contests, pony rides, and pet parades, and craft and rummage sales all in one place? This spring festival packs even more than that into its one-day celebration. | 800/455–9570.
AUG.–SEPT.: *Du Quoin State Fair.* This is a real rural state fair, with produce and livestock competitions and exhibits, as well as judgings for local arts and crafts. There's also an old-fashioned carnival midway through the fair. It all takes place the last week of August to the first week of September at the Du Quoin State Fairground at Rte. 14 and U.S. 51. | 618/542–1515.

Dining

B.J.'s Garden Inn Café. American. Most folks prefer to dig in to the buffet, but you can also choose crispy fried chicken or catfish from the menu in this simply appointed café with its cheery staff. | 11 W. Main St. | 618/542–6125 | $5–$7 | No credit cards | Breakfast also available.

To Perfection. American. Favorites to try in the spacious dining room with wood accents here are the lobster and the pasta dishes, and on the weekend, prime rib. | 1664 S. Washington St. | 618/542–2002 | $7–$30 | MC, V | No lunch Sat. Closed Sun.

Lodging

Francie's Inn. This 1908 Prairie School– and Gothic-style inn, which used to be a home for orphans, has rooms with floral linens and clawfooted tubs. The property spans 3 acres and includes rose and perennial gardens. Some baths are shared. Complimentary breakfast. No room phones, no TV in some rooms. No pets. No smoking. | 104 S. Line St. | 618/542–6686 or 877/877–2657 | fax 618/542–4834 | www.franciesinnonline.com | 5 rooms | $60–$85 | AE, D, DC, MC, V.

Oxbow Bed and Breakfast. In Pinckneyville, 12 mi northwest of Du Quoin, you can stay in a restored barn, of which there are two, or the 1929 main house, all furnished with antiques. There are recreations rooms and a pool table you can enjoy here, too. Complimentary breakfast. Indoor pool. No smoking. | 3967 Rte. 13/127, Pinckneyville | 618/357–9839 or 800/929–6888 | 6 rooms | $50–$65 | MC, V.

DUNDEE

(Nearby towns also listed: Barrington, Crystal Lake, Elgin)

Dundee (actually East Dundee and West Dundee, on either side of the Fox River) is home to Haeger Potteries, which had its beginnings as a brickworks, but today turns out art pottery. The area was first settled in the 1830s; by the late 19th century it was a vacation spot for Chicagoans. The towns' walkable shopping district, spanning a bridge over the Fox River, retains an old-fashioned appeal.

Information: Cardunal Area Chamber of Commerce and Industry | 99 W. Main St., West Dundee, 60118 | 847/426–8565 | www.cardunal.com.

Attractions

Dolphin's Cove. This amusement park is filled with fun activities. For the daring, there are two very curvy three-story water slides, and for the less adventurous, two smaller ones. You can also swim in indoor and outdoor pools, play sand volleyball, and workout in the fitness center. | 665 Barrington Ave., Carpentersville | 847/836–7946 | $7.50 | June–Sept., Mon.–Thurs. 11–7, Fri. 11–9, weekends noon–6.

Haeger Pottery Factory Outlet. Both the seconds and the top-quality specimens of this famous pottery are for sale at the factory outlet here, but you are also welcome to browse. | 7 Maiden La., West Dundee | 847/426–3441 | Free | Weekdays 10–6, weekends 11–5.

Santa's Village Theme Park. Music shows, amusement-park rides, and a petting zoo are among the many things you can enjoy in Santa's Village. | Rtes. 25 and 72, East Dundee | 847/426–6751 | www.santasvillageil.com | $15.95–$18.95; special rates for kids | May–Oct. weekdays 10–6, weekends 11–8.

Racing Rapids Action Park. You can cool down at this water park, where the slides and rides can also make your heart race. | Rtes. 25 and 72, East Dundee | 847/426–5525 | www.santasvillageil.com | $12.95; special rates for kids | Mid-June–Labor Day, daily 11–7.

ON THE CALENDAR

JULY: *Fireman's Festival.* The Dundee Fire Department sponsors a carnival and other activities during the three days, Friday through Sunday, of this mid-July fair—and all events are coordinated with what's called East Dundee Day that Saturday—when you can enjoy bike-decorating contests, bake-offs, bands, and a golden-retriever parade, where the dogs really do enjoy showing off in glasses and scarves. | 847/426–2822.

Dining

Cha Cha Cha. Mexican. Fajitas are the local favorite at this East Dundee restaurant filled with Mexican folk art and other south-of-the-border rural touches. Kids' menu. | 16 E. Main St., East Dundee | 847/428–4774 | $15–$25 | AE, D, DC, MC, V.

Duran's of Dundee. American. This restaurant is in an old house, which makes your dining on fish, steak, and chicken dishes homey and relaxed. | 8 S. River St., East Dundee | 847/428–0033 | No lunch Sat.–Mon. | $9–$40 | AE, D, DC, MC, V.

The Manor. Continental. This bustling eatery, where you can choose booth or table seating, includes tenderloin steaks, meatloaf, and roast pork on its menu. | 425 E. Main St. | 847/426–7580 | $6–$10 | AE, D, DC, MC, V | Breakfast also available.

Milk Pail. American. In addition to dining on poultry and fish at this eatery on the 30-acre Fin 'n' Feather Farm, you can tour the grounds, which include many gardens and shops. Kids' menu and Sunday buffet. | 14N 630 Rte. 25, East Dundee | 847/742–5040 | $15–$25 | AE, D, DC, MC, V.

Lodging

Ironhedge Inn Bed and Breakfast. When you stay at this opulent 1907 Victorian mansion, with its Tiffany-style windows and green velvet curtains, you are just a couple of blocks from the jogging trails that wind along the Fox River. The inn is on the National Historic Registry and is surrounded by other stunning homes on a history-filled street. Some baths are shared. Complimentary breakfast. Some in-room hot tubs, cable TV. No pets. No smoking. | 305 Oregon Ave. | 847/426–7777 | fax 847/426–5777 | www.inn-dex.net/ironhedge | 4 rooms, 1 suite | $73–$192 | AE, MC, V.

EDWARDSVILLE

MAP 6, E8

(Nearby towns also listed: Alton, Belleville, Cahokia, Collinsville, Grafton)

Two areas in Edwardsville—the St. Louis Street Historic District and the LeClaire Historic District—are on the National Register of Historic Places. Edwardsville, named in 1816 after territorial Governor Ninian Edwards, is the seat of Madison County and has a population of 24,000.

Information: Edwardsville/Glen Carbon Chamber of Commerce | 200 University Park Dr., Suite 260, 62025 | 618/656–7600.

Attractions

Madison County Historical Museum. In this eight-room 1836 Federal mansion, the history of Madison County is chronicled through exhibits of Native American and pioneer artifacts, period furnishings and costumes, and a genealogy research library. | 715 N. Main St. | 618/656–7562 | Free | Wed.–Fri. 9–4, Sun. 1–4.

Nickel Plate Depot. This 1883 depot, restored by the Goshen Preservation Alliance to its 1920s specifications, is one of the last original stations from the Nickel Plate railroad line, where you will find a collection of original waybills, reference materials on other railroads, and interactive kids' displays. | 410 LeClaire St. | 618/655–0525 | Free | By appointment only.

Southern Illinois University at Edwardsville. This university's campus on 2,660 acres of wooded, rolling hills serves a student body of 12,500 and includes the Lovejoy Library, which houses the National Ragtime and Jazz Archives. | Rte. 157 | 618/650–2000 | www.siue.edu | Free | Daily.

ON THE CALENDAR

JUNE: *Route 66 Festival.* You can get your kicks viewing and riding in vintage cars along the original Route 66 in this area, as well as dine on local vendors' fare, dig the live music, and whirl till you're dizzy on the carnival rides during this celebration. | 618/656–7600.

Dining

Andria's Countryside Restaurant. Steak. Known for its New York strip and rib-eye steaks, this converted brick ranch house hangs its walls with Ducks Unlimited prints and covers its tables in white linen. | 7415 Rte. 143 | 618/656–0281 | $12–$30 | MC, V | No lunch. Closed Sun.

Rusty's Restaurant. American. You dine beneath antique chandeliers in this restored 19th-century trading post, where veal saltimboca and steak à la Romano are favorites. Choose among daily fish specials. There's a kids' menu, buffet lunch, and Sunday brunch. Entertainment Friday and Saturday. | 1201 N. Main St. | 618/656–1113 | $10–$20 | AE, D, DC, MC, V | No lunch Sat.

Lodging

Comfort Inn. On the southeastern outskirts of Edwardsville, this motel is on a scenic bluff overlooking St. Louis, which is just a 15-minute drive from here. Complimentary Continental breakfast. In-room dataports, some microwaves, cable TV. Indoor pool. Exercise equipment. Business services. | 3080 S. Rte. 157 | 618/656–4900 or 800/228–5150 | fax 618/656–0998 | www.comfortinn.com | 71 rooms | $65–$80 | AE, D, DC, MC, V.

The Innkeeper. This modest motel is 7 mi north of Edwardsville on Route 157. Some microwaves, some refrigerators, cable TV. Pets allowed (fee). | 401 E. State St., Hamel | 618/633–2111 | fax 618/633–1965 | 23 rooms | $40–$50 | AE, D, MC, V.

EFFINGHAM

MAP 6, G8

(Nearby towns also listed: Charleston, Mattoon, Shelbyville, Vandalia)

The old National Road helped settle Effingham in the 1850s; today the city of 11,800 is a regional center for commerce and industry and the seat of Effingham County.

Information: **Effingham Convention and Visitors Bureau** | Box 643, 508 W. Fayette Ave., 62401 | 217/342–4147.

Attractions

Lake Sara. You can boat, fish for bass, or picnic and lounge on the beach at this 800-acre artificial recreational lake area. Ice fishing is possible in the winter. | Off Rte. 32/33N | 217/868–2787 | Free | Daily dawn–dusk.

ON THE CALENDAR

SEPT.: *Effingham Transportation Celebration.* Around 15,000 people attend this celebration from late Friday afternoon through Sunday night the second weekend in September, during which you can enjoy an air parade, displays of vintage cars and model railroads, a carnival, and food and crafts booths scattered throughout town. | 217/342–5310.

Dining

China Buffet. Chinese. You can partake of the buffet or order the soups, fried rice, chow mein, chicken, pork, and seafood dishes from the menu in this ethnic restaurant filled with Asian art and furnishings. | 1500 W. Fayette Ave. | 217/342–3188 | $10–$20 | MC, V.

El Rancherito. Mexican. This festive place is known for its creative servings of fajitas, chimichangas, burritos, and other south-of-the-border cuisine. Kids' menu. | 1313 Keller Dr. | 217/342–4753 | $12–$18 | AE, MC, V.

Iron Horse Café. American. This cafeteria—open around the clock every day—gets its name from the train memorabilia that fills the place, including a functional model train on a track, and is popular for its down-home cooking, such as fried chicken and roast beef. All meals à la carte. | 101 S. Merchant St. | 217/347–7191 | $3 | AE, D, DC, MC, V | Breakfast also available.

Niemerg's Steak House. American. You can join the locals who come to this family-style restaurant for the fried chicken and steak. Kids' menu. | 1410 W. Fayette Ave. | 217/342–3921 | $6–$15 | AE, DC, MC, V | No lunch.

Ole Grey Dog Bar and Grill. American. Known for the Mastiff, a gargantuan pizza with every conceivable topping, this bar and grill, washed in a colorful glow from the neon advertisements on its walls, also serves steaks. | 303 E. Fayette St. | 217/342–2035 | $7–$21 | AE, D, MC, V | Closed Sun.

Rexroat's Distinctive Dining. American. Try the steak or smoked pork loin at Rexroat's, where the oak tables are draped with linens at night but things are a bit more casual during the day. | 221 W. Jefferson St. | 217/347–5831 | $10–$27 | AE, D, DC, MC, V | No lunch Sat. Closed Sun.

Third Street Dairy Bar and Grill. American. There are no pretenses at this diner, so you can just hunker down at the counter or grab a table to try the home-cooked lasagna or coun-try-fried steak. Cinammon rolls are a favorite dessert here. | 803 N. 3rd St. | 217/342–4455 | $4–$5 | No credit cards | Breakfast also available. No dinner.

Lodging

Abe Lincoln Motel. This small motel is a basic mom-and-pop operation with no frills in downtown Effingham. Cable TV. Pets allowed. | 1108 Edgar St. | 217/342–4717 | 18 rooms | $30 | AE, D, MC, V.

Holiday Inn Express. You take exit 160 off of I–57 to reach this motel, which was previously the Baymont Inn. Complimentary Continental breakfast. Cable TV. Indoor pool. Laundry facil-ities. Business services. Some pets allowed (fee). | 1103 Ave. of Mid America | 217/342–2525 | fax 217/347–7341 | www.basshotels.com | 122 rooms, 14 suites | $75–$85 | AE, D, DC, MC, V.

Best Inns of America. Shopping and restaurants are within a mile of this motel, which is 2 mi north of the Amtrak station. Complimentary Continental breakfast. Cable TV. Pool. Some pets allowed. | 1209 N. Keller Dr. | 217/347–5141 or 877/877–6810 | www.bestinn.com | 83 rooms | $31–$50 | AE, D, DC, MC, V.

Comfort Suites. This all-suites hotel a mile from the Amtrak station. Complimentary Con-tinental breakfast. In-room data ports, microwaves, refrigerators, cable TV. Indoor pool. Sauna. Laundry facilities. Business services. Pets allowed. | 1310 W. Fayette Rd. | 217/342–3151 | fax 217/342–3555 | www.comfortsuites.com | 65 suites | $53–$99 | AE, D, DC, MC, V.

Days Inn. Just off I–57/70, this motel is within 2 mi of factory outlet shopping and a mall. Restaurant, complimentary Continental breakfast. Cable TV. Pool. Laundry services. Pets allowed. | W. Fayette Ave. | 217/342–9271 or 800/544–8313 | www.daysinn.com | 109 rooms | $34–$49 rooms, $65–$80 suites | AE, D, DC, MC, V.

Hampton Inn. Just a mile from downtown, this motel is off I–57/70. Complimentary Con-tinental breakfast. Microwaves, some refrigerators, cable TV. Indoor pool. Laundry ser-vices. Business services. Pets allowed. | 1509 Hampton Dr. | 217/342–4499 or 800/HAMPTON | fax 217/347–2828 | www.hamptoninn.com | 62 rooms | $62–$82 | AE, D, DC, MC, V.

Howard Johnson. It's too bad this HoJo didn't retain its futuristic styling of the 1950s, when it was built, but its refurbishing assures contemporary accommodations, just a mile from a large outlet mall. Complimentary Continental breakfast. In-room data ports, cable TV, in-room VCRs (and movies). Indoor pool. Pets allowed (fee). | 1606 W. Fayette Ave. | 217/342–4667 or 800/446–4656 | fax 217/342–4645 | 50 rooms | $55–$70 | AE, D, DC, MC, V.

Lincoln Lodge. A standard motel near area restaurants. Cable TV. No pets. | 2404 N. 3rd St. | 217/342–4133 | 25 rooms | $37 | AE, D, MC, V.

Paradise Inn. This plainly appointed motel is just two blocks from downtown and four blocks from a favorite local's haunt, Niemerg's Steak House. Cable TV. Pets allowed (fee). | 1000 W. Fayette Ave. | 217/342–2165 | fax 217/347–3373 | 33 rooms | $33–$39 | AE, D, DC, MC, V.

Ramada Inn–Thelma Keller Convention Center. The premises of this motel complex include a bowling alley, where you can also try your luck at off-track betting, and a ballroom in the convention center. Restaurant, bar, complimentary Continental breakfast, room service. Cable TV. Indoor pool, outdoor pool. Hot tubs. Miniature golf. Bowling, exercise equipment. Video games. Playground. Some pets allowed. | 1202 N. Kellar Dr. | 217/342–2131 | fax 217/347–8757 | www.ramada.com | 169 rooms; 8 condo units | $69–$95 | AE, D, DC, MC, V.

Super 8. You can walk to the factory outlet mall from these standard chain accommoda-tions. Complimentary Continental breakfast. Cable TV. Some pets allowed. | 1400 Thelma

Keller Ave. | 217/342–6888 or 800/800–8000 | fax 217/347–2863 | www.super8.com | 49 rooms | $43–$55 | AE, D, DC, MC, V.

Super 8. This motel is in Altamont, 14 mi southwest of Effingham. Cable TV. Playground. Laundry facilities. Pets allowed (fee). | Rte. 2, Altamont | 618/483–6300 or 800/800–8000 | fax 618/483–3323 | www.super8.com | 25 rooms | $46–$51 | AE, D, DC, MC, V.

ELGIN

(Nearby towns also listed: Barrington, Crystal Lake, Dundee, Geneva, St. Charles, Schaumburg)

This Fox River city has a long history of manufacturing such diverse products as Elgin watches and condensed milk. Today, a gambling casino dominates its downtown. The Elgin Historic District is on the National Register of Historic Places and includes examples of Queen Anne, Greek Revival, and brick row houses. Its population is 86,000.

Information: **Elgin Area Convention and Visitors Bureau** | 77 Riverside Dr., 60120 | 847/695–7540 or 800/217–5362.

Attractions

Blackhawk Forest Preserve. The 284 acres of forest here include hiking trails, boat access to the Fox River, horse trails, and picnic shelters. | 35W003 LaFox St., South Elgin | 847/741–7883 | Free | Daily dawn–dusk.

Burnidge Forest Preserve. Jogging and hiking trails and a 15-acre wetlands complex are part of this 510-acre preserve. | 14N035 Coombs Rd. | 847/695–8410 | Free | Daily 8–dusk.

Elgin Area Historical Society Museum. The exhibits here focus on the architecture and industry in Elgin, including the manufacturing of the famous Elgin watches. | 360 Park St. | 847/742–4248 | $2; special rates for senior citizens, students, and kids | Call for hours.

Fox River Trolley Museum. You can take a 3-mi trolley trip and admire the antique specimens of this mode of transport at this museum. | Rte. 31, South Elgin | 847/697–4676 | www.foxtrolley.org | Free; trolley rides $2.50, special rates for senior citizens and kids | Call for hours.

Grand Victoria Riverboat Casino. You can gamble on this immense boat, which also shows movies and has a restaurant in its pavilion. | 250 S. Grove Ave. | 847/888–1000 | Free | Daily.

Lord's Park. This city park has picnic areas, tennis courts, a pool, and a zoo on its grounds. | Grand Blvd. | 847/931–6120 | Free | Daily dawn–dusk.

Elgin Public Museum. This museum includes interactive natural history, anthropology, and aquarium exhibits. | 225 Grand Blvd. | 847/741–6655 | fax 847/931–6787 | $1; special rates for kids | Apr.–Oct., Tues.–Sat. 10–4, Sun. noon–4, closed Wed.; Nov.–Mar., weekends noon–4.

State Street Market. You can stroll around this warehouse and browse the wares in 35 cubicles, including antiques, woodcrafts, furniture, and candles. | 701 N. State St. | 847/695–3066 | Free | Tues.–Sun. 10–5.

Tyler Creek Forest Preserve. You can fish in the Fox River, ride the bike trails, and picnic in the shelters on the 53 acres of land to explore on the preserve here. | 401 Davis Rd. | 847/741–5082 | Free | Daily dawn–dusk.

Voyageurs Landing Forest Preserve. There are two boat launches, and 2,000 ft of river frontage, as well as picnic areas, throughout this 11-acre preserve. People go biking, boating, and fishing here. | Airport Rd. | 847/741–0106 | Free | Daily dawn–dusk.

JUNE: *Trolley Fest.* At the Fox River Trolley Museum, you can enjoy special demonstrations and trolley rides during this celebration. | 847/697–4676.

SEPT.: *Historic Cemetery Walk.* Costumed tour guides lead you through the Bluff City Cemetery and tell you the history of notable Elgin citizens and other significant "residents" of the gravesites here. The walk takes place the fourth Sunday of the month. | 847/742–4248.

SEPT.: *Historical House Walk.* During the second weekend in September, the Gifford Park Association sponsors a tour of about 10 historically interesting homes in a different neighborhood each year for you (and the estimated 2,500 other people who participate) to view them. | 847/741–2837.

SEPT.–MAY: *Elgin Symphony Orchestra.* There are classical, popular, and family oriented orchestral programs in this series presented at the Hemmons Theater | 847/888–4000.

NOV.–JAN.: *Touching on Traditions.* At Elgin's Lord's Park Pavilion, you can view the multicultural exhibits of 13 holidays from 59 countries. | 847/741–6655.

Dining

Prairie Rock Brewing Company. American. Parts of the stone-and-wood structure of this restored theater from the 1920s are exposed in its interior, and there is an impressive 60-ft stone chimney in the place, where New York strip or bourbon pork chops along with one of the fine ales offered here are the favorites to try. | 127 S. Grove St. | 847/622–8888 | $12–$25 | AE, D, MC, V | Closed Mon.

Lodging

Crown Plaza. You'll find the facilities here crisp and contemporary since the hotel was built in 1999. You can dine at the Bennigan's or sip a cocktail at the piano bar on the property. A courtesy shuttle takes you anywhere in the area. There is a casino, shopping mall, roller rink, and restaurants about 2 mi away. Restaurant, bar, complimentary Continental breakfast. Some minibars, some microwaves, some refrigerators, some in-room hot tubs, cable TV. Indoor pool. Exercise equipment. Laundry service. No pets. | 495 Airport Rd. | 847/488–9000 | fax 847/488–9800 | 206 rooms, 37 suites | $89–$139 | AE, D, MC, V.

Days Inn. Just off of I–90, the standard accommodations of this motel are 2 mi northeast of the Grand Victoria Riverboat casino. In-room data ports, cable TV. Indoor pool. Some hot tubs. Pets allowed. | 1585 Dundee Ave. | 847/695–2100 or 800/544–8313 | fax 847/697–9114 | www.daysinn.com | 96 rooms | $54–$149 | AE, D, DC, MC, V.

Ramada Inn. There are four shopping centers within 5 mi of this motel. Restaurant, bar, room service. In-room data ports, cable TV. Pool. Hot tub, sauna. Exercise equipment. Video games. Laundry facilities, laundry service. Business services. | 345 W. River Rd. | 847/695–5000 or 888/298–2054 | fax 847/695–6556 | 203 rooms | $59–$99 | AE, D, DC, MC, V.

ELMHURST

MAP 8, C5

(Nearby towns also listed: Downers Grove, Glen Ellyn, Itasca, La Grange, Lisle, Oak Brook, Wheaton)

This western suburb of Chicago started as a stagecoach stop in the 1840s; today, it's primarily residential with tree-lined streets and a population of 43,000.

Information: Elmhurst Chamber of Commerce and Industry | Box 752, 113 Adell Pl., 60126 | 630/834–6060 | www.elmhurstchamber.org.

Attractions

Elmhurst Art Museum. Since 1997 this starkly modern museum has featured regional contemporary artists, sculptors, and photographers, and touring exhibits of painters such as Audubon and Remington. The museum is built around a Mies van der Rohe–designed home. | 150 Cottage Hill Ave. | 630/834–0202 | www.elmhurstartmuseum.org | $3 | Tues., Thurs., Sat. 10–4; Wed., Fri., Sun. 1–4.

Elmhurst Historical Museum. The changing exhibits here focus on local, regional, and national history. The archives are open to researchers. | 120 E. Park Ave. | 630/833–1457 | fax 630/833–1326 | Free | Tues.–Sun. 1–5, and by appointment.

Lizzadro Museum of Lapidary Art. In Wilder Park, you can admire and learn about the collecting and faceting of gems and the art of stone carving from the exhibits at the Lizzadro, which includes unusual jade carvings among its holdings. | 220 Cottage Hill Ave. | 630/833–1616 | $3; special rates for senior citizens and students; free Fri. | Tues.–Sat. 10–5; Sun. 1–5.

ON THE CALENDAR

JUNE: *Elmfest.* This summer festival draws 40,000 people each of its three days, Friday through Sunday, the second weekend in June, when you can whirl on a carnival ride, dance to a local band, or gorge yourself at one of the many food stands. | 630/834–6060.

Dining

Francesca's Amici. Italian. Seafood pasta and sautéed fish in seasonal sauces are the standouts in this restaurant, where you can sit back and relax in one of Francesca's leather-and-wood booths among beautiful photographs of Italy. | 174 N. York Rd. | 630/279–7970 | $9–$23 | AE, MC, V | No lunch weekends.

Las Bellas Artes. Continental. This European café has lace curtains and antique furnishings in its dining room, where you can also enjoy afternoon tea and Sunday brunch. | 112 W. Park Ave. | 630/530–7725 | www.lasbellasartes.com | $15–$25 | MC, V | Closed Mon. No dinner Sun.

McNally's Irish Pub. Irish. Try the fish-and-chips in Guinness batter or the shepherd's pie with an expertly drawn Black-and-Tan from the red-oak bar in this pub, which has murals of Belfast on its walls and an interior similar to ornate bars in Dublin. | 122 S. York Rd. | 630/941–7100 | $5–$20 | AE, D, DC, MC, V.

Lodging

Amerisuites Elmhurst. You can really spread out and stretch your legs here, as all accommodations are suites with full sitting rooms. Complimentary Continental breakfast. Kitchenettes, microwaves, refrigerators, cable TV, in-room VCRs. Indoor pool. Business services. Pets allowed. | 410 W. Lake St. | 630/782–6300 | fax 630/782–6303 | www.amerisuites.com | 128 suites | $79–$131 | AE, D, DC, MC, V.

Courtyard by Marriott. This hotel is 2 mi from Elmhurst College, at the junction of Routes 83 and 64. Restaurant, bar. In-room data ports, cable TV. Indoor pool. Hot tub. Exercise equipment. Laundry facilities. Business services. | 370 N. Rte. 83 | 630/941–9444 | fax 630/941–3539 | www.courtyard.com | 128 rooms, 12 suites | $114; $130–$180 suites | AE, D, DC, MC, V.

Holiday Express. There are many restaurants and shops within a 5-mi radius of these standard motel rooms. Complimentary Continental breakfast. Cable TV. Outdoor pool. Driving range. No pets. | 933 S. Riverside Dr. | 630/279–0700 | fax 630/279–0131 | 102 rooms | $89–$109 | AE, D, DC, MC, V.

Holiday Inn. Just 7 mi southeast of Chicago O'Hare and 2 mi from Elmhurst College, this chain hotel has a Holidome recreation center, and a putting green. Restaurant, bar, room service. In-room data ports, cable TV. Indoor pool. Hot tub. Putting green. Exercise equipment. Game room. Laundry facilities, laundry service. Business services, airport shuttle.

Some pets allowed. | 624 N. York Rd. | 630/279–1100 or 800/707–7070 | fax 630/279–4038 | www.basshotels.com | 238 rooms | $99–$129 | AE, D, DC, MC, V.

Holiday Inn Hillside and Convention Center. In Hillside, 3 mi south of Elmhurst, these chain accommodations and convention facilities are 10 mi south of Chicago O'Hare Airport. Restaurant, bar, room service. In-room data ports, cable TV. Pool. Exercise equipment. Laundry facilities, laundry service. Business services, free parking. Pets allowed. | 4400 Frontage Rd., Hillside | 708/544–9300 | fax 708/544–9310 | www.basshotels.com | 248 rooms | $99–$119 | AE, D, DC, MC, V.

EVANSTON

(Nearby towns also listed: Chicago, Glenview, Skokie, Wilmette)

This cosmopolitan suburb of 80,000 on Chicago's northern border is home to Northwestern University (established in 1851) and easily accessible by train or rapid transit. The university offers a steady stream of concerts and lectures, but Evanston offers lots to do in town as well—restaurants, shopping, beaches, and parks. It's also the birthplace, and still the national headquarters, of the Women's Christian Temperance Union, founded there in 1855.

Information: Evanston Convention and Visitors Bureau | 1 Rotary Center, 1560 Sherman Ave., No. 860, 60201 | 847/328–1500 | www.evanston-illinois.org.

Attractions

Block Museum Outdoor Sculpture Garden. You can admire modern sculptures by such renowned artists as Miró and Hepworth as you wander on these artfully landscaped grounds. | 1967 S. Campus Dr. | 847/491–4000 | www.nwu.edu/museum | Free | Daily dawn–dusk.

Charles Gates Dawes House. You can explore this 1890s house, now a museum and National Historic Landmark, that was the home of Charles Gates Dawes, who served as Calvin Coolidge's vice president. Tours available. | 225 Greenwood St. | 847/475–3410 | www.evanstoncircle.org | $5; special rates for senior citizens and kids | Thurs.–Sun. 1–5; tours by appointment.

Frances E. Willard Home/National Woman's Christian Temperance Union. Exhibits and furnishings of this 19th-century home chronicle the life and work of the founder of this women's union, Frances E. Willard. | 1730 Chicago Ave. | 847/864–1399 | $3 | First Sun. each month 1–4, and by appointment.

Grosse Point Lighthouse. You can tour this 1873 landmark Great Lakes lighthouse, from which you have great views of Lake Michigan and the Chicago skyline. | 2601 Sheridan Rd. (at Central St.) | 847/328–6961 | $3; special rates for kids | June–Sept., weekends, weather permitting; tours 2, 3, and 4; reservations recommended.

John M. and Betty Seabury Mitchell Museum of the American Indian. Art and artifacts from many North American cultures are on display in this museum honoring the native people of this continent. | 2600 Central Park Ave. | 847/475–1030 | $5; special rates for senior citizens and kids | Tues.–Sat. 10–5, Thurs. until 8; Sun. noon–4.

Ladd Arboretum. This 17-acre arboretum has trees grouped by species and many ornamental plantings for your enjoyment. | 2024 McCormick Blvd. | 847/864–5181 | Free | Daily.
Evanston Ecology Center. On the arboretum grounds, the Ecology Center offers displays, a reference library, and a solar greenhouse. | Sept.–May, Mon.–Sat. 9–4:30; June–Aug., weekdays 9–4:30.

Levere Memorial Temple. This Gothic-style building with its stained-glass windows designed and crafted by Tiffany is the international headquarters of Sigma Alpha Epsilon. | 1856 Sheridan Rd. | 847/475–1856 | fax 847/475–2250 | Free | Tours by appointment.

Merrick Rose Garden. You can wander this serene in-town garden, which has dozens of species of roses in it. | Lake St. and Oak Ave. | Free | Daily.

Northwestern University. The stately old limestone buildings of this lakefront campus house modern classrooms, where 11,850 full-time students get their college educations. | Clark St. | 847/491–7271 | www.nwu.edu | Free | Daily.

ON THE CALENDAR

MAY: *Bach Week*. During this concert series spanning two weeks in the beginning of May, big hits and the more esoteric works by this Baroque master are performed, as well as pieces by his contemporaries, at St. Luke's Episcopal Church. | 847/945–5625.

JUNE: *Custer's Last Stand Arts and Crafts Fair*. You can join the throngs wandering this street fair the third weekend in June on Custer and Washington, which includes live performers, artisans and crafts booths, and food and drink vendors. | 847/328–2204.

Dining

Blind Faith Café and Bakery. Vegetarian. Seitan, a meat substitute, is a popular ingredient used in such favorites as the Marsala butternut squash and the Mongolian stir-fry at this restaurant filled with live plants and handprinted wall hangings. | 525 Dempster St. | 847/328–6875 | $9–$12 | AE, DC, MC, V | Breakfast also available.

Carmen's. Pizza. You can choose from dining rooms on two levels, where some seats overlook the pizza kitchen that whips up thin-crust, deep-dish, and stuffed pizzas here. | 1012 Church St. | 847/328–0031 | $9–$20 | AE, D, DC, MC, V.

The Dining Room at Kendall College Culinary School. American. Students at the Culinary School of Kendall College prepare and serve all kinds of basic fare as well as occasional special theme dinners in this dining room, where you can bring your own wine ($5 corkage fee) and there's no smoking. | 2408 Orrington Ave. | 847/866–1399 | Reservations essential | $15–$30 | AE, D, MC, V | Closed Sun. and Mon.

Flat Top Grill. Eclectic. You can create your own stir-fry combination here by ordering rice or noodles with selections from locally raised vegetables, homemade sauces, and a variety of meats, which may include specialty game. The lighting is subdued, and there is a full bar. | 707 Church St. | 847/570–0100 | $7–$11 | AE, D, DC, MC, V.

Jilly's Café. Contemporary. The menu changes seasonally, featuring dishes such as chilean sea bass, at this cozy bistro with mahogany detailing in its interior, but you can count on the rack of lamb. Early-bird specials and Sun. brunch. | 2614 Green Bay Rd. | 847/869–7636 | $9–$18 | AE, DC, MC, V | Closed Mon.

Kuni's. Japanese. This bright and airy restaurant, which includes a popular sushi bar, is known for its fresh sashimi, tempura dishes, and beef and chicken teriyaki. | 511 Main St. | 847/328–2004 | $20–$30 | AE, MC, V | Closed Tues. No lunch Sun.

Las Palmas. Mexican. Colorful Mexican textiles and artifacts create a festive atmosphere here, where the dishes to try are the snapper and the chile rellenos, and you can enjoy a harpist Thursday and Saturday. | 817 University Pl. | 847/328–2555 | $15–$25 | AE, D, DC, MC, V.

Lindo Mexico. Mexican. Just off campus, this restaurant is a favorite of students, who tout the variety of enchiladas and tacos, and the roasted snapper here. | 1934 Maple St. | 847/475–3435 | Breakfast also available | $12–$20 | AE, D, DC, MC, V.

Lucky Platter. Continental. You can get unusual pizza combos and special all-vegetable dishes in addition to the usual mix of Continental cuisine at this popular and eclectic spot. No smoking. | 514 Main St. | 847/869–4064 | Breakfast also available | $12–$22 | MC, V.

Merle's #1 Barbecue. Barbecue. Try the pulled pork or the barbecued chicken at this down-home, country-style barbecue joint, where you can also hear live music. Kids' menu. | 1727 Benson St. | 847/475–7766 | $10–$16 | AE, DC, MC, V.

New Japan Restaurant. Japanese. The simple and airy interior of this Japanese eatery makes for pleasant dining on sushi, sashimi, crab croquettes, and chicken teriyaki. | 1322–24 Chicago Ave. | 847/475–5980 | $10–$18 | AE, D, DC, MC, V | Closed Mon. No lunch Sun.

Oceanique. French. The menu highlights such specialties as king salmon and a rich bouil-labaisse, but you can also choose uniquely prepared venison, rack of lamb, or quail in this pair of Mediterranean-style dining rooms. | 505 Main St. | 847/864–3435 | $22–$32 | AE, D, DC, MC, V | Closed Sun. No lunch.

The Olive Mountain. Middle Eastern. Seated among pictures of Jordan and other Islamic countries on the marbleized walls, you can try shwarmas and kebabs made with chicken, beef, and lamb, which are specialties here. | 814 Church St. | 847/475–0380 | $8–$27 | AE, D, DC, MC, V.

Pete Miller's Steakhouse. Steak. This is a 1940s-style Chicago steak house, where you can hear live jazz every night, that also offers some seafood dishes. | 1557 Sherman Ave. | 847/328–0399 | $18–$55 | AE, MC, V.

Siam Square. Thai. You can dine among artifacts from Thailand or in an outdoor court-yard, starting with the popular spring rolls with plum sauce, which will only whet your appetite for the long list of indigenous, spicy dishes offered here. | 622 Davis St. | 847/475–0860 | $9–$15 | AE, D, DC, MC, V.

Trio. Contemporary. A seasonally changing and innovative list of meat, fish, and vegetable recipes are served up in unique ways—such as on slabs of polished stone—at this restau-rant, where you may not find the same dish twice. No smoking. | 1625 Hinman Ave. | 847/733–8746 | Jacket required | $25–$35; $75 for prix–fixe tasting menu | AE, D, DC, MC, V | No lunch, except on Friday.

Va Pensiero. Italian. Either in the dining room of the Margarita European Inn or on its patio, you can choose from among classic Italian dishes, but the favorite to try is the spaghet-tini with caramelized onions. | 1566 Oak Ave. | 847/475–7779 | $28–$38 | AE, D, DC, MC, V | No lunch. Closed Sun.

Lodging

Holiday Inn. Four blocks from Lake Michigan, this standard motel is right downtown. Restaurant, bar, room service. In-room data ports, microwaves, some refrigerators, cable TV. Pool, wading pool. Exercise equipment. Laundry service. Business services. | 1501 Sher-man Ave. | 847/491–6400 or 800/382–6786 | fax 847/328–3090 | www.basshotels.com | 159 rooms | $109–$179 | AE, D, DC, MC, V.

The Homestead. This is a sprawling 1927 Colonial. An inn since its inception, the Home-stead's rooms are furnished with period pieces. Complimentary parking at a garage half a block away. Restaurant, complimentary Continental breakfast. Some kitchenettes, some microwaves, some refrigerators, cable TV. Pets allowed. | 1625 Hinman Ave. | 847/475–3300 | fax 847/570–8100 | www.thehomestead.net | 30 rooms, 30 suites, 30 apartments | $120 rooms; $175 suites; $200–$290 apartments | AE, D, DC, MC, V.

Margarita European Inn. In central Evanston, this Georgian mansion, formerly a women's club, is now a cozy inn with a rooftop terrace, a parlor with a fireplace, and floor-to-ceil-ing arched windows. While rooms vary in size, from functional to spacious, all have antique furnishings. Twenty-five of the rooms have shared baths. The restaurant downstairs, Va Pensiero, serves some of the best Northern Italian cooking in the area. Restaurant, com-plimentary Continental breakfast. No TV in some rooms. Business services. | 1566 Oak Ave. | 847/869–2273 | fax 847/869–2353 | 45 rooms | $70–$185 | AE, DC, MC, V.

Omni Orrington. This large motel with a European-style lobby is in downtown Evanston, just a block from the Northwestern University campus. Restaurant, bar. In-room data ports, cable TV. Exercise equipment. Laundry service. Business services, parking (fee). | 1710 Orrington Ave. | 847/866–8700 or 800/THEOMNI | fax 847/866–8724 | www.omniho-tels.com | 244 rooms, 33 suites | $179–$345 | AE, D, DC, MC, V.

Widmeyer Guest House. More simple, modest, and family-style than the typical antiques-and-lace bed and breakfasts, this house is a 1918 Prairie School–style and is in a neighborhood of similar homes. The bath is shared. Complimentary Continental breakfast. Cable TV. No pets. No smoking. | 2327 Park Pl. | 847/922–7491 | fax 847/570–4891 | 2 rooms | $65 | No credit cards.

FREEPORT

MAP 6, E1

(Nearby towns also listed: Galena, Rockford)

Freeport was where the second Lincoln-Douglas debate (1858) took place; a life-size statue marks the spot today. The town of 25,900 is the seat of Stephenson County and thrives on agriculture and industry.

Information: Stephenson County Convention and Visitors Bureau | 2047 AYP Rd., 61032 | 815/233–1357 or 800/369–2955 | fax 815/233–1358 | www.stephenson-county-il.org.

Attractions

Freeport Arts Center. The seven permanent galleries here display European, Asian, and contemporary art, and a theater offers performances by local artists and programs especially geared to families. | 121 N. Harlem Ave. | 815/235–9755 | fax 815/235–6015 | $3; special rates for senior citizens and kids | Tues. 10–6, Wed.–Sun. 10–5.

Krape Park. This park has a merry-go-round, a waterfall, tennis courts, a mini-golf course, and boat rentals. | 1799 South Park Blvd. | 815/235–6114 | Free | Daily dawn–10:30 PM.

Lincoln-Douglas Debate Square. A focal point of this public park is a statue depicting the second debate between Honest Abe and Stephen Douglas in 1858, and the Freeport Doctrine on State's Rights was unveiled here. | Douglas and State Sts. | Free | Daily dusk–dawn.

Silver Creek and Stephenson Railroad Silvercreek Museum. You can take a ride back in time and can get some railroad history under your belt from the displays in this antique steam engine and train museum at S. Walnut and Lamm Roads. | 2945 S. Walnut Rd. | 815/232–2198 or 800/369–2955 | $4 train ride; $1 museum; special rates for kids | May–Oct., select weekends 11–5.

Stephenson County Historical Museum. This complex of buildings exhibiting artifacts from the county's history include an 1857 Italianate home, a log cabin, and a one-room schoolhouse. | 1440 S. Carroll Ave. | 815/232–8419 | $3; special rates for kids | Call for hours.

ON THE CALENDAR

JULY: *Steam Threshing and Antique Show.* At the Stephenson County Fairgrounds, on S. Walnut, during the last full weekend of July, from very early morning till late evening Friday, Saturday, and Sunday, you can view old-fashioned steam engines and horse-powered machines, and antique tractors, as well as witness the work of blacksmiths and sawmills. More than 140 antiques dealers have booths here. | 815/232–2350.

AUG.: *Stephenson County Fair.* Held at the county fairgrounds at 2250 S. Walnut Street the third or fourth week of the month, this old-fashioned fair includes livestock judging, carnival rides, and live entertainment. | 815/235–2918 or 800/369–2955.

Dining

Beltline Café. American. In this homey eatery in an 1890s building, you can always get breakfast and the soup of the day is not to be missed. | 325 W. South St. | 815/232–5512 | Breakfast also available. No dinner | $5–$12 | No credit cards.

Club Esquire. American. Since 1939 folks have come to the Esquire for its steaks and pork chops, and the soups and desserts made right on the premises, where photographs of the great Chicago Bears teams of the past decorate the walls. | 1121 W. Empire St. | 815/235–7404 | $7–$19 | AE, D, DC, MC, V | Closed Sun.

Lodging

AmeriHost. Bright rooms with views of the countryside are at this hotel 1 mi from downtown Freeport. Complimentary Continental breakfast. In-room safes, some refrigerators, some in-room hot tubs, cable TV. Indoor pool. Hot tub. Exercise equipment. No pets. | 1060 N. State Hwy. #26 | 815/599–8510 | fax 815/599–8610 | www.amerihostinn.com | 58 rooms, 16 suites | $69–$109 | AE, D, DC, MC, V.

Country Inn and Suites by Carlson. These standard motel rooms and suites are just off of Route 26 South, almost downtown. Complimentary Continental breakfast. In-room data ports, some microwaves, some refrigerators, cable TV. Indoor pool. Hot tub. Health club. Laundry facilities, laundry service. Business services. | 1710 S. Dirck Dr. | 815/233–3300 or 800/456–4000 | fax 815/233–3333 | 60 rooms, 6 suites | $64–$70; $90–$130 suites | AE, D, DC, MC, V.

Holiday Inn Express. This brand-new motel is 3 mi from downtown Freeport. Complimentary Continental breakfast. In-room data ports, some minibars, some in-room hot tubs, cable TV. Indoor pool. Exercise equipment. Laundry services. Business services. No pets. | 1551 Sleezer Home Rd. | 815/232–4455 | fax 815/232–5252 | 59 rooms, 6 suites | $69–$89 | AE, D, DC, MC, V.

Ramada Inn Freeport. A 10-minute drive from downtown, this Ramada is on the eastern edge of Freeport, near Route 20. Restaurant, bar, complimentary breakfast, room service. In-room data ports, some microwaves, some refrigerators, cable TV. Indoor pool. Hot tub. Gym. Video games. Laundry service. Business services. Pets allowed (fee). | 1300 E. South St. | 815/297–9700 | fax 815/297–9701 or 800/2RAMADA | www.ramada.com | 90 rooms | $56–$86 | AE, D, DC, MC, V.

Stephenson Hotel. This eight-story brick hotel in the center of the Freeport business district has both standard rooms and suites and serves its complimentary Continental breakfast weekends only. Restaurant, bar. In-room data ports, some refrigerators, cable TV, some VCRs. Exercise equipment. Laundry service. Business services. Some pets allowed (fee). | 109 S. Galena Ave. | 815/233–0300 or 888/320–7820 | fax 815/233–1599 | 73 rooms | $55; $125–$150 suites | AE, D, DC, MC, V.

GALENA

MAP 6, D1

(Nearby town also listed: Freeport)

Set in the hills of northwestern Illinois, Galena (population 3,647) is a historic lead-mining town that's enjoying a second life as a weekend getaway destination. Its 19th-century shopping district houses gift, collectibles, and antiques stores; the rest of the town has fine examples of period architecture.

Information: Galena/Jo Daviess County Convention and Visitors Bureau | 101 Bouthillier St., 61036 | 815/777–3566 or 888/8–GALENA | www.galena.org.

Attractions

Belvedere Mansion and Gardens. This immense Italianate mansion was built in 1857 and is furnished with formal Victorian pieces, and you can tour both the building and the gardens on the property. | 1008 Park Ave. | 815/777–0747 | $7; special rates for kids | Memorial Day–Oct., Sun.–Fri. 11–4, Sat. 11–5.

Dowling House. You can wander through Galena's oldest house, built in 1826, which has been restored to the period when it served as a trading post. | 220 N. Diagonal St. | 815/777–1250 | $5; combined entry with Belvedere Mansion and Gardens $10 | May–Oct., Sun.–Fri. 10–5, Sat. 10–6; Nov., Dec., Apr., weekends only.

Galena/Jo Daviess County History Museum. Permanent exhibits here include artifacts and information from Civil War history and the county's geological past, as well as seasonal displays. Introductory videos available. | 211 S. Bench St. | 815/777–9129 | $3.50; special rates for kids | Daily 9–4:30.

Grace Episcopal Church. You can visit this Gothic Revival church built in 1848 and admire its beautiful stained-glass windows and hand-carved pulpit. | Hill and Prospect Sts. | 815/777–2590 | Free | Sun. and by appointment.

Old Market House State Historic Site. On Market Square, this 1846 Greek Revival building, which you can tour, was the hub of civic and commercial life in 19th-century Galena. | 123 N. Commerce St. | 815/777–3310 | www.state.illinois.us/hpa | Free; $2 donation suggested | Thurs.–Mon. 9–noon and 1–5.

Mississippi Palisades State Park. In this park outside Savanna, 28 mi south of Galena, you can bird-watch and hike the trails—parts of which are challenging—where you will see unusual rock formations and get some spectacular views of the Mississippi River. | 16327A Rte. 84 | 815/273–2731 | Free | Daily.

Chestnut Mountain Resort. At this riverfront resort 8 mi southeast of Galena, there is a 120-room inn and 17 mi of trails that you can take on foot and by mountain bike in summer and on skis and snowshoes in winter. Night skiing on lighted trails. | 8700 W. Chestnut Rd. | 815/777–1320 or 800/397–1320 | fax 815/777–1068 | www.chestnutmtn.com | Prices vary.

PACKING IDEAS FOR COLD WEATHER

- Driving gloves
- Earmuffs
- Fanny pack
- Fleece neck gaiter
- Fleece parka
- Hats
- Lip balm
- Long underwear
- Scarf
- Shoes to wear indoors
- Ski gloves or mittens
- Ski hat
- Ski parka
- Snow boots
- Snow goggles
- Snow pants
- Sweaters
- Thermal socks
- Tissues, handkerchief
- Turtlenecks
- Wool or corduroy pants

*Excerpted from *Fodor's: How to Pack: Experts Share Their Secrets*
© 1997, by Fodor's Travel Publications

Ulysses S. Grant Home State Historic Site. You can wander through this historic house, bought for Grant by Galena's citizens after the Civil War. | 500 Bouthillier St. | 815/777–3310 | $3 suggested donation; special rates for kids | Daily 9–5.

Vinegar Hill Lead Mine and Museum. This preserved underground operation is typical of early 19th-century mining in the area, and the museum contains lead ore samples and mining tools along with information on the history of the industry. | 8885 N. Three Pines Rd. | 815/777–0855 | $5; special rates for kids | June–Aug., daily 9–5; May, Sept., Oct., weekends 9–5.

Galena Cellars Winery. You can taste and purchase the table and fruits wines at this family-run winery. | 4746 N. Ford Rd. | 815/777–3330 | www.galenacellars.com | $2.50 | Memorial Day–Oct., Fri.–Sun. 11–8.

ON THE CALENDAR

MAR.: *Irish Heritage Days.* You don't have to be Irish to win the Pot o' Gold raffle for a trip to Ireland, and you needn't be a fair daughter of Eire to win the Miss Shamrock Beauty Pageant; here all are welcome to enjoy traditional Irish food, drink, and music throughout downtown the entire weekend preceding St. Patrick's Day. | 815/777–0467.

JUNE: *June Tour of Historic Homes.* Residents of Galena literally open their doors to you the second weekend of June, when you can tour several of the architecturally and historically significant homes in the area. | 815/777–9129.

JUNE: *Stagecoach Trail Festival.* The towns of Apple River, Scales Mound, Lena, Warren, and Nora celebrate their Native American and pioneer heritage through many types of remembrances of life along the stagecoach trail in this region. It all takes place the second weekend of the month. | 800/747–9377.

JULY: *Galena Arts Festival.* You can admire and purchase the paintings submitted in this juried art show in Grant City Park held the last weekend of the month. | 815/777–2433.

SEPT.: *Ladies' Getaway Weekend.* The Chamber of Commerce sponsors tea parties, classes, and demonstrations of jewelry making, cooking, and scrapbooking the second weekend of the month. Men are welcome too. | 815/777–9050.

OCT.: *Galena Country Fair.* Columbus Day weekend, local artisans, and crafters, and performers show their stuff at this old-fashioned country fair. | 815/777–1048.

Dining

Benjamin's. American. You are surrounded by antique beer advertisements and memorabilia and photos of Galena's history in this comfy restaurant, where Italian meat loaf, penne Florentine, and rib-eye steaks are the specialties. | 103 N. Main St. | 815/777–0467 | Reservations not accepted | $10–$19 | D, MC, V.

Bubba's Seafood, Pasta, and Smokehouse. American. There are two floors at Bubba's, where you can get a taste of New Orleans–style dining; try the Cajun dishes and the hickory-smoked ribs. | 300 N. Main St. | 815/777–8030 | www.vinnyvanucchis.com | $13–$30 | AE, D, MC, V | No lunch Mon.–Thurs.

Café Italia and Twisted Taco Café. Eclectic. In a vintage building on historic Main Street, this popular café offers two distinct menus, one with an assortment of pasta dishes, and the other with such Mexican fare as tacos, enchiladas, rice and beans. Kids' menu. | 301 N. Main St. | 815/777–0033 | $10–$25 | AE, D, DC, MC, V.

★ **El Dorado Grill.** Contemporary. This simple eatery serves up unique cuisine made from locally grown produce, including a number of sublime vegetarian recipes. Other standouts are the fresh fish and game. | 219 N. Main St. | 815/777–1224 | www.eldorado-grill.com | $13–$24 | AE, D, MC, V | Closed Tues. and Wed. No lunch.

Fried Green Tomatoes. Contemporary. A variety of pasta dishes, black Angus steaks, and the eponymous vegetables—picked green, then fried—are served in the dining room of this old brick farmstead, where a pianist plays Friday and Saturday. | 1301 Irish Hollow Rd. | 815/777–3938 | www.friedgreen.com | $11–$25 | AE, MC, V | No lunch.

Grant's Place. American. Memorabilia of both the Civil War and the Yankee general–cum–president are scattered about this eatery on the second floor of the Galena Cellars winery, where you can also enjoy balcony dining. Kids' menu. | 515 S. Main St. | 815/777–3331 | $11–$20 | AE, MC, V.

Log Cabin. American. You can choose from among the all-American assortment of steaks, seafood, and chicken, plus a few Greek–inspired dishes, in the rustic log-cabin interior of this old-fashioned place. You can also enjoy a pianist Friday and Saturday. Kids' menu. | 201 N. Main St. | 815/777–0393 | Closed Mon. | $14–$18 | MC, V.

Market House Tavern Restaurant. American. In this tavern's simple black-and-white interior, you can do a little armchair traveling among the many photographs of Ireland on the walls as you dine on grilled salmon or a 12-ounce rib-eye. | 204 S. Perry St. | 815/777–0690 | $8–$33 | D, MC, V.

Perry Street Brasserie. Eclectic. The menu changes monthly, but you'll always find a mix of simple, classic dishes among more adventurous ones, such as grilled quail on Israeli couscous, at this restaurant furnished with an interesting collection of facsimiles of Medieval English brass and Celtic figures. | 124 N. Commerce St. | 815/777–3773 | Reservations essential | $15–$25 | MC, V | Closed Sun. and Mon. No lunch.

Lodging

Aldrich Guest House. Once the home of an Illinois state representative who later became a U.S. senator representing Minnesota, this old home in the historic district has antique furnishings, a library–sitting room, a fireplace, and a large porch where you can relax. Restaurant, complimentary breakfast. No room phones, TV. No kids under 12. No smoking. | 900 3rd St. | 815/777–3323 | www.aldrichguesthouse.com | 5 rooms | $85–$175 | D, MC, V.

Annie Wiggins House. This house, built in 1846, is filled with antiques and overlooks the Galena River. Complimentary Continental breakfast. No air-conditioning in some rooms, no room phones. | 1004 Park Ave. | 815/777–0336 | www.anniewiggins.com | 5 rooms | $75–$150 | AE, MC, V.

Avery Guest House. Formerly the home of a Union officer, this building dates from 1848 and is filled with antiques from that era and others. It has a small yard with a charming gazebo, and it is only one block from downtown. Complimentary breakfast. No TV in some rooms. No pets. No kids under 12. No smoking. | 606 S. Prospect St. | 815/777–3883 | fax 815/777–3889 | www.averybedandbreakfast.com | 4 rooms | $90–$115 | D, MC, V.

Belle Aire Guest House. On 11 acres, this 1836 Federal home has an impressive drive sweeping up to its front door and old-fashioned wreaths and baskets of dried flowers in its rooms. Complimentary breakfast. Some in-room hot tubs, no TV in some rooms. No pets. No smoking. | 11410 U.S. 20 W | 815/777–0893 | www.galena-bnb.com/belleaire | 3 rooms, 2 suites | $85–$165 | D, MC, V.

Best Western Quiet House Suites. The all-suites accommodations here include specialty suites with themes and fireplaces. Downhill skiing is 8 mi away. In-room data ports, some microwaves, some refrigerators, some in-room hot tubs, cable TV. Indoor-outdoor pool. Exercise equipment. Business services. Some pets allowed (fee). | 9923 U.S. 20 W | 815/777–2577 | fax 815/777–0584 | www.bestwestern.com | 42 suites | $91–$190 | AE, D, DC, MC, V.

Captain Gear Guest House. In the historic district, on 4 acres, this 1855 Federal mansion is furnished lavishly with articles from that era. Complimentary breakfast. Some in-room hot tubs, in-room VCRs, cable TV. No pets. No kids under 18. No smoking. | 1000 S. Bench St. | 815/777–0222 or 800/794–5656 | fax 815/777–3210 | www.captaingearguesthouse.com | 2 rooms, 1 suite | $155–$195 | D, MC, V.

Chestnut Mountain Resort. Ski enthusiasts can skim the bluffs overlooking the Mississippi River at this resort 8 mi southeast of Galena. Restaurant, bar, room service. Some refrigerators, cable TV, some in-room VCRs. Indoor pool. Sauna. Miniature golf. Downhill skiing.

Video games. Children's programs (4–12), playground. Laundry facilities. Business services, airport shuttle. | 8700 W. Chestnut Rd. | 815/777–1320 or 800/397–1320 | fax 815/777–1068 | www.chestnutmtn.com | 120 rooms | $87–$135 | AE, D, DC, MC, V.

Desoto House Hotel. Built in 1855, this antebellum hostelry in the historic district of town has both single and double rooms, and some suites with fireplaces. Downhill skiing is 7 mi away. Restaurant, bar. Cable TV. Business services. | 230 S. Main St. | 815/777–0090 or 800/343–6562 | fax 815/777–9529 | www.desotohouse.com | 51 rooms, 4 suites | $89–$205 | AE, D, DC, MC, V.

Eagle Ridge Inn and Resort. On 6,800 wooded acres, this lakeside resort offers outdoor activities such as canoe and pontoon-boat rentals in its marina, hayrides, sleigh rides, and trails rides, as well as a smooth sand beach for sunning. Restaurant, bar with entertainment, room service. Minibars, some refrigerators, some in-room VCRs (and movies), cable TV. Indoor pool. Hot tub, massage. Driving range, golf courses, putting green, tennis. Exercise equipment, beach, boating, bicycles. Cross-country skiing, downhill skiing. Video games. Children's programs (ages 2–16), playground. Business services, airport shuttle. | Eagle Ridge Dr. | 815/777–2444 or 800/892–2269 | fax 815/777–4502 | www.eagleridge.com | 80 rooms | $120–$279 | AE, D, DC, MC, V.

Grant Hills Motel. This motel's rooms have good views of the surrounding pastureland, and after an early outing exploring the past in historic downtown Galena, you can play horseshoes or picnic in the outdoor pavilion here. Cable TV. Outdoor pool. Volleyball. No pets. | 9372 U.S. 20 W | 815/777–2116 | fax 815/777–1856 | www.granthills.com | 34 rooms | $61–$76 | AE, D, MC, V.

Hellman Guest House. In this Queen Anne Victorian on a bluff overlooking downtown Galena, you can choose among four rooms with private baths—three with showers only—and you are served a full breakfast. Complimentary breakfast. No room phones. No kids under 13. No smoking. | 318 Hill St. | 815/777–3638 | www.galena.com/hellman | 4 rooms | $99–$149 | D, MC, V.

Logan House Inn. This antebellum inn at the north end of Galena's historic center, is one of the town's first hotels, built in 1855. Restaurant, bar, complimentary Continental breakfast. Some in-room VCRs (and movies), cable TV. | 301 N. Main St. | 815/777–0033 | fax 815/777–0049 | 6 rooms | $75–$90 | AE, D, DC, MC, V.

Palace Motel. These accommodations are in a complex made up of a standard motel and two late-19th-century homes with period details and furnishings. Cable TV, some room phones. Hot tub. Some pets allowed. | 11383 U.S. 20 W | 815/777–2043 | fax 815/777–2625 | 51 rooms | $85–$175 | AE, D, MC, V.

Park Avenue Guest House. Built in 1893, this small Queen Anne–style inn has a large wraparound porch, is furnished with antiques, and offers some rooms with fireplaces. Complimentary breakfast. Some in-room VCRs (and movies), cable TV. No kids under 12. | 208 Park Ave. | 815/777–1075 or 800/359–0743 | fax 815/777–1097 | www.galena.com/parkave | 4 rooms | $95–$125 | AE, D, MC, V.

Pine Hollow Inn. A Christmas tree farm and a babbling brook are included on this 120-acres of rolling hills a mile from town, where you can rent one of four rooms with working wood-burning fireplaces and lounge on an immense front porch. Complimentary Continental breakfast. Microwave, refrigerator. No kids under 12. No smoking. | 4700 N. Council Hill Rd. | 815/777–1071 | www.pinehollowinn.com | 5 rooms | $75–$125 | D, MC, V.

Queen Anne Guest House. Many of the furnishings in this Queen Anne house, built in 1891, are antique, and there are a library and a wraparound porch you are more than welcome to use. Complimentary Continental breakfast. No smoking. | 200 Park St. | 815/777–3849 | 4 rooms | $85–$125 | D, MC, V.

Stillman's Country Inn. In this Italianate mansion across the street from the Ulysses S. Grant Home, the rooms are filled with Victorian furnishings and some have fireplaces. Complimentary

Continental breakfast. In-room hot tubs, cable TV. No kids. | 513 Bouthillier St. | 815/777–0557 | fax 815/777–8098 | www.stillmanscountryinn.com | 7 rooms | $80–$160 | D, MC, V.

Stoney Creek Inn. Built in 1996 to resemble a hunting lodge, this inn's rooms are a combination of rustic details, such as exposed stone and wood, and modern conveniences. You can walk the ½ mi to Galena's Historic district and a golf course is 5 mi away. Complimentary breakfast. In-room data ports, some refrigerators, some in-room hot tubs, cable TV. Indoor pool. Hot tub, sauna. Exercise equipment. Video games. No pets. | 940 Galena Square Dr. | 815/777–2223 or 800/659–2220 | fax 815/777–6762 | www.stoneycreekinn.com/galena.htm | 66 rooms, 8 suites | $69–$166 | AE, D, DC, MC, V.

GALESBURG

MAP 6, D4

(Nearby towns also listed: Bishop Hill, Kewanee, Monmouth)

In 1836, Presbyterian minister George Washington Gale and some 50 followers founded this town in order to open Knox College to train ministers. Today Galesburg has 33,500 residents.

Information: **Galesburg Area Convention and Visitors Bureau** | 2163 E. Main St., 61401 | 309/343–2485 | fax 309/343–2521 | www.galesburg.org/visitors.

Attractions

Carl Sandburg State Historic Site. This three-room workers cottage is where the beloved poet was born, and his ashes are buried in its yard. You can learn details of his life, and about other local history, in the adjoining visitors center's exhibits and video presentation. | 313–331 E. 3rd St. | 309/342–2361 | www.misslink.net/sandburg | $2 donation suggested; special rates for kids | Daily 9–5.

Galesburg Railroad Museum. Here you can enjoy the restored railroad cars, train memorabilia, and history of this system of transport. | 423 Mulberry St. | 309/342–9400 | $2; special rates for kids | Memorial Day–Labor Day, Tues.–Sun. noon–5.

Knox College. This campus was founded for the training of Presbyterian ministers and houses the only remaining building from the 1858 Lincoln-Douglas debates, the Old Main. | Cherry and South Sts. | 309/343–0112 | www.knox.edu | Free | Daily.

Lake Storey Recreational Area. At the north end of town, you can boat, bike, and hike the trails in this park, which also has a beach and a water slide. | 1033 Southlake Storey Rd. | 309/345–3683 | Free | Daily.

ON THE CALENDAR
JUNE: *Railroad Days.* At this celebration of the town's railroad heritage that takes place the fourth weekend of the month, you can see antique model trains as well as ride in full-sized ones. There are also flea markets, a carnival, and a beer garden. | 309/343–2485.
AUG.: *Knox County Fair.* You can join the county folks for the livestock and produce judging, carnival rides and games on the midway, and the food and entertainment that this fair offers the first week of the month on Henderson Road. | 309/289–2714.
SEPT.: *Stearman Fly-In.* At this gathering of antique Stearman biplanes, you can gaze skyward and gasp at the formation flying, USO show, and aerial-skills competitions held at the Galesburg Airport the first weekend after Labor Day. | 309/343–2485.

Dining
Landmark Café and Crêperie. French. The specialties in this downtown bistro with exposed-brick walls and antique furnishings are paper-thin crepes, filled with assorted fillings, and

the wholesome soups. Weekend brunch. | 62 S. Seminary St. | 309/343–5376 | $5–$15 | AE, D, DC, MC, V.

Oogie's. American. Known for its prime rib and its accommodations for families, this relaxed place is also a favorite for breakfast. Kids' menu. | 1721 N. Henderson St. | 309/344–1259 | Breakfast also available | $10–$14 | D, MC, V.

Packinghouse. American. Antique scales and other memorabilia are placed throughout this restored meat-packing plant, where the menu is weighted with beef but includes a hefty salad bar. Kids' menu. | 441 Mulberry St. | 309/342–6868 | $22–$30 | AE, D, DC, MC, V.

Perkin's Family Restaurant. American. Rose-colored wallpaper with floral borders creates a warm and cheery backdrop for enjoying Perkin's basic fare, such as New York strips and pork chops. | 1850 N. Henderson St. | 309/344–5498 | $7–$12 | AE, D, DC, MC, V | Breakfast also available.

The Steak House. Steak. The steaks served in this restaurant's dinner-only, dark-paneled, candlelit dining room are from prime beef and are well-aged. | 951 N. Henderson St. | 309/343–9994 | $20–$30 | AE, D, MC, V | Closed Sun. No lunch.

Lodging

Comfort Inn. This motel has standard rooms and suites; it's 4 mi northwest of downtown Galesburg and Knox College. Complimentary Continental breakfast. Some in-room VCRs, cable TV. Business services. Pets allowed. | 907 W. Carl Sandburg Dr. | 309/344–5445 | www.comfortinn.com | 46 rooms, 6 suites | $58–$74 | AE, D, DC, MC, V.

Country Inn and Suites. Adjacent to a mall and built in 1999, this modern hotel complex still manages an inviting hominess with its wood staircase and hardwood floors in the lobby. Complimentary Continental breakfast. In-room data ports, some microwaves, some refrigerators, some in-room hot tubs, cable TV. Indoor pool. Hot tub. Exercise equipment. Video games. Business services. No pets. | 2284 Promenade Ct. | 309/344–4444 or 800/456–4000 | fax 309/344–4445 | www.countryinns.com | 52 rooms, 9 suites | $61–$135 | AE, D, DC, MC, V.

The Great House. Each of the three rooms in this stately Greek Revival inn is unique: one has a mahogany four-poster bed and a black marble fireplace, another an antique canopy bed, and the third, lots of natural light streaming across its white linens. Here, you are a scant five blocks from Main Street. Complimentary breakfast. Cable TV. No pets. No smoking. | 501 E. Losey St. | 309/342–8683 | fax 309/342–8987 | www.galesburg.net/~great | 3 rooms | $99 | MC, V.

Jumer's Continental Inn. On the east edge of town, this two-story motel's interior is appointed with such elegant details as dark-wood paneling. Restaurant, bar with entertainment, room service. Some in-room VCRs, cable TV. Indoor pool. Hot tubs, sauna. Putting green. Laundry facilities. Business services, airport shuttle. Pets allowed. | 260 S. Soangetaha St. | 309/343–7151 or 800/285–8637 | fax 309/343–7151 | www.jumers.com | 147 rooms | $50–$88 | AE, D, DC, MC, V.

Ramada Inn. You can request a room with a balcony at this seven-story motel in downtown Galesburg, four blocks from the historic district of Seminary Street and Knox College. Restaurant, bar. Some in-room VCRs (and movies), cable TV. Indoor pool. Hot tub. Business services. Pets allowed. | 29 Public Sq. | 309/343–9161 or 888/298–2054 | fax 309/343–0157 | www.ramada.com | 96 rooms | $40–$75 | AE, D, DC, MC, V.

Super 8. This modest accommodation is 5 mi east of downtown Galesburg, just off of I–74. Complimentary Continental breakfast. Indoor pool. Cable TV. Business services. Pets allowed (fee). | 737 Rte. 10 | 309/289–2100 or 800/800–8000 | fax 309/289–2132 | www.super8.com | 47 rooms | $46–$61 | AE, D, DC, MC, V.

GENEVA

(Nearby towns also listed: Aurora, Elgin, St. Charles, Wheaton)

This riverfront town of 18,900 residents offers a pleasant day of strolling and shopping; many of its stores are in historic buildings.

Information: Geneva Chamber of Commerce | 8 S. 3rd St., 60134 | 630/232–6060 | www.genevachamber.com.

Attractions

Ray Elfstrom Stadium. At this home to Kane County Cougars, a popular minor-league baseball team, you can cheer on aspiring pro ballplayers. | 34W002 Cherry La. | 630/232–8811 | $5–$8 | Daily.

Garfield Farm Museum. You can learn about the history of this 1840s teamster inn and 281-acre prairie farmstead here and cheer the fact that the place is being restored as a working farm. | 3N016 Garfield Rd., LaFox | 630/584–8485 | fax 630/584–8522 | $3 suggested donation | June–Sept., Wed., Sun. 1–4; and by appointment.

Wheeler Park. North of Geneva on Route 31, this 57-acre park has a mini-golf course, picnic shelters, a playground, and a museum. | 822 N. 1st St. | 630/232–4542 (park) or 630/208–1179 (golf) | Free | Daily.

The **Geneva Historical Society Museum,** in the park, includes four galleries that each focus on different aspects of Geneva's history. Full local research archives are available. | 400 Wheeler Dr. | 630/232–4951 | Free | Apr.–mid-Dec., Wed.–Sun. 1–4; archives by appointment.

ON THE CALENDAR

MAY: *Geneva on the River.* You can join the folks of Geneva in home-decorating seminars and workshops at local stores, as well as old-fashioned teas and carriage rides during this event held the first weekend of the month. | 630/232–6060.
JUNE: *Swedish Days.* The history of Swedish influence in the development of Geneva is celebrated with a parade and ethnic food, and arts and crafts sales and demonstrations. It takes place the third week of the month. | 630/232–6060.
SEPT.: *Fox Valley Folk Fest.* The first Sunday and Monday of September, this festival is held in Island Park—an island in the middle of the Fox River—and includes traditional American and British music performed on eight stages, an old-time barn dance, storytelling, and workshops for all ages. | 630/897–3655.
SEPT.: *Festival of the Vine.* These fall festivities include food-and-wine tastings from local restaurants, live-music performances, a car show, and regional arts and crafts booths, held the second weekend in the month. | 630/232–6060.
DEC.: *Christmas Walk.* Join Genevans the first Friday of the month during their tree-lighting ceremony, caroling, and evening stroll through downtown shops. | 630/232–6060.

Dining

302 West. Eclectic. This restaurant boasts an adventurous menu that changes daily, but you can expect to find dishes like pan-seared Key West red snapper or grilled New Zealand venison in what was once a bank, with an impressive lofty ceiling and 20-ft arched windows. | 302 W. State St. | 630/232–9302 | $20–$30 | AE, D, DC, MC, V | No lunch. Closed Sun.–Mon.

Little Traveller Atrium Café. Continental. In the enclosed atrium of a Victorian mansion, you can order tea sandwiches and watch a fashion show weekdays, as well as partake of the buffet, seafood special, or chicken salad here. | 404 S. 3rd St. | 630/232–4200 | Reservations essential for lunch buffet | $6–$10 | MC, V | No dinner. Closed Sun.

Mill Race Inn. Continental. The country-style dining room warmed by firelight looks out on the Fox River, and you can also dine in the outdoor gazebo here, where the dish to try is zucchini ravioli. Entertainment Wednesday, Friday, and weekends; Sunday brunch; and kids' menu. | 4 E. State St. | 630/232–2030 | www.themillraceinn.com | $16–$23 | AE, MC, V.

Lodging

The Herrington Inn. All the rooms in this inn overlooking the Fox River have fireplaces, whirlpool tubs, and balconies. Restaurant, bar, complimentary Continental breakfast, room service. Minibars, refrigerators, cable TV, some in-room VCRs. Hot tub. Laundry service. Business services, airport shuttle. | 15 S. River La. | 630/208–7433 | fax 630/208–8930 | www.herrington-inn.com | 40 rooms | $159–$249 | AE, D, DC, MC, V.

Oscar Swan Country Inn. This turn-of-the-century brick Colonial Revival mansion on 8 acres of wooded grounds, which includes a modernized 1836 barn popular for weddings, is filled with antiques, and some of its rooms have fireplaces and bay windows. Complimentary breakfast. Cable TV. No pets. No smoking. | 1800 W. State St. | 630/232–0173 | fax 630/232–2706 | www.oscarswan.com | 8 rooms | $119–$139 | AE, MC, V.

GLEN ELLYN

MAP 8, B6

(Nearby towns also listed: Downers Grove, Elmhurst, Lisle, Naperville, Oak Brook, Wheaton)

Although there were settlers in the Glen Ellyn area as early as the 1840s, the town wasn't incorporated until 1892. Today, this western suburb of 25,000 residents is marked by historic houses and antique stores. You can hop on the commuter train that runs through town and be in downtown Chicago in 45 minutes.

Information: **Glen Ellyn Chamber of Commerce** | 490 Pennsylvania St., 60137 | 630/469–0907 | www.glen-ellyn.com.

Attractions

Lake Ellen. The pride and joy of Glen Ellyn, this small lake is surrounded by a wooded park, lovely homes, and an old English Tudor, ivy-covered high school. | Hawthorne and Lenox Sts. | 630/469–0907 | Free | Daily dawn–dusk.

Stacy's Tavern Museum. You can marvel over the memorabilia and period furnishings in this reconstructed 1846 stagecoach stop. | 557 Geneva Rd. | 630/858–8696 | Donation suggested | Tues., Wed., Sun. 1:30–4:30.

ON THE CALENDAR
MAY: *Taste of Glen Ellyn.* This celebration of the local restaurants' cuisine includes food tastings and an old-fashioned carnival. It takes place the third weekend in the month. | 630/469–0907.
NOV.: *Holiday Walk.* You can join the townsfolk around sunset to watch the children's parade, stroll about the business district brightly decorated with lights and evergreens, listen to Christmas carols, and take a candlelight tour of Stacy's Tavern Museum. | 630/469–0907.

Dining
Bavarian Inn. German. Enjoy traditional dishes such as Wiener schnitzel or roast duck at this locally renowned restaurant, where you can also view a nice collection of German beer steins on display. | 430 Roosevelt Rd. | 630/790–0060 | $7–$12 | AE, MC, V | Closed Tues. No lunch weekends.

Greek Islands West. Greek. You could swear you're in a Mediterranean village at this restaurant in Lombard known for its fresh seafood and its Athenian lamb chops, where you can also eat out on an enclosed patio. | 300 E. 22nd St., Lombard | 630/932–4545 | $15– $25 | AE, D, DC, MC, V.

Lodging

Best Western Inn. This two-story motel is within two blocks to the nearest golf course. Complimentary Continental breakfast. In-room data ports, some in-room hot tubs, cable TV. Indoor pool. Exercise equipment. Laundry service. Business services. Pets allowed (fee). | 675 Roosevelt Rd. | 630/469–8500 or 800/448–1190 | fax 630/469–6731 | www.bestwestern.com | 122 rooms, 7 studios | $65–$175 | AE, D, DC, MC, V.

Holiday Inn. On Route 38, 2 mi south of the station for the commuter train to Chicago, this motel is within 5 mi of the campuses of College of DuPage and Wheaton College and Stacy's Tavern Museum. Restaurant, bar, room service. In-room data ports, cable TV. Pool. Laundry facilities, laundry service. Business services. Pets allowed. | 1250 Roosevelt Rd. | 630/629–6000 | fax 630/629–0025 | www.basshotels.com | 121 rooms | $99–$111 | AE, D, DC, MC, V.

GLENVIEW

MAP 8, D4

(Nearby towns also listed: Evanston, Glencoe, Northbrook, Skokie, Wilmette)

Today home to a number of large, multinational corporations—as well as many comfortable neighborhoods—this northern Chicago suburb of 38,000 residents had its origins as a farming community.

Information: **Glenview Chamber of Commerce** | 2320 Glenview Rd., 60025 | 847/724– 0900.

Attractions

Glenview Area Historical Society Museum and Coach House. You can tour this 1864 home furnished with late Victorian pieces and filled with items from everyday life in that era. The yard is a popular resting place for folks strolling about the neighborhood. | 1121 Waukegan Rd. | 847/724–2235 | Free | Sun. 1–4.

The Grove National Historic Landmark. Within this 124-acre woodland preserve, there is a restored 1856 schoolhouse, amphibian and reptile displays, and hiking trails that you can explore. Several seasonal festivals are held here. | 1421 N. Milwaukee Ave. | 847/299– 6096 | fax 847/299–0571 | Donation suggested | Weekdays 8–4:30, weekends 9–5.

Hartung's License Plate and Auto Museum. More than 150 antique cars, trucks, and tractors, as well as license plates from every state and other auto-related collections are exhibited at this museum. | 3623 W. Lake St. | 847/724–4354 | Donation suggested | Daily; hours variable.

ON THE CALENDAR

JUNE: *Glenview Street Sale.* Attended annually by nearly 35,000 people, this massive sale on the last Saturday in June includes about 100 retailers selling new discounted merchandise, rather than antiques. The sale stretches along Glenview Road between Waukegan Road and the Milwaukee Railroad. | 847/724–0900.

JULY: *Grove Heritage Days.* At the Grove National Historic Landmark, you can watch the many demonstrations of pioneer skills and Civil War reenactments during this celebration of the area's history that takes place the last weekend of the month. | 847/299–6096.

OCT.: *Grovefest.* This fall festival includes exhibits focusing on the life of the pioneers and their crafts, as well as live performances of folk music, all held on the grounds of the Grove National Historic Landmark the first Sunday of the month. | 847/299–6096.

Dining

Brasserie T. American. In Northfield, 3 mi north of Glenview, this spacious brasserie is known for its pork chops, bouillabaisse, and calves' liver dishes. | 305 S. Happ Rd., Northfield | 847/446–0444 | $15–$25 | AE, D, DC, MC, V | No lunch Sun.

Dapper's North. American. There is an extensive menu at this casual restaurant, including many beef, chicken, seafood, and pasta dishes, as well as barbecued ribs. Daily specials and kids' menu offered. | 4520 W. Lake Ave. | 847/699–0020 | $9–$12 | AE, DC, MC, V | Breakfast also available.

Dragon Inn North. Chinese. A collection of Asian artifacts tastefully peppers the dining room of this restaurant, where you can order Mandarin, Szechwan, and Hunan dishes, including moo shu pork, orange beef, and spicy shrimp sauté. | 1650 Waukegan Rd. | 847/729–8383 | $13–$20 | AE, MC, V | No lunch Sat.

Periyali Greek Taverna. Greek. Reminiscent of a Mediterranean village, the walls have been white-washed in this taverna's dining room, where the dish to try is grilled octopus. | 9860 Milwaukee Ave. | 847/296–2232 | $8–$15 | AE, D, DC, MC, V.

Willow on Wagner. American. In this informal dining room overlooking a garden and forest preserve, the local favorites are fried chicken and spaghetti au gratin. Fresh fish and other daily specials and a kids' menu are offered. | 1519 Wagner Rd. | 847/724–5100 | www.willowonwagner.com | $11–$25 | AE, D, DC, MC, V | No lunch Sun.

Lodging

Baymont Inn and Suites. This three-story motel is on the northwest border of Glenview, nearly in Northbrook and close to the Pal-Waukee Airport, just off of I–294. Complimentary Continental breakfast. In-room data ports, microwaves, some refrigerators, cable TV. Laundry facilities. Business services. Free parking. Some pets allowed. | 1625 Milwaukee Ave. | 847/635–8300 | fax 847/635–8166 | www.baymontinns.com | 142 rooms | $62–$94 | AE, D, DC, MC, V.

Courtyard by Marriott. Though the restaurant in this Marriott serves breakfast only, there are many eateries within a five-mile radius of this three-story motel on Route 21 near I–294. Restaurant, bar. In-room data ports, microwaves, some refrigerators, cable TV. Indoor pool. Hot tub. Exercise equipment. Laundry facilities, laundry service. Business services, free parking. | 1801 N. Milwaukee Ave. | 847/803–2500 | fax 847/803–2520 or 800/321–2211 | www.courtyard.com | 149 rooms, 12 suites | $109–$164 | AE, D, DC, MC, V.

Doubletree Guest Suites–O'Hare North. Nine miles north of Chicago O'Hare Airport, this all-suites hotel is across from Grove Forest Preserve and near the Golf Mill Shopping Center. Restaurant, bar. In-room data ports, microwaves, refrigerators, cable TV. Indoor pool. Hot tub. Exercise equipment. Laundry service. Business services, airport shuttle. | 1400 Milwaukee Ave. | 847/803–9800 | fax 847/803–0380 | 252 suites | $169–$199 | AE, D, DC, MC, V.

Fairfield Inn by Marriott. You take the West Lake Avenue exit off of I–294 to reach this standard three-story motel. Complimentary Continental breakfast. In-room data ports, cable TV. Pool. Business services, free parking. | 4514 Lake Ave. | 847/299–1600 | fax 847/803–9943 | www.fairfieldinn.com | 138 rooms | $49–$75 | AE, D, DC, MC, V.

Motel 6. This motel, typical of the chain known for its practicality and simplicity, is 6 mi north of town. Cable TV. Pets allowed. | 1535 Milwaukee Ave. | 847/390–7200 | fax 847/390–0845 | www.motel6.com | 111 rooms | $51–$57 | AE, D, DC, MC, V.

GRAFTON

(Nearby towns also listed: Alton, Cahokia, Collinsville, Edwardsville)

Grafton is a tiny river town of about 900 in Jersey County northwest of St. Louis, between Alton and the Missouri state line. At the confluence of the Mississippi and the Illinois rivers, it's a fine stopping-off point during foliage season and the natural flyway attracts American bald eagles, Canada geese, and blue herons. Wonderful restaurants feature freshly caught fish from the river.

Information: **Greater Alton/Twin Rivers Convention and Visitors Bureau** | 200 Piasa St., Alton 62002 | 618/465–6676 or 800/258–6645 | www.altoncvb.org.

Attractions

Center for American Archaeology. You can learn about many of the fascinating prehistoric and historic aspects of the Illinois Valley at this center in Kampsville, 30 mi northwest of Grafton. | Box 366, Market St. and Broadway, Kampsville | 618/653–4316 | www.caa-archeology.org | Free | Apr.–Nov., Mon.–Sat. 10–5, Sun. noon–5.

Chateau Ra-Ha Winery. Tastings of the estate-produced wines are offered here. | 230 E. Main St. | 618/786–3335 | Free | Mon.–Sat. 11–7, Sun. noon–7.

Père Marquette State Park. This park is known to be a great place to sight bald eagles in winter. At the union of the Mississippi and Illinois rivers, the 8,000-acre sanctuary has bike trails, hunting programs, horseback riding, hiking, picnicking, boating, fishing, and a 270-gallon aquarium. There are also educational exhibits about the wildlife and geology of the Illinois River. The park is named after the missionary Jacques Marquette ("Père" is the French "Father"), who explored the area with Louis Jolliet in 1673. Camping and lodges are available. | Rte. 100 | 618/786–3323 | Free | Daily 8 AM–9 PM.

Raging Rivers Waterpark. You can board- and body-surf in the wave pool, shoot the rapids on a river-rafting ride, and slide down the water flumes at this amusement park. | 100 Palisades Pkwy. | 800/548–7573 or 618/786–2345 | www.ragingrivers.com | $15.95; special rates for kids under 9 | Memorial Day–Labor Day, daily 10:30–8.

Dining

The Reubel. American. The central attraction in this restaurant, where you can get grilled chicken breast, burgers, and several kinds of fish, is the bar, which was used at the 1904 World's Fair. | 217 E. Main St. | 618/786–2315 | fax 618/786–2325 | $9–$12 | MC, V.

Lodging

Père Marquette Lodge and Conference Center. Ten minutes north of Grafton, this lodge and conference center are in Père Marquette State Park, on the Illinois River. Restaurant, bar, picnic area. Some in-room VCRs (and movies), cable TV. Indoor pool. Hot tub, sauna. Exercise equipment. Video games. Playground. Business services. | Rte. 100 | 618/786–2331 | 72 rooms | $67–$82 | AE, D, DC, MC, V.

The Reubel. Rooms in the 1884 main house, and in the 1990s cottages and lodges, are furnished with replicas of turn-of-the-century antiques, such as cherrywood pieces, and brass and wrought-iron beds. Some rooms have a view of the confluence of the mighty Mississippi and Illinois rivers. Complimentary Continental breakfast. Cable TV. No pets. No smoking. | 217 E. Main St. | 618/786–2315 | fax 618/786–2325 | 22 rooms, 10 cottages, 4 lodges | $69–$89; $119–$129 cottages; $109–$129 lodges | MC, V.

GRAND DETOUR

MAP 6, F2

(Nearby towns also listed: Dixon, Oregon)

The tiny hamlet of Grand Detour (population 300) sits in a C-shaped bend in the Rock River, where farm implement pioneer John Deere developed the self-cleaning steel plow that helped pioneers cultivate the prairie.

Information: **Blackhawk Waterways Convention and Visitors Bureau** | 201 N. Franklin Ave., Polo 61064 | 800/678–2108 | fax 815/946–2277 | www.blackhawkwaterwayscvb.org.

Attractions

John Deere Historic Site. In addition to the restored blacksmith shop where Deere developed the self-scouring steel plow, there are an 1830s homestead and archeological exhibits for you to explore here. | 8393 S. Main St. | 815/652–4551 | www.deere.com | $3; special rates for kids | Apr.–Oct., daily 9–5.

ON THE CALENDAR
AUG.: *Two-Cylinder Show*. Every other year, two-cylinder fanatics flock to Detour for this three-day show, when more than 80 fully restored tractors, maintained by various two-cylinder clubs, are exhibited. This affair usually takes place the first full weekend in August, in odd-numbered years (2001, 2003, etc.). | 815/652–4551.

Dining

Colonial Rose Inn Restaurant. American. This restaurant in an 1850s inn is known for its filet mignon, fresh fish, and hickory-smoked pork chops, as well as its antique bar. | 8230 S. Green St. | 815/652–4422 | $15–$30 | MC, V | Closed Sun.–Tues. No lunch.

GREENVILLE

MAP 6, F8

(Nearby towns also listed: Collinsville, Edwardsville, Vandalia)

This rural community touts its small-town charms. It has a population of 6,000 and is the seat of Bond County.

Information: **Greenville Chamber of Commerce** | 404 S. 3rd St., 62246 | 618/664–9272 or 888/862–8201 | www.greenvilleillinois.com.

Attractions

Bock Museum. On the campus of Greenville College, this museum houses much of the work of Richard Bock, a turn-of-the-century sculptor associated with Frank Lloyd Wright. | College Ave. | 618/664–6724 | fax 618/664–9841 | Free | Wed., Fri. 1–5, Sat. 10–2.

Lodging

Best Western Country View Inn. These standard accommodations are 3 mi southeast of Greenville College, at the junction of I–70 and Route 127. Complimentary Continental breakfast. Cable TV. Pool. Hot tub. Exercise equipment. Business services. Some pets allowed (fee). | RR 4, Box 163, Rte. 127 at I–70 | 618/664–3030 | www.bestwestern.com | 83 rooms | $38–$52 | AE, D, DC, MC, V.

Budget Host Inn Greenville. To reach this Budget Host, take exit 45 off of I–70, 1 mi south of Greenville College. Complimentary Continental breakfast. In-room data ports, kitchenettes, some refrigerators, cable TV. Pool. Playground. Laundry facilities. Business services, airport shuttle. Pets allowed (fee). | 1525 S St. | 618/664–1950 or 800/283–4678 | fax 618/664–1960 | www.budgethost.com | 48 rooms | $28–$69 | AE, D, MC, V.

Greenville Super 8 Motel. This modest motel is at the junction of Route 127 and I–70, 1 mi south of Greenville College. Complimentary Continental breakfast. Some refrigerators, some in-room VCRs, cable TV. Laundry facilities. Business services. | Rte. 127 and I–70 | 618/664–0800 or 800/800–8000 | fax 618/664–0845 | www.super8.com | 43 rooms | $42–$57 | AE, D, MC, V.

GURNEE

(Nearby towns also listed: Libertyville, Waukegan)

This northern Chicago suburb of 13,700 residents has grown dramatically in the past 20 years, thanks in part to Six Flags Great America and the Gurnee Mills shopping mall.

Information: Lake County Illinois Convention and Visitors Bureau | 401 N. Riverside Dr., No. 5, 60031 | 847/662–2700 or 800/LAKE–NOW.

Attractions

Gurnee Antique Center. This 24,000-square-ft building where 200 dealers sell all kinds of antiques is between Six Flags Great America and Gurnee Mills Mall, less than 1 and ½ mi from each. | 5742 Northridge Dr. | 847/782–9094 | Free | Mon.–Wed., Fri., Sat. 10–5; Thurs. 10–8; Sun. noon–5.

Gurnee Mills Mall. More than 200 retail outlets, including many discount stores, are here for your shopping pleasure. | I–94 at Rte. 132 | 847/263–7500 or 800/YES–SHOP | Free | Mon.–Sat. 10–9, Sun. 11–6.

Six Flags Great America. You can relax and get your thrills on this famous 200-acre amusement park's rides and in its many other attractions, including shows of all kinds. | Grand Ave. | 847/249–1776 | www.sixflags.com | $43; special rates for senior citizens and kids; parking $8 | May–Oct.; call for schedule.

ON THE CALENDAR

AUG.: *Gurnee Days.* Viking Park, at O'Plain and Old Grand, is the primary location for this four-day festival, which includes educational exhibits, a bike rodeo, a beach bash, a pancake breakfast, displays of students' art, talent shows, and other staged performances, but some of the activities are held at the local library, school, and police and fire houses. Admission fees for some events. | 847/249–5596.

Lodging

Baymont Inn and Suites. This motel is adjacent to Six Flags Great America and ½ mi from Gurnee Mills Mall. Complimentary Continental breakfast. In-room data ports, some microwaves, refrigerators, cable TV. Laundry facilities. Business services. Pets allowed. | 5688 N. Ridge Rd. | 847/662–7600 | fax 847/662–5300 | www.baymontinns.com | 103 rooms, 4 suites | $69–$94; $124 suites | AE, D, DC, MC, V.

Comfort Inn. Gurnee Mills Mall is right next door to this Comfort Inn, and Six Flags Great America is only a half mile from here. Complimentary Continental breakfast. Some microwaves, some refrigerators, cable TV. Indoor pool. Hot tub. | 6080 Gurnee Mills Blvd. | 847/855–8866 | www.comfortinn.com | 59 rooms, 4 suites | $69–$110; $125 suites | AE, D, DC, MC, V.

Country Inn and Suites-Gurnee. Entertainment and shopping are practically outside your door at this hotel, which is across the street from Six Flags Great America and three blocks from Gurnee Mills Mall. All rooms offer the same amenities, though suites have a sitting room with a hide-a-bed couch in them. Complimentary Continental breakfast. In-room data ports, microwaves, refrigerators, cable TV. Indoor pool. Hot tub. Laundry facilities, laundry service. Pets allowed. | 5420 Grand Ave. | 847/625–9700 or 800/456–4000 | fax 847/625–4251 | 56 rooms, 12 suites | $125–$135 | AE, D, DC, MC, V.

Fairfield Inn by Marriott. Next door to Gurnee Mills Mall, this motel is less than a mile from Six Flags Great America. Complimentary Continental breakfast. Some microwaves, refrigerators, cable TV. Indoor pool. Hot tub. Laundry services. Business services. | 6090 Gurnee Mills Blvd. | 847/855–8868 | www.fairfieldinn.com | 51 rooms, 12 suites | $69–$120; $120–$140 suites | AE, D, DC, MC, V.

Hampton Inn. Just two blocks from Six Flags Great America, this motel is also less than a mile from Gurnee Mills Mall. Complimentary Continental breakfast. In-room data ports, cable TV. Pool. Video games. Business services. | 5550 Grand Ave. | 847/662–1100 or 800/426–7866 | fax 847/662–2556 | www.hamptoninn.com | 134 rooms | $79–$99 | AE, D, DC, MC, V.

Holiday Inn. Right across from Gurnee Mills Mall and ¼ mi from Six Flags Great America, this standard inn has a Holidome recreation center. Restaurant, bar, room service. In-room data ports, cable TV. Indoor pool. Hot tub. Exercise equipment. Video games. Laundry facilities, laundry service. Business services, free parking. | 6161 W. Grand Ave. | 847/336–6300 | fax 847/336–6303 | www.basshotels.com | 223 rooms | $99–$150 | AE, D, DC, MC, V.

Sweet Basil Hill Farm. This is a Cape Cod–style house on 7½ wooded acres with an herb garden and some sheep, and it's only ⅓ mi southeast of Six Flags Great America and the outlet shops in Gurnee Mills Mall. Complimentary breakfast. In-room VCRs, cable TV. Business services. No smoking. | 15937 W. Washington St. | 847/244–3333 | fax 847/263–6693 | 3 suites; 1 cottage | $95–$175 | www.sweetbasilhill.com | AE, D, DC, MC, V.

HAVANA

(Nearby towns also listed: Lincoln, Macomb, Peoria, Petersburg)

Havana, which sits at the juncture of the Spoon and Illinois rivers, began as a fishing and steamboat center. Today, those industries have been replaced with wheatfields. Its population is 6,500.

Information: Havana Area Chamber of Commerce | 227 W. Main St., 62644 | 309/543–3528.

Attractions

Chautauqua Refuge. Birds and other wildlife are in abundance in this 4,388-acre preserve, where you can boat, fish, and hunt. Though the focal point of the refuge is Lake Chautauqua, it is bordered on the north and south by shallow lakes, on the west by the Illinois River, and on the east by a 70-ft-high bluff, all of which you can explore. | 19031 E. Rte. 2110 N | 309/535–2290 | Free | Daily dawn–dusk.

Dickson Mounds State Museum. Five mi north of Havana via Routes 78 and 97, on a hill above the Spoon and Illinois rivers, this archaeological museum's exhibits, galleries, and hands-on discovery center focus on the Native Americans who inhabited the Illinois River valley as far back as 12,000 years ago through about the 1830s. | Dickson Mounds Rd., Lewiston | 309/547–3721 | www.museum.state.il.us/ismsites/dickson | Free | Daily 8:30–5.

Illinois River National Wildlife and Fish Refuges. Home to one of the largest concentrations of waterfowl in the Illinois River valley, this refuge is 8 mi northeast of Havana. You can enjoy easy trails and a great shorebird viewing area. | Manito Rd. | 309/535–2290 | www.fws.gov/r3pao/ill_rvr | Free | Daily dawn–dusk.

ON THE CALENDAR

SEPT.: *Oktober Fest.* The weekend after Labor Day you can put on your lederhosen and polka into downtown Havana, the main part of which is closed off for all the bratwurst eating, pilsner drinking, and family entertainment that the festival offers, including the 5K Polka Pace Race on Saturday morning. | 309/543–3528.

Dining

The Lunchbox. American/Casual. This small breakfast and lunch eatery serves home-cooked soups and stews, as well as burgers and sandwiches. | 117 S. Plum St. | 309/543–4301 | $2–$6 | No credit cards | Breakfast also available. No dinner. Closed Sun.

Lodging

Red Lion Motel Lodge. This former Best Western is on Route 136, right behind Shopco Grocery Store. Now a mom-and-pop motel, it has a cookie-cutter appearance but more-personalized amenities, such as king-size water beds in two of the rooms. In-room data ports, microwaves, refrigerators, cable TV. Outdoor pool. Exercise equipment. Laundry service. Business services. | 1020 E. Laurel Ave. | 309/543–4407 | 40 rooms | $40–$50 | AE, D, DC, MC, V.

HIGHLAND PARK

MAP 6, H2

(Nearby towns also listed: Chicago, Highwood, Lake Forest, Northbrook)

The downtown area of this North Shore Chicago suburb (population 31,900) is now a lively, bustling town center anchored by Port Clinton Square, a shopping and office development.

Information: Highland Park Chamber of Commerce | 600 Central Ave., No. 205, 60035 | 847/432–0284.

Attractions

Chicago Botanic Garden. A half-mile east of I–94 in Glencoe, you can tour this 385-acre botanical marvel dotted with lagoons, including 23 gardens: rose gardens, fruit and vegetable gardens, and a Japanese garden. Educational exhibits in several buildings; tram tour. | 1000 Lake Cook Rd., Glencoe | 847/835–5440 | www.chicago-botanic.org | Free; parking $7 per car | Daily 8–sunset.

Francis Stupey Log Cabin. Built in 1847 by Francis Stupey, a German immigrant logger, this cabin is furnished with artifacts from the period. | 1750 block of St. Johns Ave. | 847/432–7090 | Weekends by appointment.

Jean Butz James Museum. You can tour this 12-room 1871 house, which has period furnishings and artifacts throughout as well as informative exhibits on local history. | 326 Central Ave. | 847/432–7090 | www.highlandpark.org/histsoc | Tues.–Fri. 10–3; weekends 2–4.

ON THE CALENDAR

JUNE–SEPT.: *Ravinia Festival.* At Green Bay and Lake Cook Roads, in an outdoor pavilion with lawn seating, you can hear the Chicago Symphony perform pop and classical music, as well as jazz and pop concerts by other performers throughout the summer. | 847/266–5100.

Dining

Café Central. French. The beef tenderloin is the dish to try at this casual bistro, where there is sidewalk-dining in summer. Kids' menu. | 455 Central Ave. | 847/266–7878 | $12–$20 | AE, D, DC, MC, V | Closed Mon. No lunch Sun.

Carlos'. Italian. Jackets are required here, but the dining room is relaxed and intimate in this restaurant in a vintage brick building, where the risotto and the salmon with mushroom canoli are favorites. | 429 Temple Ave. | 847/432–0770 | Jacket required | $35–$80 | AE, D, DC, MC, V | No lunch. Closed Tues.

Little Szechwan. Chinese. Both Mandarin and spicy Szechwan dishes are served at this ethnic eatery, where you can also eat outdoors if you wish. | 1900 1st St. | 847/433–7007 | $12–$20 | AE, DC, MC, V | No lunch Sat.

Norton's. American/Casual. In addition to the standard American fare of steaks and burgers, you can get unusually hearty salad entrées, such as the Santa Fe barbecue salad with black beans and jicama, in this dining room decked with sports and movie memorabilia, hardwood floors, and ceiling fans. | 1905 Sheridan Rd. | 847/432–3287 | $10.95–$14.95 | D, MC, V | Closed Mon. No lunch Sun.

Panda Panda. Chinese. Favorites at this Asian restaurant are the sizzling steak, the spicy Hunan lamb, and the neptune delight, which is a seafood combination. | 1825 2nd St. | 847/432–9470 | $15–$25 | AE, MC, V.

Timbers Charhouse. American. Despite its proximity to Chicago, this homey place looks like a rustic lodge, where you can get steak, chicken, and different fresh fish items daily. Kids' menu. | 295 Skokie Valley Rd. | 847/831–1400 | $12–$20 | AE, D, DC, MC, V | No lunch Sun.

Lodging
Courtyard by Marriott. Off U.S. 41, between Highland Park and Northbrook, this motel is just a 10-minute drive from the Chicago Botanic Garden. Restaurant, bar. In-room data ports, some microwaves, refrigerators, cable TV. Indoor pool. Hot tub. Laundry facilities, laundry service. Business services, free parking. | 1505 Lake Cook Rd. | 847/831–3338 or 800/321–2211 | fax 847/831–0782 | www.courtyard.com | 137 rooms, 12 suites | $109–$129; $139–$149 suites | AE, D, DC, MC, V.

HIGHWOOD

MAP 8, D2

(Nearby towns also listed: Highland Park, Lake Forest, Northbrook)

Highwood is a small Chicago North Shore community of 5,300, best known for its Italian restaurants.

Information: Highwood Chamber of Commerce | 17 Highwood Ave., 60040 | 847/433–2100.

Attractions
Highwood Veteran's Memorial. Built by local master stonemasons, this miniature version of the Washington Monument pays tribute to all the men and women of Highwood who served in this country's wars. The monument is lit throughout the night. | 17 Highwood Ave. | 847/433–2100 | Free | Daily.

ON THE CALENDAR
JULY: *Highland Festival Days*. You could call this four-day festival in downtown Highland feast-days, as it celebrates the fact that the town's 5,500 residents are served by 31 local restaurants, some of which are rated four-star. You can savor the samplings from many of these establishments as well as enjoy the carnival rides, and games, and nighttime entertainment. | 847/433–2100.

Dining
Alex's Washington Garden. Italian. Among the specialties to try at this restaurant are tortellini Alfredo, veal and asiago cheese in a creamy sauce with mushrooms; and swordfish oregenato, grilled with tomato, oregano, capers, and olive oil. | 256 Green Bay Rd. | 847/432–0309 | $12–$17 | MC, V.

Del Rio. Italian. The dishes in this quaint restaurant are primarily from the northern regions of Italy, such as the veal Del Rio, which is breaded and served with a buttery lemon sauce. Extensive wine list; valet parking. | 228 Green Bay Rd. | 847/432–4608 | $20–$32 | AE, D, DC, MC, V | No lunch.

Froggy's. French. This is an intimate, artsy café known for its ethnic recipes for rack of lamb, seafood, and chicken, and its homemade pastries. | 306 Green Bay Rd. | 847/433–7080 | $20–$30 | D, DC, MC, V | No lunch Sat. Closed Sun.

Gabriel's. Contemporary. You can watch the chefs in the open kitchen of this bistro as they prepare grilled veal, roasted lobster in ginger butter, and a must-try, the papillote of Chilean sea bass (steamed in parchment paper with vegetables). Tables are set with fresh flowers, there's seating on a grated terrace outdoors, and a wine cellar. Valet Parking. | 310 Green Bay Rd. | 847/433–0031 | $25–$35 | AE, D, DC, MC, V | No lunch. Closed Sun. and Mon.

Lodging

Clarion Hotel Moraine. This former mom-and-pop, which has both standard guest rooms and suites with sitting rooms and kitchenettes, is next door to Fort Sheridan, between Lake Forest and Highland Park. The beach and a golf course are 1 mi away, and the Ravinia Music Festival is 3 mi away. Complimentary Continental breakfast. Some kitchenettes, some microwaves, some refrigerators, cable TV. Indoor pool. Hot tub. Exercise equipment. Business services. | 700 Sheridan Rd. | 847/433–5566 | 95 rooms, 4 suites | $99–$130 | AE, D, DC, MC, V.

HINSDALE

MAP 8, C6

(Nearby towns also listed: Downers Grove, Elmhurst, La Grange, Oak Brook)

This wooded, hilly commuter community of 17,500 residents 20 miles from downtown Chicago has parks, playgrounds, and a cultural center.

Information: **Hinsdale Chamber of Commerce** | 22 E. 1st St., 60521 | 630/323–3952 | www.vil.hinsdale.il.us.

Attractions

Robert Crown Center for Health Education. Programs on health and the environment, and sex and drug education are offered here for kids from preschool-age through high school. Reservations are required. | 21 Salt Creek La. | 630/325–1900 | www.health-ed.org/ | $3.25 | Weekdays 8–1:30.

ON THE CALENDAR

FEB.: *Hinsdale Winter Carnival.* During the afternoon of the first Sunday in February, residents of Hinsdale create a winter wonderland at the Katherine Legge Memorial Lodge, where you can join in the snow games and contests, mule-drawn sleigh- and hayrides. And if you have your own cross-country skis or tube, you can also join the locals traversing the snowy slopes. | 630/789–7090.

Dining

Bailey's. Continental. A half mile west of Rte. 83, this restaurant's unusual dining spaces include an atrium, a library with a fireplace, and an open area filled with live plants, old clocks, and Monet replicas. Here you can choose from an extensive list of specials, which changes weekly, as well as the standard fare of steak, filet mignon, and chicken marsala. Sun. brunch. | 330 E. Ogden Ave., Westmont 60559 | 630/655–0440 | $5.95–$17.95 | AE, D, DC, MC, V.

Egg Harbor Café. American. This is a family-friendly breakfast and lunch place, where locals flock for the eggs Benedict. Kids' menu. | 777 N. York Rd. | 630/920–1344 | $6–$12 | AE, D, MC, V | Breakfast also available. No dinner.

Jade Dragon. Chinese. Seated in a red booth with a Chinese flower vase on the table here, you can watch the comings and goings of downtown Hinsdale while feasting on Mongolian beef with sweet and green onions over crispy rice noodles, and on sesame chicken and Szechwan-style green beans. | 43 S. Washington St. | 630/323–6959 | $3.95–$11.50 | AE, D, DC, MC, V | Closed Mon.

Sal Bute's. Mexican. Right in downtown Hinsley, you can try authentic dishes from south of the border, including grilled sea bass and fingerling potatoes, roasted corn, green beans, all drizzled with a sweet and smoky chipotle sauce or a tamarind and morita chile sauce. The restaurant's walls are hung with monthly exhibits of paintings and photographs by local artists. | 20 E. 1st St. | 630/920–8077 | $12.95–$26 | AE, D, DC, MC, V.

Lodging

Baymont Inn and Suites. In Willowbrook, 4 mi southwest of Hinsdale, this hotel is one in a cluster of four, surrounded by several Italian restaurants, 12 mi south of Midway Airport and the Brookfield Zoo. Complimentary Continental breakfast. Some refrigerators, cable TV. Business services. Some pets allowed. | 855 79th St., Willowbrook | 630/654–0077 | fax 630/654–0181 | 134 rooms | $79–$89 | AE, D, DC, MC, V.

Best Western Inn. Between Hinsdale and the Argonne National Laboratory, just off I–55, these standard accommodations are near Harvester Park. Restaurant, bar, room service. Some in-room VCRs (and movies), cable TV. Indoor pool. Laundry service. Airport shuttle, free parking. | 300 S. Frontage Rd., Burr Ridge | 630/325–2900 or 800/528–1234 | fax 630/325–8907 | www.bestwestern.com | 124 rooms | $79–$89 | AE, D, DC, MC, V.

Fairfield Inn by Marriott. In Willowbrook, 4 mi southwest of Hinsdale, this three-story motel is 15 mi southwest of Midway Airport. Complimentary Continental breakfast. Cable TV. Pool. Laundry service. Business services, free parking. | 820 79th St., Willowbrook | 630/789–6300 or 800/228–2800 | www.fairfieldinn.com | 129 rooms | $63–$81 | AE, D, DC, MC, V.

Holiday Inn. At the junction of I–55 and Route 83, 5 mi south of Hinsdale, this large motel is 13 mi west of Midway Airport. Restaurant, bar, room service. In-room data ports, some in-room VCRs (and movies), cable TV. Pool. Exercise equipment. Business services, airport shuttle, free parking. | 7800 S. Kingery Hwy., Willowbrook | 630/325–6400 or 800/HOLIDAY | fax 630/325–2362 | www.basshotels.com | 220 rooms, 5 suites | $99–$140 | AE, D, DC, MC, V.

Red Roof Inn. This standard three-story motel is 15 mi southwest of Midway Airport, in Willowbrook, which is 4 mi southwest of Hinsdale. In-room data ports, cable TV. Business services. Some pets allowed. | 7535 S. Kingery Hwy., Willowbrook | 630/323–8811 | fax 630/323–2714 | www.redroof.com | 109 rooms | $61–$82 | AE, D, DC, MC, V.

HOMEWOOD

MAP 8, E9

(Nearby towns also listed: Chicago, Oak Lawn)

Homewood is a southern suburb of Chicago of 19,300 residents. It's predominantly a commuter community (often mentioned with its neighbor, Flossmoor); its downtown area has outdoor murals on buildings.

Information: Homewood Chamber of Commerce | 1154 Ridge Rd., 60430 | 708/206–3384.

Attractions

Cook County Cheetahs. In Crestwood, 11 mi north of Homewood, you can visit the home turf of the Frontier League's Cook County Cheetahs, Haskinson Ford Field, which has a 3,400-fan capacity and includes two luxury suites, a picnic deck along the right-field line, a Tri-Vision scoreboard, and a state-of-the-art Bose sound system. | 14100 S. Kenton Ave., Crestwood | 708/489–2255 | $4–$23 | May–Aug. Call for schedule.

Midwest Carvers Museum. You can admire more than a thousand carvings and tour the woodshop, educational exhibits, and farmhouses that make up this 2-acre complex in South

Holland, 4 mi from Homewood, off Route 6. | 16234 Vincennes Ave., South Holland | 708/331–6011 | Free | Mon.–Sat. 10–4.

ON THE CALENDAR

JULY: *Homewood Days*. From noon till midnight the third weekend in July, you can join the people of Homewood celebrating in the streets—along Ridge Road and Dixie Highway—with local musicians playing during the day and more nationally renowned bands jamming throughout the evening. There are also local food vendors, sidewalk sales of crafts and kitsch, kids' games, and a car show. | 708/206–3384.

Dining

Aurelio's Pizza. Italian. You can order wine or beer to accompany the thin-crust pizza served in the dining room of this renovated warehouse that retains an appealing industrial look. Seating on a canopied deck also available. | 18162 Harwood Ave. | 708/798–8050 | $7–$14 | AE, D, DC, MC, V | No lunch weekends.

Bellagio. Italian. Hand-painted murals of pastoral scenes transport you to Italy as you dine on homemade pastas and sauces, including dishes from the country's northern region, such as the Polla Nilla—a chicken breast with bowtie pasta, mushrooms, and a combination of marinara and Alfredo sauces, served with a splash of marsala. | 18042 Martin Ave. | 708/957–1650 | $10.95–$19.95 | AE, DC, MC, V | Closed Mon. No lunch weekends.

Lodging

Ramada Limited. Lincoln Mall, River Oaks Shopping Center, and two golf courses are within a 5-mi radius of this five-story hotel. Restaurant, bar, complimentary Continental breakfast, room service. Some refrigerators, cable TV. Indoor-outdoor pool. Exercise equipment. Barbershop, beauty salon. Laundry service. Business services, airport shuttle, free parking. | 17400 S. Halsted Ave. | 708/957–1600 or 800/528–1234 | fax 708/957–1963 | www.bestwestern.com | 188 rooms | $76–$115 | AE, D, DC, MC, V.

Holiday Inn Express In Harvey, 10 mi north of Homewood, you can choose among rooms with big beds (queen- and king-size) and suites with Jacuzzis. Midway Airport is 2 mi away, and there are three casinos within an 8-mi range. Complimentary Continental breakfast, room service. In-room data ports, some kitchenettes, some microwaves, some refrigerators, some in-room hot tubs, cable TV. Exercise equipment. Laundry service. Business services. | 16900 S. Halsted Ave., Harvey | 708/331–0700 | www.basshotels.com | 61 rooms, 16 suites | $89–$122 | AE, D, DC, MC, V.

ITASCA

MAP 8, C5

(Nearby towns also listed: Elmhurst, Schaumburg)

In the 1840s, Itasca was a rural outpost. Today, it's a bustling commercial area, thick with modern high-rises and offices, in the sprawling northwestern suburbs of Chicago. Itasca's population is 8,000.

Information: Itasca Chamber of Commerce | 100 N. Walnut St., 60147 | 630/773–0835 | www.itasca.com.

Attractions

Spring Brook Nature Center. This preserve, between Catalpa Avenue and Irving Park Road, has 2 mi of trails where you can pass through a tunnel of tall prairie grass or take a 700-ft-long, 4-ft-high boardwalk over a cattail marsh. Information about what lives and grows in the preserve is provided in an information center, and you can relax in a picnic shelter or around a campfire ring here. | 130 Forest Ave. | 630/773–5572 | Free | Information Tues–Sun. 11:30–5. Park daily dawn–dusk.

ON THE CALENDAR

JULY: *Itasca Fest.* In Washington Park, you can eat, drink, and be merry during this four-day festival sponsored jointly by the Village of Itasca and the Itasca Lions Club. There are also many rides and games geared to kids, and artisans booths and evening entertainment, including live music, for all. | 630/773–0835.

Dining

Casale Cucina. Mediterranean. Next door to their carry-out pizza place, the Cucina is the Casale's full-service restaurant with classic white table linens and black-and-white family photos hanging on the walls. Try the crab-stuffed shrimp served on saffron rice, the paella for two, the shrimp farfalle al vodka, or the daily risotto or fresh fish specials. | 216 N. Walnut St. | 630/285–0840 | $9.95–$29.95 | AE, D, DC, MC, V.

Truffles. American. Best known for its barbecued ribs, this restaurant also offers a wide selection of salads, including a pineapple boat filled with chicken salad, and a salmon cold-plate. The split-level dining room is filled with mirrors and brass and baskets of flowers hanging on the walls. Sunday brunch. | 360 Rte. 53 | 630/773–0700 | $12–$18 | AE, D, DC, MC, V | Closed Sun. No lunch Sat.

Lodging

Chicago/Itasca Amerisuites. Twelve miles west of O'Hare and 6 mi from Woodfield Mall, these suites have modest kitchens, some of which have refrigerators stocked with goodies. The "taking-care-of-business" suites include office supplies, task lighting, an executive-size desk and chair, additional phone lines, and an overstuffed chair and ottoman. Free local transportation provided, within a 5-mi radius. Complimentary Continental breakfast. In-room data ports, minibars, microwaves, refrigerators, in-room VCRs, cable TV. Indoor pool. Hot tub. Exercise equipment. Laundry facilities. Business services. | 1150 Arlington Heights Rd. | 630/875–1400 or 800/833–1516 | fax 630/875–9756 | www.amerisuites.com | 128 suites | $149–$164 | AE, D, DC, MC, V.

Holiday Inn. You'll find this standard motel at the intersection of Irving Park and Rowhling roads. There are several golf courses 2 mi from the motel, and the Arlington Race Track is 7 mi away. Room service. In-room data ports, cable TV. Indoor pool. Hot tub, sauna. Exercise equipment. Video games. Laundry facilities, laundry service. Pets allowed. | 860 W. Irving Park Rd. | 630/773–2340 | fax 630/773–1077 | www.basshotels.com | 156 rooms, 4 suites | $109–$159 | AE, D, DC, MC, V.

Indian Lakes Resort. This golf-and-conference resort is in Bloomfield, between the Stratford Square shopping center and Old Town, 6 mi southwest of Itasca. Restaurant, bar, room service. In-room data ports, cable TV. Outdoor pool, indoor pool. Beauty salon, hot tub, massage. Two 18-hole golf courses, miniature golf, putting green, tennis. Gym. Video games. Business services. | 250 W. Schick Rd., Bloomingdale | 630/529–0200 or 800/334–3417 | fax 630/529–9271 | www.indianlakesresort.com | 308 rooms | $119–$179 | AE, D, DC, MC, V.

Nordic Hills Resort and Conference Center. A half mile southwest of Itasca, this nine-story tower hotel and expansive golf and conference resort are just west of I–290 and I–355. Restaurant, bar with entertainment. Cable TV. Indoor pool, outdoor pool. Hot tubs. 18-hole golf course, putting green, tennis. Basketball, bowling, exercise equipment. Cross-country skiing. Video games. Laundry service. Business services. | 1401 Nordic Rd. | 630/773–2750 or 800/487–1969 | fax 630/773–3622 | www.nordichillsresort.com | 226 rooms | $79–$159 | AE, D, DC, MC, V.

Wyndham Northwest Chicago. Just off of I–290, this 12-story hotel forms an atrium with the office park to which it is adjacent. Restaurant, bar with entertainment. In-room data ports, some minibars, cable TV. Indoor pool. Beauty salon, hot tub, massage. Tennis. Gym.

Laundry service. Business services, airport shuttle. | 400 Park Blvd. | 630/773–4000 or 800/ WYNDHAM | fax 630/773–4088 | www.wyndham.com | 408 rooms | $89–$139 | AE, D, DC, MC, V.

JACKSONVILLE

MAP 6, D7

(Nearby towns also listed: Havana, Springfield)

Settlers came to Jacksonville in the early 1820s, and Stephen A. Douglas also practiced law here. Today's population is 25,000.

Information: Jacksonville Area Visitors and Conventions Bureau | 115 W. Morton Ave., 62650-2880 | 217/243–5678 or 800/593–5678 | www.outfitters.com/illinois/morgan/jacksonville.html.

Attractions

Governor Duncan Home. At the time Duncan was elected as Illinois' governor, Vandalia was the state capital, but instead of living in the mansion there, Duncan had this Federal-style house built in Jacksonville for him and his family. The 1834 structure has many peculiarities, including the extremely shallow rises of the walnut staircase to accommodate Duncan's 4'5" wife, whom rumors claim he would pick up and set on the mantle when she was angry. | 4 Duncan Park | 217/243–5678 | $2 | Memorial Day–Labor Day, Wed. and Sat. 1–4.

Lake Jacksonville. You can boat on this 500-acre man-made lake just south of town, as well as fish and swim in it, and picnic and camp on the surrounding grounds. | 217/479-4646 (seasonal) or TDD 217/479–4611 | $1.50 (to beach) | Beach, Fri.–Sun.; boating and camping daily by reservation and permit.

ON THE CALENDAR

MAY: *Potawatomi Trail Powwow.* This Native American gathering includes traditional trading, dance competitions, and food in Jacksonville's community park. It takes place the third weekend of the month. | 800/593–5678.
SEPT.: *Fall Flea Market and Porky Days.* You can satisfy your appetites for all kinds of food, crafts, and kitsch at this flea market and fair in Central Park Plaza, held the second weekend of the month. | 815/740–2216.

Dining

Lonzerottis. Italian. The steak pepperloin (rolled in cracked peppercorns) and the pasta sampler, accompanied by a wine from the list of many regional selections, are favorites at this former train station now scattered with railroad memorabilia. You can also dine outdoors on the cobblestone sidewalk or at umbrella-covered tables on the deck. Kids' menu. | 600 E. State St. | 217/243–7151 | $7–$18 | AE, D, MC, V | Closed Sun.

Mugsy's. American. The walls have been stripped to the original brick and covered with collectibles in this landmark famed for its steaks, though the shrimp rolled in spices, then sautéed and served over rice with red-pepper sauce is a favorite here, too. | 230 Mauvais-terrie St. | 217/245–0641 | $8.99–$15.99 | AE, MC, V | Closed Sun. and Mon.

Lodging

258 Inn Bed and Breakfast. The three suites in this Victorian home on the corner of West Morton Avenue and Church Street, right in the center of town, have private baths with claw-foot tubs, and one with an oak and brass-chained toilet. Breakfast here includes an assortment of the proprietor's freshly baked breads, and you can purchase other homemade treats in her little shop on the first floor. Complimentary Continental breakfast. Some refrigerators, no room phones, TV in common area. No kids under 12. No smoking. | 258 W. Morton Ave. | 217/245–2588 | 3 suites | $65–$70 | No credit cards | Closed Dec.–May.

AmeriHost Inn. Both Mac Murray and Illinois colleges are within 3 mi of this hotel in the main business district of town. Complimentary Continental breakfast. Refrigerators, some microwaves, cable TV, some VCRs. Indoor pool. Gym. Business services. | 1709 W. Morton Ave. | 217/245–4500 | fax 217/245–0411 | www.amerihostinn.com | 58 rooms, 2 suites | $59–$69; $105–$115 suites | AE, D, DC, MC, V.

Holiday Inn. On the south edge of town, just off U.S. 67, this hotel with a Holidome recreation center is less than a mile from both Illinois and Mac Murray colleges. Restaurant, bar, room service. In-room data ports, microwaves, some refrigerators, cable TV. Indoor pool. Hot tub. Video games. Business services, free parking. Pets allowed. | 1717 W. Morton Ave. | 217/245–9571 or 800/HOLIDAY | fax 217/245–0686 | 116 rooms | $69–$100 | AE, D, DC, MC, V.

JOLIET

MAP 6, H3

(Nearby towns also listed: Aurora, Kankakee, Morris)

Joliet is on the banks of the Des Plaines River, where today several floating casinos entertain visitors. The town was named for explorer Louis Jolliet, who traveled the area in the 17th century. More recently, it's been a gritty industrial city whose base faded somewhat in the 1970s and 1980s. However, casinos are bringing life back to downtown. Today it has a population of 95,000.

Information: **Heritage Corridor Convention and Visitors Bureau** | 81 N. Chicago St., 60431 | 815/727–2323 or 800/926–2262.

Attractions

Bicentennial Park Theater/Bandshell Complex. You can enjoy concerts and other live performances in this indoor theater and outdoor music shell in the riverfront Bicentennial Park. | 201 W. Jefferson St. | 815/740–2298 | Free | Call for schedule.

***Empress* Casino Joliet.** You can gamble, eat, and drink on this floating casino, which has 1,000 slots and 18 daily gaming sessions. | Empress Dr. | 888/436–7737 | Free | Daily.

Harrah's Joliet Casino. Both a luxury yacht and a paddlewheeler are outfitted with casinos, restaurants, bars, and stages for live entertainment for you to enjoy here. | 150 N. Joliet St. | 800/HARRAHS | Free | Daily.

Pilcher Park. You can admire the wonders of nature in a greenhouse with seasonal displays, four acres of outdoor gardens, a nature center, and hiking trails in this park. | 225 W. Gougar Rd. | 815/741–7278 | Free | Daily.

Rialto Square Theatre. This restored 1920s theater offers live entertainment of all sorts, including musical and dramatic performances. | 102 N. Chicago St. | 815/726–6600 (box office) or 815/726–7171 | Free | Call for performance schedule; theater tours by appointment.

Route 66 Speedway. On old Route 66, this 240-acre multiplex is the first stadium built solely for drag racing. A state-of-the-art strip with a half mile clay oval dirt track and asphalt road course test track, the Speedway is home to demolition-derby and supercross events, (when cars smash into each other and motorcycles jump over obstacles). | 3200 S. Chicago St. | 815/722–5500 | $5–$65 | Call for schedule.

ON THE CALENDAR
JULY: *Waterway Daze.* In Bicentennial Park, along the waterway wall, you can watch the water parade and other entertainment as well as dine on the fare sold by vendors during this summer festival that takes place the third week in the month. | 815/740–2216.

OCT.: *Pumpkin Fest.* At this fall celebration held in Bicentennial Park, which during the festival is lined with pumpkins decorated by local school kids, you can compete in pumpkin-painting contests and other games, get your face painted, visit a haunted house, and partake of the offerings from many crafts, food, and beer vendors. | 815/724–3760.

DEC.: *Festival of the Gnomes.* You can find these ageless dwarves of folklore in all shapes and sizes at this winter festival held the first weekend of the month in Bicentennial Park, which includes live music, comedy, and drama, as well as vendors of food and drink, and arts and crafts. | 815/740–2216.

Dining

Ace Drive-In. Fast food. On Route 30 at Ingalls, you can either be served in your car by the carhops in white or dine at the picnic tables here. Ace makes its root beer, so the black-and-whites (root beer floats) are a must-try. | 1207 Plainfield Rd. | 815/726–7741 | $1.50–$4 | No credit cards | Closed Oct.–Mar.

Secrets. American. This casual place specializes in barbecued ribs and chicken, but other popular choices here are steak and seafood such as scallops and stuffed flounder. Entertainment Wednesday and Saturday. Kids' menu. | 2222 W. Jefferson St. | 815/744–3745 | $15–$27 | AE, D, DC, MC, V | No lunch. Closed Mon.

White Fence Farm. American. In Romeoville, 10 mi north of Joliet, this down-home eatery draws folks for its traditional Sunday-dinner fare, such as fried chicken and corn fritters. Kids' menu. | Joliet Rd., Romeoville | 815/838–1500 | $11–$18 | AE, D, DC, MC, V | No lunch except Sun. Closed Mon.

Lodging

Best Western Joliet Inn and Suites. Along I–55, just 2 mi north of I–80 and 2 mi southwest of Joliet Junior College, this motel offers sizable rooms with large desks. It's a mile from a golf course, and three from the Empress casino. Complimentary Continental breakfast. In-room data ports, some microwaves, some refrigerators, cable TV. Indoor pool. Hot tub. Exercise equipment. Laundry facilities, laundry service. Business services. | 4380 Enterprise Dr. | 815/730–7500 | fax 815/730–8400 | 34 rooms, 24 suites | $64–$79 | AE, D, DC, MC, V.

Comfort Inn–North. This Comfort Inn is 5 mi northwest of downtown Joliet, near the Louis Joliet shopping mall, 5 mi northeast of the riverboat casinos. Complimentary Continental breakfast. Some refrigerators, cable TV. Indoor pool. Hot tub. Pets allowed. | 3235 Norman Ave. | 815/436–5141 or 800/228–5150 | www.comfortinn.com | 64 rooms | $58–$72 | AE, D, DC, MC, V.

Comfort Inn–South. It is just under 2 mi to Rialto Square Theater from this Comfort Inn, which is 3 mi southwest of the heart of Joliet and offers shuttle service to the riverboat casinos and several nearby restaurants. Complimentary Continental breakfast. Some refrigerators, cable TV. Indoor pool. Hot tub. Business services. Pets allowed. | 135 S. Larkin Ave. | 815/744–1770 or 800/228–5150 | www.comfortinn.com | 67 rooms | $57–$104 | AE, D, DC, MC, V.

Manor Motel. These modest accommodations are in Channahon, 10 mi southeast of Joliet, just off of I–55. Cable TV. Pool. Business services. Pets allowed. | 23926 W. Eames Rd., Channahon | 815/467–5385 | fax 815/467–1617 | 77 rooms | $45–$53 | AE, D, DC, MC, V.

Motel 6. You take the Larkin Avenue exit, 130-B, off of I–80 to reach this standard motel. Cable TV. Laundry facilities. Business services. Some pets allowed. | 1850 McDonough Rd. | 815/729–2800 | fax 815/729–9528 | www.motel6.com | 132 rooms | $48–$53 | AE, D, DC, MC, V.

Ramada Limited. These accommodations are a mile from the Empress Casino in a commercial area. Complimentary Continental breakfast. In-room data ports, some microwaves, some refrigerators, some in-room hot tubs, cable TV. Indoor pool. Hot tub. Exercise equipment. Laundry service. | 1520 Commerce La. | 815/730–1111 | fax 815/730–1111 | www.ramada.com | 57 rooms, 13 suites | $50–$145 | AE, D, DC, MC, V.

KANKAKEE

(Nearby towns also listed: Joliet, Morris)

Early French explorers traveled the Kankakee River in 1679. Traces of their heritage can be found in Kankakee today as well as along the river utilized today by canoeists and other boaters. The name Kankakee is believed to be named by the Potawatomi Indians. Definitions are thought to be "Wolf," "Swampy Place," and "Wonderful Land." Today Kankakee has approximately 102,000 residents.

Information: Kankakee County Convention and Visitors Bureau | 1270 Larry Power Rd., Bourbonnais 60914 | 815/935–7390 or 800/74–RIVER | www.visitkankakeecounty.com.

Attractions

Historical Church Tour. By self-guided tour, you can explore the many old churches surrounding Court House Square, starting at First Presbyterian and including First Baptist, Ashbury United Methodist, St. Paul's Episcopalian, St. Patrick's Catholic, and St. Paul's Lutheran, as you traverse Indiana and Harrison avenues, between Court and Station Streets. | 371 E. Court St. (First Presbyterian Church) | 815/935–7390 (County Convention and Visitors Bureau) | Free | Call for schedule.

Kankakee Antique Mall. With its more than 100 dealers, this is the largest antiques mall in the state. | 145 S. Schuyler Ave. | 815/937–4957 | Free | Mon.–Sat. 10–6, Sun. noon–5.

Kankakee County Historical Society Museum. You can learn a lot about the history of this area from the collection of artifacts here and admire the permanent display of George Gray Barnard sculptures. | 801 S. 8th Ave. | 815/932–5279 | fax 815/932–5204 | Free | Mon.–Thurs. 10–4, weekends 1–4.

Kankakee River State Park. Eight miles northwest of Kankakee, you can camp, hunt, and bike the trails in this 3,900-acre park, from which you can also fish and canoe in the river. | Rte. 102 | 815/933–1383 | Free | Daily.

Olivet Nazarene University. A mix of beautiful old and more contemporary buildings on 165 parklike acres in Bourbonnais, 3 mi north of Kankakee, make up this small, private Christian college with 2,500 undergraduate and adult-education students. | U.S. 45/52 at Rte. 102, Bourbonnais | 815/939–5011 or 800/648–1463 | www.olivet.edu | Free | Daily.

Reed's Rental. You can arrange canoe and kayak trips on the Kankakee River through this tour company. | 907 N. Indiana Ave. | 815/932–2663 | Priced by the trip | Mid-Apr.–mid-Oct., daily.

ON THE CALENDAR

JUNE: *Kankakee River Valley Bicycle Classic.* These races in Cobb Park draw bicycling enthusiasts from all over despite the fact that it is just a one-day affair. | 800/747–4837.
JUNE–JULY: *Kankakee River Fishing Derby.* You can grab your pole and join the many anglers who ply the area's waterways for the tagged fish that are released there, and then trade the tags for prizes from local businesses. The 10-day derby starts the last week in June. | 800/747–4837.
JUNE–AUG.: *Concerts in the Park.* Thursday evenings at 6:30, you can grab a picnic and a beach towel and head to Veteran's Park at Third and Vine Streets to enjoy free musical entertainment. If it's raining, the outdoors concerts move indoors, at the National Guard Armory. | 309/852–2175.
AUG.: *Kankakee County Fair.* Livestock and produce judgings, a carnival midway with games and rides, and other entertainment are all a part of this traditional celebration at the county fairgrounds on U.S. 45/52, which takes place the first week of the month. | 815/932–6714 or 800/747–4837.

Dining

America's Bistro. American. This comfortable bistro is known for its fresh fish, chicken, pasta, and chops. | 1340 Kennedy Dr. | 815/932–6795 | $10–$18 | AE, D, MC, V.

Homestead. American. The fresh bread, chicken, steaks, and ribs are what draw folks to the three dining rooms in this vintage building. | 1230 S. East Ave. | 815/933–6214 | $9–$24 | D, MC, V.

Lodging

Days Inn. You take exit 312 from I–57 to reach this four-story motel on Route 17, a couple of miles east of town. Restaurant, bar. Cable TV. Pool. Laundry service. | 1975 E. Court St. | 815/939–7171 or 800/544–8313 | fax 815/939–7184 | www.daysinn.com | 98 rooms | $45–$70 | AE, D, DC, V.

Fairfield Inn. This three-story motel in Bourbonnais is just 5 mi east of Kankakee River State Park. Complimentary Continental breakfast. In-room data ports, some microwaves, refrigerators, cable TV. Indoor pool. Hot tub. Business services. Laundry service. | 1550 Rte. 50, Bourbonnais | 815/935–1334 or 800/228–2800 | www.fairfieldinn.com | 49 rooms, 8 suites | $65–$75; $85 suites | AE, D, DC, MC, V.

River Decks Bed and Breakfast and Garden Resort. This riverfront property includes a Frank Lloyd Wright Prairie-style home with five suites, two four-room cottages, and a private beach from which you can waterski, fish, or launch a boat. Each suite has a deck overlooking the waters of Kankakee, some with wraparound views, as well as gardens filled with beds, trellises, and arbors of perennials, among which you can wander on stone walkways. Complimentary breakfast. Some in-room VCRS, cable TV, no room phones. Beach, water sports, boating, fishing. | 494 W. River St. | 815/933–9000 | fax 815/939–4281 | www.riverdecks.com | 5 suites, 2 cottages | $75–$125 | AE, D, DC, MC, V.

KEWANEE

MAP 6, E4

(Nearby towns also listed: Bishop Hill, Galesburg, Princeton)

Founded in 1854 as a stop on the Central Military Tract Railroad (later the Chicago, Burlington, and Quincy Railroad), Kewanee takes its name from a Winnebago Indian word for prairie chicken. Today Kewanee (population 13,000) bills itself as the Hog Capital of the World and celebrates its porcine heritage every fall.

Information: **Kewanee Chamber of Commerce** | 113 E. 2nd St., 61443 | 309/852–2175, 309/852–2176 | www.kewanee-il.com.

Attractions

Historic Francis Park. You can camp and picnic in this park 3 mi east of Kewanee, as well as tour an 1890 home of brick, stone, and native wood, which has "disappearing" doors and windows and other odd features, particularly for a house with no electricity. Baseball field and playground. | U.S. 34 | 309/852–0511 | Free | Apr.–third weekend in Oct., daily 7AM–10PM.

Johnson Sauk Trail State Park. This park includes a 51-acre lake on which you can boat, a recreation area for camping and picnicking and winter sports, as well as Ryan's Historic Round Barn museum and National Historic Site. | Rte. 78 | 309/853–5589 | Free | Daily sunrise–10.

Windmont Park. You can get your exercise on this 3-acre park's exercise loop—three times around is just over a mile—and enjoy the birds that flock to the little lagoon here. Interestingly, the land was a maintenance area for trolley cars in the early 1900s. Now, in winter, Kewanee's senior citizens string tens of thousands of lights throughout the park to create a winter wonderland. | 349 Beach St. S | 309/852–2872 | Free | Closed Oct.–Apr., call for Christmas hours.

ON THE CALENDAR

JULY: *Sauk Trail Heritage Days.* The Native American heritage of this area is celebrated through demonstrations of the peoples' skills and traditions during the 4th of July weekend. You can come to an 1840s camp rendezvous, ride canoes, or participate in a Pow-Wow. | 309/852–2175.

AUG.: *Gladiolus Festival.* In Momence, 12 mi northeast of Kankakee, this height-of-summer festival includes a flower show, a parade, an old-fashioned carnival, and a flea market. The festival is held the second weekend of the month. | 815/472–6730 or 800/747–4837.

AUG.–SEPT.: *Hog Days.* On Labor Day weekend, enthusiasts of everything porcine gather to feast on the food and carnival offerings and join the parade celebrating Kewanee's status as the hog capital of the world. | 309/852–4644.

Dining

Andris Waunee Farm. American. In the three theme dining rooms here—one rustic, one sportsy, and the third Polynesian—the dishes are mostly meat, but the buffet and full menu also include seafood and other lighter fare. Kids' menu. | U.S. 34/Rte. 78 | 309/852–2481 | $7–$30 | MC, V | Closed Sun. No lunch.

The Cellar. American. Steak, ribs, catfish, and the charcoal-broiled shrimp are what lure folks to this casual below-street-level place in downtown Geneseo, 25 mi northwest of Kewanee. Sunday brunch and kids' menu. | 137 S. State St., Geneseo | 309/944–2177 | $14–$28 | AE, D, DC, MC, V | No lunch. Closed Mon.

R.J. Boar's. Barbecue. This fragrant smokehouse at the south end of town, just off of U.S. 34, has porcine kitsch and midwestern farm gadgets hanging around its dining room, where you can pig out on barbecued ribs (both beef and pork), chicken, and turkey. For less hog-wild appetites, salads, catfish, and rainbow trout can be had here. | 618 Tenney St. | 309/853–2500 | $8.99–$14.99 | AE, D, MC, V.

Lodging

Aunt Daisy's Bed and Breakfast. This 1890s Victorian home was willed by its original owners to the Catholic Church and used as a rectory until 1988. In its present incarnation as a B&B, its guest rooms have fainting couches, marble-top dressers, stained-glass windows, and sitting rooms. Common areas include a music room with a baby grand piano and a 1929 player piano, and nicely landscaped grounds, which you can enjoy from both the enclosed back porch and a pergola, where weddings are sometimes held. Golf, pool, and gym privileges are available at a local country club and YMCA. Complimentary breakfast. Refrigerators, cable TV, in-room VCRs. Library. | 223 W. Central Blvd. | 309/853–3300 or 888/422–4148 | fax 309/853–4148 | www.auntdaisy.net | 4 suites | $95 | AE, D, DC, MC, V.

Good's Furniture Bed and Breakfast. Perhaps an odd mixture–a luxurious bed-and-breakfast and a furniture business—but the store is a regional institution, and there is a separate entrance for the plush inn's accommodations. Restaurant, complimentary breakfast, room service. Cable TV. Hot tub. No smoking. | 200 N. Main St. | 309/852–5656 or 888/344–6637 | fax 309/854–5306 | www.goodsfurniture.com | 4 rooms | $85–$135 | D, MC, V.

Kewanee Motor Lodge. This standard motel is one of the newer hostelries in town. Some refrigerators, cable TV. Business services. Pets allowed (fee). | 400 S. Main St. | 309/853–4000 | 29 rooms | $42–$52 | AE, D, DC, MC, V.

LA GRANGE

MAP 6, H2

(Nearby towns also listed: Brookfield, Elmhurst, Hinsdale, Oak Brook)

This residential west suburban Chicago village of 15,300 was incorporated in 1879. Two of its neighborhoods are historic districts, with houses designed by noted architects from the late 19th and early 20th centuries such as Frank Lloyd Wright, J. C. Llewelyn, and John Van Bergen. The Holidome in nearby Countryside is said to be the world's largest.

Information: West Suburban Chamber of Commerce | 47 S. 6th Ave., 60525 | 708/352–0494 | www.westsuburbanchamber.org.

ON THE CALENDAR

JUNE: *Pet Parade.* You can cheer the costumed pets of area residents, who parade along a 1½-mi route through downtown La Grange for this humorous festivity that takes place the first Saturday of the month. | 708/352–0494.

AUG.: *Endless Summer.* Right downtown, west of La Grange Road between Burlington and Cossitt Avenues, this three-day festival, usually held the first weekend of August, celebrates the season with street vendors, live entertainment, and carnival rides. | 708/352–0494.

Dining

Al's Char House. Steak. This downtown La Grange steak house is famous for its humongous servings—an average steak here hovers around 2 pounds—and its neon sculpture out front depicting cowboys in varying positions of repose. The dining room's five subdivisions have hardwood floors and wooden booths. Kids' menu. | 32 S. La Grange Rd. | 708/354–6255 | $7.95–$19.95 | AE, D, DC, MC, V | No lunch Mon.–Sat.

Magic Wok. Chinese. Rest assured the fish you see in the tank as you enter this downtown Cantonese restaurant on West Harris Avenue, a half block off La Grange Avenue, will not be served as your whole crispy fish, a popular dish here. The chicken and shrimp with snow peas, and black, white, and straw mushrooms are favorites, too, as are the shrimp in lobster sauce. | 23 W. Harris Ave. | 708/352–2341 | $5.50–$11 | AE, D, DC, MC, V.

Marconi's. Italian. The chef in this homey restaurant, with hardwood floors and pale tan and green walls sprinkled with hand-painted leaves, prepares many of his northern Italian family recipes, including the popular roasted-in-garlic chicken Vesuvio. Marconi's is also known for its homemade desserts, so try to save room for the tiramisu or the carmel-pecan cheesecake. | 15 Calendar Ct. | 708/352–1621 | $8.95–$22.95 | AE, D, DC, MC, V | No lunch Sat. Closed Sun.

Lodging

Best Western Inn. Three miles south of La Grange, in Countryside, this motel is 4 mi from Brookfield Zoo, at the junction of I–55 North and La Grange Road, where there are also several chain restaurants. Complimentary Continental breakfast. In-room data ports, cable TV. Pool. | 5631 S. La Grange Rd., Countryside | 708/352–2480 | fax 708/354–0998 | www.best-western.com | 47 rooms | $78–$81 | AE, D, DC, MC, V.

Hampton Inn. In Countryside, 3 mi south of La Grange, these standard accommodations are 11 mi east of Midway Airport and 4 mi west of Brookfield Zoo. Complimentary Continental breakfast. In-room data ports, cable TV. Exercise equipment. Laundry service. Business services. | 6251 Joliet Rd., Countryside | 708/354–5200 or 800/426–7866 | fax 708/354–1329 | www.hampton-inn.com | 108 rooms | $85–$98 | AE, D, DC, MC, V.

Holiday Inn La Grange/Countryside. Home of the world's largest Holidome (an indoor recreational space), this seven-story Holiday Inn tower is in Countryside, 3 mi south of La Grange, 1 mi east of I–294 and a half mile off I–55. Restaurant, bar, room service. In-room data ports, cable TV. Indoor pool, wading pool. Hot tub. Exercise equipment. Video games. Laundry service. Business services. | 6201 Joliet Rd., Countryside | 708/354–4200 or 800/441–6041 | fax 708/354–4241 | www.basshotels.com | 305 rooms | $111–$119 | AE, D, DC, MC, V.

La Grange Motel. In Countryside, which is 1½ mi south of La Grange and the same distance north of I–55, this 1970s brick motel has standard accommodations with E-Z chairs and is right next to J. C. George's restaurant. In-room data ports, cable TV. Outdoor pool. No pets. | 5846 S. La Grange Rd., Countryside | 708/352–5640 | 35 rooms | $54–$75 | AE, D, DC, MC, V.

LAKE FOREST

(Nearby towns also listed: Highland Park, Highwood, Libertyville, Vernon Hills, Waukegan)

The downtown showpiece of this tiny North Shore suburb (population 18,000) is Market Square, a planned town center built in 1917. It is considered one of the first shopping districts built to accommodate the automobile.

Information: **Lake Forest/Lake Bluff Chamber of Commerce** | 695 N. Western Ave., 60045 | 847/234–4282 | fax 847/234–4297 | www.lakeforestonline.com.

Attractions
Lake Forest College. This small, private liberal-arts college has a student body of 1,200. | 555 N. Sheridan Rd. | 847/234–3100 | www.lfc.edu | Free | Daily.

ON THE CALENDAR
JULY: *Lake County Fair.* At Lake Forest Fairgrounds on Rte. 120, one block west of Rte. 45 in Gray Lake, you can join the locals celebrating their agricultural heritage at this fair held the last week of the month. Some of the fun is annual livestock and produce judgings, and at the live entertainment, and games and rides on the carnival brought in midway through the fair. | 847/223–2204.

Dining
Egg Harbor Café. American. Eggs Benedict, pancakes, and sandwiches are what this local chain restaurant with its chicken-and-egg interior is known for. Kids' menu. | 512 N. Western Ave. | 847/295–3449 | $6–$12 | AE, D, MC, V | No dinner.

English Room. Continental. The dining room looks like an English manor at this restaurant in the Deer Path Inn, where you can also eat outdoors in the courtyard or in the glassed-in porch. Popular dishes include leg of lamb, and oyster and lobster dishes. Breakfast buffet, Sunday brunch, and a kids' menu. | 255 E. Illinois St. | 847/234–2280 | Jacket suggested | $22–$33 | AE, D, DC, MC, V.

The Lantern of Lake Forest. American/Casual. Known for its build-your-own burgers, this restaurant also serves specialty burgers, including one with Swiss cheese and grilled onions served on dark rye bread. Other favorites here are the daily specials, such as Friday's perch-fry and Sunday's broasted chicken. A model train overhead races around a track among the Lantern's three dining rooms. | 768 N. Western Ave. | 847/234–9844 | $2.50–$13.95 | AE, D, DC, MC, V.

Lovells of Lake Forest. Contemporary. On the southeast corner of Waukegan Road and Glouster Crossing, this French Provincial structure, with furnishings of the same design, houses U.S. astronaut Captain Lovell and son's restaurant, where much of the astronaut's memorabilia and the famous Steed of Apollo mural are displayed. Son Lovell, the executive chef, includes on his menu roasted pheasant, rack of lamb, and several pasta and salad entrées. A bar expressly for cigar and cigarette smokers and a martini bar are a part of the premises. Banquet rooms available. Sunday brunch. | 915 S. Waukegan Rd. | 847/234–8013 | $20–$33 | AE, D, DC, MC, V | No lunch Sat.

Rigoletto. Italian. The cuisine is ultra-contemporary in this restaurant, where you can eat outside, weather permitting, or in the mirrored dining room. The menu ranges from authentic Italian dishes like the spicy penne all'arrabbiata to the chef's more original creations like grilled sea bass with a berry barbecue sauce. | 293 E. Illinois St. | 847/234–7675 | $10–$28 | AE, DC, MC, V | No lunch weekends. Closed Mon.

South Gate Café. American. This restaurant is in a converted turn-of-the-century fire station overlooking the town square, where favorites are the fresh seafood, pastas, and pizza. | 655 Forest Ave. | 847/234–8800 | www.southgatecafe.com | $10–$27 | AE, D, DC, MC, V.

Lodging

The Clarion Hotel Moraine and Conference Center. This deluxe hotel with its antiques-filled lobby is in the town of Highwood, a 700-acre national Historic Landmark District 5 minutes southeast of Lake Forest and just 5 minutes north of where the Ravinia Music Festival is held. Rooms on the hotel's east side have views of Fort Sheridan and Lake Michigan. Restaurant, bar, complimentary Continental breakfast. In-room data ports, some minibars, some refrigerators, cable TV. Outdoor pool. Hot tub. Exercise equipment. Business services. | 700 N. Sheridan Rd. | 847/433–5566 | fax 847/433–0020 | 100 rooms | $99–$169 | AE, D, DC, MC, V.

Deer Path Inn. A landmark since its completion in 1929, this three-story hotel near Lake Forest's historic Market Square shopping district has stone fireplaces, beamed ceilings, and English antique furnishings. Restaurant, complimentary breakfast, room service. In-room data ports, some microwaves, refrigerators, some in-room VCRs, cable TV. Laundry facilities. Business services, free parking. | 255 E. Illinois St. | 847/234–2280 | fax 847/234–3352 | 54 rooms, 27 suites | $110–$150; $170–$300 suites | AE, D, DC, MC, V.

LIBERTYVILLE

MAP 8, C2

(Nearby towns also listed: Grayslake, Gurnee, Lake Forest, Vernon Hills, Waukegan)

Formerly a summer vacation area, Libertyville is famous for having had both Adlai Stevenson and Marlon Brando as residents. Today, it's a suburb of Chicago with a population of about 20,000; a number of large corporate headquarters also dot the area.

Information: Libertyville, Mundelein, Vernon Hills Chamber of Commerce | 1123 S. Milwaukee Ave., 60048 | 847/680–0750 | www.libertyville.com.

Attractions

David Adler Cultural Center. You can enjoy both the design of the structure and the events in this 19th-century summer home of architect David Adler, which now hosts concerts, workshops, art exhibits, and music classes. | 1700 N. Milwaukee Ave. | 847/367–0707 | fax 847/367–0804 | Priced per event | Weekdays 9–9, Sat. 8:30–4:30.

Lambs Farm. A petting zoo, train rides, and miniature golf are some of what you can enjoy on this farm, which holds special events throughout the year, from which proceeds support the upkeep of the farm and provide training programs for adults with mental disabilites. There is also a restaurant, bakery, and pet store. | Rte. 176 at I–94, | 847/362–6774 (events hotline) or 847/362–4636 | Priced per attraction | Daily.

Main Street Area. This turn-of-the-century town was "modernized" in the 1950s but was then restored to its original grandeur by the combined efforts of the community and local and state governments, which revitalized the old downtown. | Main St. between Rte. 176 and Winchester Rd. 60048 | 847/680–0750 | Free | Daily.

ON THE CALENDAR

JUNE: *Auto Show.* This exhibition of restored antique cars is held on Church Street the last Sunday of the month. | 847/362–4636.

Dining

Café Pyrenees. French. In the Rivertree Shopping Center in Vernon Hills, you are transported to southwestern France as you walk through the doors of this country-style café with cherry-wood furnishings, where you can relish French cuisine with a Spanish influence, such as mustard seed–encrusted pork tenderloin served with sautéed apples and sweet-potato purée. All stocks, sauces, pastries, sorbets, and ice creams served here are made in-house. | 701 N. Milwaukee Ave., Vernon Hills | 847/918–8850 | $12.50–$19 | AE, D, DC, MC, V | No lunch Sat. Closed Sun. and Mon.

Gale Street Inn. American. Barbecued baby-back ribs are the house specialty in this restaurant in Mundelein, 5 mi west of Libertyville, where floor-to-ceiling windows in its maritime dining room and seating on its deck overlook Diamond Lake. Salad bar. Entertainment Friday and Saturday. | 906 Diamond Lake Rd., Mundelein | 847/566–1090 | $10–$20 | AE, D, DC, MC, V | Closed Mon.

The Lambs Country Inn. American. On Lambs Farm, this restaurant is a hit with locals for its steak, fried chicken, and salad bar, and a popular spot for Sunday brunch. Kids' menu. | Rte. 176 at I–94, | 847/362–5050 | Summers, reservations required Fri.–Sun. | No dinner weekends | $12–$18 | AE, D, DC, MC, V.

Lodging

Best Inns Of America. Thirty miles north of downtown Chicago and 6 mi from Lake Michigan, this motel is just on the edge of Libertyville. Complimentary Continental breakfast. Some refrigerators, cable TV. Pool. Pets allowed. | 1809 N. Milwaukee Ave. | 847/816–8006 | www.bestinn.com | 90 rooms | $72–$78 | AE, D, DC, MC, V.

Best Western Hitch Inn Post. At the junction of Routes 137 and 21, 2 mi west of I–94, this two-story brick motel is 5 mi south of Six Flags Great America and Gurnee Mills Mall. Restaurant, bar, complimentary Continental breakfast, room service. In-room data ports, some microwaves, refrigerators, some in-room VCRs, cable TV. Indoor pool. Hot tub. Exercise equipment. Video games. Laundry facilities, laundry service. Business services, free parking. | 1765 N. Milwaukee Ave. | 847/362–8700 | fax 847/362–8725 | www.bestwestern.com | 128 rooms | $69–$89 | AE, D, DC, MC, V.

Libertyville Travel Lodge & Suites. All rooms are spacious—with big desks, office chairs, and overstuffed couches—in these luxury accommodations just minutes from Six Flags Great America, Great Lakes Naval Base, and Gurnee Mills Mall, where rooms on the east side have views of both the Des Plaines River and the Lake County Forest Preserve. Complimentary Continental breakfast. In-room data ports, some minibars, some microwaves, some refrigerators, some in-room hot tubs, cable TV. Indoor pool. Exercise equipment, hiking. Laundry service. Business services. | 77 W. Buckley Rd. | 847/549–7878 or 888/515–6375 | fax 847/549–7898 | www.travelodgehotel.com | 73 rooms | $109–$199 | AE, D, DC, MC, V.

LINCOLN

MAP 6, F6

(Nearby towns also listed: Bloomington and Normal, Clinton, Decatur, Petersburg, Springfield)

Lincoln (population 17,000) is the county seat of Logan County and also has a thriving agribusiness community. It's the first city to be named for Abraham Lincoln—the town got its moniker in 1853, before Lincoln became a nationally known figure. Legend has it that he christened the town with juice from a watermelon.

Information: Abraham Lincoln Tourism Bureau of Logan County | 303 S. Kickapoo St., 62656 | 217/732–TOUR | www.lincolnillinois.com.

Attractions
Heritage in Flight Museum. Exhibits display memorabilia from military conflicts dating back to World War I in this building, which served as an Army training facility and POW

camp during World War II. | 1351 Airport Rd. | 217/732–3333 | www.tourism.abelink.com | Free | Daily 8–5.

Mt. Pulaski Court House State Historic Site. Twelve miles southeast of Lincoln, this red-brick Greek Revival building with a white trim, now on the National Register of Historic places, functioned as a county courthouse between 1847 and 1853, during which time Abraham Lincoln put in frequent appearances as a lawyer on the Eighth Judicial Circuit. | 113 S. Washington St., Mt. Pulaski | 217/792–3919 | Free | Tues.–Sat. noon–5.

ON THE CALENDAR

AUG.: *Lincoln Art & Balloon Fest.* During the last full weekend in August, this festival's action occurs in different places throughout town, including a flea market in Scully Park, a juried art show in Latham Park, a balloon launch from Lincoln County Fair Grounds, and a classic-car cruise around the courthouse square. There are concessions and vendors at all festival locations, and at the Fair Grounds only an entrance fee of $2. | 217/735–2385.

AUG.: *Logan County Fair.* At the county fairgrounds, off I–55 at exit 123, you can enjoy this old-fashioned fair's livestock and produce judging, carnival midway, and crafts and food vendors' offerings. It takes place the first week of the month. | 217/732–3311.

SEPT.: *Abraham Lincoln National Railsplitter Contest and Crafts Festival.* Railsplitting contests are the highlight of this autumn festival held at the county fairgrounds, but you can also enjoy other live entertainment as well as the arts, crafts, and food sold in the many booths set up here. | 217/732–2632.

Dining

Blue Dog Inn. American/Casual. While dining on steaks and seafood and surf-and-turf combinations, you can observe the present-day old-town activity from booths at the front of this canine-inspired restaurant and full bar residing on the original main street of Lincoln, which is now on the National Register of Historic Places. You can also belly-up to the bar-height tables in back. | 111 S. Sangamon St. | 217/735–1743 | $8.95–$12.95 | AE, D, MC, V.

The Restaurant at the Depot. Eclectic. A wide range of cuisine can be found in the old Lincoln train depot, including chicken breasts wrapped in ham and filled with tarragon stuffing or such Spanish dishes as *zarzuela del mar,* a fish stew, and *pincho moruno,* a seafood shish kebab. | 513 Pulaski St. | 217/735–3311 | $16–$19 | AE, D, DC, MC, V.

Lodging

Comfort Inn. These standard accommodations are 1 mi west of the Logan County fairgrounds and 3 mi west of the Amtrak station. Complimentary Continental breakfast. Microwaves, some refrigerators, some in-room VCRs, cable TV. Indoor pool. Video games. Laundry service. Business services. Pets allowed. | 2811 Woodlawn Rd. | 217/735–3960 | fax 217/735–3960 | www.comfortinn.com | 52 rooms, 6 suites | $44–$55; $60–$65 suites | AE, D, DC, MC, V.

Lincoln Super 8 Motel. These standard accommodations are just off I–55 on a stretch of road lined with fast food restaurants. Lincoln College is 2 mi away. Complimentary Continental breakfast. In-room data ports, cable TV. Indoor pool. Pets allowed. | 2809 Woodlawn Rd. | 217/732–8886 or 800/800–8000 | fax 217/732–8886 | www.super8.com | 45 rooms | $66–$101 | AE, D, DC, MC, V.

LISLE

MAP 8, B7

(Nearby towns also listed: Downers Grove, Glen Ellyn, Naperville, Oak Brook, Wheaton)

Incorporated in 1852, Lisle is a commuter community in Chicago's western suburbs. This town of 19,500 is part of the growing Illinois corridor with a high number of information technology companies and research labs.

Information: **Lisle Convention and Visitor Bureau** | 4746 Main St., 60532 | 800/733–9811 | www.lislecvb.com.

Attractions

Morton Arboretum. This 1,700-acre arboretum includes more than 30,000 plants from around the world, a world-renowned program to study trees in urban communities and to develop conservation programs for endangered plant species, 12 mi of hiking trails, and an 11-mi paved route to tour the gardens by car. Visitors center, restaurant, and coffee shop. | 4100 Rte. 53 | 630/719–2400 | www.mortonarb.org | $7 per car Thurs.–Tues.; $3 per car Wed. | Apr.–Oct., daily 7–7; Nov.–Mar., daily 7–5.

ON THE CALENDAR

JULY: *Eyes to the Skies Festival.* During the 4th of July holiday weekend, usually spanning four days, the Lisle Community Park, on Route 53 at Short Street, hosts balloon launches, a petting zoo, a crafts fair, aerial acrobats, remote-controlled airplane displays, lawn-mower races, food vendors, and nightly entertainment with fireworks. Many hotels in the area offer specials in conjunction with this festival. | 800/733–9811.

Dining

Allgaur's Grill. Contemporary. In this restaurant on the first floor of the Lisle/Naperville Hilton, you can dine on lamb chops in a bordelaise sauce served with a goat cheese tart, or horseradish-glazed salmon, or potato-encrusted sea bass. Allgaur's also offers Sunday brunch and an all-you-can-eat three-entrée Friday-night seafood buffet including crab legs, peel-and-eat shrimp, oysters on the half shell, and smoked salmon. | 3003 Corporate West Dr. | 630/505–0900 | $14–$27 | AE, D, DC, MC, V.

Arbor Hill Restaurant. Continental. A half mile west of Route 53 and central downtown, this brightly lit restaurant serves steaks, broasted chicken, stir-fry, and pasta at oak tables surrounded by oak-trimmed walls hung with houseplants. Breakfast fare includes Belgian waffles, crepes, and oven-baked apple pancakes, the house specialty. | 1920 Ogden Ave. | 630/810–0418 | $7–$11 | AE, D, DC, MC, V | Breakfast also available.

Pete and Johnny's Tavern & Grill. Contemporary. You can't miss the illuminated bold red sign with yellow letters and the red awnings at the corner of Yackley and Naper Boulevards, where once inside you find tables with black-and-white checked cloths, red napkins, and red candles. Try the half slab of baby-back ribs or the herb-roasted half chicken, served with soup or salad and potatoes sautéed in olive oil, lemon juice, garlic, and oregano. Kids' menu. | 2901 Ogden Ave. | 630/848–1900 | $8.95–$19.95 | AE, D, DC, MC, V.

Lodging

Hilton. This hotel off I–88, 27 mi from downtown Chicago, towers over its own small lake. Restaurant. In-room data ports, some refrigerators, cable TV. Indoor pool. Hot tub. Exercise equipment. Video games. Business services. | 3003 Corporate West Dr. | 630/505–0900 or 800/552–2599 | fax 630/505–8948 | www.hilton.com | 309 rooms | $94–$140 | AE, D, DC, MC, V.

Hyatt. This 13-story motel is just off of I–88 at the Route 53 exit, adjacent to the Morton Arboretum. Restaurant, bar, room service. In-room data ports, some refrigerators, some in-room VCRs, cable TV. Indoor pool. Hot tub. Exercise equipment. Laundry service. Business services. | 1400 Corporetum Dr. | 630/852–1234 or 800/223–1234 | fax 630/852–1260 | www.hyatt.com | 311 rooms | $89–$224 | AE, D, DC, MC, V.

Marriott Hickory Ridge Conference Center. Just off Route 53, this 60,000-square-ft multiplex conference center and hotel is 45 mi from Chicago. There is a golf course 2 mi away. Restaurant, bar, picnic area, room service. In-room data ports, some minibars, some refrigerators, cable TV. Indoor pool. Sauna. Golf privileges, tennis. Basketball, health club, hiking, racquetball, volleyball. Shops. Laundry facilities. Business services. | 1195 Summerhill Dr. | 630/971–5000 or 800/225–4722 | www.conferencecenters.com/chihr | 383 rooms | $189 | AE, D, DC, MC, V.

Radisson. You take the Naperville Road exit off of I–88 to reach this hotel, which includes 20,000 square ft of meeting space for workshops, banquets, and business conventions. Restaurant, bar, room service. In-room data ports, some microwaves, some in-room VCRs, cable TV. Indoor pool. Hot tub, massage. Gym. Video games. Laundry service. Business services. Some pets allowed. | 3000 Warrenville Rd. | 630/505–1000 | fax 630/505–1165 | www.radisson.com | 242 rooms | $99–$184 | AE, D, DC, MC, V.

LOCKPORT

MAP 6, H3

(Nearby towns also listed: Aurora, Joliet, Naperville)

Commissioners from the Illinois and Michigan Canal established Lockport in 1836 as their headquarters, and it became a major thoroughfare during Illinois' early settlement in the 19th century. Today the little town retains much of its historical heritage and attracts visitors who travel to see a variety of remnants—including several old locks—from its canal days. This southern suburb of Chicago has 9,400 residents.

Information: **Lockport Chamber of Commerce** | 132 E. 9th St., 60441 | 815/838–5080 | www.lockport.org/chamber.

Attractions

Gaylord Building. The I & M Canal Visitor Center, an art gallery that is a branch of the Illinois State Museum, and a hands-on history exhibit are all housed here for your enjoyment. | 200 W. 8th St. | 815/838–7400 (gallery); 815/838–4830 (visitors center) | Free | Tues.–Sat. 10–6, Sun. 12–6.

Illinois and Michigan Canal Museum. The exhibits in this museum chronicle the development, construction, and history of the I & M Canal, and other parts of the complex include the Old Stone Annex Building and the Pioneer Settlement, a re-creation of cabins, shops, and other buildings from the canal's development era. | (Canal Commissioner's office) 803 S. State St. | 815/838–5080 | Donation suggested | Daily 1–4:30.

Lockport Gallery. A branch of the Illinois State Museum, this gallery, located in the Gaylord Building, has changing exhibits, educational activities, and tours. | 200 W. 8th St. | 815/838–7400 | Free | Tues.–Sat. 10-5, Sun. noon–5.

ON THE CALENDAR

JUNE: *Old Canal Days.* Held at the junction of Routes 171 and 7, this early-summer festival includes an antiques auction, wagon and walking tours, a beer garden, live music, and a parade. It takes place the third week of the month. | 815/838–4744.

JULY: *Western Open Golf Tournament.* You can watch internationally known players who participate in the oldest tournament on the PGA tour. It's held the first weekend of the month at the Cog Hill Golf Course in Lemont, 5 mi northeast of Lockport. | 630/257–5872.

SEPT.: *Civil War Days.* The weekend following Memorial Day, the townsfolk of Lockport step back in time, building authentic tent communities in Dellwood Park, at Route 171 and Woods Drive, through which you can wander to view artifacts from the Civil War; even Abe Lincoln is there on horseback with cavalry. At night you can take candlelight tours. | 815/838–1183.

Dining

Adams Pub. Continental. One mile east of downtown, in the Clover Ridge Shopping Center, this pub and restaurant has its own smokehouse in the rear for preparing its ribs, chicken, and other barbecued meats, although you can also order such fare as pizzas and Mexican omelettes here. Part of the dining area opens up into the atrium of the shopping center, but this pub's highlight is its 1928 mahogany bar. | 1225 E. 9th St. | 815/838-0220 | $9-$13 | D, MC, V | Breakfast also available.

Public Landing. American. This restaurant is in the Gaylord Building, built in 1838 along the I & M Canal and now an Illinois Historic Landmark, and its fare includes a wide range of choices from blackened-chicken spring rolls to regional recipes for trout, as well as steaks, pasta, and seafood. Kids' menu. | 200 W. 8th St. | 815/838-6500 | $14-$30 | MC, V | Closed Mon. No lunch weekends.

Tallgrass. French. Known for its four- and five-course meals, lobster, and fine wine list, this intimate restaurant is in a restored 1895 commercial building with vintage wood paneling and original beams in its interior. | 1006 S. State St. | 815/838-5566 | Reservations essential | Jacket required | $45-$55 | MC, V | No lunch. Closed Mon. and Tues.

MACOMB

MAP 6, D5

(Nearby towns also listed: Havana, Lewiston, Nauvoo)

This western Illinois city takes its name from Gen. Alexander Macomb, a War of 1812 hero. Flour and woolen mills, and a brick manufacturing plant were some of its early industrial happenings. It has 20,000 residents today.

Information: Macomb Area Chamber of Commerce | Box 274, 61455 | 309/837-4855 | www.macomb.com/chamber.

Attractions

Argyle Lake State Park. The 90-acre lake is the focal point of this 1,700-acre park in Colchester, 7 mi west of Macomb, where there are beaver dams and more than 200 bird species to admire, as well as hiking, boating, fishing, a picnic area, and canoe rentals for your enjoyment. | 640 Argyle Park Rd., Colchester | 309/776-3422 | Free | Daily.

The Old Bailey House. This Eastlake-style Victorian structure was built in 1887 by W. S. Bailey, founder and first vice president of the Union National Bank of Macomb. Presently the basement and second floors are still used for commercial purposes, but you can wander through the first floor to admire its wood-and-iron fireplace, ornate lighting fixtures, parquet floors, and elaborate cherry staircase. | 100 S. Campbell St. | 309/833-1727 | Free | Weekdays 9-5, weekends by appointment.

Spring Lake Park. This park is 4 mi northwest of Macomb, where you can rent a boat, fish, camp, and picnic, as well as visit the nature center here. | 595 Spring Lake Rd. | 309/833-2052 | Free | Daily.

Western Illinois University. One of the largest nondoctoral universities in the country, WIU offers 47 undergraduate programs, as well as 33 graduate-degree programs, to a student body of approximately 12,500. | 1 Univ. Cir. | 309/298-1993 | www.wiu.edu | Free | Daily.

You can tour **The Biological Sciences Greenhouse,** which is made up of gardens with a variety of regional specimens. | 309/298-1004 | Free | Weekdays 8-4:30.

The **Western Illinois Museum,** which was formerly on the WIU campus but is now off-campus in downtown Macomb, exhibits artifacts from the region, including vintage clothing, farm tools, trapping implements, and articles from the Civil War, as well the re-creation of a physician's office from 1910. | 201 S. Lafayette St. | 309/833-1315 | Free | Weekdays 8-4:30; call for weekend hours.

JUNE: *Heritage Days*. This celebration of the region's history includes live entertainment and arts and crafts and food vendors among its festivities, in the heart of Macomb. The festival takes place the last weekend of the month. | 309/833–1315.

Dining

Dillons. Barbecue. Just north of Macomb's town square, on Route 67, you can satisfy barbecue and Chicago–style food cravings with home-smoked chicken and turkey, and beef and lamb gyros, among pictures of old Chicago and the Chicago stadium here. Kids' menu. | 538 N. Lafayette St. | 309/836–3647 | $5–$15 | No credit cards.

Cookie's Diner. American. Breakfast is served all day at this downtown eatery, where you can also order pasta, steak, stir-fry, and chicken-fried steak, all of which can be accompanied by a shake or a sundae from the diner's old-fashioned soda fountain. Kids' menu. | 118 S. Lafayette St. | 309/837–1180 | $4.95–$12.95 | No credit cards | Breakfast also available. No dinner Sun.

International Sandwich Shop, Inc. Delicatessen. Known for its bread, this deli bakes sweet white manna every morning, and serves 6- and 12-inch sandwiches, the most popular of which is the Italian, with bologna, salami, ham, provolone, and all the fixin's including the house's special mustard dressing. Daily and weekly specials are offered, and there are pool tables and video games in the back part of this deli's brightly lit dining area. | 711 W. Adams St. | 309/833–1910 | $2.99–$4.59 | No credit cards.

Lodging

Amerihost Inn. You are just a mile north of downtown Macomb and the Western Illinois University campus when you stay at this motel. Complimentary Continental breakfast. Cable TV. Indoor pool. Hot tub. Gym. Business services. | 1646 N. Lafayette St. | 309/837–2220 | fax 309/837–1720 | www.amerihostinn.com | 60 rooms | $72 | AE, D, DC, MC, V.

Brockway House. This 1907 home is just six blocks from Western Illinois University and only two blocks from Macomb's downtown square, and as you sit on the wraparound porch here, you can watch the town's traffic—both autos and Amish buggies—roll by. Rooms have either four-poster, canopy, or brass beds, and the house's woodwork reflects the change from a more-ornate Victorian to Prairie–style. Complimentary Continental breakfast. Some refrigerators, some in-room hot tubs, cable TV, no room phones. | 331 E. Carroll St. | 309/837–2375 | 4 rooms (2 with shared bath) | $80–$95 | MC, V.

Days Inn. This standard two-story motel is only two blocks from Western Illinois University. Restaurant, bar, complimentary Continental breakfast. In-room data ports, some microwaves, refrigerators, some in-room VCRs, cable TV. Pool, wading pool. Playground. Laundry services. Pets allowed. | 1400 N. Lafayette St. | 309/833–5511 or 800/544–8313 | fax 309/836–2926 | www.daysinn.com | 144 rooms | $45–$98; $85–$196 suites | AE, D, DC, MC, V.

Holiday Inn Express. On Route 36, a main Macomb thoroughfare, this motel is a mile from Courthouse Square. Complimentary Continental breakfast. In-room data ports, some kitchenettes, microwaves, refrigerators, some in-room VCRs, cable TV. Indoor pool. Hot tub. Laundry facilities, laundry service. Business services. | 1655 E. Jackson St. | 309/836–6700 | fax 309/833–1518 | www.basshotels.com | 50 rooms | $59–$119 | AE, D, DC, MC, V.

Pineapple Inn. You are three blocks from Courthouse Square when you stay in this 1882 Queen Anne mansion painted raspberry red with white trim and furnished with antiques. Pets can be boarded nearby. Complimentary breakfast. In-room data ports, cable TV. Laundry service. No smoking. | 204 W. Jefferson St. | 309/837–1914 | fax 309/837–6232 | www.thepineappleinn.com | 5 rooms | $79–$125 | No credit cards.

Plymouth Rock Roost & Antiques. Thirty miles southwest of Macomb, in the town of Plymouth, a village of 500 residents, this Queen Anne Victorian home is surrounded by greenery and filled with antique furnishings and quilts. The owners' antique store is just down the block. Complimentary breakfast. No TV. Hot tub. | 201 W. Summer St. | 309/458–6444 or 877/458–6444 | fax 309/458–6569 | 3 rooms (2 with shared bath) | $59 | MC, V.

WIU Union. You can stay right on campus at this hotel on the second floor of the Western Illinois University's student union building. Restaurant. In-room data ports, some microwaves, refrigerators, cable TV. Video games. Business services. | E. Murry St. | 309/298–1941 | fax 309/298–2560 | 29 rooms | $35–$55 | D, MC, V.

MARION

MAP 6, G11

(Nearby towns also listed: Benton, Carbondale, Du Quoin)

The seat of Williamson County in southern Illinois, Marion (population 16,000) is also a regional trade center for light industry, retail, and agriculture.

Information: Greater Marion Area Chamber of Commerce | 2305 W. Main St., 62959 | 618/997–6311 or 800/699–1760 | www.cc.marion.il.us.

Attractions

Crab Orchard National Wildlife Refuge. The wildlife refuge, which is 4 mi west of Marion, stretches 43,000 acres, holding three major lakes, each with groomed campground. As the wintering grounds for thousands of geese it offers plenty of opportunities for fishing and birding. | 8588 Rte. 148 | 618/997–3344, ext. 334 | fax 618/997–8961 | $2 per day; $5 per 5 days; camping fee | Daily 8–5.

Ferne Clyffe State Park. The stone landscape of the Shawnee Hills creates an ideal setting for fishing, horseback riding, hiking, and camping along its trails and nature preserve. The park is 15 mi south of Marion. | Rte. 37, Goreville | 618/995–2411 | fax 618/995–2411 | http://dnr.state.il.us/lands/landmgt/parks | Free | Daily.

Egyptian Hills Marina. Boating, fishing, water skiing, and camping are main activities at this facility, 15 mi south of Marion on the northeast side of Lake of Egypt, which has more than 100 mi of shoreline. Cabins, mobile home access, and boat rentals available. | 75 Egyptian Pkwy., Creal Springs | 618/996–3449 | Free; boat launching $3 | Mar.–Dec., Daily 6 AM–7 PM.

ON THE CALENDAR

AUG.: *Williamson County Fair.* Livestock, produce contests, entertainment, and carnival rides highlight the event. | 800/433–7399.

Dining

Benny's Italian Food. Italian. With lots of booths, tables, and a lunch counter, the restaurant is a favorite for families. Known for garlic salads. | 409 N. Market St. | 618/997–6736 | $5–$10 | AE, D, DC, MC, V | Closed Sun.

Pulley's Barbeque. Barbecue. From pictures of customers on the walls to the homemade planters by the windows, the eatery caters to its loyal patrons. Known for barbecue sliced-pork sandwiches. Vegetarian dishes, seafood, and hamburgers also offered. | 1301 E. Main St. | 618/997–5225 | No dinner Sun. Breakfast also available | $5–$10 | No credit cards.

Tony's Steak House. Steak. In the historic district of downtown Marion just off Tower Square Plaza, this steak house has white linen–draped tables with small candles. The dining room centerpiece is the prime rib island, where chefs create their house specialty, filet mignon and lobster tail. Friday night all-you-can-eat crab legs specials (Jan.–Nov.) are very popular. Kids' menu. | 105 S. Market St. | 618/993–2220 | $9–$59 | AE, D, DC, MC, V | Closed Sun. No lunch.

Lodging

Best Inns of America. This two-story beige-brick chain hotel is within walking distance of 15 restaurants and the Illinois Centre Mall. Crab Orchard National Wildlife Refuge is 3 mi away. It's off I–57, exit 54B. Complimentary Continental breakfast. Cable TV. Pool. Some microwaves, some refrigerators. | 2700 W. DeYoung St. | 618/997–9421 | fax 618/997–1581 | www.bestinn.com | 104 rooms | $46.99 | AE, D, DC, MC, V.

Best Western Airport Inn. The 1991 brown-brick chain hotel remains quiet even though it's conveniently two blocks from the Williamson County Airport and a mile from the nearby mall and restaurants. There's also a golf course a mile away. Complimentary Continental breakfast. Refrigerators, some microwaves, some in-room hot tubs, some in-room VCRs, cable TV. Pool. Business services, airport shuttle. Pets allowed (fee). | 8101 Express Dr. | 618/993–3222 | fax 618/993–8868 | www.bestwestern.com | 34 rooms, 10 suites | $55; $65–$70 suites | AE, D, DC, MC, V.

Comfort Inn. On the western edge of town, 3 mi from the Crab Orchard National Wildlife Refuge, this two-story cedar and brick hotel is 4 mi from the Williamson County Airport. Complimentary Continental breakfast. Microwaves, refrigerators, some in-room VCRs, cable TV. Pool. Exercise equipment. | 2600 W. Main St. | 618/993–6221 | fax 618/993–8964 | www.comfortinn.com | 88 rooms, 34 one-room suites | $50–$64; $58–$70 suites | AE, D, DC, MC, V.

Comfort Suites. The lobby is filled with large silk flower arrangements, complementing the green and beige modern motel. In town, it's within walking distance of restaurants and shops, and 2 mi northwest of the Illinois Centre Mall. Complimentary Continental breakfast. Microwaves, in-room date ports, cable TV. Indoor pool. Laundry service. Business services. Free parking. | 2608 W. Main St. | 618/997–9133 | fax 618/997–1005 | 64 suites | $58–$72 | AE, D, DC, MC, V.

Days Inn. Four blocks from town center on a well traveled business strip, this hotel comprising two 1970s brick buildings is 12 mi from Rend Lake and five minutes from the State Farm Rail Classic Golf Course. Complimentary Continental breakfast. Some refrigerators, cable TV. Pets allowed (fee). | 1802 Bittle Pl. | 618/997–1351 | fax 618–997–2770 | www.daysinn.com | 70 rooms | $60 | AE, D, MC, V.

Drury Inn. About 1½ mi from the town square, this classic redbrick 1996 structure overlooks Route 13 through a five-story glass wall complimented by a huge chandelier. Guests are whisked to their floor by way of glass elevator. Rooms are decorated in warm colors and have coffeemakers, irons, and ironing boards. Complimentary Continental breakfast. Cable TV. Indoor pool. Free parking. | 2706 W. DeYoung St. | 618/997–9600 | 126 rooms, 6 suites | $49.99–$90 | AE, D, DC, MC, V.

Hampton Inn. This three-story chain property is 2 mi west of downtown just off of I–57. Rooms have queen-sized beds and pleasant, modular furniture. Complimentary Continental breakfast. Microwaves, in-room data ports, cable TV. Indoor pool. Business services. Free parking. | 2710 W. DeYoung St. | 618/998–9900 | fax 618/997–8684 | 64 rooms | $57–$69 | AE, D, DC, MC, V.

Holiday Inn Express. This moderately-priced hotel just off of I–57 is 35 mi east of Southern Illinois University. There are several restaurants within walking distance. Complimentary Continental breakfast. Cable TV. Indoor pool. Free parking. | 400 Comfort Dr. | 618/998–1220 or 877/269–9551 | fax 618/998–0212 | 79 rooms | $63.50 | AE, D, DC, MC, V.

MARSHALL

MAP 6, H7

(Nearby town also listed: Charleston)

Quiet streets of renovated 19th-century buildings mark this agricultural community on the eastern border of Illinois, across from Terre Haute, Indiana. James Jones, author of *From Here to Eternity,* made his home here. The population is 4,900.

Information: Marshall Chamber of Commerce | 708 Archer Ave., 62441 | 217/826–2034.

Attractions

Lincoln Trail State Park. A beech and maple forest, this nature preserve is 3 mi outside of Marshall and has hiking and also boating on a 146-acre lake. Boat rentals are available; there's a restaurant on site. | 16985 E. 1350th Rd. | 217/826–2222, 217/826–8831 restaurant | fax 217/826–1054 | www.dnr.state.il.us | Free | Daily 6 AM–10 PM; restaurant closed Mon.

Mill Creek Park. Some 39 mi of shoreline surround this 811-acre lake. Boating, camping, fishing, horseback are popular here. It's north of 7 mi northwest of Marshall. | 20482 N. Park Entrance Rd., Clarksville | 217/889–3901 | Free. Boating and camping fee | Daily; camping Apr.–mid-Oct.

Whippoorwill Antique Mall. Opened in 1998, this mall contains 150 booths of antiques and is usually crowded with visitors. It is 20 mi west of Terra Haute just off of I-70 at exit 140. | 107 W. Trefz Dr. | 217/826–8832 | Free | Jan.–Mar., Mon.–Sat. 9–5, Sun. 12–5; Apr.–Dec., Mon.–Sat. 9–8, Sun. noon–5.

ON THE CALENDAR

SEPT.: _Fall Festival._ The annual community festival of entertainment, food, and arts and crafts, held the third weekend of September, is highlighted by a parade and car show. | 217/826–2034.

Dining

Bishop's Café. American. Seniors and farmers are regulars of this eatery, which serves comfort food such as biscuits and gravy and fried chicken. | 710 Archer Ave. | 217/826–9933 | $4–$6 | No credit cards | No dinner. Breakfast also available.

Marshall Family Restaurant. American. Serving traditional breafast favorites, homemade soups, hearty sandwiches, and the classic "bottomless" cup of coffee, this eatery has a loyal following. | 701 Archer Ave. | 217/826–3342 | $5–$15 | AE, D, DC, MC, V | No dinner Sun. Breakfast also available.

Sam's Steak House. Steak. This all-American steak house serves high quality steak in a rather fancy dining room. Start your meal with one of Sam's hearty salads. | 105 W. Trefz Dr. | 217/826–8123 | $6–$18 | AE, D, DC, MC, V | Closed Sun. and Mon.

Lodging

Archer House. Built in 1841 by Marshall's founder Colonel William B. Archer, this former stage-coach stop is the state's oldest inn and is listed on the National Register of Historic Places. Abraham Lincoln was a friend and frequent guest, and was nominated by Archer for the office of Vice President at the 1856 Republican Convention in Philadelphia. Lincoln declined, saying he was not ready to enter politics. Cable TV, no room phones. No Pets. No kids under 12. | 717 Archer Ave. | 217/826–8023 | fax 217/826–6342 | www.thearcherhouse.com | 8 rooms | $75–$225 | No credit cards.

Super 8. Built in 1993, this two-story motel affords basic accommodations with king-size or queen-size beds in each room. You'll find this motel off of I–70 at exit 147, about 2 mi from the center of Marshall. Complimentary Continental breakfast. In-room data ports, some microwaves, some in-room hot tubs, cable TV, TV in common area. Pool. Business services. No pets. | 106 E. Trefz Dr. | 217/826–8043 or 800/800–8000 | fax 217/826–8043 | www.super8.com | 38 rooms, 2 suites | $52, $79 suites | AE, D, DC, MC, V.

MATTOON

MAP 6, G7

(Nearby towns also listed: Arcola, Charleston, Effingham, Shelbyville)

Set in rural central Illinois, Mattoon is an industrial and commercial center, originally founded in 1854 as a railroad town. One of its more notable products today: bagels. The population is 18,400.

Information: **Mattoon Chamber of Commerce** | 1701 Wabash Ave., 61938 | 217/235–5661.

ON THE CALENDAR

JULY: *Bagelfest*. The world's largest bagel breakfast includes arts, crafts, vendors, and entertainment. | 217/258–6286 or 800/500–6286.

Dining

Cody's Roadhouse. Steak. This eatery is themed around an 1800s mural and such antiques as wool sock strechers and spitoons. The booths and tables are peopled with families and locals in search of the perfect steak. | 1320 Broadway Ave. E | 217/235–1200 | $6–$18 | AE, D, DC, MC, V.

El Rancherito. Mexican. A lot of college students head to this Mexican eatery for lunch, where chimichangas and fajitas are among the top offerings. Desert murals line the walls. | 808 Lakeland St. | 217/235–6566 | $4–$11 | No credit cards | Closed Sun.

Gunner Buc's Pub & Grub. American. This typical pub serves light fare from its grill and features local bands on weekends. | 3020 Lakeland St. | 217/235–0123 | $1–$3 | No credit cards.

Lodging

Fairfield Inn. Corn and bean fields surround this three-story motel just off I–57 and 2 mi from the center of town. Complimentary Continental breakfast. Some in-room data ports, microwaves, refrigerators, cable TV. Indoor pool. Hot tub. Business services. | 206 McFall Rd. | 217/234–2355 or 800/228–2800 | fax 217/234–2355 | www.fairfieldinn.com | 58 rooms, 5 suites | $67–$75 | AE, D, DC, MC, V.

Hampton Inn–Mattoon. This 1996 stucco structure is 1 mi east of downtown; there are also restaurants and shopping within walking distance. Complimentary Continental breakfast. In-room data ports, some microwaves, some refrigerators, cable TV. Indoor pool. Laundry service. Business services. | 1416 Broadway Ave. E | 217/234–4267 or 800/HAMPTON | fax 217/235–4267 | www.hampton-inn.com | 53 rooms, 8 suites | $69; $79 suites | AE, D, DC, MC, V.

Ramada Inn and Conference Center. Cross County Mall and restaurants are within walking distance of this two-story hotel off I–57. Restaurant, bar. Cable TV. Indoor and outdoor pools. Hot tub, sauna. Laundry facilities. Business services. Pets allowed. | 300 Broadway Ave. E | 217/235–0313 or 888/MATTOON | fax 217/235–6005 | www.ramada.com | 124 rooms, 2 suites | $76; $105 suite | AE, D, DC, MC, V.

MCHENRY

MAP 6, G1

(Nearby towns also listed: Crystal Lake, Richmond, Wauconda, Woodstock)

McHenry, with a population of 26,000, is a fast-growing town on the Fox River close to both Chicago and the Wisconsin border. Its array of outdoor activities inspired by the Chain O'Lakes, Moraine Hills State Park, and the Volo Bog, have made it very attractive to new residents.

Information: **McHenry Area Chamber of Commerce** | 1257 N. Green St., 60050 | 815/385–4300 | www.mchenrychamber.com.

Attractions

Moraine Hills State Park. More than 10 mi of biking, hiking, and cross-country skiing trails wind through 1,900 acres, while rented rowboats glide over the Fox River and 48-acre Lake Defiance. | 914 S. River Rd. | 815/385–1624 | fax 815/385–1653 | Free | Summer, daily 6 AM–9 PM; winter 8–5.

Volo Auto Museum and Village. Four buildings of collector cars are for sale next to several antique malls all housed within a large shopping complex 5 mi east of McHenry. | 27582 Volo Village Rd., Volo | 815/385–3644 | fax 815/385–0703 | www.volocars.com | $4.95 | Daily 10–5.

Volo Bog. Illinois' only open-water bog was created by glacial melting and as a result, unique plant life covers the 5 mi of hiking and cross-country ski trails. There's a visitor center and picnic areas. Ingleside is 10 mi northeast of McHenry. | 28478 W. Brandenburg Rd., Ingleside | 815/344–1294 | fax 815/344–1312 | Free | June–Aug., daily 8–8; Sept.–May, daily 8–4.

Dining

Jenny's at Chapel Hill Country Club. Continental. Reservations are a good idea at this restaurant known for its golf-course views and Sunday brunch. The kitchen prepares fresh-made pastries, plus numerous seafood and steak specialties. There's a bar with a large-screen TV. Salad bar. Kids' menu. | 2500 N. Chapel Hill Rd. | 815/385–0333 | Closed Mon.–Thurs. in Jan. Closed Mon., Tue. year-round. No lunch. Sun. brunch only | $8–$27 | AE, D, DC, MC, V.

Le Vichyssois. French. A little bit of Europe comes to this Midwestern community of Lakemoor (6 mi east of McHenry) in the form of this classy restaurant, where you'll find an array of French classics on the menu—the eponymous vichyssoise (hot and cold) among them. Also try salmon en croute, roast duck, veal loin, and the homemade desserts. | 220 W. Rte. 120, Lakemoor | 815/385–8221 | $16.75–$34 | DC, MC, V | Closed Mon., Tues. No lunch.

Lodging

Ramada Tamara Royale Conference Center. Expansive meeting rooms and proximity to Six Flags Amusement Park are key attributes of this three-story property. It's 2 mi south of downtown McHenry, near Northern Illinois Medical Center. Restaurant, bar with entertainment, complimentary Continental breakfast, room service. In-room data ports. Some in-room hot tubs, cable TV. Indoor pool. Hot tub. Laundry services. Business services. | 4100 Shamrock La. (Rte. 31) | 815/344–5500 | fax 815/344–5527 | www.ramada.com | 58 rooms, 4 suites | $95; $175–$225 suites | AE, D, DC, MC, V.

Super 8. This economical motel is 1 mi south of downtown McHenry and ½ mi north of Northern Illinois Hospital. There are several restaurants within ¼ mi. Complimentary Continental breakfast. In-room data ports. Cable TV, some in-room VCRs. Laundry facilities. Free parking. No pets allowed. | 110 State Rte. 31 S | 815/344–9200 | www.super8.com | 48 rooms | $48–$71.

METROPOLIS

MAP 6, G12

(Nearby towns also listed: Cairo, Marion)

Superman lives here—at least that's what the citizens of this little southern Illinois town on the Ohio River say. They've got the phone booth and a life-sized statue of the Man of Steel to bolster their claim. The town is, after all, according to postal directories, the only Metropolis in the country and citizens have built on that. This town of 6,700 is also the seat of Massac County.

Information: **Metropolis Area Chamber of Commerce** | 607 Market St., 62960 | 618/524–2714 or 800/949–5740.

Attractions

Fort Massac State Park. Illinois' first state park overlooks the Ohio River from U.S. 45. A reconstructed 18th-century fort marks the site where Gen. George Rogers Clark took part in reclaiming the Illinois Territory from the French. Living history is performed on one weekend per month (call for schedule). | 1308 E. 5th St. | 618/524–9321 | Free | Museum summer, daily 10–5:30; winter, daily 9–4:30. Grounds daily dawn–dusk.

Player's Island Casino. This riverboat casino is part of the Harrah's Casino chain. You'll find four floors of slot machines and table games. It also has a restaurant (entrees range from $10–$22), buffet, and snack bar. The casino also owns and hosts live performances at the Player's Island Theatre across the street. Children are only allowed in the buffet area. | 203 Ferry St. | 618/524–2628 or 800/929–5905 | fax 618/524–9150 | www.harrahs.com | Free | Sun.–Thurs. 9 AM–5 AM, Fri.–Sat. 9 AM–7 AM.

Super Museum. The world's largest collection of Superman memorabilia is here and includes original costumes from TV and movies, toys, original comic art, and movie props. | Superman Sq., 517 Market St. | 618/524–5518 | fax 618/524–2120 | www.supermuseum.com | $3 | Daily 9–6.

ON THE CALENDAR
JUNE: *Superman Celebration*. A Superman drama, fun run, rotary car show, and live entertainment complete this carnival. | 618/524–2714 or 800/949–5740.
NOV.–DEC.: *Christmas Holiday Lighting Display*. More than 20 elaborate displays created with colored lights. | 800/248–4373.

Dining
Farley's Cafeteria. American. For home-style cooking in a family-friendly restaurant, this is just the place to stop for dinner. You can have fried chicken, pork and dressing, catfish, meatloaf and more. The dining room is simple and pleasant with wooden tables and chairs and murals of windows on the walls. | 613 Market St. | 618/524–7226 | Wed.–Sat. No lunch | $2–$3 | AE, MC, V.

Lodging
Best Western Metropolis Inn. On U.S. 45 just off I–24, this 1980s brick building lies close to restaurants and shops, and is a 10-minute drive from the commerce of Paducah, Kentucky. The Superman Museum and Fort Massac State Park are less than 2 mi away. Complimentary Continental breakfast. Some kitchenettes, some in-room refrigerators, cable TV. Indoor pool. Pets allowed. | 2119 E. 5th St. | 618/524–3723 or 800/577–0707 | fax 618/524–2480 | www.bestwestern.com | 57 rooms | $64 | AE, D, DC, MC, V.

Comfort Inn. This standard chain property is east of downtown, a short drive from the Superman Museum and Player's Island casino. Complimentary Continental breakfast. In-room data ports, some in-room microwaves, some in-room refrigerators, some in-room hot tubs, cable TV. Indoor pool. Laundry facilities. Business services. Pets allowed (fee). | 2118 E. 5th St. | 618/524–7227 or 800/228–5150 | fax 618/524–9708 | www.comfortinn.com | 49 rooms, 3 suites | $75; $85 suites | AE, D, DC, MC, V.

Days Inn. Across from Fort Massac State Park this concrete lodge is east of downtown and within walking distance of restaurants. Restaurant. In-room data ports, some in-room hot tubs, cable TV. Pool. Laundry facilities. Business services. | 1415 E. 5th St. | 618/524–9341 or 800/DAYSINN | fax 618/524–9341 | www.daysinn.com | 44 rooms, and 2 suites | $42.70; $70–$125 suites | AE, D, DC, MC, V.

Isle of View Bed and Breakfast. This 1889 Eastlake Victorian looms high with its central tower and gingerbread detail. The house is a favorite of honeymooners as it has two rooms with king canopy beds and whirlpool tubs that face working fireplaces. There is a kitchenette with a refrigerator and microwave available to guests in the common area, and downtown restaurants are a block away. Complimentary breakfast. Some in-room hot tubs. Cable TV, room phones. Free parking. | 205 Metropolis St. | 618/524–5838 or 800/566–7491 | fax 618/524–2978 | www.Illinois-bnb.com | 5 rooms | $75–$125 | AE, D, DC, MC, V.

Old Bethlehem School Bed and Breakfast. Originally a one-room school house, this 1910 building has original hardwood floors and windows, and is rented out as a single unit.

Guest rooms are furnished with armoires and early American antiques. Horses, dogs, and kids are welcome. Guests may also request a hunting ride on the adjacent farm during deer or turkey season. You'll find it 10 mi north of downtown Metropolis near the Shawnee National Forest. Complimentary breakfast. Kitchenettes, microwaves, refrigerators. Cable TV, room phones. Free parking. No pets allowed. No smoking. | 6506 Old Marion Rd. | 618/524–4922 | www.bethlehemschools.com | 3 rooms | $85–$99 | No credit cards.

Players and Amerihost Hotel. Set next to the popular Players riverboat casino, the two-story building often hosts evening concerts. Complimentary Continental breakfast. Hot tub. Exercise equipment. Laundry facilities. Business services. | 203 E. Front St. | 618/524–5678 or 800/434–5800 | fax 618/524–2225 | www.amerihostinn.com | 112 rooms, 8 suites | $90 rooms, $110 suites | AE, D, DC, MC, V.

MOLINE

MAP 6, D3

(Nearby town also listed: Rock Island)

MOLINE

INTRO
ATTRACTIONS
DINING
LODGING

In the southwest corner of Illinois, on the Mississippi River, Moline (population 43,080) is one of the Quad Cities, along with Rock Island and also the Iowa cities of Davenport and Bettendorf. It's best known as the home of agricultural equipment manufacturer John Deere and Company. It has one of the nation's largest communities of Belgian immigrants and their descendants.

Information: Quad Cities Convention and Visitors Bureau | 2021 River Dr., 61265-1472 | 309/788–7800 or 800/747–7800 | fax 309/788–7898 | www.visitquadcities.com.

Attractions

Center for Belgian Culture. Local residents have contributed to the selection of artifacts here. | 712 18th Ave. | 309/762–0167 | Free | Wed. and Sat. 1–4.

Deere and Company. This parklike office campus was designed by architect Eero Saarinen and opened in 1964. The product display area is filled with Deere equipment. | 1 John Deere Pl. | 309/765–1000 | Free | Display building, daily 9–5:30.

EMPIRE (East Moline Playground Innovation Recreation Efforts). This playground is a favorite of families as it includes 48 play stations with wooden swings, mazes, slides and more. The area expands with a boat launch, picnic shelters, and a bike path. Adjacent to

EAGLES OVER ILLINOIS

Swallows may come back to Capistrano every year, but Illinois can do better than that. Each December and January, bald eagles winter along the Mississippi from Minnesota down to Missouri. The birds tend to congregate near locks and dams along the river; fish that come over the dam are stunned, and the birds can swoop in and scoop them up.

A number of towns along the river—Alton, Quincy, Moline, and Dubuque, Iowa, near Galena—set aside special days in January and offer lectures and special sighting programs to give people a chance to gaze at the magnificent birds. But you can also go solo; all you need are some good binoculars and warm clothing. The locks are a good place to start; many of them have areas where you can set up your own viewing spot.

© Corbis

the area is a miniature golf course and other diversions. | Rte. 84 on the East Moline/Hampton border | 309/752–1573 | Daily.

John Deere Commons. This four square block area extends from the river's edge to 4th Avenue, from 12th to 17th Streets. It's anchored by a 14,000-square-ft glass-enclosed pavilion full of past and present products, interactive stations, films on farming practices, and tractors to explore. Retailers, restaurants, a civic center, a hotel, office buildings, and a transportation center are also here. | 1400 River Dr. | 309/765–1000 | www.johndeerepavilion.com | Free | Weekdays 9–6, Sat. 10–5, Sun. noon–4.

Niabi Zoo. This 30-acre zoo with lions, elephants, petting zoo, and a miniature steam train is 15 mi southeast of Moline. | 13010 Niabi Rd., Coal Valley | 309/799–5107 | $4.25; special rates for children | Apr.–Oct., daily 9:30–5; Nov.–mid-Dec., weekdays noon–5, Sat.–Sun. 9:30–5; closed Dec. 16–April 15.

ON THE CALENDAR
FEB.–DEC.: *Belgian Waffle Breakfast.* This tradition continues the first Saturday of each month (except Jan.), 8–noon at the Center for Belgian Culture. | 309/762–0167 | $3.50.
JUNE: *Moline Riverfest.* Fireworks, concerts, and a lighted boat parade. | 309/797–0462.

Dining

C'est Michele. French. Octagonal ornately carved columns stretch from floor to two-story ceilings, and a lighted mezzanine surrounds the main floor and terrazzo floors of the 1918 Carlson Brothers building, now a top restaurant. French classics like boneless breast of duck with a raspberry sauce are among the offerings. | 1405 5th Ave. | 309/762–0585 | Reservations essential | $13.95–$24.95 | AE, DC, MC, V | Closed Sun.–Tues. No lunch.

Lodging

Best Western Airport Inn. This two-story stucco chain property lies close to Moline International Airport, a mall, and restaurants; it's 3 mi south of downtown. Complimentary Continental breakfast. Some refrigerators, some microwaves, cable TV. Indoor pool. Hot tub. Business services. Some pets allowed (fee). | 2550 52nd Ave. | 309/762–9191 or 800/528–1234 | www.bestwestern.com | 50 rooms | $89–$99 | AE, D, DC, MC, V.

Hampton Inn. This early 1980s property faces Quad City Airport and is 5 mi from downtown. Complimentary Continental breakfast. In-room data ports, cable TV. Pool. Business services, airport shuttle. Pets allowed. | 6920 27th St. | 309/762–1711 | fax 309/762–1788 | www.hampton-inn.com | 138 rooms | $85 | AE, D, DC, MC, V.

La Quinta Inn. Adjacent to the Moline International Airport and convenient to nearby Snowstar Ski Area, this Spanish-style motel sits atop a bluff overlooking Rock River. Many casinos and paddlewheelers are close by. Bender's Restaurant, just next door, is known for ribs. Complimentary Continental breakfast. In-room data ports, some refrigerators, cable TV. Pool. Laundry facilities. Business services, airport shuttle. Pets allowed. | 5450 27th St. | 309/762–9008 or 800/531–5900 | fax 309/762–2455 | www.laquinta.com | 126 rooms, 4 suites | $69–$79; $89 suites | AE, D, DC, MC, V.

MONMOUTH

MAP 6, D4

(Nearby town also listed: Galesburg)

Settled in the 1830s and now with a population of 9,600, Monmouth is set in rural west central Illinois and the surrounding area produces a variety of agricultural products. Monmouth College, a small liberal arts school, was founded here in 1853.

Information: **Monmouth Area Chamber of Commerce** | 68 Public Sq. (Box 857), 61462 | 309/734–3181 | www.misslink.net/macc/.

Attractions

Buchanan Center for the Arts. This local arts agency is complemented by an art gallery. | 64 Public Sq. | 309/734–3033 | fax 309/734–3554 | www.misslink.net/bca/ | Free | Weekdays 9–5, Sat. 9–2.

Warren County Pioneer Cemetery. Originally owned by Daniel McNeil, Monmouth's first resident, this cemetery was founded in 1833 and used for interment until 1861. During that time it became the final resting place of relatives of Wyatt Earp and soldiers who fought in the War of 1812, the Black Hawk War, and the Civil War. A complete listing of graves is available at the Warren County Library. | N. 6th St. at E. Archer Ave. | 309/734–3181 | Free | Daily dawn–dusk.

Wyatt Earp Birthplace. The refurbished home holds special events and stages reenactments four times a season. | 406 S. 3rd St. | 309/734–3181 | Free | Tours by appointment only.

ON THE CALENDAR
SEPT.: *Warren County Prime Beef Festival.* Four-wheel ATV races, livestock shows, and parades celebrate the area's cattle industry. | 309/734–3181.
DEC.: *Living Windows.* The first Friday night in December, between 5 and 9:30, the town of Monmouth begins its holiday festivities around the town square with carriage rides, a live nativity, carolers, and dazzling storefront displays. Businesses open to provide treats such as roasted chestnuts and hot cider. | 309/734–3181.

Dining

Cerar's Barnstormer. American/Casual. This restaurant, a favorite of the locals, serves fresh seafood, Angus steaks, prime rib, and chicken. Try the seafood combination platter, which includes lobster, crab legs, stuffed shrimp, and sauteed scallops. | 1201 Broadway | 309/734–9494 | $8–$28 | AE, D, DC, MC, V.

Monmouth Soda Works. American/Casual. At this turn-of-the-20th-century soda fountain with pine plank floors and church pews for booths, you can get old-fashioned sodas, sundaes with any topping imaginable, and homemade pies, such as cherry and apple dumpling, served in or on antique glassware. Some soups are homemade, too. | 112 S. 1st St. | 309/734–3221 | Closed Sun. | $2–$8 | AE, D, DC, MC, V.

Lodging

Hawthorn Inn and Suites of Monmouth. Just off Route 34 less than a mile west of Monmouth College, this corporate hotel has functional rooms and reasonable rates. The hotel is 1 mi west of the Wyatt Earp Birth Site, 4 mi west of the Monsanto Agronomy Center, and just across the street from the upscale family restaurant Cerar Barnstormer. Picnic area, complimentary breakfast. In-room data ports, some microwaves, some refrigerators, some in-room hot tubs, cable TV. Indoor pool. Hot tub. Exercise equipment. Laundry facilities. Business services. | 1200 W. Broadway | 309/734–0909 | fax 309/734–0910 | 30 rooms, 30 suites | $79–$139 | AE, D, DC, MC, V.

Meling's Motel. Seven blocks north of downtown and a 15-minute drive from Monmouth College, the stone-faced early '70s building remains independently owned. The full-scale restaurant here is known for its buffet of American favorites and homemade cakes and pies. Restaurant, bar. Cable TV. Laundry facilities. Business services. Pets allowed (fee). | 1129 N. Main St. | 309/734–2196 | fax 309/734–2127 | eva@naplecity.com | 34 rooms | $46 | AE, D, DC, MC, V.

Super 8 Motel. The late '90s brick and stucco, 2-story lodge is 1 mi northeast of downtown Monmouth and has restaurants and shopping nearby. Complimentary Continental breakfast. Some microwaves, some refrigerators, some in-room hot tubs, cable TV. Indoor pool.

Laundry facilities. | 1122 N. 6th St. 61462 | 309/734–8558 or 800/800–8000 | fax 309/734–8558 | www.super8.com | 38 rooms | $63–$100.88 | AE, D, DC, MC, V.

MONTICELLO

MAP 6, G6

(Nearby towns also listed: Bement, Champaign/Urbana)

Monticello, population 5,125, was a transportation hub in the 19th century and that heritage is commemorated today in the town's railroad museum. The town also has a strong agricultural base, particularly in corn and soybeans.

Information: **Monticello Chamber of Commerce** | Box 313, Monticello 61856-0313 | 800/952–3396 | fax 217/762–2711 | www.monticello.net.

Attractions

Monticello Railway Museum. This museum collects, preserves, and exhibits railroading materials, emphasizing central Illinois. Train rides and some special events are available. | 999 Access Rd. | 217/762–9011 or 800/952–3396 | www.prairienet.org/mrm | Free. Train rides $6; special rates for seniors and children | May–Oct., weekends 1–4.

Robert Allerton Park and Conference Center. Formal gardens, statuary, trails, and a visitor center surround the mansion now used for conferences. | 515 Old Timber Rd. | 217/762–2721 | www.monticello.net/html/montalle.htm | Free | Gardens and trails 8–dusk, visitors center 8–5.

ON THE CALENDAR
SEPT.: *Railroad Days.* Train rides and concessions create the bulk of the festival. | 217/762–9011 or 800/952–3396.

Dining
Sage City Café. Contemporary. A seasonal menu here includes exotic dishes such as black and blue, a blackened fillet mignon with a blue-cheese horseradish sauce; Cajun-style risotto with andouille, shrimp, and red beans; and ostrich grilled with sundried tomato and currant relish. The century-old brick walls are covered with scenes from Monticello's past. | 108 S. Charter St. | 217/762–7454 | $12–$16 | D, MC, V | Breakfast also available. Closed Mon. No dinner Sun.

Lodging
Best Western Monticello Gateway Inn. Built in 1997, this brick-and-wood-sided building is 1/4 mi from the railway museum, 3 mi from Robert Allerton Park, and 1 mi north of downtown. The grounds feature two small ponds with wooded areas and wildlife. Restaurant, complimentary Continental breakfast. In-room data ports, some kitchenettes, some microwaves, some refrigerators, cable TV. Indoor pool. Hot tub. Laundry service. Business services. | 805 Iron Horse Pl. | 217/762–9436 or 888/331–4600 | fax 217/762–3202 | www.bestwestern.com | 39 rooms, 2 suites | $71–$89; $118 suites | AE, D, DC, MC, V.

MORRIS

MAP 6, G3

(Nearby town also listed: Ottawa)

Set on the Illinois River, Morris is the seat of Grundy County. Surrounded by farms and an ever-increasing number of new housing subdivisions, the town population is about 12,500. Shabbona, a 19th-century Potawatomi chief, is buried east of town.

Information: **Grundy County Chamber of Commerce and Industry** | 112 E. Washington St., 60450 | 815/942–0113.

Attractions

Channahon State Park. Twenty acres invites hiking, biking, fishing, tent camping, picnicking, and snowmobiling. The park is 11 mi east of Morris in Channahon via Route 6. | 2 W. Story St. Channahon | 815/467–4271 | Free; camping fee | Daily.

Gebhard Woods State Park. Hiking, canoeing, picnicking, and camping are popular activities at this 30-acre park along the I & M Canal off Route 47. | 401 Ottawa St. | 815/942–0796 | www.imcanal.org | Free; camping fee | Daily.

Goose Lake Prairie State Natural Area. This 2,500-acre tract once used for grazing is home to bluestem Indian grass and switchgrass, and 7 mi of trails here provide good bird-watching; you might even see the rare henslow sparrow. Interpreters are available to explain the flora and fauna, if you call to arrange in advance. | 5010 N. Jugtown Rd. | 815/942–2899 | Free | Visitor Center, Mar.–Nov., daily 10–4, Dec.–Feb., Mon.–Fri. 10–4; Prairie open daily year-round.

Illinois and Michigan (I & M) Canal State Trail. This 61-mi towpath is now used for hiking, biking, and snowmobiling. It's accessed from both Gebhard Woods and Channahon state parks (*see above*). | 815/942–0796 | Free | Daily.

ON THE CALENDAR
JULY: *Dulcimer Festival.* This two-day "hammer-and-hand" festival takes place the second full weekend in July in Gebhard Woods State Park along the towpath of the I & M Canal, where you provide your own seating, such as a blanket or lawn chair. Admission to the festival is per day, per family, or for the weekend, and a shuttle provides transportation between Union Street and the park. | 815/942–0796.
SEPT.: *Grundy County Corn Festival.* Parades, a carnival, and a crafts fair flea market mark the harvest moon's arrival here. | 815/942–CORN.

Dining

Firehouse Restaurant and Brewery. Contemporary. Never actually a firehouse, this restaurant's walls are brightly painted, and a beer brewed here is called Fire Engine Red. Large windows allow you to watch the brewmasters in action, making the five beers served on tap here as well as Firehouse root beer and cream soda, which you can quaff with pulled-pork quesadillas, chicken fried steak, and nightly rotating specials. On Saturday at noon you can take a free tour of the brewing area. | 124 W. Illinois Ave. | 815/941–4700 | $7–$17 | AE, D, MC, V.

R Place. American. In the eclectically decorated truck stop, with one section equipped with booths with phones for truckers and another for families, patrons chow down on burgers, homemade baked breads, cakes, and cookies amid thousands of antiques, from dolls to model airplanes. The 4-pound Ethyl Burger is free to any brave patron who can finish it in an hour. Kids' menu. Salad bar. Open 24 hours. | 21 Romines Dr. | 815/942–3690 | $3.50–$15 | No credit cards.

Rockwell Inn. American. This century-old Victorian inn set in the country is named for Norman Rockwell, whose images hang on the walls. The bar hails from the 1893 world's fair in Chicago, and is made by Brunswick. The restaurant has a menu of prime rib, orange roughy, and is known for flaming Irish coffees. Salad bar. Pianist Fri. and Sat. evenings. Kids' menu. Sun. brunch. | 2400 W. U.S. 6 | 815/942–6224 | Reservations essential Fri. and Sat. nights and Nov.–Dec. | $9.75–$41.75 | AE, D, DC, MC, V.

Lodging

Best Western. Just off I–80, this modest hotel has average-sized rooms with modular furnishings. You'll find it 3 mi north of downtown Morris. There's a Denny's next door, and R

Place is across the street. Complimentary Continental breakfast. Refrigerators, in-room data ports, cable TV. Pool. Hot tub, sauna. Exercise equipment. Laundry facilities. Business services. | 80 Hampton St., | 815/942–9000 | fax 815/942–9000, ext.102 | www.bestwestern.com | 57 rooms, 10 suites | AE, D, DC, MC, V.

Comfort Inn. This redbrick two-story motel is less than a block from I–80, and 1½ mi north of town. R Place restaurant is within walking distance. Complimentary Continental breakfast. Some microwaves, some refrigerators, cable TV. Pool. Hot tub. Laundry service. Business services. Pets allowed. | 70 W. Gore Rd. | 815/942–1433 or 800/222–1212 | fax 815/942–1433 | www.comfortinn.com | 50 rooms | $79 | AE, D, DC, MC, V.

Holiday Inn–Morris. A mile from Grundy County Fairgrounds, this late '70s property is just off exit 112 of I–80. There's a movie theater within walking distance. Restaurant, bar. In-room data ports, cable TV. Pool. Business services. Some pets allowed. | 200 Gore Rd. | 815/942–6600 or 800/HOLIDAY | fax 815/942–8255 | www.basshotels.com | 120 rooms | $77 | AE, D, DC, MC, V.

Morris Super 8 Motel. This standard motel is just off of I–80 and Route 47, right next door to WalMart. Rooms are furnished with queen- or king-sized beds. In-room data ports, some microwaves, some refrigerators, cable TV. Laundry facilities. Business services. | 70 Green Acres Dr. | 815/942–3200 or 800/800–8000 | fax 815/942–3325 | 54 rooms, 6 suites | $48–$118 | AE, D, DC, MC, V.

MT. VERNON

MAP 6, G9

(Nearby towns also listed: Benton, Centralia, Salem)

Mt. Vernon, the county seat of Jefferson County, was settled by southerners and many of its 17,080 residents still identify with a southern heritage. You'll find southern-style restaurants are the most popular in town, and the historical society concentrates on representing scenes and artifacts from the first settlements of the area.

Information: **Mt. Vernon Convention and Visitors Bureau** | 200 Potomac Blvd. (Box 1708), 62864 | 618/242–3151 or 800/252–5464 | www.southernillinois.com.

Attractions

Jefferson County Historical Society's Historical Village and Museum. Historic buildings and memorabilia from pioneer days are displayed in this village, which includes an original working blacksmith shop, The original one-room school and general store, as well as a century-old print shop and log church. | 1411 N. 27th St. | 618/246–0033 | Free | May–Oct., weekends Sat. 10–4, Sun. 1–4.

Mitchell Museum at Cedarhurst. A single nature trail runs through this 90-acre estate with bird sanctuary. There is also a sculpture park, and a fine arts museum with late-19th- and early-20th-century works of American impressionism and a children's gallery. | Richview Rd. | 618/242–1236 | fax 618/242–9530 | www.cedarhurst.org | Free | Tues.–Sat. 10–5; Sun. 1–5.

ON THE CALENDAR

JUNE: *Blues and Ribs Fest.* In Whittington, 15 mi south of Mt. Vernon on Route 37, you can get down with the blues and fill up on ribs at the Pheasant Hollow Winery, which hosts many Saturday events such as an all-afternoon blues bash and a monthly murder/mystery dinner for only a nominal admission fee. The winery has picnic tables, but a blanket or towel to sit on is advisable. | 618/629–2302.

AUG.: *Southern Illinois Sweet Corn and Watermelon Festival.* Enjoy a parade, races, 5K run, and free corn and watermelon. | 618/242–3151 or 800/252–5464.

SEPT.: _Cedarhurst Craft Fair._ Juried fair of over 160 crafters, supplemented by entertainment, and food. | 618/242–1236.

Dining

Caroline's. Continental. This quiet, dimly lit restaurant on the first floor of the Holiday Inn sports a Southwest theme with its pale terra-cotta–like walls and pottery. The menu, however, is broad, ranging from prime rib to Mexican pizza, chicken scampi to salads, with fresh fish and shellfish often on the list of specials. | 222 Potomac Blvd. | 618/244–7100 | $6.95–$15.95 | AE, DC, MC, V.

El Rancherito. Mexican. Spicy favorites of fajitas and chimichangas warm the already festive decor of Mexican hats and art. Kids' menu. | 4303 Broadway Ave. | 618/244–6121 | $5–$10 | AE, D, DC, MC, V.

Triple E Bar-b-que. Barbecue. Not the only barbecue in town, but here you can get smoked chicken, steak, and shrimp in addition to the house specialty, ribs, which you can savor in the company of mounted bass hanging on the walls all around. | 37 Mateer Dr. | 618/244–7500 | $4.49–$7.99 | D, MC, V.

Lodging

Best Inns of America. Close to Jent Factory Outlet Mall, these accommodations are 1½ mi west of the town center in a small business district. Complimentary Continental breakfast. Cable TV. Pool. Some pets allowed. | 222 S. 44th St. | 618/244–4343 | fax 618/244–4343 | www.bestinn.com | 153 rooms | $47.99 | AE, D, DC, MC, V.

Drury Inn. Just half a block east of I–57 and I–64 this three-story 1970s concrete-and-brick structure is 2 mi from downtown. Complimentary Continental breakfast. Some microwaves, some refrigerators, cable TV. Pool. Pets allowed. | 145 N. 44th St. | 618/244–4550 or 800/378–7946 | 81 rooms | $64.99–$70.99 | AE, D, DC, MC, V.

Hampton Inn Mt. Vernon. On the west side of Mt. Vernon, just off of I–57 and I–64, this inn is one of several strung among restaurants and factory-outlet stores. In-room data ports, some microwaves, some refrigerators, some in-room hot tubs. Cable TV. Indoor pool. Hot tub. Exercise equipment. Laundry service. | 221 Potomac Blvd. | 618/244–2323 | fax 618/244–9948 | www.hamptoninn.com | 101 rooms | $71 | AE, D, DC, MC, V.

Holiday Inn. There's a sundeck and three-story atrium at this 1984 hotel 1 mi west of downtown, and it's within walking distance of the Casey Creek Golf Course. Shopping is available at the nearby Jent Factory Outlet Mall. Two restaurants, bar, room service. In-room data ports. Cable TV. Indoor pool. Hot tub, sauna. Exercise equipment. Video games. Airport shuttle. Free parking. Some pets allowed. | 222 Potomac Blvd. | 618/244–7100 or 800/243–7171 | fax 618/242–8876 | www.basshotels.com | 236 rooms | $71 | AE, D, DC, MC, V.

Mount Vernon Comfort Inn. You take exit 95 off of I–57 to reach this chain hotel, which is less than a half mile from the Jent Factory Outlet Mall. Complimentary Continental breakfast. In-room data ports, some microwaves, some refrigerators, some in-room hot tubs, cable TV. Indoor pool. Hot tub. Laundry facilities. Business services. No pets. | 201 Potomac Blvd. | 618/242–7200 | fax 618/242–9800 | 93 rooms | $55–$109 | AE, D, DC, MC, V.

Villager Premier. Guests at this four-story redbrick hostelry with extensive meeting space can enjoy a recreation atrium, complete with inside pool, exercise equipment, games, and landscaping. Restaurants are within walking distance and a shopping mall within a half mile. Restaurant, bar. In-room data ports, cable TV. Indoor pool. Hot tub. Exercise equipment. Pool table. Miniature golf. Business services. Pets allowed (fee). | 405 S. 44th St. | 618/244–3670 | fax 618/244–6904 | 135 rooms, 27 suites | $65; $99–$129 suites | AE, D, DC, MC, V.

NAPERVILLE

(Nearby towns also listed: Aurora, Downers Grove, Glen Ellyn, Lisle, Wheaton)

Chicago's suburb of Naperville was settled as a farming community and incorporated in 1857; today it's best known for its many research and high-tech industries as well as for its tremendous growth over the past 20 years—its population is now 140,000. It does, however, retain many of its older, restored buildings close to its downtown.

Information: **Naperville Area Chamber of Commerce** | 131 W. Jefferson Ave., 60540 | 630/355–4141 | www.naperville.net. **Naperville Visitors Bureau** | 212 S. Webster St., 60540 | 630/305–7701 | www.visitnaperville.net.

Attractions

Naper Settlement. This museum village re-creates the town's pioneer and Victorian past and offers various seasonal events. | 523 S. Webster St. | 630/420–6010 | fax 630/305–4044 | www.napersettlement.org | summer $6.50, winter $3.25; winter special rates for seniors and children | Call for hours.

Riverwalk. This scenic 3.5-mi redbrick pathway winds through downtown Naperville along the DuPage River. Covered bridges, fountains, and landscaping mark the way. The trail begins at Hillside Road and ends at Jefferson Avenue but can be accessed along the route; parking is available on the street and at Centennial Beach, at Rotary Hill, and at the Naperville Park District Administration Building at 320 W. Jackson Avenue. | 630/848–5000 | fax 630/848–5001 | www.napervilleparks.org | Free | Daily; Administration Building weekdays 8:30–5; Sat. 9–noon.

ON THE CALENDAR

DEC.: *Christmas Memories.* 19th-century holiday celebration in Naper Settlement. | 630/420–6010.

JULY: *Rib Fest.* "Ribbers" from all over the country flock to this 4th of July feast at Knoch Park to chow down and to compete in the contests for best ribs and best sauce; you can also hear nationally renowned bands that evening. | 630/305–7701.

Dining

Carzz Seafood Grilleria. Cajun/Creole. Near the corner of Jefferson and Washington Streets, this restaurant is known for jambalaya, shiitake mushroom–encrusted halibut with sun-dried tomato–Asiago sauce, and its torch-lit courtyard and cherry-wood-paneled dining room decked with wine posters and nautical paraphernalia. Kids' menu. | 216 S. Washington St. | 630/778–1944 | $6–$24 | AE, D, DC, MC, V | Closed Mon. No lunch weekends.

La Sorella di Francesca. Italian. This bustling trattoria is housed in what was Naperville's first city hall, where you can choose among several pasta dishes, at least three fish recipes, and a veal specialty, such as veal *sassi* sautéed veal medallions with artichokes and wild mushrooms in a brandy sauce; the menu changes weekly. | 18 W. Jefferson St. | 630/961–2706 | $9.95–$25.95 | AE, D, DC, MC, V | No lunch weekends.

Mesón Sabika. Spanish. Set on 5 acres west of the historic district, this 1847 Georgian mansion holds eight dining rooms each decorated differently with murals and regional artifacts from Spain. Tapas, paella, patatas con alioli, and queso de cabra al horno are just a few of the favorites here. Open-air dining is popular on the brick terrace garden patio. Flamenco entertainment Fri. | 1025 Aurora Ave. | 630/983–3000 | www.mesonsabika.com | $9.95–$30 | AE, DC, MC, V | No lunch Sat.

Montparnasse. French. Under the 70-ft ceiling of this 1925 former furniture factory, old Burgundy French cooking permeates. Rack of lamb is the speciality, complemented by a menu of venison, salmon, bass, and other classics. Reservations can be tough to snag on short notice. | 200 E. 5th Ave. | 630/961–8203 | www.montparnasse5thave.com | Reservations essential on weekends | $28–$32 | AE, D, DC, MC, V | No lunch Sat. Closed Sun.

Petey Z's. Italian. Nestled among small neighborhood shops directly across from the train station, this tiny bistro plays Italian music and has black-and-white photos of Italian stars on its walls. Among the many authentic dishes from the home country, try gnocchi and spinach in garlic and olive oil. | 327 Center | 630/983–5565 | $4.95–$15.95 | AE, MC, V | No lunch weekends.

Samba Room. Latin. At the southernmost Naperville downtown intersection, Chicago Ave. and Washington St., this Cuban nightclub offers Latin music and cuisine, such as paella, sugarcane beef tenderloin, grilled Chilean sea bass, and *xin xim* (sautéed chicken and shrimp with curried rice and toasted cashews). | 22 E. Chicago Ave. | 630/753–0985 | $10–$19 | AE, D, DC, MC, V.

Lodging

Chicago/Naperville Red Roof Inn. This standard three-story beige-stone chain accommodation is close to I–88, with easy access to rail transit into Chicago; it's 5 mi northwest of downtown and a 40-minute drive from Chicago. In-room data ports, cable TV. Business services. Pets allowed. | 1698 W. Diehl Rd. | 630/369–2500 or 800/REDROOF | fax 630/369–9987 | www.redroof.com | 119 rooms | $78.99 | AE, D, DC, MC, V.

Courtyard by Marriott. Convenient to area corporations and I–88, this late '80s brick structure is 3 mi north of downtown and has regular rooms or suites with kings or doubles. Restaurant, bar, room service. In-room data ports, some microwaves, some refrigerators, cable TV. Indoor pool. Hot tub. Exercise equipment. Laundry facilities. Business services. Free parking. | 1155 E. Diehl Rd. | 630/505–0550 or 800/321–2211 | fax 630/505–8337 | www.courtyard.com | 131 rooms, 16 suites | $79; $149 suites | AE, D, DC, MC, V.

Days Inn. Within walking distance of a movie theater, shopping, and restaurants, this concrete mid-'80s structure lies 2 mi northeast of downtown Naperville. Complimentary Continental breakfast. In-room data ports, microwaves, some refrigerators, cable TV. Gym. Business services. Laundry facilities. | 1350 E. Ogden Ave. | 630/369–3600 or 800/DAYSINN | fax 630/369–3643 | www.daysinn.com | 120 rooms | $59.95 | AE, D, DC, MC, V.

Exel Inn. Next to Naperville Corporate Center, this three-story redbrick late 1980s building lies within walking distance of restaurants and corporate offices. Complimentary Continental breakfast. In-room data ports, some microwaves, cable TV. Video games. Laundry facilities. Business services. Pets allowed (fee). | 1585 N. Naperville-Wheaton Rd. | 630/357–0022 or 800/367–3935 | fax 630/357–9817 | www.exelinns.com | 123 rooms | $64 | AE, D, DC, MC, V.

Fairfield Inn–Naperville. This standard hotel is right off of I–88 30 mi west of downtown Chicago. There are several large corporate offices nearby, such as Lucent Technologies and Hewlett-Packard, as well as North Central College, Wheaton College, and Benedictine University within a 5 mi radius. Complimentary Continental breakfast. In-room data ports, some microwaves, some refrigerators, some in-room hot tubs, cable TV. Indoor pool. Hot tub. Exercise equipment. Business services. | 1820 Abriter Ct. | 630/577–1820 or 800/228–2800 | www.marriott.com | 105 rooms | $79–$94 | AE, D, DC, MC, V.

Hampton Inn. Convenient to local corporate offices and equipped with two meeting rooms, the Hampton Inn lies 3 mi north of downtown, edging a business park. Complimentary Continental breakfast. In-room data ports, cable TV. Outdoor pool. Gym. Business services. | 1087 E. Diehl Rd. | 630/505–1400 or 800/426–7866 | fax 630/505–1416 | www.hampton-inn.com | 128 rooms | $94 | AE, D, DC, MC, V.

Harrison House. This Victorian home, which blends antiques with more contemporary American furnishings, is on a quiet residential street in downtown Naperville, where you can relax on the large front porch and observe the neighborhood's comings and goings. During the week a complimentary Continental breakfast is served; on the weekends there is a compli-

mentary full breakfast. Complimentary Continental breakfast. Some microwaves, some refrigerators, cable TV. | 26 N. Eagle St. | 630/420–1117 | 4 rooms | $118–$158 | AE, D, DC, MC, V.

Holiday Inn Select. The business-oriented hotel, complete with conferenceroom and banquet facilities sits in the heart of the Illinois high-tech corridor. The seven-story concrete-and-stone structure has an extended sundeck and attractive landscaping. The hotel is less than 5 mi northeast of downtown and offers free shuttle service within a few miles. Restaurant, bar. In-room data ports, room service, cable TV. Indoor pool. Gym. Video games. Business services. | 1801 N. Naper Blvd. | 630/505–4900 or 800/HOLIDAY | fax 630/505–8239 | www.holiday-inn.com | 299 rooms | $89–$119 | AE, D, DC, MC, V.

Homestead Village Guest Studios. Five minutes north of downtown Naperville, just off Washington Street, this studio-apartment compound with daily, weekly, and monthly rentals offers twice-weekly maid service and complimentary use of the nearby Power House Gym about 1 mi south of the facilities. In-room data ports, kitchenettes, cable TV. | 1827 Cedar Point Cir. | 630/577–0200 | 137 units | $79–$99 | AE, D, DC, MC, V.

Travelodge of Naperville. About 3 mi northeast of downtown, this mid-'80s building has been refurbished recently. It's in a mixed residential-commercial neighborhood, 5 mi northeast of the Morton Arboretum. In-room data ports, some refrigerators, cable TV. Exercise equipment. Laundry facilities. Business services. | 1617 Naperville Rd. | 630/505–0200 or 800/578–7878 | fax 630/505–4291 | www.travelodge.com | 104 rooms | $79 | AE, D, DC, MC, V.

Wyndham Garden. Guests at this redbrick, mid-'80s hotel built around an enclosed courtyard garden can enjoy the view from the lobby and library overlooks. It's 2 mi north of downtown. Restaurant, bar. In-room data ports, some refrigerators. Microwaves available upon request. Room service, cable TV. Indoor pool. Hot tub. Exercise equipment. Business services. | 1837 Centre Point Cir. | 630/505–3353 or 800/WYNDHAM | fax 630/505–0176 | www.wyndham.com | 143 rooms, 39 suites | $139 | AE, D, DC, MC, V.

NAUVOO

MAP 6, C5

(Nearby towns also listed: Macomb, Quincy)

In 1839, Joseph Smith, founding leader of the Church of Jesus Christ of Latter-day Saints (the Mormons) brought his followers to this spot on the Mississippi. They established

KODAK'S TIPS FOR USING LIGHTING

Daylight
- Use the changing color of daylight to establish mood
- Use light direction to enhance subjects' properties
- Match light quality to specific subjects

Dramatic Lighting
- Anticipate dramatic lighting events
- Explore before and after storms

Sunrise, Sunset, and Afterglow
- Include a simple foreground
- Exclude the sun when setting your exposure
- After sunset, wait for the afterglow to color the sky

From *Kodak Guide to Shooting Great Travel Pictures* © 2000 by Fodor's Travel Publications

a town, and by the early 1840s, the population had ballooned to 12,000. Anti-Mormon sentiment brewed in the area, though, and in 1844 Smith and his brother were murdered by a mob. The Mormons left the town and established Salt Lake City, Utah two years later. Today the population is 1,100, and Mormon groups have restored many historical sites.

Information: Nauvoo Chamber of Commerce | Mulholland and Page Sts. (Box 41), 62354 | 217/453–6648 | www.visitnauvoo.org.

Attractions

Baxter's Vineyard. Illinois' oldest winery is open for tours and tastings. | 2010 E. Parley St. | 217/453–2528 or 800/854–1396 | www.nauvoowinery.com | Free | Mon.–Sat. 9–5, Sun. 10–5.

Joseph Smith Historic Center. The visitor center has a video introduction and exhibits; the grounds include Joseph Smith's grave and log-cabin homestead, where he first lived, as well as his mansion, which was built later, and his store. | 149 Water St. | 217/453–2246 | fax 217/453–6416 | www.joseph-smith.com | Free | Mon.–Sat. 9–5, Sun. 1–5.

Nauvoo Historic District. This historic area includes a print shop, the Heber C. Kimball home, the Brigham Young home, the Wilford Woodruff home, a pioneer burial ground, and the Temple. All are fully restored with their original 1840s furnishings. | Main St. at Young St. | 217/453–2237 | fax 217/453–6348 | www.visitnauvoo.org | Free | Visitor center summer, daily 8 AM–9 PM; winter, daily 9–6. Restored buildings summer, Mon.–Sat. 9–6, Sun. 10:30–6; winter, Mon.–Sat. 9–5, Sun. noon–5.

Nauvoo State Park. 148-acre park with a nature trail and fishing lake has been landscaped to re-create what the area would have looked like 150 years ago. The park museum, staffed by the local historical society, contains 1,200 artifacts covering the history of Nauvoo. Camping and RVing welcome. | Rte. 96 | 217/453–2512 | Free; camping and RV (fee) | Grounds daily; museum May–Sept., daily 1–5.

Old Carthage Jail. This historic jail, where Joseph Smith and his brother were murdered by an armed mob, is about 23 mi southeast of Nauvoo, and is part of the Nauvoo Restoration and LDS Visitors Center. | 307 Walnut St., Carthage | 217/357–2989 | fax 217/453–6348 | www.visitnauvoo.org | Free | Summer, Mon.–Sat. 9–6, Sun. 10:30–6; winter, Mon.–Sat. 9–5, Sun. 12:30–5.

ON THE CALENDAR

JULY–AUG.: *City of Joseph* is a musical production that tells the story of Mormon founder Joseph Smith, and the history of Nauvoo. The outdoor pageant takes place across from the LDS Visitor Center. | 800/453–0022.

SEPT.: *Grape Festival.* The grape harvest is celebrated by parades downtown, a grape stomp, and live entertainment at Nauvoo State Park. | 217/453–6648.

DEC.: *Holiday Walk.* You can join the townsfolk of Nauvoo, who launch the holiday season the first Saturday in December with this annual walk downtown when shops along Mullholland St. (Route 96) offer seasonal specials, Santa comes to town, and the high school chorus goes a-caroling. | 217/453–6648.

Dining

Grandpa John's. American. This down-home place, decorated with antiques, serves a reliable menu of fried chicken, catfish, turkey, and sandwiches—as well as a lunch buffet. A specialty is homemade ham loaf. Kids' menu. | 1255 Mulholland St. | 217/453–2310 | $6 | No credit cards | Closed Jan.–Feb. No dinner.

Hotel Nauvoo. American. Tucked in the historic hotel from the town's Mormon heyday, this eatery draws people from miles around for its buffet and 40-item salad bar. The 1940s business remains an established gathering spot for families. Known for wild rice dressing. | 1290 Mulholland St. | 217/453–2211 | www.hotelnauvoo.com | $15–$22 | No credit cards | Closed Mon. No lunch Tues.–Sat., no dinner Sun.

Sunny Day Café. American. Across from the Nauvoo Family Hotel, you can enjoy the popular all-you-can-eat buffet, including the bottomless 21-item salad bar, or order meals from the traditional American menu here. | 1840 Mulholland St. | 217/453–2909 | $5.75–$8.95 | No credit cards | Closed Mon.

Lodging

Hotel Nauvoo. The historic inn of 1840 holds cozy rooms full of home-style antiques and sits within the small business district. Landscaped lawns surround the blue-brick two-story structure. Restaurant, bar. Cable TV. | 1290 Mulholland St. | 217/453–2211 | fax 217/453–6100 | www.hotelnauvoo.com | 6 rooms, 2 suites | $59.50 | No credit cards | Closed mid-Nov.–mid-Mar.

Mississippi Memories. This early '80s brick accomodation overlooks the Mississippi and has two large decks. The breakfast space is accentuated by linens, flowers, and homeade candles. This getaway in the woods has rooms packed with such comforts as robes, fresh fruit and flowers, and fresh ice water; it's 2 mi from Great River Golf Course. Complimentary breakfast. | 1 Riverview Terr. | 217/453–2771 | 4 rooms | $69–$95 | MC, V | Closed Christmas week.

Motel Nauvoo. Surrounded by birch and pine trees and manicured lawns and gardens, this independently owned '50s motel has rooms with private entrances, plus picnic tables and chairs. It's convenient to downtown Nauvoo's antique shops. Picnic area. Cable TV. | 1610 Mulholland St. | 217/453–2219 | fax 217/453–6100 | 11 rooms (8 with shower only) | $49 | D, MC, V.

Nauvoo Family Motel. Rooms are large in this independently owned, three-story modern hotel built in the Federal style. It's two blocks from the downtown area. Some in-room hot tubs, cable TV. Indoor pool. Exercise equipment. Room service, breakfast only. | 1875 Mulholland St. 62354 | 217/453–6527 or 800/416–4470 | fax 217/453–6601 | www.nauvoonet.com | 115 rooms, 17 suites | $66; $95–$100 | AE, D, MC, V.

White House Inn. You can truly make yourself at home in this inn, an 1850 two-story white brick house, where you have use of the kitchen to prepare the breakfast fixings that are supplied, and use of the gas grill on the patio for other meals. The innkeepers can be reached at the bakery across the street and are accessible via the telephone in the inn's small sitting room. Three of the rooms have private baths. Kitchen, microwave, refrigerator, cable TV, in-room VCRs, no room phones. Hot tub. | 1475 Mulholland | 217/453–6734 | 4 rooms | $50–$75 | MC, V.

NORTHBROOK

MAP 8, D3

(Nearby towns also listed: Arlington Heights, Glencoe, Glenview, Highland Park, Highwood)

Originally, this northern Chicago suburb was a milk stop called Schermerville. It was incorporated in 1901 and renamed in 1925. Today, it's largely residential and is also home to a number of national corporations. The population is 32,000.

Information: **Northbrook Chamber of Commerce and Industry** | 2002 Walters Ave., 60062 | 847/498–5555.

Attractions

Fudge Factory. This sweets shop is in the Old Temple House Motel, diagonally across from the Nauvoo Mormon Temple. Its big windows give passersby a chance to see fudge being made. | 1240 Mulholland St. | 217/453–6389 | Closed Sun.

Northbrook Court Shopping Center. Three department stores and 125 shops and cinemas, plus lots of benches for resting. | 2171 Northbrook Ct. | 847/498–1770 | Daily.

Northbrook Historical Society. The society's collection of old photos and rotating exhibits of the area's history are housed on the first two floors of this former inn, built in 1894, in which the third floor is a re-created 1890's Shermerville home. | 1776 Walters Ave. | 847/498–3404 | Donation suggested | Thurs. 10–2, Sun. 2–4.

River Trail Nature Center. Forest preserve with walking trail and nature center. | 3120 N. Milwaukee Ave. | 847/824–8360 | Free | Trail summer weekdays 8–5, weekends 8–5:30; winter, 9–4:30. Nature center, summer Mon.–Thurs. 9–4:30, weekends 9–5; winter 9–4.

ON THE CALENDAR

MAR. OR APR.: *Maple Sugar Festival.* Demonstrations of sap collecting and syrup-making; pancake breakfast. | 847/824–8360.

JUNE–JULY: *Parks Fest.* Free concerts are performed Tuesday evenings throughout June and July in the Village Green on Walters Avenue, where you can take a picnic and blanket and flop down on the grass, or purchase food from vendors, who start selling about an hour prior to prelude. | 847/291–2985.

Dining

Ceiling Zero. Continental. An old airplane hangar in Sky Harbor industrial park has been transformed into this European bistro. Try the French pepper steak, rack of lamb, and fish. | 500 Anthony Tr. | 847/272–8111 | Reservations essential Sat. | $13–$29 | AE, D, DC, MC, V | No lunch weekends.

Ed Debevic's. American. This fun, noisy diner–style eatery, straight out of *Leave It to Beaver,* is popular with teens and young families. The wisecracking waiters periodically dance on the countertops. Known for the buffet of salads, veggies, and homemade soups, as well as myriad variations of burgers and sandwiches. It's also well regarded for chili and meat loaf the way mom made it, plus desserts from the '50s-style soda shop. Deerfield is less than a mile west of Northbrook. Kids' menu. | 660 Lake Cook Rd., Deerfield | 847/945–3242 | $4.25–$8 | AE, D, MC, V.

Edwardo's. Pizza. Here you can enjoy pastas and salads in addition to the numerous pizzas offerings, including the Hawaiian, which has a sweet-and-sour sauce topped with pineapple, Canadian bacon, and chopped tomatoes, and the barbecue pizza with chicken. | 240 Skokie Blvd. | 847/272–5222 | $10–$30 | AE, D, DC, MC, V.

Francesco's Hole in the Wall. Italian. A cozy, bustling spot known for its veal shank over risotto, chicken, fresh fish, and homemade pasta. No smoking. | 254 Skokie Blvd. | 847/272–0155 | $20–$35 | No credit cards | Closed Tues. No lunch weekends.

Max and Benny's Restaurant and Deli. Delicatessens. A kosher-style restaurant with both sit-down and carry-out service, this deli serves all the classic sandwich favorites, such as brisket, stuffed cabbage, and corned beef and cabbage, plus breakfast all day. Videos show sports, and one windowed wall looks out into the mall in which Max and Benny's is located; the others boast a mural of a shtetl. | 461 Waukegan Rd. | 847/272–9490 | Breakfast also available | $11.95–$14.95 | AE, D, DC, MC, V.

Tonelli's. Italian. This homey place is famous for its thick-crust pizza, white fish, and home-made lasagna. Kids' menu. | 1038 Waukegan Rd. | 847/272–4730 | $5–$19.50 | AE, D, DC, MC, V | No lunch weekends.

Lodging

Adam's Mark Hotel. This business hotel is 9 mi from O'Hare, 9 mi from Rosemont Expo Center, and close to corporate offices. Four-story and seven-story buildings house 15 meeting rooms. A golf course is on the grounds. Restaurant, bar. Cable TV, in-room movies available. Pool. Hot tub. Exercise equipment. Business services. Airport shuttle. | 2875 N. Milwaukee Ave. | 847/298–2525 | fax 847/298–4615 | 318 rooms | $39–$199 rooms, $250–$350 suites | AE, D, DC, MC, V.

Courtyard by Marriott. Half a mile off I–294 (Lake Cook exit), 15 mi north of O'Hare, and close to local corporations, this hotel has four meeting rooms, a landscaped courtyard, and a gazebo. The restaurant here serves only breakfast, which is available 7 days a week. Restaurant, bar. In-room data ports, microwaves, some refrigerators, cable TV. Indoor pool. Hot tub. Exercise equipment. Laundry facilities. Business services. Free parking. | 800 Lake Cook Rd., Deerfield | 847/940–8222 or 800/321–2211 | fax 847/940–7741 | www.courtyard.com | 131 rooms, 14 suites | $159; $189 suites | AE, D, DC, MC, V.

Embassy Suites. This all-suites hotel is less than a mile from the commuter train station. It's in a corporate business park, 28 mi northwest of Chicago and less than a mile west of Northbrook. The hotel runs a free shuttle to businesses and restaurants within 5 mi and serves free beverages in the evening. Restaurant, bar, complimentary breakfast. In-room data ports, cable TV. Indoor pool. Hot tub, sauna. Exercise equipment. Laundry facilities. Business services. | 1445 Lake Cook Rd., Deerfield | 847/945–4500 or 800/EMBASSY | fax 847/945–8189 | www.embassysuiteschi-dfld.com | 237 suites | $224 | AE, D, DC, MC, V.

Hilton. Across from Allison Woods forest preserve, this 10-story, brick, all-suites hotel complex is on the Des Plaines River. There is a complimentary shuttle to sites within 5 mi. Restaurant, bar. In-room data ports, cable TV. Indoor pool. Hot tub. Sauna. Gym. Business services. | 2855 N. Milwaukee Ave. | 847/480–7500 or 800/445–8667 | fax 847/480–7659 | www.hilton.com | 246 suites | $99–$250 | AE, D, DC, MC, V.

Hyatt–Deerfield. Convenient to corporations, the Botanic Garden, and Ravinia, and 40 minutes from Chicago, this hotel is in a business complex 1 mi west of downtown Deerfield, which is 1 mi west of Northbrook. Restaurant, bar. In-room data ports, cable TV. Indoor pool. Hot tub. Exercise equipment. Business services. | 1750 Lake Cook Rd., Deerfield | 847/945–3400 or 800/233–1234 | fax 847/945–3563 | www.hyatt.com | 300 rooms, 1 suite | $205; $650 suite | AE, D, DC, MC, V.

Marriott Suites. This all-suites hotel is in a corporate park, less than 1 mi west of I–294 and 4 mi west of Northbrook. Restaurants and shopping are 2 mi away. Restaurant, bar. In-room data ports, microwaves, refrigerators, cable TV, some in-room VCRs. Indoor-outdoor pool. Hot tub. Exercise equipment. Laundry facilities. Business services. Some pets allowed. | 2 Parkway N, Deerfield | 847/405–9666 or 800/228–9290 | fax 847/405–0354 | 248 suites | $94–$189 | AE, D, DC, MC, V.

Red Roof Inn–Northbrook. You can find this standard chain motel north of Dundee and south of Lakecook at the Deerfield end of Northbrook along I-94. The surrounding area is fairly commercial and there is a restaurant just across the street. Some in-room data ports, some microwaves, some refrigerators, some in-room hot tubs, cable TV. Pets allowed. | 340 Waukegan Rd. | 847/205–1755 or 800/843–7663 | fax 847/205–1891 | 117 rooms, 1 suite | $45–$110 | AE, D, DC, MC, V.

Residence Inn by Marriott–Deerfield. An extended-stay hotel with 17 two-story town houses is in a quiet corporate park ¾ mi west of Northbrook. The property is geared to business training and relocation, plus family travel. Restaurants and shopping are within 2 mi; rooms have separate entries and fully equipped kitchens, and most have fireplaces.

In-room data ports, cable TV. Pool. Hot tub. Tennis. Basketball, gym, volleyball. Laundry facilities, laundry service. Business services. Free parking. Pets allowed (fee). | 530 Lake Cook Rd., Deerfield | 847/940–4644 or 800/331–3131 | fax 847/940–7639 | www.marriott.com | 128 suites | $164–$204 | AE, D, DC, MC, V.

Sheraton–North Shore. Near the Botanic Garden and Northbrook Court shopping mall, this brick hotel offers a free shuttle to spots within 5 mi. Restaurants, bar. In-room data ports, some refrigerators, cable TV. Indoor pool. Exercise equipment. Laundry facilities. | 933 Skokie Blvd. | 847/498–6500 or 800/325–3535 | fax 847/498–9558 | www.sheraton.com | 386 rooms, 3 suites | $189, $250–$550 suites | AE, D, DC, MC, V.

OAK BROOK

MAP 8, C6

(Nearby towns also listed: Downers Grove, Elmhurst, Hinsdale, LaGrange)

A southwest suburb of Chicago, Oak Brook is home to Oak Brook Center—a large, upscale shopping mall—and a number of major corporations, like McDonald's and Merrill Lynch. It's laced with hiking and bike trails and is known for its polo matches. The population is 9,087.

Information: DuPage Convention and Visitors Bureau | 915 Harger Rd., Suite 240, 60523 | 800/232–0502 | www.dupagecvb.com.

Attractions

Fullersburg Woods Environmental Center. Educational nature center with living marsh, woolly mammoth bones. | 3609 Spring Rd. | 630/850–8110 | fax 630/850–8110 | Free | Daily 9–5.

Graue Mill and Museum. The only water-powered gristmill still operating in Illinois grinds and sells corn daily. There's also an Underground Railroad station and museum. Potters, weavers, basketmakers, spinners, and tinsmiths demonstrate their work, and special events like story-telling and dulcimer playing are held every weekend. There is a Civil War encampment in September. | 3720 York Rd. | 630/655–2090 | fax 630/920–9721 | $3.75; special rates for seniors and children | Mid-Apr.–mid-Nov., Tues.–Sun. 10–4:30.

Oak Brook Center. This open-air mall on Cermak Road, at Route 83 and 22nd Street covers 2.5 million square ft, boasts five anchor stores, and houses 165 more stores and restaurants, where you can shop, eat, drink, or simply stroll. | Cermak Rd. at Rte. 83 and 22nd St. | 630/573–0700 | Free | Mon.–Sat. 10–9, Sun. 11–6.

ON THE CALENDAR

JUNE: *Highland Games.* Each year on the third Saturday in June, the Illinois St. Andrews Society organizes a day of Scottish culture held at the Oak Brook Polo Grounds, including demonstrations and competitions of piping, drumming, dancing, and Highland games, such as toss the caber (flinging a 14-ft pine tree trunk end-over-end), and a "shopping center" for all manner of Scottish goods, such as food, audiotapes, and suits of armor. Expect a modest admission fee. | 708/442–7293.

JUNE–SEPT.: *Sunday Polo.* Polo matches are held every Sunday afternoon at Oak Brook Polo Grounds, 31st Street and York Road. | 630/990–2394.

Dining

Braxton Seafood Grill. Seafood. Designed with an English port in mind, with dark oak woodwork and forest green accents, this place in Oak Brook Center is a good bet for fresh seafood, especially jumbo crab cakes and live Maine lobster. Live Dixieland band in lounge Fri.–Sat. Kids' menu. Early bird menu. | 3 Oak Brook Center | 630/574–2155 | $15–$45 | AE, D, DC, MC, V.

The Clubhouse. American. This places looks like a golf clubhouse, with TVs downstairs tuned to golf only. Photos of celebs adorn the walls, and there's a cigar bar. Upstairs is more formal, with leather chairs and velvet drapes. Try the Portobello mushroom carpaccio, and the pasta, steaks, and fish. | 298 Oak Brook Center | 630/472–0600 | Daily | $13–$28 | AE, D, DC, MC, V.

Fond de la Tour. French. Specialties here include rack of lamb, steak Diane, and Dover sole. A pianist and singer perform Fri. and Sat. | 40 N. Tower Rd. | 630/620–1500 | www.opentable.com | Reservations essential | Jacket required | $29–$55 | AE, D, DC, MC, V | Closed Sun., Mon. No lunch Sat.

J. Alexander's. Continental. On the north side of Oak Brook Center, behind the pond that often has geese paddling in it, this restaurant's interior has an exposed-brick wall, beamed ceilings, and both booths and tables at which you can dine on burgers to prime rib accompanied by a selection from the pub's many brews. | 1410 16th T. | 630/573–8160 | $8–$22 | AE, D, DC, MC, V.

Maggiano's Little Italy. Italian. You step back into mid-20th-century Europe in this dining room, with its red-checked tablecloths and walls covered by old family portraits, where you can order from the family-portions menu if you are a group of four or more, or simply order Maggiano's Italian classics—eggplant parmesan, ravioli, lasagna, veal scallopine—à la carte. | 240 Oak Brook Center | 630/368–0300 | fax 630/368–0310 | Daily | $11–$29 | AE, D, DC, MC, V.

Melting Pot. Swiss. Fondue—cheese, meat, and chocolate—is the specialty in this romantic, rustic place 1 mi north of Oakbrook. | 17 W. 633 Roosevelt Rd., Oakbrook Terrace | 630/495–5778 | www.meltingpot.net | Reservations essential | $15–$30 | AE, D, DC, MC, V | No lunch.

Morton's of Chicago. Steak. An elegant den for meat lovers about 3 mi east of Oak Brook. Prime rib and porterhouse are specialties. | 1 Westbrook Corporate Center, Westchester | 708/562–7000 | www.mortons.com | Daily for dinner | $20–$45 | AE, DC, MC, V | No lunch.

Papagus Greek Taverna. Greek. On the east side of the first level of the Oak Brook Center, next to Neiman Marcus, you can enjoy such Greek favorites as pastitsio, grilled seafood, and chops. Specialties are Greek roast chicken, braised lamb with orzo, souvlaki, and a large selection of mezedes appetizers. The dining room has wood ceilings and is adorned in stone. | 272 Oak Brook Center | 630/472–9800 | $10–$24 | AE, D, DC, MC, V.

The Pepper Mill. Continental. This formal restaurant with etched-glass windows serves pastas, steaks, and seafood with an ample choice of appetizers. The restaurant is 1 mi west of Oakbrook. Open-air dining on rose garden patio. Salad bar. Kids' menu. | 18W066 22nd St., Oakbrook Terrace | 630/620–5656 | www.peppermill.com | $5–$22.50 | AE, D, DC, MC, V | Breakfast also available.

Sylviano's Ristorante. Italian. Known for its Northern Italian–style recipes for veal, this restaurant also serves chicken and beef, and daily fish specials, in its candlelit dining room overlooking a park with trees, ponds, and a fountain. Live music Wed., Fri., and Sat. | 2809 Butterfield Rd. | 630/571–3600 | $10.95–$32.95 | AE, D, DC, MC, V | Closed Sun. No lunch Sat.

Wild Fire. Steak. A large stone grill is the focal point of the dining area in this restaurant in Oak Brook Center, next to Tiffany's and Neiman Marcus, where you can order spit-roasted chicken as well as beef grilled to your specifications. You can hear '40s swing music and admire black-and-white photos of old Chicago on the walls. There's a kids' menu, and the waiters provide crayons for diversion while you wait for your food. | 232 Oak Brook Center | 630/586–9000 | $6.95–$24.95 | AE, D, DC, MC, V.

Lodging

Clubhouse Inn & Suites. Town houses surround a garden courtyard with pool, 2 mi from Oakbrook Center shopping mall and within walking distance of restaurants. The hotel is geared to business meetings and social gatherings. Suites have two rooms, dining area, some kitchenettes, some refrigerators, some microwaves. Complimentary breakfast. In-room data ports, some kitchenettes, some microwaves, cable TV. Indoor pool. Hot tub. Laundry facilities. Business services. | 630 Pasquinelli Dr., Westmont | 630/920–2200 or 800/ CLUBINN | fax 630/920–2766 | www.clubhouseinn.com | 118 rooms, 19 suites | Rooms $119; suites $149 | AE, D, DC, MC, V.

Comfort Suites. This suburban all-suites hotel is less than 1 mi from Oakbrook Center, 3 mi from Yorktown Mall, and 5 mi from Loyola University. Children 18 and under stay free with parent. Complimentary breakfast. In-room data ports, cable TV. Indoor pool. Sauna. Exercise equipment. Laundry facilities. Business services. | 17W445 Roosevelt Rd., Oakbrook Terrace | 630/916–1000 or 800/221–5150 | fax 630/916–1068 | www.comfortinn.com | 103 suites | $119 | AE, D, DC, MC, V.

Courtyard by Marriott. A chain hotel designed for business travelers has large office areas and is close to many local corporations, including IBM and J.D. Edwards. Oak Brook Center and Yorktown Mall are a short drive. Restaurant, bar. In-room data ports, some refrigerators, cable TV. Indoor pool. Hot tub. Exercise equipment. Laundry facilities. Business services. | 6 Trans Am Plaza Dr., Oakbrook Terrace | 630/691–1500 or 800/321–2211 | fax 630/691–1518 | www.courtyard.com | 147 rooms | $129 | AE, D, DC, MC, V.

Four Point Barcelo Hotel. This business hotel is close to Oak Brook Center, a short walk to restaurants. Restaurant, bar, room service. Some microwaves, some refrigerators, cable TV. Indoor pool. Hot tub. Exercise equipment. Business services. | 17W350 22nd St., Oakbrook Terrace | 630/833–3600 or 800/325–3535 | fax 630/833–7037 | 223 rooms, 5 suites | $159 | AE, D, DC, MC, V.

Hampton Inn–Lombard. Walk to shopping and area corporations (MCI WorldCom, Ricoh) from this four-story stucco hotel, 5 mi west of Oak Brook Center and a half-mile from Yorktown Mall. Complimentary Continental breakfast. In-room data ports, cable TV. Exercise equipment. Laundry service. Business services. | 222 E. 22nd St., Lombard | 630/916–9000 or 800/HAMPTON | fax 630/916–8016 | www.hampton-inn.com | 130 rooms | $109 | AE, D, DC, MC, V.

Hampton Inn–Westchester. Brookfield Zoo is 4 mi, Fresh Meadows Golf Course is 1 mi, and Oak Brook Polo Club is 1 mi from this brick, four-story hotel. Westbrook Corporate Center is next door. You can walk to restaurants. Complimentary Continental breakfast. In-room data ports, cable TV. Exercise equipment. | 2222 Enterprise Dr., Westchester | 708/409–1000 or 800/HAMPTON | fax 708/409–1055 | www.hampton-inn.com | 112 rooms | $119 | AE, D, DC, MC, V.

Hilton Suites–Oakbrook Terrace. An all-suites, 10-story hotel with atrium, adjacent to Drury Lane Dinner Theater, in affluent Oakbrook Terrace. Complimentary cocktails and snacks in the evening. Restaurant, bar, complimentary breakfast. In-room data ports, in-room VCRs and movies, cable TV. Indoor pool. Hot tub. Exercise equipment. Business services. | 10 Drury La., Oakbrook Terrace | 630/941–0100 or 800/HILTONS | fax 630/941–0299 | www.hilton-hotels.com | 212 suites | $185 | AE, D, DC, MC, V.

Hyatt Regency–Oak Brook. A seven-story tower with the chain's trademark atrium lobby, across from Oak Brook Center and 2 mi to Metra train station. Free shuttle within 5-mi radius. Restaurants, bar, room service, cable TV. Indoor pool. Hot tub. Exercise equipment. Business services. | 1909 Spring Rd. | 630/573–1234 or 800/233–1234 | fax 630/573–1133 | www.hyatt.com | 411 rooms, 12 suites | $189–$234 | AE, D, DC, MC, V.

La Quinta. This three-story business hotel offers free local transportation weekdays to destinations within a 3-mi radius. Yorktown and Oak Brook shopping malls are 1 mi away. Complimentary Continental breakfast. In-room data ports, cable TV. Pool. Exercise equipment. Business services. Some pets allowed. | 1S666 Midwest Rd., Oakbrook Terrace | 630/495–4600 or 800/687–6667 | fax 630/495–2558 | www.laquinta.com | 150 rooms, 1 suite | $99 | AE, D, DC, MC, V.

Marriott–Oak Brook. Close to interstates and corporate headquarters, this 12-story hotel is a 20-minute ride to O'Hare. You can walk to restaurants and Oak Brook Center. Loyola University is 3 mi, the Metra station 5 mi, Fresh Meadows and Oak Brook golf courses 2 mi. Restaurant, bar, room service. In-room data ports, some microwaves, cable TV. Pool. Hot tub. Exercise equipment. Business services. | 1401 W. 22nd St. | 630/573–8555 or 800/228–9290 | fax 630/573–1026 | www.marriott.com | 335 rooms, 12 suites | $199–$224 | AE, D, DC, MC, V.

Oak Brook Hills Resort and Conference Center. This state-of-the-art, 45,000-square-ft conference center on sweeping, landscaped grounds is designed for business meetings. The interior is dark wood and marble. Oak Brook Center is 6 mi. Restaurants, bar, room service. In-room data ports, cable TV. Indoor–outdoor pools. Barbershop/beauty salon, hot tubs, saunas. 18-hole golf course. Cross-country skiing. Shops. Business services. Some pets allowed. | 3500 Midwest Rd. | 630/850–5555 or 800/445–3315 | fax 630/850–5569 | www.dolce.com | 340 rooms, 44 suites | $199; suites $450 | AE, D, DC, MC, V.

Renaissance Oak Brook Marriott. There's a rooftop pool in this 10-story luxury conference hotel and two meeting rooms on every floor. It's next to Oak Brook Center. Restaurant, bar. Room service, cable TV. Pool, wading pool. Exercise equipment. Business services. | 2100 Spring Rd. | 630/573–2800 or 800/HOTELS1 | fax 630/573–7134 | www.renaissance.com | 164 rooms, 2 suites | $184; suites $300 | AE, D, DC, MC, V.

Residence Inn by Marriott. This all-suites hotel consists of 18 two-story town homes on landscaped grounds; all units have private outside entrances and full kitchens. It is two blocks from Yorktown Mall and 2 mi west of Oak Brook. A spa and health club are nearby. Picnic area, complimentary breakfast. In-room data ports, microwaves, refrigerators, cable TV. Pool. Hot tub. Gym. Laundry facilities. Pets allowed (fee). | 2001 S. Highland Ave., Lombard | 630/629–7800 or 800/331–3131 | fax 630/629–6987 | www.marriott.com | 108 studios, 36 suites | $144; suites $174 | AE, D, DC, MC, V.

The Wyndham Drake Oak Brook Hotel. A four-story luxury hotel with an 18-hole Oak Brook Golf Course nearby. It's 10 mi from both O'Hare and Midway. Restaurant, bar. In-room data ports, some refrigerators, cable TV. Indoor–outdoor pool. Hot tub. Tennis. Gym. Business services. | 2301 York Rd. | 630/574–5700 or 800/WYNDHAM | fax 630/574–0830 | www.wyndham.com | 150 rooms, 10 suites | $159 | AE, D, DC, MC, V.

OAK LAWN

MAP 6, H3

(Nearby towns also listed: Chicago, Homewood)

This close-in southern Chicago suburb is primarily residential, although its proximity to Midway Airport makes it an appealing stopover.

Information: Oak Lawn Chamber of Commerce | 5314 W. 95th St., 60453 | 708/424–8300.

Attractions

Village Green. This popular meeting place in the center of town is home to the September festival Fall on the Green and a Veterans' Memorial. | 95th St. at Cook Ave. | 708/424–8300 | Free | Daily.

ON THE CALENDER

AUG.: *Oak Lawn Family Days.* This four-day extravaganza of carnival rides, pony rides, a petting zoo, clowns, stage shows, and food vendors is held at the Oak Lawn Pavilion at 94th Street and Oak Park Avenue the first weekend of the month, and all profits go to local Oak Lawn charities. | 708/424–8300.

SEPT.: *Fall on the Green.* The first weekend in September you can head down to the Village Green at 95th Street and Cook Avenue to hear all kinds of live music performed on two stages throughout the three days of the festival, while you dine on food from the many vendors, and drink in the beer garden. Kids' activities include an obstacle course, petting zoo, games, and pony rides. | 708/636–4400.

Dining

The Old Barn. American. In season, a fire warms this dark, cozy, wood-paneled place a couple of miles from Oak Lawn in suburban Burbank. Try lobster Bentley, prime rib, and barbecued ribs. Kids' menu. | 8100 S. Central Ave., Burbank | 708/422–5400 | $10–$23 | AE, D, DC, MC, V | No lunch weekends.

Senese's Winery Restaurant. American. Just a few blocks from the main intersection of 95th Street and Cicero Avenue, this dinner-and-comedy club has seating among old wine barrels and presses and is known for tender ribs. | 10345 Central Ave. | 708/636–5030 | $5.95–$11.95 | AE, D, DC, MC, V | Closed Mon.

Whitney's Bar and Grill. Continental. In the Oak Lawn Hilton, this tri-level dining room has floor-to-ceiling windows that overlook the hotel's landscaping, and a glass-enclosed exhibition kitchen. The grilled steaks and the beef Wellington are favorites here. | 9333 S. Cicero Ave. | 708/425–7800 | $15–$22 | AE, D, DC, MC, V | Breakfast also available.

Lodging

Baymont Inn. Midway airport is 8 mi and the Metra station is 3 mi from this three-story hotel. Four suites have hot tubs. Complimentary Continental breakfast. In–room data ports, some refrigerators, some in-room hot tubs, cable TV. Business services. Pets allowed. | 12801 S. Cicero Ave., Alsip | 708/597–3900 or 800/301–0200 | fax 708/597–3979 | www.baymont.net/alsip.com | 95 rooms, 6 suites | $70–$85; suites $85–$160 | AE, D, DC, MC, V.

Exel Inn. This standard brick motel is about 5 mi west of Oak Lawn in the industrial area of Bridgeview. Restaurants are one block, Chicago Ridge Mall is 1 ½ mi. Complimentary Continental breakfast. Some microwaves, some refrigerators, cable TV. Exercise equipment. Video games. Laundry facilities. Business services. Some pets allowed. | 9625 S. 76th Ave., Bridgeview | 708/430–1818 or 800/367–3935 | fax 708/430–1894 | www.exelinns.com | 113 rooms | $79 | AE, D, DC, MC, V.

Gateway Motel. A red neon sign beckons you from 95th Street, at the corner of Cicero Avenue, to this no-frills motel with its plain Americana style. Kitchenette units can be rented weekly. Some kitchenettes, some microwaves, some refrigerators, TV. | 4657 W. 95th St. | 708/423–4330 | 20 rooms, 7 kitchenettes | $55–$61 | AE, D, DC, MC, V.

Hampton Inn. This brick, four-story hotel is 3 mi south of Oak Lawn. Complimentary Continental breakfast. In-room data ports, some in-room hot tubs, cable TV. Indoor pool. Exercise equipment. Business services, airport shuttle. Some pets allowed. | 13330 S. Cicero Ave., Crestwood | 708/597–3330 or 800/HAMPTON | fax 708/597–3691 | www.hampton-inn.com | 115 rooms, 8 suites | $95; $150 suites | AE, D, DC, MC, V.

Hilton Oak Lawn Hotel. There's an atrium pool in this 12-story hotel, 4 mi south of Midway Airport, in the heart of Oak Lawn. The grounds are landscaped and the top floors afford views of Chicago at night. Restaurant, bar with entertainment, complimentary Continental breakfast. In-room data ports, some minibars, some refrigerators, some in-room hot tubs, some in-room VCRs, cable TV. Indoor pool. Hot tub. Exercise equipment. Business services, airport shuttle. | 9333 S. Cicero Ave. | 708/425–7800 or 800/445–9333 | fax 708/425–8111 | www.hilton.com | 173 rooms, 3 suites | $120; suites $329–$629 | AE, D, DC, MC, V.

Holiday Inn. This standard brick motel is close to three area hospitals, and 5 mi from Midway Airport. Restaurant, bar, room service. In-room data ports, cable TV. Pool. Gym. Business services, airport shuttle. | 4140 W. 95th St. | 708/425–7900 or 800/362–5529 | fax 708/425–7918 | www.basshotels.com | 138 rooms, 2 suites | $115 | AE, D, DC, MC, V.

Radisson Hotel–Alsip. This brick hotel in the heart of Alsip 5 mi southeast of Oak Lawn has landscaped grounds with trees, a courtyard, and a bocci ball court. It's 8 mi south of Midway. Free shuttle to bus station. Restaurant, bar, room service. In–room data ports, some

microwaves, cable TV. Indoor pool. Gym. Video games. Laundry facilities. Business services. Airport shuttle. Pets allowed. | 5000 W. 127th St., Alsip | 708/371–7300 or 800/333–3333 | fax 708/371–9949 | www.radisson.com | 188 rooms, 5 suites | $139; suites $200 | AE, D, DC, MC, V.

OAK PARK

MAP 6, H2

(Nearby towns also listed: Brookfield, Chicago, Riverside)

This close–in western Chicago suburb's best-known residents were Ernest Hemingway and Frank Lloyd Wright, and Oak Park provides plenty of opportunities to find out about both. The village's tree-shaded streets are lined with stately homes, including many Frank Lloyd Wright–designed beauties. A bustling downtown shopping district offers easy access to the Loop via train or rapid transit. The population is 52,000.

Information: **Oak Park Visitors Bureau** | 158 N. Forest Ave., 60301 | 708/524–7800 or 708/848–1500 | fax 708/524–7473 | www.visitoakpark.com.

Attractions

Ernest Hemingway Museum. Exhibits highlight the author's life, with special emphasis on his early years. The admission price includes the Hemingway birthplace just a block away at 339 North Oak Park Avenue. Born in 1899, Hemingway lived his first six years in this restored Queen Anne Victorian home. The site includes information about Hemingway's family and community from the period. Hours are the same as for the museum. | 200 N. Oak Park Ave., in Arts Center | 708/848–2222 | fax 708/386–8506 | www.hemingway.org | $6 | Thurs, Fri., Sun. 1–5; Sat. 10–5.

Frank Lloyd Wright Home and Studio. Guided tours are available of this 1889 studio and home of the famed architect. | 951 Chicago Ave. | 708/848–1976 | fax 708/848–1248 | www.wrightplus.org | $8 | Daily 10–5.

Oak Park Visitors Center. Check with the center for times and variations on walking tours of Oak Park and Frank Lloyd Wright buildings. | 158 N. Forest Ave. | 708/848–1500 or 708/848–1500 | fax 708/524–7473 | www.visitoakpark.com | Varies by tour | Winter, daily 10–4; summer, daily 10–5.

The Pleasant Home. This spacious residence was built in 1897 in the early Prairie style by George W. Maher, a contemporary of Frank Lloyd Wright. It's six blocks south of the Frank Lloyd Wright home and studio. | 217 S. Home Ave. | 708/383–2654 | fax 708/383–2768 | www.oprf.com/phf/tour.html | $5 | Thurs.–Sun. 12:30–3:30; tours on the hour.

Riverside. Riverside, a residential suburb about 10 mi west of Chicago, was conceived as a model suburb in the 1860s. Famed landscape architect Frederick Law Olmsted was commissioned to lay out the village, which was incorporated in 1875. Riverside is today listed as a National Historic Landmark Village, and its houses represent a wide range of architectural styles. | 27 Riverside Rd., Riverside | 708/447–2700 | fax 708/447–2704 | www.riverside-illinois.com | $3 | Weekdays 8–5; Sat. 9–noon.

Unity Temple. You can opt for self-guided or docent-guided tours (weekends only) of this Frank Lloyd Wright–designed church, built in 1908. | 875 Lake St. | 708/383–8873 | fax 708/383–7473 | www.unitytemple-utrf.org | $4; $6 for guided tour (weekends only) | Memorial Day–Labor Day, weekdays 10–5, weekends 1–4; Labor Day–Memorial Day, Daily 1–4.

ON THE CALENDAR

DEC.: *Christmas Tours.* Free guided tours of the Frank Lloyd Wright home on the second and third Saturdays. Tours led by junior interpreters (5th–10th graders) show how the Wright family celebrated Christmas. | 708/848–1976.

Dining

La Bella Pasteria. Italian. An informal downtown eatery, with exposed brick and wall sconces, specializes in pastas, chicken, seafood, and chops. | 1009 S. Marion St. | 708/524–0044 | $7–$20 | AE, D, DC, MC, V | No lunch weekends.

Philander's. American. Seafood, steaks, and oysters are favorites at this elegant bistro with wood and brass accents in turn-of-the-century style, in the beautiful old Carleton Hotel. There's nightly entertainment in the lounge. | 1120 Pleasant St. | 708/848–4250 | Reservations essential | $14–$26 | AE, D, DC, MC, V | Closed Sun. No lunch.

Lodging

Carleton of Oak Park. Built in 1903, this European-style hotel complex two blocks from the main drag of Harlem Avenue includes a three-story brick hotel and an adjoining two-story motor inn. Spa facilities and athletic equipment are complimentary for guests of the hotel at the YMCA, just a a block away. Two restaurants, bar. In-room data ports, some kitchenettes, some microwaves, some refrigerators, some in-room hot tubs, cable TV. Laundry service. | 1110 Pleasant St. | 708/848–5000 or 888/CARLETON | fax 708/848–0537 | www.carletonhotel.com | 150 rooms | $99–$200 | AE, D, DC, MC, V.

Wright's Cheney House Bed and Breakfast. This B&B is a famous brick home designed by Frank Lloyd Wright in 1903 for the Cheney family. (Mrs. Cheney later became his lover.) All furniture and fabrics were designed by Wright. It has an outdoor hot tub and cozy fireplace. You can walk to the Wright and Hemingway museums. Complimentary Continental breakfast. Kitchenettes, some in-room TVs, in-room VCRs available. | 520 N. East Ave. | 708/524–2067 | fax 708/641–3418 | 3 suites | $155 | No credit cards | Closed Jan.

OLNEY

MAP 6, H8

(Nearby towns also listed: Effingham, Salem)

Off U.S. 50 in southeastern Illinois, Olney's claim to fame is its white squirrels. A population of the albino animals has made its home here for nearly 100 years. It's also the seat of Richland County. The population is 9,000.

Information: Olney Chamber of Commerce | 201 E. Chestnut St. (Box 575), 62450 | 618/392–2241 | fax 618/392–4179 | www.olneychamber.com.

Attractions

Heritage House Museum. Volunteers of the Richland Heritage Museum Association prevented this 1874 Victorian home's destruction, and it is now fully restored and continues to be maintained by the association so that you can wander through its rooms and imagine life in that era. Among the holdings is a bed made by a man who grew up in Olney, Charlie Tripp; born without arms Charlie learned to do everything with his toes, including working a hammer and saw. | 122 W. Elm St. | 618/392–5491 | Donation suggested | Sun. 1–4.

Robert Ridgway Memorial Arboretum and Bird Sanctuary. Hundreds of varieties of plants and trees and many species of birds are represented here. A 1½-mi path winds through the acreage. | N. East St. | Free | Daily.

ON THE CALENDAR

JULY: *Richland County Fair.* Midway rides, livestock shows, and entertainment. | 618/863–2606.

SEPT.: *Olney Arts Council Fall Festival.* Arts and crafts vendors, food, and entertainment on the last Saturday of September at the City Park. | 618/395–4444.

NOV.–DEC.: *Christmas Light Display.* From Thanksgiving to New Year's Day, Olney City Park, on White Squirrel Circle at Route 130, is decorated with over 125,000 lights, and you can drive through the park to view them, making a donation at the end, if you wish. Santa makes appearances. | 618/392–4179.

Dining
Hovey's. American/Casual. This family-owned place is locally famous for its burgers and shakes, and heartwarming chili in the winter. | 410 E. Main St. | 618/395–9144 | $1.30–$2.10 | No credit cards.

Lodging
Fessel's Cabbage Rose. Four blocks north of Main Street, this three-story 1883 Gothic-and-Georgian brick structure surrounded by nearly 100 species of trees has been covered with stucco and limestone. Its interior, however, retains the original oak floors, fireplaces, and porcelain and crystal chandeliers, and is furnished with period antiques. You can lounge on the very private front porch, and relax in the garden room and the sun room here. Complimentary breakfast. No TV. Some room phones. | 409 N. Boone St. | 618/392–0218 | 5 rooms | $59–$89 | AE, MC, V | Closed Jan.

Holiday Motel. This two-story, independently owned motel is the largest in town and the only one with an indoor pool. Restaurant. Cable TV. Indoor pool. Exercise equipment. | 1300 S. West St. | 618/395–2121 | 89 rooms | $34–$50 | AE, D, MC, V.

Super 8 Motel. A two-story chain motel with interior entrances, right in town. In-room data ports, cable TV. Hot tub. | 425 Southwest St. | 618/392–7888 or 800/800–8000 | 41 rooms | $39–$54 | AE, D, DC, MC, V.

Traveler's Inn Motel. An independently owned drive-up motel in a quiet setting. Cable TV. | 1801 E. Main St. | 618/393–2186 or 800/232–0976 | 16 rooms | $30–$40 | AE, D, DC, MC, V.

OREGON

MAP 6, F2

(Nearby towns also listed: Dixon, Grand Detour, Rockford)

Set on the Rock River, Oregon attracts many visitors to several local scenic state parks. Its downtown is anchored by the beautiful Ogle County Courthouse, built in 1892, and the Soldiers' Monument, designed by Loredo Taft. The population is 4,000.

Information: **Oregon Chamber of Commerce** | 201 N. 3rd St., 61061 | 815/732–2100.

Attractions
Castle Rock State Park. Sandstone rock formations offer stunning views of the Rock River. There's also a nature preserve and lots of good hiking, picnicking, and fishing. | 1365 W. Castle Rd. | 815/732–7329 | fax 815/732–6742 | Free | Daily sunrise–sunset.

Lowden State Park. There's a 48-ft-tall Loredo Taft sculpture of a Native American at this park 2 mi north of town on Route 64 on the east side of Rock River. Taft, the renowned Illinois sculptor, was inspired to create the statue when he was a guest at Eagle's Nest, an artists' colony that had been on the site. The statue is made of reinforced concrete with a surface of cement and pink granite chips, and weighs about 100 tons. Come to the park for the views, hiking, fishing, and camping. | 1411 N. River Rd. | 815/732–6828 | Free; camping $11 per night | Daily.

Lowden-Miller State Forest. A 2,225-acre forest 3 mi south of Oregon on the Rock River. There are many miles of trails for hiking and cross-country skiing, and deer and turkey hunting in season. | Lowden and Nashua Rds. | 815/732–7329 | Free | Daily.

Ogle County Historical Society Museum. Historical artifacts of Oregon and Ogle County are displayed in this 1878 home. | 111 N. 6th St. | 815/732–6876 | Free | May–early Oct., Thurs. 9–noon, Sun. 1–4.

Oregon Public Library Art Gallery. Works by early-20th-century artists from the Eagle's Nest, a local art colony, are displayed at this library and gallery. | 300 Jefferson St. | 815/732–2724 | Free | Mon.–Thurs. 9–8, Fri.–Sat. 9–4.

Pride of Oregon. Take a 15-mi, two-hour paddleboat ride on the Rock River to see the cliffs, forests, and towns on its banks. The boat departs twice daily from Maxson Riverside Restaurant. You can also take lunch, dinner, or buffet cruises. | 1469 Illinois St. | 815/732–6761 or 800/468–4222 | www.maxsonrestaurant.com | $12 sightseeing, $24 lunch, $30 dinner, $26 Sunday buffet | Apr.–mid-Nov., Mon.–Sat. 11 AM and 6:30 PM; Sunday 11 AM and 2 PM.

Soldiers' Monument. A 1916 war memorial by sculptor Loredo Taft in Courthouse Square at 4th Street. | Free | Daily.

Stronghold Conference Center. This retreat center on 465 acres overlooks the Rock River. A 25-room mansion is used for meetings and seminars. It's open to the public the first weekend in October for an old English fair, as part of the town's Autumn on Parade. At other times you can drive through the grounds. Camping is also available. | 1922 Rte. 2 N | 815/732–6111 | fax 815/732–7325 | Free; camping fee, reservations essential | Daily 9–4.

White Pines Forest State Park. This is the nation's southernmost stand of white pine, 8 mi west of Oregon and 5 mi south of Mt. Morris. The lovely conifers, which have long, silky needles, were once common in the area, but they have mostly disappeared. Hiking on limestone bluffs, cabin accommodations (*see* Lodging, *below*), restaurant. | 6712 W. Pines Rd., Mt. Morris | 815/946–3717 (park), 815/946–3817 (cabins) | www.dnr.state.il.us | Free | Daily 8–sunset; restaurant hours vary.

ON THE CALENDAR

OCT.: *Autumn on Parade.* During the first full weekend in October, you can join the revelry in the streets of downtown Oregon, where strolling madrigal and country singers, jugglers, and a parade roll by. You can enjoy a vintage car and motorcycle show, a petting zoo, pony rides, a pig scramble, a tug-o'-war spanning the river, and a reenactment of life at the turn of the century here, too. | 815/732–2100.

Dining

La Vigna. Italian. Fine northern Italian dining known for seafood, steaks, pasta, and veal dishes. | 2190 S. Daysville Rd. | 815/732–4413 or 800/806–4982 | $9–$17 | AE, D, DC, MC, V.

Maxson Riverside Restaurant. Italian. Dine on veal marsala, chicken piccata, pasta, or prime rib, overlooking Rock River. A large luncheon buffet and dinners are served. This is also the departure point for the *Pride of Oregon* paddlewheel tours. | 1469 Rte. 2 N | 815/732–6761 or 800/468–4222 | $11.50–$16.50 | AE, D, DC, MC, V | Closed Mon. No lunch.

Lodging

Paddle Wheel Inn. The suites here have balconies with panoramic vistas of Rock River at these accommodations a mile north of town. Restaurants, complimentary Continental breakfast, room service. In-room data ports, some in-room hot tubs, cable TV, some in-room VCRs. Hot tub, sauna. Gym. | 1457 N. Illinois Rte. 2, Oregon | 815/732–4540 or 800/468–4222 | fax 815/732–3404 | www.promotion.com/bwcvb | 42 rooms, 2 suites | $99 | AE, D, DC, MC, V.

Patchwork Inn. A two-story inn with front porches on both levels was built in 1835 as a brick Greek Revival home. Abraham Lincoln ate and slept here, and you can stay in the same room, with a fireplace and period furnishings. Braided rugs and handmade quilts adorn the rooms; the parlor is Victorian. Half a block from downtown, at the intersection of Routes 64 and 2. Complimentary Continental breakfast. Some in-room hot tubs. Cable TV. | 122 N. 3rd St. | 815/732–4113 | fax 815/732–6557 | www.essex1.com/people/patchworkinn | 10 rooms | $98–$128 | D, MC, V.

Pinehill Bed and Breakfast. This 1874 Italianate country villa with front porch and period furnishings is a chocolate-lover's delight. Fresh fudge is baked daily for afternoon tea, and the library is stocked with chocolate histories and recipe books. Complimentary breakfast. No TV. | 400 Mix St. | 815/732–2067 | 4 rooms (1 with shared bath) | $125–$145 | MC, V.

White Pines Inn. Rustic cabins and a restaurant nestle the middle of 385 acres of forest in White Pines State Park, 8 mi from Oregon. The cabins were constructed in the 1930s by the Civilian Conservation Corps. They have gas fireplaces, and three cabins have four adjoining units. No cooking is allowed in or around cabins. Story-telling in summer. Reservations are essential. Restaurant. Cable TV, some in-room VCRs, in-room phones. Hiking, volleyball, fishing. Playground. | 6712 W. Pines Rd., Mt. Morris | 815/946–3817 | fax 815/946–3006 | www.whitepinesinn.com | 25 cabins | $68 | D, MC, V | Sun. before Christmas to first Fri. in March.

OTTAWA

MAP 6, G3

(Nearby towns also listed: Morris, Peru, Utica)

Ottawa sits neatly at the juncture of the Fox and Illinois rivers. The downtown has a number of historic 19th-century buildings as well as Washington Park, the town square. Farming continues to be one of the area's chief livelihoods; the town of 18,600 also has some light industry.

Information: **Ottawa Area Chamber of Commerce and Industry** | 100 W. Lafayette St., 61350 | 815/433–0084 | www.ottawa.il.us.

Attractions

Buffalo Rock State Park. The focal point of the park, 5 mi west of Ottawa, is its quintet of effigy tumuli—large-scale earthen Indian mounds representing Illinois River animals. | Dee Bennett Rd. | 815/433–2220 | Free | Daily 8 AM–sunset.

Land of Oz Corn Maze. You can drive through this amazing 10-acre maze made of maize, where the corn is at least as high as an elephant's eye, in approximately an hour, depending on how many dead ends you hit. Sponsored by the Campfire Council of North Central Illinois. | 3262 E. 1951 Rd. | 815/434–4409 or 815/434–2103 | Adults $5 | Fri. 4–sunset, weekends noon–sunset, or by appointment.

Ottawa Scouting Museum. Collections of artifacts from Boy and Girl Scouting, including uniforms, badges, handbooks, and equipment. | 1100 Canal St. | 815/431–9353 | $3, special rates for children | Tues.–Wed. | Thurs.–Mon. 10–4.

Skydive Chicago. A skydiving training and jump center that also hosts special jump events. | Skydive Chicago Airport, 3215 E. 1969th Rd. | 815/433–0000 | fax 815/433–6806 | www.skydivechicago.com | Prices vary | Jan.–Feb. weekends, 9–sunset; Mar.–Memorial Day, Wed.–Sun. 9–sunset; Memorial Day–Labor Day, daily 8–sunset; Labor Day–Dec., Wed.–Mon., 9–sunset.

William Reddick Mansion. This antebellum Italianate mansion built in 1856 now houses the Ottawa visitors center. | 100 W. Lafayette St. | 815/434–2737 or 888/OTTAWA–4 | www.visit-ottawa-il.com | Free | Weekdays 9–5, Sat. 9–4, Sun. 10–2.

ON THE CALENDAR

JUNE: *Ottawa Ethnic Festival.* A celebration of cultural heritage through music, food, and crafts, the fourth weekend of June in Washington Square Park, across from the Visitors Center. | 815/434–2737.
JULY–AUG.: *Ottawa's Riverfest Celebration.* Paddleboat races, fireworks, crafts booths, food, and musical acts the last half week of July and first full week of August. | 815/434–2737.
OCT.: *Scarecrow Festival.* During the first weekend in October, the town of Ottawa heralds fall in Washington Square Park with hayrides, a petting zoo, a chili cook-off, and

many crafts and food booths, but the highlight of the celebration is the visitors' judging of the scarecrows designed by local businesses and organizations. | 815/434–2737.

Dining

Monte's Riverside Inn. Continental. Close to but not overlooking the Illinois River, this inn offers cocktails on the deck or in the gazebo, and serves seafood, steaks, pasta, and seasonal freshwater fish in curtained booths in the dining room paneled in rustic wood. Kids' menu. | 903 E. Norris Dr. | 815/434–5000 | Reservations essential | $20–$45 | AE, MC, V | No lunch Sat.–Tues.

Woody's Steak House. Continental. In the oak-paneled dining room here, favorites to try are the Portobello steak—a center-cut beef tenderloin with grilled onions and Portobello mushrooms—and the blackened duck. Kids' menu. | 1321 N. Lasalle St. | 815/433–2400 | $10.95–$21 | MC, V | No lunch.

Lodging

Holiday Inn Express. This three-story motel is 10 mi from Starved Rock State Park, walking distance to restaurants. Complimentary Continental breakfast. In-room data ports, some microwaves, some refrigerators, cable TV. Indoor pool. Hot tub. Laundry facilities. Business services. Some pets allowed. | 120 W. Stevenson Rd. | 815/433–0029 or 800/HOLIDAY | fax 815/433–0382 | www.basshotels.com | 70 rooms, 10 suites | $85; suites $100 | AE, D, DC, MC, V.

Marcia's Bed and Breakfast. This 250-acre farmstead off I–80 via Route 71 includes a turn-of-the-century house furnished with antiques and Native American art, a private cottage reflecting the stagecoach era, a horse barn, and other outbuildings. Days you can ride the horses here and evenings warm yourself by a bonfire. Complimentary breakfast. Some kitchenettes, some microwaves, some refrigerators, no TV in some rooms. Horseback riding. | 3003 Rte. 71 | 815/434–5217 | marbb@theramp.net | 4 rooms (2 with shared bath) | $45–$95 | No credit cards.

Ottawa Comfort Inn. Starved Rock State Park, Allen Park, and Illini State Park are within 10 mi of this typical chain hotel, near restaurants and cornfields. Complimentary Continental breakfast. In-room data ports, some microwaves, some refrigerators, some in-room hot tubs, cable TV. Indoor pool. Video games. Laundry facilities. Business services. | 510 E. Etna Rd. | 815/433–9600 or 800/228–5150 | fax 815/433–9696 | www.comfortinn.com | 53 rooms, 2 suites | $63, $85 suites | AE, D, DC, MC, V.

Ottawa Inn–Starved Rock. This standard motel is convenient to the interstate and a 20-minute drive from the area's state parks. Restaurant, bar. Cable TV. Indoor pool. Hot tub. Business services. | 3000 Columbus St. | 815/434–3400 | fax 815/434–3904 | 120 rooms | $39–$98 | AE, D, DC, MC, V.

Prairie Rivers Bed and Breakfast. This three-story 1890s Queen Anne home is on a bluff overlooking the Illinois River, and here you have great views of the waterway from the front porch, a sun room, and some of the bedrooms, which include the garrett suite with 18-ft ceilings; the Queen Anne room, with a mahogany bed; and a single-occupancy maid's room, with a wrought-iron bed. You can walk down the bluff to Allen Park, where you can fish, canoe, and simply stroll. Complimentary breakfast. No room phones, no TV. Water sports, boating, fishing. | 121 E. Prospect Ave. | 815/434–3226 | 4 rooms | $50–$150 | MC, V.

PEORIA

MAP 6, E5

(Nearby towns also listed: Bloomington–Normal, Havana, Lewiston)

Peoria, as in "How will it play in Peoria?," most often stands as a symbol of the Midwest middle of the road—not exotic, not extreme. But the city has a rich historical past that's anything but bland. French explorers Jolliet and Marquette explored this area in the late 1600s, and La Salle built Fort Crèvecoeur here in 1680. In the early 1900s, Peoria claimed some fame as a world-class distillery capital, thanks to the city's good water and abundant supply of corn. Today it boasts a thriving riverfront area, museums, a symphony, parks, and colleges. The population is 115,000.

Information: Peoria Area Convention and Visitors Bureau | 456 Fulton Ave., 61602 | 309/676–0303 or 800/747–0302 | www.peoria.org.

Attractions

Bradley University. An independent and privately endowed, coeducational institution, Bradley University was founded in 1897 as Bradley Polytechnic, by Lydia Moss Bradley, in memory of her husband and children. There are now 90 undergraduate programs in five colleges, as well as 13 graduate degrees in 22 academic areas. Tours given by appointment. | 1501 Bradley Ave. | 309/676–7611 | www.bradley.edu | Free | Daily.

Contemporary Art Center of Peoria. Above the Rhythm Kitchen restaurant, on the second and third floors of a riverfront coffee warehouse, two galleries retaining the structure's original wood columns, brick walls, and hardwood floors exhibit works by emerging regional artists alongside those by nationally renowned contemporary artists. You can observe art-in-the-making in open studios here, where classes are also offered, and enjoy special events such as blues, jazz, and poetry nights hosted by the center. | 305 S.W. Water St. | 309/674–6822 | www.peoriacac.org | Free | Tues.–Sat 11–5, Sun. noon–4.

Eureka College. The most famous alum of this small arts and sciences college, 18 mi west of Peoria, is Ronald Reagan, class of '32. | 300 E. College Ave., Eureka | 309/467–3721 | fax 309/467–6325 | www.eureka.edu | Free | Daily; Ronald Reagan exhibit 10–3.

Flanagan House. Maintained by the Peoria Historical Society, this house contains period furniture from the 1800s from the Peoria area. Tours are by appointment. | 942 N.E. Glen Oak Ave. | 309/674–1921 | $4.

Forest Park Nature Center. This 500-acre preserve in Peoria Heights has 7 mi of hiking trails, a nature store, and exhibits on the natural history of forests and prairies. | 5809 Forest Park Dr. | 309/686–3360 | fax 309/686–8820 | Free | Mon.–Sat. 9–5, Sun. 1–5.

Glen Oak Park and Zoo. Centrally located in town, the park has tennis courts, playgrounds, and an amphitheater. The zoo has 100 species of exotic animals. | 2218 N. Prospect Rd. | 309/686–3365 (zoo), 309/682–1200 (park) | www.peoriaparks.org, www.peoriazoo.org | Park free, zoo $3.75 | Park daily dawn–11 PM, zoo daily 10–5.

George L. Luthy Memorial Botanical Garden. Here you can stroll through 4 acres of botanical splendor including herb, perennial, and rose gardens, and a conservatory with a collection of rain-forest plants and seasonal flower shows. | 2218 N. Prospect Rd. | 309/686–3362 | www.peoriaparks.org | Free | Mon.–Sat. 10–5, noon–5 | Donation suggested.

Jubilee College State Historic Site. One of the state's oldest educational institutions, founded in 1840, is now a museum. It's 15 mi northwest of Peoria. | 11817 Jubilee College Rd., Brimfield | 309/243–9489 | $2 suggested donation | Nov.–Feb., daily 9–4; Mar.–Oct., daily 9–5.

Jubilee College State Park. Camping, cross-country skiing, and birding are popular activities here. The park is adjacent to the college. | 13921 W. Rte. 150, Brimfield | 309/446–3758 | Free; camping fee | Daily 8 AM–10 PM.

Lakeview Museum of Arts and Science. There are changing art, science, and folk art exhibitions, a gallery of Illinois folk art, and a discovery center with hands-on art and science activities for kids. | 1125 W. Lake Ave. | 309/686–7000 | www.lakeview-museum.org | $5; special rates for seniors and children | Tues., Thurs., Fri. 11–5; Wed. 11–8; Sat. 10–5; Sun. noon–5.

Planetarium. Shows here focus on astronomy through the ages. | 1125 W. Lake Ave. | 309/686–NOVA | $1 extra in addition to museum admission | Fall–spring, weekends, call for show times.

Metamora Courthouse State Historic Site. Abraham Lincoln practiced law in this 1845 courthouse 10 mi east of Peoria. | 113 E. Partridge St., Metamora | 309/367–4470 | Suggested donation $2 | Tues.–Sat. 9–noon and 1–5.

Pettengill-Morron House. The Peoria Historical Society maintains this elegant Victorian-era house-turned-museum built in 1868. | 1212 W. Moss Ave. | 309/674–1921 | fax 309/674–1882 | $4; special rates for children | By appointment only.

Spirit of Peoria. Take sightseeing and overnight cruises on the Illinois River on an authentic paddleboat. Departs from the landing at the foot of Main Street. | 100 N.E. Water St. | 309/636–6169 or 800/676–8988 | fax 309/676–3667 | www.spiritofpeoria.com | Varies | Call for times.

Theater. Peoria's theater scene is a lively mix of professional and community productions; dinner theaters are especially popular.
Corn Stock Theatre. The company produces musicals and comedies in a tent in summer; productions move indoors to Corn Stock Theatre Center for the winter. | Bradley Park | 309/676–2196 | fax 309/676–9036 | www.cornstocktheatre.com | Varies | June–Apr.
Peoria Players. The community theater presents six plays a season. | 4300 N. University St. | 309/688–4473 | fax 309/688–4483 | www.peoriaplayers.com | Prices vary with shows | Sept.–May.

Wheels O'Time Museum. Exhibits include tractors, antique cars, fire engines, and musical instruments, 8 mi north of Peoria. | 11923 N. Knoxville Ave.; Rte. 40 | 309/243–9020 | www.wheelsotime.org | $4; special rates for children | May–Oct., Wed.–Sun. noon–5.

Wildlife Prairie Park. This 2,000-acre zoological park about 10 mi west of Peoria displays native Illinois animals such as bobcats, bison, elk, and cougars, as well as farm animals, waterfowl, and birds of prey. Hike nature trails and visit the butterfly garden and pioneer farmstead. A restaurant is housed in a renovated railroad caboose, and there are lakeside cottages. | 3826 N. Taylor Rd. | 309/676–0998 | fax 309/676–7783 | www.wildlifepark.org | $5; special rates for children | Summer, daily 9–6:30; winter, daily 9–4:30 | Dec. 12–Mar. 11.

ON THE CALENDAR

JUNE: ***Steamboat Festival.*** This annual riverfront festival includes powerboat racing, sporting events, a carnival, concerts, and kids' events. | 309/681–0696.
NOV.–DEC.: ***Historic Homes Candlelight Tours.*** The Pettengill-Morron house and the John C. Flanagan home are decorated for the holidays. Tours, music, and treats. | 309/674–1921.

Dining

Crooked Waters Brewery and Pub. Contemporary. This waterfront brewery claims no pasta and no seafood but touts its crooked waters chicken—teriyaki-style, topped with grilled provolone cheese, scallions, mushrooms, and tomatoes. Accompany this with one of the beers, ales, or lagers, and admire the river-life and brew pub memorabilia. | 330 S.W. Water St. | 309/673–2739 | $8.50–$14 | AE, D, DC, MC, V | No lunch Sun.–Thurs.

The Grill on Fulton. Contemporary. In the Twin Towers Mall across from the Civic Center, this many-windowed room offers panoramic views along with its seafood and fresh fish—such as sea bass with a horseradish crust, served with mashed potatoes, crispy leeks, and chive oil. Live jazz Fri. nights. | 456 Fulton St. | 309/674–6870 | $14.95–$34.95 | AE, D, DC, MC, V | No lunch Sat. Closed Sun.

Joe's Crab Shack. Seafood. In Joe's tin-ceilinged dining room among maritime paraphernalia or outside overlooking the river, favorites include Old Bay–seasoned crabs served with corn, parsley potatoes, and slaw, and steamed-garlic barbecue. Kids' menu. | 110 S.W. Water | 309/671–2223 | $9.99–$23 | AE, D, DC, MC, V.

Jumer's. German. Dark woodwork and massive furniture reflect the Teutonic heritage of the area, as does the menu of hearty fare in Jumer's Castle Lodge hotel. Jumer Royal Beer is brewed from an old family recipe. Also try the Wiener schnitzel, sauerbraten, or Nurnburger pork roast. Entertainment Fri. and Sat. nights. Kids' menu. | 117 N. Western Ave. | 309/673–8181 | www.jumers.com | $10–$35 | AE, D, DC, MC, V | Breakfast also available.

Lindsay's on Liberty. Contemporary. The building's past is evident in this restaurant dining room's exposed-brick walls, pressed-tin ceilings, and wood paneling, where you can savor such contemporary fare as espresso-encrusted Angus fillet or praline-glazed salmon. Sample one of the wines from the vault downstairs. | 330 Liberty St. | 309/497–3300 | $13–$25 | AE, D, MC, V | No lunch weekends.

Paparazzi. Italian. A dark, intimate café 4 mi north of downtown Peoria, with a menu of pastas, veal dishes (try the veal saltimbocca), and other meat entrées. Extensive wine list. No smoking. | 4315 W. Voss St., Peoria Heights | 309/682–5205 | Reservations essential on weekends | $6–$12 | AE, D, DC, MC, V | Closed Sun., Mon. No lunch.

Rizzi's on State. Italian. A family-owned eatery in an old riverfront building with red-checked tablecloths and a mural of the old country. Try pollo marsala, tortellini Michaelangelo, pizza, stromboli, and other favorites. | 112 State St. | 309/673–2500 | $10–$19 | AE, MC, V | Closed Sun.

Rhythm Kitchen Music Café. Café. This former warehouse on the waterfront now houses a lively eatery where you can get quiche, sandwiches, salads, and spicy entrées—such as ginger-garlic chicken—and hear live music Friday and Saturday evenings. Thursdays you can get up on stage yourself for open-mike night. | 302 S.W. Water St. | 309/676–9668 | $6–$12.95 | MC, V | Breakfast also available. Closed Sun., Mon.

Spirit of Peoria. American. One Saturday a month, you can partake of the prime-rib dinner buffet on this stern-wheeler as it paddles the river for two hours and hosts a variety of stage shows, including mystery theater and ragtime music. | 100 N.E. Water St. | 309/636–6169 or 800/676–8988 | Reservations essential | $40 | AE, D, DC, MC, V | Closed Nov.–Apr.

Lodging

AmeriSuites. This three-story all-suites hotel behind Westlake Shopping Center caters to the business traveler, with executive suites outfitted with a large desk and office amenities. Complimentary breakfast. In-room data ports, cable TV. Indoor pool. Hot tub, gym. Laundry facilities. Business services, airport shuttle. | 2701 W. Lake Ave. | 309/681–2700 | fax 309/681–2701 | 124 suites | $80–$85 | AE, DC, MC, V.

Comfort Suites. An all-suites brick hotel next to I-74, 8 minutes northwest of downtown and 8 mi to Par-A-Dice Riverboat Casino. Complimentary pass to local health club. Complimentary Continental breakfast. In-room data ports, cable TV. Indoor pool. Hot tub. Business services. Some pets allowed. | 4021 N. War Memorial Dr. | 309/688–3800 or 800/228–5150 | www.comfortinn.com | 66 suites | $80 | AE, D, DC, MC, V.

Days Inn. This two-story brick hotel 8 mi east of Peoria has two couples-oriented suites with hot tubs. It's 7 mi from Par-A-Dice Riverboat Casino. Complimentary Continental breakfast. In-room data ports, some in-room hot tubs, cable TV. Indoor pool. Hot tub. Exercise room. Laundry facilities. Business services. | 150 W. Ashland Ave., Morton | 309/266–9933 or 800/DAYSINN | fax 309/266–9933 | www.daysinn.com | 46 rooms, 12 suites | $64; $74–$135 suites | AE, D, DC, MC, V.

Fairfield Inn by Marriott. A three-story hotel, 6 mi northwest of downtown, the convention center, and the casino, in the Northwoods Mall. Free pass to local health club 2 mi away. Complimentary Continental breakfast. In-room data ports, cable TV. Pool. Laundry service. Business services. | 4203 N. War Memorial Dr. | 309/686–7600 or 800/228–2800 | fax 309/686–0686 | www.fairfieldinn.com | 135 rooms | $69 | AE, D, DC, MC, V.

Glory Hill Bed and Breakfast. On a 5-acre lot in Chillicothe, 20 mi north of Peoria, you can stay in an 1840s home visited by Lincoln, the reason there's a room here named for the man and filled with memorabilia of his time. All rooms in the house are furnished with antiques, and the large veranda is a fine place to take your breakfast. Complimentary breakfast. Some in-room hot tubs, cable TV, in-room VCRs, no room phones. Outdoor pool. | 18427 N. Old Galena Rd., Chillicothe | 309/274–4228 | fax 309/691–3125 | 2 rooms | $75–$85 | AE, D, MC, V.

Hampton Inn–East Peoria. This five-story brick hotel overlooks the Illinois River, next to Par-A-Dice casino. It's 2 mi from downtown, 2 mi from Caterpillar headquarters, 4 mi from Illinois Central College, 5 mi from Bradley University. Complimentary Continental breakfast. In-room data ports, cable TV. Indoor pool. Hot tub. Exercise equipment. Business services. Airport shuttle. | 11 Winners Way, East Peoria | 309/694–0711 or 800/HAMPTON | fax 309/694–0407 | www.hampton-inn.com | 145 rooms, 9 suites | $89; $125 suites | AE, D, DC, MC, V.

Holiday Inn City Centre. This lavishly renovated nine-story tower, one of Peoria's tallest buildings, has a convention center that accommodates up to 1,400 people. Because it's geared to business travelers, an Avis car rental and six meeting rooms are on site. Caterpillar and the civic center are a block away. Restaurant, bar. In-room data ports, some kitchenettes, cable TV. Indoor pool. Barbershop. Exercise equipment, hot tub. Video games. Business services. Airport shuttle. Pets allowed. | 500 Hamilton Blvd. | 309/674–2500 or 800/474–2501 | fax 309/674–1205 | www.basshotels.com | 306 rooms, 21 suites | $108; suites $150–$250 | AE, D, DC, MC, V.

Honolka House. Twenty miles north of Peoria, on a double city-block lot neatly landscaped and stippled with trees, this 1905 home blends its turn-of-the-century architectural details—hardwood floors, pocket doors—with more contemporary furnishings. You can enjoy the quiet neighborhood and peaceful grounds from front and back decks or from the enclosed front porch. Complimentary Continental breakfast. Cable TV, some room phones. | 721 5th St., Chillicothe | 309/274–5925 | 3 rooms | $60–$80 | MC, V.

Hotel Pere Marquette. This independently owned 12-story downtown hotel looks as spiffy and stylish as it did in 1927, when it was built. Two restaurants, bar. In-room data ports, some refrigerators, cable TV. Exercise equipment. Business services. Airport shuttle. | 501 Main St.; I–74, exit 93A from west or 92 from east | 309/637–6500 or 800/447–1676 | fax 309/637–6500 | 288 rooms, 30 suites | $109; $200–$350 suites | AE, D, DC, MC, V.

Jumer's Castle Lodge Hotel. Elaborate woodwork and European paintings grace the lobby of this four-story, half-timber hostelry, just west of town. Some rooms have fireplaces, four-poster beds, and tapestries. Restaurant, bar. In-room data ports, cable TV, in-room VCRs. Indoor pool. Sauna, hot tub. Gym. Business services. Airport shuttle. Pets allowed. | 117 N. Western Ave. | 309/673–8040 or 800/285–8637 | fax 309/673–9782 | www.jumers.com | 175 rooms | $85–$95 | AE, D, DC, MC, V.

Mark Twain Hotel–East Peoria. Gaming enthusiasts appreciate the location of this independently owned two-story hotel in East Peoria, just half a mile from the Par-A-Dice casino and a mile from downtown. Walk to shopping plaza and restaurants. Restaurant, bar, complimentary breakfast, room service. In-room data ports, cable TV. Indoor pool. Hot tub, sauna. Exercise equipment. Laundry facilities. Business services, airport shuttle. | 401 N. Main St., East Peoria | 309/699–7231 | fax 309/698–7833 | www.marktwainhotel.com | 129 rooms, 2 suites | $59–$79 | AE, D, DC, MC, V.

Par-A-Dice Hotel. Across the river from Peoria, this eight-story hotel has art deco–style rooms with river views. Its casino, with slot machines, blackjack, and roulette, is on a boat on the river about 50 yards from the hotel. A complimentary shuttle will take you if you don't feel like walking. In-room data ports, some refrigerators, some in-room hot tubs, cable TV. | 7 Blackjack Blvd., East Peoria | 309/699–7711 or 800/547–0711 | www.par-a-dice.com | 208 rooms | $79–$250 | AE, D, DC, MC, V.

Red Roof Inn. This standard two-story motel is 3 mi west of town and 3 mi from Bradley University. Two restaurants are within walking distance. Free pass to local health club. Cable TV, some in-room VCRs. Laundry service. Business services. Some pets allowed. | 4031 N. War Memorial Dr. | 309/685–3911 or 800/REDROOF | fax 309/685–3941 | www.redroof.com | 108 rooms | $58 | AE, D, DC, MC, V.

Ruth's Bed and Breakfast. On 1 acre in the farmland just outside of Peoria proper, this country-style lace-curtained B&B has two rooms upstairs that share a bath, while the downstairs room has its own; there are flower gardens in the yard. Complimentary Continental breakfast. Some microwaves, no room phones, no TV. Laundry facilities. Pets allowed. | 10205 Eva La. | 309/243–5977 | 3 rooms (2 share a bath) | $45 | No credit cards.

Signature Inn. This reasonably priced motel 4 mi west of downtown Peoria is across the street from Northwoods Mall and adjacent to a small park. Complimentary Continental breakfast. In-room data ports, cable TV, some in-room VCRs. Pool. Exercise equipment. Business services. | 4112 N. Brandywine Dr. | 309/685–2556 or 800/822–5252 | www.signature-inns.com | 124 rooms, 2 suites | $69 | AE, D, DC, MC, V.

Sleep Inn. A three-story motel with indoor entrances is geared to the business traveler. Northwoods Mall is across the street. Complimentary Continental breakfast. In-room data ports, some in-room hot tubs, cable TV. Indoor pool. Gym. Laundry facilities. Airport shuttle. Pets allowed. | 4244 Brandywine Dr. | 309/682–3322 | 72 rooms | $58–$128 | AE, D, DC, MC, V.

PERU

MAP 6, F3

(Nearby towns also listed: Morris, Ottawa, Princeton, Utica)

Construction workers on the I & M Canal settled the area around Peru in the 1830s. Twenty years later the railroads brought still more residents to the area. Today, Peru and its sister city, La Salle, provide gateways to the scenic Starved Rock area. Peru's population is 9,300.

Information: Illinois Valley Area Chamber of Commerce | 300 Bucklin St. (Box 446), La Salle 61301 | 815/223–0227 | www.ivaced.org.

Attractions

Donnelley/Depue State Wildlife Area and Complex. Spread over two counties and a mile west of Peru, this 4,200-acre refuge has nature preserves, hiking and horse trails, and waterfowl hunting. There's fishing and boating on Lake De Pue. | 1001 W. 4th St. | 815/447–2353 | Free; hunting fee | Daily dawn–dusk.

ON THE CALENDAR

MAY: *Illinois State Morel Mushroom Hunting Championship.* On the first Saturday in May, you can join mushroom lovers at the Ruby Peterson Park in Magnolia (25 mi southwest of Peru). From here you are carted off to a secret spot (which changes each year) for a two-hour hunt, after which judging and awards in many categories for the found morels occurs back at the park. | 309/364–3319.

JUNE: *Taste of Illinois Valley.* Held in Centennial Park, this two-day festival includes food sampling, live music, games, rides and more. | 815/223–7904.

JULY: *National Championship Boat Races.* Powerboats compete for national titles in these races held the last full week of the month on Lake De Pue. Evening entertainment, food, music, and a carnival are also on the agenda. There's a $2 admission. | 815/447–2848.

AUG.: *National Sweet Corn Festival.* In addition to 50 tons of roasted sweet corn, this festival, which takes places the second weekend of the month, has arts and crafts, a flea market, carnival, and beer garden with live bands. The festival is in downtown Mendota, 15 mi north of Peru. | 815/539–6507.

Dining

The Maples. Contemporary. This family-style restaurant has a soup and salad bar and a popular Sunday buffet with carved roast beef, prime ribs, steaks, and ham. Kids' menu. | 1401 Shooting Park Rd. | 815/223–1938 | $6.50–$27.95 | MC, V | No dinner Sun., closed Mon.

Red Door Inn. Continental. There are five dining rooms around an atrium (including a real train caboose made into a dining car) at this former saloon dating from the late 19th century. Erté original sculptures and paintings adorn the walls. On the menu are tableside flaming specialties (steak Diane) and seafood (1-lb lobster). Salad bar. Kids' menu. Friday night seafood buffet. | 1701 Water St. | 815/223–2500 | $14–$23 | AE, D, MC, V | No lunch weekends.

Uptown Grill. Contemporary. This restaurant has a covered, screened-in patio where you can dine on steaks, seafood, pasta dishes, fajitas, and sandwiches. It's 2 mi south of I–80. Kids' menu. | 601 1st St., La Salle | 815/224–4545 | www.uptowngrill.com | Reservations essential weekends | $12–$23.50 | AE, D, DC MC, V.

Lodging

Comfort Inn. This standard motel is 6 mi from Lake De Pue, and about 10 mi from Starved Rock. Complimentary Continental breakfast. In-room data ports, some refrigerators, some in-room hot tubs, cable TV. Pool. Laundry facilities. Business services. | 5240 Trompeter Rd. | 815/223–8585 or 800/228–5150 | fax 815/223–9292 | www.choicehotels.com | 50 rooms, 1 suite | $66, $85 suite | AE, D, DC, MC, V.

Econolodge. Right off I–80 is this two-story motel ¼ mile north of Peru. Restaurant. Some kitchenettes, cable TV. Indoor pool. Video games. Laundry facilities. Business services. Free parking. Pets allowed (fee). | 1840 May Rd. | 815/224–2500 or 800/55ECONO | fax 815/224–3693 | 104 rooms | $60 | AE, D, DC, MC, V.

Ramada Limited. These standard motel accommodations are 3 mi from downtown. It's less than a mile from the mall, as well as Wal-Mart and other chain stores. Complimentary Continental breakfast. In-room data ports, some in-room hot tubs, some in-room VCRs, cable TV. Indoor pool. Hot tub. Exercise equipment. Laundry facilities. Business services. | 4389 Venture Dr. | 815/224–9000 or 800/298–2054 | fax 815/224–9100 | www.ramada.com | 64 rooms | $63–$69 | AE, D, DC, MC, V.

Super 8. This motel is 10 mi from Starved Rock and Matthiessen state parks and 3 mi north of downtown Peru. Complimentary Continental breakfast. Some refrigerators, some microwaves, cable TV, in-room movies. Laundry facilities. Pets allowed (fee). | 1851 May Rd. | 815/223–1848 or 800/800–8000 | 61 rooms, 2 suites | $57.99, $67.99 suites | AE, D, DC, MC, V.

PETERSBURG

MAP 6, E6

(Nearby towns also listed: Havana, Jacksonville, Lincoln, Springfield)

Spoon River Anthology poet Edgar Lee Masters is buried in a cemetery here, as is Ann Rutledge, the legendary sweetheart of Abraham Lincoln. This agricultural community of 2,339 is also the seat of Menard County.

Information: Petersburg Chamber of Commerce | 125 S. 7th St., 62675 | 217/632–7363 | www.petersburgil.com.

Attractions

Edgar Lee Masters Memorial Home. The author of *Spoon River Anthology* lived in this house as a young boy; today memorabilia of his life and works is displayed here. | 8th St. and Jackson | 217/632–2187 or 217/632–2156 | Donation suggested | Memorial Day–Labor Day Tues.–Sat. 10–noon and 1–3 | Closed Sun.–Mon.; call for an appointment.

Lincoln's New Salem State Historic Site. This restored 20-building village is on the site where Lincoln spent some of his young adult years (1831–1837). Crafts and skills demonstrations take place throughout the season. Campers can stay on the grounds, which are 2 mi south of Petersburg. | Rte. 97, 2 mi south of Petersburg | 217/632–4000 | fax 217/632–4010 | www.lincolnsnewsalem.com | $2; camping $3–$11 | Daily.

Theatre in the Park. This theater offers outdoor performances of historic-themed shows and musical presentations in summer. | 800/710–9290 | $7; special rates for kids | June–Aug., Fri.–Sun. 8 PM.

ON THE CALENDAR

JULY: *Summer Festival at New Salem.* This festival has crafts demonstrations and re-creations of 19th-century life the first weekend of the month at Lincoln's New Salem State Historic Site. There's a $2 suggested donation. | 217/632–4000.

AUG.: *"Prairie Tales" at New Salem.* Story-telling performances incorporating literature, drama, and music take place the first weekend in August at Lincoln's New Salem State Historic Site. There's a $2 suggested donation. | 217/632–4000.

SEPT.: *Traditional Music Festival.* This festival offers demonstrations and performances of early 19th-century music and dancing during a weekend of the month. Folk and bluegrass shows take place throughout the village. | 217/632–4000.

OCT.: *Candlelight Tour of New Salem.* During this nighttime tour of the village, homes and pathways are illuminated with candlelit lanterns. Interpreters in period clothing are available. It's held the first weekend of the month at Lincoln's New Salem State Historic Site. A $2 donation is suggested. | 217/632–4000.

Dining

Clara's Covered Tea Room American. Chandeliers light up this Victorian-style restaurant and antique mirrors hang over the fireplace beside framed vintage prints. The menu changes daily, but frequent specials are the kishke, cream of potato soup, chicken salad, and bread pudding. | 113 S. 7th St. | 217/632–5074 | No dinner. Closed Sun. and Mon. | $3–$5 | No credit cards.

Third Berry Lincoln Tavern. Expose yourself to a central Illinois culinary extravaganza at this small town restaurant that commemorates President Lincoln (photographs of him are on the walls). Typical central Illinois fare includes the horse shoe, which is a piece of toast, with meat, french fries, and cheese sauce drizzled over the top. Also popular is the chili. Desserts aren't offered, but it's rare that anyone comes out of this downtown place hungry. | 107 S. 7th St. 62675 | No credit cards | $2–$5 | 217/632–3383.

Lodging

The Oaks Bed and Breakfast. Make advance arrangements and you can also have a seven-course dinner at this Victorian bed and breakfast. Perched on a bluff overlooking Petersburg, the inn is on 5½ oak-treed acres four blocks west of the town square. Three of the rooms have fireplaces (one has two) and all are furnished with period pieces. Murder mystery weekends take place 10 times a year. Complimentary breakfast. No room phones, no TV in some rooms. | 510 W. Sheridan Rd. | 217/632–5444 or 888/724–6257 | www.petersburgil.com | 5 rooms | $70–$130 | D, MC, V.

PRAIRIE DU ROCHER

(Nearby town also listed: Chester)

French Christmas and New Year's customs are still observed in this tiny, picturesque village of 650 residents in southern Illinois that was founded in 1722.

Information: Prairie du Rocher Village Clerk's Office | 209 Henry St., 62277 | 618/284–7171.

Attractions

Fort de Chartres. This 1720 stone fort 4 mi from town was named in honor of Louis duc de Chartres, son of the regent of France. It was the seat of the French colonial government. | 1340 Rte. 155 | 618/284–7230 | Free | Daily 9–5.

ON THE CALENDAR

JUNE: *Rendezvous.* On the first full weekend in June, you can travel back in time while wandering through the more than 450 juried living-history campsites set up at Fort de Chartres on Route 155. On the agenda are such events as gun and cannon competitions; you can also dance to live music and sample the variety of foods sold here. | 618/284–7230.

Dining

La Maison du Rocher Country Inn. French. You can satisfy your appetite for hearty fare from the Alsatian countryside, such as sausage dishes, roast pork and dressing, and highly seasoned bouillons and French onion soup, in this limestone, tile-floored dining room with wrought-iron chandeliers. | 2 Duclos St. | 618/284–3463 | $5.95–$12.95 | AE, MC, V | Breakfast also available Fri.–Sun. Closed Mon.

Lodging

La Maison du Rocher Country Inn. On Duclos at the corner of Main Street, right in the middle of town, this two-story limestone bed-and-breakfast dates to around 1885. It has oak floors and claw-foot tubs, and a four-poster cherrywood and white wrought-iron beds in its guest rooms. Complimentary breakfast. Some refrigerators. No TV. | 2 Duclos St. | 618/284–3463 | fax 618/284–3463 | 3 rooms | $55–$65 | AE, D, MC, V.

PRINCETON

(Nearby towns also listed: Bishop Hill, Kewanee, Peru)

Princeton was host to a number of Underground Railroad stops, including Owen Lovejoy Homestead and Colton Schoolhouse that you can visit today. Gift and antiques shops line the central shopping district. The town is also close to the Hennepin Canal Recreation Area, popular for fishing, hiking, and biking. It's the seat of Bureau County, and has a population of 7,200.

Information: Princeton Chamber of Commerce, Prouty Building | 435 S. Main St., 61356 | 815/875–2616 | www.princeton-il.com.

Attractions

Bureau County Historical Society Museum. This four-story museum has a genealogy library and displays from fossils and Native American artifacts to pioneer utensils and Civil War memorabilia. | 109 Park Ave. W | 815/454–2184 | Free | Wed.–Mon. 1–5.

Hennepin Canal Parkway State Park. This 104.5-mi linear park spans five counties. The park has many picnic areas, and you can also hike, ride horses, fish, bike, boat, canoe, and hunt. The visitor center is 1 mi south of I–80, just west of Route 40, 12 mi west of Princeton. | 16006 875 E. St., Sheffield | 815/454–2328 | Free | Daily.

Owen Lovejoy Homestead and Colton Schoolhouse. This former station on the Underground Railroad, 2 blocks east of Princeton, is furnished with 19th-century pieces. | 1103 E. Peru St. | 815/875–2616 | fax 815/875–1156 | $2 | May–Sept., Fri.–Sun. 1–4; and by appointment.

ON THE CALENDAR

SEPT.: *Homestead Festival.* This three-day event the second weekend of the month has tours of the Bureau County Historical Society Museum, live entertainment, a barbecue sponsored by the county pork producers, kids' activities, an ice cream social, art show, beer garden, parade, and more. | 815/875–2616.

OCT.: *Shadows of Blue and Gray.* This 700 person Civil War reenactment takes place the first weekend of October at Princeton's City-County Park. The largest reenactment in the state of Illinois, it also features a Ladies' Style Show and a Military Ball with period band. | 815/875–2616.

Dining

Blarney's Pub. American. This pub owner sponsors race cars, so there's racing paraphernalia scattered about the only place in the area where you can get a Chicago-style hot dog. Blarney's also serves burgers, grilled-cheese sandwiches, and racks of ribs, along with its many brews. | 2209 N. Main St. | 815/879–8055 | $3.95–$14.95 | D, MC, V | Closed Sun. No dinner Mon.–Wed.

Oak Room Café. Contemporary. This casual downtown café serves sandwiches, homemade soup, and pizza as well as Sunday brunch. The antiques displayed are also for sale. | 432 S. Main St. | 815/875–1363 | Daily | $3.95–$6.95 | D, MC, V | No dinner.

Prime Quarters Steak House. Steak. From the case next to the two big grills here, you can select your cut of beef, chops, or fish to go with the potato and Texas toast, also prepared on the grill, and selections from the salad bar in this restaurant dressed with oak and brass and hanging plants. You can even grill your meat yourself. | 250 E. Backbone Rd. | 815/872–3500 | $14.95 | AE, D, DC, MC, V | No lunch.

Lodging

Comfort Inn Princeton. On the north edge of town, this motel is 5 mi to antiques shopping and 8 mi to the Lovejoy Homestead. Complimentary Continental breakfast. Some microwaves, some refrigerators, cable TV. Indoor pool. Laundry facilities. Business services. No-smoking rooms. | 2200 N. Main St. | 815/872–3300 or 800/228–5150 | fax 815/872–2306 | www.comfortinn.com | 41 rooms, 2 suites | $66, $71 suites | AE, D, DC, MC, V.

Princeton Days Inn. Also in the northern part of town, this motel is 1 mi from Sherwood Antique Mall and 3 mi from the Hennepin Canal State Park. Bar, complimentary Continental breakfast. Some microwaves, some refrigerators, cable TV. Pool. Laundry facilities. Business services. Pets allowed (fee). | 2238 N. Main St. | 815/875–3371 or 800/DAYSINN | fax 815/872–1600 | www.daysinn.com | 85 rooms, 2 suites | $60, $89 suites | AE, D, DC, MC, V.

Yesterday's Memories Bed & Breakfast. This 1852 home is three blocks from Main Street where you can peruse many of Princeton's antique stores. These Victorian accommodations include the Coach House Suite with its countrified furnishings and a private bath, and the innkeepers here share organic produce from their garden with you. Complimentary breakfast. Microwave, refrigerator, no TV in some rooms. No smoking. Pets allowed. | 303 E. Peru St. | 815/872–7753 | 2 room (with shared bath), 1 suite | $65 | No credit cards.

QUINCY

(Nearby town also listed: Nauvoo)

Because of its location across the Mississippi from Missouri—Illinois was not a slave state and Missouri was—Quincy was an important stop on the Underground Railroad. Quincy was founded in 1822 by John Wood, a native New Yorker. Later, scores of German immigrants who had come to New Orleans by boat continued up the river and settled in Quincy. Today, this town of 42,000 boasts several major historical districts, including a downtown with buildings that span the period between 1850 and 1930; the East End; and German Village, settled by Quincy's early German residents.

Information: Quincy Convention and Visitors Bureau | 300 Civic Center Plaza, Suite 237, 62301 | 217/223–1000 | www.quincy-cvb.org.

Attractions

Gardner Museum of Architecture and Design. Originally the Quincy Free Public Library and Reading Room, this building was constructed in 1889. Exhibits today focus on architecture, particularly local styles. There's also a stained-glass-window gallery. | 332 Maine St. | 217/224–6873 | fax 217/224–3303 | $2; special rates for senior citizens and students | Mar.–Dec., Tues.–Sun. 1–5.

John Wood Mansion. This restored home of the former Illinois governor six blocks from downtown also has a genealogical reference library. | 425 S. 12th St. | 217/222–1835 | $2; special rates for students | June–Aug., daily 1–4; other times call for hours. Library open year-round weekdays 10-2.

Quincy Museum. Exhibits on dinosaurs, the Mississippi River, wildlife, and Native Americans trace the history of the region in this 1890s mansion five blocks east of downtown. The first floor has been restored to the period. | 1601 Maine St. | 217/224–7669 | fax 217/224–9323 | quincymuse@hotmail.com | $2; special rates for kids | Tues.–Sun. 1–5.

ON THE CALENDAR

MAY: *Dogwood Festival.* This kickoff to spring the first weekend of the month includes a parade, crafts fair, food, and other activities in Washington Park, off Maine Street. | 217/222–7980.

AUG.: *World Free-Fall Convention.* This is the largest festival of its kind in the world. Plane shows and tours, and hot-air balloon rides are some of the 10 days of events that take place at Quincy Regional Municipal Airport in the first part of the month. There are fees if you want to skydive. Prices vary, and pre-registration is recommended. | 217/222–5867.

Dining

The Pier Restaurant. Contemporary. This dining room's fountain and views of the river create a tranquil environment, where you can dine on catfish cakes or horseradish-encrusted fish as well as freshly baked pizza dough and homemade pastas covered in the Pier's special toppings. | 401 Bayview Dr. | 217/221–0020 | $8.95–$19.95 | AE, MC, V.

Tiramisu. Italian. Housed in an 1800s structure on the corner of 3rd and Hampshire streets, this restaurant has an interior reminiscent of the old country with its photographs of the Italian countryside and its warm yellow-sponged walls. Its seasonal menu changes weekly and includes such dishes as fettuccine al salmone, portobello ravioli, and rigatoni with fresh mozzarella and basil. | 137 N. 3rd St. | 217/222–9560 | $5–$18.95 | AE, MC, V | Closed Sun. No lunch Sat.

Vintage Internationale. Mediterranean. The optional seafood or fish platter is what distinguishes a seven-course from an eight-course meal at this informal, prix fixe restaurant, where exposed rafters, brick walls, and hardwood floors create a French country atmosphere. If you call in advance you can arrange to have lion and bear. There's some outside seating. | 330 S. 8th St. | 217/228–9463 | $20–$25 includes three glasses of wine | AE, D, DC, MC, V.

Lodging

The Kaufmann House Bed & Breakfast. You can enjoy views of treelined Hampshire Street from bay windows in most of the rooms in this Victorian home, built in 1885, which also has a patio, and a deck off of one of the suites, surrounded by flower gardens. All rooms have private baths. Complimentary breakfast. Some refrigerators, no room phones, TV in common area. | 1641 Hampshire St. | 217/223–2502 | 2 rooms, 1 suite | $70 | No credit cards.

Quincy Holiday Inn. Right next to the convention center, this hotel also has views of the Mississippi. Restaurant, 2 bars, complimentary breakfast, room service. In-room data ports, microwaves, refrigerators, cable TV, in-room VCRs. Indoor pool. Hot tub. Gym. Volleyball. Video games. Laundry facilities. Business services, airport shuttle. Pets allowed (fee). No-smoking rooms. | 201 S. 3rd St. | 217/222–2666 or 800/HOLIDAY | fax 217/222–3238 | www.basshotels.com | 151 rooms, 2 suites | $89.50, $139.50 suites | AE, D, DC, MC, V.

Quincy Riverside Days Inn. This downtown motel is across from the convention center and perched on a bluff overlooking the Mississippi. | 121 rooms. Restaurant, bar, complimentary breakfast. In-room data ports, some refrigerators, microwaves, cable TV. Pool. Laundry facilities. Business services. Pets allowed (fee). No-smoking rooms. | 200 Maine St. | 217/223–6610 or 800/329–7466 | fax 217/223–DAYS | www.daysinn.com | AE, D, DC, MC, V.

Travelodge. This motel a block from the Civic Center is on a bluff overlooking the Mississippi River. Complimentary Continental breakfast. Some microwaves, some refrigerators, cable TV. Pool. Laundry facilities. Business services. Pets allowed (fee). | 200 S. 3rd St. 62301 | 217/222–5620 or 800/578–7878 | fax 217/224–2582 | www.travelodge.com | 67 rooms | $58 | AE, D, DC, MC, V.

W. T. Dwire House. This turn-of-the-century Queen Anne–style home, in the heart of town by the shopping district, has hardwood floors and oak and butternut woodwork throughout, working fireplaces, a century-old marble vanity, and a collection of firefighters' memorabilia from three generations of firefighters in the family. You can relax on the brick patio or wander the grounds with its pond and fountain. Complimentary breakfast. In-room data ports, TV in common area. | 1621 Vermont St. | 217/228–2023 | fax 217/223–7176 | www.wtdwire@rnet.com | 3 rooms | $55–$75 | No credit cards.

RANTOUL

MAP 6, H5

(Nearby towns also listed: Champaign and Urbana, Clinton, Danville)

Chanute Air Force Base, which is no longer open, was built in 1917 in less than 60 days to train World War I fighter pilots—for many years it was the dominant presence in town. Today Rantoul has 15,000 residents and is geared to both industry and agriculture.

Information: **Rantoul Chamber of Commerce** | 100 W. Sangamon Ave., Suite 101, 61866 | 217/893–3323 | www.rantoulchamber.com.

Attractions

Chanute Aerospace Museum. Exhibits in this World War II hangar in southern Rantoul focus on airplanes, underground missile silos, and Rantoul history; there's also a POW room. | 1011 Pacesetter Dr., I–57, exit Rte. 136 | 217/893–1613 | fax 217/893–3970 | www.aeromuseum.org | $5; special rates for senior citizens and kids | Mon.–Sat. 10–5, Sun. noon–5.

Dining

Century Restaurant. American. This restaurant's self-proclaimed "middle-American cooking" includes an open-face hamburger served with mashed potatoes, and a rib-eye steak sandwich with fries. A neon Pepsi sign outside beckons visitors. | 105 S. Century Blvd. | 217/893–0550 | $4.25–$6.95 | AE, D, DC, MC, V | Closed Tues.

Lodging

Best Western Heritage Inn. A mile from Chanute Aerospace Museum, this motel is also 1 mi west of Rantoul and close to restaurants. Complimentary Continental breakfast. Cable TV. Pool. Hot tub, sauna. Pets allowed. | 420 S. Murray Rd. | 217/892–9292 or 800/528–1234 | fax 217/892–4318 | www.bestwestern.com | 46 rooms, 2 suites | $72.98, $88.98 suites | AE, D, DC, MC, V.

Better N Grandmas Overniters. At the end of Main Street in downtown Rantoul, this no-frills homestead is a complete anomaly at $10 per person per night. One of the three rooms in this three-floored abode can house a whole family with its five beds and one crib. Complimentary Continental breakfast. No room phones. Cable TV. | 102 S. Meyers St. 61866 | 217/893–0469 | 3 rooms (with shared bath) | $10 per person | No credit cards.

Days Inn. This motel in downtown Rantoul is close to restaurants. Bar. Cable TV. Indoor pool. Pets allowed (fee). | 801 W. Champaign St. | 217/893–0700 or 800/329–7466 | www.daysinn.com | 80 rooms, 1 suite | $49–$58, $70 suite | AE, D, DC, MC, V.

RICHMOND

MAP 6, G1

(Nearby towns also listed: Antioch, McHenry, Woodstock)

Richmond only has a few streets, but they're packed with antiques and specialty stores (quilts, candles, etc.). This little town (population 1,100), just south of the Wisconsin border and the Lake Geneva area, is a favorite destination for day-trippers from Chicago and Milwaukee.

Information: Richmond/Spring Grove Chamber of Commerce | Main St. (Box 475), 60071 | 815/678–7742 | www.Richmond-il.com.

ON THE CALENDAR

AUG.: *Richmond Round Up Days.* The last weekend in August this festival brings everyone out onto Main and Broadway in Richmond, where you can hear live blues and jazz, shops welcome browsing, and food and beer vendors go al fresco. Festivities include lots of carnival activities for kids. | 815/678–4040.

NOV.: *Christmas of Yesteryear.* Main Street and Broadway are transformed into an old-fashioned winter wonderland for Richmond's annual tree lighting ceremony on Thanksgiving weekend, which includes caroling, wagon rides, and a visit from Santa Claus. Cookies and cocoa are served to kids at the American Legion Hall on Route 173 while parents get started on their Christmas shopping. | 815/678–4040.

Dining

Dog & Suds. Fast Food. Just like in the good old days, you can drive right up and order hot dogs, hamburgers, chicken, and fries—and home-brewed root beer—from the sometimes poodle-skirted carhops here. Old-fashioned prices, too. | 11015 U.S. 12 60071 | 815/678–7011 | $1.40–$5.00 | No credit cards | Closed Oct.–Apr.

Doyle's Pub and Eatery. American/Casual. On the corner of 12th and Mill Streets, this colorful place serves its burgers, pizzas, steaks, and brews among Beatles, John Wayne, and old circus memorabilia. Once an old mill, the place has a deck you can eat on. Kids' menu. | 5604 Mill St. | 815/678–3623 | $8.95–$17.95 | AE, D, MC, V | Closed Mon.

International House of Wine and Cheese/American Café. Café. A retail wine-and-cheese deli with traditional red-and-green awnings out front, this market is also a pleasant spot to enjoy the popular Belgian waffles, panfried/oven-baked omelettes, and assortment of salads and sandwiches. | 11302 U.S. 12 | 815/678–4573 | $5–$8 | DC, MC, V | Breakfast also available. No dinner Sun.–Thurs.

Outfitters. American. Wild game such as pheasant, quail, venison, and duck, is the specialty at this restaurant, which is also a hunt club. Steaks and fresh seafood are also available. Bands perform on weekends. | 5016 Rte. 173 | 815/678–3271 | www.outfittershc.com | $10–$15 | D, MC, V.

Lodging
Days Inn. Within a few blocks of antiques shopping, this motel is in the northern part of town. It's also 5 mi to fishing, golfing, skiing, and other recreation in Chain O'Lakes and Lake Geneva. Complimentary Continental breakfast. Satellite TV. Pool. Some pets allowed (fee). | 11200 N. U.S. 12 | 815/678–4711 or 800/DaysInn | fax 815/678–4623 | www.daysinn.com | 60 rooms | $75–$110 | AE, D, DC, MC, V.

ROCKFORD

MAP 6, F1

(Nearby towns also listed: DeKalb, Freeport, Oregon)

The Rock River winds its way through downtown Rockford, which was originally christened Midway in the 1830s for its location halfway between Chicago and Galena. Rockford started as an industrial center and has remained very much of one. But this city of 140,000 is also home to a number of specialty museums, displaying everything from Illinois wildlife to Swedish artifacts; in addition, there's a lively arts scene.

Information: **Rockford Area Convention and Visitors Bureau** | 211 N. Main St., 61101-1010 | 815/963–8111 or 800/521–0849 | fax 815/963–4298 | www.gorockford.com.

Attractions
Anderson Japanese Gardens. This formal Japanese garden east of downtown has waterfalls, koi ponds, footpaths, and many peaceful nooks and crannies. | 340 Spring Creek Rd. | 815/229–9390 | www.andersongardens.org | $4; special rates for senior citizens and students | Mon.–Sat. 10–4, Sun. noon–4.

Burpee Museum of Natural History. A simulated Pennsylvania coal forest at this museum on the west side of town features fake thunderstorms to dramatize prehistoric times. Dioramas of natural history scenes, a Native American gallery, and a skeletal cast of a Tyrannosaurus rex round out the scene. | 737 N. Main St. | 815/965–3132 | fax 815/965–2703 | www.burpee.org | $4; special rates for kids | Summer, Mon.–Sat. 10–5, Sun. noon–5; fall–spring, Tues.–Sat. 10–5, Sun. noon-5.

Coronado Theatre. Built in 1927, this renovated building is a perfect example of an atmospheric old movie house and is listed on the National Register for Historic Places. Its stage has seen many great live performances from the likes of Louis Armstrong, Benny Goodman, and Jerry Seinfeld. | 314 N. Main St. | 815/968–5222 | www.coronadotheatre.com.

Davis Park at Founder's Landing. In this village green in which you can stroll and picnic, there is a larger-than-life sculpture of the region's three founders, Thatcher Blake, Germanicus Kent, and Lewis Lemon, an Alabama slave. | Wyman and Church Sts. | 815/968–5600 | Free | Daily.

Discovery Center Museum. There are more than 200 hands-on science and art exhibits, as well as an outdoor discovery park in this science and arts museum for kids a block north

KODAK'S TIPS FOR PHOTOGRAPHING LANDSCAPES AND SCENERY

Landscape
- Tell a story
- Isolate the essence of a place
- Exploit mood, weather, and lighting

Panoramas
- Use panoramic cameras for sweeping vistas
- Don't restrict yourself to horizontal shots
- Keep the horizon level

Panorama Assemblage
- Use a wide-angle or normal lens
- Let edges of pictures overlap
- Keep exposure even
- Use a tripod

Placing the Horizon
- Use low horizon placement to accent sky or clouds
- Use high placement to emphasize distance and accent foreground elements
- Try eliminating the horizon

Mountain Scenery: Scale
- Include objects of known size
- Frame distant peaks with nearby objects
- Compress space with long lenses

Mountain Scenery: Lighting
- Shoot early or late; avoid midday
- Watch for dramatic color changes
- Use exposure compensation

Tropical Beaches
- Capture expansive views
- Don't let bright sand fool your meter
- Include people

Rocky Shorelines
- Vary shutter speeds to freeze or blur wave action
- Don't overlook sea life in tidal pools
- Protect your gear from sand and sea

In the Desert
- Look for shapes and textures
- Try visiting during peak bloom periods
- Don't forget safety

Canyons
- Research the natural and social history of a locale
- Focus on a theme or geologic feature
- Budget your shooting time

Rain Forests and the Tropics
- Go for mystique with close-ups and detail shots
- Battle low light with fast films and camera supports
- Protect cameras and film from moisture and humidity

Rivers and Waterfalls
- Use slow film and long shutter speeds to blur water
- When needed, use a neutral-density filter over the lens
- Shoot from water level to heighten drama

Autumn Colors
- Plan trips for peak foliage periods
- Mix wide and close views for visual variety
- Use lighting that accents colors or creates moods

Moonlit Landscapes
- Include the moon or use only its illumination
- Exaggerate the moon's relative size with long telephoto lenses
- Expose landscapes several seconds or longer

Close-Ups
- Look for interesting details
- Use macro lenses or close-up filters
- Minimize camera shake with fast films and high shutter speeds

Caves and Caverns
- Shoot with ISO 1000+ films
- Use existing light in tourist caves
- Paint with flash in wilderness caves

From *Kodak Guide to Shooting Great Travel Pictures* © 2000 by Fodor's Travel Publications

of downtown. | 711 N. Main St. | 815/963–6769 | fax 815/968–0164 | www.discoverycenter-museum.org | $4; special rates for kids | Summer, Mon.–Sat. 10–5, Sun. noon–5; fall–spring, Mon.–Sat. 10–5, Sun. noon–5.

Erlander Home Museum. The first brick home in Rockford, this house in the center of town was built by a Swedish family in 1871. Today it's a museum run by the Swedish Historical Society, with antiques from 1890 and memorabilia from early Swedish settlers in the area. | 404 S. 3rd St. | 815/963–5559 | $3 | Sun. 2–4, or by appointment.

Forest City Queen. This large, pontoon-style boat has 45-minute narrated Rock River cruises; lunch and dinner excursions are also available. | 324 N. Madison St. | 815/987–8894 | Prices vary | June–Aug., Tues.–Fri., hourly 11–3; weekends, hourly noon–4; early Sept., weekends hourly noon–4.

Haight Village Historic District. Rockford's first downtown area and a fashionable neighborhood at the turn of the century, this stretch of East State Street is a fine example of the changes in architecture from its first settlers through its development as an industrial city. The Peterson House, now business offices, was built in 1873 and is a stunning example of the Victorian Gothic style. | E. State St. between Prospect and Longwood Sts. | 800/521–0849 | Free | Daily.

Klehm Arboretum. The Klehm Arboretum is jointly owned and operated by the Northern Illinois Botanical Society and the Winnebago County Forest Preserve, and you can peruse its 155-acre property, which includes a fountain garden and many demonstration gardens, such as butterfly, lily, Irish, herb, heritage, peony, grass, and prehistoric gardens. Guided tours and golf-cart tours available by arrangement for additional charge. | 2701 Clifton Ave. | 815/965–8146 | fax 815/965–5914 | www.klehm.org | $2 | Labor Day–Memorial Day, daily 9–4, Memorial Day–Labor Day, daily 9–8.

Magic Waters Water Park. Illinois' largest water park, 3 mi east of downtown Rockford, has a wave beach, slides, and tube rental. | 7820 N. Cherry Vale Blvd., Cherry Valley | 815/332–3260 or 800/373–1679 | www.magicwaterswaterpark.com | $16; special rates for kids and senior citizens | Memorial Day–Labor Day, daily 10–6.

Midway Village and Museum Center. Rockford's history is spotlighted in this museum on the east side of town that contains a re-created village, and industrial exhibits. | 6799 Guilford Rd. | 815/397–9112 | fax 815/397–9156 | www.midwayvillage.com | $5; special rates for kids | Call for hours.

Rock Cut State Park. In addition to some 3,000 acres of hiking and biking, this park on the north side of Rockford has fishing on two lakes, and cross-country skiing, snowmobiling, and ice fishing in winter. | 7318 Harlem Rd. | 815/885–3311 | fax 815/885–3664 | Free | Apr.–Oct., daily 6 AM–10 PM; Nov.–Mar., daily 8–5.

Rockford Art Museum. Contemporary exhibits and a permanent collection are housed in this museum along the Rock River. | 711 N. Main St. | 815/968–2787 | fax 815/968–0164 | www.rockfordartmuseum.com | Free | Tues.–Fri. 11–5, Sat. 10–5, Sun. noon–5.

Rockford Park District Trolley Station. Take a 45-minute trolley ride of downtown or a 45-minute boat excursion on the Rock River. | 324 N. Madison St. 61107 | 815/987–8894 | $3.50; special rates for kids | Call for hours.

Sand Bluff Bird Banding Station. You can see migrating birds being banded and released at this station located in the 114-acre Colored Sands Forest Preserve in Shirland. | Haas Rd., Shirland | 815/629–2671 | www.wcfpd.org | Free | Mar.–May, Aug.–Nov. Sat. dawn–dusk, Sun. noon–dusk.

Sinnissippi Gardens. These gardens in northwest Rockford about a mile from the State Street Bridge have an arboretum, seasonal floral displays, and an aviary. There's winter ice-skating on the lagoon. | 1300 N. 2nd St. | 815/987–8858 | fax 815/969–4066 | Free | Daily 9–4.

Tinker Swiss Cottage Museum. Built in 1865, this alpine-style cottage a half-mile from downtown is on the National Register of Historic Places. Inside it has elaborate woodwork, parquet floors, spiral staircases, and murals that illustrate the life of a midwestern family during America's Gilded Age. Outside is a Victorian rose garden. | 411 Kent St. | 815/964–2424 or TDD 815/963–3323 | fax 815/964–2466 | www.tinkercottage.com | $4; special rates for kids and senior citizens | Tues.–Sun.; tours at 1, 2, 3.

ON THE CALENDAR

JAN.: *Illinois State Snow Sculpting Competition.* Demonstrations and competitions (including qualifiers for the national competition) take place in Sinnissippi Park. | 815/987–8800.

MAY–OCT.: *Rockford Speedway.* Loves Park, Route 173 and Forest Hills Rd., is where NASCAR and stock-car racing and novelty racing take place at 7:30 on Wednesday and Saturday nights. | 815/633–1500.

AUG.: *Winnebago County Fair.* This county fair at the Winnebago County Fairgrounds in Pecatonica runs the second week of the month, with rides, livestock, food, and entertainment. Admission is $6. | 815/239–1642.

SEPT.: *On the Waterfront Festival.* If you are in Rockford over Labor Day weekend you can get swept up into this annual merrymaking, with its 10 venues, nearly continuous music, more than 55 international food booths, hands-on activities for kids, and arts-and-crafts marketplace, mainly on State Street but spanning 30 blocks through town. In addition to admission, you purchase food and drink tickets, and there are parking fees, but a shuttle bus travels among many hotels. Admission is $8 in advance, $12 at the door. Kids under 5 free. | 815/964–4388.

SEPT.: *Rockford Art Museum Festival.* Some 200 artists from all over the country show their work the second weekend after Labor Day at this open-air fine arts fair on the banks of the Rock River. There's a $3 entrance fee. | 815/968–2787.

SEPT.–JUNE: *New American Theater.* This two-stage Equity theater downtown offers a full season of comedies, dramas, musicals, and kids' shows throughout the year (except July and August). | 815/964–8023.

Dining

Bacchus. Mediterranean. In the river district four blocks east of the river, you can enjoy wood-grilled lamb and ostrich, fresh seafood, pastas, and other vegetarian dishes, either in the glow of Bacchus's blue ceiling underlit by blacklights above the copper-accented dining room or by the waterfall-fountain in the enclosed outdoor patio. | 515 E. State St. | 815/968–9463 | fax 815/968–9490 | $11–$30 | AE, D, DC, MC, V | Closed Mon.

Café Patou. French. This country bistro in southeast Rockford serves crepes, as well as Italian fare, including pasta dishes and a special personal gourmet pizza known as flat bread. Live jazz Fri. and Sat. Kids' menu. | 3929 Broadway | 815/227–4100 | $11–$28 | AE, D, DC, MC, V | Closed Sun. No lunch Sat.–Mon.

Cliffbreakers River Restaurant. Continental. Two-hundred-year-old gold French pillars, an Italian fountain, and French doors grace the entry of this restaurant, where you can watch the Rock River through a wall of leaded-glass windows as you enjoy seafood and steaks in its antique-filled dining room. Sun. brunch | 700 W. Riverside Blvd. | 815/282–3033 | $15.95–$40 | AE, D, DC, MC, V.

Giovanni's. Contemporary. An extensive cognac list and seafood, steak, and veal dishes, and tournedo of beef are on tap at this dining spot. Bar. | 610 N. Bell School Rd. | 815/398–6411 | www.geodine.com | $14–$26 | AE, D, DC, MC, V | Closed Sun. No lunch Sat.

Great Wall Chinese Restaurant. Chinese. On the Mandarin and Szechuan menu at this restaurant on the east side of town are such dishes as moo shu pork, black bean chicken, and Great Wall steak. Sun. brunch buffet. | 4228 E. State St. | 815/226–0982 | $6.50–$12 | AE, D, MC, V.

Lucern's Fondue and Spirits. French. It is fondue start-to-finish in this restored Victorian house, built in 1895 as a wedding present, where the most-requested seating is by the fireplace or in the upstairs bay windows. To start, try fruits or bread to dip in cheese fondue, move on to entrée fondues—beef, chicken, shrimp, lobster, or scallops—and finish off with a chocolate fondue. | 845 N. Church St. | 815/968–2665 | $19–$28 | AE, D, MC, V | No lunch.

Octane InterLounge. Contemporary. On the pedestrian mall of Rockford's Main Street, this "lounge" has no computers despite its name, and it is made cozy by the tangerine walls, a big blue-velvet couch, and artsy light fixtures in the dining area, where you can nibble pita laced in hummus or chips dipped in mango or banana salsa, and gorge on one of the Pacific Rim–inspired entrées. Coffee and muffins from 7 AM on and live jazz weekends. | 124 N. Main St. | 815/965–4012 | $8.95–$13.95 | AE, D, MC, V | Closed Sun. No dinner Mon.

Stockholm Inn. Scandinavian. You can slide into a booth or sit at a table to enjoy Swedish specialties, including *kaldolmar* (Swedish stuffed cabbage), which are served alongside American fare at this Scandinavian inn in eastside Rockford. Swedish pancakes are a run-away breakfast favorite here, and a kids' menu is available. | 2420 Carles St. | 815/397–3534 | $6.20–$7.95 | DC, MC, V | Breakfast also available. No lunch or dinner weekends.

Trattoria Fantini. Italian. Ten blocks north of downtown Rockford, this chalet with a big fireplace and Italian linens serves duck roasted prepared in a wood-burning oven, and made-to-order pastas. Other favorites here are the wood-fired pizzas and the risotto. | 815 Marchesano Dr. | 815/961–3674 | $6.95–$22 | AE, D, DC, MC, V | Closed Sun. No lunch Sat. and Memorial Day–Sept.

Lodging

The Barn of Rockford. To the east of Rockford and easily from I–90, this 1880s barn has original wood beams, posts, and pegs. The stairwells are lined with quilts, some of which are made by the owners, who also have a quilting business. You are encouraged to explore the entire barn when you stay here, including the old corn bed, which is now an indoor lap pool, and you are served breakfast by candlelight. Dinner offered by arrangement. Complimentary breakfast. TV in common area. Indoor pool. | 6786 Guilford Rd. | 815/395–8535 or 888/378–1729 | www.barnrkfd@juno.com | 4 rooms | $65–$95 | D, MC, V.

Best Western Clock Tower Resort and Conference Center. This expansive resort and conference center about 5 mi east of Rockford sits on 27 acres. Fitness, dining, shopping, and theater facilities are all on the grounds. It's 3 mi to Magic Waters Water Park and Cherry Vale shopping mall. Two restaurants, bar with entertainment, picnic area, room service. In-room data ports, some refrigerators, some in-room hot tubs, cable TV. Indoor pool, 2 outdoor pools, 2 wading pools. Hot tubs. Indoor tennis. Gym. Shops, video games. Playground. Laundry facilities. Business services, airport shuttle. | 7801 E. State St. | 815/398–6000 or 800/358–7666 | fax 815/398–0443 | www.clocktowerresort.com | 252 rooms, 20 suites | $103–$200, $200 suites | AE, D, DC, MC, V.

Best Western Colonial Inn. Next to Rockford College, this motel is 4 mi east of downtown. Some refrigerators, some microwaves, some in-room hot tubs, cable TV. Indoor pool. Hot tub. Exercise equipment. Business services. Pets allowed (fee). | 4850 E. State St. | 815/398–5050 or 800/528–1234 | fax 815/398–8180 | www.bestwestern.com | 84 rooms, 10 suites | $96, $105–$170 suites | AE, D, DC, MC, V.

Cliffbreakers River Suites and Conference Center. This establishment's motto is "the only thing we overlook is the Rock River." Nevertheless, some rooms actually look out over the parking lot, but each room has 12-ft ceilings and a sitting room separate from the bedroom. Restaurant, complimentary Continental breakfast, room service. In-room data ports, microwaves, refrigerators, cable TV. Indoor pool. Sauna. Exercise equipment. Laundry facilities. Game room. Business services. | 700 W. Riverside Blvd. | 815/282–3033 | fax 815/637–4704 | www.cliffbreakers.com | 104 rooms | $99–$200 | AE, D, DC, MC, V.

Comfort Inn. About 10 mi east of downtown, this motel is 3 mi to the Cherry Vale shopping mall and close to restaurants. Complimentary Continental breakfast. In-room data ports. Some microwaves, some refrigerators, cable TV. Indoor pool. Hot tub. Business services. Some pets allowed. | 7392 Argus Dr. | 815/398–7061 or 800/228–5150 | www.comfortinn.com | 54 rooms, 10 suites | $79, $89 suites | AE, D, DC, MC, V.

Courtyard Rockford by Marriott. This hotel is 1 mi from Magic Waters Water Park, 8 mi from downtown, and less than a mile from Cherry Vale shopping mall. Golf is 5 mi away. Restaurant (open for breakfast only), bar. In-room data ports, some microwaves, some refigerators, cable TV. Indoor pool. Hot tub. Exercise equipment. Laundry facilities. Business services. | 7676 E. State St. | 815/397–6222 or 800/321–2211 | fax 815/397–6254 | www.courtyard.com | 147 rooms, 11 suites | $94, $120 suites | AE, D, DC, MC, V.

Exel Inn. About 10 mi east of downtown, this motel is also 3 mi from Cherry Valley Mall and 2 mi from Magic Waters Water Park. Complimentary Continental breakfast. In-room data ports, microwaves (fee), refrigerators (fee), cable TV. Gym. Laundry facilities. Business services. Some pets allowed. | 220 S. Lyford Rd. | 815/332–4915 or 800/367–3935 | fax 815/332–4843 | www.exelinns.com | 100 rooms, 1 suite | $65, $125 suite | AE, D, DC, MC, V.

Fairfield Inn. This motel is 1 mi to Cherry Valley shopping mall and 7 mi east of downtown. Complimentary Continental breakfast. In-room data ports, cable TV. Pool. Business services. | 7712 Potawatomi Trail | 815/397–8000 or 800/228–2800 | fax 815/397–8183 | www.fairfieldinn.com | 135 rooms | $79 | AE, D, DC, MC, V.

Fox Run Bed & Breakfast Inn. Three blocks from the hospital, on the corner of Sauber and North Rockton, this grand East Lake home was built in 1878. It's filled with family heirlooms and furnished has an original gentleman's parlor—now a unisex sitting room where you can luxuriate amid warm honey oak and stained-glass bookcases. There's also a baby grand piano and in many rooms claw-foot tubs. Some pets allowed by arrangement. Complimentary breakfast. No room phones, TV and VCR in common area. | 2815 N. Rockton Ave. | 815/963–8151 | fax 815/963–0158 | www.foxrun@xta.com | www.foxrunbedandbreakfast.com | 5 rooms | $108–$116 | AE, D, MC, V.

Hampton Inn. About 7 mi east of downtown, this motel is next to I–90. Complimentary Continental breakfast. In-room data ports, microwaves (fee), refrigerators (fee), cable TV. Indoor pool. Hot tub. Exercise equipment. Laundry service. Business services. | 615 Clark Dr. | 815/229–0404 or 800/HAMPTON | fax 815/229–0175 | www.hampton-inn.com | 122 rooms | $89 | AE, D, DC, MC, V.

Holiday Inn. This hostelry is 8 mi east of downtown and 1 mi north of Magic Waters Water Park. Restaurants are less than a mile from the hotel and a movie theater is three blocks away. Restaurant, bar, room service. In-room data ports, some in-room hot tubs, cable TV. Indoor pool. Barbershop/beauty salon, hot tub. Exercise equipment. Video games. Business services, airport shuttle. | 7550 E. State St. | 815/398–2200 or 800/383–7829 | fax 815/229–3122 | www.basshotels.com/holiday-inn | 198 rooms, 4 suites | $99 | AE, D, DC, MC, V.

Howard Johnson. Rockford's largest indoor pool is at this motel 1 mi north of Rockford Airport. Restaurant, bar. In-room data ports, cable TV. Indoor pool. Hot tub. Tennis. Exercise equipment. Video games. Playground. Laundry facilities. Business services, airport shuttle. | 3909 S. 11th St. | 815/397–9000 or 800/446–4656 | fax 815/397–4669 | www.hojo.com | 146 rooms | $79 | AE, D, DC, MC, V.

Red Roof Inn. This motel is 2 mi north of Magic Waters Water Park and 7 mi east of downtown. Some in-room data ports, some microwaves, some refrigerators, cable TV. Business services. Pets allowed. | 7434 E. State St. | 815/398–9750 or 800/REDROOF | fax 815/398–9761 | www.redroof.com | 108 rooms | $55.99–$65.99 | AE, D, DC, MC, V.

Residence Inn by Marriott. One block west of I–90, this all-suite hotel is 7 mi east of downtown and about a mile from shopping and restaurants. Complimentary Continental breakfast. In-room data ports, kitchenettes, cable TV. Indoor pool. Hot tub. Exercise equipment. Laundry facilities. Business services. Pets allowed (fee). | 7542 Colosseum Dr. | 815/227–0013 or 800/331–3131 | fax 815/227–0013 | www.residenceinn.com | 94 rooms | $94–$135 | AE, D, DC, MC, V.

Riverhouse Bed & Breakfast. In Machesney, just 7 mi north of Rockford, you can rough it in a tepee with a chimenea firepot and portable toilets or enjoy a more pampered homestay at this riverside abode, where common areas are full of frontier collectibles. Two resident cats here can be invited into or repelled from your dwelling. Complimentary breakfast. Some refrigerators, some in-room hot tubs, cable TV, some in-room VCRs, some room phones. Outdoor pool. Hot tub. Volleyball. Business services. No kids under 8. | 11052 Ventura Blvd., Machesney Park | 815/636–1884 | fax 815/636–1884 | 2 suites, 1 tepee | $95–$185 | MC, V | Teepee closed seasonally.

Sweden House Lodge. Just 3 mi west of I–90, this motel 4 mi east of downtown is along the Rock River. Complimentary Continental breakfast. In-room data ports, cable TV. Indoor pool. Hot tub. Exercise equipment. Business services. Some pets allowed (fee). | 4605 E. State St. | 815/398–4130 or 800/886–4138 | fax 815/398–9203 | www.swedenhouselodge.com | 105 rooms, 2 suites | $51–$61 | AE, D, DC, MC, V.

Victorian Veranda. Five miles west of Rockford on a rural 4-acre lot in Winnebago, this B&B dates to 1865 and contains a mix of contemporary and antique furnishings. There's also a 180-ft wraparound porch with swings, wicker furniture, and glass-topped tables. Two of the five rooms have private balconies overlooking the surrounding property where you can play horseshoes, volleyball, and croquet. The innkeepers share their kitchen and telephone with you. Complimentary breakfast. No room phones, TV in common area. | 8430 W. State Rd., Winnebago | 815/963–1337 | fax 815/963–6595 | www.bbonline.com/il/veranda | 5 rooms | $60–$85 | MC, V.

Villager Lodge. Four miles north of Anderson Garden, these accommodations include four apartments should you choose to stay awhile and a shuttle service that will take you to most Rockford destinations. Continental breakfast. Microwaves, refrigerators, cable TV. Outdoor pool. Laundry facilities. Business services. | 4404 E. State St. | 815/399–1890 or 800/399–3580 | fax 815/399–1898 | www.villagerrockford.com | 106 rooms, 4 apartments | $38.99–$51.75; call for apartment rates | AE, D, DC, MC, V.

ROCK ISLAND

MAP 6, D3

(Nearby towns also listed: Bishop Hill, Galesburg, Kewanee, Moline, Monmouth)

In its early days Rock Island was a steamboat center on the Mississippi; later, railroads also boosted its growth. (The Chicago and Rock Island Railroad Line, in fact, built the first railroad bridge across the Mississippi at Rock Island.) One of the largest Union military prisons was housed on an island in the river during the Civil War. Today the city of 40,630 concentrates on trade and transportation.

Information:**Quad Cities Convention and Visitors Bureau** | 2021 River Dr., Moline 61265 | 309/788–7800 or 800/747–7800 | fax 309/788–7898 | www.visitquadcities.com.

Attractions
Black Hawk State Historic Site. This popular Quad City park 10 blocks south of downtown is on 208 acres. It has a dedicated nature area, hiking trails, and a museum. The latter interprets daily life of the Sauk and Fox tribes during the 18th and 19th centuries. | 1510 46th Ave. | 309/788–0177 (park) or 309/788–9536 (museum) | Park, free; museum, donation suggested | Park, daily sunrise–10 PM. Museum Mar.-Oct., daily 9–noon and 1–5; Nov.–Feb. 9–noon and 1–4.

Mississippi River Visitor Center. The center has an observation deck over the river and video and displays that focus on commercial navigation. Take the Rock Island Viaduct from Route 92. | West end, Arsenal Island | 309/794–5338 | fax 309/794–5741 | www.mvr.usace.army.mil/ missriver | Free | Mid-May–mid-Sept., daily 9–9; mid-Sept.–mid-May, daily 9–5.

Quad City Botanical Center. These gardens in the center of town have a tropical conservatory, a waterfall, and walkways over water. | 2525 4th Ave. | 309/794–0991 | fax 309/794–1572 | www.qcbotanicalgardens.org | $3.50; special rates for senior citizens and kids | Mon.–Sat. 10–5, Sun. 1–5.

Rock Island Arsenal. This manufacturing arsenal began production after the Civil War. Today it includes a museum with a firearms collection, a blockhouse replica of Fort Armstrong, and a national cemetery. Take the Rock Island Viaduct from Route 92. | Building 60, North Ave. and Gillespie | 309/782–5021 | fax 309/782–3598 | www.quadcities.com/cvb/museum.htm | Free | Daily 10–4.

ON THE CALENDAR
JUNE–AUG.: *Genesius Guild.* Free open-air presentations of classical drama, including Greek tragedies in mask, and ballet, are performed weekends at 8 PM from mid-June to mid-August in Lincoln Park (38th St. and 11th Ave.). | 309/788–7113 or 309/786–5420.
JULY: County Fair and Rodeo. This agricultural fair held in East Molina, has cattle, sheep, and horse judging, as well as flower, vegetable, and fine art and craft awards. At the rodeo you can see roping, bronc-riding, barrel-racing, and other equestrian competitions. In addition to the food and novelties vendors, there's a midway with rides and games for kids of all ages. Although parking and gate entry are free, there's a charge for the grandstand events. | 309/796–1620.

Dining
Hunter's Club. American/Casual. True to its reputation for having offered the first charbroiled burger in the quad cities, the Club remains famous for its burgers, including three-cheese, barbecue, and bacon varieties, but it also serves steaks, catfish, and prime rib. Regulars say the dining room in this two-story 100-ft-long brick building erected in 1933 adjacent to the downtown district reminds them of a Chicago-style pub. | 2107 4th Ave. | 309/786–9880 | $5–$12.95 | AE, D, MC, V | Closed Sun.

Le Figaro. French. Expect a meal at this downtown French restaurant to be leisurely (at least two hours) and the staff to be friendly and willing to make recommendations. Le Figaro has an extensive wine list and serves classic haute cuisine including foie gras, filet mignon, lamb chops Provençale, Dover sole, and frogs' legs. | 1708 2nd Ave. | 309/786–4944 | $15–$40 | AE, D, MC, V | No lunch.

Rock Island Brewing Co. American. This restaurant and pub takes its live entertainment seriously. Snack on sandwiches, burgers, and salads as you listen to local bands playing everything from rock to reggae. | 1815 2nd Ave. | 309/793–1999 | www.ribco.com | $2–$6 | AE, D, MC, V | Closed Sun.

Lodging
Four Points Sheraton. One block from the Mississippi River and right in downtown, this hotel is in the heart of the entertainment district, with clubs, a casino, and restaurants in abundance. Some of the rooms have river views. Restaurant, bar, room service. In-room data ports, cable TV. Indoor pool. Massage. Gym. Laundry service. | 226 17th St. | 309/794–1212 | 172 rooms | $64–$95 | AE, D, DC, MC, V.

Potter House Bed and Breakfast. This restored 1907 Colonial Revival mansion five blocks from the Mississippi was commissioned by Mrs. Potter after her husband's death when she became publisher of the Rock Island newspaper, the *Argus*. It has six fireplaces, a glass solarium, stained-glass windows, and a mahogany-paneled dining room. Complimentary breakfast. Cable TV. | 1906 7th Ave. | 309/788–1906 or 800/747–0339 | fax 309/794–3947 | www.qconline.com/potterhouse | 5 rooms | $75–$95 | AE, MC, V.

Top O'The Morning Bed & Breakfast. This Prairie School brick home with wrought-iron gates used to be the country estate of a former Rock Island railroad president. On a hill overlooking the Mississippi River, it's on 3 acres dotted with fruit trees and gardens. There is a fireplace in the common room. Complimentary breakfast. No pets. No smoking. | 1505 19th Ave. | 309/786–3513 | 3 rooms | $60–$100 | No credit cards.

Victorian Inn Bed & Breakfast. Antiques fill this Victorian house-turned-inn, built in 1876. It's seven blocks south of downtown in a residential historic district. Complimentary beverages and snacks are available. Complimentary breakfast. Cable TV, no room phones. | 702 20th St. | 309/788–7068 or 800/728–7068 | 5 rooms (4 with shower only) | $75–$85 | AE, MC, V.

ST. CHARLES

MAP 6, G2

(Nearby towns also listed: Aurora, Elgin, Geneva, Wheaton)

St. Charles was first settled in the 1830s; its Fox River location attracted settlers who used the waterway to help power lumber and grist mills. The city was also the site of Franklin Medical Institute, the first medical school in Illinois. Today, St. Charles is primarily residential (population 25,000), although the downtown is filled with antiques shops and malls, as well as boutiques, restaurants, and specialty shops.

Information: St. Charles Convention and Visitors Bureau | 311 N. 2nd St., Suite 100, 60174 | 630/377–6161 or 800/777/4373 | www.visitstcharles.com.

Attractions

Durant-Peterson House. On the LeRoy Oakes Forest Preserve, you can really step back in time in this two-story brick home—now a living-history museum where even the docents wear period dress—which is the oldest remaining dwelling constructed by this area's first settlers. Built in 1843 by a St. Charles brickmason and now fully restored and furnished with original period furnishings, it is on the National Register of Historic Places. | Dean St. west of Randall Rd. | 630/377–6424 | $1 suggested donation | June-Oct., Thurs. and Sun. 1–4, Nov.–May by appointment.

Kane County Flea Market. More than 1,000 vendors sell their wares at this flea market that takes over the Kane County Fairgrounds on the first Sunday and preceding Saturday of every month. The fairgrounds are on the west side of St. Charles between Route 64 and Route 38. | Randall Rd. | 630/377–2252 | www2.pair.com/kaneflea/index.htm | $5; free kids 12 and under | Sat. noon–5, Sun. 7–4.

Pottawatomie Park. This preserve stretches along the Fox River and has paddlewheel boat rides, pedal boat rentals, a pool, golf, miniature golf, and playgrounds. | 8 North Ave. | 630/584–1885 | fax 630/584–7413 | www.st-charlesparks.org | $5 | Daily 7 AM–11 PM.
Saint Charles Belle II and *Fox River Queen.* You can pick up river cruises on either of these two paddlewheel boats. On weekdays board at bottom of hill in the lower parking area in the park for a one-hour cruise; on weekends board in the picnic area for a 50-minute ride. | 630/584–2334 | $5 | June–Aug., daily 3:30; May, Sept.–mid-Oct., Sat. 2–4, Sun. 2–5.

ON THE CALENDAR

JUNE: *Pride of the Fox River Fest.* This free family festival the second weekend of the month focuses on river themes; events include dragon boat races, live music, a carnival, and a craft show. It takes place at various venues downtown and along the river. | 630/377–6161 or 800/777–4373.

© 2000 Visa U.S.A. Inc.

When it Comes to Getting Cash at an ATM, Same Thing.

Whether you're in Yosemite or Yemen, using your Visa® card or ATM card with the PLUS symbol is the easiest and most convenient way to get cash. Even if your bank is in Minneapolis and you're in Miami, Visa/PLUS ATMs make getting cash so easy, you'll feel right at home. After all, Visa/PLUS ATMs are open 24 hours a day, 7 days a week, rain or shine. And if you need help finding one of Visa's 627,000 ATMs in 127 countries worldwide, visit **visa.com/pd/atm**. We'll make finding an ATM as easy as finding the Eiffel Tower, the Pyramids or even the Grand Canyon.

It's Everywhere You Want To Be®

Woodfield
World
Class
Shopping

Chicago's Premier Shopping and Entertainment Center

Prepare to be delighted at Chicago's favorite shopping center, Woodfield. With the most distinctive collection of shopping, dining and entertainment, it's no wonder Chicago's visitors voted it their favorite suburban attraction in 2000. Surround yourself with fashion, food and fun at Woodfield's 300 stores including:

Marshall Field's	Timberland
Nordstrom	Woolrich
Lord & Taylor	Build-a-Bear Workshop™
JCPenney	Brooks Brothers
Sears	Sharper Image
Abercrombie & Fitch	bebe
J. Crew	Coach
Sephora	Rainforest Café
Fossil	NASCAR Silicon Motor
Steve Madden	Speedway
Guess?	Mars 2112

World Class Shopping hotel packages available, call 1-800-847-9590 for more information.

To find out about things to do in our area, contact the Greater Woodfield Convention and Visitors Bureau at 1-800-VISIT-GW.

www.shopwoodfield.com

AUG.: *Downtown Fox Rox and Cord on Blues Fest.* This weekend's events are actually the combination of two festivals occupying all of downtown St. Charles and both banks of the river. The Fox Rox includes tent and sidewalk sales, craft exhibitions, kids' activities, and live music, while the Cord on Blues stages local and nationally renowned artists—mainly blues bands but with an eclectic smattering of others. Daily admission charges for the Cord on Blues fest. | 800/777–4373 or 630/377–6161.

OCT.: *Scarecrow Festival.* Arts, crafts, and entertainment happen throughout downtown the second full weekend of the month. | 630/377–6161 or 800/777–4373.

Dining

Erik and Me Riverside Restaurant. Scandinavian. Try the *frikadeller* (pork meatballs served with potatoes, homemade red cabbage, and pickled cucumber)—a Danish specialty in this riverfront restaurant, where you can sit out on the deck to really enjoy the water, though there are river views from inside. Sun. brunch. | 1 W. Illinois St. | 630/377–9222 | $11.95–$19.95 | AE, D, DC, MC, V.

The Filling Station Pub and Grill. Contemporary. Named for the filling station that once occupied this 1930s building downtown, this place is furnished with memorabilia from that period and place. It serves casual fare—burgers and Tex-Mex favorites. Kids' menu. | 300 W. Main St. | 630/584–4414 | www.filling-station.com | Reservations not accepted | $4.95–$12.95 | AE, D, DC, MC, V.

Francesca's By The River. Italian. This trattoria on Route 31, two blocks south of Route 64, presents the recipes of northern Italy—namely Rome and the surrounding areas of Tuscany, Umbria, and Lazio. Try *pesce al funghi* (sautéed fish-of-the-day with wild mushrooms, spinach, tomatoes, and herbs) and granchi escarole (sautéed soft-shell crabs with capers, escarole, garlic, tomato, and lemon balsamic). Francesca's has sister restaurants in Chicago, Naperville, and Northbrook. | 200 S. 2nd St. | 630/587–8221 | $15–$30 | AE, MC, V | No lunch weekends.

Lodging

Best Western Inn. A mile east of downtown, this hostelry is 2 mi from Potowatomie State Park, and 3 mi from shopping and area restaurants. Complimentary Continental breakfast. Refrigerators, cable TV. Outdoor pool. Exercise equipment. Laundry facilities. Business services. | 1635 E. Main St. | 630/584–4550 or 800/WESTERN | fax 630/584–5221 | www.bestwestern.com | 54 rooms | $75–$89 | AE, D, DC, MC, V.

Days Inn. This motel is 2 mi east of the town center. In-room data ports, some kitchenettes, cable TV. Indoor pool. Gym. Business services. | 100 S. Tyler Rd. | 630/513–6500 or 800/DAYSINN | fax 630/513–6501 | www.daysinn.com | 49 rooms; 2 suites | $80, $150 suites | AE, D, DC, MC, V.

Hotel Baker. This 1920s hotel on the Fox River downtown hosted political and show business celebrites from when it first opened in 1928 through mid-century. It then became a senior citizens home until 1996 when new owners restored the hotel to its previous grandeur (some of the original period furnishings remain). Restaurant, bar, complimentary Continental breakfast, room service. In-room data ports, some kitchenettes, some minibars, cable TV, in-room VCRs. Hot tubs (in suites). Gym. Laundry service. Business services. No smoking. | 100 W. Main St. | 630/584–2100 | fax 630/443–0795 | www.hotelbaker.com | 41 rooms, 12 suites | $199, $279–$600 suites | AE, D, DC, MC, V.

The Oscar Swan Country Inn. On 8 acres in Geneva, 2 mi south of St. Charles, this gentleman's farm and country retreat was built for Chicago banker Oscar Swan in 1902 and is now a popular spot for breakfast meetings, weddings, and quiet getaways, where you can roam the gardens and the old carriage house, and relax on the patios and in the gazebo. Some kitchenettes, some refrigerators. Outdoor pool. | 1800 W. State St., Geneva | 630/232–0173 | www.oscarswan.com | 8 rooms | $88–$139 | AE, MC, V.

Villa Batavia. Adjacent to the Fox River bike path in Batavia, 5 mi south of St. Charles, this large-frame home is on 7 wooded acres and has floor-to-ceiling windows so you can enjoy the view. The oldest part of the house, built in 1844, is Greek Revival–style and subsequent additions are Italianate. Two guest rooms have fireplaces, and the suite has a sitting room and library. Complimentary breakfast. Cable TV. | 1430 S. Batavia Ave., Batavia | 630/406–8182 | 2 rooms, 1 suite | $85–$150 | D, MC, V.

SALEM

MAP 6, G9

(Nearby towns also listed: Centralia, Mt. Vernon, Vandalia)

In the early 1800s Salem was a stagecoach stop. A hundred years later it was an oil town, and in the late 1930s, Salem had the second-largest oil field in the country. William Jennings Bryan was born here, and Miracle Whip salad dressing was invented in Salem. Today the town has a population of 7,500.

Information: Salem Chamber of Commerce | 615 W. Main St., 62881 | 618/548–3010 | www.salemilchamber.com.

Attractions

Halfway Tavern. This reconstructed stagecoach stop is halfway between St. Louis, Missouri, and Vincennes, Indiana, and 7 mi east of Salem. Abraham Lincoln often stopped here. | U.S. 50 | Free | Daily.

Ingram's Log Cabin Village. In the northern part of Kinmundy, this compound of 16 authentic log cabins—most built before 1860—is 12 mi north of Salem. | Rte. 37, Kinmundy | 618/547–7123 | $1.25; special rates for kids | Mid-Apr.–mid-Nov., daily 10–4.

One-Room Schoolhouse. This restored 19th-century schoolhouse on the campus of Salem Community High School is 1 mi north of downtown Salem on Rte. 37. | Route 37, Salem, 62881 | 618/548–2499 | Free | Call for hours.

Statue of William Jennings Bryan. Originally dedicated in 1934, this statue created by Gutzon Borglum, sculptor of Mount Rushmore, was moved to its present location in Salem in 1961. | N. Broadway (across from Bryan Park) | 618/548–3010 | Free | Daily.

Stephen A. Forbes State Park. A 585-acre lake with beach, boating, fishing, hunting, horseback riding (no rentals available), and three campgrounds, are all in 3,100-acre park about 15 mi east of Salem. | 6924 Omega Rd., Kinmundy | 618/547–3381 | fax 618/547–9884 | Free; camping fee | Daily.

William Jennings Bryan Birthplace/Museum. Exhibits at this museum four blocks south of the courthouse square include artifacts from Bryan's life. | 408 S. Broadway | 618/548–7791 | Free | Fri.–Wed. 1–5.

ON THE CALENDAR

JULY–AUG.: *Marion County Fair.* Livestock judging, midway rides and games, food and entertainment take place at this week-long event in the fairgrounds on the south side of Salem. Admission $2. | 618/548–1251.

SEPT.: *Days Fest.* This three-day event, most of which takes place on the courthouse lawn, celebrates the soap *Days of Our Lives* and the town of Salem, where the soap takes place. You can play a Days trivia contest, enter the look-alike competitions, and go to the dinner dance and brunch—all with stars of *Days*. Tickets sold per event and there are several free events. | 618/548–3010.

Dining

Sweeny's Diner and Old Fashioned Ice Cream Parlor. American. You can take a trip down memory lane in this neon-wrapped diner with its '50s memorabilia, cobalt-blue porcelain and stainless-steel ice-cream fountain, and the front half of a '57 Chevy at the entrance. With your burger and fries, try one of the shakes, such as the Candyman and the Peppermint Twist, which are always accompanied by the remainder in its stainless blender canister. Weekend all-you-can-eat selections served. | 101 E. Main St. | 618/548–4520 | $3.50–$9.95 | AE, MC, V.

Lodging

Comfort Inn. Ten minutes west of Salem, these standard accommodations are a block away from an industrial park surrounded by several other chain hotels. Complimentary Continental breakfast. Some microwaves, some refrigerators, some in-room hot tubs, cable TV. Indoor pool. Laundry facilities, laundry service. Business services. | 1800 W. Main St. | 618/548–2177 | www.comfortinn.com | 35 rooms, 30 suites | $49–$69 | AE, D, DC, MC, V.

SCHAUMBURG

MAP 8, B4

(Nearby towns also listed: Arlington Heights, Barrington, Elgin, Itasca)

This northwest Chicago suburb has grown from farm fields to high-rises in the last 30 years—spurred in part by the presence of Woodfield Mall. Today it has 75,000 residents.

Information: Greater Woodfield Convention and Visitors Bureau | 1430 N. Meacham Rd., Suite 1400, 60173 | 847/605–1010 | www.chicagonorthwest.com.

Attractions

Chicago Athenaeum Museum-Schaumburg. A satellite of the Chicago branch of the Athenaeum, the Schaumburg is dedicated to the art of design in all disciplines—architecture, industrial and product design, graphics, and urban planning—and has a sculpture park within walking distance of the museum. | 190 S. Roselle Rd. | 847/895–3950 | fax 847/295–3951 | Adults $3, sculpture garden free | Weds.–Fri. 11–6, weekends noon–5.

Lynfred Winery. Owner Fred Koehler has won national awards and local acclaim for his winery housed in a restored Victorian mansion 5 mi from Schaumburg. | 15 S. Roselle Rd., Roselle | 630/529–WINE or 888/298–WINE | fax 630/529–4971 | www.lynfredwinery.com | Free; 7 tastings for $4 | Daily 10–7, tours on weekends.

Prairie Center for the Performing Arts. This 442-seat performing arts center in downtown Schaumburg hosts concerts and plays. | 201 Schaumburg Ct. | 847/895–3600 or TDD 847/895–3638 | fax 847/895–1837 | www.ci.schaumburg.il.us | Prices vary with shows | Box office weekdays 9–4.

Woodfield Mall. This is one of the largest enclosed retail shopping centers in the United States; it includes more than 300 stores and restaurants. The mall is 25 mi northwest of Chicago. | Rte. 53 and Golf Rd. | 847/330–0035 or TTY 800/322–9721 | fax 847/330–0251 | www.taubman.com | Daily.

ON THE CALENDAR

JUNE–JULY: *Free Street Theater.* From mid-June to late July, you can pack a picnic and a blanket and enjoy this series of plays performed in different locations throughout the parks of Schaumburg. | 847/490–7015.

Dining

Curradh. Irish. In this Irish pub on the south perimeter of the Woodfield Mall, you can quaff stouts and single-malt whiskey while watching soccer on TV—a contrast to the bric-a-brac and dark wood-bars imported from Ireland—eating burgers, pastas, and Irish fare such as boxtys (potato pancakes). Live music Thurs.–Sun. Kids' menu. | 1700 Woodfield Rd. | 847/706–1700 | $7.99–$16.99 | AE, D, DC, MC, V.

Maggiano's Little Italy. Italian. This restaurant across Woodfield Road from the Woodfield Mall has a big outdoor fountain, linen cloths and candles on the tables, photos of Italian celebrities on the walls, and crooners like Old Blue Eyes on the sound system, setting the mood for dining on linguine, lasagna, seafood, and steak. | 1901 Woodfield Rd. | 847/240–5600 | $15–$20 | AE, D, DC, MC, V | No lunch weekends.

Martin's of Chicago-Schaumburg. Continental. Filet mignon with bearnaise sauce is a favorite in this dimly lit, wood-trimmed dining room admired for its stunning floral arrangements. Martin's sometimes offers a popular Cajun rib-eye in addition to seafood, chicken, fish, and a remarkable vegetable plate. | 1470 McConnor Pkwy. | 847/413–8771 | $19–$32 | AE, MC, V | No lunch.

Prairie Rock Brewing Company. American/Casual. If you sit at the bar you might see the brewmaster at work preparing the six Prairie Rock brews served on tap here, such as the exclusively brewed Vanilla Cream Ale and Ambitious Amber, or one of the monthly specials. In the dining room's rustic old-brick, wood-ceilinged dining room with red-stained cedar-topped tables, you can choose among steaks, chops, and the popular shrimp Boursin pasta. You can also get a sandwich at the Prairie Rock Market and sit in the outside beer garden. Kids' menu. | 1385 N. Meachan Rd. | 847/605–9900 | $8–$26 | AE, D, DC, MC, V.

Ron Santo's American Rotisserie. Contemporary. Mementoes of the former Cubs star fill the room in this sports bar-restaurant across the street from Motorola and 5 minutes from I-90. On the menu is wood-roasted chicken, ribs, sandwiches, pasta, and pizza. Kids' menu. | 1925 N. Meacham Rd. | 847/397–2676 | $5.75–$16.95 | AE, DC, MC, V.

Stir Crazy Café. Pan-Asian. You can take a break from shopping at Woodfield and duck into this colorful spot, on the ground floor of the mall, serving cuisine from China, Japan, Thailand, and Vietnam. A favorite to try is the create-your-own-stir-fry, which allows you to choose from a selection of veggies, a meat, and rice or noodles. | 5 Woodfield Mall, Suite G-129 | 847/330–1200 | $7.95–$13.95 | AE, D | No lunch weekends.

Timpano Italian Chop House. Italian. When you enter this eatery on the southeast perimeter of the Woodfield Mall, you feel you've stepped into a '50s Italian supper club—ceiling fans, big plants, Frank Sinatra tunes—where "bone-in" cuts of beef are the speciality, but you can also choose chicken, seafood, veal, and salad. Or try the shrimp fra diablo, which is a firey combination of shrimp, garlic, white wine, asparagus, spinach, pine nuts, goat cheese, and diablo sauce over fettuccine. | 1695 E. Golf Rd. | 847/517–8866 | $12–$40 | AE, D, DC, MC, V.

Lodging

Chicago-Schaumburg Drury Inn. Adjacent to a Denny's, a Bennigan's, and a Wendy's, this hotel is just off the intersection of I-290 and Higgins Road and a block and a half south of the Woodfield Mall. Complimentary Continental breakfast. In-room data ports, some microwaves, some refrigerators, cable TV. Indoor pool. Exercise equipment. Laundry facilities. Business services. | 600 N. Maringale Rd. | 847/517–7737 or 800/378–7946 | www.druryinn.com | 125 rooms | $98–$108 | AE, D, DC, MC, V.

Country Inn & Suites-Carlson. Two miles west of the Woodfield Mall, on the corner of Remington and Roselle Roads, this inn has a lobby with a fireplace, wood floors, and a beamed ceiling, and all rooms have feather bedding. You can splurge here and get a Jacuzzi suite with a fireplace. Complimentary Continental breakfast. In-room data ports, microwaves, refrigerators, some in-room hot tubs, cable TV, and in-room movies. Indoor pool, hot tub.

Exercise room. Laundry facilities. Business services. | 1401 N. Roselle Rd. | 847/839–1010 | fax 847/839–1212 | 49 rooms, 24 suites | $89–$169 | AE, D, DC, MC, V.

Embassy Suites. Across from Motorola, this all-suites accommodations is 1½-mi north of the Woodfield Mall. Restaurant, bar, complimentary breakfast, room service. In-room data ports, microwaves, refrigerators, cable TV. Indoor pool, pond. Hot tub. Exercise equipment. Laundry facilities. Business services. | 1939 N. Meacham Rd. | 847/397–1313 or 800/EMBASSY | fax 847/397–9007 | 209 suites | $199 | AE, D, DC, MC, V.

Hampton Inn. These standard accommodations 45 minutes north of downtown Chicago are two blocks from the Woodfield Mall. Complimentary Continental breakfast, room service. In-room data ports, cable TV. Exercise equipment. Laundry service. | 1300 E. Higgins Rd. | 847/619–1000 or 800/426–7866 | fax 847/619–1019 | www.hampton-inn.com | 128 rooms | $119 | AE, D, DC, MC, V.

Holiday Inn. On the north side of Schaumburg, this hostelry is a half-hour from O'Hare International Airport. Restaurant. Bar. Complimentary Continental breakfast, room service. In-room data ports, microwaves, refrigerators, cable TV. Pool. Exercise room. Laundry service. Business services. Some pets allowed. | 1550 N. Roselle Rd. | 847/310–0500 or 877/289–8443 | fax 847/312–0579 | www.holidayinnschaumburg.com | 141 rooms, 2 suites | $159.95, $199.95 suites | AE, D, DC, MC, V.

Homewood Suites. This extended-stay hotel is where visitors to local corporations make their home. It's 1 mi west of Woodfield Mall and 13 mi west of O'Hare International Airport. Picnic area, complimentary Continental breakfast. In-room data ports, kitchenettes, microwaves, cable TV, in-room VCRs (and movies). Pool. Hot tub. Basketball, exercise equipment. Laundry facilities. Business services. Some pets allowed (fee). | 815 E. American La. | 847/605–0400 or 800/CALLHOME | fax 847/619–0990 | www.homewood-suites.com | 108 suites | $159 | AE, D, DC, MC, V.

Hyatt Regency Woodfield. This five-story hostelry is across the street from the Woodfield Mall. Restaurant, bar. In-room data ports, refrigerators, cable TV, in-room VCRs. Outdoor and indoor pools. Barbershop, hot tub. Exercise equipment. Business services. | 1800 E. Golf Rd. | 847/605–1234 or 800/233–1234 | fax 847/605–0328 | www.hyatt.com | 469 rooms | $99–$205 | AE, D, DC, MC, V.

La Quinta Motor Inn. One block west of I–290, this stucco motel is in south Schaumburg and 3 blocks north of downtown. Complimentary Continental breakfast. In-room data ports, cable TV. Outdoor pool. Laundry services. Pets allowed. | 1730 E. Higgins Rd. | 847/517–8484 or 800/687–6667 | fax 847/517–4477 | www.laquinta.com | 127 rooms | $109 | AE, D, DC, MC, V.

Marriott. This 14-story tower is 1 mi south of Woodfield Mall; a shuttle to the mall is provided. Restaurant, bar. In-room data ports. microwaves, refrigerators, cable TV, in-room VCRs (fee). Indoor-outdoor pool. Pond. Hot tub. Exercise equipment. Laundry facilities. Business services. Some pets allowed. | 50 N. Martingale Rd. | 847/240–0100 or 800/228–9290 | fax 847/240–2388 | www.marriott.com | 394 rooms, 4 suites | $99–$174 | AE, D, DC, MC, V.

Radisson. At the northeast tip of Schaumburg, this motel is right next door to TGI Friday's. Complimentary shuttle serves both the O'Hare Airport and the Woodfield Mall. In-room data ports. Outdoor pool. Hot tub. Exercise equipment. Video games. Business services. Airport shuttle. | 1725 E. Algonquin Rd. | 847/397–1500 | www.radisson.com | 200 rooms | $59–$259 | AE, D, DC, MC, V.

Red Roof Inn. Located in Hoffman Estates, this motel is 3 mi northwest of Schaumburg. In-room data ports, some microwaves, some refrigerators, cable TV. Business services. Pets allowed. | 2500 Hassell Rd., Hoffman Estates | 847/885–7877 or 800/REDROOF | fax 847/885–8616 | www.redroof.com | 118 rooms | $65.99–$68.99 | AE, D, DC, MC, V.

Wyndham Garden Hotel. This hotel is in the Schaumburg business district and just over a mile from Woodfield Mall. Restaurant, bar, complimentary breakfast, evening room ser-

vice. In-room data ports, cable TV. Refrigerators. Indoor pool. Hot tub. Exercise equipment. Laundry service. Business services. | 800 National Pkwy. | 847/605–9222 or 800/WYNDHAM | fax 847/605–9240 | www.wyndham.com | 188 rooms, 1 suite | $135 | AE, D, DC, MC, V.

SHELBYVILLE

MAP 6, G7

(Nearby towns also listed: Decatur, Effingham, Mattoon)

Shelbyville was originally settled in the 1830s, its growth fueled by railroads and coal mining (the latter foundered during the Depression). Today, it's a thriving agricultural center with 5,000 residents and the Shelby County seat.

Information: **Shelby County Office of Tourism** | 315 E. Main St., 62565 | 217/774–2244 | www.lakeshelbyville.com.

Attractions

Shelby County Illinois Historical and Genealogical Society. Housed in the old Shelbyville jail, built in 1892, the society's research library and plethora of artifacts are available for you to explore. | S. 1st and S. Washington Sts. | 217/774–2260 or 217/774–4082 | www.shelbycohistgen.org | Free | Nov.–Mar. Mon., Fri., and Sat. 10–4; Apr.–Oct. Mon.-Sat 10–4.

ON THE CALENDAR
NOV.–JAN.: *Shelby County Victorian Splendor Lights Festival.* This holiday celebration with lights, parades, Christmas tree decorating, and live nativity scenes takes place sporadically during the winter season. | 217/774–2244.

Dining
Guys Steakhouse Steak. This family-style restaurant has five separate rooms, including a lounge and a pizza shop. This is one of the few restaurants that can successfully serve everything from pizza to prime rib, though it's especially famous for smoked ribs. Try the walleye, ribeye, filet mignon, chicken, or pork chops. On weekends, enjoy an all-you-can-eat buffet. | 1000 W. Main St. | 217/774–2714 | $6–$15 | AE, MC, V.

Stoney's Long Branch. Continental. This restaurant on the corner of Main and Morgan has pressed-tin ceilings and hardwood floors, and its rib-eye steak is a longstanding favorite. A bear-skin rug and a mounted tuna hang on one wall, and Harley Davidson paraphernalia covers another. Kids menu. | 203 E. Main St. | 217/774–1700 | $7.95–$18.95 | AE, MC, V | Closed Sun. No lunch Sat.

Lodging
Country Charm Bed & Breakfast. Three blocks from town on a three-lot plot, this yellow farmhouse trimmed in green was built by the Gregorys, friends of Lincoln, in 1858. It boasts rooms appointed with respect to their names, the Lincoln, the Brass, the Treasure, and the Patchwork. Complimentary breakfast. TV in common area. | 314 S. Cedar St. | 800/600–5352 | www.shelbyville-il.net/countrycharm | 4 rooms (2 with shared bath) | $50–$55 | No credit cards.

Eagle Creek Resort and Conference Center. This 34,000-acre golf resort is in Eagle Creek State Park on the shores of Lake Shelbyville. The furnishings are handcrafted by local Amish artists, and the suites have fireplaces. Two restaurants, bar, room service. Some microwaves, some refrigerators, cable TV. Indoor-outdoor pool. Hot tub. Eighteen-hole golf course, miniature golf, tennis. Exercise equipment, hiking, boating. Video games. Playground. Laundry facilities. Business services. | Eagle Creek State Park, Findlay, IL 62534 | 217/756–3456 or 800/876–3245 | www.eaglecreekresort.com | 138 rooms, 10 suites | $119–$149, $165 suites | AE, D, DC, MC, V.

Shelby Historic House and Inn. One of the four buildings (the Tallman House) at this Victorian-style property in the center of town is on the National Register of Historic Places; the other three were built 1965–1997 in similar style. Complimentary breakfast. In-room data ports, cable TV. | 800 W. Main St. | 217/774–3991 or 800/342–9978 | www.shelbyinn.com | 45 rooms | $62–$78 | AE, D, DC, MC, V.

SKOKIE

MAP 8, D4

(Nearby towns also listed: Chicago, Evanston, Glenview, Wilmette)

Until the 1940s, Skokie was a rural village known as Niles Center. Today, it still calls itself a village, but it's a blend of corporate offices, vibrant retail, and pleasant neighborhoods in north suburban Chicago, and the population has blossomed to 60,000.

Information: **Skokie Chamber of Commerce** | 5002–5006 Oakton St., 60077 | 847/673–0240 | fax 847/673–0249 | www.skokiechamber.org.

Attractions

SKOKIE

INTRO
ATTRACTIONS
DINING
LODGING

Holocaust Museum. This museum a mile from downtown is also the research center for the Holocaust Memorial Foundation of Illinois. | 4255 Main St. | 847/677–4640 | fax 847/677–4684 | Free | Mon.–Thurs. 9–4:30, Fri. 9–3, Sun. noon–4.

North Shore Center for the Performing Arts. Two theaters make up this performing arts complex: Northlight Theater and Centre East Production. It's one block south of the Old Orchard Shopping Center. | 9501 Skokie Blvd. | 847/637–6300 (box office) or 847/679–9501 | fax 847/679–1879 | www.skokienet.org/nscpas/ | Prices vary with shows | Call for hours.

Skokie Heritage Museum. This museum in a fire engine house built in the 1880s traces Skokie's roots as a pioneering community in the 19th century. It's one block west of downtown Skokie. | 8031 Floral Ave. | 847/677–6672 | fax 847/674–8959 | www.skokieparkdistrict.org | Free | Tues.–Sat. noon–4.

ON THE CALENDAR

JUNE: *Brandeis University Used Book Sale.* This tent sale at the Old Orchard Shopping Center has a half-million used books for purchase. It runs the second week of the month. | 847/724–9715.

MAY: *Festival of Cultures.* A festival of over 20 different cultures, including European, Asian, and Native American, has music, dancers, food, and folk art on tap at Oakton Park. | 847/674–1500, ext.0.

Dining

Don's Fishmarket and Tavern. Seafood. There are two dining rooms at this restaurant—many a proposal has been made at "Don's Mantle"—serving mainly seafood dishes (grilled salmon, swordfish, and tuna). There's also a casual tavern with karaoke on Wednesday nights with seafood, pasta, and Mexican dishes. Kids' menu. Early-bird dinners. | 9335 Skokie Blvd. | 847/677–3424 | www.donsfishmarket.com | Reservations essential | $5.95–$12.95 Tavern; $15.95–$39.95 Fishmarket | AE, D, DC, MC, V | No lunch Sat. in Fishmarket. No lunch Sun.

Maggiano's Little Italy. Italian. It's busy (you can expect to wait) in this restaurant in the Old Orchard Shopping Center that feels straight out of Little Italy in the 1940s. There's a sidewalk café for outdoor dining. Specialties from southern Italy include mostaccioli, roast chicken with rosemary, and shells with roasted vegetables. | 175 Old Orchard Rd. | 847/933–9555 | www.maggianos.com | $10.95–$27.95 | AE, D, DC, MC, V.

Myron and Phil's. American. This North Shore fixture 2 mi south of Lincolnwood serves seafood, Romanian skirt steak, and ribs. Piano bar Wed.–Sat. | 3900 W. Devon Ave., Lincolnwood | 847/677–6663 | $12.95–$42 | AE, D, DC, MC, V | No lunch weekends.

Lodging

Days Inn. Eight miles west of Skokie, this motel is in a residential and business district. Complimentary Continental breakfast. Some in-room data ports, some kitchenettes, some microwaves, some refrigerators, cable TV. Business services. No-smoking rooms. | 6450 W. Touhy Ave., Niles | 847/647–7700 or 800/DAYSINN | fax 847–647–7716 | www.daysinn.com | 140 rooms, 10 suites | $84–$94, $129–$153 suites | AE, D, DC, MC, V.

Doubletree. This 12-story hotel is next to the North Shore Center for the Performing Arts and across the street from the Old Orchard Shopping Center. Restaurant, bar, room service. In-room data ports, microwaves, refrigerators, cable TV, in-room VCRs. Indoor-outdoor pool. Exercise equipment. Business services. | 9599 Skokie Blvd. | 847/679–7000 or 800/222–TREE | fax 847/679–9841 | www.doubletreehotels.com | 368 rooms, 11 suites | $114–$159, $169 suites | AE, D, DC, MC, V.

Hampton Inn & Suites. Across Eden's Expressway from the Old Orchard Shopping Center in the heart of Chicago's North Shore, this hotel has drivers available day and night to tote you gratis (within a 5-mi radius) to local restaurants and sites you won't want to miss. Complimentary breakfast. In-room data ports, microwaves, refrigerators, some in-room hot tubs, cable TV, in-room VCRs. Indoor pool. Hot tub, sauna. Exercise equipment. Laundry facilities, laundry service. | 5201 Old Orchard Rd. | 847/583–1111 or 800/426–7866 | fax 847/583–0300 | www.hampton-inn.com | 225 rooms | $119–$179 | AE,D,DC,V.

Holiday Inn North Shore. The Holidome and Recreational Center at this hotel 12 mi from downtown Chicago has all sorts of sports activities and expansive meeting spaces. Restaurant, bar, room service. In-room data ports, microwaves, refrigerators, cable TV. Indoor pool. Hot tub. Sauna. Exercise equipment. Video games. Laundry facilities. Some pets allowed. | 5300 W. Touhy Ave. | 847/679–8900 or 888/221–1298 | fax 847/679–7447 | www.basshotels.com | 243 rooms | $99–$179 | AE, D, DC, MC, V.

Howard Johnson Hotel–Skokie. This hotel in northern Skokie is a block from the North Shore Center for Performing Arts and two blocks from Old Orchard shopping mall. Restaurant, bar, complimentary breakfast buffet. In-room data ports, microwaves, refrigerators, cable TV. Indoor pool. Hot tub. Sauna. Exercise equipment. Business services. Pets allowed. | 9333 Skokie Blvd. | 847/679–4200 or 800/654–2000 | fax 847/679–4218 | www.hojo.com | 134 rooms | $133 | AE, D, DC, MC, V.

Thrift Lodge. In Niles, 2 mi west of Skokie, these basic accommodations are 15 mi from O'Hare Airport. In-room data ports, cable TV. | 7247 Waukegan Rd., Niles | 847/647–1913 | 75 rooms | $60 | AE, D, DC, V.

SPRINGFIELD

MAP 6, E6

(Nearby towns also listed: Lincoln, Jacksonville, Petersburg)

Springfield is awash in history. With good reason, of course: Abraham Lincoln was a supporter of moving the state capital here in 1837; he lived here for 24 years; he married, bought a house, raised a family, practiced law, and served in the legislature here; was elected president while he lived here; and is buried here. It's possible to see places where every one of these activities occurred, which alone would make Springfield a popular destination.

But Springfield also lives very much in the present. It's Illinois' capital, and every year thousands come to see the ornate state capitol building, tour the Governor's Mansion, and browse in the Illinois State Museum and the Illinois Historical Library.

Beyond that, Springfield is simply a good-sized American city with many activities unrelated to its historical past and its civic present. It has a zoo; museums; numerous parks; a city lake with beaches, fishing, and boating; shopping malls and downtown specialty shops; and a healthy selection of restaurants. There are also concerts, theater, art exhibitions, and the state fair in this city of 115,000.

Information: Springfield Convention and Visitors Bureau | 109 N. 7th St., 62701 | 217/789–2360 or 800/545–7300 | www.springfield.il.us.visit.

TRANSPORTATION

Airports: Capital Airport; 1200 Capital Airport Dr., I–55, Springfield 62707 | 217/788–1060 | fax 217/788–8056 | www.flyspi.com.
Rail Passenger Service: Amtrak: Amtrak | Jefferson and Washington Sts. | 800/USA–RAIL or locally 217/753–2013 | amtrak.com | www.amtrak.com.

WALKING TOURS

Springfield—Without Lincoln (4–5 hours)

Don't try to see all of Springfield in one day; instead visit the city's government and recreational sites one day, and save the next for Abe. Start at the **State Capitol;** take a look at the rotunda or keep an eye on the legislature if it's in session. From here, walk down 2nd Street and take a right on Edwards to the **Illinois State Museum,** which exhibits cultural and natural artifacts from the state's past.

After browsing in the museum, go back to 2nd, take a right, and walk down to Lawrence. One block to the left is the **Dana–Thomas House,** the Prairie-style mansion designed by Frank Lloyd Wright for Springfield resident Susan Lawrence Dana in 1903. After seeing Mr. Wright's distinctive furniture and glasswork, you can walk back to Cook, take a right, and walk over to 5th Street, past the home of poet Vachel Lindsay at No. 603. Continue on another block to another home—that of the Illinois governor, the **Executive Mansion.**

Two blocks farther east on Edwards is the **Oliver P. Parks Telephone Museum;** one block farther down on 6th is the Grand Army of the Republic Memorial Museum, a trove of Civil War artifacts. If you've still got some steam left, hike seven blocks north on 6th to the **Springfield Children's Museum.**

THE INCREDIBLE MOVING CAPITAL

Illinois has had three capitals since its inception—in fact, it had all three in the first 20 years of existence.

The first was at the Mississippi River town of Kaskaskia, which had been the capital of the Illinois Territory. However, delegates ratifying the new state constitution asked for a more centrally located seat of government, and two years later, the capital was moved to Vandalia.

Vandalia went through several capitol buildings during its 19-year run as capital. One was hastily constructed after Vandalia was named capital; it burned three years later. Another was constructed and used for 13 more years. By the mid-1830s, though, the rapidly growing upstate counties were pressing for a more centrally located capital. Vandalia built a brand-new building to try to keep the capital in town, but Springfield won out in 1839.

© Corbis

Springfield—With Lincoln (3–4 hours)

The logical place to start a Lincoln tour is at the **Lincoln Home National Historic Site** at 8th and Jackson. After you've seen where he lived, you can stop by where he worked; walk north on 7th Street to Monroe Street; turn left and go two blocks to the **Lincoln–Herndon Law Offices.** Conveniently for Honest Abe and his partner, the offices are right across the street from the **Old State Capitol State Historic Site,** where Lincoln worked, read, and spoke. The work paid the bills—and you can see Lincoln's account ledger with the Springfield Marine and Fire Insurance Company. It's on display at the **Bank One building,** one block east at 6th and Washington. Go a block south to Adams and follow Adams east three blocks to 9th Street. Take a right, and one block in is the **Lincoln Depot,** from which Lincoln left Springfield as president-elect, bound for Washington, DC.

Attractions

ART AND ARCHITECTURE

Dana–Thomas House State Historic Site. This Frank Lloyd Wright—designed mansion two blocks south of the Governor's Mansion has original furniture, light fixtures, and windows. | 301 E. Lawrence Ave. | 217/782–6776 | $3 (suggested) | Wed.–Sun. 9–4.

Daughters of Union Veterans of the Civil War National Headquarters. Civil War records of both the Union and Confederate armies are on display at this museum. Four blocks from downtown. There are also exhibits of Civil War artifacts. | 503 S. Walnut St. | 217/544–0616 | Free | Weekdays 9–noon and 1–4; and by appointment.

Edwards Place. This restored 1830s Italianate mansion 6 blocks north of downtown Springfield is now home to Springfield Art Association Tours (history of the building and its furnishings), an art gallery, and the Michael Victor II Art Library. | 700 N. 4th St. | 217/523–2631 | fax 217/523–3866 | Donation suggested to house and gallery; library free | Tours by appointment; call ahead for gallery and library hours.

Executive Mansion. Three levels of the Illinois' governor's home are open viewing. | 410 E. Jackson St. | 217/782–6450 | fax 217/782–2771 | www.state.il.us | Free | Tues., Thurs. 9:30–11 and 2–3:30; Sat. 9:30–11.

Lincoln Ledger. Lincoln had to pay bills like everyone else and you can view his original account ledger with Springfield Marine and Fire Insurance at Bank One, which was formerly Springfield Marine Bank. | 6th at Washington Sts. | 217/525–9600 | Weekdays 9–5 | Free.

New State Capitol. This center for state government west of downtown was built from 1868 to 1888. When the Illinois House and Senate are in session, you can watch the proceedings from galleries. | 2nd St. and Capitol Ave. | 217/782–2099 | Free | Daily.

Capitol Complex Visitors Center. Information on Springfield sites and other Illinois attractions is available here. | 425 S. College St. | 217/524–6620 | Free | Mon. 9–3, Tues.–Fri. 8–4:30, Sat. 9–4.

Illinois State Museum. The bones of an Ice Age mastodon and natural and cultural treasures from around the state are on display here. | Spring and Edwards Sts. | 217/782–7386 | fax 217/782–1254 | www.museum.state.il.us | Free | Mon.–Sat. 8:30–5; Sun. noon–5.

CULTURE, EDUCATION, AND HISTORY

Illinois Korean War Memorial. In the Oakridge Cemetery, adjoining property to that on which the state's Vietnam Veterans Memorial resides, this circular, gray granite monument, dedicated in May 1988, pays tribute to the 1,748 citizens of Illinois killed in action in the Korean War. Encircled by the wall are a bell representing liberty and statues of military figures in uniforms of the army, navy, air force, and marines. | 1500 Monument Ave. 62702 | 217/782–2717 | Free | Daily.

Illinois Vietnam Veterans Memorial. A black-and-gray granite structure topped by an eternal flame honors the 2,972 citizens of Illinois who served in the Vietnam War and died or are still missing. Inscribed below the flame are hymns of the army, navy, air force, marines, and coast guard. | 1500 Monument Ave. | 217/782–2717 | Free | Daily.

Lincoln Pew. You can visit Abe and Mary Lincoln's family pew in Springfield's first church, the First Presbyterian Church, built in 1830, directly across the street from the Lincoln Library. | 7th St. (at Capitol) | 217/528–4311 | Free | June–Sept., weekdays 10–4.

Lincoln Shrines. Abe Lincoln's presence is a big part of this town—nowhere more so than in the buildings where he lived and worked. You can visit many of them that are still around.

Lincoln Depot. Lincoln bid farewell to Springfield at this depot as he left for Washington, DC in 1861. You can look at two restored waiting rooms (one for women and one for the luggage and tobacco-spitting men), displays of people and places close to Lincoln, and an audiovisual show that re-creates the 12-day trip to his inauguration. | Monroe St. | 217/544–8695 or 217/788–1356 | Free | Apr.–Aug., daily 10–4.

Lincoln–Herndon Law Office Building. Lincoln practiced law at this office downtown from 1843–1852. Visits to the building are by guided tours only and include a video and a stop at a re-created 1846 post office. | 1 Old State Capitol Plaza, 6th and Adams Sts. | 217/785–7289 | $2 suggested donation | Mar.–Oct., daily 9–5; Nov.–Feb., daily 9–4.

Lincoln Home National Historic Site. Just three blocks from the town square is the only home Lincoln ever owned. An exhibit on the Lincoln family is on display here. | Visitor center, 426 S. 7th St. | 217/492–4241, ext. 221 | fax 217/492–4648 | www.nps.gov/liho | Free | March–Oct. 1, daily 8–6; Oct.–March 1, daily 8–5.

Lincoln Tomb State Historic Site. This tomb in the Oak Ridge Cemetery is the final resting place of the Lincoln family. It's 16 blocks north of the Old State Capitol. | 1500 Monument Ave. | 217/782–2717 | fax 217/524–3738 | Free | Mar.–Oct., daily 9–5, Nov.–Feb., daily 9–4.

Old State Capitol State Historic Site. Lincoln worked in this building for 23 years, trying cases and using its law library. He made his famous "House Divided" speech in its Hall of Representatives. | 1 Old State Capitol Plaza | 217/785–7960 | fax 217/557–0282 | $2 suggested donation | Mar.–Oct., daily 9–5, Nov.–Feb., daily 9–4.

MUSEUMS

Oliver P. Parks Telephone Museum. Exhibits on the history of the telephone are on display at this museum a block south of the Lincoln Home National Historic Site. | 529 S. 7th St. | 217/789–5303 | fax 217/789–5510 | Free | Weekdays 9–4:30.

Springfield Children's Museum. Kids and adults alike can enjoy the exhibits on art, architecture, health, and nature at this museum a block east of the Old State Capitol. | 619 E. Washington St. | 217/789–0679 | fax 217/789–0682 | $3 | Mon., Wed., Fri. 10–4, Thurs. 10–7; weekends 11–4.

PARKS, NATURAL AREAS, AND OUTDOOR RECREATION

Lincoln Memorial Garden and Nature Center. Wooded trails (five for hiking) and a nature center are 10 mi south of Springfield, on the south bank of Lake Springfield. | 2301 E. Lake Dr. | 217/529–1111 | fax 217/529–0134 | www.lmgnc.com | Free | Garden, daily dawn–dusk; nature center, Tues.–Sat. 10–4, Sun. 1–4.

OTHER POINTS OF INTEREST

Henson Robinson Zoo. More than 33 species of rare and exotic animals are at this local zoo 4 mi southeast of town on Lake Springfield. | 1100 E. Lake Dr. | 217/753–6217 | fax 217/529–8748 | www.hensonrobinsonzoo.org | $2.50; special rates for kids | Late Mar.–mid-Oct., weekdays 10–5, weekends 10–6.

Washington Park Botanical Gardens. The domed conservatory in this 20-acre park is one of central Illinois' major horticultural attractions, and the surrounding grounds, which you can stroll while the sun is up, include seasonal display beds, rose and shade gardens, a rockery, and perennial borders. | 1740 W. Fayette Ave. | 217/753–6228 | Free | Grounds daily sunrise–sunset. Domed conservatory weekdays noon–4, weekends noon–5.

Thomas Rees Memorial Carillon. Visit the bell tower or attend a carillon concert throughout the summer here at Washington Park. | Fayette Ave. and Chatham Rd. | 217/753–6219 | fax 217/529–8748 | $2; special rates for students | June–Aug., tours Tues.–Sun. noon–8, concerts Sun. 3 and 7; Wed. 7.

ON THE CALENDAR

FEB.–MAR.: *Maple Syrup Time.* Demonstrations of maple syrup–making from sap gathering to sugaring down take place weekends from the middle of February to the middle of March at the Lincoln Memorial Garden and Nature Center. The center is 10 mi south of Springfield on the south bank of Lake Springfield. | 217/529–1111.

JUNE: *International Carillon Festival.* Carillon artists from all over the world perform at evening concerts at the Thomas Rees Memorial Carillon in Washington Park. There's a $2 admission charge; special rates for students. | 217/753–6219.

JUNE: *Washington Street Jazz.* A fund-raiser for the Arts Council, this open-air festival, which in inclement weather moves inside the National City Bank, is a one-night extravaganza featuring jazz bands, food, and drink. Although seats are set up around the stage, you can copy the locals who bring lawnchairs for maximum comfort. | 217/753–3519, ext. 10.

JUNE–JULY: *Municipal Band Concerts.* The community band performs outdoor concerts in the evening several times a week at Douglas Park, 1 mi north of downtown. | 217/789–2360.

JUNE–AUG.: *114th Infantry Retreat Ceremony.* Illinois Vounteer Infantry wear authentic period clothing for this event in Lincoln Tomb State Historic Site in Oak Ridge Cemetery. It takes place on Tuesday evenings. | 217/782–2717.

JUNE–AUG.: *Springfield Muni Opera.* A volunteer community theater performs musicals outdoors throughout the summer on Lake Shore Drive. Take I–55 south, exit Stevenson. Seating charges are $8 reserved, $6 general; special rates for senior citizens, students, and kids. | 217/793–6864.

AUG.: *Illinois State Fair.* This annual fair showcases livestock and produce from all over the state, as well as nationally known performers, and plenty of food, rides, and exhibits. It all happens at the State Fairgrounds (I–55, exit 100) the first two weeks of the month from 7AM–midnight. There's a $3 entrance fee; kids 12 and under free. | 217/782–6661.

SEPT.: *Ethnic Festival.* Food, exhibits, and entertainment from different cultural groups (varies from year to year) all happen at this free festival that takes place at the State Fairgrounds (I–55, exit 100) Labor Day weekend. | 217/529–8189.

SEPT.: *LPGA State Farm Rail Classic.* This annual women's golf tournament at the Rail Golf Club (I–55, exit 105) Labor Day weekend attracts some 150 international professional players. Tickets are $18 in advance, $20 at the gate; special rates for kids. | 217/528–5742.

SEPT.: *Springfield Air Rendezvous.* At Springfield's airfield on Capital Airport Drive, this celebration usually held the third weekend of the month starts with a Friday evening hangar party followed by a twilight show of fireworks and flying. Saturday and Sunday you can marvel at the continuous shows of aerobatics in different types of planes, and peruse the many displays that chronical aeronautical history, including the plane's role in the military. Free activities for kids, in the "children's village." | 900 Capital Airport Dr. Suite 220, 62707 | 217/789–4400.

Dining

Arturo's. Continental. Pasta, seafood (salmon and crab Napoleon), and meat dishes (osso buco, beef Wellington, and prime ribs) fill out the menu at this dining spot across from the Governor's Mansion. Live entertainment Fri. and Sat. in the piano lounge. | 517 S. 4th St. | 217/522–5359 | $10–$21 | AE, D, DC, MC, V | Closed Sun. No lunch Sat.

Augie's Front Burner. Contemporary. Chef-owner Augie describes his cooking in this airy artsy place on the west side of the old state capitol plaza as "American with an attitude," offering such innovations as macadamia nut–encrusted salmon and pan-roasted ostrich fillet. | 2 W. Old State Capitol Plaza | 217/544–6979 | $12–$21 | AE, D, DC, MC, V | Closed Sun. No lunch Sat.

Café Brio. Eclectic. Recipes from Mexico, the Caribbean, and the Mediterranean make up this colorful restaurant's menu, where the margaritas are made with fresh lime juice. Try the rotolo, a puff pastry filled with mushrooms, three cheeses, and basil pesto, served atop a roasted tomato and kalamata olive sauce. Weekend brunch. | 524 E. Monroe St. | 217/544–0574 | $10–$18 | AE, MC, V | No dinner Sun.

Chesapeake Seafood House. Seafood. You can order steak and barbecued ribs as well as fish (baked orange roughy and fried whole catfish) in this restored 19th-century mansion on the outskirts of town. There are kids' items on the menu. | 3045 Clear Lake Ave. | 217/522–5220 | $10–$45 | AE, D, DC, MC, V | No lunch Sat, closed Sun.

Gumbo Ya Ya's. Cajun/Creole. In addition to its spicy gumbo, jambalaya, and shrimp etoufée, this lively place on the 30th floor of the Hilton serves up live entertainment weekends, and you can get seafood, chicken, and steaks grilled, bronzed, or blackened here. Kids' menu. | 700 E. Adams St. | 217/789–1530 | $9.95–$19.95 | AE, D, DC, MC, V | No lunch. Closed Sun.

Maldaner's. Contemporary. Established in 1883, this is the oldest restaurant in Springfield (it's been at this location in the center of town for more than a century). Legislators, lobbyists, businesspeople, and tourists come here for the beef Wellington and pistachio-roasted salmon. Other menu items include grilled rib-eye, filet of beef, portobello mushrooms, roasted chicken, and rack of lamb. You can dine on the sidewalk in summer.

SPRINGFIELD AND CENTRAL ILLINOIS

Springfield has always been a popular touring destination—for families and for history buffs. But the Central Illinois region around it also has attractions for those with other interests—outdoor activities, shopping, or just scenery-gazing.

The capital, of course, is the center of it all, particularly with its concentration of Lincoln sites. But a number of visiting spots relate to Springfield's status as the capital, including the State Capitol building itself; the Executive Mansion, where the governor lives; and the Illinois State Museum.

But if you feel you've overdone the history, the city has a number of other museums—a kids' museum and a telephone museum among them—where you can lay off the Lincoln for a while. Springfield also has a zoo, a botanic garden, a wildlife sanctuary, and a variety of parks and gardens. There's a water park and amusement park for the kids, and Lake Springfield, which is ringed with public parks. Downtown Springfield offers shopping—particularly in the historic district, where stores are likely to be housed in restored buildings—and restaurants.

A little farther afield, there are numerous small towns to explore—some with Lincoln connections, some with other historical significance. Petersburg is the home of Lincoln's New Salem State Historical Site; a little to the south is the Clayville Rural Life Center, which offers demonstrations of 19th-century frontier life.

The Illinois River and Spoon River valleys, about 50 mi northwest, provide scenery, and several fish and wildlife areas lie between Springfield and the Illinois River. There's also the Dickson Mounds Museum, near Lewiston, which focuses on early Native American ceremonial mounds.

© Artville

| 222 S. 6th St. | 217/522–4313 | www.maldaners.com | $12.50–$18.50 | AE, MC, V | Closed Sun. No lunch Sat., no dinner Mon.

Sebastian's. Eclectic. This late 1800s painted-brick establishment is sandwiched between the old and new capital buildings. You can eat in the candlelit dining room, with its brass fixtures and a terrazzo fountain, or take the marble staircase down into the bar and sit at the marble-top tables. Try the shrimp stuffed with jack cheese and chipotle dipping sauce, a signature dish that lures diners from miles away. | 221 S. 5th St. | 217/789–8988 | $11.95–$17.95 | AE, D, DC, MC, V | No lunch. Closed Sun.

Lodging

INEXPENSIVE

Best Inns of America. This motel is 10 mi south of Capital Airport. Complimentary Continental breakfast. In-room data ports, cable TV, in-room VCRs. Pool. Laundry facilities. Some pets allowed. | 500 N. 1st St. | 217/522–1100 or 800/237–8466 | fax 217/753–8589 | www.bestinn.com | 91 rooms | $48–$64 | AE, D, DC, MC, V.

Days Inn. Just two blocks west of Lake Springfield is this modern motel in the southeast section of town. It has free shuttle service to Capital Airport and the train station. Picnic area, complimentary Continental breakfast. Some in-room data ports, some microwaves, some refrigerators, cable TV. Pool. Laundry services. Business services, airport shuttle. Pets allowed (fee). | 3000 Stevenson Dr. | 217/529–0171 or 800/DAYSINN | fax 217/529–9431 | www.daysinn.com | 153 rooms | $68 | AE, D, DC, MC, V.

Red Roof Inn. This motel is 2 mi east of downtown and 3 mi north of Lake Springfield. In-room data ports, cable TV. Business services. Pets allowed. | 3200 Singer Ave. | 217/753–4302 or 800/THEROOF | fax 217/753–4391 | www.redroof.com | 108 rooms | $55.99 | AE, D, DC, MC, V.

Super 8–South. These basic accommodations are 4 mi south of downtown. Some microwaves, some refrigerators, cable TV. Laundry facilities. Business services. Some pets allowed. | 3675 S. 6th St. | 217/529–8898 | fax 217/529 4354 | 122 rooms | $36–$65 | AE, D, DC, MC, V.

MODERATE

Comfort Inn. This hotel is 8 mi southwest of downtown Springfield. Complimentary Continental breakfast. In-room data ports, some microwaves, some refrigerators, cable TV. Indoor pool. Hot tub. Some pets allowed. | 3442 Freedom Dr. | 217/787–2250 or 800/228–5150 | www.comfortinn.com | 51 rooms, 15 suites | $59, $72 suites | AE, D, DC, MC, V.

© Artville

A CANAL RUNS THROUGH IT

The Illinois and Michigan Canal brought life to Illinois; now Illinois is bringing it back to life.

The canal, which opened in 1848, was a vital link for shipping goods from the Great Lakes to the Gulf of Mexico. It stretched from the South Side of Chicago to La Salle, where barges would join up with the Illinois River, which took them to the Mississippi.

However, the railroads made the canal less vital, and it finally closed in the 1930s. But in the early 1980s, the canal was declared a national heritage corridor, and the canal got a new purpose. Today, bike trails and hiking paths follow the course of the waterway (which looks like little more than a stream in some spots), and commercial buildings that once lined the canal have been restored to their canal-days condition.

Country Dreams Bed & Breakfast. Ten miles east of Springfield on 16 acres in rural Rochester, this contemporary old-farmhouse-style home has vaulted ceilings, alcoves, cushioned windowseats, and a wraparound porch, where you can sit and look out on the surrounding farmland and fruit trees. Full breakfast weekends. No kids under 12. Complimentary Continental breakfast. Cable TV, some room phones. | 3410 Park La., Rochester | 217/498–9210 | www.countrydreams.com | 4 rooms | $75–$145 | AE, D, MC, V.

Hampton Inn. This standard motel is 2 mi east of downtown. Complimentary Continental breakfast. Cable TV. Indoor pool. Hot tub. Exercise equipment. Business services. Free parking. | 3185 S. Dirksen Pkwy. | 217/529–1100 or 800/HAMPTON | fax 217/529–1105 | www.hampton-inn.com | 123 rooms | $76 | AE, D, DC, MC, V.

Henry Mischler House Bed & Breakfast. Across from the Lincoln Home National Historic Site, this inn has hand-carved oak banisters, Victorian wallpaper, and lace curtains. The rooms are all furnished with antiques; all have private baths, though some require a short walk down the hall. Complimentary breakfast. Cable TV, room phones. No pets. | 802 E. Edwards St., 62703 | 217/525–2660 | www.mischlerhouse.com | 4 rooms, 1 suite | $75–$95 | AE, D, MC, V.

Mansion View Inn and Suites. At this white-shuttered hotel with motel-like outdoor entrances in the heart of the state's capital complex, you are directly across from the Executive Mansion and your room rental includes a free pass to the YMCA here. Restaurant, bar, complimentary Continental breakfast. In-room data ports, some in-room hot tubs, cable TV. Laundry facilities. Airport shuttle, free parking. | 529 S. 4th St. | 217/544–7411 or 800/252–1083 | fax 217/544–6211 | www.bestwestern.com/mansionview | 93 rooms | $75–$129 | AE, D, DC, MC, V.

Ramada Inn–South Plaza. This hotel is in a quiet, old residential neighborhood 2 mi south of downtown. Restaurant, bar. In-room data ports, some microwaves, some refrigerators (in suites), cable TV. Pool. Laundry facilities. Business services. Airport shuttle. Parking (fee). Some pets allowed (fee). | 625 E. St. Joseph St. | 217/529–7131 or 877/529–7131 | fax 217/529–7160 | www.ramada.com | 108 rooms, 6 suites | $62, $150 suites | AE, D, DC, MC, V.

Ramada Limited–North. This hotel overlooking a pond is 2 mi northeast of downtown. Complimentary Continental breakfast. Some microwaves, some refrigerators, cable TV. Indoor pool. Exercise equipment. Laundry facilities. Business services, airport shuttle, free parking. | 3281 Northfield Dr. | 217/523–4000 or 800/272–6232 | fax 217/523–4080 | www.ramada.com | 93 rooms, 4 suites | $71–$76, $100–$150 suites | AE, D, DC, MC, V.

EXPENSIVE

Courtyard by Marriott. Five miles southwest of downtown, this hotel is also 6 mi southwest of the medical centers. Restaurant (breakfast only), bar. In-room data ports, microwaves, refrigerators, cable TV. Indoor pool. Hot tub. Exercise room. Laundry facilities. Business services. Free parking. | 3462 Freedom Dr. | 217/793–5300 or 800/321–2211 | www.courtyard.com | 75 rooms, 3 suites | $85, $110 suites | AE, D, DC, MC, V.

Hilton–Springfield. This downtown 30-story tower with views of the city is across the street from the convention center. Three restaurants, bars with entertainment. In-room data ports, cable TV. Indoor pool. Barbershop/beauty salon. Gym. Business services. Airport shuttle. | 700 E. Adams St. | 217/789–1530 or 800/HILTONS | fax 217/789–0709 | www.hilton.com | 358 rooms, 10 suites | $144, $300–$550 suites | AE, D, DC, MC, V.

Inn at 835 Bed & Breakfast. In the heart of Springfield's historic district, on the old Route 66, this inn's rooms are furnished with antiques, such as brass and four-poster beds and claw-foot tubs, and have verandas and ceiling fans. Select wines are served in the sitting room evenings. Complimentary breakfast. Some in-room hot tubs, cable TV, in-room phones. Video games. Laundry facilities. | 835 S. 2nd St. | 888/217–4835 | www.innat835.com | 8 rooms, 2 suites | Rooms $109–$149, suites $169–$189 | AE, D, MC, V.

Renaissance Springfield Hotel. This 12-story hostelry is in historic downtown Springfield. Restaurant, bar, room service. In-room data ports, some refrigerators, cable TV. Indoor pool. Hot tub. Exercise equipment. Video games. Business services. Airport shuttle. Park-

SPRINGFIELD

INTRO
ATTRACTIONS
DINING
LODGING

ing (fee). | 701 E. Adams St. | 217/544–8800 or 800/HOTELS1 | fax 217/544–9607 | www.marriott.com | 314 rooms, 2 suites | $152, $304 suites | AE, D, DC, MC, V.

UNION

MAP 6, G1

(Nearby towns also listed: Rockford, Woodstock)

There are three historical museums in this small (population 650), quiet, and rural town.

Information: **Marengo–Union Chamber of Commerce** | 116 S. State St., Marengo 60152 | 815/568–6680 | www.merengo-union.com.

Attractions

Donley's Wild West Town. This re-creation of a western village 3 mi south of Union includes pony rides, gold panning, and reenactments. | U.S. 20 and S. Union Rd. | 815/923–2214 | fax 815/923–2253 | www.wildwesttown.com | $10, kids under 3 free | Memorial Day–Labor Day, daily 10–6; Apr.–May, Sept.–Oct., weekends 10–6.

Illinois Railway Museum. Restored trains, rides, and theme weekends are on tap at this rail museum just east of town. | 7000 Olson Rd. | 815/923–4391 or 800/BIG–RAIL | www.irm.org | $6–$9, special rates for senior citizens and kids | Memorial Day–Labor Day, weekdays 10–4, weekends 10–5; call for hours after Labor Day–Oct.

McHenry County Historical Museum. This downtown museum houses artifacts from county history and a research library with books on local history, genealogy, and civil war diaries. Also here is a one-room schoohouse and a log cabin. | 6422 Main St. | 815/923–2267 | fax 815/923–2271 | www.crystallakenet.org/mchs | Museum $3, $2 for senior citizens and students | Museum, May–Oct., Tues.–Fri. and Sun. 1–4; library, by appointment.

ON THE CALENDAR
JUNE: *Antique Music Show and Sale.* A show and sale of antique instruments and other music-related items take place in Donley's Wild West Town the second weekend of the month. There's an $8 admission charge. | 815/923–8000.
JULY: *Heritage Fair.* This outdoor fair with an auction, pioneer demonstrations, and a museum open house is at the McHenry County Historical Society the second Sunday of the month. | 815/923–2267.

Dining

Checkers. American. Folks drive from miles around to this busy place for the chicken, which is steam-fried with Checker's secret spices, the ¾-pound Checker burger, and the daily specials. These include a Friday-night fish-fry and Monday's barbecued ribs. You can also dine outside May through October. | 6524 Main St. | 815/923–2000 | $7.95–$18.95 | No credit cards | Closed Sun.

Lodging

Sunset Motel. In Morengo on West Grant Highway, right off U.S. 20, this small basic motel is the closest lodging to Union, which hasn't any. Cable TV. | 22116 W. Grant Hwy. | 815/568–7525 | 10 rooms | $37.50 | MC, V.

UTICA

MAP 6, F3

(Nearby towns also listed: Morris, Ottawa, Peru, Princeton)

Built as a canal town in the 1830s, today Utica (population 900) is the gateway to Starved Rock State Park, as well as to boating and water activities on the Illinois River.

Information: **Illinois Valley Area Chamber of Commerce and Economic Development** | 300 Bucklin St. (Box 446), La Salle 61301 | 815/223–0227 | www.ivaced.org.

Attractions

Illinois Waterway Visitor Center. You can get up-close views of the Illinois River lock and exhibits on Illinois waterways at this center 2 mi east of Utica. | 950 N. 27th Rd. | 815/667–4054 | fax 815/667–4954 | www.mvr.usace.army.mil/illwwyvc | Free | Fall–spring, daily 9–5; summer, daily 9–8.

I & M Canal State Trail. You can hike, bike, and snowmobile on the 61-mi network of trails between Rockdale and La Salle, which you can access in Buffalo Rock State Park or off Canal Street in Utica. No open fires are allowed, and you can camp only in designated areas. | Buffalo Rock State Park, Dee Bennett Rd and County Rd 34, Ottawa, 61350 | 815/942–0796 | Free | Daily.

La Salle County Historical Museum. This small museum in downtown Utica contains memorabilia from the area. | Canal and Mill Sts. | 815/667–4861 | fax 815/667–5121 | www.lasallecountymuseum.org | $1; special rates for kids | Apr.–mid-Dec., Wed.–Fri. 10–4, weekends noon–4; Mid-Dec.–Mar., Fri.–Sun. noon–4.

Matthiessen State Park. Bluffs, canyons, and cascading waterfalls dot this park 2 mi south of Utica on Route 178. There's also hiking, fishing, cross-country skiing, and a horse campground. | Rte. 178 | 815/667–4868 or 815/667–4906 | fax 815/667–5353 | www.dnr.state.il.us | Free | Park daily 7 AM–10 PM; visitor center weekdays 9–5, weekends 9–6.

Starved Rock State Park. Punctuated with bluffs, canyons, and waterfalls, Starved Rock has spectacular views of the Illinois River. Activities here at one of the state's most popular sites include paddleboat rides, canoe rental, horseback riding, hiking, and camping (reservations essential May–Oct.). A lodge and restaurant are on the grounds. The park is 1 mi south of Utica on Route 178. | Rte. 178 | 815/667–4726 or 815/667–4906 | fax 815/667–5353 | www.dnr.state.il.us | Free | Park daily 5:30 AM–10 PM; Visitor Center weekdays 9–5, weekends 9–6.

ON THE CALENDAR

JAN.: *Winter Wilderness Weekend.* Guided hikes take you through Starved Rock State Park to frozen waterfalls and other winter sights. Hikes leave from the visitor center one weekend in mid-month at 9AM and 1PM each day. | 815/667–4906.

FEB.: *Cross-Country Ski Weekend.* The first weekend in February is when you can take a guided cross-country ski trip through Matthiessen and Starved Rock State Parks. The excursion leaves from Matthiessen each day at 9 AM and 1 PM. | 815/667–4906.

MAY: *Wildflower Pilgrimage.* Guided hikes through Starved Rock State Park to view the area's wildflowers depart from the visitor center the first weekend of May at 9AM and 1PM each day. | 815/667–4906.

JUNE: *Montreal Canoe Weekend.* You can take a ride in a 34-ft voyageur canoe that's a replica of one used by the French to explore North America. The trip starts from Point Shelter at the east end of Starved Rock State and goes the second weekend of the month 11–3. | 815/667–4906.

SEPT.: *Valley Carvers Woodcarving Expo.* This judged and juried show and sale takes place one weekend in late September at the Starved Rock Lodge, 5 mi south of Utica. Thirty-five carvers from seven states exhibit here. | 815/672–7101.

OCT.: *Burgoo Festival.* Locals claim there are no domestic animals left in the area after this festival, which pays homage to the pioneers' thick meat stew by the Historical Society's cooking up a 150-gallon facsimile to serve on the second Sunday in October, rain or shine. This is Utica's largest fund-raiser for their museum complex. After you fill up on stew, you can wander the village to enjoy the bands, Civil War reenactments, and the wares of more than 250 crafts vendors. | 815/667–4861.

Dining

Cajun Connection. Cajun. Owner Ron McFarlaine grew up in Louisiana and brought his own recipes north to this casual Cajun restaurant that features alligator, gumbo, jumbo shrimp, and jambalaya. | 2954 Rte. 178 | 815/667–9855 | $8–$15 | MC, V | Mon.–Wed.

Duffy's. Eclectic. A traditional Irish pub, Duffy's menu changes daily: Monday is All-American with burgers and ribs; Tuesday is Italian; Wednesday is Mexican; Thursday is Irish; and Friday features an all-you-can-eat fish fry. | 101 Mill St. | 815/667–4324 | $5–$10 | AE, D, MC, V.

Lodging

Brightwood Inn. Each room in this peaceful inn, within the confines of Matthiessen State Park, is decorated differently from floral patterns and wicker furniture to dark green interiors and canopied beds. Each room has a queen-size bed and fireplace, and three of the rooms have private balconies. Dinner is served in the dining room Thursday–Sunday. It's 2 mi from Starved Rock State Park. Complimentary breakfast, cable TV, in-room VCRs. | 2407 N. Rte. 178 | 815/667–4600 | 8 rooms | $90–$185 | AE, D, MC, V.

Lander's House. A mile from Starved Rock State Park, this country house offers rooms with natural wood furniture and checked quilts in the main house or intimate cottages with a Jacuzzi, fireplace, and private screened in porch in a converted 108 year old barn. Complimentary breakfast. No room phones. Some in-room hot tubs. TV in common area. | 115 E. Church St. | 815/667–5170 | 7 rooms | $90–$185. Rooms $139, cottages $279 | MC, V.

Starved Rock Inn. At this small country inn 2 mi north of Starved Rock State Park, just a block off I-80, all the rooms have queen-size beds and log headboards. Cable TV. | Rtes. 178 and 6 | 815/667–4550 | 8 rooms | $45 | AE, D, MC, D, V.

Starved Rock Lodge and Conference Center. This hostelry in the eponymous park is convenient to all its facilities and activities. The wood-shingled buildings are on Rte. 178, 2½ mi south of downtown Utica. Restaurant, bar, coffee shop. In-room data ports, cable TV, in-room VCRs (and movies). Indoor pool, wading pool. Hot tub, 2 saunas. Business services. | Rte. 178 and Rte. 71 | 815/667–4211 or 800/868–7625 | fax 815/667–4455 | www.starvedrocklodge.com | 94 rooms | $95 | AE, D, DC, MC, V.

VANDALIA

MAP 6, F8

(Nearby towns also listed: Effingham, Salem)

Vandalia was the second capital of Illinois, until the legislature moved to Springfield in 1839. The 1836 Vandalia Statehouse, where Abraham Lincoln first practiced as a legislator, still stands. Today the town of 6,100 is home to a variety of businesses and industry.

Information: Vandalia Chamber of Commerce | 1408 N. 5th St. (Box 238), 62471 | 618/283–2728.

Attractions

Fayette County Museum. On Main Street, just north of the State House, this early Gothic Revival building, originally the First Presbyterian Church, is on the National Register of Historic Places and houses artifacts of the first European settlers of Vandalia, who were from Germany. | 301 W. Main St. | 618/283–4866 | Donations suggested | Mon.–Sat. 10–4.

Little Brick House Museum. This 1860 house has period furnishings. | 621 St. Clair St. | 618/283–0667 or 618/283–4866 | $3; special rates for kids | By appointment.

Ramsey Lake State Park. Horseback riding (no rentals though), hunting, camping, boating, and fishing are some of the activities in this 1,960-acre park 13 mi north of Vandalia on U.S. 51. | State Park Rd. | 618/423–2215 | fax 618/423–2766 | Free | Daily.

Vandalia Statehouse State Historic Site. Both Lincoln and Stephen Douglas served in the state legislature when it met in this 1830s state capitol building. | 315 W. Gallatin St. | 618/283–1161 | Free | Call for hours.

JUNE: *Grande Levée.* Father's Day weekend, Vandalia turns back its clock to the early 1800s, when it was the capital of Illinois, by decorating shop windows, donning costumes, and selling wares all in the style of that era. Street vendors, including trappers, wood-carvers, and blacksmiths, get into the act, following the Friday night kick-off ham-and-bean dinner cooked over an open flame in a cast-iron stove. Sunday's closing activities include a reenactment of the Lincoln-Douglas debate. | 618/283–1161.

Dining

Cuppy's Old Fashioned Soda Fountain and Café. American. Abe's pioneer salad, a variation on the Cobb, is a favorite in this old-fashioned café with its small soda fountain, black-and-white tiled floors, heart-back chairs, and cabinets from a 1924 drugstore, but a shake and a grilled-cheese fit the bill here, too. | 402 W. Gallatin St. 62471 | 618/283–0080 | $1.50–$4.50 | AE, D, V | Closed Sun. No dinner.

The Depot Restaurant and Lounge. American. In the depot that once served two railroads, this 1923 building even has an old caboose you can check out before or after you try this restaurant's *railroad spikes,* which are sautéed mushrooms in wine, garlic, and fresh herbs; and a *club car,* assorted breaded appetizers with dipping sauce. Some nights dinner is accompanied by a pianist on the grand piano, and you can join the karaoke crowd in the lounge. | 107 S. 6th St. 62471 | 618/283–1918 | $5.95–$24 | AE, D, DC, MC, V.

Gallatin St. Grille. Continental. All entrées here are served with the restaurant's signature home-baked flour pot bread, and you can join the locals who return again and again for the fettuccine Alfredo, which you eat at tables made quite homey by a small lamp on each. | 524 W. Gallatin St. | 618/283–0023 | $6.95–$18.95 | No credit cards | No lunch Sat. Closed Sun. and Mon.

Lodging

Beau-Meade House Bed & Breakfast. Six blocks from town, this 1860s folk Victorian house resembles the Lincoln Home in Springfield, sporting an upper parade, and lower front and back porches, where you can enjoy your breakfast or afternoon tea. Inside, the staircase is similar to that in the historic Little Brick House, and you can bathe in a claw-foot tub. Complimentary breakfast. TV in common area. Pond. Fishing. | 606 N. 6th St. | 618/283–1826 | 1 room | $80–$90 | No credit cards.

Brazle Haus Bed & Breakfast. Innkeepers of this Alpine-style home in one corner of a 100-acre farm in Brownstow, 17 mi west of Vandalia, give you free range of the kitchen, and ask that you relax—in front of their fire or on the wraparound porch or beside the farm's pond—when you stay in one of their two guest rooms, which share a bath. Complimentary breakfast. TV in common area. Pond. | Rte. 1, Brownstow | 618/347–2207 | 2 rooms (with shared bath) | $45–$50 | No credit cards.

Days Inn. This motel is 2 mi north of downtown and convenient to area golf courses (Vandalia Country Club is 3 mi away) and antiques shopping (5 mi from town). Complimentary Continental breakfast. In-room data ports, some microwaves, some refrigerators, cable TV. Pool. Video games. Pets allowed. | 1920 Kennedy Blvd. | 618/283–4400 or 800/DAYSINN | fax 618/283–4240 | www.daysinn.com | 83 rooms, 10 suites | $57.95 | AE, D, DC, MC, V.

Jay's. This family-run, two-story hostelry a block southwest of I–70 has a restaurant and bar next door. Some microwaves, refrigerators. Cable TV. Pets allowed. | 720 Gochenour St. | 618/283–1200 | fax 618/283–4588 | 21 rooms | AE, D, DC, MC, V.

Ramada Limited. Two miles west of downtown, this hostelry is next to I–70. Complimentary breakfast, room service (from adjacent restaurant). In-room data ports, some microwaves, some refrigerators, cable TV. Pool. Exercise equipment. Laundry service. Business services. Pets allowed. | 2707 Veterans Ave. | 618/283–1400 or 800/2RAMADA | fax 618/283–3465 | www.ramada.com | 55 rooms, 5 suites | $62.95, $87.95 suites | AE, D, DC, MC, V.

VANDALIA

INTRO
ATTRACTIONS
DINING
LODGING

Travelodge. This stucco motel is 1 mi north of downtown and has truck and RV parking. Complimentary Continental breakfast. In-room data ports, some microwaves, some refrigerators. Cable TV. Pool. Playground. Business services. Airport shuttle. Pets allowed (fee). | 1500 N. 6th St. | 618/283–2363 or 800/578–7878 | fax 618/283–2363 | www.travelodge.com | 48 rooms | $59.95 | AE, D, DC, MC, V.

VERNON HILLS

MAP 8, C3

(Nearby towns also listed: Grayslake, Lake Forest, Libertyville)

Vernon Hills is a bustling Chicago suburb with easy access to the Loop via a Metra commuter line. This northern community has a population of 26,000.

Information: **Green Oaks, Libertyville, Mundelein, Vernon Hills Chamber of Commerce** | 1123 S. Milwaukee Ave., Libertyville 60048 | 847/680–0750 | www.glmv.org.

Attractions

Cuneo Museum and Gardens. This opulent Venetian-style mansion a quarter of mile north of the center of town, was built in 1914. On display inside are Italian paintings, Flemish tapestries, porcelain, Oriental rugs, and Continental furnishings. Outside is a formal rose garden and antique statuary. | 1350 N. Milwaukee Ave. | 847/362–3042 | fax 847/362–4130 | $10; special rates for senior citizens, students, and kids | Grounds Feb.–Dec., Tues.–Sun. 10–5; tours Feb.–Dec., Tues.–Sat. 11–3:30.

ON THE CALENDAR

NOV.–DEC.: *A Winter Wonderland.* More than 80,000 people flock to the Cuneo Museum and Gardens on Lakeview Parkway to take this mile-and-a-half drive through displays of twinkling lights and animated scenes, including Reindeer Row, Candycane Lane, and Zooland, the opening of which the day after Thanksgiving marks the official beginning of the holiday season in Vernon Hills. Closed Christmas Eve, Christmas Day, and New Years. | 847/367–3725.

Dining

Café Pyrenees French. This café is decorated with framed lithographs and prints of southwestern France. Try the seafood ravioli or the duck confit. An array of fresh fish is served daily—the dover sole and grilled salmon are especially popular. The restaurant is in the Rivertree Court Shopping Center. | Rte. 21 at Rte. 60 | 847/918–8850 | Closed Mon. | $12–$20 | AE, D, MC, V.

Gilardi's. Italian. Art Deco furnishings in this turn-of-the-century mansion 5 mi south of downtown complement the fresh seafood and eight-finger cavatelli on the menu. There's entertainment on Friday and Saturday. | 23397 N. U.S. 45 | 847/634–1811 | Reservations essential | $11–$23 | AE, D, DC, MC, V | No lunch weekends.

Lodging

Amerisuites of Vernon Hills. Forty minutes north of Chicago and 8 mi from Gurnee Mills Shopping Mall, this all-suites hotel has a number of special suites with large desks, office supplies, speaker phones, and multiple phone lines, particularly welcome when you are traveling on business. Complimentary Continental breakfast. Some in-room data ports, minibars, microwaves, refrigerators, cable TV, VCRs. Indoor pool. Exercise equipment. Laundry facilities. | 450 N. Milwaukee Ave. | 847/918–1400 or 800/833–1516 | fax 847/918–1474 | www.amerisuites.com | 128 suites | $139–$154 | AE, D, DC, MC, V.

Hawthorn Suites. This corporate hotel is surrounded by malls, and many restaurants. The rooms are very spacious, and you can relax in front of the fireplace in the airy lobby. Complimentary Continental breakfast. In-room data ports, cable TV. Indoor pool. Hot tub. Gym. Laundry facilities. | 975 N. Lakeview Pkwy. | 847/367–8031 | fax 847/367–8039 | 120 rooms | $89–$130.

Homestead Guest Studios. Designed with the extended stay traveler in mind, each suite has a full-size kitchen and separate workspace with oversized desk. Fourteen miles from Six Flags America and 3 mi from Cuneo Museum. In-room data ports, cable TV. Laundry facilities. Business services. Pets allowed (fee). | 675 Woodland Pkwy. | 847/955–1111 or 800/888–STAYHSB | fax 847/955–0446 | $89 | AE, D, DC, MC, V.

WAUCONDA

MAP 6, G1

(Nearby towns also listed: Barrington, Crystal Lake, McHenry)

On the shores of Bangs Lake, Wauconda (incorporated in 1877) once hosted Chicagoans eager for a vacation away from the city. Today, the town (population 8,000) is home to the Lake County Discovery Museum, as well as a number of forest preserves and parks.

Information: Wauconda Chamber of Commerce | 100 N. Main St., 60084 | 847/526–5580.

Attractions

Lake County Discovery Museum. In addition to exhibits that highlight regional history, there's an extensive archive of postcards at this museum in the Lakewood Forest Preserve. There's also a vortex roller coaster theater that has an 11-minute simulated roller coaster ride that takes you from the Ice Age to the 21st century. | 27277 Forest Preserve Dr. | 847/526–7878 | fax 847/367–6642 | www.co.lake.il.us/forest/education.htm | $5; special rates for kids | Mon.–Sat. 11–4:40, Sun. 1–4:30.

ON THE CALENDAR

SEPT.: *Applefest/Pig Roast.* These three days of feasting and live music, pony rides, hayrides, and apple picking to herald the harvest season are always held the weekend before Labor Day, at Breedan's Wauconda Orchards, 1201 Gossell Road, ending with the pig roast on Sunday. But the music and hayrides continue weekends through the end of October. Activities are individually priced. | 847/526–8553 or 800/36–APPLE.

Dining

Biloxi Grill. Southern. Seafood gumbo, barbecued shrimp, and berry cobblers are on tap at this restaurant that has lakefront views from the dining room and deck. The restaurant is a mile east of downtown. | 313 E. Liberty St. | 847/526–2420 | Reservations essential weekends | $9.95–$23.95 | AE, D, DC, MC, V | No lunch. Closed Mon.

Spasso. Italian. Linguine with seafood and ravioli with butternut squash are among the draws at this trattoria one block west of Route 12. | 614 W. Liberty St. | 847/526–4215 | $20–$28 | AE, D, DC, MC, V.

Lodging

Wauconda Motel. Less than a mile from town, this small motel on eight acres is the only place in town to rest your head. Cable TV. | 26671 N. U.S. 12 | 847/526–2101 | 10 rooms | $55–$60 | AE, D, MC, V.

WAUKEGAN

MAP 6, H1

(Nearby towns also listed: Gurnee, Lake Forest)

This industrial North Shore city on Lake Michigan was incorporated in 1841 and is the county seat of Lake County. It's also the birthplace of 1950s violinist-comic Jack Benny and sci-fi author Ray Bradbury.

Information: Lake County, Illinois Convention and Visitors Bureau | 401 N. Riverside Dr., Suite 5, Gurnee 60031 | 847/662–2700 or 800/LAKENOW | www.lakecounty.org.

Attractions

Illinois Beach State Park. Hiking and biking trails through a nature preserve and along a beachfront, a swimming beach, camping, tours of sand dunes, volleyball, horseshoes, and a lodge (call 847/625-7300 for reservations) are included on 6 mi of grounds 3 mi north of Waukegan off Sheridan Road on Wadsworth. | Lake Front, Zion | 847/662–4811 | fax 847/662–6433 | www.dnr.state.il.us | Free; camping fee | Daily dawn–8 PM.

ON THE CALENDAR
JULY: *Waukegan's Heritage Fest.* After Waukegan's Independence Day parade, you can head over to Bowen Park, at Sheridan Road and Greenwood Avenue, for a day of opera and dance performances, baseball games, a bean bag toss, arts and crafts shows, and the highly anticipated greased-watermelon roll. | 847/360–4700.

Dining

Madison Ave. Contemporary. In this 1890s structure with a contemporary facade, you have broad views of the harbor through floor-to-ceiling windows in its dining room, where you can choose from among steak, pasta, fish, and chicken dishes, though the prime rib is a local favorite. | 34 N. Sheridan Rd. | 847/662–6090 | $9.95–$16.95 | AE, D, DC, MC, V | No lunch weekends.

Mathon's. Seafood. You can get chicken and steaks as well as fresh fish in this wood-paneled eatery with a seafaring theme right on Lake Michigan. Kids' menu. Bar. | 6 E. Clayton St. | 847/662–3610 | $14–$50 | AE, D, DC, MC, V | Closed Sun.–Mon.

Potesta's. Italian. Three miles east of downtown, this cheery restaurant has booth and table seating and serves pasta and pizza; lasagna is a favorite. | 434 S. Green Bay Rd. | 847/662–0602 | $5.50–$8.95 | AE, D, MC, V.

Saddle Ridge. Continental. Steaks and chops are served up alongside pasta, such as penne gorgonzola, in this restaurant done up in a western theme with tack and other saddleshop gear. You can join the karaoke in the lounge here Tuesdays through Saturdays. Sunday brunch and menus for kids and senior citizens are offered, too. | 200 N. Green Bay Rd. | 847/336–4696 | $8.95–$18.95 | AE, D, DC, MC, V | Breakfast also available.

Lodging

Best Inns of America. This motel is 12 blocks east of downtown. Complimentary Continental breakfast. In-room data ports, some microwaves, some refrigerators, cable TV. Pool. Some pets allowed (fee). | 31 N. Green Bay Rd. | 847/336–9000 or 800/BESTINN | fax 847/336–9000 | www.bestinn.com | 89 rooms | $78.99–$89.99 | AE, D, DC, MC, V.

Comfort Inn. Two miles west of downtown, this standard motel is 6 mi north of Illinois Beach State Park. Complimentary Continental breakfast. Cable TV. Video games. Business services. | 3031 Belvidere Rd. | 847/623–1400 or 800/228–5150 | fax 847/623–0686 | www.comfortinn.com | 64 rooms | $75 | AE, D, DC, MC, V.

Courtyard by Marriott. True to its name, this hostelry 5 mi west of downtown has an interior courtyard with a pool. Restaurant (breakfast only), bar. In-room data ports, some refrigerators, cable TV. Indoor pool. Hot tub. Exercise equipment. Laundry facilities. Business services, free parking. | 800 Lakehurst Rd. | 847/689–8000 or 800/321–2211 | fax 847/689–0135 | www.courtyard.com | 137 rooms, 12 suites | $109, $149 suites | AE, D, DC, MC, V.

Candlewood Suites. These suites are either studios or one-bedroom accommodations. All have cooking facilities, so you can prepare meals in your room with ingredients from Candlewood Cupboard, which is on the premises, if you wish. In-room data ports, kichenettes, microwaves, refrigerators, cable TV, and VCRs. Exercise equipment. Laundry facilities. | 1151 S. Waukegan Rd. | 847/578–5250 or 800/946–6200 | fax 847/578–5256 | www.candlewoodsuites.com | 122 units | $115–$135 | AE, D, DC, MC, V.

Holiday Inn Express. This motel is 3 mi southwest of downtown. Complimentary Continental breakfast. In-room data ports, some refrigerators, cable TV, in-room VCRs (and movies). Video games. Business services. | 619 S. Green Bay Rd. | 847/662–3200 or 800/465–4329 | fax 847/662–7275 | www.basshotels.com | 87 rooms | $89 | AE, D, DC, MC, V.

Illinois Beach Resort and Conference Center. Inside Illinois Beach State Park is this three-story hostelry on the Lake Michigan shore. Suites and balcony rooms have a lakeside view. There's a private beach. Restaurant, bar, picnic area. Cable TV. Indoor pool. Hot tubs. Gym. Beach. Video games. Playground. | 1 Lake Front Dr. | 847/625–7300 | fax 847/625–0665 | www.ilresorts.com | 84 rooms, 8 suites | $119–$149, $220–$275 suites | AE, D, DC, MC, V.

Ramada Inn. This hostelry is 3 mi west of downtown. Restaurant, bar, room service. In-room data ports. Some microwaves, some refrigerators, cable TV. Indoor pool. Hot tub, sauna. Exercise equipment. Video games. Laundry service. Business services. | 200 N. Green Bay Rd. | 847/244–2400 or 800/2RAMADA | fax 847/249–9716 | www.ramadainnwaukegan.com | 173 rooms, 12 suites | $105, $120 suites | AE, D, DC, MC, V.

Super 8. This standard motel is 3 mi west of downtown. Complimentary Continental breakfast. Some in-room data ports. Some microwaves, some refrigerators. Cable TV. Laundry facilities. Business services. Pets allowed (fee). | 630 N. Green Bay Rd. | 847/249–2388 or 800/800–8000 | fax 847/249–0975 | 59 rooms, 2 suites | $77.99, $139.99 suites | AE, D, DC, MC, V.

Waukegan Days Inn. Directly across from the Waukegan Region Airport, this two-story motel is equidistant from both Chicago and Milwaukee. Complimentary Continental breakfast, room service. Some kitchenettes, microwaves, some refrigerators, some in-room hot tubs, cable TV. Laundry service. | 3633 N. Lewis Ave. | 847/249–7778 or 800/544–8313 | fax 847/249–4970 | www.daysinn.com | 79 rooms | $59–$116 | AE, DC, MC, V.

WHEATON

MAP 6, G2

(Nearby towns also listed: Downers Grove, Geneva, Glen Ellyn, Lisle, Naperville, St. Charles)

Settled in the 1830s, Wheaton became the county seat in 1868. Evangelist Billy Graham hails from here; this residential Chicago suburb of 55,755 residents is also home to Wheaton College.

Information: Wheaton Chamber of Commerce | 108 E. Wesley St., 60187 | 630/668–2739 | www.wheatonchamber.org.

Attractions

Cantigny. Colonel Robert McCormick, the late publisher of the Chicago Tribune, owned this 500-acre estate on the southwest side of town. It contains not only his mansion and other museums, but 15 acres of gardens (including many formal designs and a rose garden), and the graves of McCormick and his wife. | 1 S. 151 Winfield Rd. | 630/668–5161 | fax 630/260–1860 | www.cantignypark.com | Free, parking $5 | Call for hours.

At the **First Division Museum** you can find military displays of wars in which the First Division fought. | 1 S. 151 Winfield Rd. | 630/260–8161 | www.rrmtf.org/firstdivision.

The **Robert R. McCormick Museum** is in an 1896 mansion, the former home and gardens of the *Chicago Tribune* publisher. Its 35 rooms contain European antiques, paintings, rare books, and Asian art that McCormick gathered in his world travels. | 1 S. 151 Winfield Rd. | 630/260–8159.

Cosley Zoo. Visit Illinois native species as well as domestic farm animals at this local zoo on the north side of town, just over the train tracks. | 1356 N. Gary Ave. | 630/665–5534 | fax 630/260–6408 | www.wheatonparkdistrict.com | Donation suggested | Call for hours.

Du Page County Historical Museum. Housed in a Richardson Romanesque building, this downtown museum traces county history from settlement to present. There's also a costume gallery, interactive exhibits, and a railroad exhibit. | 102 E. Wesley St. | 630/682–7343 | fax 630/682–6549 | www.co.dupage.il.us/museum/ | Free | Mon., Wed., Fri.–Sat 10–4; Sun. 1–4.

Lincoln Marsh. This 139-acre park of wetland prairies and oak savanna includes trails through and over the marsh on a boardwalk, ponds, strategic viewpoints, a picnic shelter, and the Lincoln March Teams Course, a carefully designed "challenge course" to develop team fundamentals, such as communication, trust, and support. From the trails here there is access to the Prairie Path, which runs from Chicago to Aurora. | Harrison Ave. at Pierce Ave. | 630/871–2810 | Free | Dawn–dusk.

Wheaton College. Billy Graham is an alum of this small Christian liberal arts college. | 500 E. College Ave. | 630/752–5000 | fax 630/752–5998 | www.wheaton.edu | Free | Daily.
Billy Graham Center Museum. Exhibits here trace the history of Christianity in America. | 630/752–5909 | fax 630/752–5916 | www.wheaton.edu/bgc/museum | $2 suggested donation | Mon.–Sat. 9:30–5:30, Sun. 1–5.
Marion E. Wade Center. This is a major research collection of seven British authors now housed in the Wheaton College Library. | 630/752–5908 | fax 630/752–7855 | www.wheaton.edu/learnres/wade | Free | Weekdays 9–noon and 1–4, call for Sat. hours.

Morton Arboretum. This arboretum is dedicated to collecting and studying plants from around the world in order to learn and then share the resulting knowledge about them through its extensive education programs. World renowned, this research program is on 1,700 acres and has more than 3,000 plants on view, which you can see either on foot or by riding the Acorn Express, an open-air tram, through the property. | 1740 W. Fayette Ave. | 630/968–0074 or 630/719–2400 (24-hr. hotline), or 630/719–7955 (Bloom 'n Color hotline) | $7 per car, $3 Wed. Additional fee for tram | Apr.–Oct., daily 7–7; Oct–Apr. 7–dusk.

ON THE CALENDAR

JULY: *Du Page County Fair.* Carnival rides, food, exhibits, and entertainment happen at the fairgrounds off Route 38 on the west side of town the last full week of the month. Admission is $5; special rates for senior citizens and kids. | 630/668–6636.
SEPT.: *Autumn Fest.* A carnival, entertainment, kids' tent, food, and crafts are the focus of this festival in Memorial Park downtown that takes place the third weekend of the month. The carnival is a couple of blocks away in a parking lot on Main and Liberty. | 630/668–6464.
OCT.: *Heritage Tour.* Each year, five homes built between 1800 and 1900 are selected and decorated in a special-occasion or holiday theme for this event, which includes narrated tours of each home, for which maps and tickets can be purchased at the Wheaton History Center at 606 North Main Street. For an additional fee, you can lunch at the Arrowhead Golf Club, where local chefs share cooking and table design tips. Group rates available. | 630/682–9472.

Dining

Front Street Cocina. Mexican. Famous for spicy fajitas, burritos, and carne asada, Front Street prides itself on authenticity. Green and red Mexican decorations and artifacts line the restaurant's walls, while lively Latin music plays in the background. Kids' menu. | 112 N. Hale St. | 630/668–2837 | $6–$12 | AE, D, DC, MC, V.

120 Ocean Place. Seafood. This restaurant is in an old chapel, built in 1928, complete with stained-glass windows and cathedral ceilings, where you can purr over your fresh wild fish—no farm-raised varieties here—either indoors or out. Of course the menu changes with availability of certain fish, but try the cornmeal-crusted whitefish, if you can. | 120 N. Hale St. | 847/336–9690 | $15–$24 | AE, D, DC, MC, V | No lunch weekends.

Lodging

Wheaton Inn. Four blocks from town and the train station, this inn serves a hearty breakfast on its back patio, and offers afternoon wine-and-cheese receptions, and pre-bedtime cookies and milk. Each room has its own Williamsburg color scheme and coordinated furnishings. Complimentary breakfast. Some in-room hot tubs, cable TV. | 301 W. Roosevelt Rd. | 630/690–2600 or 800/447–4667 | fax 630/690–2623 | www.wheatoninn.com | 16 rooms | $145–$225 | AE, D, DC, MC, V.

WHEELING

MAP 8, C4

WHEELING

INTRO
ATTRACTIONS
DINING
LODGING

(Nearby towns also listed: Arlington Heights, Barrington, Northbrook)

By the time Wheeling was incorporated in 1894, it had become known for its restaurant row along Milwaukee Avenue. Today it is still lined with eating establishments both casual and exclusive. Wheeling has a population of 32,000.

Information: Wheeling–Prospect Heights Area Chamber of Commerce and Industry | 395 E. Dundee Rd., 60090 | 847/541–0170 | www.wphchamber.com.

Attractions

Indian Trails Public Library. Serving both the Wheeling and Buffalo Grove communities, this library offers special youth and teen services as well as community outreach programs, and through reciprocal agreements with other libraries in the system you can access their catalogues through the internet services here. | 355 S. Schoenbeck Rd. | 847/459–4100 or 847/459–5271 (after hours) or 847/459–5271 (TDD) | Free | Weekdays 9–9, Sat. 9–5, Sun. 1–5. Summer closed Sun.

ON THE CALENDAR

JULY: *Taste of Wheeling.* In the field in front of the Park District Building at 327 Dundee Road, you can feast and frolic with the locals during this culinary 4th of July celebration, when Wheeling restaurateurs set up food booths and musicians and other local performers entertain. There's also a parade during the day and a fireworks finale at dusk. | 847/465–3333.

Dining

Aspen Grille. Contemporary. This place with high-beam ceilings a couple of miles from Wheeling looks like something you'd expect to find in the eponymous Rocky Mountain Ski resort. You can also dine outside on a patio overlooking a pond. Sliced beef tenderloin, mustard chicken, and wood-burning oven pizza are just a few of the menu samplings. Kids' menu. | 250 Marriott Dr., Lincolnshire | 847/634–0700 | $4.95–$21.95 | AE, D, DC, MC, V.

Bob Chinn's Crab House. Seafood. A New England–style nautical motif in this large, bustling dining room on Restaurant Row prepares diners for soft-shell and stone crabs, and at least six varieties of fresh fish daily. Salad bar, raw bar. Kids' menu. | 393 S. Milwaukee Ave. | 847/520–3633 | www.bobchinns.com | $12.95–$89.95 | AE, D, DC, MC, V.

Crawdaddy Bayou. Cajun/Creole. This combination dining room/general store on the north side of town puts you right into Cajun country. The store sells the requisite seasonings and other items, and the restaurant serves boiled crawfish, chicken and smoked sausage gumbo, and etoufée. There's also a screened-in porch on a bayou. Entertainment Thurs.–Sat. Kids' menu. | 412 N. Milwaukee Ave. | 847/520–4800 | www.crawdaddybayou.com | Reservations essential | $8.95–$24.95 | AE, D, DC, MC, V | Closed Mon. No lunch weekends.

Don Roth's Blackhawk. Contemporary. Memorabilia from Don Roth's original—and now-shuttered—landmark in downtown Chicago, including posters and other memorabilia from the Big Band era, are on display at this dining spot in a turn-of-the-century building. Outside is a garden patio where you can feast on steaks and prime rib, fresh fish (Boston scrod), chicken, and a spinning salad bowl. | 61 N. Milwaukee Ave. | 847/537–5800 | www.theblackhawk.com | Reservations essential | $16.95–$29.95 | AE, D, DC, MC, V | Closed lunch.

Le Français. French. This charmer on the east side of town, two blocks south of Dundee is nationally known for its traditional French fare—foie gras, caviar, pâté, lobster bisque, smoked salmon, and lobster ravioli. The menu changes frequently. | 269 S. Milwaukee Ave. | 847/541–7470 | Reservations essential | Jacket required (dinner) | $28.50–$38.50 | AE, D, DC, MC, V | Closed Sun. No lunch.

94th Aero Squadron. American. You can watch the runways at Palwaukee airport from the large picture windows at this dining spot in the very southern part of Wheeling. It's also loaded with antiques and collectibles dating from World War I and has a cabaret/lounge with a large dance floor for twirling on weekends. Outdoor patios have firepits. Specialties include sizzling steak prime top sirloin and country market chicken. Kids' menu. Sun. brunch. | 1070 S. Milwaukee Ave. | 847/459–3700 | Reservations essential | $11–$22 | AE, D, DC, MC, V | No lunch Sat.

Weber Grill. American. This casual, rustic room with an exhibition kitchen located a block north of Lake Cook serves steak (a 20-ounce summit strip) and barbecued ribs cooked on a Weber-kettle grill. Bar. Kids' menu. | 920 N. Milwaukee Ave. | 847/215–0996 | www.webergrillrestaurant.com | Reservations essential | $12.95–$26.95 | AE, D, DC, MC, V | No lunch weekends.

Lodging

Courtyard by Marriott. In nearby Lincolnshire, this hotel is 4 mi south of Wheeling Restaurant (breakfast only), bar. In-room data ports, some microwaves, some refrigerators, cable TV. Indoor pool. Hot tub. Exercise equipment. Laundry facilities and services. Business services. | 505 Milwaukee Ave., Lincolnshire | 847/634–9555 or 800/321–2211 | fax 847/634–8320 | www.courtyard.com | 133 rooms, 12 suites | $139–$169, $159–$189 suites | AE, D, DC, MC, V.

Exel Inn. This motel is a half mile south of downtown Wheeling. Complimentary Continental breakfast. In-room data ports, microwaves, refrigerators, cable TV. Video games. Laundry facilities. Business services. Some pets allowed. | 540 N. Milwaukee Ave., Prospect Heights | 847/459–0545 or 800/367–3935 | fax 847/459–8639 | www.exelinns.com | 121 rooms, 2 suites | $65, $90 suites | AE, D, DC, MC, V.

Hawthorn Suites. This all-suite hotel is 5 mi south of Wheeling in Lincolnshire. There's a free light dinner buffet Mon.–Thurs. Complimentary breakfast. Kitchenettes, microwaves, cable TV. Indoor pool. Hot tub. Exercise equipment. Laundry facilities. Business services. Some pets allowed (fee). | 10 Westminster Way, Lincolnshire | 847/945–9300 or 800/527–1133 | fax 847/945–0013 | www.hawthorn.com | 125 suites | $139 | AE, D, DC, MC, V.

Marriott's Lincolnshire Resort. A 900-seat theater-in-the-round that mounts musical comedies anchors this sprawling resort 3 mi south of downtown Wheeling. Some rooms have a view of the lake. Two restaurants, bars with entertainment, room service. Some microwaves, refrigerators. Cable TV. Two pools (1 indoor). Hot tub, massage. 18-hole golf course, putting green. Tennis. Gym, boating. Video games. Playground. Laundry facilities. Business services. Some pets allowed (fee). | 10 Marriott Dr., Lincolnshire | 847/634–0100 or 800/228–9290 | fax 847/634–1278 | www.marriott.com | 384 rooms, 6 suites | $133–$209, $325 suites | AE, D, DC, MC, V.

Olde Court Inn. At the corner of Milwaukee and Dundee, this brick motel is a straightforward no frills establishment. Some kitchenettes, some microwaves, some refrigerators, cable TV. Hot tub. | 374 Milwaukee Ave. 60090 | 847/537–2800 | 32 rooms | $50–$55 | AE, D, DC, MC, V.

Palwaukee Inn. Within a few blocks of the several restaurants on Milwaukee Avenue here, this motel is 1 mi east of downtown Wheeling and housed in a building with a bowling alley. Complimentary breakfast. In-room data ports, cable TV. Exercise equipment. Laundry facilities. | 1090 S. Milwaukee Ave. | 847/537–9100 | 144 rooms | $95 | AE, D, DC, MC, V.

WILMETTE

(Nearby towns also listed: Evanston, Glenview, Northbrook, Skokie)

This residential North Shore suburb of Chicago has pleasant parks and beaches and a cozy, walkable downtown. The town was originally settled in the 1830s, and is named after French-Canadian settler Antoine Ouilmette. The population is 22,000.

Information: Wilmette Chamber of Commerce | 1150 Wilmette Ave., 60091 | 847/251–3800.

Attractions

Baha'i House of Worship. Architecturally striking, this domed building right on Sheridan Road about three blocks south of town that took 40 years to build is on the National Register of Historic Places. There are educational displays on the lower level and gardens. | Sheridan Rd. and Linden Ave. | 847/853–2300 | Free | Fall–spring, daily 10–5; summer, daily 10–10.

Gillson Park. This 59-acre park on Lake Michigan a few blocks east of town has ice-skating, tennis, sailing, a beach, picnicking, and summer theater. | Sheridan Rd. and Michigan Ave. | 847/256–6100 | fax 847/256–7908 | www.wilmettepark.org | Free | Daily.

Kohl Children's Museum. Interactive exhibits at this hands-on museum less than a mile from town help kids 1 to 10 understand science, commerce, and history. | 165 Green Bay Rd. | 847/256–6056 | fax 847/256–5438 | www.kohlchildrensmuseum.org | $5; special rates for senior citizens and kids | Mon.–Sat 9–5, Sun. noon–5.

Wilmette Historical Museum. Exhibits at this museum in the center of town focus on Wilmette history. Archives and a library are on the premises. | 609 Ridge Rd. | 847/853–7666 | fax 847/853–7706 | www.wilmette.com | Free | Sept.–July, Tues., Thurs. 10–4, Wed., Sun. 1–4.

ON THE CALENDAR
JUNE–JULY: *Wilmette Community Sidewalk Sale.* You can find many bargains during this rain-or-shine event in the Village Hall of downtown Wilmette where vendors set up shop in outdoor booths and sell their wares, and musicians, magicians, and artisans entertain. Kids' diversions, too. It all takes place the third weekend in either June or July. | 847/251–2700.

Dining

Akai Hana. Japanese. In a strip mall across from Eden's Plaza, just off of I–94, this restaurant specializes in sushi, sashimi, tempura, and teriyaki; try the salmon teriyaki. | 3223 W. Lake Ave. | 847/251–0384 | $10–$19 | AE, D, DC, MC, V.

Bêtise. French. Local art enriches this airy, open space in the Plaza del Lago shopping center at the north end of Wilmette along the lake front. Specialties include steak and pommes frites, fresh seafood, and rack of lamb. Dishes at the Sunday brunch change weekly. | 1515 N. Sheridan Rd. | 847/853–1711 | Reservations essential | $14.95–$24.95 | AE, D, DC, MC, V.

Convito Italiano. Italian. This friendly restaurant in the Plaza del Lago shopping center has an outdoor canopied terrace with hanging plants. On the menu is pasta, salads, fish, chicken, and veal. | 1515 N. Sheridan Rd. | 847/251–3654 | www.convitoitaliano.com | $7.99–$16.99 | AE, D, DC, MC, V.

Tanglewood. Contemporary. Dine outside in a brick courtyard with ivy and flowers or inside this former laundry factory with 20-ft-high windows; it was built in 1898 and is in downtown Winnetka, 4 mi north of Wilmette. Long Island duck and salmon with corn cakes are two of the food draws. | 566 Chestnut St., Winnetka | 847/441–4600 | Reservations essential on weekends | $18.95–$26.95 | AE, MC, V | Closed Sun.–Mon.

Walker Bros. Original Pancake House. American. This homey eatery at the south end of Wilmette buzzes on weekends with area residents tucking into platters of all kinds of griddle cakes. A specialty is oven-baked apple pancakes. Kids' menu. | 153 Green Bay Rd. | 847/251–6000 | Breakfast also served | Reservations not accepted | $5–$8 | D, MC, V.

WOODSTOCK

MAP 6, G1

(Nearby towns also listed: Crystal Lake, McHenry, Richmond, Union)

Woodstock's got a real, old-fashioned town square complete with a white gazebo, and ringed with shops and an 1890s opera house. The 1992 movie *Groundhog Day* was filmed here, and every February, the 18,250 residents celebrate with tours, sales, and, of course, a screening of the film.

Information: Woodstock Chamber of Commerce and Industry | 136 Cass St., 60098 | 815/338–2436 | fax 815/338–2927 | www.woodstockilchamber.com.

Attractions

Chester Gould–Dick Tracy Museum. Exhibits at this downtown museum highlight the life and work of Woodstock native Chester Gould, creator of Dick Tracy. | 101 N. Johnson St. | 815/338–8281 | Free | Feb.–Dec., Thurs.–Sat. 11–5, Sun. 1–5; Jan., Thurs.–Sat. 11–5.

Old Court House Arts Center. The Old Court House, built in 1857 and vacated in 1972, is now home to an art gallery with revolving exhibits. There's an annual show of women's artwork, sponsored by the Northwest Arts Council, in March and April. | 101 N. Johnson St. | 815/338–4525 | Thurs.–Sat. 11–5, Sun. 1–5. Closed Mon.–Weds.

Woodstock Opera House. This restored 1890s opera house on Woodstock Square hosts concerts, plays, and dance performances. | 121 Van Buren St. | 815/338–5300 | fax 815/334–2287 | www.woodstock-il.com | Prices vary with events | Box office weekdays 9–5, Sat. 1–5, and during performances.

© Corbis

BOVINE INSPIRATION

She's not exactly the Statue of Liberty drawing you to New York Harbor—but Harmilda is every bit as recognizable and every bit as welcoming to residents who live in and around the northern Illinois town of Harvard.

Harmilda is a life-sized fiberglass cow that stands at the head of Harvard's main street greeting visitors coming into town. Harvard was once a milk-producing center and hosts the Milk Days festival every year; Harmilda was created as part of the celebration. She stood on a pedestal in the middle of the street for years, but a road widening brought her closer to earth; now she has her own little square, with a cheerful country scene painted in behind her. And her name? That's HARvard MILk DAys.

JUNE: *Dick Tracy Days.* Band concerts, a drum and bugle corps pageant, and a parade are some of the activities at this festival that takes place for five days near the end of the month in Woodstock Square. The parade is free; there's a $10 charge for the drum and bugle corps pageant; special rates for senior citizens and kids. | 815/338–2436.
AUG.: *Mozart Festival.* Symphony performances of works by Mozart and his contemporaries are given at the Woodstock Opera House the last weekend in July and first two weekends of August. | 815/338–5300.
OCT.: *Annual Autumn Drive.* During the third weekend in October, you can visit approximately 16 farms along Garden Valley Road and take part in a variety of activities—fall harvests of pumpkin and squash; and sale of art, antiques, crafts, and food. | 815/568–8823.

Dining

Deeter's. German. Wiener schnitzel, roast duck, fillet goulash, fresh seafood, steaks, and chops are on the menu here, as you'd expect given the alpine-Bavarian pictures. There's entertainment Friday–Sunday at this restaurant in west Woodstock. Kids' menu. | 15105 U.S. 14 | 815/338–6550 | $8.95–$31.95 | D, MC, V | Closed Mon. No lunch.

Harvest Moon Café. Contemporary. Work by local artists hangs in this café on Woodstock Square. Menu samplings include grilled salmon, pasta, tenderloin, and wild game. Kids' menu. | 113 S. Benton St. | 815/334–9166 | Reservations essential | $14–$23 | AE, D, DC, MC, V | Closed Sun.–Mon.

Lodging

Bundling Board Inn. This Queen Anne–style home bordered by flowerbeds and with a porch swing out front is in an old, residential neighborhood two blocks from the Opera House and the historic square. You have use of the kitchen here. Complimentary breakfast. Laundry facilities. | 220 E. South St. | 815/338–7054 | fax 815/568–5243 | 6 rooms | $75–$100 | D, MC, V.

Days Inn. This motel is a mile from Woodstock Square and the opera house. Complimentary Continental breakfast. Some in-room data ports, some microwaves, some refrigerators, cable TV. Indoor pool. Hot tub. Business services. | 990 Lake Ave. | 815/338–0629 or 800/DAYSINN | fax 815/338–0895 | www.daysinn.com | 40 rooms, 4 suites | $66.75, $106.75 suites | AE, D, DC, MC, V.

Holiday Inn Express. This motel 1 mi south of downtown has a 24-hour coffee and juice bar. Complimentary Continental breakfast. In-room data ports, some microwaves, some refrigerators, cable TV. Indoor pool. Hot tub. Gym. Laundry facilities, laundry service. Business services. | 1785 S. Eastwood Dr. | 815/334–9600 or 800/HOLIDAY | fax 815/334–9614 | www.basshotels.com | 47 rooms, 4 suites | $79, $95–$105 suites.

Iowa

In the 1989 Academy Award–winning movie *Field of Dreams*, Ray Liotta, as Shoeless Joe Jackson, asked, "Is this Heaven?" to which Kevin Costner replied, "No . . . it's Iowa." The line is legendary in this state, perhaps because it finally put into words what many residents of this fertile land have long believed—that if Iowa isn't heaven, it's pretty close.

Iowa takes its name from a Native American word meaning "beautiful land" and the soil here, among the most fertile, wisely managed, and lucrative on the planet, is the greatest of many riches in the state. Iowa's 100,000 family farms produce more pork, beef, and grain than any other state in the union. Each year, the average Iowa farm grows enough food to feed 279 people.

Iowa's farm economy is supported by the state's many small towns. Clean, wide, tree-lined streets, courthouse squares, and corner cafés are omnipresent and farmers who make their living feeding the world are proud and wholesome to the point of stereotype. The peaceful images captured on canvas by native son Grant Wood are as real today as they were in the 1930s and '40s when Grant was painting.

Education is a top priority for Iowans. More than half of the state budget is dedicated to public education, and in return Iowa consistently sees its population ranked among the most literate of the 50 states. Three world-class universities and 62 public and private colleges attract and retain top faculty and students. Iowa Public Television is regarded as a national leader in using state-of-the-art technology to make learning opportunities easily accessible. And nearly every community can boast about its art center, museum, or community music group. Arts festivals, galleries, and cultural events across the state attract large, appreciative audiences.

The residents of neighboring states often joke that Iowa stands for "Idiots Out Walking Around." Iowans enjoy the joke, for they know that little could be further from the truth. The population as a whole is well read and aware of the world beyond Iowa's borders. It may be for these reasons that the nation looks to Iowa every four years to

CAPITAL: DES MOINES	POPULATION: 2,913,000	AREA: 55,965 SQUARE MI
BORDERS: IL, MO, NE, SD, MN, WI	TIME ZONE: CENTRAL	POSTAL ABBREVIATION: IA
WEB SITE: WWW.STATE.IA.US/TOURISM.		

host the first presidential caucuses and that often during national crisis, the opinions of Iowans are reported as indicators of the nation's pulse.

Iowans—along with the University of Iowa's sports teams—are known as "Hawkeyes," a name which can be traced rather ironically to a Sauk Indian chief named Black Hawk, who led a three-month-long uprising to protest the westward expansion of white settlement in the early 1800s. It was the treaty signed after Chief Black Hawk's defeat which opened the eastern portion of this "beautiful land" to white settlement.

History

In 1673 when French-Canadian explorers Louis Joliet and Father James Marquette arrived in what is today the state of Iowa, the Ioway, a Native American tribe originally from the Great Lakes, were living along many of the tributaries to the Mississippi. The next hundred years saw the arrival of Sauk and Fox Indians pushed out of Wisconsin and Illinois by white settlers, along with French-Canadian explorers like Julien Dubuque. But by the 1840s it was the white explorers and settlers who controlled the land. The Ioway chose not to resist white settlement and in 1838, they abandoned their land here and moved west; by the end of the next decade most of the Sauk and Fox Indians had followed.

The Louisiana Purchase of 1803 incorporated what would become Iowa into the United States, and in 1805 the government sent Zebulon Pike to explore and select locations suitable for military posts. In those early years, Iowa's political status changed frequently. Initially the area was made a part of the Missouri Territory, then the Michigan Territory, and then the Wisconsin Territory. But as each of those territories became a state, Iowa found itself returned to a kind of limbo without any official government.

In 1838, six years after the Black Hawk War, the Territory of Iowa was established, and Burlington was made its first capital. In response to the growing number of settlers in regions north of Burlington the territorial capital moved to Iowa City in 1842. Construction began on the capitol building, which is now the centerpiece of the University of Iowa, and the state was officially welcomed into the Union as a free state on December 28, 1846. But Iowa City's reign as capital was short-lived. In 1857, again responding to a population shift and the demand for a more centrally located state government, the legislature moved the capital to Des Moines.

From 1846 to 1848, more than 70,000 Mormons crossed Iowa on their way from Illinois to Utah. Original campfire rocks and wagon ruts can be seen today in parts of southern Iowa where the Mormons battled the Iowan elements at the beginning of their journey.

The settlers of Iowa came primarily from Ohio, Indiana, and Pennsylvania. Most were farmers who sought to settle and work the land. Before the 20th century, 85% of the state was open, virgin prairie but this changed quickly with the arrival of five railroad lines in the 1860s–80s. The railroads made markets in the east far more accessible and agriculture far more profitable.

IA Timeline

12,000 BC	450 BC	1673	1682
Glaciers form the Iowa Lakes Region in northwestern Iowa.	Woodland Indian culture flourishes; Woodland Indians begin to build effigy mounds.	Marquette and Joliet explore the Mississippi River, reaching it via the Wisconsin River.	French explorer Robert Cavelier sieur de La Salle explores the northern Mississippi River valley, claiming Iowa for France.

It is ironic that the only U.S. president born in Iowa took office during the most difficult time in agriculture history. Although the forces that created the Great Depression were already in motion before Herbert Hoover of West Branch, Iowa, took office in 1929, he was the recipient of much public hostility and frustration, particularly from those in his home state.

INTRODUCTION
HISTORY
REGIONS
WHEN TO VISIT
STATE'S GREATS
RULES OF THE ROAD
DRIVING TOURS

Farm foreclosures reached record numbers in 1930, resulting in the formation of the Farm Holiday Association in Newton, Iowa, in 1931. Today the FHA is the leading government agency providing financial assistance to farmers during lean economic times. The Granger Association and other agriculture co-ops also began in Iowa during this period.

Since the farm crisis of the 1980s (when bumper crops and falling world prices created a similar economic condition), state leaders have worked to diversify the state's economy. Although Iowa is still the nation's leader in agriculture production, manufacturing is now the leading industry in Iowa, creating a more stable economy for the region.

Regions

1. WESTERN

Oh, the famous names that have called these rolling prairies home—Andy Williams, Donna Reed, Abigail Van Buren (Dear Abby) and Ann Landers, Harry Reasoner, Johnny Carson, Glenn Miller, and Frank Phillips of Phillips Petroleum. The Great Plains begin here, and little imagination is required to envision the trials of the pioneers crossing this land by foot and wagon. Today many people travel to western Iowa to see the impressive Loess Hills, a geographical phenomenon of steep hills created by windblown soil found only here and in China. Others come to northwest Iowa for the beautiful lakes region where, among the

15,000 acres of water, there is one of only three blue-water lakes in the world. West Okoboji Lake was formed by a glacier, and the clarity of its water combined with its depth (136 ft) allows it to reflect the blue of the sky.

Towns listed: Algona, Anita, Atlantic, Avoca, Carroll, Cedar Rapids, Cherokee, Clarinda, Clear Lake, Council Bluffs, Creston, Denison, Elk Horn, Emmetsburg, Estherville, Fairfield, Le Mars, Missouri Valley, Newton, Okoboji, Onawa, Pocahontas, Red Oak, Sheldon, Shenandoah, Sioux City, Spencer, Spirit Lake, Storm Lake, Washington, West Bend.

2. CENTRAL

Central Iowa is dominated by the metropolitan area of Des Moines. Although less than a half-million people live in the metroplex, it is the largest urban center in the state and is accessible from most other areas of Iowa in less than three hours. The six covered bridges of Madison County, made famous in Robert Waller's best-selling novel

1788	1803	1805	1813	1832
Julien Dubuque discovers lead ore in the region, resulting in an influx of white settlers.	The Louisiana Purchase brings Iowa into the Union.	Zebulon Pike maps the upper Mississippi River valley for the federal government.	The U.S. Army abandons and burns Fort Madison, unable to protect it from harassment by Sauk Indians led by Chief Black Hawk.	The Black Hawk War in Illinois ends, and eastern Iowa is opened to white settlement.

and the Clint Eastwood movie it inspired, are just 30 minutes south of Des Moines. Central Iowa is also home to the Boone and Scenic Valley Railroad, near Boone. Visitors can learn about the railroad's impact on Iowa's overall development, as well as enjoy a relaxing tour of the natural wonders of this "beautiful land."

Towns listed: Adel, Ames, Boone, Cedar Falls, Centerville, Chariton, Charles City, Des Moines, Fort Dodge, Garner, Grinnell, Hampton, Humboldt, Indianola, Lamoni, Marshalltown, Mason City, Osceola, Oskaloosa, Pella, Van Meter, Waverly, Webster City, Winterset.

3. EASTERN
The land and the early history of eastern Iowa were shaped by the Mississippi River and its tributaries. Rolling hills, valleys, and the area's many rivers and streams create beautiful vistas and today entice outdoor enthusiasts to days of hiking, fishing, and canoeing. It was along these rivers that the Ioway Indians lived and later these same valleys saw the first white settlements. This part of the state was home to Iowa's first territorial capital (in Burlington), its first state capital (in Iowa City), its first railway line (from Davenport to Iowa City), and its first university (in Iowa City).

Towns listed: Amana Colonies, Anamosa, Bettendorf, Burlington, Clinton, Davenport, Decorah, Dubuque, Dyersville, Fort Madison, Iowa City, Kalona, Keokuk, Keosauqua, Maquoketa, Marquette, Mount Pleasant, Muscatine, Ottumwa, Spillville, Strawberry Point, Waterloo, West Branch, West Union.

When to Visit
Iowa is a four-seasons state, with each season virtually equal in length and intensity. Summers can be hot and humid. Temperatures, which run the same across much of the state, frequently approach 100°F and the state's record high was well above that— 118°F on July 20, 1934, in Keokuk. But even the hottest days are often cooled down with a quick thunderstorm, creating evenings of croaking frogs and pleasant breezes. Relative humidity in July and August runs at 85%–90% on the eastern side of the state along the Mississippi River, and about 10% less in the northwest. Sioux City in the northwest corner gets considerably less rain than cities in the eastern half of Iowa. This, of course, is good news for those choosing to vacation in the lakes region of northwest Iowa.

Winter can be harsh, even downright wicked, in Iowa. From December to March, all precautions should be taken when traveling within even the most populated parts of the state. The record low was -47°F on February 3, 1996, in Elkader. Most of Iowa's interstate rest areas are equipped with monitors that display current weather and travel conditions. It is not uncommon for Interstate 80 to be closed on several occasions throughout the winter due to heavy snow, particularly west of Des Moines.

There are two types of winter storms in Iowa. The most common is the "Alberta Clipper," which sweeps in a southeasterly direction from Canada and brings very cold temperatures but little snowfall. The "Colorado Lows" are usually early and late winter

1838	1838	1842	Dec. 28, 1846	1847
The Ioway sell their Ioway lands and move west.	Territory of Iowa is established with Burlington as capital.	Iowa City named new territorial capital and construction begins on the Old Capitol Building.	Iowa becomes the 29th state in the Union.	University of Iowa, the first public institution of higher learning in the state, is founded.

INTRODUCTION
HISTORY
REGIONS
WHEN TO VISIT
STATE'S GREATS
RULES OF THE ROAD
DRIVING TOURS

storms that carry a lot of moisture from the Gulf of Mexico, and dump large amounts of heavy wet snow and freezing rain on the state.

Spring and fall are wonderful times to visit. Springtime brings the refreshing sight and smell of newly turned soil as farmers prepare their fields for crops. And in fall the golden fields complement the autumnal colors of the trees. Spring and fall tornadoes are not as common in Iowa as they are in states to its south, but lightning and thunderstorms can cause trouble and in spring the many rivers that bring life to Iowa's farmland can overflow their banks and claim the land as their own.

CLIMATE CHART

Average High/Low Temperatures (°F) and Monthly Precipitation (in inches)

	JAN.	FEB.	MAR.	APR.	MAY	JUN.
SIOUX CITY	27/7	33/14	46/26	62/38	73/50	82/60
	.5	.7	2.0	2.3	3.6	3.7
	JUL.	AUG.	SEPT.	OCT.	NOV.	DEC.
	86/65	83/62	75/52	64/40	46/26	31/13
	3.2	2.9	2.8	1.9	1.1	.7
	JAN.	FEB.	MAR.	APR.	MAY	JUN.
DES MOINES	28/10	34/16	47/27	61/40	73/51	82/61
	.56	1.1	2.33	3.36	3.66	4.46
	JUL.	AUG.	SEPT.	OCT.	NOV.	DEC.
	86/66	84/63	75/54	64/42	48/29	32/16
	3.78	4.20	3.53	2.62	1.79	1.32
	JAN.	FEB.	MAR.	APR.	MAY	JUN.
DAVENPORT	28/11	34/16	47/28	61/39	72/50	82/60
	1.5	1.2	3	3.9	4.3	4.2
	JUL.	AUG.	SEPT.	OCT.	NOV.	DEC.
	86/65	84/62	76/53	64/42	48/31	33/17
	4.9	4.2	4.0	2.9	2.5	2.2

FESTIVALS AND SEASONAL EVENTS

WINTER

Nov.–Feb.: **Winterfest.** Winter can get mighty wicked in western Iowa, but that doesn't stop the people of Council Bluffs from celebrating the unique opportunities of the season with ice sculptures, an ice-fishing contest, and snowball softball as well as lighted trees, houses, and sculptures in the park. | 712/325–1000 or 877/330–9638.

1855
The Amana Colonies are founded on 26,000 acres near Iowa City.

1856
First bridge across the Mississippi River is completed at Davenport and the Davenport–Iowa City train line is opened.

1857
State capital is moved from Iowa City to Des Moines.

1867
First railroad across the state is completed.

1868
Black lawyer Alexander Clark wins a case before the Iowa State Supreme Court, arguing that his daughter has been unjustly denied the right to attend a public high school based on her race.

Dec.: **It's a Wonderful Life Festival.** Visit Denison during the holidays to celebrate this classic movie made famous in part by hometown hero Donna Reed. Live performances of the story, as well as the original big screen version, can be seen at the Donna Reed Performing Arts Center. Gingerbread house decorating contests, hayrides, and Christmas caroling turn this tiny Iowa town into the much celebrated, yet mythical, Bedford Falls. | 712/263–3334.

Feb.: **Winter Dance Party.** Dance the night away in memory of the legendary rock-and-roll musician Buddy Holly who died in a 1959 plane crash in a frozen field near Clear Lake. You can actually dance all weekend if you like at the Surf Ballroom, the site of their last performance. Events around the area celebrate this performer's musical legend. | 515/357–2159 or 515/357–6151.

Mar./Oct.: **Waverly Midwest Horse Sale.** Whether or not you're in need of a good horse to work the fields, you'll be amazed at the size and grandeur of the huge draft horses auctioned in Waverly. The frenetic pace of the auction combined with the energy and vitality of the animals and their owners is entertainment enough, but good food and a thorough education about the role of work horses in today's agricultural environment are added bonuses. | 319/352–2804.

SPRING

Apr.: **Drake Relays.** Some of the greatest athletes in the country, both professional and amateur, gather at Drake University in Des Moines for three days of competition in track-and-field events. The competition includes high-school and college-level athletes, but scouts, sports superstars, and other recognizable personalities are often found in the stands. | 515/271–2115.

May: **Pella Tulip Time.** The Dutch community of Pella bursts with color as hundreds of thousands of tulip bulbs come into their glory. Street scrubbings, dancing, arts festivals, and the celebration of many Dutch customs are highlights of this three-day event held each Mother's Day. | 641/628–4311.

May: **Snake Alley Criterium Bicycle Races.** On Memorial Day weekend in Burlington, some of the best bicyclists in the world ride what many consider to be the most crooked street in the country. Within 275 ft, the street has five half-curves, two

1929	1931	1959	1979	1980s
Iowa native Herbert Hoover becomes president.	The Farm Holiday Association (FHA) is formed to protect farmers from foreclosure during the Great Depression.	Soviet premier Nikita Khrushchev visits farms in western Iowa.	Pope John Paul II visits Des Moines, his only visit to a U.S. city west of the Mississippi.	Record low commodity prices and high interest rates result in record high farm foreclosures and a new direction for the agricultural economy of Iowa.

quarter-curves, and drops 58 ft. Sometimes cyclists travel up and down this road as many as 20 times to win cash prizes. A pancake breakfast for participants and spectators starts the day. | 319/752–0015 or 800/827–4837.

INTRODUCTION
HISTORY
REGIONS
WHEN TO VISIT
STATE'S GREATS
RULES OF THE ROAD
DRIVING TOURS

SUMMER

June: **TrekFest in Riverside.** If you miss it this year, come back next year, or anytime in the next 200 years. This is a big birthday party held the last week in June, where Trekkies from around the globe celebrate the impending birth of Star Trek Captain James T. Kirk in the year 2228. During the 1970s, a Riverside resident and Star Trek fan wrote the producers of the television show asking that Riverside, near Kalona, be officially designated as the future birthplace of Captain Kirk. The producers agreed. A 20-ft spaceship, the USS *Riverside,* has been built in anticipation of Captain Kirk's arrival. | 319/648–5475.

July: **Bix Beiderbecke Memorial Jazz Festival.** Bix Beiderbecke's contribution to jazz is celebrated in four days of events that include a 7-mi run, porch parties, satellite concerts, and live performances in LeClaire Park on the riverfront in Davenport. Jam sessions are held in hotels, bars, and ballrooms around the Quad Cities. | 319/324–7170.

AUTUMN

Sept.: **Clay County Fair.** Spencer, a community of about 11,000 residents, swells to more than 300,000 as visitors from around the world come for the largest commercial agriculture exhibit anywhere in the country. Hotels are booked a year in advance. | 712/262–4740.

Oct.: **Madison County Covered Bridge Festival.** Autumn is the best time to drive through the Iowa countryside in search of the six covered bridges made famous by the novel and Clint Eastwood movie *The Bridges of Madison County,* which was filmed here. During the second full weekend in October, the tiny town of Winterset is jammed with nearly 100,000 people during this two-day festival, the only fund-raiser for the restoration of the historic bridges. Food stands, music, crafts, and tours of the bridges are part of the weekend festivities. Many couples choose this time to exchange or renew marriage vows on the Roseman Bridge. | 800/298–6119.

1993
The Great Flood of '93 devastates much of Iowa. Hundreds are left homeless and thousands of acres of fertile farmland are destroyed.

1996
The State of Iowa celebrates its sesquicentennial.

State's Greats

The **Loess Hills** of western Iowa is a unique geographical feature, found only in Iowa and China. Thousands of years ago, harsh winter winds blew the loose Missouri River silt into windswept dunes or hills. Today the dunes are called the Loess (pronounced *luss*) Hills and extend along the Missouri River from Sioux City to the Missouri border. Clay for Sioux City's first brick buildings came from these hills, and today the area offers some of the most scenic driving in the Midwest.

The western part of the state also includes Iowa's Great Lakes—**East Okoboji Lake, West Okoboji Lake,** and **Spirit Lake**—which together equal approximately 15,000 acres of water. **West Okoboji** is one of only three blue-water lakes in the world. (The others are Lake Geneva in Switzerland and Lake Louise in Canada.) West Okoboji is a glacial lake, created by the Wisconsin Glacier nearly 14,000 years ago. Because it's on Iowa's highest point of land little runoff enters the 136-ft-deep lake. Instead, deep water springs provide much of the clear, blue water with a unique thermocline. The water at the surface of the lake changes temperature with the seasons and averages approximately 75°F in summer while water in the depths of the lake remains at about 45°F. When the seasons change and the top layers of water cool, they sink, creating the appearance that the lake is turning over, and debris that rises from the bottom of the lake can be seen for days.

The **locks and dams** system along the Mississippi River is a testament to the demands of river travel and surviving life along this great body of water. The locks and dams system was designed to keep the river open for navigation in winter and to minimize flooding at other times. Because the water does not freeze, American bald eagles congregate in the areas near locks to search for fish and other sustenance. People also congregate along these dams for fishing, bird-watching, and viewing the great barges coming and going through a complicated system of water control.

Beaches, Forests, and Parks

Iowa's best beaches are found in the Great Lakes region in the northern part of the state in the resort community of Okoboji. Sand bars along the Missouri and Mississippi riverbanks, however, also make good picnic and sunning spots.

Iowa has four major state forests and six smaller units totaling more than 40,000 acres of tree-covered land, as well as 76 state parks with more than 5,700 campsites. **Stephens State Forest,** near Chariton, is the largest, with more than 13,000 acres of white and red oak, hickory, and several species of softwood and coniferous trees. This forest is one of the most popular wild turkey hunting areas in the state; it is also the site of the first successful wild turkey stocking. There is no fee for entrance to any state-owned property, although a minimal fee is charged for overnight camping.

Culture, History, and the Arts

The county and town museums of Iowa are often worth exploring in order to gain a better understanding of Iowa's history. The principal museums in the larger cities include the **Des Moines Art Center** known for its European and American paintings and sculptures, the **University of Iowa's Museum of Natural History** in Iowa City, and the **Putnam Museum of History and Natural Science** in Davenport; both the Museum of Natural History and the Putnam Museum have exhibits for adults and children. Smaller towns also have exceptional museums, such as Cherokee's **Sanford Museum and Planetarium,** which has archaeology, astronomy, and geology exhibits, and Marshalltown's **Fisher Art Gallery** with its ceramics and Impressionist and post-Impressionist paintings.

History lovers will appreciate time spent at the **Amana Colonies.** These seven villages were founded in eastern Iowa in 1855 and residents maintained a communal lifestyle until 1932. All seven of the Amana Colonies are designated as National Historic Landmarks. You can also follow a section of the **Lewis and Clark Trail,** a section of the **Mormon Trail,** and Iowa's own **Dragoon Trail,** each of which offers an incredible story

INTRODUCTION
HISTORY
REGIONS
WHEN TO VISIT
STATE'S GREATS
RULES OF THE ROAD
DRIVING TOURS

of people looking to make a home in this land. The Lewis and Clark Trail follows the path those explorers took up the Missouri River in 1804 as they began their search for a passage to the Pacific. The Dragoon Trail follows the Des Moines River and the path taken by cavalry soldiers establishing the first U.S. forts in the territory after the 1832 Black Hawk Purchase. And the Mormon Trail tracks the route taken by tens of thousands of Mormons across southern Iowa during the mid-1800s on their journey from Illinois to Utah.

Sports

Many will tell you that the only sports in this state are ones with the gold-and-black Hawkeye as their symbol. Fanaticism surrounding the **University of Iowa's** football, basketball, and wrestling teams cannot be topped. Events are sold out years in advance, and many services literally shut down on game day so that employees may enjoy the game on TV. Numerous national championships and bowl game appearances reinforce the quality of and pride taken in the University of Iowa's sports programs.

Although no professional sports team makes its home in the Hawkeye state, AA and AAA farm teams for the Chicago Cubs, St. Louis Cardinals, Kansas City Royals, and Minnesota Twins are found throughout the state and draw healthy crowds of appreciative baseball fans.

Bicycling is big in Iowa, perhaps because of the success of the *Des Moines Register's* **Annual Great Bike Ride Across Iowa (RAGBRAI).** Several small towns and counties host their own regional rides (some on tandem bikes or unicycles) and always welcome visitors to participate. The abandoned railroad beds that crisscross the state have been converted into wonderful biking trails and many state parks and forests accommodate bicyclists as well.

Other Points of Interest

Madison County is the undisputed "Covered Bridge Capital of Iowa," serving as home to six of Iowa's 10 **covered bridges.** Two of the other covered bridges are in Marion County near Knoxville, while one is near Carlisle in Warren County, and the oldest one is near Keokuk, in the southeastern part of the state.

State Parks

Admission to state parks in Iowa is free, although there are separate camping fees. For more information, contact individual parks or the **Department of Natural Resources** | Wallace State Office Building, Des Moines | 515/281–8368 | www.state.ia.us/parks.

Rules of the Road

License requirements: To drive in Iowa, you must be at least 17 years old, although an instruction permit is possible at age 14, and an intermediate license may be granted at age 16.

Right turn on red: Right turns on red are allowed in Iowa after coming to a full and complete stop, unless otherwise posted.

Seat belt and helmet laws: The driver and front seat occupants must wear a seat belt. Children under the age of three are required to be in a car safety seat. Children between the ages of three and six must be in either a car safety seat or a seat belt. Helmets are not required.

Speed limits: The speed limit on rural Iowa interstates is 65 mph. In urban areas and on secondary roads, the speed limit is 55 mph, unless otherwise posted. Mopeds that operate over 25 mph are illegal in Iowa.

For more information: Contact the **Iowa Motor Vehicle Information Center** at | 800/532–1121.

Iowa's Mormon Trail Driving Tour

FROM MONTROSE TO COUNCIL BLUFFS, "THE SOUTHERN ROUTE"

Distance: approximately 300 mi   Time: 2–5 days
Breaks: Consider spending the night in Winterset and taking your time to visit the covered bridges of Madison County.

From 1846 to 1869, more than 70,000 Mormons, fleeing from violence and religious persecution in Illinois, crossed the southern edge of Iowa at the beginning of their journey to a "New Zion" in Utah. A marked auto route begins in Council Bluffs and continues 1,600 mi across Nebraska and Wyoming to the Great Salt Lake. The true beginning of the journey, however, is in Lee County, on the eastern side of Iowa, on the banks of the Mississippi River, where the first Mormon wagon landed on February 4, 1846. The Mormons' footpath through Iowa crossed 12 counties, giving the state a place in what has become known as the largest human migration in U.S. history. The trail testifies to the endurance of people inspired by faith and a belief that life would be better in the American West. The driving route covering the Mormon Trail in Iowa closely follows Route 2, taking you through panoramic countryside dotted with silos, barns, and charming communities, all of which are representative of Iowa today.

❶ The first Mormon wagons were ferried across a narrow point in the Mississippi River to Montrose Landing at **Riverview Park.** Montrose is approximately halfway between

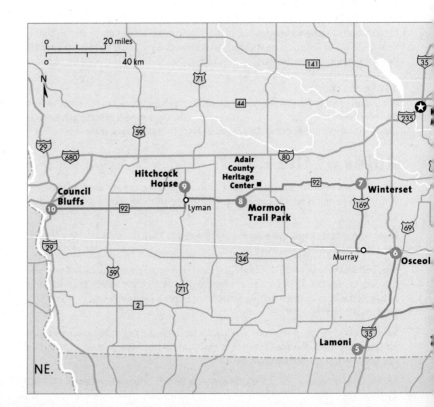

INTRODUCTION
HISTORY
REGIONS
WHEN TO VISIT
STATE'S GREATS
RULES OF THE ROAD
DRIVING TOURS

Fort Madison and Keokuk on U.S. 61. Riverview Park is on Route 404, 1 mi east of town. An interpretive panel marks the site. A brown wagon-wheel panel is the road sign that today marks the route heading west.

Nine miles west on Route J72 near the town of Argyle was the encampment of Sugar Creek, where 2,000 Mormons spent the first winter. They organized into companies and, led by Brigham Young, headed west to what is today Route 2.

From Argyle follow W62 to Route 2 and **Bonaparte.** The Mormons crossed the Des Moines River at Bonaparte, just downstream from the current bridge. The area has been well preserved; even the stepping stones used to cross the river remain.

❷ Near Bonaparte is the historic community of Bentonsport, along Route J40. In the **Bentonsport National Historic District** you'll find crafters and artisans working as they would have at the time of the Mormon crossing, as well as buildings that were constructed by Mormons, a 19th-century iron bridge, and the remains of old mills along the Des Moines River.

❸ Continue west on Route 2 to Bloomfield and stop at the **Davis County Welcome Center** where you will receive help obtaining permission to visit original wagon ruts on private property in nearby Drakesville. Ruts from thousands of wagons can still be seen in this area, but you must obtain permission before visiting them. Take U.S. 63 to Route 273 to reach Drakesville, where you will also find a cabin that Mormons built in 1846.

Return to Route 2 after your visit to Drakesville and continue west. The Mormons crossed the Chariton River and for 10 days camped very close to where Route 2 crosses

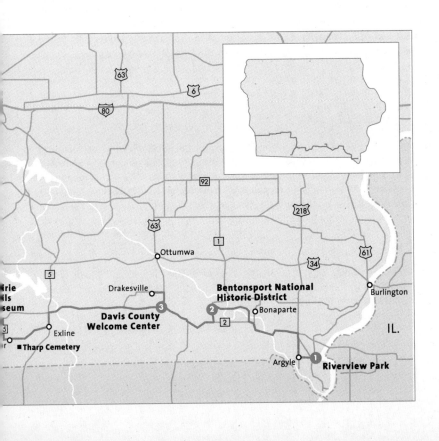

it today. This campsite is marked by another interpretive panel and cemetery. Turn south at Route 5 to Exline Junction and follow the clearly marked brown wagon-wheel signs to Seymour.

❹ Southeast of Seymour is the site of Tharp Cemetery where the hymn "Come, Come Ye Saints" was written. The Reorganized Church of Jesus Christ of Latter Day Saints (RLDS) considers this one of the most significant sites along the Mormon Trail. From Seymour, drive north on Route 55 back to Route 2, then west again to reach the town of Corydon, where the **Prairie Trails Museum** tells the story of the Mormon encampment here, complete with an ox-drawn wagon.

❺ Drive west on Route 2 until you reach Interstate 35. Take Interstate 35 south and get off at exit 4 for **Lamoni,** where the RLDS established Graceland College in 1895.

❻ From Lamoni, take Interstate 35 north to **Osceola** and turn west on U.S. 34 to the town of Murray, where a log cabin and wagon ruts may be seen. A few miles west of Murray, turn north on U.S. 169 to Beulah Cemetery, then turn west and follow signs to what was known as Mt. Pisgah, where nearly 300 people died at the Mormons' first winter camp.

❼ Follow U.S. 169 north to **Winterset** and, for a slight diversion, take a few hours to explore the six covered bridges of Madison County. The Madison County Chamber of Commerce has maps that allow you to drive yourself, or, if you prefer, they can set up a chartered trip.

❽ From Winterset, follow Route 92 west to Bridgewater, where the 160-acre **Mormon Trail Park** contains original wagon ruts and numerous types of grasses native to the trail. The **Adair County Heritage Center** in Greenfield also has trail markers used by the Mormons.

❾ Continue west on Route 92 to Lyman, then north 2 mi on U.S. 71 to Lewis, where Brigham Young crossed the Nishnabotna River. The ferry house is being restored, as is the **Hitchcock House,** which the Mormons built in 1856 as a station on the Underground Railroad.

❿ Take Route 71 south back to Route 92 west and on to **Council Bluffs,** where the Mormons first saw the Missouri River. Because of diminishing supplies and physical weakness, 10,000 people camped here on the banks of the Missouri River for six months, in preparation for the larger journey ahead of them. Pottawattamie County's Kanesville Tabernacle is perhaps the most significant part of the Mormon Trail, since it was here that Brigham Young was elected president of the Mormon church. At Mosquito Creek, near the Iowa School for the Deaf, are several markers commemorating the Mormon encampment.

To return to Montrose from Council Bluffs, drive east on Route 92 until you reach U.S. 59. Take U.S. 59 south until you reach Route 2. Take Route 2 east until you reach U.S. 61. Take U.S. 61 south to Montrose.

The Iowa Great River Road Driving Tour

FROM NEW ALBIN TO KEOKUK

INTRODUCTION
HISTORY
REGIONS
WHEN TO VISIT
STATE'S GREATS
RULES OF THE ROAD
DRIVING TOURS

Distance: 237 mi   Time: 3 days

Breaks: Consider stopping overnight in Dubuque, Bettendorf or Davenport, and Burlington.

The Great River Road is a 3,000-mi network of federal, state, and county roads that parallel the Mississippi River on both sides, from Canada to the Gulf of Mexico. The upper Mississippi River, dominated by Iowa countryside, offers spectacular scenery, charming communities, and interpretive centers on the influence the Great River has had on life here. The green paddle-wheel symbol found on maps and road signs is known throughout the region as the symbol of the Great River Road.

❶ This driving tour may begin where the Mississippi River enters Iowa from Minnesota on Route 26 at New Albin, a quiet little town known only for the state boundary marker there. It is in this area of dense forests and fertile farmland that the upper Iowa River flows into the Mississippi River.

❷ Continue 11 mi south on Route 26 to Lansing, the first scenic spot at which you should stop to take a look at a region known locally as Little Switzerland. During the Ice Age when great glaciers carved out the Mississippi River valley, the hills in northeastern Iowa were not flattened like those in much of the area. From Mt. Hosmer Park, you can see for miles into Wisconsin and Minnesota. You can also take a paddle-wheeler ride in the shallow backwaters of the Mississippi on **Backwater Cruises.**

❸ Leaving Lansing, the Great River Road departs Route 26 for a county road, X52, which is clearly marked with road signs. Within a few miles, you come to the village of Harper's Ferry, which is home to the 9,000-acre **Yellow River State Forest.** With additional access to approximately 3,000 acres of Mississippi River backwater, this is a great place to visit if you enjoy hunting, fishing, or hiking.

❹ Farther south on the road rejoins Route 26 and you'll come to the twin communities of **Marquette** and **McGregor.** Iowa's only National Monument, **Effigy Mounds,** is in this area. Here you'll see some 200 burial and ceremonial mounds created by prehistoric Native Americans between 500 BC and AD 1300. Effigy Mounds also has several hiking trails that provide views of the many tiny islands that make up the upper Mississippi River valley.

Marquette is named for the French Canadian explorer who, along with Louis Joliet, journeyed down the Mississippi River in the 1670s. Marquette is home to **Pikes Peak State Park,** which contains the highest bluff along the 1,100-mi path of the Great River. From the top of this 500-ft bluff, the confluence of the Wisconsin River and the mighty Mississippi may be seen to the south. To the north, there is a breathtaking view of the twin suspension bridges that connect Iowa and Wisconsin.

Adjacent to Marquette is McGregor, a community of historic homes with a business district filled with antiques and other shops. Here you may wish to divert from the Great River Road for a jaunt around the **River Bluffs Scenic Byway,** which will take you along hilly U.S. 18 through Gunder, Clermont, and West Union. If you think Iowa is all flat farmland, this 40-mi roller-coaster journey will certainly prove you wrong.

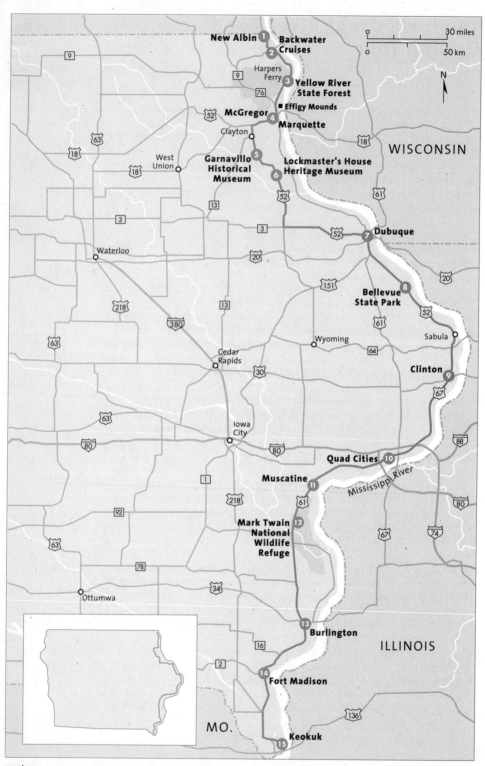

New Albin **1**

**Backwater
Cruises** **2**

Harpers
Ferry **9**

3 **Yellow River
State Forest**

76

■ **Effigy Mounds**

52 **McGregor** **4**

Marquette

Clayton

WISCONSIN

18

5 **Garnavillo
Historical
Museum**

6 **Lockmaster's House
Heritage Museum**

West
Union **18**

63

18

52

61

13

3

3 **52** **7** **Dubuque**

20

Waterloo **20**

151

8 **Bellevue
State Park**

52

218

13

61

20

88

63

380

Wyoming

64

Sabula

Cedar
Rapids

30

Clinton **9**

67

63

Iowa
City

80 **80**

Quad Cities **10**

88

1

Muscatine **11**

218

61

Mississippi River

80

92

12 **Mark Twain
National
Wildlife
Refuge**

67

74

63

78

34

Ottumwa

13 **Burlington**

16 **ILLINOIS**

2

14 **Fort Madison**

MO.

136

15 **Keokuk**

30 miles

50 km

N

INTRODUCTION
HISTORY
REGIONS
WHEN TO VISIT
STATE'S GREATS
RULES OF THE ROAD
DRIVING TOURS

⑤ You may continue on Route 26 where your next stop is the historic fishing village of Clayton, followed by Garnavillo, where you'll find numerous Native American artifacts in the **Garnavillo Historical Museum.**

⑥ At Guttenberg, Route 26 becomes one with U.S. 52 for a few miles. Get out of the car at Guttenberg, take a quick mile-long walk through River Park, and see the activities at Lock and Dam 10. The **Lockmaster's House Heritage Museum** is one of the few left along the river, providing a look inside the lives of those who built the lock and dam system. Guttenberg also has an art gallery and microbrewery, as well as several shops and restaurants in its historic downtown square.

⑦ About 20 mi south of Guttenberg along U.S. 52 is **Dubuque.** Depending on the number of stops you've made along the way, Dubuque may be your first overnight stay. You'll find numerous B&Bs and a surprisingly wide variety of restaurants here. There's also plenty to do in Dubuque. The **Mississippi River Museum,** the **Dubuque Art Center, Crystal Lake Cave,** and trolley and carriage rides are among the city's many offerings. Depending upon the season, you can go skiing at **Sundown Mountain Ski Area** or drive west on U.S. 20 to Dyersville and play baseball at the *Field of Dreams* **Movie Site** baseball field.

⑧ Leaving Dubuque along U.S. 52, you'll come to the Luxembourger community of St. Donatus. Also on U.S. 52, in nearby Bellevue you can visit the butterfly garden at **Bellevue State Park.** The **Grant Wood Scenic Byway** is another diversion from the river. This 30-mi drive along Route 64 passes through the towns of Andrew, Maquoketa, and Preston. You may, however, decide to just continue driving south from Bellevue along U.S. 52 to Sabula, the only Iowa town situated on an island.

⑨ At Sabula, the Great River Road becomes U.S. 67, on which you should continue south to **Clinton. Eagle Point Park** is worth stopping to see, as it provides a view of the widest part of the Mississippi River, an impressive 3-mi span of water. A casino and a showboat are docked in Clinton, but be sure to save time for the arboretum and museum as well.

⑩ From Clinton, continue south on U.S. 67 into the **Quad Cities** (**Davenport** and **Bettendorf, Iowa,** and **Rock Island** and **Moline, Illinois**). More riverboats and walking trails dominate the riverfront, along with Lock and Dam 15. Take time to drive onto **Arsenal Island** (*see* Illinois for full listings) for a visit to the **Rock Island Arsenal Museum** and the **Mississippi River Visitor's Center.** Activities are numerous in the Quad Cities; you could chose to spend several days here or continue south on U.S. 61 to Muscatine, driving through great camping and boating communities such as Buffalo, Montpelier, and Fairport.

⑪ **Muscatine** is at a bend in the river where clam shells collect; the resulting business of manufacturing pearl buttons put Muscatine on the map at the turn of the last century. Muscatine's **Mark Twain Overlook** provides one of the best views of the river during the course of this driving tour. Be sure to bring your camera for shots of the bald eagles, tugboats, or the immense power of the Mississippi River.

⑫ Just south of Muscatine on U.S. 61 you'll enter Louisa County, with its **Mark Twain National Wildlife Refuge.** The refuge is marshy and filled with wetlands, a place enjoyed in the past by the Native Americans for hunting and fishing. In Toolesboro, you'll find a series of Native American burial mounds and a museum of Oneota culture.

⑬ From Toolesboro, the Great River Road moves inland a few miles until you reach **Burlington,** 25 mi to the south on Route 99. The **Point of Burlington Welcome Center** is on the riverfront in a 1928 building that once served the city and the commercial barge traffic stopping here.

⑭ The Great River Road returns to U.S. 61 at Burlington. Twenty miles south of Burlington on U.S. 61 is **Fort Madison,** the site of a full-scale replica of the old fort and a new museum dedicated to the Great Flood of 1993. Fort Madison also has a working railroad museum, a winery, and access to the Mormon Trail.

⑮ The Great River Road continues 25 mi south along U.S. 61 to **Keokuk,** the last town in Iowa before the road enters northeast Missouri. Another of the locks and dams is in Keokuk, as is the **George M. Verity Riverboat Museum,** a **National Cemetery,** and **Rand Park,** which overlooks the river and is the burial site of Chief Keokuk.

To return to New Albin, take U.S. 218 north out of Keokuk. U.S. 218 north becomes Interstate 380 around Iowa City. Take Interstate 380 into Cedar Rapids, then take U.S. 151 out of Cedar Rapids to Route 13 north. Take Route 13 north to U.S. 52 and then take U.S. 52 to U.S. 18 east into Marquette. From Marquette you can follow the Great River Road again. Take Route 76 north to Route 364, then Route X52 to Route 26, which you'll pick up around Lansing. Route 26 will bring you back to New Albin.

ADEL

MAP 3, D4

(Nearby towns also listed: Des Moines, Van Meter, Winterset)

Adel was settled in the 1860s and is now the seat of Dallas County. Its turn-of-the-20th-century French château–style courthouse and clock tower are listed on the National Register of Historic Places and you'll find brick streets and restored historic homes here as well. The 34-mi bicycle trail known as the Raccoon River Valley Trail passes through Adel on its way from Waukee to Yale.

Information: **Main Street Adel** | 1129 Main St., Box 73, 50003 | 515/993–5472.

Attractions

Dallas County Courthouse. Built in 1902, this French château–style building has a 128-ft clock tower and is on the National Register of Historic Places. | 201 N. 8th St. | 515/993–5472 | Free | Daily 8–5.

Raccoon River Trail. You can bike or walk along this 34-mi trail from Waukee to Yale, which is part of Iowa's rails-to-trails project and follows what was once a Union Pacific freight line. There's an entrance to the trail with a parking area on North 9th Street just one block west of Highway 169 in town. | N. 9th St. | 515/993–4205 | Free | Daily.

ON THE CALENDAR

AUG.: *Sweet Corn Festival.* Free corn on the cob, parades, live entertainment, children's games, and a street dance are all part of this festival held on the town square. | 515/993–5472.

OCT.: *Halloween Party.* Pumpkin decorating, a costume contest, and treats for children are part of this old-fashioned event on the town square. | 515/993–5472.

Dining

Patrick's Restaurant. American. This humble small-town café serves steak and eggs, chicken, and pasta. Prime rib is the house favorite and breakfast is served all day. | 111 N. 9th St. | 515/993–3884 | $5 | No credit cards | Closed Sun.

Lodging

Grey Goose B&B. This 1920s farmhouse with a wraparound porch is furnished with antiques and country furniture and sits on 40 acres of land northwest of town. Complimentary breakfast. Pond. Hiking, fishing. | 1740 290th St. | 515/833–2338 | 3 rooms (2 with shared bath) | $55–$65 | No credit cards.

ALGONA

(Nearby town also listed: Emmetsburg)

Surrounded by thousands of acres of the most productive farmland in the world, Algona could very well be a poster town for Iowa at large. Although this town of 6,000 is primarily an agricultural community, three Fortune 500 companies are here, providing economic diversity and stability. High-school sports, adult rugby, and fishing dominate Algona's social life.

Information: Algona Area Chamber of Commerce | 123 E. State St., 50511 | 515/295–7201 | www.algona.org.

Attractions

Algona Nativity Scene. This concrete-and-plaster Nativity scene was designed and built by German prisoners of war held in Algona during World War II. Publicly displayed from the first Sunday in December until the end of the month, it can be seen by appointment during the rest of the year. | Kossuth County Fairgrounds | 515/295–7201 | Free | Dec., Mon.–Fri. 2 PM–9 PM, Sat.–Sun. noon–9 PM.

Ambrose A. Call State Park. 1½ mi south of town out in the gently rolling farmland near the east fork of the Des Moines River, this 138-acre park of rugged hills and thick virgin timber offers sheltered picnic areas, several miles of hiking trails, and both modern and primitive campsites. | Rte. 1 | 515/295–3669 | www.state.ia.us/parks | Free | Daily.

Smith Lake Park. This 120-acre park 3 mi north of town has camping and fishing sites and a 55-acre catfish-stocked lake, complete with two designated swimming areas and plenty of room for sailing or electric trolling motorboats. | U.S. 169 | 515/295–2138 | Free | Daily.

ON THE CALENDAR

AUG.: *Kossuth County Fair.* This weeklong event at the Kossuth County Fairgrounds includes 4-H projects, a carnival, and stage shows with juggling, magic, and music. | 515/295–7201.

OCT.: *Autumnfest Craft Show.* More than 150 regional crafters sell their work during this one-day event, held in the gymnasiums of both Algona high schools, as well as the Knights of Columbus Hall on State Street. | 515/295–7201.

Dining

Chrome Country Inn. American. This large, lively restaurant specializes in Swiss steaks, sauerkraut, and sausages any way you like them. Try the country meat loaf for a flavorful treat. | Intersection of Hwys. 18 and 169 | 515/295–9174 | $7 | AE, MC, V.

Sister Sarah's. Contemporary. This restaurant on the eastern edge of town doubles as an art gallery, so you can consider buying one of the paintings on the wall while enjoying prime rib or honey jalapeño pork chops. The dining room has booths and tables, or you can dine alfresco in the beer garden out back or on the expansive, Southern-style front porch. Salad bar. Kids' menu. | Hwy. 18 E | 515/295–7757 | $7–$15 | D, MC, V | Closed Sun., Mon.

Lodging

AmericInn. Just ½ mi west of downtown Algona on Highway 18, this chain motel has a spacious lobby with a fireplace. Cable TV. Pool. | 600 Hwy. 18 W | 515/295–3333 or 800/634–3444 | fax 515/295–9215 | www.americinn.com | 41 rooms | $68–$106 | AE, D, DC, MC, V.

Burr Oak. This low, steel-sided motel 3 mi south of town is perfect if you're looking for quiet rural surroundings and aren't too hung up on frills and amenities. Rooms are immaculate but smallish with furnishings from the late 1970s. Complimentary Continental breakfast. Cable TV. | 1903B U.S. 169 S | 515/295–7213 | fax 515/295–2979 | www.burroakmotel.com | 42 rooms | $42 | AE, D, DC, MC, V.

Heartland Bed and Breakfast. Built in 1913 with hardwood floors, leaded-glass windows, and an Italian marble fireplace for the sitting room, this was the home of Algona's first surgeon. Guest rooms have delicate lace curtains and acres of polished wood. For those who are tempted, massages are available across the street and you'll be just one block from Main Street's movie theater, tea room, shops, and restaurants. Complimentary breakfast. Cable TV, room phones, in-room data ports. | 400 E. Nebraska St., | 515/295–9445 | 4 rooms | $75 | MC, V.

© Corbis

ALGONA POW NATIVITY

It wasn't *Hogan's Heroes* by any stretch of the imagination. It was a World War II POW camp for nearly 9,000 German soldiers in rural Iowa. During the Christmas season of 1944 Eduard Kaib, a noncommissioned officer in the German Army, was a long way from home and feeling quite homesick, so he and five fellow prisoners talked their guards into allowing them to build a Nativity scene.

The Germans fashioned figures of concrete on a wire frame and finished them with hand carving in plaster, paying for all the materials with their allowances. The Nativity began with Baby Jesus in a straw-filled crib and grew over the next two years to include 60 figures, built to half size, which were displayed at the edge of camp for the public to enjoy.

When the war was over and the camp disbanded, the Junior Chamber of Commerce asked Mr. Kaib to allow his creation to remain as a permanent exhibit in Algona. A new building was constructed, lighting added, and a recording of "Silent Night" was made to accompany the scene.

Mr. Kaib died in 1988, having returned to Iowa once after the war to visit the people of Algona and the Nativity he left them. Each December thousands of people come to Algona to view the Nativity. Special appointments can be made at other times of the year by calling 515/295–7163. In accordance with Mr. Kaib's wishes, there is no charge.

AMANA COLONIES

(Nearby towns also listed: Cedar Rapids, Iowa City)

A trip to the Amana Colonies is a must for those who want to experience Iowa fully. Each year, nearly 1.5 million people visit the seven villages (Amana, High Amana, Middle Amana, South Amana, West Amana, East Amana, and Homestead), which are collectively designated a National Historic Landmark. The colonies were settled by members of the Community of True Inspiration escaping religious persecution in Germany and Switzerland. In 1842 approximately 800 members of the community came to the New World, first settling in Buffalo, New York, and later purchasing 26,000 acres from private and government sources at $1.25 an acre in the Iowa River valley.

After the Amanites' communal lifestyle ended in 1932, free enterprise led to the production of the Amana stoves, refrigerators, and other appliances found in many American homes. The business has since been sold to a holding company in Texas but you can shop and find great bargains at several of the original Amana appliance stores while learning the history of this innovative economic undertaking.

A trip to the Amana Colonies can be a family vacation, a romantic getaway, or a fun destination with friends. The community has live theater, great food, B&B inns, golf, and plenty of shopping.

Information: Amana Colonies Convention and Visitors Bureau | 39 38th Ave., 52203 | 319/622–7622 or 800/579–2294 | accvb@netins.net | www.amanacolonies.com.

Attractions

Amana Arts Guild Center. Special exhibits and demonstrations in quilting, basket and rug making, pottery throwing, and more are offered throughout the season. You can also buy quilts here. | Rte. 220, High Amana | 319/622–3678 | www.amanacolonies.com | Free | May–Sept., Wed.–Sun. 10:30–4:30; Oct., weekends 10:30–4:30.

Communal Agriculture Museum. Displays antique agricultural instruments used long ago on Amana's communal farms. | 505 P St., South Amana | 319/622–3567 | www.amana-colonies.com | $5 ticket to all 4 of Amana's historical museums | May–Sept., Mon.–Sat. 10–5, Sun. noon–5.

Communal Kitchen and Cooper Shop Museum. Amana's only intact communal kitchen tells the story of pre-1930s life here with original cooking utensils and supplies. The former village barrel-making shop is adjacent. | 103 26th Ave., Middle Amana | 319/622–3567 | www.amanacolonies.com | $5 ticket to all 4 of Amana's historical museums | May–Oct., Mon.–Sat. 9–5, Sun. noon–5.

Community Church Museum. Built in 1865, this is the only one of seven Amana village churches that visitors can tour. It's 5 mi east of South Amana. | 4210 V St., Homestead | 319/622–3567 | www.amanacolonies.com | $5 ticket to all 4 of Amana's historical museums | May–Oct., Mon.–Sat. 10–5, Sun. noon–5.

Museum of Amana History. This museum, housed in three 19th-century buildings, has won national awards for authenticity in portraying life in this communal society. | 4310 220th Tr., Amana | 319/622–3567 | www.amanacolonies.com | $5 ticket to all 4 of Amana's historical museums | Mid-Apr.–mid-Nov., Mon.–Sat. 10–5, Sun. noon–5.

Old Broom and Basket Shop. Watch while quality brooms and baskets are made before your eyes, or purchase completed items on the shelves. | 618 8th Ave., West Amana | 319/622–3315 | www.jeonet.com/amanas | Free | June–Aug., Mon.–Sat. 9–5, Sun. 11–4.

Old Creamery Theatre Company. Since 1971 live professional theater has been offered here every weekend. | 39 38th Ave., Amana | 800/352–6262 | Admission varies per show | Apr.–mid-Dec., Wed.–Sun.

South Amana Barn Museum. This horse barn now contains a collection of miniature buildings depicting the history of rural America. | Hwy. 220,South Amana | 319/622–3058 | barnmus@aol.com | www.amanacolonies.com | $3 | Apr.–Oct., daily 9–5.

Tanger Outlet Center. This mall is 15 mi south of the Amana Colonies near Interstate 80 at exit 220 and has more than 60 stores including outlets for Nike, Brooks Brothers, Polo, and Levi. | 1991 O'Donnel Rd.,Williamsburg | 319/668–2885 | Free | Mon.–Sat. 9–9, Sun. noon–9.

ON THE CALENDAR

APR.: *Midwest Natural Basketry Fest.* Learn about basket weaving from the masters at this weekend event in High Amana. | 1210 G St., High Amana | 319/622–7622.

JUNE: *Splinterfest Woodcrafter's Festival.* More than 150 wood-carving specialists demonstrate their skill and sell goods at this outdoor event just off Interstate 80 at exit 225. | 319/622–7622.

NOV.: *Fall Fibre Show and Sale.* Clothing, decorative pieces, and other warm and fuzzy goodies are available at this event in High Amana. | 1210 G St., High Amana | 319/622–7622.

Dining

Amana Barn Restaurant. German. This casual, rustic restaurant in a restored barn has country decor. Ceiling beams, wagon wheels, and strategically placed antiques highlight the area's history. The Barn is known for sauerbraten, schnitzel, and local dishes such as Iowa ham and beef. Family-style service. Kids' menu. Sunday brunch. | 4709 220th Trail, Amana | 319/622–3214 | $8–$15 | AE, D, MC, V | Limited fall and winter hrs.

Brick Haus Restaurant. German. Vintage photos of the original German and Dutch families who settled Amana cover the walls here and a large collection of antique German plates give a sense of life in the Amana Colonies in days gone by. Try the *Wiener schnitzel mit spaetzle.* Kids' menu. Beer and wine only. No smoking. | 728 47th Ave., Amana | 319/622–3278 | $10–$20 | AE, MC, V.

Colony Inn Restaurant. German. Sauerbraten and jaeger schnitzel are among the specialty dishes offered at this lively eatery that has been serving since 1935. Vintage photographs of colony residents and antique farm tools decorate the walls. | 741 47th Ave., Amana | 319/622–6270 or 800/227–3471 | $13 | AE, D, MC, V.

Colony Village. German. Open since 1967, this Williamsburg restaurant (about 15 mi south of the colonies) has made a name for itself with its amazing selection of baked goods. Sit in a cozy booth or gather around one of the large tables in the restaurant's dining area and enjoy traditional family-style German dishes from Wiener schnitzel and sauerbraten to rhubarb pie and cinnamon-pecan rolls. | 2224 U Ave., Williamsburg | 319/668–1223 | $10–$20 | AE, D, DC, MC, V.

Homestead Kitchen. German. This restaurant recalls Amana's original communal kitchens, with its family-style service and wooden benches at long tables. Specialties are basic, hearty German fare, like schnitzel and bratwurst. Meal portions are beyond generous—plan to share. Kids' menu. Beer and wine only. | 3146 U.S. 6 Tr., Homestead | 319/622–3203 | $7–$12 | No credit cards.

Lady Di's Tea Room. American/Casual. Dine on homemade soup or quiche or a sandwich made to order in this modest two-room café decorated with an eclectic mix of antiques and old hats. | 4444 V St., Homestead | 319/622–3338 | Reservations required for dinner | $6 | No credit cards | Closed Sun., Mon.

Ox Yoke Inn. German. A photo history of the inn, which was built in 1873, adorns the walls here while the tables sport blue-checked tablecloths and fresh flowers and a taxidermied bear oversees the goings-on. The menu features traditional German specialties including Wiener schnitzel, sauerbraten, chicken schnitzel, and jager schnitzel. The rhubarb custard pie is not to be missed. Family-style service. Kids' menu. Sunday brunch. | 4420 220th Tr. (Main St.), Amana | 319/622–3441 | $8–$20 | AE, D, DC, MC, V | Closed Mon. Dec.–Mar.

Ronneburg Restaurant. German. The decor of this good-size restaurant reflects its namesake medieval castle in Hesse, Germany, with its red-checked table cloths, red-glass lanterns, and early 19th-century-styled furnishings. The sauerbraten (with potato dumplings) is a favorite dish, as is Iowa-raised round beef marinated in local wine and spices. Family-style service. | 4408 220th Tr. (Main St.), Amana | 319/622–3641 | $8–$15 | D, MC, V.

Zuber's. American. Memorabilia from the current owner's professional baseball career embellish this inn established in the late 1800s. The kitchen is known for its oven-baked steak. Family-style. Kids' menu. | 2206 V St., Homestead | 319/622–3911 | $10–$15 | AE, D, MC, V.

Lodging

Best Western Quiet House Suites. Fifteen miles southwest of Amana and directly across from the Tanger outlet mall, this hotel looks like a rambling, multilevel house. The spacious guest rooms have large windows and each is decorated with a different local or area theme. Complimentary Continental breakfast. Cable TV. Indoor-outdoor pool. Hot tub. Exercise equipment. Business services. Pets allowed (fee). | 1708 N. Highland St., Williamsburg | 319/668–9777 or 800/528–1234 | fax 319/668–9770 | www.bestwestern.com | 33 rooms, 7 suites | $101, $145 suites | AE, D, DC, MC, V.

Comfort Inn. This chain hotel is 9 mi from the Amana Colonies and 5 mi west of the Tanger Shopping Outlet. There are several restaurants across the highway. Cable TV. Pool. | I–80 (exit 225), Amana | 319/668–2700 or 800/228–5150 | fax 319/668–2725 | comfortamana@earthlink.net | www.choicehotels.com | 61 rooms | $78 | AE, D, DC, MC, V.

Days Inn. About 10 mi from the Amana Colonies and 5 mi. south of the Tanger Shopping Outlet, this motel offers rooms with two doubles or a king-size bed. Complimentary Continental breakfast. Cable TV. | 2214 U Ave.(exit 225 off I–80), Williamsburg | 319/668–2097 or 800/325–2525 | www.daysinn.com | 115 rooms | $60–$75 | AE, D, DC, MC, V.

Die Heimat Country Inn. Built in 1854, this former stagecoach stop in Homestead incorporates hand-pieced quilts as decoration and also as very practical covers on the inn's four-poster canopy beds. Complimentary breakfast. Some refrigerators, in-room TVs. Some pets allowed (fee). | 4430 V St., Homestead | 319/622–3937 | 18 rooms | $70–$100 | D, MC, V.

Dusk to Dawn. Built in 1868 as one of the early communal houses for the Amana colonies, this building is now a gracious B&B with an all-weather Jacuzzi, spacious back deck, and a greenhouse/sunroom. Picnic area, complimentary Continental breakfast. Microwaves available, cable TV, no room phones. Hot tub. No smoking. | 2616 K St., Middle Amana | 319/622–3029, 800/669–5773 reservations | 7 rooms (4 with shower only) | $62–$68 | AE, D, MC, V.

Guest House Motor Inn. This wood-frame motor inn on Amana's main street has antique cherry-wood beds and patch-work quilts in all the rooms. Park in front of your room for easy arrival and departure. Cable TV. | 4712 220th Tr., Amana | 319/622–3599 | 38 rooms | $50 | AE, D, MC, V.

Holiday Inn. Next to Little Amana and an Iowa Welcome Center, this hotel is just 7 mi from the Colonies and 18 mi from Iowa City. The hotel boasts a large lobby with vaulted ceilings and a dozen or so couches and chairs for lounging and instead of generic, modular motel furnishings, the rooms here are decorated with antique reproductions in a variety of fine woods. Restaurant, bar, room service. Cable TV. Pool. Hot tub. Exercise equipment. Playground. Laundry facilities. Business services. Pets allowed. | 2211 U Ave., Williamsburg | 319/668–1175 or 800/465–4329 | fax 319/668–2853 | www.amanaholidayinn.com | 155 rooms | $65–$100 | AE, D, DC, MC, V.

My Little Inn. This small, single-story inn, 10 minutes from the Colonies on a commercial strip just off I-80 at exit 225, prides itself on small-town courtesy. There are three German restaurants, including Colony Village, right next door. In-room microwaves, refrigerators, TV. | 2208 U Ave., Williamsburg | 319/668–9667 | 6 rooms | $40–$55 | D, MC, V.

Ramada Limited. Just off Interstate 80 at exit 220, this basic hotel is ½ mi from the Tanger Shopping Outlet and 15 mi from the Amanas. Complimentary Continental breakfast. Cable TV. Exercise equipment. | 122 Hawkeye Dr., Williamsburg | 319/668–1000 or 800/272–6232 | fax 319/668–1000 | www.ramada.com | 40 rooms | $72 | AE, D, DC, MC, V.

Rawson's B&B. You'll find exposed beams and brick walls, period furnishings and fabrics, and lavish baths in this historic building that was a kitchen workers' dormitory during Homestead's days of communal living. Complimentary breakfast. TVs, VCRs. Some hot-tubs. | 4424 V St., Homestead | 319/622–6035 | 4 rooms | $65–$119 | MC, V.

Super 8. This standard motel is in Williamsburg, within sight of the Tanger Shopping Outlet and 15 mi from the Amana Colonies. Complimentary Continental breakfast. Cable TV. Business services. Some pets allowed (fee). | 2228 U Ave., Williamsburg | 319/668–2800 or 800/800–8000 | fax 319/668–2800 | www.super8.com | 63 rooms | $57 | AE, D, DC, MC, V.

AMES

MAP 3, D4

(Nearby town also listed: Boone)

This All-America City (a title awarded by the National Civic League) just north of Des Moines was named after railroad promoter Congressman Oakes Ames in 1864. Iowa State University was founded here in 1858 as one of the nation's first land-grant colleges. Today the university employs nearly 13,000 people and is the primary economic force in this town of 48,000. It's also the reason you'll find a number of art galleries, museums, and theaters in town.

Information: **Ames Chamber of Commerce** | 213 Duff Ave., 50010-6676 | 515/232–2310 | www.chamber.ames.ia.us.

Attractions

Iowa Arboretum. There are hundreds of cultivated trees, shrubs, and flowers to enjoy in this "Library of Living Plants" 20 minutes southwest of Ames in nearby Madrid. | 1875 Peach Ave., Madrid | 515/795–3216 | $2 | Daily dawn–dusk.

Iowa State University. Established as the Iowa Agricultural College in 1858, Iowa State today has one of the best veterinary medicine and chemistry programs in the country. George Washington Carver was a student and faculty member here. | Elwood Dr. | 515/294–4111 | www.iastate.edu | Free | Daily.

More than 50 carillon bells sound daily in the **Campanile,** a brick and terra-cotta clock tower on campus. | Union Dr. | 515/294–4111 | Free | Daily.

A self-guided walking tour of the **Christian Petersen Sculptures,** 12 large public sculptures created by the Denmark-born artist while in-residence from 1934 to 1955, begins at Memorial Union on the central campus. | Memorial Union | 515/294–3342 | www.museums.iastate.edu | $1 for guidebook.

The first building constructed on the ISU campus, now known as the **Farm House Museum,** is a National Historic Landmark and contains more than 6,000 antiques and pieces of Victorian art. | Knoll Rd. | 515/294–3342 | www.museums.iastate.edu | Free | Weekdays noon–4, Sun. 1–4.

Eight **Grant Wood Murals** surround the first floor of the university's Parks Library. The collection includes one of the Iowa artist's most famous works, "Breaking the Prairie Sod."

| Morrill Rd. | 515/294–3342 | www.museums.iastate.edu | Free | Mon.–Sat. 7 AM–midnight, Sun. 11–11.

The **Iowa State Center,** a sprawling campus conference, sports, and performing arts center, is often the site of national political forums. | South of Lincoln Way between Beach Ave. and Elwood Dr. | 515/294–3347 or 877/843–2368 | fax 515/294–3349 | www.center.ias-tate.edu | Admission varies per event | Hrs vary per event.

The **Reiman Gardens** on the south edge of campus are used as teaching gardens. | 1407 Elwood Dr. | 515/294–2710 | www.reimangardens.iastate.edu | Free | Daily dawn–dusk.

Resource Recovery Plant. Founded in 1975, this facility was the first municipally owned recycling plant in the country and a vital step in the development of a nationwide con-sciousness for recycling. | 110 Center Ave. | 515/239–5137 | Free | Open for tours Wed.

ON THE CALENDAR
JULY: *Iowa State Games.* A statewide sports festival for amateur athletes of all ages. | 515/292–3251.

JULY: *Midnight Madness.* Begun in 1972, this event features both celebrity and ama-teur runners competing in various road races, including a speed walk, bike ride, kids' race, 5K, and 10K. All events take place at midnight. | 515/292–0133.

AUG.: *Octagon Art Festival.* The work of over 100 midwestern artists and craftspeople is on display and for sale at this yearly event held in ISU's Hilton Coliseum. | 515/232–5331.

Dining
Aunt Maude's. Seafood. Fresh swordfish, salmon, and mahimahi are flown in three times a week to this upscale restaurant with linen tablecloths and original oil paintings on the walls. | 547 Main St. | 515/233–4136 | $15–$30 | AE, MC, V | No lunch weekends.

Broiler Steakhouse. Steak. Beef dishes and red wine are the order of the day here. Fresh-cut roses from the restaurant's own greenhouse—which also supplies the kitchen with herbs—decorate the linen-draped tables. Kids' menu. | 6008 W. Lincoln Way | 515/292–2516 | $10–$20 | AE, D, DC, MC, V.

Elwell's Chef's Inn. American. This restaurant is known for its prime rib and Iowa-raised steaks in a family-with-kids-friendly atmosphere. Kids' menu, earlybird dinners. Sunday brunch. | 6100 W. Lincoln Way | 515/292–4454 | $8–$15 | AE, D, DC, MC, V.

Hickory Park. American. A staple of Ames and ISU life for three decades since it was estab-lished in 1970, Hickory Park first made a name for itself by barbecuing anything that moved and serving truly monumental ice-cream sundaes and it's still known locally for fantastic BBQ sandwiches and a dessert list longer than the entrée menu. The multiple dining areas have tin ceilings and old church pews for seats. Kids' menu. | 1404 S. Duff St. | 515/232–8940 | $5–$15 | AE, D, MC, V.

Lucullan's. Italian. This family restaurant in the historic downtown area serves a range of dishes from steak and fresh flown-in salmon to the house specialty Cajun pasta and offers free dessert for kids under 12 and those celebrating birthdays. Large windows in the dining area look out onto an outdoor courtyard and historic Main Street. There's also a downstairs sports bar. Kids' menu. | 400 Main St. | 515/232–8484 | $9–$15 | AE, D, MC, V.

Lodging
Baymont Inn and Suites. This chain hotel on the south edge of town less than 5 mi from the interstate and Iowa State University prides itself on fast, cheerful service and spacious rooms. A convenience store and deli are within walking distance and several restaurants and shopping areas are just a short drive away. Complimentary Continental breakfast. Some refrig-erators, cable TV. Pool. Hot tub. Exercise equipment. Pets allowed. | 2500 Elwood Dr. | 515/296–2500 | fax 515/296–2874 | www.baymontinns.com | 88 rooms | $72 | AE, D, DC, MC, V.

Best Western Starlite Village. This hotel is in a rural area 1 mi east of Ames off I-35. All rooms look out onto an indoor pool/atrium area, either through sliding deck-level glass doors or from railed balconies. Restaurant, bar, room service. Cable TV, in-room VCRs available. Pool. Hot tub. Free parking. Pets allowed. | 2601 E. 13th St. | 515/232–9260 or 800/903–0009 | fax 515/232–9260 | www.bestwestern.com | 130 rooms | $64 | AE, D, DC, MC, V.

Comfort Inn. Visible from the interstate, this motel in the middle of a corporate park in southeast Ames is still a quiet haven after a day visiting the ISU campus or shouting yourself hoarse at a Cyclones game. The motel is just 4 mi east of ISU and is within walking distance of several restaurants and other hotels. Complimentary Continental breakfast. Some refrigerators, cable TV. Pool. Hot tub. Business services. Pets allowed (fee). | 1605 S. Dayton Ave. | 515/232–0689 or 800/221–2222 | fax 515/232–0689 | www.choicehotels.com | 52 rooms, 6 suites | $55–$85 | AE, D, DC, MC, V.

Country Inn and Suites of Ames. This chain hotel just off of Highway 30, about 2 mi from town and the university, offers country hospitality. Complimentary Continental breakfast. Pool. Exercise equipment. | 2605 S.E. 16th St. | 515/233–3935 | www.countryinns.com | 78 rooms | $79 | AE, D, DC, MC, V.

Hampton Inn. This hotel is 3 mi east of downtown and 7 mi east of ISU. Restaurants and bars are a few minutes' drive away. Restaurant. Cable TV. Gym. Laundry facilities, laundry services. | 1400 S. Dayton Ave. | 515/239–9999 or 800/426–7866 | fax 515/239–6015 | www.hamptoninn-suites.com | 78 rooms | $80 | AE, D, DC, MC, V.

Heartland Inn. Iowa State Cyclones pennants, posters, and other memorabilia decorate the lobby and common area of this hotel. Rooms are large with standard furnishings. The hotel is 5 mi east of ISU and is just one highway exit west of a large shopping area with a theater and several restaurants. Complimentary Continental breakfast. Cable TV. Sauna. | 2600 S.E. 16th Ave. | 515/233–6060 or 800/334–3277 | fax 515/233–1911 | 87 rooms | $60–$66 | AE, D, DC, MC, V.

Holiday Inn Gateway Center. Popular with parents in town for sports events and ISU functions, this hotel is just 1½ mi south of ISU in southwest Ames and sits on 17 acres of lush countryside and manicured grounds. Rooms are very quiet and furnished with antique reproduction pieces. Beds all have feather pillows. Restaurant, bar, room service. Some in-room data ports, cable TV, in-room VCRs available. Pool. Hot tub, sauna. Business services, airport shuttle. | 2100 Green Hills Dr. | 515/292–8600 or 800/465–4329 | fax 515/292–4446 | www.holidayinn.com | 188 rooms | $100 | AE, D, DC, MC, V.

Howard Johnson Express Inn. This hotel is 2 mi south of the university in the southwest part of Ames off Highway 69 and offers shuttle service to and from town for those who don't want to drive. There are several restaurants and a theater within walking distance. In-room data ports, cable TV. Pool. | 1709 S. Duff | 515/232–8363 or 800/798–8363 | 73 rooms | $60 | AE, D, MC, V.

Ramada Inn. This downtown hotel is just off the Iowa State University campus and within easy walking distance of theaters, nightclubs, bowling, restaurants, and shopping. The lobby resembles a hunt club with its wood panels, hanging lamps, and large flagstone fireplace. Restaurant, bar, complimentary Continental breakfast, room service. Cable TV. Pool. | 1206 S. Duff St. | 515/232–3410 or 800/272–6232 | fax 515/232–6036 | www.ramada.com | 103 rooms | $68–$85 | AE, D, DC, MC, V.

University Inn. This small, quaint hotel is only ¼ mi from downtown Ames within easy walking distance of shopping, movies, and people-watching. The lobby is spacious with large windows and high ceilings. Guest rooms are outfitted with blond furnishings. Complimentary Continental breakfast. In-room data ports, cable TV. Business services. | 229 S. Duff St. | 515/232–0280 or 800/422–5250 | fax 515/232–4578 | 47 rooms | $60–$75 | AE, D, MC, V.

ANAMOSA

(Nearby town also listed: Cedar Rapids)

Irish immigrants first settled in the Wapsipinicon River valley in the mid 1800s, carving homes and a community from the stone bluffs over the river. In 1891 artist Grant Wood, who would become the area's most famous resident, was born on an Anamosa farm. Wood's painting was inspired by the Iowa landscape, and many of his works are displayed during the art festival held in his honor here each June. He is buried in Anamosa's Riverside Cemetery.

Information: Grant Wood Country Tourism | 124 E. Main St., 52205 | 319/462–4101.

Attractions
Grant Wood Tourism Center and Gallery. You can watch a movie about Grant Wood's life, see photographs of the art colonies he ran, and see original murals he painted for the Old Chieftain Hotel in Council Bluffs here. | 124 E. Main St. | 319/462–4267 | Free | Mon.–Sat. 10–4, Sun. 1–4.

Riverside Cemetery. Here you can pay tribute to Grant Wood in his final resting place. | Cemetery Rd. | 319/462–4267 | Free | Daily, dawn–dusk.

Wapsipinicon State Park. The sandstone and limestone bluffs in this 251-acre park immediately northeast of town are covered with moss and columbine. If you hike along the bluffs you'll find rocky natural staircases, crevices, and two caves. One, Horse Thief Cave, is the legendary hideout of a pair of 19th-century horse thieves. The park also maintains a riverside boat launch for fishing and several campsites. | 21301 Rte. E34 | 319/462–2761 | www.state.ia.us/parks | Free | Daily.

ON THE CALENDAR
JUNE: *Grant Wood Art Festival.* An extensive exhibit of original paintings by Grant Wood, a juried show for artists and entertainers, hands-on workshops for children and adults, and performances by local actors and musicians celebrate the talents of Anamosa's famous son in nearby Stone City, where Grant Wood ran several summer art colonies. | 319/462–3988.

Dining
Opera House. American. Housed in a former opera house from the 1800s and catering to a mixed crowd of tourists and local folks, this restaurant has excellent breakfasts; homemade soups and sandwiches at lunch; and steaks, fish, and pasta for dinner. No alcohol is served. | 221 W. Main St. | 319/462–2302 | $5–$7 | AE, MC, V.

Lodging
Super 8 Hotel. This chain hotel is 1½ mi east of downtown next to a restaurant and lounge. Complimentary Continental breakfast. Cable TV. | 110 Grant Wood Dr. | 319/462–3888 or 800/800–8000 | www.super8.com | 35 rooms | $56 | AE, D, MC, V.

ANITA

(Nearby towns also listed: Atlantic, Avoca)

The way some people tell it, the story of how Anita got its name is a long one but suffice it to say that back in the 1860s several railroad construction workers ate in a local hotel

ANITA

INTRO
ATTRACTIONS
DINING
LODGING

where the owner's niece was named Anita. Today, visitors frequent Lake Anita State Park, an excellent fishing and mushrooming park in the northeast of Cass County. Anita is known for two very special trees. One grew next to—and eventually engulfed—a field plow with its trunk, and the other is growing right in the middle of a country road just north of town. Be sure to ask about them when you're in the area.

Information: **City of Anita** | 744 Main St., 50020 | 712/762–3746 or 712/762–3387.

Attractions
Lake Anita State Park. Iowa's soft, rolling Loess Hills, the product of windblown silt from the Missouri River, are not to be missed and this 942-acre park is a great place to explore these unique geological formations. The park has several self-guided nature trails, camping sites, and a 171-acre man-made lake where you can swim or fish. | 55111 650th St. | 712/762–3564 | www.state.ia.us/park | Free | Daily.

Dining
Nick's Sports Club. American. Steaks and prime rib fill the plates and baseball and football memorabilia from local and pro teams line the walls here. | 870 Main St. | 712/762–3355 | $10–$25 | MC, V.

Lodging
Anita Grand Motel. This small downtown 1950s motel is within walking distance of several restaurants and is 1½ mi from Lake Anita State Park. Cable TV. | 1203 White Pole Rd. | 712/762–3508 | 10 rooms | $40 | No credit cards.

ATLANTIC

MAP 3, C5

(Nearby town also listed: Avoca)

Like many western communities, Atlantic was founded in anticipation of the railroad passing through. Growth fueled by the railroad soon resulted in Atlantic's becoming the seat of Cass County. With its wide expanses and rolling hills, two impressive golf couses have flourished here, and Atlantic is now known as the golf capital of Iowa.

Information: **Atlantic Area Chamber of Commerce** | 614 Chestnut St., 50022 | 712/243–3017 or 877/283–2124 | atlantic@netins.net | www.atlanticiowa.com.

Attractions
Hitchcock House. This former station on the Underground Railroad in Hitchcock Park, 1 mi west of town, was built by Mormons in 1856 and is listed on the National Register of Historic Places. | 63748 567th Ln., Lewis | 712/769–2323 | $1 | Mid-Apr.–mid-Oct., 1–5; closed Thurs.

Nishna Hills Golf Club. This 18-hole professional-level course in the south part of town is semi-private. | 1400 E. 14th St. | 712/243–9931 | $15-$20 | Daily, 8 AM–dusk.

ON THE CALENDAR
AUG.: *AtlanticFest.* Food, music, and southwest Iowa's largest craft show. | 877/283–2124. **SEPT.: *Coca-Cola Days.*** There's a parade, a barbecue, golf, and displays from 150 collectors of Coca-Cola memorabilia at this downtown festival. | 877/283–2124.

Dining
La Casa Grande. Mexican. Taco Tuesdays are a highlight in this colorful eatery decorated with clay pots. Kids' menu. | 500 W. 7th St. | 712/243–4326 | $8–$10 | No credit cards.

Pine's Steakhouse Steak. They've been serving steaks from the grill at this large, busy restaurant since 1939. | 1500 E. 7th St. | 712/243–3606 | $8–$12 | AE, D, MC, V | Closed Sun.

Lodging

A-Ford-O Motel. This one-story economy motel is eight blocks from downtown and is across the street from a bar and a restaurant. Cable TV. | 610 W.7th St. | 712/243–1412 | 12 rooms | $31 | AE, MC, V.

Chestnut Charm. This 1898 Victorian mansion was built by a local timber baron and is largely intact, boasting stained- and leaded-glass windows, hardwood floors, marble fireplaces, and original linen wall-coverings. There's a gazebo and fountained courtyard on the grounds. Complimentary breakfast. Some in-room microwaves and refrigerators, in-room hot tubs, no TV in some rooms, no phone in some rooms. No kids. No smoking. | 1409 Chestnut St. | 712/243–5652 | info@chestnutcharm.org | www.chestnutcharm.org | 5 rooms (1 with shower only), 1 cottage | $70–$140, $175–$250 cottage | MC, V.

Econo Lodge. This basic motor inn with reasonably spacious rooms surrounding a pool is in a rural area 8 mi north of town off I-80 at exit 60. There's a Country Kitchen Restaurant within walking distance. Cable TV. Pool. Pets allowed. | 64968 Boston Rd. | 712/243–4067 | fax 712/243–1713 | www.hotelchoice.com | $28 | AE, D, DC, MC, V.

S.F. Martin House B&B. Rooms in this downtown 1873 Victorian are furnished in period style. There is an on-site restaurant that serves homemade food as well as wine and beer. Complimentary breakfast. Cable TV. | 419 Poplar | 712/243–5589 | 4 rooms | $50 | No credit cards.

Super 8. This downtown, drive-up motel is within easy walking distance of Atlantic's restaurants and shops. Restaurant, complimentary Continental breakfast. In-room data ports, cable TV. Pool. Hot tub. Exercise equipment. Business services. | 1902 E. 7th St. | 712/243–4723 or 800/800–8000 | fax 712/243–2864 | www.super8.com | 59 rooms | $55 | AE, D, DC, MC, V.

AVOCA

MAP 3, B4

(Nearby town also listed: Atlantic)

Avoca's claim to fame is that television talk-show host Johnny Carson lived here for about five years as a child and has since donated money to both the library and the historical society of this community. This is an agricultural community and the people of Avoca follow the corn and soybean markets on a daily basis, knowing that the slightest fluctuation in prices may make the difference between a good year and a bad year. The town today takes great pride in its community resources, such as its schools, parks, and golf course.

Information: Avoca City Hall | 201 N. Elm St., Box 219, 51521 | 712/343–2424.

Attractions

Prairie Rose State Park. This 680-acre park, 11 mi northeast of Avoca in nearby Harlan, is popular for fishing, hiking, and camping. | County Rd. M47 | 712/773–2701 | www.state.ia.us/parks | Free | Daily.

Sweet Vale of Avoca Museum. More than 75 mounted animal heads from all over the world are a part of the exhibits here. | 504 N. Elm St. | 712/343–2477 | Donations accepted | Memorial Day–Labor Day, daily 1–4.

ON THE CALENDAR
MAY: *Avenue of Flags.* Flags from around the world are displayed in a ceremony commemorating American veterans at various cemeteries. | 712/343–6358.

SEPT.: *Country Music Festival*. Pickin' and grinnin' are billed as the highlights of this weeklong musical gathering of musicians playing public-domain tunes on the Pottawattamie Fairgrounds. | 712/343–6358.

Dining

Ember's Restaurant. American. This restaurant cooks up chicken, steaks, and sandwiches for a large crowd consisting mostly of locals. The Philly cheesesteak and cheeseburgers are favorites. | 1817 N. Lavista Heights Rd. | 712/343–2419 | $6 | No credit cards.

Lodging

Avoca Motel. This 1970s-era motel is on the edge of town within, walking distance of restaurants and bars. Cable TV. | 104 Lavista Heights Rd. | 712/343–2424 | 20 rooms | $40 | AE, MC, V.

Capri. This simple motel offers small but well-maintained rooms in a quiet rural setting less than a mile north of downtown. Cable TV. Pets allowed. | 110 E. Pershing St. | 712/343–6301 | 26 rooms | $41–$55 | AE, D, MC, V.

BETTENDORF

MAP 3, H4

(Nearby towns also listed: Clinton, Davenport)

Originally incorporated as Gilbertown, Bettendorf was renamed for two German brothers who founded an iron wagon business on the Mississippi riverfront that greatly accelerated the growth of the community. The "quiet sister" of the Quad Cities (which also includes Davenport, Iowa, and Rock Island and Moline, Illinois), Bettendorf is primarily a residential community with beautiful riverfront access. Taken together, the Quad Cities cover three counties in eastern Iowa and northwestern Illinois and have a population of almost 400,000. Although neighboring Moline was hit hard during the farm crisis of the 1980s, an established industrial base kept the economy of Bettendorf stable.

Information: **Bettendorf Chamber of Commerce** | 2117 State St., 52722 | 319/355–4753 | www.bettendorfchamber.com.

Attractions

Buffalo Bill Cody Homestead. Buffalo and longhorn cattle graze around the 1847 family home of this famous frontiersman, about 12 mi northeast of town. | 28050 230th Ave., Princeton | 319/225–2981 | $2 | Apr.–Oct., daily 9–5; Nov.–Mar. by appointment.

Family Museum of Arts and Science. Touch a tornado, make a cloud, or hop through a rabbit hole at this hands-on museum for kids. | 2900 Learning Campus Dr. | 319/344–4106 | fax 319/344–4164 | www.familymuseum.org | $4 | Mon. noon–8, Tues.–Thurs. 9–8, Fri.–Sat. 9–5, Sun. noon–5.

Isle of Capri. One of the world's largest riverboat casinos, just east of Interstate 74, includes Roger Craig's Sports Bar, which contains one of the Midwest's largest collections of rare sports memorabilia. | 1777 Isle Pwy. | 319/359–7280 or 800/724–5825 | www.isleofcaprircasino.com | Daily 24 hrs.

Splash Landing. This public water park features a baby pool and water games, play structures, and water slides for older kids. | Intersection of 23rd St. and Middle Rd. | 319/344–4113 | $3 | June, July, Aug.

ON THE CALENDAR

JULY: *Independence Day Parade*. The Quad Cities' best 4th of July parade and festival with a large fireworks display and floats sponsored by various community businesses and organizations. | 319/355–4753.

Dining

Bennigan's. American. Attached to the Holiday Inn, this restaurant caters to travelers as well as locals, and offers steaks, burgers, and seafood along with more adventurous dishes like stir fry. There's also a bar with a billiards table. | 909 Middle Rd. | 319/355–4761 | $7 | AE, MC, V.

Happy Joe's. Pizza. This festive family favorite has 12 locations throughout the Midwest. The dining area includes a few large tables as well as more intimate booths. The chain's specialty is pizza, but you can also order spaghetti by the bucket and finish it all off with Joe's homemade ice cream. Kids' menu. | 2430 Spruce Hills Dr. | 319/359–5457 | $6–$15 | AE, MC, V.

Jumer's. German. Mounted deer heads decorate this dining room known for its braised lamb shank. Pianist during dinner hours. Kids' menu. | 900 Spruce Hills Dr. | 319/359–1607 | $15–$45 | AE, DC, MC, V.

Old Chicago. Pizza. Deep-dish Chicago-style pizza is a favorite at this sports-theme restaurant but many customers come for the selection of 110 beers, 30 of which are on tap. | 3030 Utica Rich Rd. | 319/355–9494 | $7 | AE, DC, MC, V.

Stubbs Eddy. Continental. A large antique bar, mirrors, and gas lighting give this dining room known for filet mignon, barbecued ribs, and fresh seafood its river-town-of-yore ambience. Entertainment Thursday–Saturday evenings. Kids' menu. | 1716 State St. | 319/355–0073 | $17–$40 | AE, MC, V | Closed Sun.

Waterfront Deli. Delicatessen. This local deli specializes in sandwiches like the popular cardiac (turkey salad on wheat). | 1020 State St. | 319/359–4300 | $5 | No credit cards | Closed Sun.

Lodging

Abbey Hotel. Built in 1914 to house a cloistered Carmelite monastery, this formidable Romanesque structure on a bluff overlooking the Mississippi River is now on the National Register of Historic Places. Fawn-and-beige guest rooms have Italian marble bathrooms, and tall arched windows overlook the river or the hotel's manicured grounds and sparkling swimming pool. Immediately outside Bettendorf proper, the hotel is ½ mi off Interstate 74 at exit 4. Bar, complimentary breakfast, room service. In-room data ports, cable TV, in-room VCRs available. Pool. Exercise equipment. Business services, airport shuttle. No smoking. | 1401 Central Ave. | 319/355–0291, 800/438–7535 reservations | fax 319/355–7647 | www.theabbeyhotel.com | 19 rooms | $99–$149 | AE, D, DC, MC, V.

City Center Motel. This downtown motel is just off of Interstate 74 and close to the city's casinos. Cable TV. | 1138 State St. | 319/355–0268 | 30 rooms | $42 | AE, D, MC, V.

Courtyard by Marriott. This chain hotel, 2 mi from several riverboat casinos and 5 mi from the convention center, caters to business travelers. The hotel has a spacious, low-lit lobby set about with sofas and comfortable lounge chairs. Rooms are equipped with desks and lighted work areas. Restaurant, bar, room service. In-room data ports, microwaves available, some refrigerators, cable TV. Pool. Hot tub. Exercise equipment. Laundry facilities. Business services. | 895 Golden Valley Dr. | 319/355–3999 | fax 319/355–0308 | www.marriott.com | 108 rooms | $84 | AE, D, DC, MC, V.

Econo Lodge-Quad Cities. This chain motel is within 5 mi of both the Duck Creek and North Park malls in a commercial area with plenty of shopping and restaurants within walking distance. Complimentary Continental breakfast. Cable TV. Pool. Playground. Business services. Some pets allowed. | 2205 Kimberly Rd. | 319/355–6471 | fax 319/359–0559 | www.hotelchoice.com | 65 rooms | $60–80 | AE, D, DC, MC, V.

Heartland Inn. This chain hotel is within walking distance of dining, shopping, movie theaters, and three large casinos and offers a complimentary dinner on Wednesday nights. Complimentary Continental breakfast. Microwaves available. Pool. Sauna. Health club. Laundry facilities. Business services. Free parking. | 815 Golden Valley Dr. | 319/355–6336 or 800/334–3277 ext. 14 | fax 319/355–0039 | 85 rooms | $65 | AE, D, DC, MC, V.

Holiday Inn. This chain hotel is right across the street from Duck Creek Mall and just 5 mi from the Quad Cities airport in Moline. Restaurant, bar, room service. In-room data ports, cable TV. Pool. Exercise equipment. Laundry facilities. Business services, airport shuttle. | 909 Middle Rd. | 319/355–4761 or 800/465–4329 | fax 319/355–5572 | www.holidayinn.com | 150 rooms, 10 suites | $70–$75 | AE, D, DC, MC, V.

Jumer's Castle Lodge. This massive stone hotel with a nine-story tower section and sharply pitched roof looks like a European castle set down on the banks of the Mississippi. And the opulent, medieval feel isn't just on the outside: guest rooms are finished in custom-made woodwork with deep marble fireplaces, one-of-a-kind tapestries, scores of rich oil paintings, and heavily draped four-poster oak beds. Restaurant, 2 bars (with entertainment). Cable TV. 2 pools. Hot tub. Putting green. Exercise equipment. Playground. Business services, airport shuttle. Some pets allowed (fee). | 900 Spruce Hills Dr. | 319/359–7141 or 800/285–8637 | fax 319/359–5537 | www.jumers.com | 161 rooms, 49 suites | $91, $94–$140 suites | AE, D, DC, MC, V.

Signature Inn. Rooms are furnished with antique reproductions and have locally themed art prints on the walls at this upscale chain hotel in a residential area 10 minutes from downtown and 15 minutes from the riverfront or the Quad Cities Airport in Moline. Complimentary breakfast. In-room data ports, microwaves, refrigerators, cable TV. Pool. Exercise equipment. Health club. Business services, airport shuttle. | 3020 Utica Ridge Rd. | 319/355–7575 | fax 319/355–7575 | 119 rooms, 4 suites | $77 | AE, D, DC, MC, V.

Super 8. This chain hotel is 2 mi south of downtown and within walking distance of restaurants and bars. Complimentary Continental breakfast. Cable TV. Pool. | 890 Golden Valley Dr. | 319/355–7341 or 800/800–8000 | www.super8.com | 38 rooms | $65–$85 | AE, D, MC, V.

Twin Bridges Motor Inn. Some rooms have balconies at this motor inn just two blocks from the river and the *Isle of Capri* Casino. The downtown area is a few miles away, but there are several 24-hour restaurants within walking distance. Restaurant, bar. Cable TV. Pool. | 221 15th St. | 319/355–6451 | 70 rooms | $35 | AE, D, MC, V.

BOONE

MAP 3, D3

(Nearby town also listed: Ames)

Boone's roots are in coal mining, agriculture, and the railroads. It's home to the Kate Shelley High Bridge, the highest and longest double-track railroad bridge in the country, named for a local girl who became a national heroine in 1881 when she braved a violent storm to save a trainload of people from certain derailment and death at a washed-out bridge. Mamie Doud Eisenhower also was born here in 1896, and her home is one of the town's attractions.

Information: Boone Area Chamber of Commerce | 806 7th St., 50036 | 515/432–3342 or 800/266–6312 | www.booneiowa.com.

Attractions

Boone and Scenic Valley Railroad. In 2½ hours you'll travel just 15 mi from Boone to nearby Fraser, but speed isn't the point on this train ride through some of Iowa's most scenic woods and farmland. You'll be traveling back in history in historic rail cars pulled by a steam locomotive on weekends and a diesel locomotive on weekdays. | 225 10th St. | 515/432–4249 | www.scenic-valleyrr.com | $10 | Departure times: Memorial Day–Oct., weekdays 1:30, weekends 11, 1:30, 4.

Boone County Historical Center. This former Masonic temple, built in 1907, houses exhibits on Kate Shelley's dramatic story, the coal mining history of the region, and local wildlife. Traveling exhibits are also featured throughout the year. | 602 Story St. | 515/432–1907 | $2 | Weekdays 1–5.

Kate Shelley High Bridge. You'll find this 2,685-ft long bridge, named for local heroine Kate Shelley, 3 mi west of town and 185 ft above the Des Moines River. | J Ave. | 515/432–3342 | Free | Daily.

Kate Shelley Railroad Museum and Park. Exhibits and a video (shown in a Rock Island Rocket passenger car) in this restored railroad depot in nearby Moingona focus on Kate Shelley's story as well as railroad history. | 1198 232nd St., Moingona | 515/432–1907 | Free | Apr.–Oct., Sat.–Sun. 9–6.

Ledges State Park. This 1,200-acre park 6 mi south of Boone contains sandstone cliffs and crags up to 75 ft high, as well as an excellent system of hiking trails. If you'd rather not navigate the precipices themselves, you might consider canoeing or fishing on the Des Moines River, which flows through the park. | 1519 250th St., Madrid | 515/432–1852 | www.state.ia.us/parks | Free | Daily.

Mamie Doud Eisenhower Birthplace. The birthplace of President Eisenhower's First Lady showcases the bed she was born in and the cars she owned during the presidency, as well as home furnishings and photos. | 709 Carroll St. | 515/432–1896 | $3 | June–Oct., daily 10–5; Apr.–May, Tues.–Sun. 1–5; also by appointment.

ON THE CALENDAR
JULY: *Iowa Municipal Band Festival.* Bands from across the state perform in Herman Park. | 800/266–6312.
SEPT.: *Pufferbilly Days.* This celebration of the town's railroad heritage includes a spike-driving contest, handcar races, and a model train display. | 800/266–6312.

Dining
Colorado Grill. American. There's a drive-up window here, but if you use it you'll miss the wonderful photos of the Rocky Mountains, snowshoes, skis, and other staples of Colorado life displayed on the walls of this grill known for smoked meats, prime rib, and turkey. Kids' menu. | 1514 S. Marshall St. | 515/433–7020 | $8–$12 | MC, V.

Gables and Gardens. Contemporary. Housed in a Victorian mansion, this restaurant serves only lunch and offers such dishes as fruited chicken salad. | 721 Carroll St. | 515/432–9601 | $7 | MC, V | Closed weekends. No dinner.

Lodging
AmeriHost Inn. This chain hotel is in a commercial area 2 mi south of downtown and features a large lobby area with overstuffed lounge chairs and guest rooms with wood-beamed ceilings. Complimentary Continental breakfast. In-room data ports, cable TV. Pool. Hot tub. Exercise equipment. | 1745 S.E. Marshall St. | 515/432–8168 | fax 515/432–8175 | www.amerihostinn.com | 60 rooms | $69 | AE, D, MC, V.

Bluebird B&B. This 1918 home is furnished with antiques and a vintage clothing display dating back to the 1800s. It is 2 mi south of town and a short drive from Ledges State Park and the Iowa Arboretum. Complimentary breakfast. | 1372 Peony La. | 515/432–5057 | 2 rooms (with shared bath) | $60 | No credit cards.

Hancock House Bed and Breakfast. This 1915 home on the south side of town has Mission-style oak woodwork, 19th-century antiques, and hand-pieced quilts. Guest rooms are done in a subdued, nonfrilly country style with antique furnishings and lots of light. Complimentary breakfast. | 1004 Hancock Dr. | 515/432–4089 | www.booneiowa.com | 2 rooms | $55–$60 | No credit cards.

Super 8. This chain hotel is on the edge of town within walking distance of several restaurants and just a quarter mile from the Boone and Scenic Valley Railroad. Complimentary Continental breakfast. Cable TV. | 1715 S. Storage St. | 515/432–3342 or 800/800–8000 | www.super8.com | 56 rooms | $59 | AE, D, DC, MC, V.

BURLINGTON

MAP 3, G5

(Nearby town also listed: Fort Madison)

As the first territorial capital of Iowa, Burlington and the German immigrants who settled here were central to much of this region's development. Today, historic buildings perched on bluffs overlooking the Mississippi River preserve something of the town's 19th-century past; manufacturing is the primary source of employment and one of the upper Mississippi's 29 locks and dams is here.

Information: Burlington Area Convention and Tourism Bureau | 807 Jefferson St., Box 6, 52601 | 319/752–6365 or 800/827–4837 | www.visit.burlington.ia.us.

Attractions

Apple Trees Historical Museum. In the former home of prominent businessman Charles Perkins, in Perkins Park, this museum houses a growing collection of Burlington memorabilia, Native American artifacts, and other displays. | 1616 Dill St. | 319/753–2449 | Free | May–Oct., weekends 1:30–4:30, weekday tours by appointment.

Crapo and Dankwardt Parks. These parks in the southeast corner of the city cover more than 100 acres on the west bank of the Mississippi River. | Great River Rd. | 319/753–8110 or 319/753–8117 | www.visit.burlington.ia.us | Free | Daily.
In Crapo Park you'll find **Hawkeye Log Cabin,** a small, one-room cabin on a bluff overlooking the Mississippi River. The cabin was built in the early 1900s as a clubhouse for a local pioneer society and is now a museum with examples of pioneer-era furniture and tools used in this area. | Great River Rd. | 319/753–2449 | Free | May–Oct., weekends 1:30–4:30, weekday tours by appointment.

Geode State Park. Geodes, with their hollow centers and sparkling quartz crystals, are Iowa's state rock and they can be found in this park 12 mi west of Burlington in relative profusion. If you are not a rockhound you may enjoy the supervised swimming beach which rims Lake Geode, known for excellent bluegill and crappie fishing, or the park's hiking and camping. | Rtes. 79/J2O | 319/392–4601 | www.state.ia.us/parks | Free | Daily.

Grandpa Bill's Farm. This family fun park on a 100-year-old farm 13 mi north of Burlington includes hayrides, an animal barn, and mazes. Autumn- and Christmas-theme shows are presented in the Country Barn Theater in season, and the adjacent 7 Ponds Park has a water slide, a sandy beach for swimming, and a 30-acre lake fully stocked with fish. | U.S. 61, Sperry | 319/985–2262 | $5 | June–late Aug., daily; May and late Aug.–Oct., weekends.

Heritage Hill National Historic District. Nearly 160 buildings in various architectural styles provide a sense of local history. | North of downtown, between Washington and High Sts. | 800/827–4837 | Daily.
The original part of the historic home called **Phelps House** was built in 1851. Some original furnishings remain in the six-story Italianate-style structure, as well as other artifacts of local history. | 521 Columbia St. | 319/753–2449 | $2 | May–Oct., weekends 1:30–4:30.
Some people call **Snake Alley,** a shortcut from Heritage Hill to downtown, the crookedest street in the world. | North of downtown, between Washington and High Sts. | 800/827–4837 | Daily.

Mosquito Park. Named for its size, this ½-acre park is on a bluff overlooking the Mississippi River, just north of downtown. Though small, it has one of the area's most beautiful views. | 3rd and Franklin Sts. | 319/753–8117 | Free | Daily.

Point of Burlington Welcome Center. The center offers tourist information and displays of local history in a historic 1928 building on the Mississippi River. | 400 N. Front St. | 319/752–8731 | Mon.–Sat. 9–5, Sun. 10–5.

ON THE CALENDAR
MAY: *Snake Alley Criterium Bicycle Races.* Bicyclists race down what locals claim is the world's most crooked street on Memorial Day weekend. | 319/752–0015 or 800/827–4837. **JUNE:** *Burlington Steamboat Days and the American Music Festival.* This three-day riverfront music festival attracts more than 100,000 people each year. In addition to big-name touring acts, the festival books bluegrass, country, western, and jazz ensembles. Fireworks light the sky on the last night of the event, and during the day there are amusement-park rides and a vast array of food merchants. | 319/754–4334.

Dining
Big Muddy's. American. This converted historic freight depot has a stunning view of the river. BBQ ribs are a hot menu item, or try the steaks or seafood. | 710 N. Front St. | 319/753–1699 | $12 | AE, D, DC, MC, V.

Martini's. Eclectic. A cherry-wood and brick interior and overstuffed chairs set the ambience for this bustling restaurant at the Best Western Pizzaz Motor Inn. Everything from Thai food to brick-oven pizza to steaks is served here to a mixed crowd of hotel guests and locals. Sunday brunch. | 3003 Weingard Dr. | 319/753–2291 | $12 | AE, D, DC, MC, V.

Lodging
Best Western Pizazz Motor Inn. Burlington's only full-service hotel is in the northwest corner of town, just north of U.S. 34 and U.S. 61. Most guest rooms are either poolside or have balconies overlooking the three-story indoor pool atrium, which encloses a heated swimming pool and two attached hot tubs. There's also a game room. Restaurant *(see* Martini's, *above)*, bar (with entertainment), complimentary Continental breakfast, room service. In-room data ports, cable TV, in-room VCR, and movies. Pool. Barbershop, beauty salon, hot tub. Exercise equipment. Laundry facilities. Business services, airport shuttle. Pets allowed. | 3001 Winegard Dr. | 319/753–2223 or 800/528–1234 | fax 319/753–2224 | www.bestwestern.com | 151 rooms | $72 | AE, D, DC, MC, V.

Comfort Inn. This quiet, unassuming chain motel is on a commercial street only 2 mi east of Snake Alley and the Mississippi River with plenty of shops and restaurants within walking distance. Complimentary Continental breakfast. In-room data ports, cable TV. Pool. Business services. Pets allowed. | 3051 Kirkwood | 319/753–0000 or 800/221–2222 | fax 319/753–0000 ext. 301 | www.comfortinn.com | 52 rooms | $46 | AE, D, DC, MC, V.

Fairfield Inn by Marriott. This chain hotel is 2 mi from a shopping mile and within walking distance of restaurants and bars. Complimentary Continental breakfast. Cable TV. Pool. | 1213 N. Roosevelt | 319/754–0000 | www.marriott.com | 63 rooms | $65 | AE, D, DC, MC, V.

Holiday Inn Express. This basic suburban hotel is 5 mi west of downtown within easy walking distance of riverfront shopping and dining. Complimentary Continental breakfast. Microwaves and refrigerators available, cable TV. Pool. Exercise equipment. Business services. | 1605 N. Roosevelt Ave. | 319/752–0000 or 800/465–4329 | fax 319/754–1111 | burlexpress@yahoo.com | www.holidayinn.com | 52 rooms, 24 suites | $52–$73 | AE, D, DC, MC, V.

Super 8. This stucco building is a ½-mi walk from the river. Guest rooms with king and queen-size beds also have recliners. Complimentary Continental breakfast. Microwaves available, cable TV. | 3001 Kirkwood | 319/752–9806 or 800/800–8000 | fax 319/752–9806 | www.super8.com | 62 rooms | $49–$57 | AE, D, DC, MC, V.

CARROLL

(Nearby town also listed: Denison)

This city was named after Maryland's Charles Carroll, the longest-lived signer of the Declaration of Independence and the only one to include the location of his home (so that King George would not mistake which Charles Carroll was declaring his independence). At a Chamber of Commerce Banquet in 1959, Senator John F. Kennedy of Massachusetts addressed a crowd of 500, which crammed into the Saint Peter and Saint Paul auditorium and spilled over into the school's auditorium. Senator Kennedy spent the night at The Villa, a restored mansion, which now has a room dedicated to him.

Information: Carroll Chamber of Commerce | 223 W. 5th St., Box 307, 51401 | 712/792–4383 | cchamber@netins.net | www.carrolliowa.com.

Attractions

Black Hawk State Park. Formed thousands of years ago by a glacier, 957-acre Black Hawk Lake is popular with fishermen in search of bluegills, sunfish, and several types of bass. The park, which is 23 mi northwest of Carroll, has lakeside picnic areas and in winter offers ice-skating, cross-country skiing, and ice-fishing. | 228 S. Blossom, Lake View | 712/657–8712 | www.state.ia.us/parks | Free | Daily.

Chicago North Western Railroad Depot. This 1896 Victorian Romanesque railroad depot has been completely preserved. There is an adjacent railroad park. | N. Carroll and 5th St. | 712/792–4383 | Free | By appointment.

Swan Lake State Park. You'll find a 115-acre lake, a farmstead museum, and three wildlife exhibits at this 510-acre park just 2 mi south of town. | 22811 Swan Lake Dr. | 712/792–4614 | www.state.ia.us/parks | Daily.

ON THE CALENDAR

JUNE: *B.A.C.C.I. (Bike Around Carroll County, Iowa).* A weekend bike ride through the county with an overnight stay in the Swan Lake Park. | 712/792–4383.
JULY: *Carroll County Fair.* This classic small-town country fair features nightly musical entertainment and 4-H exhibits on the fairgrounds in nearby Coon Rapids. | 712/684–5610.
NOV.–DEC.: *Holiday Animated Lighting Extravaganza.* From Thanksgiving through Christmas Swan Lake Campground plays host to an expo of light sculptures including miniature churches and Santa's reindeer. | 712/792–1335.

Dining

Four Seasons Restaurant. American. This large, friendly roadside eatery on the northern edge of town offers an all-you-can-eat lunch buffet featuring dishes like lasagna, Swiss steaks, and chicken over rice. At dinner, the tablecloths come out and the atmosphere is a bit more formal. Sunday brunch. | Hwy. 71 N | 712/792–4383 | $7 | AE, MC, V.

Tony's. American. People come to this family-style eatery, with checkered tablecloths and a wood plank floor for burgers, prime rib, and chicken-fried steak. Salad bar. Kids' menu. Sunday brunch. | 601 Walnut St. | 712/792–3792 | $6–$12 | AE, D, DC, MC, V.

Lodging

Burke Inn. This motel is on the eastern edge of town, just 1 mi from Swan Lake and within walking distance of restaurants and bars. Complimentary Continental breakfast. Cable TV. | 1225 Plaza Dr. | 712/792–4383 or 800/348–5156 | 41 rooms | $52 | AE, D, DC, MC, V.

Carrollton Inn. This brick hotel is right next to a park in a residential area on the north side of town. Restaurant, bar, room service. Cable TV, in-room VCR, and movies available.

Pool. Beauty salon. Hot tub, sauna. Laundry facilities. | 1730 U.S. 71 N | 712/792–5600 or 800/798–3535 | fax 712/792–5600 | 87 rooms | $58 | AE, D, DC, MC, V.

Garst Farm Resort. Soviet Premier Nikita Khrushchev once visited this 4,500-acre river valley and working farm to learn more about Iowa farming from agricultural innovator Roswell Garst. The farm has several guest houses as well as a 120-year-old farmhouse still occupied by Garst family descendants. As a guest you can camp, hike, mountain bike, go horseback riding, or canoe down the river that flows through the property. Complimentary breakfast. Hot tub. Horseback riding, boating, fishing, bicycles. Sleigh rides. | 1390 U.S. 141 | 712/684–2964 | fax 712/684–2887 | gresort@pionet.net | www.farmresort.com | 5 rooms, 2 cottages | $60–$110, $120 cottages | AE, MC, V.

The Villa Lodge. This small downtown hotel in a restored 1918 mansion was John F. Kennedy's choice when he was in town campaigning and today you can stay in the Kennedy suite where his picture is on the wall. There are lovely architectural details throughout and some rooms have marble fireplaces. In-room TVs. | 220 W. 7th St. | 712/792–5335 | 10 rooms | $40–$54 | MC, V.

CEDAR FALLS

MAP 3, F3

(Nearby towns also listed: Waterloo, Waverly)

In March 1845, William Sturgis, his brother-in-law, and their families built a small group of log cabins here on the banks of the Cedar River. This settlement was originally called Sturgis Falls, but became Cedar Falls in 1849. In 1876 the Iowa State Normal School was founded here to train public school teachers. Eventually the school became the University of Northern Iowa and today it has 13,000 students studying a variety of subjects.

Information: **Cedar Falls Chamber of Commerce** | 10 Main St., Box 367, 50613-0367 | 319/266–3593 or 800/845–1955 | www.cedarnet.org/cf.tourism.

Attractions

Black Hawk Park. This 1,768-acre park along the Cedar River 1½ mi north of Cedar Falls has boat access, picnic area, and an archery and shooting range. | 2410 W. Lone Tree Rd. | 319/266–6813 | Free | Daily.

Cedar Falls Historical Society Victorian Home Museum. This 1860s Civil War–era home has antique furnishings, clothing, and memorabilia documenting the area's early history. | 308 W. 3rd. St. | 319/266–5149 | Donations accepted | Wed.–Sat. 10–4, Sun. 1–4.

George Wyth House. This prairie-style residence was built in 1907. The Wyth family moved in in the mid-1920s and gave the house its Art Deco interior. The third floor now houses a museum telling the story of the Viking Pump Company, which still operates in the Cedar Falls area. | 303 Franklin St. | 319/266–5149 or 319/277–8817 | Donations accepted | Apr.–Dec., Sun. 2–4; also by appointment.

George Wyth Memorial State Park. More than 200 species of birds have been spotted in this National Urban Wildlife Sanctuary named for a local conservationist and businessman just east of Cedar Falls on Route 218. | 3659 Wyth Rd. | 319/232–5505 | www.state.ia.us/parks | Free | Daily.

Ice House Museum. Built in 1921, this circular structure once housed an ice business. Today ice harvest equipment is on display. | 1st and Franklin Sts. | 319/266–5149 or 319/277–7448 | Free | May–Oct., Wed., weekends 1–4:30.

Little Red School. Built in 1909, this former one-room schoolhouse shows kids what school was like in the olden days. There are old books, a potbellied stove, and turn-of-the-last-century furnishings. | 1st and Clay Sts. | 319/266–5149 | Free | May–Oct., Wed., weekends 1–4.

University of Northern Iowa. Approximately 13,000 students attend this public university founded in 1876. You can pick up a campus walking-tour guide at Gilchrist Hall. | College St. between 23rd St. and University Ave. | 319/273–2761 or 319/273–2281 | www.uni.edu | Free | Daily.

The **Gallery of Art,** in Kamerick Art Building–South, has a permanent collection of 1,500 photographs and contemporary art pieces, including several works by Andy Warhol. | 27th St. and Hudson Rd. | 319/273–2077 | Free | Weekdays 9–4:30; weekends 1–4:30.

ON THE CALENDAR
JUNE: *Sturgis Falls Days Celebration.* This celebration includes a parade, carnival, talent contest, and more than 20 bands filling Overman, Tourist, and Island Parks. | 319/266–3593.
JUNE–SEPT.: *Band concerts.* You can have a picnic and listen to local talent on the second Saturday of each month in Overman Park. | 319/266–6813.

Dining
Olde Broom Factory. American. Housed in a renovated 1862 broom factory with high ceilings and exposed rafters, this restaurant offers a few excellent Cajun dishes, but is better known for its prime rib, steaks, and pasta. Kids' menu. Sunday brunch. | 110 N. Main St. | 319/268–0877 | $8–$20 | AE, D, DC, MC, V.

Lodging
Holiday Inn University Plaza. Within sight of the University of Northern Iowa campus, this hotel often hosts UNI parents or those in town for UNI sporting events. Restaurant, bar, room service. Cable TV. Pool. Hot tub, sauna. Exercise equipment. Laundry facilities. Business services, airport shuttle. Pets allowed. | 5826 University Ave. | 319/277–2230 or 800/465–4329 | fax 319/277–0364 | www.holidayinn.com | 182 rooms | $65–$120 | AE, D, DC, MC, V.

University Inn. This motel is 3½ mi west of the university campus and about 4 mi southwest of downtown on a quiet residential street with one restaurant in walking distance. Complimentary Continental breakfast. Cable TV. Pool. Hot tub. | 4711 University Ave. | 319/277–1412 | 65 rooms | $50 | AE, D, DC, MC, V.

Villager Lodge. This simple, brick hotel is located in a quiet, mostly residential district about 5 mi from the Waterloo airport and within easy walking distance of Cedar Falls's downtown business district. Complimentary Continental breakfast. Some microwaves and refrigerators, some in-room data ports, cable TV. Pool. Hot tub, sauna. Business services. | 4410 University Ave. | 319/277–1550 | fax 319/277–8947 | 96 rooms | $60–$65 | AE, D, DC, MC, V.

CEDAR RAPIDS

MAP 3, G4

(Nearby town also listed: Amana Colonies)

Early settlers of this area included farmers from Germany and Czechoslovakia who took advantage of the region's rich soil to produce bumper crops of corn and oats. Railroad connections to the Chicago market proved lucrative, and soon a little company called Quaker Oats was born. The Quaker Oats cereal manufacturing plant here is the largest in the world, and on some days you can smell the Cap'n Crunch being made. In addition to Quaker Oats, more than 20 Fortune 500 companies make their home in Cedar Rapids.

Information: **Cedar Rapids Area Chamber of Commerce** | 424 1st Ave. NE, Box 74860, 52401 | 319/398–5317 | www.cedarrapids.org.

Attractions

Brucemore Mansion. This lovely Queen Anne–style house with its many-peaked, slate-tiled roof, pillared porch, cavernous Great Hall, and a dramatic grand staircase was built between 1884 and 1886 on 26 parklike acres. Today the mansion is a center for culture and the arts hosting outdoor performances in summer and various events and festivals throughout the year. It is also known for its beautiful gardens. | 2160 Linden Dr. SE (I–380, exit 22), | 319/362–7375 | www.brucemore.org | $5 | Feb.–Dec., Tues.–Sat. 10–3, Sun. noon–3.

Cedar Rapids Museum of Art. Eight galleries house more than 5,000 works here, including the world's largest collection of Grant Wood, Marvin D. Cone, and Mauricio Lasansky pieces. Also on view is a changing series of exhibitions which sometimes include sculpture, painting, and installation works. | 410 3rd Ave. SE | 319/366–7503 | www.crma.org | $4 | Tues., Wed., Fri., Sat. 10–4; Thurs. 10–7; Sun. noon–4.

Coe College. In 1851 Daniel Coe, a farmer in New York's Catskills, gave Presbyterian pastor Williston Jones $1,500 to found what would become Coe College. Today the college offers a liberal arts education to 1,200 students, half of whom are the first in their families to attend college. In the 1850s the campus was on the outskirts of town, but today this former farmland is just 8 blocks from downtown. | 1220 1st Ave. NE | 319/399–8000 or 800 332–8404 | www.coe.edu | Free | Daily.

Cornell College. Like Coe College, Cornell College in nearby Mt. Vernon was founded in 1851, in this case by Methodist preacher George Bryant Bowman. The college was named for William Wesley Cornell, a prosperous New York Methodist and distant cousin of Ezra Cornell who would later found Cornell University. The first building on the hillside campus of Cornell College was completed in 1853 and today the campus in its entirety is listed on the National Register of Historic Places. | 600 1st St. W, Mt. Vernon | 319/895–4000 | www.cornell-iowa.edu | Free | Daily.

CSPS. In a typical season this independent, nonprofit contemporary arts center, housed in a former Czech social hall from the 1890s, hosts 12 art exhibits in its two galleries and up to 65 different musicians, dancers, and performance artists in its 150-seat theater. | 1103 3rd St. SE | 319/364–1580 | www.legionarts.org | Galleries: free | Galleries open Wed.–Sun., 11–6.

Czech Village. Nearly a third of Cedar Rapid's population is of Czech origin and that's reflected in this collection of stores and shops near downtown which sell handcrafted Czech and Slovak costumes, glassware, art, music, and other folk items. | 16th Ave. | 319/286–6011 | Free | Daily.

Within the village you'll find the **National Czech and Slovak Museum and Library** with a collection of more than 5,000 artifacts related to Czech and Slovak history and culture. There are ethnic costumes, old maps, crafts, Czech books and newspapers, and a restored late 19th-century immigrant home. | 30 16th Ave. | 319/362–8500 | www.ncsml.org | $5 | Tues.–Sat. 9:30–4, Sun. noon–4.

Granger House Museum. This beautifully restored 19th-century home once belonged to a prosperous middle-class businessman, Earl Granger, and now houses a superior collection of antique furnishings, many original to the home. | 970 10th St., Marion | 319/337–6672 | Free | Call for appointment.

Indian Creek Nature Center. You can follow nature trails or visit a learning center at this 210-acre prairie and woodland preserve. | 6665 Otis Rd. SE | 319/362–0664 | Free | Daily 9–4.

Iowa Masonic Library and Museum. This gleaming white marble building houses the world's most complete Masonic library as well as pioneer, military, and Native American artifacts. | 813 1st Ave. SE | 319/365–1438 | Free | Weekdays 8–5, Sat. by appointment.

CEDAR RAPIDS

INTRO
ATTRACTIONS
DINING
LODGING

Palisades-Kepler State Park. This 840-acre park 12 mi east of town on U.S. 30 has dramatic river bluffs, deep ravines, majestic hardwood trees, a large variety of wildflowers, and an abundance of wildlife. | 700 Kepler Dr. | 319/895–6039 | www.state.ia.us/parks | Free | Daily.

Paramount Theatre. Built in 1928, the intimate Paramount Theatre is a lovely venue for speakers, fine-art performances, concerts, and plays. | 123 3rd Ave. SE | 319/398–5211 or 319/366–8203 | www.uscellularcenter.com.

Science Station. Three floors of hands-on galleries allow kids to explore science and technology in the former Central Fire Station. There are exhibits focused on robotics, space travel, volcano eruptions, and more. | 427 1st St. SE | 319/366–0968 | $3.75 | Daily 9–4.

U.S. Cellular Center. Concerts, family shows, trade shows, conventions, sporting events, antique shows, and arts-and-crafts fairs are held here. | 370 1st Ave. NE | 319/398–5211 | www.uscellularcenter.com.

ON THE CALENDAR

MAR.: *Maple Syrup Festival.* A tasty demonstration and sale at the Indian Creek Nature Center. | 319/362–0664.
APRIL: *Czech and Slovak Easter Celebration.* An old-world celebration of the Easter Holy Season includes costume and parades in the Czech Village. | 319/362–8500.
JUNE/JULY: *Cedar Rapids Freedom Festival.* Thousands of people take part in this city-wide, two week celebration of the fourth of July. There are special exhibits at area museums, fun runs, sailboat and cardboard boat regattas, concerts, a barbecue, a parade, and, of course, fireworks. Daily schedules of events are posted on the festival's website. | 319/365–8313 | www.freedomfestival.com.

Dining

Al and Irene's BBQ. Barbecue. This casual restaurant on the northeast side of town specializes in pork-back country-style ribs. | 2020 N. Town La. NE, | 319/393–6242 | $8–$13 | AE, MC, V | Closed Mon.

Bennigan's. American. This large, busy restaurant serves steaks, salads, and sandwiches. Try the Monte Cristo sandwich stuffed with melted Swiss and ham. There are booths and tables and the walls are adorned with antiques. | 4444 1st Ave. NE | 319/378–8015 | $6–$16 | AE, D, DC, MC, V.

Cedar Brewing Company. American/Casual. This grill and sports bar has 19 televisions, including two with large screens. Four kinds of beer, including the popular Golden Hawk lager, are brewed on site and the kitchen smokes its own chicken and ribs. Sunday brunch. | 500 Blairs Ferry Rd. NE | 319/378–9090 | $6–$15 | AE, D, MC, V.

Folktales Bar and Grill. American/Casual. Steaks and burgers straight from the grill are the house favorites in this large restaurant, frequented by local folks. | 2245 Blair's Ferry Rd. | 319/294–0020 | $7–$14 | AE, D, DC, MC, V.

Gringo's Mexican Restaurant. Mexican. This large, lively restaurant has a full bar with excellent margaritas. The grilled chicken fajitas smothered in salsa are a house favorite. | 207 1st Ave. SE | 319/363–1000 | $7–$12 | AE, MC, V.

Happy Chef. American/Casual. Seafood, chops, and steaks are standard fare at this 24-hour restaurant in the southwest part of town. You can order up breakfast at anytime, night or day. | 365 33rd Ave. | 319/365–4087 | $7–$12 | AE, MC, V.

North County Steakhouse. Steak. This grill-your-own restaurant features two large grills where you can make sure you have it the way you like it. Antlers and deer trophies adorn the walls. | 1140 Blair's Ferry NE | 319/378–3970 | $15 | AE, D, DC, MC, V | No lunch.

RJ Boars of Cedar Rapids. Barbecue. This establishment takes BBQ seriously—sculptures and paintings of pigs hang on the walls and stand throughout the restaurant. Try the baby-back ribs. | 4801 1st Ave. SE | 319/377–8900 | $8–$15 | AE, D, MC, V.

Royal Fork Buffet. American/Casual. This huge restaurant seats 380 and has a buffet that changes daily. Ribs, chicken, roast beef, and baked ham are just a few of the many mainstays at this family-oriented establishment. | 2745 Blair's Ferry Rd. NE | 319/378–9916 | $8 | AE, MC, V.

Tommy's Marion. American/Casual. A brass and wood bar gives a warm feel to this casual eatery. BBQ ribs are a popular choice and the weekend breakfast buffet is worth a visit. | 1107 7th Ave. | 319/373–0414 | $7–$15 | AE, D, DC, MC, V | No dinner Sun.

Vernon Inn–The Greek Place. Greek. Favorites here are the moussaka, the stuffed grape leaves, and of course, for dessert, the baklava. | 2663 Mt. Vernon Rd. SE | 319/366–7817 | $12 | AE, D, MC, V | Closed Sun.

Lodging

Belmont Hill B&B. This serene 1880 brick Victorian carriage house is on extensive wooded grounds with a fountain and a terrace five minutes from downtown. Rooms are furnished with antiques, and TVs are available upon request. Complimentary breakfast. In-room data ports. | 1525 Cherokee Dr. NW | 319/366–1343 | fax 319/366–1351 | www.belmonthill.com | 3 rooms | $99–$150 | MC, V.

Best Western Cooper's Mill. This downtown chain motel is within walking distance of the convention center, Paramount Theater, and the federal building. Restaurant, bar, room service. In-room data ports, cable TV. Pool. Hot tub. Business services. Laundry services. Pets allowed (fee). | 100 F Ave. NW | 319/366–5323 or 800/858–5511 | fax 319/366–5323 | www.bestwestern.com | 86 rooms | $70 | AE, D, DC, MC, V.

Best Western Longbranch. This chain hotel is just two blocks from the area's largest shopping mall and three multiscreen movie theaters. Restaurant, 2 bars (with entertainment), room service. In-room data ports, cable TV, in-room VCRs available. Pool. Business services, airport shuttle, free parking. | 90 Twixtown Rd. NE | 319/377–6386 or 800/528–1234 | fax 319/377–3686 | www.bestwestern.com | 106 rooms | $72 | AE, D, DC, MC, V.

Cedar Rapids Inn and Convention Center. This independently run horseshoe-shape hotel is 3 mi from the interstate and the airport and encloses a "fun dome" with a pool, hot tub, and playground facility. Some rooms face outward with a view of the surrounding buildings and countryside, and others look out onto the dome area. Restaurant, bar, room service. In-room data ports, cable TV. Pool. Hot tub, sauna. Laundry facilities. Business services, airport shuttle, free parking. Pets allowed. | 2501 Williams Blvd. SW | 319/365–9441 | fax 319/365–0255 | 184 rooms | $65–$75 | AE, D, DC, MC, V.

Collins Plaza. Rooms at this hotel in the northern part of town are large and open onto a tree-filled atrium with a waterfall. Lindale Mall and dozens of restaurants are less than a mile away. Restaurant, bar (with entertainment). In-room data ports, refrigerators, cable TV. Pool. Hot tub. Exercise equipment. Laundry facilities. Business services, airport shuttle, free Parking. | 1200 Collins Rd. NE | 319/393–6600 or 800/541–1067 | fax 319/393–2308 | 221 rooms, 85 suites | $75–$101, $120–$145 suites | AE, D, DC, MC, V.

Comfort Inn–North. Rooms are spacious and have large windows at this chain motel north of downtown next to Noelridge Park. Lindale Mall is a mile away. Complimentary Continental breakfast. In-room data ports, some refrigerators, cable TV. Exercise equipment. Business services, free parking. Some pets allowed. | 5055 Rockwell Dr. | 319/393–8247 or 800/221–2222 | fax 319/393–8247 | www.comfortinn.com | 59 rooms | $76 | AE, D, DC, MC, V.

Comfort Inn–South. Slightly more removed from the thick of things than its northern counterpart, the Comfort Inn South is about 5 mi from downtown, but has easy access to Interstate 380 and is a quieter place to stay. Complimentary Continental breakfast. Cable TV.

Exercise equipment. Free parking. Pets allowed. | 390 33rd Ave. SW | 319/363–7934 or 800/221–2222 | fax 319/363–7934 | www.comfortinn.com | 60 rooms | $60 | AE, D, DC, MC, V.

Crown Plaza Five Seasons. This upscale hotel is right downtown and caters to business travelers visiting for conventions. There are marble tables in the lobby and oak crown molding in the guest rooms. Restaurant, bar, room service. In-room data ports, cable TV. Pool. Exercise equipment. Business services, airport shuttle, parking (fee). | 350 1st Ave. NE | 319/363–8161 | fax 319/363–3804 | www.crownplaza.com | 275 rooms, 2 suites | $99–$145 | AE, D, DC, MC, V.

Days Inn. This motel is about 5 mi southwest of downtown and 3 mi from Interstate 380 and the airport, in a commercial area with plenty of shops and restaurants. The lobby is done in a country-home theme, with wooden chairs, Formica dinette tables, and sprays of dried wildflowers on the walls. Complimentary Continental breakfast. In-room data ports, some refrigerators, cable TV. Pool. Hot tub. Business services, airport shuttle, free parking. Pets allowed (fee). | 3245 Southgate Pl. SW | 319/365–4339 or 800/325–2525 | fax 319/365–4339 | www.daysinn.com | 40 rooms, 8 suites | $60 | AE, D, DC, MC, V.

Econo Lodge. This standard motel, built in 1992, is 6 mi south of downtown in a commercial area with plenty of shopping and places to eat within walking distance. Complimentary Continental breakfast. Cable TV. Pool. Laundry facilities. Free parking. Pets allowed. | 622 33rd Ave. SW | 319/363–8888 | fax 319/363–7504 | www.choicehotels.com | 50 rooms | $65 | AE, D, DC, MC, V.

Exel Inn. This cream-and-mint-green building is 5 mi south of downtown in a commercial area with many other hotels and restaurants nearby. Complimentary Continental breakfast. In-room data ports, cable TV. Laundry service. Business services, free parking. Pets allowed (fee). | 616 33rd Ave. SW | 319/366–2475 | fax 319/366–5712 | www.exelinns.com | 120 rooms | $42 | AE, D, DC, MC, V.

Fairfield Inn by Marriott. This hotel is about 10 mi south of the downtown area in a commercial area with several restaurants, shops, and other hotels nearby. Guest rooms have wall sconces to provide diffuse lighting and pastel art prints on the walls. Complimentary Continental breakfast. In-room data ports, cable TV. Pool. Laundry facilities. Business services, free parking. | 3243 Southridge Dr. SW | 319/364–2000 | fax 319/364–2000 | www.marriott.com | 105 rooms | $68 | AE, D, DC, MC, V.

Hampton Inn. This downtown hotel, just off Interstate 380, is within easy walking distance of the Czech Village. Rooms have work spaces and freestanding lamps. Complimentary Continental breakfast. Cable TV, in-room VCR (and movies) available. Pool. Hot tub. Exercise equipment. Laundry facilities. Business services. Free parking. | 3265 6th St. SW | 319/364–8144 or 800/426–7866 | fax 319/399–1877 | www.hamptoninn.com | 106 rooms | $79 | AE, D, DC, MC, V.

Heartland Inn. This pleasant country-style motel with local craft items in the lobby is 5 mi north of downtown along a commercial strip with other hotels. Several restaurants are within walking distance. Complimentary Continental breakfast. Cable TV. Pool, sauna. Exercise equipment. Business services. | 3315 Southgate Ct. SW | 319/362–9012 or 800/334–3277 | fax 319/362–9694 | 113 rooms, 30 suites | $70 | AE, D, DC, MC, V.

Holiday Inn Express. This chain hotel is a five-minute drive from downtown. There are several restaurants and bars as well as a few other businesses within walking distance, but the surrounding area is fairly rural. Complimentary Continental breakfast. Cable TV. Pool. | 1230 Collins Rd. NE | 319/294–9407 or 800/465–4329 | www.holidayinn.com | 83 rooms | $81 | AE, D, DC, MC, V.

Howard Johnson's Airport Express. This hotel is in a rural area about 10 mi south of downtown and five minutes from the airport. Complimentary Continental breakfast. Cable TV. Pool. Hot tub. Airport shuttle. | 9100 Atlantic Dr. SW | 319/363–3789 | 72 rooms | $86 | AE, D, DC, MC, V.

Joy in the Morning. This B&B in a 1910 Victorian listed in the National Historic Register is about five minutes from downtown. Rooms feature antiques and king-size beds. Complimentary Continental breakfast. Cable TV. Hot tub. | 1809 2nd Ave. SE | 319/363–9731 or 800/363–5093 | 3 rooms | $75–$95 | AE, D, MC, V.

Residence Inn by Marriott. This chain hotel is on a commercial street 10 minutes northeast of downtown. Complimentary Continental breakfast. Cable TV. Pool. Hot tub.v | 1900 Dodge Rd. NE | 319/395–0111 | www.marriott.com | $115–$130 | AE, D, DC, MC, V.

Sheraton Four Points. This elegant hotel is about halfway between the airport and the downtown area in a commercial neighborhood with plenty of restaurants within walking distance. The lobby sets the tone here with its marble floors, 16-ft ceilings, crystal chandeliers, and large fireplace. Restaurant, bar (with entertainment), room service. In-room data ports, cable TV. Pool. Hot tub, sauna. Exercise equipment. Business services, airport shuttle, free parking. Pets allowed. | 525 33rd Ave. SW | 319/366–8671 | fax 319/362–1420 | www.sheraton.com | 153 rooms, 4 suites | $119 | AE, D, DC, MC, V.

Super 8. A few miles southwest of downtown, this hotel is in a commercial area near restaurants and three blocks from its other half, the Super 8 West. There are several restaurants and bars within walking distance. Complimentary Continental breakfast. Cable TV. | 400 33rd Ave. SW | 319/363–1755 or 800/800–8000 | fax 319/363–1755 | www.super8.com | 62 rooms | $58 | AE, D, DC, MC, V.

Super 8 West. This chain motel is a few miles southwest of downtown close to the Hawkeye Downs Racetrack. There are several restaurants and bars within walking distance. Complimentary Continental breakfast. Cable TV. | 720 33rd Ave. SW | 319/362–6002 or 800/800–8000 | www.super8.com | 61 rooms | $65 | AE, D, DC, MC, V.

Red Roof Inn. This white stucco chain motel is 3 mi south of downtown and visible from Interstate 380. Cable TV. | 3325 Southgate Ct | 319/366–7523 | fax 319/366–7639 | www.redroof.com | 108 rooms | $48 | AE, D, DC, MC.

CENTERVILLE

MAP 3, E6

(Nearby town also listed: Chariton)

Sauk and Fox Indians were the first inhabitants of this area but in the early 1840s white settlement began. The historic Mormon Trail passes through this community and while coal mining played an important role in Centerville's development, the 11,000-acre Rathbun Lake, which was developed by the Army Corps of Engineers in the late 1960s, provides most of the area's attractions today.

Information: Centerville Area Chamber of Commerce | 128 N. 12th St., 52544 | 641/437–4102 or 800/611–3800 | cntrvlle@lisco.net | www.centerville-ia.com.

Attractions

Appanoose County Coal Mining Museum. Housed in a post office building from 1903, this small museum contains area artifacts dating as far back as the first white settlement here in 1843. There's also a display of maps and artifacts from the Mormon Trail of 1846 and an exhaustive research library. | 100 W. Maple St. | 641/856–8040 | Donations accepted | Sun. 1–4.

Rathbun Lake. One of the largest bodies of water in Iowa, this manmade, 11,000-acre lake 8 mi northwest of Centerville offers a wide variety of recreational activities from sailing to waterskiing to fishing for crappie, walleye, and channel catfish. | Rte. 142 | 641/647–2464 | Free | Daily.

At the **Rathbun Fish Hatchery,** just below the Rathbun Dam at the eastern end of the lake, you can observe the hatchery from elevated walkways, visit an aquarium, or watch audiovisual presentations about fish production. | 15053 Hatchery Pl | 641/647–2406 | Free | Weekdays, 8–3:30.

Along the north shore of the lake you'll find the 828-acre **Honey Creek State Park** with its rolling, timbered hills. To reach the park from Centerville, take Route 5 North to Route 42, Route 42 West to 160th Ave., then head south. The park has hiking trails, boat launches, and 155 camp sites. | 12194 Honey Creek Pl., Moravia | 641/724–3739 | www.state.ia.us/parks | Free | Daily.

Sharon Bluffs State Park. This 144-acre state park divided by the Chariton River includes an elk and deer reserve. It's 3 mi east on Route 2, then 1 mi south. | 25100 520th St. | 641/856–8528 | fax 641/437–4850 | www.state.ia.us/parks | Free | Daily.

ON THE CALENDAR
JULY: *Croatian Fest.* Native costumes, ethnic foods, and a polka mass on the courthouse lawn in city square. | 515/437–7327.

SEPT.: *Pancake Days.* More than 25,000 people attend this festival sponsored by the merchants' association on the courthouse lawn in city square. Twenty-six giant griddles produce more than 80,000 pancakes to feed the hungry masses. Plain cakes are free— gourmet cakes come at a small price. | 800/611–3800.

Dining
The Continental. American/Casual. Housed inside a restored historic turn-of-the-last-century hotel with authentic antique telephones, safes, and a barbershop, this restaurant offers a menu of steaks and seafood. The grilled salmon is a popular choice. | 217 N. 13th St. | 641/437–1025 | $9 | AE, D, DC, MC, V.

Green Circle. American. You'll be surrounded by gold-framed mirrors and large picture windows looking out onto a landscaped garden with a waterfall and fishponds at this family-style restaurant which offers such standards as steak and lasagna. | 22984 Hwy. 5 | 641/437–4472 | $8–$15 | AE, D, MC, V.

Lodging
Don Elen. This economy motel is three blocks from downtown, within walking distance of restaurants and bars. Complimentary Continental breakfast. Cable TV. | 920 E. Maple Dr. | 641/437–1025 | 25 rooms | $33–$41 | AE, D, DC, MC, V.

Super 8. This brown-brick, chain motel is right next door to a multiscreen movie theater and 6 mi from Rathbun Lake. Complimentary Continental breakfast. Cable TV. Business services. | 1021 N. 18th St. | 641/856–8888 ext. 102 or 800/800–8000 | fax 641/856–8888 ext. 102 | www.super8.com | 41 rooms | $54 | AE, D, DC, MC, V.

CHARITON

MAP 3, E5

(Nearby town also listed: Osceola)

Named for the French fur trader who founded this town as a trading post on the west side of the state, Chariton was home to Mormons during the difficult winter of 1846, as they were making their way from Illinois to Utah. Although primarily an agricultural community, Chariton is now home to Hy-Vee, the Midwest's largest food chain distribution center.

Information: **Chariton Chamber of Commerce** | 104 N. Grand St., Box 488, 50049 | 641/774–4059.

Attractions

Cinder Path. This abandoned railroad right-of-way west of Chariton has been reborn as a 13-mi biking and walking path with covered bridges, towers, and scenic rest areas. The path begins on the west end of Chariton on Business Highway 34 and ends in the town of Humiston in adjacent Wayne County. | Rte. 34 | 515/774–2438 | Daily.

John L. Lewis Museum of Mining and Labor. Dedicated to the life of a United Mine Workers' president, this museum 10 mi west of Chariton includes early mining tools and a miniature coal-mining town. | 102 Division St., Lucas | 641/766–6831 | $1 | Mid-Apr.–mid-Oct., Tues.–Sat. 9–3.

Lucas County Historical Society Museum. A historic home, school, and church re-create life in Lucas County in the late 1800s. | 123 17th St. | 641/774–4464 | Free | June–Oct., Tues.–Fri., Sun. 1–4.

Prairie Trails Museum of Wayne County. This small museum 18 mi south of Chariton contains more than 90,000 items, including a bank safe robbed by Jesse James and an ox-drawn wagon from the Mormon Trail. | 515 E. Jefferson, Corydon | 641/872–2211 | Donations accepted | Apr.–Oct., daily 1–5.

Red Haw State Park. This park 1 mi east of town contains a 649-acre forest filled with hawthorn, oak, maple, and pine trees, and a 72-acre lake for swimming, boating, ice-skating, and snowmobiling. | RR 1 | 641/774–5632 | www.state.ia.us/parks | Free | Daily.

Stephens State Forest. This state forest 12 mi southwest of Chariton boasts a 30-mi network of trails for horseback riding and hiking through 9,000 plus acres of tall prairie grass and hardwood timber. Keep an eye out for white-tail deer, fox, and opossum. | Hwy. 34 W, 10 mi from Chariton | 641/774–5632 | www.state.ia.us | Free | Daily.

ON THE CALENDAR

JUNE: *Old Fashioned Saturday.* This daylong downtown event includes a barbecue, bluegrass music jamboree, 60-mi bike ride, and an antiques show. | 641/774–4059.
OCT.: *Pumpkin Patch Festival.* Good ol' farm fun 12 mi north of Chariton at Pierce's Pumpkin Patch with hayrides, hay-bale mazes, and chain-saw wood carving. Pick out the best pumpkin for Halloween, too. | 2491 Hwy. 14 | 641/862–3398.

Dining

Donna's Place. American/Casual. This warm, friendly, family-style café serves homemade bread and great cheeseburgers. | 101 N. Main St. | 641/774–8597 | $5 | No credit cards | Breakfast also available Mon.–Sat.; no dinner.

Smokewagon Grill. American/Casual. This family-friendly eatery known for pizza, steak, and meat sandwiches is done in Old West style, complete with an actual chuck wagon. Antique guns, roping, and branding irons hang on the walls. Salad bar. Kids' menu. | 131 N. Main St. | 641/774–8111 | $5–$10 | No credit cards | Closed Sun.

Lodging

Royal Rest Motel. This basic motel is just east of downtown Chariton in a commercial area and offers spacious rooms and drive-up parking. There are several restaurants within walking distance. Complimentary Continental breakfast. Cable TV. Business services. | 137 Grace Ave. | 641/774–5961 | 27 rooms | $42 | AE, D, MC, V.

Super 8. This chain hotel is 1/4 mi from Red Haw State park, on the eastern edge of town. There's a restaurant with a bar right next door. Complimentary Continental breakfast. Cable TV. Hot tub. | 169 E. Grace St. | 641/774–8888 or 800/800–8000 | www.super8.com | 35 rooms | $56–$66 | AE, D, DC, MC, V.

CHARLES CITY

(Nearby towns also listed: Mason City, Waverly)

Founded on the Cedar River in 1860 and named after an early settler's son, this small settlement was soon named the seat of Floyd County. In 1866 Charles City became home to Carrie Lane Chapman Catt, one of the nation's pioneers for women's rights. Her home is among the many structures the community has restored and seen placed on the National Register of Historic Places.

Information: Charles City Area Chamber of Commerce | 610 S. Grand Ave., 50616 | 641/228–4234 | ccchamber@fiai.net | www.charlescitychamber.com.

Attractions

Carrie Lane Chapman Catt Childhood Home. This 1866 brick farmhouse 2 mi south of town was home to the women's rights leader. Carrie's room is furnished with her own belongings; elsewhere you'll find information on her life and work. | 2379 Timber Ave. | 641/228–3336 | www.catt.org | Donations accepted | Daily.

Floyd County Historical Society Museum. A pioneer log cabin, a tractor from 1901, and a popcorn wagon from 1910 are just some of the historical artifacts you'll find here. | 500 Gilbert St. | 641/228–1099 | $2 | May–Sept., weekdays 9–4:30, Sat. 1–4; Oct.–Apr., weekdays 9–4:30; also by appointment.

Little Brown Church in the Vale. In 1857, before there was a church here, this spot in the Iowa countryside 11 mi south of Charles City inspired the gospel favorite "The Church in the Wildwood." Seven years later, a little church, painted brown because it was an inexpensive color at the time, was dedicated on the spot and the hymn was sung publicly for the first time. Today the church is popular for weddings, baptisms, and vow renewals. | 2730 Cheyenne Ave., Nashua | 641/435–2027 | www.littlebrownchurch.org | Donations accepted | Weekdays 10–4, Sun. worship 10:30 AM.

ON THE CALENDAR

JUNE: *Music In Motion.* Groups from around the region converge on Comet Field for northern Iowa's only drum and bugle corps competition held the third Saturday of June. | 641/220–0019.

AUG.: *Art-A-Fest.* This art fair and celebration held the third Saturday of August in Central Park showcases artists from the Midwest. | 641/228–6284.

Dining

Brooks. American/Casual. Burgers and thick shakes are the order of the day at this diner-themed restaurant with an old-fashioned soda fountain and comfy booths in the Cedar Mall. Kids' menu. | 102 Cedar Mall | 641/228–7162 | $4–$6 | AE, D, DC, MC, V.

J. P. Sisson's. American. This sports-theme bar and grill has plenty of Jets memorablia around as well as collector's items like a signed pair of Muhammad Ali's boxing gloves. Sandwiches and fries are popular items, as are the lunch specials like meat loaf and mashed potatoes with gravy. | 101 N. Jackson St. | 641/228–5387 | $5–$10 | AE, MC, V.

Lodging

Hartwood Inn. This quiet lodging with basic rooms overlooks the Cedar River and is within easy walking distance of a park. Complimentary Continental breakfast. Cable TV. Pool. Laundry facilities. Some pets allowed. | 1312 Gilbert St. | 515/228–4352 or 800/972–2335 | fax 515/228–2672 | www.imalodging.com | 35 rooms | $45 | AE, D, DC, MC, V.

Sherman House B&B. This 1888 home is right in town within walking distance of shops and restaurants. There are views of the Cedar River from the main sitting room and the two-room Sherman suite has a hot tub, fireplace, and a view of the city. Complimentary breakfast. Cable TV. | 800 Gilbert St. | 641/228–6831 | klaartz@fiai.net | www.bestinns.net/atway/ia/sherman.html | 5 rooms | $100–$150 | D, MC, V.

CHEROKEE

MAP 3, B2

(Nearby town also listed: Storm Lake)

Cherokee Indians never lived in this community, so no one knows why the founders chose the name. The Little Sioux River runs through Cherokee and has carved out beautiful bluffs and red quartz rocks in the surrounding county. This part of western Iowa contains fertile farmland and is home to large meatpacking businesses.

Information: Cherokee Chamber of Commerce | 228 W. Main St., 51012 | 712/225–6414 | www.cofccherokee@ncn.net.

Attractions

Koser Spring Lake Park. This 15-acre spring-fed lake and the 100-acre city park on the Little Sioux River that surrounds it are ideal for fishing and camping. A 1.2-mi blacktop walking trail circles the lake. | 530 W. Bluff St. | 712/225–2715 | Free | Daily.

Sanford Museum and Planetarium. Permanent exhibits document northwest Iowa's history and prehistory. The planetarium, which hosts monthly programs on the night sky, was the first in the state. | 117 E. Willow St. | 712/225–3922 | Free | Weekdays 9–5, weekends noon–5.

ON THE CALENDAR

JUNE: *Cherokee Rodeo.* Thousands attend this three-day Professional Rodeo Cowboy Association (PRCA) event at the Cherokee Fairgrounds on Highway 59, the biggest attraction in town. | 712/225–6414.
JULY: *Cherokee County Fair.* A week of concerts, carnival rides, and agriculture exhibits at the Cherokee Fairgrounds. | 712/225–6414.

Dining

Danny's Sports Bar. American/Casual. This bar and grill is popular for its $5 steak. Weekend lunch buffets include BBQ ribs, soup, and salad bar with a sundae bar for dessert. There are multiple televisions for watching games. | 1013 S. 2nd St. | 712/225–4556 | $5–$9 | AE, D, MC, V.

Lodging

Best Western La Grand Hacienda. Guest rooms at this chain hotel in a commercial area 1 mi north of downtown on Hwy. 59 are large enough to be comfortable for families. Restaurant, complimentary Continental breakfast, room service. In-room data ports, cable TV, in-room VCR (and movies) available. Pool. Hot tub. Business services. | 1401 N. 2nd St. | 712/225–5701 or 800/528–1234 | fax 712/225–3926 | www.bestwestern.com | 55 rooms | $60 | AE, D, DC, MC, V.

Prairie Path Lodge. This B&B is 2 mi northeast of town on 20 acres of native wild prairie. A log cottage and cedar lodge house cozy rooms, one with a TV. Complimentary breakfast. | 5148 S Ave. | 712/225–4940 or 800/409–4940 | cofccherokee@ncn.net | 2 rooms | $65–$95 | No credit cards.

Skyline Motel. This quiet downtown motel is within walking distance of restaurants and local attractions. Cable TV. | 768 N. 2nd St. | 712/225–2544 | 21 rooms | $40 | AE, MC, V.

Super 8. Locally themed art prints decorate the walls at this basic motel which is next door to the Best Western. Cable TV. Exercise equipment. | 1400 N. 2nd St. | 712/225–4278 or 800/ 800–8000 | fax 712/225–4678 | www.super8.com | 30 rooms | $45–$57 | AE, D, DC, MC, V.

CLARINDA

MAP 3, C6

(Nearby town also listed: Shenandoah)

This small town gave birth to two American cultural icons: big-band leader Glenn Miller and 4-H. Both Glenn Miller's home and the Goldenrod School, where rural school teacher Jessie Field founded 4-H, are among the sights here. Clarinda is also known locally for its broad, lighted central boulevard, which is popular with joggers and is often used for festivals.

Information: **Clarinda Association of Business and Industry** | 200 S. 15th St., 51632 | 712/ 542–2166.

Attractions

Lake of Three Fires State Park. About 20 minutes northeast of Clarinda you'll find the 85-acre Lake of Three Fires. The lake is nearly a mile long and half a mile wide and its scenic inlets make it ideal for fishing and boating. About 691 acres of woodland with trails for horseback riding, hiking, and wild berry ring the lake. | 2303 Rte. 49, Bedford | 712/523–2700 | www.state.ia.us/parks | Free | Daily.

Nodaway Valley Historical Museum. What was once the Goldenrod School, birthplace of the first 4-H program, is now a museum. The displays on local history include original-press Glenn Miller records and old military pins and uniforms. | 1600 S. 16th St. | 712/542–3073 | Donations accepted | Tues.–Sun. 1–4:30.

ON THE CALENDAR
JUNE: *Glenn Miller Festival.* Big bands from around the country perform at Clarinda High School in honor of this hometown legend. | 712/542–2461.
OCT.: *Craft Carnival.* Crafters from around the area sell their products at the Page County Fairgrounds. | 712/542–2166.

Dining

Ice House. American. This restaurant has three large rooms: one is a sports bar, the other two are for casual family meat-and-potatoes dining. | 922 E. Washington St. | 712/542–4010 | $10 | AE, D, MC, V | Closed Sun.

J. Bruner's. American. White wicker furnishings and fresh flowers give this restaurant a fresh, garden feel. Try one of the steaks or a tasty, classic hamburger. Kids' menu. | 1100 E. Washington St. | 712/542–3364 | $6–$10 | AE, D, MC, V | Closed Mon.

Lodging

Celebrity Inn. This modern inn is decorated with a professional baseball theme, with framed photos and stats of Cardinal shortstop Ozzie Smith, who once played on a farm team here. More photos and autographs adorn the guest rooms. In-room data ports, cable TV. | 1323 S. 16th St. | 712/542–5178 | fax 712/542–5085 | 36 rooms | $42 | AE, D, MC, V.

Super 8. This chain hotel on the southern edge of town is about a mile from the Glenn Miller Birthplace Home and within walking distance of several bars. Complimentary Continental breakfast. In-room data ports, some in-room hot tubs, cable TV. Pool. Hot tub. Gym. | 1203 S. 12th St. | 712/542–6333 or 800/800–8000 | www.super8.com | 40 rooms | $55–$60 | AE, D, DC, MC, V.

CLEAR LAKE

MAP 3, E2

(Nearby towns also listed: Garner, Mason City)

In the fall of 1850, early explorers came here based on reports of a beautiful lake; today visitors come for the same reason. The 3,600-acre spring-fed Clear Lake is the third largest in Iowa and is a major recreational resource. The area is also well known among rock-and-roll aficionados as the site of the last concert Buddy Holly gave before he died nearby in a 1959 plane crash. Tourism based on outdoor activities such as hunting and fishing has become a major force in the region's economy, as has the historic downtown shopping area with its many antiques and specialty stores.

Information: **Clear Lake Convention and Visitors Bureau** | 205 Main St., Box 188, 50428 | 515/357–2159 or 800/285–5338 | chamber@netins.net | www.clearlakeiowa.com.

Attractions

Clear Lake Fire Museum. Turn-of-the-last-century fire-fighting equipment, including 12 trucks, and a memorial to all firefighters who have served the city. | 112 N. 6th St. | 515/357–2613 | Free | Memorial Day–Labor Day, weekends 10–4.

Clear Lake State Park. This 55-acre state park on the southeast shore of 3,600-acre Clear Lake is 2 mi south of town and has facilities for swimming, boating, fishing, and sailing. A 3-acre island in the middle of the lake, accessible only by boat, is a great place for a picnic. | 2730 S. Lakeview Dr. | 515/357–4212 | www.state.ia.us/parks | Free | Daily.

Lady of the Lake. This authentic stern-wheeler provides 2 hour cruises around the lake and departs from Clear Lake City Park right downtown. | 1500 S. Shore Dr. | 515/357–2243 | $10 | Cruises May–Oct., Mon.–Thurs. 7 PM; Fri. 7 PM and 9:30 PM; Sat. 2, 4:30, 7, 9:30; Sun. 2, 4:30, 7.

McIntosh Woods State Park. This 62-acre park on the northwest shore of Clear Lake is one of the major boating access points for the lake. In the summer there is beach access for swimming. | 1200 E. Lake St., Ventura | 515/829–3847 | www.state.ia.us | Free | Daily.

Surf Ballroom. Buddy Holly gave his last show here; his successors still perform here. | 460 N. Shore Dr. | 515/357–6151 | fax 515/357–6822 | www.clearlakeiowa.com/surf.htm | Free | Mon.–Sat. 9–4.

ON THE CALENDAR

FEB.: *Winter Dance Party.* Events around the area—culminating in a bash at the Surf Ballroom—pay tribute to late great musician Buddy Holly and his final show at the Surf. | 515/357–2159 or 515/357–6151.

MAY: *International May Festival.* Music, dance, and food from various cultures as well as kid's rides, and talent competitions. | 515/357–2159.

JULY: *Antique/Classic Wooden Boat Show.* Antique and restored wooden boats are displayed on both land and water in Clear Lake City Park. | 515/357–2164.

Dining

Boathouse Bar and Grill. American. Steaks and seafood are the specialties at this upscale, nautical-themed restaurant, but sandwiches and pizza are popular too. | 468 N. Shore Dr. | 641/357–8688 | $9–$16 | MC, V | Closed Sun. No lunch.

Ge-Jo's by the Lake. Italian. Founded by the current owner's grandmother in the 1950s and named after the founder's grandsons, Gene and Joseph, this restaurant is known for pasta dishes, meatball sandwiches, and its fabulous lake views. Open-air dining on the front deck and on the grass with a view of the lake and park nearby. Kids' menu. | 12 N. 3rd St. | 515/357–8288 | fax 515/357–8483 | $8–$10 | MC, V | Closed Mon., Tues.

Martha's. American. This lunch-counter café is a friendly local gathering place serving such dishes as hot beef and meat loaf. | 305 Main Ave. | 641/357–8720 | $3–$5 | No credit cards | Closed Sun. No dinner. Breakfast also available.

Sandbar. American. Steaks, fish, and sandwiches are popular fare here but many people really come for the homemade pies served in this converted Victorian home. | 211 N. 4th St. | 641/357–3733 | $4–$7 | AE, D, MC, V | Closed Mon., Tues.

Lodging

AmericInn. This chain hotel is 1 mi northeast of town and just a few miles from the airport. It is within walking distance of several restaurants and bars. Complimentary Continental breakfast. Cable TV. Pool. | 1406 N. 25th St. | 641/357–8954 or 800/634–3444 | www.americinn.com | 48 rooms | $72 | AE, D, DC, MC, V.

Best Western Holiday Lodge. The immediate surroundings are nothing special here, but this hotel is just a mile from downtown and the lake. Inside you'll find a brass-and-oak bar and lounge and guest rooms with upholstered wing chairs and well-lit work areas. Restaurant, bar, complimentary Continental breakfast, room service. Cable TV. Pool. Hot tub, sauna. Airport shuttle. Pets allowed. | 2023 7th Ave. N | 515/357–5253 or 800/528–1234 | fax 515/357–8153 | www.bestwestern.com | 136 rooms | $55–$62 | AE, D, DC, MC, V.

Budget Inn. This basic motor inn is within a mile of the lake in a commercial area with several fast food establishments within walking distance. Complimentary Continental breakfast. Cable TV. Pool. Playground. Pets allowed. | 1306 N. 25th St. | 515/357–8700 | fax 515/357–8811 | 60 rooms | $50 | AE, D, DC, MC, V.

Heartland Inn. This small but pleasant hotel has just 30 rooms, but all have lakefront exposure. The lobby is proportionally small but functional, with a few chairs and magazine tables to keep you occupied. The inn also has a dock leading out into the lake with benches at the end for romantic sunset appreciation. In-room data ports, some refrigerators, cable TV. Lake. Dock. | 1603 S. Shore Dr. | 641/357–5123 or 800/334–3277 | fax 515/357–2228 | 30 rooms | $59–$139 | AE, D, DC, MC, V.

Hilltop Motel. This economy motel, built in 1944, is next door to the Surf Ballroom six blocks west of downtown and within walking distance of restaurants and bars. Cable TV. Pool. | 10 Allens Alley | 641/357–8720 | 21 rooms | $35 | No credit cards.

Lake Country Inn. This is a mom-and-pop drive-up-to-your-room motel with friendly, small-town service. Many of Clear Lake's most popular restaurants are less than 1/2 mi away. Complimentary breakfast. Some kitchenettes, cable TV. Pets allowed. | 518 Hwy. 18 W | 641/357–2184 | loopsia@aol.com | www.netmation.com/lci | 28 rooms | $40 | AE, D, MC, V.

Larch Pine Inn. This 1875 Victorian B&B with a screened-in wraparound porch is a block from the lake, 2 blocks from Boathouse Bar and Grill and Ge-Jo's by the Lake (*see above*), and 3 blocks from downtown. In addition to a guest parlor there's a guest kitchenette. Complimentary breakfast. TV in common area. | 401 N. 3rd St. | 641/357–7854 | 3 rooms | $85 | AE, D, MC, V.

CLINTON

MAP 3, I4

(Nearby town also listed: Maquoketa)

This pleasant community on a wide bend in the Mississippi River was known as the "Lumber Capital of the World" during the construction boom that took place in this region in the late 1800s. Today you'll find several riverfront parks, beautiful Victorian homes and impressive buildings in the old business district, and a brand-new children's museum celebrating the antics of Clinton native and longtime Ringling Brothers clown, Felix Adler.

TOP TIPS FOR TRAVELERS

Smart Sightseeings

Don't plan your visit in your hotel room. Don't wait until you pull into town to decide how to spend your days. It's inevitable that there will be much more to see and do than you'll have time for: choose sights in advance.

Organize your touring. Note the places that most interest you on a map, and visit places that are near each other during the same morning or afternoon.

Start the day well equipped. Leave your hotel in the morning with everything you need for the day—maps, medicines, extra film, your guidebook, rain gear, and another layer of clothing in case the weather turns cooler.

Tour museums early. If you're there when the doors open you'll have an intimate experience of the collection.

Easy does it. See museums in the mornings, when you're fresh, and visit sit-down attractions later on. Take breaks before you need them.

Strike up a conversation. Only curmudgeons don't respond to a smile and a polite request for information. Most people appreciate your interest in their home town. And your conversations may end up being your most vivid memories.

Get lost. When you do, you never know what you'll find—but you can count on it being memorable. Use your guidebook to help you get back on track. Build wandering-around time into every day.

Quit before you're tired. There's no point in seeing that one extra sight if you're too exhausted to enjoy it.

Take your mother's advice. Go to the bathroom when you have the chance. You never know what lies ahead.

Hotel How-Tos

How to get a deal. After you've chosen a likely candidate or two, phone them directly and price a room for your travel dates. Then call the hotel's toll-free number and ask the same questions. Also try consolidators and hotel-room discounters. You won't hear the same rates twice. On the spot, make a reservation as soon as you are quoted a price you want to pay.

Promises, promises. If you have special requests, make them when you reserve. Get written confirmation of any promises.

Settle in. Upon arriving, make sure everything works—lights and lamps, TV and radio, sink, tub, shower, and anything else that matters. Report any problems immediately. And don't wait until you need extra pillows or blankets or an ironing board to call housekeeping. Also check out the fire emergency instructions. Know where to find the fire exits, and make sure your companions do, too.

If you need to complain. Be polite but firm. Explain the problem to the person in charge. Suggest a course of action. If you aren't satisfied, repeat your requests to the manager. Document everything: Take pictures and keep a written record of who you've spoken with, when, and what was said. Contact your travel agent, if he made the reservations.

Know the score. When you go out, take your hotel's business cards (one for everyone in your party). If you have extras, you can give them out to new acquaintances who want to call you.

Tip up front. For special services, a tip or partial tip in advance can work wonders.

Use all the hotel resources A concierge can make difficult things easy. But a desk clerk, bellhop, or other hotel employee who's friendly, smart, and ambitious can often steer you straight as well. A gratuity is in order if the advice is helpful.

© Artville

Information: **Clinton Area Convention and Visitor's Bureau** | 333 4th Ave. S, Box 1024, 52733 | 319/242–5702 or 800/828–5702.

Attractions

Bickelhaupt Arboretum. Fourteen acres of labeled trees, shrubs, and perennials as well as a medicinal plant display. | 340 S. 14th St. | 319/242–4771 | Free | Daily, dawn–dusk.

Eagle Point Park. A scenic road winds through this 205-acre park overlooking the Mississippi River at the northern edge of town, taking you past ball fields and a picnic area to a three-story stone observation tower built in the 1930s by the WPA. | U.S. 67 | 319/243–1260 | Free | Daily.

Felix Adler Museum. There are some Adler memorabilia here, but the main point of this museum is fun learning. There's a minigolf course, a rabbit house with live bunnies, a giant bubble machine, a dress-up corner, face-painting, and balloon-animal-making demonstrations. | 216 5th Ave. S | 319/243–3356 | $1 | Thurs.–Sat., 10–4.

Riverview Park. A 65-acre riverfront park with a band shell and picnic facilities. | 6th Ave. N | 319/243–1260 | Free | Daily.

Named for the actress born here, the **Lillian Russell Theatre** is aboard the *City of Clinton* showboat, a permanently dry-docked paddle wheeler that's home to Clinton's summer-stock theater. | 309 Riverview Dr. | 319/242–6760 | Admission varies | June–Aug.

Also docked at Riverview Park is the ***Mississippi Belle II,*** a 40-ft cruising riverboat with gambling and entertainment aboard. Children are not allowed on the boat but may stay at a day care center on the premises until 4pm for a $10 charge. | 311 Riverview Dr. | 319/243–9000 or 800/457–9975 | Free | Daily 24 hrs.

Valley Oaks Golf Club. *Golf Digest* considers this challenging 18-hole course a particularly good value. | 3330 Harts Mill Rd. | 319/242–7221 | Apr.–Oct.

ON THE CALENDAR

FEB.: *B-b-rrrry Scurry.* Locals break out the thermal undies for a 4-mi run/walk, snow golfing, bicycling, and ice fishing. | 319/244–7001.
JUNE: *Felix Adler Clown Festival.* Clinton's best-loved native son was Felix Adler, a Ringling Brothers clown, and this event celebrates his profession. There are children's games, displays of clown and circus artifacts, workshops for aspiring clowns, and a clown parade. | 319/242–7895.

Dining

The Unicorn. Contemporary. Expect to be served slightly unexpected dishes like the Duke of Earl sandwich with turkey, melted Swiss, asparagus, and curry sauce in this redbrick Victorian. | 1004 N. 2nd St. | 319/242–7355 | $7–$14 | AE, D, MC, V.

Upper Mississippi Brewing Company. American. This historic brewing house, built in the early 1900s, now serves steak, ribs, and specialty sandwiches. And don't forget to try the frothy house brew. | 132 6th Ave. S | 319/241–1275 | $7 | AE, D, DC, MC, V.

Lodging

Best Western Frontier Motor Inn. This motel is in an industrial area in the southwestern part of town 3 mi from the airport, and caters to business travelers, with large work surfaces and lots of light in guest rooms. Restaurant, bar, room service. Some refrigerators, cable TV. Pool. Hot tub. Exercise equipment. Business services. Some pets allowed. | 2300 Lincolnway | 319/242–7112 or 800/528–1234 | fax 319/242–7117 | www.bestwestern.com | 117 rooms | $58 | AE, D, DC, MC, V.

Country Inn. This hotel is on a commercial strip at the western edge of town, within walking distance of several bars and restaurants. Restaurant, bar, complimentary Continental breakfast. Cable TV. Pool. Hot tub. | 2224 Lincolnway | 319/244–9922 | 64 rooms | $79–$94 | AE, D, DC, MC, V.

Ramada Inn. There are river-theme art prints in the rooms of this chain hotel in a commercial area 5 mi west of the downtown riverfront. There's also a game room with a pool table. Restaurant, bar, room service. Some refrigerators and microwaves, cable TV, in-room movies available. Pool. Business services. No pets. | 1522 Lincolnway | 319/243–8841 or 800/272–6232 | fax 319/242–6202 | www.ramada.com | 115 rooms | $64 | AE, D, DC, MC, V.

Super 8. This chain motel offers basic rooms on the same commercial strip as most of Clinton's other lodging options. Complimentary Continental breakfast. Cable TV. In-room movies available. Business services. | 1711 Lincolnway | 319/242–8870 or 800/800–8000 | fax 319/242–8870 | www.super8.com | 63 rooms | $44 | AE, D, DC, MC, V.

Timber Motel. This economy motel on the western edge of town is on a commercial strip with other motels, Wal-Mart, and several restaurants and bars. Complimentary Continental breakfast. Cable TV. | 2225 Lincolnway | 319/243–6901 | 27 rooms | $43 | AE, D, MC, V.

Travelodge. This chain hotel is just two blocks from the river and three blocks from Clinton's downtown shopping and dining. Some rooms have riverviews. Complimentary breakfast. Some refrigerators, cable TV. Pool. Pets allowed. | 302 6th Ave. S | 319/243–4730 | fax 319/243–4732 | www.travelodge.com | 51 rooms | $48–$60 | AE, DC, MC, V.

COUNCIL BLUFFS

MAP 3, B5

(Nearby town also listed: Missouri Valley)

The name Council Bluffs comes from a famous meeting, or council, that explorers Lewis and Clark held here in 1804 on the bluffs high above the Missouri River with the Missouri and Oto Indians, in order to gain knowledge of the area and permission to move through their territory. Some years later in the mid-1800s, the Mormon Trail led 30,000 Mormons through this then lawless city, and their influence is seen in numerous schools, libraries, and other buildings they established throughout the region. Today health care and food processing, along with legalized gambling, have become the area's primary economic engines. If you are visiting Council Bluffs, you may want to cross the river and visit Omaha, Nebraska, as well.

Information: Council Bluffs Chamber of Commerce | 7 N. 6th St., Box 1565, 51502 | 712/325–6171 or 800/228–6878 | www.councilbluffsiowa.com.

Attractions

Confederate Air Force Museum. This airport hangar at Council Bluffs Airport has authentic World War II fighter planes on display including a P-51 Mustang as well as flight and aviation exhibits. | Old Hwy. 6 | 712/322–2435 | Free | Wed. 6–9 pm, Sat. 9–4, or by appointment.

Golden Spike. This 56-ft gold-leafed concrete spike was erected in 1939 in conjunction with the premier of the film *Union Pacific* to memorialize Council Bluffs's role in the race to connect the Union Pacific and Central Pacific railroad lines in 1869. Council Bluffs native Grenville Dodge played a large role in the building of the railroad and Abe Lincoln declared Council Bluffs as the Eastern terminus of the line. | 21st St. and 9th Ave. | 800/228–6878 | Free | Daily.

Historic General Dodge House. This Victorian house–turned–museum was built in 1869 and was home to Grenville Mellen Dodge, chief engineer of the first transcontinental railroad, a Civil War general in charge of spies, a congressman, a close friend to President Lincoln, and an advisers to Presidents Grant, McKinley, Roosevelt, and Taft. | 605 3rd St. | 712/322–2406 | $3 | Feb.–Dec., Tues.–Sat. 10–5, Sun. 1–5.

Historic Pottawattamie County Jail. Nicknamed the "squirrel cage jail," this is one of only three Lazy Susan jails remaining in the nation. The three-story cellblock, which was built in 1885, rotates, confining prisoners by stone walls instead of bars. | 226 Pearl St. | 712/323–2509 | $3 | Apr.–Sept., Sat. 10–4, Sun. noon–4, or by appointment.

Kanesville Tabernacle. This log cabin is where Brigham Young was elected president of the Church of Jesus Christ of Latter-Day Saints in 1847. | 222 E. Broadway | 712/322–0500 | Free | Mar.–Sept., daily 9–7; Oct.–Feb., daily 10–5.

Lake Manawa State Park. Lake Manawa, an oxbow lake 1 mi south of town, was formed in the 1880s when a portion of the river channel was cut off by the meandering Missouri River. Today it's surrounded by a 1,500-acre park. | 1100 S. Shore Dr. | 712/366–0220 | www.state.ia.us/parks | Free | Daily.

Lewis and Clark Monument. A monument dedicated to Lewis and Clark's famous expedition with an expansive view of the Missouri River valley. | A962 Monument Rd. | 712/328–4650 | Free | Daily.

Lincoln Monument. Raised in 1911 on the spot where the president stood, this monument honors Abraham Lincoln's efforts to hasten the westward expansion of the railroad. | Lafayette and Oakland Aves | 800/228–6878 | Free | Daily.

Mormon Trail Memorial. This monument in Bayliss Park is one of several around Council Bluffs honoring the Mormon Trail. | Pearl St. and 1st Ave. | 712/325–1000 or 800/228–6878 | Free.

National Western Historic Trails Center. In this small but exhaustive museum, multimedia exhibits use photos, film, interactive maps, and sculpture to document the Lewis and Clark, Mormon, Oregon, and California trails. You can also participate in activities designed to re-create everyday life experiences for early area settlers. | 3434 Richard Downing Ave. | 712/366–4900 | Free | May–Sept., daily 9–6; Oct.–Apr., daily 9–5.

RailsWest Railroad Museum. An 1899 Rock Island Railroad Depot is home to this museum and its collection which includes historic photos, a handcar, a post office car, a caboose, steam locomotives, and a complete model railroad town. | 1512 S. Main St. | 712/323–5182 | $3 | Tues.–Sat. 10–4; Sun. 1–5; closed Sept.–Apr.

Casinos. There are two riverboat casinos in town—*Ameristar* and *Harveys*. Both have slot machines, table games, and restaurants going 24 hours a day. Bluffs Run Casino offers live greyhound racing as well as slots. | *Ameristar:* 2200 River Rd; *Harveys:* One Harvey Blvd.; Bluffs Run: 2701 23rd Ave. | *Ameristar:* 712/328–8888 or 800/700–1012; *Harveys:* 712/329–6000 or 800/373–5825; Bluffs Run: 712/323–2500 or 800/238–2946 | Free | Daily.

Ruth Anne Dodge Memorial. A graceful bronze angel by renowned artist Daniel Chester French, who also sculpted Washington's Lincoln Memorial, honors Mrs. Dodge, wife of Grenville Dodge and one of early Council Bluffs's prominent citizens. If you explore Fairview Cemetery you'll also find the graves of many Mormon pioneers and Amelia Bloomer, who designed the first "trousers" for women. | N. 2nd and Lafayette Aves. | Free | Daily.

ON THE CALENDAR

JUNE: *Renaissance Faire of the Midlands.* Jousting, magic, stage performances, and costumed characters take over the wooded campus of Iowa Western Community College for a weekend. | 402/330–8446 or 712/328–4992.

NOV.–FEB.: *Winterfest.* Ice sculptures, snowball softball, and an ice-fishing contest, as well as lighted trees, cabins, and sculptures liven up the cold winter months in Bayliss Park. | 712/325–1000 or 800/228–6878.

Dining

Beverlee's. Contemporary. This upscale restaurant on the 12th floor of Harveys Casino has a panoramic view of the river and the Omaha skyline. Steak Diane, Caesar salads, and the flaming desserts are favorites here. Sunday brunch. | One Harveys Blvd. | 712/329–6000 | $16–$25 | AE, D, DC, MC, V | No lunch.

Landing Steakhouse. Steak. This superb steak house in the Bluffs Run Casino features prime rib and grilled filet mignon. | 2701 23rd Ave. | 712/325–1700 | $9–$14 | AE, D, DC, MC, V | No lunch.

Szechwan Chinese Restaurant. Chinese. This busy restaurant has a wide selection including many vegetarian and seafood dishes. The lunch special includes soup; try the kung pao chicken. | 2612 W. Broadway | 712/325–1782 | $4–$10 | MC, V | Closed Mon.

Veranda Buffet. American. This Ameristar Casino Hotel buffet features meat-and-potatoes fare. | 2200 River Rd. | 712/328–8888 | $7 | AE, D, DC, MC, V.

Lodging

Ameristar Casino Hotel. This Queen Anne–style hotel on the riverfront has marble floors and fountains in the lobby and is operated in conjunction with a riverboat casino with 1,000 slot machines and 40 table games. Restaurant, bar, room service. Some in-room hot tubs, cable TV, in-room VCRs available. Indoor-outdoor pool. Hot tub. Exercise equipment. Business services. Children's programs (ages 6 weeks–12 years. | 2200 River Rd. | 712/328–8888 | fax 712/328–8882 | www.ameristars.com | 160 rooms | $85–$155 | AE, D, DC, MC, V.

Best Western-Metro Inn and Suites. This chain hotel is 1 mi from downtown Omaha and 5 mi from such Council Bluff sites as the Golden Spike and General Dodge House (*see above*). Rooms have beamed ceilings, work spaces, and partially separated sleeping areas. Restaurant, complimentary Continental breakfast. In-room data ports, microwaves in suites, refrigerators, cable TV. Pool. Video games. Business services, airport shuttle. Pets allowed. | 3537 W. Broadway | 712/328–3171 or 800/528–1234 | fax 712/328–2205 | www.bestwestern.com | 89 rooms, 43 suites | $68 rooms, $79 suites | AE, D, DC, MC, V.

Comfort Suites of Council Bluffs. This chain hotel is right downtown. Complimentary Continental breakfast. Cable TV. Pool. Hot tub. | 1801 S. 35th St. | 712/323–9760 | 66 rooms | $89–$159 | AE, D, DC, MC, V.

Econo Lodge. Most rooms have wonderful views of the Missouri River in this basic, no-frills motel. The lodge is only a mile from the General Dodge House (*see above*). Complimentary Continental breakfast. Some refrigerators, cable TV. Exercise equipment. Laundry facilities. Business services. | 3208 S. 7th St. | 712/366–9699 | fax 712/366–6129 | www.hotelchoice.com | 60 rooms | $52 | AE, D, DC, MC, V.

Fairfield Inn by Marriott. This basic chain hotel is only ½ mi from the 18-hole Fox Run Golf Course, and is within walking distance of shopping and dining areas. Complimentary Continental breakfast. Cable TV, in-room VCRs available. Pool. Hot tub. Business services. | 520 30th Ave. | 712/366–1330 | fax 712/366–1330 | www.marriott.com | 62 rooms | $64 | AE, D, DC, MC, V.

Heartland Inn. This chain motel is in a commercial area with restaurants and a mall within walking distance. Complimentary Continental breakfast. Microwaves available, cable TV. Hot tub, sauna. Business services. | 1000 Woodbury Ave. | 712/322–8400 or 800/334–3277 | fax 712/322–4022 | 89 rooms | $60 | AE, D, DC, MC, V.

Interstate Inn. This downtown motel is within walking distance of several restaurants and bars. Complimentary Continental breakfast. Cable TV. | 2717 S. 24th St. | 718/328–8899 | 166 rooms | $45 | AE, D, DC, MC, V.

Motel 6 Council Bluffs. This chain hotel is just off Interstate 80 at exit 3 about 2½ mi south of downtown. There are several restaurants within walking distance and a mall just across the interstate. Pool. | 3032 S. Expressway Dr. | 712/366–2405 | 84 rooms | $33–$39 | AE, D, DC, MC, V.

Western Inn. This small, independently operated establishment has drive-up rooms and easy access to Interstate 80. Complimentary Continental breakfast, cable TV. Pool. Hot tub. Business services. | 1842 Madison Ave. | 712/322–4499 or 800/322–1842 | 51 rooms | $62 | AE, D, DC, MC, V.

CRESTON

(Nearby towns also listed: Osceola, Winterset)

Creston's name derives from its place as the high point, or crest, of the Burlington Railroad line between the Mississippi and Missouri rivers. The impressive depot built in 1899 now serves as the town's city hall, and many town activities take place there. Trains still roll through town 24 times a day, hauling products from nearby manufacturing plants, as well as grain and livestock for southwest Iowa's farms.

Information: Creston Chamber of Commerce | 208 W. Taylor, Box 471, 50801 | 515/782–7021 | www.mddc.com/chamber.

Attractions

Green Valley State Park. This 990-acre park 2½ mi north of town off Route 25 is a popular family picnicking and swimming area. You can also hike, fish, and water-ski here. | 1480 130th St. | 515/782–5131 | www.state.ia.us/parks | Free | Daily.

Mt. Pisgah Mormon National Monument. Mormon leader Parley Pratt stopped with his followers just south of what is now Lorimor 20 mi northeast of Creston in winter 1846. They sought shelter in log cabins and caves, but hundreds did not survive at this, their first winter camp on the Mormon Trail. | Beulah Cemetery and Hwy. 169 | 515/782–4405 | Free | Daily.

Union County Visitors Center. This visitors center is housed in a renovated 1931 Phillips 66 gas station. | 636 New York Ave. | 515/782–4405 | Free | Apr.–Oct., weekdays, 1–5.

ON THE CALENDAR
SEPT.: *Creston Hot-Air Balloon Days.* Nearly 50 balloons take to the skies over the Municipal Airport during this event. You can bring a picnic and watch the competition. | 515/782–7021.

Dining

Windrow Restaurant and Sports Bar. American. Steaks, burgers, and prime rib are served in this bar and grill that boasts seven TVs, including one large-screen. | 402 Taylor St., | 515/782–5014 | $5–$12 | D, MC, V.

Lodging

Berning Motor Inn. This quiet, brick motor inn in the heart of town has a large grandfather clock in the lobby and simply furnished rooms. Restaurant, bar. Cable TV. Exercise equipment. Business services. | 301 W. Adams St. | 515/782–7001 | fax 515/782–7415 | 48 rooms | $45 | AE, MC, V.

Moonlight Motel. This quiet 1950s motel is just a few blocks from the visitors center and within walking distance of restaurants and bars. Cable TV. | 704 New York Ave. | 515/782–4422 | 10 rooms | $39 | AE, D, MC, V.

Super 8. This 1970s chain motel is 1 mi from Creston's downtown shopping district and restaurants. In-room data ports, cable TV. Business services. | 804 W. Taylor St. | 515/782–6541 or 800/800–8000 | fax 515/782–9941 | www.super8.com | 83 rooms | $49–$65 | AE, D, DC, MC, V.

DAVENPORT

(Nearby towns also listed: Bettendorf, Muscatine)

Davenport today is the largest of the Quad Cities (Davenport and Bettendorf in Iowa, and Rock Island and Moline in Illinois), but in the early 1800s its growth as a white settlement was slow, due to bitter conflicts with Native Americans. The city's location at a wide bend of the Mississippi River where the mighty waters run west rather than south, however, eventually ensured its growth, as steamboat traffic and the transportation of agricultural products from eastern Iowa contributed to its overall development. It was on this stretch of river that Dam 15 of the Mississippi's 29 locks and dams was built in 1933, controlling the current of the water and opening up endless recreational opportunities more common to a lake community than to a river port. One of the country's first riverboat casinos opened here in 1991, establishing Davenport as the country's primary bus-tour destination for that year. An attractive riverfront park on the broad banks of the Mississippi River is the focal point of many activities in the Quad Cities area.

Information: Davenport Chamber of Commerce | 102 S. Harrison St., 52801 | 319/322–1706 | www.quadcities.com/davenport.

Attractions

Davenport Museum of Art. Opened in 1925, this is one of the oldest museums in the region and has works by Grant Wood and Thomas Hart Benton, European old masters, and rotating pieces by area artists on loan from local galleries. | 1737 W. 12th St. | 319/326–7804 | fax 319/326–7876 | www.art-dma.org | Admission varies per exhibit | Tues.–Sat. 10–4:30, Sun. 1–4:30.

Fejervary Park. This park overlooks the Mississippi River and includes Davenport's zoo with over 200 animal species. | 1900 Telegraph Rd. | 319/326–7812 | Free | Apr.–Oct., daily dawn–dusk.

Palmer College of Chiropractic. This first college of chiropractic education was started by the profession's founder, David D. Palmer. | 1000 Brady St. | 319/884–5676 | www.palmer.edu | Free | Daily.

President Riverboat Casino. This National Historic Landmark riverboat opened as the first riverboat casino on the Mississippi River in 1991. Cruises are available in warm weather. | 212 Brady St. | 800/262–8711 | www.prescasino.com | Free | Daily 24 hrs.

Putnam Museum of History and Natural Science. Founded in 1867, this is one of the oldest museums west of the Mississippi. Highlights of the collection include a 3,000-year-old mummy and an exhibit entitled, "Black Earth, Big River," documenting the environmental history of the region. By the summer of 2001, the museum also plans to have an IMAX theater. | 1717 W. 12th St. | 319/324–1933 | www.putnam.org | $4 | Tues.–Fri. 9–5, Sat. 10–5, Sun. noon–5.

Scott County Park. You can watch for wildlife, swim, or cross-country ski at this 1,500-acre park 8 mi north of town. | 19251 N. 290th St. | 319/381–1114 | Free | Daily.

Vander Veer Botanical Park. A botanical center and 1,800-variety rose garden with a duck pond that's used for ice-skating in winter. | E. Central Park Ave. | 319/326–7818 | Free | Daily.

Walnut Grove Pioneer Village. Once a stagecoach stop, this 3-acre village 8 mi north of town is now home to 18 historic buildings, including a one-room schoolhouse, a blacksmith shop, and a grocery store. | 18817 290th St., Long Grove | 319/285–9903 | Free | Apr.–Oct., daily dusk–dawn.

ON THE CALENDAR

JUNE: *Quad Cities Air Show.* One of the premier air shows in the country at Davenport Municipal Airport. | 800/747–7800.

JULY: *Bix Beiderbecke Memorial Jazz Festival.* A four-day jazz festival in LeClaire Park on the riverfront celebrating the life of this Davenport native. | 319/324–7170.

JULY: *Mississippi Valley Blues Festival.* A three-day event on the riverfront in LeClaire Park with simultaneous performances on two stages and free workshops for musicians of all levels. | 319/322–1706.

NOV.: *Festival of Trees.* One of the largest tree festivals in the nation kicks off the holiday season with lighted evergreens, decorated shop windows, and a giant helium-filled balloon parade downtown. | 319/322–1706.

Dining

Christie's. Continental. This small restaurant is housed in a 19th-century Victorian home filled with antiques and oil paintings. Specialties include crab cakes and Black Angus beef tenderloin. | 2207 E. 12th St. | 319/323–2822 | $13–$25 | AE, D, DC, MC, V | Closed Sun.

The Dock. Seafood. Almost every table has a panoramic view of the Mississippi thanks to this riverfront restaurant's floor-to-ceiling windows. A particularly tasty dish here is the fresh-grilled salmon, brushed with Chef Ron's special barbecue glaze and served with a fresh salad and tomato corn relish. Kids' menu. Sunday brunch. | 125 S. Perry St. | 319/322–5331 | $20–$25 | AE, D, DC, MC, V.

Filling Station. American/Casual. This fun, family-oriented restaurant in an old service station full of jukeboxes and pinball machines is known for triple-decker burgers smothered with toppings and served with the best fries in town. | 305 E. 35th St. | 319/391–6954 | $5–$15 | MC, V.

Iowa-80 Kitchen. American. This is a classic truck stop complete with big rigs, campers, and the occasional motorcycle convoy. It specializes in comfort food that will stick to your ribs—and your arteries. Try the breaded pork tenderloin with mashed potatoes and white (or brown) gravy. Salad bar. Open 24 hours. | 395 W. Iowa 80 Rd. | 319/284–6965 | $6–$8 | D, MC, V | Breakfast also available.

Iowa Machine Shed. American. Country artifacts, including old saw blades and miniature trucks and tractors, decorate this restaurant, the oldest of six machine sheds. Waitstaff wear plaid shirts and denim overalls and food is served family-style, with more-than generous portions. Try the pot roast or the chicken-fried steak—and plan to share. Salad bar. Kids' menu. | 7250 Northwest Blvd. | 319/391–2427 | $12–$20 | AE, D, DC, MC, V.

Rudy's Tacos. Mexican. A Quad City favorite known for its support of local sports teams and its great chimichangas, enchiladas, tacos, and tostadas. Kids' menu. | 4334 N. Brady | 319/386–2475 | $5–$7 | DC, MC, V.

Thunder Bay Grille. American. Not surprisingly, this restaurant which is designed to resemble a northern hunting lodge, with fishing and hunting gear on the walls and a massive, two-story stone fireplace, is known for its fish and steak. Kids' menu. Saturday and Sunday brunch. | 6511 Brady St. | 319/386–2722 | $10–$25 | AE, D, DC, MC, V.

Lodging

Best Western Steeplegate Inn. Many rooms in this centrally located chain hotel look out onto an atrium with an indoor pool, a hot tub, a lounge with umbrellas and bistro seating, and a pool table. Restaurant, bar (with entertainment), room service. Some refrigerators and microwaves, cable TV. Pool. Hot tub. Exercise equipment. Business services, airport shuttle. Pets allowed (fee). | 100 W. 76th St. | 319/386–6900 or 800/528–1234 | fax 319/388–9955 | www.bestwestern.com | 121 rooms | $75–$85 | AE, D, DC, MC, V.

Bishop's House Inn. Built in the 1870s, this Italianate B&B has four parlors, hardwood oak floors, and original stained-glass panels. All rooms have private bathrooms and are furnished with antiques. Complimentary Continental breakfast. Some in-room hot tubs, some in-room TVs. TV in common area. No pets. No kids under 12. No smoking. | 527 Brady St. | 319/322–8303 | 4 rooms, 1 suite | $65–$90, $140 suite | MC, V.

Clarion Hotel. Most rooms in this downtown hotel four blocks from the riverfront and President Casino have views of the Mississippi's lock and dam system. Restaurant, bar, complimentary Continental breakfast, room service. In-room data ports, refrigerators, microwaves, cable TV. 2 pools. Hot tub, sauna. Gym. Laundry facilities, laundry services. Business services, airport shuttle. | 227 Le Claire St. | 319/324–1921 | fax 319/324–9621 | www.hotel-choice.com | 150 rooms | $65–$75 | AE, D, DC, MC, V.

Comfort Inn. On the western edge of Davenport, away from the river but close to Interstate 80, this chain motel caters primarily to business travelers and those just passing through town. Complimentary Continental breakfast. Microwaves available, in-room VCRs available. Exercise equipment. Business services. Some pets allowed. | 7222 Northwest Blvd. | 319/391–8222 or 800/221–2222 | fax 319/391–1595 | www.comfortinn.com | 89 rooms | $54–$60 | AE, D, DC, MC, V.

Davenport Country Inn and Suites. Popular with business travelers, this hotel is in a commerical area off Highway 61, 10 mi north of downtown. Complimentary Continental breakfast. In-room data ports, some microwaves, some refrigerators, cable TV. Pool. Pets allowed. | 140 E. 55th St. | 319/388–6444 | www.countryinns.com | 49 rooms, 15 suites | $79–$99, $105–$125 suites | D, DC, MC, V.

Days Inn. This chain motel is 1½ mi north of town along a commercial stretch of highway with several chain and fast-food restaurants close by. Complimentary Continental breakfast. In-room data ports, some refrigerators, cable TV, in-room VCRs available. Pool. Hot tub. Exercise equipment. Business services. | 101 W. 65th St. | 319/388–9999 or 800/325–2525 | fax 319/388–9999 | www.daysinn.com | 64 rooms, 7 suites | $58 | AE, D, DC, MC, V.

Days Inn. You can reach Davenport's river casinos or the huge Northpark Mall in five minutes from this chain motel. Most rooms have comfy recliners and some overlook the pool area. Complimentary Continental breakfast. Cable TV. Pool. Beauty salon, hot tub, spa. Exercise room. Laundry service. Business services. Some pets allowed. | 3202 E. Kimberly Rd. | 319/355–1190 or 800/325–2525 | fax 319/355–1190 | www.daysinn.com | 65 rooms | $58 | AE, D, DC, MC, V.

Exel Inn. This basic, just-passing-through motel is only ¼ mi from Northpark Mall and ½ mi from Interstate 80. Complimentary Continental breakfast. In-room data ports, cable TV. | 6310 Brady St. N | 319/386–6350 | fax 319/388–1548 | www.exelinns.com | 103 rooms | $52 | AE, D, DC, MC, V.

Fairfield Inn by Marriott. This hotel is on the west side of the Quad Cities about 3 mi from the riverfront. Guest rooms are equipped for business travelers, with desks that have lamps and phone jacks built in. Complimentary Continental breakfast. Refrigerators in suites, cable TV. Pool. Hot tub. Business services. | 3206 E. Kimberly Rd. | 319/355–2264 | fax 319/355–2264 | www.marriott.com | 62 rooms | $63–$73 | AE, D, DC, MC, V.

Fulton's Landing. This huge, stone-and-brick Greek Revival mansion, now a B&B, has leaded-glass windows, carved woodwork, arching ceilings, and original fixtures and a perfect spot on a bluff overlooking the Mississippi. Guest rooms are furnished entirely with antique pieces. Kids are welcome with prior arrangement. Complimentary breakfast. Cable TV, in-room VCRs available. No pets. No smoking. | 1206 E. River Dr. | 319/322–4069 | fax 319/322–8186 | www.flinthills.com/atway/ia/fulton | 5 rooms | $60–$125 | AE, MC, V.

Hampton Inn. Rooms are basic, but some have views of the city at this chain hotel on the western edge of town 3 mi from the riverfront. Complimentary Continental breakfast. In-room data ports, cable TV. Pool. Exercise equipment. Business services, airport shuttle. Some pets allowed. | 3330 E. Kimberly Rd. | 319/359–3921 or 800/426–7866 | fax 319/359–1912 | www.hamptoninn.com | 132 rooms | $55 | AE, D, DC, MC, V.

Heartland Inn. Another chain hotel on the western edge of town near the Northpark Mall and adjacent theaters, 3 mi from the riverfront. Complimentary Continental breakfast. Cable TV. Pool, sauna. Business services. No pets. | 6605 N. Brady | 319/386–8336 or 800/334–3277 or 800/334–3277 | fax 319/386–6005 | 86 rooms | $62–$70 | AE, D, DC, MC, V.

Holiday Inn. This hotel is 5 mi north of downtown Davenport on Hwy. 61 about 5 minutes from several fast-food and restaurants and shopping. Bar, room service. Cable TV. Pool. Miniature golf. Exercise equipment. Business services, airport shuttle. | 5202 Brady St. | 319/391–1230 or 800/465–4329 | fax 319/391–6715 | www.holidayinn.com | 295 rooms | $68–$88 | AE, D, DC, MC, V.

President Casino's Blackhawk Hotel. This 1915 hotel with marble floors, oak and walnut woodwork, and guest rooms furnished with antique reproduction and fluffy duvets is now on the National Register of Historic Places. It is operated by President's Casino, which is just two blocks up the street. Restaurant, bar. Microwaves available. Barbershop, beauty salon. Exercise equipment. Business services, airport shuttle. | 200 E. 3rd St. | 319/328–6000 | fax 319/328–6047 | www.prescasino.com | 189 rooms | $85 | AE, D, DC, MC, V.

Radisson Quad City Plaza. Frequented by business travelers, this hotel is in the heart of downtown near office buildings and shopping. Restaurant, bar. In-room data ports, cable TV. Pool. Gym. Laundry service. Business services, airport shuttle. | 111 E. 2nd St. (at Brady St.) | 319/322–9200 | fax 319/322–9939 | www.radisson.com | 203 rooms, 18 suites | $76–$119, $159 suites | AE, D, DC, MC, V.

Residence Inn by Marriott. This all-suite hotel is frequented by business travelers and is 1 mi from Northpark and 5 mi from River Center. Complimentary Continental breakfast. Kitchenettes, microwaves, refrigerators, cable TV. Pool. Hot tub, spa. Gym. Laundry facilities. Business services. | 120 E. 55th St. | 319/391–8877 or 800/331–3131 | www.residenceinn.com | 78 suites | $89–$139 | AE, D, DC, MC, V.

Super 8. This no-frills motel is across the street from the Northpark Mall and within 5 mi of Davenport's river casinos. Complimentary Continental breakfast. Microwaves available, cable TV. Business services. Pets allowed. | 410 E. 65th St. | 319/388–9810 or 800/800–8000 | fax 319/388–9810 | www.super8.com | 61 rooms | $54 | AE, D, DC, MC, V.

DECORAH

MAP 3, G1

(Nearby town also listed: Spillville)

Immigrants from several Scandinavian countries were attracted to this part of northeast Iowa because of the potential the Iowa River offered for various trades. Today the Iowa River attracts canoeists and fishing enthusiasts in the warm months. The rolling hills and wooded countryside are also popular for various outdoor activities.

Information: **Decorah Area Chamber of Commerce** | 300 W. Water, 52101 | 319/382–3990 or 800/463–4692 | www.decorah-iowa.com.

Attractions

Fort Atkinson State Preserve. A military fort dating from the mid-1800s is the focal point of this 5-acre nature preserve 16 mi southwest of town. | 9026 Ivy Rd. | 319/425–4161 | www.state.ia.us/parks | Free | Daily.

Hayden Prairie. A National Natural Landmark, this 240-acre black-soil prairie near Chester on the border with Minnesota is a piece of living history, a look at what the Eastern Great Plains once were. Late May or late summer see the most wildflowers. | County V26 | 515/281–5145 | Free | Daily.

Laura Ingalls Wilder Park and Museum. Charles Ingalls, father of author Laura Ingalls Wilder, moved his family to Burr Oaks, 12 mi south of Decorah, in 1876. There he managed a hotel where the family lived. Today the hotel is the only childhood home of Laura Ingalls Wilder still standing. It features guided tours highlighting how the family lived, period furniture, and items and letters belonging to her. | 3603 236th Ave., Burr Oak | 319/735–5916 | www.decorah-iowa.com/tourism_destinations.idc | $4 | May–Oct., daily 10–5.

Seed Savers Exchange and Heritage Farm. This site is the headquarters of a nonprofit organization devoted to documenting and preserving "heirloom" varieties of fruits and vegetables that might otherwise vanish. On display are examples of over 3,600 varieties of beans, 1,200 different peppers, and 450 strains of corn, to name only a few. Tour the breathtaking 170-acre "living museum" and organic Preservation Gardens, or stroll through the Historic Orchard for what many claim is a spiritual experience. | 3076 N. Winn Rd. | 319/382–5990 | Free | May–Oct., Mon.–Sat. 9–4:30.

Upper Iowa River. The 40-mi stretch of the Iowa River in the extreme northeastern corner of the state is filled with canoeists and trout fishers every summer. | Bordered by Rtes. 150 and 52 | 800/463–4692.

Vesterheim, the Norwegian-American Museum. This historic downtown complex includes a Norwegian farmhouse, pioneer homes, a church from North Dakota, and displays of woodcarving, early farming tools, folk costumes, and boats. | 523 W. Water St. | 319/382–9681 | $5 | May–Oct., daily 9–5; Nov.–Apr., daily 10–4.

ON THE CALENDAR

JAN.–FEB.: *Winter Fest.* Ice sculpting, skiing, snow-fort building, and more. | 319/382–3990.

JULY: *Nordic Fest.* Celebrates the area's Scandinavian heritage with food, dance, a parade, and craft demonstrations. | 319/382–3990 or 800/382–3378.

Dining

Stone Hearth Inn. American. A large stone fireplace anchors this dining room decorated with old saw blades, barn artifacts, and tin signage. The food is hearty Midwestern fare. Try the breaded pork loin, or perhaps the prime rib. Kids' menu. Sunday brunch. | 811 Commerce Dr. | 319/382–4614 | $8–$14 | AE, D, MC, V.

Victorian Rose Restaurant. Contemporary. Chef Robin Hernaez combines locally grown organic vegetables with steak, chicken, pasta, and seafood for diners in this palm-filled formal dining room at the Hotel Winneshiek. | 104 E. Water St. | 319/382–4164 | $8–$28 | AE, D, DC, MC, V | Breakfast also available.

Lodging

Heartland Inn. You'll find stuffed pheasant trophies, reflecting the popularity of local hunting and fishing, in the lobby here along with special snacks on week nights—popcorn on Mondays, fresh-baked cookies Tuesday through Thursday. Friday nights from May to October bring the Manager's Social, with beverages and a barbecue. Complimentary Continental breakfast. Cable TV. Pool, exercise equipment. | 705 Commerce Dr. | 319/382–2269 or 800/334–3277 | fax 319/382–4767 | 58 rooms | $50 | AE, D, DC, MC, V.

Hotel Winneshiek. Built in 1905, this Victorian hotel was restored and reopened in spring 2000. Furnishings are reproductions or antiques, and you can have high tea or cocktails in the octagonal lobby by the fireplace. Restaurant *(see* Victorian Rose Restaurant, *above),* bar. Some refrigerators, cable TV. Shops. Laundry service. | 104 E. Water St. | 319/382–4164 | fax 319/382–4189 | www.hotelwinn.com | 26 rooms, 5 suites | $105–$160, $145–$195 suites | AE, D, DC, MC, V.

Super 8. This basic facility is within easy walking distance of Decorah's dining and nightlife destinations. Complimentary Continental breakfast. In-room data ports, cable TV, in-room

VCRs available. Laundry facilities. Business services. Pets allowed. | 810 Hwy. 9 E | 319/382–8771 or 800/800–8000 | fax 319/382–8771 | www.super8.com | 60 rooms | $45–$56 | AE, D, DC, MC, V.

DENISON

MAP 3, B3

(Nearby towns also listed: Carroll, Onawa)

Denison's motto, "It's a Wonderful Life," builds on the acclaim this little town received when native daughter Donna Reed starred in the 1946 classic holiday film. Today thousands of performing arts students receive training at the Donna Reed Festival and Workshop, through her foundation and local theater.

Information: Denison Chamber of Commerce | 109 N. 14th St., 51442 | 712/263–5621 | dsnchamber@frontiernet.com.

Attractions

Donna Reed Center for the Performing Arts. Named after the famous Iowan actress and filled with photos and mementos from her life, this 1914 Germanie Opera House hosts films, theatrical productions, and community gatherings. The Donna Reed Festival held here raises funds for performing arts scholarships. | 1305 Broadway | 712/263–3334 | www.donna-reed.org | $2 | Weekdays 9–4, weekends by appointment.

W. A. McHenry House. The Oscar Donna Reed won for "From Here to Eternity" is on display along with other memorabilia related to Crawford County and Iowa history in this 1885 Victorian home. | 1428 1st Ave. N | 712/263–3806 | $2 | Wed., Thurs., Sun. 1–4:30, and by appointment.

Yellow Smoke Park. This 321-acre park is just outside town and offers hiking, swimming, canoeing, sailing, and fishing. | 2237 Yellow Smoke Rd. | 712/263–3409 | Free | Daily.

ON THE CALENDAR

JUNE: *Donna Reed Festival for the Performing Arts.* Dozens of showbiz professionals, from casting directors to actors to acting coaches, come to town for a week of workshops, live performances, and autograph sessions. Take a minicourse on how to audition for stage or screen, improve you stage presence, or learn to market yourself in the fast-paced, cutthroat world of Hollywood. | 712/263–3334.

DEC.: *It's a Wonderful Life Festival.* Live performances of the story made famous in the movie, as well as gingerbread-house-decorating competitions, hayrides, and lighting displays. | 712/263–3334.

Dining

Cronk's. American. Iowa's oldest restaurant, this meat-and-potatoes favorite opened for business in 1929. Local arts-and-crafts pieces, ornate clocks, and dried flowers on the walls give this eatery a country-casual feel. Try a chicken-fried steak or pork tenderloin sandwich. Salad bar. Sunday brunch. | 812 4th Ave. S | 712/263–4191 | $6–$15 | AE, MC, V.

Family Table. American/Casual. You can order the largest pancakes in Crawford County all day at this family restaurant three blocks south of downtown. Savory dishes range from New York strip and rib-eye steaks to Tex-Mex fare such as taco salads. | Hwy. 30 and 12th Ave. S | 712/263–6300 | Breakfast also available | $4–$11.

Lodging

Ho-Hum Motel. All of the rooms at this small motel six blocks southwest of downtown contain 19th-century antiques. Some microwaves, some refrigerators, cable TV. Pets allowed. | 916 4th Ave. S (Hwy. 30) | 712/263–3843 | 12 rooms | $32–$34 | AE, D, MC, V.

Super 8. Rooms are bright and airy at this small-town chain motel on the west end of town where Highways 30, 59, and 141 meet. Restaurants and shopping are just a few minutes up the highway. Complimentary Continental breakfast. Cable TV. | 502 Boyer Valley Rd. | 712/263–5081 or 800/800–8000 | fax 712/263–2898 | www.super8.com | 40 rooms | $30–$40 | AE, D, DC, MC, V.

DES MOINES

MAP 3, E4

(Nearby town also listed: Indianola)

Iowa's capital city is at the fork of the Raccoon and Des Moines rivers. The Native Americans called the Des Moines river "Moingonia," meaning "river of the mounds." French explorers who traveled through the area translated the name to "La Rivière des Moines." A great source of irritation for Iowans is the mispronunciation of Des Moines (you don't pronounce either "s"). In 1857, with Iowa's population moving west, centrally located Des Moines succeeded Iowa City as the state's capital. Today the city is home to 200,000, nearly 60 insurance companies (making it the third-largest insurance center in the world), the highly respected *Des Moines Register,* an unusual 3½-mi downtown skywalk system, and several fine museums and galleries. Outside Iowa, Des Moines may be best known for the attention it receives during the presidential caucuses every four years.

Information: Greater Des Moines Convention and Visitors Bureau | 405 6th Ave., Suite 201, 50309 | 515/286–4960 or 800/451–2625 | www.desmoinescvb.com.

NEIGHBORHOODS

Valley Junction. If you like browsing around in antique and specialty shops, you'll probably want to visit Valley Junction in the former railroad district of West Des Moines. Bounded by Grand Avenue on the north and Railroad Avenue on the south, Valley Junction's six square blocks are filled with cozy cafés and shops that have taken up residence in the area's historic buildings.

Court Avenue District. If you are looking for nightlife, plan to spend a few hours downtown in the area known as the Court Avenue District. Bounded by 5th Avenue on the west and 1st Street on the east, this section of Court Avenue is filled with comedy clubs, retail shops, restaurants, and hot spots for live music and dancing, all in some of the city's oldest commercial buildings. If you like farmers' markets, plan to be here on a Saturday morning between May and October for one of the best in the country.

Sherman Hills National Historic District. Since the 1870s, Sherman Hills has held a prominent place in the city's social, cultural, and architectural life. Built as a residential area by Des Moines's top business leaders of the 1800s, the five-block neighborhood, bounded by 15th Street on the east, Olive Street to the north, Woodland Avenue to the south, and 20th Street on the west, has been designated a National Historic District and boasts the greatest remaining concentration of late-19th-century architecture in Des Moines.

TRANSPORTATION INFORMATION

Des Moines International Airport | 5800 Fleur Dr.; I–35/80 south to Army Post Rd., then east 3 mi | 515/256–5100.
Bus Lines: Jefferson Bus Lines (515/283–0074).
Intra-city Transit: Des Moines Metropolitan Transit Authority (515/283–8100) or **Para-Transit,** for people with disabilities (515/283–8136).

Attractions

ART AND ARCHITECTURE

Hoyt Sherman Place. Hoyt Sherman, a pioneer businessman, built this home complete with its own theater in 1877. Today it's a showcase for antiques and fine arts. | 1501 Woodland Ave. | 515/243–0913 | Free | Weekdays 8–4.

Jordan House. This 1848 Victorian home was built by James Jordan, the first white settler in West Des Moines. It served as a major stopping and supply point on the Underground Railroad and now boasts 16 refurbished period rooms as well as displays on the Underground Railroad in Iowa. | 2001 Fuller Rd., West Des Moines | 515/225–1286 | Free | Wed. and weekends 1–5.

Salisbury House. This 42-room Tudor mansion on 11 wooded acres 3 mi west of downtown is a replica of King's House in Salisbury, England, and displays, among other things, period furniture and a 16th-century suit of armor. | 4025 Tonawanda Dr. (I–235, 42nd St. exit) | 515/274–1777 | www.salisburyhouse.org | $5 | Tours Mar.–Nov., Tues.–Sat. 11 and 2; closed Jan.–Feb.

State Capitol. You can't miss the 275-ft gold-leafed dome of the capitol, built in 1886 of limestone, granite, and sandstone, and if you are intrigued by government or architecture you won't want to miss the tours given hourly. Highlights include the stunning law library and the collection of first-lady dolls. On the grounds outside you'll find memorials to the soldiers who have lost their lives in America's wars. | E. 12th St. and Grand Ave. | 515/281–5591 | Free | Weekdays 8–5.

Terrace Hill. Built to overlook downtown Des Moines by the state's first millionaire, this grand 1869 Victorian home with a formal Victorian garden is now the Iowa governor's mansion. | 2300 Grand Ave. | 515/281–3604 | $5 | Mar.–Dec., Tues.–Sat. 10–1:30.

Wallace House. This 1882 Italianate Victorian was home to agriculture and conservation leader Henry Wallace and it now has exhibits on his life as well as turn-of-the-last-century photos of Des Moines. | 756 16th St. | 515/243–7063 | Donations accepted; fee for large groups.

BEACHES, PARKS, AND NATURAL SITES

Des Moines Botanical Center. Extensive gardens and a weatherproof conservatory on the east bank of the Des Moines River house one of the largest collections of plants in the Midwest. | 909 E. River Dr. | 515/323–8900 | $1.50 | Mon.–Thurs. 10–6, Fri. 10–9, weekends 10–5.

Walnut Creek National Wildlife Refuge. You'll find 8,600 acres of tallgrass prairie, elk and bison, hiking trails, and a prairie education center in this National Wildlife Refuge 20 mi east of Des Moines. | 9981 Pacific St., Prairie City | 515/994–3400 | Free | Tues.–Sat. 9–4, Sun. noon–5.

CULTURE, EDUCATION, AND HISTORY

Civic Center. This performance center is home to several arts events in Des Moines. It is also the site of Des Moines's presidential caucuses every four years. | 221 Walnut St. | 515/243–0766 | www.civiccenter.org | Admission varies per event | Weekdays 10–4:30.

Drake University. Founded in 1881 on a 120-acre campus, this private university offers 70 undergraduate majors. | 2507 University Ave. | 515/271–2011 | www.drake.edu.

Heritage Village. This village on the Iowa Fairgrounds showcases barns, churches, a barbershop, and a general store, all filled with pioneer artifacts. | 400 E. 14th St. | 515/262–3111 | www.iowastatefair.org | $7; free with admission to Iowa State Fair | During Iowa State Fair wk in July, 9–9.

MUSEUMS

Des Moines Art Center. This museum, the largest in Iowa, was designed by Eliel Saarinen, I. M. Pei, and Richard Meier. The collection includes paintings by Picasso and Warhol, sculpture by Oldenberg and Rodin, and a small gallery of African art. Behind the center is beautiful Greenwood Park, which provides a gorgeous woodland setting for a post-museum picnic or frisbee game. | 4700 Grand Ave. | 515/277–4405 | $4; free on Thurs. | Weekdays 10–6, Sat. 10–5, Sun. noon–5.

Iowa Historical Building. This dramatic granite-and-glass building, completed in 1987, is right next to the capitol. It has an interactive exhibit on the pioneer settlement of Iowa and an exhibit on the state's natural history as well as traveling exhibits. | 600 E. Locust St. | 515/281–5111 | www.state.ia.us/government/dca | Free | Tues.–Sat. 9–4:30, Sun. noon–4:30; also open Mon. May–Aug. 9–4:30.

Living History Farms. Three hundred years of Iowa's agricultural history come alive through the gardens, livestock exhibits, and hands-on activities at five period farm sites on this 600-acre museum. Visit a 1700 Ioway Indian village, an 1850 pioneer farm, a 1875 town, a 1900 farm, and a 20th-century crop center. | 2600 N.W. 11th St. (I–80, exit 125), Urbandale | 515/278–2400 | www.lhf.org | $10 | May–late Oct., daily 9–5.

Polk County Heritage Gallery. Built in 1908, this former post office now hosts art shows and cultural exhibits. | 111 Court Ave. | 515/286–3215 | Admission varies per exhibit | Weekdays 11–4:30, Sat. 9–12; closed between exhibits.

Science Center of Iowa. Hands-on scientific exhibits illustrate basic physics concepts like gravity, electricity, and momentum and showcase indigenous Iowa wildlife, while the planetarium offers astronomy presentations and a laser-light show. | 4500 Grand Ave. (in Greenwood Park) | 515/274–4138 | www.sciowa.org | $3.50 | Mon.–Sat. 10–5, Sun. noon–5.

SPORTS AND RECREATION

Adventureland Park. Four roller coasters and the new Inverter which swings riders through a harrowing series of loop-the-loops high above the ground are among the more than 100 rides, shows, and attractions at this theme park. | 3225 Adventureland Dr. | 515/266–2121 | www.adventureland-usa.com | $22 | June–Aug., Mon.–Thurs. 10–9, Fri.–Sun. 10–10; May and Sept., weekends 10–7.

Jester Park Golf Course. *Golf Digest* includes this 18-hole course about 15 mi northwest of Des Moines in nearby Granger on its list of good value courses. | R.R. 1, Granger | 515/999–2903 | Apr.–Oct.

Prairie Meadows Racetrack and Casino. Live horse racing in spring and fall 10 mi east of town. | 1 Prairie Meadows Dr. (I–80, exit 142), Altoona | 515/967–1000 or 800/325–9015 | www.prairiemeadows.com | Free | Daily 24 hrs.

White Water University. A water park with a wave pool, tube rides, and twin-engine go-carts. | 5401 E. University St. | 515/265–4904 | $14 | Memorial Day–Labor Day, daily 10–7.

OTHER POINTS OF INTEREST

Blank Park Zoo. More than 800 animals call this 22-acre park home. Among them are lions, tigers, snow leopards, giraffes, zebra, antelope, and penguins. Children especially enjoy the zoo's "contact areas" where they can interact with animals face-to-face. | 7401 S.W. 9th St. | 515/285–4722 or 515/285–2676 | $4.50 | May–mid-Oct., daily 10–5.

ON THE CALENDAR

FEB.: *Skywalk Open Golf Tournament.* Proceeds from this unusual 18-hole miniature golf tournament held in the city's downtown skywalk system benefit local charities. | 515/243–6625.

APR.: *Drake Relays.* Competitors from 740 high schools and colleges, as well as professional and Olympic athletes, compete in this nationally recognized track and field event at Drake University. | 515/271–2115.

JUNE: *Art in the Park.* The best artists and craftspeople in the country come to the fairgrounds for a party and sale. | 515/277–4405.

AUG.: *Iowa State Fair.* Widely held to be the best state fair in the country, this event is a riot of activity, including big-name nightly entertainment, livestock and agriculture exhibits, crafts from around the state, and a midway full of harrowing amusement-park rides. Check out state fair fixtures like the Butter Cow and the live reptile exhibit. | 515/262–3111.

SEPT.: *Festival Europa.* Every year a different country is featured and official ambassadors from 20 European nations host dinners and other cultural events in the Capitol Square Atrium and on downtown Nolan Plaza. | 515/282–8269.

DEC.: *Holiday and Ivy Tour.* Three homes in the Sherman Hill Historic District host holiday festivities, including caroling, candlelight tours, and holiday teas. | 515/244–0507.

WALKING TOURS

Sherman Hill National Historic District (approximately 2 hours)

Begin at the headquarters of the Sherman Hill Association, the **Wallace House,** at 756 16th Street. The house operates as a historical center and meeting facility, interpreting the architectural and social significance of the district. Turn right and go less than a half block to Center Street, then turn right again and look for **1511 Center Street.** This 1883 Victorian was built at an original cost of $10,000 and saved from demolition in the 1970s by a prominent local doctor. Continue in the same direction on Center Street to 15th Street. Turn right and walk three blocks to the **Hoyt Sherman Place** at 1501 Woodland. Built in 1877 and now on the National Register of Historic Places, this home includes original marble fireplaces, parquet floors, and a unique umbrella room for the top hats and capes of Victorian guests. Tours of the home's interior require reservations (515/244–0507). Leaving the **Hoyt Sherman Place,** turn right walk one block west on Woodland Avenue to 16th Street. Look for **618 16th Street,** a Craftsman duplex built in 1902 and still under renovation. You may rest for a while in the garden gazebo and watch the work progress or continue two more blocks on Woodland to the **Chat Noir Café,** a restored home from 1885 that now serves as a favorite spot for food and beverages. Continue in the same direction on Woodland for two more blocks to the intersection of Woodland and 20th Street. The home at **640 20th Street** is in the Victorian Italianate style and was built in 1878 by Dr. Edwin Carter, a prominent local physician. It now operates as the **Carter House Inn.** Ornate curved staircases, pocket doors, and a vintage kitchen are treats you'll find on a tour inside. From the **Carter House,** turn right and walk one block north on 20th Street, crossing Pleasant Street. The 1903 Craftsman at **717 20th Street** was intended to be a side-by-side duplex, but the second half was never completed. Continue walking north on 20th Street to Center Street. Turn right on Center Street and walk four blocks and you are back at the **Wallace House.**

Dining

INEXPENSIVE

Drake Diner. American/Casual. Students love this chrome-and-neon diner. Just off the Drake campus and up the block from the Varsity Theater, this is a great place to grab coffee or a tasty dessert after a movie. Most menu items here are winners, but particularly scrumptious are the more-than-generous burgers and old-fashioned milk shakes. Kids' menu. | 1111 25th St. | 515/277–1111 | $6–$10 | AE, DC, D, MC, V.

Mustard's. American. Barbecued ribs are the speciality at this brewpub 5 mi west of downtown. The dining area is decorated with antiques, old tin signage, and sports memorabilia. Beer only. | 6612 University Ave., Windsor Heights | 515/274–9307 | $5–$7 | D, MC, V.

Nacho Mamma's. Southwestern. This downtown eatery known for homemade tortillas can be a little rowdy and a lot of fun. Sandwiched in between two other Court Avenue nightspots, the interior is narrow but lofty. Live cacti dominate the rangy-but-festive cantina decor. Open-air dining on sidewalk patio. Kids' menu. | 216 Court Ave. | 515/280–6262 | $6–$11 | AE, DC, MC, V.

MODERATE

China Wok. Chinese. Asian art sets the scene for dishes such as chicken and shrimp doused in piquant hoisin sauce. If you're less adventuresome, the Mongolian beef will do you right. | 1960 Grand Ave., Suite 23, West Des Moines | 515/223–8408 | $8–$17 | AE, D, DC, MC, V.

Christopher's. Italian. Soft lighting, dark wood paneling, and linen tablecloths set the mood in this intimate spot north of downtown. Favorite menu items range from deep-fried onion rings to escargot royale or homemade pasta. Kids' menu. | 2816 Beaver Ave. | 515/274–3694 | $8–$20 | AE, D, DC, MC, V | Closed Sun.

El Patio. Mexican. The colorful rooms in this converted bungalow west of downtown are full of southwestern artifacts and diners enjoying authentic Mexican food that can be very hot. Try the cheese-drenched enchiladas inside or on the covered patio. | 611 37th St. | 515/274–2303 | $16 | AE, MC, V | No lunch.

House of Hunan. Chinese. The dining area decor of this Urbandale restaurant involves brass calligraphic characters, calligraphy scrolls, mirrors, and Asian artwork. The sweet-and-sour chicken here will shame any you've had before. Buffet during lunch. | 6810 Douglas Ave. | 515/276–5556 | Reservations essential Fri.–Sat. | $8–$14 | AE, D, DC, MC, V.

India Cafe. Indian. Indian art hangs on the peach-color walls in this Parkwood Plaza eatery, and the menu includes such classic Indian dishes as mild tandoori chicken, a range of curries, and for the more adventurous, spicy vindaloo dishes. | Parkwood Plaza, 86th and Douglas Sts., Urbandale | 515/278–2929 | $10–$20 | AE, MC, V.

Iowa Machine Shed. American. One of six privately owned Machine Shed restaurants, this one—like its brethren—has antique farm equipment on the raw wood paneling walls. Food here is not for the fat-and-cholesterol-conscious. Portions of such dishes as stuffed pork chops and roast pork loin are massive and just about everything has seen the inside of the fry vat. | 11151 Hickman Rd., Urbandale | 515/270–6818 | $12–$20 | AE, D, DC, MC, V.

Maxie's. American. The owner's passion is antique cars, and photos of classic Corvettes and Mustangs embellish the walls here. The menu proffers carefully prepared American favorites like hot wings, burgers, and such. Kids' menu. | 1311 Grand Ave., West Des Moines | 515/223–1463 | $11–$14 | AE, D, DC, MC, V | Closed Sun.

Ohana Steakhouse. Japanese. Translucent paper screens and tatami mats transport you to another, more tranquil space as you dine on fresh, made-to-order Japanese-style steaks and seafood. Kids' menu. | 2900 University Ave., West Des Moines | 515/225–3325 | $11–$18 | AE, D, MC, V | Closed Mon.

SpaghettiWorks. Italian. For many locals this relaxed downtown spaghetti specialist with its casual lounge full of overstuffed chairs is a place for an evening out, not just a quick dinner. All sauces are made on the premises. Open-air dining is available on an iron-railed patio to the side of the main restaurant. The neighborhood's old railroad station and 1920s-era warehouses give the place a pleasantly rumpled feel. Salad bar. Live music every Monday night, comedy acts Friday–Saturday. Kids' menu. | 310 Court Ave. | 515/243–2195 | $8–$20 | AE, DC, MC, V.

EXPENSIVE

Café Su. Chinese. Dine on contemporary interpretations of Eastern classics in a bright, airy dining area lit with huge white-paper lanterns and decorated with an ever-changing array of local art. Su's has a healthy selection of red and white wines and the staff is attentive and knowledgeable. Lemon chicken is a favorite, as is Mongolian beef or the crabmeat Rangoon. | 225 Fifth St., Valley Junction | 515/274–5102 | $10–$22 | AE, D, MC, V | Closed Sun.

Chat Noir Café. Contemporary. Mismatched antique tables and chairs are arranged throughout several velvet-draped salons in this restored 1855 Victorian home. Try the incomparable muffuletta sandwich, a New Orleans concoction involving ham, Genoa salami, provolone cheese, and a special olive salad made at the Chat. If that's not quite

DES MOINES

INTRO
ATTRACTIONS
DINING
LODGING

what you had in mind, try a crêpe with Nutella and bananas or just have some tea. At dinner be sure to check specials featuring fresh fish and steak. | 644 18th St. | 515/244–1353 | $13–$20 | AE, D, DC, MC, V | Closed Sun., Mon. and late Dec.–mid Jan.

China Palace. Chinese. Candlelight and a tuxedoed waitstaff at this Hunan and Szechuan specialist in Clock Tower Square make for a more formal dining experience than at many Chinese restaurants. Massive mirrors and gold-leafed dragons give the dining area an opulent—if somewhat dated—appearance. This is the place to take your parents-of-a-certain-age on Sunday night. American style Sunday brunch. | 2800 University Ave., West Des Moines | 515/225–2800 | Jacket required | $10–$22 | AE, D, DC, MC, V.

Jesse's Embers. American. The open-pit grill and family-style service in this small dining room west of downtown make it a local favorite. It goes without saying that steak is king here, but if you'd rather, go with one of Jesse's incomparable burgers. | 3301 Ingersoll Dr. | 515/255–6011 | Reservations not accepted | $15–$22 | AE, MC, V | Closed Sun.

Splash. Seafood. Established in 1998, this fabulous spot has been dubbed "the most ambitious restaurant in Des Moines" by local food critics. Right downtown, Splash boasts an jaw-dropping four-story atrium, a huge undersea-inspired abstract mural, an 11-ft mako shark on one wall, a 275-pound blue marlin on another, and 1,000 gallons' worth of saltwater aquariums filled with coral and tropical fish. As for the food, Splash turns out contemporary and classic preparations of the freshest seafood. Try the mahimahi crusted with cashews and tropical fruit salsa with caramelized onion–and–garlic mashed potatoes. | 303 Locust St. | 515/244–5686 | $10–$30 | AE, D, DC, MC, V | Closed Sun.

Waterfront Seafood Market. Seafood. Although this restaurant is in a mini mall in West Des Moines, miles from any moving bodies of water, it is one of the only places in town for so-fresh-it's-still-wigglin' fish and seafood. Pick a lobster from the on-site rock pool, or sample something from the Market's raw bar. Kids' menu. | 2900 University Ave., West Des Moines | 515/223–5106 | $10–$22 | AE, D, MC, V | Closed Sun.

VERY EXPENSIVE

Anna's. Continental. This downtown favorite in the Hotel Savery with large chandeliers, a wall of wine bottles, and an elevated bar is known for prime rib, steak, and seafood. | 401 Locust St. | 515/244–2151 | Reservations essential | Jacket required | $22–$36 | AE, D, DC, MC, V | No lunch.

Lodging

INEXPENSIVE

Archer Motel. This motel off Highway 65 is within 1 mi of Adventureland and Prairie Meadows Racetrack and Casino, and about 8 mi northeast of downtown. Cable TV. Pool. Pets allowed. | 4965 Hubbell Ave. (Hwy. 65, exit 141) | 515/265–0368 | 29 rooms | $36–$50 | AE, D, DC, MC, V.

MODERATE

Airport Comfort Inn. This chain hotel is near the airport, on the south side of town, about 3 mi from downtown. Complimentary Continental breakfast. In-room data ports, refrigerator in suites, cable TV. Pool. Hot tub. Business services, airport shuttle. Some pets allowed. | 5231 Fleur Dr. | 515/287–3434 | fax 515/287–3434 | www.comfortinn.com | 55 rooms, 16 suites | $65 rooms, $75 suites | AE, D, DC, MC, V.

Airport Inn. This motel is on a commercial strip 2 mi from the airport, 4 mi from Interstate 35, and 6 mi from Interstate 80. Complimentary Continental breakfast. Cable TV. Pool. Laundry facilities. Business services, airport shuttle, free parking. Pets allowed. | 1810 Army Post Rd. | 515/287–6464 | fax 515/287–5818 | 145 rooms | $65–$77 | AE, D, DC, MC, V.

Best Inn. Locally themed art prints dominate the lobby of this chain motel 2 mi from Merle Hay Mall and 12 mi from the heart of downtown. Rooms are basic but spacious. Complimentary Continental breakfast. Microwaves available, cable TV. Pool. Hot tub. Business services. Pets allowed. | 5050 Merle Hay Rd., Johnston | 515/270–1111 or 800/237–8466 | fax 515/331–2142 | www.bestinns.com | 92 rooms, 14 suites | $63 rooms, $77 suites | AE, D, DC, MC, V.

Best Western Starlite Village. This chain hotel is about 10 mi north of downtown in the town of Ankeny, almost halfway to Ames and Iowa State University. It's just off I–35 in a commercial area among other hotels and several restaurants. Restaurant, bar. Cable TV. Business services. Some pets allowed. | 133 S.E. Delaware, Ankeny | 515/964–1717 | fax 515/964–8781 | www.bestwestern.com | 116 rooms | $63–$68 | AE, D, DC, MC, V.

Best Western Walnut Creek. A mainstay in the business district for 25 years, this hotel at the corner of Office Park Road is 7 mi west of downtown. Bar, complimentary Continental breakfast. Some microwaves, some refrigerators, cable TV. Pool. Hot tub. Free parking. No pets. | 1258 8th St., West Des Moines | 515/223–1212 or 800/792–5688 | fax 515/223–1235 | www.bestwestern.com | 63 rooms, 1 suite | $59–$75 rooms, $110 suite | AE, D, DC, MC, V.

Carter House Inn. This 1878 Italianate Victorian B&B is in the historic Sherman Hill District, within walking distance of the Chat Noir Café and most of the area's historic homes. Guest rooms are furnished with period antiques and a gourmet breakfast is served every morning. Complimentary breakfast. No room phones, no TV, cable TV and VCR in common area. | 640 20th St. | 515/288–7850 | 4 rooms | $50–$65 | AE, MC, V.

Chase Suites. This hotel is on the outskirts of town, off Interstate 80 in the residential suburbs of West Des Moines and you'll need your car when you are exploring local attractions. There's a Thursday-night poolside barbecue from June to September and free beverages in the lobby on weeknights. Picnic area, complimentary Continental breakfast. In-room data ports, kitchenettes, microwaves available, cable TV. Pool. Hot tub. Exercise equipment. Laundry facilities. Business services, free parking. Pets allowed (fee). | 11428 Forest Ave., Clive | 515/223–7700 | fax 515/223–7222 | 112 suites | $64 | AE, D, DC, MC, V.

Executive Inn. This no-frills West Des Moines hotel caters to business travelers. Rooms have desks with good lighting and large windows. There's plenty of shopping at the Valley West Mall next door and convenient eating at several chain restaurants within walking distance. Restaurant, bar, complimentary Continental breakfast, room service. Refrigerators and microwaves available, cable TV, in-room VCR and movies available. Indoor-outdoor pool. Hot tub. Exercise equipment. Business services. | 3530 Westown Pkwy., West Des Moines | 515/225–1144 | fax 515/225–6463 | 100 rooms, 2 suites | $58 rooms, $64–$75 suites | AE, D, DC, MC, V.

Fairfield Inn by Marriott. Rooms are large enough to accommodate families with kids at this chain hotel right off Interstate 80 and Interstate 35 at exit 124. The setting isn't picturesque, but you're just 1 mi from Valley West Mall and more than a dozen West Des Moines restaurants. Complimentary Continental breakfast. Cable TV. Pool. Business services. | 1600 114th St. | 515/226–1600 | fax 515/226–1600 | www.marriott.com | 135 rooms | $55–$60 | AE, D, DC, MC, V.

Hampton Inn. This chain hotel is 7 mi south of downtown and just across the street from the airport in a residential area. The South Ridge and Valley West Malls are within a 15-minute drive. Fresh-baked cookies are free in the lobby daily 5–8 PM. Ice cream is available on weeknights, too. Complimentary Continental breakfast. In-room data ports, cable TV. Pool. Exercise equipment. Business services, airport shuttle, free parking. | 5001 Fleur Dr. | 515/287–7300 | fax 515/287–6343 | www.hamptoninn.com | 122 rooms | $58 | AE, D, DC, MC, V.

Heartland Inn. This motel is on the west side of town about 5 min from the Valley West Mall and is surrounded by restaurants. Rooms are done in what could be called "motor inn traditional"—which is to say, somewhat nondescript, faux-wood furniture, bedside wall-bracket lamps, and floral bedspreads. Complimentary Continental breakfast. Microwaves available, cable TV. Hot tub, sauna. Business services. Some pets allowed (fee). | 11414 Forest Ave. | 515/226–0414 | fax 515/226–9769 | 87 rooms | $55 | AE, D, DC, MC, V.

Holiday Inn Express at Drake. This hotel is just off the Drake University campus and its brick facade blends nicely with the university buildings. Guest rooms are furnished with simple antique reproductions. Complimentary Continental breakfast. Microwaves available, cable TV. Business services. | 1140 24th St. | 515/255–4000 | fax 515/255–1192 | www.hiexpress.ocm | 52 rooms | $70 | AE, D, DC, MC, V.

Inn at Merle Hay. This hotel, on a quiet suburban road near a commercial strip with a wide variety of chain and fast-food restaurants, is 12 mi northwest of downtown in Johnston. It boasts a small library in the lobby and an adjacent retro diner with bright lime, yellow, and orange furnishings (accessible via the hotel lobby and from the street). Restaurant, bar. Microwaves available, cable TV. Pool. Hot tub. Business services, airport shuttle. Pets allowed (fee). | 5055 Merle Hay Rd., Johnston | 515/276–5411 or 800/643–1197 | fax 515/276–0696 | knapp@dwx.com | www.knapphotels.com | 146 rooms | $59–$71 | AE, D, DC, MC, V.

Kirkwood Civic Center. Built in 1930, this historic hotel has original wall-mounted telephones and chandeliers in the lobby. Guest rooms have an updated-but-cozy feel. Restaurant. Some in-room hot tubs, cable TV. Business services. | 400 Walnut St. | 515/244–9191 or 800/798–9191 | fax 515/282–7004 | 150 rooms | $45–$79 | AE, D, DC, MC, V.

Motel 6-East. This chain motel is 10 mi east of downtown, and 5 mi east of the Adventureland Park and Prairie Meadows Racetrack in Altoona. Cable TV. Pool. Business services. Pets allowed. | 3225 Adventureland Dr., Altoona | 515/967–5252 | fax 515/957–8637 | www.motel6.com | 116 rooms | $48–$58 | AE, D, DC, MC, V.

Quality Inn and Suites. This chain hotel on a commercial strip just off I-80 about a mile north of Merle Hay Mall and 10 minutes from downtown has traditional, country-home style furnishings. Restaurant, complimentary Continental breakfast. Microwaves available, cable TV. Indoor-outdoor pool. Hot tub. Exercise equipment. Laundry facilities. Business services. | 4995 Merle Hay Rd. | 515/278–2381 | fax 515/278–9760 | www.qualityinn.com | 120 rooms | $52–$76 | AE, D, DC, MC, V.

Sheraton Four Points. Trees and flowering bushes surround this upscale hotel in the suburbs 20 mi west of downtown. Restaurant, bar, room service. In-room data ports, cable TV. Pool, wading pool. Hot tub, sauna. Laundry facilities. Business services, airport shuttle, free parking. Pets allowed. | 11040 Hickman Rd. | 515/278–5575 | fax 515/278–4078 | www.sheratoninns.com | 161 rooms | $69 | AE, D, DC, MC, V.

Travelodge. Just off Interstate 35 and across the street from the Merle Hay Mall in West Des Moines, this basic motel is within easy driving distance of most major area attractions, but things in this neighborhood are a bit spread out so you will need to use your car to explore. Microwaves available, cable TV. Business services. | 5626 Douglas Ave. | 515/278–1601 | fax 515/278–9816 | www.travelodge.com | 46 rooms | $52 | AE, D, DC, MC, V.

EXPENSIVE

Adventureland Inn. This hotel, next to and owned by the Adventureland amusement park, is filled with sculptures and prints of brightly colored carousel horses. Restaurant, bar (with entertainment), room service. Cable TV. Pool. Playground. Business services. | I-80 at Hwy 165, exit 142 | 515/265–7321 | fax 515/265–3506 | www.adventureland-usa.com | 130 rooms, 4 suites | $80–$95 rooms, $135 suites | AE, D, DC, MC, V.

Comfort Suites. This chain hotel is adjacent to Living History Farms and the Heritage Village west of Des Moines. Bar, complimentary Continental breakfast. Refrigerators, cable TV. Pool. Hot tub. Exercise equipment. Video games. Business services. | 11167 Hickman Rd., Urbandale | 515/276–1126 | fax 515/276–8969 | www.hoari.com | 101 rooms | $89–$104 | AE, D, DC, MC, V.

Courtyard by Marriott. In a commercial neighborhood 7 mi west of downtown, this chain hotel is frequented by business travelers. On weekends, you can get a package deal for two people which includes complimentary breakfast. Restaurant. Some microwaves, some refrigerators, cable TV. Pool. Hot tub. Gym. Laundry facilities. | 1520 N.W. 114th St. | 515/225–12222 or 800/321–2211 | fax 515/245–3773 | www.marriott.com | 102 rooms, 6 suites | $59–$95 rooms, $119 suites | AE, D, DC, MC, V.

Holiday Inn–Airport. Overstuffed chairs fill the spacious lobby of this motel 5 mi south of downtown near the airport and Army Post Road. South Ridge Mall is only about ¼ mi away, and dozens of chain and independent restaurants dot both Fleur Drive and Army Post Road. Restaurant, bar, complimentary Continental breakfast, room service. In-room data ports, microwaves available, cable TV, in-room VCRs available. Pool. Hot tub. Exercise equipment. Business services, airport shuttle, free parking. | 6111 Fleur Dr. | 515/287–2400 | fax 515/287–4811 | www.basshotels.com/holiday-inn | 227 rooms | $89–$99 | AE, D, DC, MC, V.

Holiday Inn–Downtown. The lobby of this downtown hotel has 15-ft ceilings and comfortable lounge chairs. Rooms are large and most have an excellent view of the city's skyline. Restaurant, bar. Cable TV, in-room movies available. Pool. Business services, airport shuttle. | 1050 6th Ave. | 515/283–0151 | fax 515/283–0151 | www.holidayinn.com | 253 rooms | $89 | AE, D, DC, MC, V.

Mussell Inn. This 1950s three-story brick B&B is on a residential block 3 mi west of downtown. Some rooms have private entrances, wet bars, decks, and fireplaces. A garden and lawn furniture surround the outdoor pool which has a whirlpool. Complimentary breakfast. Cable TV. Some microwaves, some refrigerators. Pool. Basketball. Free parking. No pets. No smoking. | 3705 Colby Ave. (between 66th St. and 68th St.) | 515/274–4329 | www.ia-bedand-breakfast-inns.com | 3 rooms | $65–$85 | No credit cards.

Sleep Inn at Living History Farms. This hotel is 5 mi west of downtown right next to the Living History Farms, which you can see from the lobby. The large indoor pool and whirlpool are in a two-story atrium, and there's a recreation room with pool tables. Complimentary Continental breakfast. Some microwaves, some refrigerators, cable TV. Pool. Hot tub. Laundry facilities. Pets allowed (fee). | 11211 Hickman Rd. (I–80/I–35, exit 125), Urbandale | 515/270–2424 | fax 515/270–2424 | www.hoari.com | 107 rooms, 3 suites, 2 two-bedroom conference suites | $69–$89 rooms, $99–$119 suites, $149–$179 conference suites | AE, D, DC, MC, V.

University Park Holiday Inn. Frequented by business travelers, this hotel is 6 mi west of downtown, near the financial district. Restaurant, bar. In-room data ports, some in-room hot tubs, cable TV. Pool. Sauna. Gym. Laundry facilities, laundry service. Business services, airport shuttle, free parking. Pets allowed (fee). | 1800 50th St. (I–80, exit 126), West Des Moines | 515/223–1800 or 800/HOLIDAY | 226 rooms, 62 suites | $89–$99 rooms, $99–$109 suites | AE, D, DC, MC, V.

Valley West Inn. This motel is next to Valley West Mall in suburban West Des Moines. You'll find a half dozen restaurants within easy walking distance. Restaurant. Cable TV. Pool. | 3535 Westown Pkwy. | 515/225–2524 or 800/833–6755 | fax 515/225–9058 | www.knappho-tels.com | 136 rooms | $70–$100 | AE, D, MC, V.

VERY EXPENSIVE

Butler House on Grand. Less than 3 mi from downtown, this this 1923 Tudor mansion B&B is across the street from the Des Moines Art Center and Greenwood Park. Rooms have been furnished by local artists. In fine weather you can sit in the courtyard by the pond, and in poor weather by the fireplace in the living room. Complimentary breakfast. In-room data ports, some in-room hot tubs, cable TV. No smoking. | 4507 Grand Ave. | 515/255–4096 | www.butlerhouseongrand.com | 6 rooms, 1 suite | $90–$120 rooms, $130–$140 suite | AE, D, MC, V.

Des Moines Marriott. This hotel in the heart of the downtown financial district is connected to Des Moines's skywalks. It caters mostly to those in town for business, but the large rooms and commanding view of downtown make it a nice choice for anyone. 4 restaurants, bar. Cable TV, in-room VCRs available. Pool. Barbershop, beauty salon, hot tub. Exercise equipment. Business services, airport shuttle, free parking. Some pets allowed. | 700 Grand | 515/245–5500 | fax 515/245–5567 | www.marriott.com | 415 rooms | $79–$169 | AE, D, DC, MC, V.

Embassy Suites on the River. This all-suites hotel is built around a soaring atrium with glass elevators, a six-story waterfall, and tropical plants. Suites have separate sleeping and living areas furnished with sleek, modern furniture. Restaurant, bar (with entertainment), complimentary breakfast, room service. Microwaves, refrigerators, cable TV, in-room VCRs available. Pool. Hot tub. Exercise equipment. Laundry facilities. Business services, airport shuttle. | 101 E. Locust St. | 515/244–1700 | fax 515/244–2537 | www.embassysuites.com | 234 suites | $109–$144 | AE, D, DC, MC, V.

Fort Des Moines. Built in 1919, this downtown hotel has played host to some of the world's most noted dignitaries, among them Nikita Khrushchev and Woodrow Wilson. Elvis Presley spent a night here on his way through town, and eccentric musician Tiny Tim made the hotel his home for 34 years. The hotel's history and guest list earned it a place on the National Register of Historic Places. Walnut and marble figure largely in both the lobby and guest rooms. Restaurant, bar. In-room data ports, refrigerators in some suites, cable TV. Pool. Hot tub. Exercise equipment. Business services, airport shuttle. Pets allowed. | 1000 Walnut St. | 515/243–1161 or 800/532–1466 | fax 515/243–4317 | www.hotelfortdesmoines.com | 242 rooms, 56 suites | $109–$159 rooms, $130–$350 suites | AE, D, DC, MC, V.

Hotel Savery. This stately downtown hotel was built in 1919 and now boasts a day spa and a link to the downtown skywalk system. Most of the lobby's furnishings are original, including the gas lights, antique mirrors, and front desk. 2 restaurants (*see* Anna's, *above*), bar, room service. Some kitchenettes, cable TV. Pool. Beauty salon, hot tub. Exercise equipment. Airport shuttle. Some pets allowed. | 401 Locust St. | 515/244–2151 or 800/798–2151 | fax 515/244–1408 | 224 rooms | $119–$145 | AE, D, DC, MC, V.

Wildwood Lodge. A massive stone fireplace and rough-hewn furnishings fill the lobby of this rustic resort 10 mi from downtown. Guest rooms feature wildlife photos, and some also have their own fireplaces. Bar, complimentary Continental breakfast. In-room data ports, microwaves available, cable TV, in-room VCRs available. Pool. Hot tub. Exercise equipment. Business services. | 11431 Forest Ave., Clive | 515/222–9876 or 800/728–1223 | fax 515/222–9876 | www.hoari.com | 94 rooms, 10 suites | $80–$115 rooms, $130–$250 suites | AE, D, DC, MC, V.

DUBUQUE

MAP 3, H3

(Nearby town also listed: Dyersville)

Built into the bluffs overlooking the Mississippi River, Dubuque is widely known for the elevators, cable cars, and steep stone staircases that take pedestrians from one street level to another as well as its meatpacking and heavy farm equipment industries. Today the city is home to several private colleges, riverboat casinos, a museum that documents river history, and tree-lined streets filled with elaborate Victorian homes, many of which are now B&Bs.

Information: **Dubuque Area Chamber of Commerce** | 770 Town Clock Plaza, Box 705, 52004 | 319/557–9200 or 800/798–8844 | www.dubuquechamber.com.

Attractions

Bellevue State Park. Tall cliffs in this 700-acre park 26 mi south just beyond the town of Bellevue afford fine views of the Mississippi River. You'll also find wooded walking trails, a butterfly sanctuary, and a nature center. | 24668 Hwy. 52 | 319/872–3243 or 319/872–4019 | www.state.ia.us/parks | Free | Daily.

Cathedral Square. Across from St. Raphael's Cathedral, this quaint corner of town is home to small specialty shops and the 4th Street Elevator, which is the shortest, steepest public transit vehicle in the world. | 2nd and Bluff Sts. | 800/798–8844.

Clarke College. A four-year Catholic liberal arts institution founded in 1843 by the nuns of the Sisters of Charity order. | 1550 Clarke Dr. | 319/588–6318 | www.clarke.edu | Free | Daily.

Crystal Lake Cave. Discovered in 1868, this cave is about 5 mi south of town, off Highway 52. It contains a "chapel room" and unusual geological formations like cave flowers and soda straws. | 7699 Crystal Lake Cave Dr. | 319/556–6451 or 319/872–4111 | $8 | Memorial Day–Labor Day daily 9–6; Labor Day–mid-Oct. weekdays 11–5, weekends 9–5.

Czipar's Orchard. You can see how 25 different varieties of apples are picked, polished, and packaged at this family- owned and -operated apple orchard 4 mi south of downtown on Highway 52. | 8562 Hwy. 52 S | 319/582–7476 | Free | Sept.–Oct., daily.

Diamond Jo Casino. This cruising paddleboat casino offers dining, entertainment, and gambling as it travels 5 mi up the river. | 3rd St. at Ice Harbor | 319/583–7005 or 800/582–5956 | www.diamondjo.com | Mon.–Tues. 7 AM–2 AM, Wed.–Thurs. 7 AM–4 AM, Fri.–Sun. 24 hrs.

Dubuque Arboretum and Botanical Gardens. This 50-acre area of Marshall Park, 2 mi from downtown, includes all-American rose gardens, water gardens, prairie grasses and wildflowers, and "Seed Savers Display Gardens," highlighting pioneers' efforts to preserve seeds for planting along the trail. | 3800 Arboretum Dr. | 319/556–2100 | Donations accepted | May–Nov., daily dawn–dusk.

Dubuque Art Center. This small but impressive art museum has won several architectural awards for its renovation of the 1970s bank building it now occupies. Glass-curtain walls look out onto downtown Dubuque's Washington Park. Inside local and regional artwork including the second-largest collection of Grant Wood pieces in the country and traveling exhibits are on display. | 701 Locust St. | 319/557–1851 | Tues.–Fri. 10–5, weekends 1–4 | Donations accepted.

Dubuque County Courthouse/Old County Jail. The beautiful solid-oak furnished North Courtroom of Dubuque's 1893, twin gold-domed courthouse has been featured in two short-lived TV series and in the film *Take This Job and Shove It.* The adjacent jail predates the Civil War and is one of only two examples of Egyptian jail architecture in the United States (the other being The Tombs in New York). The first murderer in Iowa history was held in this jail, and it was packed with Confederate soldiers during the Civil War. | 720 Central Ave. | 319/589–4432 | Weekdays 8–4:30.

Dubuque Greyhound Park and Casino. This casino on the banks of the Mississippi River has 600 slot machines open year-round and greyhound racing May through October. | 1855 Greyhound Park Dr. | 319/582–3647 | Free | Daily.

Dubuque Welcome Center. You'll find a museum with displays of prehistoric and Native American artifacts, local historical exhibits, and an observation deck looking out onto the Mississippi at this converted warehouse. | 400 E. 3rd St., Ice Harbor | 319/556–4372 or 800/798–8844 | www.dubuque.org/attracts | Free | Daily 10–5.

Eagle Point Park. This 164-acre park in the northeast corner of the city overlooks the Mississippi River and provides spectacular views of Iowa, Wisconsin, and Illinois. | Shiras Ave. | 319/589–4263 | $1 per car | May–Oct., daily.

The east side of the park offers some of the best views of **General Zebulon Pike Lock and Dam.** Completed in 1937, this Mississippi dam measures 4,818 ft in length and has 16 gates. The dam itself is just off Hawthorn Street and can be toured on summer Sundays. | 319/582–0881 | Free | Memorial–Labor Day, tours Sun. 2 PM.

Fenelon Place Elevator. Traveling just 296 ft while elevating passengers 189 ft, this is the world's shortest, steepest railway. Built in 1882 and now providing both transportation and a wonderful view, this lift is also known as the Fourth Street Elevator. | 512 Fenelon Pl | 319/582–6496 | www.mall.mwci.net/fenplco | $1.50 | Apr.–Nov., daily 8 AM–10 PM.

Five Flags Theater. This historic theater has been a place of public entertainment since 1840. The current building, the third incarnation of this playhouse, was built around 1915 after the second theater burned, and presents entertainment including nationally recognized musicians, traveling drama groups, and old-time live radio. | 4th and Main Sts. | 319/589–4254 | Admission varies per event.

Grand Opera House. In its glory days this 1889 theater hosted Ethel Barrymore, George M. Cohan, Lillian Russell, and Sarah Bernhardt. Today repertory productions are offered here year-round. | 135 8th St. | 319/588–1305 | Admission varies per show.

Grant Wood Scenic Byway (East End). Pass through tiny towns like Monmouth (pop. 167) and stop to view the majestic expanse of rolling Iowa farmland and the Mississippi River valley along a series of county roads and highways named for the famed Iowa artist. The route stretches from Bellevue, 26 mi south of Dubuque, to Anamosa. You can get a brochure describing the route from the Iowa Division of Tourism. | 319/872–5830.

Heritage Trail. You'll find a trailhead for this 26-mi biking and hiking trail that follows a retired railroad bed to Dyersville 2 mi north of town. | Hwy. 52 N | 319/556–6745 | $1 | Daily.

Loras College. This four-year Catholic liberal arts college has 1,700 students and the third-largest private library in Iowa. | 1450 Alta Vista St. | 319/588–7100 | www.loras.edu.

Mathias Ham House Historic Site. This stately country villa below Eagle Point Park reflects the golden era of steamboat wealth in Dubuque and the opulence of the lead-mining magnate who once owned it. | 2241 Lincoln Ave. | 319/583–2812 or 319/557–9545 | $3.50 | May–Oct., daily 10–5.

The Meadows Golf Club. *Golf Digest* includes this 18-hole course on the west side of Dubuque in its list of good value courses. | 15766 Clover Ln. | 319/583–7385 | Mar.–Dec., daily; Jan.–Feb, Fri.–Sat.

Mines of Spain Recreation Area. A National Historic Landmark, this 1,380-acre park contains a prairie woodland preserve, an interpretive nature center, steep limestone bluffs, nature trails, and the remnants of 1800s-era lead mines. | 8999 Bellevue Heights | 319/556–0620 | Free | Daily.

On the park's high bluffs overlooking the Mississippi River you'll also find the **Julien Dubuque Monument** honoring the city's founder. | Julien Dubuque Dr. | 319/556–0620 | Free | Daily.

Mississippi River Museum. Float on a simulated log raft, pilot a riverboat, and explore a boatbuilding shop as you learn about 300 years of river history in this riverfront museum complex. You may get a little wet and lost in the fog during *River of Dreams,* an atmospheric film (involving split screens and fog machines) that tells the history of life on the river. While you are at the museum be sure to climb aboard the 277-ft Sidewheeler *William M. Black,* which once served as a dredge boat along the river. | 300 3rd St. | 319/557–9545 | $6 | Daily 10–5:30.

Old Shot Tower. A memorial to the munitions industry that flourished here in the early days of Dubuque. | River and Tower Sts. | 319/557–9200 | Free | Daily.

Rustic Hills Carriage Tours. This horse-drawn carriage tour takes in Dubuque's historic attractions, including the Mathias Ham House and Cable Car Square. | 4th and Bluff Sts. | 319/556–6341 | $10 per person; $8 each with 4 people or more; $25 per couple. Maximum of 6 adults per carriage | Daily 10–5.

Spirit of Dubuque. A double-decker paddle wheeler in Ice Harbor, in the Port of Dubuque, offering dinner cruises, dancing, and musical entertainment. | 3rd St. | 319/583–8093 or 800/747–8093 | www.spiritofdubuque.com | $9–$34 | May–Oct., departs from Ice Harbor hourly 10–6:30.

Sundown Mountain Ski Area. You'll find 22 trails through cedar forests and a 475-ft vertical drop (the highest in Iowa) here 5 mi west of town. | 17017 Asbury Rd. | 319/556–6676 or 888/786–3686 | www.webfire.com/sundown | Lift passes $5–$30 | Dec.–Mar.

Town Clock. Originally erected in 1873 atop a building north of Main Street, the clock was moved to the downtown mall in 1971. | 7th and Main St. | 319/557–9200 | Free | Daily.

Trolleys of Dubuque, Inc. Old-fashioned trolleys depart from the welcome center and take you to all the sights of Dubuque. | 400 E. 3rd St., Ice Harbor | 319/582–0077 or 800/408–0077 | $7.50 | Apr.–Oct., daily departure 12:30.

University of Dubuque. A private, coeducational liberal arts university and Presbyterian theological seminary founded in 1852. | 2000 University Ave. | 319/589–3000 or 319/589–3200 | www.dbq.edu | Weekdays tours by appointment.

ON THE CALENDAR
JUNE–SEPT.: *Dubuque . . . And All That Jazz!* A different professional jazz band from the Midwest plays one Friday night during each summer month downtown at Town Clock Plaza off Locust St. | 319/588–9400.

Dining

Betty Jane's Candies. Café. Family-owned and -operated since 1938, this candy shop is famous for homemade chocolates, particularly the "gremlin," a caramel, pecan, and chocolate confection. You can also choose from 66 flavors of homemade ice cream. In addition to this shop 2 mi northwest of downtown there are three others in town which only sell candy. | 3049 Ashbury Rd. | 319/582–4668 | $12–$14/pound | MC, V.

Breitbach's Country Dining. American. This restaurant 20 mi north of town hasn't changed much since its founding in 1852. It looks like a rambling farmhouse straight out of Grant Wood; it's equally homey inside with its old photos, lace curtains, and checkered tablecloths. On the menu: chicken-fried steak, Iowa pork chops with homemade applesauce, and creamy hand-mashed potatoes. | 563 Balltown Rd., Balltown | 319/552–2220 | $8–$10 | No credit cards.

Carlos O'Kelley's. Southwestern. Fajitas, chimichangas, and flavored margaritas are the draw at this eatery just off North Arterial in a new commerical development on the west side of town. Antique banjos and old radios adorn the walls. | 1355 Associates Dr. | 319/583–0088 | $5–$11 | AE, D, DC, MC, V.

Dempsey's Steakhouse. Steak. Much of the art on the walls of this casual, downtown Irish pub/restaurant known for steak and pasta is for sale. Kids' menu. | 395 W. 9th and Bluff Sts. | 319/582–7057 | $9–$16 | AE, MC, V | Closed Sun. No lunch Sat.

Garden Room Café. American/Casual. You can choose from daily soup, salad, and lunch specials here and enjoy the indoor garden underneath a solarium. | 801 Davis Ave. | 319/582–5100 | $5–$7 | MC, V | Closed weekends. No dinner.

Mario's. Italian. Italian opera and movie posters hang throughout this cozy, downtown eatery. House specialties include rich-but-delicious fettuccine alfredo, veal scaloppine, and chicken marsala. Kids' menu. | 1298 Main St. | 319/556–9424 | $7–$20 | AE, DC, MC, V | Closed Sun.

Pickerman's of Dubuque. American/Casual. In the new commercial district in the western part of town, this country-theme establishment serves 12 different warm sandwiches, salads, and soups. | 3301 Pennsylvania Ave. | 319/582–4908 | $5–$6 | No credit cards | Closed Sun.

Yen Ching. Chinese. Lanterns, paper walls, and Asian art set the scene for Mandarin and Hunan fare such as almond chicken, spicy chicken, and perennial favorite Mongolian beef. | 926 Main St. | 319/556–2574 | $7–$10 | AE, D, DC, MC, V | Closed Sun.

Lodging

Best Western Dubuque Inn. This basic motel is on a commercial street 3½ mi from Dubuque's waterfront and 5 mi from the Wacker Plaza, Plaza 20, and Kennedy Mall shopping areas. Restaurant, bar, complimentary breakfast, room service. In-room data ports, some refrigerators and microwaves. Pool. Hot tub, sauna. Business services, airport shuttle, free parking. | 3434 Dodge St. (Hwy. 20) | 319/556–7760 | fax 319/556–4003 | www.best-western.com | 155 rooms | $81–$105 | AE, D, DC, MC, V.

DUBUQUE

INTRO
ATTRACTIONS
DINING
LODGING

Best Western Midway. Rooms are comfortable but unremarkable at this hotel just 1½ mi from the Mississippi. Restaurant, bar, picnic area, complimentary breakfast weekdays, room service. In-room data ports, some refrigerators, cable TV, in-room VCRs (and movies). Pool. Hot tub. Exercise equipment. Business services, airport shuttle. Some pets allowed. | 3100 Dodge St. | 319/557–8000 | fax 319/557–7692 | www.bestwestern.com | 151 rooms | $75–$99 | AE, D, DC, MC, V.

Comfort Inn. This smallish hotel on Dubuque's main drag does a brisk business with tourists on weekends and is primarily filled with businesspeople during the week. It's only a half mile to the Kennedy Mall and less than 3 mi to the big riverboat casinos. Rooms have large work areas for business travelers. Complimentary Continental breakfast. In-room data ports, refrigerators and microwaves in suites, cable TV. Pool. Hot tub. Business services. Pets allowed. | 4055 Dodge St. | 319/556–3006 | fax 319/556–3006 | www.comfortinn.com | 52 rooms, 14 suites | $50 rooms, $65 suites | AE, D, DC, MC, V.

Days Inn. Built against the limestone cliffs of the Mississippi River, this motel has pleasant, unassuming rooms with great water views. Restaurant, bar, picnic area, complimentary Continental breakfast. Refrigerators and microwaves in suites, in-room VCRs available. Pool. Exercise equipment. Business services, airport shuttle. Pets allowed. | 1111 Dodge St. | 319/583–3297 | fax 319/583–5900 | www.daysinn.com | 154 rooms | $55–$75 | AE, D, DC, MC, V.

Four Mounds Inn Bed and Breakfast. On 65 acres of Mississippi bluff land once inhabited by Woodland Indians, this B&B gets its name from the four ancient Native American burial mounds on the property. The mansion itself was designed in 1908 by architect Lawrence Buck in the Mission style. Its only suite has a fireplace and views of the Mississippi River. A cabin built in 1956 is also available for rental. TV in common area. Hiking. Laundry facilities. Business services. No pets. No smoking. | 4900 Peru Rd. | 319/557–7292 | www.fourmounds.com | 5 rooms, 1 suite, 1 cabin | $85–$95 rooms, $125 suite, $150 cabin | AE, D, DC, MC, V.

Hancock House. This meticulously restored lavender Victorian home perches halfway up a bluff in the 11th Street Historic District overlooking downtown. The large front porch sports swings and comfy deck furniture. You'll sleep in wood or brass four-poster beds, look outdoors through lace-draped windows, read by the light of Tiffany lamps, and you may have your own fireplace. The inn's second-floor turret has a great view of the river. Complimentary breakfast. Some in-room hot tubs. No TV in some rooms. | 1105 Grove Terr. | 319/557–8989 | fax 319/583–0813 | www.thehancockhouse.com | 19 rooms | $89–$200 | AE, D, MC, V.

Heartland Inn. This white-stucco motel 5 mi from downtown overlooks the river, and many rooms have spectacular views of the Mississippi and its bluffs. Complimentary Continental breakfast, cable TV. Hot tub, sauna. Laundry facilities. Business services. No pets. | 4025 McDonald Dr. | 319/582–3752 or 800/334–3277 ext. 12 | fax 319/582–0113 | 88 rooms | $65–$80 | AE, D, DC, MC, V.

Holiday Inn. A freestanding fireplace dominates the spacious lobby of this downtown hotel. Some rooms have excellent views of city and the area's surrounding bluffs. Restaurant, bar, room service. Some refrigerators, cable TV. Pool. Hot tub. Exercise equipment. Business services, airport shuttle. Some pets allowed. | 450 Main St. | 319/556–2000 | fax 319/556–2303 | www.basshotels.com/holiday-inn | 173 rooms | $89–$145 | AE, D, DC, MC, V.

Julien Inn. For over 100 years, this grande dame of downtown Dubuque and its ballroom have been host to the area's greatest events, including political rallies, celebrity weddings, and centennial celebrations. Restaurant, bar. Exercise equipment. Business services, airport shuttle. | 200 Main St. | 319/556–4200 or 800/798–7098 | fax 319/582–5023 | 145 rooms | $55–$70 | AE, D, DC, MC, V.

Lighthouse Valleyview Bed and Breakfast. The grounds of this B&B feature an Oriental garden and overlook the Mississippi River. From the top of a 61-ft lighthouse added on to this 1960's house by owners Bill and Jo Ann, you can see up to 48 mi away and into three states—Illinois, Wisconsin, and Iowa. If you stay here you'll be less than 3 mi from the Heritage Nature Trail and about 3½ mi west of downtown. Complimentary breakfast. Refrigerators. Pool. Hot tub, sauna. Gym. Library. No pets. | 15937 Lore Mound Rd. | 319/583–7327 or 800/407–7023 | www.lighthousevalleyview.com | 3 rooms, 1 two-bedroom suite | $75–$90 rooms, $150 suite | AE, D, MC, V.

Mandolin Inn. Named for a stained-glass picture depicting St. Cecilia, the patron saint of musicians, holding a mandolin, this former home of financier Nicholas Schrup was built in 1908 and today is filled with the sounds of classical music. You can enjoy views of the bluff from the Queen Anne porch which has Italian tile and wicker furniture. Breakfast is served in the dining room which is filled with oil paintings and an Italian-tile fireplace. Complimentary Continental breakfast. Cable TV, some in-room VCRs. No pets. No smoking. | 199 Loras Blvd. | 319/556–0069 or 800/524–7986 | www.mandolininn.com | 7 rooms, 1 two-bedroom suite | $75 rooms with shared bath, $95–$125 rooms with private bath, $135 suite | AE, D, MC, V.

Redstone Inn. Built in 1894 by a prominent Dubuque industrialist, this Victorian mansion offers 15 rooms furnished with antiques and marble fireplaces. The façade is clad in red quartz from local quarries and Cable Car square is just a few blocks away. Complimentary Continental breakfast. In-room data ports, cable TV. Hot tub. Business services. No smoking. | 504 Bluff St. | 319/582–1894 | fax 319/582–1893 | 15 rooms | $75–$175 | AE, MC, V.

Richard's House Bed and Breakfast. This 1883 Victorian mansion in Jackson Park has its original stained-glass windows and other details. In addition to antique furnishings, most rooms have working fireplaces and private bathrooms. Complimentary breakfast. No air-conditioning, no room phones, no TV. Laundry facilities. No pets. | 1492 Locust St. | 319/557–1492 | 6 rooms, 1 suite | $45–$65 rooms with shared bath, $60–$90 rooms with private bath, $95–$105 library suite, $160 2–room suite | AE, D, DC, MC, V.

Super 8. This simple but adequate motel is on the west edge of town, away from the river and closer to Interstate 80. Complimentary Continental breakfast. Cable TV. Business services. Some pets allowed. | 2730 Dodge St. | 319/582–8898 | fax 319/582–8898 | www.super8.com | 61 rooms | $45–$56 | AE, D, DC, MC, V.

DYERSVILLE

INTRO
ATTRACTIONS
DINING
LODGING

DYERSVILLE

MAP 3, H3

(Nearby town also listed: Dubuque)

Remember the line from the movie *Field of Dreams*, when Ray Liotta asks Kevin Costner, "Is this Heaven?" In reality, it was Dyersville, Iowa. You can still bat at the field carved in the corn, just as it appeared in the 1989 film. Dyersville also carries the self-bestowed title of Farm Toy Capital of the World, because manufacturers like Ertl, Scale Models, Spec Cast, and Toy Factory are here.

Information: **Dyersville Area Chamber of Commerce** | 1100 16th Ave. Ct. SE, 52040 | 319/875–2311 | www.dyersville.org.

Attractions

Field of Dreams **Movie Site.** The 1989 Academy Award–nominated movie was shot here 3 mi northeast of town. Run the bases, play catch, or cheer from the bleachers, just as Kevin Costner did. Bring your own bat and glove. | 29001 Lansing Rd. | 319/875–6012 | Free | Apr.–Nov., daily 9–6.

National Farm Toy Museum. All the farm toys you vroom-vroom-vroomed with as a child are available to play with once again on the front porch of this farmhouse located at the intersection of U.S. Highway 20 and State Highway 136. | 1110 16th Ave. SE | 319/875–2727 | www.dyersville.org | $4 | Daily 8–7.

St. Francis Xavier Basilica. One of only 33 basilicas in the country, this is one of the finest examples of Gothic architecture in the Midwest. It's at the corner of 3rd and 1st Sts. near the park. | 104 3rd St. SW | 319/875–7325 | Donations accepted | Daily 8–5. Tours by appointment ($1 per person) or self-guided tour (free).

ON THE CALENDAR
AUG.: *Field of Dreams Festival*. Run bases in the field where dreams really do come true. | 319/875–6012 or 800/443–8981.

Dining
The Palace. American/Casual. This old-fashioned saloon and bar in the heart of downtown is popular for such comfort food as roasted chicken, stews, and soups. In fair weather on Friday nights you can grill your own steaks outside on the deck. | 149 1st Ave. East | 319/875–2284 | $4–$6 | No credit cards.

Lodging
Comfort Inn Dyersville. This chain hotel is in a commercial area right off Highway 20 at exit 294 about 1 mi south of downtown. Complimentary Continental breakfast. Some in-room data ports, some microwaves, some refrigerators, cable TV. Pool. Hot tub. Gym. Video games. Laundry facilities. Pets allowed (fee). | 527 16th Ave. SE | 319/875–7700 or 800/228–5150 | www.comfortinnhotels.com | 46 rooms, 4 suites | $60–$87 rooms, $80–$148 suites | AE, D, DC, MC, V.

ELK HORN

MAP 3, C4

(Nearby towns also listed: Atlantic, Avoca, Anita, Walnut)

One look at the Elk Horn's 60-ft-tall imported Danish windmill and you know what this small town and its even smaller sister city Kimballton are all about. The site of the largest Danish rural settlement in the United States, these villages—founded in the late 1800s—proudly pay homage to their heritage with Scandinavian attractions, food, crafts, and festivals.

Information: Danish Windmill and Welcome Center | 4038 Main St., 51531 | 800/451–7960.

Attractions
Bedstemor's House. Listed on the National Register of Historic Places and operated by the Danish Immigrant Museum, this 1908 house reflects how life was lived by a Danish immigrant grandmother and her family during the early 20th century. | 2105 College St. | 712/764–7001 | $2 | May–Sept., Mon.–Sat. 10–4, Sun. 1–4.

Danish Immigrant Museum. This Elk Horn museum explores the history of the region's Danish community. | 2212 Washington St. | 712/764–7001 | $3 | Memorial Day–Labor Day, Mon.–Sat. 9–6, Sun. noon–5; Sept.–May, Mon.–Sat. 9–5, Sun. noon–5.

Danish Windmill Museum. You can take a guided tour of this 60-ft windmill built in 1848 in Denmark and brought to Elk Horn in the 1970s and learn how it uses wind power to grind wheat and rye. | 4038 Main St. | 712/764–7472 or 800/451–7960 | $2 | Memorial Day–Labor Day, Mon.–Sat. 8–7, Sun. 10–7; Sept.–May, Mon.–Sat. 9–5, Sun. noon–5.

ON THE CALENDAR
MAY: *Tivoli Fest*. This downtown Memorial Day festival is named after Denmark's Tivoli Gardens and includes a parade, entertainment, crafts, and such Danish food as *aebleskiver* (pancakes) and *medisterpolse* (sausage). | 800/451–7960.

OCT.: *State Hand Corn Husking Contest.* State and national competitors try their hands at husking corn the old-fashioned way in a field just outside Kimballton the second weekend in October. | 712/773–2117.

NOV.: *Julefest.* The weekend after Thanksgiving brings a Danish Christmas with displays of Danish crafts and food in Elk Horn and neighboring Kimballton. | 800/451–7960.

Dining

Danish Inn. Danish. This low-key restaurant near the windmill serves a daily buffet with American and Danish food. | 4116 S. Main St. | 712/764–4251 | $6–13 | No credit cards | Closed Mon.

Simply Sweet. American. This lunch spot just north of the windmill serves homemade soups, bread, pie, ice cream, and candies. | 2104 Elm St. | 712/764–4030 | $2–$4 | MC, V | Closed weekends. No dinner.

Village Texaco and Café. American. This gas station/café serves lunch and dinner specials, from soup and a sandwich to a beef-and-noodle dinner. | 4020 Main St. | 712/764–2816 | $7–$14 | AE, D, DC, MC, V.

Lodging

AmericInn of Elkhorn. Rooms and suites are decorated with a Scandinavian touch at this redbrick motel ½ mi from downtown. Kids under 12 stay free. Complimentary Continental breakfast. In-room data ports, some in-room hot tubs, cable TV. Pool. | 4037 Main St. | 712/764–4000 or 800/634–3444 | 30 rooms, 3 whirlpool suites | $54–$116 | AE, D, DC, MC, V.

Hansen's Kro. You'll be served a full Danish breakfast with Danish pancakes, meats, and cheeses at this downtown B&B in a modern 1970s house filled with Danish pictures, books, and maps. Complimentary breakfast. Cable TV. | 2113 Park St. | 712/764–2052 or 800/606–2052 | 1 room, 1 suite | $55 | No credit cards.

Joy's Morning Glory B&B. Breakfast (Danish, of course) is served in the dining room, on the porch, or in the back garden of this 1912 wood home. There's a windmill in the backyard and rockers on the front porch. Complimentary breakfast. TV and phone in common area. No kids. | 4308 Main St. | 712/764–5631 or 888/776–5631 | 3 rooms (with shared bath) | $45–$60 | No credit cards | Closed Jan.–Feb.

Our House B&B. This 1930s-style white wooden cottage has a quaint front porch and is right downtown. Complimentary breakfast. Phone in common area, in-room cable TV. | 2007 Washington St. | 712/764–4111 | 1 room | $45 | No credit cards.

EMMETSBURG

MAP 3, C2

(Nearby towns also listed: Spencer, West Bend)

This farming community in northwest Iowa was settled by Irish immigrants in search of freedom and financial success in the mid-1800s. Their community was named after Robert Emmet, an Irish patriot and champion of human rights. Today Emmetsburg continues to celebrate its heritage as the "Emerald Island of Iowa." A statue of Robert Emmet stands in the courthouse square and you can kiss a Blarney stone nearby.

Information: Emmetsburg Chamber of Commerce | 1013 Broadway, 50536 | 712/852–2283.

Attractions

Kearney State Park. On the shores of the 1,000-acre Five Island Lake, this park is just 1 mi north of downtown and is great for camping, picnicking, and fishing. | N. Lawler St. | 712/852–4030 | www.state.ia.us/parks | Free | Daily.

Victorian Museum on Main. This Victorian home was built in 1883 as a wedding gift from a prominent businessman to his daughter. Its woodwork and lead and stained-glass windows are particularly fine. | 1703 E. Main St. | 712/852–2283 | Donations accepted | Call for appointment.

ON THE CALENDAR

MAR.: *St. Patrick's Day Celebration.* Irish Mass and Irish stew are a small part of this weeklong celebration. A member of the Irish Parliament is always welcomed as the parade grand marshal. Visitors can contribute to the nonprofit St. Patrick's Association and receive a commemorative "can of blarney" and an official "100% Irish" membership card. | 712/852–4326.

DEC.: *Scandinavian Tea.* The Lutheran church hosts this holiday tea, complete with costumes, handcrafted items, and traditional Scandinavian foods. | 712/852–4450.

Dining

Dublin's Food and Spirits. American/Casual. This casual pub 1 mi west of downtown features seafood sautées, steaks, and a big selection of Australian, American, and Chilean wines as well as 50 beers. There's a built-in antique liquor case in the bar area. | 3639 450th Ave. | 712/852–2214 | $6–$18 | AE, MC, V | Closed Sun., Mon. No lunch.

Lodging

Ima Suburban Motel. This drive-up motel with basic rooms and free popcorn and fresh coffee in the office is 1½ mi northwest of town and five minutes from Five Island Lake. Cable TV. | 3635 450th. Ave. | 712/852–2626 | fax 712/852–2821 | 27 rooms | $43–$55 | AE, D, MC, V.

Lucky Charm Motel. This single-story motel is 500 yards of the Des Moines River and seven blocks from Five Island Lake. For hunters there's a game room in back. Some refrigerators, some in-room hot tubs, cable TV. Laundry facilities. Pets allowed. | 3681 450th Ave. | 712/852–3640 | 12 rooms | $34 | AE, D, MC, V.

Queen Marie Victorian B&B. An Emmetsburg lumberman built this Victorian with its carved oak staircase and wide front porch in 1890. The inn is in a quiet residential neighborhood within easy walking distance of Five Islands Lake and downtown antiques shops. Complimentary breakfast. Cable TV, no room phones. No smoking. | 707 Harrison St. | 712/852–4700 or 800/238–9485 | fax 712/852–3090 | www.nwiowabb.com | 5 rooms (2 with shared bath) | $45–$55 | MC, V.

ESTHERVILLE

MAP 3, C1

(Nearby towns also listed: Okoboji, Spirit Lake)

This community along the Iowa–Minnesota border is named after Esther Ridley, who in the early 1860s was the first white woman to settle in these parts. Most people in the community can trace their roots to Scandinavia, Germany, or Ireland and still make their living on the farm, or in the related meatpacking industry. The biggest day in local history was May 10, 1879, when a meteor weighing 437 pounds fell to the earth in a farm field not far from town. Pieces of the meteor are on display at the local library, and at museums around the world.

Information: Estherville Chamber of Commerce | 801 Central Ave., 51334 | 712/362–3541 | echamber@ncn.net | www.ncn.net/echamber.

Attractions

Fort Defiance State Park. Named for the military fort that once stood nearby, this small prairie with native grasses and flowers is 2 mi west of town. | 1500 Harpen St. | 712/362–2078 | www.state.ia.us/parks | Free | Daily.

Peterson Point Historic Farmsite. At this historic farmstead 12 mi southeast of Estherville you'll get to see and touch a bit of the pioneer past. The original 1866 log cabin and 1897 barn built by Norwegian immigrants have been restored. Other buildings include a blacksmithery and a carpenter shop. | County Rd. N40 (east of Wallingford) | 712/362–3541 | Free | Daily.

ON THE CALENDAR

FEB.: *Winter Sports Festival.* The Snow and Ice Sculpture Contest is the most popular activity celebrating the cold at this downtown festival. | 712/362–3541.
AUG.: *Sweet Corn Days.* A downtown carnival and festival celebrates the ripening of sweet corn which is sold by farmers throughout the area. | 712/362–3541.

Dining

Village Wok. Chinese. The only Chinese restaurant in town is just ½ mi north of downtown. You can choose from a lunch or dinner buffet or select from the menu. | 6 N. 16th St. | 712/362–4430 | $4–$8 | No credit cards | Closed Sun.

Lodging

Super 8 Estherville. This chain motel is right on Highway 9 on the eastern edge of town, 10 blocks from downtown. You can help yourself to coffee, tea, and hot chocolate in the lobby and there's a tanning bed in the weight room. Some microwaves, some refrigerators, some in-room hot tubs, cable TV. Sauna. Gym. | 1919 Central Ave. | 712/362–2400 | www.super8.com | 29 rooms, 5 suites | $50–$55 rooms, $53–$86 suites | AE, D, DC, MC, V.

FAIRFIELD

MAP 3, G5

(Nearby towns also listed: Mount Pleasant, Ottumwa)

Fairfield is like many pleasant Iowa communities—its population is small, about 10,000, and its economy is dependent upon agriculture and its supporting industries. The first white settlers came to this area in the 1840s, and the first Iowa State Fair was held here in 1854. The community is well preserved, and more than a dozen of its buildings are on the National Register of Historic Places. What's surprising about Fairfield is that it's home to the Maharishi University of Management, which incorporates transcendental meditation into its daily curriculum.

Information: **Fairfield Chamber of Commerce** | 204 W. Broadway, 52556 | 515/472–2111 | fbphipps@fairfieldiowa.com | www.fairfieldiowa.com.

Attractions

Jefferson County Park. Hiking and biking trails draw most visitors to this park. There's also a nature center and aquarium. | 2003 Libertyville Rd. | 515/472–4421 | Free | Daily.

Maharishi University of Management. Founded in 1971, this university incorporates a holistic approach to education of the mind and spirit. The school's goal is to graduate students able to manage their lives successfully in both the public and private spheres. About 500 students from more than 90 countries work toward undergraduate or advanced degrees. | 1000 N. 4th St. | 515/472–1110 | www.mum.edu | Free | Weekdays 8–5.

Water Works Park. This city park on the north edge of town contains the Bonnifield Cabin, the 1838 log home of the country's first white settlers. | On B St., north edge of town | 319/472–6193 | Free | Daily.

JUNE: *Vintage Dodge Power Wagon Rally.* Fans of Dodge trucks demonstrate the vehicles' power in this three-day event. | 515/472–4665.

NOV.: *Holiday Lighting on the Square.* Thousands of people turn out the night after Thanksgiving as the town is lit for the holidays and dedicated to a special individual of the community. | 515/472–2111.

Dining

India Cafe. Indian. This restaurant in the center of town serves authentic Indian vegetarian and meat dishes. | 50 W. Burlington St. | 515/472–1792 | $6–$8 | AE, MC, V.

Lodging

Best Western. This basic lodging is centrally located between the area's largest parks. It's 2 mi from Jefferson County Park, 15 mi from Lake Darling, and 20 mi from Lacey-Keosauqua State Park. Restaurant, complimentary Continental breakfast. Cable TV. Pool. Hot tub. Some pets allowed. | 2200 W. Burlington St. | 515/472–2200 | fax 515/472–7642 | www.bestwestern.com | 52 rooms | $62–$75 | AE, D, DC, MC, V.

Economy Inn. Simple pine pieces furnish the guest rooms and lobby of this downtown motel. Cable TV. | 2701 W. Burlington St. | 515/472–4161 | fax 515/472–4161 | 42 rooms | $43 | AE, D, MC, V.

Super 8. This single-story motel is 1½ mi west of downtown in a commercial area right on Highway 34. Complimentary Continental breakfast. In-room phones, cable TV. Pool. | 3001 W. Burlington Ave. | 641/469–2000 or 800/800–8000 | www.super8.com | 45 rooms | $69–$90 | AE, D, DC, MC, V.

FORT DODGE

MAP 3, D3

(Nearby towns also listed: Humboldt, Webster City)

The United States Dragoons, the nation's first mounted military units, first explored this area in 1835 and built a military fort here a few years later. Although original structures no longer exist, a museum, frontier village, and walking tour tell the history of life here in the 19th century. Today Fort Dodge is a tranquil agricultural community surrounded by some of the most fertile farmland in the world, where people celebrate the successes of their high-school basketball team, good hunting and fishing, and a bountiful harvest.

Information: **Fort Dodge Convention and Visitors Bureau** | 1406 Central Ave., 50501 | 515/573–4282 or 888/573–4282 | www.fortdodgecvb.com.

Attractions

Blanden Memorial Art Museum. Founded in 1930 by a former Fort Dodge mayor in memory of his wife, this was Iowa's first art museum. Its impressive collection includes Oriental, African, European, and early 20th-century American works by such masters as Calder and Henry Moore. | 920 3rd Ave. S | 515/573–2316 | Free | Tues., Wed., Fri. 10–5; Thurs. 10–8:30, weekends 1–5.

Dolliver Memorial State Park. The highlight of this park, 10 mi south of Fort Dodge, is a group of sandstone formations called the "Copperas beds" which include a 100-ft bluff on Prairie Creek that is more than 150 million years old. | 2757 Dolliver Park Ave. | 515/359–2539 | www.state.ia.us/parks | Free | Daily.

Fort Museum and Frontier Village. This impressive recreation of Fort Williams, an 1860s garrison meant to protect settlers from Indians, includes an elaborate frontier village with seven original buildings and five replicas; displays of American Indian, pioneer, and military artifacts; and the National Museum of Veterinary Medicine. | Business Hwy. 20 and Museum Rd. | 515/573–4231 | www.dodgenet.com | $4 | May–Oct., daily 9–6; Nov.–Apr. by appointment.

After visiting the fort you might want to follow the **Dragoon Trail,** a scenic drive along the Des Moines River that begins at the Fort Museum and follows the path of the U.S. Dragoons followed as they explored this area in 1835. Upon completion of their 1,100-mi march, the Dragoons recommended what is today the city of Fort Dodge as one of two sites for future military posts. | Free | Daily.

John F. Kennedy Memorial Park. Swimming, fishing, and a golf course 5 mi north of town. | Rte. P56 | 515/576–4258 | Free | Daily.

Twin Lakes State Park. This small, heavily-wooded, 100-acre state park is on the shore of one of two natural lakes about 30 mi west of town. | Rte. 124 | 712/657–8712 | www.state.ia.us/parks | Free | Daily.

Webster County Courthouse. This 1902 building, now on the National Registry of Historic Places, has lovely marble wainscoting, murals, ornate plaster work, and oak furnishings. | 701 Central Ave. | 515/573–7175 | Free | Weekdays 8–5.

ON THE CALENDAR

JUNE: *Frontier Days.* The days of the dragoons come to life at the Fort Museum. | 515/573–4231.

SEPT.: *Skydive Convention.* Learn about skydiving, try it yourself, or just watch others at the Fort Dodge Regional Airport. | 515/955–5500.

OCT.: *Applefest.* Take a hayrack ride to a giant pumpkin patch, wander through a cornfield maze, visit a quilt show, or sample apple pies, caramel apples, apple crisp, apple preserves, and homemade apple cider at Community Apple Orchards in the northwest corner of the Fort Dodge airport. | 515/573–8212.

Dining

Marvin Gardens. American. This restaurant was named and decorated with Monopoly in mind and you'll find paraphernalia from the game throughout the dining room. Steaks are the main draw here, but the menu also offers sandwiches, seafood, and pasta. Sunday brunch. | 809 Central Ave. | 515/955–5333 | $5–$16 | AE, D, DC, MC, V.

Mineral City. American. This eatery offers steak, pasta, chops, and sandwiches served amid mining artifacts and old photos of miners which reflect the area's history as the biggest supplier of gypsum in the United States. Sunday brunch features the Cardiff Giant Skillet. | 2621 5th Ave. S | 515/955–8514 | $6–$18 | AE, D, DC, MC, V.

Lodging

Best Western Starlite Village. This otherwise unassuming hotel's main selling point is its Olympic-size indoor pool. If you stay here you'll be 3 mi from the airport and 8 mi from the Fort Museum. Restaurant, bar, room service. Cable TV. Pool. Hot tub. | 1518 3rd Ave. NW | 515/573–7177 | fax 515/573–3999 | www.bestwestern.com | 120 rooms | $62–$70 | AE, D, DC, MC, V.

Budget Host Inn Ft. Dodge. This chain hotel is next to the Fort Dodge Museum, off Highway 169 2 mi east of downtown. Restaurant. In-room data ports, some microwaves, some refrigerators, some in-room hot tubs. Pool. Hot tub. Gym. Video games. Laundry facilities, laundry service. Pets allowed. | 116 Kenyon Rd. | 515/955–8501 | www.budgethostinn.com | 109 rooms, 1 suite | $47–$55 rooms, $90 suite | AE, D, DC, MC, V.

Comfort Inn. This hotel is just across the street from the Crossroads Mall, one of the area's larger shopping malls, and 1½ mi from downtown Fort Dodge. Complimentary Continental breakfast. Some refrigerators, cable TV. Pool. Hot tub. | 2938 5th Ave. S | 515/573–3731 | fax 515/573–3751 | www.comfortinn.com | 48 rooms | $51 | AE, D, DC, MC, V.

Holiday Inn. This chain hotel is just a mile from downtown Fort Dodge, within easy walking distance of a number of popular restaurants, and just six blocks from the city's Fort Dodge historic site. Restaurant, bar, room service. Cable TV. Pool. Hot tub. Playground. | 2001 U.S. 169 S | 515/955–3621 | fax 515/955–3643 | www.basshotels.com/holiday-inn | 94 rooms | $65 | AE, D, DC, MC, V.

Towers Motel. This single-story motel is 2 mi west of downtown, ½ mi east of the Ft. Dodge Museum, and 1½ mi north of the Ft. Dodge Fairgrounds. Refrigerators, cable TV. Laundry facilities. Pets allowed (fee). | 324 Kenyon Rd. (Hwy. 20 W) | 515/955–8575 | 50 rooms | $32 | AE, D, MC, V.

FORT MADISON

MAP 3, G6

(Nearby towns also listed: Burlington, Keokuk)

Fort Madison was the first military post in the upper Mississippi region and home to the 1st Regiment U.S. Infantry from 1808 to 1813. In 1813 the fort was abandoned after harassment from Sauk Indian chief Black Hawk and his men and it wasn't until 1833 that settlers returned and a town began to grow here. The old fort was not excavated until the 1960s; remains were found when digging for a new parking garage began. Several small manufacturing plants flourish here today alongside a riverboat casino, and the state penitentiary is here as well.

Information: **River Bend Regional Tourism Bureau** | 933 Ave. H, Box 425, 52627 | 319/372–5472 or 800/210–8687.

Attractions

Catfish Bend Riverboat Casino. This 19th-century stern-wheel riverboat is now a full-service casino. | 902 Riverview Park | 319/372–2946 | Free | Mon.–Tues. 8 AM–2 AM, Wed.–Sun. 24 hrs.

Central Park. On 10th Street and Avenue E, this manicured public park with a gazebo and fountain was funded and built in 1889 to rid the town of the unsavory behavior the area had once attracted. Today arts-and-crafts festivals are held here and every Sunday evening the city band plays under the gazebo. | 10th St. and Ave. E | 319/372–5472 | Free | Daily dawn–dusk.

Flood Museum. Through TV footage, newspaper clippings, and photos this museum focuses on some recent history—the Mississippi flood of 1993. | 814 10th St. | 319/372–7661 | $2 | Memorial Day–Labor Day, Wed.–Sat. noon–4.

Lee County Courthouse. Built in the early 1800s, this is the oldest Iowa courthouse in continuous use. | 701 Ave. F | 319/372–3523 | Free | Weekdays 8–4:30.

Old Settler's Park. The site of the annually held Christmas Walk, this public park has a replica of the original copper-top gazebo. | 5th St. and Ave. D | 319/372–5472 | Free | Daily, dawn–dusk.

River View Park. This park on the eastern edge of town offers river access, a marina, and an ice-skating rink. | At junction of Hwy. 61 and 6th St. | 319/372–7700 | Free | May–Sept., daily.

Inside the park you'll also find **Old Fort Madison,** a replica of the first military fort west of the Mississippi. There are daily military reenactments in summer and you can participate in hands-on learning activities like candle making and basketry. | 319/372–6318 | www.fort-madison.net/oldfort/ | $3 | Memorial Day–Labor Day, daily; Sept.–Oct., weekends.

Rodeo Park. This 250-acre park 1 mi north of town offers hiking trails, picnic areas, and primitive campsites. It's also home to the Fort Madison Tri-State Rodeo each September. | Rte. 88 | 319/372–7700 | Free | Apr.–Oct., daily.

Sante Fe Depot Historic Museum and Complex. Donated by the Sante Fe and Burlington Railroad, this museum houses 100 years of railroad history and the world's largest Sheaffer pen collection. | 9th and Ave. H | 319/372–7661 | $2 | Apr.–Sept., daily.

Santa Fe Railway Bridge. This bridge from the 1830s on the east edge of town is the largest doubledeck swingspan bridge in the country and turns on its axis. It's still functioning as a railway and an automobile bridge and there's a $1 toll as you cross from Iowa into Illinois. | East edge of town | 800/210–8687 | $1 | Daily.

Shimek State Forest. These 10,000 acres 25 mi west of Fort Madison belong to the last standing uncut forest in Iowa. | Rte. 2 | 319/878–3811 | Free | Daily.

ON THE CALENDAR

SEPT.: *Tri-State Rodeo.* Big-name country-and-western recording artists perform at this event which boasts roping and riding events, a parade with hundreds of horses and riders, food booths, a beauty pageant, and historical reenactments. | 319/372–2550 or 800/369–3211.

OCT.: *Old Fort Candlelight Tour.* Characters from Old Fort Madison's past come to life by candlelight. | 319/372–5472.

FORT MADISON

INTRO
ATTRACTIONS
DINING
LODGING

Dining

Ivy Bake Shop. Café. Breakfast treats at this gourmet bakery and café include blackberry scones, rhubarb brunch cake, cinnamon and pecan rolls, and a variety of muffins. Lunches feature quiches, pasta dishes, salads, soups, and sandwiches such as chicken salad or fresh veggies with basil pesto mayonnaise on homemade white bread. You can sip specialty coffee drinks, homemade lemonade, and brewed teas all day on the screened-in porch along Avenue G. | 622 7th St. | 319/372–9939 | $1–$6 | No credit cards | No dinner.

Lodging

Ivy Manor Bed & Breakfast. Rooms in this ivy-covered downtown 1860s house two blocks from the Mississippi River have Victorian wallpaper, walnut antiques, and white wicker furniture. In summer the flower garden next to the pool is full of pink begonias which can be seen from the breakfast sunporch and it's worth noting that baked goods come from the owner's Ivy Bake Shop. Complimentary Continental breakfast. Some room phones, TV in common area. Pool. No pets. No kids under 12. No smoking. | 804 Ave. F | 319/372–7380 | 3 rooms | $85 | AE, MC, V.

Kingsley Inn. This 1860s inn (with a modern two-story smoked-glass atrium addition) overlooks the Mississippi River and is just 100 yards from Old Fort Madison. Inside you'll find a mix of antiques, antique reproductions, and modern furnishings. Complimentary breakfast. Microwaves available, cable TV. Some in-room hot tubs. | 707 Ave. H | 319/372–7074 or 800/441–2327 | fax 319/372–7096 | www.kingsleyinn.com | 14 rooms | $75–$135 | AE, D, DC, MC, V.

Madison Inn. The owners' vacation photos adorn this homey mom-and-pop motel with pine furnishings and all queen-size beds 1½ mi east of downtown. Complimentary Continental breakfast. In-room data ports, cable TV. Business services. Some pets allowed (fee). | 3440 Ave. L | 319/372–7740 or 800/728–7316 | fax 319/372–1315 | www.madisoninn.com | 20 rooms | $45–$50 | AE, D, DC, MC, V.

GARNER

(Nearby towns also listed: Clear Lake, Mason City)

Named after a civil engineer with the Rock Island Railroad, Garner is most famous for three brothers who once lived here—Henry, August, and Fred Duesenberg. In the 1880s the brothers opened a bicycle shop in Garner and established a large bike-riding club. The brothers soon became interested in the horseless carriage and eventually built their own line of automobiles bearing their surname. Garner's present-day economy has more to do with corn production than automobiles.

Information: Garner Chamber of Commerce | 415 State St., 50438 | 515/923–3993.

Attractions

Pilot Knob State Park and Recreation Area. Pilot Knob is the second-highest point in Iowa. Its 1,450-ft elevation allowed early pioneers to map a path across the plains (hence its name) and today provides great views of the most fertile farming region in the world. The park also includes a 4-acre floating bog called (ominously enough) Dead Man's Lake, which is home to dozens of flowering plant and waterfowl species. The park is about 15 mi north of Garner. | Rte. 332 near Forest City | 515/581–4835 | www.state.ia.us/parks | Free | Daily.

Rice Lake State Park. This park 20 mi north of Garner surrounds Rice Lake and contains a nice picnic shelter and lots of open areas for Frisbee. | 2148 340th St. | 515/581–4835 | Free | Daily.

ON THE CALENDAR
JULY: *Duesey Days Celebration.* Three days of food, music, and classic car shows. | 515/923–3993.

Dining

Candy's Tea House. American. This downtown restaurant resembles an English cottage and specializes in tea luncheons, but also serves salads, hot dishes such as baked chicken breast with creamy asparagus sauce, soups, and homemade pies and cakes. Groups of eight or more can reserve two weeks in advance to have dinner here on any evening year-round except Sunday. | 315 Maben Ave. | 641/923–2670 | Reservations essential | $7–$9 | No credit cards | Closed Sun., Mon., and Fri.; closed Sat.–Mon. June–Sept. No dinner Oct.–May.

Lodging

R-Motel. This two-building motel at the junction of Highways 18 and 69, in a commerical district less than a mile from downtown, is the only lodging in town. It is 7 mi west of the closest point of Clear Lake. Cable TV. Pets allowed. | 785 Hwy. 18 W | 641/923–2823 | 21 rooms | $30–$45 | AE, D, MC, V.

GRINNELL

(Nearby towns also listed: Marshalltown, Newton)

In its early days in the mid-1850s, Grinnell was an unofficial stop on the Underground Railroad. The town has twice been listed in Norman Crampton's book, *The 100 Best Small Towns in America,* perhaps because of its tree-lined streets, historic homes, and the good reputation of Grinnell College.

Information: **Grinnell Area Chamber of Commerce** | 833 4th Ave., Box 538, 50112 | 515/236-6555 | www.padiowa.org.

Attractions

Brenton Bank—Poweshiek County. This 1914 bank was designed by renowned architect Louis Sullivan and is now listed on the National Register of Historic Places. | 833 4th Ave. | 515/236-7575 | Free | Weekdays 9–5.

Carroll Pumpkin Farm. This working farm north of town has special weekend events including hay wagon rides, a corn maze, pumpkin catapults, and cider-making demonstrations. | 224 400th Ave. | 515/236-7043 | $3.50 | Oct., Mon.–Sat. 10–7, Sun. 1–7.

Grinnell College. This private, coeducational college was founded in 1846 and has around 1,300 students. Grinnell stresses imaginative, analytical approaches to teaching and studying the liberal arts. | 1233 Park St. | 515/269-4000 | www.grinnell.edu | Free | Daily.

Grinnell Historical Museum. This Victorian mansion displays memorabilia from J. B. Grinnell, the town founder, who was famously told by the journalist Horace Greely, "Go West, young man, go West—and grow up with the country!" Other exhibits document the life and times of another well-known local son, Billy "the Bird Man" Robinson, who was an aviation pioneer. | 1125 Broad St. | 515/236-3252 | Donations accepted | June–Aug., Tues.–Sun. 1–4; Sept.–May, Sat. 1–4.

Rock Creek State Park. With more than 600 acres, Rock Creek Lake is the third-largest lake in Iowa under state stewardship. Its 15 mi of shoreline include many sandy beaches and there's good swimming and fishing. | 5627 Rock Creek E | 515/236-3722 | www.state.ia.us/parks | Free | Daily.

ON THE CALENDAR

SEPT.: *Happy Days.* This downtown, Labor Day weekend festival includes sidewalk sales, a carnival, and food booths. | 319/372-5472.

Dining

Depot Crossing. American. You can get anything from sandwiches to steaks but the pork scaloppine is especially popular at this converted 1893 railroad depot. Chandeliers now hang from the high vaulted ceilings and old photos of trains and depots adorn the walls. | 1014 3rd Ave. | 515/236-6886 | $12–$17 | AE, D, MC, V.

Kelcy's. American. This homey place sports bright, flowered wallpaper, lace curtains, and plants, and offers traditional American cuisine from steaks to sandwiches and salads. Be sure to try the grilled apricot pork chop. | 812 6th Ave. | 515/236-3132 | $10–$14 | D, MC, V | Closed Sun.

Lodging

Carriage House B&B. This Victorian B&B with a wraparound porch is right next to Grinnell College and within walking distance of downtown shops and restaurants. Complimentary breakfast. In-room TVs. Some in-room hot tubs. | 1133 Broad St. | 515/236-7520 | 5 rooms | $50–$70 | MC, V.

Clayton Farms B&B. This working farm 10 minutes from town has a pond for fishing or paddling around and 2,000 acres for hunting. Complimentary breakfast. TV in common area. Pond. Boating, fishing. | 621 Newburg Rd. | 515/236-3011 | 3 rooms (2 with shared bath) | $60–$70 | MC, V | Closed Jan.–Mar.

Days Inn. This white stucco hotel with a red-tile roof is just off Interstate 80, on a commercial strip 2 mi south of town. Complimentary Continental breakfast. Cable TV. Pool. Pets allowed (fee). | 1902 West St. | 515/236-6710 | fax 515/236-5783 | www.daysinn.com | 41 rooms | $55 | AE, D, DC, MC, V.

Super 8. Another chain motel just off Interstate 80 2 mi south of town. Complimentary Continental breakfast. Cable TV. Some pets allowed. | 2111 West St. S | 515/236–7888 | fax 515/236–7888 | www.super8.com | 53 rooms | $58–$62 | AE, D, DC, MC, V.

HAMPTON

(Nearby town also listed: Waverly)

This predominantly rural northern Iowa community, the seat of Franklin County since 1856, was hit hard by the agriculture crisis of the 1980s but has bounced back since establishing a cottage industry base, with more than 150 specialty shops in the community. The Hampton Main Street Association is active in historic preservation, and a number of events support the fund-raising efforts that make this preservation possible.

Information: Hampton Area Chamber of Commerce | 5 1st St. SW, 50441 | 515/456–5668 | www.hamptoniowa.org.

Attractions

Beed's Lake State Park. This state park just outside of town contains a 170-ft spillway of multicolored stone, which cascades water through a dam and gristmill. There's a sand beach to one side of the spillway that's perfect for swimming. | 1422 165th St. | 515/456–2047 | www.state.ia.us/parks | Free | Daily.

Midwest Prairie Candles. This candle-making factory is one of 19 cottage industries on Main Street. | 1518 Rte. 65 N | 515/456–4515 | Free | Weekdays 9–5, Sat. 9–4.

ON THE CALENDAR
JUNE: *Main Street Car Show.* More than 20 classes of vintage cars on display downtown. | 515/456–5668.
AUG.: *Sister Friend Weekend.* A weekend of events—such as garden lunches, yoga classes, and wine tastings—designed specifically for women of all ages. | 515/456–5668.

Dining

Betty's Cafe. American. Homemade mashed potatoes, gravy, pies, and breads are served with midwestern friendliness at simple booths and counter seats at this downtown restaurant. | 19 N. Federal St. | 515/456–4233 | $4–$8 | No credit cards | Closed Sun.

Lodging

AmericInn. Rooms are simple but adequate and there's a game room with a pool table in this chain motel in downtown Hampton. Complimentary Continental breakfast. Cable TV. Pool. Hot tub, sauna. | 702 Central Ave. W | 515/456–5559 | fax 515/456–5539 | www.americinn.com | 41 rooms | $62–$75 | AE, D, MC, V.

Gold Key. This single-story brick motel is 2 mi north of downtown in a rural farming area. Restaurant. Cable TV. Pets allowed. | 1570 B Hwy. 65 | 515/456–2566 | fax 515/456–3622 | 20 rooms | $44 | AE, D, DC, MC, V.

Hampton Motel. This motel is seven blocks east of downtown, right on Highway 3. Rooms have parking right outside the door. In-room microwaves, refrigerators, cable TV, in-room VCRs, no room phones. No pets. | 816 Central Ave. W, | 515/456–3680 | 15 rooms | $44–$47 | AE, D, MC, V.

HUMBOLDT

(Nearby town also listed: Fort Dodge)

Named after German scientist and writer Baron von Humboldt, this little community was founded by religious liberals who admired von Humboldt's works and hoped to establish a Christian college here. That plan failed around 1900 due to a dispute over taxes. Humboldt County is proudest of its two famous citizens—the late CBS news anchor Harry Reasoner and world-champion wrestler Frank Gotch, both of whom grew up on local farms. The community of Humboldt reflects the founders' vision of wide, tree-lined streets, beautiful parks, good schools, and well-attended churches.

Information: Humboldt/Dakota City Area Chamber | 29 S. 5th St., Box 247, 50548 | 515/332–1481.

Attractions

Frank A. Gotch Park. Named for the world-champion wrestler who was born and raised here, this 67-acre park 3 mi southeast of town offers camping, canoeing, and fishing. | 2568 Gotch Park Rd. | 515/332–4087 | Free | Daily.

Humboldt County Historical Museum. This museum complex 1 mi east of Humboldt on the edge of Dakota City contains a log cabin, a mill farm, and a schoolhouse from the 1880s, as well as a doctor's office, post office, and tinsmith shop. | 905 1st Ave. N | 515/332–5280 | $2 | May–Sept., Mon.–Tues. 10–4, Thurs.–Sat. 10–4, Sun. 1–4:30.

Joe Sheldon Park. This 81-acre park and wildlife area 2 mi west of the junction of Highways 169 and 3 offers a boat ramp, fishing, and 28 campsites. | 2210 Sheldon Park Rd. for campsites, 2250 Sheldon Park Rd. for boat ramp and lake | 515/332–4087 | Free | Daily.

Three Rivers Trail. You can walk, bike, cross-country ski, or drive your snowmobile along this crushed limestone trail which runs from Eagle Grove (east of Humboldt) to Rolfe (northwest of Humboldt) along 32 mi of the old Chicago Northwest Railroad route and the eastern and western branches of the Des Moines River. The trail can be joined downtown at Sumner Avenue by the train depot. | Sumner Ave. | 515/332–4087 | Free | Daily dawn–dusk.

ON THE CALENDAR

MAY: *Annual Lake Nokomis Buckskinners Rendezvous Days.* If you're in town over Mother's Day weekend you can experience life in the early 1800s, the time of the buckskinners, in Joe Sheldon Park. Demonstrations include fire-starting with flint and steel, hawk and knife throws, trap setting, and black-powder shoots. | 515/332–1481.

JULY: *ABATE Freedom Rally.* More than 6,000 Harley motorcyclists attend concerts and events in Sheldon Park coordinated by ABATE (American Bikers Aimed Towards Education), an organization concerned with cyclists' rights and safety issues. | 515/332–1481.

SEPT.: *Midwest Polka Fest.* More than 3,000 dancers show up at the Humboldt County Fairgrounds and turn Humboldt into the polka capital of Iowa each Labor Day weekend. | 515/332–1481.

Dining

Cedar Room. American/Casual. Soup, sandwiches, stand-out cheeseburgers, and homemade pies are the mainstays at this eatery six blocks south of downtown on Highway 169. | 600 13th St. S | 515/332–4210 | $2–$6 | AE, D, DC, MC, V | Breakfast also available; no dinner.

Lodging

Broadway Inn. This simple, downtown motel prides itself on friendly small-town service. Complimentary Continental breakfast. Cable TV. | 812 N. 13th St. | 515/332–3545 | 38 rooms | $43 | AE, D, MC, V.

Corner Inn. This small hotel, with its meticulously kept flower beds out front, is right on the town's main intersection. The lobby and guest rooms are simply furnished. Cable TV. Pets allowed. | 1004 N. 13th St. | 515/332–1672 | 22 rooms | $36–$40 | AE, D, MC, V.

Super 8 Humboldt. This chain motel 2 mi northwest of downtown has some suites with fold-out couches. Complimentary Continental breakfast. Some microwaves, some refrigerators, cable TV. Pets allowed (fee). | 1520 10th Ave. N | 712/476–9389 or 800/800–8000 | 28 rooms, 5 suites | $52–$67 rooms, $57–$74 suites | AE, D, DC, MC, V.

INDIANOLA

MAP 3, E5

(Nearby towns also listed: Des Moines, Winterset)

In 1849 Colonel Paris Henderson and others who were hired to do land appraisals in this area saw an article in the *New York Sun.* about Indianola, Texas. They liked the name and decided to use it for the town they founded here. By 1863 Indianola had grown enough to become a city. Following the farm crisis of the 1980s, civic leaders banded together to develop a strong industrial base in the community, which now includes a large cement mixing facility and an agriculture replacement parts business. Equal effort has been put forth in maintaining and developing an impressive parks-and-recs program that draws visitors from surrounding communities for activities and outings.

Information: **Indianola Chamber of Commerce** | 515 N. Jefferson, 50125 | 515/961–6269 | chamber@indianolachamber.com | www.indianola.ia.us.

Attractions

Buxton Park Arboretum. A formal perennial and rose garden, an interpretive tree tour, and Victorian gazebo near the northern edge of the Simpson College campus. | N. Buxton and W. Girard Sts. | 515/961–9420 | Free | Daily.

Lake Ahquabi State Park. This 770-acre park 6 mi south of town offers swimming, boating, fishing, and a self-guided nature trail. The lakeside concessionaire rents canoes, kayaks, and paddleboats and sells snacks, firewood, and fish bait. | 1650 118th Ave. | 515/961–7101 | www.state.ia.us/parks | Free | Daily.

National Balloon Museum. Artifacts showcase more than 200 years of hot-air ballooning. | 1601 N. Jefferson St. | 515/961–3714 | Donations accepted | Weekdays 10–4, weekends 1–4; closed Jan.

Simpson College. Founded in 1860 by the Methodist Church, the college offers degrees in music and other liberal arts. | N. Buxton St. and W. Clinton Ave. | 515/961–1606 or 800/362–2454 | www.simpson.edu | Free | Daily.

ON THE CALENDAR
JUNE–JULY: *Des Moines Metro Opera Summer Festival.* Since 1972 the Des Moines Opera has traveled to Indianola to perform in the Blank Performing Arts Center, at Simpson College. | 515/961–6221.
JULY–AUG.: *National Balloon Classic.* More than 100 professional balloonists demonstrate their skills during this event. | 515/961–8415.

Dining

Corner Sundry. Café. This old-fashioned soda fountain bar on the southwest corner of Town Square has been serving phosphates, ice-cream sodas, malts, sundaes, cookies, candy, and flavored cokes for three generations. They still use the original malt machine from the 1950s. You won't find any substantial food here, but in the morning you can stop by for coffee and donuts. | 101 N. Buxton St. | 515/961–9029 | $1–$3 | No credit cards | Closed Sun. No dinner.

Cottage Inn. American. Blue valances frame the windows of this homey café filled with fresh flowers. Sample the hot beef tenderloins, homemade onion rings, and pies. | 302 S. Jefferson St. | 515/961–3137 | $5–$10 | No credit cards | Closed Sun.

Lodging

Apple Tree Inn. This spacious brick hotel is on a grassy hill overlooking downtown. Cable TV. Business services. | 1215 N. Jefferson St. | 515/961–0551 or 800/961–0551 | fax 515/961–0555 | 60 rooms | $50–$65 | AE, D, DC, MC, V.

Summerset Inn and Winery. This small, secluded inn with a stone fireplace and vaulted ceilings is surrounded by an oak forest and Iowa's largest vineyard. You can visit the winery. Complimentary breakfast. Hiking. | 1507 Fairfax Rd. | 515/961–3545 | 4 rooms | $85–$120 | MC, V.

Super 8 Indianola. This chain motel is on Highways 65/69, less than 1 mi south of downtown. Complimentary Continental breakfast. Cable TV. Pool. | 1710 N. Jefferson St. | 515/961–0058 or 800/800–8000 | www.super8.com | 44 rooms | $56–$74 | AE, D, DC, MC, V.

LITERARY LIGHTS ON THE PRAIRIE

The best-selling 1992 novel *The Bridges of Madison County* introduced millions of readers to Iowa's rural Madison County, 37 mi south of Des Moines. But the state's true literary hub is 114 mi west of Des Moines in the bustling college town of Iowa City. This is the home of one of the nation's most prestigious creative writing programs—the Iowa Writers' Workshop at the University of Iowa—and the nationally known independent bookstore Prairie Lights.

For seven decades, novelists and poets have flocked to Iowa City. Flannery O'Connor, John Irving, Robert Bly, Wallace Stegner, and Jane Smiley were Workshop students. Kurt Vonnegut, Jr., John Cheever, Raymond Carver, Philip Roth, Robert Lowell, and Robert Penn Warren taught there. The first creative writing program of its kind in the nation, Iowa has produced a dozen Pulitzer Prize winners, three recent Poet Laureates, and many winners of the National Book Award.

Many workshop writers hang out at Prairie Lights—which has remained very much a light on the prairie since it opened in 1978. A two-story hip-modern building amidst 19th-century storefronts housing boutiques, ethnic restaurants, and cafés, Prairie Lights is the place to spot a famous author—or buy a book by one. Prairie Lights owner Jim Harris and his staff (which often includes Workshop students) pride themselves in leading customers to great writing by the famous and not-yet-famous alike.

And if you're lucky, you may just stumble upon a reading—dozens of writers read their work at Prairie Lights each year. If you can't be there in person, tune in on Iowa public radio to "Live from Prairie Lights"—a statewide broadcast that brings great books to farmers in combines, city commuters, and travelers barreling across Iowa on Interstate 80.

© Corbis

IOWA CITY

MAP 3, G4

(Nearby towns also listed: Amana Colonies, Cedar Rapids, Kalona, West Branch)

Iowa City was surveyed and lots were sold for the new territorial capital in 1839. In 1846 when Iowa gained statehood, the town was named the first state capital, and a year later the University of Iowa was founded here. Today the university is home to nearly 30,000 students, one of the largest university-owned teaching hospitals in the nation, the famed Writers' Workshop, and, of course, the Hawkeye football and basketball programs that draw hundreds of thousands of sports fans each year. This is a real university town and there's always something going on. If you want to find out what's happening during your visit, pick up a copy of the free weekly paper *The Icon* or peruse the downtown bulletin boards and their fliers announcing lectures, concerts, and readings. The neighboring town of Coralville, though an independent urban entity, often gets mentioned in the same breath as Iowa City because the two towns are practically conjoined.

Information: Iowa City/Coralville Convention and Visitors Bureau | 408 1st Ave., Coralville 52241 | 319/337–6592 or 800/283–6592 | cvb@icccvb.org | www.icccvb.org.

NEIGHBORHOODS

Northside. Between 1850 and 1930, the small cottages, large gardens, and brick-lined streets of Northside were home to many University of Iowa faculty members. In recent years, however, lots have been subdivided and additional buildings have been constructed in this neighborhood, which is bounded east and west by Dodge and Dubuque streets, and north and south by Brown and Jefferson streets. University students now nearly fill the area, which is under consideration as an Iowa City Historic Preservation District.

Summit Street District. The first homes built on the gentle ridge in south-central Iowa City were begun in 1860, and more than half of the remaining homes were completed by 1910. The broad, tree-lined Summit Street, the heavily wooded lots, and the large front yards make this neighborhood feel like a park. Architectural styles include Classical, Italianate, French, Gothic, Victorian, and neo-Georgian, to name a few. The Summit Street District was named to the National Register of Historic Places in 1973.

Woodlawn. Only 14 homes make up this neighborhood at the east end of Iowa Avenue, which was originally part of the master plan of a capital city. The governor's mansion was to have been built on these spacious lots, but after the capital moved to Des Moines in 1857, the area was divided and sold for residential lots. Queen Anne– and Italianate-style architecture dominates this distinctive neighborhood.

TRANSPORTATION INFORMATION

Airports: Eastern Iowa Airport (2121 Wright Bros. Blvd., Cedar Rapids; 20 mi north on I–380 | 319/362–8336).

Bus Lines: Greyhound (319/337–2552).

Intra-city Transit: Iowa City Transit Service (319/351–5151) or **Coralville Transit Service** (319/351–7711).

Attractions

ART AND ARCHITECTURE

Old Capitol. Guided tours are available of this National Historic Landmark which served as the territorial capitol, then as the first state capitol for Iowa. Today its Greek Revival columns and dome are a symbol of the university. | Clinton St. and Iowa Ave. | 319/335–0548 | www.uiowa.edu/oldcap | Free | Daily.

Plum Grove. Built in 1844, this Greek Revival house is the former home of Robert Lucas, Iowa's first territorial governor. | 1030 Carroll St. | 319/337–6846 | $2 | Apr.–Nov., Wed.–Sat. 1–5.

BEACHES, PARKS, AND NATURAL SITES

Coralville Lake. This man-made lake 6 mi north of town is popular for water sports. After extensive flooding in 1993, a large fossil deposit was exposed in an area now known as the Devonian Fossil Gorge. | Dubuque St. north of I–80 | 319/338–3543 | Free | Daily 8–4.

Lake MacBride State Park. Named for a professor of botany at the University of Iowa, this 2,180-acre park 15 mi northwest of town has everything from native prairie to a Frisbee golf course. | 3525 Rte. 382 NE, Solon | 319/644–2200 | www.state.ia.us/parks | Free | Daily.

CULTURE, EDUCATION, AND HISTORY

Riverside Theater. Iowa City's only professional theater company produces plays from the classics to world premieres in an intimate setting. | 213 N. Gilbert St. | 319/338–7672 | www.riversidetheatre.org | $17 | Daily.

University of Iowa. This four-year public university in the center of the city flanks the Iowa River with most of the liberal arts buildings on the east side and all the law and medicine facilities on the west. The UI is internationally known for its medical school, writing program, and sports teams. There's a visitors center in the Memorial Union lobby. | Iowa Memorial Union, Madison and Jefferson Sts. | 319/335–3500 | www.uiowa.edu | Free | Daily.

The university is a member of the Big Ten Conference and **Carver-Hawkeye Arena** is home to Hawkeye basketball and wrestling. The arena seats 15,500 and is nearly 10 stories high. Because of its unique ceiling support design, there isn't a bad seat in the house. | Elliott Dr. | 319/335–9410.

The **Medical Museum,** at the University of Iowa Hospitals and Clinics, Patient and Visitor Activities Center, displays medical artifacts and historic photographs documenting advances in patient care from ancient times to the present. | 200 Hawkins Dr, 8th fl | 319/356–7106 | www.vh.org | Free | Weekdays 8–5, weekends 1–4.

MUSEUMS

Iowa Children's Museum. Explore 28,000 square ft of hands-on learning landscapes and minds-on programming. The museum includes interactive exhibits that encourage communication and teamwork. | 1451 Coral Ridge Ave. (in Coral Ridge Mall), Coralville | 315/625–6255 | iowachildren'smuseum.org | $4.50 | Tues.–Fri. 11–8, weekends 11–6.

Museum of Art. Major 20th-century artists such as Picasso, Matisse, and Chagall are part of the permanent collection of this University museum in the Iowa Arts Complex, on the west bank of the Iowa River. Its African art collection is one of the best in the country. | 150 N. Riverside Dr. | 319/335–1727 | www.uiowa.edu/~collect | Free | Tues.–Sat. 10–5, Sun. 11–4.

Museum of Natural History. The premier exhibit in this University museum on the east campus in MacBride Hall is "Native Cultures of Iowa," tracing human history in Iowa from the hunters of the Ice Age to an 1845 Meskwaki Indian lodge. | Clinton St. and Iowa Ave. | 319/335–0481 | Free | Mon.–Sat. 9:30–4:30, Sun. 12:30–4:30.

SHOPPING

Prairie Lights Bookstore. One of the country's leading independent bookstores, Prairie Lights is an Iowa City institution. The bookstore's series of readings, which are free and often feature Writers' Workshop graduates or teachers, is broadcast live on local public radio. You can also just browse or enjoy a coffee in the upstairs café. | 15 Dubuque St. | 319/337–2681 | Free | Mon.–Sat. 9 AM–10 PM, Sun. 9 AM–6 PM.

JUNE: *Iowa Arts Festival.* Artists throughout the Midwest sign up years in advance to be in this juried show. | 319/337–7944.

WALKING TOURS
Woodlawn (approximately 1½ hours)
Begin at **1011 Woodlawn,** an Italianate-style residence typical of many homes built in Iowa City in the 1880s. Turn right and walk to the next house at **No. 1025,** a private home built in 1891 in the stick style of architecture, which is characterized by wood construction and boxy projections like bay windows and towers. Continuing to your right, the next two homes, at **No. 1033** and **No. 1041,** are built in the Italianate style, circa 1865 and 1878. The next home to your right, **No. 1047,** is also Italianate but incorporates the Gothic elements of high peaks and stone entries. The character of the neighborhood shifts to the 20th century at **No. 1049,** a World War I–era, one-story bungalow with a picket fence and gracious gardens. The modern-day trend continues as you continue right around the oval street at **No. 1050,** a 1950s ranch home. **No. 1042–44** is a massive structure built in 1880 and covering two of the already large lots in an eclectic style that includes Victorian, Gothic, and Queen Anne characteristics. Queen Anne is very distinctly the style at **No. 1036,** a beautifully restored 2½-story mansion built in 1895 complete with two turrets, a wide veranda, and detailed spindle work. Moving on around the oval street to the right, **No. 1024** represents the Italianate period of 1845–85 with its low-pitched roof and square pillared veranda. **No. 1010** was built in 1926 and stands apart in the neighborhood as the only true Tudor, with characteristic timber and plaster motifs and trim. The last home in this classic neighborhood (an Italianate home built in 1883) is across Evans Street and a half block to the right. **19 Evans Street** was originally at 1010 Woodlawn, but was moved in 1926 when the Tudor was built. When visiting Woodlawn, parking is available on Iowa Avenue and neighboring streets. Parking space on the narrow, oval drive of Woodlawn is reserved for residents, whose privacy should be respected.

Dining

INEXPENSIVE
Bread Garden Bakery and Café. Delicatessen. This downtown bakery and specialty sandwich shop makes everything—from their delicious breads, to their cakes, and six daily soup specials—from scratch. | 224 S. Clinton St. at Dubuque St. | 319/354–4246 | $6–10 | AE, D, DC, MC, V | Breakfast also available; no dinner.

MODERATE
The Brewery. Continental. Housed in a late 1800s factory building with huge arched windows and sky-high vaulted ceilings, The Brewery is arguably the most beautiful restaurant in Iowa City. Behind the polished oak bar you'll see the copper brewing tanks that produce the numerous house beers. Seating is almost exclusively in high-backed, dark-wood booths facing linen-draped tables. The Brewery's claim to fame is its perfect filet mignon, but everything here from the baguettes to the herbed butter is worth sampling. | 521 S. Gilbert St. | 319/356–6900 | $13–$20 | AE, MC, V.

Devotay. Mediterranean. This sunny little restaurant on a tree-lined downtown block has huge windows, charmingly mismatched tables and chairs, and locally made ceramic dishware. Try some of the *tapas,* a Spanish word for small dishes meant to be enjoyed by the whole table, like bacon-wrapped dates in maple-chipotle syrup. For the main course, the *paella,* a savory blend of saffron rice, duck sausage, and shellfish, can't be beat. | 117 N. Linn St. | 319/354–1001 | $6–$15 | AE, D, DC, MC, V.

Gringo's. Mexican. Seating is almost entirely in booths separated by stained-glass partitions at this chain eatery with exposed brick walls and antique wooden statues of saints on the Pedestrian Mall in the heart of downtown. Try the steak fajitas, served in a still-sizzling skillet, or the popular seafood enchiladas—shrimp and crabmeat wrapped in a tortilla, doused with white clam sauce and topped with shredded cheese. | 115 E. College St. | 319/338–3000 | $9–$16 | AE, D, MC, V.

The Mekong. Vietnamese. Try the spicy lemongrass chicken or the asparagus chicken at this small, casual family-run restaurant in Coralville. | 222 1st Ave., Coralville | 319/337–9910 | $6–$12 | D, MC, V.

The Mill. American/Casual. Try the palace special pizza at this favorite graduate student hangout that features a great schedule of live music. Offerings are eclectic—there's everything from fusion jazz to local folk and bluegrass artists including local legend Greg Brown who plays here every few months. Tuesday nights there's an old-time music jam session. | 120 E. Burlington St. | 319/351–9529 | $7–$13 | MC, V.

Motley Cow Café. Contemporary. Try the savory crêpes, or perhaps the falafel on an organic whole-wheat pita, served with a salad of organic field greens and fresh vinaigrette at this small café in one of Iowa City's not-quite-downtown shopping/dining niches. No two tables or chairs are the same here, work by local artists adorn the walls, and food is prepared in an open kitchen area. | 327 E. Market St. | 319/688–9177 | Mon.–Sat. 11 AM–midnight, Sun. 8 AM–noon. Breakfast Sun. only | $10–$12 | D, MC, V.

The Sanctuary. American. You'll find better than average pub food, the best beer selection in Iowa (there are over 200 beers on offer), and live music (mostly regional and local jazz artists) on Friday and Saturday nights at this casual downtown eatery. This is also one of the latest-serving restaurants in town. | 405 S. Gilbert St. | 319/351–5692 | $8–$15 | AE, D, MC, V.

EXPENSIVE

Giovanni's. Italian. This restaurant on the downtown Pedestrian Mall was nearly destroyed by a fire in early 1999, but its soaring ceilings, exposed brick walls, large, abstract paintings and tasteful bands of neon lighting are now back. Try the much-loved pasta pacifica, which mixes shrimp, scallops, and clams in a white-wine glacé with a rich tomato-onion sauce and angel-hair pasta. | 109 E. College St. | 319/338–5967 | $10–$25 | AE, D, DC, MC, V | No lunch Sun.

Linn Street Café. Contemporary. You can expect an outstanding meal at this small, elegant downtown restaurant that has been praised in *Wine Spectator* and is considered by some locals to be the closest thing in town to New York dining. The chef favors regional produce and offers entrées such as mustard-seed-encrusted loin of lamb. | 121 N. Linn St. | 319/337–7370 | $15–$24 | AE, D, MC, V | Closed Sun. No lunch.

126. Contemporary. There's a fabulous wine bar downstairs, a full bar upstairs, an exhibition kitchen, French café windows that can be opened in fair weather, and live music on Friday and Saturday nights at this recent addition to Iowa City's restaurant scene. The menu changes daily but you're likely to find dishes like beef tenderloin with porcini mushrooms or pan-seared trout in a white wine and herb sauce. | 126 E. Washington St. | 319/887–1909 | $25–$40 | AE, D, DC, MC, V.

Lodging

INEXPENSIVE

Haverkamp's Linn Street Homestay B&B. This antiques-filled 1908 Edwardian home with a large covered front porch is within walking distance of downtown and the university. Complimentary breakfast. In-room TVs. | 619 Linn St. | 319/337–4363 | fax 319/354–7057 | havbb@soli.inav.net | 3 rooms (with shared bath) | $45–$50 | No credit cards.

MODERATE

Hampton Inn. This 1990s hotel on a commercial strip just off Interstate 80 in Coralville caters primarily to businesspeople and those in town for university functions. Restaurant, complimentary Continental breakfast. In-room data ports, some refrigerators and microwaves, cable TV. Pool. Hot tub. Gym. Business services. | 1200 1st Ave., Coralville | 319/351–6600 | fax 319/351–3928 | www.hamptoninn.com | 115 rooms | $65 | AE, D, DC, MC, V.

Heartland Inn. Rooms at this Coralville chain hotel are furnished with cherry-oak antique reproductions and locally themed art prints. The hotel is on a busy street with its back to the Iowa River. Complimentary Continental breakfast. In-room data ports, in-room hot tubs in suites, cable TV, in-room VCRs available. Pool. Gym. Business services. | 87 2nd St., Coralville | 319/351–8132 | fax 319/351–2916 | 155 rooms, 14 suites | $73 rooms, $125–$215 suites | AE, D, DC, MC, V.

Historic Phillips House. This B&B is right on the University of Iowa campus overlooking the Iowa River. There are six fireplaces in the house, lots of antiques, as well as a sauna and outdoor hot tub. Some rooms share a bath. Complimentary breakfast. TV in common area. Hot tub, sauna. | 721 N. Linn St. | 319/337–3223 | 4 rooms | $65 | No credit cards.

Super 8. Basic lodging just off Interstate 80 on a commercial strip in Coralville. Complimentary Continental breakfast. Microwaves available, cable TV. Business services. | 611 1st Ave., Coralville | 319/337–8388 | fax 319/337–4327 | www.super8.com | 87 rooms | $58 | AE, D, DC, MC, V.

EXPENSIVE

Brown Street Inn. The pillared porch of this 1913 cottage-style mansion overlooks the weathered cobblestones of historic, tree-lined Brown Street. Rooms are done in a Shaker-transitional style, blending pencil-post beds and simple, nonfussy furnishings with luxurious antique Persian carpets. Complimentary breakfast. In-room data ports, some minibars, some refrigerators, cable TV. Exercise equipment. Laundry facilities. Business services. No pets. No smoking. | 430 Brown St. | 319/338–0435 | fax 319/351–8271 | www.ia.net/~brown430 | 5 rooms | $69–$99 | AE, MC, V.

Golden Haug. This 1919 mission-style B&B is within easy walking distance of downtown shops and restaurants as well as the university. All rooms have ceiling fans and unique features such as a claw-foot tub or a fireplace; some have hot tubs. Complimentary breakfast. Cable TV. Free parking. No pets. No smoking. | 517 E. Washington | 319/338–6452 | 2 rooms, 3 suites | $79–$99 rooms, $109–$125 suites | No credit cards.

VERY EXPENSIVE

Bella Vista. This B&B is on the historic north side overlooking the Iowa River and the university's Hancher Auditorium. The 1920s-era house is filled with antiques and international artifacts collected by the globe-trotting innkeeper. Complimentary breakfast. Cable TV. | 2 Bella Vista Pl | 319/524–3888 | 2 rooms (with shared bath), 3 suites | $70–$125 | AE, MC, V.

Iowa House Hotel. Housed in the Iowa Memorial Union, the Iowa House literally sits atop the hub of university activity. Many rooms look out onto the Iowa River, others onto the grassy expanse of Hubbard Park, where you may see students playing a pickup game of football, lacrosse, soccer, or mud wrestling, depending on the season. The hotel lobby is entirely paneled in oak and houses a UI Homecoming button collection donated to the school in 1967. Rooms and hallways are hung with scores of pieces by Iowa artists, many of them UI graduates and faculty. Restaurant. Cable TV. In-room data ports. Gym. Business services, free parking. No smoking. | 121 Iowa Memorial Union, Jefferson and Madison Sts. | 319/335–3513 or 800/553–IOWA | fax 319/335–0497 | 100 rooms | $75–$180 | AE, D, MC, V.

Sheraton Iowa City Hotel. This hotel is right on the downtown Pedestrian Mall, making it one of the most convenient places to stay. The lobby is quiet with diffuse lighting and a sunken lounge area. Rooms have polished-oak furnishings and some have views of the Ped Mall fountain. There's also a game room with pinball and foosball. Restaurant, bar, room service. Some refrigerators, cable TV. Pool. Hot tub. Gym. Business services, airport shuttle. No pets. | 210 S. Dubuque St. | 319/337–4058 | fax 319/337–9045 | 234 rooms | $109–$145 | AE, D, DC, MC, V.

KALONA

(Nearby towns also listed: Iowa City, Muscatine)

Known as the "Quilt Capital of Iowa" by quilting enthusiasts around the Midwest, this little town is home to the largest Amish settlement west of the Mississippi. The town's name comes from a famous bull sire who was bred here around 1900. Kalona is a haven for antiques and crafts lovers and is appreciated for its home cooking and simple living.

Information: Kalona Area Chamber of Commerce | Box 615, 52247 | 319/656–2660 | chamber@kctc.net | www.kctc.net/chamber.

Attractions
Kalona Historical Village. This cluster of 14 historical buildings just west of downtown includes a log house, a Victorian home, a country store, a one-room school, a church, and the Iowa Mennonite Museum and Archives. | 411 9th St. | 319/656–2660 | $6 | June–Nov., Mon.–Sat. 9:30–4; Dec.–May, Mon.–Sat. 11–3.

Kalona Quilt and Textile Museum. Exhibits quilts and textiles from the 1800s through the mid-1900s. | 515 B Ave. | 319/656–2240 | $3 | Mon.–Sat. 11–3.

ON THE CALENDAR
JUNE: *TrekFest in Riverside.* A celebration of the anticipated birth of Star Trek Captain James T. Kirk in the year 2228 in the nearby town of Riverside. | 319/648–3501.
SEPT.: *Kalona Fall Festival.* A variety of skilled demonstrations, old-time crafts, entertainment, and food at the Kalona Historical Village. | 319/656–2660.
SEPT.: *Prints Charming Quilt Show.* This is one of the largest quilt shows in the nation and draws both quilt makers and quilt buyers. | 319/656–2660.

Dining
Parlor Café. Delicatessen. This downtown eatery offers deli sandwiches, homemade soups, and hot meat dishes for lunch. | 125 4th St. | 319/656–2550 | $3–$5 | No credit cards | Breakfast also available; closed Sun.; no dinner.

Lodging
Carriage House Bed and Breakfast. Rooms are furnished with antiques at this B&B in the countryside 1 mi west of Kalona. Complimentary breakfast. No pets. No smoking. | 1140 Larch Ave. | 319/656–3824 | www.carriagehousebnb.com | 3 rooms | $70 | MC, V.

KEOKUK

(Nearby town also listed: Fort Madison)

During the Civil War the Union Army sent quite a number of its wounded soldiers to a medical facility here. Some of those who did not survive were buried in the town's national cemetery, one of the country's original 12. This river town was one of Mark Twain's favorites to visit and today has an impressive historic downtown. Just as it did in Mark Twain's time, the river continues to influence the economic life of Keokuk through a hydroelectric power plant and grain-shipping facility on the riverfront.

Information: Keokuk Area Convention and Tourism Bureau | 329 Main St., 52632 | 319/524–5599 or 800/383–1219 | www.cdm-sites.com/kact.

Attractions

George M. Verity Riverboat Museum. You can visit the crew quarters or the pilot house of this dry-docked paddle-wheel steamboat in Victory Park which also has exhibits on old-time life on the river. | 1st St. at Water St. | 319/524–4765 | $3 | Memorial Day–Labor Day, daily 9–5.

Grand Avenue. The Keokuk Convention and Tourism Bureau offers a "Walking Tour of Grand Avenue" map which will guide you past the beautiful homes on Grand and Orleans avenues—prestigious addresses for Keokuk's elite during the late 1800s and early 1900s. | Grand and Orleans Aves. | 319/524–5599 | Free | Daily.

Keokuk Dam. At 12,000 ft, lock and dam No. 19 is the longest on the Mississippi. It's a great place to watch barges and other boats navigate a lock system or to watch for eagles in winter. | End of N. Water St. | 319/524–4091 or 319/524–9660 | Free | Memorial Day–Labor Day, tours daily 11 AM.

National Cemetery. Built in the 1860s, this is one of America's 12 original national cemeteries, and the only one in Iowa. There's a large Civil War section. | 1701 J St. | 319/524–5193 | Free | Daily.

Rand Park. Community flower gardens, a fountain, and the burial site of Chief Keokuk, the city's Sauk/Fox namesake, fill this city park overlooking the Mississippi River. | Between N. 14th and N. 17th Sts. | 800/383–1289 | Free | Daily.

Samuel F. Miller House Museum. This 1859 Federal-style house once belonged to Samuel Miller, a local attorney appointed to the Supreme Court by Abraham Lincoln. Today the house is filled with period antiques and exhibits on local history. | 318 N. 5th St. | 319/524–7283 or 800/383–1289 | $1 | Fri.–Sun. 1–4:30, or by appointment.

ON THE CALENDAR

JAN.: *Bald Eagle Appreciation Days.* Watch for and learn about bald eagles nesting and feeding along the river. | 800/383–1219.

APR.: *Civil War Reenactment.* Actors portray Civil War soldiers in Kilbourne Park, and you can touch a Civil War cannon and learn details of battles fought by Iowa regiments. | 800/383–1219.

DEC.: *City of Christmas.* Throughout the month, you can see over 150,000 lights on 100 Christmas scenes throughout Rand Park. Toyland, Santa's Barn, and the Nativity scene are just some of the traditional displays. | 319/524–5599 or 800/383–1219.

Dining

Hawkeye Restaurant. American. Barbecued ribs, barbecued prime rib, and chops are among the favorites at this eatery 2 mi north of town but you can also get catfish, shrimp, and lobster. While you wait for your dinner, you can enjoy any of the 12 different microbrews on tap or study the period photos of Keokuk on the walls. The lounge is open until 1 AM. | 105 N. Park Dr. | 319/524–7549 | $5–$35 | AE, D, MC, V | Closed Sun.

Lodging

Holiday Inn Express. This downtown chain hotel is 4 blocks from the riverfront. Complimentary Continental breakfast. In-room data ports, cable TV. Pool. Hot tub. Exercise equipment. Business services. | 4th and Main Sts. | 319/524–8000 | fax 319/524–4114 | holidayi@interl.net | www.basshotels.com/holiday-inn | 80 rooms | $62–$79 | AE, D, DC, MC, V.

River's Edge B&B. There's a porch overlooking the river, two guest rooms have water views, and one looks out on an eagle's nest at this B&B. A fireside parlor offers cozy winter seating. Complimentary breakfast. Pool. No pets. | 611 Grand Ave. | 319/524–1700 | 3 rooms | $75–$110 | MC, V.

KEOSAUQUA

(Nearby towns also listed: Fairfield, Fort Madison, Keokuk, Mount Pleasant)

Keosauqua is among a handful of tiny riverfront communities including Bentonsport, Bonaparte, Cantril, and Farmington known as the Villages of Van Buren that thrived during the mid-19th century. Today, these slow-paced, quiet communities along the banks of the Des Moines River offer restored historic districts with old-world-style lodging and stores selling antiques, local crafts, and artwork, plus a state park, forest, and lake.

Information: Villages of Van Buren Inc. | Box 9, Keosauqua, 52565 | 319/293–7111 or 800/868–7822 | villages@800-tourvbc.com.

Attractions
Bentonsport National Historic District. Numerous artists and craftspeople have opened shops in the 10 historic buildings of this once-thriving community 12 mi south of Keosauqua. | Rte. J40, Bentonsport | 319/592–3579 | Free | Apr.–Oct., daily.

Bonaparte National Historic District. The old mills in this historic town 20 mi southeast of Keosauqua are now shops selling antiques and collectibles. The well-known Bonaparte Retreat Restaurant is also here. | Rte. J40, Bonaparte | 319/592–3400 | Apr.–Oct., daily.

Lacey-Keosauqua State Park. The hills, bluffs, and valleys of this 1,653-acre park wind along the Des Moines River on the historic Mormon Trail. The park is adjacent to Lake Sugema, a large man-made lake. | Hwy. 1 | 319/293–3502 | www.state.ia.us/parks | Free | Daily.

ON THE CALENDAR
OCT.: *Forest Craft & Scenic Drive Festival.* All the villages of Van Buren take part in this festival the second full weekend of October during peak autumn leaf season. There are arts-and-crafts exhibits, a juried woodcraft show, a quilt show, a lumberjack show featuring log rolling and axe throwing, a carnival, and a parade. | 800/868–7822.

Dining
Bonaparte Retreat Restaurant. American. Built in the 19th century, this four-story redbrick gristmill in Bonaparte's National Historic District serves steak, pork chops, and seafood from scallops to salmon in a dining room featuring exposed brick walls, hardwood floors, and wildlife prints. | 713 Front St., Bonaparte | 319/592–3339 | $8–$16 | AE, MC, V | Closed Sun.

Bridge Café and Supper Club. American. The two laid-back dining rooms of this café/supper club serve fried chicken, catfish, and country-style ribs as individual entrées or as part of an all-you-can eat buffet dinner. | 101 Olive St., Farmington | 319/878–3315 | $9–$22 | No credit cards | Closed Sun., Mon., Tues. No dinner.

Red Barn Bistro. American. Fresh-cut steaks and surf-and-turf are the order of the day at this eatery in a modern steel barn in the farm country just outside town. Inside the feeling is rustic with wood siding and beams salvaged from an old barn, and cast-iron skillets and farm saws hanging on the walls above booths and tables. | 21268 Fir Ave. | 319/293–6154 | $7–$13 | No credit cards | Closed Mon., Tues.

Lodging

Hotel Manning B&B and Motor Inn. You'll find B&B accommodations in this graceful 19th-century redbrick hotel with its antiques-filled rooms and wide veranda overlooking the Des Moines River. There's also an adjacent modern motel. In hotel: complimentary breakfast. Phones and TV in common area. In motel: room phones, cable TV. | 100 Van Buren St., | 319/293–3232 or 800/728–2718 | fax 319/293–9960 | www.netins.net/showcase/manning | Hotel: 18 rooms (8 with shared bath); motel: 19 rooms | $35–$72 | D, MC, V.

Mansion Inn B&B. Built in 1884, this yellow-brick mansion with pillars and a large front porch looks like it belongs in the South. Complimentary breakfast. TV in common area. | 500 Henry St. | 319/293–2511 or 800/646–0166 | fax 319/293–6449 | www.mansion-inn.com/ | 5 rooms (2 with shared bath) | $60–$75 | MC, V.

Mason House Inn. Rooms are furnished with antiques and a cookie jar at this landmark steamboat river inn was built in Bentonsport in the 1800s by Mormons and visited by Abe Lincoln and Mark Twain. Complimentary breakfast. Phones and TV in common area. | R.R. 2 Box 237, Bentonsport | 319/592–3133 or 800/592–3133 | showcase.netins.net/web/bentonsport/ | 9 rooms | $64–$79 | MC, V.

LAMONI

(Nearby town also listed: Osceola)

Lamoni is the name of a good king in the Book of Mormon. For a short time, Joseph Smith III, son of the founder of Mormonism and leader of the Reorganized Church of Jesus Christ of Latter Day Saints, lived in this southern Iowa community. In addition to founding Graceland University, a four-year private college attended by Olympic gold medalist Bruce Jenner, the church built a number of distinctive homes and buildings. Lamoni is home to Iowa's oldest quilt guild, and people drive for hours to buy quilts here.

Information: City of Lamoni | 190 S. Chestnut St., 50140 | 515/784–6311 | www.lamoni-iowa.com.

Attractions

Graceland University. Members of the Reorganized Church of Jesus Christ of Latter Day Saints founded this four-year private liberal arts college in 1895. | 1 University Pl | 515/784–5000 | www.graceland.edu | Free | Daily.

Liberty Hall Historic Center. This Victorian mansion was once home to Joseph Smith III and now tells the story of the establishment of the Reorganized Church after his father's assassination and the departure of Brigham Young and his followers for Utah. | 1300 W. Main St. | 515/784–6133 | Free | Tues.–Sat. 10–4; Sun. 1:30–4; closed late Dec.–Jan.

ON THE CALENDAR

MAR.: *Southern Iowa Quilt Show.* Designers of more than 500 quilts show and sell their work, and demonstrate their skills. | 515/784–6311.
DEC.: *Christmas Lighted Parade.* Holiday parade, caroling, and tours of festively decorated homes. | 515/784–6311.

Dining

Quilt Country Restaurant. American. This restaurant, named for the quilt country that surrounds it, is right across from the Iowa Welcome Center and 1¼ mi east of downtown. Amid antiques, you'll be served homemade dishes such as ham and beans with corn bread, barbecued ribs, fried chicken, and fresh pies and cakes. Breakfast includes country skillets and pancakes. | Intersection of U.S. 69 and I–35 | 515/784–6342 | $7–$8 | AE, D, MC, V | Closed Mon., Tues. No dinner Sun.

Lodging

Super 8 Lamoni. This motel is near Graceland University and Nine Eagles State Park. You'll find king-size beds in some rooms, and in the morning you can have coffee, toast, and orange juice in the lobby. Cable TV. No pets. | Intersection of U.S. 69 and I–35 | 641/784–7500 or 800/800–8000 | fax 515/784–7500 ext. 102 | www.super8.com | 30 rooms | $52–$55 | AE, D, DC, MC, V.

LE MARS

MAP 3, B2

(Nearby town also listed: Sioux City)

According to the Iowa legislature, Le Mars is the "Ice Cream Capital of the World." As home to Wells/Blue Bunny Ice Cream, more ice cream is produced in Le Mars than in any other town in the world. The town is also a Main Street Iowa city, participating in the National Historic Trust for downtown preservation.

Information: Le Mars Area Chamber of Commerce | 50 Central Ave. SE, 51031 | 712/546–8821.

Attractions

Ice Cream Capitol of the World Visitors Center and Museum. Come to the only interactive museum in the United States dedicated to the history of ice cream. | 16 5th Ave. NW | 712/546–4090 | www.bluebunny.com | $3 | Mon.–Sat. 9–6, Sun. 1–5.

Plymouth County Historical Museum. This small museum houses antique carriages, tools, and musical instruments. Other on-site exhibits include a log cabin, a schoolroom, and barber and beauty shops. | 335 1st Ave. SW | 712/546–7002 | Donations accepted | Tues.–Sun. 1–5.

ON THE CALENDAR

JULY: *Ice Cream Days.* Celebrating the town's status as the ice-cream capital of the world, this event includes ice-cream-cone relays and the building of the world's largest ice-cream sundae. | 712/546–8821.
AUG.: *Plymouth County Fair.* One of the biggest county fairs in the state, with a midway, concerts, and livestock shows all on the county fairgrounds. | 712/546–8821.
DEC.: *Lighted Christmas Parade.* This early December festival features more than 100 decorated Christmas trees, horse-drawn carriage and sleigh rides, and a parade. | 712/546–4090.

Dining

Archie's Waeside. American. This is one of the few restaurants in the country to dry-age carcass beef on the premises, an ongoing practice at Archie's for 50 years. You can also try a variety of seafood dishes. | 224 4th Ave. NE | 712/546–7011 | $8–$20 | AE, D, MC, V | Closed Sun., Mon. No lunch.

Lodging

Amber Inn. This basic one-story motel is just off Highway 75 about 2 mi south of town. Complimentary Continental breakfast. Cable TV. Business services. Pets allowed. | 635 8th Ave., SW | 712/546–7066 or 800/338–0298 | fax 712/548–4058 | www.geocities.com/amberinn | 70 rooms | $45 | AE, D, MC, V.

AmeriHost Inn. This hotel is in a commerical area off of U.S. 75, about 1 mi southwest of downtown Le Mars and the Ice-Cream Capitol of the World Visitor Center. Complimentary

Continental breakfast, in-room data ports, in-room safes, some microwaves, some refrigerators, cable TV. Pool. Hot tub, sauna. Gym. Laundry service. No pets. | 1314 12th St. SW | 712/548-4910 or 800/434-5800 | fax 712/548-4488 | 178@amerihostinn.com | www.amerihostinn.com | 56 rooms, 7 suites | $64-$69 rooms, $119-$129 suites | AE, D, DC, MC, V.

Super 8. This unassuming motel on the southwest side of town is a stone's throw from the Blue Bunny ice-cream plant. The parking lot has room enough for RVs and trucks, and there is a lobby-side breakfast nook and a freestanding restaurant next door. Complimentary Continental breakfast. Cable TV. Hot tub. Business services. | 1201 Hawkeye Ave. SW | 712/546-8800 | fax 712/546-8800 | www.super8.com | 60 rooms | $42-$51 | AE, D, DC, MC, V.

MAQUOKETA

MAP 3, H3

(Nearby towns also listed: Anamosa, Clinton)

Founded on the banks of the Maquoketa River in 1838, Maquoketa is known for its beautiful tree-lined streets, strong agricultural base, nearby Maquoketa Caves State Park, and an antiques show and sale each summer. The town's name is a Sauk and Fox Indian word which translates roughly into "Bear River."

Information: **Maquoketa Area Chamber of Commerce** | 117 S. Main, 52060 | 319/652-4602 | chamber.maquoketa.net.

Attractions

Costello's Old Mill Gallery. This 1867 stone gristmill a mile east of town now displays the work of midwestern artists. | 22095 Rte. 64 | 319/652-3351 | Free | Wed.–Sat. 10–5.

Hurstville Lime Kilns. In the 1870s, before the advent of concrete, these kilns were used to produce lime for area construction. Today they sit on a wooded bluff above a street that is a registered historic district north of town. | U.S. 61 | 319/652-4602 | Free | Daily.

Jackson County Historical Museum. County artifacts, including old agricultural equipment and a machine shed, along with a small historical research center. | 1212 E. Quarry St. | 319/652-5020 | Donations accepted | Tues.–Sun. 10–4, Mon. by appointment.

Maquoketa Caves State Park. There are six limestone caves along with a natural bridge, a balancing rock, and areas for picnicking at this park 6 mi northwest of town on Route 428. | 10970 98th St. | 319/652-5833 | www.state.ia.us/parks | Free | Daily.

Old City Hall Art Gallery. This stone-and-brick building, now a downtown art gallery, has served as a fire station, a police station, and as city hall. | 121 S. Olive St. | 319/652-3405 | Free | May–Dec., daily 11–4 or by appointment.

ON THE CALENDAR

JULY: *Banowetz Antique Show and Sale.* The biggest antiques show and sale in the Midwest draws thousands of collectors and dealers. | 319/652-2359.
OCT.: *Octoberfest of Bands.* A parade and field competition brings together some of the best high-school bands in the area. | 319/652-4602.

Dining

Decker Hotel Restaurant. American. You can dine on a formally presented prime rib or fish dinner or choose from a selection of healthful sandwiches and salads at this relaxed restaurant. On Sunday, enjoy a large brunch buffet, with fixings such as crêpes, quiches, puff pastries, hash browns, and eggs. | 128 N. Main St. | 319/652-6654 | $5-$17 | AE, D, DC, MC, V | Closed Mon. No dinner Sun.

Lodging

Decker Hotel. This 1875 Italianate hotel is furnished with Victorian and reproduction antiques. It is one block north of Platte Street, within walking distance of several art galleries, movie theaters, and shops. Restaurant, some microwaves, some refrigerators, some in-room hot tubs, cable TV, some in-room VCRs, room phones. No pets. No smoking. | 128 N. Main St. | 319/652–6654 | fax 319/652–6384 | 11 rooms, 7 suites | $55–$65 rooms, $95–$125 suites | AE, D, DC, MC, V.

Squiers Manor. Built in 1882, this Queen Anne–style mansion was the first home in Maquoketa to get electricity and running water. Much of the cherry and walnut woodwork is original, and there are antiques throughout. Most rooms have whirlpools. Complimentary breakfast. Some in-room hot tubs. Some in-room TVs. | 418 W. Pleasant St. | 319/652–6961 | fax 319/652–5995 | inkeeper@squiersmanor.com | www.squiersmanor.com | 8 rooms (2 with shower only), 3 suites | $75–$110 | AE, MC, V.

MARQUETTE

MAP 3, G2

(Nearby town also listed: West Union)

Known as North McGregor in its early days, Marquette started as a supply point for the railroad linking Chicago and Minneapolis/St. Paul. Both Marquette and its adjacent community of McGregor were destroyed by floods in 1896 and 1916. It was after the latter flood that North McGregor was renamed Marquette, in honor of the priest who first explored the upper Mississippi in 1673. The river still dominates life in Marquette, especially since the arrival of a riverboat casino. Also on the riverfront is AgriGrain Marketing, a primary employer in the area, which buys and ships by barge more than 40 million bushels of corn and soybeans each year.

Information: **McGregor–Marquette Chamber of Commerce** | 146 Main St., Box 105, McGregor, 52157 | 319/873–2186 or 800/896–0910 | www.netins.net/showcase/mmcofc.

Attractions

Backwater Cruises. Tour the shallow backwaters of the upper Mississippi on a 49-passenger paddle wheeler from Lansing, about 30 mi upriver from Marquette. | Front and Main Sts., Lansing | 319/544–4989 | $9 | Mid-May–mid-Oct., weekends; call for hrs.

Effigy Mounds National Monument. The 1,481-acre monument 3 mi north of Marquette contains 191 known prehistoric mounds built by the Woodland Indians in the shape of animals or in conical and linear shapes as well as numerous scenic hiking trails. | 151 Hwy. 76 | 319/873–3491 | www.nps.gov/efmo | $2 per person, $4 maximum charge per car | Daily 8–4:30.

Garnavillo Historical Museum. This little museum houses prehistoric and Native American artifacts in Garnavillo, about 12 mi south of Marquette. | Washington and Centre Sts., Garnavillo | 319/964–2191 | Free | Memorial Day–Labor Day, weekends 1–5 or by appointment.

Lockmaster's House Heritage Museum. The only remaining lockmaster's house on the Mississippi is now a museum in Guttenberg about 21 mi southeast of Marquette. It displays period furnishings and photos and provides insight into the lives of those who built the lock and dam system. | Lock and Dam La., Guttenberg | 319/252–1531 | Free | Memorial Day–mid-Oct., Tues.–Sun. noon–4.

Miss Marquette **Riverboat Casino Resort.** This riverboat casino offers all the usual gambling choices—slots, poker, blackjack, and roulette. | 100 Anti-monopoly St. | 319/873–3531 | Free | Fri.–Sun. 24 hrs, Mon.–Thurs. 9–3.

Pikes Peak State Park. You'll have a clear view of Wisconsin and Illinois from the park, on the highest bluff of the Mississippi, 5 mi southeast of town. | 15316 Great River Rd. | 319/873–2341 | www.state.ia.us/parks | Free | Daily.

River Bluffs Scenic Byway (East End). A hilly, roller coaster of a drive through numerous small towns. | Start on Main St. in MacGregor and head south for Pikes Peak | 319/873–2186 or 800/896–0910.

Spook Cave and Campground. Guided boat tours through Spook Cave are offered at the base of a 90-ft limestone bluff about 10 mi north of town. You can also picnic, camp, and swim. | 13299 Spook Cave Rd. | 319/873–2144 | $7 | May–Oct., daily.

Yellow River State Forest. This 8,503-acre forest 11 mi north of Marquette offers hiking, hunting, cross-country skiing, and more. The forest's Paint Creek Unit has the most acreage and recreational opportunities. | 729 State Forest Rd., Harpers Ferry | 319/586–2254 | Free | Daily.

ON THE CALENDAR
JUNE: *Hobo Festival.* A day of crafts, food, and costumes. | 319/873–2186.
SEPT.: *Labor Day Celebration.* This farewell-to-summer minifestival features a parade, musical performances, helicopter and hot-air balloon rides, and a vintage-car show. | 319/873–2186.

Dining
Alexander Café. American. This comfortable spot 1 mi south of Marquette boasts oversize chairs and large windows with fine river views. It's known for Friday-night fish fries and Saturday steak specials. | 213 Main St., McGregor | 319/873–3838 | $8–$12 | No credit cards.

Lodging
Alexander Hotel. This is the second-oldest hotel in Iowa. Each guest room is unique, but all retain the old-time flavor of the town. Downtown Marquette is just 1 mi away and Effigy Mountain State Park is just 3 mi south of the hotel. Restaurant, 2 bars. Some microwaves, some refrigerators, cable TV, no room phones. No pets. | 213 Main St., McGregor | 319/873–3454 | 9 rooms | $60–$70 | AE, MC, V.

Holiday Shores. On wooded bluffs with a view of the Mississippi, this motel is about 1 mi south of Marquette. Rooms are simply furnished. Cable TV. Pool. Hot tub. | 110 Front St., McGregor | 319/873–3449 | fax 319/873–3328 | 33 rooms | $55–$80 | D, MC, V.

Port of Marquette. This unassuming white clapboard motel on a cliff atop the Mississippi is part of the Miss Marquette Casino. Complimentary breakfast. Cable TV. Dock. Business services. | 30325 128th St. | 319/873–3477 or 800/496–8238 | fax 319/873–3479 | www.miss-marquette.com | 23 rooms, 1 suite | $50–$79 rooms, $150 suite | D, MC, V.

MARSHALLTOWN

MAP 3, E3

(Nearby town also listed: Grinnell)

Founded in 1853, this central Iowa community was one of two Iowa towns named Marshall; hence a few years after its founding, "town" was added to its name. Before the turn of the 20th century, baseball hall-of-famer Adrian "Cap" Anson was born here and played for the city league. Shortly after that, a resident named Dave Lennox began a company that eventually became Lennox Heating and Air Conditioning, the largest such company in the Midwest and one of the dominant forces in the economic base of Marshalltown.

Information: **Marshalltown Convention and Visitors Bureau** | 709 S. Center St., 50158 | 641/753–6645 or 800/697–3155 | www.marshalltown.org.

Attractions

Appleberry Farm. This is a working orchard and farm with crafts, cider, and homegrown dried flowers for sale. | 2402 W. Main St. | 515/752–8443 | Free | June–Oct., daily 9–7.

Big Treehouse. This 11-level tree house complete with sound effects, music, and gardens is the result of one man's hobby. | 2370 Shady Oaks Rd. | 515/752–2946 | $2 | Tours by appointment.

Fisher Art Gallery. Known for its permanent collection of ceramics and Impressionist and Postimpressionist paintings, this gallery also offers features regional artists in temporary exhibits. | 709 S. Center St. | 515/753–9013 | Free | Daily 11–5.

Glick-Sower House. This 1860 home is filled with 19th-century domestic items, such as kitchen utensils, sewing and washing machines, and other appliances. | 201 E. State St. | 515/752–6664 | Free | Apr.–Oct., Sat. 1–3; groups by appointment year-round.

Matthew Edel Blacksmith Shop. This blacksmith shop 10 mi south of town was operated by German immigrant Matthew Edel from 1883 until 1940. | 214 1st St., Haverhill | 515/752–6664 | Donations accepted | Memorial Day–Labor Day, daily noon–4.

Riverview Park. This 70-acre park has a swimming pool, campground, and access to a trail that's good for biking, walking, and jogging. | N. 3rd Ave. and Woodland Dr. | 515/754–5715 | Free | Daily.

ON THE CALENDAR

JULY: *Art Fair.* More than 60 regional artists display and sell their work at Fisher Community Center. | 515/753–9013.
JULY: *State High School Baseball Tournament.* Four days of the best in boys high-school baseball at Marshalltown High School. | 515/754–1142.

Dining

Caddyshack Pub and Restaurant. American. This popular dining spot in the American Legion Hall is affiliated with the American Legion but is open to the public, and serves such dishes as homemade pork tenderloins and onion rings. | 1301 S. 6th St. | 515/753–3212 | $6–$10 | MC, V | Closed Sun.

Fields Bar and Grill. American. Steaks and sandwiches are served all day at this casual restaurant in the center of the downtown area. | 2013 S. Center St. | 641/753–1099 | $5–$16 | AE, D, DC, MC, V.

Lodging

Best Western Regency Inn. This chain hotel caters to business travelers and is on a commercial street 5 mi north of downtown near several restaurants. Restaurant, bar, room service. Cable TV. Pool. Hot tub. Airport shuttle. | 3303 S. Center St. | 515/752–6321 | fax 515/752–4412 | www.bestwestern.com | 161 rooms | $65–$89 | AE, D, DC, MC, V.

Comfort Inn. This no-frills lodging is 3 mi south of downtown and the same distance from several antiques shopping malls and the Meskwaki Casino. Complimentary Continental breakfast. Cable TV. Pool. Hot tub. Business services. Pets allowed (fee). | 2613 S. Center St. | 515/752–6000 | fax 515/752–8762 | www.comfortinn.com | 62 rooms | $55 | AE, D, DC, MC, V.

Marshalltown AmericInn and Suites. This motel is in a commercial area 3 mi north of downtown. The Grand Suites have two rooms with a fireplace, a kitchen, and a hot tub. Complimentary Continental breakfast, in-room data ports, cable TV, room phones, TV in common area. Pool. Hot tub. Video games. Laundry facilities. No pets. | 115 Iowa Ave. W | 641/752–4844 or 800/634–3444 | fax 641/753–7714 | www.americinn.com | 46 rooms, 4 suites | $59–$67 rooms, $100–$122 suites | AE, D, DC, MC, V.

Super 8. This brick motel is 5 mi south of downtown, less than 5 mi from nearby shops and casinos, and within a block or two of several restaurants. Cable TV. Business services. | 3014 S. Center St. | 515/753–8181 | fax 515/753–8181 | www.super8.com | 61 rooms | $38–$55 | AE, D, MC, V.

MASON CITY

MAP 3, E2

(Nearby town also listed: Clear Lake)

Winnebago and Sioux Indians were the first to call northern Iowa home, but two men by the name of John Long (founder of Mason City) and John Biford were the first white settlers to join them in 1853. In the early 20th century, Mason City became home to Meredith Willson, author of the novel and award-winning musical *The Music Man*. Frank Lloyd Wright designed buildings here, and a number of other buildings feature Victorian- and Queen Anne–style architecture.

Information: **Mason City Convention and Visitors Bureau** | 15 W. State St., 50402-1128 | 641/423–5724 or 800/423–5724 | cvb@masoncityia.com | www.masoncityia.com.

Attractions

Cerro Gordo Wind Farm. Eight miles west of Mason City, this wind farm consists of 55 wind energy turbines. The wind farm viewing area is on Route S14. | 10586 Balsam Ave., Ventura | 641/829–3933 | www.masoncitytourism.com | Free | Daily.

Charles H. MacNider Museum. This Tudor-style mansion was donated to the city by the decorated World War I general and displays a collection of 19th- and 20th-century American art, a collection of puppets, and a variety of temporary exhibits. | 303 2nd St. SE | 515/421–3666 | Free | Tues., Thurs. 10–9; Mon., Wed., Fri., Sat. 10–5; Sun. 1–5.

Here you will also find the small **Meredith Willson Footbridge,** which spans Willow Creek and is on the town's historical walking tour.

Frank Lloyd Wright Stockman House. Famed architect Frank Lloyd Wright designed this building in 1908 for the town's first doctor. This was the first building in Iowa that Wright designed in the Prairie style. | 530 1st St. NE | 515/423–1923 | www.radiopark.com/stockmanhouse | $3 | June–Oct., Sat. 10–5, Sun. 1–5.

Kinney Pioneer Museum. Fossils, dolls, a soda shop, a log cabin, a blacksmith shop, and antique cars are on display at this museum 7 mi west of town at the entrance to Municipal Airport. | 9184-G 265th St. | 641/423–1258 or 641/357–2980 | $2.50 | May–Sept., Wed.–Sun. 1–5.

Lime Creek Nature Center. You'll find 4 mi of walking trails through 400 acres of restored prairie as well as a nature center with displays of live and stuffed birds, mammals, fish, and insects here. | 3501 Lime Creek Rd. | 515/423–5309 | Free | Daily.

Margaret M. MacNider/East Park. An arch bridge replica from the movie *The Music Man* and a life-size locomotive for you to examine are among the attractions here. | 841 Birch Dr. | 515/421–3673 | Free | Daily.

Meredith Willson Boyhood Home. The 1902 birthplace of the man who wrote *The Music Man*. | 314 S. Pennsylvania Ave. | 515/423–3534 | $3 | May–Oct., Fri.–Sun. 1–4.

Van Horn's Antique Truck Museum. There's a large display of commercial vehicles, circus equipment, and antique gas pumps at this site 2 mi north of town. | 15272 North St. | 515/423–0550 or 515/423–9066 | $5 | May–Sept., Mon.–Sat. 9–4, Sun. 11–4.

JULY: *North Iowa Fair.* A draft-horse show is this fair's biggest event, drawing breeders and aficionados from around the country. | 515/423–3811.

AUG.: *Snowmobile Grass Drag Races.* People haul out their snowmobiles in the off-season with this unusual event. | 515/423–5724.

Dining

Chandler's Eatery and Pub. Eclectic. At this Chicago-chop-house/California-grill-style restaurant, you can have such local favorites as the London broil with Chandler's sauce and lighter fare like salads and sandwiches. A number of different cheesecakes are sure to satisfy your sweet tooth. | 1617 S. Monroe St. | 641/421–1525 | $4–$20 | AE, D, MC, V | Closed Sun., Mon.

Lodging

Comfort Inn. This modest lodging is right next to the hospital and the local mall. Complimentary Continental breakfast. Some refrigerators, cable TV. Pool. Hot tub. | 410 5th St. SW | 515/423–4444 | fax 515/424–5358 | www.comfortinn.com | 60 rooms | $42 | AE, D, DC, MC, V.

Days Inn. This modest chain hotel is within walking distance of the lake, which may afford you some pleasant views around sunset. Complimentary Continental breakfast. Cable TV. Business services. Pets allowed. | 2301 4th St. SW | 515/424–0210 | fax 515/424–0210 | www.daysinn.com | 58 rooms | $48 | AE, D, DC, MC, V.

Mason City Super 8. Built in 1999, this motel has large guest rooms with cherry furnishings. If you stay here, you'll be just 2 mi west of downtown, on U.S. 122, near the Frank Lloyd Wright Architectural Museum, the Antique Fire Station Museum, and the *Lady of the Lake* paddle-wheel excursion boat. Complimentary Continental breakfast. Room phones, cable TV. No pets. | 3010 4th St. SW | 641/423–8855 or 800/800–8000 | www.super8.com | 57 rooms | $59–$79 | AE, D, DC, MC, V.

Super 8. Just off Interstate 35 at its junction with B 35, this interstate motel is near the Mason City Municipal Airport. Complimentary Continental breakfast. Cable TV. | B-35 and I-35, exit 193 | 515/357–7521 | fax 515/357–5999 | www.super8.com | 60 rooms | $38–$55 | AE, D, DC, MC, V.

MISSOURI VALLEY

MAP 3, B4

(Nearby town also listed: Council Bluffs)

Settlers from Tennessee were the first whites to make a home in this part of southwestern Iowa in the 1850s. The town's location on the Missouri River and the expansion of three railroads into the Missouri Valley ensured its growth and stability in its early years. But the river also presents a constant threat, with at least six floods all but destroying the town since its founding. Missouri Valley is at the heart of two scenic byways in Iowa and is not far from the DeSoto National Wildlife Refuge.

Information: **Missouri Valley Chamber of Commerce** | 400 E. Erie St., 51555 | 712/642–2553 | www.missourivalley.com.

Attractions

DeSoto National Wildlife Refuge. This 7,800-acre refuge is 6 mi west of town on a major flyway for migrating ducks, geese, and other waterfowl that make use of the refuge as a rest stop in October and November. You'll also find the Steamship *Bertrand* displayed here and you can see what this supply boat for the Montana goldfields was carrying when she sank on the Missouri in 1864. | 1434 316th La. | 712/642–4121 or 712/642–2772 | $3 per vehicle | Daily dawn–dusk.

Harrison County Historical Village/Welcome Center. More than 10,000 items, including household and farm equipment, are on display in five vintage buildings, among them a log cabin and a schoolhouse 3 mi northeast of town on Highway 30. | 2931 Monroe Ave. | 712/642–2114 | $2 | Apr.–Nov., Mon.–Sat. 9–5, Sun. noon–5.

Loess Hills Scenic Byway. This network of designated two-lane roads stretches for 225 mi through 17,190 acres of rugged, hilly land shaped thousands of years ago in the wake of retreating glaciers and now declared a National Scenic Byway. The hills were created from fine, powdery soil whipped into snowdriftlike formations by primordial winds. Hills such as these exist only in one other place in the world—the Huang He river valley in China. Maps of the Byway, which begins about 3 mi east of town, are available at Iowa welcome centers. | Rte. 183 | 712/642–2114 | Free | Daily dawn–dusk.

© Corbis

IOWA'S "GLACIAL FLOUR"

What do western Iowa and Shaanxi, China, have in common? They're the only places to find a remarkable geological formation—windswept, oddly shaped mini-mountains made of thick layers of loess. Pronounced "luss," loess is German for loose river silt. Iowa's Loess Hills rise 200 ft above the flat plains, forming a narrow band of rough and jagged bluffs along the Missouri River that stretches 200 mi from the Missouri border north to just past Sioux City.

Some small Loess Hills towns are reaching out to tourists with new amenities and low-key attractions. Conservationists—eager to preserve the fragile hills from too much development—also have mobilized to get federal protection for the area. In 1999, Washington lawmakers authorized a study to determine if the Loess Hills should become a national park.

It all began during the Ice Age when glaciers ground rock in their path into a fine, powderlike sediment known as "glacial flour" that ended up on the Missouri River floodplain. Fierce winds later picked up this sediment and dropped it into thick piles that became the Loess Hills. Erosion by wind and water created some of the Loess Hill's stranger formations, from bumpy ridge crests that resemble an animal's back to slope indentations that look like steps made by an animal.

While Iowa waits to see if its Loess Hills go national, visitors should check out the Pioneer Forest Overlook, a hilltop observation deck built in 1997 near Preparation Canyon State Park, just west of the small town of Moorhead. Built on a spot where five ridges converge, this large wooden deck offers a spectacular panoramic view of what looks like a rippling checkerboard of flat fields, wooded hills, and steep ridges. To see more by car, bicycle, or on foot, pick up a free map that details several scenic loops at the Loess Hills Hospitality Association's visitor center in Moorhead off Highway 183.

Museum of Religious Arts. A wax depiction of the Last Supper, a chapel, and other artifacts on display at this museum 5 mi north of town near Logan reflect the history and culture of various faiths. | 2697 Niagara Tr. | 712/644–3888 | Donations accepted | Weekdays 10–6:30.

Wilson Island State Recreation Area. You'll find camping, primitive cabins, interpretive nature trails, stream fishing, and boat access to the Missouri at this recreation area 12 mi south of town. | Rte. 362 | 712/642–2069 | www.state.ia.us/parks | $4–$9 for camping.

ON THE CALENDAR
JUNE: *Western Iowa Gospel Sing.* More than 30 gospel groups and entertainers perform in the Missouri Valley City Park during this three-day event. | 712/642–2553.
OCT.: *Halloween Parade.* More than 400 ghosts and goblins parade through the streets en route to an apple-bobbing festival. | 712/642–2553.

Dining
Izzy's Place. American. For home-style cooking 24 hours a day, this is the place to go. You'll find your comfort-food favorites here: chicken-fried steak, hamburgers, onion rings, and french fries. Izzy's also serves breakfast foods, like omelets and pancakes, all day. Open 24 hrs. | 514 E. Erie St. | 712/642–4954 | $2–$6 | No credit cards.

Lodging
Days Inn. This motel is off Interstate 29 at exit 75, 1 mi east of downtown Missouri Valley. You'll find several restaurants and shops nearby. Complimentary Continental breakfast. Some refrigerators, in-room TVs. Pool. Hot tub. Gym. Pets allowed (fee). | 1967 Rte. 30 | 712/642–4788 | fax 712/642–3813 | www.daysinn.com | 48 rooms | $60–$85 | AE, D, DC, MC, V.

MOUNT PLEASANT

MAP 3, G5

(Nearby town also listed: Fairfield)

When settlers founded this community in 1835, they were so captivated by this hillside land on a bend of Big Creek that Mount Pleasant seemed the only suitable name. This community of 8,000 has maintained its pleasant reputation through 150 years of agriculture and industrial growth by developing 230 acres of parkland and a strong library system and school district.

Information: Henry County Tourism Association | 502 W. Washington St., Mount Pleasant, 52641 | 319/385–2460 or 800/421–4282 | hcta@lisco.net.

Attractions
Iowa Wesleyan College. This four-year liberal arts college, founded in 1842 by the Methodist Church, pioneered a unique Real World Learning program. | 601 N. Main St. | 319/385–6215 or 319/385–8021 | fax 319/385–6296 | www.iwc.edu | Free | Daily.

Midwest Old Threshers Heritage Museum. At this site south of town you can explore agriculture history through steam engines, gas-burning engines, an exhibit on women's contributions to the family farm, and demonstrations of farm life from the 1840s to 1930. | 1887 Threshers Rd. | 319/385–8937 | $3; kids free | May–Sept., daily by appointment.

Oakland Mills Park. The Skunk River and many hiking trails crisscross this 104-acre park 4 mi south of town. There's a nature center and historic wagon bridge now used by pedestrians. | U.S. 34 | 319/986–5067 | Free | Daily.

Swedish American Museum. Here you'll learn the story of the Swedish immigration through exhibits portraying family life, farming practices, social and business activities, and major events of the community. The museum, which is 10 mi north of Mt. Pleasant, has a library containing genealogical and historical materials. | James Ave. off Hwy. 218 | 319/254–2317 | Free | Mon., Tues., Thurs.–Sat. 9–4.

Theatre Museum of Repertoire Americana. This celebration of the days of traveling vaude-ville and minstrel shows showcases old sets and scenery, costumes, scripts, and musical scores. | 405 E. Threshers Rd. | 319/385–9432 | $3; kids free | Memorial Day–Labor Day, Tues.–Sun. 10–4:30; Sept.–May, weekdays 1–4.

ON THE CALENDAR

SEPT.: *Midwest Old Settlers and Threshers Reunion.* This weeklong countywide cele-bration of the history of agriculture includes corn-shucking contests, steam engine shows, and lye soap making. | 319/385–8937.

DEC.: *Holiday Stroll.* Wander past the festive live and stationery window displays in storefront windows around Central Park in downtown Mt. Pleasant or take a horse-drawn carriage ride during this evening event. | 319/385–3101.

Dining

Iris Restaurant and Lounge. American. Just 1½ mi west of downtown on Highway 34 West, this restaurant and lounge owned by state representative Dave Heaton is known for its French onion soup. You can get anything from sandwiches to lobster dinners here, and for Sunday's buffet brunch the owner has been known to make rhubarb pies. | 915 W. Washington St. | 319/385–2241 | $6–$25 | AE, D, MC, V.

Lodging

Dover House. This B&B is in a residential neighborhood 10 mi east of downtown. The 1913 house has an eclectic array of antique and French provincial furnishings. The guest suite has a brass bed, full kitchen, sitting area, and private bathroom. Complimentary break-fast. Refrigerator, cable TV, room phones. No pets. No smoking. | 205 E. Main St., New Lon-don, off Hwy. 34 | 319/367–5893 | 1 suite | $65 | No credit cards.

Heartland Inn. Photos and framed newspaper clippings line the lobby and hallways of this motel 2 mi north of town. Complimentary Continental breakfast. Cable TV. Pool. Hot tub, sauna. Business services. Pets allowed. | Hwy. 218 N | 319/385–2102 | fax 319/385–3223 | 59 rooms | $57–$65 | AE, D, DC, MC, V.

Super 8. This basic chain motel is 2 mi east of Iowa Wesleyan College and next door to two popular restaurants. Complimentary Continental breakfast. Microwaves available, cable TV. Business services. | 1000 N. Grand Ave. | 319/385–8888 | fax 319/385–8888 | www.super8.com | 55 rooms | $50 | AE, D, DC, MC, V.

MUSCATINE

MAP 3, G4

(Nearby towns also listed: Bettendorf, Davenport)

No one agrees on where the name "Muscatine" came from. Some say it comes from the Mascoutin Indians who lived in the area; others believe it came from the Native American word that means "fiery nation" or "burning island." In any case that's what the town was called by the 1850s when German immigrants made use of the fresh-water mussel shells in the Mississippi to build an enduring business of pearl button manufacturing.

Information: **Muscatine Convention and Visitors Bureau** | 319 E. 2nd St., 52761 | 319/263–8895 | visitorinfo@muscatine.com | www.muscatine.com.

Attractions

Mark Twain National Wildlife Refuge. Two of the four separate divisions of this refuge are south of Muscatine on County Route X61. Both the Big Timber Division (which is 10 mi south of town) and the Louisa Division (which is 14 mi south of town) are part of one of the most important flyways in the country, and offer wildlife observation, hiking trails, educational programs, and more. The Louisa Division closes for four and a half months each year so migrating birds will not be disturbed. | Rte. X61 | 319/523–6982 | Free | Big Timber: daily dawn–dusk; Louisa: Feb.–Sept. 15, daily dawn–dusk.

Mark Twain Overlook. A commemorative plaque with a quote from the great author marks an expansive view of the river he wrote about. | Hwy. 92 and Business U.S. 61 | 319/263–8895 | Free | Daily 24 hrs.

Muscatine Art Center. A 1908 Edwardian mansion houses French Impressionist works and historical decorative arts. | 1314 Mulberry Ave. | 319/263–8282 | Free | Tues.–Fri. 10–5, Thurs. 7 PM–9 PM, weekends 1–5.

Muscatine Municipal Golf Course. A well-maintained 18-hole course. | 1820 Rte. 38 N | 319/263–4735 | $9–$11 | Mar.–Nov.

Pearl Button Museum. Pearl button manufacturing put this town on the map in the late 1800s and at the turn of the last century Muscatine produced a third of the world's buttons. Learn about the industry's past, present, and future here. | 206 W. 2nd St. | 319/263–8895 | Free | Sat. 1–3 or by appointment.

Saulsbury Bridge Recreation Area. This 675-acre county park has a nature center, hunting and fishing areas, and a canoe transport service. | 2007 Saulsbury Rd. | 319/649–3379 or 319/264–5922 | Free | Apr.–Oct., daily; Nov.–Mar., Sun.–Fri.

Shady Creek Recreation Area. The Army Corps of Engineers manages this 16-acre area 7 mi east of town on the Mississippi River where you'll find 53 modern campsites and a boat ramp. | 1611 2nd Ave. | 319/263–7913 | www.mvr.usace.army.mil/missriver/rec.htm | Free | Daily.

Wildcat Den State Park. One of the focal points of this park 12 mi east of Muscatine is the Pine Creek Grist Mill. Built in 1848, the mill is on the National Register of Historic Places. | 1884 Wildcat Den Rd. | 319/263–4337 | www.state.ia.us/parks | Free | Daily.

ON THE CALENDAR

JAN.: *Ragtime Weekend.* Silent movies, ragtime concerts, and 1920s antiques. | 319/263–8895.
AUG.: *Great River Days.* Three days of food, crafts, a golf tournament, and a fishing tournament. | 319/263–8895.

Dining

McDuff's. American/Casual. This casual pub is on the corner of Iowa Avenue in the heart of downtown. You can get cheeseburgers and butterflied pork chop sandwiches for lunch; for dinner the menu offerings are mostly steaks, Iowa chops, and catfish. | 101 W. Mississippi Dr. | 319/262–4030 | $4–$15 | MC, V | Closed Sun.

Lodging

Econo Lodge Fantasuite Hotel. This hotel is on the northern edge of town within walking distance of a few popular restaurants and within easy driving distance of several more. Restaurant, bar, room service. Some in-room hot tubs, cable TV. Pool. Laundry facilities. Business services. | 2402 Park Ave. | 319/264–3337 or 800/234–7829 | fax 319/263–0413 | 74 rooms, 17 hot tub suites | $52–$55 | AE, D, DC, MC, V.

Holiday Inn. This hotel 5 mi northeast of town is built around a central atrium with a waterfall and a miniature pond. There are several restaurants within a mile. Restaurant, bar, room service. In-room data ports, some refrigerators, cable TV. Pool, wading pool. Hot tub, sauna.

Exercise equipment. Laundry facilities. Business services. Pets allowed (fee.). | 2915 N. U.S. 61 | 319/264–5550 | fax 319/264–0451 | www.basshotels.com/holiday-inn | 112 rooms | $68– $89 | AE, D, DC, MC, V.

Muscatine Super 8. This chain motel 3 mi northwest of downtown has interior corridors. Complimentary Continental breakfast. Some microwaves, some refrigerators, cable TV. | 2900 N. Hwy 61 | 319/263–9100 or 800/800–8000 | 63 rooms | $45–$60 | AE, D, DC, MC, V.

NEWTON

(Nearby town also listed: Grinnell)

Founded in 1850, Newton is best known for a resident named Fred Maytag, who started making washing machines here in 1893. Today the Maytag Corporation is the world's leader in laundry appliances and continues to make its home alongside the 14,000 residents of Newton. The philanthropic efforts of the Maytag family and the Maytag Foundation have led to the creation of hospitals, parks, golf courses, churches, and other community structures, all enriching the fabric of this community.

Information: **Newton Convention and Visitors Bureau** | 113 1st Ave., 50208 | 515/792– 0299 or 800/798–0299 | www.newton-iowa.com.

Attractions
Fred Maytag Park. This 40-acre park contains a swimming pool and a band shell. | 301 S. 11th Ave. W | 515/792–1470 | Free | June–Aug., daily.

International Wrestling Institute. The focus of the museum in this training facility is the history of amateur and professional wrestling. There's a wrestling ring, Olympic uniforms and flags, a video room, and training equipment. | 1690 W. 19th St. S | 515/791–1516 | $3 | Tues.–Sat. 10–5.

Jasper County Historical Museum. Victorian and 1930s-era homes, a church, a school, a post office, and a Maytag display are included in this complex that tells the story of Jasper County. | 1700 S. 15th Ave. W | 515/792–9118 | $2 | May–Sept., daily 1–4:30.

Maytag Dairy Farms. This farm ¼ mi north of Maytag plant is known for its Maytag blue cheese and contains historic artifacts of the cheese industry. | 2282 E. 8th St. N | 641/792– 1133 | Free | Weekdays 8–5.

Trainland, USA. This operating toy-train museum 12 mi west of town puts you in the conductor's seat with an interactive animation center. | 3135 Rte. 117 N, Colfax | 515/674–3813 | $4.50 | Memorial Day–Labor Day, daily 10–6.

ON THE CALENDAR
JAN.: *Crow Day.* This one-day festival heralds the return of the birds to their winter rookery just outside town. You can take a bus tour to the rookery, go to a dance, and watch the crowning of the Newton Crow Queen. | 515/792–0299.
JULY: *Blue Festival.* Showcases Maytag blue cheese with art, music, and a golf tournament in Fred Maytag Park. | 515/792–0299.
JULY: *Newton Air Show.* Aerobatics, skydivers, ground displays, and more at Newton Airport. | 515/792–0299.

Dining
La Corsette Maison Inn. Continental. This restaurant is housed in a 1911 Mission-style mansion that is now a B&B. Even as a nonguest, you can enjoy dinner served in the gracious dining room by tuxedoed waiters with soothing music from the baby grand piano in the parlor. Particularly tasty: the farmer's frittata, a breakfast dish involving bacon, onion,

new potatoes, and both cheddar and Swiss cheese, or the mushrooms stuffed with ham, cloves, mozzarella, parmesan, and pine nuts. Reservations must be made 48 hours in advance. No smoking. One seating per day, usually 7 PM; call for schedule. | 629 1st Ave. | 515/792–6833 | Reservations essential | Jacket required | $45–$85 | AE, MC, V.

Lodging

Aerie Glen Bed and Breakfast. This rambling, contemporary Tudor house is on 8 wooded acres in Lambs Grove, just outside Newton proper. Choose the Cardinal Suite for skylights in cathedral ceilings, a king-size bed, and a private entrance, or stay in the cottage for total privacy, a fireplace, and a two-person hot tub. Complimentary breakfast. In-room hot tubs. Pool. No pets. No kids under 14. No smoking. | 2364 1st Ave. W, Lambs Grove | 515/792–9032 | fax 515/791–7917 | www.midiowa.com/aerieglen | 3 rooms, 1 cottage | $79–$100 rooms, $190 cottage | D, MC, V.

Best Western Newton Inn. Immediately south of Interstate 80, this motel is known for its indoor family recreation area which boasts a junior-Olympic-size indoor pool, an oversize whirlpool, two cedar-wood saunas, indoor putting green and picnic area, Ping-Pong tables, and a video-game arcade. There's also a sundeck on the roof. Restaurant, bar. Cable TV, in-room VCRs available. Pool. Hot tub. Putting green. Gym. Business services. Pets allowed. | 2000 W. 18th St. S | 515/792–4200 | fax 515/792–0108 | www.bestwestern.com | 118 rooms | $65 | AE, D, DC, MC, V.

Days Inn. This hotel is 2 mi south of town near the interstate but surrounded by cornfields. Guest rooms are spacious and very quiet. Complimentary Continental breakfast. Cable TV. Business services. Pets allowed. | 1605 W. 19th St. S | 641/792–2330 | fax 641/792–1045 | www.daysinn.com | 59 rooms | $50–$75 | AE, D, DC, MC, V.

Holiday Inn Express. Just off Interstate 80 at exit 164, this no-frills hotel is about 1 mi away from the Jasper County Museum and the International Wrestling Museum. In-room data ports. Cable TV. Pool. Hot tub. Laundry service. Business services. | 1700 W. 19th St. S | 515/792–7722 or 888/249–1468 | fax 515/792–1787 | www.basshotels.com/hiexpress | 60 rooms | $59–$70 | AE, D, DC, MC, V.

La Corsette Maison. This downtown inn was built as a private home in 1911 and has been called one of the best examples of Arts-and-Crafts style architecture anywhere in the country. All the woodwork and lighting fixtures are original, and the furnishings and wall treatments reflect the building's history. In warmer months, the inn's expansive porch, with its wicker furniture, flowers, and commanding view of the manicured grounds, is the place to be. Restaurant, complimentary breakfast. No TV in some rooms. Business services. No smoking. | 629 1st Ave. E | 515/792–6833 | fax 515/292–6597 | www.innbook.com | 7 rooms | $80 | AE, MC, V.

Super 8. This motel is in a commercial area 2 mi northwest of downtown. The breakfast nook is well-equipped, and there are several restaurants within walking distance. Complimentary Continental breakfast. Cable TV. Business services. | 1635 S. 12th Ave. W | 515/792–8868 | fax 515/792–8868 | www.super8.com | 43 rooms | $45 | AE, D, DC, MC, V.

OKOBOJI

MAP 3, C1

(Nearby towns also listed: Spencer, Spirit Lake)

The Lakota Sioux Indian word for the large blue-water lake here and the town at its banks means "reeds" or "rushes," as the lakeshore was once covered by them. Okoboji is situated between East and West Okoboji Lakes, which together cover more than 5,000 acres. The town is a vacation haven during hot summers, as well as a popular winter sports destination. On the western shore of the lake is Arnold's Park, a large recreation complex that includes an amusement park and other tourist attractions. Arnold's Park can be reached easily from Okoboji itself via a 280-yard bridge.

Information: **Okoboji Tourism Association** | 243 W. Broadway, Arnold's Park 51331 | 800/270–2574 | www.okoboji.com.

Attractions

Arnold's Park Amusement Park. This park was already 14 years old in 1929 when the Coaster, its wooden roller coaster, was installed. The Coaster now competes for attention with several dozen other rides and attractions, but it's still a star attraction. | Hwy. 71 and Lake St. | 712/332–2183 | www.arnoldspark.com | Memorial Day–Labor Day daily 10 AM–11 PM | $14.

Boji Bay Water Park. This large amusement complex just north of town includes four water slides, a wave pool, the Lazy River rafting ride, and a wading pool for small children. | 2207 Okoboji Ave., Milford | 712/338–2473 | $14 | Memorial Day–Labor Day, daily 11:30–6.

East Okoboji Lake. This 1,835-acre natural lake on the east edge of town is one of 13 lakes known as Iowa's Great Lakes—it has boat ramps, swimming, fishing, and picnic tables. | Hwy. 71 | 800/270–2574 | www.state.ia.us.

Gull Point State Park. This shady 160-acre park on the shore of West Okoboji Lake 6 mi southwest of town is small but lovely with several beaches, marshes inhabited by diverse flora and fauna, hiking trails, and the best campground in the lakes region. | 1500 Harpen St. | 712/337–3211 | www.state.ia.us/parks | Free | Daily.

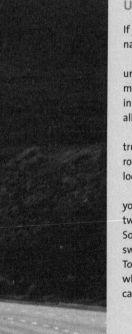

© Corbis

UNIVERSITY OF OKOBOJI

If you visit Okoboji you're sure to see bumper stickers, T-shirts, caps, visors, and pennants proclaiming the merits of the University of Okoboji.

The sports teams are legendary: the football team, the Phantoms, remains undefeated, and tickets are hard to come by. During football season, it's not uncommon for the Phantoms to play the University of Iowa, Nebraska, and Notre Dame all in one day. All tickets are sold for seats on the 50-yard line and proceeds benefit an all-weather dome over West Okoboji Lake.

The philosophy at Okoboji is simple: books and lectures are not necessary for a true learning experience. University of Okoboji students work toward degrees in roller coaster engineering and human anatomy, both acquired by grueling hours at local parks and beaches.

You see, there isn't really a University of Okoboji. The university is a joke, and if you don't go along with it, you'll really upset the administration, which consists of two brothers and a friend with a great imagination and lots of community spirit. Sometime in the mid-1980s, they began printing T-shirts, bumper stickers, and sweatshirts with the university logo, with proceeds benefiting community causes. Today, alumni chapters across the country boast loyalty to this imaginary university where everyone graduates at the top of the class. If you visit Okoboji, you too can call yourself an alum.

Higgins Museum. This banking museum displays national bank notes from 1863 to 1935, paying particular attention to those from Iowa, Nebraska, Minnesota, and South Dakota. The museum also houses between 16,000 and 20,000 turn-of-the-last-century Iowa-themed photo postcards. | 1509 Sanborn Ave. | 712/332–5859 | Free | May–Sept., Tues.–Sun. 11–5.

Iowa Great Lakes Maritime Museum. This attraction includes restored wooden boats and other nautical memorabilia in Arnold's Park. Two short multimedia presentations illustrate the natural and nautical history of the Iowa Great Lakes region. | 243 Broadway | 712/332–5264 | www.okobojimuseum.org | Free | Memorial Day–Labor Day, daily 10–8.

Pikes Point State Park. You'll find an unguarded beach on the east side of West Okoboji Lake and numerous picnic sites, including one sheltered site, at this park 3 mi east of town. | 1500 Harpen St. | 712/337–3211 | www.state.ia.us/parks | Free | Daily.

West Okoboji Lake. The state's deepest natural lake and the second largest of Iowa's Great Lakes, this is one of only three blue-water lakes in the world. (The other two being Lake Geneva in Switzerland and Lake Lorraine in Canada.) Fishing, boating, and water sports are all popular here. | Hwy. 71 | 800/270–2574 | www.state.ia.us.

ON THE CALENDAR

MAY: *Blue Water Music Festival.* Musicians from around the region representing diverse styles play for free all weekend. | 800/270–2574.

JUNE–AUG.: *Okoboji Summer Theater.* Students from Stephens College in Columbia, Missouri, earn credits by performing a different show every week here in summer. | 712/332–7773.

Dining

Crescent Beach Restaurant. American. Dock your boat at this restaurant's slip and enter a large front dining room set with deep-green linens and crystal goblets. The menu offers many choices, but especially popular is the Wednesday-night fish fry, with all-you-can-eat battered perch fillets. Piano music accompanies dinners nightly. | 1620 Lakeshore Dr. on W. Lake Okoboji, Wahpeton | 712/337–3351 | $7–$15 | AE, D, MC, V.

Dry Dock. American. Video equipment at this casual Arnold's Park gathering spot simulcast live pictures of lake activity, and people sailing, swimming, or waterskiing often pass by on the water to wave. The restaurant is decorated in a casual nautical theme and is known for its excellent, juicy burgers. | Hwy. 71, Arnold's Park | 712/332–9449 | $6–$12 | AE, D, MC, V.

Stars and Stripes. American. This Americana-filled restaurant serves salads and sandwiches at lunch, pub fare like stews and heartier sandwiches in mid-afternoon, and entrées ranging from fettuccine alfredo to jumbo shrimp to sirloin in the evening. In fine weather, dine on the terrace. | 3301 Lakeshore Dr. | 712/332–2113 | $10–$20 | AE, D, DC, MC, V | Breakfast also available.

Lodging

AmericInn Motel and Suites. This chain motel is on U.S. 71, adjacent to the Brooks Golf Club and near several area restaurants, parks, and golf courses. Complimentary Continental breakfast. In-room data ports. Cable TV. Pool. Hot tub, sauna. Laundry facilities. Business services. | 1005 Brooks Park Dr. | 712/332–9000 or 800/634–3444 | fax 712/332–9724 | www.americinn.com | 61 rooms | $75–$219 | AE, D, MC, V.

Country Club Motel. Rooms are simple at this one-story, L-shape motel centered around a pool and surrounded on three sides by trees but you'll be just half a block from Lake Okoboji and a public boat ramp. Picnic area. Some kitchenettes, cable TV. Pool. Business services. Pets allowed. | 1107 Sanborn Ave. | 712/332–5617 or 800/831–5615 | fax 712/332–7705 | 40 rooms, 13 suites | $60–$99 rooms, $119 suites | AE, D, DC, MC, V.

Fillenwarth Beach. This resort on West Okoboji Lake caters to outdoor enthusiasts. Wood-frame buildings are nestled into a wooded hillside, and all rooms have balconies with lake views. The resort also offers lake cruises, boat trips, and a host of other, nonwatery, activities. Picnic area. Cable TV, in-room VCRs. Indoor-outdoor pool. Tennis. Beach, dock, water sports, boating. Business services, airport shuttle. Children's programs (ages 2 and up), playground. Pets allowed. | 87 Lake Shore Dr., Arnold's Park | 712/332–5646 | fax 712/332–5646 | www.fillenwarthbeach.com | 15 cottages (fit up to 18 people), 75 apartments | $88–$480 cottages, $120–$216 apartments | No credit cards | Closed Oct.–Apr.

Four Seasons Resort. A nautical motif dominates this resort on West Okoboji Lake—there's lots of brass, sea blue, seashells, and lighthouses. The property has its own boating jetties, beach, marina, and lakefront walking paths. Some rooms have balconies with lake views Restaurant, bar, picnic area. Cable TV. Beach. Pets allowed. | 3333 U.S. 71, Arnold's Park | 712/332–2103 or 800/876–2103 | 32 rooms | $75–$115 | AE, MC, V.

The Inn. This is an old-school resort, complete with balconies, patios, bathhouses on the beach, and a social director to coordinate activities in summer. Rooms have pine log furniture and wildlife prints. Restaurant, bar (with entertainment), room service. Kitchenettes, refrigerators, cable TV. 2 pools. Driving range, 9-hole golf course, putting green, tennis. Docks, boating. Playground, children's programs (ages 4 and up). Business services. | 3301 Lakeshore Dr. | 712/332–2113 | fax 712/332–2714 | 131 one- and two-bedroom apartments) | $110–$300 | AE, D, MC, V | Closed Oct.–Apr.

Village East Resort. This resort on Lake Okoboji offers fine lake and golf course views. Guest rooms have antique reproduction furnishings. Two restaurants are adjacent to the resort. Restaurant, bar. Cable TV, in-room VCRs available. 2 pools. Beauty salon, hot tub, sauna. 18-hole golf course, tennis. Gym. Cross-country skiing. Playground. Business services. Pets allowed. | 1405 Hwy. 71 | 712/332–2161 or 800/727–4561 | fax 712/332–7727 | 95 rooms, 4 suites | $149–$164 rooms, $225 suites | AE, D, DC, MC, V.

Wild Rose of Okoboji. Guest rooms in this modern Victorian-style home on the north end of town are cozy and bright, with plush furnishings, spacious balconies, and fireplaces in some rooms. The house has a 3½-acre back garden and the lake is just 5 min away by bicycle. Complimentary breakfast. Some in-room hot tubs, cable TV. | 2329 170th St. | 712/332–9986 | fax 712/332–6069 | www.wildroseresort.com | 12 rooms | $100–$130 | AE, D, MC, V.

ONAWA

MAP 3, B3

(Nearby town also listed: Denison)

The word "Onawa" comes from an old Ojibway love song that was incorporated into Henry Wadsworth Longfellow's poem "Song of Hiawatha." Onawa means "wide-awake," and whether by coincidence or design, this town is known for its wide streets and alert citizenry. The greatest contribution an Onawa resident has made to society came about when schoolteacher Christian Nelson, who worked part-time at an ice-cream store, created the Eskimo Pie and chocolate-covered ice-cream bar in 1920. The world hasn't been the same since.

Information: Onawa Chamber of Commerce | 1009 Iowa Ave., Box 238, 51040 | 712/423–1801 | chamber@onawa.com | www.onawa.com.

Attractions

Casino Omaha. This large casino has slot machines, blackjack, and a half dozen other ways to part you with your vacation funds. A buffet is available for refueling between big-money jackpots. | 1 Blackbird Bend Blvd. | 712/423–3700 or 800/858–8238 | Free | Mon.–Thurs. 8 PM–2 AM, Fri.–Sun. open 24 hrs.

Lewis and Clark State Park. You'll find a full-size replica of Lewis and Clark's expedition keelboat at this 30-plus-acre park on the shores of Blue Lake 3 mi northwest of town. There are also picnic grounds with fireplaces and tables. | 21914 Park Loop | 712/423–2829 | www.state.ia.us/parks | Free | Daily.

ON THE CALENDAR
JUNE: *Lewis and Clark Festival.* An authentic 1800s encampment with buckskinners and traders, music, and informational programs, in Lewis and Clark State Park. | 712/423–1801.
AUG.: *Onabike.* This bicycle trip around Monona County lasts a couple of hours or a couple of days, depending on how fast you ride. | 712/423–1801.

Dining
Onawa Café. American. This classic American diner has been serving since the mid-1930s. Sit in a booth, at a table, or on a stool at the original sandwich counter and try the most popular menu item by far—the hot beef sandwich, a heap of beef, gravy, and mashed potatoes atop two slices of white bread. | 811 Iowa Ave. | 712/423–3123 | $4–$5 | No credit cards.

Lodging
Country Homestead Bed and Breakfast. This antiques-filled B&B is 7 mi east of Onawa in nearby Turin. The house is on a foothill near the Loess Hills. Complimentary breakfast. No TVs. | 22133 Larpenteur Memorial Rd., Turin | 712/353–6772 | dlzahrt@pionet.net | 2 rooms (1 with shared bath) | $55–$85 | No credit cards.

Super 8. This chain hotel is 2 mi west of Onawa in a commercial area; several restaurants are within walking distance. Picnic area. Cable TV. Pets allowed. | 22868 Filbert Ave. | 712/423–2101 | fax 712/423–3480 | www.super8.com | 80 rooms | $40 | AE, D, DC, MC, V.

OSCEOLA

MAP 3, D5

(Nearby towns also listed: Chariton, Lamoni)

Founded in 1851, just five years after Iowa became a state, Osceola has changed little over time. At its founding, 3,100 people called this south-central community home; today approximately 4,500 people live here. Fishing, hunting, and other outdoor activities, necessities of life in the 1850s, are spare-time pursuits nowadays; there are also good schools, health services, and community organizations.

Information: **Osceola Chamber of Commerce** | Box 1, 50213 | 515/342–4200.

Attractions
John Lewis Mining and Labor Museum. Just east of Osceola in nearby Lucas you'll find this museum which celebrates the story of John L. Lewis who entered the area's coal mines in 1896 at age 16 and went on to become one of the most powerful labor leaders in the country. | 102 Dividsion St., Lucas | 515/766–6831 | Apr.–Oct., Tues.–Sat.

Melcher-Dallas Museum of Military History. Uniforms, maps, helmets, flags, and firearms from the 1800s to present day are on display. | 123 Main St. | 515/947–4506 | Donations accepted | Daily 3:30–6, or by appointment.

Nine Eagles State Park. Trees that are more than 300 years old shade the bridle and hiking trails of this 1,100-acre park 35 mi southeast of town. | R.R. 1, Davis City | 515/442–2855 | www.state.ia.us/parks | Free | Daily.

OSCEOLA

INTRO
ATTRACTIONS
DINING
LODGING

JULY: *Fourth of July Celebration.* This old-fashioned carnival and ice-cream social is held on the courthouse grounds on the town square. Fireworks follow the festivities. | 515/342–4200.

Dining

Redman's Pizza and Steakhouse. American. Wildlife photos, hunting artifacts, and heavy wooden furniture decorate this rustic downtown eatery on the square. Redman's is known for its hand-ground hamburgers, barbecue, and its homemade pizza sauce and dough. Kids' menu. | 123 S. Main St. | 515/342–6116 | $5–$13 | No credit cards | Closed Sun.

Lodging

AmericInn. This motel is eight minutes from downtown Osceola at the intersection of Interstate 35 and Highway 34. Two fast-food restaurants are next door to the inn. Complimentary Continental breakfast. Cable TV. Pool. Spa. Business services. | 111 Ariel Cir | 641/342–9400 | fax 641/342–7285 | 45 rooms | $65–$127 | AE, D, MC, V.

Days Inn. Guest rooms in this standard motel 2 mi west of town are large enough to accommodate desks and lounge chairs. In-room data ports, cable TV. Pool. Business services. | 710 Warren Ave. | 515/342–6666 | fax 515/342–6408 | www.daysinn.com | 45 rooms | $48–$65 | AE, D, DC, MC, V.

OSKALOOSA

MAP 3, F5

(Nearby towns also listed: Ottumwa, Pella)

Founded in 1844 by William Canfield and named for a Creek Indian princess, Oskaloosa was soon chosen as the seat of Mahaska County. Large deposits of bituminous coal in the area brought wealth to Oskaloosa. The coal has been mined out, but fertile land remains and agriculture is now the town's economic base of Oskaloosa's economy.

Information: **Oskaloosa Chamber of Commerce** | 124 N. Market, 52577 | 515/672–2591 | www.oskaloosa.ia.us.

Attractions

Lake Keomah State Park. This 84-acre lake 5 mi east of town has modern campsites, picnic lodges, and hiking trails. | 2720 Keomah La. | 515/673–6975 | www.state.ia.us/parks | Free | Daily.

Nelson Pioneer Farm and Craft Museum. A mule cemetery, a stagecoach stop, a voting house, and several buildings from a working farm of the 19th century are on display at this site about 5 mi northeast of downtown. | 2294 Oxford Ave. | 515/672–2989 | $4 | May–Oct., Tues.–Sun. 10–4:30, Sun. 1–4:30.

Oskaloosa Bandstand. This ceramic-tile bandstand in the center of the city square was dedicated in 1912, though the Oskaloosa Municipal Band has been playing there since 1864. | City square | Free | Daily.

JUNE: *Art on the Square.* More than 70 local and national artists sell their work on the town square during one of Iowa's most respected juried art shows, held annually on the second Saturday of the month. | 515/672–2596.
JULY: *Southern Iowa Fair.* This fair has 4-H and livestock shows, as well as the largest antique farm machinery display in Iowa. | 515/673–7004.

AUG.: *Oskaloosa Bluegrass Festival.* Thousands of people come to hear local, regional, and national bluegrass performers during this four-day event, held at the Southern Iowa Fairgrounds. To secure a campsite on the fairgrounds, book well in advance. | 515/ 673–7004.

Dining

Jaarsma Bakery. Bakery. This is strictly a bakery, not a sit-down spot, but it's well worth a visit. Try Dutch-influenced baked goods and sweets or standards like a cinnamon-pecan sticky bun. | 210 A Ave. E | 515/673–6415 | $1–$3 | No credit cards | Closed Sun.

Karen's Kafe. American. Sit at the counter or in a booth and try the pork tenderloins, meat loaf, or homemade pies at this casual eatery. | 216 S. Market St. | 515/673–5306 | $4–$6 | No credit cards.

The Peppertree. American. This family-owned restaurant can seat up to 425 people in booths or at larger white-oak tables. Big windows allow in lots of light and make for a cheerful interior. Try the 1½-inch-thick New York strip steak topped with demi-glacé and cracked peppercorns. | U.S. 63 N | 515/673–9191 | $15–$23 | AE, D, MC, V.

Lodging

Comfort Inn. This motel offers basic rooms near the intersection of U.S 63 and Route 92, slightly east of Oskaloosa proper. Continental breakfast. In-room data ports, cable TV. Pool. Business services. | 2401 A Ave. W | 641/672–0375 | fax 515/673–8527 | www.comfortinn.com | 46 rooms | $40–$150 | AE, D, DC, MC, V.

Red Carpet Inn. Large flower beds welcome you to this motel on 3 acres of well-tended grounds 2 mi north of downtown. Guest rooms are plain—but this motel offers you on-site bird-cleaning and -dressing services, in case you're too beat after a day of hunting pheasant in the nearby timber to pluck your own trophy. Complimentary Continental breakfast. Cable TV. Pool. Basketball. Pets allowed. | 2278 U.S. 63 N | 515/673–8641 | fax 515/673–4111 | www.reservahost.com | 41 rooms | $46 | AE, D, MC, V.

Rodeway Inn Mahaska. Named for an Indian chief, this hotel is close to Vennard College. Rooms are simply done with dark-wood furnishings. Picnic area. Refrigerators, cable TV. Playground. Business services. | 1315 A Ave. E | 515/673–8351 | fax 515/673–8351 | www.hotel-choice.com | 42 rooms | $50–$64 | AE, D, DC, MC, V.

Super 8. This otherwise-typical motel 2 mi east of downtown offers a "breakfast toast bar" with a variety of breads, spreads, and preserves for you to toast to your heart's content in the morning. Cable TV. Business services. | 306 S. 17th St. | 515/673–8481 | fax 515/673–8481 | www.super8.com | 51 rooms, 4 suites | $50 | AE, D, DC, MC, V.

Traveler Budget Inn. Rooms are spacious in this motel 1½mi east of downtown. In-room data ports, cable TV. Laundry facilities. | 1210 A Ave. E | 515/673–8333 | fax 515/673–5483 | 27 rooms | $35–$40 | AE, D, MC, V.

OTTUMWA

MAP 3, F5

(Nearby town also listed: Oskaloosa)

The little southeastern Iowa town of Ottumwa received international recognition during the 1970s as the home of Radar O'Reilly of the hit television show *M*A*S*H*. The town's name is a Native American word meaning "Land of Rippling Waters." Although very much a modern community with a strong agriculture-related business base, Ottumwa remains quiet and somewhat innocent—the kind of place you might expect Radar O'Reilly to call home.

Information: **Ottumwa Area Chamber of Commerce** | 217 E. Main, Box 308, 52501 | 515/682–3465.

Attractions

Airpower Museum. Models, photographs, and 20 aircraft from various periods including World War II are featured at a 30-acre antique airfield 10 mi west of town. | 22001 Bluegrass Rd. | 515/938–2773 | Free; donations accepted | Weekdays 9–5, Sat. 10–5, Sun. 1–5.

The Beach—Ottumwa. A water park with a wave pool, a 340-ft body slide, kayaks, sand volleyball, basketball, and an indoor tube slide. | 101 Church St. | 515/682–7873 | www.ci.ottumwa.ia.us/beach/ | $9 | Memorial Day–Labor Day, daily 11–6.

Davis County Welcome Center. This welcome center in a 1910 home, with tourist information and crafts made by the local Amish community, is about 18 mi south of town. | 301 N. Washington St., Bloomfield | 515/664–1104 | Jan.–Mar., Mon.–Sat. 10–4, Sun. 1–5; Apr.–Dec., Mon.–Sat. 9–5, Sun. 1–5.

John Deere Ottumwa Works. Retired employees lead hour-long tours that show how hay-processing equipment is made. | 928 E. Vine St. | 515/683–2394 | www.deere.com | Free | Weekdays 8–5.

Lake Wapello State Park. With 89 modern camping sites and scenic rolling woodlands, this 1,150 acre park about 12 mi southwest of Ottumwa is often referred to as the "country club" of Iowa parks. | R.R. 1, Drakesville | 515/722–3371 | www.state.ia.us/parks | Free | Daily.

Ottumwa Park. A wooded bike trail surrounds a 5-acre lake, and there's a campground and baseball fields. | Junction of Hwys. 34 and 63 | 515/682–1307 | Free | Apr.–mid-Oct., daily.

ON THE CALENDAR

JULY: *Ottumwa Pro Balloon Races.* More than 100 hot-air balloonists fill the sky and demonstrate their skills in Ottumwa Park. | 515/684–8838.
AUG.: *Southeast Iowa Swiftwater Festival.* This event in Sycamore Park includes duck races, paper sailboat races, and more. | 515/682–3465.

Dining

Fisherman's Bay. American. Life preservers, replicas of old ships, and large fish tanks set the scene at this eatery northwest of town, known for its seafood and french fries. Salad bar. Kids' menu. | 221 N. Wapello St. | 515/682–6325 | $12–$18 | AE, D, MC, V.

Lodging

Fairfield Inn by Marriott. Slightly north of town, near the John Deere Works, this hotel caters to business travelers in town on errands involving the local John Deere and Cargill industries. Complimentary Continental breakfast. Microwaves available, some refrigerators, cable TV. Pool. Hot tub. Laundry facilities. | 2813 N. Court St. | 515/682–0000 | fax 515/682–0000 | www.marriott.com | 63 rooms | $62 | AE, D, DC, MC, V.

Guest House. One of the two guest rooms in this antiques-filled 1890 Queen Anne home occupies the house's towerlike turret; the other is octagonal in shape. You'll also find a sizable collection of heirloom dolls here. Complimentary breakfast. No room phones. | 645 Court St. | 515/684–8893 | 2 rooms | $75–$95 | No credit cards.

Heartland Inn. This 1990s redbrick hotel is primarily frequented by business travelers. There are always free popcorn and fresh-baked cookies in the lobby, and there's a complimentary dinner on Wednesday evenings. Complimentary Continental breakfast. In-room data ports, cable TV. Pool. Hot tub, sauna. Laundry facilities. Business services. No pets. | 125 W. Joseph Ave. | 515/682–8526 | fax 515/682–7124 | www.heartlandinns.com | 88 rooms | $65–$70 | AE, D, DC, MC, V.

Super 8. This chain hotel is adjacent to an 18-hole golf course 5 mi north of downtown. Guest rooms offer large, comfortable recliners strategically placed relative to the TV. Complimentary Continental breakfast. Cable TV. Pool. Hot tub, sauna. Laundry facilities. | 2823 N. Court Rd. | 515/684–5055 | fax 515/682–6622 | www.super8.com | 62 rooms | $38–$54 | AE, D, DC, MC, V.

PELLA

(Nearby town also listed: Oskaloosa)

Although the Scottish and the English were the first white settlers in this community, the town's identity was established with the arrival of 800 Dutch settlers in 1847. Legendary lawman Wyatt Earp spent much of his childhood here, and his home is now one of the town's seven museums. Most visitors arrive in Pella in spring to see the tulip blossoms, but the historical village and shops on the town square make for an enjoyable visit any time.

Information: Pella Tourism | 518 Franklin St., 50219 | 515/628–2626 | www.pella.org.

Attractions

Central College. Founded as a Baptist institution in 1853, this four-year liberal arts college became affiliated with the Reformed Church in America in 1916. | 812 University St. | 515/628–9000 | www.central.edu | Free | Daily.

Klokkenspel at Franklin Place. This clock ½ block east of the town square has eight mechanical figures that perform to a 147-bell carillon on the hour. | 627 Franklin St. | 515/628–2626 | Free | Daily.

Lake Red Rock. With 19,000 acres of water from the Des Moines River, this is Iowa's largest man-made lake. It's 4½ mi southwest of town. | 1105 Hwy. T15 | 515/828–7522 | Free | Daily.

Pella Historical Village Museum. This museum is made up of 21 historical buildings nestled in a courtyard east of the town square. The buildings include Wyatt Earp's boyhood home, a gristmill, a church, and a bakery. | 507 Franklin St. | 515/628–4311 | $5 | Apr.–Dec., Mon.–Sat. 9–5; Jan.–Mar., weekdays 9–5.

Pella Opera House. Built in 1900, this totally restored performance space has retained its stained-glass windows and original, ornate, pressed-tin ceilings. The Opera House hosts a variety of cultural events throughout the year. | 611 Franklin St. | 515/628–8625 | Free; performances $5–$20 | Mon.–Sat. 11–4. Box office: weekdays 9–5.

Scholte House. The elegant Dutch mansion, north of Central Park and home of one of the city's founders, contains 23 rooms with Italian and French furnishings, as well as gardens with thousands of tulips and other flowers. | 728 Washington St. | 515/628–3684 or 515/628–2409 | $3.50 | Mon.–Sat. 1–4:30; also by appointment.

ON THE CALENDAR

MAY: *Pella Tulip Time.* 30,000 or 40,000 people flock to Pella for parades, street scrubbing, and tens of thousands of blooming tulips. | 515/628–4311.

NOV.: *Sinterklaas Parade and Celebration.* Watch Sinterklaas himself, the Dutch incarnation of old St. Nick, ride into town on a ship at this post-Thanksgiving event. A party at the Pella Opera House follows the parade. | 641/628–4311.

Dining

de Snoepwinkel. American. Come to "the sweet shop" for light lunch fare—sandwiches, soups, and homemade desserts—or for the candy. The dining area is decorated with Dutch memorabilia and antiques. | 605 Franklin St. | 641/628–1222 | $4–$6 | D, MC, V | No dinner.

Lodging

Clover Leaf Bed and Breakfast. This 1892 home is completely restored and furnished with turn-of-the-last-century antiques. Each room contains a brass-and-oak bed and a claw-foot bathtub. Complimentary breakfast. | 314 Washington St. | 515/628–9045 | 4 rooms (with shared baths) | $58 | MC, V.

Dutch Mill Inn. This elegant lodging is directly across the street from Caldwell Park and boasts a distinctly Dutch-themed decor. Exposed timbers support the structure and the lobby and grounds are set about with Pella's famous tulips. Restaurant, complimentary breakfast. Microwave and refrigerator in common area. Cable TV. No smoking. | 205 Oskaloosa St. | 515/628–1060 | fax 515/628–8958 | www.pellaiowa.com/dutchmillinn | 17 rooms | $42–$50 | AE, D, DC, MC, V.

Super 8. This chain motel is on a commercial street 2 mi west of downtown. Cable TV. Laundry facilities. Business services. | 105 E. Oskaloosa St. | 515/628–8181 | fax 515/628–8181 | www.super8.com | 41 rooms | $44–$59 | AE, D, DC, MC, V.

POCAHONTAS

MAP 3, C2

(Nearby towns also listed: Humboldt, Storm Lake)

Established in the fall of 1870, this little town is named for the Indian princess Pocahontas. It is the seat of Pocahontas County, a rich agricultural area of northwestern Iowa. Although just 2,000 people call Pocahontas home today, the community has a number of civic, social, and cultural organizations that provide activities throughout the year.

Information: **Pocahontas Chamber of Commerce** | 101 2nd Ave. SW, 50574 | 712/335–4841 | www.scdc@ncn.net.

Attractions

Saints Peter and Paul Catholic Church. The first church built in this county is now on the National Register of Historic Places. | 102 2nd Ave. NW | 712/335–3864 | Free | Daily.

ON THE CALENDAR

JULY: *Pocahontas County Fair.* Four days of livestock shows, carnival rides, food, and entertainment on the county fairgrounds. | 712/335–3864.

Dining

The Chateau. American. For upscale dining in a casual, come-as-you-are environment, try this huge dining room. Prime rib and the chicken Oscar (with hollandaise sauce, crab, and asparagus) are popular entrées. You can also dine or just have drinks in the adjacent lounge, where you'll find a jukebox and a dance floor. Sunday brunch buffet. | 12 N.W. 7th St. | 712/335–4501 | $8–$14 | MC, V | Closed Mon. No dinner Sun.

Mary's Café. American. Mary is famous for her homemade pies—try the pecan or any one of the fruit pies. You can eat breakfast all day here. For lunch and dinner, folks come for the pressure-cooked chicken, barbecued pork, and goulash. The café is at the junction of Routes 3 and 4. Kids' menu. | 12 S.W. 7th St. | 712/335–3175 | $2–$6 | No credit cards.

Lodging

Chief Motel. Building on the Native American heritage of the region, this motel, which is 4 blocks west of downtown, displays Native American artwork in the lobby and in many rooms. Complimentary Continental breakfast. Some kitchenettes, cable TV. | 801 W. Elm St. | 712/335–3395 | 38 rooms | $46 | AE, D, DC, MC, V.

RED OAK

(Nearby towns also listed: Clarinda, Shenandoah)

Travel and tourism experts often call this community of 6,000 the Williamsburg of the Midwest because there are so many restored turn-of-the-last-century homes. The river, railroad, and stagecoach brought travelers and investors from all points; the result has been a diverse community with a rich heritage, which is clearly seen on any walking tour of the town.

Information: **Red Oak Chamber of Commerce** | 405 Reed St., 51566 | 712/623–4821 | www.redoak.heartland.net/local/rocchamber.

Attractions

Montgomery County Historical Center. Exhibits at this local history museum change periodically and have included displays devoted to the first Iowans, the area's agricultural history, and prairie ecology. | 2700 N. 4th St. | 712/623–2289 | Free | Tues.–Sun. 1–5.

Viking Lake State Park. You'll find a 160-acre lake popular for catfish and bass fishing at this 800-acre park 12 mi east of town. | 2780 Viking Lake Rd. | 712/829–2235 | www.state.ia.us/parks | Free | Daily.

ON THE CALENDAR

JUNE: *Junction Days.* A street dance, parade, and carnival celebrate the town's heritage. | 712/623–4821.
AUG.: *Old Car Days.* More than 200 antique cars and their owners fill the streets and town square. | 712/623–4821.

Dining

Red Lion Café. American. This gathering spot is a long-standing local favorite, with booths and tables, fresh flowers, and lots of plants. On the menu: soups and sandwiches. Kids' menu. | 203 Coolbaugh St. | 712/623–9545 | $5–$10 | D, MC, V.

Lodging

House on Hammond Hill Bed and Breakfast. This small but beautiful B&B is housed in a Queen Anne home with original stained-glass windows and fireplaces, and lacy curtains and offers guests a two-room suite. Complimentary breakfast. | 811 Hammond St. | 712/623–9269 | 1 suite | $85 | MC, V.

Red Coach Inn. You can expect a quiet night's sleep in this semirural motel just outside Red Oak. Restaurant, bar, complimentary Continental breakfast, room service. Cable TV, in-room VCRs available. Pool. Business services, free parking. | 1200 Senate Ave. | 712/623–4864 or 800/544–6002 | fax 712/623–2389 | 74 rooms | $40 | AE, D, DC, MC, V.

Super 8. Guest rooms at this chain motel a few minutes from the center of town have large windows and are decorated in autumn tones. Several restaurants are nearby. Complimentary Continental breakfast. In-room data ports, cable TV. Pool. Laundry facilities. Business services. | 800 Senate Ave. | 712/623–6919 | fax 712/623–6929 | www.super8.com | 40 rooms | $43–$100 | AE, D, DC, MC, V.

SHELDON

(Nearby town also listed: Spencer)

Sheldon is a farming community in the extreme northwest of Iowa. Settled by German and Dutch immigrants, it is now home to approximately 5,000 people. The Sheldon High School Summer Theater is the only high-school repertory in Iowa (and one of just a few in the nation); it presents a different play each week for most of June and July.

Information: **Sheldon Community Development Corp.** | 416 9th St., Box 276, 51202 | 712/324–4602 | www.scdc@ncn.net.

Attractions

Sheldon High School Summer Repertory Theater. In operation for almost 30 years, this acclaimed community theater program stages a variety of plays (and a musical every two years) performed by high-school students and directed by college students. Buy tickets at the door every Thursday, Friday, and Saturday for six weeks during June and July. | 1700 E. 4th St. | 712/324–2501 | fax 712/324–5607 | $3–$4.

Sheldon Prairie Museum. Contains the Sheldon Hall of Fame and historical artifacts of local significance. | 10th and 4th Ave. | 712/324–4482 | Free | Mon.–Sat. 2–4.

ON THE CALENDAR
JULY: *Fourth of July Celebration.* An old-fashioned ice-cream social highlights the long weekend. | 712/324–4602.
SEPT.: *Sheldon Celebration Days.* Parades, crafts, food booths, and music are offered all weekend long. | 712/324–4602.

Dining

Kinbrae South. American. This restaurant is reminiscent of an old-school dinner club, with brick and wood walls, white linens, and wooden captain's chairs. The menu is known among locals for its beef cuts—try the prime rib or the sirloin. A soup and salad buffet is available during the lunch hour, and a champagne brunch is served on Sunday. | 1111 2nd Ave. | 712/324–4411 | $10–$20 | D, MC, V.

Lodging

Iron Horse Inn. This inn is across the street from the old train depot and there's a railroad motif to the decor—with crossing guards in the lobby and the headlights and photos of old trains throughout. Restaurant, bar, complimentary Continental breakfast. Cable TV. | 1111 S. Rte. 60 | 712/324–5353 | 33 rooms | $50 | AE, D, DC, MC, V.

Super 8. This redbrick chain hotel 8 blocks north of downtown has a comfortable lounge area with overstuffed sofas and chairs and a large fireplace. Complimentary Continental breakfast. In-room data ports, cable TV. Pool. Hot tub. Laundry services. Business services. | 210 N. 2nd Ave. | 712/324–8400 | fax 712/374–8352 | www.super8.com | 40 rooms | $47–$99 | AE, D, DC, MC, V.

SHENANDOAH

(Nearby towns also listed: Clarinda, Red Oak)

In 1870 this town was christened Shenandoah because of its resemblance to the valley of the same name in Virginia. A decade later a man named David Lake began a small tree and seed business which eventually grew to become Earl May Nurseries.

Shenandoah now has more than 5,000 acres of growing fields for tree and shrub nurseries, earning it the title among nursery and garden enthusiasts as the "Seed and Nursery Center of the World."

Information: Shenandoah Chamber and Industry Association | 301 Maple, Box 38, 51601 | 712/246–3455 | chamber@shenessex.heartland.net.

Attractions

Greater Shenandoah Historical Museum. Artifacts and diorama detail the Mormon experience during their temporary settlement in Iowa en route from Illinois to Utah in the 1850s. | 405 Sheridan St. | 712/246–1669 | Free | Wed., Fri., Sun. 1–4.

ON THE CALENDAR

JULY: Continental Amateur Baseball World Series. Teams of 11-year-olds from all over North America compete at all area ball fields during this weeklong event. | 712/246–3455.
SEPT.: ShenFest. Parades, pageants, a car show, and a carnival. | 712/246–3455.

Dining

Country Inn Restaurant. American. This rustic-style restaurant has shelves of antique kitchen utensils on the walls and hearty, traditional food. You'll find steaks and seafood, plus a soup-and-salad bar. Daily specials range from porcupine meatballs (meatballs made with sticky rice) to the 12-ounce rib-eye steak. This restaurant is a favorite of older Shenandoah residents. | 1503 W. Sheridan St., Rte. 59 | 712/246–1550 | $7–$15 | AE, D, DC, MC, V | Breakfast also available; closed Mon.; no dinner Sun.

Mondo's. American. This family-style restaurant, a local favorite, is the the only one in town that serves breakfast all day. Harvest-theme pictures and stuffed pigs hang on the walls. For lunch or dinner, try the pressure-cooked chicken or the chicken-fried steak. Save room for homemade desserts: fruit, cream, and meringue pies; ice-cream shakes; cinnamon rolls; and strawberry shortcake à la mode. | 309 S. Fremont St. | 712/246–1325 | $4–$6 | No credit cards.

Lodging

Country Inn. Though independently run, this motel 3 blocks west of downtown has something of a chain-property feel and caters primarily to business travelers and those just passing through. Restaurant, bar, complimentary Continental breakfast, room service. Cable TV. Pool. Business services, airport shuttle. Pets allowed. | 1503 Sheridan Ave. | 712/246–1550 | fax 712/246–4773 | 65 rooms | $50 | AE, D, DC, MC, V.

Days Inn. Guest rooms are spacious but unremarkable at this chain hotel on a commercial street 6 blocks west of downtown. Complimentary Continental breakfast. Refrigerators, cable TV. | 108 N. Fremont St. | 712/246–5733 | fax 712/246–2230 | www.daysinn.com | 33 rooms | $48 | AE, D, DC, MC, V.

59er Motel and Executive Suites. This small roadside motor inn is in a busy commercial area on the north end of town at the intersection of Hwy 59 and Mishnah Rd. There is a campground run by the motel just behind the facilities. Restaurant. Cable TV. In-room phones, in-room data ports. Business services. | 1148 Rte. 59 | 712/246–2925 | 10 rooms, 5 suites | $40–$75 | AE, D, DC MC, V.

SIOUX CITY

MAP 3, A3

(Nearby town also listed: Le Mars)

This part of western Iowa is known as Siouxland, although it was once inhabited by tribes of Omaha and Ponca Indians, as well as the Sioux. The only member of the Lewis and Clark expedition to die on the journey did so here in 1804 and is buried on a hill overlooking the Missouri River. Meatpacking is Sioux City's primary industry—it is home to three national companies. The Sue Bee Honey Company and Gateway 2000 Computers can are based here as well. But Sioux City may be best known for the famous twin sisters who graduated from its public school system—Esther and Pauline Friedman, better known as Dear Abby and Ann Landers.

Information: **Sioux City Convention Bureau** | 801 4th St., 51101 | 712/279–4800 or 800/593–2228 | www.siouxlan.com.

Attractions

Battle Hill Museum of Natural History. This private museum houses a range of displays from exotic taxidermied skins to enormous cases of fossils and prehistoric artifacts. You'll see skeletons, shells, and dozens of preserved animal specimens, including bears and zebras. | Rte. 175 E, Battle Creek | 712/365–4414 | bhmuseum@pionet.net | Free | June–Aug., Sun. 1–5 and by appointment year-round.

Belle of Sioux City. A riverboat casino with cruises and entertainment. | 100 Larsen Park Dr. | 712/255–0080 or 800/424–0080 | Free | May–Aug., daily cruises at 10 AM; casino open 24 hrs year-round.

Dorothy Pecaut Nature Center. This nature center includes fascinating exhibits on the geology and biology of the Loess Hills. | 4500 Sioux River Rd. | 712/258–0838 | Free | Tues.–Sat. 9–5; Sun. 1–5.

Historic 4th Street. You'll find 15 buildings built between 1889 and 1915, many in the Richardsonian Romanesque style then popular, on the two blocks of 4th Street between Iowa and Virginia streets. | 4th St. between Iowa and Virginia Sts. | 712/279–4800 | Free | Daily.

Morningside College. This four-year liberal-arts college affiliated with the Methodist Church has approximately 1,000 students. | 1501 Morningside Ave. | 712/274–5000 or 800/831–0806 | www.morningside.edu | Free | Daily.

Sergeant Floyd Monument. This monument on the east bank of the Missouri River, the first registered historic landmark in the nation, is dedicated to the only man to die on the Lewis and Clark expedition. | Glenn Ave. at U.S. 75 | 800/593–2228 | Free | Daily.

Sergeant Floyd Welcome Center and Museum. A U.S. Army Corps of Engineers diesel inspection ship turned river transportation museum, this black-red-and-white three-story boat houses artifacts dating from the Lewis and Clark expedition, scale models of Missouri River steamboats, and Iowa's only professional model shipbuilding shop. | 1000 Larsen Park Rd. | 712/279–4840 | www.sioux-city.org/museum | Free | May–Sept., daily 8–6; Oct.–Apr., daily 9–5.

Sioux City Art Center. This small but well-appointed museum, begun as a WPA project during the Depression, has a 900-piece permanent collection, a hands-on children's gallery, and a three-story atrium. The on-site gift shop offers exquisite blown-glass pieces and books on art for young and old. | 225 Nebraska St. | 712/279–6272 | www.sc-artcenter.com | Free | Tues.–Sun. 10–5.

Sioux City Public Museum. Built in 1890 from pink quartzite, this 23-room Romanesque mansion today houses pioneer and Civil War artifacts, Plains and Woodland Indian artifacts, and natural-history displays. | 2901 Jackson St. | 712/279–6174 | www.sioux-city.org/museum | Free | Tues.–Sat. 9–5, Sun. 1–5.

Stone State Park. Hiking trails crisscross 1,069 acres of Loess Hills, formed by windblown deposits in the northwest part of city. | 5001 Talbot Rd. | 712/255–4698 or 712/258–0838 | www.state.ia.us/parks | Free | Daily dawn–dusk.

Trinity Heights. A life-size wooden carving of the Last Supper and a 30-ft steel statue of Mary surrounded by walkways and gardens. | 2509 33rd St. | 712/239–8670 | Free | Daily dawn–dusk.

Woodbury County Courthouse. Completed in 1918, this courthouse is still in use and is also on the National Register of Historic Places. | 620 Douglas St. | 712/279–6109 | Free | Weekdays 8–5.

ON THE CALENDAR

JUNE: *Waterfest Weekend.* This bash celebrates the mighty Missouri and all the fun that can be had in, on, and around it. Events include waterskiing expositions, a volleyball tournament, a car show, live concerts, and a 5-km run for charity. | 402/494–1307 or 800/793–6327.

JULY: *River-Cade Festival.* A parade, a carnival, stage shows, and other entertainment are featured in this weeklong celebration in riverfront Chautauqua Park. | 712/277–4226.

JULY: *Saturday in the Park.* Hours of music, food, games, and fireworks at the band shell in Grandview Park. | 800/593–2228.

Dining

Bluestem. Contemporary. Low lighting, a swanky interior, and live music set the tone at this restaurant in Sioux City's historic 4th Street district. Try the pan-seared Chilean salmon fillet rolled in sesame, sunflower, and poppy seeds. The bar is known for its well-executed martinis and wide variety of imported and domestic beers. | 1012 4th St. | 712/279–8060 | $10–$21 | AE, MC, V.

Green Gables. American. Hand-painted murals of scenes from the 1920s decorate this historic building. On the menu: Iowa Black Angus steaks and chicken dishes. Kids' menu. | 1800 Pierce St. | 712/258–4246 | $9–$12 | AE, DC, MC, V.

RAGBRAI

Many small towns in Iowa will boast that they have hosted RAGBRAI, which stands for the *Register's* Annual Great Bike Ride Across Iowa. It's a term you need to know if you are going to spend any time in Iowa, especially if you plan to be here in late July.

RAGBRAI started in 1973 with a challenge between a features writer and a columnist at the *Des Moines Register,* both avid bicyclists, to ride across the state and write about what they saw. In their articles and columns, they invited anybody who wanted to join them to meet on the banks of the Missouri River in Sioux City on August 26th. Approximately 300 people showed up. Six days later, 141 riders dipped their toes in the Mississippi River in Davenport, and a state tradition was born.

The following year 2,700 riders showed up. The route changed, and the basic requirement that riders begin by dipping their rear tire in the Missouri River and end by dipping their front tire in the Mississippi River was added. The *Des Moines Register* holds a contest each year to determine RAGBRAI's route, and small communities vie for the opportunity to host this village on wheels, with its now almost 10,000 participants.

Bicyclists from all over the world have pedaled in RAGBRAI. For safety reasons, the Highway Patrol limits the number of participants, so, if you are interested in riding, put your name on the waiting list now.

© Corbis

Hunan Palace. Chinese. Bamboo trinkets, a goldfish pond, and soft lighting set the scene for excellent Mongolian beef, sweet-and-sour chicken, and steamed rice with seared veggies at this restaurant in the Mayfair Shopping Mall. | 4280 Sergeant Rd. | 712/274–2336 | $8–$16 | AE, D, MC, V.

Victorian Opera Company. American. This establishment serves lunch in a high, tin-ceilinged dining area with hardwood floors and arched windows. Try the homemade soups, the country quiche, or the innovative chicken-chile lasagna, and don't miss the restaurant's own hot almond tea. | 1021 4th St. | 712/255–4821 | $5–$7 | MC, V | No dinner.

Lodging

AmericInn Sioux City. This chain motel offers standard rooms just off Interstate 29, a short distance from the Missouri River and downtown Sioux City. In-room data ports, cable TV. Pool. Hot tub. Laundry facilities. Business services. | 4230 S. Lewis Blvd. | 712/255–1800 | fax 712/255–1800 | www.americinn.com | 58 rooms | $62–$130 | AE, D, DC, MC, V.

Best Western City Center. Local art fills the bright, spacious lobby in this downtown hotel. Guest rooms are primarily equipped for business travelers—they're soundproof and spacious with large work spaces. Bar, complimentary breakfast. Cable TV. Pool. Laundry facilities. Business services, airport shuttle. Some pets allowed. | 130 Nebraska St. | 712/277–1550 | fax 712/277–1120 | www.bestwestern.com | 114 rooms | $59 | AE, D, DC, MC, V.

Comfort Inn. This basic, no-frills hotel is right next to the Southern Hills Mall. Complimentary Continental breakfast. In-room data ports, cable TV. Pool. Hot tub. Business services. | 4202 S. Lakeport St. | 712/274–1300 | fax 712/274–7592 | www.comfortinn.com | 70 rooms | $52 | AE, D, DC, MC, V.

Days Inn. This chain motel 5 mi south of downtown caters to business travelers and rooms have large, well-lit desks. Complimentary Continental breakfast. In-room data ports, cable TV. Pool. Hot tub. Laundry services. Business services. | 3000 Singing Hills Blvd. | 712/258–8000 | fax 712/252–1323 | www.daysinn.com | 56 rooms | $45–$105 | AE, D, DC, MC, V.

English Mansion B&B. This 1894 landmark mansion is on a residential street in a historical district on the near north side of downtown. In addition to breakfast, you'll be offered complimentary dessert here in the evenings. Complimentary breakfast. In-room data ports, some in-room hot tubs, cable TV. Business services. | 1525 Douglas | 712/277–1386 | 4 rooms (2 with shared bath) | $70–$150 | AE, D, MC, V.

Hilton Sioux City. Most rooms in this 12-story downtown hotel have commanding views of the Missouri River. Others look out on the downtown area. Restaurant, bar. In-room data ports, cable TV, in-room VCRs available. Pool. Exercise equipment. Business services, airport shuttle. | 707 4th St. | 712/277–4101 | fax 712/277–3168 | www.hilton.com | 193 rooms | $79–$99 | AE, D, DC, MC, V.

Holiday Inn Express. Guest rooms at this chain hotel 4 mi south of downtown are done up with knotty wood trim and illuminated by brass and ceramic floor-and-table lamps. Complimentary Continental breakfast. In-room data ports, cable TV, in-room VCR (and movies) available. Hot tub. Exercise equipment. Business services. | 4230 S. Lakeport St. | 712/274–1400 | fax 712/276–2136 | www.basshotels.com/holiday-inn | 58 rooms | $55 | AE, D, DC, MC, V.

Palmer House. This simple, independent motel is just outside of town. Restaurant, complimentary Continental breakfast. Cable TV. Pool. Laundry facilities. Business services. Pets allowed. | 3440 E. Gordon Dr. | 712/276–4221 or 800/833–4221 | fax 712/276–9535 | 60 rooms | $43–$60 | AE, D, DC, MC, V.

Super 8. This standard chain hotel is less than 1 mi from Western Iowa Tech and Morningside College and within 4 mi of the Sioux City Arts and Public Museums. Complimentary Continental breakfast. Cable TV. Pets allowed. | 4307 Stone Ave. | 712/274–1520 | fax 712/274–1520 | www.super8.com | 60 rooms | $36–$65 | AE, D, DC, MC, V.

SPENCER

(Nearby towns also listed: Okoboji, Spirit Lake)

Settled in 1859, Spencer became the seat of Clay County in 1871. Today it is home to what is considered the best county fair in the world, with more than a quarter of a million visitors attending the nine-day event each September.

Information: Spencer Association of Business and Industry | 122 W. 5th St., Box 7937, 51301-7937 | 712/262–5680.

Attractions

Oneota State Park. These rugged 120 acres, about 15 mi southwest of town, are used primarily by backwoods hikers. | 1500 Harpen St., Peterson | 712/337–3211 | Free | Daily.

River View Park. You can picnic on the landscaped lawns of this 60-acre park, or hike on its well-maintained nature trails. You'll also find an aquatic center and an eight-court tennis facility here. | 612 47th St. SE | 712/264–7260 | Free; aquatic center $3 | Daily dawn–dusk. Aquatic center: May–Sept., daily 12:30 PM–8:30 PM.

ON THE CALENDAR

APR./NOV.: *Clay Country Flair.* More than 100 regional artisans and craftspeople sell their wares at this twice-annual arts-and-crafts show. Past exhibitors have displayed wood carving, Victorian-decorated Christmas trees, painted emu eggs, and handmade candles. | 712/262–5680.

JUNE: *Flagfest Summer Festival.* A three-day patriotic event. | 712/262–5680.

SEPT.: *Clay County Fair.* Considered the best county fair in the world, this event is not to be missed. Few towns the size of Spencer manage to attract entertainment and events on the scale of what happens here every year. Past fairs have featured acts as diverse as "Weird Al" Yankovich, Def Leppard, Kenny Rogers, and Alabama—all in one week. Other attractions have included traditional music of the Andes mountains, huge classic car shows, and Blaze, the balloon-blowing goat. The fair is also home to the Midwest's largest agricultural machinery exhibit. | 712/262–4740.

Dining

Grand Diner. American. You can sit in a booth or at the counter here and soak in the glow of a bygone era as you enjoy an excellent burger and fries or perhaps a bowl of homemade chicken noodle soup. | 208 Grand Ave. | 712/262–4404 | $5–$7 | AE, D, MC, V.

Hu Pei Chinese Restaurant. Chinese. This small establishment has all the usual trappings—red-and-gold lanterns, balsa-wood chopsticks in paper sleeves, and a little Buddha by the cash register. The extensive menu features such favorites as sweet-and-sour chicken/pork/shrimp, crab Rangoon, and both lo and chow mein. | 419 11th St. SW | 712/262–4442 | $5–$10 | AE, D, MC, V.

Stub's Ranch Kitchen. American. A horse harness, cowboy hats, branding irons, and barbed wire decorate this eatery 2 mi southwest of town. This is a great place to stop for a hearty steak-and-potatoes dinner or a hand-patted burger. Salad bar. Buffet. Beer and wine only. | 1700 11th Ave. SW | 712/262–2154 | $4–$8 | No credit cards.

Lodging

AmericInn. Like others of its ilk, this motel is a no-fuss overnight option. Rooms here are big enough to accommodate a rollaway bed or two, and you'll be just 5 min from the Clay County Fairgrounds. In-room data ports, cable TV. Pool, hot tub. Laundry services. Business services. Pets allowed. | 1005 13th St. SW | 712/262–7525 | fax 712/262–7514 | 46 rooms | $59–$122 | AE, D, DC, MC, V.

Hannah Marie Country Inn. This charming, country-casual B&B is comprised of two houses connected by a veranda. One house was built in 1907, the other in 1910. Guest rooms have themes, from South Sea Island, to African Safari, to, of course, Victorian. Behind the inn itself is a labyrinth made of cypress mulch and strategically planted rows of chives which you can try to find your way through. Complimentary breakfast. In-room hot tubs. No room phones. No TV. | 4070 U.S. 71, 4 mi south of Spencer | 712/262–1286 or 800/972–1286 | fax 712/262–3294 | www.nwiowabb.com | 6 rooms | $79–$120 | MC, V.

The Hotel. This 1920s redbrick building has stained glass, fine woodwork, and many antiques originally from other buildings in the area. Restaurant, bar, room service. Some refrigerators, cable TV. Business services, airport shuttle. | 605 Grand Ave. | 712/262–2010 | fax 712/262–5610 | 41 rooms (35 with shower only) | $33–$69 | AE, D, DC, MC, V.

Iron Horse. Scenes from the early days of the railroad decorate the lobby and rooms of this independently run motel. Old silvery prints of steam engines and even older tintypes and daguerreotypes adorn the walls. Cable TV. | 14 11th St. SE | 712/262–3720 | fax 712/262–4538 | 94 rooms | $46 | AE, D, DC, MC, V.

Plaza I. This bright motel with large picture windows is less than 3 mi from local parks, theaters, and restaurants. Guest rooms are done in a country-home style with pale pastel carpets, drapes, and bedspreads. Complimentary Continental breakfast. In-room data ports, cable TV. Business services. | 102 11th St. SW Plaza | 712/262–6100 or 800/369–3891 | fax 712/262–5742 | 58 rooms | $46–$55 | AE, D, DC, MC, V.

Super 8. This chain motel is 1 mi from downtown, 5 mi from the fairgrounds, and within 4 mi of all the area museums and a shopping mall. Cable TV. | 209 11th St. | 712/262–8500 | fax 712/262–8500 | www.super8.com | 50 rooms | $36–$44 | AE, D, DC, MC, V.

SPILLVILLE

MAP 3, F2

(Nearby towns also listed: Decorah, West Union)

A German immigrant named Spielman founded this village in 1854, but in the 1800s its population was predominantly Czech. Music has always played an important role in this community; the band shell in the park hosts many musical events, and the visit of composer Antonín Dvořák in summer 1893 has never been forgotten. Dvořák, who chose the town for a summer retreat after a winter in New York, worked on his *New World* symphony here and enjoyed the company of his compatriots.

Information: **Spillville Tourism** | Box 258, 52168 | 319/562–3569 | ketourism@salamander.com.

Attractions
Antonín Dvořák Memorial. A statue of the great composer stands in Riverside Park where he came for relaxation and inspiration. | Bridge St. and Hwy. 325 (on the extreme east side of town) | 319/562–3569 | Daily.

Bily Clock Museum. Hundreds of hand-carved clocks made by two brothers, including clocks for Charles Lindbergh and Antonín Dvořák are housed in this smallish downtown building where Dvořák lived in the summer of 1893. | 323 S. Main St. | 319/562–3569 or 319/562–3627 | Donations accepted | May–Oct., daily 8:30–5; call ahead for hrs rest of year.

ON THE CALENDAR
JULY: *Polkafest.* This bash celebrates all things polka with music, dance competitions, Czech food, and plenty of *lederhosen.* | 319/562–3569.

Dining

Old World Restaurant. American. This dining spot occupies the basement level of the Hotel Iowa. The dining room walls are covered with an Old English landscape mural, and the table linens contrast sharply with the abundance of dark, polished wood. Try the shrimp scampi and the scallops marinara. | 401 Main St. | 319/526–3996 | $6–$15 | AE, D, MC, V.

Lodging

Hotel Iowa. This historic 1913 building in the heart of Spillville is primarily a residential hotel. The lobby has an air of faded elegance, and guest rooms are all done differently with contemporary furnishings. If you stay here you'll be within walking distance of the Bily Clock Museum and other downtown attractions. Restaurant. Some cable TV. Laundry facilities. Business services. | 401 Main St. | 319/524–1451 | fax 319/524–4042 | 5 rooms | $35 | No credit cards.

Taylor-Made Bed and Breakfast. The 11 Taylor children worked together to help their mother develop this B&B filled with homemade quilts, family antiques, photos, and toys. Complimentary breakfast. | 330 Main St. | 319/562–3958 | 4 rooms | $55–$69 | No credit cards.

SPIRIT LAKE

(Nearby towns also listed: Estherville, Okoboji, Spencer)

According to Native American legend, Spirit Lake is guarded by evil spirits, and in the 19th-century Native Americans avoided crossing the 5,600-acre lake by canoe. White men, however, did not believe the legend and quickly learned that they could make a buck by carrying passengers across the lake, from one point to another. To this day, boats are popular on the lake and in the community, which is a summer and winter resort.

Information: Iowa Great Lakes Chamber of Commerce | Box 9, Arnold's Park, 51331 | 712/332–2107 or 800/839–9987.

Attractions

Mini-Wakan State Park. This 10-acre park on the north shore of Spirit Lake off Route 276 offers a boat ramp and fishing sites. | 1500 Harpen Rd. | 712/337–3211 | www.state.ia.us/parks | Free | Daily.

Spirit Lake. At 5,600 acres this is the largest natural lake in Iowa and on its north edge it crosses into Minnesota. Access is at Marble Beach, 3 mi northwest of town, or Mini-Wakan State Park. | Rte. 276 | 800/839–9987 | Free | Daily.

Spirit Lake Fish Hatchery. This state-operated facility 1 mi north of Spirit Lake hatches and rears walleyes and muskie for stocking the area lakes. | 122 252nd Ave. | 712/336–1840 | fax 712/336–0921 | Free | Weekdays 8–5.

ON THE CALENDAR

JUNE: *Cruise-In.* Owners of 1950s-era cars grease back their hair, have a burger and shake, cruise up and down Main Street, and listen to the oldies. | 712/336–4978.
JUNE: *Main Sailabration.* There are parades, crafts shows, and food, and the lake fills up with sailboats. | 712/336–4978.

Dining

Sillbilly's. American. This family restaurant on Lake Okoboji serves a wide array of steak, pasta, and seafood dishes. The dining area has a relaxed, seminautical theme, and seating is mostly at tables large enough to accommodate diners with children. | 2608 22nd St. | 712/336–2362 | $5–$13 | MC, V.

Lodging

Beaches Resort. This family-oriented resort at the northern end of West Lake Okoboji offers clapboard cottages and complimentary s'mores on the beach each evening. Restaurant, picnic area. Refrigerators, kitchenettes, cable TV, no room phones. Lake. Beach, 2 docks, boating. Children's programs, playground. Laundry facilities. No pets. | 15109 215th Ave. | 712/336–2230 | 6 cottages, 5 apartments, 1 house | $89–$159 | D, MC, V.

Francis Hospitality Manor. Built by a U.S. Senator in 1912, and used as a hospital in the 1940s and '50s, this Greek Revival home now serves as a gracious B&B. Lunch is served to both guests and the public in the lofty parlor area. The front porch is perfect for sipping tea and relaxing. Complimentary breakfast. No room phones. No TV. | 608 Lake St. | 712/336–4345 | 4 rooms | $75–$95 | No credit cards.

STORM LAKE

MAP 3, C2

(Nearby town also listed: Cherokee)

In 1855 a small group of surveyors spent the night camping with an old trapper on the shore of a lake. The trapper asked what the name of the lake was; the surveyors said there was none and that he could name it. That night a storm blew through and tore down the camp; it was thus that the lake and town were named. Today Storm Lake is a popular recreational spot in northwest Iowa, but food processing and metal fabrication are the town's economic base.

Information: Storm Lake Chamber of Commerce | 119 W. 6th St., Box 584, 50588 | 712/732–3780 | slc@nwiowa.com | www.stormlake.org.

Attractions

Andy Williams Birthplace. See the home where this Emmy and Grammy Award winner was born and the piano on which he learned to play 22 mi south of Storm Lake. | 102 E. 1st St., Wall Lake | 712/664–2119 | Donations accepted | Memorial Day–Labor Day, weekends 10–2; by appointment rest of of year.

Buena Vista County Historical Museum. Sports, games, and a recreation exhibit, as well as artifacts of the county's history. | 214 W. 5th St. | 712/732–4955 | Donations accepted | Daily 1–4:30.

Harker House. This 1875 French mansard cottage–style home was the first all-brick house in town. | 328 Lake Ave. | 712/732–3267 | Donations accepted | June–Aug., Sun. 1–4:30.

Living Heritage Tree Museum. One of the largest living-tree museums in the country is here in Sunset Park. According to the museum, a seedling or tree cutting "must be documented and linked to a historic person, place or events" in order to be considered for placement within the museum. One of the more notable trees in the museum is the "Moon Tree"—a sycamore that went to the moon as a seed on one of the Apollo missions. | W. Lakeshore Dr. | 712/732–3780 | Free | Daily dawn–dusk.

Storm Lake. At 3,200 acres, this is Iowa's fourth-largest natural lake. There are usually good sailing conditions and you'll also find a 5-mi recreation trail by the lake. | 1001 Sunrise Park Rd. | 712/732–8023 | Free | Daily.

ON THE CALENDAR

JULY: *Star-Spangled Spectacular.* Parades, crafts, food, and children's activities along the lakefront. | 712/732–3780 | July 4th.

SEPT.: *Balloon Days.* More than 50 balloonists and thousands of spectators participate in this weeklong event at the airport, north of town. You'll find parachuting and aerobatic acts throughout the weekend. | 712/732–3780.

SEPT.: *Windfest.* Hosted by the Iowa Department of Natural Resources, this festival held on the Buena Vista Fairgrounds focuses on environmental education with displays of solar and battery-powered cars, craftspeople selling windsocks, wind chimes, and other air-related wares, lots of eco-friendly booths set up by local businesses and environmentalist groups, and tours of the local wind farm. | 712/732–3780.

NOV.–DEC.: *Santa's Castle.* The country's largest animated holiday window display is in the original Carnegie Library building on Erie Street. | 712/732–3780.

Dining
Baker's Court. American. This casual, family-oriented restaurant has something for everyone. Entrées include a grilled breast of chicken glazed with a honey-mustard sauce, or the beef Oscar, beef tenderloin on an English muffin, topped with asparagus and hollandaise sauce. At the start of the meal you can visit the soup-and-salad bar and at the end there's an ice-cream bar, with a dozen different flavors and do-it-yourself toppings. | Rte. 7 W | 712/732–6298 | $6–$13 | AE, MC, V.

Lakeshore Restaurant. American. Boating artifacts and photographs decorate this popular gathering spot for locals and tourists. Check out the steaks, the seafood, and the ice-cream buffet—an all-you-care-to-eat, create-your-own-flavor frozen confection bar. | 1520 N. Lake Ave. | 712/732–9800 | $12–$35 | MC, V.

Lodging
AmeriHost Motel. This redbrick and stained-wood lodging is 1 mi from the lake's recreation area and the Buena Vista County Historical Museum. Complimentary Continental breakfast. In-room data ports, in-room safes, cable TV. Pool. Hot tub. Gym. Business services. | 1726 Lake Ave. | 712/732–1000 | fax 712/732–7056 | 141@amerihostinn.com | 60 rooms | $50–$64 | AE, D, DC, MC, V.

Sail-Inn. Anchors, life preservers, and bottled boats set a nautical tone at this hotel. If you stay here you'll be less than 2 mi from the lake. Complimentary Continental breakfast. In-room data ports, some refrigerators, some in-room hot tubs, cable TV. Laundry facilities. Business services. | 1015 E. Lakeshore Dr. | 712/732–1160 | fax 712/732–9441 | 44 rooms | $30–$55 | AE, D, MC, V.

STRAWBERRY POINT

MAP 3, G2

(Nearby town also listed: Dubuque)

Strawberry Point, known as Little Switzerland because of the heritage of this area's first white settlers, was named by railroad workers who found wild strawberries on the town's hillsides. The world's largest strawberry (made of fiberglass), measuring 15 ft high and 12 ft across, can be found at City Hall. Hotels and homes built in the early 1900s, as well as a drugstore with a real soda fountain, are part of this town's charm.

Information: Strawberry Point Chamber of Commerce | Box 404, 52076 | 319/933–2260 | www.strawberrypt.com.

Attractions
Backbone State Park. Iowa's first state park was founded in 1919 4 mi southwest of Strawberry Point and has 1,750 acres of camping, fishing, hiking, and climbing. | 1347 129th St. | 319/924–2527 | www.state.ia.us/parks | Free | Daily.

Brush Creek Canyon Preserve. This remote and rugged 212-acre preserve is for hikers only. If you venture there, expect to see a wide variety of plants and animals, some of them on the endangered species list. | 1025 Ivy Rd., Arlington | 319/425–4161 | Free | Daily dawn–dusk.

Wilder Memorial Museum. The eclectic collection here includes more than 750 heirloom dolls dating back to the 1700s, an extensive collection of arrowheads, prehistoric stone tools, Revolutionary and Civil War–era artifacts, and a vast collection of miniature toy tractors. | 123 W. Mission St. | 319/933–4615 | $3 | Memorial Day–Labor Day, daily 10–4; May, Sept.– Oct., weekends 10–4.

World's Biggest Strawberry. This fiberglass fruit was erected in 1957 to pay homage to the town's namesake and mark the entrance to City Hall. The 15-ft-tall statue has weathered gale-force winds, political upheaval, and rust problems aplenty, yet still stands as proudly today as it did the day it was constructed. | 111 Commercial St. at City Hall | Free | Daily.

ON THE CALENDAR

JUNE: *Strawberry Days.* This celebration of the berry harvest includes a parade, a craft show, a carnival and dance, a 60-mi bike race, a basketball tournament, a big chicken barbecue, and free strawberries and ice cream. | 319/933–2260.

JULY: *Bluegrass Festival.* Regional bands and musicians play at a natural amphitheater in a wooded area about 2 mi south of town. | 319/427–5386.

Dining

Franklin Coffee Shop. American. You can sit at the counter, at a booth, or at a table in this turn-of-the-last-century building. The burgers are pretty tasty, but save room for the homemade pies and bread. | 102 Elkader St. | 319/933–4788 | $6–$9 | MC, V.

Lodging

Franklin Hotel. This small downtown redbrick hotel was built in 1902 and is now on the National Register of Historic Places. The lobby has oak woodwork, a high tin ceiling, and old crystal chandeliers. Guest rooms are furnished with functional, nonfussy antiques. No room phones. | 102 Elkader St. | 319/933–4788 | 7 rooms | $65 | MC, V.

Ivy Rose Inn. This quaint B&B is within walking distance of downtown and is only a five-minute drive from Backbone Ridge State Park. You'll have a private entrance to your room. Complimentary breakfast. No room phones, no TV. | 624 Commercial St. | 319/933–4485 | 4 rooms | $65–$75 | MC, V.

VAN METER

MAP 3, D4

(Nearby towns also listed: Des Moines, Indianola, Winterset)

Van Meter is a small, rural community with 1,000 residents west of Des Moines. Early settlers came from Holland, via homesteads in Virginia and Kentucky. Originally called Lik-Skillet, the town was renamed in 1868 for Jacob Rhodes Van Meter, a local farmer and businessman who served as a captain in the Civil War and whose descendants still live in town. There's a museum here celebrating the career of Baseball Hall of Famer Bob Feller, but otherwise this is a town focused on those who live here, not those who are passing through.

Information: **Van Meter City Hall** | Box 160, 50261 | 515/996–2644.

Attractions

Bob Feller Hometown Exhibit. Displays memorabilia from this baseball Hall of Famer's career with the Cleveland Indians. | 310 Mill St. | 515/996–2806 | $2 | Mon.–Sat. 10–5, Sun. noon–4.

JUNE: *Kids Day.* Hosted by the Van Meter Volunteer Fire Department, this one-day event celebrates the community's children with a parade, games, and other activities. | 319/233–8431.

Dining
Coon River Bar and Grill. American. This place is essentially a bar with a kitchen. The dining area is also the drinking and pool-shooting area, just right if you're in the mood for Hank Williams on the jukebox. The kitchen offers hearty pub food—things like hot wings or a burger basket. | 415 Grant St. | 515/996–9400 | $5–$7 | MC, V.

WALNUT

MAP 3, C4

(Nearby towns also listed: Anita, Atlantic, Avoca, Elk Horn)

Known as "Iowa's Antique City," Walnut features about 250 antiques dealers showing their wares in 21 small shops and sprawling antiques malls near a short stretch of redbrick road aptly named Antique City Drive.

Information: Walnut Welcome Center | 607 Highland St., 51577 | 712/784–2100 | www.netins.net/showcase/walnutia.

Attractions
Antique City Drive. Crystal, china, fine furniture, and silverware from years past are sold in buildings that include a former lumberyard, motel, mill, livery, and appliance store. | Antique City Dr. | 712/784–2100 | Free | Daily.

Prairie Rose State Park. Deer, heron, and geese grace this 680-acre park 8 mi north of Walnut. You'll also find hiking trails and a 218-acre man-made lake offering swimming, fishing, boating, and a sandy beach. | 680 Rd. M47, Harlan | 712/773–2701 | www.state.ia.us/parks | Free | Daily.

JUNE: *AMVETS Antique Show and Walk.* Over 400 antiques dealers from Iowa and beyond set up shop in downtown Walnut for three days on Father's Day weekend. | 712/784–2100.
NOV.: *Annual Antique Christmas Walk.* This downtown event features antiques dealers from Iowa and Nebraska, horse-drawn carriage rides, strolling carolers, and a community bazaar on Thanksgiving weekend. | 712/784–2100.

Dining
Aunt B's Kitchen. American. Aunt B's serves "down-home" daily specials like smothered chicken breast with potatoes and gravy as well as sandwiches and casseroles in a wood-and-brick building painted green with a white picket fence. | 221 Antique City Dr. | 712/784–3681 | $8–$13 | No credit cards.

Sandy's Food and Spirits. American. Sandy's is part-bar and part-restaurant, specializing in pork tenderloin and "real meat" specials with mashed potatoes and gravy. | 213 Antique City Dr. | 712/784–2190 | $6–$13 | No credit cards.

Villager Restaurant. American. This former chain restaurant just off Interstate 80 is now independently owned and is known for its hearty buffets and broasted chicken (chicken cooked in a pressure-cooker.) | 2117 Antique City Dr. | 712/784–2200 | $5–$11 | D, MC, V.

Lodging

Antique City Inn B&B. This 1911 white wooden house with a wraparound porch (plus swing), a living room with French doors and wood baseboards, and a one-room carriage house is within easy walking distance of many antiques stores. Complimentary breakfast. Some room phones, no TV in some rooms, TV in common area. No kids under 12. | 400 Antique City Dr. | 712/784–3722 | fax 712/784–4242 | 6 rooms (3 with half-baths) | $45–$55 | AE, D, DC, MC, V.

Clark's Country Inn B&B. Family heirlooms and oak woodwork fill the living and dining rooms of this 1912 home. If you stay here you'll be just four blocks from antiques shops. Complimentary breakfast. Cable TV, VCR, no room phones. No kids under 13. No smoking. | 701 Walnut St. | 712/784–3010 | 3 rooms | $55 | MC, V.

Walnut Super 8 Motel. This basic chain motel is just off Interstate 80 at exit 46. Kids 12 and under stay free. In-room data ports, some in-room hot tubs, cable TV. Pool. Laundry facilities. Some pets allowed. | 2109 Antique City Dr. | 712/784–2221 | fax 712/784–3961 | 51 rooms | $39–$60 | AE, D, DC, MC, V.

WASHINGTON

MAP 3, G5

(Nearby towns also listed: Iowa City, Kalona)

Washington can claim several vintage homes and buildings on the National Register of Historic Places, but it's the nearby rivers and parkland that draw outdoor enthusiasts to town.

Information: Washington County Touristry Committee | 212 N. Iowa Ave., 52353 | 319/653–3272 | washcofc@lisco.com | wash.ia-chamber@se-iowa.net.

Attractions

Alexander Young Log Cabin. This 1840 log cabin in Sunset Park has been fully restored and an area of prairie grass planted nearby. | Main and 4th Sts. | 319/694–2323 | Free | June–Aug., Sun. 1–5.

Lake Darling State Park. You can camp, swim, and fish around the park's 2½-mi-long manmade lake 11 mi southwest of town. | Rte. 78 | 319/694–2323 | www.state.ia.us/parks | Free | Daily.

ON THE CALENDAR

MAY: *Keep on Track.* Displays of race cars in the town square plus face painting, clowns, and dunking booths. | 319/653–3272.

JUNE: *Washington Arts Festival.* Music, food, live entertainment, and an art show downtown, on the square. | 319/653–3272.

Dining

Winga's. American. A traditional small-town café on the north side of the square with counter service and a handful of tables and booths. On the menu: meat loaf, fried chicken, and pork chops. | 12 N. Main St. | 319/653–2093 | $6–$10 | No credit cards | Closed Mon.

Lodging

Hawkeye Motel. This relaxed motel, named after the University of Iowa mascot, proudly displays football memorabilia and locally themed art prints. Cable TV. | 1320 W. Madison St. | 319/653–7510 or 800/639–4295 | fax 319/653–7531 | 15 rooms | $30–$40 | D, MC, V.

Super 8. This motel has a spacious lobby with big windows looking out onto the countryside 1 mi outside Washington. A 13-mi-long nature trail leads off from the grounds. Bar.

In-room data ports, cable TV. Laundry facilities. Business services. | 119 Westview Dr. | 319/653–6621 | fax 319/653–6621 | 56 rooms | $42–$64 | AE, D, DC, MC, V.

WATERLOO

(Nearby town also listed: Cedar Falls)

Before white settlement in 1845, the Black Hawk Indians made their home in this part of the Cedar River valley. The Cedar River valley has some of the richest farming soil in Iowa, which is one reason the University of Northern Iowa's agriculture program is so popular. A large John Deere factory is also here.

Information: Waterloo Convention and Visitor's Bureau | 215 E. 4th St., Box 1587, 50704 | 319/233–8350 or 800/728–8431 | www.waterloocvb.org.

Attractions

Bluedorn Imaginarium. A hands-on discovery center allows children to explore physics, light, sound, and momentum. You can ride a human-size gyroscope—a spinning turntable platform that demonstrates angular momentum—or draw a light-picture in the air with a laser spirograph. | 322 Washington St. | 319/324–6357 | groutmuseum@cedarnet.org | $2.50 | Tues.–Sat. 10–6.

Cedar Rock/The Walter Residence. Completed in 1950, this was one of the last homes Frank Lloyd Wright designed. Its owner, Lowell Walter, left it to the people of Iowa in 1981. Cedar Rock is about 25 mi east of Waterloo in Quasqueton. | 2615 Quasqueton Diag. Blvd., Quasqueton | 319/934–3572 | $3 | May–Oct., Tues.–Sun. 11–5.

Cedar Valley Arboretum and Botanical Gardens. Twenty-four acres of land are being developed in an ongoing project to create a community garden of native plants, flowers, and trees. | 1927 E. Orange Rd. | 319/226–4966 | Free | Tours by appointment.

Grout Museum of History and Science. Established in 1956, this museum focuses on the area's natural and human history. | 503 South St. | 319/234–6357 | groutmuseum@cedarnet.org | $3.50 | Tues.–Sat. 10–4.

John Deere Waterloo Works. You can tour four John Deere plants and see the entire tractor production process from design to finished product, the assembly of the engine and tractors, and the casting of parts and components. | 3500 E. Donald St. | 319/292–7801 or 319/292–7697 | www.deere.com | Free | Weekdays 8–5.

Rensselaer Russell House Museum. This mid-Victorian Italianate brick home, which housed four generations of the Russell family, has its original furnishings and period gardens. | 520 W. 3rd St. | 319/233–0262 | $2.50 | Tues.–Sun. 10–4; limited hrs in Dec.

Waterloo Community Playhouse. This theater group has been given Iowa's Top Performing Arts Organization Award and has an international reputation for its productions of new plays. | 225 Commercial St. | 319/235–0367 or 319/291–4494 | www.waterloocvb.org | Admission varies per production.

Waterloo Museum of Art. Displays American decorative art and folk art, as well as one of the nation's largest public collections of Haitian art. | 225 Commercial St. | 319/291–4490 | www.wplwloo.lib.ia.us/waterloo | Free | Daily 10–5.

ON THE CALENDAR

MAY: *My Waterloo Days Festival*. A specially constructed cultural village tells the community's story. There's also a hot-air balloon rally, a Renaissance fair, and fireworks. | 319/233–8431 or 800/728–8431.

AUG.: _Old Time Power Show._ Antique farm equipment, tractor pulls, parades, and demonstrations. | 319/987–2380.

Dining

Boardwalk Deli. Deli. This fabulous little downtown sandwich shop has exposed brick walls punctuated with historical newspaper clippings, movie posters, and rock-and-roll memorabilia and serves sloppy joes beyond compare. The cold-cut sandwiches and hot subs are also excellent. | 206 E. 4th St. | 319/233–9160 | $5–$6 | MC, V.

Brown Bottle. Italian. Despite ivory table linens and low lighting, this restaurant remains relaxed and comfortably casual. Folks in shorts and sandals socialize alongside businesspeople in suits. One specialty is the chicken Dijon, topped with melted mozzarella cheese, green peppers, and onions. The Bottle also serves popular sandwiches and pizzas. | 209 W. 5th St. | 319/232–3014 | $7–$13 | AE, D, DC, MC, V.

China Jade. Chinese. This busy, in-and-out spot is popular with students and specializes in Szechuan, Hunan, and Cantonese cuisine. The dining area is set with simple, bare tables. Try the General Tso's chicken, or possibly share a very generous serving of hot-and-sour soup. | 3840 University Ave. | 319/232–7715 | $5–$12 | AE, MC, V.

Goose Creek Truck Plaza. American. If you're passing through this plaza to refuel, you might consider joining the long-distance truckers who stop to indulge in such classic roadhouse fare as open-faced meat sandwiches with mashed potatoes and gravy. | 2424 Ranchero Rd. | 319/234–2424 | $5–$7 | AE, D, MC, V.

R. J. Boar's. Barbecue. Bare-wood planks and strategically placed TVs set the scene in this casual smokehouse that gets rather noisy during peak hours. The food focus here is on hearty meat sandwiches—the kind of meal you want to eat when you're cheering on a college football game or boxing match. Try the pulled-pork sandwich—it's a heap of deep-seasoned meat piled on a fresh kaiser roll. | 3821 University Ave. | 319/833–5500 | $4–$6 | AE, D, MC, V.

Lodging

Best Western Starlite Village. This 11-story tower 2 blocks from downtown rises like a skyscraper in an otherwise uninterrupted landscape of fields, barns, and homes. Rooms are spacious but basic, and all enjoy an excellent view of the city. Restaurant, bar. In-room data ports, cable TV. Pool. Business services, airport shuttle. Pets allowed. | 214 Washington St. | 319/235–0321 | fax 319/235–6343 | www.bestwestern.com | 215 rooms | $88 | AE, D, DC, MC, V.

Fairfield Inn by Marriott. This pink- and white-brick hotel 5 mi south of downtown is right next to a shopping center. Rooms have work spaces and sitting areas separated from the sleeping area by low, wood-trimmed partitions. Complimentary Continental breakfast. Cable TV. Pool. Hot tub. Some pets allowed. | 2011 La Porte Rd. | 319/234–5452 | fax 319/234–5452 | www.marriott.com | 57 rooms | $72 | AE, D, DC, MC, V.

Grand Hotel Waterloo. A dozen brightly colored flags mark the front of this downtown hotel. Guest rooms are full of light from large, ground-floor windows. Complimentary Continental breakfast. In-room data ports, cable TV. Pool. Exercise equipment. Laundry services. Business services. Pets allowed. | 300 W. Mullan Ave. | 319/234–7791 or 877/928–3756 | grandhotel@earthdome.com | www.grandhotelwaterloo.com | fax 319/234–1727 | 96 rooms | $45 | AE, D, MC, V.

Heartland Inn. The standard chain hotel is in a commercial area near the Crossroads Mall 3 mi from downtown. There are several restaurants and fast-food establishments within walking distance. Complimentary Continental breakfast. In-room data ports, cable TV. Exercise equipment. Business services. Pets allowed (fee). | 1809 LaPorte Rd. | 319/235–4461 or 800/334–3277 | fax 319/235–0907 | 118 rooms | $62 | AE, D, DC, MC, V.

Holiday Inn-Convention Center. This 10-story high-rise hotel with a soaring glass atrium in the lobby is right in the center of Waterloo, and a skywalk connects the inn to an adjacent parking garage. Rooms have large work spaces. Restaurant, dining room, bar (with entertainment). In-room data ports, some refrigerators, cable TV. Pool. Hot tub. Airport shuttle. Pets allowed. | 205 W. 4th St. | 319/233–7560 | fax 319/236–9590 | www.basshotels.com/holiday-inn | 229 rooms | $85–$105 | AE, D, DC, MC, V.

Quality Inn. This chain hotel is just 1½ blocks from the Waterloo Convention Center. Bar, complimentary Continental breakfast. In-room data ports, microwaves, refrigerators, some in-room hot tubs, cable TV. Laundry service. Business services. Pets allowed. | 226 W. 5th St. | 319/235–0301 or 800/228–5151 | fax 319/234–4837 | www.qualityinn.com | 50 rooms, 17 suites | $60–$72 rooms, $80–$144 suites | AE, D, DC, MC, V.

Super 8. This brown-and-white, faux-exposed-timber chain hotel is adjacent to the Crossroads Shopping Center 2 mi from the center of town. Complimentary Continental breakfast. Cable TV. Some pets allowed. | 1825 LaPorte Rd. | 319/233–1800 | fax 319/233–1800 | www.super8.com | 62 rooms | $46–$50 | AE, D, DC, MC, V.

WAVERLY

(Nearby towns also listed: Cedar Falls, Waterloo)

Founded by German immigrants on what was once a Winnebago Indian Reservation, this town has a large number of Italianate-style homes and buildings. Each spring and fall it hosts the largest draft horse sale in North America. The town is also in the process of developing a bike trail on an old railroad bed as a part of Iowa's "Rails-to-Trails" project. Following the lead of many Iowa communities, Waverly has diversified its economy to include finance, business, and industry, as well as agriculture.

Information: Waverly Main Street Chamber | 118 W. Bremer Ave., 50677 | 800/251–0360 | waverly@sbt.net.

Attractions

Wartburg College. A four-year liberal-arts college founded in 1852 by the Evangelical Lutheran Church of America. | 222 9th St. NW | 319/352–8200 | www.wartburg.edu | Free | Daily.

Waverly House and Bremer County Historical Museum. You can learn the story of Bremer County and the community of Waverly through photos, artifacts, and an ever-changing roster of exhibits, in this compact museum. | 422 W. Bremer Ave. | 319/352–2738 | Free | Mon.–Sat. 1:30–4, Sun. 2–4.

ON THE CALENDAR

MAR., OCT.: *Waverly Midwest Horse Sale.* This is North America's largest sale of draft horses, driving teams, equipment, and tack. Nearly 20,000 prospective horse buyers come from far and wide to bid on animals. | 319/352–2804.

Dining

Abe Downing's Steak House. American. A fireplace warms the dining room at this local favorite. On the menu: Iowa beef, in the form of steaks, ribs, burgers, and hearty beef stew. Kids' menu. | 1900 Heritage Way | 319/352–5050 | $15–$30 | AE, D, DC, MC, V.

The Tassel. American. This restaurant is known for its vast buffet, which has a different theme every weekend. Depending on availability and season, you might find seafood, or perhaps a western-flavor spread, with hot wings, fried chicken, and grits. Regardless of what's on the buffet, you can still order favorites like prime rib and pork chops from the menu. | Rte. 3 W | 319/352–5330 | $6–$10 | AE, D, DC, MC, V.

Lodging

Star Motel. This single-story drive-up is a picture of classic American road-trip history. The smallish rooms with older furnishings bring to mind a bygone era before the rise of the corporate hotel chain. Restaurant. | 3303 E. Bremer St. | 319/352–4434 | 33 rooms | $40 | AE, D, MC, V.

Super 8. The lobby of this brick-and-siding motel 1 mi southwest of downtown is decked out with overstuffed chairs, a couple of couches, and an adjacent breakfast nook with an ever-burbling coffeepot and a microwave. Some in-room hot tubs, in-room data ports, cable TV. Sauna. Gym. Laundry services. Business services. | 301 13th Ave. SW | 319/352–0888 | fax 319/352–0888 | www.super8.com | 43 rooms | $42–$99 | AE, D, DC, MC, V.

WEBSTER CITY

MAP 3, D3

(Nearby town also listed: Fort Dodge)

In the rolling hills of the Boone River valley, Webster City is a typical Iowa town with tree-lined streets, homey festivals, and good high-school basketball. The Boone River is good for fishing and swimming. Webster City was home to two great writers—Nobel Prize–winner Clark Mollenhoff, author of *Game Plan for Disaster,* and MacKinlay Kantor, who won a Pulitzer Prize for the Civil War drama *Andersonville.*

Information: Webster City Chamber of Commerce | 628 2nd St., Box 310, 50595 | 515/832–2564 or 800/535–8341 | wcabi@ncn.net | www.ncn.net/~wcabi.

Attractions

Country Relics Little Village and Homestead. Restored farm machinery and other antiques fill two buildings. A small country church on the site, 10 mi south of town, is still used for weddings. | 3290 Briggs Woods Rd. | 515/826–3491 | $3 | May–Oct., daily 10–4.

Depot Museum Complex. This 9-acre complex includes two 1854 log cabins, a family cemetery, and Native American artifacts such as arrowheads, pottery, and artwork. The depot's ticket office and waiting room contain original furnishings and artifacts such as stamps, schedules, and a log book. | Superior Ave. and Ohio Ave. | 515/832–2847 | $2 | May–Sept., daily 10–5.

Kendall Young Library. Built in 1905, this structure is a beautiful example of Beaux Arts architecture, with a tiled roof, a portico supported by white columns, and manicured grounds. Inside, you'll find extensive exhibits, including a Foster doll collection, a sculpture collection, and hundreds of historic and prehistoric artifacts. | 1201 Wilson Ave. | 515/832–9100 | Free | Weekdays 9–5, Sat. 10–5.

ON THE CALENDAR
JULY: *Raspberry Festival.* This festival celebrates the area's fruit harvest with bands, carnivals, crafts, and tasty raspberry pies, cobblers, and preserves. | 515/832–2564.
SEPT.: *Doodle Bug Festival and Reunion.* Highlights of this three-day event at the county fairgrounds include a Webster City Cruisers parade, a quilt show, and a woodcarvers' show. | 515/832–2564.

Dining

Second Street Emporium. Steak. This upscale restaurant is in a turn-of-the-last-century building that used to be a downtown theater in the 1920s. Now there's an air of rustic elegance with stained-glass windows, pressed-tin ceilings, and crisp linens. The Emporium's hand-cut Black Angus steaks are its pride and joy, and the restaurant also maintains an excellent wine list and a selection of imported beers. | 615 2nd St. | 515/832–3463 | $12–$17 | AE, D, MC, V.

Lodging

Best Western Norseman Inn. Rooms are spacious enough to sleep a family comfortably at this small, brick motel. Bar, complimentary Continental breakfast. Cable TV. Pets allowed. | 3086 220th St., Williams | 515/854–2281 | fax 515/854–2447 | www.bestwestern.com | 33 rooms | $50 | AE, D, DC, MC, V.

Executive Inn. This unremarkable hotel in a busy commercial area ¾ mi from the center of town caters to business travelers. Complimentary Continental breakfast. Cable TV. Pool. | 1700 Superior St. | 515/832–3631 or 800/322–3631 | fax 515/832–6830 | 39 rooms | $50 | AE, D, DC, MC, V.

Super 8. This motel is 1 mi west of the center of town at the junction of U.S. 20 and U.S. 27, a few minutes' drive from several restaurants. In-room data ports, cable TV. Pool. Laundry facilities. Business services. Pets allowed. | 305 Closz Dr. | 515/832–2000 | fax 515/832–2000 | www.super8.com | 44 rooms | $43–$58 | AE, D, DC, MC, V.

WEST BEND

MAP 3, D2

(Nearby towns also listed: Algona, Emmetsburg)

Palo Alto County's first white settlement was named for its location in the West Bend of the Des Moines River. West Bend's historical society has remained active over the years, restoring a one-room schoolhouse and maintaining Iowa's only sod house. Most visitors come to West Bend to visit the Grotto of the Redemption, which covers an area equal to a city block and depicts man's fall from grace in a series of vignettes picked out in semiprecious stones.

Information: West Bend Economic Development | Box 111, 50597 | 515/887–4721.

Attractions

Grotto of the Redemption. Each year more than 100,000 people visit this grotto, which covers an area equivalent to a city block. Via a series of nine vignettes, the Grotto depicts scenes from the life of Christ. Begun in 1912, its mortar towers, battlements, and steeples encrusted with minerals, crystals, and semiprecious stones are still taking shape. | 300 N. Broadway | 515/887–2371 | Donations accepted | Weekdays 9–4; guided tours June–mid-Oct.; also by appointment; Sun. mass 9 AM.

Historic Sod House and School House Museum. Here you can tour both an early pioneer-era sod house and a one-room schoolhouse, as well as a collection of antique farm equipment. | 1st Ave. SW | 515/887–4721 | Free | Tours available by appointment May–Aug.

ON THE CALENDAR
JULY: *Fourth of July Celebration.* This community celebration includes a large fireworks display. | 515/887–2371.

Dining

Grotto Restaurant. American. You'll find this very casual restaurant, on the grounds of the Grotto of the Redemption, serving up comfort foods like meat loaf, roast beef, and macaroni-and-cheese in a cafeteria-style dining area. | 300 W. Broadway | 515/887–2371 | $5–$7 | D, MC, V.

Lodging

West Bend Motel. This humble, single-story motel is proud of its down-home friendly service at the desk and is right in town about a block from the Grotto. Cable TV. Pets allowed. | 13 4th Ave. | 515/887–3611 | 18 rooms | $36 | D, MC, V.

WEST BRANCH

MAP 3, G4

(Nearby towns also listed: Cedar Rapids, Iowa City, Kalona, Muscatine)

This pleasant town is particularly proud of its native son, Depression-era U.S. President Herbert Hoover. Hoover's official presidential library is here on sprawling well-tended grounds with restored buildings, including the cottage in which Hoover was born and the Quaker meetinghouse his family attended. The nearby downtown, a National Historic District, offers interesting shops and restaurants.

Information: **West Branch Chamber of Commerce** | Box 365, 52358 | 319/643–2111.

Attractions

Herbert Hoover National Historic Site. You'll find the birthplace and grave site of the "Great Humanitarian" and 31st American president here, along with Hoover's father's blacksmith shop, an 1850s schoolhouse, the Quaker meetinghouse the Hoover family attended, and 76 acres of restored tallgrass prairie. | 110 Parkside Dr. | 319/643–2541 | www.nps.gov/heho | $2 | Daily 9–5.

The **Herbert Hoover Presidential Library-Museum** highlights various aspects of Hoover's public service career, including the 57 nations where his hunger program was implemented and Wall Street circa 1929. | 319/643–5301 | www.hoover.nara.gov | $2 | Daily 9–5.

Secrest 1883 Octagonal Barn. One of the nation's oldest and largest round barns, this building—listed on the National Register of Historic Places—has a 75-ft high bell-shape roof and is part of a 10-acre, mid-1800s farmstead near Downey, 4 mi south of West Branch on County Road X30. | County Rd. X30 | 319/643–2260 | Tours by appointment only; $6 | Daily.

ON THE CALENDAR

AUG.: *Hoover Fest.* Historic reenactments, food, and music celebrate the birth and legacy of the only Iowan to become president of the United States. | 319/643–5301.

Dining

Fox Run Golf and Country Club. American. This bar-and-grill in the clubhouse of a public golf course serves sandwiches, steak, chicken, and fish dinners. | 19 Greenview La. | 319/643–2100 | Apr.–Nov. nightly; Dec.–Mar. Fri. only. No lunch | $4–13 | MC, V.

Herb and Lou's. American/Casual. Named after President Herbert Hoover and his wife, this downtown restaurant and bar serves pizza and deli sandwiches. | 105 N. Downey St. | 319/643–9408 | $5–$20 | No credit cards | Closed Sun.

Heyn Quarter Steak House. Steak. Grill your own steak at this downtown dinner-only spot. Kids' menu. | 102 W. Main St. | 319/643–5420 | $8–$17 | AE, D, MC, V | Closed Mon.

Lodging

Econo Lodge Motel. A basic motel just off Interstate 80 at exit 259 in West Liberty, about 5 mi from West Branch. Kids stay free. Complimentary Continental breakfast. Cable TV. Pool. Some pets allowed. | 1943 Garfield Ave., West Liberty | 319/627–2171 or 888/589–5007 | fax 319/627–4982 | 35 rooms | $48–$55 | AE, D, DC, MC, V.

Presidential Motor Inn. Pictures of Herbert Hoover hang in each room of this basic motel. Microwaves available, refrigerators, cable TV. Laundry facilities. Some pets allowed. | 711 S. Downey Rd. | 319/643–2526 | fax 319/643–5166 | 38 rooms | $42 | AE, D, DC, MC, V.

WEST UNION

(Nearby towns also listed: Marquette, Spillville)

West Union is the seat of Fayette County and its three-story stone courthouse is one of the most beautiful in the Midwest with its brass and marble fittings inside. Many of the town's activities center around the courthouse square and its many fountains. The community is civic minded; the Lions, Rotary, Knights of Columbus, and volunteer fire department provide a lively calendar of fairs, festivals, and fund-raisers.

Information: West Union Chamber of Commerce | 101 N. Vine St., Box 71, 52175 | 319/422–3070 | www.westunion.com.

Attractions

Montauk. This 1870s brick-and-limestone Italianate mansion on 46 acres overlooking the Turkey River 9 mi northeast of town near Clermont was home to Iowa's 12th governor. Its original furnishings include Tiffany lamps, a large collection of paintings, and Italian statues. | Hwy. 18 | 319/423–7173 | $3 | May–Oct., daily noon–4.

Volga River State Recreation Area. This 5,400-acre park in Iowa's Little Switzerland 6 mi south of town is heavily wooded and has great fishing in Frog Hollow Lake. The park also offers equestrian trails, snowmobiling, and cross-country skiing. | 9026 Ivy Rd. | 319/425–4161 | www.state.ia.us/parks | Free | Daily.

ON THE CALENDAR

JUNE: *Dairy/Agriculture Days.* This weekend-long celebration honors the farm and dairy industries that fuel this community. A parade, children's games, a magician, comedy performances, and live music are among the Dairy Days events. | 319/422–3070.

Dining

Town House Cafe. American. A West Union institution for 25 years, this family-oriented restaurant serves "Granny's cooking" in a formal dining room and a front room with booth and counter service. Hot beef and noodles is a favorite here, but the casseroles are popular too. Antique dresses, bonnets, kitchenware, and knickknacks decorate the interior. Come early because the café closes at 8. | 131 N. Vine St. | 319/422–9255 | $6–$7 | No credit cards | No dinner weekends.

Lodging

Butler House Bed and Breakfast. Built in 1891 on a small hill, this stately Victorian home has vaulted ceilings, ornate moldings, stained glass, and solid oak everything. Today, it also has five guest rooms lit with original fixtures and furnished with period antiques. Complimentary breakfast. No room phones, cable TV. | 214 W. Maple St. | 319/422–5944 | 5 rooms | $45–$70 | MC, V.

Lilac Motel. This motel on the edge of town was named for the fragrant bushes that bloom outside in spring. Passes for the city pool are available to guests. Complimentary Continental breakfast. In-room data ports, cable TV. | 310 U.S. 150 N | 319/422–3861 | fax 319/422–5465 | 27 rooms | $47 | AE, D, DC, MC, V.

WINTERSET

(Nearby town also listed: Indianola)

Winterset was originally to be named Summerset, but when founders met to vote on the name the day was unusually cold, thus the last-minute change. The state's largest poultry production facility, producing more than 1 million eggs a day, is nearby, and many of the cornfields around Winterset produce grain for the chickens. The birthplace of screen legend John Wayne, this town has gained even greater notice in recent years, as its six covered bridges are the center of the novel and the movie *The Bridges of Madison County*. Tourists flock here to see both the bridges and the movie site.

Information: **Madison County Chamber of Commerce** | 73 Jefferson St., Winterset, 50273 | 515/462–1185 or 800/298–6119 | www.madisoncounty.com.

Attractions

Adair County Heritage Center. This historical museum on 10 acres some 24 mi west of Winterset includes a schoolhouse, a church, the birthplace of Governor George Wilson, and more. | Rte. 92 W, Greenfield | 515/743–2232 | $3 | May–Oct. 1, daily 1–4:30 or by appointment.

Covered bridges. The county's six covered bridges, reminders of a long-ago era, were featured in the novel and movie *The Bridges of Madison County*. Maps for a self-guided tour are available at the Madison County Chamber of Commerce on the town square. | 73 Jefferson St. | 515/462–1185 or 800/298–6119 | Free | May–Oct., Mon.–Fri. 9–5, Sat. 9–4, Sun. 11–4; Nov.–Apr., Mon.–Fri. 9–4:30.

Francesca's House. This farmhouse 16 mi north of Winterset lay abandoned in the middle of a field of tall grass for 35 years before it was rediscovered by movie producers and totally restored for the *Bridges* film. Today, the house remains as it appeared in the movie. You're welcome to climb into the bathtub Clint Eastwood used. | 3271 130th St., Cumming | 515/981–5268 | $4 | May–Oct. daily.

John Wayne Birthplace. The tiny four-room home the star lived in until age three is filled with movie memorabilia and antiques. | 224 S. 2nd St. | 515/462–1044 | www.johnwaynebirthplace.org | $2.50 | Daily 10–4:30.

Madison County Museum and Complex. This 18-acre complex of 13 buildings—among them a one-room schoolhouse, a fire station, and exhibit halls—tells the story of Madison County. | 815 S. 2nd Ave. | 515/462–2134 | $3 | Mon.–Sat. 11–4 (May–Oct., also Sun. 1–5); also by appointment.

Winterset City Park. Occupying the eastern corner of town, City Park features Clark's Tower—a medieval-looking limestone structure perched on a hill overlooking the Middle River valley. Built in 1937 to honor the area's first settlers, the tower stands 25 ft high and can be reached by car in dry weather or by a brisk hike on foot. | Park entrance: 9th and South Sts. | 515/462–3258 | Free | Daily.

ON THE CALENDAR

JUNE: *National Skillet-Throwing Contest*. Battle for points by knocking the head off a dummy with a cast-iron skillet, in Macksburg, 15 mi southwest of Winterset. | 515/768–2471.
AUG.: *Madison County Fair*. A rodeo and figure-eight races are part of this very traditional Iowa county fair held at the Madison County Fairgrounds on Summit Street. | 800/298–6119.
OCT.: *Madison County Covered Bridge Festival*. Civil War reenactments, live music, sheep-shearing demos, potters, quilters, jugglers, and buckskinners, as well as crafts, food, and music to raise money to maintain and restore the county's famous and historic covered bridges. | 515/462–1185 or 800/298–6119.

NOV.: *Festival of Lights.* Held at twilight the day after Thanksgiving, this festival welcomes the holiday season with a parade of illuminated floats. | 515/462–1185 or 800/298–6119 | chamber@dwx.com.

Dining

Espresso Yourself. American. Barn-red wallpaper and mismatched antique tables set the scene for fabulous focaccia sandwiches (try the Southwestern chicken), homemade soups, and freshly made desserts. Of course, you can get tea, coffee, and Italian sodas as well, but it's the sandwiches and soups that have made this place a hit for lunch. | 122 N. 1st Ave. | 515/462–5962 | $4–$6 | No credit cards | Closed Sun. No dinner.

Northside Café. American. Quaint doesn't begin to describe the bygone-era charm of the Northside. Established in 1876, this little joint on the courthouse square has a lunch counter complete with swivel stools and chipped Formica. The meat loaf, fried chicken, and pork chops make the café a favorite among locals, but its role in Clint Eastwood's *The Bridges of Madison County* draws tourists. | 61 W. Jefferson St. | 515/462–1523 | $4–$9 | No credit cards.

Lodging

Summerset House. This gorgeous Victorian mansion is in a quiet residential neighborhood two blocks from town square and five blocks from the John Wayne Birthplace (*see above*). Guest rooms are done in a tasteful blend of antique and contemporary furnishings, and the inn's tearoom serves lunch on weekdays and dinner by arrangement. Complimentary breakfast. In-room TVs, no room phones. | 204 W. Washington St. | 515/462–9014 | 4 rooms | $65–$110 | No credit cards.

Village View Motel. This white-sided motel on the north edge of town provides guests with maps of the county's famous bridges. Rooms are small and basic, but the motel is within easy walking distance of the town square. Cable TV, in-room VCRs available. Pets allowed. | 711 E. Hwy. 92 | 515/462–1218 or 800/862–1218 | fax 515/462–1231 | www.madisoncounty.com | 16 rooms | $43 | AE, D, DC, MC, V.

Missouri

Missouri is the nation's 15th-largest state, and the third most populous west of the Mississippi River, ranking behind California and Texas. Steelville, a small town some 50 mi southwest of St. Louis, is the population center of the United States, according to the Census Bureau, and the geographic center of the country is just a bit farther west in neighboring Kansas.

Its central position, along with its great rivers, lakes, and waterways, has shaped much of Missouri's past, and continues to define its present. The ancient Mississippi marks the state's eastern border and it was that river that brought early explorers Father Jacques Marquette, Louis Jolliet, and Pierre Laclède to these lands. Ste. Genevieve, St. Louis, Hannibal, and Cape Girardeau were all founded on the banks of the Mississippi which still serves as one of the nation's most important waterways.

The younger Missouri River comes down the northwest edge then cuts through the center of the state dividing the glaciated plains of the north from the more rugged Ozarks to the south. It was the Missouri that carried Lewis and Clark north as they began their exploration of the American West and its banks saw the rise of Kansas City, Jefferson City, St. Joseph, and St. Charles as well as the backs of the 19th-century wagon trains heading west.

Once frequented by steamboats, the Mississippi and the Missouri are now home to riverboat gambling, a controversial part of Missouri's well-developed tourism industry. Elsewhere in the state a wealth of lakes, rivers, and caves provide opportunities for recreation, and for development.

For all its rivers have offered the state, they are not always a force for development and growth as the Great Flood of 1993 revealed. No state suffered more than Missouri which saw more than $20 billion worth of damage. Many towns, some miles from today's riverbanks, have markers indicating the height of water levels that year and extraor-

CAPITAL: JEFFERSON CITY	POPULATION: 5,402,000	AREA: 69,674 SQUARE MI
BORDERS: IL, TN, AR, OK, KS, NE, IA	TIME ZONE: CENTRAL	POSTAL ABBREVIATION: MO
WEB SITE: WWW.MISSOURITOURISM.ORG		

dinary stories of heroism and effort in the face of rising waters abound throughout these communities.

Nicknamed the Show-Me State, Missouri is said to be full of residents as stubborn as the mule that has been named the state animal. No one knows exactly when or where this reputation and expression originated, but much of the credit for popularizing them both goes to Congressman Willard Duncan Vandiver of Cape Girardeau County. During an 1899 speech to Philadelphia's Five O'Clock Club, Vandiver questioned the accuracy of an earlier speaker's remarks, concluding with the phrase, "I'm from Missouri and you've got to show me." The expression soon caught the public fancy, and Missourians liked the idea of being tough-minded demanders of proof.

Proof of Missouri's contributions to the larger culture of the nation include the novels of Samuel Clemens (a.k.a. Mark Twain), the poetry of T. S. Eliot, the agricultural ideas of George Washington Carver, President Harry S Truman's years of leadership, the journalistic tradition of Hungarian immigrant Joseph Pulitzer and native son Walter Cronkite, and J. C. Penney's stores.

History

When Father Jacques Marquette and Louis Jolliet descended the Mississippi from the north in 1673, Missouri's earliest settled inhabitants, the people of the Woodland and Mississippi cultures, had already mysteriously disappeared. In their place, early European explorers encountered relatively recent migrants to the area. There were Sauk, Fox, and Illinois Indians, all Algonquian tribes, in the northeast and the Siouan Osage, Oto, Iowa, and Missouri tribes elsewhere in the state. Although the state took its name from the Missouri, a series of treaties in the first years of the 19th century obliged the Indians to cede their lands in the region to white settlers and today there are no organized tribes left in Missouri. The French were the first Europeans to claim sovereignty of the region as part of the Louisiana Territory and the land passed through Spanish hands, then back to the French before becoming part of the United States.

Lead mining played an important role in Missouri's early development. Galena, a lead ore, was first discovered in 1701 near Potosi, and began to be mined in earnest in 1720 upon the discovery of significant deposits at Mine La Motte, on the state's eastern border. One of the first commercial endeavors in Missouri, mining continues to be a major enterprise today. The 1700s also saw the establishment of permanent settlements at Ste. Genevieve and St. Louis on the Mississippi River. Because of its excellent location at the spot where the Missouri River flows into the Mississippi, St. Louis became the largest settlement in the state, and today is one of the nation's larger cities.

Thomas Jefferson authorized the purchase of the Louisiana Territory in April 1803 for $11,000. Missouri was named a first-class territory in 1805 and in 1818 applied for statehood. The Union, however, was already embroiled in the political debate over slavery, which became an issue in the state's admission. Maine was also being considered for statehood, and both Maine and Missouri wanted to enter as free states. This did not sit well with southern congressmen, who saw the imbalance as politically unfa-

MO Timeline

8,000 BC	1000	1400	1541
Prehistoric nomadic tribes hunt in what will one day be Missouri.	The Woodland and Mississippian cultures inhabit the fertile floodplains of the Missouri, Mississippi, and Illinois rivers.	The Mississippian culture mysteriously declines.	Spanish explorers led by Hernando de Soto venture into southeast Missouri.

INTRODUCTION

HISTORY

REGIONS

WHEN TO VISIT

STATE'S GREATS

RULES OF THE ROAD

DRIVING TOURS

vorable. The famous Missouri Compromise was then proposed, which allowed Maine to enter as a free state and Missouri to enter as a slave state in 1821.

During the Civil War, Missouri was the one slave state which did not secede from the Union. But its place as a border state in the conflict and the mixed allegiances of the state's population meant it saw fierce battles and guerrilla activity. The war devastated industries such as wine making and tobacco production, which have only recently been reintroduced as powerful economic forces.

The westward movement of American settlers in the 19th century also helped define Missouri. Trading posts in St. Louis, Kansas City, Arrow Rock, Independence, and St. Joseph outfitted wagon trains heading west and these cities were often the last bastions of civilization settlers saw as they made their way through the plains and mountains to the West Coast. Without the innovation and courage provided by the riders of the Pony Express, many of those pioneers would have remained cut off from Eastern relatives and businesses.

Missouri entered the 20th century as proud host of the 1904 World Fair, then halfway through the century saw the first Missourian, Harry S Truman, elected to the White House.

Regions

1. ST. LOUIS AND METRO AREA

The streets and buildings of St. Louis stand as testament to some of Missouri's oldest history. Founded in 1764 by Pierre Laclède, a French trader from New Orleans, the city first belonged to the Spanish and the French before passing into the hands of the young American nation in 1803, and the Catholic influence has been strong throughout the city's history. Today St. Louis is one of the country's most diverse cities, with pockets of ethnicity celebrated in all corners. In the 1950s and '60s St. Louis proper suffered from urban decay as the county around it prospered, but programs in recent years have brought a renewal to much of the city's inner core. Illinois, just across the river, is easily accessible from the metro area.

Towns listed: Clayton, St. Charles, St. Louis, Wentzville

2. KANSAS CITY AND METRO AREA

For what many consider to be a cowboy town, perhaps best known for its steaks, its barbecue, and its past as a trailhead for the wagon trains carrying settlers to the American West, Kansas City and its surrounding communities have a surprisingly cosmopolitan, even European, feel evident in their architecture and arts. Although the city's premiere social event, the Belle of the American Royal, has its roots in a cattle show, the city is

1673	**1701**	**1730s**	**1735**	**1764**
French explorers Marquette and Jolliet canoe down the Mississippi River.	Lead ore is discovered near Potosi.	The Osage Indians dominate all tribes in the Missouri region.	First white settlement in what will become Missouri is established at Ste. Genevieve.	St. Louis is founded.

also known for its wide boulevards, its many fountains, the Nelson-Atkins Museum of Art, and the State Ballet.

Towns listed: Blue Springs, Excelsior Springs, Harrisonville, Independence, Kansas City, Liberty, Parkville, Weston

3. THE OZARKS

The rugged Ozark hills stretch from central Missouri through the southern part of the state. Famed for the beauty of its forests, thousands of acres of which are preserved in the Mark Twain National Forest, as well as its pristine lakes, rivers, and streams, the region is now also home to Branson. With 27 theaters, Branson is second only to Nashville as a venue for country-music shows. A trip to the Ozarks offers something for everyone—family entertainment, water sports, history, shopping, and the ever-present beauty of the hills.

Towns listed: Branson, Camdenton, Carthage, Clinton, Lake Ozark, Mount Vernon, Nevada, Osage Beach, Rolla, Springfield, Stockton, Sullivan, Van Buren, Waynesville

4. THE BOOTHEEL

The rolling forested hills of the Ozarks begin to dissipate as you move south out of Cape Girardeau into Missouri's bootheel and the flat floodplains of the Mississippi. What was once wet prairie and bottomland forests has long since been converted into farmland and the Old South heritage of the area is evidenced by the rice, cotton, peaches, and soybeans that are the mainstays of economic life here.

Towns listed: Cape Girardeau, New Madrid, Poplar Bluff, Sikeston

5. THE PONY EXPRESS REGION

Nineteenth-century America's western frontier began in Missouri's northwest regions, and reminders of that history are dotted throughout the many towns, villages, rolling hills, and riverways of this area. Notables who have come from this part of Missouri include J. C. Penney, Jesse James, Dale Carnegie, and Walter Cronkite. Fields, forests, and marshes offer an abundance of opportunities for hunters and wildlife enthusiasts.

Towns listed: Bethany, Cameron, Jamesport, Mound City, St. Joseph

When to Visit

Missouri experiences all four seasons and while each inevitably brings a number of pleasant days and evenings, each also has the potential for extreme or serious weather conditions. The mid-state community of Warsaw has recorded Missouri's most extreme

1803	1804	1808	1811–12	1817
Thomas Jefferson authorizes the purchase of the Louisiana Territory, which includes what will become Missouri.	Lewis and Clark travel up the Missouri in search of a waterway to the Pacific.	The Osage Indians sign a treaty relinquishing some of their lands in Missouri. They will sign a second treaty relinquishing more land in 1825.	The worst earthquake in the young American nation's history, registering an estimated 8.8 on the Richter scale, shakes the region for three months, and is centered in New Madrid.	The first steamboat arrives in St. Louis.

INTRODUCTION
HISTORY
REGIONS
WHEN TO VISIT
STATE'S GREATS
RULES OF THE ROAD
DRIVING TOURS

temperatures. In July 1954, Warsaw reached 118°F, and in February 1905, the same town saw the state's record low at −40°F. More typically, the average daily temperature in January varies from 25°F in the northwest to 34°F in the southeast Missouri bootheel. Average daily temperatures in summer range from 78°F to 80°F across the state. A July day is likely to be quite humid. The temperature may be around 66°F just before sunrise, and then reach 85°F or 90°F by mid-afternoon, but a summer spell of 100+°F temperatures is not uncommon either.

Missouri is in the midst of "tornado alley," and the months of March, April, and May are when weather conditions are most conducive to tornadoes. Southeast Missouri sees an average annual precipitation of 47 inches, most of which falls in spring and autumn. Northwest Missouri is noticeably drier with just 36 inches of precipitation on average, much of which comes during summer. But spring thunderstorms throughout the state frequently contain high winds and damaging hail and you'd do well to pay attention to weather warnings while visiting this time of year.

Autumn is usually wonderful in Missouri, despite some rainy days now and then. The lower humidity and cooler temperatures dry many crops, turning the fields vibrant shades of gold and brown. Allergy sufferers should note that mold and pollen counts reach their highest points in September, but the fields, the colorful trees throughout the state, and birds migrating south make late September and October a delightful time to visit any part of Missouri.

CLIMATE CHART

Average high/low temperatures (°F) and monthly precipitation (in inches)

	JAN.	FEB.	MAR.	APR.	MAY	JUN.
ST. LOUIS	40/23	44/25	53/32	66/44	75/53	85/63
	1.7	2.1	3.3	3.5	3.5	3.7

	JUL.	AUG.	SEPT.	OCT.	NOV.	DEC.
	89/67	87/66	81/58	70/47	54/35	43/27
	3.6	2.5	2.7	2.7	2.5	2.2

	JAN.	FEB.	MAR.	APR.	MAY	JUN.
KANSAS CITY	42/12	46/19	58/30	63/46	74/58	83/68
	1.8	1.5	2.8	3.1	5.4	4.7

	JUL.	AUG.	SEPT.	OCT.	NOV.	DEC.
	90/72	87/70	67/61	65/47	52/35	46/13
	4.4	4.1	4.8	3.4	1.4	1.5

1818	1821	1821	1831	
Missouri applies for statehood.	French fur trader François Choteau establishes a post at what will become Kansas City.	Missouri is admitted as the 24th state in the Union.	Mormon leader Joseph Smith, Jr. names Independence as the promised land for Mormons and many of his followers move to the area. But the Mormons are not welcomed	and by 1839 they are gone.

FESTIVALS AND SEASONAL EVENTS

WINTER

Nov.   **Mid-America Holiday Parade.** The Midwest's largest holiday parade fills downtown St. Louis on Thanksgiving morning. | 314/286–4086.

Dec.   **Christmas on the River.** Santa arrives by riverboat to be met by a 1,000-voice children's choir, fireworks choreographed to Christmas carols, and a crowd of 15,000 people at Parkville's annual town lighting ceremony. | 816/505–2227.

Ozark Mountain Christmas and Branson Area Festival of Lights. The Branson/Table Rock Lake area celebrates with more than 15 mi of sparkling lights and special holiday music shows. | 417/334–4084 or 800/214–3661 | www.bransonchamber.com.

SPRING

Mar.   **St. Patrick's Day Parade.** One of the largest in the nation, this St. Patrick's Day event begins in downtown Kansas City and proceeds north. The parade is not always held on the 17th. | 816/931–7373.

Apr.   **Dogwood Festivals.** Festivals honoring the beauty of dogwood trees in bloom are held in several towns including Camdenton as dogwoods in the Ozarks burst into bloom. | 573/346–2227 or 800/769–1004.

SUMMER

July   **National Tom Sawyer Days.** Since the 1950s, Mark Twain fans have traveled from around the globe to Samuel Clemens's hometown of Hannibal to participate in this four-day event which falls around Independence day and features a fence-painting contest, a frog-jumping contest, a Tom and Becky look-alike contest, and more. | 573/221–2477 | www.hanmo.com/hcvb.

Aug.   **U.S. Balloon Classic.** Balloons, food, musical entertainment, and a visit from Ronald McDonald are part of this fund-raiser in Columbia for the Ronald McDonald house. | 573/814–4000.

AUTUMN

Sept.   **St. Louis Art Fair.** More than 100,000 people turn out to view artwork created in various mediums and displayed at this fair in Clayton. | 314/863–0278.

1835	1836	1860	early 1860s	1864
Samuel Langhorne Clemens (a.k.a. Mark Twain) is born in Florida, Missouri.	The Sauk, Fox, and other Indian tribes give up the last of their land claims in Missouri with the Platte Purchase.	The first Pony Express departs from St. Joseph.	George Washington Carver is born into slavery on a farm near Diamond, Missouri.	The Battle of Westport, the last major Civil War battle west of the Mississippi, is fought near Kansas City.

INTRODUCTION
HISTORY
REGIONS
WHEN TO VISIT
STATE'S GREATS
RULES OF THE ROAD
DRIVING TOURS

| Sept., Oct. | **Festival of America.** For nearly forty years the country's best glass blowers, basket weavers, candlemakers, and others have been showing off their traditional skills during this eight-week festival at Silver Dollar City. | 417/336–7171 or 800/952–6626 | www.silverdollarcity.com. |
| Oct. | **Octoberfest.** Come for the wine and beer, and enjoy the party in Hermann, where wineries were born and reborn in Missouri. | 573/486–2744 or 800/932–8687 | www.hermannmo.com. |

State's Greats

There are many reasons to visit Missouri, but the state's natural beauty is perhaps its main draw. From its 5,000 caves to its bucolic lakes, rivers, and streams, to its rolling hills that accommodate hunting and camping, Missouri's natural gifts rival those of the most scenic spots in the nation. History buffs are also drawn to Missouri for the role it played in the westward expansion of the nation, its pivotal role in the Civil War, and the legacy left behind by native son President Harry S Truman. And those travelers seeking inspiration and entertainment via the fine arts, spectacular architecture, and spirited sporting debates will not be disappointed either.

Beaches, Forests, and Parks

The **Mark Twain National Forest** in southern and central Missouri is the state's only forest. Myriad rivers, streams, and lakes ideal for floating and fishing can be found across its 1½ million acres. The forest's seven designated wilderness areas, which cover more than 63,000 acres, are essential to maintaining the natural, undisturbed beauty of the state. More than 175 species of birds call the forest home, as well as 50 species of mammals and 70 species of amphibians and reptiles.

Throughout the Mark Twain National Forest runs the **Ozark National Scenic Riverways** featuring the first two rivers in the United States to receive federal protection.

Other parks not to be missed include **Lake of the Ozarks State Park,** the largest in the state and by far the best for a variety of activities from water sports to hiking, camping, and trail riding, and **Onondaga Cave State Park,** where the scenery is almost entirely underground (camping and other resources are available above ground).

Culture, History, and the Arts

For many people around the world Tom Sawyer and Huck Finn are Missouri's most familiar ambassadors. Although in many ways the state is more sophisticated than those barefoot, imaginary characters, their simplicity and innocence does capture something of the life of the state's many small towns. Tom and Huck's creator, Mark Twain, is Missouri's most prominent cultural figure, but Thomas Hart Benton, George Caleb Bing-

1882 Notorious bank robber Jesse James is shot and killed by Robert Ford in St. Joseph.

1931 Bagnell Dam is completed, creating electricity for the mid-Missouri region, and recreational activities for the nation.

1945 Upon the death of Franklin D. Roosevelt, Vice President (and Missouri native) Harry S. Truman becomes the 33rd President of the United States.

1965 The St. Louis Arch is completed.

1993 The Great Flood of '93 sends the Missouri and Mississippi rivers and their tributaries out of their banks, devastating homes, towns, and farmland.

ham, and Sam Butcher all received inspiration from the landscape and people of Missouri as well. Their works are displayed in numerous museums, such as the **Nelson-Atkins Museum of Art** in Kansas City and the **St. Louis Art Museum.**

Missouri cannot be experienced without visiting one of the dozens of towns with National Historic Districts. Fayette, Rocheport, and Kimmswick are among those towns where the streets, homes, and businesses rather than any monument or museum tell the story of this state and the people who lived here. Civil War buffs will appreciate the historic sites around the state relating to the war, especially "Bloody Hill" at the **Wilson's Creek National Battlefield,** site of the first major Civil War battle west of the Mississippi. Military aficionados will also appreciate the state's museums featuring Generals Pershing and Bradley.

Sports

The great outdoors is celebrated throughout the state of Missouri, but perhaps no statewide effort is more impressive than the **Katy Trail.** The former Missouri/Kansas/Texas railroad corridor stretches 235 mi across the state and now offers bicycling, walking, and hiking paths through a variety of natural landscapes and along the scenic path of the Missouri River. Although parts of the trail are still under construction, many towns, including St. Charles, Hermann, Rocheport, and Sedalia, already have trailheads. If you travel the trail, you'll find that the small towns and businesses snuggled up along the old railroad corridor provide a unique glimpse into Missouri's past and present.

Special as it is, the Katy Trail is just one of innumerable options in Missouri. Hiking, camping, fishing, boating, and waterskiing are available in all corners of the state. Canoeing and spelunking draw hundreds of participants each year, and the business of outfitting canoers is well developed throughout the Ozarks. Turkey and deer hunting is at its best in central Missouri, as is pheasant, quail, and duck hunting in the northwest.

Golfing enthusiasts can find their fill on the 12 courses at Lake of the Ozarks, as well as at quality courses across the state, including Tom Watson's first personally designed course in the nation, located in Parkville, just north of Kansas City.

Fans of pro sports will not be disappointed either. Baseball's American League has a home at The K, home of the Kansas City Royals, and the National League has its place at Busch Stadium with the St. Louis Cardinals. Rams and Chiefs football is among the most exciting in the country, as is hockey with the St. Louis Blues. Only basketball is missing a professional team in the Show-Me State, but college basketball at the Hearnes Center at the University of Missouri-Columbia never fails to draw a crowd.

Other Points of Interest

The 1920s hydroelectric engineering project that became known as **Bagnell Dam** continues to define central Missouri today. The $30 million project harnessed the power of the Osage River and created more than 20,000 jobs in the midst of the Great Depression. The dam is 2,543 ft long and 148 ft high, and holds back 650 billion gallons of water. The dam's economic influence on the state is immeasurable. In addition to

1994
Missouri native Sheryl Crow wins three of her seven Grammy Awards for her debut album, "Tuesday Night Music Club."

2000
The St. Louis Rams beat the Tennessee Titans to win Super Bowl XXXIV.

generating hundreds of thousands of hours of electrical energy each year, the dam draws virtually the same number of tourists to the lakes region it created for relaxation, exercise, and shopping. Tourism, the state's third-largest industry, would certainly be less of a force without Bagnell Dam.

INTRODUCTION
HISTORY
REGIONS
WHEN TO VISIT
STATE'S GREATS
RULES OF THE ROAD
DRIVING TOURS

Rules of the Road

License requirements: To drive in Missouri, you must be at least 16 years old and have a valid driver's license.

Right turn on red: You may turn right on red anywhere in the state, after a full and complete stop, unless otherwise posted.

Seat belt and helmet laws: Missouri requires all front-seat occupants in cars and persons under 18 years of age operating or riding in a truck to wear safety belts. Children ages 4 to 16 must be secured in a safety belt. All kids under age 4 must be in a child safety seat. These laws include passengers in cars, trucks, vans, and buses manufactured with safety belts. They do not include taxi cabs and commercial buses. Missouri does not require motorcycle and bicycle riders to wear a helmet.

Speed limits: The speed limit on most Missouri interstates is 70 mph, except where posted in and around large cities. The speed limit on state highways is 65 mph, except where posted. Be sure to check speed limit signs carefully.

For more information: Contact the State Department of Motor Vehicles at 573/526–3669.

Missouri Caves Driving Tour

FROM HANNIBAL TO BRANSON

Distance: 275 mi   Time: 2–4 days
Breaks: Stop in Branson for a show or at any of the wineries along the route. Rocheport is a good halfway point with several bed-and-breakfast inns to choose from for the night.

Jesse James used Missouri's caves for hiding stolen treasure and more recently some young couples have chosen to marry under their dripping stalactites, but even if you don't have such dramatic plans you shouldn't overlook Missouri's 5,000 caves. Only Tennessee has more caves, and there not as many are open to the public.

Missouri's caves can be accessed by foot, boat, or vehicle, so people of all ages and physical abilities can enjoy them. Some offer true wilderness experiences while others have been developed for tourism, or as storage facilities, office space, and even restaurants and schools. When visiting any cave, remember to bring a light jacket and/or wear long pants. The average temperature of the caves is a constant 55°F.

❶ The first cave to open for public tours was the **Mark Twain Cave** (1 mi south of Hannibal on Rte. 79) in 1886, and it's a logical starting point for a driving tour of Missouri caves. Tom Sawyer and Becky Thatcher were lost in this cave, which is now a National Historic Landmark. "No man knew the cave; that was an impossible thing. Most of the young men knew a portion of it, and it was not customary to venture beyond the known portion. Tom Sawyer knew as much of the cave as anyone," Twain wrote. An experienced guide will escort you on a one-hour tour featuring points of interest mentioned in Mark Twain's writings. Walkways are level and smooth and there are no steps. Persons of any age can easily make the tour.

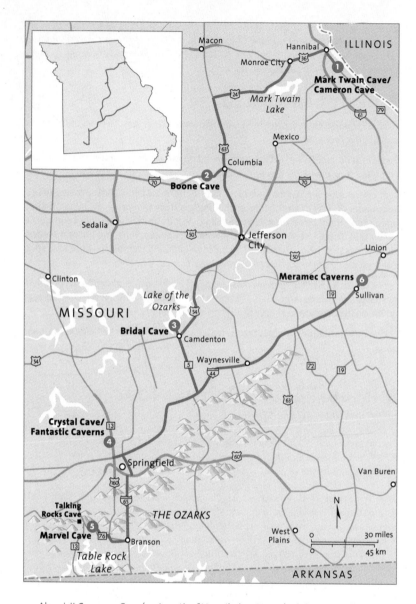

Also visit **Cameron Cave** (1 mi south of Hannibal on Rte. 79) while in Hannibal, particularly in summer when lantern tours are offered. Cameron is Missouri's newest cave, first discovered in 1925 and opened to the public in 1976. Your tour is conducted by a guide because Cameron Cave is an unbelievably complex maze-type cave. The tour lasts 1¼ hours, and several visitors on the tour will be given a lantern to carry.

❷ Many consider the entrance to **Boone Cave** (U.S. 36 to U.S. 24 to U.S. 63 to I–70, 9 mi west of Columbia on I–70, approximately 2 mi south of exit 115) to be the most picturesque of any cave in the state. The two-story opening is set in a valley with streams running out of the cave through the valley. The picnic grounds that also serve the Katy Trail make this a nice afternoon stop.

INTRODUCTION
HISTORY
REGIONS
WHEN TO VISIT
STATE'S GREATS
RULES OF THE ROAD
DRIVING TOURS

③ While vacationing at the Lake of the Ozarks, thousands of boaters choose to visit **Bridal Cave** (I–70 to U.S. 63 to U.S. 54, 2 mi north of Camdenton on Rte. 5, then 1½ mi on Lake Rd. 5–88) in their boats. If you don't have aquatic transportation, you can take the path the Osage Indians did by foot to the wedding chapel, mystery lake, and massive onyx formations. Don't be surprised if you happen upon a wedding in progress. A hundred or more are held here each year and uninvited guests are welcomed and expected. Rated as one of the three most scenic caverns in America, Bridal Cave contains more onyx formations per square foot than any other show cave.

④ The Springfield area has two caves worthy of a visit. **Crystal Cave** (Rte. 5 to I–44 south to exit 80B, then 5 mi north on Hwy. H) is renowned for Indian symbols and fossil crinoids. It's been open to the public for more than 100 years, but the owners have worked hard to keep the cave as natural as possible. Although some lighting has been added, the one-hour tour is mostly flashlight and lantern lit.

Then **Fantastic Caverns** (Hwy. H south back to I–44, I–44 west to exit 77, then follow signs north on Rte. 13) is the only all-riding cave tour to be had. Jeeps follow the route cut by rivers and reveal more than most people can find in a walking tour. Lower levels not accessible to visitors are home to creatures such as the Ozark cave-fish, bristly cave crayfish, and grotto salamander, all of which are tiny, white, and blind after countless generations of living in darkness. A hydrologist explains all of this and more on the 50-minute tour.

⑤ **Marvel Cave** (Hwy. 13 south back to I–44 east to U.S. 65 south to Rte. 76 west) is a part of Branson's Silver Dollar City theme park, and is Missouri's deepest cave at more than 500 ft. The Cathedral Room is 20 stories high, but you don't have to walk back to the top. A tram car will take you. This cave is a National Historic Landmark.

Silver Dollar City also once held claim to **Talking Rocks Cave** (½ mi south of Branson West on Rte. 13), and they tried to do something funky with loudspeakers and echoes, but it didn't work. It is now privately owned and considered Missouri's most beautiful cave. It takes a little effort, however—265 steps up and 265 steps down. There's a beautiful 400-acre nature area above ground and if you're afraid of bats, this is the cave for you. Talking Rocks Cave is one of the few caves where bats don't make a home.

⑥ To return to Hannibal, retrace your steps north on U.S. 65 to Interstate 44 and travel northeast to Sullivan and one last stop at the **Meramec Caverns** (5 mi east of Sullivan on I–44, exit 230, then 3 mi south through La Jolla Park; follow signs), which was the first major cave discovery in the state and a hideout for the Jesse James gang. Continue on Interstate 44 into St. Louis, following U.S. 61 back to Hannibal.

Spring Dogwood/Fall Foliage Tour of the Ozarks Driving Tour

IN THE FORSYTH AREA

Distance: 75 mi   Time: 2 hours minimum; all day maximum
Breaks: Take a break at any of the numerous scenic overlooks, where a picnic lunch would be pleasant or try lunch at the Wagon Wheel Restaurant.

The blossoming of dogwoods in spring here is often compared to the cherry blossoms blooming in Japan. A carpet of blossoms covers the hills in late April. Or make this same journey in October to see the explosion of fiery colors of autumn.

● Begin at Forsyth (Rte. 76 and U.S. 160, 10 mi northwest of Branson), the seat of Taney County. Travel west on U.S. 160, to Route H. Go north about 4 mi. Stop and visit the fire tower for a more spectacular view. From 150 ft high, you can see into the hills of Arkansas and miles beyond, but you have to climb the steps here. There's no elevator. About 13 mi north of the fire tower, you'll find a picnic area and rest rooms.

● At the intersection of Route H and Route 125, turn southwest or right on Route 125. You will pass through several little towns and scenic creeks, and end up in Bradleyville, where you will find restaurants, groceries, and service stations.

● Continue on Route 125 about 5 mi to the 12,300-acre **Hercules Glades Wilderness Area,** one of eight protected wilderness areas in the state. If you need to stretch your legs a bit, hike a mile or so on the more than 42 mi of trails that originate here, but remember to watch out for poisonous snakes. On very clear days, when the humidity is low, you can see the St. Francis Mountains in the distance, 40 mi away. Containing rugged and inaccessible terrain, the St. Francis Mountains were one of the last areas settled in the Ozarks. They were also once the domain of the Cherokee Nation.

● Continue south on Route 125 and turn west or right on Route 160. This takes you through the village of Kissee Mills, which hosts only a gas station and convenience store. Head west at U.S. 160 and pass the Taney County Health Center and keep your eyes open for any of the many activities that happen here on a regular basis. You'll be welcome. You are now back in Forsyth, the beginning point of this drive.

● Before moving on, visit **Shadow Rock Park** (½ mi west of Branson on U.S. 160), at the mouth of Swan Creek and Bull Shoals. If you choose springtime for this drive, don't forget a rod and reel for the white bass that Bull Shoals is known for. Or drive over to the Powersite Dam that separates Taneycomo from Bull Shoals. There's no tour, but visitors are welcome to walk along the top and picnic in the area below the dam.

ARROW ROCK

(Nearby towns also listed: Columbia, Rocheport)

Stroll down Main Street in Arrow Rock and you'll find yourself back in the 19th century. A working blacksmith shop, a gunsmith shop that has operated continuously since 1840, and a host of century-old buildings and businesses set Arrow Rock apart. The town's bed-and-breakfast inns, many in authentic log cabins, are a popular weekend destination for people from St. Louis and Kansas City, but even if you only have a few hours this town is worth a visit.

Information: **Historic Arrow Rock Council** | Box 15, 65320 | 660/837–3335 | www.arrowrock.org.

Attractions

Arrow Rock State Historic Site. This historic site marks the spot where the Sante Fe Trail crossed the Missouri and today offers nature trails and camp sites in addition to several historic buildings. | 4th St. and Van Buren | 660/837–3330 | www.arrowrock.org | Free | June–Aug., daily 10–5; Sept.–Nov. and Mar.–May, daily 10–4; Dec.–Feb., Fri.–Sun. 10–4.

George Caleb Bingham House. This 1840s home, once lived in by local artist George Caleb Bingham, a portrait and political painter of the mid 1880s, is especially interesting. | 100 High St. | 660/837–3231 | $4 | June–Aug., Mon.–Sat. 9–5, Sun. noon–5; Apr., May, Sept., Oct., Sat. 9–5, Sun. noon–5.

Houston Tavern. Built in 1834, this place is still operating as a working tavern. It's now run by the state and is a nice place to get a bite to eat. | 302 Main St. | 660/837–3200 | Free | May–Sept., Tues.–Sun.; Oct.–Dec. and Apr., weekends.

Van Meter State Park. Black walnut trees and wildflowers surround an Indian village site from 10,000 BC. To reach the park take Route 41 north to Route 122 and head west 5 mi until you see signs for the park. | Rte. 122, Miami | 660/886–7537 | www.dnr.state.mo.us/parks.htm | Free | Daily 7–10; visitor center Thurs.–Mon. 10–4.

SIGHTSEEING TOURS/TOUR COMPANIES

Friends of Arrow Rock Tours. Choose from two one-hour guided walking tours of four to five historic buildings dating from the 1830s to the Victorian era, such as the 1834 Houston Tavern, an 1875 gunsmith shop, the Dr. Sappington Medical Museum, the J. P. Sites Gun Shop, and the 1868 I. O. O. F. (Independent Order of Odd Fellows) Lodge Hall. | 309 Main St. | 660/837–3231 | www.friendsar.org | $4 | June–Aug., Mon.–Sat.; Apr.–May and Sept.–Oct., weekends; tours begin at 10, 11:30, 1:30, 3, 4.

ON THE CALENDAR

JUNE–OCT.: *Lyceum Theatre Productions.* A lively theater production is presented on weekends throughout the summer and early fall in a late-19th-century church on High Street. | 660/837–3311 | www.lyceumtheatre.org.

OCT.: *Arrow Rock Heritage Crafts Festival.* Costumed craftspeople demonstrate their prowess in such 19th-century skills as basket making, wood carving, and quilting in several historic buildings along Main Street on the second weekend of the month. | 660/837–3231.

Dining

Evergreen Restaurant. German. Built in the 1800s, this Italianate Revival home is now a restaurant known for their German smoked pork loin as well as their steaks. | Rte. 41, Box 125 | 660/837–3251 | Reservations essential | $16–$20 | No credit cards.

Grandma D's Café. American. Enjoy dining in an old schoolhouse surrounded by antiques and unique gifts. The café specializes in grilled chicken, pork, and steak dinners, stir-fry, sandwiches, salads, homemade soups, and desserts. It's 1½ blocks west of U.S. 41 south. | 704 Van Buren St. | 660/837–3335 | $4–$9 | No credit cards.

Lodging

Borgman's Bed and Breakfast. This national landmark was built in the 1850s by a relative of the artist George Caleb Bingham. Complimentary breakfast. TV in common area. | 706 Van Buren | 660/837–3350 | 4 rooms | $55–$60 | No credit cards.

Down Over Inn Bed and Breakfast. This blue-painted 1912 bungalow in the center of town has a wraparound porch complete with swing. The sprawling main house and an adjacent cottage provide comfortable and quiet overnight accommodations. Each room has a private bath, and the inn operates a shop that sells Missouri gift baskets. Complimentary breakfast. No room phones, no TV, TV in common area. | 602 Main St. | 660/837–3268 | www.go-native.com/inns/0199.html | 5 rooms, 1 cottage | $60–$85 rooms, $95 cottage | D, MC, V.

Miss Nellie's Bed and Breakfast. This 1853 home is filled with antiques and surrounded by huge elm trees. It's also decorated with original watercolors by the owner and some nationally recognized artists. Children are welcome. No room phones, no TV. | 633 Main St. | 660/837–3280 or 800/795–2797 | 2 rooms | $50 | No credit cards.

BETHANY

MAP 12, A2

(Nearby towns also listed: Cameron, Jamesport, St. Joseph)

For a short time at the beginning of its history, this town near the Iowa border was called Dallas. Early residents didn't feel that name conveyed the area's potential for growth, though, so in January 1860, they debated other names, held a vote, and settled on the new name Bethany. A steam mill and the arrival of the railroad in the 1890s brought some growth, but despite its new name Bethany never really saw the boom it hoped for and today it is a pleasant agricultural community of 3,000.

Information: Bethany Chamber of Commerce | 116 N. 16th St., Box 202, 64424 | 660/425–6358 | lynnmcl@netin.net | www.net.ins.net/showcase/bethany.

Attractions

Edna Cuddy Memorial House and Gardens. This 1882 pink brick house, designed by French architect Edmund Eckel in the Italian style with tall windows and lots of light, is full of period furnishings. | 1218 Main St. | 660/425–6811 or 660/425–4613 | $2 | May–Oct., by appointment.

ON THE CALENDAR

DEC.: *Christmas in the Park.* A lighted Christmas parade to the mayor's tree in Bethany Memorial Park, a live nativity scene in the park, and a snow princess contest are highlights of this celebration held on the first Saturday of the month. | 660/425–6358.

Dining

Toot Toots/Cattlemen's. American. You'll feel like you're in a train car in this family-style restaurant known for fried chicken and roast beef. Buffet. | 3101 Miller Rd. | 660/425–7001 | $5–$12 | MC, V.

Lodging

Family Budget Inn. This one-level inn is on a commercial strip just off Interstate 35 at exit 92. Picnic area. Cable TV. Pool. Business services. Pets allowed. | 4014 Miller Rd. | 660/425–7915 | fax 660/425–3697 | 78 rooms | $40–$60 | AE, D, DC, MC, V.

Super 8 Motel. This chain motel is just a few blocks off Interstate 35 at exit 92. Complimentary Continental breakfast. Cable TV. | 600 S. 37th St. | 660/425–8881 or 800/800–8000 | fax 660/425–8099 | www.super8.com | 49 rooms | $50–$60 | AE, D, MC, V.

BLUE SPRINGS

(Nearby towns also listed: Independence, Kansas City, Lexington, Liberty)

Named for the springs used as watering holes for wagon trains on their westward journey, Blue Springs is now a prosperous, affluent suburb of Kansas City known for its good schools, community spirit, and great parks and recreation program. Fourteen parks cover 300 acres in town, but the crowning "natural" jewel of Blue Springs is the 1,000-acre Burr Oaks Woods, which includes hiking trails and an aquarium.

Information: Blue Springs Chamber of Commerce | 1000 S.W. Main St., 64015 | 816/229–8558 | fax 816/229–1244 | chamber@bluesprings.com | Mon.–Fri. 8–5.

Attractions

Burr Oak Woods Conservation Nature Center. The Missouri Department of Conservation operates this 1,071-acre area of prairie, glades, forest, ponds, and streams. It includes sheer ravines that plunge 100 ft, forested hillsides strewn with giant limestone boulders, five hiking trails, and several picnic areas. The 15,000-square-ft nature center includes a 3,000-gallon aquarium stocked with native fish, reptiles, and amphibians. The forest is 1 mi north of Interstate 70 on Route 7. | 1401 N.W. Park | 816/228–3766 | www.conservation.state.mo.us/areas/natareas | Free | State forest, daily dawn–dusk; nature center, Mon.–Sat. 8–5, Sun. noon–5.

Lone Jack Battlefield, Museum, and Cemetery. Union and Confederate soldiers who fought and died here are buried in the cemetery and remembered in a memorial. The museum has displays and dioramas depicting the battle. To reach Lone Jack, take Route 7 south to U.S. 50, then U.S. 50 east. | 301 S. Bynum Rd., Lone Jack | 816/566–2272 | Free | Apr.–Oct., weekdays 9–5, Sat. 9–4, Sun. 1–5; Nov.–Mar., Sat. 9–4, Sun. 1–4.

Fleming Park. A great place to come with children, the park, which is southwest of town, offers access to the 970-acre Lake Jacomo, as well as to the 720-acre Blue Springs lake and beach. | 22807 Woods Chapel Rd. | 816/795–8200 | www.co.jackson.mo.us.com | Free | Daily.

Missouri Town 1855. This reconstruction of an 1800s town, with more than 30 original buildings and staff dressed in period costume, is in Fleming Park. | 8010 E. Park Rd. | 816/524–8770 or 816/795–8200 ext. 1260 | $3 | Mar. 16–Nov. 14, Wed.–Sun 9–4:30; Nov. 15–Mar. 15, Sat.–Sun. 9–4:30.

ON THE CALENDAR

SEPT.: *Blue Springs Fall Fun Fest.* This weekend festival features entertainment on two stages, a parade, and more than 200 food and craft booths. | 816/228–6322.

Dining

Clancy's Café and Pub. American. The menu ranges from burgers and chicken strips to large salads and steaks at this casual local favorite. You can dine indoors or on the patio overlooking the café's volleyball courts. | 3000 N.W. Outer Rd. | 816/229–2233 | $5–$13 | AE, D, MC, V | Closed Sun.

Marina Grog and Galley. Seafood. You don't have to see the menu here to know that seafood is the house specialty. The 1,500-gallon saltwater aquarium gives that away even before you sit down. Open-air dining overlooking lake. Kids' menu. | 22A N. Lake Shore Dr., Lake Lotawana | 816/578–5511 | $15–$44 | AE, D, MC, V | Closed Mon. Labor Day–Memorial Day.

Lodging

American Inn. This basic motel is just off the interstate at exit 18 near the sports stadiums. Some in-room data ports. Pool. | 3300 W. Jefferson St. | 816/228–1080 | fax 816/228–1080 | 170 rooms | $34–$40 | AE, D, DC, MC, V.

Ramada Limited. Spacious rooms overlook a small pond with a fishing beach at this resortlike hotel. Restaurant, complimentary Continental breakfast. Cable TV. Pool. Exercise room. Fishing. Laundry facilities. Pets allowed. | 1110 N. Rte. 7 | 816/229–6363 or 800/272–6232 | fax 816/228–7299 | www.ramada.com | 137 rooms | $50–$85 | AE, DC, MC, V.

Sleep Inn. This 1998 brick motel is 15 mi from downtown Blue Springs. Complimentary Continental breakfast. In-room data ports, cable TV. Pool. Hot tub. Gym. Business services. | 1020 S.E. Blue Pkwy., Lees Summit | 816/554–7600 or 800/753–3746 | fax 816/554–7011 | www.choice-hotels.com | 63 rooms, 8 suites | $62–$110 | AE, D, DC, MC, V.

BONNE TERRE

MAP 12, E5

(Nearby towns also listed: Farmington, Pilot Knob, Ste. Genevieve)

Named for the lead-bearing "good earth" of the area, Bonne Terre is the oldest and largest mining district in the United States. Here you can walk the passageways of the world's largest man-made cavern or scuba dive in a billion-gallon underground lake. You'll also find several state parks and part of Missouri's Mark Twain National Forest nearby.

Information: **Bonne Terre Chamber of Commerce** | 11 S.W. Main St., Box 175, 63628 | 573/358–4000 or 888/358–7350.

Attractions

Bonne Terre Mine. Bonne Terre offers walking tours of the country's largest man-made caverns, boat tours on weekends, and scuba diving. | Rte. 47 at Park and Allen Sts. | 573/358–2148 | www.2dive.com | $12; $17.50 for boat tours | Apr.–Oct., walking tours daily on the ½ hr starting at 10:30, last tour at 3:30; Nov.–Mar., Fri.–Sun. 10:30–3:30, Mon. 10:30–12:30; boat tours weekends.

Mark Twain National Forest. More than 1½ million acres of national forest includes hundreds of trails for hikers, separate trails for bikers and ATV users, 16 lakes, and 14 floatable streams. | 401 Fairgrounds Rd., Rolla | 573/364–4621 | www.fs.fed.us/r9/marktwain | Free | Daily dawn–dusk.

St. Francois State Park. Many a float trip has begun at the Big River put-in point here, located amid the rugged Pike Run Hills. | 8920 U.S. 67 N | 573/358–2173 | www.dnr.state.mo.us/parks | Free | Daily.

Washington State Park. You can canoe, fish, swim, and see rock carvings by prehistoric Native Americans at this park some twenty miles north of town. Those interested in an overnight stay will find furnished cabins. | Rte. 21, DeSoto | 636/586–2995 | www.dnr.state.mo.us/parks | Free | Apr.–Memorial Day and Labor Day–Nov., daily 8–5; Memorial Day–Labor Day, daily 8–8.

ON THE CALENDAR
JULY: *Chautauqua Festival.* This three-day celebration of historical story telling takes place under a large tent in mid-July and also features local musicians. | 573/358–4000.

Dining
Crossroads Restaurant and Lounge. American. This neighborhood tavern is known for prime rib and seafood, particularly pasta dishes incorporating shrimp. | 2 W. School St. | 573/358–8820 | $6–$15 | MC, V | Closed Sun.

Homestead Restaurant. American. Home-style cooking is the specialty at this family restaurant. The dinner buffet is piled high with fried chicken, baked fish, and beef and noodles. | 1024 Rte. K | 573/358–7277 | $4–$11 | D, MC, V | Closed Mon.

Lodging
Red Cedar Lodge. New to the community in 1998, this rustic lodge is easily accessible, but blends in well with the rolling hills and countryside that surround it. Restaurant, complimentary Continental breakfast. Cable TV. | 7036 S. Hwy. 67 | 573/358–8900 | fax 573/358–7700 | 48 rooms | $30–$50 | AE, D, MC, V.

Super 8 Motel. This redbrick motel is on a commercial street one mi from the Bonne Terre Mines and downtown. Complimentary Continental breakfast. In-room data ports, cable TV. | 8 Northwood Dr. | 573/358–5888 or 800/800–8000 | fax 573/358–1049 | www.super8.com | 40 rooms, 12 suites | $52–$60 | AE, D, DC, MC, V.

Victorian Veranda Bed and Breakfast. This large Victorian home has a wraparound porch. Rooms have antiques and private baths. Complimentary breakfast. No TV. | 207 E. School St. | 573/358–1134 or 800/343–1134 | 4 rooms | $70–$95 | D, MC, V.

BRANSON

MAP 12, B6

(Nearby towns also listed: Cassville, Joplin, Kimberling City, Mount Vernon, Springfield)

Until the mid-1980s, Branson was a sleepy little spot in the middle of the Missouri Ozarks, known primarily as a good fishing destination and the region of Harold Bell Wright's turn-of-the-20th-century best-selling novel, *The Shepherd of the Hills.* A few local entertainers opened stage shows for the enjoyment of visitors in the 1960s, but the entertainment explosion officially began when Roy Clark and Japanese violinist Shoji Tabuchi opened theaters here 20 years later. Now the beauty of the hills and lakes and the talents of some of the world's best entertainers make Branson one of the top vacation destinations in America with more than 5 million people and all too many cars arriving in town each year.

Information: **Branson Convention and Visitor's Bureau** | Box 1897, 65615 | 417/334–4136 | www.bransoncvb.com.

Attractions
Branson Scenic Railway. A restored depot is the launching point for a railroad ride through the Ozark Mountains. | 206 E. Main St. | 417/334–6110 or 800/2-TRAIN-2 | www.bransontrain.com | $19.75, $42 dinner train | Mid-Mar.–Dec., Mon.–Sat. 9, 11:30, and 2; June–July and October, Mon.–Sat. 9, 11:30, 2, and 5.

College of the Ozarks. This liberal arts college has no admission fees. The students work for their education at the fruitcake and jelly kitchens and gifts stores, which are open to the public. | Point Lookout | 417/334–6411 | www.cofo.edu/ | Free | Daily.

Edwards Mill. Students operate this working gristmill that grinds corn into cornmeal on a daily basis. | Point Lookout | 417/334–6411 | Free | Jan.–mid-Dec., Mon.–Sat. 9–4.

Ralph Foster Museum. This museum showcases the history of the Ozarks region via Native American artifacts, an art gallery, and more. | Point Lookout | 417/334–6411 | $4.50 | Jan.–mid-Dec., Mon.–Sat. 9–4:30).

Entertainment shows. The main reason so many people come to the Branson area is the music shows. From early morning to late at night some of the country's best musicians provide family entertainment and enjoyment.

Andy Williams Moon River Theatre. This was the first theater in town to offer variety entertainment. This museum has an extensive selection of Andy's personal art collection, and features performances by Andy Williams himself. | 2500 W. Rte. 76 | 417/334–4500 or 800/666–6094 | $25 | Apr.–mid-Dec. .

Baldknobbers Hillbilly Jamboree. Here you'll find comedy, gospel, and country music. | 2835 W. Rte. 76 | 417/334–4528 | $20 | Mar.–mid-Dec., Mon.–Sat. Train whistles and comedy are mixed together in the family entertainment show at **BoxCar Willie Theater.** | 3454 W. Rte. 76 | 417/334–8696 or 800/942–4626 | www.boxcarwillie.com | $20 | Apr.–mid-Dec., Mon.–Sat. The **Celebrity Theater** features The Platters and Philip Wellford. | 3425 W. Rte. 76 | 417/334–0076 | $21 | Apr.–mid-Dec., Mon.–Sat. **Elvis and the Superstars Show** is Branson's top tribute show, and a treat for Elvis fans. | 205 S. Commercial | 417/336–2112 or 800/ELVIS–95 | $20 | Mid-Feb.–mid-Jan., Fri.–Tues. The **Grand Palace** has a southern mansion–style 4,000-seat auditorium, and is one of the most lavish theaters in the country. The Radio City Rockettes perform here in Nov. and early Dec. | 2700 W. Rte. 76 | 800/884–4536 or 800/246–9940 | www.silverdollarcity.com | Daily. Flying blimps, laser lights, and other spectacular effects combine with music and comedy at the **Jim Stafford Theatre.** | 3440 W. Rte. 76 | 417/335–8080 | www.jimstafford.com | $28 | Feb.–mid-Dec. The magic show at **Kirby Van Burch Mystical Palace** includes illusions and white tigers. | 470 Rte. 248 | 417/337–7140 | $25 | Mar.–Dec., Tues.–Sun. The **Lawrence Welk Show** at the Champagne Theater in the Welk Resort Center features the Lennon Sisters, Jo Ann Castle, and lots of polka. | 1984 Rte. 165 | 417/337–7469 or 800/505–9355 | www.welkresort.com | $33 | Mar.–mid-Dec. Mel Tillis sings his hits and performs with his children, including country music star Pam Tillis, at the **Mel Tillis Theater.** | 2527 Rte. 248 | 417/335–6635 | www.meltillis.com | $31 | Tues.–Sat.; Special holiday schedule Nov.–Dec. Besides shows with the family, Andrew Lloyd Weber musicals are often performed at the **Osmond Family Theater.** | 3216 W. Rte. 76 | 417/336–6100 | www.osmond.net | $28–$30 | Mar.–mid-Dec., Mon.–Sat. **Presleys' Country Jubilee** is a rousing mixture of country and gospel music mixed with comedy and musical talent. Features four generations of Presleys, with no relation to Elvis. | 2920 W. Rte. 76 | 417/334–4874 | $20 | Mar.–Dec., Mon.–Sat. The popular religious shows, *The Promise* and *Two from Galilee*, are performed at the **Promise Theater.** | 755 Gretna Rd. | 417/336–4202 or 800/687–4752 | www.thepromise.com | $28 | Apr.–mid-Dec., Mon.–Sat. A flag-waving, patriotic tribute to veterans and Americana shares the theater with Al Brumley's Memory Valley Show and others at **76 Music Hall.** | 1945 W. Rte. 76 | 417/335–2484 | $18 | Daily. A Japanese-born country music star's fiddle-playing show at the **Shoji Tabuchi Theatre** is one of Branson's best. Take your camera to the rest rooms, where you can play billiards. | 3260 Rte. 248 | 417/334–7469 | $36 | Mid-Mar.–mid-Dec. At the **Waltzing Waters Theatre** Frederick Antonio plays two grand pianos simultaneously, while 40,000 gallons of water are choreographed by a fountaineer who interprets Antonio's music. | 3617 W. Rte. 76 | 417/334–4144 or 800/276–7284 | $12 | Daily. Jim Nabors, the musical Lowe family of Utah, and the Incredible Acrobats of China alternate performances at the **Wayne Newton Theater.** | 464 Rte. 248 | 417/335–2000 | $23 | Mid-Apr.–mid-Dec.

Hercules Glades Wilderness Area. One of eight protected wilderness areas in the state, these 12,300 acres are home to white-tailed deer, raccoon, numerous song birds, and road runners. When hiking the trails, watch out for the poisonous snakes that also call this place

ONE LAST TRAVEL TIP:

Pack an easy way to reach the world.

Wherever you travel, the MCI WorldCom Card℠ is the easiest way to stay in touch. You can use it to call to and from more than 125 countries worldwide. And you can earn bonus miles every time you use your card. So go ahead, travel the world. MCI WorldCom℠ makes it even more rewarding. For additional access codes, visit **www.wcom.com/worldphone.**

EASY TO CALL WORLDWIDE

1. Just dial the WorldPhone® access number of the country you're calling from.
2. Dial or give the operator your MCI WorldCom Card number.
3. Dial or give the number you're calling.

Canada	1-800-888-8000
Mexico	01-800-021-8000
United States	1-800-888-8000

EARN FREQUENT FLIER MILES

Limit of one bonus program per customer. All airline program rules and conditions apply. © 2000 WorldCom, Inc. All Rights Reserved. The names, logos, and taglines identifying WorldCom's products and services are proprietary marks of WorldCom, Inc. or its subsidiaries. All third party marks are the proprietary marks of their respective owners.

6 "I'm thirsty"'s, 9 "Are we there yet"'s, 3 "I don't feel good"'s,
1 car class upgrade.
At least something's going your way.

Hertz rents Fords and other fine cars. ® REG. U.S. PAT. OFF. © HERTZ SYSTEM INC., 2000/005-00

Make your next road trip more comfortable with a free one-class upgrade from Hertz.

Let's face it, a long road trip isn't always sunshine and roses. But with Hertz, you get a free one car class upgrade to make things a little more bearable. You'll also choose from a variety of vehicles with child seats, Optional Protection Plans, 24-Hour Emergency Roadside Assistance, and the convenience of NeverLost®, the in-car navigation system that provides visual and audio prompts to give you turn-by-turn guidance to your destination. In a word: it's everything you need for your next road trip. Call your travel agent or Hertz at **1-800-654-2210** and mention PC# **906404** or check us out at **hertz.com** or AOL Keyword: **hertz**. Peace of mind. Another reason nobody does it exactly like Hertz.

Hertz
exactly.®

Offer available on standard and leisure daily, weekend and weekly rentals at participating locations through March 31, 2003. Upgrade subject to larger car availability at time of rental. Upgrades apply to car classes B-F (compact 4-door through full-size). Max. upgrade to class G (premium). Offer cannot be combined with any other offer, discount or promotion. Minimum rental age for this offer is 25. Blackout periods apply. Standard rental qualifications, rental period and return restrictions must be met. Advance reservations are required.

home. There's an entrance to the wilderness area northeast of Branson on Route 160. | Rte. 160 | 417/683–4428 | www.gorp.com/gorp/resource | Free | Daily.

Ripley's Believe It or Not! Museum. View collections and exhibits of the unusual and bizarre. | 3326 Rte. 76 | 417/337–5460 or 800/998–4418 | $12 | Daily 9–11.

Shadow Rock Park. This 20-acre park at the mouth of Swan Creek, 1 mi east of Forsyth, is a popular picnic site and a good place to wade in the stream on a hot summer day. | U.S. 160 | 417/546–2876 | Free | Daily.

Shepherd of the Hills. The homestead includes the Harold Bell Wright museum, a petting zoo, Clydesdale-drawn wagon rides, and Inspiration Tower. | 5586 W. Rte. 76 | 417/334–4191 | www.oldmatt.com | $15 | Apr.–Oct., Mon.–Sat. 9–5; tours 10, noon, 2, and 4. Evening performances at the **Outdoor Theater** tell the story of the Ozark Mountain people. | 5586 W. Rte. 76 | 417/334–4191 | $19 | May–Oct., daily).

Shepherd of the Hills Trout Hatchery. This state-operated facility raises rainbow and brown trout. | 483 Hatcher Rd. | 417/334–4865 | Free | Labor Day–Memorial Day, daily 9–5; Memorial Day–Labor Day, daily 9–6.

Silver Dollar City. Named the world's top theme park in 1999 by industry professionals, this 1880s-style park 5 mi west of Branson on Route 76 offers train and wagon rides, water rides, hands-on crafts with more than 100 crafts people, and music shows. | Rte. 76 | 417/338–2611 or 800/952–6626 | www.silverdollarcity.com | $34 | Apr., May, Tues.–Sun. 9–7; June–Aug., daily 9–7; Sept., Oct., Tues.–Sun. 9:30–6; Nov., Dec., Wed.–Sun. 1–10. Missouri's deepest cave, **Marvel Cave** is within Silver Dollar City. Admission to the cave is included in park admission.

Stone Hill Winery. Take Route 76 west out of Branson to Route 165 south to reach this winery which offers free tours. | 601 Rte. 165 | 417/334–1897 | Free | Mon.–Sat. 8:30–dusk; Sun. 11–6.

Table Rock Dam and Lake. Table Rock Dam is located on the main stream of the White River, about 6 mi southwest of Branson. The dam was built as part of an effort to generate electricity, decrease flooding, and provide recreation opportunities. Construction of the dam was completed in 1958 at a cost of $66 million. | 5272 Rte. 165 | 417/334–4101 | www.tablerocklake.org | Free | Visitors center: Apr.–Oct., daily 9–5; Mar., Nov., Dec., weekends 9–5. Tours: Apr.–Oct., daily hourly except noon; Mar., Nov., Dec., weekends hourly except noon.

Table Rock State Park. This 356-acre park sits on the edge of the lake for which it is named, and offers scuba diving, camping, and fishing. | 5272 Hwy. 165 W | 417/334–4704 | www.dnr.state.mo.us/dsp | Free | Nov.–Mar., daily 7:30–4; Apr.–May and Sept.–Oct., daily 7:30–9; June–Aug., daily 7:30–9.

Talking Rocks Cave. Guided tours through this cave, considered one of Missouri's most beautiful, reveal the unusual auditory phenomenon that inspired its name. | Rte. 13, past Hwy. 76 | 417/272–3366 | $10 | Hrs vary; closed Jan.

White Water. This 12-acre amusement park offers the largest variety of water activities and slides in the Ozarks. | 3505 W. Rte. 76 | 417/334–7487 or 800/952–6626 | $19–$25 | Mid- to late May and Aug.–Labor Day, daily 10–6; June–July, daily 9–8.

SIGHTSEEING TOURS/TOUR COMPANIES

Lake Queen **Cruises.** Branson's music theaters began as a source of entertainment for the outdoor enthusiasts who visited the southern Ozarks but the lake and mountain scenery here is an attraction in itself and the focus of numerous tours. *Lake Queen* offers 1½-hour breakfast, lunch, and dinner cruises along Lake Taneycomo. Each cruise has a full buffet and live musical entertainment. | 280 N. Lake Dr. | 417/334–3015 | $18–$23 dinner cruise, $11 sightseeing | Apr.–Dec., daily 9, 12:30, 2:30, and 5.

Polynesian Princess. There's a tropical flavor in both the food and entertainment on these 1½-hour breakfast, sightseeing, and dinner cruises that leave from Gages Long Creek

Marina. | 1358 Long Creek Rd. | 417/337–8366 or 800/653–6288 | $16–$29 | May–Oct., Tues.–Sun. 9 [breakfast], 5 and 8 [dinner].

"Ride the Ducks." Converted military vehicles carry you through the streets and across the lake. Kids have a chance to drive, and everyone gets a set of duck lips. | 2320 W. Rte. 76 | 417/334–3825 | $15 | Mar.–Dec., daily.

Sammy Lane Pirate Cruise. This tour departs from the foot of Main Street and includes an attack by pirates, and, in a quieter moment, an opportunity to feed the ducks and geese on the lake. | 280 N. Lake Dr. | 417/334–3015 | $11 | Mid-Apr.–Sept., daily.

Showboat Branson Belle. A cruise around Table Rock Lake aboard this 700-seat paddleboat includes freshly prepared meals and excellent entertainment. Cruises are approximately 2–2½ hours long. | 4800 Rte. 165 | 417/336–7171 or 800/227–8587 | $38 | Apr.–Dec., Mon.–Sat. 11, 4:30, and 8.

Table Rock Helicopters. For a different perspective on the area, try flying over the area's dams and lakes. There are four flights per day. | 3309 W. Rte. 76 | 417/334–6102 or 800/298–UFLY | $19–$30 | www.tablerockhelicopters.com | Mar.–Nov., daily; Dec., first 2 weekends only.

ON THE CALENDAR

MAY: *Branson Remembers.* A special city-wide Memorial Day weekend tribute to those lost in service to the country. | 417/337–8387.

MAY: *Plumb Nellie Days.* This hillbilly festival including pet parade, children's games, and crafts takes place downtown over the third weekend in May. | 417/334–1548 or 888/322–2786.

AUG.: *Oldtime Fiddle Contest.* Fiddlers from all over the United States compete for cash and prizes on the 3rd Sat. in August in downtown Branson. | 417/334–1548 or 888/322–2786 | www.branson.com/dbma.

SEPT.–OCT.: *Festival of America.* The country's best glass blowers, basket weavers, woodworkers, candle makers, and other traditional craftspeople show off their stuff during this eight-week festival held in Silver Dollar City. | 417/336–7171 or 800/952–6626 | www.silverdollarcity.com.

NOV.–DEC.: *Ozark Mountain Christmas and Branson Area Festival of Lights.* This two-month-long event includes more than 15 mi of lights sparkling throughout the Branson/Table Rock Lake area, and music shows showcasing the holiday's finest. | 800/214–3661 or 417/334–4084 | www.bransonchamber.com.

DEC.: *Adoration Parade.* A parade down Commercial Street precedes the lighting of the nativity scene atop Mt. Branson on the first Sunday in December. | 417/334–4136 or 800/214–3661 | www.bransonchamber.com.

Dining

Buckingham's Restaurant and Oasis. American. Buckingham's is perfect for special occasions; it serves traditional steak, seafood, and pasta dishes, and unusual entrées like quail. The staff will prepare some dishes tableside. The restaurant's big-game motif includes a mural of safari animals and a hand-carved cherry bar in the lounge. | 2820 W. Rte. 76 | 417/337–7777 | $15–$29 | AE, D, MC, V.

Candlestick Inn. American. Some of the most popular dishes at this inn on top of Mt. Branson include the beef Wellington and roasted rack of lamb. Kids' menu. | 127 Taney St. | 417/334–3633 | $18–$42 | AE, D, MC, V.

Contrary Mary's. American. This bright and airy restaurant resembles a country garden, right down to the live plants. It serves freshly prepared home-style food, including chicken-fried steak, baked ham, pork chops, and pasta, and it specializes in fresh-baked desserts. | 3292 Shepherd of the Hills Expressway | 417/334–7700 | $7–$16 | AE, D, MC, V.

Dimitris. Continental. This floating restaurant boasts an extensive wine list to complement its fresh fish and exceptional views of Lake Taneycomo. Kids' menu. | 500 E. Main St. | 417/334–0888 | $20–$31 | AE, D, DC, MC, V | Closed Jan.

Friendship House. American. On the campus of the College of the Ozarks, Friendship House is known for catfish and fried chicken. Sunday brunch. No smoking. | College of the Ozarks, Point Lookout | 417/334–6411 | $7–$11 | AE, D, MC, V.

Hard Luck Diner. American. Fashioned after a 1950s diner, this family restaurant serves thick burgers, malts, and fries. Kids' menu. | 2820 W. Rte. 76, Grand Village Shopping Mall | 417/336–7217 | $5–$10 | AE, MC, V | Breakfast also available.

Hillside Inn. Mexican. This family-style restaurant 9 mi from Branson's theaters is known for such Mexican family-style dishes as chicken fajitas and enchilada platters. Kids' menu. | Main St., Rockaway Beach | 417/561–8252 | $6–$9 | No credit cards | Breakfast also available.

Home Cannery. American. Home-canned goods decorate the walls and shelves of this family-friendly restaurant just a few blocks from Branson's theaters. Specialties include beef dishes and a marinated chicken breast served with mushrooms, peppers, onions, and mozzarella cheese. Kids' menu. No smoking. | 1810 W. Rte. 76 | 417/334–5756 | $4–$11 | AE, MC, V | Closed late Dec.–Mar.

Mr. G's. Italian. Dishes range from Chicago-style pizza to various pastas at this informal downtown restaurant. | 202 N. Commercial Dr. | 417/335–8156 | $8–$15 | D, MC, V | Closed Jan.

Paradise Grill. American. The Paradise Grill is a casual restaurant, with an old-fashioned feel and home-style fare, including burgers cooked on a cast-iron grill, mesquite-smoked barbecue rib dinners, and fresh-baked cheesecake. | 3250 Shepherd of the Hills Expressway | 417/334–5405 | $8–$15 | AE, D, MC, V.

Peppercorn's. American. This restaurant occupies a Colonial-style clapboard building and has tall paned windows and a bright setting. It serves buffets with freshly prepared entrées, fruits, and vegetables, and fresh-baked bread and desserts. The regular menu includes inventive dishes like cashew chicken. | 2421 W. Rte. 76 | 417/335–6699 | $7–$19 | AE, D, MC, V.

Sadie's Sideboard and Smokehouse. American. Choose from a menu known especially for its barbecue offerings or from a huge buffet at this spacious and friendly family restaurant. The buffet is available for breakfast, lunch, and dinner, and includes turkey, catfish, and ham. Kids' menu. | 2230 W. Rte. 76 | 417/334–3619 | $5–$11 | AE, D, MC, V | Closed mid-Dec.–Feb.

Two Sisters Midtown Diner. American. The breakfast, lunch, and dinner buffet at this retro diner includes baked fish, chicken, and ham. A full menu of sandwiches, soups, and other home-style fare is also available. Kids' menu. | 1580 W. Rte. 76 | 417/334–1206 | $4–$11 | AE, D, MC, V.

Uncle Joe's Bar-B-Q. American. Country eating in a country-music town. Tables have red-checkered tablecloths and the most popular dish is the hickory-smoked ribs and ham. Kids' menu. No smoking. | 2819 W. Rte. 76 | 417/334–4548 | $8–$24 | D, DC, MC, V | Closed mid-Dec.–late Jan.

Wagon Wheel Restaurant. American. BLTs are one of the most popular items on a menu built around homemade soups and sandwiches. Kids' menu. | 20262 U.S. 160, Forsyth | 417/546–4219 | $5–$10 | D, MC, V | Breakfast also available; closed Sun.

Lodging

Baymont Inn & Suites. Suites with interior corridors are the specialty of this hotel. Its central location provides easy access to the town's theaters and restaurants. Restaurant, bar, complimentary Continental breakfast. Cable TV. Pool. Tennis. Exercise room. | 2375 Green Mountain Dr. | 417/336–6161 | fax 417/336–2449 | 86 rooms | $58–$108 | AE, D, DC, MC, V.

Best Western Mountain Oak Lodge. This chain hotel runs a shuttle to the Silver Dollar City amusement park which is just ½ mi away. It's convenient to other area attractions and you'll find a pool table as well as video games in its game room. Restaurant, complimentary Continental breakfast, room service. Cable TV. Pool, wading pool. Hot tub. Video games. Laundry facilities. | Rte. 76 at Notch, Box 1059, Branson West | 417/338–2141 or 800/528–1234 | fax 417/338–8320 | bransonlodge@pcis.net | www.bestwestern.com | 146 rooms | $50–$74 | AE, D, DC, MC, V | Closed Jan.–Feb.

Big Cedar. This lakeside resort is owned by Bass Pro Shops and is designed with anglers in mind. There's a fishing pond for kids, and the two-story marina on Table Rock Lake has a cut-out floor for fish viewing and feeding. There's a tackle shop, of course, and guides as well as boats (from simple canoes to party barges) are available. Also on the grounds: a 1-mi jogging trail; a 2-mi nature trail; a 3-par, 9-hole Jack Nicklaus Signature golf course; and horse, carriage, and wagon rides. Accommodations are in one of three lodge buildings, or in cabins. Some rooms and cabins have balconies, kitchens, fireplaces, or Jacuzzis. Bar (with entertainment), dining room, room service. Cable TV. Pool, lake, pond. Massage, sauna, spa. 9-hole golf course, miniature golf, two tennis courts. Gym, horseback riding, water sports, boating. Children's programs (ages 4–12), playground. Laundry facilities. Business services. | 612 Devil's Pool Rd.,Ridgedale | 417/335–2777 | fax 417/335–2340 | bigcedar@big-cedar.com | www.big-cedar.com | 224 rooms, 11 suites in 3 buildings, 81 cabins | $125–$229, $225–$450 suites, $349–$599 cottages | AE, D, MC, V.

Branson Hotel. This small hotel, built at the turn of the 20th century, is decorated with antiques from the Victorian era. Complimentary breakfast. Cable TV. No smoking. | 214 W. Main St. | 417/335–6104 | 9 rooms | $95–$105 | MC, V | Closed Jan., Feb.

Branson House. A wide porch welcomes visitors to this turn-of-the-20th-century home with six rooms, each decorated with a different theme. Four rooms have baths with showers only. Complimentary breakfast. No room phones, TV in common area. No kids under 10. | 120 4th St. | 417/334–0959 | 6 rooms | $65–$90 | AE, MC, V | Closed Jan.

Branson Inn. This rustic hotel near the College of the Ozarks has two theaters on the premises. Picnic area with grills, complimentary Continental breakfast. Cable TV. Pool, wading pool. Hot tub. Business services. | 448 Rte. 248 | 417/334–5121 | fax 417/334–6039 | 276 rooms | $55–$61 | AE, D, DC, MC, V.

Briarwood. Rustic in feel but equipped with modern conveniences, these wood-paneled cottages sit on a wooded property on Lake Taneycomo. Cable TV. Pool. Dock, boating, fishing. Video games. Playground. | 1685 Lake Shore Dr. | 417/334–3929 | fax 417/334–1324 | 16 kitchen cottages | $46–$63 1–bedroom cottages, $63–$74 2–bedroom cottages, $115–$150 3–bedroom cottages | No credit cards | Closed Nov.–Mar.

Clarion at Fall Creek Resort. Each of the condos rented out through Clarion across the approximately 150 acres of Fall Creek Resort is decorated slightly differently since each is individually owned, but all have full kitchens and sofa sleepers. Some have views of Lake Taneycomo. If you stay here, you'll be 2½ mi from the main strip on Route 76. The restaurant is open only for breakfast. Restaurant, picnic area. Cable TV. 5 pools, 3 ponds, 2 wading pools. 1 indoor and 2 outdoor hot tubs. Miniature golf, tennis. Gym, volleyball, boating. 2 playgrounds. Laundry facilities. Business services. | 1 Fall Creek Dr. | 417/334–6404 or 800/562–6636 | fax 417/335–4652 | 108 rooms, 8 studios, 100 condos | $79 studios, $109 1–bedroom condos, $139 2–bedroom condos, $229 3–bedroom condos | AE, D, DC, MC, V.

Days Inn. Located in the heart of Branson's Theater District, this inn is within 1 mi of 15 theaters and is convenient to area shopping, dining, and attractions. Restaurant, complimentary Continental breakfast. Cable TV. Pool, wading pool. Hot tub. Playground. Business services. Pets allowed (fee). | 3524 Keeter St. | 417/334–5544 or 800/329–7466 | fax 417/334–2935 | www.daysinn.com | 425 rooms | $60–$130 | AE, D, DC, MC, V.

Dogwood Inn. This simple brick motel is built on a hill one mi outside of town on Route 76. Restaurant, bar (with entertainment). In-room data ports, cable TV. Pool, wading pool.

Hot tub. Laundry facilities. Business services. | 1420 W. Rte. 76 | 417/334–5101 | fax 417/334–0789 | 210 room, 10 suites | $45–$65, $95–$125 suites | AE, D, DC, MC, V.

Foxborough Inn. Just a few blocks off Route 76, this inn is within spitting distance of Branson's theaters. Complimentary Continental breakfast. Cable TV. Pool. Laundry facilities. Business services. | 235 Expressway La. | 417/335–4369 or 800/335–4369 | fax 417/335–5043 | www.foxboroughinn.com | 175 rooms | $65–$90 | AE, D, DC, MC, V.

Gazebo Inn. This pink Victorian-style inn is on Country Music Boulevard next to the Andy Williams Moon River Theatre. Complimentary Continental breakfast. Cable TV. Pool. No smoking. | 2424 Rte. 76 | 417/335–3826 or 800/873–7990 | fax 417/335–3889 | 73 rooms, 14 suites | $40–$75, $60–$132 suites | AE, D, MC, V.

Green Gables Inn. This two-story motel is behind the Andy Williams Theater and the Grand Palace. Cable TV. Pool. | 2400 Green Mountain Dr. | 417/335–3400 | fax 417/336–3486 | 54 rooms | $43–$58 | AE, D, DC, MC, V.

Hampton Inn–West. This hotel on Branson's main drag is surrounded by restaurants, shops, and other hotels. It's close to Branson's theaters and approximately 5 mi from Silver Dollar City. Complimentary Continental breakfast. Cable TV. Pool. Hot tub. Business services. | 3695 Rte. 76 | 417/337–5762 or 800/426–7866 | fax 417/337–8733 | www.hamptoninn.com | 103 rooms, 7 suites | $60–$73, $90–$113 suites | AE, D, DC, MC, V.

Holiday Hills Resort. This modern condominium resort designed for the upscale golf or tennis enthusiast offers nightly rentals of one-, two-, or three-bedroom condo units with kitchenettes and laundry facilities. Kitchenettes, cable TV. 2 pools. Hot tub. 18-hole golf, 2 tennis courts. Basketball. Laundry facilities. | 630 E. Rockford Dr. | 417/334–4013 or 800/225–2422 | michele@holidayhills.com | www.holidayhills.com | 80 condos | $89–$109 1 bedroom, $109–$139 2 bedrooms, $179 3 bedrooms | AE, D, MC, V.

Holiday Inn Express Central. Built in the mid-1990s, this chain motel is a block off Branson's main strip and 3–5 mi from the town's many theaters. Complimentary Continental breakfast. Cable TV. Pool. Hot tub. Laundry facilities. Business services. | 2801 Green Mountain | 417/336–2100 or 800/465–4329 | fax 417/336–6319 | www.basshotels.com/holiday-inn | 120 rooms, 10 suites | $40–$165 | AE, D, DC, MC, V.

Holiday Inn Express. Though not on the main strip, this chain motel, which offers hot tubs in all rooms, is close to area theaters, shopping, and restaurants. Complimentary Continental breakfast. In-room hot tubs. Cable TV. Pool. Business services. No smoking. | 1000 W. Main St. | 417/334–1985 | fax 417/334–1984 | www.basshotels.com/holiday-inn | 90 rooms, 20 suites | $77–$95 | AE, D, DC, MC, V.

Indian Point Resorts. There are lots of outdoor activities, including swimming, badminton, horseshoes, and boating, at this lakeside lodge 2 ½ mi from Silver Dollar City. Kitchenettes, some in-room hot tubs, in-room TV. Dock, boating, fishing. Playground. Laundry facilities. | Indian Point Rd. | 417/338–2250 | fax 417/338–3507 | 24 rooms, 26 two-bedroom suites, 5 three-bedroom suites | $75–$165 | AE, D, DC, MC, V | Closed Jan.–mid-Mar.

Lodge of the Ozarks. Home to the Celebrity Theatre, this lodge aims for an upscale English feel, with wood trim and decorative tile throughout. Restaurant, bar (with entertainment), complimentary Continental breakfast. Some refrigerators, cable TV. Pool. Barbershop, beauty salon, hot tub, massage. Business services. | 3431 W. Highway 76 | 417/334–7535 or 800/655–7330 | fax 417/334–6861 | www.bransonlodging.net | 190 rooms | $89 | AE, D, MC, V.

Magnolia Inn. This big white inn with pink and purple shutters was built in the early 1990s and is just ¼ mi from the main strip on Route 76. Cable TV. Pool. Barbershop, beauty salon, hot tub. Laundry facilities. Business services. | 3311 Shepherd of the Hills Expressway, Rte. 248 | 417/334–2300 or 800/222–7239 | fax 417/336–4165 | 152 rooms, 12 suites | $50–$95 | AE, D, MC, V.

Melody Lane Inn. A large natural stone fireplace welcomes visitors in the lobby of this centrally located inn that's within walking distance of half a dozen Branson theaters. Complimentary Continental breakfast. Cable TV. Pool. Hot tub. Laundry facilities. Business services. | 2821 W. Rte. 76 | 417/334–8598 or 800/338–8598 | fax 417/334–3799 | 140 rooms, 1 suite | $60–$70, $140–$170 suite | AE, D, MC, V | Closed Jan.–Feb.

Palace Inn. This centrally located, upscale hotel, built in the early 1990s, is right next to the Grand Village Shopping Center and within walking distance of half a dozen theaters including the Grand Palace, which is just two doors away. Restaurant, bar, complimentary Continental breakfast. Some refrigerators, cable TV. 2 pools. Barbershop, beauty salon, hot tub, massage. Laundry facilities. Business services, airport shuttle. | 2820 W. Rte. 76 | 417/334–7666 or 800/725–2236 | fax 417/334–7720 | 154 rooms, 12 suites | $88, $120–$225 suites | AE, D, DC, MC, V.

Pointe Royale Resort. Below the bluffs of Lake Taneycomo just downstream from Table Rock Lake Dam, this modern lakeside condominium resort has one-, two-, or three-bedroom condos each with a patio or deck, a fully equipped kitchen, and a washer and dryer. 2 restaurants, 2 bars, picnic area. Kitchenettes, cable TV, in-room VCRs. 2 pools. 18-hole golf course, putting green, 2 tennis courts. Business services. | 158A Pointe Royale Dr. | 417/334–5614 or 800/962–4710 | fax 417/334–5620 | www.pointeroyale.com | 275 condos | $97 1–bedroom condos, $146–$159 2–bedroom condos, $205–$225 3–bedroom condos, $285 4–bedroom condos | AE, D, DC, MC, V.

Radisson. You can easily walk to several theaters including the Grand Palace and the Andy Williams Moon River Theatre from this upscale chain hotel. Restaurant, bar. In-room data ports, cable TV. 2 pools. Barbershop, beauty salon, hot tub. Gym. Business services. | 120 Wildwood Dr. S | 417/335–5767 | fax 417/335–7979 | 500 rooms, 26 suites | $90, $160–$180 suites | AE, D, DC, MC, V.

Ramada Inn Limited. Built on 17 acres of wooded, landscaped land and once known as Shadowbrook, this is one of Branson's older motels. You can drive right up to your room and you'll be just across the street from Dixie Stampede. Complimentary Continental breakfast. Cable TV. Pool. Laundry facilities. Business services. | 1610 Rte. 76, Branson | 417/334–4173 or 800/641–4600 | fax 417/339–3046 | www.ramada.com | 298 rooms | $60–$88 | AE, D, MC, V.

Ramada Inn. This Ramada offers simple rooms on Branson's main drag. Restaurant, complimentary Continental breakfast. In-room TV. 2 pools. Laundry facilities. Business services. | 1700 W. Rte. 76 | 417/334–1000 or 800/641–4106 | fax 417/339–3046 | www.ramada.com | 395 rooms | $75 | AE, D, MC, V.

Residence Inn by Marriott. These apartment-style accommodations are perfect for long-term stays. Studio, one-, and two-bedroom units are available. The inn is behind the Grand Palace. Complimentary Continental breakfast. Kitchenettes, cable TV. 2 pools. Hot tub. Basketball, exercise room. | 280 Wildwood Dr. S | 417/336–4077 or 800/331–3131 | fax 417/336–5837 | www.residenceinn.com | 85 rooms | $69–$94 | AE, D, DC, MC, V.

Rodeway Inn. This huge inn sits on the side of a hill on two landscaped acres 4 mi from Silver Dollar City, across the street from the IMAX theater, and within walking distance of the Branson USA Theme Park. Complimentary Continental breakfast. Cable TV. Pool. Hot tub. | 3601 Shepherd of the Hills Expressway | 417/334–8694 | fax 417/334–1037 | 95 rooms | $60–$70 | AE, D, DC, MC, V.

Settle Inn. The exterior of this inn is designed to bring Camelot to mind. Inside there are 32 theme rooms that range from Early England to Greek Mythology to the Wild West. Restaurant, bar, complimentary breakfast, room service. Cable TV. 2 pools. Hot tub, sauna. Gym. Video games. Laundry facilities. Business services. Pets allowed (fee). | 3050 Green Mountain Dr. | 417/335–4700 or 800/677–6906 | fax 417/336–1226 | www.bransonsettleinn.com | 300 rooms, 40 suites | $70–$130 | AE, D, MC, V.

Southern Oaks Inn. Across from the Shoji Tabuchi Theater and close by the IMAX theater and Country Tonite, this motor inn prides itself on its friendly staff. Complimentary Continental breakfast. Some in-room refrigerators, some in-room hot tubs, cable TV. 2 pools.

Hot tub. Laundry facilities. Business services. | 3295 Shepherd of the Hills Expressway | 417/335–8108 or 800/324–8752 | fax 417/335–8861 | www.southernoaksinn.com | 148 rooms, 4 suites | $60, $89–99 suites | AE, D, MC, V.

Taneycomo Motor Lodge. Just across the street from Lake Taneycomo and 9 mi from Branson's theaters, this motel is popular with trout fishermen and families. Cable TV. Pool, lake. Dock, boating, fishing. | 2518 Hwy. 76, Rockaway Beach | 417/561–4141 | devoted.to/taneycomomotorlodge | 27 rooms | $50 | AE, D, MC, V.

Travelodge. This chain hotel offers affordable rooms and is located midway between the Osmond Family Theater and the Welk Resort Center. Complimentary Continental breakfast. Cable TV. Pool. Business services. | 3102 Falls Pkwy. | 417/334–7523 | fax 417/336–2495 | 81 rooms | $60 | AE, D, DC, MC, V.

Turkey Creek Ranch. The cottages at this modern, landscaped resort on 400 acres on Bull Shoals Lake all have kitchens and range in size from one to four bedrooms. Restaurant. 2 pools, wading pool. Hot tub. Putting green, tennis. Horseback riding, docks, boating. Playground. Laundry facilities. | HC 3, Theodosia | 417/273–4362 | 24 kitchen cottages | $87–$158 | No credit cards.

Welk Resort Center and Champagne Theater. Rooms at the Welk Resort, which is 3 mi from Branson's theaters, have contemporary furnishings, country-style accents, and luxurious baths. The center is home to the Lawrence Welk Variety Show and its 20-piece orchestra. Restaurant, bar, complimentary Continental breakfast. Pool. Hot tub. Volleyball. Pets allowed. | 1984 Rte. 165 | 417/336–3575 or 800/505–9355 | fax 417/336–6573 | 160 rooms | $94–$99 | AE, D, MC, V.

CAMDENTON

MAP 12, C5

(Nearby towns also listed: Lake Ozark, Lebanon, Osage Beach, Rolla, Waynesville)

Flanked by the Big and Little Niangua rivers, and known as the "Hub City," Camdenton is the most centrally located of all lake communities. Home of dozens of family-oriented resorts, great fishing, and waterskiing, Camdenton is nonetheless on one of the quieter areas of lake waters.

Information: Camdenton Chamber of Commerce | Box 1375, 65020–1375 | 573/346–2227 or 800/769–1004 | www.odd.net/ozarks/chamber.

Attractions

Bridal Cave. Weddings are conducted year-round in this cave 2 mi north of town used by the Osage Indians for the same purpose. | Lake Rd. 5-88 | 573/346–2676 | $12 | Daily, 9–6.

Camden County Museum. A small collection focusing on how early county residents lived is housed in the abandoned Linn Creek School. The town of Linn Creek was relocated when the Bagley Dam was built. Classrooms contain themed exhibits on weaving, vintage and antique household furnishings, tools, and banking. | Box 19, N. U.S. 54, Linn Creek | 573/346–7191 | Free | May–Oct., Tues.–Fri. 10–4.

Ha Ha Tonka State Park. The remains of a 60-year-old castle, a natural bridge, springs, and caves invite exploration in this 2,993-acre park set on the limestone bluffs overlooking Lake of the Ozarks. There's a 7-mi hiking trail, 2 docks, and facilities for fishing. Take U.S. 54 to D Road to reach the park. | D Rd. | 573/346–2986 | www.dnr.state.mo.us/dsp | Free | Daily 8–dusk.

Pomme de Terre State Park. Camp, swim, hike, or fish for muskie in one of the many coves of Pomme de Terre Lake. You can reach the park by taking U.S. 64 to exit 64B. | Pittsburg | 417/852–4291 | www.dnr.state.mo.us/dsp | Free | Daily.

MAR.: *Products and Service Show.* More than 230 exhibitors show off products from the Show-Me State in this two-day event in mid-March at the Lake Expo Center in Osage Beach. | 800/769–1004 | www.camdentonchamber.com.

APR.: *Dogwood Festivals.* For more than fifty years Camdenton has hosted a weekend celebration of the beauty of dogwoods in bloom. Visit Ha Ha Tonka State Park to see the trees or enjoy the music, juried craft show, carnival, and parade in town. | 573/346–2227 or 800/769–1004.

Dining
Barons Bistro. Contemporary. Barons specializes in American and European cuisine, served with lake views. Prime rib, steaks, and seafood top the menu, and some dishes are prepared tableside. | 5-88 Lake Rd. | 573/346–6369 | $5–$19 | AE, DC, MC, V | No lunch.

Lodging
Castleview Bed and Breakfast. Four-poster beds and marble-top tables furnish this Victorian-style clapboard home next to the Ha Ha Tonka State Park. All rooms have private baths. Complimentary breakfast. TVs in rooms and common areas. | Rural Route 1, Box 183M, Highway D | 573/346–9818 or 877/346–9818 | allers@usmo.com | www.lakelinks.com/castleview | 4 rooms | $90–$95 | MC, V.

Old Kinderhook Resort. The lake's only gated community, this 638-acre resort has an 18-hole Tom Weiskopf golf course as well as lake access. 3 restaurants. Cable TV. Pool. 18-hole golf course. Dock, boating, fishing. Playground. | 5480 Lake Rd. | 573/346–3952 | fax 573/346–3958 | 38 cottages | $125–$250 | AE, D, MC, V.

Rippling Waters Resort. Rustic cottages on the lakefront. Picnic area. Kitchenettes, cable TV. Dock, boating. Video games. Playground. Laundry facilities. | Rte. 80, Box 123 | 573/346–2642 | 15 cottages | $50–$115 | MC, V | Closed Dec.–Feb.

CAMERON

MAP 12, A3

(Nearby towns also listed: Bethany, Chillicothe, Excelsior Springs, Jamesport, Kearney, St. Joseph)

Founded in 1855, Cameron today calls itself "the Crossroads of the Nation" because of its location at the junction of Interstate 35 and U.S. 36. If you don't have time to drive through town, you can get a quick taste of Cameron's past at the McDonalds just off Interstate 35 at exit 54, which has photos of old homes, schools, and other spots around the area on display.

Information: **Cameron Chamber of Commerce** | 205 S. Main St., 64429 | 816/632–2005 | chamber@cameron.net | www.cameron.net/city.

Attractions
Pony Express Region Tourist Information Center. This center provides information on all of Missouri, as well as Iowa, Kansas, South Dakota, and Nebraska. There's another center in St. Joseph. | I–35 and U.S. 36 at Cameron | 816/232–1839 or 816/632–546 | Apr.–Oct., daily 8:30–4:30.

Wallace State Park. This park 6 mi south of Cameron offers one of the best examples of a presettlement forests, along with camping, hiking, and fishing. | 10621 N.E. Hwy. 121 | 816/632–3745 | www.dnr.state.mo.us/dsp | Free | Daily.

JUNE–SEPT.: *Municipal Band Concerts*. The city band plays each Thursday evening from Memorial Day through Labor Day downtown at McCorkle Park. | 816/632–2005.
JULY: *Country Days*. Barbecue, crafts, and watermelon-eating contests highlight this Chamber of Commerce–sponsored celebration at McCorkle Park. | 816/632–2005.

Dining

Breadeaux Pizza. Pizza. Pizza with homemade crust is the specialty of the house. Pasta dishes are also available. | 225 E. 3rd St. | 816/632–7472 | $7–$15 | No credit cards.

MacNamara's. American. A Colonial-style restaurant serving such standards as fried chicken, steak, and seafood. Salad bar. Kids' menu. | 933 N. Walnut | 816/632–6110 | $9–$17 | AE, D, DC, MC, V.

Lodging

Best Western Acorn Inn. This redbrick Colonial-style motel is ¼ mi from I-35 on U.S. 36 near the birthplace of Jesse James and several antiques malls. Complimentary Continental breakfast. In-room data ports, cable TV. Pool. Pets allowed. | I-35 and U.S. 36 | 816/632–2187 or 800/607–2288 | fax 816/632–2523 | www.bestwestern.com | 40 rooms | $51–$64 | AE, D, DC, MC, V.

Econo Lodge. This downtown chain hotel is within walking distance of Cameron's restaurants and shops. Complimentary Continental breakfast. Cable TV. Pool. Pets allowed. | 220 E. Grand | 816/632–6571 | 36 rooms | $35–$65 | AE, D, DC, MC, V.

Holiday Inn Express. On the edge of town next to a supermarket and a Wal-Mart, this chain motel is 6 mi from Wallace State Park. Complimentary Continental breakfast. Cable TV. Pool. Gym. | 601 E. Bryon Rd. | 816/632–6666 or 800/465–4329 | www.basshotels.com/holiday-inn | 47 rooms | $49–$59 | AE, D, DC, MC, V.

CAPE GIRARDEAU

MAP 12, F5

(Nearby towns also listed: Farmington, Poplar Bluff, Ste. Genevieve, Sikeston)

"The City of Roses on the River" gets its nickname from the nationally accredited rose test garden in the city's Capaha Park, but its true name comes from a French trading post established on a rock overlook in 1733. Some locals call the town "the Cape," but mostly people know it as Cape, the home of Southeast Missouri State University, Rush Limbaugh, and the Cherokee Indian Trail of Tears.

Information: Cape Girardeau Chamber of Commerce | 1267 Mt. Auburn Rd., Box 98, 63702 | 573/335–3312 | www.capechamber.com.

Attractions

Bollinger Mill State Historic Site. A nice place for picnics, the covered bridge here is one of only four remaining in the state. Turn off Hwy 34 onto Hwy OO, then take Hwy HH to the site. | Hwy HH, Burfordville | 573/243–4591 | www.dnr.state.mo.us/dsp | $2 | Mon.–Sat. 10–4, Sun. noon–4.

Cape River Heritage Museum. The first state flag was created here and is on display along with exhibits by famous residents. | 538 Independence St. | 573/334–0405 | $2 | Mar.–Dec., Mon.–Sat. 11–4; also by appointment.

Cape Rock Park. The original site of the trading post that became a city, this park has scenic overlooks of the Mississippi River and picnic spots. | Eastern end of Cape Rock Dr. | 573/335–3312 | www.rosecity.net/caperock.html | Free | Daily.

Court of Common Pleas Building. A dungeon in the basement held Union prisoners during the Civil War. | Spanish and Themis Sts. | 573/335–2802 or 800/777–0068 | Free | Weekdays 8–4.

Glenn House. Decorated slate fireplaces, stenciled ceilings, and fine woodwork are highlights of this 1883 home. | 325 S. Spanish St. | 573/334–1177 | $3 | Apr.–Dec., weekends 1–4; tours by appointment.

Jurrock's Park Zoo and Pet Shop. Get close to unusual spiders, alligators, turtles, lizards, and other reptiles at this hands-on reptile specialty zoo and park. | 853 S. Kingshighway | 573/332–7006 | rosecity.net/jurrocks_park/index.html | $3 | Mon.–Fri. 10–6; Sat. 10–8.

Old Lorimier Cemetery. More than 1,100 grave sites—including those of notable local residents—mark this 200-year-old cemetery. The cemetery was named for Major Louis Lorimier, who established a trading post in the area. The site spreads across 5 acres on a hill overlooking the Mississippi River. | 500 N. Fountain St. | 573/334–0405 | Free | Daily 7–sunset.

Old St. Vincent's Church. Built in the 1850s, this church is right on the riverfront. | Main St. and William St. | 573/335–9347 | Free | Sun. mass 10; tours by appointment.

Rose Display Garden. A nationally accredited rose test garden since 1953, there are more than 200 varieties of roses here and more than 1,000 plants. | Capaha Park, Perry Ave. | 573/335–4124 | www.rosecity.net/rosegard.html | Free | Daily.

Trail of Tears State Park. More than 16,000 Cherokee Indians camped here in the winter of 1830 on their forced march from Tennessee to Oklahoma. Today, this state park offers hiking, camping, fishing, and swimming. | 429 Moccasin Springs Rd., Jackson | 573/334–1711 | www.mobot.org/stateparks/tears.html | Free | Apr.–Sept., Mon.–Sat. 9–5, Sun. noon–5; Oct., Wed.–Sat. 9–5, Sun. noon–5; Nov.–Mar., Fri., Sat. 10–4, Sun. noon–4.

SIGHTSEEING TOURS/TOUR COMPANIES

St. Louis Iron Mountain and Southern Railway. Tours of the countryside on trains from the early to mid-1900s. Also offered are dinner and murder-mystery excursions. | 252 E. Jackson Blvd., Jackson | 573/243–1688 or 800/455–RAIL | $12.50–$37 | Wed.–Sun., 9–5.

ON THE CALENDAR

JULY: *Cape Girardeau Regional Air Festival.* With a full arena of civilian and military aerial aerobatics and displays, this weekend-long event in early or mid-July draws thousands to the airport south of town. | 573/335–1631 or 800/777–0068.

Dining

BG's Olde Tyme Deli and Saloon. American. Imagine a cross between a sports bar/movie restaurant and an old-fashioned saloon. That's what you have here, and they are serving deli foods and lots of potato skins. Salad bar. Kids' menu. | 205 S. Plaza Way | 573/335–8860 | $6–$12 | AE, D, DC, MC, V.

Broussard's Cajun Cuisine. Cajun. This place looks like it's ready for Mardi Gras every day. There's New Orleans jazz playing and dishes include such bayou favorites as shrimp Creole or jambalaya. Live music Friday and Saturday. Sunday brunch. | 120 N. Main St. | 573/334–7235 | $6–$15 | AE, D, MC, V.

Royale N'Orleans Restaurant. Cajun. The New Orleans French Quarter is the inspiration for this restaurant, whose extensive menu includes steaks, fresh seafood, and Cajun specialties. Reservations are recommended. | 300 Broadway St. | 573/335–8191 | $10–$26 | AE, MC, V | No lunch.

Lodging

Bellevue Bed and Breakfast. Original woodwork, stenciled ceilings, and period furnishings are some of the highlights of this downtown 1891 Victorian home 10 minutes' walk from the Mississippi. All rooms have private baths. Complimentary breakfast. TVs in rooms and common areas, some in-room hot tubs. | 312 Bellevue St. | 573/335–3302 or 800/768–6822 | fax 573/332–7752 | bellevuebb@compuserve.com | www.bbonline.com/mo/bellevue | 4 rooms | $70 | AE, D, DC, MC, V.

Drury Lodge. This chain motel just off I-55 at exit 96 about 10 minutes from downtown is especially proud of its restaurant which is good enough to draw locals as well as serving guests. Restaurant, bar, complimentary breakfast, room service. Cable TV. Pool, wading pool. Gym. Playground. Business services. Some pets allowed. | 104 S. Vantage Rd. | 573/334–7151 or 800/325–8300 | fax 573/334–7151 | www.druryinn.com | 139 rooms | $68–$75 | AE, D, DC, MC, V.

Hampton Inn. Near the airport, 4 mi west of downtown, this chain motel is just across the street from several restaurants. Complimentary Continental breakfast. Cable TV. Business services. Some pets allowed. | 103 Cape West Pkwy. | 573/651–3000 or 800/426–7866 | fax 573/651–0882 | www.hamptoninn.com | 80 rooms | $60–$90 | AE, D, DC, MC, V.

Holiday Inn West Park. This chain hotel is 1 mi from the Southeast Missouri State University campus and a nearby mall. The hotel has several meeting rooms available to business travelers. Restaurant, bar, room service. In-room data ports, cable TV. 2 pools, wading pool. Sauna. Gym. Laundry facilities. Business services. Pets allowed. | 3257 William St. | 573/334–4491 or 800/465–4329 | fax 573/334–7459 | www.basshotels.com/holiday-inn | 186 rooms | $82–$88 | AE, D, DC, MC, V.

Pear Tree Inn. This chain hotel is within walking distance of a shopping mall and movie theater. Complimentary Continental breakfast. Cable TV. Pool, wading pool. Business services. Some pets allowed. | 3248 William St. | 573/334–3000 | 78 rooms | $55–$65 | AE, D, DC, MC, V.

Victorian Inn of Cape Girardeau. This motel is right off Interstate 55 at exit 96 on a commercial strip with lots of chain restaurants. Despite its name it has a contemporary, not Victorian, look. Refrigerators, cable TV. 2 hot tubs. Pets allowed. | 3265 William St. | 573/651–4486 | fax 573/651–3970 | 133 rooms | $65–$95 | AE, D, DC, MC, V.

CARTHAGE

MAP 12, A6

(Nearby towns also listed: Joplin, Lamar, Mount Vernon, Nevada, Springfield)

Large deposits of zinc and lead in the area meant Carthage had more millionaires per capita than any city in the United States at the end of the 19th century. The ornate homes the millionaires left behind are a treat to see. However, these days more visitors end up at the Precious Moments Chapel Center just outside town than they do inside the city limits. Also nearby is the site where George Washington Carver was born.

Information: **Carthage Chamber of Commerce** | 107 E. 3rd St., 64836 | 417/358–2373 | www.carthagenow.com.

Attractions
Battle of Carthage Civil War Museum. This museum houses artifacts from the 1861 Civil War battle and features an elaborate mural painted by local artist Andy Thomas. | 205 E. Grant St. | 417/237–7060 | Free | Mon.–Sat. 8:30–5, Sun. 1–5.

George Washington Carver National Monument. This park pays tribute to Carver's achievements and distinction as a scientist, educator, and humanitarian. The site of Carver's birth is marked, although the original cabin no longer stands. | 5646 Carver Rd., Diamond | 417/325–4151 | Free | Daily 9–5.

Jasper County Courthouse. Constructed of locally quarried stone in 1894, this courthouse includes the bicentennial mural *Forged in Fire* by Lowell Davis, celebrating the history of the city. | Courthouse Sq. | 417/358–2373 or 800/404–0421 | www.carthagenow.com | Free | Weekdays 8:30–4:30.

Old Cabin Shop/1842 Log Courthouse. The authentic 1830s cabin of the George Hornback family, which later served as the first Jasper County Courthouse, now presents an intriguing vision of early settlers' lives. On display across the street in the Old Cabin Shop is a large collection of Native American artifacts and a gun collection. | 155 N. Black Powder Lane | 417/358–6720 or 800/799–6720 | www.oldcabinshop.com | Free | Weekdays 11–4.

Powers Museum. This local history museum hosts many traveling exhibits. | 1617 Oak St. | 417/358–2667 | Donations accepted | Mar.–Dec. 23, Tues.–Sat. 10–5, Sun. 1–5.

Precious Moments Chapel Center. Sam Butcher, the creator of the Precious Moments figurines, has constructed a chapel, garden, and fountain show here. He is often on site painting and signing autographs. | 4321 Chapel Rd. | 417/358–7599 or 800/543–7975 | www.preciousmoments.com | Donations accepted | Daily, 9–9.

ON THE CALENDAR

MAY: *City Wide Garage Sale.* The first weekend in May affords treasure hunters the opportunity to find great bargains at garage and lawn sales across town. | 417/358–2191.
OCT.: *Maple Leaf Celebration.* Organized walks, parades, and home tours celebrate the hundreds of colorful trees throughout the city on the third Saturday of the month. | 417/358–2373.

Dining

Bam-Boo Gardens. Chinese. This restaurant, with its oriental lanterns and white linen tablecloths, offers a full hot and cold buffet with such dishes as broccoli beef and sweet-and-sour chicken. | 102 N. Garrison | 417/358–1611 | Reservations not accepted Fri., Sat. | $7–$10 | MC, V | Closed Sun.

C. D.'s Pancake Hut. American. The extensive breakfast menu at this restaurant includes a variety of pancakes and omelets. The lunch menu includes sandwiches and homemade soups. | 301 S. Garrison St. | 417/358–9807 | $4–$8 | No credit cards | Closed Mon. No dinner.

Ranch House. Steak. This casual steak house serves steaks, catfish, and other seafood dinners. Kids' menu. | 2937 S. Grand Ave. | 417/359–5200 | $11–$27 | AE, D, MC, V | Closed Mon.

Lodging

Best Western Precious Moments Hotel. This redbrick Colonial-style hotel 3 miles west of the Precious Moments complex was designed and decorated by Precious Moments creator Samuel J. Butcher in 1995 and showcases one-of-a-kind Precious Moments artwork and a Precious Moments gift shop. Complimentary Continental breakfast. Cable TV. Pool. Laundry facilities. | 2701 Hazel Ave. | 417/359–5900 or 800/551–7676 | www.preciousmoments.com | fax 417/359–5240 | 121 rooms | $47–$73 | AE, D, DC, MC, V.

Days Inn. This chain motel sits on a quiet commercial street at the south end of town 3 mi from the Precious Moments Chapel Center. Complimentary Continental breakfast. Some in-room data ports, cable TV. Business services. | 2244 Grand Ave. | 417/358–2499 or 888/454–2499 | fax 417/358–2499 | www.daysinn.com | 40 rooms | $45–$65 | AE, D, DC, MC, V.

Econo Lodge. Some rooms have inside entrances, some outside entrances at this chain motel on a commercial street 1 mi from downtown. Complimentary Continental breakfast. Cable TV. Pool. Hot tub. | 1441 W. Central Ave. | 417/358–3900 | fax 417/358–6839 | 82 rooms | $52–$60 | AE, D, DC, MC, V.

Grand Avenue Bed and Breakfast. This lovely Queen Anne Victorian was built in 1893 and still retains its original woodwork and stained-glass windows. Rooms are named in honor of such authors as Mark Twain and Charles Dickens. Most popular is the Laura Ingalls Wilder room which has a fireplace as well as a selection of Wilder's books. Complimentary breakfast. Some room phones, no TV in some rooms. Pool. No smoking. | 1615 Grand Ave. | 417/358–7265 or 888/380–6786 | fax 417/358–7265 | reservation@grand–avenue.com | www.grand-avenue.com | 4 rooms | $79–$99 | AE, D, MC, V.

Super 8 Motel. This chain motel, built in 1998, is ½ mile from Interstate 71. Complimentary Continental breakfast. Cable TV. | 416 W. Fir Rd. | 417/359–9000 or 800/800–8000 | fax 417/359–9099 | www.super8.com | 56 rooms | $47–$59 | AE, D, DC, MC, V.

CASSVILLE

MAP 12, B6

(Nearby towns also listed: Branson, Joplin, Kimberling City, Mount Vernon)

The first telegraph line to cross the state came through Cassville in 1859. For that reason, Union and Confederate soldiers fought heavily in the area, and for a short time, Cassville was the Confederate capital of Missouri. Today, hunters know the area to be a haven for deer, quail, squirrel, duck, and wild turkey.

Information: Cassville Chamber of Commerce | 504 Main St., 65625-1418 | 417/847–2814.

CASSVILLE

INTRO
ATTRACTIONS
DINING
LODGING

Attractions

Eagle Forest and Coyote Gardens. See coyotes, hawks, and eagles at this private wildlife refuge with a small nature center on-site. | Rte. 86, Eagle Rock | 417/271–3964 | Free | Thurs.–Sun. 10–6.

Piney Creek Wilderness Area. The Piney Creek Wilderness area, a part of the Mark Twain National Forest, includes 13 mi of trails on old forest roads. | 248 E. Rte. 112 | 417/847–2144 | www.fs.fed.us/r9/marktwain | Free | Daily.

Roaring River State Park. More than 20,000 gallons of water rush from a spring into the Roaring River every day at this state park that offers hiking and fishing 7 mi south of Cassville. | Rte. 112 | 417/847–2539 or 417/847–2330 | www.dnr.state.mo.us/parks.htm | Free | Mar.–Oct., daily.

ON THE CALENDAR
APR.: *Dogwood Car and Truck Festival.* Vintage cars and trucks are displayed under a canopy of dogwoods just south of town at Roaring River State Park on the third weekend of the month. | 417/847–2814.

APR., SEPT.: *Spring and Fall Trout Derby.* Compete with more than 4,000 other fishermen for cash prizes at Roaring River State Park. | 417/847–2814.

Dining
Dave's Café. American. This homey café with red-checked curtains and tablecloths is known for breaded chicken and pork cutlets, homemade pies, and cinnamon rolls. Sunday buffet. Kids' menu. | HC 81, Box 8002 | 417/847–3535 | $6–$10 | MC, V | Closed Sat.

Rib House. Barbecue. Barbecued rib dinners are the specialty at this rustic family eatery, but steaks and other meats smoked on the premises are also available. The restaurant is at the junction of Routes 112 and 248, near the Roaring River State Park. Kids' menu. | Rte. 112 at Rte. 248 | 417/847–3600 | $5–$15 | AE, D, MC, V | Closed Mon.

Lodging

Rainbow Motel. This facility has clean cottages surrounded by plenty of lawn space and fresh flowers. Cable TV. Pool. | 1301 Old Hwy. 37 | 417/847–2234 | 10 rooms | $40 | AE, D, DC, MC, V.

Roaring River Inn. Operated by the Missouri Department of Natural Resources in Roaring River State Park, this rustic lodge and the surrounding wood cabins have such modern amenities as air-conditioning and kitchenettes. Restaurant. Kitchenettes, cable TV. Pool. | Rte. 112 | 417/847–2330 | fax 417/847–5667 | 26 double rooms, 26 cabins, 2 suites | $72–$93, $88 cabins, $110 suites | AE, D, MC, V.

Super 8 Motel. This two-story motel built in 1993 is 7 mi from the Roaring River State Park on Highway 37. Cable TV. Pool. Pets allowed. | 101 S. Hwy 37 | 417/847–4888 or 800/800–8000 | fax 417/847–4888 | www.super8.com | 46 rooms | $49–$56 | AE, D, DC, MC, V.

CHILLICOTHE

MAP 12, B2

(Nearby towns also listed: Cameron, Jamesport, Macon)

Founded in 1837, the seat of Livingston County was named for an old Shawnee Indian village. The word *Chillicothe* means "our big town," and although just under 9,000 people call Chillicothe home, it has many amenities of a larger area. The downtown, renovated in the 1990s, features several historical murals on the sides of buildings. Nearby Laclede is even smaller, but earned a place in the nation's history as the home of World War I's General John J. Pershing.

Information: **Chillicothe Chamber of Commerce** | 514 Washington St., Box 407, 64601-0407 | 660/646–4050 | cacc@greenhills.net | www.chillicothemo.com.

Attractions

General John J. Pershing Boyhood Home State Historic Site. Take U.S. 36 east to Route 5 north to reach the birthplace of the highest-ranking U.S. military officer in history, along with the one-room schoolhouse in which he was taught. | Rte. 5, Laclede | 660/963–2525 | www.dnr.state.mo.us/dsp | $2 | Nov.–Mar., Mon.–Sat. 8–4; Apr., Oct., Mon.–Sat. 8–4, Sun. noon–5; May–Sept., Mon.–Sat. 8–4, Sun. noon–6.

Grand River Historical Society and Museum. The museum showcases local history with artifacts, paintings, themed exhibits, and occasional special programs. | 1401 Forest Dr. | 660/646–1341 | Free | Apr.–Oct., Tues. and Sun. 1–4.

Pershing State Park. A wetland area and shady campgrounds pay tribute to General John Pershing, a World War I commander born in this area. | Rte. 130, Laclede | 660/963–2299 | www.dnr.state.mo.us/dsp | Free | Daily.

Swan Lake National Wildlife Refuge. You can see a wide variety of wildlife on these 10,000 acres which are about 20 mi outside of Chillicothe in nearby Sumner. Hunting and fishing are allowed during certain seasons. | Rte. 139, Sumner | 660/856–3323 | Free | Mar.–mid-Oct., weekdays 7:30–4.

ON THE CALENDAR

JULY: *Freedom Festival.* Fireworks and live local entertainment celebrate Independence Day in Simpson Park. | 660/646–4050.

SEPT.: *Chautauqua in the Park.* A juried arts-and-crafts festival with food, clowns, and a petting zoo in Simson Park the weekend after Labor Day. | 660/646–4050.

Dining

Country Kitchen. American. The restaurant's country motif complements its varied menu of freshly prepared sandwiches, salads, soups, and home-style dinners. A breakfast buffet is served on weekends. | 1029 S. Washington St. | 660/646–6500 | $4–$16 | D, MC, V.

Harlow's. American/Casual. Named for movie star Jean Harlow, this establishment's Art Deco theme is enhanced with posters, photos, and memorabilia celebrating the actress's life. Harlow's specializes in hand-cut steaks and seafood. | 609 Jackson St. | 660/646–6812 | $7–$15 | AE, D, MC, V | Closed Sun., Mon. No lunch.

Lodging

Best Western Inn. This chain hotel is set in a commercial area near several restaurants. Complimentary Continental breakfast. In-room data ports, refrigerators, cable TV. Pool. Business services. Pets allowed (fee). | 1020 S. Washington St. | 660/646–0572 or 800/990–9150 | fax 660/646–1274 | www.bestwestern.com | 60 rooms, 6 suites in 2 buildings | $50–$85 | AE, D, DC, MC, V.

Grand River Inn. This brick hotel is within walking distance of several restaurants and shops including a Wal-Mart. Restaurant, bar, complimentary Continental breakfast, room service. In-room data ports, some refrigerators, cable TV. Pool. Hot tub, sauna. Business services. Some pets allowed. | 606 W. Business 36 | 660/646–6590 | 60 rooms, 5 suites | $58–$79, $83–$92 suites | AE, D, DC, MC, V.

Super 8 Motel. Built in 1995, this chain motel is off Highway 36 at the Industrial Road Exit. Complimentary Continental breakfast. Cable TV. Pets allowed. | 580 Old Highway 36 E | 660/646–7888 or 800/800–8000 | fax 660/646–2531 | www.super8.com | 56 rooms | $50 | AE, D, DC, MC, V.

Travel Inn Motel. This older, single-story motel is on the edge of town, at the junction of Routes 36 and 65. Cable TV. | 1024 Rte. 36 W | 660/646–0784 | 25 rooms | $45–$58 | AE, D, MC, V.

CLAYTON

MAP 13, C6

(Nearby towns also listed: St. Charles, St. Louis)

This St. Louis suburb is primarily a business district with wide, shaded streets, bountiful flower beds, and discreet office complexes ten to fifteen minutes from downtown. Art galleries, restaurants, and shops keep the area lively in the evening. Clayton is also the home to artist and author Mary Englebreit, who can often be seen on the streets of her hometown.

Information: Clayton Chamber of Commerce | 225 S. Meramec Ave., Suite 300, 63105-1909 | 314/726–3033 | www.claytonchamber.org.

Attractions

Clayton Row Antique District. Browse eight shops selling a wide selection of fine American and European antiques including furniture, china, jewelry, decorative arts, and other items. | 7700 to 7800 blocks of Clayton Rd. | 314/726–3033 | Free | Mon.–Sat. 10–6, Sun. 1–5.

Craft Alliance Gallery. Functional, contemporary art in clay, metal, wood fiber, and glass by regional and national artists. | 6640 Delmar Blvd. | 314/725–1177 | Free | Weekdays 10–6 (Tues. and Thurs. until 8), Sat. 10–5, Sun. noon–6. Education Center weekdays 9–5.

ON THE CALENDAR

JUNE: *Taste of Clayton.* A food tasting on the city streets, featuring the creations of Clayton's top chefs. | 314/863–0249.

CLAYTON

INTRO
ATTRACTIONS
DINING
LODGING

SEPT.: *St. Louis Art Fair.* More than 100,000 people come to Clayton's central business district the weekend after Labor Day to see art created in a wide range of mediums. | 314/863-0278 | www.saintlouisartfair.com.

Dining

Annie Gunn's. Irish. This Irish pub has open-air dining on a patio with a wood-burning fireplace and a garden view. Some of the featured foods here are jumbo smoked shrimp, extra-large steaks, and a variety of smoked meats. For dessert the bread pudding is a must-have. Annie's offers private dinners for six to eight people called "snugs." Kids' menu. | 16806 Chesterfield Airport Rd., Chesterfield | 636/532-7684 | $15-$30 | AE, DC, MC, V | Closed Mon.

Benedetto's. Italian. Candelabras and fine china set the tone at this restaurant known for pasta and veal dishes. | 10411 Clayton Rd., Frontenac | 314/432-8585 | Jacket and tie | $16-$23 | AE, D, DC, MC, V.

Café Provençal. French. The seasonally inspired menu changes daily at this intimate bistro where you may find such dishes as bouillabaisse or roast chicken. | 34 N. Central Ave. | 314/725-2755 | $15 | AE, DC, MC, V.

Candicci's. Italian. Try such dishes as langusto supremo, fettuccine with shellfish, and a lobster tail in a creamy lobster/pesto sauce, inside by candlelight or outside surrounded by flowers and a decorative wrought-iron fence. Live music Tuesday–Thursday 6:30–9:30. Kids' menu. | 12513 Olive St., Creve Coeur | 314/878-5858 | $11-$25 | AE, D, DC, MC, V.

Cardwell's. Contemporary. Such house specialties as grilled Atlantic salmon and veal chops are served on marble-top tables or outdoors on a patio with a view of neighborhood streets and gardens. | 8100 Maryland Ave. | 314/726-5055 | $18-$30 | AE, DC, MC, V | Closed Sun.

Crazy Fish Fresh Grill. American. This grill features eclectic aquatic artwork on the walls and such dishes as shrimp and voodoo pasta, shrimp served with black linguine in a jalapeño cream sauce, and Cajun beef tenderloin. There's a small patio with four outdoor tables. Kids' menu. | 15 N. Meramec Ave. | 314/726-2111 | $10-$25 | AE, D, DC, MC, V.

Daniele. Continental. Known for seafood, steak, veal, and prime rib. Sunday brunch. No smoking. | 216 N. Meramec Ave. | 314/721-0101 | Jacket and tie | $13-$19 | AE, D, DC, MC, V | No dinner Sun.

Fio's La Fourchette. French. Fio himself runs the kitchen at this candlelit bistro, where you can get seconds (and thirds) of any dish. The pink interior is accented with artificial flower arrangements, and the menu focuses on game and vegetarian options. | 7515 Forsyth Ave. | 314/863-6866 | Reservations essential | $15-$40 | AE, DC, MC, V | Closed Sun.–Tues. No lunch.

J. Buck's. American. Basic cuts of grilled beef, pork, and fish—as well as salads and sandwiches—are served at this eatery named for St. Louis sportscaster Jack Buck. It's a popular after-work spot for the younger crowd. | 101 S. Hanley Rd. | 314/725-4700 | $7-$12 | D, MC, V | Closed Sun.

Portobella. Contemporary. Modern art and marble floors set the tone at this restaurant serving such dishes as porcini-encrusted sea bass, grilled beef tenderloin with white truffle oil, or roasted halibut with lemon garlic. | 15 N. Central Ave. | 314/725-6588 | $14-$27 | AE, D, DC, MC, V | Closed Sun.

Remy's Kitchen and Wine Bar. Continental. Chose one of 35 wines served by the glass or 65 served by the bottle to accompany such house specialties as filet mignon or frito misto, a combination of calamari, scallops, and rock shrimp flash-fried and served with a mustard vinaigrette, in a dining room decorated with posters of different wines and a border of quotes from famous wine connoisseurs. Outdoor dining on a patio. No smoking in restaurant only. | 222 S. Bemiston Rd. | 314/726-5757 | www.remyskitchen.net | $10-$18 | AE, D, DC, MC, V | Closed Sun.

Lodging

Daniele. A steaming pot of coffee will be delivered to your room shortly after your wake-up call at this European-style hotel near Washington University. Rooms are furnished with antique reproductions. Restaurant (*see* Daniele, *above*), bar, complimentary Continental breakfast. In-room data ports, some refrigerators, cable TV. Pool. Business services, airport shuttle, free parking. Pets allowed. | 216 N. Meramac Ave. | 314/721–0101 or 800/325–8302 | fax 314/721–0609 | 82 rooms, 5 suites | $129, $250 1–bedroom suites, $500 2–bedroom suites, $800 3–bedroom suites | AE, D, DC, MC, V.

Das Gast Haus Nadler. Built as a farmhouse in 1904 and later enlarged, this guest house has a game room with bumper pool and a gym. Restaurant, complimentary breakfast. No room phones. Hot tub. Gym. | 125 Defiance Rd., Defiance | 636/987–2200 | 4 rooms (all with shared bath) | $70–$90 | MC, V.

Radisson. This chain hotel is in a business district 20 minutes from downtown St. Louis and just five minutes from the Galleria mall, the St. Louis Zoo, and the St. Louis Science Center. Restaurant, bar, complimentary Continental breakfast. In-room data ports, refrigerators, cable TV. Pool. Hot tub. Gym. Video games. Business services, airport shuttle. | 7750 Carondelet Ave. | 314/726–5400 | fax 314/719–1126 | www.radisson.com/stlouismo_clayton | 194 rooms, 11 honeymoon suites | $129, $139 suites | AE, D, DC, MC, V.

Ritz-Carlton, St. Louis. Museum-quality oil paintings line the halls of this luxury hotel. Each room has a balcony and marble bath and some have views of the St. Louis skyline. Restaurant, bar (with entertainment), room service. In-room data ports, minibars, some microwaves, some refrigerators, cable TV. Pool. Hot tub, massage. Gym. Business services, parking (fee). | 100 Carondelet Plaza | 314/863–6300 or 800/241–3333 | fax 314/863–3524 | www.ritzcarlton.com | 301 rooms, 34 suites | $219–$289 rooms, $299–$400 suites, $2,000 presidential suite | AE, D, DC, MC, V.

Seven Gables. This historic 1926 Tudor-style building was converted into a luxury hotel with parquet floors, oriental rugs, and French country antiques in 1986. Now on the National Register of Historic Places, it's 10 minutes from downtown and surrounded by office buildings, ritzy shops and galleries, and fine eateries. You can find the menus for its own restaurants on-line. 3 restaurants, bar, room service. Cable TV. Parking (fee). | 26 N. Meramec Ave. | 314/863–8400 or 800/433–6590 | fax 314/863–8846 | gm@sevengablesinn.com | www.sevengablesinn.com | 32 rooms | $145 and up | AE, D, DC, MC, V.

Sheraton Clayton Plaza Hotel. A spacious lobby, concierge service, free airport transportation, and large rooms distinguish this hotel, which is 9 mi from Lambert International Airport. Restaurant, bar, room service. Cable TV. Pool. Barbershop, beauty salon. Exercise room. Shop. Airport shuttle. | 7730 Bonhomme Ave. | 314/863–0400 or 800/325–3535 | fax 314/863–8513 | www.sheraton.com | 253 rooms | $149–$169 | AE, D, DC, MC, V.

CLINTON

MAP 12, B4

(Nearby towns also listed: Harrisonville, Nevada, Sedalia)

Just about an hour southeast of metropolitan Kansas City, Clinton is in the heart of lake country. Truman Lake is Missouri's largest, with more than 55,000 acres of fishing, primarily crappie and largemouth bass. Clinton is also one of the anchors of Missouri's rails-to-trails long-distance hiking and biking path known as the KATY trail.

Information: Clinton Chamber of Commerce | 200 S. Main St., 64735-1123 | 660/885–8166 or 800/222–5251 | infor@clintonmo.com | www.clintonmo.com.

Attractions

Harry S Truman State Park. This 1,044-acre park on a peninsula features rolling hills, plains, hiking trails, campgrounds, and access to Truman Lake. | H.C.R. 66, on County UU, Warsaw | 660/438–7711 | www.dnr.state.mo.us/dsp | Free | Daily.

Henry County Historical Society Museum and Cultural Arts Center. The former Anheuser-Busch building now houses war relics, documentation of genealogies, an art gallery, and an 1850s log home. | 203 W. Franklin St. | 660/885–8414 | Wed.–Sat. $3, Tues. by donation | Apr.–Dec., Tues.–Sat., limited hrs; also by appointment.

Katy Trail State Park. This long-distance hiking and cycling trail is built along the the former corridor of the Missouri-Kansas-Texas (MKT) Railroad, also known as "Katy." The trail and park extends from Clinton to St. Charles, passing through 26 towns and crossing 225 mi of farmland that was once prairie. You'll find a map of the whole trail, with directions to trailheads and information about parking, food, and lodging along the way, at the trail's website. An area between Calhoun and Clinton is being restored to tallgrass prairie. | The Clinton trailhead is at Green St. where Route 52 and Route 7 separate | 660/882–8196 or 800/334–6946 | www.katytrailstatepark.com | Free | Daily dawn–dusk.

ON THE CALENDAR

NOV.: *Festival of Lights.* Thanksgiving weekend brings more than 100 displays around historic Courthouse Square. | 660/885–2121.

Dining

Ernesto's Restaurante. Italian. Pasta and pizza specialties are served at this casual family eatery. American fare is also available. | 109 S. Washington St. | 660/885–9280 | $7–$16 | D, MC, V | Closed Sun., Mon.

Uchie's. American. This restaurant has a country feel and such homey dishes as chicken-fried steak and fried chicken. Salad bar. Kids' menu. | 127 W. Franklin St. | 660/885–3262 | $6–$10 | AE, D, MC, V | Closed Sun.

© Corbis

ARE YOU A TIGHTWAD?

Just about 15 mi east of Clinton on Route 7, right on the shores of Truman Lake, is the little town of Tightwad. Only 50 people live there, but they are proud to call themselves "tightwads." No one really remembers how the town got its name, but you can only imagine the personality of the founding father, right?

The big tourist attraction in Tightwad is the Tightwad National Bank, just recently bought out by United Missouri Banks. The bank manager gets several phone calls a month from people out of state wanting to open an account at the Tightwad Bank. People from 20 states and three countries have accounts here—an incredible number for a small branch bank.

The other tourist attraction, located in the same facility as the bank, is the Tightwad Post Office—which is a popular place for people to have their income tax returns mailed on April 15. People drive for miles just to have their pictures taken in Tightwad, and the city has been featured in the *Wall Street Journal* and *Fortune*, and, of course, it has been the focus of jokes on the *David Letterman Show*.

Lodging

Best Western Colonial Motel. This older L-shape motel at the junction of Routes 13 and 7 is white-painted brick with black trim. Its rooms are modest, comfortable, and well maintained. Restaurant, complimentary Continental breakfast. In-room data ports, cable TV. Pool. | 13 E. Franklin St. | 660/885–2206 or 800/528–1234 | fax 660/885–2206 | www.bestwestern.com | 32 rooms | $45–$69 | AE, D, MC, V.

Days Inn. There are several restaurants within walking distance of this chain motel 2 mi northwest of downtown. In-room data ports, cable TV. Pool. Hot tub. Business services. | Rte. 7 and Rives Rd. | 660/885–6901 or 800/329–7466 | fax 660/885–5978 | www.daysinn.com | 100 rooms | $79 | AE, D, MC, V.

Hickory Hollow Resort. The rustic cabins at this fishing lodge are 1 mi from the shores of Truman Lake. The game room has pool tables as well as video games and there's a sleeping lodge available for groups of 12. TVs in all cabins and in common areas. Pool. Basketball. Video games. | 158 S.E. Hwy. PP, Tightwad | 660/477–3413 | fax 660/477–3413 | hhollow@gateway.net | www.trumanlake.com | 15 cabins, RV park | $45–$65 | AE, D MC, V.

COLUMBIA

MAP 12, C3

(Nearby towns also listed: Arrow Rock, Fulton, Hermann, Jefferson City, Mexico, Moberly, Rocheport)

Founded in 1819, Columbia is home to the 25,000-plus students at the University of Missouri–Columbia and is dominated by university activities and events. Because of its central location and easy access to Interstate 70, most state conventions and conferences are held in the area. Columbia is also a great place for shopping, concerts, and a walk in the Shelter Insurance Gardens on Broadway.

Information: **Columbia Chamber of Commerce** | 300 S. Providence, Box 1016, 65205 | 573/874–1132 | chamber.columbia.mo.us.

Attractions

Boone Cave. You'll find picturesque picnic facilities outside this small cave. | 1307 S. Roby Farm Rd. | 573/698–2283 | Free | Daily.

Nifong Park. The park includes walking trails, the 1855 Maple Wood home, and a fine arts gallery, all operated by the Boone County Historical Society. | Off U.S. 63 at Nifong Blvd. and Ponderosa Dr. | 573/874–7460 | Free | Daily.

Shelter Gardens. This 6-acre public garden on the grounds of Shelter Insurance Company, featuring roses, cacti, conifers, and specialty gardens, is popular for weddings and serves as the site for free summer concerts. | 1817 W. Broadway | 573/214–4715 | Free | Daily, dawn–dusk.

State Historical Society of Missouri. The historical society houses and exhibits collections of genealogical material, historical manuscripts, journals, diaries, and photographs. Reference and newspaper libraries are available. Thomas Hart Benton paintings are displayed throughout. | 1020 Lowry St. | 573/882–7083 | Free | Weekdays 8–4:30, Sat. 9–4:30.

Stephens College. This women's college was established in 1833 and seeks to address the changing needs and roles of women in society. | 1200 E. Broadway | 573/442–2211 or 573/876–7111 | fax 573/876–7248 | www.stephens.edu | Free | Sept.–May.

University of Missouri–Columbia. Founded in 1839 as the first state university west of the Mississippi, "Mizzou" is known internationally for its journalism program, agriculture, and veterinary science and medicine. In the 1960s, campuses were added in St. Louis and Kansas City. The university is recognized visually by the four quad columns and the legendary paw print of the Missouri Tigers. | S. 6th St. between Stewart Rd. and Elm St. | 573/882–6333 or

573/882–2121 | www.missouri.edu | Free | Weekdays. Named after the 13th president of the University of Missouri, the **Elmer Ellis Library,** MU's main library, occupies a central block on campus facing Lowry Mall. The State Historical Society and Western Historical Manuscripts are on the ground floor. | 9th St. and Lowry Mall between Memorial Union and Jesse Hall | 573/882–4701 | Free | Mon.–Thurs. 7:30 AM–midnight, Fri. 7:30 AM–9 PM, Sat. 9–9, Sun. noon–midnight. There are several wonderful museums and research facilities at the university. The galleries of the **Museum of Art and Archaeology** house 13,000 pieces of art and artifacts from six continents and five millennia. | Pickard Hall, on Francis Quadrangle | 573/882–3591 | Free | Tues.–Wed. and Fri. 9–5, Thurs. 9–5 and 6–9, weekends noon–5. The **Museum of Anthropology** is the only anthropology museum in the state of Missouri and has more than 100 million objects. | Swallow Hall, on Francis Quadrangle | 573/882–3764 | Free | weekdays 9–4. The **Research Reactor Facility** provides a high-flux neutron source that is used in the research work of many campus departments as well as by medical researchers and visitors from other universities and from industry. | Providence Rd., in University Research Park | 573/882–4211 | Free | Tues.–Fri., appointment required. The **Botany Greenhouses and Herbarium** houses a live and dried plant collection that is used for student study and research and is open to the public. | Tucker Hall, off Hitt St. | 573/882–6888 | Free | weekdays, appointment required. Also on campus is the **Edison Electric Dynamo,** one of only three electrical generators of its kind left in the world built by Thomas Edison. | S. 6th St. between Stewart Rd. and Elm | 573/882–4375 | Free | weekdays 8–6.

ON THE CALENDAR

JUNE: *J. W. Boone Ragtime Festival.* This celebration of the music and history of the county's founding father is held on the second Sun. and Mon. of the month outside the Boone County Courthouse. | 573/445–2539 | blindboone.missouri.org/festival.html.
JULY: *Show-Me State Games.* Venues across the city host events in 32 different sports during this Olympic-style sports festival for Missouri's amateur athletes, the last two weekends of the month. | 573/882–2101 | www.smsg.org.
AUG.: *U.S. Balloon Cellular Classic.* This Boone County Fairgrounds fund-raiser for the Ronald McDonald house, held the last weekend of the month, includes balloons, food, musical entertainment, and a visit from Ronald McDonald. | 573/814–4000 | www.uscellularballoonclassic.com.

Dining

Alexander's Steakhouse. Steak. Grill your own steaks over Alexander's charcoal grill, or order from the menu, which includes prime rib and seafood. This casual restaurant is off Interstate 70 at exit 124 south. | 301 N. Stadium Blvd. | 573/445–1282 | $11–$19 | AE, D, DC, MC, V | No lunch.

Blue Cactus Café. Mexican. This eatery off Interstate 70 at exit 126 south is a casual, lively café with brightly colored Mexican cantina accents. The menu includes American and Mexican specialties. | 3915 S. Providence Rd. | 573/443–2583 | $5–$12 | AE, D, DC, MC, V | Closed Mon.

Boone Tavern. Continental. This tavern in the heart of town is decorated with historical photos of Columbia. Try the chicken cordon bleu or steak. There's open-air dining in a gazebo with a view of the courthouse. Kids' menu. Sunday brunch. | 811 E. Walnut St. | 573/442–5123 | $10–$25 | AE, D, DC, MC, V.

Flat Branch Pub and Brewing. American/Casual. There's a casual atmosphere in this pub that serves 15 different beers, pizzas, and such special dishes as chicken *fuente* (chicken, onions, and peppers rolled in a flour tortilla with a spicy enchilada sauce, cheddar and jack cheese, olives, tomatoes, and scallions). Open-air dining on the pub's landscaped grounds. Kids' menu. | 115 S. 5th St. | 573/499–0400 | $5–$13 | AE, D, DC, MC, V.

Lodging

Best Western Columbia. This chain hotel is on the east side of town at the junction of Interstate 70 and U.S. 63, about 10 minutes' drive from the University of Missouri. Restaurant, bar. Cable TV. Pool. Business services. | 3100 I–70 Dr. | 573/474–6161 or 800/528–1234 | fax 573/474–9323 | www.bestwestern.com | 125 rooms | $55–$65 | AE, D, DC, MC, V.

Campus Inn. This simple motel is within walking distance of the University of Missouri campus. Restaurant, bar. Cable TV. Pool. Business services. | 1112 Stadium Blvd. | 573/449–2731 | fax 573/449–6691 | 98 rooms | $68–$72 | AE, D, DC, MC, V.

Columbia Dome. This chain hotel is a 10-minute drive from the University of Missouri. Restaurant, bar, room service. Cable TV. Pool. Hot tub. Gym. Some pets allowed. | 1612 N. Providence Rd. | 573/449–2491 | fax 573/874–6720 | 142 rooms | $80 | AE, D, DC, MC, V.

Comfort Inn. This older, two-story inn is 4 mi from the University of Missouri and 5 mi from parks and lakes. Restaurant, bar, complimentary Continental breakfast. Cable TV. Pool. Business services. | 901 Conley Rd. | 573/443–4141 or 800/221–2222 | fax 573/443–4141 | 122 rooms | $59–$79 | AE, D, DC, MC, V.

Holiday Inn Executive Center. This Holiday Inn claims to have the biggest hotel gym in the Midwest. Five miles from the University of Missouri, the hotel is just across the street from a shopping mall. Restaurant, bar, room service. In-room data ports, cable TV. 2 pools. Beauty salon, hot tub. Gym. Business services. Pets allowed. | 2200 I–70 Dr. SW | 573/445–8531 or 800/465–4329 | fax 573/445–7607 | www.basshotels.com/holiday-inn | 311 rooms, 11 suites | $90, $135 suites | AE, D, DC, MC, V.

Super 8. Built in the mid-80s, this chain motel is 3 miles from the University of Missouri and within walking distance of several chain restaurants. Complimentary Continental breakfast. Cable TV. Business services. | 3216 Clark La. | 573/474–8488 or 800/800–8000 | fax 573/474–4180 | www.super8.com | 75 rooms | $55 | AE, D, DC, MC, V.

Travelodge. This chain motel is 4 mi from the University of Missouri and 2 mi from Boone County Fairgrounds. Complimentary Continental breakfast, picnic area. Some refrigerators, cable TV. Pool. Laundry facilities. Business services. Some pets allowed (fee). | 900 Vandiver Dr. | 573/449–1065 | fax 573/442–6266 | 164 rooms | $50–$70 | AE, D, DC, MC, V.

EXCELSIOR SPRINGS

MAP 12, A3

(Nearby towns also listed: Cameron, Kansas City, Kearney, Lexington, Liberty)

In the early years of the 20th century, people came from around the world to experience the healing and therapeutic powers of Excelsior Springs. Marilyn Monroe swore by them, as did Presidents Franklin Roosevelt and Harry Truman. Whether you stay for a few hours or a few days, you'll find plenty of personal pampering along with a dash of history here.

Information: **Excelsior Springs Economic Development** | 101 E. Broadway, 64204 | 816/630–6161 or 800/386–2529 | www.exsmo.com.

Attractions

Claybrook Plantation. Built in 1855, this home was briefly occupied by Mary James Barr, the daughter of Jesse James. | 21011 Jesse James Farm Rd. | 816/628–6065 | Free | June–Aug., weekends 9–4; Halloween and Christmas, call for hrs.

Excelsior Springs Historical Museum. A 30-year collection in a former bank building includes household items, pictures, and stories from the late 1800s to the early 1900s. | 101 E. Broadway | 816/630–3712 | $1 | Weekdays 9–noon and 1–4, weekends and evenings by appointment.

Hall of Waters. A range of massage and spa treatment packages is offered here at a resort boasting the world's largest water bar and garden. | 201 E. Broadway | 816/630–0753 | Free;

baths (steam, sitz, light vapor, and bubble tub) $15; aromatherapy bath $25; mud wraps $75, body shampoos $40, and salt scrubs $50; massages $35–$85 | Weekdays 9–5, weekends 10–5.

Smithville Lake and Jerry Litton Visitor Center. With more than 175 mi of shoreline and 7,200 acres of water, Smithville Lake is ideal for boating, fishing, swimming, waterskiing, and inner-tubing. Amenities include two full-service marinas, two swimming beaches, and camping facilities. The visitor center near the dam has exhibits and a 100-gallon aquarium full of native fish. | Rte. C, Smithville | 816/532–0174 | www.mrk.usace.army.mil/smithville/fish.htm | Free; camping fee | Visitors center: Apr., weekdays 8–4, weekends noon–4; May–Sept., daily 8–4; Oct–Mar., weekdays 8–4.

Watkins Woolen Mill State Historic Site and Park. Built in 1860, this woolen mill still has its original machinery. Take Interstate 35 to Highway 92 to Exit 26 to reach the site and the surrounding park. | 26600 Park Road North, Lawson | 816/296–3357 site, 816/580–3387 camping | www.dnr.state.mo.us/dsp | $2 | Mon.–Sat. 10–4; Sun. 11–4.

ON THE CALENDAR

SEPT.: *Waterfest.* This citywide weekend celebration of the springs that made the town famous, includes a parade, a carnival, and gospel music. | 816/630–6161.
OCT.: *Scarecrows on Parade.* The city provides the straw, but you'll need to bring clothing, a hat, and any accessories you want to create an award-winning scarecrow at the Hall of Waters. | 816/630–0753.

Dining

Mill Inn Restaurant. American. Chicken, ribs, and meat loaf are served up family-style on red-checked tablecloths. Kids' menu. Sunday brunch. | 415 St. Louis Blvd. | 816/637–8008 | $5–$13 | No credit cards.

Wabash BBQ. Barbecue. This converted historic train depot is known for smoked turkey, ham, ribs, brisket, and pork roast. Kids' menu. | 646 S. Kansas City Ave. | 816/630–7700 | $5–$18 | AE, D, MC, V.

Lodging

Elms Resort. Situated on 16 acres of wooded hills, this resort was first opened in 1888 as a wellness/mineral springs spa and became a favorite destination for Franklin Roosevelt and Harry Truman. 2 restaurants, 2 bars, room service. In-room data ports, some in-room safes, cable TV, in-room VCRs. 2 pools. Beauty salon, 2 hot tubs, massage, sauna, spa, steam room. Gym, volleyball, bicycles. Business services. | 401 Regent St. | 816/630–5500 or 800/

CAR RENTAL TIPS

- ❏ Review auto insurance policy to find out what it covers when you're away from home.
- ❏ Know the local traffic laws.
- ❏ Jot down make, model, color, and license plate number of rental car and carry the information with you.
- ❏ Locate gas tank—make sure gas cap is on and can be opened.

- ❏ Check trunk for spare and jack.
- ❏ Test the ignition—make sure you know how to remove the key.
- ❏ Test the horn, headlights, blinkers, and windshield wipers.

*Excerpted from *Fodor's: How to Pack: Experts Share Their Secrets*
© 1997, by Fodor's Travel Publications

843–3567 | fax 816/630–5380 | www.elmsresort.com | 152 rooms, 42 suites | $119–$149, $149–$340 suites; private floors available | AE, D, DC, MC, V.

Inn at Crescent Lake. This restored 1915 Georgian Colonial–style mansion sits on 22 secluded acres. Rooms are spacious and elegantly furnished, with luxurious private baths, and the grounds include two crescent-shape ponds and walking paths. The innkeepers are graduates of the French Culinary Institute in New York City and guests can arrange to be served dinner with advance notice. No TV in rooms, TV in common area. | 1261 St. Louis Ave. | 816/630–6745 | fax 816/630–9326 | www.crescentinn.com | 5 rooms, 2 suites | $135–$165 rooms, $185–$195 suites | AE, D, DC, MC, V.

Monterey Motel. This centrally located downtown motel was built in 1950 and has Spanish-style architecture and well-landscaped grounds. Cable TV. Pets allowed. | 217 Concourse | 816/630–0099 | fax 816/637–3171 | 56 rooms | $60 | AE, D, DC, MC, V.

Super 8. This chain motel built in 1994 is 3 mi from Highway 435 off exit 41b and is near several chain restaurants. Complimentary Continental breakfast. Cable TV. Business services. | 112 Cuttings Dr., Smithville | 816/532–3088 or 800/800–8000 | fax 816/873–3502 | www.super8.com | 55 rooms | $41–$76 | AE, D, DC, MC, V.

FARMINGTON

MAP 12, E5

(Nearby towns also listed: Bonne Terre, Cape Girardeau, Pilot Knob, Ste. Genevieve)

Like many towns in east-central Missouri, Farmington owes its birth and development to mining in "them thar hills." Today, in many ways it's a typical small town, though the spectacular surrounding countryside and easy access to Mark Twain National Forest and several state parks give it special appeal. Wander into town on any Friday or Saturday night in the fall, and you might witness some of the best high school football in the state downtown at Farmington High School.

Information: Farmington Chamber of Commerce | 302 N. Washington, Box 191, 63640 | 573/756–3615 | fxnet.missouri.org/econdev | Mon.–Fri. 8–5.

Attractions
Eagle Lake Golf Club. This 18-hole course, opened in 1993, has challenging greens. | 4215 Hunt Rd. | 573/756–6660 | Year-round.

St. Joe State Park. The 8,000-acre park sits in the heart of the "Lead Belt," where much of the nation's lead ore was mined in the early 1900s. During the ore-extraction process, sand flats were formed. Today the area caters to off-road vehicles and also has areas for swimming, cycling, camping, hiking, fishing, boating, and picnicking. | 2800 Pimville Rd., Park Hills | 573/431–1069 or 800/334–6946 | www.dnr.state.mo.us/parks | Free | Daily dawn–dusk.

ON THE CALENDAR
MAR.: *Trivia Night.* This team trivia competition, held the first Saturday of the month, offers cash prizes for local charities. | 573/756–3615.
AUG.: *Downtown Farmington Backyard Barbecue.* On the fourth Saturday of the month, the streets around Long Park in downtown Farmington are filled with good smells and crafts. | 573/756–3615.

Dining
Plank Road Inn. American. This big, homey restaurant is in town and caters to families. Expect generous servings of home-style fare, such as barbecue and fried chicken. Steaks and fried fish are also served, and a dinner buffet is available on weekends. | 606 E. Karsh Rd. | 573/756–8893 | $6–$14 | MC, V.

Lodging

Super 8 Motel. This basic motel, built in 1995, is on a commercial strip with several restaurants just off Highway 67 at Exit 32. Complimentary Continental breakfast. Cable TV. Pool. Pets allowed. | 930 Valley Creek Dr. | 573/756–0344 or 800/800–8000 | fax 573/760–0846 | www.super8.com | 60 rooms | $44–$52 | AE, D, DC, MC, V.

FULTON

MAP 12, D4

(Nearby towns also listed: Columbia, Hermann, Jefferson City, Mexico, Moberly, Wentzville)

Fulton is a town with plenty of history. As the Winston Churchill Memorial at Westminster College attests, this is where Churchill delivered his famous "Iron Curtain" speech in March 1946. In a nod to that speech and the changes in Europe, pieces of the then recently demolished Berlin Wall were shipped here in 1989. Fulton is also county seat for what is sometimes called the Kingdom of Callaway, so named because this Missouri county wanted no part of the bloody Civil War and preferred to secede from both North and South.

Information: **Kingdom of Callaway Chamber of Commerce** | 409 Court St., 65251 | 573/642–3055 or 800/257–3554 | www.kits.net/~cocommer.

Attractions

Auto World Museum. Rare cars, vintage fire trucks and tractors, plus 200 model cars and trucks are all on display under one roof. To reach the museum, take the Business 54 exit off of Highway 54. | 1920 N. Bluff St., Fulton | 573/642–2080 | www.automuseumbybacker.com | $5.50 | April– Nov., Mon.–Sat. 10–4, Sun. 12:30–4; other months by reservation.

Helen Stephens Olympic Display, William Woods University. An exhibit of memorabilia traces the life and athletic feats of Fulton native Helen Stephens. The displays include the gold medals she won in the 1936 Olympic Games. | 200 W. 12th St. | 573/642–2251 | Free | Daily 8–6.

Little Dixie Lake Conservation Area. You can enjoy bird-watching, hiking, and fishing at this 6,000-acre area. | 1821 State Rd. RA, Millersburg | 573/592–4080 | Free | Daily 4 AM–10 PM.

Westminster College. Founded in 1851, this small liberal arts college has about 700 students. | 7th St. | 573/642–3361 | www.westminster-mo.edu | Weekdays. The Church of St. Mary the Virgin, Aldermanbury, England, which dates from the 12th century and once stood in London where it was gutted by a German bomb during World War II has been restored in this mid-Missouri town, on the Westminster College campus, and is the central part of the **Winston Churchill Memorial and Library,** delivery site of Churchill's famed "Iron Curtain" speech. | 501 Westminster Ave. | 573/592–5369 | www.wcmo.edu | $5 | Daily 10–4:30. Adjacent to the Churchill Memorial is *Breakthrough,* created from pieces of the Berlin Wall brought to the campus by sculptress Edwina Sands, the granddaughter of Winston Churchill. | 501 Westminster Ave. | 573/592–5222 | Free | Daily.

ON THE CALENDAR

SEPT.: *Callaway Heritage Festival.* This one-day outdoor celebration features traditional craft makers such as basket weavers and soap makers, children's events, and musical entertainment. | 573/642–3055 or 800/257–3554.
SEPT.: *Jazz in the Park.* Jazz musicians entertain in Veterans Park on the third Saturday of the month. | 573/642–4177.

Dining

Sir Winston's. American. Appropriately, Sir Winston's has an English pub atmosphere but the food has more of a southern feel with smoke-house specialties and lemon-pepper catfish. | 1205 S. Business Hwy 54 | 573/642–7733 | www.sirwinstons.com | $8–$14 | AE, D, DC, MC, V | Closed Sun.

Lodging

Amerihost Inn Fulton. This brick hotel is one mi from downtown just off Highway 54 at the Highway F exit and is surrounded by woods. Complimentary Continental breakfast. Cable TV. Pool. Hot tub. | 556 Amerihost Dr. | 573/642–0077 or 800/434–5800 | fax 573/642–6465 | 62 rooms | $69 | AE, D, MC, V.

Loganberry Inn Bed and Breakfast. This 1899 Victorian home, just steps from the Churchill Memorial, once hosted Margaret Thatcher. Complimentary breakfast. Cable TV. Gym. Business services. | 310 W. 7th St. | 573/642–9229 or 888/866–6661 | 6 rooms | $75–$85 | MC, V.

Romancing the Past Bed and Breakfast. An 1868 Queen Anne–style home with rose gardens and antiques is on a quiet side street within walking distance of Westminster College and several antiques shops. Complimentary breakfast. No TV in rooms, TV in common area. Hot tub. Bicycles. | 830 Court St. | 573/592–1996 | www.bbonline.com/mo/romance | 4 rooms | $85–$105 | MC, V.

HANNIBAL

MAP 12, D3

(Nearby towns also listed: Kirksville, Macon, Mexico, Monroe City, Wentzville)

Founded in 1818, Hannibal is known worldwide as the boyhood home of author Mark Twain. He once said, "All that goes to make the me in me is this small Missouri village." Steamboats still dock at the riverfront, and much of the historic downtown looks exactly as it did in Twain's day, although since the Great Flood of 1993, a flood wall protects the area from the mighty Mississippi River that Twain so loved.

Information: Hannibal Convention and Visitor's Bureau | 505 N. 3rd St., 63401 | 573/221–2477 | www.chamber.hannibal.mo.us.

Attractions

Adventures of Tom Sawyer Diorama Museum. The story of Tom Sawyer is reconstructed in 16 hand-carved miniature scenes from the book. | 323 N. Main St. | 573/221–3525 | $1 | Daily.

Becky Thatcher House. Mark Twain's sweetheart Laura Hawkins lived in this house in the 1840s. | 209–211 Hill St. | 573/221–0822 or 800/731–0822 | Free | Daily.

Cameron Cave. You can explore the interconnecting mazes of this memorable cave just south of Hannibal on a lantern-lit tour. | Rte. 79 | 573/221–1656 or 800/527–0304 | $10 | Early July–Labor Day, daily 8–8; Labor Day–early Nov., daily 9–5; early Nov.–early July, daily 9–4.

Haunted House on Hill Street. A wax museum with 28 life-size, hand-carved characters from Mark Twain's world in the haunted house he wrote about. | 215 Hill St. | 573/221–2220 | $3 | Mar.–Nov., daily 9–5.

Mark Twain Cave. This cave, just south of Hannibal on Route 79, is where Tom and Becky were lost, and where Injun Joe hid his treasure. There's a one-hour guided tour and a seven-minute video. | Rte. 79 | 800/527–1656 | $12 | July 4–Labor Day, daily 8–8; Labor Day–Nov. 1, daily 9–5; Nov. 2–July 3, daily 9–4.

★ **Mark Twain Museum and Boyhood Home.** The original two-story home in which Samuel Clemens spent much of his childhood is at the center of this site. | 208 Hill St. | 573/221–

9010 | $5 | June–Aug., daily 8–6; Mar., Mon.–Sat. 9–4, Sun. noon–4; May, daily 8–5; Apr., Sept., and Oct., daily 9–5; Nov.–Feb., Mon.–Sat. 10–4, Sun. noon–4. You can also tour **John M. Clemens Law Office,** where Mark Twain's father, who was Hannibal's justice of the peace in 1841, carried on his law practice. | 208 Hill St. | 573/221–9010 | June–Aug., daily 8–6; Mar., Mon.–Sat. 9–4, Sun. noon–4; May, daily 8–5; Apr., Sept., and Oct., daily 9–5; Nov.–Feb., Mon.–Sat. 10–4, Sun. noon–4. **Pilaster House and Grant's Drugstore** was the temporary home of the Clemens family in 1847. This is where Judge Clemens died. | 208 Hill St. | 573/221–9010 | June–Aug., daily 8–6; Mar., Mon.–Sat. 9–4, Sun. noon–4; May, daily 8–5; Apr., Sept., and Oct., daily 9–5; Nov.–Feb., Mon.–Sat. 10–4, Sun. noon–4. At the **Museum Annex** a video presentation provides insight into Samuel Clemens's life. | 415 N. Main St. | 573/221–9603 | June–Aug., daily 8–6; Mar., Mon.–Sat. 9–4, Sun. noon–4; May, daily 8–5; Apr., Sept., and Oct., daily 9–5; Nov.–Feb., Mon.–Sat. 10–4, Sun. noon–4.

Molly Brown House. This is where the unsinkable daughter of Irish immigrants was born. | U.S. 36 and Denkler's Alley | 573/221–2100 | $3 | June–Aug., daily 9:30–6; Apr., May, Sept., Oct., weekends 10–5; Nov.–Dec., group tours by appointment.

Optical Science Center and Museum. This 4,000-square-ft museum contains exhibits on vision, sight, and optics, a computerized light show, and hands-on displays. | 214 N. Main St. | 573/221–2020 | $2–$3.50 | Mid-Mar.–Oct., Mon.–Sat. 10–6, Sun. noon–6.

Riverview Park. This 400-acre park off Route 36 has scenic overlooks, hiking trails, picnic areas, and, of course, a statue of Mark Twain. | 2000 Harrison Hill | 573/221–0154 | Free | Daily 6 AM–10 PM.

Rockcliffe Mansion. This 32-room mansion on the river was the site of Mark Twain's last visit to Hannibal when he greeted 300 friends from the area. | 1000 Bird St. | 573/221–4140 | $5 | Mar.–Nov., daily 9:30–5; Dec.–Feb., daily 11:30–3.

Sawyers Creek. Enjoy an 18-hole miniature golf course, an arcade, and bumper boats at this fun park on the banks of the Mississippi River. Additional attractions include a huge year-round Christmas shop and a restaurant. | 11011 Rte. 79 S | 573/221–8221 | www.sawyerscreek.com | Prices for rides vary | Feb.–Dec., daily 10–8.

Tom and Huck Statue. Dedicated in 1926, this is believed to be the first statue in the country to honor fictional characters. | Main St. | Free | Daily.

SIGHTSEEING TOURS/TOUR COMPANIES

Hannibal Trolley. This old-fashioned trolley allows you to disembark and embark at several sites around town and is a good way to tour the historic district. | 220 N. Main St. | 573/221–1161 | $7 | Mid-Apr.–Oct., daily 9–5; Nov.–Apr. 15, by appointment.

Mark Twain **Riverboat Excursions.** These one-hour sightseeing cruises on the river Twain loved most depart from the foot of Center Street. | Box 288, Hannibal | 573/221–3222 or 800/621–2322 | www.marktwainriverboat.com. | $9; dinner cruises $26 | Memorial Day–Labor Day, daily, 11, 1:30, 4, 6:30; May, Sept., Oct. daily 1:30.

Twainland Express. You'll get an overview of the history of the area as you ride this custom-designed "train" on wheels through the historic parts of Hannibal and to the Mark Twain Cave. | 400 N. 3rd St. | 573/221–5593 | $7 | June–Aug., daily 10, noon, 1:30, and 3; Apr., May, Sept., and Oct., weekends 10, noon, 1:30, and 3.

ON THE CALENDAR

JULY: *National Tom Sawyer Days.* Fans have traveled from around the globe to Samuel Clemens's (a.k.a. Mark Twain's) hometown of Hannibal since the 1950s to participate in the fence-painting contest; the frog-jumping contest; the Tom and Becky look-alike contest; and more held each year on the July 4th weekend. | 573/221–2477.
OCT.: *Autumn Historic Folklife Festival.* On the third weekend of the month North

Main St. is transformed and storytellers, musicians, and artists will take you back to Mark Twain's world of the mid-1800s. | 573/221–6545.

NOV.: *Doll Show.* Teddy bears, antique dolls, and doll clothing are a part of the show and sale held at Hannibal Inn that raises money for the Shriner's Hospital. | 573/221–6610.

Dining

Hucks Homestead. American/Casual. Fill up at Huck's all-you-can-eat dinner buffet, which includes salads, hot entrées, and a dessert bar or try the house specialty: fried catfish. This huge restaurant is perfect for relaxed family dining. Dinner theater packages are available during the summer. | 14009 Clemens Dr., New London | 573/985–5961 | $7–$15 | AE, D, DC, MC, V | No lunch.

Logue's. American. Antique farm implements create a country feel at this homey establishment where you can order breakfast all day or enjoy other midwestern home cooking. Kids' menu. | 121 Huckleberry Heights Dr. | 573/248–1854 | $5–$10 | No credit cards.

LulaBelle's. American.Enjoy sandwiches, entrée salads, and homemade soups served in the dining room of a restored 1917 home. This quaint eatery re-creates the atmosphere of a Victorian tearoom. | 111 Bird St. | 573/221–6662 or 800/882–4890 | $9–$17 | D, MC, V | Closed Sun.

Lodging

Best Western Hotel Clemens. This downtown hotel within walking distance of many of Hannibal's museums has a three-story atrium with water fountains. Complimentary Continental breakfast. Cable TV. Pool. Hot tub. Gym. Laundry facilities. Business services, airport shuttle. | 401 N. 3rd St. | 573/248–1150 or 800/528–1234 | fax 573/248–1155 | www.bestwestern.com | 78 rooms | $67–$70 | AE, D, DC, MC, V.

Comfort Inn. This chain motel built in 1995 is behind Logue's Restaurant and has a woodland setting, though it's only 3 mi from Hannibal's historic district. Complimentary Continental breakfast. Cable TV. Pool. Hot tub. Exercise room. | 123 Huckleberry Dr. | 573/221–9988 or 800/221–2222 | fax 573/221–7382 | 48 rooms | $39–$99 | AE, D, DC, MC, V.

Fifth Street Mansion. This antiques-filled B&B in an 1858 home is within walking distance of the riverfront, Hannibal's historic district, and numerous shops and restaurants. And if you don't feel like walking anywhere, there are front and back porches and a back porch swing where you can sit and relax. Complimentary breakfast. No TV in rooms, TV in common area. Library. | 213 S. 5th St. | 573/221–0445 or 800/874–5661 | fax 573/221–3335 | 7 rooms | $65–$95 | AE, D, MC, V.

Garth Woodside Mansion. Mark Twain once stayed in this lovely home surrounded by 33 acres of rolling lawns, gardens, and trails. Complimentary breakfast. No room phones, no TV. No smoking. | 11069 New London Rd. | 573/221–2789 | garth@nemonet.com | www.garth-mansion.com | 8 rooms | $83–135 | D, MC, V.

Super 8. This chain motel 2 mi from Hannibal's historic district is across the street from Logue's Restaurant and next to a city park. Complimentary Continental breakfast. Cable TV. Pool. Business services. | 120 Huckleberry Heights Dr. | 573/221–5863 or 800/800–8000 | fax 573/221–5478 | www.super8.com | 59 rooms | $52 | AE, D, DC, MC, V.

Travelodge. This older basic motel is the best economy value lodging in the area, and it's only four blocks from the historic district. Amenities include a grassy picnic area and barbecue grill. Complimentary Continental breakfast. Cable TV. Pool. Business services. | 502 Mark Twain Ave. | 573/221–4100 | 42 rooms | $34–$75 | AE, D, DC, MC, V.

HARRISONVILLE

MAP 12, A4

(Nearby towns also listed: Clinton, Kansas City, Nevada)

Harrisonville, on the southern edge of metropolitan Kansas City, has the feel of a small town where everybody knows everybody and visitors are welcome. The towns-people are proud of their history as a Union outpost during the Civil War and of their town square with its antiques shops and café.

Information:**Harrisonville Chamber of Commerce** | 400 E. Mechanic, 64701 | 816/380–5271 | www.harrisonville.org.

Attractions

Sharp–Hopper Log Cabin. This was the only home in the county to survive destruction when a Civil War general ordered that all homes be destroyed to cut off guerrilla activities into free-state Kansas. | 400 E. Mechanic | 816/887–9323 | Free | Daily by appointment.

ON THE CALENDAR
SEPT.: *Cass County Barbecue Cook-Off.* Locals and visitors are invited to fire up the grill or smoker for prizes and great eats at the Mill-Walk Mall on the second weekend of the month. | 816/380–5271.

Dining

Pearl Street Grill. American. You can order up a hearty breakfast or lunch any day of the week and dinner on Thursday, Friday, or Saturday at this Harrisonville institution right on the town square. Try the biscuits and gravy for breakfast, grilled or deli sandwiches with homemade chips or fries for lunch, and dinner specials including prime rib on Friday nights. | 201 Pearl St. | 816/380–1121 | $8–$15 | AE, D, DC, MC, V.

Lodging

Best Western. There are several restaurants within walking distance of this chain motel 1 ½ mi from downtown and 35 mi from Worlds of Fun theme park. Complimentary Continental breakfast. In-room data ports, some refrigerators, cable TV. Pool. Playground. | 2201 Rockhaven Rd. | 816/884–3200 or 800/528–1234 | fax 816/884–3200 | www.bestwestern.com | 45 rooms | $45 | AE, D, DC, MC, V.

Budget Host Caravan Motel. This older motel on the edge of town has small but well-maintained rooms. Complimentary Continental breakfast. Some refrigerators, cable TV. Pool. Playground. | 1705 N. Rte. 291 | 816/884–4100 | 24 rooms | $31–$49 | AE, D, DC, MC, V.

HERMANN

MAP 12, D4

(Nearby towns also listed: Columbia, Fulton, Mexico, Wentzville)

Founded in 1836 by the German Settlement Society of Philadelphia (whose members were appalled at the loss of native customs and language among their countrymen in America), Hermann was intended to be a self-supporting refuge for German heritage and traditions. Like the Rhine River region of Germany, the area the Society chose for their town was teeming with grapevines, and for many years wine production was the area's main industry.

Information:**Hermann Visitor's Bureau** | 312 Schiller St., Box 104, 65041 | 573/486–2744 or 800/932–8687 | www.hermannmo.com.

Attractions

Cady Studio and Gallery. Artists Jack and Chris Cady design and hook primitive wool rugs. Their work also includes greeting cards inspired by German traditions, primitive floor cloths, garden sculptures, and paintings. | 179 Rte. 100 E | 573/486–3886 | www.pelzenichol-haus.com | Free | Weekdays 10–4, Sat. 10–6.

Corn Cob Pipe Museum. If you pass through the town of Washington on your way to or from St. Louis it's well worth your time to stop in this little museum which showcases what was once a big industry in the area. | 400 W. Front St. | 636/239–2109 | Free | Weekdays 8–4:30.

Deutschheim State Historic Site. Two homes and a winery preserve the history of the original German immigrants who came to this area. | 109 W. 2nd St. | 573/486–2200 | www.dnr.state.mo.us/dsp | Free | Tours daily 9:30, 11:15, 1, and 2:30.

Graham Cave State Park. Radiocarbon dating of the sandstone cliffs in this 357-acre park has revealed that people lived here more than 10,000 years ago. The park has camping sites as well as hiking trails and playgrounds. | 217 Hwy. TT, Montgomery City | 573/564–3476 | www.dnr.state.mo.us/dsp | Free | Daily.

Hermannhof Winery. The world's largest wine hall is part of a national historic site that dates to 1852. | 330 E. 1st St. | 573/486–5959 | Free | Sun.–Thurs. 10–5, Fri., Sat. 11–6.

Historic Hermann Museum. Located in an old school building, this museum tells the story of local German settlement. | 312 Schiller St. | 573/486–2017 | $2 | Apr.–Oct., Mon.–Wed., Fri., Sat. 10–4, Sun. noon–4.

White House Hotel Museum. Located near the old train station, this four-story hotel from the 1880s has been partially restored as a B&B inn and museum. | 232 Wharf St. | 573/486–3200 | Free | Apr.–mid-Nov., call for hrs.

Stone Hill Winery. Before the Civil War and days of prohibition this was the second-largest winery in the country. Today it produces 155,000 award-winning gallons annually. | 1110 Stone Hill Hwy. | 573/486–2120 or 800/909–9463 | www.wine-mo.com | Free | Weekdays 8:30–7, Sat. 8:30–8, Sun. 10:30–6.

Wohlt House 1884 Christmas Store and Gift Store. The Christmas store showcases an extensive selection of country- and Victorian-style Christmas ornaments, decorations,

INTRO
ATTRACTIONS
DINING
LODGING

THE CORN COB PIPE CAPITAL OF THE WORLD

About an hour's drive west of St. Louis in Franklin County, the town of Washington, once known as the Corn Cob Pipe Capital of the World, lies in the heart of Missouri's wine country. If you find yourself here you should be sure not to miss the Corn Cob Pipe Museum.

The museum is housed in a three-story brick building next to the railroad tracks along with the Missouri Meerschaum Company, which still makes 5,000 corn cob pipes a day for customers around the world. Here in the "Nostalgia Room" you can see old-fashioned pipes and production equipment. In the mid-1800s the pipes were a popular commodity and in 1894, a Dutch immigrant woodworker named Henry Tibbe became the first person to patent a process to mass-produce them. It was Tibbe who founded the Missouri Meerschaum Company and when several other manufacturers set up competing establishments over the years, Washington earned its nickname as the Corn Cob Pipe Capital of the World. The businesses thrived into the mid-1900s, but today, only the Missouri Meerschaum Company, with its 50 employees and 18 styles of pipes, remains.

© Corbis

silk wreaths, santas, angels, and other gifts. The gift store carries candles, glassware, decorator items, swags, picture frames, and doilies. | 415 E. 1st St. | 573/486–2394 or 877/339–0390 | Free | Mon.–Sat. 9–5.

AUG.: *Grape Stomp.* Take your shoes off and get your toes purple at Stone Hill Winery the second Saturday of the month. | 573/486–2221.
OCT.: *Octoberfest.* All four weekends in October see special events at the wineries and other venues in town. Come for the wine and beer and enjoy the party. | 800/932–8687.
DEC.: *Kristkindl Market.* The first weekend of the month brings carolers, hot cider, and an old-world style German holiday market to Stone Hill Winery. | 800/932–8687.

Dining

American Bounty. Contemporary. From the dining room or the patio, diners here have a view of the Missouri River. Try chicken coated in oats and sunflower seeds, grilled strip steak, or potato-encrusted chicken breast. Kids' menu. No smoking. | 430 W. Front St., Washington | 636/390–2150 | $14–$20 | AE, D, DC, MC, V | Closed Mon.

Char-Tony's. Italian. Try the linguine *tuttomare* (with shrimp, crab, clams, and mushrooms in your choice of sauce), or the chicken *Palermo* (charbroiled chicken breast in a butter-wine sauce with Parmesan cheese, peas, and mushrooms). Open-air dining with a garden view of the river. | 116 W. Front St., Washington | 636/239–2111 | $8–$19 | AE, D, MC, V | Closed Sun. and Mon.; no lunch on Sat.

Montague's. Barbecue. Mesquite-smoked barbecue with homemade sauce is Montague's specialty, but sandwiches are also available at this cozy storefront café. | 301 Schiller St. | 573/486–2035 | $2–$10 | D, MC, V | Closed Tues., Wed.

Reiff House. Contemporary. For romantic, candlelit dinners, try this 19th-century brick town house. Five-course gourmet dinner specialties include Maryland crab cakes, bay scallops with wine-celery sauce, and flank steak. Dinner is served each evening at 6 and 7:30, and reservations are required. On Friday and Saturday, you can enjoy Reiff House's outdoor Biergarten from 11 to 6, featuring bratwurst, wine, and brew. | 306 Market St. | 800/482–2994 or 573/486–2994 | Dinner $37.50 per person | D, MC, V | Closed Sun.

Vintage 1847. Contemporary. Six former horse stalls have been transformed into booths in the renovated 1840s horse stables on the grounds of the Stone Hill Winery that serves as home for this restaurant. Some great regulars on the menu are the peanut shrimp appetizer and the Wiener schnitzel entrée. Kids' menu. | 1110 Stone Hill Hwy. | 573/486–3479 | Reservations essential Sat. | $16–$21 | AE, D, DC, MC, V.

Lodging

Esther's Ausblick. The dining room, a screened-in gazebo, and two guest rooms in this 1940s riverside home have water views. Each room is decorated with different antiques. Complimentary breakfast. No room phones, no TV in rooms, TV in common area. Hot tub. Business services. No smoking. | 236 W. 2nd St. | 573/486–2170 | 4 rooms | $67–$75 | No credit cards.

German Haus Inn and Suites. This inn, just half a block from the Missouri River bridge, consists of two adjacent 1847 brick buildings that have been converted into handsomely adorned lodgings. Some rooms are quite large, and many have views. Complimentary breakfast. Refrigerators, cable TV. Hot tub. | 113 N. Market St. | 573/486–2222 or 888/942–PLAY | fax 573/486–4244 | 24 rooms | $45–$125 | AE, MC, V.

Hermann Hill Vineyard and Inn. Vineyards surround this elegantly furnished four-story inn, and its bluff location makes for an extensive valley view. The rooms are spacious. Complimentary breakfast. Cable TV. Exercise room. | 714 Wein St. | 573/486–4455 | fax 573/486–5373 | 5 rooms | $125–$225 | AE, D, MC, V.

Hermann Motel. This basic motel is located on one of Hermann's main streets within walking distance of Hermann's downtown sites. Cable TV. | 112 E. 10th St. | 573/486–3131 | fax 573/486–4244 | 24 rooms | $45 | AE, D, MC, V.

Lewis and Clark Inn. Twenty-eight miles east of Hermann on the banks of the Missouri River, this brick inn built in 1985 is in the midst of Missouri's wine country and just 20 minutes from Six Flags. Complimentary Continental breakfast. Cable TV. Business services. | 6054 Rte. 100, Washington | 636/239–0111 | fax 636/239–3657 | lwsclark@fidnet.com | www.justabouttown.com | 50 rooms | $55 | AE, D, DC, MC, V.

Lindenhof Bed and Breakfast. This 1850s B&B is in the very small town of Augusta, in the wine country about halfway between Hermann and St. Louis. Rooms are furnished with antiques. Complimentary breakfast. Cable TV. Hot tub. No smoking. | 5596 Walnut St., Augusta | 636/228–4617 | 4 rooms | $120, $135 room with basket of "goodies" and a bottle of wine from a local winery | MC, V.

Montague's Bed and Breakfast. Montague's simple rooms occupy the upper floors of a restored 1869 brick building downtown and have Shaker-style furnishings. The first floor of the building houses the innkeeper's casual barbecue eatery, and there's a bookstore next door. Complimentary breakfast. Cable TV. Library. | 301 Schiller St. | 573/486–2035 | 2 rooms | $85 | MC, V.

Nestle Inn Guest House. This big brick bungalow sits on a quiet bluff overlooking the Missouri River, near the wineries. Inside you can relax in comfortable sofas and wing-back chairs. The rooms have modern baths. Complimentary breakfast. Cable TV. No smoking. | 215 W. 2nd St. | 573/486–5893 or 888/841–STAY | www.nestleinn.com | 4 rooms | $115–$125 | MC, V.

Pelze Nichol Haus Bed and Breakfast. This 1800s German farmstead, which includes a smokehouse, German gardens, a wine cellar, and a barn as well as a guest house, is on the National Register of Historic Places. A primitive Christmas collection pays tribute to the B&B's name and Father Nicholas. Complimentary breakfast. No room phones, no TV. No smoking. | 179 Rte. 100 E | 573/486–3886 | www.pelzenicholhaus.com | 2 rooms | $92 | D, MC, V.

Schwegmann House. This 1861 inn has period furnishings and river views. Complimentary breakfast. Business services. No kids allowed Friday or Saturday. No smoking. | 438 W. Front St., Washington | 636/239–5025 or 800/949–2262 | fax 573/239–3920 | www.schwegmannhouse.com | 9 rooms | $85–$150 | AE, MC, V.

Windhomme Hill. If they are so inclined, visitors can lend a hand in the kitchen at this turn-of-the-20th-century inn that offers a complimentary dinner as well as breakfast. Rooms are decorated in a tastefully eclectic fashion. Complimentary breakfast and dinner. Pool. Hot tub. Bicycles. No kids. No smoking. | 301 Schomberg Rd., Marthasville | 636/932–4234 or 800/633–0582 | fax 636/932–4809 | windhill@socket.net | 6 rooms (2 with shared bath) | $165 | AE, MC, V.

INDEPENDENCE

MAP 12, A3

(Nearby towns also listed: Blue Springs, Kansas City, Lexington, Liberty)

The first settlers arrived in what would become Independence in 1827 and the town grew in tandem with nearby Kansas City. Like Kansas City, Independence was a starting point for those heading to the American West via the Santa Fe, California, and Oregon trails. In the 1920s the town proved itself to be a different sort of starting point when a country lawyer by the name of Harry S Truman opened a law office here. Today you can stop in at the Harry S Truman Library and Museum, as well as numerous other historic spots in the area.

Information:**Independence Chamber of Commerce** | 210 W. Truman Rd., 64050 | 816/
252–4745 | www.independencechamber.com.

Attractions

Bingham–Waggoner Estate. This 1855 home belonged to artist George Caleb Bingham and
was remodeled in the 1890s by the Waggoner family. There are memorabilia from both
families. | 313 W. Pacific Ave. | 816/461–3491 | $3 | Apr.–Oct., Mon.–Sat. 10–4, Sun. 11–4.

1859 Marshal's Home and Jail Museum. You can visit this restored 19th-century country
jail and marshal's living quarters or a one-room schoolhouse also on the site. | 217 N. Main
St. | 816/252–1892 | $3 | Apr.–Oct., Mon.–Sat. 10–5, Sun. 1–4; Mar., Nov., Dec., Tues.–Sat. 10–4,
Sun. 1–4.

Fort Osage. This 1808 fur-trading fort high above the Missouri River offers a living history
program and tours. You can reach the fort, which is about 14 mi northeast of Independence,
by taking U.S. 24 to Buckner, then heading north to Sibley. From Sibley follow signs for the
fort. | 105 Osage St. | 816/795–8200 or 816/249–5737 | $5 | Apr.–Nov., Wed.–Sun. 9–4:30; Dec.–
Mar., weekends 9–4:30.

George Owens Nature Park. A fishing lake, shady picnic areas, and hiking trails are some
of the highlights of this 85-acre city park. | 1601 Speck Rd. | 816/257–1760 | Free | Daily
dawn–dusk.

Harry S Truman Courtroom and Office Museum. This is the law office Truman worked in
before starting his political career. | Jackson County Courthouse, 112 W. Lexington | 816/795–
8200 or 816/881–4467; 816/795–8200 ext. 1264 (for tours) | $2 | Mar.–Dec., Fri., Sat. 9–4:30;
tours by appointment.

Harry S Truman Library and Museum. The official library of the 33rd president includes
such memorabilia as his famous "The Buck Stops Here" desk plate and the newspaper pro-
claiming "Dewey Defeats Truman." | 500 W. U.S. 24 | 816/833–1225 museum, 816/833–1400
library | www.trumanlibrary.org | $5 | Daily 9–5 (Thurs. until 9).

Harry S Truman National Historic Site (Truman House). The 33rd president of the United
States and his wife Bess moved to this home in 1919. The Victorian-style house, which had
been in the first lady's family, became known as the Summer White House. | 219 N. Delaware
St. | 816/254–9929 or 816/254–2720 | www.nps.gov/hstr/ | $2 | Tues.–Sun. 9–4:45.

National Frontier Trails Center. Through films, diaries, and exhibits including covered
wagons and period artifacts, you can experience the adventures and hardships of the pio-
neers. | 318 W. Pacific | 816/325–7575 | $3.50 | Mon.–Sat. 9–4:30, Sun. 12:30–4:30.

Pioneer Spring Cabin. This is an 1850s log cabin furnished as it would have been in the
late 1800s. | Truman Rd. and Noland Rd. | 816/325–7111 | Free | Apr.–Oct., weekdays 10–2.

Powell Gardens. This 835-acre garden includes waterfalls, perennials, and instruction pro-
grams. | 1609 N.W. U.S. 50, Kingsville | 816/697–2600 | $4 | Apr.–Oct., weekends 9–6; Nov.–
Mar., weekends 9–5.

Truman Farm Home. Only 5 acres and the family home remain of the original 600 acres
where the president worked from 1906 to 1917. Take Interstate 435 to U.S. 71 south to the
Blue Ridge Blvd exit. The farm is 1/2 mile from the exit. | 12301 Blue Ridge Blvd., Grandview
| 816/254–2720 | www.nps.gov/hstr | Free | Grounds are always open; tours: May–Aug., Fri.–
Sun. 9:30–4.

Vaile Mansion. If you've visited Pioneer Spring Cabin, this opulent 1881 mansion is a
chance to see how the other half lived. | 1500 N. Liberty | 816/325–7430 or 816/325–7111 | $3
| Apr.–Oct., Mon.–Sat. 10–4, Sun. 1–4.

World Headquarters Complex, Reorganized Church of Jesus Christ of Latter Day Saints. Organ
recitals, using some of the world's largest pipe organs, with more than 6,500 pipes, are offered
here. A 15-minute daily prayer for peace service begins at 12:30 PM, and children are invited

to the Peace Pavilion for interactive programs dedicated to the concept of peace. | 1001 W. Walnut St. | 816/833–1000 | www.rlds.org | Free | Mon.–Sat. 9–4:30, Sun. 1–4:30.

ON THE CALENDAR
SEPT.: *Santa–Cali–Gon Days.* Crafts, food, and music in Truman Square celebrate the history of the wagon trains that began their journeys here at this Labor Day weekend event. | 816/252–4745.
OCT.: *Independence Halloween Parade.* On the Saturday preceding Halloween (or Halloween itself if it falls on a Sat.), children and adults are invited to enjoy this annual event in Independence Square. Various clubs, organizations, and businesses participate. | 816/252–4745.

Dining
Courthouse Exchange Restaurant and Lounge. American/Casual. Enjoy steaks, chicken florentine, pasta primavera, seafood, and sandwiches in this spacious, traditional restaurant. It's downtown, near the courthouse. | 113 W. Lexington St. | 816/252–0344 | $9–$23 | D, DC, MC, V.

Garozzo's Due. Italian. Autographed pictures of celebrities fill the walls at this restaurant serving such dishes as Chicken spiedini (chicken breaded, skewered, charbroiled, then finished with olive oil, garlic, lemon, and herbs). Kids' menu. | 12801 E. U.S. 40 | 816/737–2400 | $10–$25 | AE, D, DC, MC, V.

Rheinland. German. German music and a large collection of beer steins and plates complement such popular German dishes as sauerbraten. Entertainment on weekends. Kids' menu. Beer and wine only. | 208 N. Main St. | 816/461–5383 | $10–$22 | AE, D, DC, MC, V | Closed Sun.

Tippin's. American. You can enjoy a quiche, a burger, shepherd's pie, or chicken fingers in this modern, airy restaurant with booths for dining and floor-to-ceiling windows. Kids' menu. | 2931 S. Noland Rd. | 816/252–8890 | $8–$15 | AE, D, DC, MC, V.

V's Italiano Ristorante. Italian. Entrées such as lasagna and fettuccine alfredo served by candlelight. Buffet lunch. Kids' menu. Sunday brunch. | 10819 E. U.S. 40 | 816/353–1241 | $9–$22 | AE, D, DC, MC, V.

Lodging
Adams Mark Hotel. This high-rise hotel is across from the Truman Sports Complex and has comfortable and spacious rooms. 2 restaurants, bar, room service. In-room data ports, cable TV. 2 pools. Hot tub, sauna. Laundry service. Business services, free parking. | 9103 E. 39th St. | 816/737–0200 | fax 816/373–3312 | 374 rooms | $99–$129 | AE, D, DC, MC, V.

Howard Johnson. This 1960s HoJo is just minutes away from two local malls with several restaurant options and a 15-minute drive to either the Harry S Truman Library and Museum or the Worlds of Fun theme park. Complimentary Continental breakfast. In-room refrigerators, cable TV. 2 pools. Hot tub, 2 saunas. Business services. Pets allowed. | 4200 S. Noland Rd. | 816/373–8856 or 800/338–3752 | fax 816/373–3312 | 171 rooms, 2 suites | $80–$90 | AE, D, DC, MC, V.

Red Roof Inn. This chain hotel, built in 1975, is a 15-min drive from Truman's home. Cable TV. Business services. Pets allowed. | 13712 E. 42nd Terr. | 816/373–2800 or 800/RED–ROOF | fax 816/373–0067 | www.redroof.com | 108 rooms | $50–$75 | AE, D, DC, MC, V.

Serendipity Bed and Breakfast. Antique walnut furniture, antique rugs, and period lighting evoke the stately past of this three-story brick home built in 1887. Collections of Victorian children's books, toys, china, and glassware add to the flavor. An overnight stay comes with a 1920s car ride (weather permitting) and if you stay here you'll be just three blocks from the National Frontier Trails Center. Complimentary breakfast. In-room TV. Laundry facilities. Pets allowed. | 116 S. Pleasant St. | 816/833–4719 or 800/203–4299 | fax 816/833–4719 | www.bbhost.com/serendipitybb | 6 rooms | $45–$85 | D, MC, V.

Woodstock Bed and Breakfast. From the Wedgewood Suite, with its sleigh bed and col-lection of Wedgewood plates, to the Blue Oasis with a Balinese teak marriage bed with a handmade canopy, wheels, and a secret compartment, each named room or suite in this B&B has a distinct character. Complimentary breakfast. In-room refrigerators, some in-room hot tubs, cable TV, in-room VCRs. Airport shuttle. No smoking. | 1212 W. Lexington St. | 816/833–2233 or 800/276–5202 | www.independence-missouri.com | 8 rooms, 3 suites | $69–$185 | AE, D, MC, V.

JAMESPORT

MAP 12, B2

(Nearby towns also listed: Bethany, Cameron, Chillicothe, Kearney)

Long just a sleepy farming community, Jamesport took on a new life in the 1950s when seven Amish families bought land near town and established what has become the largest Amish settlement in Missouri, with more than 1,200 people. Today the town is full of antiques and crafts stores, and bakeries and restaurants run by the Mennon-ites, who have also settled in the area.

Information: **Jamesport Society** | Box 215, 64648 | 660/684–6146 | www.jamesport-mo.com.

Attractions

1889 Squirrel Cage Jail. This octagon-shape jail was one of only three built in the coun-try. The cellblock rotates, and prisoners are confined by stone walls instead of bars. Because there is no way out of this type of jail, prisoners have, in the past, died in fires, and the jails are therefore no longer made. | W. Jackson St., Gallatin | 660/663–2154 | Free | May–Aug., Wed.–Fri. 9–4; Sept.–Apr., by appointment.

J. C. Penney Boyhood Home and Museum. Penney's three-room childhood home has been moved to town from its farm site and now is just a block from the museum explaining his contribution to American retailing. | 312 N. Davis St., Hamilton | 816/583–2168 | $3 home; museum free | Weekdays 8–4, Sat. 1–5.

ON THE CALENDAR
FEB.: *Winter Festival.* No matter what the weather, this downtown arts-and-crafts show with demonstrations of spinning, weaving, quilting, and more goes on. | 660/684–6146.
MAY: *May Days Festival.* Jamesport celebrates Mother's Day weekend with a car show, flea market, and crafts show. | 660/684–6146.
SEPT.: *Heritage Days.* Demonstrations of such old-time arts and skills as horseshoeing and spinning are held in Festival Park downtown on the last weekend of the month. | 660/684–6146.

Dining
Gingerich Dutch Pantry. American. This Amish restaurant has cedar walls and white wooden tables and serves traditional American fare like hamburgers, fried chicken, and mashed pota-toes. The real specialty is the Amish dinner: roast beef, mashed potatoes, schnitzel beans, and pepper slaw. | Hwy. F and Main St. | 660/684–6212 | $6–$8 | AE, D, MC, V | Closed Sun.

Lodging
Country Colonial Bed and Breakfast. This 1865 white clapboard B&B was originally constructed as a hotel. Antiques fill the rooms; the Veranda Room has a canopy bed adorned with lace and a copper bath, not to mention access to the lovely second-story verandah. Activities include tours of the Amish countryside in the proprietors' horse and carriage. Complimentary

breakfast. No room phones, TV in common area. No pets. No kids under 12. No smoking. | 106 E. Main St. | 660/684–6711 or 800/579–9248 | fax 660/684–6682 | info@jamesport-mo.com | www.jamesport-mo.com/countrycolonialnl | 3 rooms | $65–$85 | D, MC, V.

JEFFERSON CITY

MAP 12, C4

(Nearby towns also listed: Columbia, Fulton, Lake Ozark, Osage Beach)

The town planners who began building Jefferson City, known as "Jeff" or "Jeff City" to most Missourians, in the 1820s always had it in mind that this would be the state capital. In fact, they completed the first capitol building in 1826. But for nearly 100 years, until a vote of the people settled the squabble in 1911, towns all over mid-Missouri competed for the right to be home to the state government.

During the Civil War, Jeff City, like Missouri itself, was divided in sympathy. Governor Claiborn Fox Jackson called for secession but then had to flee when General Nathaniel Lyon claimed the city for the Union. Jefferson City was slow in recovering from the war, and not until the 1880s did industry find its way here. Electric lights were installed, a waterworks system was completed, and in 1896 a bridge was built across the Missouri River. This structure was replaced in 1955 by the bridge now in use. In 1991, to accommodate increased traffic, the old bridge was refurbished, and a new bridge was built in mirror image.

JEFFERSON CITY

INTRO
ATTRACTIONS
DINING
LODGING

TRANSPORTATION INFORMATION

Airports: Corporate and private aircraft provide the majority of traffic at the small **Jefferson City Memorial Airport** (501 Airport Rd. | 573/534–6469), located near the capital. General and corporate aviation use **Columbia Regional Airport** (1100 S. Airport Dr., Columbia | 573/874–7508), which is serviced by commuter airlines flying to St. Louis, Chicago, Kansas City, and Dallas.

Jefferson City's **Amtrak** station is one block from the capitol building, and is one of four stops in Missouri (101 Jefferson St. | 800/872–0008).
Intra-city Transit: Jefferson City Transit (573/634–6477) serves the capitol district and downtown area, and also provides service to Osage Beach.

Information: **Jefferson City Chamber of Commerce and Tourism** | 213 Adams St., Box 776 | 573/634–3616 | www.visitjeffersoncity.org.

ART AND ARCHITECTURE

Governor's Mansion. This landmark has been the home to first families for more than 100 years and is a highlight of any tour to the capital city. | 100 Madison St. | 573/751–4141 | www.jcchamber.org | Free | Jan.–July and Sept.–Nov., Tues., Thurs. 10–noon; tours by appointment.

Jefferson Landing State Historic Site. This is one of the few remaining 19th-century river landings. Two buildings tell of the time when this was a busy point of commerce that kept Jefferson City alive. | 100 block of Jefferson St. | 573/751–3475 | www.dnr.state.mo.us/dsp | Free | Daily 10–4.

State Capitol. High on a bluff and visible for miles, this is the third building to house the legislature in Jefferson City. There are Thomas Hart Benton murals on the first floor and a statue of Ceres, the goddess of agriculture, adorns the dome. Tours are conducted hourly. | High St. | 573/751–4127 | www.jcchamber.org/dtsites | Free | Daily 8–5. Civil War artifacts, Jesse James memorabilia, and other fascinating features of state history fill half of the **Missouri State Museum** on the first floor of the capitol. The remaining section is devoted to the state's natural resources. | High St. | 573/751–4127 | Free | Daily 8–5.

BEACHES, PARKS, AND NATURAL SIGHTS

Lake of the Ozarks. The Lake of the Ozarks was formed with the creation of Bagnell Dam in 1932. The lake stretches 92 mi across central Missouri, creating unequaled fishing, boating, and outdoor sports opportunities. The central location of this 54,000-acre lake and the 1,150 mi of wooded shoreline make it a popular vacation destination. | 5815 Rte. 54, (shoreline information booth) | 573/348–1599 or 800/386–5253 | www.funlake.com | Free | Daily; information booth weekdays 8–5.

CULTURE, EDUCATION, AND HISTORY

Missouri State Information Center. Houses numerous records and archives, as well as the state library and the Wolfner Library for the Blind. | 600 W. Main St. | 573/751–2000 | Free | Weekdays 8–5.

Veterans Memorial. A row of obelisks, together with a waterfall and pool, commemorates the sacrifice made by soldiers in each of the national wars. The memorial is behind the capitol, beside the river. | Riverside of the Capitol Complex | 573/751–2854 | Free | Daily.

MUSEUMS

Cole County Historical Society Museum. A display of inaugural ball gowns of the First Ladies of Missouri is the highlight here. | 109 Madison St. | 573/635–1850 | $2 | Feb.–Dec., Tues.–Sat. 1–3; tours by appointment.

ON THE CALENDAR

MAR.: *Spring Ice Show.* Ice dancers perform at Washington Park Ice Arena, mid-Missouri's only indoor ice rink, during this 3-day-long festival. | 573/634–6482.
DEC.: *Candlelight Tours of the Governor's Mansion.* The governor's home is decorated for the holidays and open to the public for two days early in December. | 573/751–7929.

WALKING TOUR

Capitol District (approximately 3 hrs)
This tour begins at the focal point of Jefferson City, the **State Capitol,** located at Broadway and High Street. Guided tours are given every day on the hour, and you are free to explore the museum on the first floor on your own. If you do not take a tour of the building, at least take time to admire the Thomas Hart Benton murals on the walls in the capitol foyer.

From the front steps of the capitol, turn right for a view of the All Missouri Veterans Memorial. Dedicated in 1991, the memorial features a limestone colonnade, terraced waterfall, and reflecting pool. If you take a few steps farther to your right, you will enter the grounds of the **Jefferson Landing State Historic Site.** Two buildings here, the Lohman Building and the Union Hotel, stand as a record of the time when this was a vital river landing that contributed to the growth of the city.

After touring the landing site, return to the grounds' front entrance and turn right. You will see the Governor's Gardens, a public garden filled with roses, sculptures, and walking paths. The backdrop of this beautiful garden is the **Governor's Mansion,** a Renaissance Revival mansion built in 1871. Tours are offered only on Thursdays, or by appointment.

Continuing to your right and crossing Madison Street, you will come to the **Cole County Historical Society Museum,** 109 Madison Street. Many items relevant to the county's development—from Civil War artifacts to inaugural ball gowns—are on display here.

At this point, retrace your steps back along east Capitol Drive three blocks until you intersect Broadway. Turn left one block to High Street and turn left again. Here you will find the Harry S Truman Office Building. For a soft drink or light refreshment, visit the cafeteria in the lobby and relax in the three-story atrium.

Leaving the office building, continue left on High Street to Missouri Boulevard. Turn right on Missouri and travel one block to West Main Street. Turn left and go to the **Missouri State Information Center,** located at 600 West Main Street, where you will find numerous records and archives, the state library, and the Wolfner Library for the Blind.

Upon leaving the Information Center, turn to your right and return to the parking lot in front of the **State Capitol** building where your tour started.

Dining

INEXPENSIVE

Veit's. American. Settle in to a meal of fried chicken, ham, or roast beef at this onetime 1920s truck stop that still has old-fashioned gas pumps outside for decoration and pictures of past owners on the walls. Kids' menu. | 2001 Missouri Blvd. | 573/635–1213 | $8–$15 | AE, D, DC, MC, V | Closed Sun.

MODERATE

Top of the Round. American. This hotel restaurant with wraparound windows designed to provide panoramic views of the city and capitol building from the 13th floor serves such standards as prime rib, smoked chicken, and smoked biscuits. Kids' menu. Sunday brunch. | 422 Monroe | 573/636–5101, ext. 2127 | $13–$15 | AE, D, DC, MC, V.

EXPENSIVE

Madison's Café. Italian. A relaxed restaurant with antique furnishings serving such nightly specials as chicken *agee,* chicken served in a piccata sauce with fresh mushrooms, cheese, ham, fresh broccoli, and a touch of red pepper, and an exceptional Châteaubriand for two. Kids' menu. | 216 Madison St. | 573/634–2988 | $14–$45 | AE, D, DC, MC, V | Closed Sun.

Lodging

MODERATE

Best Western Inn. This chain hotel, owned and operated by the same family for two generations, is a 5-minute drive from downtown. Restaurant, bar (with entertainment), complimentary Continental breakfast, room service. In-room data ports, cable TV. Pool. Hot tub. Gym. Laundry service. Business services. | 1937 Christy Dr. | 573/635–4175 or 800/528–1234 | fax 573/635–6769 | www.bestwestern.com/innjeffersoncity | 79 rooms, 5 suites | $69–$100 | AE, D, DC, MC, V.

Hotel de Ville. Just four blocks from the State Capitol and Jeff City's business district this European-style hotel with a New Orleans flair was built in 1967 and renovated in 2000. Restaurant, bar, room service. Cable TV. Pool. Business services. | 319 W. Miller St. | 573/636–5231 | fax 573/636–5260 | 98 rooms | $73 | AE, D, DC, MC, V.

Huber's Ferry Bed and Breakfast. Hospitality is lavished on you at this B&B, which is perched on a bluff overlooking the Osage and Maries rivers (12 mi east of Jefferson City). This 1881 home was built by one of the area's early German settlers and is on the National Register of Historic Places. The rooms are appointed with antiques and are graced with fresh flowers. Manicured lawns and lush gardens surround the inn. Complimentary breakfast. No room phones, TV in common area. No pets. No smoking. | Junction of Hwys. 50 east and 635; Country Rd. 501 | 573/455–2979 or 877/454–2979 | fax 573/455–9806 | 4 rooms | $65–$80 | D, MC, V.

Jefferson Inn. Floral wallpaper, lace curtains, and handsome antiques give this inn a Victorian flourish. Upon your arrival you will be served complimentary drinks and snacks in front of the common room's brick-and-marble fireplace. The inn is just six blocks from the capitol. Complimentary breakfast. Cable TV, in-room VCRs, some room phones. Hot tub. Pets allowed. No kids under 6. No smoking. | 801 High St. | 573/635–7196 or 800/530–5009 | jeffersoninn@aol.com | 4 rooms | $65–$125 | AE, D, MC, V.

Ramada Inn. This chain hotel is on a commercial strip about a five-minute drive from Jefferson City's business district and the State Capitol. Restaurant, bar (with entertainment), room service. Some refrigerators, cable TV. Pool. Gym. Business services, airport shuttle. Pets allowed. | 1510 Jefferson St. | 573/635–7171 or 800/272–6232 | fax 573/635–8006 | www.ramada.com | 233 rooms, 7 suites | $70–$140 | AE, D, DC, MC, V.

EXPENSIVE
Holiday Inn Express. This is one of a number of hotels on a commercial strip a five-minute drive from the State Capitol. Complimentary Continental breakfast. Microwaves, refrigerators, cable TV. Pool. Hot tub, sauna. Gym. | 1716 Jefferson St. | 573/634–4040 or 800/465–4329 | fax 573/634–4200 | www.basshotels.com/holiday-inn | 67 rooms, 3 suites | $80, $155 suites | AE, D, DC, MC, V.

VERY EXPENSIVE
Capitol Plaza. This upscale hotel, with its nine-story atrium and seven-story cascading waterfall, is popular with legislators, and has a great view of the Truman office building. Restaurant, bar (with entertainment), room service. In-room data ports, refrigerators, cable TV. Pool. Gym. Business services. | 415 W. McCarty | 573/635–1234 or 800/338–8088 | fax 573/635–4565 | www.jqhhotels.com | 255 rooms, 40 suites | $99–$250 | AE, D, DC, MC, V.

JOPLIN

MAP 12, A6

(Nearby towns also listed: Branson, Carthage, Cassville, Kimberling City, Lamar, Mount Vernon, Nevada, Springfield)

Although incorporated in 1873, Joplin had to wait until 1946 to find its place on the country's cultural map. That year saw the release of Bobby Troop's song "Route 66," which included Joplin in the refrain. The city gets a lot of mileage from its central location on the famed highway, but the area is also filled with Civil War history and Bonnie and Clyde lore, and is the birthplace of Thomas Hart Benton.

Information: **Joplin Chamber of Commerce** | Box 1178, 64802 | 417/624–4150 or 800/657–2534 | www.usachamber.com/joplin.

Attractions
Grand Falls. Grand Falls, part of Shoal Creek, is Missouri's only continuously running waterfall. The falls, which are in the 166-acre McCleland Prak, are a perfect place for picnicking, fishing, or just relaxing. | Riverside Dr. | 800/657–2534 | free | Daily.

Missouri Southern State College. Founded in 1937, this college offers a liberal-arts education and each year hosts an international piano competition. | 3950 E. Newman Rd. | 417/625–9300 or 417/623–0183 | www.mssc.edu | Free | Weekdays 8–5.

Museum Complex. Surrounded by a golf course and park, the two museums here offer a detailed look at early life in and around Joplin. | Schifferdecker Ave. and W. 7th St. | 417/623–2341. Exhibits at the **Tri-State Mineral Museum** tell the story of local lead and zinc mining. | Schifferdecker Ave. and W. 7th St. | 417/623–2341 | Donations accepted | Tues.–Sat. 9–4, Sun. 1–4. The **Dorothea B. Hoover Historical Museum** houses an extensive doll collection that helps portray the founding of Joplin and the Victorian period. | Schifferdecker Ave. and W. 7th St. | 417/623–1180 | Free | Mid-Jan.–mid-Dec., Tues.–Sat. 9–4, Sun. 1–4.

Post Memorial Art Reference Library. Reference books on art, architecture, and antiques make up the bulk of this collection. There's also a permanent display of antiques donated by the Post family. | 300 Main St. | 417/782–7678 | Free | Mon. and Thurs. 9:30–7:30, Tues., Wed., Fri., and Sat. 9:30–5:30.

Thomas Hart Benton Exhibit. Benton's autobiographical mural *Joplin at the Turn of the Century, 1896–1906.* | Municipal Bldg., 303 E. 3rd St. | 417/624–0820 | Free | Weekdays 8–5.

APR., NOV.: *A Touch of Country Arts and Crafts Show.* Twice a year, over the first weekend in April and the third weekend in November, some of the best historic crafts are demonstrated and sold here at Hammond's Trade Center. | 405/262–8666 | www.joplincbb.com.

SEPT.: *Heartland Doll Show and Sale.* Antique, handmade, and brand-name dolls, as well as doll clothes and furniture, are displayed in Hammond's Trade Center the last Sat. of the month. | 417/625–4789.

OCT.: *Barnyard Days.* This outdoor arts-and-crafts festival held the first weekend of the month at the Circle R Ranch, 9 mi south of Joplin on Highway 71, features vendor booths set up in barns, while outside there are demonstrations, a crafts show, and musical performances. | 417/451–3399.

Dining

Club 609. Contemporary. Exposed brick walls and hardwood floors add to the charm of this restaurant that occupies an old storefront. The eclectic menu includes lobster, sandwiches, salads, and the menu's most popular item: steak Oscar, a fillet topped with crabmeat, asparagus, and béarnaise sauce. | 609 Main St. | 417/623–6090 | $10–$25 | AE, D, MC, V | Closed Sun.

Kitchen Pass. American. Kansas City strip steaks and orange roughy (a white fish) served in a casual country atmosphere. Kids' menu. | 1212 Main St. | 417/624–9095 | $8–$15 | AE, MC, V | Closed Sun.

Red Onion Café. American/Casual. Set in a historic building, the dining room has 18-ft ceilings with exposed duct work, windows on all sides, and architectural artifacts on the walls. The menu includes pastas, steaks, bruschettas, and most popular of all: fried chicken salad. | 203 E. 4th St. | 417/623–1004 | $8–$15 | AE, MC, V | Closed Sun.

Wilder's Fine Foods Since 1929. Italian. A tin ceiling and vintage-looking menus emphasize the history of this restaurant known for such dishes as lobster ravioli and rack of New Zealand deer. | 1216 Main St. | 417/623–2058 | $13–$32 | AE, MC, V | Closed Sun.

Lodging

Baymont Inn and Suites of Joplin. This hotel is just off Interstate 44, 7 mi from downtown. It is surrounded by chain restaurants. In-room data ports, some microwaves, some refrigerators, some in-room hot tubs, cable TV. Pool. Hot tub. Gym. Pets allowed. | 3510 S. Range Line Rd. | 417/623–0000 or 800/301–0200 | 80 rooms | $62–$130 | AE, D, DC, MC, V.

Best Western Hallmark Inn. You can walk to several restaurants and area shops from this chain hotel, built in the 1970s. Offers standard, affordable rooms. In-room data ports, refrigerators available, cable TV. Pool. Playground. Business services, airport shuttle. Pets allowed. | 3600 Range Line Rd. | 417/624–8400 or 800/528–1234 | fax 417/781–5625 | www.bestwestern.com | 96 rooms | $40–$65 | AE, D, DC, MC, V.

Comfort Inn and Suites of Joplin. Just off Interstate 44 at exit 8B, this hotel is within walking distance of many restaurants. Complimentary Continental breakfast. In-room data ports, microwaves, refrigerators, some in-room hot tubs, cable TV. Pool. Gym. No pets. | 3400 S. Range Line Rd. | 417/627–0400 or 800/228–5150 | 80 rooms | $49–$169 | AE, D, DC, MC, V.

Drury Inn. This chain hotel built in 1990 is on a commercial strip within walking distance of an antiques mall and approximately 20 mi from Precious Moments Chapel Center. Complimentary Continental breakfast. In-room data ports, some in-room refrigerators, cable TV. Pool. Hot tub. Business services. Some pets allowed. | 3601 Range Line Rd. | 417/781–8000 or 800/325–8300 | www.druryinn.com | 109 rooms | $55–$90 | AE, D, DC, MC, V.

Hampton Inn Joplin. Just ½ mi from Interstate 44, this three-story chain hotel is in Joplin's commercial district, near the convention center. Restaurants and shops are within walking distance. Complimentary Continental breakfast. Some refrigerators, cable TV. Pool. Gym. Laundry service. Pets allowed. | 3107 E. 36th St. | 417/659–9900 or 800/426–7866 | fax 417/659–9901 | www.hamptoninn.com | 89 rooms | $75–$86 | AE, D, DC, MC, V.

Holiday Inn Hotel and Convention Center. This chain hotel is on a landscaped property on a commercial strip, and is just 3 mi from Missouri Southern State College. Restaurant, bar, room service. In-room data ports, cable TV. 2 pools. 2 hot tubs, sauna. Gym. Business services, airport shuttle. Some pets allowed. | 3615 Range Line Rd. | 417/782–1000 or 800/465–4329 | fax 417/623–4093 | www.basshotels.com/holiday-inn | 264 rooms, 8 suites | $65–$135 | AE, D, DC, MC, V.

Ramada Inn. Built in 1970 and renovated in 2000, this chain hotel is one of several on a commercial strip 2 mi southeast of downtown. Restaurant, bar, room service. In-room data ports, cable TV. 2 pools. Hot tub, sauna. Tennis court. Playground. Business services, airport shuttle. Pets allowed (fee). | 3320 Range Line Rd. | 417/781–0500 or 800/272–6232 | fax 417/781–9388 | www.ramada.com | 171 rooms | $54–$75 | AE, D, DC, MC, V.

Westwood. This wood-frame hotel is close to the hospital and 1 mi west of downtown. Cable TV. Pool. Laundry facilities. Pets allowed. | 1700 W. 30th St. | 417/782–7212 | fax 417/624–0265 | www.westwoodmotel.com | 33 rooms | $30–$45 | AE, D, MC, V.

KANSAS CITY

MAP 12, A3

(Nearby towns also listed: Blue Springs, Excelsior Springs, Harrisonville, Independence, Kearney, Lexington, Liberty, Parkville, Weston)

Kansas City is known as the "Heart of America," centrally located within 250 mi of both the geographic and population centers of the nation. Famous for steaks, barbecue, and the stockyards it once housed, Kansas City is also known to have more boulevards than Paris and more working fountains than any city but Rome. A fountain of some fashion is incorporated into the design of virtually all commercial building projects in Kansas City, giving Kansas City a second nickname as "The City of Fountains."

Established as a fur trading post in 1821, Kansas City played a major role in American history as a gateway for pioneers heading west along the Oregon, California, and Santa Fe trails. In the mid-1800s, settlers, missionaries, and traders began their overland journeys here or from nearby Independence and Westport. Several Civil War battles were fought here, and the 33rd president of the United States, Harry S Truman, began his political career here. Jazz musicians Charlie Parker and Duke Ellington played in the nightclubs of the 18th and Vine District, Walt Disney first sketched Mickey Mouse in a Kansas City garage, and Joyce Hall made his first greeting card here. Kansas City today is a vibrant, diverse place with a healthy mixture of art and agriculture, sports and technology, cowboys and haute couture. Those factors, combined with midwestern values, affordable housing, and variable seasons, make Kansas City one of the most livable cities in the country.

NEIGHBORHOODS

The **River Market** has been a central part of Kansas City since riverboats docked here on their way to the frontier. The first market house was opened in 1858 and today remains a popular destination on Saturday mornings for fresh produce and Sundays for art fairs. Trendy loft apartments in historic warehouses are drawing a young population back to the River Market. The district, located between 5th Street and the riverfront, is home to Kansas City's newest park dedicated in 1998, several brewpubs and ethnic restaurants, and the Arabia Steamboat Museum.

18th and Vine was in its heyday in the 1920s when Kansas City jazz made a name for itself. But, like much of the urban core, 18th and Vine fell into shambles in the late 1960s and '70s. Although devoted musicians would still make their way to the famous Blue Room, few others ventured to the area. However, restoration of the historic area began in the 1990s with the opening of the Jazz and Negro Leagues Baseball Museum, and with the making of the movie *Kansas City*, which focused on the music industry here.

When 19th-century settlers headed west, **Westport,** a tiny outpost miles from Kansas City and Independence, was often an important stop along the way. Here they outfitted their wagons for what lay ahead. In 1899, the growth of Kansas City overtook the town, but it retained its own character. Today, Westport is a vital arts and entertainment district for the metropolitan area. Art and poster galleries, trendy boutiques, and classic restaurants blend in harmoniously with rowdy bars, concert halls, and comedy clubs between Southwest Trafficway and Main, just north of the Plaza.

The **Plaza/Ward Parkway** area is home to some of Kansas City's most interesting architecture and certainly the city's oldest money. Designed in the 1920s, the J. C. Nichols Country Club Plaza remains one of the nation's premiere outdoor shopping districts. The Spanish-style architecture, reflective of Seville, Spain, is decorated for the holidays each year and draws hundreds of thousands of tourists. Some of Kansas City's most beautiful fountains are in this area, as is an abundance of outdoor art and fine restaurants.

TRANSPORTATION INFORMATION

Airports: Kansas City International Airport is located 15 mi north of downtown and is consistently ranked as one of the easiest major airports in which to make connections. | I–29 and I–435 | 816/243–5237.

Airport Transportation: KCI Shuttle is a van service between KCI and area hotels. | 816/ 243–5000.

Bus Lines: The Metro provides bus service to Jackson, Clay, Platte, and Wyandotte counties. | 816/221–0660 | www.kcata.org.

Information: **Convention and Visitor's Bureau of Greater Kansas City** | 1100 Main St., #2550 | 816/221–5242 | www.visitkc.com.

HEART FOREST

As you approach the Kansas City International Airport by air, you are greeted by a true symbol of America's heartland—the Heart Forest, a 22-acre heart-shape forest just south of the airport.

The Heart Forest, a project of the Kansas City Community Foundation, symbolizes a community that cares for each other and cares for the environment. Begun on Earth Day 1990, the Heart Forest now has more than 5,000 seedling trees growing toward maturity. Surrounded by a carpet of native grasses and wildflowers, the Heart Forest is visible for miles as passengers circle Kansas City.

Each Earth Day, and on dozens of weekends each year, volunteers clear out weeds and debris, remove dead trees, and every year plant new seedlings to continue the forest's growth.

© Corbis

Attractions

ART AND ARCHITECTURE

Cathedral of the Immaculate Conception. This Romanesque basilica and its gold-leaf dome can be seen for miles around Kansas City. | 411 W. 11th St. | 816/842–0146 | Free.

Folly Theatre. Once a burlesque hall and home to traveling vaudeville acts, the Folly today is home to more respectable forms of stage entertainment. | 300 W. 12th St. | 816/842–5500.

Grace and Holy Trinity Cathedral. It took seven years to build this church, beginning in 1887. The 72-ft-high bell tower was not completed until 1938. | 415 W. 13th St. | 816/474–8260 | Free | Daily.

Lyric Theater. First built as an Ararat Shrine Temple, this theater now hosts musical and dramatic productions. The local ABC television affiliate is located in the lower level of the building. | 222 W. 11th St. | 816/471–4933.

Thomas Hart Benton Home and Studio State Historic Site. Missouri's most noted artist lived in this home for nearly 40 years. | 3616 Belleview | 816/931–5722 | $2 | Mon.–Sat. 10–4, Sun. noon–5.

CULTURE, EDUCATION, AND HISTORY

Coates House Hotel. Once the most elegant hotel in Kansas City, the Coates House is now home to small offices and apartments. | 1005 Broadway | Free.

Fire Station No. 2. Law offices now occupy what was once the home of horse-drawn fire equipment and the Kansas City Fire Department. | 1020 Central | Free.

★ **Liberty Memorial.** A 217-ft tower and museum on a hill at the northern border of Penn Valley Park commemorate those who served in World War I. Renovations of the tower and museum began in May of 2000 and are expected to keep them closed closed until spring 2002; in the meanwhile the museum's collection can be seen at the Town Pavilion, at 12th and Main streets. | 100 W. 26th St. | 816/513–7500 | $2 | Tues.–Sun., 9:30–4:30.

Union Cemetery. Guided tours are provided hourly at this Civil War cemetery where more than 1,000 Union soldiers are buried. | 227 E. 28th St. Terr. | 816/561–6630 or 816/221–4373 | Free | Mon.–Sat. 8:30–3:30.

University of Missouri–Kansas City. This suburban campus of the University of Missouri system is home to the Henry Bloch Business School, the Missouri Repertory Theatre, and the State Ballet of Missouri. | 5100 Rockhill Rd. | 816/235–1576, 816/235–8652 tours | www.umkc.edu | Free | Tours by appointment.

MUSEUMS

American Jazz Museum. Interactive displays tell the story of jazz and its masters: Duke Ellington, Ella Fitzgerald, and Charlie Parker, among others. Hundreds of CDs are available for your listening enjoyment at the interactive studio and sound library. | 1616 E. 18th St. | 816/474–8463 | www.americanjazzmuseum.com | $6 | Tues.–Sat. 9–6, Sun. noon–6.

American Royal Museum and Visitor's Center. Museum of Kansas City history, agriculture, and the American Royal—the city's famed rodeo, horse, and livestock show. | 1701 American Royal Ct. | 816/221–9800 | www.americanroyal.com | $2–$3 | Daily 10–4.

***Arabia* Steamboat Museum.** A local family discovered 200 tons of sunken treasures of a pre–Civil War steamboat, buried in a field near the Missouri River. | 400 Grand Ave. | 816/471–4030 | $7.50 | Mon.–Sat. 10–6, Sun. noon–5.

John Wornall House Museum. This 1858 antebellum frontier home was restored to period style in honor of John Wornall, a prominent Kansas City citizen. | 146 W. 61st Terr. | 816/444–1858 | $3 | Tues.–Sat. 10–4, Sun. 1–4.

Kansas City Art Institute. The student gallery at this institution displays creative works in all mediums. | 4415 Warwick Blvd. | 816/472–4852 | www.kcai.edu | Free | Mon.–Fri., 8:30–5.

Kansas City Museum. The Challenger Learning Center and planetarium are popular attractions, as are exhibits and programs on science and technology. | 3218 Gladstone Blvd. | 816/483–8300 | www.kcmuseum.com | $2–$5 | Tues.–Sat. 9:30–4:30, Sun. noon–4:30.

Kemper Museum of Contemporary Art and Design. The works of Georgia O'Keeffe, Philip Pearlstein, and Robert Motherwell form the core of the collection in Kansas City's newest museum. | 4420 Warwick Blvd. | 816/561–3737 | www.kemperart.org | Free | Tues.–Thurs. 10–4, Fri. 10–9, Sat. 10–5, Sun. 11–5.

Negro Leagues Baseball Museum. Finally bringing recognition to the fascinating history of the Negro Leagues, this museum includes interactive displays, allowing you to actually hit against the likes of Satchel Paige and Buck O'Neal. | 1616 E. 18th St. | 816/221–1920 | $6 | Tues.–Sat. 9–6, Sun. noon–6.

★ **Nelson-Atkins Museum of Art.** Ranked among the top 15 museums in the country, the Nelson's prestige is based on its Asian collection and works of Monet. The Henry Moore Sculpture Garden graces the massive south lawn. | 4525 Oak St. | 816/751–1278 | www.nelson-atkins.org | $5, free Sat. | Tues.–Thurs. 10–4, Fri. 10–9, Sat. 10–5, Sun. 1–5.

Toy and Miniature Museum of Kansas City. More than 100 antique dolls and houses, toys, and other special exhibits. | 5235 Oak St. | 816/333–2055 | $4 | Mid-Sept.–Aug., Wed.–Sat. 10–4, Sun. 1–4.

SHOPPING

Antiques, Art and Design Center. This shopping district just west of the Country Club Plaza offers two square blocks of elegant antiques and gifts. | 45th St. and State Line | 816/531–4414 | Free | Tues.–Sat. 10–5.

City Market. Some of Kansas City's earliest history happened in this market, which is now the site of numerous ethnic shops and restaurants. | 20 E. 5th St., Grand St. exit off I–35 | 816/842–1271 | www.kc-citymarket.com | Free | Weekdays 10–5, weekends 7–4.

Country Club Plaza. The Country Club Plaza was designed in 1922 as the nation's first suburban shopping district and includes numerous fountains, sculptures, and murals, many with a Spanish influence. (The plaza was designed to resemble Seville, Spain.) More than 300,000 people show up on Thanksgiving night for the annual holiday lighting ceremony, which features more than 45 mi of Christmas lights. | 47th St. between Nichols Pkwy. and Madison Ave. | 816/753–0100 | www.kansascity.com | Free | Daily.

Crown Center. Something is always happening in this trendy three-story shopping center owned and operated by Hallmark Cards, Inc. There are musicals, parades, and holiday decorations. The covered ice terrace draws crowds in winter, as do the free outdoor Friday-evening concerts in summer. Two major hotels adjoin the facility. | 2450 Grand Ave., Pershing | 816/274–8444 | www.crowncenter.com | Free | Mon.–Sat. 10–6 (Thurs., Fri. until 9), Sun. noon–5. At the **Hallmark Visitors Center** you learn about the history of the greeting card business, the impact of the Hallmark Hall of Fame television specials, and more. | 2450 Grand Ave., Pershing | 816/274–5672 | Free | Weekdays 9–5, Sat. 9:30–4:30; closed early Jan. You will also find the **Kaleidoscope,** a hands-on kids' center operated entirely by Hallmark employee volunteers to encourage creativity in young people. | 2501 McGee St. | 816/274–8300 or 816/274–8301 | Free | Mon.–Sat., session hours vary. Another highlight for children is the **Coterie–Kansas City's Family Theatre,** where kids' programs are featured in an environment that encourages creativity. | 2450 Grand Ave., Pershing | 816/474–6552 | $6 | Weekdays 10–4, weekends call for hrs.

Hunt Midwest Subtropolis. This is one of the more unusual business parks in the world. More than 60 businesses are located in the 10-million-square-ft limestone underground. Tours and visitors are welcome. | 8300 N.E. Underground Dr. | 816/455–2500 | Free | Weekdays 8:30–5.

Westport Square. Once a stop for wagon trains heading west, this is now the place for clubs, trendy shops, galleries, and ethnic restaurants, plus the celebration of any major event in Kansas City. | 4123 Mill St. | 816/756–2789 | Free | Daily.

SPORTS AND RECREATION

American League (AL) Baseball–Kansas City Royals. Kauffman Stadium, home of the 1985 World Series Champions, was remodeled in 1999 and is famous for the fountains that light up after a home run. | Truman Sports Complex, I–70 and the Blue Ridge Cutoff | 816/921–8000 | www.kcroyals.com | $7–$17.

Benjamin Ranch. Trail, hay, and sleigh rides are a part of the fun here, as well as the junior rodeo and other seasonal activities. | 6401 E. 87th St. | 816/761–5055 | Free; horseback riding, $15 | Apr.–Nov., daily 8–5.

International Hockey League (IHL)–Kansas City Blades. This International Hockey League team has fared well against more established competition. | 1800 Gennesse St.; Kemper Arena | 816/842–5233 | www.kcblades.com | $10–$18 | Oct.–Apr.

Kansas City Wizards. The Wiz debuted in Kansas City in 1995 and local soccer fans have been excited to see them lead the league in conference titles and scoring most seasons since. | 706 Broadway | 816/472–4625 | www.kcwizards.com | $15 | Mar.–Sept.

National Football League (NFL)–Kansas City Chiefs. If you're interested in attending a game, you'd better plan on standing in line early, because this city is crazy about its football team. Arrowhead Stadium holds 70,000 and is always sold out. | One Arrowhead Dr., I–70 to the Truman Sports Complex | 816/924–9300 | www.kcchiefs.com | $45–$75 | Aug.–Dec.

Oceans of Fun. The Caribbean Cooler and the Surf City Wave Pool are highlights at this family water park. | 8300 N.E. Parvin Rd. | 816/454–4545 | www.worldsoffun.com | $24 | Memorial Day–Labor Day, daily 10–7.

Riverboat Gambling. Both the Argosy and Harrah's casinos operate gambling facilities on boats moored in the Missouri River. | Argosy: 777 N.W. Argosy Rd., Riverside; Harrah's: 1 Riverboat Dr., North Kansas City | 816/746–3100 Argosy, 816/472–7777 Harrah's | Free | Argosy: Sun.–Thur., 8 AM–5 AM; Sat., Sun. 24 hrs. Harrah's: Sun.–Mon, 11 AM–3 AM, Fri.–Sat., 9AM–4 AM.

★ **Worlds of Fun.** This entertainment park is home to the world's longest wooden roller coaster, the TimberWolf, as well as dozens of other rides and attractions. | 4545 Worlds of Fun Ave. | 816/454–4545 | $34 | Memorial Day–3rd weekend in Aug., Sun.–Thurs 10–10, Fri. and Sat. 10 AM–midnight; Apr.–Memorial Day and after 3rd weekend in Aug.–mid-Oct., weekends 10–8.

SIGHTSEEING TOURS/TOUR COMPANIES

Fiesta Cruises. The newest addition to the many Country Club Plaza attractions, these boats cruise the Brush Creek area. | Wyandotte and Ward Pkwy. | 816/741–1302 or 888/741–2628 | $6.50 | Mar.–Dec., Mon.–Sat. 11–9, Sun. 1–9.

Heritage Hikes. The Historic Kansas City Foundation provides guided walking tours that include access to many historic homes and buildings otherwise not open to the public. | 201 Westport Rd. | 816/931–8448 | Tours by appointment.

Kansas City Trolley. Lively narrated tours take you to a dozen Kansas City stopping points. There are pickup spots at Crown Center, Steamboat *Arabia*, Country Club Plaza, and other major attractions. | 816/221–3399 | $10 | Mon.–Thurs. 10–10, Fri.–Sun. 10–6.

OTHER POINTS OF INTEREST

Barney Allis Plaza. This spacious outdoor plaza is in the heart of the convention area and is the site of many celebrations and events in the city. | Between 12th and 13th Sts., and Central and Wyandotte | Free | Daily.

Board of Trade. From the gallery, watch the price of grains and other commodities fluctuate by the second, or visit an exhibit documenting the history of the Board. | 4800 Main St. | 816/753–7500 | Free | Weekdays 8:30–3:30.

Kansas City Zoological Gardens. The IMAX theater and the African exhibit make this zoo worth an afternoon's visit. | 6700 Zoo Dr. | 816/513–5700 | $6 | Daily 9–5.

ON THE CALENDAR

MAR.: *St. Patrick's Day Parade.* One of the largest in the nation, this St. Patrick's Day event is not always held on the 17th. The route begins in downtown Kansas City and proceeds north. | 816/931–7373.

JULY: *Kansas City Blues and Jazz Fest.* On the third weekend of the month three stages at Penn Valley Park host more than 40 local, regional, and international musicians including some of the biggest in the business. Past performers include Al Green, David Sanborn, Etta James, and George Benson. Educational workshops are offered as well. | 800/530–5266.

SEPT.: *Westport Art Fair.* On the first weekend of the month local artists fill Pennsylvania Avenue from Westport Road to Archibald Road with their work, displaying paintings, sculptures, jewelry, glassware, and more. | 816/756–2789.

OCT., NOV.: *American Royal.* This monthlong livestock and horse show and rodeo starts the first week of October and runs into the second week of November. | 816/221–9800.

NOV.–JAN.: *Plaza Lighting.* More than 42 mi of lights outlining Country Club Plaza are turned on Thanksgiving night and kept lighted through mid-January. | 816/753–0100.

WALKING TOURS

Art and Architecture of the Country Club Plaza (approximately 3–4 hrs)

The starting point of this Country Club Plaza tour is the much photographed **J. C. Nichols Memorial Fountain,** located at the intersection of J. C. Nichols Parkway and 47th Street. Dedicated to the developer of the Country Club Plaza, this fountain was sculpted in Paris by Henri Greber in 1910, and dedicated in Kansas City in 1960. Step south across 47th Street, turning left at the tennis courts to the statue of ***Massasoit,*** the Native American who befriended the Pilgrims. Cyrus Edwin Dallin was the sculptor. Retrace your steps across 47th Street and notice the traffic circle at 47th and J. C. Nichols Parkway. **Seville Light** is an exact replica of a theatrical fountain found in Seville, Spain, Kansas City's sister city. At this same intersection, look high and to the south for a view of **Giralda Tower,** the plaza's tallest tower, similar to one in Seville. The tower is home to carillon bells and the statue of ***Faith,*** sculpted by Bernhard Zuckerman. On the north side of the intersection, you will find the **Shepherd Fountain,** first acquired by the J. C. Nichols Company in 1948, but rededicated at this site in 1991. Moving west along 47th Street, a courtyard at 47th and Wyandotte is home to the **Fountain of Bacchus,** in honor of the Greek god. This 1911 sculpture was acquired from the Bromsgrove Guild in Worcestershire, England. While walking through the plaza, take note of the street lights, which were molded after those on Market Street in San Francisco. Turn left on Wyandotte, traveling a half block to Nichols Road. On the northwest corner is a statue of ***Ruth,*** an original by Pasquale Romanelli of Florence. Continue to travel west on Nichols Road to the intersection of Central Street. Turn right on Central Street, and look at the wall on your right. Along the lower level of this parking garage is a mural entitled ***Spanish Bullfight.*** The mural was created in Seville, Spain, specifically for this space. Returning to 47th Street, look up at the clock to your right. The three faces of this **Clock Tower** are Spanish scenes depicted in ceramic tile by artist Carolyne Payne. At the intersection of Wornall and 47th Street is the **Fountain of Neptune,** sculpted in England in 1911. To the right of this fountain is another impressive mural, ***Panorama of the Americas,*** a 1964 creation of Kansas City artist John Podrebarac. And just to the left of Neptune is a **Bronze Boar,** from the Marinelli Studios of Florence. Rub his nose for good luck, as nearly everyone walking the plaza does at one time or another. Retrace your steps down Central Street, past the bullfighting mural, to the corner of Central Street and Nichols Road. There in the northwest corner are two fountains, **Boy and Frog,** made of Verona marble, and **Allen Memorial Fountain,** in honor of a Nichols family relative. A few steps farther west on Nichols Road brings you to the intersection of Broadway, as well as the **Pool of Four Fauns,** which is from Brindisi, Italy, and was dedicated here in 1928. Turn left on Broadway, crossing Nichols Road, and you will see **Mermaid Pool,** a 300-year-old fountain with inlaid ceramic tile. Toss a few coins in the pool to benefit the children's hospital in Kansas City. Continue south on Broadway, looking for *Pamona,* goddess of the vineyards, by Donatello Gabrielli, dedicated in 1969. You are now at the intersection of Broadway and Ward Parkway, where you should turn left. Look into the median of Ward Parkway. There you will see *New Friends,* a bronze statue commemorating the 75th anniversary of the Country Club Plaza. Turning left, now walking east on Ward Parkway, you will encounter *Monkey Business,* a sculpture by Mark Lundeen, depicting an organ grinder and his pet monkey. Travel a few steps on to the east and you will find a bronze plaque in the sidewalk. The plaque comes from an editorial cartoon in *The Kansas City Star,* following the death of J. C. Nichols in 1950. Continue two blocks along Ward Parkway to J. C. Nichols Parkway. Turn left and walk two blocks where you will see the **J. C. Nichols Memorial Fountain,** where this walking tour began.

Dining

INEXPENSIVE

André's Confiserie Suisse. Swiss. Swiss favorites such as quiche lorraine, bread and cheese casserole, cheese pie, and chocolate torte served in a chalet-style building 15 min. south of downtown. No smoking. | 5018 Main St. | 816/561–3440 | $10.25 | AE, DC, MC, V | Closed Sun. No dinner Mon.

★ **Arthur Bryant's.** Barbecue. Although the city is packed with barbecue joints, this is a local favorite. The flavorful ribs and chops make up for whatever the eatery, 3 mi southeast of downtown, lacks in decor. Although there may be a line to order, it is well worth the wait. | 1727 Brooklyn Ave. | 816/231–1123 | $7–$16 | AE, MC, V.

Berliner Bear. German. Maps of Europe, ethnic costumes, and German plates adorn the walls while such dishes as Wiener Schnitzel and jaegerschnitzel, a pork cutlet served in wine sauce with peppers and onions, fill the tables and the diners here. You'll need to drive about 15 minutes south of downtown to reach this eatery. | 7815 Wornall | 816/444–2828 | $8–$13 | D, DC, MC, V | Closed Sun., Mon.

Canyon Café. Southwestern. This spacious two-level restaurant in the Westport Plaza area has 35-ft ceilings, arched windows, and old southwestern artifacts and offers such entrées as chile-rubbed tuna and choice cut steaks. Live Latin jazz on Wednesday and Sunday. Kids' menu. | 4626 Broadway | 816/561–6111 | $8–$20 | AE, D, DC, MC, V.

Chappell's Restuarant and Sports Mueseum. American. This downtown restaurant, best known for meat entrées like the shrimp and prime rib combination, serves lighter sandwiches and soups as well and houses the country's largest private collection of sports memorabilia. Kids' menu. | 323 Armour Rd., North Kansas City | 816/421–0002 | $6–$17 | AE, D, DC, MC, V | Closed Sun.

Classic Cup Sidewalk Café. Contemporary. With its Art Deco style and dishes such as Thai chicken pizza and beef medallions, this Westport Plaza area café aims for casual chic. Open-air dining on a back deck. Kids' menu. Sunday brunch. | 301 W. 47th St. | 816/753–1840 | $6–$25 | AE, D, MC, V.

Corner Restaurant. American/Casual. Sitting at a busy Westport corner, this quaint eatery serves a variety of sandwiches, salads, and breakfast items, the most popular of which are the "scramblefuls" and "potatofuls" (fried eggs or potatoes cooked with your choice of extras). | 4059 Broadway | 816/931–6630 | $2–$6 | No credit cards | No dinner.

D'Bronx. Delicatessen. You'll find this Kansas City eatery, ranked as the top deli in the nation in a survey by Zagat's, in a late 1800s building with tin ceiling, exposed brick walls, and old marble tables 10 minutes south of downtown. Pastrami sandwiches and hand-tossed pizzas share space on the menu with lasagnas, salads, and a famous apple pie. There's another D'Bronx in the Crown Center Shopping Mall at 2450 Grand. | 3904 Bell St. | 816/531–0550 | $5–$12 | AE, D, MC, V.

Harry's Bar and Tables. Contemporary. Two real favorites here are the salmon salad and the Kansas City strip steak. Open-air dining on a patio, bar, and two-level deck. Entertainment on the weekends. | 501 Westport Rd., Westport | 816/561–3950 | $6–$14 | AE, D, DC, MC, V.

Italian Gardens. Italian. Pasta is the specialty at this downtown Kansas City landmark in business since the 1920s. Kids' menu. | 1110 Baltimore | 816/221–9311 | $8–$16 | AE, D, DC, MC, V | Closed Sun.

Jazz. Cajun. Traditional Cajun fare mixes with a variety of specialty pastas at this lively and boisterous downtown eatery. Neon lights together with zydeco, blues, and jazz performances give it the appeal of a Bourbon Street nightspot. Live music is presented Wednesday through Sunday nights. | 1823 W. 39th St. | 816/531–5556 | $6–$12 | AE, D, DC, MC, V.

K. C. Masterpiece. Barbecue. Celebrity pictures hanging on the wall testify to the reputation of this restaurant's barbecue sauce which is sold around the world. Try the baby-back ribs. Kids' menu. | 4747 Wyandotte St. | 816/531–3332 | $9–$23 | AE, D, DC, MC, V.

Milano. Italian. Pasta, gourmet pizzas, and grilled dishes are the specialties here. Set in a glass atrium, the dining room has a view of Crown Center. | 2450 Grand Ave. | 816/426–1130 | $9–$19 | AE, D, DC, MC, V.

O'Dowd's Little Dublin. Irish. This pub 15 minutes south of downtown in the Country Club Plaza, offers such Irish specialties as County Cork stuffed pork loin, stuffed with bread crumbs, apples, celery, and peppers, or good ol' fish-and-chips. Open-air dining on a rooftop deck. Celtic music Sundays and Mondays; blues Tuesdays and Thursdays. | 4742 Pennsylvania Ave. | 816/561–2700 | $8–$15 | AE, D, DC, MC, V.

Otto's Malt Shop. American. Otto's 1950s theme extends from the furnishings to the food. Among the many burgers on the menu is the Fat Boy, a burger with jalapeños, cheese, and egg—enormously popular. And don't leave without trying one of the malts. | 3903 Wyoming St. | 816/756–1010 | $3–$6 | No credit cards | Breakfast also available.

Sharp's. American/Casual. Sharp's, downtown at the Brookside Plaza, boasts of an extensive menu of 150 items. It serves, for example, pastas, pizzas, steaks, stir-fries, and sautéed shrimp. The large, marble-topped bar is a popular place for drinks. | 128 W. 63rd St. | 816/333–4355 | $10–$16 | AE, MC, V | Breakfast also available.

Stephenson's Apple Farm. American. Stephenson's started as a fruit stand in 1900. Now it's a country-style restaurant known for its all-American menu. Try the hickory-smoked chicken or brisket. Open-air dining. Kids' menu. Sunday brunch. | 16401 E. U.S. 40 | 816/373–5400 | $7–$20 | AE, D, DC, MC, V.

Tasso's. Greek. This traditional Greek restaurant 15 min. south of downtown is known for lamb and beef kabobs. Entertainment. Kids' menu. | 8411 Wornall Rd. | 816/363–4776 | $10–$16 | AE, MC, V | Closed Sun., Mon.

MODERATE

Café Allegro. Continental. A romantic spot 10 minutes south of downtown serving such dishes as tuna tartare and rack of lamb. No smoking. | 1815 W. 39th St. | 816/561–3663 | $20–$28 | AE, DC, MC, V | Closed Sun.

Café Barcelona. Spanish. Try such Spanish specialties as paella or chicken chorizo (chicken, peppers, and chorizo sausage in a wine sauce), in a downtown dining room with a terracotta tile floor and a distinctly Spanish feel. Open-air dining on a patio with a view of downtown Kansas City. Entertainment Saturday. | 520 Southwest Blvd. | 816/471–4944 | $11–$25 | AE, D, DC, MC, V | Closed Sun.

Californos. Contemporary. Try the beef tenderloin or salmon at this laid-back restaurant with a California feel in trendy Westport, 10 minutes south of downtown. Open-air dining on multilevel, terraced decks. Pianist Saturday evenings. | 4124 Pennsylvania Ave. | 816/531–7878 | $11–$22 | AE, DC, MC, V | Closed Sun.

Cascone's. Italian. Celebrity photos line the walls of this intimate dining room on the north side of the city. Kids' menu. | 3733 N. Oak | 816/454–7977 | Jacket and tie | $18–$40 | AE, D, DC, MC, V.

EBT. Continental. Dishes including herb-encrusted swordfish and pepper steak are offered in what was once the atrium of an old-fashioned department store in South Kansas City. You can see the old elevator cages, now set amid palm trees and linen-covered tables. | 1310 Carondelet Dr. | 816/942–8870 | $19–$30 | AE, D, DC, MC, V | Closed Sun.

Figlio. Italian. The pasta served here is homemade daily. Other specialties include the Spiedini Dimanzo, a marinated tenderloin skewered with grilled vegetables. The upstairs dining room has a view of Country Club Plaza's Horse Fountain. Open-air dining. Kids' menu. Sunday brunch. | 209 W. 46th Terr. | 816/561–0505 | $8–$25 | AE, D, DC, MC, V.

Garozzo's. Italian. A casual dining room with celebrity autographs on the wall offers such dishes as tortellini Gina (tortellini stuffed with prosciutto, cheese, and beef), and chicken Spiedini (skewered chicken rolled in bread crumbs and grilled with your choice of marinade). | 526 Harrison | 816/221–2455 | $9–$25 | AE, D, DC, MC, V | Closed Sun.

Golden Ox. Steak. A steak house with a western atmosphere. Kids' menu. | 1600 Gennesse St. | 816/842–2866 | $10–$30 | AE, D, DC, MC, V.

Grand Street Café. Continental. Fresh fish, pizza, and pasta along with specialties such as the 47th Street chop, a sautéed pork chop with bacon mashed potatoes and homemade applesauce on top, are served in an English setting with a botanical theme in this café at the east end of Country Club Plaza. There are no walls separating the kitchen from the dining room, so you can see your food being prepared. Open-air dining. Kids' menu. Sunday brunch. | 4740 Grand Ave. | 816/561–8000 | $6–$27 | AE, D, DC, MC, V.

Hereford House. American. A Kansas City classic for steaks and barbecue with a western theme. Kids' menu. Free valet parking. | 2 E. 20th St. | 816/842–1080 | $14–$42 | AE, D, DC, MC, V.

Jess and Jim's Steak House. Steak. A casual western restaurant 15 minutes south of downtown known for its fillets. Kids' menu. | 517 E. 135th St. | 816/941–9499 | $12–$35 | AE, D, DC, MC, V.

Lidia's. Italian. Glass chandeliers hang from the vaulted ceiling of this 1891 freight warehouse just north of downtown. The menu selections are numerous and include Italian favorites like osso buco, calamari, and a pasta sampler. Try the fricos—cheese crêpes filled with shrimp, leeks, and potatoes. Reservations are essential on weekends. | 101 W. 22nd St. | 816/221–3722 | $12–$29 | AE, DC, MC, V.

Macaluso's. Italian/Continental. Rack of lamb and veal with white wine, butter, lemon, and capers are specialties at this casual, intimate spot a few minutes west of downtown. | 1403 W. 39th St. | 816/561–0100 | $18–$30 | AE, D, DC, MC, V | Closed Sun.

Metropolis American Grill. Contemporary. Specialties such as rosemary-scented smoked rack of lamb and wild mushroom strudel served in a Westport dining room with high-tech decor and pin-point lighting. | 303 Westport Rd., Westport | 816/753–1550 | $18–$25 | AE, D, DC, MC, V | Closed Sun.

Paradise Grill. Contemporary. A brightly decorated restaurant 20 minutes north of downtown serving such dishes as Paradise roasted chicken, roasted with honey and thyme then served with wild mushrooms and pepperjack scalloped potatoes. Kids' menu. | 5225 N.W. 64th St. | 816/587–9888 | $13–$22 | AE, D, DC, MC, V.

Raphael Dining Room. Continental. This roomy European-style dining room in Country Club Plaza is known for rack of lamb and such daily specials as fresh Chilean sea bass panfried and served with a sun-dried tomato cream sauce. Entertainment weekends. | 325 Ward Pkwy. | 816/756–3800 | $16–$30 | AE, D, DC, MC, V | Closed Sun.

Shiraz. Contemporary. Known for their roasted garlic-encrusted rack of lamb, this downtown restaurant has a casual atmosphere and eclectic decor, including brick walls, an open kitchen, and local art showings. | 320 Southwest Blvd. | 816/472–0015 | $12–$23 | AE, D, DC, MC, V | Closed Sun.

Smuggler's. Continental. Favorite entrées in this large, spacious dining room 5 minutes northeast of downtown include prime rib and cognac pepper steak. Salad bar. Entertainment most nights. | 1650 Universal Plaza Dr. | 816/483–0400 | $13–$24 | AE, D, DC, MC, V.

Velvet Dog. Italian. A supper club 5 minutes south of downtown that serves sandwiches, pizza, and pastas. Open-air dining. | 400 E. 31st St. | 816/753–9990 | $22–$45 | AE, D, DC, MC, V.

EXPENSIVE

Majestic Steakhouse. Steak. This historic midtown restaurant, in business since the early 1900s, still has its original hardwood floors and carved tin ceiling. Be sure to try the 34-ounce T-bone steak. | 931 Broadway | 816/471–8484 | $16–$42 | AE, D, DC, MC, V.

Papagallo. Continental. Paintings by local artists, linen table cloths, and candles set the tone at this intimate midtown restaurant praised in *Food and Wine Magazine* as among the best restaurants in Missouri. The extensive menu includes steaks, kebabs, veal marsala, and fresh seafood specials. Entertainment weekends. | 3535 Broadway | 816/756–3227 | $22–$45 | AE, D, DC, MC, V | Closed Sun., Mon.

★ **Plaza III The Steakhouse.** Steak. This classic steak house in Country Club Plaza is known for beef and veal chops as well as fresh seafood. Entertainment. Kids' menu. | 4749 Pennsylvania Ave. | 816/753–0000 | $18–$35 | AE, D, DC, MC, V.

Savoy Grill. Continental. In business since 1903, this old-world-style restaurant is known for lobster and such seafood specialties as blackened salmon, and for steaks. | 219 W. 9th St. | 816/842–3890 | $17–$53 | AE, D, DC, MC, V.

VERY EXPENSIVE

American Restaurant. Contemporary. Contemporary and traditional American dishes such as rib-eye steak and chicken breast with Thai peanut sauce and jasmine rice served in a midtown dining room with broad views of the Kansas City skyline. Pianist. | 2450 Grand Ave. | 816/426–1133 | $40–$65 | AE, D, DC, MC, V | Closed Sun.

Fedora Café and Bar. Contemporary. This downtown bistro has some unusual specialties including the ostrich rossini (ostrich fillets served with foie gras). | 210 W. 47th St. | 816/561–6565 | Jacket and tie | $40–$60 | AE, D, DC, MC, V.

Le Fou Frog. Contemporary. The menu at this River City Market area eatery offers three pages of classic French dishes with a contemporary spin, including daily specials and such favorite as the fillet stuffed with lobster and Boursin cheese sabayon. | 400 E. 5th St. | 816/474–6060 | Jacket required | $35–$60 | AE, D, DC, MC, V | Closed Mon., Tues.

Ruth's Chris Steakhouse. Steak. A dark wood–paneled downtown restaurant known for its fillets. Free valet parking. | 700 W. 47th St. | 816/531–4800 | $19–$58 | AE, D, DC, MC, V.

Lodging

INEXPENSIVE

Adam's Mark. Built in 1974, this cement high-rise hotel is across the street from the Truman sports complex. Sports fans will appreciate the statue of the baseball player Casey in the lobby. Restaurant, bar (with entertainment). In-room data ports, cable TV. 2 pools. Hot tub. Gym. Laundry facilities. Business services. | 9103 E. 39th St. | 816/737–0200 or 800/444–2326 | fax 816/737–4713 | www.adamsmark.com | 374 rooms | $89–$159 | AE, D, DC, MC, V.

Baymont Inn. This chain hotel is close to Kansas City's business district and less than 20 minutes from the Kansas City International Airport. It has a homey atmosphere complete with a fireplace in the lounge. Complimentary Continental breakfast. In-room data ports, cable TV. Business services. Some pets allowed. | 2214 Taney | 816/221–1200 | fax 816/471–6207 | www.baymontinn.com | 94 rooms, 8 suites | $70–$90 | AE, D, DC, MC, V.

Best Western Banister Hotel. This 1940s chain hotel sports Western theme paintings and a rustic decor. There's a restaurant across the street and Banister Mall is one exit away on the highway. Bar. In-room data ports, cable TV. Pool. Business services. | 6101 E. 87th St. | 816/765–4331 or 800/528–1234 | fax 816/765–9786 | www.bestwestern.com | 237 rooms, 3 suites | $70, $150 suites | AE, D, DC, MC, V.

Best Western Country Inn KCI Airport. Rooms at this chain hotel on a commercial strip five minutes from Kansas City International Airport have outside entrances. Complimentary Continental breakfast. In-room data ports. Business services, airport shuttle. | 11900 Plaza Circle | 816/464–2002 or 800/528–1234 | fax 816/464–2002 | www.bestwestern.com | 43 rooms | $68 | AE, D, DC, MC, V.

Best Western Country Inn. This chain hotel is on a commercial strip ½ mi from the Worlds of Fun theme park. Complimentary Continental breakfast. In-room data ports, cable TV. Pool. Business services. | 7100 N.E. Parvin Rd. | 816/453–3355 or 800/528–1234 | fax 816/453–0242 | www.bestwestern.com | 86 rooms | $68 | AE, D, DC, MC, V.

Best Western Seville Plaza. This chain hotel is four blocks from the Nelson-Atkins Museum of Art and within walking distance of area shopping, bars, and clubs. Complimentary Continental breakfast. In-room data ports, refrigerators, cable TV. Hot tub. Business services, free parking. | 4309 Main St. | 816/561–9600 or 800/528–1234 | fax 816/561–4677 | www.bestwestern.com | 77 rooms | $79–$109 | AE, D, DC, MC, V.

Chase Suites at KCI. This all-suites hotel is 3½ mi from Kansas City International Airport. Complimentary Continental breakfast. In-room data ports, kitchenettes, cable TV. Pool, wading pool. Hot tub. Gym. Laundry facilities. Business services, airport shuttle, free parking. Some pets allowed (fee). | 9900 N.W. Prairie View Rd. | 816/891–9009 | fax 816/891–8623 | www.woodfinsuitehotels.com | 112 suites | $69–$139 | AE, D, DC, MC, V.

Doanleigh Wallagh. There is a park with tennis courts across the street from this Georgian Federalist–style mansion which is just 1 mi from Crown Center. The owners offer complimentary wine and hors d'oeuvres in the evening. Complimentary breakfast. In-room data ports, cable TV. Hot tub. Business services. No smoking. | 217 E. 37th St. | 816/753–2667 | fax 816/531–5185 | 5 rooms | $105–$160 | AE, D, MC, V.

Dome Ridge Bed and Breakfast. The main attractions of this unique B&B are its forest setting and distinct geodesic dome architecture. Beneath the dome's many glass pentagons and hexagons are four guest rooms, three with private baths. A deck encircles the entire dome, providing ample access to the wooded landscape. The B&B is surrounded by 17 thickly wooded acres and is just outside the city limits. Complimentary breakfast. Some in-room hot tubs, cable TV, in-room VCRs (and movies), no room phones. Hot tub, spa. Hiking. No pets. No kids under 18. No smoking. | 14360 N.W. Walker Rd. | 816/532–4074 | fax 816/532–0992 | wnfaust@aol.com | 4 rooms | $70–$95 | No credit cards.

Drury Inn Kansas City/Stadium. Across the street from the sports complex, this chain hotel is just off Interstate 70 at exit 9. Reserve your room well in advance of any sporting event. Complimentary Continental breakfast. Some refrigerators, cable TV. Pool. Gym. Free parking. No pets. | 3830 Blue Ridge Cutoff | 816/923–3000 or 800/325–8300 | fax 816/923–3000 | www.druryinn.com | 133 rooms | $79–$89 | AE, D, DC, MC, V.

Embassy Suites. This chain hotel is 4 mi from Kansas City International Airport. Restaurant, bar (with entertainment), complimentary breakfast, room service. In-room data ports, microwaves, refrigerators, cable TV. Pool. Hot tub. Gym. Laundry facilities. Business services, airport shuttle. | 7640 N.W. Tiffany Springs Pkwy. | 816/891–7788 | fax 816/891–7513 | www.embassy-suites.com | 236 suites | $85–$144 | AE, D, DC, MC, V.

Hampton Inn Kansas City Airport. A mile south of the airport, this four-story hotel is just off the 112th Street exit of Interstate 29. Complimentary Continental breakfast. Some refrigerators, cable TV. Pool. Gym. Laundry service. Airport shuttle. No pets. | 11212 N. Newark Circle | 816/464–5454 or 800/426–7866 | fax 816/464–5416 | www.hamptoninn.com | 120 rooms | $82–$87 | AE, D, DC, MC, V.

Hampton Inn Kansas City Worlds of Fun/Executive Plaza. Two miles south of both the riverboat casinos and Worlds of Fun theme park, this hotel stands at the Executive Park Office Complex, just west of Interstate 435 at exit 57. Complimentary Continental breakfast. Some refrigerators, cable TV. Pool. Gym. Laundry service. Business services. No pets. | 1051 N. Cambridge | 816/483–7900 or 800/426–7866 | fax 816/483–8887 | www.hamptoninn.com | 134 rooms | $89 | AE, D, DC, MC, V.

Hampton Inn and Suites–Country Club Plaza. This chain inn is only a stroll away from Country Club Plaza's many shops, theaters, and restaurants. Complimentary Continental breakfast. Some refrigerators, cable TV. Pool. Gym. Laundry service. Business services, free parking. No pets. | 4600 Summit | 816/448–4600 or 800/426–7866 | fax 816/448–4610 | www.hamptoninn.com | 203 rooms | $109–$119 | AE, D, DC, MC, V.

Hilton–Airport. This Hilton is 3 mi from the airport, and about a 20-minute drive to the casinos and sports complex. Restaurant, bar, room service. In-room data ports, cable TV. Indoor-outdoor pool. Hot tub. 2 tennis courts. Gym. Laundry facilities. Business services, airport shuttle. | 8801 N.W. 112th St. | 816/891–8900 | fax 816/891–8030 | 347 rooms | $150 | AE, D, DC, MC, V.

Historic Suites. The flagship building of this upscale hotel nestled in the historic Wholesale and Garment District was built in 1889 as the Builders and Traders Exchange. Two other turn-of-the-20th-century pressed-brick and stone buildings complete the hotel which is just blocks from City Market, 2 mi from Crown Center shops and restaurants, and 5 mi from Country Club Plaza. Complimentary Continental breakfast. In-room data ports, microwaves, cable TV. Pool. Hot tub. Gym. Laundry facilities. Business services. | 612 Central St. | 816/842–6544 or 800/733–0612 | fax 816/842–0656 | www.historicsuites.com | 39 studios, 100 suites | $99–$120 studios, $120–$130 suites (with living room) | AE, D, DC, MC, V.

Holiday Inn Airport. This chain hotel is 2 mi from the airport. Restaurant, bar, room service. In-room data ports, some refrigerators, cable TV. Pool. Gym. Laundry facilities. Business services, airport shuttle, free parking. | 11832 Plaza Circle | 816/464–2345 or 800/465–4329 | fax 816/464–2543 | www.basshotels.com/holiday-inn | 196 rooms | $89–$125 | AE, D, DC, MC, V.

Holiday Inn Citi Centre. This historic downtown Kansas City hotel was built in 1925 in a style reminiscent of Europe's grand hotels with mahogany, Italian marble, and brass throughout. Restaurant, room service. Some microwaves, some refrigerators, cable TV. Gym. Business services. | 1215 Wyandotte St. | 816/471–1333 or 800/465–4329 | fax 816/283–0541 | www.basshotels.com/holiday-inn | 186 rooms | $109–$119 | AE, D, DC, MC, V.

Holiday Inn Express—Westport Plaza. Five minutes from the plaza, this six-story chain inn stands in the middle of Westport. In-room data ports, some refrigerators, cable TV. Laundry service. Business services, free parking. No pets. | 801 Westport Rd. | 816/931–1000 or 800/465–4329 | fax 816/561–0447 | www.basshotels.com | 109 rooms | $84–$104 | AE, D, DC, MC, V.

Holiday Inn Northeast. This chain hotel with a holidome is across the street from Worlds of Fun theme park. Restaurant, bar, room service. In-room data ports, cable TV. Pool. Hot tub, sauna. Laundry facilities. Business services, free parking. | 7333 N.E. Parvin Rd. | 816/455–1060 or 800/465–4329 | fax 816/455–0250 | www.basshotels.com/holiday-inn | 167 rooms | $105 | AE, D, DC, MC, V.

Holiday Inn–Sports Complex. You are right in the sports complex and just 4 mi from the zoo and 8 mi from Worlds of Fun theme park at this chain hotel. Restaurant, bar, room service. Some in-room data ports, cable TV. Pool. Hot tub. Gym. Laundry facilities. Business services, free parking. | 4011 Blue Ridge Cutoff | 816/353–5300 or 800/465–4329 | fax 816/353–1199 | www.basshotels.com/holiday-inn | 164 rooms | $79–$149 | AE, D, DC, MC, V.

Marriott–Airport. This chain hotel is right at the airport, just ¼ mi from the terminals and 15 mi from downtown. Restaurant, bar, picnic area, room service. In-room data ports, cable TV. Pool. Hot tub, sauna. Gym. Laundry facilities. Business services, airport shuttle, free parking. Pets allowed. | 775 Brasilia Ave. | 816/464–2200 | fax 816/464–5915 | www.marriott.com | 382 rooms | $124 | AE, D, DC, MC, V.

Marriott Country Club Plaza. This high-rise chain hotel is within easy walking distance of Country Club Plaza. Restaurant, bar. In-room data ports, some refrigerators, cable TV. Pool. Hot tub. Gym. Business services. | 4445 Main St. | 816/531–3000 | fax 816/531–3007 | 296 rooms, 28 suites | $129–$149, $150–$305 suites | AE, D, DC, MC, V.

Park Place. Some rooms in this 1970s motel in an industrial park a five-minute drive from Worlds of Fun theme park have views of a small lake. Restaurant, bar (with entertainment), complimentary Continental breakfast. In-room data ports, some refrigerators, cable TV. Indoor-outdoor pool. Gym. Business services, free parking. Some pets allowed. | 1601 N. Universal Ave. | 816/483–9900 or 800/821–8532 | fax 816/231–1418 | 227 rooms, 115 suites | $79–$89, $119 suites | AE, D, DC, MC, V.

Quarterage Hotel. This contemporary brick hotel with oak- and brass-trimmed lobby is in the Westport Historic District. The Nelson-Atkins Museum of Art and Country Club Plaza are within a five-minute drive, and the Kansas City Art Institute and the Bartle Hall Convention Center are 10–15 minutes away. Complimentary breakfast buffet. Refrigerators, cable TV. Hot tub. Business services, free parking. | 560 Westport Rd. | 816/931–0001 or 800/942–4233 | fax 816/931–8891 | www.quarteragehotel.com | 123 rooms, 8 suites | $89–$159 | AE, D, DC, MC, V.

Savoy Bed and Breakfast. Downtown in the garment district, this B&B was built as a hotel in 1888, and still has original tile floors and tin ceilings. You can walk to the convention center, which is just three blocks away. Restaurant, bar, complimentary breakfast. Cable TV. In-room data ports. Business services, free parking. | 219 W. 9th St. | 816/842–3575 | 22 suites | $79–$120 | AE, D, DC, MC, V.

Southmoreland. Rooms in this 1913 Colonial Revival–style mansion honor notable Kansas City citizens. The Thomas Hart Benton Room has Mission oak furniture favored by the artist, and the Satchel Paige Room resembles a sportsman's lodge. Complimentary breakfast. In-room data ports, no TV in rooms, TV in common area. Business services, free parking. | 116 E. 46th St. | 816/531–7979 | fax 816/531–2407 | 12 rooms | $100–$235 | AE, MC, V.

Wyndham Garden. This chain hotel is a five-minute drive from Kansas City International Airport in an area of hotels and airport businesses. Some refrigerators, cable TV. Pool. Hot tub. Gym. Laundry facilities. Business services, airport shuttle, free parking. | 11828 N.W. Plaza Circle | 816/464–2423 or 800/258–2466 | fax 816/464–2560 | www.wyndham.com | 138 rooms, 8 suites | $105, $124 suites | AE, D, DC, MC, V.

MODERATE

Doubletree. This downtown Kansas City hotel, renovated in 1997, has a Midwestern Mission style. It's within walking distance of the theater and business districts, and its circular Penthouse Ballroom, used for special events, offers memorable views of the city skyline. Restaurant, bar. In-room data ports, some microwaves, refrigerators, cable TV. Pool. Gym. Business services. | 1301 Wyandotte St. | 816/474–6664 | fax 816/474–0424 | www.doubletreehotels.com | 289 rooms, 99 suites | $169, $199 suites | AE, D, DC, MC, V.

Kansas City Marriott Downtown. This downtown hotel which caters to business travelers is within walking distance of several city museums and casinos. 2 restaurants, 2 bars (with entertainment). In-room data ports, minibars, cable TV. Pool. Gym. Business services. | 200 W. 12th St. | 816/421–6800 | fax 816/855–4418 | www.marriott.com | 983 rooms, 34 suites | $149–$179 rooms, $200 studio suites, $325–$600 suites | AE, D, DC, MC, V.

LaFontaine Inn. This 1910 Colonial is 1 block from Nelson-Atkins Museum and the Kemper Museum and 6 blocks from the Country Club Plaza. The rooms have been individually decorated, and each has a distinctive character. The Summer Room, for example, has a private deck with a hot tub, while the Winter Room has its own wood-burning fireplace. Antiques, hardwood floors, and chandeliers add to the charm. Complimentary breakfast. In-room data ports, some in-room hot tubs, some in-room VCRs, TV in common area. No pets. No smoking. | 4320 Oak St. | 816/753–4434 or 888/832–6000 | fax 816/756–3665 | lionel@lafontaine.com | www.lafontainebb.com | 5 rooms | $125–$159 | AE, D, MC, V.

★ **Raphael.** Built in 1927 as an apartment house, this U-shape hotel faces Country Club Plaza and aims for a European feel. Restaurant, bar, complimentary Continental breakfast in rooms, room service. In-room data ports, minibars, refrigerators, cable TV. Business services, free parking. | 325 Ward Pkwy. | 816/756–3800 or 800/821–5343 | fax 816/802–2131 | 27 rooms, 96 suites | $119–$195 | AE, D, DC, MC, V.

Sheraton Suites. This 18-story pink hotel is in Country Club Plaza. Restaurant, bar. In-room data ports, refrigerators, cable TV. Indoor-outdoor pool. Hot tub. Gym. Laundry facilities. Business services, free parking. | 770 W. 47th St. | 816/931–4400 or 800/325–3535 | fax 816/516–7330 | www.sheraton.com | 258 suites | $179–$240 | AE, D, DC, MC, V.

EXPENSIVE

Fairmont Kansas City at the Plaza. This luxury hotel with a marble and mahogany lobby and marble baths and crystal fixtures in guest rooms was built in 1969 close by the Country Club Plaza. The Nelson-Atkins Museum of Art, the Kansas City Art Institute, and Crown Center are 10 minutes away. Restaurant, bar (with entertainment), room service. In-room data ports, minibars, refrigerators, cable TV. Pool, wading pool. Massage. Gym. Business services. Valet parking (fee). | 401 Ward Pkwy. | 816/756–1500 or 800/241–3333 | fax 816/756–1635 | www.fairmont.com | 344 rooms, 22 suites | $139–$199 rooms, $239–$1,500 suites | AE, D, DC, MC, V.

Hyatt Regency Crown Center. This chain hotel is connected to Crown Center and is near such area attractions as the *Arabia* Steamboat Museum. 3 restaurants, sports bar, room service. In-room data ports, minibars, cable TV. Pool. Hot tub. 2 tennis courts. Gym. Business services. | 2345 McGee St. | 816/421–1234 | fax 816/435–4190 | www.hyatt.com | 681 rooms, 40 suites | $109–$170 rooms, $300 1–bedroom suites, $400 2–bedroom suites, $500 3–bedroom suites, $575 2–bedroom suites with dining room, $800 deluxe suite/parlor, $950 deluxe 2–bedroom suite | AE, D, DC, MC, V.

Westin Crown Center. Just 1 mi from Worlds of Fun theme park and the Nelson-Atkins Museum of Art, this hotel is attached to the Crown Center shopping mall. Restaurants, bar (with entertainment), room service. In-room data ports, refrigerators, cable TV. Pool. Barbershop, beauty salon, hot tub. 2 tennis courts. Gym. Kids' programs (ages 6–12). Business services. Pets allowed. | 1 Pershing Rd. | 816/474–4400 or 800/228–3000 | fax 816/391–4438 | www.westin.com | 725 rooms, 45 suites | $200–$245 rooms, $350–$400 1–bedroom suites, $500–$550 2–bedroom suites, $1,500 presidential suite | AE, D, DC, MC, V.

KEARNEY

MAP 12, A3

(Nearby towns also listed: Cameron, Excelsior Springs, Kansas City, Jamesport, Liberty)

Pronounced Car-Knee, this little town north of Kansas City draws visitors from around the world to the birthplace and grave of bank robber Jesse James. But if you're not into celebrating criminal activity, a drive through Kearney reveals some beautiful antebellum homes and great antiques shops. Stop by the state's oldest woolen mill at Watkins Mill State Park, just north of town.

Information: **Kearney Chamber of Commerce** | 100 E. Washington St., 64060 | 816/628–4229 | kearneymo.com/index1.html.

Attractions

Jesse James' Farm. This quiet, unassuming frame house was the birthplace of the country's most notorious bank robber, and was his burial place until 1900 when he was moved to a public cemetery. | 21216 Jesse James Farm Rd. | 816/628–6065 | $5.50 | May–Sept., daily 9–4; Oct.–Apr., weekdays 9–4, weekends noon–4.

Watkins Mill State Park. This 818-acre park is right next to Watkins Woolen Mill State Historical Site. There's a small lake where you can fish, boat, or swim and a paved trail on the lake's shore that's perfect for biking. | Clay County MM | 816/560–3387 | Free | Daily, dawn to dusk.

Watkins Woolen Mill State Historic Site. Waltus L. Watkins opened his woolen mill here in 1860 and its original machinery is preserved to this day. Stop by the vistors center for information about the hour-long tours of the mill, or for information on tours of Mr. Watkins's home. | Clay County MM | 816/296–3357 | $2 | Daily, 8–4:30.

ON THE CALENDAR

SEPT.: *Jesse James Festival.* Ride with the James Gang during reenactments of bank robberies, learn to rope and shoot, and enjoy crafts, food, and a little bit of melodrama at Kearney Festival Grounds on the second weekend of the month. | 800/386–2529.
DEC.: *Christmas at Mt. Gilead.* The town's 1850s one-room schoolhouse is decorated by the public and is the center of a holiday celebration on the first or second weekend in December. | 816/628–6065.

Dining

Clem's Country Café. American. Old pictures, bulls' horns, and barbed wire ornament the walls of this eatery, where local residents come for the home cooking. Specialties include fried chicken, meat loaf, and burgers. | 123 E. Washington St. | 816/628–4044 | $3–$5 | MC, V | Breakfast also available.

Lodging

Western Way Bed and Breakfast. This B&B is part of a 55-acre working horse ranch, 4 mi northwest of Kearney. The serene landscape is perfect for hikes, watching wildlife, and communing with nature. You can even go on a horse-drawn carriage ride, weather permitting. Some in-room hot tubs, no room phones, no TV. Pond. Hot tub. Hiking, fishing. No pets. No kids under 12. No smoking. | 13606 Henson Rd., Holt | 816/628–5686 | othehill@flash-net.com | 3 rooms | $80–$95 | No credit cards.

KIMBERLING CITY

(Nearby towns also listed: Branson, Cassville, Joplin, Springfield)

Kimberling City is the anchor point for much activity along Table Rock Lake and in the Table Rock Lake Area. About 850 mi of shoreline was created when this arm of the White River was brought under control in 1958. The water here is crystal clear, and you'll find many sheltered coves that hide bass, catfish, and crappie. Numerous marinas, resorts, and private homes fill the area, but the 53,000 acres of clear water never seem too full for yet another fishing boat, Jet Ski, or sailboat.

Information: Kimberling City Chamber of Commerce | Box 495, 65686 | 417/739–2564 or 800/742–4667 | trichcamber@tablerocklake.org | www.tablerocklake.com/chamber.

Attractions

Port of Kimberling Marina and Campground. Camp, rent boats, and play tennis or basketball at this marina and campground. The beach is great for swimming, too. | Lake Rd. 13-40 | 417/739–2315 or 800/439–3500 | $5, camping fee $9–$19 | March 15–Nov., daily 8am–6pm; Dec.–Feb., Mon.–Fri. 8 AM–5 PM.

ON THE CALENDAR

JULY: *Fireburst.* Enjoy this July 4th fireworks display over Table Rock Lake from a boat, a car, or on foot. The fireworks conclude a day of music, food, and more. | Downtown Kimberling City | 417/739–2564.
NOV., DEC.: *Port of Lights.* The Port of Kimberling is outlined with more than 1½ mi of lights for the holiday season. | 417/739–2564.

Dining

Ahoys Food and Spirits. Seafood. Dock your boat and dine in your swimsuit at this casual restaurant at the Kimberling Inn. You can eat either inside or on a deck overlooking Table Rock Lake. The dining room is almost entirely windowed—ensuring a good view of the water from your table—and the menu includes sandwiches, burgers, and popular entrées. Try the fried catfish sandwich or the grilled amberjack. | Hwy. 13 | 417/739–4311 or 800/833–5551 | $5–$15 | AE, MC, V.

Pier Restaurant. American/Casual. This restaurant, the more elegant of the two dinner eateries at the Kimberling Inn, has expansive views of Table Rock Lake. It serves a range of steak, seafood, and pasta dishes. The prime rib and daily fish specials are the local favorites. | Hwy. 13 | 417/739–4311 or 800/833–5551 | $10–$25 | AE, MC, V | No lunch.

Top of the Rock Restaurant. Continental. Though the wood-fired pizza, fresh pasta specialties, and thick steaks are top-notch, the best thing about the restaurant is its beautiful dining room, which overlooks Table Rock Lake. | 612 Devil's Pool Rd., Ridgedale | 417/339–5023 | $10–$25 | AE, D, MC, V.

Lodging

Bittersweet Resort. This resort, about 10 mi west of Silver Dollar City, offers a dozen free-standing cottages ranging in size from one to three bedrooms along 1,000 ft of wooded lakefront. Kitchenettes, microwaves, cable TV. Pool. Docks, boating. Playground. | Lake Rd. 300, D-2 | 417/739–4492 | fax 417/739–4899 | bittersweet@tri-lakes.net | www.bittersweet-resort.com | 12 cottages | $50 1–room cottages, $67 1–bedroom cottages, $73 2–bedroom cottages, $95–$150 3–bedroom cottages | MC, V.

Cove Resort. This resort on Table Rock Lake has both cottages and motel rooms. The cottages have fully equipped kitchens, and some of the wood-paneled motel rooms have views of the lake. There is a restaurant on the premises and one across the street. Restaurant, bar. Cable TV, no room phones. Pool. Dock, boating, fishing. Playground. Pets allowed ($5 fee). | Hwy. 13 | 417/739–4341 or 800/739–COVE | candymnt@aol.com | www.tablerock-lake.net/lodging/coveresort | 22 rooms, 16 cottages | $55 | AE, D, MC, V.

Kimberling Inn Resort and Conference Center. This lakeside resort is on the quiet side of Branson, 8 mi from Silver Dollar City and 13 mi from the theaters. The largest resort on Table Rock Lake, it offers motel rooms, condos, and time shares, some with views of the water. 4 restaurants, 4 bars. Cable TV. 4 pools, lake. Hot tub, sauna, steam room. Miniature golf, tennis. Health club. Beach, dock, boating. Playground. Laundry service. Business services. | Rte. 13, Box 159B | 417/739–4311 or 800/833–5551 | fax 417/739–5174 | 300 rooms | $70–$160 | AE, D, DC, MC, V.

Table Rock Chalet Resort. Enjoy the lake, relax in the outdoor hot tub, and play volleyball or horseshoes while staying in one of this resort's modern cabins. In-room TV. Outdoor hot tub. Volleyball. | 4497 State Hwy. H, Lampe | 800/995–3307 | www.tablerockchalet.com | 13 rooms | $48 2– to 4–person cabins, $70 4– to 6–person cabins | MC, V.

KIRKSVILLE

MAP 12, C2

(Nearby towns also listed: Hannibal, Macon)

Much of the activity in Kirksville, which was founded in 1891, revolves around Truman State University, noted as one of the best educational values in the United States. The Kohlenberg Lyceum Series brings a number of renowned artistic events to town. At the other end of the spectrum, the facilities at the fairgrounds draw stock car races, livestock shows, and sporting events.

Information: **Kirksville Chamber of Commerce** | 304 S. Franklin, Box 251, 63501 | 660/665–3766 | kvacoc@kvmo.net | www.kirksvillechamber.com.

Attractions

Adair County Historical Museum. A historic 1916 building that once housed a women's social club now displays a variety of items from Adair County's past. Exhibits include a chair built by Andrew T. Still, the American founder of osteopathy, and an original 1860 John Deere planter. | 211 S. Elson St. | 660/665–6502 | Donation | Wed.–Fri. 1–4.

Thousand Hills State Park. A 573-acre lake is the center of this park, nestled in the rolling hills of northeastern Missouri 2½ mi from town. Take Route 6 to Route 157 South to reach the park. | Rte. 157 | 660/665–6995 | www.dnr.state.mo.us/dsp | Free | Daily.

Truman State University. Founded as Northeast Missouri State University in 1867, Truman State University is now home to 6,300 students. | 110 E. Normal St. | 660/785–4000 | www.truman.edu | Free | Weekdays.

ON THE CALENDAR

MAY, OCT.: *Blue Grass Festival.* Twice a year, bluegrass musicians from around the country converge on the Northeast Fairgrounds on Route 11 for a weekend of entertainment and competition. | 660/665–7450.
SEPT.–APR.: *Kohlenberg Lyceum Series.* Performances ranging from jazz concerts of ice-skating exhibitions are given once a month during the school year on the Truman State University campus. | 660/785–4016.
OCT.: *Northeast Missouri Antique Show/Sale.* An impressive collection of everything antique, from automobiles to dishware, is displayed at the Northest Fairgrounds on Route 11 on the third weekend of the month. | 660/665–6637.

Dining

Ailerons. Continental. This casual spot with aeronautical decor and a menu of sandwiches, pizzas, and potato skins is popular with students. | 2523 Business Hwy. 63 S | 660/665–6700 | $12–$25 | MC, V.

Minn's. Contemporary. Fresh flowers, candlelight, and linen set the tone at this cozy, relaxed restaurant. | 216 N. Franklin St. | 660/665–2842 | Jacket required | $22–$40 | AE, MC, V | Closed Sun.

Lodging

Budget Host Village Inn. This chain motel is just a two-minute walk from Truman State University. Cable TV. Business services. Some pets allowed. | 1304 S. Baltimore St. | 660/665–3722 | fax 660/665–8277 | 30 rooms | $48 | AE, D, DC, MC, V.

Days Inn. This chain motel is on the outskirts of town 2 mi from Truman State University. The game room has pool tables as well as video games. Restaurant, bar, complimentary breakfast buffet, room service. Cable TV. Pool. Hot tub. Video games. Business services. | S. Business Hwy. 63 | 660/665–8244 or 800/329–7466 | www.daysinn.com | 105 rooms | $59–$65 | AE, D, DC, MC, V.

Holiday Inn Express. This three-story chain hotel, adjacent to several restaurants and shops, is 1 mi from downtown, just off Highway 63. Complimentary Continental breakfast. In-room data ports, some microwaves, some refrigerators, some in-room hot tubs, cable TV. Pool. Hot tub. No pets. | 2702 S. Business Hwy. 63 | 660/627–1100 or 800/465–4329 | fax 660/627–5876 | www.basshotels.com/holiday-inn | 63 rooms | $62–$110 | AE, D, DC, MC, V.

Kirksville Comfort Inn. This two-story hotel is on Highway 63, across the street from the Wal-Mart Super Center. Complimentary Continental breakfast. Some microwaves, some refrigerators, cable TV. Hot tub. Pets allowed. | 2209 N. Baltimore St./Hwy. 63 | 660/665–2205 or 800/228–5150 | fax 660/665–2205 | 47 rooms | $50–$75 | AE, D, DC, MC, V.

Super 8. This chain motel is 1 mi from Truman State University and just next door to Kirksville Country Club where out-of-towners can play golf. Cable TV. | 1101 Country Club Dr. | 660/665–8826 or 800/800–8000 | fax 660/665–8826 | www.super8.com | 64 rooms | $42 | AE, D, DC, MC, V.

LAKE OZARK

MAP 12, C4

(Nearby towns also listed: Camdenton, Jefferson City, Osage Beach)

On the west side of Bagnell Dam is the relatively young city of Lake Ozark. The first mile, known to area residents and visitors alike as "The Strip," houses boutiques, crafts, souvenirs, T-shirt shops, restaurants, and arcades and amusements, plus dozens of family resorts and motels.

Information: Lake Ozark Chamber of Commerce | 3502 Bagnell Dam Blvd., Box 1510, 65049 | 573/365–3002 | www.odd.net/ozarks.

Attractions

Bagnell Dam and Museum. The Lake of the Ozarks was created with the damming of the Osage River in the 1920s. The dam itself is 2,543 ft long and 148 ft high, and holds back 650 billion gallons of water. To reach the dam take U.S. 54 and Route W. | 1 Willmore La. | 573/365–3002 | Free | Visitor center weekdays 9–4:30, weekends 10–3.

Jacob's Cave. You'll see reflective pools and sponge work on a walk along the paved paths at this cave 25 mi from Lake Ozark in nearby Versailles. | County Rd. TT, Versailles | 573/378–4374 | $10 | Daily 9–5.

SIGHTSEEING TOURS/TOUR COMPANIES

Casino Pier. Lunch and dinner tours of Lake of the Ozarks. | 1046 Bagnell Dam Blvd. | 573/365–2020 | $19 | Memorial Day–Labor Day, daily 9–7; Apr.–Memorial Day and Labor Day–Oct., call for schedule.

Paddlewheeler *Tom Sawyer* Excursion Boat. Tours of Lake of the Ozarks aboard a replica of an 1800s riverboat. | 1006 Bagnell Dam Blvd. | 573/365–3300 | $10 | Apr.–Oct., daily 10–9.

ON THE CALENDAR

MAY: *Magic Dragon Street Meet Nationals.* Seven hundred street rods, customs, street machines, motorcycles, and more meet for Missouri's largest festival of its kind at the Columbia College Exposition Center on the first weekend of the month. | www.odd.net/ozarks/carshow/ | 573/365–3663.

SEPT.: *Hillbilly Fair.* Crafts, music, and a parade all held at the Laurie Fairgrounds on Silvey Road on the third weekend of the month. | 573/374–8776.

SEPT.: *Mountain Man Festival.* Encampment of tents, tepees, and trading posts take you back to the days of explorers and Native Americans in the early 1800s at the American Legion Campground at the foot of Bagnell Dam on the third weekend of the month. | 573/348–2128 or 800/451–4117.

OCT.: *Turkey Festival.* A 5K turkey trot, a turkey egg toss, and frozen turkey bowling are among the activities that celebrate the area's prominence as a turkey producer on the second Saturday of the month on Maple Street in nearby Eldon. | 573/392–3752.

Dining

Bentley's Restaurant and Pub. English. This classic English pub has wood beams, rubbed etchings on the walls, and a menu featuring four cuts of prime rib and daily fish specials. Kids' menu. | Business Rte. 54 | 573/365–5301 | $13–$39 | AE, D, DC, MC, V | Closed Sun. and Jan.–Feb. No lunch.

Blue Heron. Seafood. The glass-enclosed patio at this hilltop restaurant faces Lake Ozark and affords a panoramic view of the water and surrounding country. Veal and steak dishes complement the many seafood items on the menu. Try the batter-fried lobster, an innovative dish first made here. | Business Rte. 54 and Rte. HH | 573/365–4646 | $20–$40 | AE, D, MC, V | Closed Sun., Mon. and Dec.–Mar. No lunch.

J. B. Hooks. Contemporary. Built on a cliff with a view of Lake Ozark, this restaurant offers such entrées as Steak Neptune, a beef tenderloin stuffed with shrimp and crabmeat then charbroiled and topped with asparagus spears and a béarnaise sauce. Open-air dining. Raw bar. | 2260 Bagnell Dam Blvd. | 573/365–3255 | $16–$55 | AE, D, DC, MC, V.

Riverside Inn. American. Opened in 1923 as a single-room café, the restaurant has since grown to its present size of nine dining rooms. The original menu of fried chicken has been augmented with steaks and fish entrées such as salmon and trout. The eatery is on the Finley River and is adorned throughout with art by the original owner. | 2629 N. Riverside Rd. | 417/581–7051 | $15–$40 | AE, D, DC, MC, V | Closed Sun., Mon. No lunch.

Lodging

Barn Again Bed and Breakfast. The guest rooms of this rustic B&B are in what was the milking parlor of a dairy barn. Another, adjacent barn houses a common area. Converted by local Amish craftsmen, the barns have an authentic Ozark flavor. On 5 acres just at the edge of town, this is a quiet spot to reconnect with nature. Complimentary breakfast. No air-conditioning, refrigerators, no TV. Pool, pond. Basketball. No pets. No kids under 10. No smoking. | 904 W. Church St. | 417/581–2276 or 877/462–2276 | www.bbim.org | 4 rooms | $89–$109 | D, MC, V.

Bass Point Resort. This family-owned 25-acre resort has 35 cottages, many with patios and lake views, and ½ mi of gently sloping shoreline. The owners are proud that 90% of their customers are repeat visitors. Picnic area. Kitchenettes, microwaves, cable TV, no room phones.

2 pools. Tennis court. Water sports, boating. Video games. Playground. Laundry facilities. | Rte. 1, Box 127, Sunrise Beach | 573/374–5205 | fax 573/374–0545 | www.basspoint.com | 35 cottages | $90–$175 | D, MC, V | Closed Nov.–Apr.

Dear's Rest Bed and Breakfast. This Amish-built home is on a ridge overlooking the Ozark Mountains. It is surrounded by dogwoods, hickories, and oaks, and part of the property abuts the Mark Twain National Forest. Because of its proximity to the forest, the B&B often plays host to wandering deer and raccoons. Inside, a fireplace, full kitchen, and large living room are nestled beneath a high, rough-hewn beam ceiling. In-room VCRs (and movies). Hot tub. No pets. No smoking. | 1408 Capp Hill Ranch Rd. | 417/581–3839 or 800/LUV–2BNB | stay@dearsrest.com | www.dearsrest.com | 1 room | $95 | D, MC, V.

Holiday Inn Sun Spree Resort. This large Lake of the Ozarks resort is next door to Port Arrowhead marina and 4 mi from town. Restaurant, bar, complimentary Continental breakfast, room service. In-room data ports, microwaves, cable TV. 3 pools. Hot tub. Miniature golf. Gym. Video games. Children's programs, playground. Laundry facilities. Business services. Pets allowed. | Business Rte. 54, Box 1930 | 573/365–2334 or 800/465–4329 | fax 573/365–6887 | www.funlake.com | 213 rooms | $125–$145 | AE, D, DC, MC, V.

Lodge of Four Seasons. This golf resort nestled on the shoreline of Lake of the Ozarks has hotel rooms as well as two- and three-bedroom condos for nightly or weekly rental. There are golfing, fishing, spa, and b&b packages and an "adventure club" for kids. 4 restaurants, 2 bars, room service. Cable TV, in-room VCRs available. 5 pools (1 indoor-outdoor), wading pool. Hot tub, spa. Driving range, 3 18-hole golf courses, putting greens, tennis court. Bowling, gym, beach, water sports, boating. Video games. Kids' programs (ages 2–16), playground. Business services, airport shuttle. | Rte. HH | 573/365–3000 or 888/265–5500 | fax 573/365–8525 | www.4seasonsresort.com | 304 rooms in 5 buildings, 110 condos | $189–$239 rooms, $229–$275 2–bedroom condos, $299–$350 3–bedroom condos | AE, D, DC, MC, V.

LAMAR

MAP 12, A5

(Nearby towns also listed: Carthage, Joplin, Nevada, Stockton)

Although the residents didn't know it at the time, tiny Lamar had a big day on May 8, 1884, when Harry S Truman was born here. Before that time Wyatt Earp was the sheriff, and Native Americans and buffalo roamed the prairie. Today, you might visit Lamar when fishing at nearby Lake Stockton.

Information: Lamar Chamber of Commerce | 110 W. 11th St., Box 228, 64759 | 417/682–3595 | www.bartoncounty.com.

Attractions

Harry S Truman Birthplace State Historic Site. The only Missourian ever elected president lived here with his family in 1884. | 1009 Truman Ave. | 417/682–2279 | www.dnr.state.mo.us/dsp | Free | Mon.–Sat. 10–4, Sun. noon–4.

Prairie State Park. The native prairie grass featured here once covered most of the state. | 128 N.W. 150 La., off U.S. 160, Liberal | 417/843–6711 | www.dnr.state.mo.us/dsp | Free | Daily; visitors center Tues.–Sat. 8:30–5, Sun. 1–5.

Stilabower Public Observatory. Search the skies on Tuesday, Thursday, and Saturday nights when this observatory, one of the few in the country that is accessible to kids and the disabled, is open to the public by appointment. | 6th and Maple Sts. | 417/682–3929 | Free | Tues., Thurs., Sat. nights by appointment.

JUNE: *Truman Days.* The town celebrates the birth of its most famous citizen with vendors, crafts, food, and more on the town square the last Saturday in June. | 417/682–3595.

AUG.: *Lamar Free Fair.* For most visitors the highlight of this weeklong event at the end of August, billed as Missouri's largest fair that's free of admission, is a carnival around Barton County Square. | 417/682–3595.

SEPT.–OCT.: *Prairie Jubilee.* This fall festival is held in late September or early October every other year at Prairie State Park in nearby Liberal on Missouri's largest remaining tallgrass prairie and includes storytelling, music, guided hikes, and more. | 417/682–3595.

Dining

Blue Top Restaurant. American. This small café just off Highway 71 serves traditional diner fare to its loyal local following. The breakfast biscuits and hot dinner rolls should not be missed; also try the fried chicken. | 57 S.E. 1st La. | 417/682–5080 | $5–$10 | MC, V | Breakfast also available.

Lodging

Best Western Blue Top Inn. This chain motel is 1½ mi from Truman's birthplace and home. There are several restaurants within walking distance. Complimentary Continental breakfast. Cable TV. Pool. | 65 S.E. 1st La. | 417/682–3333 or 800/528–1234 | fax 417/682–3336 | www.bestwestern.com | 25 rooms | $42 | AE, D, DC, MC, V.

Lamar Super 8. Every room at this chain motel has a queen- or king-size bed, and complimentary popcorn is served every evening. It's at the junction of Highways 71 and 160. Complimentary Continental breakfast. Some minibars, some in-room hot tubs, cable TV. Pool. Gym. Laundry facilities. Business services. No pets. | 45 S.E. 1st La. | 417/682–6888 or 800/800–8000 | fax 417/682–3510 | www.super8.com | 57 rooms | $47–$57 | AE, D, DC, MC, V.

LEBANON

MAP 12, C5

(Nearby towns also listed: Camdenton, Osage Beach, Rolla, Sullivan, Waynesville)

Founded in 1849, the community of Lebanon was first called Wyota, after a local Indian tribe. Later, a respected minister asked that the town be renamed after his hometown in Tennessee. This area in the Ozarks is rich in natural beauty and there's good hunting and fishing, making Lebanon a great spot for a vacation or retirement.

Information: **Lebanon Chamber of Commerce** | 334 S. Washington St., 65536 | 417/588–3256 | lebanon.missouri.org/.

Attractions

Bennett Spring State Park. Twelve miles west of Lebanon, this 3,100-acre park sees nearly 100 million gallons of emerald-green water rush from the spring and flow into the Niangua River every day. This section of the Niangua is one of the best stretches of river for canoeing in the state. The park also offers 12 miles of hiking trails and 189 campsites. | Hwy. 64A | 417/532–4338 or 417/532–4307 | www.dnr.state.mo.us/dsp | Free | Mar.–Oct., daily; office Mon.–Thurs. 9–6:30, Fri. 9 AM–10 PM, Sat. 9–9, Sun. 10–6:30.

Laclede County Museum. Exhibits here include antique furniture and household appliances, photos of the Laclede County area, and more. | 262 Adams St. | 417/588–2441 | 50¢ suggested | May–Oct., weekdays and 3rd Sat. of each month 10–3.

Walnut Bowl. Whiskey and wine barrels are manufactured and sold here, along with other wooden products such as picture frames, bowls, and knife cases. Half-hour tours are given every hour on the hour from 9 until 2. | 1100 S. Jefferson | 417/532–6186 | Free | Daily 9–6.

JUNE: *Hillbilly Days.* A crosscut saw competition as well as skillet throwing, apple bob-bing, and nail-driving contests are held at Bennett Spring State Park on Father's Day weekend. | 417/588–3256.

JUNE: *National Breeders Cup Fox Trotters Horse Show.* Fox trotters from all over the country compete in this event at the Cowan Civic Center Fairgrounds. | 417/588–3256.

Dining

Stonegate Station. Eclectic. You'll find a wide range of dishes here—everything from steak and seafood to Mexican and Italian specialties. Kids' menu. No smoking. | 1475 S. Jefferson St. | 417/588–1387 | $7–$19 | AE, D, MC, V.

Lodging

Bennett Spring Inn. This all-suites hotel built in 1995 is in a rustic setting within walking distance of Bennet State Park and several restaurants. Complimentary Continental break-fast. Kitchenettes, cable TV. Pool. Hot tub. Basketball. | 11525 Rte. 64 | 417/588–9110 or 800/478–7688 | fax 417/588–3174 | 55 rooms | $52–$75 | AE, D, MC, V | Closed Jan.

Best Western Wyota Inn. This highway motel is 12 mi from Bennett Spring State Park. Restau-rant, complimentary Continental breakfast. Cable TV. Pool. Laundry facilities. Some pets allowed. | 1225 Mill Creek Rd. | 417/532–6171 or 800/528–1234 | fax 417/532–6174 | www.best-western.com | 52 rooms | $55 | AE, D, DC, MC, V.

Fort Niangua River Resort. Modern log cabins equipped with air-conditioning, kitch-enettes, and fireplaces share space with camping and RV facilities along ½ mi of Niangua River frontage 2 mi from Bennett Springs State Park. You can arrange canoe rentals here with shuttle service for three- to eight-hour floats along the Niangua. Kitchenettes. Pool. Basketball, volleyball, water sports. Video games. Laundry service. | Rte. 16, Box 1020, Lebanon | 417/532–4377 | fax 417/588–7066 | www.missouri.net/fortniangua | 17 cabins | $35–$60 | D, MC, V.

Hampton Inn. Right off Interstate 44 at exit 127, this three-story hotel is 3 miles west of downtown. Several restaurants are within walking distance. Complimentary Continental breakfast. Some refrigerators, some in-room hot tubs, cable TV. Pool. Gym. Business ser-

MISSOURI'S FLOURISHING COOPERAGE INDUSTRY

While you're traveling through the Missouri Ozarks, you will surely marvel at the beautiful scenery, especially the magnificent oak trees growing along the rolling terrain. What you may not be aware of is the nearly 500 million acres of limestone covered with a thin layer of topsoil that make up the Ozarks.

Vegetation of any kind, particularly oak trees on the north slopes of the Ozark hills, must struggle to gain and maintain a foothold. This struggle for life results in oak trees averaging 20 to 25 rings per inch, which makes great wine and whiskey barrels. The denser the rings, the more organic compounds are present in the wood, which contribute to the overall flavor of the product.

World Cooperage, located in Lebanon, produces about 140,000 barrels for the wine industry each year and more than a half million for whiskey, all using Mis-souri-harvested white oak. A major producer of domestic wines in the 1840s, the Missouri wine industry was all but obliterated during the Civil War and the days of Prohibition. The use of Missouri oak in the cooperage industry is an important step in rebuilding the reputation of Missouri as a serious factor in the U.S. wine market.

© Corbis

vices. No pets. | 930 Ivey La. | 417/533–3100 or 800/426–7866 | fax 417/533–5858 | www.hamptoninn.com | 64 rooms | $72–$82 | AE, D, DC, MC, V.

Quality Inn. This chain motel, built in 1984, is 2 mi from downtown. Restaurant, bar, complimentary Continental breakfast, room service. Cable TV. Pool. Laundry facilities. Business services. Pets allowed. | 2071 W. Elm St. | 417/532–7111 | fax 417/532–7005 | 82 rooms | $65 | AE, D, DC, MC, V.

Sand Spring Resort. This large tree-filled property provides opportunities for hiking, swimming, and enjoying nature. Because of its location adjacent to the Bennett Spring State Park and the Niangua River, the resort also is the perfect spot for fishing. Occasional fishing seminars are held at the resort. Restaurant. Some kitchenettes, some microwaves, some refrigerators, cable TV. Pool. Sauna. Hiking, boating, fishing. Pets allowed ($10 fee). | Rte. 16 | 417/532–5857 or 800/543–FISH | www.sandspringresort.com | 52 rooms | $42–$67 | MC, V.

LEXINGTON

MAP 12, B3

(Nearby towns also listed: Blue Springs, Excelsior Springs, Independence, Kansas City, Liberty)

Founded in 1822 by settlers from Lexington, Kentucky, today Lexington is one of Missouri's largest producers of apples. A Civil War cannonball embedded in the county courthouse is one of the many reminders of the battles fought in this town, but apple orchards, B&Bs, and great antiques are what draw visitors to Lexington. When the weather is good, something is happening downtown just about every weekend, whether a cooking demonstration, a parade of the nearby Wentworth Military Academy cadets, or Jesse James returning to rob the bank.

Information: Lexington Tourism Bureau | Box 132, 64067 | 660/259–4711 | www.historiclexington.com.

Attractions

Battle of Lexington State Historic Site. This is one of the few Civil War battlefields that has never been cultivated; as a result the outlines of the trenches used by Missouri State Guard troops and Union troops in one of the state's major Civil War battles in 1861 are still visible. Guided tours begin on the hour and you'll have a chance to see a field hospital as well as the battlefield itself. | N. 16th St. | 660/259–4654 | www.dnr.state.mo.us/dsp | $2 | Tours Apr. 15–Oct., Mon.–Sat. 10–4, Sun. noon–6; Nov., Dec., Wed.–Sat. 10–4, Sun. noon–6.

Lafayette County Courthouse. A Civil War cannonball can still be seen lodged in one of the pillars of the building. | 1001 Main St. | 660/259–4315 | Free | Weekdays 8:30–4:30.

Lexington Historical Museum. Erected in 1846 as a church, this building now houses Pony Express, Civil War, and pioneer exhibits. | 112 S. 13th St. | 660/259–6313 | $1 | Wed.–Sun. 10–4; closed Mon., Tues.

Log House Museum. This original log house was occupied by several prominent local families over the years. | Main St. at Broadway | 660/259–4711 | $1 | Wed.–Sat., Sun. afternoons; also by appointment.

Madonna of the Trail. A monument to pioneer women, dedicated by Harry S Truman. | Main St. at Broadway and Highland Ave. | 660/259–3082 | Free | Daily.

Shirkey Golf Club. This semiprivate 18-hole course opened in 1969. It's longer and more difficult than it appears. | 901 Wollard Blvd., Richmond | 816/470–2582 | Year-round.

MAY: *Dogwood Homes Tour.* Five antebellum homes are open for show on the third weekend of the month. | 660/259–4711.

Dining

Franny's Gourmet. Delicatessen. This lovely deli in an 1840s storefront has its original tin ceiling, exposed brick walls, and hardwood floors. Its sandwiches are made with freshly baked breads, and its soups are homemade. Try the chile and follow it with ice cream. Amish and Mennonite jarred foods are available for purchase. | 1109 Main St. | 660/259–4008 | $3–$7 | AE, D, DC, MC, V | Closed Sun. No dinner.

Zachariah's. Contemporary. Candlelight, linen tablecloths, and crystal set the stage for the select choice of steaks, seafood, and chicken dishes served at Zachariah's. In the 1870s, the restaurant was a bank, which explains its magnificent 35-ft ceilings. Try the prime rib or Maine blue crab. | 1012 Main St. | 660/259–3633 | $12–$16 | AE, D, MC, V | No lunch Sat.–Mon., no dinner Sun.–Wed.

Lodging

Inn on Main. This inn, built in the 1870s, features deluxe rooms filled with antiques, such as four-poster beds and settee couches. The inn is family friendly, and the proprietor welcomes parents and kids. As a guest, you will be welcome to use the amenities at the Lady of Lexington Bed and Breakfast. Complimentary breakfast. Microwaves, refrigerators, cable TV. No pets. No smoking. | 920½ Main St. | 660/259–4593 or 877/894–6914 | 4 rooms | $85–$95 | AE, D, MC, V.

Lady of Lexington Bed and Breakfast. Complimentary flowers, sherry, and fruit await your arrival at this luxurious B&B in the center of Lexington. The Victorian home, built in 1841, is surrounded by a garden and manicured lawns, and the guest rooms are appointed with antiques and original art. Complimentary breakfast. Cable TV, no room phones. Pond. Hot tub. No pets. No kids under 12. No smoking. | 905 Franklin Ave. | 660/259–4593 or 877/894–6914 | www.ladyoflexb-b.com | 3 rooms | $75–$95 | AE, D, MC, V.

Lexington Inn. Built in 1969, this brick inn is 1 mi from Battle of Lexington State Historic site and Wentworth Military Academy. Restaurant, bar (with entertainment). Cable TV. Pool. Laundry facilities. Business services. Pets allowed (fee). | 1078 N. Outer Rd. W | 660/259–4641 or 800/289–4641 | 60 rooms | $45–$75 | AE, D, DC, MC, V.

Victorianne Bed and Breakfast. Located in the historic district, this Queen Anne brick home was built in 1885 and has gingerbread trim, a wide porch, and turrets. Rooms are furnished in antiques and have fireplaces. Complimentary Continental breakfast. No room phones. Outdoor hot tub. | 1522 South St. | 660/259–2868 | 3 rooms | $75–$85 | MC, V.

LIBERTY

MAP 12, A3

(Nearby towns also listed: Blue Springs, Excelsior Springs, Independence, Kansas City, Kearney, Lexington, Parkville, Weston)

Visit the site of Jesse James's first daylight bank robbery on the town square in Liberty, then have lunch or dinner at the locally famous Hardware Café, in the original 1840s building of a hardware store. Liberty leaders have done a commendable job of maintaining and restoring historic buildings, artifacts, and traditions, making the community an appealing home for residents and a pleasant day-trip destination for travelers from Kansas City.

Information: Liberty Chamber of Commerce | 9 S. Leonard St., 64069–2320 | 816/781–5200 | www.ci.liberty.mo.us/chamber/welcome.htm.

Attractions

Jesse James Bank Museum. This small facility on the town square was the site of the first daytime bank robbery in the country. | 103 N. Water St. | 816/781–4458 | $4 | Mon.–Sat. 9–4.

ON THE CALENDAR

SEPT.: *Fall Festival.* An 8K run, classic car show, and tour of historic homes by lantern light held the fourth weekend of the month. | 816/781–5200.

NOV.: *Holiday Homes Tour.* Tours of six historical homes decorated for the holidays are offered over Thanksgiving weekend. | 816/792–3359.

Dining

Fork N' Spoon Café. American. Down-home fare like catfish, prime rib, and chicken-fried steak is the hallmark of this storefront eatery, whose cozy dining room is filled with antiques. The café is just west of Liberty's town square. | 12 W. Kansas Ave. | 816/792–0707 | $5–$11 | AE, D, DC, MC, V | Breakfast also available.

Hardware Café. American. Named to reflect the history of the building it's housed in, this casual place seats about 125 and is known for its fried chicken and desserts. | 5 E. Kansas Ave. | 816/792–3500 | $7–$13 | D, MC, V | Closed Sun. No dinner Mon.

Lodging

Dougherty House 1880 Bed and Breakfast. Original art-glass windows, period antiques, a gazebo, and lush gardens are just some of the charms of this 1880 Queen Anne. The four guest rooms, two with private baths, are elaborately decorated, and the grounds contain a bridged fishpond. The B&B is in the historic district, just off the town square and within walking distance to Liberty's many attractions. Complimentary breakfast. Some in-room VCRs, no room phones, no TV in some rooms. Pond. Business services. No pets. No kids under 18. No smoking. | 302 N. Water St. | 816/792–4888 | www.doughertyhouse.com | 4 rooms | $75–$85 | AE, MC, V.

James Inn Bed and Breakfast. This romantic turn-of-the-20th-century inn was built as a church in the early 1800s and is now filled with antiques. It's two blocks from historic Liberty Square. Complimentary breakfast. Cable TV. In-room hot tubs, massage. Business services. | 342 N. Water St. | 816/781–3677 | 4 rooms | $135 | AE, MC, V.

Wynbrick Inn Bed and Breakfast. This 1928 brick home with a slate roof and an acre of attractively landscaped grounds has five guest rooms, each decorated in an antique theme. Complimentary Continental breakfast. No TV in rooms. Business services. | 1701 Wynbrick Dr. | 816/781–4900 | fax 816/781–0840 | 5 rooms | $80–$125 | AE, D, MC, V.

MACON

MAP 12, C2

(Nearby towns also listed: Chillicothe, Hannibal, Kirksville, Moberly, Monroe City)

If you enjoy hunting, you'll know that Macon County is the best place in Missouri for deer and turkey hunters. The nearby Thomas Hill Wildlife Area, with more than 10,000 acres of lakes and forest land, also provides for fishing, hiking, and waterskiing.

Information: **Macon Chamber of Commerce** | 218 N. Rollins, #102A, 63552 | 660/385–2811 | www.macc.istmacon.net.

Attractions

Long Branch State Park. Wooded areas and restored prairie grass make this a pleasant camping and picnicking spot. Take U.S. 36 west to reach the park. | 28615 Visitor Center Rd. | 660/773–5229 | www.dnr.state.mo.us/dsp | Free | Daily.

Thomas Hill Wildlife Area. Offers primitive camping, hunting, and fishing about 10 mi southwest of Macon. Take U.S. 36 west to Route 3 South. | Rte. 3 | 660/785–2420 | Free | Daily.

ON THE CALENDAR
SEPT.: *Pepsi Show-Me Show Down.* Macon County Park hosts one of the nation's largest Grand National Truck and Tractor Pulls in late September. | 660/385–2811.
SEPT.: *Exotic Animal Sale.* Lions, tigers, and bears are among the many critters auctioned worldwide through the Lolli Brothers Livestock Auction held the last weekend of the month at the Livestock Market in Macon. | 660/385–2516.

Dining
Gaslight Room. American. Gaslight lamps and candles set the tone in this dining room. House specialties include prime rib and Kansas City strip steak. Salad bar. Entertainment Friday and Saturday. Sunday brunch. | 203 N. Rollins | 660/385–4013 | $5–$25 | AE, D, DC, MC, V.

Long Branch. American. Steaks, pork chops, and such desserts as turtle pie (a confection of caramel, chocolate, and pecans) are served in a dining room adorned with saddles, branding irons, and roping awards. Salad bar. Buffet (dinner). Sunday brunch. | 28855 Sunset Dr. | 660/385–4600 | $5–$18 | AE, D, DC, MC, V.

Pear Tree. Steak. Famous for its outstanding steaks, this antiques-filled restaurant 4 mi west of Macon is the place to go for any special occasion. All the steaks are delicious, but try the prime rib; it's legendary. Chops, seafood, and poultry options fill out the menu. | 222 N. Macon St., Bevier | 660/773–6666 | $14–$22 | AE, D, MC, V | Closed Sun., Mon. No lunch.

Lodging
Best Western Inn. This older chain hotel is across the street from a Lake Longbranch and within walking distance of several antiques stores. In-room data ports, cable TV. Pool. Business services. Some pets allowed. | 28933 Sunset Dr. | 660/385–2125 or 800/528–1234 | www.bestwestern.com | 46 rooms | $55 | AE, D, DC, MC, V.

St. Agnes Hall Bed and Breakfast. This brick home was built in the 1840s and was once a girls' boarding school. The rooms are graced with family heirlooms and antiques, which accent the building's heritage. The grounds include period gardens and decks. Complimentary breakfast. No room phones. Hot tub. Pets allowed. No smoking. | 502 Jackson | 660/385–2774 | fax 660/385–4436 | 3 rooms | $68–$95 | AE, D, MC, V.

MEXICO

MAP 12, D3

(Nearby towns also listed: Columbia, Fulton, Hannibal, Hermann, Moberly, Monroe City)

In the early days of the 20th century, Mexico was world renowned for its saddle-horse trade and firebrick industry. Today, Mexico has one of the most diverse economies of any Missouri small town, with an advanced technology center to rival the nearby University of Missouri–Columbia. But locals are perhaps most proud of their distinction as perennial host to the Miss Missouri Pageant.

Information: Mexico Chamber of Commerce | 100 W. Jackson St., Box 56, 65265 | 573/581–2765 or 800/581–2765 | www.mexico-chamber.org.

Attractions
Advanced Technology Center. This technology center is a cooperative effort of Linn State Technical College, Moberly Area Community College, the city of Mexico, and University of Missouri. | 2900 Doreli La. | 573/582–0817 | Free | Mon.–Thurs. 8 AM–9 PM, Fri. 8–5.

Graceland: Audrain County Historical Society Museum. As the birthplace of the American saddle horse, this antebellum home has artifacts from the American Saddle Horse Association. | 501 S. Muldrow St. | 573/581–3910 | $2 | Mar.–Dec., Tues.–Fri. and Sun. 2–5, Sat. 1–4.

ON THE CALENDAR

JUNE: *Miss Missouri Pageant.* For almost 30 years, Mexico has been home to the Miss Missouri Pageant, in which talented women vie for scholarships. The pageant is held the second weekend of the month at the Missouri Military Academy. | 573/581–0654.

Dining

G and D Steak House. Steak. A casual steak house with booths as well as tables, cafeteria service, and a salad bar. | Hwy. 54 south | 573/581–0171 | $5–$13 | AE, D, DC, MC, V.

Golden Corral. Steak. Sirloin steaks in inch-thick cuts and rib eyes are the most popular items at this downtown restaurant. The menu also contains seafood options, and a seafood buffet is served on Friday nights. Enjoy your meal in the dining room's pleasant solarium. | 650 W. Jackson St. | 573/581–5347 | $6–$9 | AE, D, MC, V.

Lodging

Holiday Inn Express Mexico. Three miles south of Mexico's downtown, this hotel is on Highway 54 South, 13 mi north of Interstate 70. Complimentary Continental breakfast. In-room data ports, some refrigerators, some in-room hot tubs, cable TV. Pool. Hot tub. Gym. Laundry service. Business services. No pets. | 3602 S. Clark St./Hwy. 54 S | 573/582–0700 or 800/465–4329 | fax 573/582–0725 | www.basshotels.com | 47 rooms | $59–$100 | AE, D, DC, MC, V.

MOBERLY

MAP 12, C3

(Nearby towns also listed: Columbia, Fulton, Macon, Mexico, Monroe City)

Moberly's claim to fame is that General Omar Bradley, the five-star World War II general, was born nearby and was educated in Moberly Public Schools. The downtown Randolph County Historical Center and a memorial in Rothwell Park are worth your time. While in the area, watch for horse-drawn carriages belonging to the Amish who live about 5 mi south of Moberly along U.S. 63.

Information: **Moberly Chamber of Commerce** | 211 W. Reed St., Box 602, 65270-0602 | 660/263–6070 | www.moberlymo.com/chamber.

Attractions

Randolph County Historical Center. General Omar Bradley memorabilia, genealogy, and research are on display. | 223 N. Clark | 660/263–9396 | Free | Mon. 10–noon, Thurs. 1–3, Sat. 9–noon.

Randolph County Railroad Museum. Train cars and train memorabilia are featured. | 100 block of N. Sturgen St. | 660/263–9396 | Free | Sun. 1–4, and by appointment.

Rothwell City Park. In addition to a statue honoring General Omar Bradley, this 447-acre park has fishing, camping, walking trails, and paddle boats. | 109 Clark | 660/263–6757 | Free | Daily.

Shepard Valley Pecan Farm. This working farm has more than 8,000 pecan trees as well as 600 buffalo and large flocks of Canada geese in the fall. Take U.S. Hwy 63 North to Route 24 West to reach the farm. | Clifton Hill | 660/261–4567 | Free | Daily.

JUNE: *Randolph County Flywheel Reunion.* For three or four days in mid-June the fairgrounds at Sutliss Stadium in nearby Huntsville host displays of old tractors, tractor pulls, and nightly entertainment. | 660/263–6070.

SEPT.: *Native American Pow Wow.* Native Americans display crafts, culture, and history in Rothwell Park on the second weekend of the month. | 660/263–6070.

NOV.: *Randolph County Craft Show.* This two-day craft show, held in Moberly Area Community College over the third weekend of the month, is the oldest in the state. | 660/263–6070.

Dining

CC Sawyers. American/Casual. Steaks are cooked over an open wood pit at this casual restaurant and lounge. | 104 Wightman St. | 660/263–7744 | $10–$33 | MC, V | No lunch.

Reed Street Café. American. Everything from omelets and Belgian waffles to Reuben sandwiches and country ham dinners are served at this storefront café in downtown Moberly. All the dishes are homemade, including the cinnamon rolls, cream puffs, and desserts. | 407 W. Reed St. | 660/263–1810 | $3–$6 | No credit cards | No dinner.

Lodging

Ramada Inn of Moberly. One of the region's only full-service hotels, the Ramada is 1 ½ mi from downtown in a quiet commercial area. 2 restaurants, room service. Some refrigerators, cable TV. Pool. Hot tub. Airport shuttle. Pets allowed ($30 fee). | 1200 Hwy. 24 E | 660/263–6540 or 888/298–2054 | fax 660/263–0092 | www.the.ramada.com | 98 rooms | $69–$105 | AE, D, DC, MC, V.

MONROE CITY

MAP 12, D3

(Nearby towns also listed: Hannibal, Macon, Mexico, Moberly)

This town at the entrance to Mark Twain Lake caters to hunters and fishermen. The lake is home to Missouri's largest bass fishing tournament each year, but antiques shops, the historic St. Jude's Episcopal Church, and Mark Twain's birthplace are draws as well.

Information: **Monroe City Chamber of Commerce** | Box 22, 63456 | 573/735–4391.

Attractions

Mark Twain State Park. The 18,600-acre Mark Twain Lake was created when the Salt River was dammed. Today you can camp, picnic, hike, or fish in a 2,775-acre park on its shores. | Hwy. 107 | 573/565–3440 | www.dnr.state.mo.us/dsp | Free | Daily. While you are in the park you can also visit **Mark Twain Birthplace State Historic Site** and see the two-room cabin where the famous author was born. There's a modern museum surrounding the cabin with lots of Mark Twain memorabilia and a handwritten manuscript for *The Adventures of Tom Sawyer.* | County Rd. U (off Hwy. 107) | 573/565–3449 | $1.75 | Mon.–Sat. 10–4, Sun. 11–5.

St. Jude's Episcopal Church. Founded in 1855, this is no longer a working church. The building itself is currently closed to the public, but the city is working to have it declared a historic building and to offer tours. | N. Main St. | 573/735–4391.

Union Covered Bridge State Historic Site. Built in 1871 to span the Elk Fork of the Salt River, the bridge served travelers on the Paris–Fayette Road through Monroe County for 99 years and is one of three covered bridges remaining in the state. To reach the bridge, take U.S 24 West 5 mi beyond Paris, then head south on Highway C. | Hwy. C in Monroe County | 573/565–3449 | www.dnr.state.mo.us/dsp | Free | Daily.

ON THE CALENDAR
JULY: *Mark Twain Rodeo.* Held at the Clarence Cannon Dam on Mark Twain Lake on July 4th weekend, this event draws cowboys from across the state. | 573/735–4391.
SEPT.: *Missouri Mule Days.* Mule races, jumps, and other festivities at Mark Twain Lake celebrate Missouri's state animal on the last weekend of the month. | 800/735–4391.

Dining

Broadway on the Lake. American. Dine and see a musical revue at this restaurant and the-ater. The dinner/theater package includes a four-entrée buffet with roast sirloin, pasta, or pork roast. Or you can order from the menu, which includes hamburgers, steaks, and many other selections. The restaurant is 10 mi south of Monroe City and 8 mi north of Perry. | 19941 Hwy. J | 573/735–9208 | $20–$26 | AE, MC, V | Closed Jan.–Mar. No lunch.

Junction. Steak. Junction serves a wide range of steak entrées—sirloins, rib eyes, prime ribs, and K.C. strips—as well as catfish sandwiches, smoked turkey sandwiches, and sal-ads. It is just outside Perry, 15 mi south of Monroe City, and is a favorite prom-night des-tination for local kids. | 28840 Hwy. 19, Perry | 573/565–3620 | $4–$14 | AE, D, MC, V | Breakfast also available.

Railway Steakhouse and Lounge. Steak. This steak house serves a variety of entrées, such as crab legs, shrimp Alfredo, and cheeseburgers, in addition to the traditional range of steaks. Its name comes from its location right next to the railroad tracks in the middle of Mon-roe City. Kids' menu. | 101 N. Main St. | 573/735–3539 | $10–$17 | AE, D, MC, V.

Lodging

Bel-Air Motel. This one-level motel is 12 mi from Mark Twain Lake and has an area in the parking lot for boats. Cable TV. Refrigerators. | 501 U.S. Business Rte. 36, Box 247 | 573/735–4549 | 21 rooms | $23–$46 | AE, D, MC, V.

Harbor Inn Motel and Condos. Fish to your heart's content in this motel's four small lakes, or travel the 1½ mi to Mark Twain Lake. The barbecue grills, fish-cleaning stations, and kids' playground make the Harbor Inn Motel a great place for families who enjoy the outdoors. Picnic area. Some microwaves, some refrigerators, cable TV. Pool, lake. Hot tub. Volleyball, beach, fishing. Playground. Business services. No pets. | 18552 Harbortown Rd./Rte. J | 573/735–4988 | www.riverbnd.com/harborinn | 40 rooms | $44–$50 | D, MC, V.

Monroe City Inn. This hotel is within walking distance of several fast-food restaurants and is 1½ mi from a local golf course. It has a game room with video games, pool tables, and foozball. Cable TV. Pool. Hot tub. Some pets allowed (fee). | 3 Gateway Sq. | 573/735–4200 | fax 573/735–3493 | 47 rooms | $40–$55 | AE, D, DC, MC, V.

Rainbow. This motel was built in 1988 on a commercial strip about ½ mi from downtown. There are several fast-food restaurants within walking distance. Cable TV. Pool. | 308 5th St. | 573/735–4526 | 20 rooms | $38 | AE, D, MC, V.

Red Barn Inn. This rustic red barn on Mark Twain Lake has its original exposed-beam ceil-ings, hardwood floors, and staircase. Its three guest rooms, with two shared baths, are com-fortably furnished and ornamented with country quilts and lace curtains. The barn also houses a gift shop, where you can purchase handcrafted gifts, coffees, and souvenirs. You are welcome to explore the 2 acres of countryside surrounding the inn. Picnic area, com-plimentary breakfast. No room phones, TV in common area. Hot tub, outdoor hot tub. Gym, hiking, fishing. Shops, library. No pets. No smoking. | 22748 Joanna Dr., Perry | 573/565–9612 | redbarnn@dstream.net | www.redbarninn.com | 3 rooms (with shared bath) | $55 | MC, V.

MOUND CITY

(Nearby town also listed: St. Joseph)

Known and named for its trail of unusual red-rock creations, left by departing glaciers, Mound City is popular with wildlife lovers. The Squaw Creek National Wildlife Refuge is a major stopping point for snow geese and bald eagles on the migration each fall. The State Theater on State Street draws a good crowd to productions throughout the year, and restored homes and buildings add charm to the community.

Information: Mound City Hall | P.O. Box 215, 205 East 6th St., 64470 | 660/442–3447.

Attractions

Big Lake State Park. The Missouri River carved this park hundreds of years ago, creating a perfect spot for bird-watching and fishing. | Rte. 118 southwest to Rte. 111 south, Bigelow | 660/442–3770 | www.dnr.state.mo.us/dsp | Free | Daily.

Squaw Creek National Wildlife Refuge. Hundreds of thousands of ducks and geese stop at this 7,178-acre refuge in the fall and spring migrations. You may also see bald eagles here. Take Interstate 29 south to exit 79, then U.S. 159 west. | U.S. 159 S | 660/442–3187 | Free | Refuge daily dawn–dusk; visitors contact station Oct.–Nov., weekdays 7:30–4, weekends 10–4; Dec.–Sept., weekdays only, 7:30–4.

State Theater. Local and national companies offer a variety of live performances throughout the year. Musical performances range from classical to bluegrass. | 510 State St. | 660/442–5909 or 660/442–5423.

ON THE CALENDAR

JULY–SEPT.: *Lotus Blooms.* Photographers and others enjoy the beauty of the American water lily in bloom at the Squaw Creek Wildlife Refuge from mid-July through early September. | 660/442–3187.

SEPT.: *Market Square Days.* This Labor Day Weekend festival celebrates the farmers' market at the town square. | 660/442–3702.

Dining

Quackers Bar and Grill. American. This low-key local hangout with a hunting motif is known for pizza, burgers, and tenderloin sandwiches. | 1012 State St. | 660/442–5502 | $5–$16 | AE, D, MC, V | Closed Sun.

Lodging

Audrey's Motel. Many people who come to view the area's wildlife stay at this low-key motel on Highway 59 North. Rooms have queen-size beds. Restaurants and shops are two blocks away. Complimentary Continental breakfast. Some microwaves, some refrigerators, cable TV. Pets allowed. | 1211 State St. | 660/442–3191 | 30 rooms | $40–$45 | AE, D, MC, V.

Big Lake State Park Resort. This rustic lodge and the surrounding cabins are in the midst of Big Lake State Park, near Squaw Creek Wildlife Refuge. All cabins and rooms have views of the lake and all cabins have fireplaces. Restaurant. Pool. | 200 Lake Shore Dr., Craig | 660/442–5432 | 11 rooms, 5 suites, 8 cabins | $45 rooms, $60 suites, $75 cabins | MC, V.

Historic Hugh Montgomery Bed and Breakfast. This downtown Victorian home, built in 1881, has a lovely porch, a walnut staircase, stained glass, and period antiques. Complimentary Continental breakfast. Cable TV. Hot tub. No pets. No kids. No smoking. | 410 E. 6th St. | 660/442–5634 | www.bbonline.com/mo/hhmh/ | 5 rooms | $55–$85 | MC, V.

MOUNT VERNON

MAP 12, B6

(Nearby towns also listed: Branson, Carthage, Cassville, Joplin, Springfield)

For many people Mount Vernon is just a town on the way to Branson, but it's worth your time to visit. Author Harold Bell Wright once lived here, as did the Hopewell, Kickapoo, and Delaware tribes, and you may enjoy searching for arrowheads around the areas.

Information: Mount Vernon Chamber of Commerce | 425 E. Mount Vernon Blvd., Box 373, 65712 | 417/466–7654 | www.mtvernonchamber.com.

Attractions

Mt. Vernon Courthouse. Construction of the grand courthouse began in 1900, even before Mt. Vernon's streets were paved. The imposing four-story structure is crowned with a clock tower, which chimes on the hour. | Town Sq. | 417/466–2638 | free | Weekdays, 9–5.

ON THE CALENDAR

OCT.: *Apple Butter Makin' Days.* Apple butter and cider made the old-fashioned way, plus arts and crafts on the town square on the second weekend of the month. | 417/466–7654.

Dining

Country Pride Restaurant. American. This roadside eatery augments its traditional diner fare with southern favorites. The seafood buffet is a popular attraction on Friday and Saturday evenings. The restaurant, off East Business Loop Interstate 44 at exit 46, is open around the clock. | 1080 Mt. Vernon Blvd. | 417/466–3639 | $5–$12 | AE, D, MC, V | Breakfast also available.

McClure's Plantation Restaurant. American. This large, old-fashioned establishment with stained glass throughout serves such standards as fried chicken and roast beef. Kids' menu. | 109 Market St. | 417/466–4708 | $3–$5 | No credit cards | Closed weekends. No dinner.

Lodging

Bel-Aire Motor Inn. This older one-level motel is across the street from several fast-food restaurants. Picnic area. Cable TV. Pool. | 900 E. Mount Vernon Blvd. | 417/466–2111 | www.bestwestern.com | 43 rooms | $50 | AE, D, DC, MC, V.

Budget Host Ranch. You can walk to several fast-food restaurants from this older chain motel. Picnic area. Cable TV. Pool. Some pets allowed. | 1015 E. Mount Vernon Blvd. | 417/466–2125 | fax 417/466–4440 | 21 rooms | $36–$52 | AE, D, MC, V.

McCanse House Bed and Breakfast. Period antiques like four-poster mahogany beds take you back to the Victorian era in which this home was built. A wraparound porch and English garden surround the B&B. In addition to a sumptuous gourmet breakfast, the proprietors also serve a complimentary dessert each evening, such as blackberry wine cake or crêpes. Complimentary breakfast. No room phones, TV in common area. Library. No pets. No kids under 12. No smoking. | 406 S. McCanse St. | 417/466–4867 | mccansehouse@aol.com | www.mccansehouse.com | 3 rooms | $80 | D, MC, V.

NEVADA

(Nearby towns also listed: Carthage, Clinton, Harrisonville, Joplin, Lamar, Springfield, Stockton)

The seat of Vernon County is pronounced Na-VAY-da by locals. It was founded in the 1850s then completely burned to the ground by Union troops in 1863 in an attempt to disperse bushwhackers, those southern guerrillas who created such trouble for the North. Later, in the early 20th century, a School of Magnetic Healing attracted patients from around the world.

Information: **Nevada Chamber of Commerce** | 110 S. Adams St., 64772 | 417/667–5300 | www.nevada-mo.com.

Attractions

Bushwhacker Historical Museum. This museum contains historical exhibits on Vernon County, a Civil War exhibit, a military exhibit, an early-1900s home and doctor's office, and an Osage Indian exhibit. | 212 W. Walnut St. | 417/667–9602 | $3 | May–Oct., Mon.–Sat. 10–4.

Old Jail. This is the oldest building in town to have survived a burning by federal troops. | 231 N. Main St. | 417/667–5841 | $3 | May–Sept., Tues.–Sun. 10–4; Oct., weekends 10–4.

Schell Osage Wildlife Area. You can reach this 8,633-acre conservation area, which offers hunting, camping, and fishing, by taking U.S. 54 East to State Road AA North to State Road RA East. | State Rd RA | 417/432–3414 | Free | Daily.

ON THE CALENDAR
JUNE: *Bushwhacker Days.* Nevada was burned during the Civil War, and this festival celebrates its rebuilding and rebirth. Courthouse Square hosts two evenings and one full day of live entertainment and a quilt and craft show over Father's Day weekend. | 417/667–5300.
DEC.: *Vernon County Christmas Parade.* Possibly the largest and most beautiful parade on the prairie, this event celebrates the holiday season and is sponsored by the business community to kick off Christmas shopping the first weekend of December. | 417/667–5300.

Dining

El Sambre. Mexican. Such typical Mexican dishes as fajitas and burritos are served in a spot with a south-of-the-border look. Kids' menu. | 1402 W. Austin Blvd. | 417/667–8242 | $8–$12 | AE, D, MC, V.

54 Café. American. Breakfast is always available at this restaurant across from Vernon County's fairgrounds. T-bone steaks, cod, and hamburgers are some of the many home-cooked items that fill the menu. Kids' menu. | 540 N. Subway Blvd. | 417/667–2405 | $3–$7 | AE, D, MC, V | Breakfast also available.

J. T. Maloney's. American. A friendly staff serves prime rib, chicken, and seafood in a Western-rustic atmosphere. Kids' menu. | 2117 E. Austin Blvd. | 417/667–7719 | $5–$13 | AE, D, MC, V.

Lodging

Comfort Inn. This chain hotel is on a commercial strip along with a truck stop, a Wal-Mart, and a Burger King. Complimentary Continental breakfast. Cable TV. Some pets allowed (fee). | 2345 Marvel Dr. | 417/667–6777 or 800/221–2222 | fax 417/667–6135 | 46 rooms | $62 | AE, D, DC, MC, V.

Country Inns and Suites. Just off Highway 71 on the eastern edge of town, this chain motel provides complimentary cookies, candy, and fruit in the lobby 24 hours a day.

Complimentary Continental breakfast. In-room data ports, some microwaves, some refrigerators, some in-room hot tubs, cable TV. Pool. Hot tub, massage. Gym. Laundry facilities. No pets. | 2520 E. Austin Blvd. | 417/667–9292 or 800/456–4000 | fax 417/667–2549 | www.countryinns.com | 45 rooms, 9 suites | $60–$75 | AE, D, DC, MC, V.

Rambler Motel. This older motel is 1½ mi north of downtown and within walking distance of a movie theater. Complimentary Continental breakfast. Cable TV. Pool. | 1401 E. Austin Blvd. | 417/667–3351 | fax 417/667–3390 | 53 rooms | $46 | AE, D, DC, MC, V.

Ramsey's Nevada. All rooms at this single-level motel have outside entrances and extra-large bathrooms. There are several fast-food restaurants within walking distance. Some refrigerators, cable TV. Pool. | 1514 E. Austin Blvd. | 417/667–5273 | 30 rooms | $44 | AE, D, DC, MC, V.

71 Motel. Restaurants surround this motor inn in the older, northern end of town, on Business Highway 71 and just blocks from Highway 54. Cable TV. No pets. | 400 N. Osage Blvd. | 417/667–3331 | 11 rooms | $31 | MC, V.

Super 8. A standard chain motel within walking distance of a small restaurant. Complimentary Continental breakfast. Cable TV. Pool. Hot tub. Laundry facilities. Business services. Pets allowed. | 2301 E. Austin Blvd. | 417/667–8888 or 800/800–8000 | fax 417/667–8883 | www.super8.com | 60 rooms | $50 | AE, D, DC, MC, V.

NEW MADRID

MAP 12, F6

(Nearby towns also listed: Poplar Bluff, Sikeston)

If you're a student of seismic activity, you know New Madrid (pronounced MAD-rid). One of the most intense earthquakes ever to hit North America shook this area for about three months in 1811–12. The Mississippi River flowed backward, and craters, sand blows, and fissures opened that can still be seen today. Today New Madrid, which was incorporated in 1803, is worth a stop off the interstate to view the Mississippi River from the county's observation deck.

Information: **New Madrid Economic Development and Tourism** | 560 Mott St., 63869 | 573/748–2866 | www.new-madrid.mo.us.

Attractions

Hunter-Dawson State Historic Site. This 15-room antebellum home reflects the splendor of the fine mansions once common along the great river road. | 101 Dawson Rd. | 573/748–5340 | $2 | Tours Mon.–Sat. 10–4, Sun. noon–4.

New Madrid Historical Museum. Exhibits here record the history of the most intense earthquake to shake North America, and tell the story of the exploration days of the French, the Civil War, and riverboat traders. | 1 Main St. | 573/748–5944 | $1 | Mon.–Sat. 9–4, Sun. noon–4.

ON THE CALENDAR

JULY: *Farm Fair Day.* Popcorn, rice, and fruit are used to teach about agriculture in the bootheel on the third Thursday in July at the Welcome Center at milemarker 42 on the northbound side of I-55. | 573/643–2654.

DEC.: *Hunter-Dawson House Victorian Christmas.* Missouri's southernmost historical attraction is dressed for the holidays on the second weekend of the month. | 573/748–5242 or 573/748–5340.

Dining

Rosie's Bar and Grill. American. Local favorite Rosie's is right in the center of town and is a quaint place to soak in New Madrid's flavors. The menu has hamburgers, steaks, and fried chicken. | Hwy. 61 | 573/748–7771 | $5–$13 | MC, V | Breakfast also available.

Lodging
Marston/New Madrid Super 8 Motel. This chain motel is in the middle of a cotton field just off Interstate 55 at exit 40, 5 mi south of New Madrid. Cable TV. Business services. Pets allowed. | 501 S.E. Outer Rd., Marston | 573/643–9888 or 800/800–8000 | fax 573/643–9025 | www.super8.com | 63 rooms | $41–$61 | AE, D, DC, MC, V.

OSAGE BEACH

MAP 12, C5

(Nearby towns also listed: Camdenton, Jefferson City, Lake Ozark, Lebanon, Rolla, Waynesville)

Southwest of Lake Ozark on U.S. 54 is Osage Beach, an 8-mi-long community that has become a shopping destination for visitors throughout the Midwest. Picturesque Factory Outlet Village has more than 110 top-name manufacturers' stores, as well as movie theaters and restaurants. Osage Beach is one of several small communities that make up the Lake Ozark area, and activities in the communities overlap. Versailles, Ozark, Sunrise Beach, Osage Beach, Eldon, Gravois Mills, and Camdenton all combine to serve as a summer home for thousands of outdoor enthusiasts and a real home for a few year-round residents.

Information: Lake Area Chamber of Commerce | 3502 Bagnell Dam Blvd., Box 1510, Lake Ozark 65049 | 573/365–3002 or 800/451–4117 | www.odd.net/ozarks.

Attractions
Big Shot Family Action Park. Go-carts, bumper cars, and an arcade keep everybody in the family entertained. | Rte. 2, Linn Creek | 573/346–6111 | Pay per ride | Memorial Day–Labor Day, 10–midnight; Labor Day–Oct., 10–5.

Big Surf Water Park. A space-bowl ride and a wave pool are highlights here. New to the park in 2000 was Tropical Splash Island, a special area for children age six and under. | Hwy. 54, Linn Creek | 573/346–6111 | $20 | Memorial Day–Labor Day, daily 10–7.

Factory Outlet Village. More than 110 top-name manufacturers have outlet stores here. There are also movie theaters and restaurants. | 4540 Hwy. 54 | 573/348–2065 | Free | Mar.–Dec., daily.

House of Butterflies. Live butterflies from around the world. | Lake Rd. 54-63, Osage Beach | 573/348–0088 | $5 | Apr.–Dec., daily 10–6.

Lake of the Ozarks State Park. Missouri's largest state park features Angel Showers, a waterfall in Ozark Caverns. There are also two swimming beaches, several boat-launch areas, cave tours, hiking trails, horseback riding trails, and camp sites. | Hwy. 42 | 573/348–2694 | www.dnr.state.mo.us/dsp | Free | Daily.

Dining
Brass Door Restaurant and Lounge. Contemporary. Favorites here include the prime rib and the batter-fried lobster. Entertainment Fridays and Saturdays. Kids' menu. | 5167 U.S. 54 | 573/348–9229 | $11–$50 | AE, D, MC, V | No lunch.

Domenico's at the Lake. Eclectic. This large upscale restaurant is known for its Friday and Saturday all-you-can-eat prime rib special. Other dishes, such as the shrimp fontina and shrimp made with tomatoes and mushrooms in a garlic and olive oil sauce over a bed of angel-hair pasta, are Italian-inspired. Kids' menu. | 4737 U.S. 54 | 573/348–5335 | $7–$34 | D, DC, MC, V | Closed Super Bowl Sun. No lunch.

Happy Fisherman. Seafood. While dominated by such fish dishes as all-you-can-eat catfish or Honduran and Mexican rock shrimp, this restaurant also offers chicken and steak.

Salad bar. Kids' menu. | 4767 U.S. 54 | 573/348–3311 | $10–$26 | AE, D, MC, V | Closed mid-Dec.–mid-Jan.

Imo's Pizza. Pizza. Sandwiches, salads, and a few pasta dishes are available at this roadside restaurant, but it specializes in St. Louis–style (thin-crust) pizza. Try the deluxe with sausage, mushrooms, green peppers, onions, and bacon. | 4344 Hwy. 54 | 573/348–6766 | $5–$15 | AE, D, MC, V.

Lil' Rizzo's Italian Restaurant. Italian. Mismatched tables and chairs and three-dimensional paintings contribute to this funky eatery's ambience. Pizzas, pastas, and steaks are some of the menu options; try the chicken *modiga* (breaded chicken cooked with bacon and mushrooms in a white wine sauce and served over angel-hair pasta). The restaurant is in the town's factory outlet mall. | 929 Chef St. | 573/302–1500 | $8–$20 | AE, D, MC, V.

Potted Steer. Contemporary. Known for steaks, batter-fried lobster, and a wine list praised in *Wine Spectator,* this casual spot at the west end of Grand Glaze Bridge has a view of the Lake of the Ozarks. | U.S. 54 | 573/348–5053 | Reservations not accepted | $25–$35 | AE, D, MC, V | Closed Sun. and Dec.–Feb. No lunch.

Vista Grande. Mexican. Piñatas brighten up this restaurant that serves such fare as chimichangas or a Grande Combination Platter with a taste of all the restaurant's most popular dishes across from Factory Outlet Village. Kids' menu. | 4579 U.S. 54 | 573/348–1231 | $4–$15 | AE, D, MC, V.

Lodging

Dogwood Hills Golf Club and Resort Inn. Built around an 18-hole golf course in the foothills of the Ozarks, this resort which offers individual rooms or four-bedroom condo villas on the fairway is just 1 mi from the Lake of the Ozarks. Golf and golf school packages are offered. Bar, dining room. Some refrigerators, cable TV. Pool. Hot tub. Driving range, 18-hole golf course, putting green. Business services. | 1252 State Rd. KK | 573/348–1735 or 800/220–6571 | fax 573/348–0014 | www.dogwoodhillsresort.com | 47 rooms, 4 fairway villas | $72–$97 rooms, $253–373 villas | AE, D, DC, MC, V | Closed Nov.–Feb.

Gray's Country Home Bed and Breakfast. Tall trees encircle this romantic B&B, whose charms include a wide wraparound porch. Antiques complement the quaint details of the rooms, each of which has a private entrance. One room has a private porch and hot tub, while the other, Dolly's Suite, contains an eclectic assortment of dolls. The lodging is 2 mi east of Osage Beach. Complimentary breakfast. No room phones. No pets. No kids under 18. No smoking. | 24 High Ridge Ct., Kaiser | 573/348–5564 | www.countryhome.odd.net | 2 rooms | $89–$110 | MC, V.

Inn at Grand Glaize. You'll find a fireplace, leather couches, and a view of the Lake of the Ozarks in the lounge, and lake views in most rooms at this resort. There's also a marina with boat rentals. Restaurant, bar, room service. Some refrigerators, cable TV. Pool, wading pool. Hot tub, sauna. Tennis. Gym, boating, fishing. Video games. Business services. | 5142 Hwy. 54 | 573/348–4731 | fax 573/348–4694 | www.innatgrandglaize.com | 151 rooms, 4 suites | $139–$225 | AE, D, DC, MC, V.

Inn at Harbour Ridge. Surrounded by mammoth oaks trees, this B&B is adjacent to a 55-acre state forest. The inn, built in 1999, has the appeal of a country home; the screened-in porch, where you can eat breakfast, has a cathedral ceiling and overlooks the Lake of the Ozarks. Rooms are individually appointed and have either a private patio or a private deck that looks across a wild field to the lake; some rooms have fireplaces. Complimentary breakfast. Some in-room hot tubs, cable TV, in-room VCRs, no room phones. Hot tub. No pets. No smoking. | Lake Rd. KK–33 | 573/302–0411 or 877/744–6020 | info@harbour-ridgeinn.com | www.harbourridgeinn.com | 4 rooms | $95–$115 | D, MC, V.

Kalfran Lodge. This lakeside resort has 2,000 ft of shoreline and offers a wide range of lodging on its 20 acres, from rustic rock cottages to motel units to one-, two-, or three-bedroom apartments. Each unit has a balcony or porch and most have lake views. All cottages and apartments are equipped with kitchenettes. Picnic area. Refrigerators, cable TV. 2 pools, 2 wading pools. Tennis. Docks, water sports, boating, fishing. Playground. Laundry facilities. | 1091 Kalfran Dr. | 573/348–2266 or 800/417–2266 | www.funlake.com/accommodations/kalfran | 12 rooms, 44 apartments/cottages | $64–$81, $54–$130 apartments/cottages | MC, V | Closed Nov.–Mar.

The Knolls. Premium condominiums on a secluded, wooded peninsula with a view of the Lake of the Ozarks. Picnic area. Some in-room hot tubs, cable TV. 2 pools. Tennis. Dock, water sports, boating, fishing. Playground. Business services. | Baydey Peak Rd. U.S. KK 25 | 573/348–2236 or 800/648–0339 | fax 573/348–7198 | www.funlake.com/accommodations/knolls_rental | 50 condos | $208–$245 1–bedroom condos, $240–$255 2–bedroom condos, $345–$399 3–bedroom condos, $432 4–bedroom condos | AE, D, MC, V.

Lake Chateau. Every room has a view of the water at this English Tudor–style lakeside resort. Restaurant, picnic area. Cable TV. 2 pools. Hot tub. Beach, dock. Playground. Laundry facilities. Business services. | 5066 Hwy. 54 | 573/348–2791 or 888/333–6927 | fax 573/348–1340 | www.lakeozark.com/lakechateau/ | 49 rooms | $79–$89 | AE, D, DC, MC, V.

★ **Marriott's Tan-Tar-A Resort, Golf Club and Spa.** One of the premiere destinations in the lake community, this upscale resort has 420 acres of lakeside property, a marina, a 27-hole golf course, a well-regarded restaurant, and in-room fireplaces. 4 restaurants, 3 bars, room service. Some kitchenettes, in-room microwaves, in-room refrigerators, cable TV. 5 pools, 2 wading pools. Barbershop, beauty salon, hot tub. Driving range, 27-hole golf course, miniature golf, putting green, tennis. Bowling, gym, racquetball, beach, water sports, boating, fishing. Ice-skating. Shops. Kids' programs, playground. Laundry facilities. Business services. | State Rd. KK | 573/348–3131 or 800/826–8272 | fax 573/348–3206 | www.tan-tar-a.com | 930 rooms, 287 suites | $86–$96 rooms, $132 1–bedroom suites, $212 2–bedroom suites, $283 3–bedroom suites, $364 4–bedroom suites, $445 5–bedroom suites, $526 6–bedroom suites | AE, D, DC, MC, V.

Osage Village. This Victorian-style inn is right next to Factory Outlet Village with its restaurants, movie theater, and more than 100 outlet stores. Complimentary Continental breakfast. Some refrigerators, cable TV. Pool. Hot tub. | 4616 Hwy. 54 | 573/348–5207 | www.funlake.com/accommodations/osagevillage/ | 40 rooms, 13 suites | $85–$150 | AE, D, MC, V.

Point Breeze Resort. This family resort is on 7 acres of land and is surrounded by water on three sides. Picnic area. Kitchenettes, cable TV. Pool, lake, wading pool. Tennis. Dock, boating. Playground. | 1166 Jeffries Rd. | 573/348–2929 | www.funlake.com/accommodations/pointbreeze | 35 rooms | $61–$86 | No credit cards | Closed Nov.–Mar.

Quail's Nest. This resortlike lodging in the heart of Osage Beach sits on 4 acres of landscaped lawns, ponds, pools, waterfalls, and flower beds. At least seven restaurants are within easy walking distance, and a popular outlet mall stands next door. A private path takes you directly to the mall. Complimentary Continental breakfast. Some refrigerators, some in-room hot tubs, cable TV. Indoor-outdoor pool. Hot tub. No pets. | 4644 Hwy. 54 | 573/348–2834 or 800/700–1006 | www.quailsnest.com | 55 rooms, 4 suites | $86–$150 | AE, D, MC, V.

SeaScape Resort. All the rooms in this lakefront resort have lakeview balconies and kitchenettes. Units have from one to four bedrooms, and the resort has a recreation room and a playground, which makes it a good place to bring the kids. Kitchenettes, refrigerators, cable TV, no room phones. Pool. Dock, fishing. Video games. Playground. Pets allowed. | 1359 SeaScape La. | 573/348–2620 | info@seascaperesort.net | www.seascaperesort.net | 23 rooms | $48–$75 | AE, D, MC, V.

Summerset Inn Resort and Villas. All rooms have water views at this 5-acre lakefront resort. Picnic area. Some kitchenettes, no room phones, cable TV. Pool, wading pool. Hot tub. Fishing. Video games. Playground. Laundry facilities. | 1165 Jeffries Rd. | 573/348–5073 | fax 573/348–4676 | www.funlake.com | 30 rooms | $64–$265 | No credit cards | Closed Nov.–Mar.

PARKVILLE

MAP 12, A3

(Nearby towns also listed: Kansas City, Liberty, Weston)

Founded in 1849 by Colonel George S. Park, Parkville remains much as it was 100 years ago. Although some of the historic downtown was destroyed in the Great Flood of 1993, many buildings have survived for 150 years. Craft and antiques shops and restaurants make Parkville a popular day-trip destination in metropolitan Kansas City.

Information: Main Street Parkville Association | 102 Main St., 64152 | 816/505–2227 | www.parkvillemo.com.

Attractions

English Landing Park. You can reach this 3-mi walking trail along the banks of the Missouri River at the end of Main Street. | Main St. at the river | 816/505–2227 | www.parkvillemo.com | Free | Daily.

Park College Underground. This private, nonsectarian Christian college was founded in 1875. Since 1982, much of its campus, including the McAfee Memorial Library, lies underground in the limestone caves of the area. | 8700 N.W. River Park Dr. | 816/741–2000 | www.park.edu | Free.

ON THE CALENDAR

JUNE: *Parkville Jazz and Fine Arts Festival.* Jazz musicians from metropolitan Kansas City fill the lawn at Park College overlooking the Missouri River bottom, and fine artists compete for prizes on the third weekend of the month. | 816/505–2227 | www.parkvillemo.com.
DEC.: *Christmas on the River.* The town's lighting ceremony on the Park College Campus on the first weekend of December includes a 1,000-voice children's choir, Santa's arrival by riverboat, and fireworks choreographed to Christmas carols. A crowd of 15,000 usually shows up. | 816/505–2227 | www.parkvillemo.com.

Dining

Stone Canyon Pizza. Pizza. This gourmet pizza spot is popular with locals including students from nearby Park College. | 15 Main St. | 816/746–8686 | $5–$18 | MC, V.

Lodging

Basswood Country Resort. Once a fish hatchery, this French country–style resort on 78 wooded acres became a private fishing club frequented by Harry S Truman among others in the 1940s. Complimentary breakfast. Kitchenettes, some in-room hot tubs, in-room TV/VCRs. Pool, lake. Hot tub. Volleyball, fishing. Laundry facilities. | 15880 Interurban Rd. | 816/858–5556 | fax 816/858–5556 | www.basswoodresort.com | 6 suites, 4 two-bedroom cottages | $79–$99 suites, $119–$149 2–bedroom cottages | AE, D, MC, V.

Down to Earth Lifestyles. Despite being only 15 minutes from downtown Kansas City and 12 mi from Kansas City International Airport, you're definitely in the country on this 86-acre farm 4 mi northwest of downtown Parkville. A patio off the modern farmhouse provides views of cows, horses, ducks, and a pond. The common room has a piano, color TV, board games, and books. TV in common area. Pool, pond. Laundry facilities. | 12500 N.W. Crooked Rd. | 816/891–1018 | 4 rooms | $79–$89 | No credit cards.

PILOT KNOB

(Nearby towns also listed: Bonne Terre, Farmington)

The rugged St. Francis Mountains in which Pilot Knob is located are considered to be the oldest mountains in the country. Iron ore hauled from Pilot Knob Mountain brought white men to the area and led to the construction of Fort Davidson, now a historic site and the location of numerous Civil War reenactments and other encampments each year.

Information: **Arcadia Valley Chamber of Commerce** | 301 S. Main St., Ironton 63650 | 573/546-7117.

Attractions

Elephant Rocks State Park. Giant granite rocks a billion years old stand end-to-end like a train of red circus elephants in this 129-acre state park 4 mi north of Pilot Knob on Route 21. | Rte. 21, Graniteville | 573/546-3454 | www.dnr.state.mo.us/dsp | Free | Daily dawn–dusk.

Fort Davidson State Historic Site. More than 1,000 Confederate soldiers and 200 Union soldiers were wounded or killed in the Battle of Pilot Knob here in 1864. In addition to the 37-acre battlefield, there is a visitors center with exhibits on the battle. | Hwy. V (just off Hwy. 21) | 573/546-3454 | Free | Mon.–Sat. 10-4, Sun. 11-5.

Johnson's Shut-Ins State Park. This 8,478-acre state park 30 mi southwest of Pilot Knob boasts canyonlike gorges cut by the currents of the Black River. The park offers swimming, camping, hiking and horseback trails, fishing, and picnicking. | Hwy. N; Rte. 21 north to Graniteville to Hwy. N | 573/546-2450 | www.dnr.state.mo.us/dsp | Free | Daily.

Sam A. Baker State Park. Unspoiled wilderness and clear streams make this 5167-acre park halfway between Pilot Knob and Poplar Bluff a popular family camping area. In addition there are great spots for fishing and hiking, and canoe rentals are available. | Patterson | 573/856-4411 or 573/856-4223 | www.dnr.state.mo.us/dsp | Free | Apr.–Oct., daily.

ON THE CALENDAR

MAY: *Our Town Tomorrow Festival.* Music, food, carnival, and auction on the courthouse lawn in mid-May. | 573/546-7117.

SEPT.: *Days Gone By Festival.* Demonstrations of vanishing arts, a tractor show, and an old trade demonstration take place the first weekend after Labor Day at the Ironton Fairgrounds. | 573/546-7117.

Dining

Kozy Korner Café. American. Home-style cooking in a country atmosphere. Be sure to try the plate lunch and the pies. Kids' menu. | 201 S. Main St., Ironton | 573/546-7739 | $4–$10 | No credit cards | Closed Sun.

Lodging

Fort Davidson Motel. This one-story, drive-up motel in central Pilot Knob is across the street from Fort Davidson Park, site of the Battle of Fort Davidson in 1864. Some in-room hot tubs. Cable TV. Pool. | Hwy. 21 and V St. | 573/546-7427 | 21 rooms | $40 | AE, D, MC, V.

Wilderness Lodge. This 1927 lodge, built by the side of the Black River, has water views, as do the 1970s log cabins surrounding it. Some rooms have fireplaces. Guests also have access to the lodge's woodland trails on 1,200 acres bordering the river. 3 dining rooms, bar, complimentary breakfast and dinner. Air-conditioning, refrigerators. Pool. Tennis. Beach, water sports. Playground. Business services. | Peola Rd., Lesterville | 573/637-2295 | fax 573/637-2504 | www.wildernesslodgeresort.com | 27 cottages | $138 | AE, D, DC, MC, V.

POPLAR BLUFF

(Nearby towns also listed: Cape Girardeau, New Madrid, Sikeston, Van Buren)

Founded in 1819, Poplar Bluff gets its name from the dense growth of tulip poplar trees that grow on this bluff above the Black River. Numerous local rivers, lakes, and wooded areas make the town a hub for outdoor activities such as hunting, fishing, and camping. One of the city's more famous residents, Hollywood producer Linda Bloodworth Thomason, also makes sure Poplar Bluff gets attention by mentioning her hometown in as many scripts as possible.

Information: **Poplar Bluff Chamber of Commerce** | 1111 W. Pine St., Box 3986, 63902 | 573/785–7761 | www.ims-1.com/~pbchamber.

Attractions

Margaret Harwell Art Museum. Local and regional art of all media are on display here, but the museum's highlight is "Parisian Trousseau for a Missouri Bride," a collection of the 1898-era clothing of Ann Trotter West, presented with a scholarly perspective. | 421 N. Main St. | 573/686–8002 | www.mham.org | Free | Tue.–Fri., 12–4; weekends, 1–4.

Mark Twain National Forest. A 37-mi section of the Ozark Trail System originates in the Poplar Bluff District of the forest. You can start a hike at one of six marked trailheads with parking lots along Highway 172, Rte. 67, and Forest Road. | Hwy. 172 | 573/785–1475 | www.fs.fed.us/r9 | Free | Weekdays.

Wappapello State Park. One of the best hiking spots in the state, this park also boasts a great fishing lake. To reach the park take U.S. 67 North to Route 172 East. | Rte. 172, Williamsville | 573/297–3232 | www.dnr.state.mo.us/dsp | Free | Daily.

ON THE CALENDAR

JAN.: *Ag Expo.* This two-day event held the third weekend of January at the Black River Coliseum on 5th Street showcases the agricultural process and culture in the bootheel. | 573/686–8064.

APR.: *Black Powder Rendezvous.* Greenville Recreation Area hosts a rendezvous of folks taking on the roles of pre-1840s fur trappers in various competitions, including a fire-starting contest over the third weekend in April. | 573/222–8562.

Dining

Hickory Hogg's Barbecue. Barbecue. Pork spareribs are the specialty of this very popular lunch and dinner destination, though the on-site smoker also turns out barbecued chicken breasts, beef brisket, and pork steaks. Southern-fried catfish and okra are also served. The restaurant is in a brick building west of downtown. | 826 W. Pine St. | 573/778–0700 | $5–$8 | AE, MC, V | Closed Sun.

Patricia's Tea Room. Tea. Victorian sensibilities dominate this quaint spot in nearby Dexter. Stop by for afternoon tea, or choose from the lunch menu of salads, soups, and sandwiches. | 529 N. Walnut St., Dexter | 573/624–6887 | $4–$6 | AE, D, MC, V | Closed Sun. No dinner.

Tower Restaurant. American. It's hard to avoid ordering something deep fried at this greasy spoon. But it's easy to get a feel for the town while listening to the conversations of the locals who sit and sip from their bottomless cups of coffee. It's open 24 hours. | U.S. 67 | 573/785–5731 | $4–$7 | MC, V.

Lodging

Comfort Inn. This chain hotel is 2 mi from the Margaret Harwell Art Museum and adjacent to Three Rivers Community College. Complimentary Continental breakfast. Cable TV.

Pool. | 2582 Westwood Blvd. N (U.S. 67 N) | 573/686–5200 or 800/221–2222 | fax 573/686–5655 | 58 rooms | $70 | AE, D, DC, MC, V.

Drury Inn. This 1980s chain hotel is just 2 mi from Mark Twain National Forest. Convenient to local transportation and area attractions, including a museum and city parks. Complimentary breakfast. In-room data ports, cable TV. Indoor-outdoor pool. Business services. Some pets allowed. | 2220 Westwood Blvd. N (U.S. 67 N) | 573/686–2451 or 800/325–8300 | fax 573/686–2451 | www.druryinn.com | 78 rooms | $65–$71 | AE, D, DC, MC, V.

Ramada Inn. This chain hotel is less than a 30-minute drive from Wappapello Lake, and about 45 mi from Big Springs, one of the largest springs in the country. Restaurant, bar (with entertainment), complimentary breakfast, room service. Cable TV. Pool. Pets allowed. | 2115 N. Westwood Blvd. (U.S. 67 N) | 573/785–7711 or 800/272–6232 | fax 573/785–5215 | www.ramada.com | 143 rooms | $55 | AE, D, DC, MC, V.

Super 8. This chain hotel is approximately 15 mi from Wappapello State Park and Wappapello Lake. Complimentary Continental breakfast. Cable TV. | 2831 N. Westwood Blvd. (U.S. 67 N) | 573/785–0176 or 800/800–8000 | fax 573/785–2865 | www.super8.com | 63 rooms | $68 | AE, D, DC, MC, V.

ROCHEPORT

MAP 12, C3

(Nearby towns also listed: Arrow Rock, Columbia)

Founded in 1836 as a ferry crossing on the Missouri River, Rocheport was a thriving river port for nearly a century. With the decline of river traffic and the increase in automobiles, however, Rocheport was left by the wayside. Today the town is home to fewer than 300 people. Perhaps in part because development passed it by, there are still many historic buildings in town and, in fact, the entire town is listed on the National Register of Historic Places. In addition to being an access point for the Katy Trail, Rocheport is a haven for antiques shops and art galleries.

Information: Convention and Visitors Bureau | 300 S. Providence, Columbia 65201 | 573/875–1231 | www.visitcolumbiamo.com.

Attractions

Katy Trail State Park. You'll find a trailhead and access to the long-distance rails-to-trails biking and hiking path known as the Katy Trail right in town at 1st Street. There are other trailheads in Clinton, Sedalia, Hermann, and St. Charles. | Box 166, Boonville | 660/882–8196 | www.mostateparks.com/katytrail | Free | Daily.

Les Bourgeois' Vineyard and Winery. Enjoy a spectacular view of the Missouri River valley while sampling wines, cheeses, and fruits. | Hwy. BB at I–70 | 573/698–2300 | Free | Daily 11–6.

ON THE CALENDAR
NOV.: *Holiday Open House.* Downtown businesses host sales and Christmas festivities over three weekends late in the month. | 573/875–1231.

Dining

Bistro at Les Bourgeois' Winery. Contemporary. This bistro, popular with locals and tourists alike, caters to those looking for vegetarian and healthy options. | 12847 W. Hwy. BB | 573/698–2300 | $6–$15 | AE, D, MC, V.

Trailside Café and Bicycle. American. At this café/bicycle shop, you can choose which bike to pedal down the Katy Trail while you wait for your hamburger to come off the grill. | 407 Pike St. | 573/698–2702 | $5 | MC, V.

Lodging

Katy O'Neil Bed & Breakfast. This modest Victorian B&B was built in 1880 and is on the National Register of Historic Places, but its most popular room is actually a detached converted railroad boxcar. Enjoy the lent bikes and easy access to the Katy bike trail or the common room with jumbo TV and DVD player. No TV in some rooms. Outdoor hot tub. Bicycles. | 101 Lewis St. | 573/698–2453 | 3 rooms, 1 converted railroad boxcar | $40–$95 | MC, V.

School House Bed and Breakfast. Guest rooms are decorated with antiques and chalkboards in this refurbished 1914 schoolhouse within walking distance of several restaurants and antiques shops and just a mile from the Katy Trail. Complimentary breakfast. No TV in rooms, TV in common area. | 504 3rd. St. | 573/698–2022 | www.schoolhousebandb.com | 10 rooms | $85–$205 | D, MC, V.

Yates House Bed and Breakfast. This antiques-filled B&B, modeled after an 1850s home, is on a quiet street one block from the Katy Trail. Complimentary breakfast. Some in-rooms TVs, TV in common area. Library. | 305 2nd St. | 573/698–2129 | www.yateshouse.com | 5 rooms, 1 suite | $110–$205 | D, MC, V.

ROLLA

MAP 12, D5

(Nearby towns also listed: Camdenton, Lebanon, Osage Beach, Sullivan, Waynesville)

Another of Missouri's Route 66 cities, Rolla first gained significance as a railroad center in the early 1800s, which then made it an integral part of the state's activities during the Civil War. The railroads still play an important role in Rolla's economy, as do the University of Missouri–Rolla and Fort Leonard Wood military base nearby.

Information: **Rolla Chamber of Commerce** | 1301 Kingshighway, Box 823, 65402 | 573/364–3577 or 888/809–3817 | www.rollanet.org/~commerce.

Attractions

Mark Twain National Forests. You'll find an entrance to the forest 12 mi south of Rolla on U.S. 63. The land here was shaped by the erosion of streams and rivers and as a result this area offers great hiking. | U.S. 63 | 573/364–4621 | www.fs.fed.us/r9 | Free | Daily.

Memoryville, USA. You can watch the restoration of old cars here. There's also a gallery of local artwork. | U.S. 63 | 573/364–1810 | $3.25 | Weekdays 8–6, weekends 9–5.

Meramec Spring Park and Remains of Old Ironworks. This 860-acre park 20 mi from Rolla includes the fifth-largest spring in the state, two museums (one focused on the history of the park, the other on agricultural history), and the remains of an old ironworks furnace, which is the center of a two-day celebration each October. To reach the park take Interstate 44 East to St. James, then Route 8 Southeast. | 21880 Meramec Spring Dr. | 573/265–7387 or 573/265–7124 | $3 per car | Mar.–Oct., daily dawn–dusk.

Montauk State Park. Over 40,000 gallons of water pour from Montauk Springs and meet with Pigeon Creek to form the Current River here. To reach this park, a winter nesting spot for bald eagles, take U.S. 63 South to Licking, then Route 137 South to County Road VV. | Salem | 573/548–2201 or 573/548–2434 | www.dnr.state.mo.us/dsp | Free | Daily.

Museum of Missouri Geology. Displays present fossils, dinosaurs, mineral specimens, and other artifacts discovered in the state. | 111 Fairgrounds Rd., in Buehler Park | 573/368–2118 | fax 573/368–2111 | www.dnr.state.mo.us/geology | Free | Weekdays 8–5.

Old Phelps County Jail. Historically important because of its use in the Civil War, this two-story, limestone block jail was built in 1860. | Park St. and 3rd St. | 573/364–5977 | Free | May–Sept., Sun., 1–4.

Phelps County Museum. Artifacts from the county's pioneers and Civil War memorabilia are displayed in an 1830s-era log cabin, providing information on the early economy and society of the region. | 302 3rd St. | 573/364–5977 | Free | May–Sept., Sun., 1–4.

St. James Winery. To reach this award-winning winery which offers tours and tastings, take Interstate 44 East out of Rolla to the St. James exit then head east on State Road B. | 540 Sydney St. | 573/265–7912 | fax 573/265–6200 | www.stjameswine.com | Free | Apr.–Oct., Mon.–Sat. 8–7, Sun. 11–7; Nov.–Mar., Mon.–Sat. 8–6, Sun. 11–6.

University of Missouri–Rolla. UMR students rank in the top 1% of ACT scores in the country and the emphasis this institution places on engineering and science is evident in several sites on campus. | 1870 Miner Circle | 573/341–4328 | www.umr.edu | Free | Daily. The **UMR Nuclear Reactor,** in operation since 1961, was the first nuclear reactor built in Missouri, and serves as a facility for research and training. | 1870 Miner Circle | 573/341–4236 | Free | Sept.–July, weekdays: appointment required. **UM–Rolla Stonehenge** is a half-scale reproduction of England's famous attraction and worth a look if you're nearby. | St. Patrick's La. | 573/341–4328 | www.umr.edu | Free | Daily.

ON THE CALENDAR
MAR.: *St. Patrick's Day Celebration.* Held by the University of Missouri–Rolla on St. Patrick's Day, this celebration is one of the biggest in the country. There's a parade, of course, and even the street is painted green. | 573/364–3577.
JULY: *Route 66 Summerfest.* A one-day celebration held the second Staurday of July in downtown Rolla on Pine Street featuring live entertainment, sporting events, and a display and sale of arts and crafts. | 573/364–3577.
OCT.: *Arts and Crafts Festival.* A one-day festival held on Pine Street the first Saturday of the month featuring handmade arts and crafts. | 573/364–3577.
OCT.: *Old Ironworks Days.* A two-day celebration at Meramec Spring Park featuring 1850s-era craft demonstrators held the second weekend of October. | 573/265–7124.

Dining
Alex's Pizza Palace. Eclectic. In business since 1964, this combination Italian/Greek restaurant is known for homemade pasta, lasagna, spinach pie, souvlaki, and baklava. | 128 W. 8th St. | 573/364–2669 | $7–$10 | AE, D, MC, V.

Good Therapy Coffee Shoppe & Restaurant. American. In addition to the usual lattes and cappuccinos, salads, burgers, and entrées are served. The Stroganoff Van Kaiser—a hamburger with cream cheese, onions, mushrooms, garlic, and sour cream—is the specialty. | 205 W. 11th St. | 573/368–4141 | $4–$25 | No credit cards.

Johnny's Smoke Stak. Barbecue. This casual, homey restaurant with large booths just off Route 72 is known for its smoked meats. Salad bar. Kids' menu. Sunday buffet. | 201 W. Hwy. 72 | 573/364–4838 | $6–$12 | AE, DC, MC, V.

Lodging
Best Western Coachlight. This chain hotel is approximately 5 mi from the University of Missouri–Rolla campus and 2 mi from downtown. Complimentary Continental breakfast. In-room data ports, some refrigerators, cable TV. Pool. Playground. Pets allowed. | 1403 Martin Spring Dr. | 573/341–2511 or 800/528–1234 | fax 573/368–3055 | www.bestwestern.com | 88 rooms | $60 | AE, D, DC, MC, V.

Drury Inn. This chain hotel is just a block from the University of Missouri–Rolla. Complimentary Continental breakfast. Cable TV. Pool. Business services. Pets allowed. | 2006 N. Bishop Ave. | 573/364–4000 or 800/325–8300 | fax 573/364–4000 | www.druryinn.com | 86 rooms | $60–$75 | AE, D, DC, MC, V.

A Miner Indulgence Bed & Breakfast. Despite the antiques—including oddballs such as a corn shucker and an invalid chair—that fill this B&B, the brick home is contemporary and has modern amenities. You can roam the property's 4 acres of woods, which once served as a Civil War campground. Complimentary breakfast. TV in common area. Pool. Hot tub. | 13750 Martin Spring Dr. | 573/364–0680 | www.bbonline.com/mo/miner | 2 rooms | $65 | AE, MC, V.

Rosati Winery Bed & Breakfast. When checking in to this B&B on the grounds of the 4M Vineyards, you'll receive a complimentary bottle of locally produced grape juice. The 1920s Colonial home has a porch and patio, and all guest rooms have private baths. Complimentary breakfast. No TV. Hiking. No kids under 12. | 22050 State Rd. KK, St. James | 573/265–6892 | fax 573/265–6804 | 4 rooms | $70–$75 | AE, D, MC, V.

Zeno's Motel. This motel on an access road alongside the interstate has a candlelit dining room and large banquet facilities popular for local meetings and receptions. Restaurant, bar. In-room data ports, cable TV. 2 pools. Hot tub. Business services. | 1621 Martin Spring Dr. | 573/364–1301 | fax 573/364–1301 | 50 rooms | $56–$65 | AE, D, DC, MC, V.

ST. CHARLES

MAP 12, E4

(Nearby towns also listed: Clayton, St. Louis, Wentzville)

Founded in 1769 as Les Petites Côtes ("The Little Hills") on the banks of the Missouri River, St. Charles was Missouri's first capital. Despite serious damage during the Great Flood of 1993, Old Town St. Charles—St. Charles's historic district—today looks much like it would have 200 or more years ago with redbrick streets, gas lamps, and more than 50 original buildings. Today, however, there are lots of outdoor cafés, restaurants, and specialty shops along streets that provide a splendid, unobstructed view of the river that first brought life to the city.

Information: **St. Charles Convention and Visitor's Bureau** | 230 S. Main St., 63301 | 636/946–7776 or 800/366–2427 | www.historicstcharles.com.

Attractions

Goldenrod **Showboat.** This restored 1909 riverboat, a National Historic Landmark, provides dinner and professional Broadway entertainment. | 1000 Riverside Dr. | 636/946–2020 | $22–$31.

Lindenwood University. Lindenwood is the oldest college or university west of the Mississippi, and the tree-filled campus houses a 3,000-seat performance hall, a cultural center, and Sibley Hall, a building on the National Historic Register. | 209 S. Kingshighway | 636/949–4949 | www.lindenwood.edu | Free | Daily.

St. Charles Historic District. Covering more than 10 blocks along the Missouri River this district of cobblestoned streets is filled with restaurants, cafés, and shops. | 400 N. Main–900 S. Main, visitors center at 230 S. Main | 636/946–7776 or 800/373–7007 | www.historicstcharles.com | Free | Daily. Of particular interest is the **First Missouri State Capitol State Historic Site** where Missouri's first legislators met from 1841 to 1846. | 200–216 S. Main St. | 636/940–3322 | www.dnr.state.mo.us/dsp | $2 | Daily. The **Lewis and Clark Center** offers exhibits and dioramas that portray the beginning of the Lewis and Clark expedition. | 701 Riverside Dr. | 636/947–3199 | www.nps.gov | $1 | Daily 10:30–4:30.

ON THE CALENDAR

MAY: *Heritage Days.* This reenactment of the events of 1804, prior to Lewis and Clark's embarking on their famed exploration, includes a parade with fife-and-drum corps, Sunday-morning church service, a demonstration of weapons, a skillet throw, an encampment, boat replicas, and 19th-century crafts and food, all at Frontier Park on the third weekend of May. | 636/946–7776.

MAY–SEPT.: *Music on Main.* Take your lawn chairs and settle in to enjoy food and music on Main Street the third Wednesday of each month. | 636/946–7776.

AUG.: *Festival of the Little Hills.* The largest festival of the year, this event draws more than 300,000 people during the third weekend of the month. More than 300 craft booths are set up along historic Main Street and in Frontier Park, and demonstrations are offered by some craftspeople and artisans. There are also numerous food and beverage booths, as well as live music and other entertainment. | 636/946–7776.

SEPT.: *Mosaics—Festival for the Arts.* This major arts festival, held the third weekend of September on North Main Street, brings renowned artists from across the country to exhibit and sell their paintings, sculptures, jewelry, and more. You'll also find food, live entertainment, and a children's area. | 636/946–7776.

Dining

Miss Aimee B's. Tea. The homemade desserts are popular at this tearoom, which serves breakfast and lunch in a house built in 1865. If the weather's nice, try the outdoor seating. Dinner for large groups by reservation. | 837 First Capitol Dr. | 636/946–4202 | $5–$8 | No credit cards | Closed Sun.; no dinner.

Paul Manno's Café. Italian. Try the veal marsala or pasta dishes served in a casual dining room with columns, plants, and linen tablecloths. | 75 Forum Center, Chesterfield | 314/878–1274 | $10–$20 | AE, D, DC, MC, V.

St. Charles Vintage House and Wine Garden. German. Set in an old winery from the 1860s, this restaurant offers such specialties as sauerbraten, Wiener Schnitzel, and potato pancakes. Open-air dining on three terraces with views of the gardens. Kids' menu. Sunday brunch. | 1219 S. Main St. | 636/946–7155 | $10–$15 | AE, D, DC, MC, V | Closed Mon.

Trailhead Brewing Company. American. Visit this renovated mill and enjoy its selection of handcrafted brews. The menu includes a variety of smoked and grilled items. | 921 S. Riverside Dr. | 636/946–2739 | $10–$20 | AE, D, MC, V.

Lodging

Boone's Lick Trail Inn. This Federal-style inn with a galleried porch was built in the 1840s. It is within walking distance of the Katy Trail, downtown shops and museums, and the Missouri River. During duck hunting season, the owner will guide guests interested in hunting. Complimentary full breakfast. Cable TV. No smoking. | 1000 S. Main St. | 636/947–7000 | fax 636/946–2637 | www.booneslick.com | 6 rooms | $95–$175 | AE, D, DC, MC, V.

Days Inn. You can pose for a picture of yourself sitting in the lap of a bear (actually a large chair) outside this motel. There are restaurants within walking distance, riverboat casinos 3 mi away, and a game room with a foozball table. Complimentary Continental breakfast. Some in-room data ports, cable TV. Pool. Hot tub. Gym. Video games. Laundry facilities. Business services, airport shuttle. | 1500 S. 5th St. | 636/946–1000 or 800/332–3448 | fax 636/723–6670 | www.daysinn.com | 170 rooms, 4 suites | $68–$75 | AE, D, DC, MC, V.

Fairfield Inn by Marriott. This chain hotel is on a busy street 7 mi from St. Charles's historic downtown. Complimentary Continental breakfast. In-room data ports, cable TV. Pool. Business services, free parking. | 9079 Dunn Rd., Hazelwood | 314/731–7700 | fax 314/731–1898 | www.marriott.com | 135 rooms | $99–$115 | AE, D, DC, MC, V.

Hampton Inn. This chain hotel is 4 mi from St. Charles's historic district and local casinos. Complimentary Continental breakfast. Cable TV. Pool. Hot tub. Gym. Business services. | 3720 W. Clay St. | 636/947–6800 or 800/426–7866 | fax 636/947–0020 | www.hampton-inn.com | 123 rooms | $69 | AE, D, DC, MC, V.

Holiday Inn–St. Peters. Five miles from St. Charles's historic district and within a 30-minute drive to local wineries, this hotel has a holidome with an indoor pool, game room, weight room, and sauna, as well as a dinner theater. Restaurant, bar (with entertainment), room service. Some refrigerators, cable TV. Indoor-outdoor pool. Hot tub, sauna. Gym. Video games. Laundry facilities. Airport shuttle. | 4221 S. Outer Rd., St. Peters | 636/928–1500 or 800/465–4329 | www.basshotels.com/holiday-inn | 199 rooms | $90–$101 | AE, D, DC, MC, V.

Mueller House B&B. A plethora of shops and restaurants are within walking distance of this restored French Victorian, which dates from the early 1900s. One room has a private bath; the other two share a bath and Jacuzzi. Complimentary breakfast. Cable TV. | 710 N. 5th St. | 636/947–1228 | 3 rooms (2 with shared bath) | $85–$110 | AE, D, MC, V.

New Motel 6 St. Charles. This chain motel is on a commercial strip 4 mi west of historic downtown St. Charles and within walking distance of several fast-food spots. Some refrigerators, cable TV. Pool. Pets allowed. | 3800 Harry S Truman Blvd. | 636/925–2020 or 800/843–5644 | fax 636/946–3480 | 109 rooms | $46–$50 | AE, D, DC, MC, V.

Old Elm Tree Inn. Period antiques grace this Queen Anne built in 1904 by the editor of the *St. Charles Banner.* The wraparound verandah, library, and formal living room with fireplace are especially inviting. All guest rooms have private baths. Complimentary breakfast. Refrigerators, cable TV. | 1717 Elm St. | 636/947–4843 | www.oldelmtreeinn.com | 3 rooms | $95–$120 | AE, MC, V.

ST. JOSEPH

MAP 12, A2

(Nearby towns also listed: Bethany, Cameron, Mound City, Weston)

Founded in 1826 and affectionately known as St. Jo to folks in the region, this All-American City award winner is best known as the home of the Pony Express, the place where Jesse James was killed, and the former site of stockyards filled with pork and beef (which left a legacy of great restaurants). The town has some beautiful homes, now turned into B&Bs in the historic Patee Town area, which is anchored by the Patee House Museum.

Information: **St. Joseph Chamber of Commerce** | 3003 Frederick Ave., 64506 | 816/232–4461 | chamber@saintjoseph.com | www.saintjoseph.com.

Attractions

Albrecht-Kemper Museum of Art. Exhibits works from the 18th, 19th, and 20th centuries. | 2818 Frederick Blvd. | 816/233–7003 | $3 | Tues.–Sat. 10–4, Sun. 1–4.

Glore Psychiatric Museum. Exhibits document the history of more than 400 years of psychiatric treatment. | St. Joseph State Hospital, 3406 Frederick Ave. | 816/387–2310 or 877/387–2310 | Free | Mon.–Sat. 9–5, Sun. 1–5.

Jesse James's Home. The picture James was straightening when he was shot in the back still hangs a little crooked. | 1202 Penn St. | 816/232–8206 | $2 | Weekdays 10–4, Sat. 10–5, Sun. 1–5.

Knea-Von Black Archives. The small museum houses displays on African-American leaders, scientists, and civil rights activists, plus it has a re-created Underground Railroad stop. | 1901 Messanie St. | 816/233–6211 or 816/364–0240 | $1 | By appointment only.

Lovers' Lane. Immortalized by Eugene Field in the poem "Lovers Lane, Saint Jo," this winding street lined with impressive early-20th-century homes was just a country lane when the poet courted his future wife, Julia Comstock, from his horse and buggy. | 8th St. between Ashland St. and Grand Ave. | Free | Daily.

Missouri Theater. This renovated 1927 movie palace hosts a number of professional touring groups throughout the year. | 717 Edmund St. | 816/271–4628 | Donations accepted (tours); $8–$20 (performances) | Daily, appointment required for tours.

Patee House Museum. This was once a main Pony Express office and now houses a number of historical artifacts, including a toy train from the 1860s which circles the house. | 1202 Penn St. | 816/232–8206 | $3.50 | Apr.–Oct., weekdays 10–4, Sat. 10–5, Sun. 1–5; Nov.–Jan., Sat. 10–4, Sun. 1–4.

Pony Express Museum. You can visit the stables where the Pony Express riders began their journey to Sacramento. | 914 Penn St. | 816/279–5059 or 800/530–5930 | $3 | Mon.–Sat. 9–5, Sun. 1–5.

Pony Express Region Tourist Information Center. Particularly full of information on St. Joseph, this center provides information on all of Missouri, as well as Iowa, Kansas, South Dakota, and Nebraska. Another center is located in Cameron. | I–29 and Frederick | 816/232–1839 | Apr.–Oct., daily 8:30–4:30.

Robidoux Row Museum. Named for the city founder, these row houses date to the 1840s. | 3rd St. at Poulin St. | 816/232–5861 | $1.50 | Feb.–Dec., Tues.–Fri. noon–4, Sat. 1–4.

St. Joseph Museum. This 19th-century mansion is now a museum that focuses on Native American and natural history, as well as local, state, and regional history. | 1100 Charles St. | 816/232–8471 | $2 | Mon.–Sat. 9–5, Sun. 1–5.

Society of Memories Doll Museum. Seven rooms display more than 600 dolls dating from 1840. | 1115 S. 12th St. | 816/233–1420 | $2 | Tues.–Sat. 11:30–4:30, Sun. 1–4.

SIGHTSEEING TOURS/TOUR COMPANIES

First Street Trolley. This colorful trolley system provides narrated tours around the museum district. | 12th St. at Penn St. | 816/233–6700 or 800/785–0360 | $3.50 | May–Oct., Mon.–Sat. 9–5.

ON THE CALENDAR

APR.: *Pony Express Anniversary/Jesse James Weekend.* The Pony Express was born and Jesse James died on April 3, although 22 years apart. To commemorate these events, every April 3rd horses fill the streets in a Pony Express ride, and guns sound the death of the bank robber. There are also children's events, cowboy poetry and music, and more at the Pony Express Museum. | 816/279–5059.

AUG.: *Trails West!* This arts festival held the third weekend of August in the Civic Center Park includes juried fine-arts competitions, displays by folk artists and crafters, and food vendors, as well as a hands-on children's art area. | 816/233–0231 or 800/216–7080.

Dining

Barbosa's Castillo. Mexican. Try the pork, chicken, or beef burritos, or the combination plate which samples the most popular dishes on the menu at this Mexican eatery set in a historic home with English oak wood paneling throughout. | 906 Sylvanie St. | 816/233–4970 | $12–$18 | AE, D, DC, MC, V | Closed Sun.

Belt Brewery. American. Complement your meal with a handcrafted wheat ale, raspberry-wheat ale, American pale ale, American amber ale, or stout at this brewpub. | 2317 N. Belt Hwy. | 816/676–2739 | $6–$15 | MC, V.

The Deli. Delicatessen. Try the mesquite-smoked meats, salads, or St. Brendan's Irish Cream cheesecake at this old-world deli. Kids' menu. | 2316 N. Belt Hwy. | 816/279–3354 | $6–$8 | No credit cards | Closed Sun.

36th Street Food and Drink Company. Contemporary. There are linen napkins and fresh flowers on the tables at this elegant but still casual eatery best known for ribs, steaks, pasta, and seafood. | 501 N. Belt Hwy. | 816/364–1564 | $6–$31 | AE, D, MC, V | Closed Sun.

Lodging

Comfort Suites. This three-story chain hotel is adjacent to a Cracker Barrel restaurant and the East Hills Shopping Center. Complimentary Continental breakfast. Some in-room hot tubs. Cable TV. Laundry service. | 917 N. Woodbine Rd. | 816/232–6557 | 66 rooms | $69–$109 | AE, D, DC, MC, V.

Days Inn. This chain motel 5 mi from the downtown historic district sits on a river bluff above the Missouri but rooms do not have river views. Restaurant, bar, complimentary breakfast, room service. Cable TV. Pool. Business services. | 4312 Frederick Ave. | 816/279–1671 or 800/329–7466 | fax 816/279–6729 | www.daysinn.com | 100 rooms | $55 | AE, D, DC, MC, V.

Drury Inn. This chain hotel is across the street from a mall and a 10-minute drive from the Pony Express Memorial and Jesse James's Home. Complimentary Continental breakfast. In-room data ports, cable TV. Pool. Gym. Business services. Pets allowed. | 4213 Frederick Blvd. | 816/364–4700 or 800/325–8300 | fax 816/364–4700 | www.druryinn.com | 134 rooms | $75 | AE, D, DC, MC, V.

Harding House Bed and Breakfast. This American foursquare home was built in 1905 right downtown. It has oak woodwork and beveled glass windows throughout, along with many antiques. Complimentary breakfast. No in-room phones, no TV, TV in common area. | 219 N. 20th St. | 816/232–7020 | fax 816/232–5467 | www.stjomo.com | 4 rooms | $55–$65 | AE, MC, V.

Holiday Inn–Downtown. This older downtown hotel is within walking distance of restaurants and antiques shops and just 3 mi from the Pony Express Memorial and Jesse James's Home. Restaurant, bar, room service. Some refrigerators, cable TV. Pool. Hot tub, sauna. Business services. Pets allowed. | 102 S. 3rd St. | 816/279–8000 or 800/465–4329 | fax 816/279–1484 | www.basshotels.com/holiday-inn | 170 rooms, 5 suites | $78–$95 rooms, $135–$211 suites | AE, D, DC, MC, V.

Ramada Inn. This chain hotel is within walking distance of a strip mall and several restaurants and is 15 minutes away from area casinos. Restaurants, bar, complimentary Continental breakfast. Cable TV. Pool. Hot tub. Laundry facilities. Business services. Pets allowed. | 4016 Frederick Blvd. | 816/233–6192 or 800/272–6232 | fax 816/233–6001 | www.ramada.com | 163 rooms, 5 suites | $65–$90 | AE, D, DC, MC, V.

Shakespeare Chateau Bed & Breakfast. More than 40 stained-glass windows adorn this 1885 Victorian mansion. Antique furniture fills the seven guest rooms, some of which have hot tubs. Complimentary breakfast. No TV in some rooms. TV in common area. Some in-room hot tubs. | 809 Hall St. | 816/232–2667 | fax 877/894–6914 | 7 rooms | $100–$150 | AE, D, MC, V.

ST. LOUIS

MAP 12, E4

(Nearby towns also listed: Clayton, St. Charles, Wentzville)

New Orleans fur trader Pierre Laclède selected an ideal location for the new settlement of St. Louis in 1764 in what had just become Spanish Colonial territory. Positioned as it was where the Missouri River met the Mississippi, the young St. Louis quickly surpassed the growth of its downstream neighbor, Ste. Genevieve.

St. Louis is known as the Gateway to the West and certainly that was true for Lewis and Clark. It was here that they provisioned their famous expedition. And in the years that followed St. Louis became a manufacturing center for wagons, guns, blankets, saddles, and everything the pioneer would need on a journey west. By 1860, the population was more than 160,000. Because of its size and location, St. Louis became a center for government offices and financial trade. The 1904 World's Fair brought increasing growth and global diversification to the St. Louis marketplace.

The Roman Catholic Church dominated the religious life of early St. Louis, and remains a powerful voice in the city's and state's religious, social, and political debates. The city is now also home to such corporations as Anheuser-Busch and McDonnell Douglas. The city's educational institutions, including Washington University and St. Louis University, are global leaders in scientific and social research. Forest Park's Muni Opera is the largest open-air theater in the nation, and the St. Louis Art Museum is world renowned.

St. Louis has many faces, but the city is indisputably a baseball town. Since the St. Louis Browns placed first in the major leagues in 1885, and the Cardinals won their first World Series title in 1926, fanatic love of their team has not diminished in the people of this city. Other sports come and go in this town, but St. Louisans remain loyal to their baseball.

NEIGHBORHOODS

The Hill is known for its incredible restaurants—mostly Italian—and simple old-world charm. The neighborhood, which was settled in the 1900s, is bounded by Hampton Avenue on the west and Kingshighway on the east, just south of Interstate 44. You'll know when you've reached the Hill because the fireplugs are painted the green, white, and red of the Italian flag. Baseball legends Yogi Berra and Joe Garagiola grew up playing stickball on these streets, but today you are more likely to see a game of bocce—Italian lawn bowling—played at local pubs and homes.

Soulard is a French neighborhood, bounded by the Mississippi River to the east and Interstate 55 to the north and west. There are many reasons to come to Soulard,

WEDNESDAYS AT ST. RAYMOND'S

If you're looking for a good lunch after sightseeing in downtown St. Louis, you've got lots of great choices, thanks in part to the Italian, German, and Greek immigrants who came in the 1800s and started a tradition of fine eating establishments. But if it's a Wednesday and you're in the mood to experience something a little different, you might head to St. Raymond's Hall, a church hall across the street from the Ralston Purina Headquarters in the La Salle Park neighborhood, a five-minute drive southwest of the Gateway Arch.

St. Raymond's is an Eastern Rite Catholic Church founded in 1898. But for three hours on Wednesdays, from 11 until 2, it's a favorite lunch spot for city aldermen, judges, lawyers, factory workers, housewives, and children.

A large community of Lebanese, some 375–385 families, form the base of the church membership and in the 1960s, to raise funds for the upkeep of the church, an all-volunteer group had the idea of serving a cafeteria-style lunch once a week. Parishioners prepare Lebanese specialties like meat-and-spinach pies; grape-leaf rolls; kibbi aras, a deep-fried mixture of ground beef, cracked wheat, onions, and spices; and pita bread and dish them out along with some American standards.

The very reasonable prices—the most expensive item on the menu is chicken and dumplings at $3.75—the freshly prepared food, and the unique atmosphere draw a steady and diverse clientele. There will probably be a line when you arrive, but don't worry. It moves quickly.

© Corbis

including the Bastille Day celebrations and Mardi Gras, but since 1779, St. Louisans have been coming here for the fresh produce, baked goods, and exotic spices offered Wednesday through Saturday at Soulard Market.

The Central West End, between Forest Park and Page Avenue, is a chic neighborhood filled with trendy boutiques, cozy sidewalk cafés, and numerous galleries. Many of the turn-of-the-20th-century homes are on display during the annual Greek Festival, held during Labor Day weekend. St. Louisans often stop here after work for a drink or dinner, but the Cathedral Basilica of Saint Louis and the collection of mosaic art inside are worth a visit as well.

TRANSPORTATION INFORMATION

Airports: Lambert–St. Louis International Airport sits on 2,000 acres of land in the northern suburbs of St. Louis. It is the eighth-busiest airport in North America, with more than 1,500 passengers arriving and departing each day. | Exit 235C on I-70 | 314/426–8000 | www.lambert-stlouis.com.

Airport Transportation: MetroLink, St. Louis's light-rail mass transportation system, links major attractions and runs between the airport and downtown daily. | 314/231–2345.

Intra-city Transit: The ShuttleBug/Shuttle Bee system serves the Central West End, Forest Park, and Clayton from the Forest Park MetroLink Station. | 314/231–2345.

Information: **St. Louis Convention and Visitor's Commission** | 1 Metropolitan Sq. | 314/421–1023 or 800/916–0092 | www.st-louis-cvc.com.

Attractions

ART AND ARCHITECTURE

Fox Theatre. Once the second-largest theater in the country and now listed on the National Register of Historic Places, the Fox seats 4,500 people and presents major shows and concerts. | 527 N. Grand Blvd. | 314/534–1111.

Grandel Theatre. Originally built as a Congregational Church in 1884, this Romanesque-style building was renovated in 1992 to host performing-arts shows. | 3610 Grandel Sq. | 314/534–1834.

Jazz at the Bistro. Located in the Bistro Restaurant, this venue hosts the best mainstream jazz acts in St. Louis. | 3536 Washington Ave. | 314/534–3663.

Powell Symphony Hall. Built in 1925 as the St. Louis Theater (a vaudeville house and movie theater), and rechristened as Powell Symphony Hall after extensive renovations in the late 1960s, this is the home of the St. Louis Symphony Orchestra. | 718 N. Grand Blvd. | 314/533–2500 | www.slso.org.

The Sheldon. This concert hall, designed in 1912, is renowned for its performance-flattering acoustics. | 3648 Washington Ave. | 314/533–9900.

Sun Theatre. This circa-1913 structure includes an elaborate facade with three garlanded archways and classical grotesque masks. | 3627 Grandel Sq. | 314/533–0802.

BEACHES, PARKS, AND NATURAL SIGHTS

Dr. Edmund A. Babler Memorial State Park. You can rent bicycles or hire horses for a ride in this park which includes a memorial to a renowned St. Louis surgeon. | 800 Guy Park Dr. (off Rte. 109), Wildwood | 636/458–3813 | www.dnr.state.mo.us/dsp | Free | Apr.–Oct., daily 7 AM–9 PM; Nov.–Mar., daily 7–6.

Edgar M. Queeny Park. This county park is popular for picnics and has an indoor recreation complex, an outdoor pool, and an ice-skating rink. | 1723 Mason Rd., off U.S. 40 | 314/615–7275 | Free | Daily.

Forest Park. This park on the western edge of town was the site of the 1904 World's Fair and is the epicenter of hundreds of activities and events held in St. Louis each year. | Forest Park Blvd. | 314/289–5300 | Free | Daily. In the southeast part of the park you'll find the **St. Louis Science Center.** The center has an OMNIMAX theater, as well as life-size animated dinosaurs and exhibits showcasing technology and the environment. | 5050 Oakland Ave. | 314/289–4400 or 800/456–7572 | www.slsc.org | Free | Sat.–Thurs. 9–5, Fri. 9–9. If you're looking for state history or background information on the park and the 1904 World's Fair, try the **History Museum—Missouri Historical Society.** | Jefferson Memorial Bldg., 5700 Lindell Blvd. | 314/746–4599 | Free | Tues. 9:30–8:30, Wed.–Sun. 9:30–5. **The St. Louis Art Museum** was the fine-arts palace during the 1904 World's Fair. Today the museum is known particularly for its pre-Columbian and German expressionist collections. | 1 Fine Arts Dr. | 314/721–0072 | Free | Tues. 1:30–8:30, Wed.–Sun. 10–5. Thousands of animals roam in outdoor and indoor displays in **St. Louis Zoological Park,** one of the oldest zoos in the country. | 1 Government Dr. | 314/781–0900 | www.stlzoo.org/home | Free | Daily 9–5. Green thumbs might want to make a quick stop at the **Jewel Box Floral Conservatory,** which houses a variety of plants and tropicals, as well as a big greenhouse with a waterfall and fountains. | 5600 Clayton Ave. | 314/531–0080 | 50¢ | Daily 9–5. Skating enthusiasts might try a spin around the **Steinberg Memorial Skating Rink** before leaving the park. | 401 N. Jefferson Dr. | 314/361–5103 | $6 | June–Sept., Nov.–Mar., Mon.–Thurs. 10–10, Fri. 10 AM–11 PM, Sat. 9 AM–11 PM, Sun. 9–9.

Laumeier Sculpture Park. The wooded trails of this 116-acre park lead you through a collection of more than 65 outdoor sculptures in a variety of styles. | 12580 Rott Rd. | 314/821–1209 | www.st-louis-cvc.com | Free | Daily 7 AM–½ hr past sunset; museum Tues.–Sat. 10–5, Sun. noon–5.

Lone Elk Park. Part of this county park is drive-through only, because of roaming animals. It contains bison and deer and has a bird section. | Rte. 141 | 314/615–7275 | Free | Daily.

Mastodon State Park. A mastodon skeleton was excavated at the site of this 425-acre state park 20 mi south of St. Louis popular now for hiking and picnicking. The skeleton is replicated in a museum here, which includes other fossils and ancient artifacts as well. | 1050 Museum Dr. (exit 186 off I-55), Imperial | 636/464–2976 | www.dnr.state.mo.us/dsp | Free | Mon.–Sat. 9–4:30, Sun. noon–4:30.

Missouri Botanical Gardens. A popular spot for weddings and nature walks, the gardens host a number of special events and activities throughout the year. | 4344 Shaw Blvd. | 314/577–5100 or 800/642–8842 | www.mobot.org | $5 | Daily. While you are in the gardens you can visit **Tower Grove House,** the country home of Henry Shaw, founder of the botanical gardens. | 4344 Shaw Blvd. | 314/577–5150 | $2 | Feb.–Dec., daily 10–4.

CULTURE, EDUCATION, AND HISTORY

Earth Ways Home. The Missouri Botanical Gardens and Mid American Energy Resources partnered to create an environmental education center together in this historic Victorian home in the Grand Boulevard Arts District. | 3617 Grandel Sq. | 314/553–1996 | Free | Tours by appointment.

Jefferson National Expansion Memorial Park. This 91-acre park, established in 1935, is home to St. Louis's famous Gateway Arch as well as the Museum of Westward Expansion and the Old Courthouse, which is two blocks away from the Arch. | Memorial Dr. | 314/655–1700 | www.nps.gov/jeff/ | Free | Daily. Don't miss the ride to the top of the 630-ft stainless-steel **Gateway Arch.** The Arch was designed in the 1940s and built in 1966 to celebrate the city's part in America's westward expansion. To reach the top, you'll take a specially designed tram with capsule cars that rotate on the tracks as they move up the Arch's curve. | Memorial Dr. | 314/655–1700 | $2 | Memorial Day–Labor Day, daily 8 AM–10 PM; Labor Day–Memorial Day, daily 9–6. Below the Arch you'll find the **Museum of Westward Expansion,** which has exhibits on the Lewis and Clark expedition, Native Americans, and animals of the west. | Memorial Dr. | 314/655–1700 | www.nps.gov/jeff/ | $2 | Memorial Day–Labor Day, daily 8

AM–10 PM; Labor Day–Memorial Day, daily 9–6. The courtrooms in the **Old Courthouse** have seen some momentous legal arguments. Dred Scott began the process of suing for his freedom here in 1847 and in 1872 the court heard arguments that a woman named Virginia Minor, and indeed all American women, were constitutionally entitled to the vote. Today one courtroom has been restored to its 19th-century appearance and a second to its 1910 appearance. Adjacent galleries showcase the area's Spanish and French history. | 11 N. 4th St. | 314/655–1700 | Free | Daily 8–4:30.

Jefferson Barracks Historical Park. A military base from 1826 to 1946, this park is now filled with historical buildings, museums, and artifacts. | 533 Grant Rd. | 314/544–5714 | Free | Tues.–Sun. dawn–dusk.

Laclede's Landing. Horse-drawn carriages clatter over cobblestone streets past 19th-century brick warehouses in a historic nine-square-block neighborhood northwest of the Gateway Arch. The restored buildings are now filled with restaurants, galleries, shops, and nightspots. | 1st, 2nd, and 3rd Sts. between Washington and Carr | 314/241–5875 | Free | Daily.

Saint Louis University. This Catholic Jesuit institution is known worldwide for its science research and healthcare facilities. | 221 N. Grand Blvd. | 314/977–2537 or 800/758–3678 | www.slu.edu | Free | Daily. History and art lovers shouldn't miss the **Samuel Cupples House.** The 1888 mansion is listed on the National Register of Historic Places, and is filled with Tiffany glass and decorative art. | 3673 W. Pine Blvd. | 314/977–3025 | $4 | Tues–Sat, 11–4). The **Museum of Contemporary Religious Art** houses the world's most renowned collection of interfaith contemporary art. | 3700 John E. Connelly Mall | 314/977–7170 | Free | Tues.–Sun. 11–4.

Washington University. Founded in 1853, "Wash U" is an independent university known internationally for excellence in teaching and research. | Hoyt Dr. | 314/935–5000 | www.wustl.edu/ | Free | Daily. Established in 1881, the **Washington University Gallery of Art** has more than 3,000 pieces of art, including European and American paintings and sculptures | Steinberg Hall, 1 Brookings Dr. | 314/935–5490 | Free | Weekdays 10–4:30, weekends 1–5.

MUSEUMS

American Kennel Club Museum of the Dog. Dog-related art, special exhibits, videos, and educational programs in a Greek Revival mansion. | 1721 S. Mason Rd. | 314/821–3647 | $3 | Tues.–Sat. 9–5, Sun. noon–5.

DeMenil Mansion and Museum. Greek Revival architecture and period furnishings are the attractions here. | 3352 DeMenil Pl. | 314/771–5828 | $4 | Tues.–Sat. 10–4.

Eugene Field House and Toy Museum. The birthplace of poet Eugene Field now houses valued old toys. | 634 S. Broadway | 314/421–4689 | $3 | Wed.–Sat. 10–4, Sun. noon–4.

Forum for Contemporary Art. A noncollecting museum in the Grand Boulevard Arts District for contemporary art and the expression of ideas. | 3540 Washington Ave. | 314/353–4660 | Free | Weekdays 10–5.

International Bowling Museum and Hall of Fame/St. Louis Cardinals Hall of Fame Museum. Memorabilia celebrating the legends of Cardinal baseball share space with a 1920s bowling lane, a bowling pin car on display, and computers that allow you to play and learn about the sport of bowling. | 111 Stadium Plaza | 314/231–6340 | www.bowlingmuseum.com | $6 | Nov.–Apr., daily 11–4; May–Oct., daily 9–5.

Magic House, St. Louis Children's Museum. More than 80 hands-on exhibits and activities—including one that literally makes your hair stand on end. | 516 S. Kirkwood Rd. | 314/822–8900 | www.magichouse.com | $5.50 | Labor Day–Memorial Day, Tues.–Thurs. noon–5:30, Fri. noon–9, Sat. 9:30–5:30, Sun. 11–5:30; Memorial Day–Labor Day, Mon.–Thurs. and Sat. 9:30–5:30, Fri. 9:30–9, Sun. 11–5:30.

Museum of Transportation. You are welcome to climb on the world's largest collection of locomotives, railway cars, aircraft, carriages, and other vehicles here. | 3015 Barrett Station Rd., Kirkwood | 314/965–7998 | $4 | Daily 9–5.

Portfolio Gallery and Education Center. Two floors of this building feature work by prominent African-American artists; a third floor is used as a student art gallery. | 3514 Delmar Blvd. | 314/533–3323 | Free | Weekdays 9–5, Sat. 1–4.

St. Louis Holocaust Museum. Photos and artifacts from local Holocaust survivors tell the story of pre-Nazi Jewish life in Europe, the Holocaust, and the resettlement of Jews. | 12 Millstone Campus Dr. | 314/432–0020 | Free | Mon.–Thurs. 9:30–4:30, Fri. 9:30–4, Sun. 10–4.

Soldiers' Memorial Military Museum. Military memorabilia from as far back as the 1800s are on display. | 1315 Chestnut St. | 314/622–4550 | Free | Daily 9–4:30.

Vaughn Cultural Center. This cultural center in the Grand Boulevard Arts District offers educational programs for children, African art exhibits, and poetry and dramatic readings. | 3701 Grandel Sq. | 314/615–3632 | Admission varies | Daily 9–5.

RELIGION AND SPIRITUALITY

Cathedral of St. Louis. It took seven years to build this Romanesque basilica, which now houses the world's largest collection of mosaics. | 4431 Lindell Blvd. | 314/533–2824 | Free | Labor Day–Memorial Day, daily 6:30–6; Memorial Day–Labor Day, daily 6 AM–7 PM.

Christ Church Cathedral. The oldest Episcopal church west of the Mississippi is on the National Register of Historic Places. | 1210 Locust St. | 314/231–3454 | Free | Weekdays 9–4, Sun. 8–4.

Old Cathedral. Daily masses are held in this Catholic Church, St. Louis's oldest, built in the early 1800s. | 209 Walnut St. | 314/231–3250 | Free | Sun.–Fri. 6:30 AM–5 PM.

SHOPPING

St. Louis Centre. This shopping center has four floors and approximately 80 stores. | 515 N. 6th St. | 314/231–5913 | Free | Mon.–Sat. 10–6, Sun. noon–5.

St. Louis Union Station. Once the world's largest train station, this was one of the first stations in the country to be restored as a shopping center. | Market St. | 314/421–6655 or 314/421–4314 | Free | Daily.

West Port Plaza. This 42-acre entertainment complex features music, restaurants, a comedy club, a sing-along piano club, and two hotels. | West Port Plaza Dr. (Page exit off Hwy. 270) | 314/576–7100 | Free | Daily.

SPORTS AND RECREATION

Grant's Farm. A cabin once lived in by Ulysses S. Grant is now the center of an animal farm where you can touch elephants and Clydesdale horses. | 10501 Gravois Rd. | 314/843–1700 | www.grantsfarm.com | $4 | Mid-April–Oct., days and hours vary according to season.

Hidden Valley Ski Area. Follow Interstate 44 West to Highway 109 North to Alt Road to reach these five intermediate and three beginner ski trails with 2 chair lifts and a rope tow and a cozy lodge. Night skiing is offered every evening. | 17409 Hidden Valley Rd., Eureka | 636/938–5373, 636/938–6999 for snow conditions | www.hiddenvalleyski.com/ | Admission varies | Dec.–Mar.

National Football League (NFL)—St. Louis Rams. Since 1995 when professional football returned to the city, the Rams have played in the Transworld Dome downtown. | Transworld Dome, between Cole St., Broadway, and Convention Plaza | 314/982–7267 | www.stlouis-rams.com | $32–$55 | Aug.–Dec.

National Hockey League (NHL)—St. Louis Blues. Almost as popular as the baseball team, the St. Louis Blues regularly make it to the Stanley Cup play-offs and draw big crowds to Keil Center. | Keil Center, 1401 Clark Ave. | 314/622–2500 | www.stlouisblues.com | $15–$80 | Sept.–Apr.

National League (NL) Baseball St. Louis Cardinals. Since 1885, St. Louisans have supported the St. Louis Cardinals with sell-out crowds. | Busch Stadium, between Walnut, Spruce, Broadway, and Stadium Plaza | 314/421–3060 | www.stlouiscardinals.com | $8–$70 | Apr.–Oct.

President Casino on the Admiral. The historic *Admiral* riverboat, a riverfront feature for generations, was remade into a casino in 1994 when riverboat gambling was legalized. | 50 Lenore K. Sullivan St. | 314/622–3000 | $2 | Sun.–Thurs. 8 AM–4 AM, Fri. and Sat. 24 hrs.

Purina Farms. There are live animals to pet here and hands-on activities promoting the proper care of animals. To reach the farm take Interstate 44 to the Gray Summit exit, then follow Route 100 to Country Road MM. | 314/982–3232 | www.purina.com/commun/ | Free | Memorial Day–Labor Day, Tues.–Sun. 9:30–3; Mid-Mar.–Memorial Day and Labor Day–mid-Nov., Wed.–Fri. 9:30–1, weekends 9:30–3; reservations required.

Six Flags St. Louis. Since the 1960s, this theme park has entertained with haunted houses, log rides, and roller coasters. | Six Flags Allentown Rd., Eureka | 636/938–4800 | www.sixflags.com | $25–$30 | Apr.–Oct., Fri. 5 PM–11 PM, Sat. 11–10, Sun. 11–8.

SIGHTSEEING TOURS/TOUR COMPANIES

***Delta Queen* and *Mississippi Queen*.** America's only authentic paddle-wheel steamboats offering overnight trips begin cruises lasting from three to 14 nights from the riverfront. | Dock below Gateway Arch | 800/543–1949 | $500–$2035 | Daily.

Gateway Riverboat Cruises. The *Tom Sawyer* and *Becky Thatcher* are docked here, providing the longest-running sightseeing excursions of the St. Louis riverfront, including Dixieland jazz dinner cruises. | Dock below Gateway Arch | 314/621–4040 or 800/878–7411 | $9–$32 | Mar.–Dec.

OTHER POINTS OF INTEREST

Anheuser–Busch, Inc. The Clydesdale stables and the free samples are the highlights of this tour of the brewery, cellar, and packaging plant. | 12th and Lynch Sts. | 314/577–2626 | www.budweisertours.com | Free | Tours Mon.–Sat. 9–5, Sun. 11:30–5.

ON THE CALENDAR

FEB.: *Missouri WineFest*. Two days of wine tastings in West Port Plaza mid-month. | 314/576–7100.

FEB.: *Soulard Mardi Gras*. A ten-day street celebration in the Soulard neighborhood. | 314/773–6767.

APR.: *Blueberry Hill Dart Tournament*. This international tournament, held in the University City Loop, is one of the biggest dart tournaments in the country. It's not for amateurs, but it's fun to watch. | 314/727–0880.

MAY: *Great St. Louis Kite Festival*. Kites fill the sky during this one-day, mid-month event in Forest Park. | 314/367–7275.

JULY: *Fair Saint Louis*. Join a million people under the Arch and on the riverfront for 4th of July weekend air shows, headliner entertainment, educational displays and exhibits, fireworks, and more. | 314/434–3434.

AUG.: *Moonlight Ramble*. A nighttime bicycle ride that begins in front of Soldier's Memorial and continues through the streets of downtown St. Louis on the third weekend of August. | 314/644–4660.

AUG.: *Great Forest Park Balloon Race*. They don't go fast or far, but they look great. This weekend-long event held late in the month also includes sky diving, a Frisbee exhibition, a photo contest, and a balloon race. | 314/993–2468.

OCT.: *Marching Band Festival*. Nearly 100 high school bands compete in this event held at the Transworld Dome on the third Saturday of October. | 314/342–5000.

NOV.: *Mid-America Holiday Parade*. The Midwest's largest holiday parade fills the downtown area on Thanksgiving morning. | 314/286–4086.

DEC.: *Cherokee Street Antique District Cookie Walk.* More than 40 antiques and collectibles shops on Jefferson and Cherokee streets serve fresh-baked holiday cookies the first weekend of December. | 314/773–8810.

WALKING TOUR

Grand Center Arts and Education District (approximately 2- 4 hrs)

Bordered by Delmar Boulevard on the north, Lindell and St. Louis University on the south, Grand Boulevard is the core of St. Louis's Education District. Since the mid-1800s, Grand Center has been recognized as a premiere residential and artistic center of St. Louis. In the late 20th century, the area experienced a massive renovation of homes, theaters, and galleries and it now attracts more than 1 million visitors to 1,200 events annually. Begin this walking tour at the intersection of Grand and Delmar Boulevards, where plenty of parking is available. Note the 1930s-era neon parking signs, especially impressive after dark. Dramatic lighting elsewhere throughout the district—but particularly at the Fox Theatre and Powell Hall—also reflects the influence of the 1930s on this neighborhood.

The first site on this tour is the **Portfolio Gallery and Education Center,** at 3514 Delmar Boulevard. Built in 1890, this Romanesque Victorian house–turned–gallery (1989) displays visual arts by African-American artists. Turn right on Delmar to reach Grand Boulevard then turn left to find the **Powell Symphony Hall,** at 718 North Grand Boulevard. The building, patterned after a chapel at the Palace of Versailles, was first opened as a movie theater in 1923. It is now home to the St. Louis Symphony, America's second-oldest orchestra, which performs more than 100 concerts each year. Continue on Grand Boulevard and make a right on Grandel Square. At 3617 Grandel Square you will find the **Earth Ways Home,** a Victorian residence–turned–environmental education center. Tours are given by appointment. Just a few steps past the Earth Ways Home is the **Sun Theatre.** Built in 1913 as a German-language theater, the remodeled 1,500-seat auditorium hosts numerous stage and musical performances throughout the year. Directly across the street from the Sun is **Grandel Theatre.** Built in 1884 as a Congregational Church in the Romanesque Revival style, the Grandel is now used by several traveling performance companies, including the St. Louis Shakespeare Company and the St. Louis Black Repertory Company. Continue west on Grandel Square to the **Vaughn Cultural Center,** at 3701 Grandel Square. Home to the Urban League of metropolitan St. Louis, the Vaughn highlights works of African-American artists and hosts poetry readings and oral performances. Retracing your steps to the intersection of Grand Boulevard and Grandel Square, note *Tilted Plane,* an environmental sculpture by James Turrell. Turn right, or south, and walk along Grand Boulevard to Washington Avenue. Turn left and you will come across **Jazz at the Bistro,** at 3536 Washington Avenue. The best of St. Louis jazz performs here for 18 weeks from September through May. Adjacent to Jazz at the Bistro is the **Forum for Contemporary Art,** which hosts numerous public dialogues, collaborative art events, and education programs to promote contemporary art. Return to Grand Boulevard for a visit to the **Fox Theatre,** at 527 North Grand Boulevard. Listed on the National Register of Historic Places, the "Fabulous Fox," as St. Louisans call it, was built in 1920 in the Siamese-Byzantine style. The 4,500-seat auditorium is dominated by a 2,000-pound glass chandelier. The Fox hosts musicals, concerts, and comedy performances. Head west on Washington Avenue to Number 3716, the **Sheldon.** Opened in 1912, the 728-seat concert hall is renowned for its acoustics and often hosts classical and operatic performances. Next door to the Sheldon is the **Pulitzer Foundation for the Arts.** Opened in 2000, the foundation promotes the relationship between art and architecture in a unique structure designed by Japanese architect Tadao Ando. Retrace your steps on Washington Avenue to Grand Boulevard. Turn south (or to the right), and enter the campus of St. Louis University. On the John Connelly Mall, you will find the **Samuel Cupples House,** built in 1888 and listed on the National Register of Historic Places. Tiffany windows, purple Colorado sandstone, and elegant exterior ornamentation highlight this 42-room mansion. Return to Grand Boulevard and travel north to your original parking spot near the **Portfolio Gallery and Education Center.**

Dining

INEXPENSIVE

Balaban's. Eclectic. This Central West End restaurant is decorated with vintage wine posters and offers a wide-ranging menu featuring such dishes as barbecued salmon and *ligorian* shrimp pasta (linguine with sun-dried tomatoes and feta in a cream sauce). Kids' menu. Sunday brunch. | 405 N. Euclid Ave. | 314/361–8085 | $11–$25 | AE, D, DC, MC, V.

Bar Italia. Italian. The specialty at this Central West End spot is homemade tortellini. Large picture windows offer a view of Maryland Plaza. Open-air dining on a patio with views of the plaza's fountains. Kids' menu. | 13 Maryland Plaza | 314/361–7010 | $13–$23 | AE, D, DC, MC, V | Closed Mon.

Barn Deli. Delicatessen. Salad and sandwich deli standards served with country style in a converted barn in Florissant. | 180 Dunn Rd., Florissant | 314/838–3670 | $4–$6 | AE, DC, MC, V | Closed Sun.

Bevo Mill. German. A large stone fireplace, a working windmill, and a hand-painted tile mural attest to the history of this 1916 building in the southern part of the city. Try the sauerbraten or the beef Rouladen. Kids' menu. Early-bird specials. Sunday brunch. | 4749 Gravois Ave. | 314/481–2626 | $12–$16 | AE, DC, MC, V.

★ **Big Sky Café.** American. An eclectic collection of Americana fills this café known for smoked mozzarella ravioli and braised artichokes or the grilled rainbow trout with orange maple glaze, and garlic mashed potatoes voted the best by the *Riverfront Times*. Voted one of the 25 best restaurants in St. Louis by Zagat's. Open-air dining on an outside patio. | 47 S. Old Orchard, Webster Groves | 314/962–5757 | $12–$18 | AE, D, DC, MC, V.

★ **Blueberry Hill.** American/Casual. This large University City restaurant, known best for its burgers, soups, and charcoal-grilled dishes, is filled with Americana. Entertainment weekends. | 6504 Delmar Blvd. | 314/727–0880 | Reservations not accepted Fri., Sun. | $5–$10 | AE, D, DC, MC, V.

Bruno's Little Italy. This southern Italian eatery on The Hill offers such dishes as stuffed tenderloin, beef tenderloin stuffed with seafood and served with a cognac sauce, and veal milanese. | 5901 Southwest Ave. | 314/781–5988 | $15–$20 | AE, D, DC, MC, V | Closed Mon.

Café Campagnard. French. Modern cuisine—with an emphasis on seafood—fills the menu, and the mussels in curry sauce are particularly well regarded. Though the restaurant is in a strip mall in the far suburbs, the plain, whitewashed interior adds a touch of class. | 403 Layfette Center, Manchester | 636/256–3949 | Reservations essential | $10–$20 | AE, D, DC, MC, V | Closed Sun. No lunch.

Charlie Gitto's. Italian. Pictures of such baseball greats as Joe DiMaggio line the walls at this downtown sports bar–cum–restaurant known for salads. Kids' menu. | 207 N. 6th St. | 314/436–2828 | $6–$16 | AE, D, DC, MC, V | Closed Sun.

China Royal. Chinese. This Hazelwood restaurant serves Cantonese and Szechuan cuisine, including such delicacies as crispy fried eggplant and jumbo shrimp in honey sauce. Dim sum is offered on Sunday. | 5911 N. Lindbergh, Hazelwood | 314/731–1313 | $10–$15 | AE, D, DC, MC, V.

Chuy Arzola's. Mexican. This bright, casual neighborhood establishment serves such Mexican standards as chicken fajitas. | 6405 Clayton Ave., Dogtown | 314/644–4430 | $5–$17 | D, MC, V.

Cicero's. Italian. The most popular dish in this large restaurant west of downtown in University City is the cheese baked alamara, a seafood pasta made with cavatelli, shrimp, and crab in a cream sauce topped with cheese and baked. Black-and-white photographs adorn the walls. Open-air dining. Live music. Kids' menu. | 6691 Delmar Blvd., University City | 314/862–0009 | $6–$12 | AE, MC, V.

Cowan's Restaurant. American. The down-home cooking at this casual café means lots of deep frying and American cheese, as well as massive slices of meringue pies that you might have to work at to finish. | 114 Elm St., Washington | 636/239–3213 | $4–$6 | No credit cards | Breakfast also available.

Cravings. Contemporary. This French bistro, known for savory tarts and curry chicken salad, occupies an 80-year-old building in Webster Groves that still has its original tin ceilings. No smoking. | 8149 Big Bend, Webster Groves | 314/961–3534 | $11–$22 | MC, V | Closed Sun., Mon.

Crown Candy Kitchen. American. Known for sandwiches, chile, ice cream, and especially homemade candy, this restaurant is decorated in a 1930s style with Coca-Cola memorabilia. | 1401 St. Louis Ave. | 314/621–9650 | Reservations not accepted | $4–$10 | AE, D, MC, V.

★ **Cunetto House of Pasta.** Italian. More than 30 kinds of pasta, including the favorite seafood linguine *tuttomare*, are served here at one of St. Louis's most popular restaurants on The Hill. | 5453 Magnolia Ave. | 314/781–1135 | $8–$18 | AE, DC, MC, V.

Frazer's Traveling Brown Bag. Eclectic. Frazer's serves a very up-to-date version of comfort food; try the endive, pear, gorgonzola, and walnut salad, or the roast beef and mashed potatoes. The restaurant is across Interstate 55 from the Budweiser brewery 3 mi south of downtown. | 1811 Pestalozzi St. | 314/773–8646 | $6–$12 | AE, D, MC, V | Closed Sun. No lunch.

Gino's. Italian. Try the rigatoni lobster (served with baby lobster tails, pine nuts, mushrooms, tomatoes, basil, garlic, and a splash of cream) or stuffed pork (a pork tenderloin stuffed with bacon, spinach, mozzarella, tomatoes, and garlic served in a white wine sauce) at this eatery on The Hill that caters to families. Kids' menu. | 4502 Hampton Ave. | 314/351–4187, 314/351–5364 reservations | $12–$20 | AE, MC, V | Closed Mon.

Giuseppe's. Italian. Such dishes as breaded spiedini (rolled slices of beef filled with Italian stuffing and breaded outside) and chicken liver and onions served in a casual, old-world Italian atmosphere. Kids' menu. | 4141 S. Grand Blvd., South St. Louis | 314/832–3779 | $8–$19 | AE, DC, MC, V | Closed Mon.

Hacienda. Mexican. Order the wet burrito or the create-a-platter where you choose your own combination of dishes at this bright Mexican eatery west of downtown. Open-air dining. Kids' menu. | 9748 Manchester Rd., Rock Hill | 314/962–7100 | $9–$20 | AE, D, DC, MC, V.

Hannegan's. American. This Laclede's Landing dining room is a replica of the Senate dining room in Washington, D.C. One of the chef's most popular dishes is the stuffed double-rib pork chop. Sidewalk open-air dining. Entertainment weekends. Kids' menu. | 719 N. 2nd St. | 314/241–8877 | $10–$18 | AE, D, DC, MC, V.

Harvest. Contemporary. Harvest's menu mixes traditional favorites (the best onion rings in town) with the unexpected (duck breast with cassoulet). Enjoy the bright interior of this former ice-cream parlor. | 1059 S. Big Bend Blvd., Richmond Heights | 314/645–3522 | Reservations essential | $10–$15 | AE, D, MC, V | Closed Mon. No lunch.

Helen Fitzgerald's. Irish. A 300-gallon fish tank is the centerpiece of this casual dining room serving homemade pizza, chicken wings, and Irish beef stew. | 3660 S. Lindbergh Blvd., Sappington | 314/984–0026 | $4–$8 | AE, D, MC, V.

House of India. Indian. Indian art and tapestries adorn the walls at this University City eatery serving such dishes as chicken *tikkamafla*, a boneless chicken breast cooked in a tomato cream gravy. Buffet. No smoking. | 8501 Delmar Blvd. | 314/567–6850 | $7–$14 | AE, D, DC, MC, V.

J. F. Sanfilippo's. Italian. This casual downtown trattoria with murals of Italy adorning the walls offers such entrées as the rigatoni Giuseppe, rigatoni with fresh tomatoes, vodka, and shallots in a spicy cream sauce. Kids' menu. | 705 N. Broadway | 314/621–7213 | $7–$21 | AE, D, DC, MC, V | Closed Sun.

John D. McGurk's. Irish. Traditional Irish music and one of the largest beer and ale selections in the state complement the menu of corned beef and cabbage with soda bread, beef and lamb stew, and other Irish standards at this Soulard eatery. Kids' menu. | 1200 Russell Blvd. | 314/776–8309 | $5–$18 | AE, D, DC, MC, V.

Joseph's Italian Café. Italian. Try the veal marsala or one of the pastas in this sleek downtown lunch spot featuring the owner's black-and-white photography collection and tables supported by aluminum camera tripods. Sidewalk open-air dining. No smoking. | 107 N. 6th St. | 314/421–6366 | $9–$13 | AE, D, DC, MC, V | Open for weekday lunches only, dinner for private parties. No lunch weekends.

King Louie's. American/Casual. Locals swear by the Guinness beef stew, but you can also try a delicate sandwich or couscous in the casual surroundings of this former brewery and dairy a few miles west of downtown. | 3800 Chouteau Ave. | 314/865–3662 | $5–$10 | MC, V | Closed Sun. No lunch Sat.

Kreis's. Continental. There are landscapes on the walls at this Frontenac restaurant best known for prime rib but also offering fresh seafood. | 535 S. Lindbergh, Frontenac | 314/993–0735 | $16–$22 | AE, DC, MC, V.

La Sala. Mexican. "La sala" translates as "living room" and with its big, comfortable chairs and casual atmosphere this downtown eatery, known for chicken fajitas, salsa, margaritas, and Caesar salad, lives up to its name. | 513 Olive St. | 314/231–5620 | $5–$13 | AE, D, DC, MC, V | Closed weekends, except during baseball season.

Lombardo's Trattoria. Italian. Try one of the seafood specials or the steak and lobster combo in this downtown trattoria with a separate jazz room. Entertainment on weekends. | 201 S. 20th St. | 314/621–0666 | $10–$26 | AE, D, DC, MC, V | Closed Sun.

Mai Lee. Pan-Asian. Vietnamese and Chinese dishes dominate the menu here. Try the chicken with hot chile sauce. | 8440 Delmar Blvd., University City | 314/993–3754 | $6–$16 | D, MC, V | Closed Mon.

Mama Campisi's. Italian. As pictures on the wall attest, both Bob Hope and President Clinton have dined in this casual, family restaurant on The Hill that serves a wide range of Italian dishes including chicken spiedini, chicken breast stuffed with fontenella and provel cheeses, tomatoes, and prosciutto ham in white wine or lemon butter sauce, or old-fashioned spaghetti and meatballs. | 2132 Edwards St. | 314/771–1797 | $5–$20 | AE, D, DC, MC, V | Closed Mon., Tues.

Mandarin House. Chinese. This Mandarin House, a fancier version of the Union Station restaurant, is 10 mi northwest of downtown. The decor is built around a fishpond and a tapestry of the Great Wall and specialties include Mandarin beef, Chinese vegetable soup, and crabmeat soup. Sunday brunch. | 9150 Overland Plaza | 314/427–8070 | $7–$15 | AE, D, MC, V.

Mandarin House. Chinese. Known for Szechuan and Peking dishes such as crispy duck and sesame chicken, this Chinese eatery west of downtown in Union Station has Chinese paintings on the walls and an open kitchen so you'll be able to see your food being prepared. Buffet lunch. | 194 Union Station | 314/621–6888 | $8–$15 | AE, D, DC, MC, V.

Marciano's. Italian. One of the specialties at this West Port Plaza spot is beef Marciano, beef medallions in a white wine, lemon, and butter sauce with mushrooms and prosciutto. Open-air dining overlooking a fountain. Kids' menu. | 333 West Port Plaza | 314/878–8180 | $8–$18 | AE, D, DC, MC, V.

Museum Café. Continental. This café, in the St. Louis Art Museum, is done entirely in black and white and overlooks the museum's sculpture park. It offers salads, such dishes as grilled halibut and barbecue pork riblets, and an extensive dessert menu. Kids' menu. Sunday brunch. | 1 Fine Arts Dr. | 314/721–5325 | $7–$9 | D, DC, MC, V | Closed Mon.

Pasta House Company. Italian. As its name suggests, this Frontenac restaurant specializes in pasta. Try the toasted ravioli. | 295 Plaza Frontenac, Frontenac | 314/569–3040 | $10–$20 | AE, D, DC, MC, V.

Patrick's. American. Such dishes as prime rib and sautéed chicken served in an Art Deco dining room with floor-to-ceiling windows overlooking West Port Plaza. Open-air dining on a large patio. DJs and live music all week. Kids' menu. | 342 West Port Plaza | 314/878–6767 | $12–$26 | AE, DC, MC, V.

Pueblo Nuevo. Contemporary. Choose between the green café room and red dining room, and feast on contemporary creations like tuna tartare with wasabi and roast chicken with a tomato vinaigrette. | 7401 N. Lindbergh Blvd., Hazelwood | 314/831–6885 | $10–$15 | AE, D, MC, V.

St. Louis Brewery and Tap Room. British. You can see 30 different beers being brewed at this downtown brewery/tap room. In addition to tasting any of these beers you can try British or German dishes including, of course, fish-and-chips in a building now on the National Register of Historic Buildings. | 2100 Locust St. | 314/241–2337 | $5–$12 | AE, D, DC, MC, V.

Saleem's. Middle Eastern. In business since 1974, this University City restaurant's decor is defined by Middle-Eastern artifacts and paintings. Try the hummus and shish-taouk (chicken shish kabobs). | 6501 Delmar Blvd. | 314/721–7947 | Reservations essential for large groups | $7–$18 | D, MC, V | Closed Sun.

Sunflower Café. Italian. Big potted sunflowers set the tone in this casual West End café known for pizza and pasta. Sidewalk open-air dining. No smoking. | 5513 Pershing Ave. | 314/367–6800 | $8–$15 | AE, D, DC, MC, V | Closed Sun.

Thai Café. Thai. A well-known dish at this University City café decorated with Thai art is the fried shrimp with fresh pepper and garlic sauce. No smoking. | 6170 Delmar Blvd. | 314/862–6868 | $7–$12 | AE, D, DC, MC, V | Closed Sun.

Trattoria Marcella. Italian. Lobster risotto is a favorite at this homey Italian restaurant on The Hill. Open-air sidewalk dining. | 3600 Watson Rd. | 314/352–7706 | Jacket required | $9–$15 | AE, DC, MC, V | Closed Sun., Mon.

Zia's. Italian. This casual family restaurant on The Hill serves such dishes as Chicken spiedini, stuffed breast of chicken stuffed with cheeses, tomatoes, and prosciutto, and pasta *tuttomare*, in a white garlic sauce with shrimp, scallops, and clams. It also offers open-air sidewalk dining. | 5256 Wilson Ave. | 314/776–0020 | $9–$20 | AE, D, DC, MC, V | Closed Sun.

Zoe Pan Asia. Pan-Asian. Seafood dishes are the specialty at this chic, darkly lit joint. | 4735 McPherson Ave. | 314/361–0013 | $10–$15 | AE, MC, V | No lunch weekends.

MODERATE

Bristol Seafood Bar and Grill. Continental. Stained-glass windows, dark wood, and low lighting set the atmosphere at this grill known for mesquite-grilled seafood, steak, and fish. Kids' menu. Sunday brunch. | 11801 Olive Blvd., Creve Coeur | 314/567–0272 | fax 314/567–9228 | $15–$35 | AE, D, DC, MC, V.

Busch's Grove. Continental. There's a country-club feel to this wood-paneled dining room, with dog and bird prints throughout, serving prime rib and steaks. Open-air dining. Bar (with entertainment). Kids' menu. | 9160 Clayton Rd., Ladue | 314/993–0011 | $15–$40 | AE, DC, MC, V | Closed Sun., Mon.

Café de France. French. High ceilings, chandeliers, linen, and classic dishes such as duck à l'orange define this downtown restaurant. | 410 Olive St. | 314/231–2204 | Jacket required | $17–$25 | AE, D, DC, MC, V | Closed Sun.

Café Napoli. Italian. Fresh pasta and seafood are the mainstays of this popular lunch spot for movers and shakers, though the veal chop is also highly acclaimed. | 7754 Forsyth Blvd., Clayton | 314/863–5731 | $15–$25 | AE, D, DC, MC, V | Closed Sun. No lunch Sat.

Carmine's Steakhouse. Steak. Try the 28-ounce porterhouse or the bone-in strip steak at this historic Drury Plaza steak house. Outdoor dining. Kids' menu. | 20 S. 4th St. | 314/241–1631 | $16–$32 | AE, D, DC, MC, V | Closed Sun.

Cheshire Inn. American. Weather permitting, you can take a carriage ride before or after dinner on Friday or Saturday. On the border between Clayton and Richmond Heights, this inn, with its Old English architecture and decor, is known for prime rib, steak, and fresh seafood. Live piano music. Kids' menu. Saturday and Sunday brunch. | 7036 Clayton Ave. | 314/647–7300 | $14–$28 | AE, D, DC, MC, V.

Frank Papa's. Italian. Try the fried escarole or stuffed veal chop with roasted garlic cream sauce at this relaxed restaurant in a country setting. In addition to seating in the main dining room, there are tables in the wine cellar. | 2241 S. Brentwood Blvd., Brentwood | 314/961–3344 | $13–$30 | AE, D, DC, MC, V | Closed Sun.

Giovanni's Little Place. Italian. This Ballwin eatery is owned by the same restaurateur as Giovanni's on Shaw Avenue on The Hill. The most popular dish here is the osso buco original, a veal shank with fresh vegetable served over Arborio rice. | 14560 Manchester Rd., Winchester Plaza Center, Ballwin | 636/227–7230 | $15–$34 | AE, D, DC, MC, V.

GP Agostino's. Italian. Chandeliers and waiters in tuxedos set the tone at this restaurant that's about a half hour west of St. Louis. Try the *costoletta* cabernet, veal chop in a cabernet sauvignon cream sauce with mushroom caps and scallops. Sunday brunch February–July. | 15846 Manchester Rd., Ellisville | 636/391–5480 | $15–$25 | AE, D, DC, MC, V.

Harry's. Contemporary. This downtown restaurant has a beautiful view of the St. Louis skyline through its arched windows. Try one of the seafood dishes or the smoke house ribs. Open-air dining. Entertainment some nights. | 2144 Market St. | 314/421–6969 | $15–$33 | AE, D, DC, MC, V.

Schneithorst's Hofamberg Inn. German. German antiques and a stein collection help set a Bavarian atmosphere that complements such standards as sauerbraten. Open-air dining on a biergarten patio surrounded by gardens. Kids' menu. Early-bird dinners. Sunday brunch. | 1600 S. Lindbergh Blvd., Ladue | 314/993–5600 | $15–$30 | AE, D, DC, MC, V.

Sidney Street Café. Contemporary. Housed in a restored storefront with hardwood floors and exposed brick walls, this tiered dining room serves such dishes as Szechuan tuna and Tuscan-style sea bass. There is an enclosed courtyard for year-round dining. | 2000 Sidney St. | 314/771–5777 | $16–$24 | AE, D, DC, MC, V | Closed Sun., Mon.

Tornatore's. Italian. Known for seafood and Sicilian veal chops, this multilevel restaurant west of downtown has modern art on the walls, high-backed chairs, and an etched glass–panel room divider. | 12315 Natural Bridge Rd., off I-270 | 314/739–6644 | $15–$25 | AE, D, DC, MC, V | Closed Sun. No lunch Sat.

Zinnia. Contemporary. In keeping with its name this restaurant features lots of fresh flowers as well as lovely floral wall murals. Be sure to try the trout Zinnia, trout encrusted in pecans, sesame seeds, and pine nuts. Open-air dining on a patio with view of gardens. | 7491 Big Bend Blvd., Webster Groves | 314/962–0572 | $15–$25 | AE, D, MC, V | Closed Mon.

EXPENSIVE

Blue Water Grill. Seafood. The fresh seafood dishes at this eatery in the western part of town have a southwestern/Mexican flair. Open-air dining. | 343 S. Kirkland Rd. | 314/821–5757 | $25–$32 | AE, D, DC, MC, V | Closed Sun.

Charcoal House. Steak. Steak by George, a 9-ounce fillet topped with onion rings, is a popular dish at this Clayton steak and seafood spot with an old-world feel. | 9855 Manchester Rd. | 314/968–4842 | Reservations not accepted Fri., Sat. | $15–$42 | AE, MC, V | Closed Sun.

Gian Peppe's. Italian. You'll find fresh flowers on the tables in this small restaurant on The Hill that specializes in marsala dishes. | 2126 Marconi Ave. | 314/772–3303 | Jacket required | $25–$35 | AE, DC, MC, V | Closed Sun. No lunch.

Giovanni's. Italian. Crystal chandeliers, oil paintings, and damask linen set the tone at this Italian spot on The Hill. | 5201 Shaw Ave. | 314/772–5958 | $17–$40 | AE, D, DC, MC, V | Closed Sun. No lunch.

Kemoll's. Italian. Waiters in tuxedos and low lighting set the tone at this downtown spot. Try the filet Douglas, medallions of beef tenderloins in a cognac cream sauce with South African lobster. Early-bird dinners. | 1 Metropolitan Sq. | 314/421–0555 | $17–$40 | AE, D, DC, MC, V.

Lombardo's. Italian. Seafood, steak, and pasta in a casual setting in the northern part of the city near the airport. | 10488 Natural Bridge Rd., off I–170 | 314/429–5151 | $20–$30 | AE, D, DC, MC, V | Closed Sun.

Lorusso's Cucina. Italian. Risotto, veal, and tenderloin *mudega,* marinated tenderloin medallions, breaded and charbroiled, in white wine garlic sauce, are specialties at this eatery on The Hill. The kitchen is open so you can see your food being prepared. Entertainment weekends. | 3121 Watson Rd. | 314/647–6222 | $25–$35 | AE, D, DC, MC, V.

Lynch Street Bistro. Contemporary. Try the Cajun fusilli or the pork porterhouse glazed with sweet horseradish and grain mustard at this Soulard eatery in a turn-of-the-20th-century brick, ironwork, tile, and glass building. Open-air dining on a patio and deck with a full service bar and a view of the Anheuser-Busch brewery house across the street. Entertainment Thur., Fri., Sat. | 1031 Lynch St. | 314/772–5777 | $20–$30 | AE, DC, MC, V | Closed Sun.

Malmaison. French. Named after Josephine Bonaparte's house in France, this restaurant, housed in a converted 1843 dairy barn, retains its old wooden beams, many windows, and rustic feel. Try the stuffed roasted quail or the seasonal fresh seafood and wild game. Open-air dining with a view of the gardens and a fountain. | St. Albans Rd., St. Albans | 636/458–0131 | $18–$26 | AE, MC, V | Closed Mon., Tues.

Mike Shannon's. American. Named for the legendary Cardinals baseball announcer, this downtown spot is filled with sports memorabilia and photographs and serves such standards as steak and seafood. | 100 N. 7th St. at Chestnut St. | 314/421–1540 | $18–$30 | AE, D, DC, MC, V.

Once Upon a Vine. Contemporary. This eclectic eatery in the southern part of the city boasts a wine list with more than 100 offerings and such dishes as grilled sushi-grade tuna with wasabi wrapped in shredded taro root, and muscovy duck breast with poached pears in raspberry sauce. Huge picture windows give a view of English walking gardens across the street. Open-air street-side dining. Kids' menu. No smoking. | 3559 Arsenal St. | 314/776–2828 | $12–$22 | AE, D, DC, MC, V | Closed Sun.

Tony's. Italian. Three generations of the Bommarito family have run this downtown favorite known for prime veal and beef, fresh seafood, homemade pasta, and attentive service. | 410 Market St. | 314/231–7007 | Jacket required | $20–$35 | AE, D, DC, MC, V | Closed Sun.

VERY EXPENSIVE

Al's. Italian. There's an old-fashioned feel to this downtown dining room known for steak, fish, lamb, and veal dishes. | 1200 N. 1st St. | 314/421–6399 | Jacket required | $30–$50 | AE, MC, V | Closed Sun.

Dierdorf and Hart's. Steak. This West Port Plaza eatery is owned by football greats Dan Dierdorf and Jim Hart and is known for its steaks and seafood. | 323 West Port Plaza | 314/878–1801 | $30–$50 | AE, D, DC, MC, V.

ST. LOUIS

INTRO
ATTRACTIONS
DINING
LODGING

Dominic's. Italian. Tuxedo-clad waiters prepare such dishes as scampi à la griglia and veal piccata, in a white wine lemon sauce, tableside at this elegant Italian eatery on The Hill. | 5101 Wilson Ave. | 314/771–1632 | $20–$50 | AE, D, DC, MC, V | Closed Sun.

Faust's. Continental. Baroque mirrors, candles, and white tablecloths grace this elegant downtown dining room in the Adams Mark Hotel. Specialties include the pecan-crusted Colorado lamb with wild rice pancakes and a bourbon-rosemary glaze, the pineapple rum duck, twice roasted Peking-style, and the classic chateaubriand. Kids' menu. | 4th and Chestnut Sts. | 314/342–4690 | Jacket required | $50–$80 | AE, D, DC, MC, V.

The Grill. American. As the name suggests, this elegant hotel restaurant in the Ritz-Carlton specializes in grilled dishes. Try the sea bass. Kids' menu. | 100 Carondelet Plaza, Ritz-Carlton Hotel | 314/863–6300 | $25–$45 | AE, D, DC, MC, V.

John Mineo's. Italian. Daily fresh fish specials and veal marsala are popular choices in this elegant, candlelit restaurant west of downtown. | 13490 Clayton Rd., Town and Country | 314/434–5244 | Jacket required | $30–$40 | AE, D, DC, MC, V | Closed Sun.

Riddle Penultimate. Eclectic. There are more than 350 wines to choose from on the extensive wine list here. The menu offers such dishes as shrimp Sara, shrimp with garlic and mushrooms in a port wine, artichoke, and tomato cream sauce. The work of local artists adorns the walls. Open-air dining. Entertainment. | 6307 Delmar Blvd., University City | 314/725–6985 | $12–$20 | AE, DC, MC, V | Closed Mon.

Robata of Japan. Japanese. This Westport Plaza restaurant on the 12th floor of an office building is a Japanese-style steak house specializing in beef and chicken dishes including flying chicken, which is prepared at the table. Kids' menu. | 111 West Port Plaza | 314/434–1007 | $13–$26 | AE, D, DC, MC, V.

Seventh Inn. Continental. Pepper steak with fried spinach is just one of more than 150 entrées you'll find on the menu here, including numerous fresh seafood dishes. Many dishes are prepared or finished table-side. Entertainment on weekends. Kids' menu. | 100 Seven Trails, Ballwin | 636/227–6686 | Jacket required | $21–$45 | AE, D, DC, MC, V | Closed Sun., Mon.

Lodging

INEXPENSIVE

Best Western Airport Inn. This hotel is right at the airport, just ⅛ mi from the terminals and 18 mi from downtown. Complimentary Continental breakfast. In-room data ports, cable TV. Pool. Laundry facilities. Business services, airport shuttle, free parking. | 10232 Natural Bridge Rd., Woodson Terr. | 314/427–5955 or 800/528–1234 | fax 314/427–3079 | www.bestwestern.com | 130 rooms, 6 suites | $60–$79 | AE, D, DC, MC, V.

Brewers House B&B. There's a great view of the St. Louis skyline from the outdoor hot tub of this mid-19th-century Tudor-style row house just south of downtown in the Soulard area. Each room has a king-size bed and some have fireplaces. Complimentary breakfast. Cable TV. Outdoor hot tub. Free parking. | 1829 Lami St. | 888/767–4665 | 4 rooms | $70–$75 | MC, V, AE.

Carousel Motor Hotel. This hotel, 5 mi west of downtown near Interstate 70, has basic rooms with two full-size beds or one king-size bed. Cable TV. Free parking. | 3930 N. Kingshighway Blvd. | 314/383–1626 | 55 rooms | $38 | AE, D, MC, V.

Deluxe Motel. This one-story, drive-up motel is just 10 mi from the Arch. Cable TV. Free parking. | 4531 Natural Bridge Ave. | 314/385–5131 | 17 rooms | $40 | MC, V.

MODERATE

Best Western 55 South Inn. This chain hotel is in a commercial area 5 mi south of downtown and 10 mi from St. Louis University. Some in-room hot tubs, cable TV. Pool. Laundry service. Business services, free parking. | 6224 Heimos Industrial Park Dr. | 314/416–7639 or 800/528–1234 | www.bestwestern.com | 89 rooms | $72–$135 | AE, D, DC, MC, V.

Cheshire Inn and Lodge. This Tudor-style hotel, built in 1969, is within walking distance of Forest Park and the zoo and is a five-minute drive from Union Station or Busch Stadium. Restaurant (see Cheshire Inn), bar (with entertainment), complimentary Continental breakfast weekdays, room service. In-room data ports, some refrigerators, some in-room hot tubs, cable TV. Pool. Business services, free parking. | 6300 Clayton Rd. | 314/647–7300 or 800/325–7378 | fax 314/647–0442 | www.cheshirelodge.com | 106 rooms, 15 suites | $91–$101 rooms, $150 suites | AE, D, DC, MC, V.

Courtyard by Marriott. This downtown hotel, built in 1990, is three blocks from Union Station and just over a mile from the Gateway Arch. In-room data ports, cable TV. Pool. Hot tub. Gym. Laundry service. Business services, free parking. | 2340 Market St. | 314/241–9111 | fax 314/241–8113 | www.marriott.com | 139 rooms, 12 suites | $119–$125 rooms, $150–$165 suites | AE, D, DC, MC, V.

Doubletree Club Hotel. Built in 1998, this hotel is just ½ mi from the airport and 6 mi from St. Charles's historic area. Restaurant, bar. In-room data ports, cable TV. Pool. Gym. Business services, airport shuttle, free parking. | 9600 Natural Bridge Rd. | 314/427–7600 | fax 314/427–1614 | www.clubhotelstl.com | 197 rooms | $159 | AE, D, DC, MC, V.

Drury Inn. This chain hotel is just three blocks from Lambert–St. Louis International Airport, and approximately a 20-minute drive from St. Charles's historic district. There are several restaurants within walking distance. Complimentary Continental breakfast. In-room data ports, cable TV. Pool. Hot tub. Business services, airport shuttle, free parking. Some pets allowed. | 10490 Natural Bridge Rd. | 314/423–7700 or 800/325–8300 | fax 314/423–7700 | www.druryinn.com | 173 rooms, 10 suites | $93–$126 | AE, D, DC, MC, V.

Drury Inn-Convention Center. You can walk to the Gateway Arch or Laclede's Landing from this hotel which is adjacent to the convention center and stadiums in a historic building known as the Union Market in the mid-1800s when it was built. Complimentary Continental breakfast. In-room data ports, some microwaves, some refrigerators, cable TV. Pool. Hot tub. Business services, free parking. Some pets allowed. | 711 N. Broadway | 314/231–8100 or 800/325–8300 | fax 314/621–6568 | www.druryinn.com | 178 rooms | $90–$125 | AE, D, DC, MC, V.

Embassy Suites. This hotel is right in Laclede's Landing, within easy walking distance of downtown restaurants, shops, gambling and sights. Restaurant, bar, complimentary breakfast. In-room data ports, microwaves, refrigerators, cable TV. Pool, wading pool. Hot tub. Gym. Video games. Laundry service. Business services, free parking. | 901 N. 1st St. | 314/241–4200 | fax 314/241–6513 | www.embassy-suites.com | 297 suites | $119–$189 | AE, D, DC, MC, V.

Embassy Suites–Airport. This all-suites hotel is in a commercial area 2 mi from the airport, and is a short drive away from several restaurants. Restaurant, bar, complimentary breakfast. In-room data ports, microwaves, refrigerators, cable TV. Pool. Hot tub. Gym. Laundry facilities. Business services, airport shuttle, free parking. | 11237 Lone Eagle Dr., Bridgeton | 314/739–8929 | fax 314/739–6355 | www.embassy-suites.com | 159 suites | $159 | AE, D, DC, MC, V.

Hampton Inn. You can walk to the Gateway Arch from this downtown hotel. Restaurant, bar, complimentary Continental breakfast. In-room data ports, cable TV. Pool. Hot tub. Gym. Laundry facilities. Business services, free parking. Some pets allowed. | 2211 Market St. | 314/241–3200 or 800/426–7866 | fax 314/241–9351 | www.hamptoninn-suites.com | 229 rooms, 10 suites | $99–$139 rooms, $149–$159 suites | AE, D, DC, MC, V.

Hilton. Set on 14 acres of landscaped grounds adjacent to the airport, this hotel is 2 mi from the University of Missouri and 6 mi from Forest Park. Restaurant, bars. In-room data ports, microwaves, some refrigerators, cable TV. Pool. Hot tub. Gym. Laundry facilities. Business services, airport shuttle, free parking. | 10330 Natural Bridge Rd., Woodson Terrace | 314/426–5500 | fax 314/426–3429 | www.hilton.com | 220 rooms | $95–$150 | AE, D, DC, MC, V.

Hilton–Frontenac. This hotel, set on 8 acres in an upscale residential neighborhood, within walking distance of shopping and restaurants, aims for a European feel. Restaurant, bar, room service. In-room data ports, cable TV. Pool. Barbershop. Gym. Business services, airport shuttle, free parking. | 1335 S. Lindbergh Blvd. | 314/993–1100 | fax 314/993–8546 | www.hilton.com | 264 rooms, 10 suites, 18 parlor suites | $119 rooms, $129–$169 suites, $195 parlor suites | AE, D, DC, MC, V.

Holiday Inn–Airport North. This chain hotel is 1 mi from the airport and 6 mi from historic St. Charles. The game room here has Ping-Pong and a pool table as well as video games. Restaurant, bar. In-room data ports, room service, cable TV. Pool, wading pool. Hot tub. Gym. Video games. Laundry facilities. Business services, airport shuttle, free parking. | 4545 N. Lindbergh Blvd. | 314/731–2100 or 800/465–4329 | fax 314/731–4970 | www.basshotels.com/holiday-inn | 392 rooms | $99 | AE, D, DC, MC, V.

Holiday Inn Airport–Oakland Park. The second of two Holiday Inns within a mile of the airport, this one is just south of the airport. Restaurant, bar, room service. In-room data ports, cable TV. Pool. Hot tub. Gym. Laundry facilities. Business services, airport shuttle, free parking. | 4505 Woodson Rd. | 314/427–4700 or 800/465–4329 | fax 314/656–1656 | stlop@aol.com | www.basshotels.com/holiday-inn | 156 rooms, 13 suites | $115 rooms, $145 suites | AE, D, DC, MC, V.

Holiday Inn–Airport West. This Holiday Inn is halfway between the airport and West Port Plaza, just 5 mi from each. Restaurant, bar, room service. In-room data ports, some refrigerators, cable TV. Pool. Hot tub. Gym. Video games. Laundry facilities. Business services, airport shuttle, free valet parking. Pets allowed. | 3551 Pennridge Dr., Bridgeton | 314/291–5100 or 800/465–4329 | fax 314/291–1307 | www.basshotels.com/holiday-inn | 249 rooms | $110 | AE, D, DC, MC, V.

Holiday Inn–Forest Park. This chain hotel is on The Hill, 6 mi from the downtown area, and 1 mi south of Forest Park. Restaurant, bar, room service. In-room data ports, cable TV. Pool. Business services. Pets allowed. | 5915 Wilson Ave. | 314/645–0700 or 800/465–4329 | fax 314/645–0700 | www.basshotels.com/holiday-inn | 119 rooms | $95–$130 | AE, D, DC, MC, V.

Holiday Inn–Southwest. This Holiday Inn is just off the highway, 15 minutes southwest of downtown on Interstate 44. It's 2 mi from Webster University and 10 mi from Washington University. Restaurant, bar (with entertainment), room service. In-room data ports, some refrigerators, cable TV. 2 pools. Gym. Business services, free parking. | 10709 Watson Rd. | 314/821–6600 or 800/465–4329 | fax 314/821–3471 | www.basshotels.com/holiday-inn | 213 rooms | $95–$149 | AE, D, DC, MC, V.

Marriott Pavilion. This high-rise hotel is across the street from the St. Louis Cardinals' Busch Stadium, and two blocks from the Gateway Arch. Restaurant, bar. In-room data ports, cable TV. Pool. Hot tub. Gym. Laundry facilities. Business services, parking (fee). | 1 Broadway | 314/421–1776 | fax 314/331–9029 | www.marriott.com/marriott | 672 rooms, 11 suites | $99–$189 | AE, D, DC, MC, V.

Omni Majestic. This downtown St. Louis hotel, built in 1913, is listed on the National Register of Historic Buildings and is within walking distance of Forest Park. Restaurant. In-room data ports, cable TV. Gym. Laundry service. Business services, airport shuttle, free valet parking. | 1019 Pine St. | 314/436–2355 | fax 314/436–0223 | www.omnihotels.com | 91 rooms, 2 suites | $99–$159 rooms, $350 suites | AE, D, DC, MC, V.

Radisson Hotel and Suites in Downtown St. Louis. This high-rise hotel is within easy walking distance of the Gateway Arch, Laclede's Landing, Busch Stadium, and other downtown attractions. Restaurant, bar. In-room data ports, some kitchenettes, cable TV. Pool. Gym. Business services. | 200 N. 4th St. | 314/621–8200 | fax 314/621–8073 | www.radisson.com | 338 rooms, 116 suites | $99 rooms, $159–$179 suites | AE, D, DC, MC, V.

Radisson St. Louis Airport. Two miles from the airport, this hotel is built around an eight-story, glass-enclosed atrium with waterfalls and glass elevators. Restaurant, bar. In-room data ports, cable TV. Pool. Hot tub. Gym. Business services, airport shuttle, free parking. | 11228 Lone Eagle Dr., Bridgeton | 314/291–6700 | fax 314/770–1205 | 353 rooms, 16 suites | $125 | AE, D, DC, MC, V.

Renaissance Airport. This airport hotel, just 1 mi from the terminals on a strip of hotels, offers a shuttle to Union Station downtown. Restaurant, bar, room service. In-room data ports, some microwaves, cable TV. 2 pools. Hot tub. Gym. Business services, airport shuttle, parking (fee). | 9801 Natural Bridge Rd. | 314/429–1100 | fax 314/429–3625 | renhtl@primary.net | 394 rooms, 23 suites | $125–$155 | www.renaissancehotels.com | AE, D, DC, MC, V.

Residence Inn by Marriott. You can walk to Westport Plaza from this chain hotel. Historic St. Charles and the airport are each less than 10 mi away. Complimentary Continental breakfast. In-room data ports, kitchenettes, microwaves, refrigerators, cable TV, in-room movies. Pool. Hot tub. Laundry facilities. Business services, airport shuttle. Some pets allowed (fee). | 1881 Craigshire Dr. | 314/469–0060 | fax 314/469–3751 | www.marriott.com | 128 suites | $99–$160 | AE, D, DC, MC, V.

Sheraton–West Port Inn. Part of the West Port Plaza entertainment complex, this hotel was built to resemble a Swiss chalet and has a small lake out back. Restaurant, bar (with entertainment). In-room data ports, cable TV. Pool. Business services, airport shuttle, free parking. | 191 West Port Plaza | 314/878–1500 or 800/325–3535 | fax 314/878–2837 | www.sheraton.com | 293 rooms, 7 suites | $129–$159 rooms, $189 1–bedroom suites, $350 2–bedroom suites | AE, D, DC, MC, V.

Summerfield Suites. This West Port hotel 45 minutes west of downtown has seven different buildings as well as basketball and tennis facilities on its landscaped grounds. Picnic area, complimentary Continental breakfast. In-room data ports, microwaves, cable TV, in-room VCRs. Pool. Hot tub. Gym. Laundry facilities. Business services, airport shuttle, free parking. Some pets allowed (fee). | 1855 Craigshire Rd. | 314/878–1555 or 800/833–4353 | fax 314/878–9203 | 106 suites in 7 buildings | $139 1–bedroom suites, $159 2–bedroom suites | AE, D, DC, MC, V.

EXPENSIVE

Adam's Mark. This hotel is designed around a three-story atrium with arched windows and a pair of larger-than-life bronze horses created in Italy. Designed as an office building in 1900, the building became a hotel in 1983 and is within easy walking distance of Laclede's Landing. 2 restaurants, 4 bars (with entertainment), room service. In-room data ports, some refrigerators, cable TV. 2 pools. Barbershop, beauty salon, hot tub. Gym. Laundry service. Business services, parking (fee). | 4th and Chestnut Sts. | 314/241–7400 or 800/444–2326 | fax 314/241–6618 | www.adamsmark.com | 813 rooms, 97 suites | $150–$245 rooms, $340–$900 suites | AE, D, DC, MC, V.

Chase Park Plaza. Glamour and opulence are in abundance at this 1920s showplace. All rooms are suites with kitchenettes, but if you don't feel like cooking, the Tenderloin Room restaurant is just off the lobby. Restaurant. Cable TV. Business services, free parking. | 212 N. Kingshighway Blvd. | 314/633–1000 | 78 rooms | $149–$209 | AE, D, DC, MC, V.

Doubletree Hotel and Conference Center. Twenty minutes from downtown or the airport, this hotel is geared toward business travelers and is in an area of offices, with some restaurants and shops in walking distance. Restaurant, bar. In-room data ports, cable TV. 2 pools, wading pool. Hot tub. Tennis. Gym. Kids' programs (ages 1–13). Business services. | 16625 Swingley Ridge Rd., Chesterfield | 636/532–5000 | fax 636/532–9984 | www.doubletreehotels.com/ | 223 rooms, 5 suites | $140 rooms, $175–$275 suites | AE, D, DC, MC, V.

★ **Drury Inn Union Station.** Built as a YMCA in the early 1900s, this historic building with lead-glass windows and marble columns has charm and a great location across from Union Station. Restaurant, bar, complimentary Continental breakfast. In-room data ports, some refrigerators, cable TV. Pool. Hot tub. Gym. Laundry facilities. Free parking. Some pets allowed. | 201 S. 20th St. | 314/231–3900 or 800/325–8300 | fax 314/231–3900 | www.druryinn.com | 176 rooms, 20 suites | $125–$150 | AE, D, DC, MC, V.

Marriott–Airport. A full-service hotel right at the airport. Restaurant, bars. In-room data ports, cable TV. 2 pools (1 indoor-outdoor). Hot tub. 2 tennis courts. Gym. Laundry facilities. Business services, airport shuttle. | I–70 at Lambert–St. Louis International Airport | 314/423–9700 | fax 314/423–0213 | www.marriott.com | 601 rooms | $145–$205 | AE, D, DC, MC, V.

Mayfair. This historic downtown hotel with marble floors, crystal chandeliers, stained glass, and a hand-operated elevator has hosted such legends as Cary Grant, John Barrymore, Harry Truman, and Irving Berlin since it opened in 1925. Guest rooms are quite large. Restaurant, bar, room service. In-room data ports, cable TV. Gym. Business services, parking (fee). | 806 St. Charles St. | 314/421–2500 or 800/996–3426 | fax 314/421–0770 | www.wyndham.com | 52 rooms, 130 suites | $99–$214 rooms, $109–$234 suites | AE, D, DC, MC, V.

Regal Riverfront. The three-story glass lobby of this late-1960s downtown hotel just a block from Busch Stadium has a view of the Gateway Arch. A revolving restaurant on the 28th floor also has wonderful downtown views. Restaurant, bar, complimentary breakfast with suites. In-room data ports, some kitchenettes, cable TV. 2 pools, wading pool. Gym. Laundry facilities. Business services. | 200 S. 4th St. | 314/241–9500 or 800/325–7353 | fax 314/241–9977 | regalstl@accessus.net | www.regal-hotels.com/stlouis | 780 rooms, 22 suites | $109–$139 rooms. $349 1–bedroom suites, $500 2–bedroom suites, $1,000 2–bedroom presidential suite | AE, D, DC, MC, V.

Sheraton Plaza. One of two hotels attached to the 42-acre West Port Plaza entertainment complex. Restaurant, bar. In-room data ports, cable TV. Pool. Hot tub, sauna. Gym. Business services, airport shuttle, free parking. | 900 West Port Plaza | 314/434–5010 or 800/325–3535 | fax 314/434–0140 | www.sheraton.com | 209 rooms, 7 suites | $129–$159 rooms, $189–$350 suites | AE, D, DC, MC, V.

VERY EXPENSIVE

Hyatt Regency St. Louis at Union Station. The vaulted ceilings of what was once the grand concourse of the Union Station train terminal now shelter the lobby of this distinctive hotel with a wonderful downtown location and beautiful rooms. Restaurants, bar. In-room data ports, some refrigerators, cable TV. Pool. Gym. Business services, parking (fee). | 1 St. Louis Union Station | 314/231–1234 | fax 314/923–3970 | www.hyattstlouis.com | 522 rooms, 16 suites | $225–$290 rooms, $275 junior suites, $350–$375 1–bedroom with living room suites, $925 presidential suite | AE, D, DC, MC, V.

STE. GENEVIEVE

MAP 12, E5

(Nearby towns also listed: Bonne Terre, Cape Girardeau, Farmington)

Founded in 1735, locals call the first white settlement on the western bank of the Mississippi "Ste. Gen." The fur traders and lead miners who first came to this area built magnificent homes and businesses, many of which are now B&Bs, antiques shops, and galleries. Take a ride on a ferry across the Mississippi River into Illinois, stop by the River Visitor's Center, or enjoy wine at a number of sidewalk cafés. The area is filled with antiques and nostalgia.

Information: **Ste. Genevieve Tourist Information Office** | 66 S. Main St., 63670 | 573/883–7097 or 800/373–7007.

Attractions

Bolduc House Museum. A restored French Colonial home shares the secrets of herb cooking in the bake house. | 125 S. Main St. | 573/883–3105 | $1.50 | Apr.–Nov., Mon.–Sat. 10–4, Sun. 11–5.

Felix Valle Home State Historic Site. Built in 1818, this home represents the American influence on what was at first a French settlement. | 198 Merchant St. | 573/883–7102 | www.dnr.state.mo.us/dsp | $2 | Mon.–Sat. 10–4, Sun. noon–5.

Guibourd-Valle House. This two-story French Colonial built in 1806 has the original Great Norman truss still intact. Well-maintained formal gardens are in back. | 1 N. 4th St. | 573/883–7544 | $3 | Apr.–Oct., daily 10–5; Nov.–Mar., daily noon–4.

Ste. Genevieve Museum. There's a display on the Saline Creek Salt Works, the state's first industry, as well as French and Spanish artifacts dating to the beginning of Ste. Gen in this history museum. | Merchant St. and Daubourg | 573/883–3461 | $1.50 | Apr.–Oct., Mon.–Sat. 9–4, Sun. 11–4; Nov.–Mar., daily noon–4.

SIGHTSEEING TOURS/TOUR COMPANIES

Modoc Ferry Rides. You'll feel the powerful current of the Mississippi River if you ride this ferry to the historic villages across the river in Illinois. | N. Main St. | 573/883–7415 | $1 per person, $7 per vehicle | Mon.–Sat. 6–6, Sun. 9–6.

ON THE CALENDAR

FEB.: *King's Ball.* At this 200-year-old event to select the king and queen of Ste. Genevieve, held now at the VFW Hall on Memorial Drive early in the month, young men line up for a piece of cake baked with one bean in it. The man who gets the bean is made king, and he in turn chooses his queen. | 573/883–7097.

TOWER ROCK

Driving south out of Ste. Genevieve on U.S. 61, you come to the town of Perryville. Nothing much there, so go on south to the intersection of Route A and turn east to the little town of Wittenberg. Wittenberg is a German town with not much more than a gas station and a café, but you can catch a ferryboat across the Mississippi River into the Illinois town of Grand Tower.

What's in the river between the two towns is interesting. Jutting 100 ft straight up from the overpowering current of the river, the tiny island park of Tower Rock is a virtual Alcatraz, except on this island you will find bald eagles and other birds making their home in the scraggly oak and pine trees atop the quarter acre of Devonian area limestone.

Listed on the National Register of Historic Places, written about by Mark Twain, and protected by the Missouri Department of Conservation, Tower Rock Island is the smallest park in the United States maintained by state and federal funding. French missionaries once erected a cross on the island, Native Americans performed wedding ceremonies there, and troubled lovers have leapt to their death from its rocky heights. Only during low water in the Mississippi River is the island accessible by a small land bridge from the Missouri banks.

© Corbis

JULY: *Ste. Genevieve County Fair.* A three-day, mid-month fair at the Ste. Genevieve fairgrounds with 4-H competitions, prizes for the children, games, and food stands. | 573/883–7097.

OCT.: *Fall Harvest Fest.* Balloon ascents, crafts, and entertainment in Ste. Genevieve's historic District the third week in October. | 573/883–7097.

Dining

Anvil Saloon. American. The interior of this restaurant, housed in a mid-19th-century building, mimics the saloons you've seen in old western movies. Popular dishes include the fried chicken and the steaks. There are also some German specialties on the menu. | 46 S. 3rd St. | 573/883–7323 | $7–$18 | AE, D, MC, V.

Bogy House Eclectic. The menu here is quite contemporary with such dishes as grilled vegetable pasta and chimichangas, but the decor with its antiques and Victorian colors reflects the setting, a house built in 1810. Open-air dining. Kids' menu. No smoking. | 163 Merchant St. | 573/883–5647 | $6–$16 | AE, D, DC, MC, V.

Old Brick House. American. This casual dining establishment occupies the oldest brick building west of the Mississippi. Be sure to try the fried chicken or steak with onion rings and the coconut cream pie. Salad bar. Buffet. Kids' menu. | 90 S. 3rd St. | 573/883–2724 | $7–$16 | MC, V.

Sainte Genevieve Winery. Delicatessen. Though it's not exactly a restaurant, this deli is a great place to pick up meats, cheeses, fresh fruit, and a bottle or two of local wine to enjoy in the park, or on the winery's front porch. | 245 Merchant St. | 573/883–2800 | Daily, 11–5 | Free | D, MC, V.

Lodging

Creole House. Built in 1983 to resemble the traditional French Creole homes of the area, the inn has a large wraparound porch, a traditional parlor room with a library, an indoor pool, and more than 2 acres of grounds. Complimentary breakfast. Cable TV. Some in-room hot tubs. Pool. | 339 St. Mary's Rd. | 573/883–7171 or 800/275–6041 | www.creolehousebb.com | 5 rooms | $95–$135 | AE, D, MC, V.

Main Street Inn. A hotel since 1882, this brick building is surrounded by an herb and flower garden. Inside you'll find traditional furniture and antiques, vintage linens, high ceilings, tall windows with lace curtains, and refinished original wood floors. Complimentary breakfast. Some in-room data ports, some in-room hot tubs, some in-room cable TV, some in-room VCRs. Business services. No kids under 13. No smoking. | 221 N. Main St. | 573/883–9199 or 800/918–9199 | info@mainstreetinnbb.com | www.mainstreetinnbb.com | 8 rooms | $85–$125 | AE, D, MC, V.

Ste. Gemme Beauvais. Tea is served at tea time and wine and hors d'oeuvres are served in the evening in this small inn. The interior is decorated in Victorian style with antique furnishings, and outside there is a formal garden with a gazebo. Complimentary breakfast. Some in-room hot tubs, cable TV, in-room VCRs, no room phones. Business services. | 78 N. Main St. | 573/883–5744 or 800/818–5744 | fax 314/883–3899 | 9 rooms | $89–$179 | MC, V.

Somewhere Inn Time. Built in 1900, this white, wooden family home with red shutters was renovated in 1993. The complimentary breakfast may include a wake-up casserole, apple lasagna, an oven omelet, or fresh sausage. Complimentary breakfast. Cable TV in some rooms. Hot tub. | 383 Jefferson St. | 573/883–9397 | 4 rooms | $95–$125 | AE, D, MC, V.

Southern Hotel. Built in 1790 in the Federal style, this was once the finest hotel between St. Louis and New Orleans. Original woodwork and stained glass have been preserved and the hotel is filled with antiques, including old-fashioned claw-foot tubs in each bathroom. Complimentary breakfast. No room phones, no TV in rooms. No kids under 13. No smoking. | 146 S. 3rd St. | 573/883–3493 or 800/275–1412 | fax 573/883–9612 | www.southernhotelbb.com | 8 rooms | $83–$138 | AE, D, MC, V.

SEDALIA

(Nearby town also listed: Clinton)

Most Missourians know Sedalia only as the home to the state fair each August, but because of the time Scott Joplin spent here, a number of homes and buildings have been preserved, making this town a surprisingly pleasant stop for antiques, cultural events, and a bit of history. There's also access to Missouri's Katy Trail.

Information: Sedalia Chamber of Commerce | 113 E. 4th St., 65301 | 660/826–2222 | www.sedalia.mo.us.

Attractions

Bothwell Lodge State Historic Site. High on a hill overlooking U.S. 65, this lodge was once the home of state senator and philanthropist, John H. Bothwell (1848–1929). Now the 247 surrounding acres are open for picnicking and hiking. | U.S. 65 N | 660/827–0510 | www.dnr.state.mo.us/dsp | $2 lodge tour | Park daily dawn–dusk; tours daily 10–4.

Knob Noster State Park. Take U.S. 50 West to Route 132 South to reach this park which boasts a small wetland and prairielike savannah. | Knob Noster | 660/563–2463 | www.dnr.state.mo.us/dsp | Free | Daily dawn–dusk.

Pettis County Courthouse. This 1924 neoclassical building lends a noble air to Sedalia. | 415 S. Ohio Ave. | 660/826–4892 | Free | Weekdays 8–4.

Sedalia Ragtime Archives. Scott Joplin (1867–1917) spent only a few years of his life in Sedalia, but the town has become a center for resources on his life, and on ragtime music in general. | State Fair Community College Library, Maple Leaf room, 3201 W. 16th St. | 660/530–5800 | www.scottjoplin.org | Free | Weekdays 9–5.

State Fair Motor Speedway. In summer, locals flock to this ½-mi dirt track to see sprint cars and dragsters try to beat the clock. | 2503 W. 16th St. | 660/826–1600 or 800/499–7223 | www.sedalia-racing.com | Admission varies by event | Call for race times.

ON THE CALENDAR

MAY: *Scott Joplin Ragtime Festival.* Silent movies, a cabaret, and concerts by ragtime musicians at Liberty Center on State Fair Boulevard over Memorial Day weekend. | 660/826–2271.

JULY: *Missouri State Pow Wow.* This intertribal Native American gathering offers a weekend of cultural activities, dancing, food, arts and crafts, poetry, and painting on the west campground of the fairgrounds in mid-July. | 660/826–5608.

AUG.: *Missouri State Fair.* Livestock shows, a midway carnival, and concerts take over the Missouri State Fairgrounds for ten days early in the month. | 660/530–5600.

Dining

Around the Fireside. American. A family restaurant with a homey feel known for steaks and seafood. Kids' menu. | 1975 W. Broadway | 660/826–9743 | $7–$25 | AE, D, DC, MC, V.

Del-Amici. Italian. Del-Amici, Italian for "among friends," serves traditional steaks, seafood, and pasta on the ground level of the Hotel Bothwell. | 103 E. 4th St. | 660/826–5588 | $10–$20 | AE, D, MC, V.

Steak and Schnitzel House. German. Wagon-wheel chandeliers and old barn beams set the tone in this converted restaurant with Bavarian decor. Specialties include the haus schnitzel, fresh pork tenderloins smothered in a brown gravy with mushrooms served over a bed of spätzle. Kids' menu. | 100 S. Maple, Cole Camp | 660/668–3080 | $5–$15 | MC, V.

Lodging

Best Western State Fair Motor Inn. The state fairgrounds are just ½ mi from this motel. Restaurant, bar, room service. Cable TV. Pool, wading pool. Hot tub. Putting green. Gym. Video games. Laundry facilities. Business services, airport shuttle. Pets allowed. | 3120 S. Limit U.S. 65 | 660/826–6100 or 800/528–1234 | fax 660/827–3850 | www.bestwestern.com | 119 rooms | $50–$70 | AE, D, DC, MC, V.

Hotel Bothwell. Operating in downtown Sedalia since 1927, this upscale hotel prides itself on its beautiful architecture and preserved interior. Rooms range from basic sleeping accommodations to deluxe suites. Restaurant. Cable TV. Business services. | 103 E. 4th St. | 660/826–5588 | fax 660/826–0395 | www.hotelbothwell.com | 48 rooms | $89–$199 | AE, D, MC, V.

Ramada Inn. This Ramada is on a commercial strip approximately 1 mi from the state fairgrounds. Restaurant, bar, complimentary Continental breakfast, room service. Cable TV. Pool. Business services. | 3501 W. Broadway | 660/826–8400 or 800/272–6232 | fax 660/826–1230 | www.ramada.com | 125 rooms | $80–$100 | AE, D, DC, MC, V.

SIKESTON

MAP 12, F6

(Nearby towns also listed: Cape Girardeau, New Madrid, Poplar Bluff)

For a small country town in the middle of nowhere, Sikeston boasts a number of cultural greats: the largest community theater between St. Louis and Memphis, the largest library in the state outside of St. Louis and Kansas City, and impressive architecture on the downtown square. But Sikeston is most famous for Lambert's Café, advertised on interstate billboards for hundreds of miles as the "home of throwed rolls." Really! Just remember to duck!

Information: **Sikeston Chamber of Commerce** | 1 Industrial Dr., 63801 | 573/471–2498 | www.sikeston.com.

© Corbis

THROWED ROLLS?

The signs appear along the interstate as far away as Abilene, Kansas, tempting and teasing you with the promise of throwed rolls. It's not an advertising gimmick. It's the real thing.

The signs are for Lambert's Café, which opened in 1942 with eight tables and nine counter stools and a menu of fried okra, turnips, macaroni and tomatoes, and lots of homemade pies and rolls. Heaping helpings are offered fresh out of the pot until you are full. "You didn't order fried okra? Well here, just try some anyway," as they dump some on your plate.

The roll throwing started in 1976 when, during a lunch rush, Norman Lambert didn't have time to get to all of the tables with fresh baked rolls, so he just kind of tossed a few to some of the regular customers. Today, employees at Lambert's Café throw rolls across 10,000 square ft of restaurant, and, although most of them actually get to where they're supposed to be going, you should still keep a heads-up while eating, or you might just get whopped by a throwed roll.

Attractions

Bent Creek Golf Course. This 18-hole course right next to Bent Creek and 38 mi from Sikeston opened in 1990. | 1 Bent Creek Dr., Jackson | 573/243–6060 | Daily.

ON THE CALENDAR

AUG.: *Jaycee Bootheel Rodeo.* Missouri's largest rodeo, and one of the nation's top five. Includes live country-western music nightly. | 573/471–2498.

AUG.: *Redneck Bar-B-Que Cook-off.* Chefs and amateur cooks from the area compete to make the best ribs and beans—with samples provided, of course—at this cook-off held in conjunction with the Jaycee Bootheel Rodeo. | 573/471–2498.

SEPT.: *Cotton Carnival.* This tribute to a primary agriculture resource in the bootheel held late in September in the parking lot of the River Birch Mall on South Kingshighway includes games, rides, musical entertainment, and a parade. | 573/471–2498.

Dining

Dexter Bar-B-Que. Barbecue. All of Dexter's menu items are smoked on-site, and the specialty is St. Louis–style loin-back ribs. The restaurant is in a brick building downtown. | 124 N. Main St. | 573/471–6676 | $5–$12 | MC, V.

Fisherman's Net. Seafood. Entwined fishing nets are draped from the ceiling and seashells and fisherman's paraphernalia are on display throughout this restaurant known especially for its catfish. Kids' menu. | 915 Kingsway Plaza | 573/471–8102 | $8–$15 | AE, D, MC, V | Closed Sun.

Lambert's Café. Southern. Beside the famous "throwed rolls," this country café features down-home southern cooking and is filled with antiques and pictures of Missouri's state animal—the mule. Drinks are served in extra-large mugs. Entertainment Thursday–Sunday. Kids' menu. | 2515 E. Malone Ave. | 573/471–4261 | $7–$15 | No credit cards.

Lodging

Best Western Coach House Inn. At the junction of Interstate 55 and U.S 62 and just ½ mi from Lambert's Café and their famous "throwed rolls." Restaurant, bar (with entertainment), complimentary Continental breakfast, room service. In-room data ports, microwaves, refrigerators, cable TV. Pool. Gym. Video games. Laundry services. Business services. Some pets allowed. | 220 S. Interstate Dr. | 573/471–9700 or 800/528–1234 | fax 573/471–4285 | www.bestwestern.com | 63 suites | $70 | AE, D, DC, MC, V.

Country Hearth Inn of Sikeston. This modern hotel is next to the Sikeston Factory Outlet Mall and within walking distance of Lambert's Café. A special golf package includes two nights' lodging and two 18-hole rounds at the nearby Bootheel Golf Club. Complimentary breakfast. Some in-room hot tubs, cable TV. Business services. | 100 Matthews La. | 573/472–4400 or 888/294–6496 | fax 573/472–3782 | www.countryhearth.com/hotels/mo-sikeston.htm | 40 rooms | $40–$125 | AE, D, DC, MC, V.

Drury Inn. This chain hotel off Interstate 55 at exit 60 is in a commercial area with outlet shopping and restaurants within easy walking distance. Convenient also to Sikeston Memorial Airport. Complimentary Continental breakfast. Some microwaves, some refrigerators, cable TV. Indoor-outdoor pool. Hot tub. Business services. Some pets allowed. | 2602 E. Malone St. | 573/471–4100 or 800/325–8300 | fax 573/471–4100 | www.druryinn.com | 78 rooms | $75–$88 | AE, D, DC, MC, V.

Sikeston House Bed & Breakfast. Innkeepers Ken and Vicki Rubenacker are avid antiques collectors and have furnished their turn-of-the-20th-century Victorian accordingly. No fewer than 174 acorns are carved into the oak staircase that leads to this B&B's two guest rooms, both with private baths. Complimentary breakfast. Cable TV. | 427 S. Kingshighway | 573/471–2501 | www.visitsikeston-miner.com/kleinhousebb | 2 rooms | $65 | MC, V.

SPRINGFIELD

MAP 12, B6

(Nearby towns also listed: Branson, Carthage, Joplin, Kimberling City, Mount Vernon, Nevada)

Springfield is officially recognized as the birthplace of America's Main Street—Route 66—the first completely paved transcontinental highway in America, stretching from the Great Lakes to the Pacific Coast. The city's past also includes major Civil War battles, railroads, and gun battles with Wild Bill Hickock. Today, the Queen City of the Ozarks is home to Southwest Missouri State University, the world headquarters of the Assembly of God Church, and a number of private religious colleges. And it's on the path you might take to Branson.

Information: **Springfield Chamber of Commerce** | 202 S. John Q. Hammons Pkwy., Box 1687, 65801 | 417/862–5567 | www.springfieldmo.org.

Attractions

Bass Pro Shops Outdoor World Showroom and Fish and Wildlife Museum. This is not just a place to shop; there's also a 4-acre indoor museum of wild animals from around the world (some are alive, others have been preserved in a taxidermy studio you can visit). | 1935 S. Campbell Ave. | 417/887–7334 | www.outdoor-world.com | Free | Mon.–Sat. 7 AM–10 PM, Sun. 9–6.

Crystal Cave. From Springfield take Glenstone St. to Highway H north to reach this cave with its great variety of formations, including black stalactites and crystals. | 7225 N. Crystal Cave La. | 417/833–9599 | $5 | Daily 9–1:15.

Dickerson Park Zoo. More than 300 wild animals, including Asian elephants and cheetahs, call this park home. | 3043 N. Fort St. | 417/864–1800 | $4 | Daily 9–5.

Exotic Animal Paradise. Nearly 3,000 wild animals and rare birds roam free here; you have to stay in your car. | 124 Jungle Dr. (exit 88 off I–44 east), Strafford | 417/859–2016 | $10 | Daily 8–dusk.

Fantastic Caverns. Take a jeep ride along the path of an ancient underground river. To reach the caverns take Interstate 44 to Route 13 north. | 4872 N. Farm Rd. 125 | 417/833–2010 | www.fantastic-caverns.com | $14.50 | May–Oct., daily 8–6.

History Museum. Hands-on exhibits of the area's history change several times during the year. | City Hall, 840 Boonville | 417/864–1976 | Free | Tues.–Sat. 10–4:30.

Laura Ingalls Wilder–Rose Wilder Lane Museum and Home. This house, east of Springfield in nearby Mansfield, is where the "Little House" books were written and where Laura, Almonzo, and Rose made their home. | 3068 Hwy. A, Mansfield | 417/924–3626 | $6 | Mar.–Oct., Mon.–Sat. 9–5, Sun. 12:30–5:30.

Milwood Golf and Racquet Club. This hilly 18-hole course opened in 1996. | 3701 Milwood Dr. | 417/889–4200 | Daily.

Missouri Sports Hall of Fame. Interactive computer stations allow you to play a simulated game of football with some of the state's best athletes. | 5051 Highland Springs Blvd. | 417/889–3100 | $5 | Mon.–Sat. 10–4, Sun. noon–4.

Southwest Missouri State University. More than 18,000 students call themselves SMSU Bears. Founded in 1905 as a teaching college, SMSU is now recognized for its emphasis on professional education, the performing arts, health care, and business and economic development. | 901 S. National | 417/836–5000 | www.smsu.edu | Free | Daily.

Springfield Art Museum. Work by regional and national artists is on display here. | 1111 E. Brookside Dr. | 417/837–5700 | Free | Tues.–Sat. 9–5, Sun. 1–5.

Springfield National Cemetery. Heroes from all America's wars are buried here, including hundreds from the Wilson's Creek Civil War Battle. | 1702 E. Seminole St. | 417/881–9499 | Daily dawn–dusk.

Wilson's Creek National Battlefield. This was the site of the first major Civil War battle west of the Mississippi. The battle took place in 1861 and involved nearly 5,000 Union troops and 10,000 Confederate troops. | 6424 W. Farm Rd. 182, Republic | 417/732–2662 | www.nps.gov/wicr | $4 | Daily 8–5.

ON THE CALENDAR

MAY: *Walnut Street Arts Fest.* A colorful celebration of the visual and performing arts with jazz, folk, and classical music recitals early in the month. | 417/869–8380.
JUNE: *Route 66 Country Music Festival.* A three-day, mid-month music and camping festival featuring big-name national acts. | 417/865–6700 or 800/678–8767.
NOV., DEC.: *Festival of Lights.* A trail of illuminated 6-ft snowflakes runs through the heart of the city along historic Commercial Street, down National Street to Walnut Street, and over to Republic Road throughout November and December. | 800/678–8767.

Dining

Aunt Martha's Pancake House. American. Pancakes are always available at this Springfield institution that has been serving for more than a quarter-century; local residents swear by them. Burgers and sandwiches round out the menu. | 1700 E. Cherokee St. | 417/881–3505 | $3–$6 | No credit cards | Breakfast also available; no dinner Sun.

Catfish House. Southern. Farm-raised catfish, smoked ribs, steaks, crab legs, and even frog legs are available here. If you can't decide what to order, sidle up to the 55-item food bar. | 930 N. Glenstone Ave. | 417/865–3700 | $5–$10 | AE, D, MC, V.

Coyote's Adobe Café and Bar. Tex-Mex. Choose from the 15 varieties of chicken wings, or have tacos, burritos, enchiladas, and the like. In summer, the small outdoor patio is a nice place to sip a margarita. | 1742 S. Glenstone Ave. | 417/889–7120 | $5–$10 | D, MC, V.

Diamond Head. Pan-Asian. Hawaiian ceiling lamps and Asian art decorate this Chinese/Polynesian eatery. Buffet. Kids' menu. | 2734 S. Campbell Ave. | 417/883–9581 | $5–$15 | AE, D, DC, MC, V.

J. Parrino's. Italian. This family-style restaurant was designed to resemble an outdoor café in Italy. Some dishes to try are the mostaccioli noodles baked with mozzarella in a red and white sauce, or the penne di mare (penne with shrimp and scallops baked in a lobster sauce). Kids' menu. | 1550 E. Battlefield | 417/882–1808 | $7–$16 | AE, D, DC, MC, V.

Le Mirabelle. French. Veal, roast duckling, and fresh seafood dishes served in a French country atmosphere. | 2620 S. Glenstone Ave. | 417/883–2550 | $15–$25 | AE, DC, MC, V | Closed Sun.

Mrs. O'Mealley's. American. This family-oriented place, known for salads and fried chicken, seats about 300 people at tables and booths. All food is served cafeteria style. | 210 E. Sunshine St. | 417/881–7770 | $5–$12 | AE, D, MC, V.

Shady Inn. Steak. Built in 1947, this restaurant is still run by its founders and is well known for its prime rib. Entertainment. Kids' menu. | 524 W. Sunshine St. | 417/862–0369 | $13–$25 | AE, DC, MC, V | Closed Sun.

Lodging

Best Western Deerfield Inn. This chain motel is in a residential neighborhood 2 mi from local shopping and restaurants and 5 mi from Southwest Missouri State University. Complimentary Continental breakfast. Cable TV. Pool. Business services, free parking. | 3343 E. Battlefield St. | 417/887–2323 or 800/528–1234 | fax 417/887–1242 | www.bestwestern.com | 103 rooms | $70 | AE, D, DC, MC, V.

Best Western Route 66 Rail Haven. This was the first Best Western in the United States when it opened in 1938 on attractively landscaped grounds on historic Route 66. Complimentary Continental breakfast. In-room data ports, some refrigerators, cable TV. Pool. Hot tub. Business services, free parking. Some pets allowed. | 203 S. Glenstone St. | 417/866–1963 or 800/528–1234 | www.bestwestern.com | 81 rooms, 12 suites | $65 rooms, $85–$105 suites | AE, D, DC, MC, V.

Clarion. A full-service hotel in the center of Springfield's entertainment and shopping district. Restaurant, bar, room service. In-room data ports, some refrigerators, cable TV. Pool. Business services, airport shuttle, free parking. Some pets allowed (fee). | 3333 S. Glenstone St. | 417/883–6550 | fax 417/887–1823 | 195 rooms | $70–$90 | AE, D, DC, MC, V.

Econo Lodge. This chain motel is two blocks off Interstate 44 at exit 80A. It is 1 mi from Baptist Bible College and 3 mi from Southwest Missouri State University. Complimentary Continental breakfast. Cable TV. Pool. Free parking. | 2611 N. Glenstone St. | 417/864–3565 | fax 417/865–0567 | 122 rooms | $50 | AE, D, DC, MC, V.

Econo Lodge You'll be 6 mi from Dickerson Park Zoo and 1 mi from Fantastic Caverns if you stay here. Complimentary Continental breakfast. Cable TV. Business services. | 2808 N. Kansas St. | 417/869–5600 | fax 417/869–3421 | 83 rooms | $45 | AE, D, DC, MC, V.

GuestHouse Suites. This all-suites hotel on a quiet street within walking distance of local restaurants and shops is 2 mi from Southwest Missouri State University and 10 mi from Wilson's Creek National Battlefield. Picnic area, complimentary Continental breakfast. Kitchenettes, cable TV. Pool. Hot tub. Laundry facilities. Business services, free parking. Some pets allowed (fee). | 1550 E. Raynell Pl. | 417/883–7300 | fax 417/520–7900 | www.guesthouse3.com | 80 suites | $89 | AE, D, DC, MC, V.

Hampton Inn–East. This chain hotel is just off U.S. 65 at exit 82A with a residential area to one side and an industrial area to the other. Complimentary Continental breakfast. In-room data ports, cable TV. Pool. Hot tub. Gym. Business services. | 222 N. Ingram Mill Rd. | 417/863–1440 or 800/426–7866 | fax 417/863–2215 | www.hamptoninn-suites.com | 99 rooms | $73 | AE, D, DC, MC, V.

Holiday Inn North. Built around an atrium with an indoor waterfall, this hotel is five minutes from Southwest Missouri State University and 10 minutes from downtown in a business area. Restaurant, bar, room service. In-room data ports, some refrigerators, cable TV. Pool. Hot tub. Gym. Business services, airport shuttle, free parking. | 2720 N. Glenstone St. | 417/865–8600 or 800/465–4329 | fax 417/862–9415 | www.basshotels.com/holiday-inn | 188 rooms, 36 suites | $90 rooms, $100–$250 suites | AE, D, DC, MC, V.

Holiday Inn University Plaza and Convention Center. This downtown hotel has over 21,000 ft of meeting space in addition to its guest rooms. Restaurant, bar (with entertainment), room service. In-room data ports, some refrigerators, cable TV. 2 pools. Barbershop, beauty salon, hot tub. 2 tennis courts. Gym. Laundry facilities. Business services, airport shuttle. Some pets allowed. | 333 John Q. Hammons Pkwy. | 417/864–7333 or 800/465–4329 | fax 417/831–5893 | www.basshotels.com/holiday-inn | 271 rooms, 33 suites | $89–$99 rooms, $129–$143 suites | AE, D, DC, MC, V.

Mansion at Elfindale. This ornate inn, complete with a chapel, was built in 1892 and still has its original stained-glass windows. It's on a quiet street in the southwestern part of town. Complimentary Continental breakfast. No smoking, TV and VCR in common area. Business services, free parking. | 1701 S. Fort St. | 417/831–5400 or 800/443–0237 | fax 417/831–5415 | 13 suites, 1 tower suite | $85–$110 suites, $135 tower suite | AE, D, MC, V.

Microtel Inn Springfield. Housed in a modern building that looks more like apartments than a hotel, this inn is near several restaurants and 2 mi from the airport and fairgrounds. Complimentary Continental breakfast. Cable TV. Business services, free parking. | 3125 N. Kentwood Ave. | 417/833–1500 or 800/414–2027 | 54 rooms | $40–$47 | AE, D, DC, MC, V.

Plainview Inn. It's not unusual to see red fox or deer roaming this modern home's 15 acres of woods. The inn is about a 10-minute drive from downtown. Some in-room hot tubs, TV in common area. Pool, pond. Basketball. | 2219 W. Plainview Rd. | 417/886–5082 or 800/974–9747 | www.usagetaways.com/mo/plainview | 3 rooms | $60–$75 | MC, V.

Ramada Inn. This chain hotel is on a commercial strip 5 mi from downtown. Restaurant, bar (with entertainment), complimentary breakfast. Some in-room data ports, some refrigerators, cable TV. Pool. Business services, airport shuttle. Pets allowed. | 2820 N. Glenstone St. | 417/869–3900 or 800/707–0326 | fax 417/865–5378 | www.ramada.com | 130 rooms | $75 | AE, D, DC, MC, V.

Sheraton Hawthorne Park. This chain hotel is on a commercial street near the Bass Pro shop. Restaurant, bar. In-room data ports, cable TV. Indoor-outdoor pool. Hot tub, sauna. Laundry facilities. Business services, airport shuttle. Some pets allowed (fee). | 2431 N. Glenstone St. | 417/831–3131 or 800/325–3535 | fax 417/831–9786 | www.sheraton.com | 203 rooms | $104 | AE, D, DC, MC, V.

Sleep Inn Springfield. This chain hotel is 5 mi from downtown in a business district. Complimentary Continental breakfast. In-room data ports, cable TV. Pool. Outdoor hot tub. | 233 E. Camino Alto | 417/886–2464 or 800/753–3746 | www.choicehotels.com | 107 rooms | $59–$94 | AE, D, DC, MC, V.

Virginia Rose Bed and Breakfast. Ten acres of grounds surround this 1906 farmhouse and barn in the middle of a subdivision. The B&B has period furnishings and accents, and is 1 mi from the Bass Pro Outdoor World, 3 mi from the Springfield History Museum, and 7 mi from Wilson Creek National Battlefield. Complimentary breakfast. TV with VCR in common area. | 317 E. Glenwood St. | 417/883–0693 or 800/345–1412 | www.bbonline.com/mo/virginiarose | 3 rooms, 1 suite | $50–$60 rooms, $90 suite | AE, D, MC, V.

Walnut Street Inn. A downtown turn-of-the-20th-century building with period furnishings and fireplaces in some rooms, this was Springfield's first B&B and was ranked among the best in the country by *Country Inns Magazine*. Complimentary breakfast. Cable TV, some in-room hot tubs. No smoking. | 900 E. Walnut St. | 417/864–6346 or 800/593–6346 | fax 417/864–6184 | stay@walnutstreetinn.com | www.walnutstreetinn.com | 14 rooms | $84–$159 | AE, D, DC, MC, V.

Wooden Horse Bed and Breakfast. Large and elaborate breakfasts are the pride of this B&B, a modern, brick, ranch-style home in nearby Nixa. Both rooms are air-conditioned and have private baths. Complimentary breakfast. In-room data ports. TV in common area. Outdoor hot tub. | 1007 W. Sterling Ct., Nixa | 417/724–8756 or 800/724–8756 | www.nixa.com/chamber/woodenhorse | 2 rooms | $60–$85 | No credit cards.

STOCKTON

MAP 12, B5

(Nearby towns also listed: Lamar, Nevada)

This area was home to Osage Indians before the French began to explore Missouri in the 1700s, and it has been home to an abundance of wildlife from time immemorial. The town switched names several times in its early years and was totally wiped off the map during the Civil War. But with the creation of Stockton Lake in the 1960s, the town resurfaced to become a remote retirement and vacation village.

Information: Stockton Area Chamber of Commerce | Box 410, 65785 | 417/276–5213.

Attractions

General Sweeney's Museum. Fifty-two exhibits focus on the Civil War west of the Mississippi River, and include uniforms, weapons, diaries, and an interesting display on wartime medical practices. | 5228 S. State Hwy. ZZ, Republic | 417/732–1224 | $3.50 | Wed.–Sun., 10–5; closed Nov.–Feb.

Stockton State Park. Winds coming across the Springfield plateau make Stockton Lake, a part of this park, the best sailing lake in the state. | Rte. 215, Dadeville | 417/276–4259 | www.dnr.state.mo.us/parks.htm | Free | Daily.

ON THE CALENDAR
JAN.: *Eagle Days.* Sponsored by the Army Corps of Engineers and the Department of Conservation, this well-organized outing for viewing bald eagles meets at the Orleans Trail Marina or the Stockton State Park Marina the first Saturday in January. | 417/276–3113.
SEPT.: *Black Walnut Festival.* A parade, music, and food booths celebrate the harvest of this local crop. | 417/276–5213.

Dining
Country Corner Café. American. Known for great hamburgers made from Black Angus beef and fried-chicken specials on Tuesday, this casual country café also has daily lunch specials. | 1225 Rte. 39 S | 417/276–5411 | $5–$10 | No credit cards | Breakfast also available.

House of Chong Lee. Korean. The hot scallion chicken is the specialty here, but a variety of Korean and Chinese dishes are served. Hamburgers and french fries are also available. | 504 RB Rd. | 417/276–5747 | $5–$10 | No credit cards.

Lodging
Cedar Oak Lodge. Just south of Stockton, this picturesque resort is two blocks from the lake and offers golfing, fishing, and boating. Some kitchenettes. Pool. 9-hole golf course, miniature golf. Volleyball, boating, fishing. | Rte. 4 | 417/276–3193 | 27 rooms, 8 kitchenette rooms | $44 rooms, $52–$70 kitchenette rooms | AE, MC, V.

Holliday Motel. Outdoor grills, picnic tables, and electric boat hookups abound at this motel, which is only a five-minute drive from a Stockton Lake public boat ramp. Single, double, and connecting rooms are available. Cable TV. Pool. | 400 E. Hwy. 32 | 417/276–4443 | stocktonlake@stocktonlake.net | 20 rooms | $28–$35 | AE, D, MC, V.

Owl Haven Resort. You have a choice of standard rooms or family units with kitchenettes at this lakefront resort. Picnic area. Cable TV. Pool, lake. Spa. Fishing. Playground. | Lake Rd. RB | 417/276–4907 | 10 rooms, 10 suites | $33 rooms, $43–$70 suites | AE, MC, V.

SULLIVAN

MAP 12, D4

(Nearby towns also listed: Lebanon, Rolla)

Known as the "Gateway to the Ozarks," the little town of Sullivan is just that. Located on historic Route 66, Sullivan is a short drive from caves, canoe streams, wine country, and other attractions of the Missouri Ozarks. The town's historic downtown square is a fun stroll for antiques and great eats, and it still has a two-screen movie house where shows are less than $2.

Information: **Sullivan Chamber of Commerce** | Box 536, 63080 | 573/468–3314 | www.ne3.com/vs.

Attractions
Jesse James Wax Museum. The museum curator and tour guide doesn't accept the idea that Jesse James was felled by Robert Ford's bullet in 1882; he'll explain why he believes James in fact passed away at age 103 in 1952. Pay your money and believe it or not. | S. Service Rd., Stanton (exit 230 off I-44) | 573/927–5233 | $5 | May–Sept., daily 9–6.

Meramec Caverns. This was the first major cave discovery in Missouri and the hideout of Jesse James. | Hwy. west (exit 230 off I–44), Stanton | 573/468–3166 | www.americascave.com | $12 | Nov.–Jan., daily 9–4; Mar. and Oct., daily 9–5; Apr. and Sept., daily 9–6; May and June, daily 9–7; July–Labor Day, daily 9–7:30.

Meramec Cinema I & II. First-run flicks are shown at this classic, small-town, two-screen movie theater. Tickets are only $2.50, and popcorn and soda refills are free. | I–44 and S. Service Rd. | 573/468–6244 | $2.50 | Daily.

Meramec State Park. This a popular canoeing and spelunking spot with more than 30 caves and many miles of river in the 6,896-acre park. | 2800 S. Hwy. 185 (exit 226 off I–44), Sullivan | 573/468–6072 | www.dnr.state.mo.us/dsp | Free | Daily.

Onondaga Cave State Park. You can swim, fish, or canoe in the Meramec River or explore some of the most spectacular caves in the country here. Tours of the cave are available for a fee. | 7556 Hwy. H (Leasburg exit off I–44), Leasburg | 314/245–6600 or 314/245–6576 | www.dnr.state.mo.us/dsp | Free | Mar.–Oct., daily.

ON THE CALENDAR

MAR., APR.: *Easter Eve and Sunrise Services at Meramec Caverns.* Missouri's largest cave is the setting for this celebration on Easter eve and Easter morning. | 573/468–2283.

Dining

Country Market Restaurant. American. Order from the menu or hit the buffet at this diner just off Interstate 44. The fried chicken is particularly popular, but steaks, pasta, and sandwiches are also available. | 825 N. Loop Dr. | 573/860–8900 | $5–$8 | AE, D, MC, V | Breakfast also available.

Du Kum In. American. There are lacey linen curtains on the windows and and a large plate collection on the walls, giving this restaurant, known for fried chicken, steaks, burgers, and homemade pies, a country feel. | 101 Grande Center | 573/468–6114 | $7–$12 | MC, V | Closed Mon., Tues.

Homer's Bar-B-Que. Barbecue. Pork steaks are the specialty at Homer's, a small restaurant with a rustic interior and knickknacks on the walls. Ribs, chicken, and beef brisket are also available. | 639 Fisher Dr. | 573/468–4393 | $5–$10 | No credit cards | Closed Sun., Mon.

Lodging

Budget Lodging. At the junction of Interstate 44 and Route 47, 15 minutes from Meramec or Onondaga State Park and 20 minutes from Six Flags, this hotel aims to make you feel at home with lace curtains and flowers in the windows. Complimentary Continental breakfast. Cable TV. Pool. Laundry facilities. Business services. Pets allowed (fee). | 866 S. Outer Rd., St. Clair | 636/629–1000 or 800/958–4354 | fax 636/629–1000 | www.stclairmo.com/budgetlodging | 68 rooms, 2 suites | $79 rooms, $129–$179 suites | AE, D, DC, MC, V.

Econo Lodge. This one-story, roadside motel is about 2 mi from Sullivan's downtown. There's a restaurant and several stores within walking distance. Complimentary Continental breakfast. Cable TV. Pool. | 307 N. Service Rd. | 573/468–3136 | fax 573/860–3136 | 45 rooms | $29–$49 | AE, D, DC, MC, V.

Family Motor Inn. This four-building complex is 2 mi from downtown. Some kitchenettes, cable TV. Pool. Hot tub. Laundry facilities. Business services. Pets allowed (fee). | 209 N. Service Rd. | 573/468–4119 | fax 573/468–3891 | 63 rooms | $55 | AE, D, DC, MC, V.

Ramada Inn. Ramada's 3-acre property is just 5 mi from the Meramec Caverns. An outdoor pool, basketball court, volleyball area, horseshoe pit, and picnic area are among the amenities. Cable TV. Pool. Basketball, volleyball. | 309 N. Service Rd. | 573/468–4172 or 800/272–6232 | www.ramada.com | 80 rooms | $40–$55 | AE, D, DC, MC, V.

Wildflower Inn. If you walk around the 43-acre grounds of this inn you may well see wild turkeys and white-tailed deer. All rooms have private baths. In-room TVs. | 2739 Hwy. D, Bourbon | 573/468–7975 | www.ne3.com/flowers | 4 rooms | $75–$85 | MC, V.

VAN BUREN

MAP 12, E6

(Nearby town also listed: Poplar Bluff)

One of the country's largest springs, Big Springs, is just outside of Van Buren in Ozark National Scenic Riverways park, and is certainly worth a stop. Although many tourists come to this area for the floating and canoeing on the Current River, the picturesque downtown square and limestone courthouse are worth a visit too.

Information: **Van Buren Chamber of Commerce** | Box 356, 63965 | 573/323–4782 or 800/692–7582.

Attractions

Clearwater Lake. This 1,600-acre lake is a popular spot for boating, waterskiing, and especially for fishing for black and white bass, catfish, and crappie. Take U.S. 60 East, to Route 34 North, to County Road HH, near Piedmont. | River Road Park | 573/223–7777 | Free | Daily.

Hay Hollow Stables. One of several places offering guided trail rides through the Ozark countryside. | County Rd. 504 F, Eminence | 573/226–3916 | $15 | Mar.–Oct., daily 9–6.

Ozark National Scenic Riverways. In 1964, Congress enacted legislation protecting 80,785 acres of pristine river country along the Current and the Jack's Fork Rivers. Both rivers, which are classified as class 1 in the park, offer good swimming, tubing, canoeing, and trout and bass fishing. In addition to the rivers, there are campsites, more than 300 caves, and numerous springs including Big Springs within the park. There is access to the rivers from Routes 17, 19, 21, or 106. | Off U.S. 60 | 573/323–4236 | www.nps.gov/ozar/ | Free | Daily.

SIGHTSEEING TOURS/TOUR COMPANIES

River's Edge Glass Bottom Boats. These rides provide a glimpse of aquatic life in the crystal-clear Current and Jack's Fork rivers. | Calm Acres Dr., Eminence | 573/226–3233 | $25/hr | Mar.–Oct., daily 9–5.

ON THE CALENDAR

MAY: *Big Springs Arts and Crafts Festival.* A two-day event on the courthouse lawn. | 573/323–4782.
OCT.: *Fall Festival.* Crafts, food, and music on the courthouse lawn. | 573/323–4782.

Dining

Float Stream Café. American. This small-town café specializes in such comfort food as fried chicken, homemade rolls, and homemade pies. | 102 Main St. | 573/323–9606 | $6–$10 | AE, D, MC, V.

Lodging

Hawthorne Motel. This 1959 stucco motel, decorated in a country motif, is right in the center of downtown Van Buren. Cable TV. Pool. Pets allowed. | 1029 Business Hwy. 60 | 573/323–4274 | 26 rooms | $38–$58 | MC, V.

Smalley's Motel. Basic, comfortable rooms are available at this one-story motel in downtown Van Buren. Also, two- to six-hour tube floats on the Current River can be arranged. Cable TV. Pool. Picnic tables. Pets allowed. | 702 Main St. | 573/323–4263 or 800/727–4263 | dsmalley@semo.net | 18 rooms | $36 | AE, D, MC, V.

WAYNESVILLE

(Nearby towns also listed: Camdenton, Lebanon, Osage Beach, Rolla)

A big green rock formation that looks like a frog, the result of rock blasting to form the highway leading to Waynesville, garners more attention than just about anything in this community of 3,600 people. Adjacent to Fort Leonard Wood and the Fort McClellan Military Police School, Waynesville has greatly influenced the military marketplace. An old stagecoach stop and Civil War battle sites make the town an interesting stop for history lovers.

Information: Waynesville Chamber of Commerce | 688 Old Rte. 66, St. Robert 65583 | 573/336–5121 or 800/447–4617 | www.jobe.net/chamber.

Attractions
Army Engineer Museum. Exhibits on land mine warfare, tactical bridging, demolitions and explosives, and topographic engineering. | Bldg. 1607, Fort Leonard Wood (exit 161 of I–44) | 573/341–5039 | Free | Weekdays 8–4, Sat. 10–4.

Jonco Diversified. Watch the custom creation of wooden awards and plaques made from walnut, oak, and cherry trees harvested in the area and shipped around the world. | 24610 Rte. 17 | 573/774–6451 | Free | Weekdays.

Old Stagecoach Stop. In its 140-year history this building has served as a hotel, a stagecoach stop, and a Civil War hospital. | Lynn St. (on Waynesville Square) | 573/774–5363 | Free | Apr.–Oct., Wed. and Sat., or by appt.

Onyx Mountain Caverns. An underground river, a Wood Indian Culture room, and bear beds dug for hibernation set this cave, which is on the National Register of Historic Places, apart from many others in the state. | 14705 PD 8541 (exit 169 off I–44), Newburg | 573/762–3341 | $7.75 | Daily 8–5.

Pulaski County Museum. The museum is housed within the 1904 county courthouse and focuses on settler life in Pulaski County. Exhibits include blacksmith and carpentry tools, quilts, school materials, and Civil War items. | 301 W. Historic 66th | 573/774–3288 | Free | By appointment.

ON THE CALENDAR
DEC.: *Christmas Parade.* This parade, held the first Sunday in December, features area high school bands and organizations. | 573/336–5121.

Dining
Aussie Jack's. Contemporary. This casual dining room sports a hand-painted mural, white oak woodwork, and Australian steaks and seafood. Kids' menu. | 141 St. Robert Blvd., St. Roberts | 573/336–2447 | $15–$55 | AE, D, DC, MC, V.

Benton Street Café. American. Known for soups and salads, this café occupies a historic house with creaking floors and local history on the walls. Open-air dining on a patio with a view of courthouse square. Kids' menu. | 103 N. Benton St. | 573/774–6268 | $3–$5 | No credit cards | Closed weekends. No dinner.

Lodging
Best Western Montis Inn. This chain hotel is on a commercial strip 8 mi from downtown Waynesville. Complimentary Continental breakfast. Some kitchenettes, some microwaves, some refrigerators, cable TV. Pool. Laundry facilities. Business services. Some pets allowed. | 14086 Hwy. Z, St. Roberts | 573/336–4299 or 800/528–1234 or 800/528–1234 | fax 573/336–2872 | www.bestwestern.com | 45 rooms | $55–$60 | AE, D, DC, MC, V.

Days Inn. All rooms have a 25-inch TV, microwave, refrigerator, and hair dryer. Movie rentals also are available at this two-story hotel, which is just off Interstate 44. Complimentary Continental breakfast. In-room data ports, microwaves, refrigerators, cable TV. Pool. | 14125 Hwy. Z | 573/336–5556 or 800/544–8313 | fax 573/336–3918 | www.daysinn.com | 35 rooms | $32–$72 | AE, D, DC, MC, V.

Fortwood Inn. This modern hotel has brightly lit, comfortable rooms with premium movie channels. It's 5 mi from Waynesville, 6 mi from the Mark Twain National Forest, and near several antiques shops and restaurants. Cable TV. Pool. Video games. Business services. | 25755 Hwy. 17 | 573/774–3600 | fax 573/774–3601 | 50 rooms | $36 | AE, D, DC, MC, V.

Home Place Bed and Breakfast. This turn-of-the-20th-century Victorian home with a fireplace, a wide porch, and landscaped gardens is on a downtown, residential street on a circular bluff overlooking the springs. Complimentary breakfast. TV in common area. | 302 S. Benton St. | 573/774–6637 | 3 rooms | $65–$75 | MC, V.

Ramada Inn. This chain hotel is 2 mi from Waynesville's downtown just off I–44 at exit 161. Restaurant, bar. In-room data ports, some in-room hot tubs, cable TV. 2 pools. Beauty salon, hot tub. Gym. Video games. Business services. Pets allowed. | I–44, Exit 161 | 573/336–3121 or 800/272–6232 | fax 573/336–4752 | www.ramada.com | 82 rooms | $65–$105 | AE, D, DC, MC, V.

WENTZVILLE

MAP 12, D4

(Nearby towns also listed: Fulton, Hannibal, Hermann, St. Charles, St. Louis)

This town is named for Erasmus L. Wentz, an engineer of the North Missouri Railroad and good friend of the man who donated land and money for the development of Wentzville. Tobacco production was essential to the growth of Wentzville, but today the largest employer is General Motors, which provides more than 6,000 jobs to area residents.

Information: **Wentzville Chamber of Commerce** | 101 Mall Pkwy., Box 11, 63385 | 636/327–6914 | www.wentzvillemo.org.

Attractions

Cuivre River State Park. This park offers a 55-acre lake, prairie grass, hardwood forests, and group camping 15 mi north of Wentzville. | 678 Rte. 147, Troy | 636/528–7247 | www.dnr.state.mo.us/dsp | Free | Daily.

Daniel Boone Home. Daniel Boone lived in this four-story Georgian-style home from 1803 to 1820. Today it's furnished with period antiques. | 1868 Hwy. F, Defiance | 636/798–2005 | $7 | Apr.–Oct., daily 9–6; Nov. and Mar., daily 11–4.

Rotary Park. The 72-acre park has a 5-acre lake, two picnic pavilions, a horse arena, sand volleyball courts, horseshoe pits, and an amphitheater. | W. Meyer Rd. | 636/327–7665 | Free | Daily.

ON THE CALENDAR

JULY: *St. Charles County Fair.* The third week of July brings six days of carnival rides, crafts, livestock shows, and concerts. | 636/327–5101.

Dining

Kwan Yin Restaurant. Chinese. Cantonese cuisine and chicken dishes are the specialties at this restaurant named for the Chinese goddess of kindness and decorated with Asian lamps and paintings. Kids' menu. | 1603 W. Pearce Blvd. | 636/327–8000 | $5–$10 | MC, V.

Lodging

Holiday Inn. This hotel is just off Interstate 70 at exit 212 in an area of office buildings. Restaurant, bar. In-room data ports, room service, cable TV. Pool. Business services. Some pets allowed. | 900 Corporate Pkwy. | 636/327–7001 or 800/465–4329 | fax 636/327–7019 | www.basshotels.com/holiday-inn | 138 rooms | $80–$109 | AE, D, DC, MC, V.

Super 8 Motel Wentzville. This basic two-story chain motel has an outdoor swimming pool, a video-game room, and car plug-ins for cold winter nights. Cable TV. Pool. Video games. | 4 Pantera Dr. | 636/327–5300 or 800/800–8000 | fax 636/639–1147 | www.super8.com | 62 rooms | $40–$50 | AE, D, DC, MC, V.

WEST PLAINS

MAP 12, D6

(Nearby towns also listed: Poplar Bluff, Van Buren)

Settlement of this part of south-central Missouri began around 1840, and by 1860, 150 people called West Plains home. During the Civil War, this town was burned to the ground and residents didn't begin to rebuild until the 1880s. It is now the largest town in a 100-mi radius, with more than 9,000 inhabitants. Many people find their way to West Plains for the extensive genealogical society records at the library here.

Information: West Plains Chamber of Commerce | 401 Jefferson Ave., 65775 | 417/256–4433 | www.wpchamber.com.

Attractions

Dawt Mill. Built in 1897, Dawt is the only water-powered gristmill on the North Fork River, and one of four mills in the West Plains area. To reach the mill take Route 160 west 26 mi to County Road PP. | 318 County Road PP, Tecumseh | 417/284–3540 | Free | Daily 8–5.

Flea Market. Find bargains galore at the Heart of the Ozarks Fairgrounds. | 417/256–2198 | Free | 1st and 3rd weekends of each month, 8–5.

West Plains Public Library. There's a special room for the genealogy collection here, which incorporates the records of the South Central Missouri Genealogy Society. | 417/256–4775 | Free | Mon., Wed., Fri., Sat., 9–5; Tues., Thur. 9–6.

ON THE CALENDAR

DEC.: *Optimist Club Arts and Crafts Show.* A two-day arts-and-crafts show (no food stands) held in the Civic Center the first weekend in December. | 417/256–4433.

Dining

Casa Deliciosa. Tex-Mex. The chef, brought in from Amarillo, Texas, makes all the food from scratch, including the just-fried chips and fresh salsa. Fajitas are a popular choice at this strip-mall restaurant. | 1504 Porter Wagoner Blvd. | 417/257–1693 | $5–$9 | AE, D, MC, V | Closed Sun., Mon.

Kenny's Walleye and Catfish House. Seafood. Customers say Kenny's has the best breakfast in town, but it also serves lunch and dinner. Try the farm-raised catfish or imported walleye. The restaurant is just five blocks from the town square. | 805 Porter Wagoner Rd. | 417/256–1538 | $5–$9 | AE, D, MC, V | Breakfast also available; closed Sun.

Lodging

Best Western Grand Villa. This three-story chain hotel with meeting rooms and an exercise room is adjacent to the 24-hour Huddle House restaurant. Cable TV. Pool. Business services. | 220 U.S. Hwy. 63 | 417/257–2711 or 800/528–1234 | www.bestwestern.com | 60 rooms | $39–$65 | AE, D, DC, MC, V.

Pinebrook Lodge Bed and Breakfast. The three-tiered porch is the most impressive feature of this converted and restored health resort, which was originally built in 1924. The B&B is on 100 acres in the Ozark Mountains. Four of the seven guest rooms have private baths. Complimentary breakfast. | 791 State Rte. T | 417/257–7769 or 888/892–7699 | 7 rooms | $60–$85 | No credit cards.

Ramada Inn. You can walk to Mark Twain National Forest from this hotel which is 1 mi outside town. Restaurant, bar, room service, cable TV. Pool. Laundry facilities. Business services. Pets allowed (fee). | 1301 Preacher Row | 417/256–8191 or 800/272–6232 | fax 417/256–8069 | www.ramada.com | 81 rooms | $57 | AE, D, DC, MC, V.

Zanoni Mill Bed and Breakfast. This is a modern home and working ranch located at the edge of an old pioneer village founded by ancestors of the current owners. Complimentary breakfast. Pool, lake. Hot tub. Fishing. | HC 78 Box 1010, Zanoni | 417/679–4050 | 4 rooms | $65–$70 | No credit cards.

WESTON

MAP 12, A3

(Nearby towns also listed: Kansas City, Liberty, Parkville, St. Joseph)

Weston was founded in 1837 and its role as a 19th-century river port has earned the entire town a designation as a National Historic District. If you love antiques, crafts, and hearty home-cooked meals, you'll love spending hours wandering the streets and alleys here. In autumn, stop by the barn at the end of Main Street and see if the tobacco auction is taking place.

Information: **Weston Development Company** | 502 Main St., 64098 | 816/640–2909 | www.ci.weston.mo.us.

Attractions
Ben Ferrell Museum. This minimansion is an exact replica of the Governor's Mansion in Jefferson City. There are also exhibits on the growth of Platte County. | 3rd St. at Ferrel St., Platte City | 816/431–5121 | www.co.platte.mo.us | $1 | Apr.–Oct., Tues.–Sat. noon–4.

Historical Museum. Dioramas and displays cover the history of Platte County from prehistoric days to World War II. | 601 Main St. | 816/640–2650 | Free | Mid-Mar.–mid-Dec., Tues.–Sat. 1–4, Sun. 1:30–5.

Lewis and Clark State Park. Lewis and Clark found the banks of Sugar Lake to be an ideal spot for bird-watching when they first explored here. Many people today would agree. The park is about 20 mi northwest of Weston. | Rte. 138, Rushville | 816/579–5564 | www.dnr.state.mo.us/dsp | Free | Daily.

Pirtle's Weston Winery. Owner Patrice Pirtle is as spirited as the product she makes and sells in a former Lutheran Church. | 502 Spring St. | 816/640–5728 | Free | Mon.–Thurs. 10–6, Fri. and Sat. 10–7, Sun. 11–6.

Price/Loyles Tour House. An 1857 Daniel Boone family heritage home filled with 160 years of original family furnishings. | 718 Spring St. | 816/640–2383 | $3.50 | Sat. 10–4; also by appointment.

Red Barn Farm. This working farm offers hayrides as well as educational tours focused on crop production and livestock. | 16300 Wilkerson Rd. | 816/386–5437 | $3 | Apr.–Nov., daily 10–6.

Snow Creek Ski Area. This ski area offers nine intermediate trails and two beginner trails and begins making artificial snow in December. | Rte. 45 north at Snow Creek Dr. | 816/640–2200 | Admission varies | Dec.–Mar.

Weston Bend State Park. The 1,133-acre park features picnic tables and shelter houses, a campground, hiking and biking trails, and a scenic overlook of the Missouri River. | Rte. 45, Weston | 816/640–5443 | www.dnr.state.mo.us/dsp | Free | Daily.

ON THE CALENDAR
OCT.: *Apple Fest.* This harvest celebration closes down Main St. for two days early in the month. | 816/640–2909.
DEC.: *Christmas Candlelight Homes Tour.* Six antebellum homes decorated for the holidays, plus carriage rides and street carolers on the first weekend in December. | 816/640–2909.

Dining
America Bowman. Irish. This is the town's oldest restaurant and it's filled with historic Irish decorations. Be sure to try the bangers, an Irish form of sausage. Entertainment weekends. | 500 Welt St. | 816/640–5235 | $10–$16 | D, MC, V | Closed Mon.

Vineyards Restaurant. Continental. Modern dishes and an extensive wine list await you at this small but romantic restaurant, though you'll have to brave the cramped dining area to get them. | 505 Spring St. | 816/640–5588 | Reservations essential | $15–$25 | MC, V.

Lodging
Hatchery House. This Federal-style home built in 1845 is near downtown antiques shops and historic attractions. All four guest rooms have private baths, and the two-course country breakfast is complimentary. Complimentary breakfast. | 618 Short St. | 816/640–5700 | 4 rooms | $90–$100 | MC, V.

Inn at Weston Landing. This small inn is on a residential street right downtown and has large rooms filled with antiques. Complimentary breakfast. Cable TV in common area. | 500 Welt St. | 816/640–5788 | 4 rooms | $90 | D, MC, V.

Wisconsin

Beer, brats, cheese, and spectacular scenery—those are among the joys of Wisconsin. The name, Wisconsin, is derived from an Ojibwa term meaning "gathering of the waters" or "place of the beaver." Miners who settled here in the 1800s built their homes by digging into the hillside like badgers, hence the nickname, "the badger state."

Also known as "America's Dairyland," Wisconsin supplies much of America with milk and cheese. Though dairy farming was once the state's primary economic activity, it has been superseded by industry producing industrial machinery and equipment, paper products, electronic equipment, and fabricated metal products. Beer brewing, however, is one of the state's oldest industries and it continues to play a role in the local culture and economy with both large and micro breweries throughout the state.

Most of Wisconsin's landscape was formed some 10,000 years ago by a great glacier. It left in its wake many lakes, prairies, and some of America's finest examples of glacial topography. Wisconsin is 320 mi long, 295 mi wide, and covers 34.8 million acres of land and 1.1 million acres of water. It has has 15,000 lakes, 12,624 rivers and streams covering 44,000 mi. There are 11 state forests, 2 national forests, 43 state parks, 5 state recreation areas, and 25 state trails. Millions visit each year from neighboring states—Minnesota, Illinois, Iowa, and Michigan—as well as from farther afield. Popular outdoor activities include hiking, bicycling, bird-watching, snowmobiling, skiing, ice-sculpting, and bowling or golfing on ice.

Wisconsin is a showcase for Midwestern fall foliage; the Door County and Kettle Moraine regions are two of the best areas to leaf-peep. Kettle Moraine, a large area of rolling hills, valleys, and dense forests extends 100 mi from north to south. In Door County, quaint towns line a long, thin limestone peninsula; with more than 200 mi of shoreline frontage and spectacular scenery, it is a nature-lover's haven.

CAPITAL: MADISON	POPULATION: 5,169,700	AREA: 56,153 SQUARE MI
BORDERS: MN, MI, IA, AND IL	TIME ZONE: CENTRAL	POSTAL ABBREVIATION: WI
WEB SITE: WWW.TOURISM.STATE.WI.US.		

Wisconsin Dells, along the Wisconsin River, is the state's prime tourist attraction, visited in all seasons. Glacially sculpted cliffs rise 100 ft above the water, and there are many family attractions.

Milwaukee, Wisconsin's largest city, offers both big-city amenities and small-town charm. Milwaukee's zoo and museum are among the best in the country, and the city includes top-notch art centers and galleries, as well as rambling parks and spectacular gardens. Milwaukee is a city of neighborhoods; some, like Concordia and Brewers Hill, are filled with large, historic homes that have been painstakingly restored.

From spring to late summer, a constant stream of large festivals celebrates immigrant heritage along the lakefront in Milwaukee. Each features lively entertainment and immense quantities of food, including Wisconsin's famous cheeses and beers. Tucked between the ethnic festivals is Summerfest, an 11-day event that attracts nearly a million visitors to hear concerts by the likes of Tina Turner, Pearl Jam, James Taylor, Bonnie Raitt, John Mellencamp, Sting, and the Temptations. In addition to these large festivals, county fairs and festivals punctuate the calendar in small towns throughout the state from spring to fall. There's a scattering of festivals in winter as well.

Madison, the state's capital, is a bustling college town with lots to see and do. It offers great shopping, historic homes, and spectacular botanical gardens. The scenery outside the city center is lovely.

Wisconsin is an ethnic mosaic; immigrants from Germany, Poland, Ireland, and other countries settled here in large numbers. Ethnic restaurants abound all over the state, especially in Milwaukee. Fabulous German restaurants can be found within walking distance of one another, and Polish restaurants where family members' traditional meals have been served for generations are also common. Numerous Serbian eateries make you feel as if you're dining abroad.

Excellent restaurants serving contemporary American cuisine in all price ranges can also be found. President Bill Clinton and West German Chancellor Helmut Kohl once lunched at Miss Katie's Diner, a casual 1950s-style restaurant. Clinton also once stopped at another popular '50s-style eatery called Leon's Frozen Custard Drive-In; it is believed to be the prototype for the TV series *Happy Days*.

Famous people that have called Wisconsin home include architect Frank Lloyd Wright, Israeli prime minister Golda Meir, pianist Liberace, actor and director Orson Welles, actor Spencer Tracy, authors Laura Ingalls Wilder and Edna Ferber, magician Harry Houdini, artist Georgia O'Keeffe, and progressive reformer Robert M. La Follette, Sr.

Wisconsin has much to offer including brilliant foliage, harvests, and festivals, big-city concerts, professional spectator sports, museums, historic sites, and wine and brewery tours.

History

About 20,000 Native Americans lived within the parameters of present-day Wisconsin when the French arrived and began exploring the area in the 17th century. Although the French bestowed names and created trading posts, they left relatively little mark

Timeline

1634	1666	1673	1701
Jean Nicolet reaches Wisconsin while searching for the Northwest Passage.	Nicholas Perrot opens fur trade with Wisconsin Indians.	Louis Jolliet and Father Jacques Marquette discover Mississippi River.	Fox Indian War begins

on Wisconsin, as they were more interested in the fur trade than agricultural settlement and were never present in large numbers.

The earliest explorers to the area included: Jean Nicolet, the first known European to reach Wisconsin when he landed in Green Bay in 1634 while looking for the Northwest Passage; Nicholas Perrot, who opened fur trade with Wisconsin Native Americans in 1666; and Louis Jolliet and Father Jacques Marquette, who discovered the Mississippi River in 1673.

In 1763 Wisconsin became part of British colonial territory when the Treaty of Paris was signed, ending the French and Indian War. Despite the change, the area remained largely unaffected. French traders continued to work in the area, and British traders began to appear. The first permanent settlement wasn't established, however, until 1764, when Charles Langlade settled at Green Bay.

In 1783, under the same Paris treaty, the British ceded Wisconsin to the United States. Despite the treaty, Wisconsin retained its British influence until after the War of 1812, when the American army established control. At that time, Native American title to the southeastern half of the state was gradually extinguished, and most of the Native Americans living in the area were moved across the Mississippi.

Lead mining brought the first large numbers of settlers to Wisconsin, and also ended the dominance of the area's fur-trade economy. Nearly half of the almost 12,000 people who lived in the territory were residents of the lead-mining district in the southwestern part of the state.

Wisconsin was made part of the Northwest Territory in 1787, part of the Indiana Territory in 1800, the Illinois Territory in 1809, and the Michigan Territory in 1818. On April 20, 1836, President Andrew Jackson signed an act creating the Territory of Wisconsin.

In 1846 Congress passed an act that would enable Wisconsin to become a state, and the first Constitutional Convention met in Madison. On May 29, 1848, President James K. Polk signed a bill to make Wisconsin a state.

After statehood, heavy immigration continued, and Wisconsin remained largely agricultural with wheat as the primary crop. During that time, slavery, banking laws, and temperance were major issues.

By 1850, Wisconsin's population had reached 305,000, with about half of the new settlers coming from New York and New England; the rest were primarily immigrants from England, Scotland, Ireland, Germany, and Scandinavia.

As political parties developed, the Democrats originally proved dominant. Despite the number of foreign immigrants and a shift from Democratic to Republican control, most political leaders continued to have ties to the northeastern United States. New York state laws and institutions provided models for much of the activity of Wisconsin's early legislative sessions; it wasn't until after the Civil War that Wisconsin became a modern political and economic entity.

Following the Civil War, heavy immigration continued, with the majority of immigrants coming from the same countries as in the pre–Civil War era; at the end of the century, however, Polish immigrants arrived in Wisconsin in large numbers.

1738	1763	1764	1774	1783
Fox Indian War ends.	Treaty of Paris signed; Wisconsin becomes part of British colonial territory.	Charles Langlade settles at Green Bay, the state's first permanent settlement.	Quebec Act makes Wisconsin part of the Province of Quebec.	Paris Peace Treaty signed, Wisconsin becomes territory of the United States.

During this time the Republican Party stayed in control of the state's government but was challenged by Grangers, Populists, Socialists, and Temperance candidates, as well as the Democratic Party and its own Republican dissidents. Temperance, the use of foreign languages in schools, railroad regulation, and currency reform were major issues throughout the state.

Wheat gradually declined in importance, as more fertile lands were opened to cultivation in the north and west. In the 1880s and '90s, dairying became the primary agricultural industry in the land, and from the 1870s through the 1890s, lumbering prospered in the northern half of the state. The lumber industry reached its peak from 1888 to 1893, when it accounted for a fourth of all wages paid in the state.

By the end of the lumber era, Milwaukee and the southeastern half of the state had developed a thriving heavy-machinery industry. Paper making, tanning, and brewing also became industry leaders.

The start of the 20th century—often referred to as the Progressive Era—found reform movements sweeping the country and Wisconsin in a role that gave the state national fame. Although Republicans still dominated the state legislature, Progressive and Stalwart factions fought for control of the party, and Milwaukee consistently returned a strong Socialist contingent to the legislature.

The Wisconsin Progressive Party was formed in 1934 but dissolved in 1946. With the demise of the Progressives, the Democratic Party began a slow resurgence, and large-scale European immigration seemed to end. Ethnic groups retained strong individual identities, however, and remained a significant force in the politics and culture of the state. In 1948 Wisconsin celebrated 100 years of statehood.

During the course of the first half of the 20th century, heavy-machinery manufacturing, dairying, and the making of paper products became Wisconsin's leading economic activities. Lumber and beer became less important, as the last virgin forests in the northern half of the state were cut and Prohibition had a grip on the country from 1920 to 1933.

In the mid-20th century, significant numbers of African-Americans began to appear in the state's urban areas. With their arrival, discrimination in housing and employment became matters of concern. Other important issues involved the growth in size of state government, radicalism on university campuses, welfare programs, and environmental questions.

In 1998 Wisconsin celebrated its sesquicentennial. Today Wisconsin is known as the birthplace of the Republican Party, and the home of Robert M. La Follette, Sr., founder of the Progressive movement.

Regions

1. GREAT LAKES

The Great Lakes region consists of two areas, one on Lake Michigan and one on Lake Superior.

1787	1795	1800	1809	1815
Wisconsin becomes part of the Northwest Territory.	Jacques Vieau establishes trading posts at Kewaunee, Manitowoc, and Sheboygan. Made headquarters at Milwaukee.	Wisconsin becomes part of the Indiana Territory.	Wisconsin becomes part of the Illinois Territory.	War with England concluded; Fort McKay abandoned by British.

INTRODUCTION
HISTORY
REGIONS
WHEN TO VISIT
STATE'S GREATS
PARK INFORMATION
RULES OF THE ROAD
DRIVING TOURS

At the southern end of the **Lake Michigan** area, there are high clay bluffs with sand and pebble beaches, which are great for recreation. To the north, the coast has two prominent geographic features: the Door County peninsula and Green Bay (the second-largest bay in the Great Lakes). The Door County peninsula has more miles of shoreline, more state parks, and more lighthouses than any other county in the United States. The peninsula's limestone bluffs, sand beaches, rural farms, islands, parks, and picturesque towns attract tourists throughout the year, but most heavily from spring to fall. When cherry and apple trees blossom in spring, finding a place to stay in this popular spot may be difficult and planning ahead is the way to go.

Towns listed: Algoma, Baileys Harbor, Egg Harbor, Ellison Bay, Ephraim, Fish Creek, Green Bay, Kenosha, Manitowoc, Marinette, Oconto, Peshtigo, Port Washington, Racine, Sheboygan, Sister Bay, Sturgeon Bay, Two Rivers, Washington Island.

The **Lake Superior** area lies along the state's far northern boundary and runs along the western end of Lake Superior's pristine shoreline, where the unspoiled Apostle Islands hover above Bayfield Peninsula. At the far western end of the shoreline, Lake Superior has a deep-water harbor that is an international inland ocean port linked to the Atlantic Ocean by the St. Lawrence Seaway. A 4-mi-long sand bar in the harbor is ideal for bird-watching, particularly the spring and fall migrations. There are also fine sand beaches, an unspoiled landscape, 431 lakes, and the state's tallest waterfall—65-ft-high Big Manitou Falls in Pattison State Park. Farther east, Bayfield and Madeline Island are small, picturesque spots ideal for a quiet getaway any time of the year. Bayfield is also the gateway to the Apostle Islands National Lakeshore, an area that has 22 coastal islands with lighthouses, sea caves, hiking trails, and sparkling blue waters. A ferry takes you from Bayfield to Madeline Island, which is home to Big Bay State Park, a picturesque area with cliffs and remote campsites.

Towns listed: Ashland, Bayfield, Superior.

2. NORTHWOODS

The Northwoods region includes nearly the top third of the state, beginning directly under the Lake Superior area of the Great Lakes region and extending to the state's borders to the east and west. This large region has some of the state's most beautiful forests, lakes, and waterways. Northwoods is the place to go if you want fresh air and to enjoy nature at its most spectacular.

The cities and towns within this region are many. Although some are miles apart, all share the same natural beauty. The Northwoods region includes prairie landscapes, wetlands, large wildlife areas, acres of untouched woods, waterfalls, lakes and rivers, and plenty of recreational areas.

The Northwoods city of Rhinelander has more than 230 lakes within a 12-mi radius. The greater Minocqua area is part of the

1818	**1825**	**1832**	**1833**	**1836**
Wisconsin becomes part of the Michigan Territory; Solomon Juneau buys trading posts of Jacques Vieau at Milwaukee.	1825 Indian Treaty establishes tribal boundaries.	Black Hawk War.	Land treaty with Indians clears southern Wisconsin land titles. First Wisconsin newspaper, the *Green Bay Intelligence,* established.	Act creating the Territory of Wisconsin signed by President Andrew Jackson.

Lakeland Area of Vilas and Oneida counties. The more than 3,200 lakes, streams, and ponds in the two counties draw water-sports enthusiasts. There is world-class fishing, boating, and waterskiing, hiking, biking, cross-country skiing, and snowmobiling in the greater Minocqua Area.

The town of Eagle River is a classic Northwoods vacation spot. Located on a chain of 28 lakes (the largest freshwater chain in the world), Eagle River is noted for its clear, cool lakes filled with game fish. The ice-cream parlors, candy stores, and other shops are also popular.

Towns listed: Antigo, Cable, Crandon, Eagle River, Hayward, Hurley, Lac du Flambeau, Ladysmith, Manitowish Waters, Minocqua, Park Falls, Rhinelander, Rice Lake, St. Germain, Sayner, Spooner, Three Lakes, Woodruff.

3. CENTRAL WISCONSIN

Located directly in the center of Wisconsin, this region is studded with small towns and cities that are surrounded by rugged natural beauty. The area, much of it once involved in the lumber industry, stretches from the western edge of the state to the east, where it abuts the Lake Michigan area of the Great Lakes region.

The Chippewa River runs northeast to southwest in Wisconsin's central region, and the Eau Claire River runs from east to west. Eau Claire, located at the junction of these two rivers, has bike and walking trails with stunning views. Menomonie, a former lumber town on the Red Cedar River, is a popular spot for antiques lovers, and the downtown area has beautifully restored historic homes. Menomonie is the gateway to the Red Cedar State Trail, a 14-mi hiking and biking route that includes an 846-ft-long former railroad bridge. Wausau evolved from an 1800s lumbering town on the Wisconsin River into a thriving city with a diverse commercial and industrial base. Wausau has a historic district, and Rib Mountain (one of the oldest geologic formations on earth) is just south of town.

Waupaca, located on the Crystal River, is a great home base for fishing and water expeditions. Nearby Chain of Lakes, a string of 22 interconnected lakes, is ideal for boating and swimming. Larger cities in Central Wisconsin include Oshkosh, Fond du Lac, and Appleton.

Towns listed: Antigo, Appleton, Black River Falls, Chippewa Falls, Eau Claire, Elkhart Lake, Fond du Lac, Green Lake, Marshfield, Menasha, Menomonie, Neenah, Oshkosh, Shawano, Stevens Point, Tomah, Waupaca, Waupun, Wausau, Wautoma, Wisconsin Rapids.

4. SOUTHERN WISCONSIN

The southern third of the state has landscape unlike any other part of Wisconsin; rock formations, steep hills, hidden valleys, ravines filled with ferns, and an abundance of woodland flowers. The widest variety of towns can be found in this region, from the tiny, quiet Mount Horeb to bustling Wisconsin Dells. In Mount Horeb, the town's Scan-

1836	1841	1846	1847	1848
Capital located at Belmont. Henry Dodge appointed Governor by President Andrew Jackson. First session of legislature. Madison chosen as permanent capital.	James D. Doty appointed Governor by President John Tyler.	Congress passes enabling act for admission of Wisconsin as state. First Constitutional Convention meets in Madison.	Census population 210,546. First Constitution rejected by people. Second Constitutional Convention.	Second Constitution adopted, President James K. Polk signs bill making Wisconsin a state. Legislature meets, Governor Nelson Dewey inaugurated. Large scale German immigration begins.

INTRODUCTION
HISTORY
REGIONS
WHEN TO VISIT
STATE'S GREATS
PARK INFORMATION
RULES OF THE ROAD
DRIVING TOURS

dinavian heritage is apparent, especially on Main Street, where there are life-size, carved wooden trolls.

Dozens of spots that fall somewhere between small 'burbs and busy vacation sites exist throughout southern Wisconsin. Mineral Point's main street is reminiscent of a Cornish village, as miners from Cornwall, England, were among the first to settle the area. New Glarus, known as Wisconsin's Little Switzerland, honors its Swiss founders by nurturing Swiss customs and showcasing Swiss crafts and cuisine. Wisconsin Dells, the state's family vacation spot, is also in the southern region, as is Kettle Moraine, a geologic corridor carved by glaciers that runs for 100 mi north and south.

A visit to the small town of Cedarburg, not far from Milwaukee, is like taking a step back in time. The town's main street is lined with antiques stores, "painted ladies," and limestone-and-cream city brick buildings dating from the mid-19th to early 20th century. Cedarburg's downtown area is listed on the National Register of Historic Places, and a nearby residential area is listed on both the national and state registers.

Towns listed: Baraboo, Beloit, Burlington, Cedarburg, Delafield, Delavan, Dodgeville, East Troy, Elkhorn, Fontana, Fort Atkinson, Galesville, Janesville, Lake Geneva, Mauston, Menomonee Falls, Mineral Point, Monroe, Mount Horeb, New Glarus, Oconomowoc, Platteville, Prairie du Sac, Reedsburg, Richland Center, Sparta, Spring Green, Tomah, Watertown, Waukesha, Wauwatosa, West Bend, Wisconsin Dells.

5. MISSISSIPPI RIVER REGION

The course of the Mississippi River defines much of the western border of Wisconsin, known as the Mississippi River Region, as it spills through the southern and central parts of the state. Throughout the Mississippi River Region you can find magnificent bluffs, rolling countryside, and river towns on the banks of the Mississippi. Cassville, one of the first river towns established in Wisconsin, is a crossing point at the river. The wooded bluffs, parkland, and broad expanse of the river in Cassville provide an ideal habitat for eagles. South of Cassville, in Potosi, you will see one of Wisconsin's oldest lead mines. Prairie du Chien, at the confluence of the Wisconsin and Mississippi rivers, is a picturesque river town.

La Crosse, a larger yet charming city, spreads from the edge of the river to the base of steep bluffs. The city's Main Street ends at a 570-ft bluff. From the summit you can see Wisconsin, Minnesota, and Iowa. Smaller towns such as Alma and Pepin attract those who want quiet getaways. Alma has just two streets, but they stretch for 7 mi along the banks of the Mississippi River. Here you'll enjoy stairway streets that head up river bluffs and a main street lined with historic buildings. Pepin sits on the edge of a strikingly wide expanse of the Mississippi known as Lake Pepin. Pepin is famous as the hometown of author Laura Ingalls Wilder.

Towns listed: Bagley, Cassville, Galesville, Hudson, La Crosse, Prairie du Chien, St. Croix Falls.

1854	1861	1871	1901	1910
Republican Party named in Ripon, first class graduates at state university and Wisconsin Supreme Court declares Fugitive Slave Law of 1850 unconstitutional.	Beginning of Civil War; governor calls for volunteers for military service. Office of county superintendent of schools created.	Peshtigo fire burns much of six counties in northeast Wisconsin resulting in more than 1,000 deaths.	First Wisconsin-born governor, Robert M. La Follette, inaugurated.	Milwaukee elects Emil Seidel first Socialist mayor. Eau Claire first Wisconsin city to adopt commission form of government.

6. MILWAUKEE AREA

In the southern part of the state, Milwaukee (and a few surrounding towns) and Wisconsin's capital city of Madison is the state's smallest, yet busiest region.

A small-town atmosphere prevails in Milwaukee, located along the southeastern border of the state. More a collection of neighborhoods than a city, Milwaukee has modern steel-and-glass high-rises in much of the downtown area, and well-kept 19th-century buildings. First settled by the Potowatomi tribe and later by French fur traders in the late 18th century, Milwaukee boomed in the 1840s with the arrival of German brewers, whose influence is still apparent.

Madison combines big-city culture and small-town charm. The center of the city is dominated by the State Capitol, which resembles the Capitol in Washington, D.C. From spring to fall, area farmers transform Capitol Square on Saturday mornings into an open-air market that should not be missed. A college town, Madison is also a great place to shop—especially on State Street, where trendy boutiques mix with bustling coffee shops. Madison is also a good jumping-off point for day trips to dozens of nearby communities.

Towns listed: Menomonee Falls, Milwaukee, Brookfield, Delafield, Madison

When to Visit

Your interests will determine when you visit Wisconsin. June through August are best if you want to lounge in the sand and play in the water, and spring and fall are good if you enjoy hiking, biking, shopping, and touring.

Wisconsin generally has short, mild summers and long, cold winters, although regions near Lake Michigan are less extreme. Typical January temperatures range from 9°F in northern Wisconsin to 18°F in the southeast. Average temperatures in July range from 67°F in north central Wisconsin to 72°F in the southwest. However, some summers, when the normal temperature should be in the 80s, the thermostat registers a humid 90°F for days, then plummets into the 70s. In winter, when weather forecasters say the average temperature should be in the teens, you can have a mini heat wave with temperatures rising to the 50s. It's been known to snow in late April and to rain at Christmas. One thing you can count on is that the farther north you go in winter, the colder it is likely to get and the more snow you'll see.

Wisconsin usually gets a good amount of rain. The average annual precipitation ranges from 30.60 inches in east-central Wisconsin, near Lake Michigan, to 32.49 inches in the southeast.

1924	1934	1946	1948	1967
La Follette wins Wisconsin's vote for president as Progressive Party candidate. Reforestation amendment to state constitution adopted.	Wisconsin Progressive Party forms.	Wisconsin Progressive Party dissolves and rejoins Republican Party.	Centennial year celebrated.	Racial rioting in Milwaukee, marathon marches demonstrate for Milwaukee open-housing ordinance. Anti-war protests at the University of Wisconsin in Madison culminate in riot with injuries.

INTRODUCTION
HISTORY
REGIONS
WHEN TO VISIT
STATE'S GREATS
PARK INFORMATION
RULES OF THE ROAD
DRIVING TOURS

CLIMATE CHART
Average High/Low Temperatures (°F) and Monthly Precipitation (in inches)

	JAN.	FEB.	MAR.	APR.	MAY	JUNE
GREEN BAY	22.8/5.8	27.1/9.5	38.5/21.4	54/33.9	67.2/43.7	75.5/53.5
	1.15	1.03	2.05	2.40	2.82	3.39
	JULY	**AUG.**	**SEPT.**	**OCT.**	**NOV.**	**DEC.**
	80.5/58.9	77.5/56.8	69.1/48.8	57.4/38.5	42/26.8	27.7/12.5
	3.10	3.50	3.47	2.23	2.16	1.53

	JAN.	FEB.	MAR.	APR.	MAY	JUNE
LA CROSSE	23.5/5.3	29.6/10.1	42.1/23.6	58.5/37	70.9/48.1	79.8/57.1
	0.93	0.90	1.98	2.88	3.26	3.90
	JULY	**AUG.**	**SEPT.**	**OCT.**	**NOV.**	**DEC.**
	84.5/62.3	81.6/59.9	72.4/51.2	60.2/40.2	43.4/27.7	28.1/12.5
	3.79	3.92	3.79	2.20	1.73	1.27

	JAN.	FEB.	MAR.	APR.	MAY	JUNE
MADISON	24.8/7.2	30.1/11.1	41.5/23	56.7/34.1	68.9/44.2	78.2/54.2
	1.07	1.08	2.17	2.86	3.14	3.66
	JULY	**AUG.**	**SEPT.**	**OCT.**	**NOV.**	**DEC.**
	82.4/59.5	79.6/56.9	71.5/48.2	59.9/37.7	44/26.7	29.8/13.5
	3.39	4.04	3.37	2.17	2.09	1.84

	JAN.	FEB.	MAR.	APR.	MAY	JUNE
MILWAUKEE	27.4/12.3	32/16.4	43.3/26.7	57.1/37.1	69.9/47	79.7/56.7
	1.44	1.22	2.16	3.20	2.77	3.17
	JULY	**AUG.**	**SEPT.**	**OCT.**	**NOV.**	**DEC.**
	84.3/62.7	82/61.2	73.9/53.6	61.1/42.9	46.6/31.5	32.6/18.5
	3.39	3.62	3.52	2.34	2.28	2.00

	JAN.	FEB.	MAR.	APR.	MAY	JUNE
RHINELANDER	20.9/0.7	26.3/2.2	37.8/15.2	53/29.3	66.7/40.6	74.8/50.2
	1.07	0.78	1.46	2.36	3.20	3.80
	JULY	**AUG.**	**SEPT.**	**OCT.**	**NOV.**	**DEC.**
	79.8/55.6	76.5/53.1	66.6/44.7	55/34.6	38.5/22.2	24.5/6.4
	3.44	4.34	4.25	2.56	1.88	1.42

FESTIVALS AND SEASONAL EVENTS
WINTER

Jan.   **World Championship Snowmobile Derby.** This Eagle River event held the third weekend in January at the Derby Racetrack 1 mi north of town includes a snowmobile competition with several classes, a motorcycle race on ice, vendors, food, entertainment, and fireworks. | 715/479–4424.

1981
U.S. Supreme Court rules against Wisconsin's historic open primary.

1998
Wisconsin celebrates sesquicentennial.

Feb. **American Birkebeiner.** More than 7,000 people from around the world participate in this 52K cross-country ski race on the last Saturday of the month. The race begins at the Cable Union airport in Cable and ends in downtown Hayward. There is a shorter event on the same day, a 26K race called the Kortelopet, which also starts at the Cable Union Airport and finishes at the Telemark Resort in Cable. | 800/533–7454 | www.birkie.com.

SPRING

May **Chocolate City Festival.** Burlington's chocolate extravaganza the weekend after Mother's Day includes chocolate and non-chocolate foods, as well as a carnival, animal acts, live entertainment, displays, an art fair, and a children's area all at the Chocolate Fest Grounds right in town. | 262/763–6044.

May **Festival of Blossoms.** This monthlong county-wide celebration of spring features blossoming orchards, daffodils, and wildflowers and special events in Egg Harbor and other Door County towns. | 920/743–4456 | www.doorcountyvacations.com.

SUMMER

June **Stone and Century House Tour.** This driving tour of homes held the first weekend in June begins in Cedarburg and features homes in Ozaukee and Washington counties that are more than 100 years old. Many of the homes include antiques and art displays, as well as collectibles. | 800/237–2874.

June **Boerner in Bloom.** As 50,000 roses bloom, Hales Corners celebrates spring with garden walks, workshops, lectures, demonstrations, music, and food in the Boerner BotanicalGardens. | 414/529–1870.

June–July **Summerfest.** Milwaukee's largest festival with top-name entertainment has earned the "World's Largest Music Festival" listing in the *Guinness Book of World Records.* Eleven entertainment stages feature more than 2,500 national, regional, and local acts at the Henry Maier Festival Park. | 414/273–2680 or 800/837–3378.

June–Oct. **Peninsula Players.** America's oldest professional resident summer theater group offers performances in an outdoor pavilion in Fish Creek. | 920/868–3287.

July **Art Fair on the Square.** Madison's Capitol Square art fair held the second weekend in July attracts 100,000 people each year and includes local and national juried artists as well as entertainment. | 800/373–6376.

July **Great Circus Parade.** This historic parade winds its way through downtown Milwaukee with more than 50 historic circus wagons, hundreds of horses, clowns, elephants, and marching bands on the second Sunday in July. | 414/273–7222 or 608/356–8341.

July **Riverfest.** In Beloit, at the Riverside Park, this music festival features more than 50 bands, arts, crafts, food, a carnival, a lumberjack show, and helicopter and hot-air balloon rides. | 608/365–4838 | 2nd weekend July.

INTRODUCTION
HISTORY
REGIONS
WHEN TO VISIT
STATE'S GREATS
PARK INFORMATION
RULES OF THE ROAD
DRIVING TOURS

| July–Aug. | **EAA AirVenture Oshkosh.** At the Whittman Regional Airport in Oshkosh, the world's largest sport aviation event draws more than 800,000 people and 11,000 airplanes each summer. | 800/236–4800 | Starts last Wed. in July and runs for 7 days. |
| Aug. | **Wisconsin State Fair.** In Milwaukee, this large fair includes a carnival, live entertainment, food booths, arts, crafts, farm animals, children's activities, and body-building and weight-lifting competitions. In West Allis, bounded by Interstate 94, Greenfield Avenue, and 76th and 84th streets. | 414/266–7000 | Starts first Thurs. in Aug. and runs 11 days. |

AUTUMN

Sept.	**Cornish Festival and Taste of Mineral Point.** In Mineral Point, this annual festival features Celtic entertainment, a taste of local restaurants, including the area's famous Cornish pasties, and *figgyhobbin*, a raisin-filled baked dessert. There are also bus tours of the Mineral Point Historic District. U.S. 151 to downtown	888/764–6894	Last weekend (Fri.–Sun.) Sept.
Sept.	**Wine and Harvest Festival.** In the Historic Downtown District of Cedarburg, this annual wine festival attracts 30,000–40,000 people and includes grape stomping, a grape-seed spitting contest, farmers' market, scarecrow contest, music, food samples, and craft shows.	262/377–9620	3rd weekend in Sept.
Sept.	**Wisconsin State Cow Chip Throw.** At Marion Park in Prairie du Sac, this family event features cow-chip tosses for fun and prizes, a beer garden, a children's parade, live music, breakfast, chip chucking for children, and an arts-and-crafts fair.	800/683–2453	Labor Day.
Nov.	**Holiday Folk Fair.** At the Wisconsin State Fair Park in Milwaukee, this ethnic festival offers a wide variety of food, music, demonstrations, and dancing.	414/225–6225	Weekend (Fri.–Sun.) before Thanksgiving.

State's Greats

The city of Milwaukee has an abundance of great ethnic restaurants, a top-notch zoo, a wide variety of museums, beautiful gardens, parks, historic sights, and art venues. Equally impressive are the city's quaint neighborhoods and shopping areas. The state capital of Madison is much the same, only on a slightly smaller scale.

For a restful holiday surrounded by nature's bounty, head away from Milwaukee or Madison in just about any direction and you will find charming little towns. A great way to see the natural beauty is to station yourself in a rural small town and tour the surrounding countryside at a leisurely pace.

For outdoor winter fun, head north to check out the large cities and small towns. The farther north you go, the more snow you will find.

Beaches, Forests, and Parks

With 15,000 lakes, great beaches can be found throughout Wisconsin. Madison and Lake Geneva have among the most beautiful lakes, and the most striking beaches are in Madison and Door County. Near the center of the state is **Wisconsin Dells,** a destination popular with families as it has many fine water parks, water rides, and water-related entertainment. During peak season you're likely to find crowds, but the area's highlights are sure to outweigh any inconvenience you'll encounter. If you prefer your water in more casual, genteel surroundings, head north to **Door County**; the charming little towns along the peninsula are either on or near the water and offer beautiful vistas with lighthouses, acres of flowering fruit trees, historical attractions, museums, and quiet campgrounds.

Door County is home to a number of great parks. **Peninsula State Park** covers 3,776 acres and over 6 mi of shoreline, and **Whitefish Dunes State Park** has a mile of sandy beach and 863 acres of forest and dunes on rugged Lake Michigan's shore. **Rock Island State Park** has about 900 acres and 6 mi of shoreline. Other popular parks include **Devil's Lake State Park** in Baraboo, a great spot for campers, with 406 campsites. Hikers will love it, too, as it is also home to 25 mi of hiking trails. Its 18 mi of cross-country ski trails also make it a good choice for winter vacationers who enjoy being outdoors. Located atop mounds that have been a southwestern Wisconsin landmark since pioneer days, **Blue Mound State Park** north of Madison has beautiful scenery. From an observation tower, you can see miles and miles of the area's striking countryside.

Forests are plentiful in Wisconsin, especially in the northern part of the state. One of the most beautiful is **Kettle Moraine State Forest,** which is actually divided into northern and southern units. Together, the units cover 47,000 square mi where you can jog, hike, and bike. Wisconsin's largest forest is **Northern Highland–American Legion State Forest** in Iron and Vilas counties, located north of Rhinelander. In this 222,728-acre forest where you can camp, hike, and cross-country ski, there are 875 campsites, 12 mi of self-guided nature trails, 400 mi of snowmobile trails, and 42 mi of cross-country ski trails. You can also fish in one of the forest's many pristine lakes.

Culture, History, and the Arts

Wisconsinites relish their heritage, as evidenced by the state's numerous restored villages, homes, and museums. **Old World Wisconsin,** in Eagle, has 65 buildings that reflect the state's German, Polish, Scandinavian, and Yankee heritage. **Pendarvis State Historical Site,** in Mineral Point, offers tours of historic homes once owned by Cornish lead miners in the 1830s and '40s. **Heritage Hill State Park,** a state park operated by the Wisconsin Department of Natural Resources, is a 40-acre complex made of 25 furnished, historic buildings grouped into pioneer, small-town, military, and agricultural theme areas.

Native American heritage can be seen in 11 areas of Wisconsin, where tribes have established museums and other sites offering a glimpse into their past. The **Arvid E. Miller Memorial Library Museum,** just northwest of Oneida at Bowler, has historical documents, a pre-European collection of Native American baskets, and beadwork. The nearby **Menomonee Logging Camp Museum,** at Keshena, has seven log buildings with more than 20,000 artifacts from Wisconsin's logging industry. To the west, near Webster, is **Forts Folle Avoine Historic Park,** a reconstructed fur trading post.

Much can be learned about African-American heritage at the **America's Black Holocaust Museum** and the **Wisconsin Black Historical Society Museum,** both in Milwaukee. A wide variety of information on African-American history can be gleaned at the former; the latter is smaller and has limited hours so is perhaps best if you are looking for additional information. The **Racine County Heritage Museum** in southeastern Wisconsin houses a permanent Civil War exhibit, and the **Wisconsin Veterans Museum** in Madison has exhibits showcasing the military contributions of Wisconsin veterans.

Wisconsin has many great museums, including those that highlight transportation. Green Bay's **National Railroad Museum** has 75 pieces of antique railroad rolling stock, some of which were part of General Dwight D. Eisenhower's personal command train from World War II. The **Wisconsin National Guard Memorial Library and Museum** in Camp Douglas has army and air guard units, and the **Hartford Heritage Auto**

INTRODUCTION
HISTORY
REGIONS
WHEN TO VISIT
STATE'S GREATS
PARK INFORMATION
RULES OF THE ROAD
DRIVING TOURS

Museum in Hartford has the largest collection of antique cars and trucks in the state (including the rare Kissel, built in Hartford from 1906 to 1931).

Maritime museums are also common in Wisconsin, the most noteworthy being the **Door County Maritime Museum** in Sturgeon Bay, where a 20,000-square-ft building highlights the region's rich marine heritage.

Wisconsin is also home to many beautiful historic mansions built by prominent residents of years past. **Hearthstone Historic House Museum** in Appleton has nine fireplaces and stained-glass windows, and the **Charles A. Grignon Mansion** in Kaukauna was built in the last days of Wisconsin's fur-trade era. The **Marcus Sears Bell Farmstead** is an 1884 Italianate farmhouse and is the centerpiece of the New Richmond Heritage Center. Some towns have entire areas that are historic districts. Exchange Square, in Brodhead, has structures important to the post–Civil War era; the **Historic District in Mineral Point** has more than 500 structures; and the town of **Cedarburg,** near Milwaukee, has two historic areas. The historic areas in both Mineral Point and Cedarburg have beautiful historic homes, buildings, and antiques stores. Cedarburg is home to mid-19th to early 20th-century buildings, many of which are made of limestone and cream city brick. The Historic District in Mineral Point has 1830s stone cottages.

Historic buildings that focus on the arts are also numerous. The **Grand Opera House** in Oshkosh and the Mabel Tainter Theater (part of the **Mabel Tainter Memorial**) in Menomonie reflect the architecture and opulence of the Victorian era. Built in 1889, the Mabel Tainter Memorial has a restored theater, reading room, and exhibit gallery, as well as a full performing-arts season. The restored Grand Opera House also hosts performances.

Sports

Few states can claim more opportunities for outdoor activities than Wisconsin. There are hundreds of miles of trails for casual, long-distance, and mountain bikers, spots where hikers and climbers are sure to get a challenging workout, and scenic areas where a leisurely walk is the best way to take in the spectacular view.

No matter what your pace, one of the best areas for traveling on foot is the **Ice Age Trail,** which has 600 mi of trail open to walkers, hikers, and runners. The trail rambles through 31 counties, beginning on the shores of Green Bay and ending at the Dalles of the St. Croix River at Wisconsin's western border. At any point along the trail, you're sure to find a spectacular view of the countryside. The trail, which was carved by glaciers more than 10,000 years ago, is also the site of 20 nature-related athletic events held each year.

If you like rock climbing or rafting Wisconsin has some challenges for you. Experienced rock climbers come from out of state to hone their skills at **Devil's Lake State Park** in Baraboo (a famous climbing area with 500-ft bluffs). Both the Wolf and Red rivers in the White Lake area have great areas for rafting, as do the Menomonie and Peshtigo rivers in Marinette County.

If you want a sport that's a bit less challenging, visit Somerset, near Hudson (called the Tubing Capital of the World), where you can splash your way down the Apple River in an inner tube. You can also choose to take a marked canoe trail that winds through the Mississippi River backwaters from **Wyalusing State Park,** near Bagley.

With Wisconsin's many lakes, and the Mississippi River along its western border, there are plenty of opportunities for fishing, waterskiing, boating, and swimming. You can rent small to large water craft in many Wisconsin vacation areas, but you can also use your own in some parts of the state. Take a leisurely tour down the Mississippi River on an authentic steam-driven paddle wheeler from La Crosse, or take a fishing trip on a chain of seven small spring-fed lakes called the **Trempealeau Lakes.** If you are looking to simply relax along a shoreline with spectacular scenery, the **Door County peninsula** is a great option with its quaint towns and many lighthouses.

Wisconsin is the place to be for both summer and winter fishing. In the Hayward and Minocqua areas, muskie fishing is extremely popular, and the little town of Potosi, along Wisconsin's Great River Road, calls itself Wisconsin's Catfish Capital. Other great spots for fishing are scattered throughout the state, but most are located in northern and central Wisconsin. Of course, where there is an abundance of fish, there is sure to be a fishing tournament. In winter, enthusiasts vie for a wide variety of fish (such as perch, northern, and walleye) from sheltered ice shanties, or brave the elements without shelter. Depending on the area, at different times of the year spear fishing for rough fish is also popular.

Generally speaking, winter in Wisconsin is a wonderland for the sports enthusiast. There are excellent ski hills, mile upon mile of groomed trails for cross-country skiers and snowmobilers, and some lakes that are safe to walk, skate, snowmobile, and even drive on.

Rules of the Road

License requirements: To drive in Wisconsin, you must be at least 16 years old and have a valid driver's license. Residents of Canada and most other countries may drive as long as they have a valid license from their home country.

Right turn on red: In most of Wisconsin you can make a right turn at a red light after coming to a full stop. At some intersections, "no turn on red light" signs are posted.

Seat belt and helmet laws: Drivers and passengers must wear seat belts at all times. Children under age four must use a federally approved child safety seat. Adult motorcyclists do not have to wear helmets, but those driving or riding on motorcycles who are under the age of 18 do. Bikers must also drive with their lights on.

Speed limits: Speed limits in Wisconsin vary widely. On expressways they can range from 50 to 65 mph, and on highways from 40 to 55 mph. In residential areas, posted speed limits can range from 25 to 40 mph. In areas where there are schools, signs are often posted indicating speed limits of 15 to 20 mph when children are present. Be sure to check signs carefully, and don't drink and drive in Wisconsin, as police aggressively pursue drunk drivers.

For more information: Contact the Department of Transportation, Division of Motor Vehicles at 414/266–1000.

Park Information

STATE PARKS
Annual admission for all state parks in Wisconsin is $25, $18 for Wisconsin residents. For more information, contact the **Wisconsin Department of Natural Resources.** | 101 S. Webster St, Madison | 608/266–2621.

Lake Michigan Circle Tour Driving Tour
FROM KENOSHA TO GREEN BAY

Distance: 80 mi   Time: 2 to 3 days

Breaks: Stop overnight in Sturgeon Bay as you enter Door County. Or check out pretty little Fish Creek, on the Green Bay side of the Door County peninsula, it's another good place to overnight.

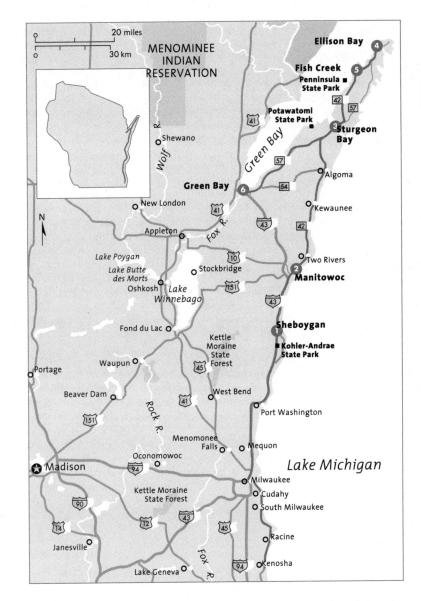

INTRODUCTION
HISTORY
REGIONS
WHEN TO VISIT
STATE'S GREATS
PARK INFORMATION
RULES OF THE ROAD
DRIVING TOURS

This tour is part of the Great Lakes Circle Tour. You'll be traveling northward along the Lake Michigan shoreline, where you'll find fishing, sailing, swimming, and spectacular views. If you take this trip in spring or fall, the views will be breathtaking, especially as you pass through Door County; in this part of the state, cherry and apple blossoms are abundant in spring, and fall color is spectacular.

This tour starts in Kenosha, which is north of the Wisconsin–Illinois border on Route 32. From there it heads to Milwaukee. Because of its size, Milwaukee is best visited on its own. If you take this tour in winter, you may find a good number of sights and businesses closed for the season, especially those located farther north; seeing this area's natural beauty—especially after a snowfall—will more than make up for a missed restaurant or museum.

❶ **Sheboygan** is nationally known for its sausage and is a great place for bratwurst. **Kohler-Andrae State Park** has a mile-long beach good for camping, swimming, sunning, and beachcombing, as well as acres of sand dunes, and four hiking trails.

❷ **Manitowoc** has a wide variety of maritime attractions as well as a historic village. **Wisconsin Maritime Museum** is the largest maritime museum on the Great Lakes, with 21,000 square ft of displays. **Pinecrest Historical Village** is a 60-acre outdoor museum with more than 20 authentically restored buildings from the Manitowoc County area, circa 1900. The village includes a gallery of changing exhibits and a nature trail.

❸ **Sturgeon Bay** is the first Door County city you come to and also the largest. It is one of the largest shipbuilding ports on the Great Lakes. Sturgeon Bay has a downtown historic district as well as a residential historic district. The **Door County Chamber of Commerce** can provide a guide for tours of the districts. At the **Sturgeon Bay Brew and Pub,** in the old railroad station on the west end of downtown, you can sample a frosty local beer and watch beer being made. **Potawatomi State Park** is known for great camping and picnicking, and offers a great view of the county from its observation platform.

❹ The small coastal village of **Ellison Bay** is the perfect jumping-off point for visits to Gills Rock and/or Washington Island—both located at the tip of the peninsula. The **Washington Island Ferry Line** departs year-round from Northport Pier, which is on the peninsula. Vehicle tours of the island are offered by the **Viking Tour Train** and **Cherry Train Tours.**

❺ In **Fish Creek** you will find a village full of historic inns, shops, restaurants, and artists' galleries. **Peninsula Players** is the oldest professional resident summer theater company in the country. The southern entrance to **Peninsula State Park** is near town. At this park you can camp, hike, bicycle, cross-country ski, snowmobile, and play golf.

❻ There's plenty to do in the big city of **Green Bay,** especially if you're a football fan or a railroad buff. The **Green Bay Packer Hall of Fame** honors the greats of the green and gold, and offers tours of Lambeau Field. The **National Railroad Museum** has more than 70 railroad cars and locomotives, and is one of the largest rail museums in America.

To return to the start of your tour, take Interstate 43 to **Milwaukee,** then take Interstate 94 to **Kenosha.**

The Great River Road along Route 35

FROM CASSVILLE TO HUDSON

Distance: 300 mi   Time: 2 days
Breaks: Consider an overnight in La Crosse, the largest city on this tour.

This tour, which covers Wisconsin's portion of the Great River Road, takes you along the state's western border, past bluffs and river towns along the Mississippi. You can start in Dickeyville, a small town at the southwest corner of Wisconsin just across the river from Dubuque, Iowa, and head north toward St. Croix Falls, a rustic town near the Minnesota border. Just follow the white-and-green "Wisconsin's Great River Road" signs. This tour is best taken when the weather is nice so you can enjoy the river, parks, and recreation areas.

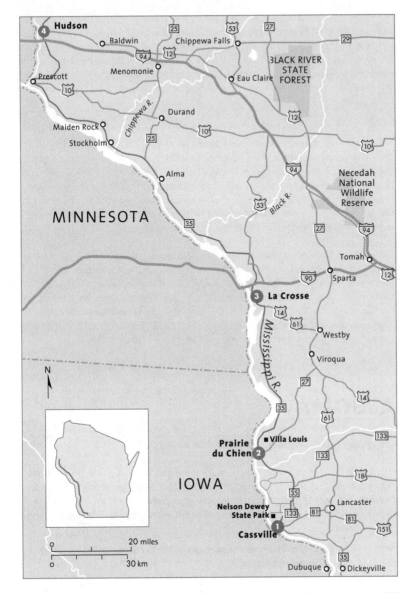

❶ Quiet **Cassville** (From Rte. 35, follow Rte. 133 west into town), which once made a bid to become Wisconsin's territorial capital, is a great spot to relax and enjoy the river. **Riverside Park** is the departure point for the **Cassville Car Ferry,** which will take you across the river. About a mile away is **Nelson Dewey State Park,** where bald eagles can be seen. There are also wooded family campsites, scenic picnic areas, and spectacular views of the river from soaring, tree-lined bluffs. At nearby **Stonefield State Historic Site,** the State Historical Society's museum of agricultural history and village, you can stroll through the town square in a re-created 1890s rural village and visit with costumed merchants and tradesmen in period shops. Across the road is the home of Wisconsin's first governor, Nelson Dewey. The grounds include five original buildings and authentic furnishings.

❷ The rustic town of **Prairie du Chien** has plenty for nature lovers and history buffs. The main attraction is **Villa Louis,** a Victorian country estate built by the family of fur trader Hercules Dousman. The villa is on the banks of the Mississippi River. **La Riviere Park** (South and east of town on Vineyard Coulee Rd.) has nature trails, rare native prairie plants, rustic camping, and an equestrian campground. Stop at the Wisconsin Travel Information Center between April 1 and October 31 for more information on area attractions.

❸ The large city of **La Crosse** (Take I–90 east off Rte. 35) has small-town charm and a wide variety of things to see and do—from brewery tours to leisurely boat rides. Get details on what's happening at the Wisconsin Travel Information Center in La Crosse on Interstate 90 east, about a mile east of the Mississippi River. For a panoramic view of the city, river, and surrounding countryside, go to **Grandad Bluff**—a park at the end of Main Street that sits about 500 ft above the river. At **Riverside Amusement Park** you can board the paddlewheel steamer *Julia Belle Swain,* a floating palace with the amenities of the riverboats of the past. The *Julia Belle Swain* offers one- and two-day excursions.

❹ The town of **Hudson** was named for its physical resemblance to the Hudson River valley in New York. Here you will find history, the arts, an impressive park, and even a greyhound racing track in a world-class facility. The **Octagon House,** a Victorian-style home built in 1855, includes period furnishings. The **Phipps Center for the Arts** has professional theatrical productions and cultural exhibits. **Willow River State Park** has a nature center, prairie remnants, a trout stream, dams, lakes, a sandy beach, and a campground. The **St. Croix Meadows Greyhound Park** has greyhound racing.

To return to the start of your tour, follow the same route back along Route 35.

ALGOMA

MAP 11, F4

(Nearby towns also listed: Green Bay, Sturgeon Bay)

Settled in 1818 and once a large commercial fishing port, Algoma is now home of one of the state's largest charter fishing fleets. The historic character of this fishing port unfolds with a walk through its charming downtown and waterfront districts. From Algoma's beachfront boardwalk you can see a century-old red lighthouse at the end of a breakwater.

Information**Algoma Area Chamber of Commerce** | 1226 Lake St., 54201 | 800/498–4888 | aacofc@itol.com | www.algoma.org.

Attractions

Ahnapee State Trail. More than 15 mi of trail, the Ahnapee runs from Algoma along the river to Sturgeon Bay. Great for biking, walking, and snowmobiling. There's a visitor center at the lake. | Lake St. | 920/487–2041 or 800/498–4888 | Free | Daily.

Kewaunee County Historical Museum. This museum 10 mi south of Algoma in Kewaunee's Court House Square covers local and maritime history. | 613 Dodge St., Kewaunee | 920/388–4410 | $2 | Memorial Day–Labor Day, daily 9–4:30; Labor Day–Memorial Day, by appointment.

Von Stiehl Winery. Located in a vintage brewery building, this winery founded in 1965 makes wines following the old German method. Wine tours and tastings, with more than 20 wines to sample, are offered. Food products, such as wine mustards, wine cheese, and wine sausage, are available. | 115 Navarino St. | 920/487–5208 or 800/955–5208 | www.von-stiehl.com | $2; special rates for senior citizens; children under 16 free | May–Oct., daily 9–5; Nov.–Dec., daily 11–5; Jan.–Apr., daily 11–4.

Zillmer's Antique Farming Center. This museum, five minutes north of town, details local agricultural history with its restored mid-19th-century farmstead buildings and extensive collection of antique tractors and farm equipment. There is also a petting zoo. | E. 7437 Kennedy Rd. | 920/487–5785 | $4, $2 children | Memorial Day–Labor Day, Tues.–Sat. 10–4.

ON THE CALENDAR

AUG.: *Shanty Days Celebration of the Lake.* This three-day family festival is held downtown the second weekend in August and includes a book sale, a parade, a street market, entertainment, children's events, food tents, arts, crafts, fireworks, and a 5K fun run/walk. | 800/498–4888.

Dining

Captain's Table. Seafood. Nautical memorabilia fills the two dining rooms here and the salad bar is in a rowboat. It's popular for breakfast as well as for fresh fish lunches and dinners. Kids' menu. | 133 N. Water St. | 920/487–5304 | $7–$16 | No credit cards | Breakfast available; no dinner Dec.–Mar.

Lodging

Algoma Beach Motel. On the edge of town in a quiet residential neighborhood, this motel has simply furnished lakeshore rooms and condo units, all have water views that are especially beautiful at sunrise. You can grill out on the private beach, have a bonfire, or take a stroll down the town boardwalk. Picnic area. Some kitchenettes, cable TV. Beach. Some pets allowed. | 1500 Lake St. | 920/487–2828 | 28 rooms, 4 condos | $70–$119 rooms, $219 condos | AE, D, DC, MC, V.

Amberwood Inn. This antiques-furnished 1920s Cape Cod–style home has five large suites overlooking Lake Michigan. Each has French doors leading to its own lakefront deck. Breakfast is served in your room or the dining room. There's a 300-ft private beach. Picnic area, complimentary breakfast. Cable TV. Hot tub, sauna. Beach. | N7136 Rte. 42, Lakeshore Dr. | 920/487–3471 | www.amberwoodinn.com | 5 suites | $80–$115 | MC, V.

ANTIGO

MAP 11, D3

(Nearby towns also listed: Crandon, Rhinelander)

Wisconsin is the world leader in the production of ginseng and in Antigo are fields covered by slatted wooden roofs, which shelter the ginseng crop. The silt loam of the Antigo Flats is so rich that Wisconsin actually christened it as an "official state" soil. Antigo also has a fishing plant that can be toured, as well as historic buildings. Antigo was founded in 1876.

Information **Antigo Area Chamber of Commerce** | 329 Superior St., Box 339, 54409-0339 | 888/526–4523 | antigocc@newnorth.net | www.newnorth.net/antigo.chamber.

Attractions

F. A. Deleglise Cabin. This historic cabin, on the grounds of the former downtown public library, was originally built for the Antigo founder, Francis Deleglise; inside are period furnishings. | 7th and Superior Sts. | 715/627–4464 | Free | May–Oct., weekdays 9:30–3:30, weekends 10–3; closed Tues.

Sheldon's Inc. Free guided tours allow you to watch as workers hand craft the world's num-ber-one fishing lure. | 626 Center St. | 715/623–2382 | Free | Weekdays tours 9:15, 10:15, 11:15, 1:30, 2:30, 3:30.

ON THE CALENDAR

FEB.: *North American Snowmobile Championship.* Snowmobile riders from across the country compete in this snowmobile race at the Langlade county fairgrounds. | 888/526–4523.

AUG.: *Ambassadors Art & Craft Show.* Artisans and craftsmen from around the state gather to show and sell their works at the Langlade county fairgrounds the third week-end of the month. | Sat. and Sun. 10–3 | 888/526–4523.

Dining

Blackjack Steak House. Steak. Just outside the city limits, this casual, black-wood-sided restau-rant is known for its steak, prime rib, and fish. Salad bar. Kids' menu. Sun. brunch. | 800 S. Superior St. | 715/623–2514 | $6–$25 | AE, DC, MC, V | No lunch Sat.

The Refuge. American/Casual. Mounted replicas of state record-breaking fish adorn the bar while a fireplace creates a cozy dining room. You can choose from a variety of inven-tive sandwiches, pizzas, and signature pastas, such as the tequila lime pasta with cilantro, sweet peppers, and chicken. | 410 Hwy. 64 E | 715/623–2249 | $6–$17 | AE, D, MC, V.

Lodging

Cutlass Motor Lodge. This single-level motel is in a commercial neighborhood ½ mile from the center of town and 3 mi from the fairgrounds. There is a game room with a pool table and pinball machines. Restaurant, bar. Cable TV, some in-room hot tubs. Pool. Cross-coun-try skiing, downhill skiing. Business services. | 915 S. Superior St. | 715/623–4185 or 800/CUT-LASS | fax 715/623–6096 | 49 rooms | $49–$69 | MC, V.

Good Nite Inn. You can snowmobile right up to the door of your room at this locally owned, roadside motel; the Blackjack Steak House is just two doors away. Cable TV. Snow-mobiling. | 836 S. Superior St. | 715/623–7657 | 17 rooms | $45–$57 | MC, V.

APPLETON

MAP 11, E5

(Nearby towns also listed: Menasha, Neenah)

Settled in 1848 and the largest of the Fox Cities, Appleton was the hometown of magi-cian Harry Houdini, and the site of the world's first home to be lighted by a central hydroelectric station (now the Hearthstone Historic House Museum). In 1994, Apple-ton built a new baseball stadium as the home field for the Wisconsin Timber Rattlers, a Class A farm team for the Seattle Mariners.

Information: **Fox Cities Convention and Visitors Bureau** | 3433 W. College Ave., 54914 | 800/236–6673 | tourism@foxcities.org | www.foxcities.org.

Attractions

Appleton Brewing Company. This is one of the first microbreweries in the state. Call ahead to schedule a tour and one of the brewers will guide you through the brewery and tell you all about the process. Twelve signature beers are available on tap in the adjoin-ing pub. | 1004 S. Oneida St. | 920/735–0507 | Free | Tours by appointment.

Charles A. Grignon Mansion. Nine miles east of Appleton on the banks of the Fox River, the home was built by a French fur trader in the late 1830s. Costumed guides lead tours of this Greek Revival home. | 1313 Augustine St., Kaukauna | 920/766–3122 | $4; special rates for children, senior citizens, and groups | June–Aug., Tues.–Sun.; Sept.–May, by appointment; open some weeks during Christmas season.

Gordon Bubolz Nature Preserve. Eight miles of hiking and cross-country skiing trails allow you to explore this 762-acre preserve, home to deer, snakes, rabbits, and other wildlife. The Nature Center has exhibits of fossils, preserved plants, and stuffed animals. | 4815 N. Lynndale Dr. | 920/731–6041 | Free | Trails daily; nature center Tues.–Fri. 8–4, Sat. 11–4:30, Sun. 12:30–4.

Hearthstone Historic House Museum. This Victorian-era mansion near the southwest edge of downtown Appleton was the first in the world to be lighted by power generated by a central hydroelectric station. Its period "electroliers" were designed by Thomas Edison. There are stained-glass windows, beautifully carved woodwork, and nine fireplaces outlined in rare Minton tiles. | 625 W. Prospect Ave. | 920/730–8204 | $4; special rates for children | Tues.–Fri. 10–4, Sun. 1–4; special hrs. by appointment and for group tours.

Lawrence University. Founded in 1847, the university is home to 1,200 students, the Wriston Art Center, and the Music-Drama Center. Tours are available. | 706 E. College Ave. | 920/832–7000 | Free | Daily during academic season.

Performances at the **Music-Drama Center** (920/832–6614) include chamber music, orchestra recitals, and jazz.

The **Wriston Art Center** has a whimsical architectural design with a glassed cathedral entrance, a spiral galleria, and an outdoor amphitheater. The center features artwork in a variety of mediums by senior university art majors. | 920/832–6621 | Free | Sept.–June, Tues.–Sat.

New London Public Museum. This small museum 20 mi west of Appleton contains Native American artifacts dating from prehistoric times to the turn of the 20th century. There is also an African collection with artwork and artifacts, and displays showcasing local and regional history. Group tours and discussions available. | 406 S. Pearl St., New London | 920/982–8520 | Free | Weekdays 9–5.

Outagamie Museum. Exhibits here detail the life and work of Wisconsin native Harry Houdini. Also featured are local and county history from the early 1800s to 1960s. | 330 E. College Ave. | 920/735–9370 or 920/733–8445 | www.houdinihistory.org | $4; special rates for children, senior citizens, families, and groups | Mon.–Sat. 10–5, Sun. noon–5.

Vande Walle's Candies. In addition to candy, this store at the intersection of U.S. 10 and U.S. 41, behind the Fox River Mall, sells freshly baked goods and ice cream. Tours of the candy-making facility are offered. | 400 Mall Dr. | 920/738–7799 | Free | Mon.–Sat. 7–9, Sun. 7–6; tours weekdays 8–4.

Wolf River Trips. Starting 20 mi west of Appleton in New London, you can explore the Wolf River by canoe or tube. Tour packages and rentals are available. | E8041 Rte. X, New London | 920/982–2458 | Admission varies | May–Labor Day.

ON THE CALENDAR
JUNE: *Flag Day Parade.* Bands and floats parade through downtown. | 800/236–6673.

Dining

Champagne Charlie's. Cajun/Creole. This place is famous for its blackened catfish and other Cajun specialities, created by a chatty chef who often makes the rounds of the dining room. The room is accented with washboards, tubs, and other southern memorabilia. | 211 W. College Ave. | 920/991–1148 | $15–$20 | AE, D, MC, V | Closed Sun. No lunch Sat.

George's Steak House. Steak. This dark-paneled steak house a mile north of downtown serves broiled seafood and steaks. Piano bar. Kids' menu. | 2208 S. Memorial Dr. | 920/733–4939 | $12–$43 | AE, D, DC, MC, V | Closed Sun.

Mongo's Mongolian BBQ. Eclectic. Choose your own ingredients from the buffet of meats, vegetables, and sauces in the dusky, candlelit dining room and then watch as the cooks grill your meal. There is a bar and lounge upstairs, and a pillow room where you can sit on the floor to feast. | 231 W. Franklin St. | 920/730–8304 | $7 lunch, $13 dinner | AE, MC, V | Closed Sun. No lunch Sat.

Peggy's. Contemporary. Order from the bright-colored chalk board behind the coffee bar in this loud and lively dining room filled with mismatched wooden chairs. On the menu are inventive salads and wraps, and a variety of espresso coffee creations. | 125 E. College Ave. | 920/830–1971 | $10–$25 | MC, V | Closed Sun. No dinner Mon.

Queen Bee. American. You'll eat on vintage Formica tables in this diner which serves breakfast all day and salads, burgers, and fries for lunch. Try the "whitey" omelet with onions, green peppers, ham, and hash browns all stuffed inside the omelet. | 225 E. College Ave. | 920/739–8207 | $5–$10 | No credit cards | Closed Sun. No dinner.

Victoria's. Italian. Hand-painted murals of Italy adorn this local favorite known for its enormous portions. You can mix and match pastas and sauces; also on the menu are seafood and veal dishes. Try the chicken Marco Polo with artichoke hearts, mushrooms, mozzarella, and wine sauce over linguine. | 503 W. College Ave. | 920/730–9595 | $8–$17 | AE, D, DC, MC, V.

Lodging

Best Western Midway Hotel. This hotel is surrounded by lakes, parks, and golf courses and is just 5 mi from the airport. It has a domed atrium filled with tropical plants and a pub and restaurant popular with locals. Complimentary breakfast weekdays. Restaurant, bar, room service. In-room data ports, cable TV. Pool. Hot tub. Gym. Business services, airport shuttle. Some pets allowed. | 3033 W. College Ave. (Rte. 125) | 920/731–4141 | fax 920/731–6343 | www.bestwestern.com | 105 rooms | $82–$122 | AE, D, DC, MC, V.

Exel Inn. This chain hotel is in the heart of the city just two blocks from Fox Valley Mall. There is one whirlpool suite. Complimentary Continental breakfast. In-room data ports, microwaves, refrigerators, some in-room hot tubs, cable TV. Gym. Business services. Some pets allowed. | 210 N. Westhill Blvd. | 920/733–5551 | fax 920/733–7199 | www.exelinns.com | 105 rooms | $58–$95 | AE, D, DC, MC, V.

Franklin Street Inn. This 1898 Queen Anne in the historic city park area has lots of antiques, an oak staircase and woodwork, old-fashioned gardens, and a wraparound porch. Complimentary breakfast. Cable TV in common area. No smoking. | 318 E. Franklin St. | 920/739–3702 or 888/993–1711 | 4 rooms | $80–$140 | AE, MC, V.

Gathering Place Bed & Breakfast. This English country-style house is in a quiet residential neighborhood. Curl up by the living-room fireplace, or get cozy in the down bedding in your guest room. Breakfast is served in the formal dining room under an antique brass chandelier which was a wedding gift to the owner's great grandmother. Complimentary breakfast. No pets. No kids under 12. No smoking. | 808 W. Front St. | 920/731–4418 | 3 rooms (2 with shared bath) | $90–$110 | No credit cards.

Hilton Garden Inn. This modern five-story hotel across the street from a convention hall and only five minutes from downtown Appleton caters to business travelers. Rooms have night views of lighted downtown. Restaurant. In-room data ports, microwaves, refrigerators, cable TV. Pool. Hot tub. Gym. Business services. | 720 Eisenhower Dr., Kimberly | 920/730–1900 | 125 rooms | $150–$190 | AE, D, DC, MC, V.

Holiday Inn. Under 2 mi from the Outagamie County Airport in a business area, this glass-and-marble-embellished hotel offers a shuttle to the nearby Fox Valley Mall and poolside service at the covered pool. Restaurant, bar. In-room data ports, microwaves in suites, refrigerators, cable TV, in-room VCRs available. Pool. Hot tub, massage. Gym. Cross-country skiing. Laundry facilities. Business services, airport shuttle. | 150 Nicolet Rd. | 920/735–9955 | fax 920/735–0309 | www.basshotels.com/holiday-inn | 228 rooms | $60–$114 | AE, D, DC, MC, V.

Inn at River Crossing Bed & Breakfast. The owners of this charming home three blocks from Lawrence University and two blocks from downtown shopping and dining welcome guests to relax on the large veranda and enjoy the gardens. The Rose Room has a private porch. Complimentary breakfast. No TV in some rooms. | 931 E. College Ave. | 920/991–0038 | 4 rooms (2 with shared bath) | $95–$170 | MC, V.

Paper Valley Hotel and Conference Center. This elegant hotel with a conference center is in the downtown area near shopping and restaurants. 2 restaurants, bar (with entertainment). In-room data ports, some microwaves, some refrigerators, cable TV, in-room VCRs available. Pool. Barbershop, beauty salon, hot tub, sauna. Miniature golf. Gym. Video games. Business services, airport shuttle. | 333 W. College Ave. (Rte. 125) | 920/733–8000 or 800/ 242–3499 | fax 920/733–9220 | papervalley@montclairhotels.com | www.montclairhotels.com | 394 rooms | $99–$119 | AE, D, DC, MC, V.

Queen Anne Bed & Breakfast. This century-old Victorian with a large front porch and lush green backyard is in a quiet, residential neighborhood three blocks from Lawrence University and near downtown dining and nightlife. All rooms have period furnishings. Complimentary breakfast. TV in common area. | 837 E. College Ave. | 920/831–9903 | 3 rooms (2 with shared bath), 1 suite | $85–$105 rooms, $150 suite | MC, V.

Ramada Inn. This modern hotel, 1 mi from downtown, has an Aztec motif throughout from its stone exterior to its large outdoor mural; western art and cacti accent the lobby. Bar, complimentary breakfast. Some refrigerators, cable TV, in-room VCRs and movies available. Pool. Hot tub. Gym. Laundry facilities. Business services, airport shuttle. Some pets allowed. | 200 N. Perkins St. | 920/730–0495 | fax 920/730–2957 | www.ramada.com | 91 rooms | $70– $115 | AE, D, DC, MC, V.

Road Star Inn. This inn on the outskirts of town—part of a local chain—is just a block from U.S. 41. Pets may stay in smoking rooms only. Complimentary Continental breakfast. Cable TV. Pets allowed. | 3623 W. College Ave. (Rte. 125) | 920/731–5271 or 920/731–5271 | fax 920/ 731–0227 | 102 rooms | $42–$63 | AE, D, MC, V.

Solie Home Bed and Breakfast. This early 1900s stucco home in a quiet residential neighborhood has cozy rooms with decorative woodwork and some antiques. Complimentary breakfast. Cable TV in common area. Cross-country skiing. No smoking. | 914 E. Hancock St. | 920/733–0863 | 3 rooms | $75–$125 | No credit cards.

Woodfield Suites. This modern brick all-suites hotel, 1 mi from downtown, has a forest-green-and-mahogany interior. Two restaurants flank either side. Complimentary cocktails. Complimentary Continental breakfast. In-room data ports, refrigerators, cable TV, in-room VCRs available. 2 pools. Hot tub, sauna. Tennis. Bowling, gym. Video games. Laundry service. Business services, airport shuttle. | 3730 W. College Ave. (Rte. 125) | 920/734–7777 or 800/ 338–0008 | fax 920/734–0049 | 98 rooms | $97–$107 | AE, D, DC, MC, V.

ASHLAND

MAP 11, C2

(Nearby towns also listed: Bayfield, Hurley, Superior)

This pretty town, founded in 1854, is at the foot of Lake Superior's Chequamegon Bay where there is a port for Great Lakes ships. You can fish in the bay, and in the trout streams and inland lakes; note that license and stamp are required. The town used to be a center for brownstone quarrying and you'll see historic brownstone buildings throughout the area. The City Hall is on the National Register of Historic Places. The town is also a gateway to the Apostle Islands.

Information Ashland Area Chamber of Commerce | 805 W. Lakeshore Dr., Box 746, 54806-0746 | 800/284–9484 | ashchamb@win.bright.net | www.visitashland.com.

Attractions

Copper Falls State Park. This park 23 mi southeast of Ashland has canyons, streams, a lake, and two waterfalls—Copper Falls and Brownstone Falls. It offers hiking, lake swimming, a beach, a large picnic area, and campgrounds. | Junction of Rtes. 13 and 169, Mellen | 715/274-5123 | www.dnr.state.wi.us/org/land/parks | $7 nonresidents, $5 residents | Daily.

Lake Superior Big Top Chautauqua. This huge tent theater in nearby Washburn seats 780 and produces a full schedule of concerts, plays, lectures, and original historical musicals celebrating the history the Great Lakes region. | 101 Bayfield St., Washburn | 888/244-8368 | www.bigtop.org | Prices vary with shows | Memorial Day–Labor Day.

Northland College. One of the first academic institutions in the state, this college was founded in 1892 as the North Wisconsin Academy, and was officially recognized as a college in 1906. Affiliated with the United Church of Christ, the college now has an enrollment of about 850 students. Tours are available. | Ellis Ave. | 715/682-1699 | Free | Sept.–May, daily.

ON THE CALENDAR

APR.: *Scandinavian Heritage Day.* Cultural displays, ethnic foods, and traditional music and dancing celebrate the region's Scandinavian heritage at the Bay Area Civic Center. | 800/284-9484.

JULY: *Bay Days Festival.* Arts, crafts, games, food, and live entertainment in Memorial Park; off-road bike races and a 10K run on the third weekend in July. | 800/284-9484.

© Corbis

SUPPER CLUBS

If you're looking for good steaks and friendly people, check out some of Wisconsin's "supper clubs."

The term "supper club," probably coined in the early part of the century, is particular to Wisconsin, according to Edward Lump of the Wisconsin Restaurant Association, located in Madison. Lump and others associated with the restaurant industry say you seldom, if ever, see the word used outside the state.

According to Lump, the term hails back to the days when the neighborhood tavern was the community gathering place. The setting was social, and relaxed with a "everyone knows your name" atmosphere. When the taverns started serving food, they labeled their establishments "supper clubs."

Though once fairly common throughout Wisconsin, the number of supper clubs has dwindled. Today they exist mainly in rural areas in the northern part of the state. The farther north you go, and the more rural the area, the more supper clubs you are likely to find. Few, if any, can be found in the state's larger cities such as Milwaukee and Madison.

The supper clubs that remain are established businesses that are privately owned and operated. Members of the community gather there to socialize and celebrate. Supper clubs serve both drink and food, and generally have white tablecloths and standard menus with several good-quality steak, chops, and fish dishes. Supper clubs are good choices for Friday-night fish fries and Sunday brunches. While you generally won't find gourmet meals or upscale deli items at a supper club, you will find good-quality food at a reasonable price.

Dining

Breakwater Café. American/Casual. You can order breakfast all day in this well-lit family restaurant overlooking Lake Superior and the Breakwater Lighthouse. The huge menu includes sandwiches, steaks, pastas, salads, and skillet breakfasts. Try the everything omelet. | 1808 E. Lake Shore Dr. | 715/682–8388 | $5–$8 | MC, V.

Golden Glow Café. American/Casual. People from all walks of life convene at this lively downtown spot. The standard fare includes daily specials such as beef sandwiches. Lunch and dinner combos include soup, salad, beverage, and ice cream. Don't miss the famous century-old Brown's velvet ice cream. | 519 W. Main St. | 715/682–2838 | $7–$9 | No credit cards | Breakfast also available; no dinner Sat., Sun.

Hillmor Supper Club. Continental. This supper club is tucked away in the woods, 4 mi south of Ashland. You can watch deer feeding outside a large bay window in the hunting-theme dining room with wicker baskets, wildlife pictures, and guns on the walls. Meal choices include filet mignon, shrimp, or pasta dishes like fettuccine alfredo. Salad bar. | Hwy. 13 S | 715/682–5711 | $10–$15 | MC, V | Closed Mon.

Hotel Chequamegon. Continental. You can choose to sit in Molly Cooper's Lounge or in Sirtoli's elegant dining room with linen napkins and tablecloths. The menu includes a wide variety of local seafood, pasta, and steak specialties. Try the bay sampler which includes several types of Lake Superior fish. | 101 W. Lake Shore Dr. | 715/682–9095 | $8–$17 | AE, D, DC, MC, V | Breakfast also available.

Lodging

Ashland Motel. Across the street from Lake Superior, you can walk to the beach from this small, no-frills motel. All rooms have lake views. In winter there's access to snowmobiling trails. Restaurant. Some microwaves, some refrigerators, cable TV. Snowmobiling. | 2300 West Lakeshore Dr. | 920/991–0038 | www.theashland.com | 34 rooms | $30–$59 | AE, D, MC, V.

Best Western Holiday House. This modern hotel on the shore of Lake Superior overlooks Chequamegon Bay. 2 restaurants, bar. Cable TV. Pool. Hot tub, sauna. Business services. Some pets allowed. | 30600 U.S. 2 | 715/682–5235 | fax 715/682–4730 | www.bestwestern.com | 65 rooms | $69–$99 | AE, D, DC, MC, V.

Hotel Chequamegon. A bright white building with green canopies, this downtown Victorian-style hotel is easy to spot. The broad porch faces the marina. The lobby has antiques and there's a fireplace in the parlor. Restaurant, bar, dining room. Some kitchenettes, some refrigerators, in-room hot tubs, cable TV. Pool. Hot tub, sauna. Business services. | 101 W. Lake Shore Dr. | 715/682–9095 or 800/946–5555 | fax 715/682–9410 | hotel@win.bright.net | www.dockernet.com/~hotelc/ | 65 rooms | $90–$149 | AE, D, MC, V.

Lake Aire Inn. Some second-floor rooms in this downtown brick hotel have lake views. Restaurants and shopping are within easy walking distance. In-room data ports, TV in common area. Business services. | 101 E. Lake Shore Dr. | 888/666–2088 | www.lakeaireinn.com | 20 rooms, 6 suites | $60–$65 rooms, $75 suites | AE, D, MC, V.

Residenz Bed and Breakfast. This historic home was built in 1889 by Senator Lamoreau. All rooms have antiques and private baths. Complimentary breakfast. No smoking. | 723 Chapple Ave. | 715/682–2425 | fax 715/682–4572 | therez@win.bright.net | www.wbba.org | 3 rooms | $60–$70 | No credit cards.

Super 8. This modern brick motel is across the road from Lake Superior, and about ½ mi from downtown on a busy shop-lined street. In-room data ports, microwaves available, cable TV. Pool. Hot tub. Laundry facilities. Business services. Some pets allowed. | 1610 Lake Shore Dr. | 715/682–9377 | fax 715/682–9377 | www.super8.com | 70 rooms | $63–$86 | AE, D, DC, MC, V.

BAGLEY

(Nearby towns also listed: Cassville, Prairie du Chien)

The beautiful Grant County countryside is the backdrop for this small town. Wyalusing State Park in Bagley has a campground on a bluff 500 ft above the Mississippi and Wisconsin rivers. Hike the trails and you'll see dramatic views of the rivers and quite possibly spot scarlet tanagers and wild turkeys as they are among the more than 100 bird species that can be seen here. In town, you can visit several museums, tour cheese factories, and browse antiques shops.

Information: **Grant County Chamber of Commerce, Grant County/UWEX Office** | Box 5157, Adams 53813-0031 | 608/339-6997 | wicip.uwplatt.edu/grant/tourism.

Attractions
River of Lakes Resort. This is a great place to fish and boat on the Mississippi River. Motorboat, rowboat, and canoe rentals are available. There are also 150 campsites, a playground, a grocery store, and a bait shop on-site. | 132A Packer Dr. | 608/996-2275 | Free | Mid-Apr.–mid-Oct., daily 7 AM–10 PM.

ON THE CALENDAR
FEB.: *Candlelight Ski/Sweetheart Stroll.* On the Saturday nearest Valentine's Day, you can take your favorite valentine for a 1½-mi sweetheart ski/stroll along a candlelit forest trail in Wyalusing State Park. Includes refreshments and a bonfire. | 800/732-1673.

Dining
Bagley Hotel Restaurant. American. On the ground floor of the 1912 Bagley Hotel, this restaurant is accented with old barn boards, a collection of miniature antique cars, and an old-fashioned wood and brass bar. On the menu: seafood platters, burgers, and hot beef special. Buffet. | 175 S. Main St. | 608/996-2241 | $8–$12 | No credit cards.

Lodging
Bagley Hotel. This hostelry, built in 1912, is the centerpiece of downtown. The bright, comfortable rooms are on the second floor above the restaurant. Restaurant. No TV. No smoking. | 175 Bagley Ave. | 608/996-2241 | 7 rooms (all with shared bath) | $25–$30 | MC, V.

BAILEYS HARBOR

(Nearby towns also listed: Egg Harbor, Ellison Bay, Ephraim)

Settled in 1851, this Door County town is on the shores of Lake Michigan. Thousands of acres of wetlands and wilderness, much of it in wildlife preserves, is picture perfect for bird-watching, hiking, and fishing. Charter fishing for lunker salmon and brown trout is especially popular here.

Information: **Door County Chamber of Commerce** | Box 406, Sturgeon Bay 54235-0406 | 920/743-4456 or 800/527-3529 | door@mail.wiscnet.net | www.doorcountyvacations.com.

Attractions
Bjorklunden Chapel. Inside are ornate Norwegian hand-carved woodwork and murals. Guided tours given Monday and Wednesday from 1 to 4. | 7603 Chapel La., off Lakeshore Dr. | 920/839-2216 | $3 | June–Aug., Mon., Wed.

Maxwelton Braes Golf Resort. The 18-hole course is partially wooded, but with few water hazards so it's a good course for golfers of all abilities. The resort's dining room has panoramic views and a large fireplace. Golf/dinner packages available. | 7670 Hwy. 57 | 920/839–2321 | Apr.–Nov.

ON THE CALENDAR
APR.: *Baileys Harbor Brown Trout Tournament.* At this annual event held the last weekend in April, contestants can fish from boats or from the dock. The event includes prizes and an awards ceremony. | 920/839–2366 | www.baileyharbor.com.
JULY: *Lions Club Celebration.* This Fourth of July party begins with a morning parade, followed by arts and crafts, and food stands with live entertainment throughout the day. Fireworks in the evening. | 920/839–2366.

Dining

Common House. Contemporary. This 1850s wood-frame restaurant was originally a hardware store. Inside you'll find original hardwood floors, tin ceilings, and an authentic woodstove. Many dishes use products from Wisconsin including steak au bleu, a grilled fillet served on an eggplant crouton topped with Wisconsin blue cheese sauce, or the roasted pork tenderloin presented with Door County fruit chutney and an apple-cider reduction. Kids' menu. | 8041 Main St. | 920/839–2708 | $11–$36 | D, MC, V | No lunch.

Gordon Lodge Restaurant. Continental. The dining experience varies depending on the day at this Lake Michigan waterfront restaurant. On Monday and Friday, a traditional fish boil is prepared and served in the dining room which has a garden setting. On Tuesday, dinner is served on the Top Deck with its magnificent water view; the standard menu includes quail, duck, salmon, and pork dishes. All other days dinner is served in the dining room using the standard menu. | 1420 Pine Dr. | 920/839–2331 | $17–$25 | AE, D, MC, V | Breakfast also available; no lunch.

Sandpiper. American. This small, modern restaurant on the north end of town is painted bright blue and accented with magenta and yellow. The building is divided into two parts: one is a rustic family-style restaurant specializing in home-cooked German food and known for liver and onions and pork roasts; the other is a casual restaurant specializing in fish boils. Murals of Door County line the walls. Kids' menu. | 8166 Rte. 57 | 920/839–2528 | Reservations not accepted | $9–$13 | MC, V | Breakfast also available; closed Nov.–Mar.

Tundra House. American. Green Bay Packers memorabilia fills this supper club with a 100-inch screen TV for watching games. Steaks, seafood, vegetarian dishes, and Italian entrées are offered and hand-tossed pizzas are made to order. | 6301 Rte. 57, Jacksonport | 920/823–2542 | $8–$17 | D, MC, V | No lunch Sept.–June.

Weisgerbers Cornerstone Pub. American. This downtown family restaurant is filled with Green Bay Packer memorabilia in honor of the owner's father who played for the team over 50 years ago. The dining room serves steaks, chicken, and burgers, and there is a separate bar. | 8123 Hwy. 57 | 920/839–9001 | $11–$19 | AE, D, MC, V.

Lodging

Baileys Harbor Yacht Club Resort. The prominent stone fireplace, overstuffed sofas, and vaulted, wood-paneled ceiling of the lobby set the tone of this resort between the Lake Michigan waterfront and a 1,000-acre wildlife preserve. Rooms in the three buildings all have hardwood furniture; some have whirlpool tubs and private porches. Some kitchenettes, cable TV. Indoor-outdoor pool. Sauna. Tennis. Dock. | 8150 Ridges Rd. | 920/839–2336 | 44 rooms, 20 suites | $119–$149 rooms, $199–$223 suites | AE, D, MC, V.

Blacksmith Inn. This renovated 1912 half-timber inn is on the waterfront and every room has a view of the lake. The inn has fireplaces, a sand beach, and, in keeping with its name, a working blacksmith shop. Complimentary Continental breakfast. In-room hot tubs, in-

BAILEYS HARBOR

INTRO
ATTRACTIONS
DINING
LODGING

room VCRs. No smoking. | 8152 Rte. 57 | 920/839–9222 or 800/769–8619 | fax 920/839–9356 | blcksmth@mail.wiscnet.net | www.theblacksmithinn.com | 15 rooms | $155–$185 | MC, V.

Gordon Lodge. Open since 1928, this resort hotel is in an evergreen forest bordered by the waters of Lake Michigan and North Bay with scenic views from every room. Bar (with entertainment), dining room, complimentary breakfast. Some microwaves, refrigerators, cable TV. Pool. Putting green, tennis. Gym, beach, boating, fishing, bicycles. Business services. | 1420 Pine Dr. | 920/839–2331 or 800/830–6235 | fax 920/839–2450 | www.gordonlodge.com | 20 rooms in lodge, 9 villas, 11 cottages | $112–$226 | AE, D, MC, V.

Inn at Bailey's Harbor. This downtown hotel is right on the shore of Lake Michigan. No air-conditioning in some rooms, some refrigerators, no room phones. Pool. Sauna. Beach, boating. | 8040 Rte. 57 | 920/839–2345 or 800/503–5959 | fax 920/839–9203 | 39 rooms | $72–$120 | D, MC, V | Closed Nov.–Apr.

Journey's End Motel. This small motel built in the early 1980s is tucked away $\frac{1}{2}$ mi from the harbor on 3$\frac{1}{2}$ acres of rolling, landscaped grounds. You can picnic, grill out, or have a bonfire and enjoy the quiet countryside. Refrigerators, cable TV. Some pets allowed. | 8271 Journey's End La. | 920/839–2887 | 10 rooms | $60–$72 | MC, V.

New Yardley Inn. This bed-and-breakfast built in 1997 is set on 10 acres in Peninsula Center. Rooms are large and casual, and there are many large windows, a screened-in porch, and some fireplaces. There is one wheelchair-accessible suite. Complimentary breakfast. No smoking. | 3360 Rte. E, between Egg Harbor and Bailey Harbor | 920/839–9487 or 888/492–7353 | fax 920/839–9487 | www.newyardleyinn.com | 3 rooms | $130–$175 | D, MC, V.

Potter's Door Inn. This 140-year-old log home is just a five-minute drive from either shore of the peninsula. It has two cozy guest rooms and is on 25 acres of land. The innkeeper's husband has a pottery studio on the property. TV and phones in common area. Cross-country skiing. | 9528 Hwy. 57 | 920/839–2003 | 2 rooms | $70–$85 | MC, V.

Stones on German Road. This rustic B&B is on 10 acres of woods on a quiet country road. It has a partial fieldstone exterior, a solarium, a gathering room with a stone fireplace, and a deck and patio overlooking a wildflower garden. Complimentary breakfast. No smoking. | 2557 German Rd. | 920/854–2407 | fax 920/854–2407 | estone@mail.doorcounty-wi.com | www.stonesdoorcountybnb.com | 3 rooms | $100 | MC, V.

BARABOO

MAP 11, C6

(Nearby towns also listed: Portage, Wisconsin Dells)

Founded in 1830 and located just 13 mi south of Wisconsin Dells, the Ringling Brothers' hometown is famous for Circus World Museum, which has the world's largest collection of circus memorabilia. Baraboo is also the home of the International Crane Foundation, which protects and displays a mating pair of all 15 crane species. Devil's Lake State Park is just outside of town. When driving into Baraboo, you'll notice the surrounding Baraboo Bluffs, a canoe-shape formation of "Baraboo" quartzite which encloses the city. The surrounding landscape is flat because a glacier leveled the area during prehistoric times, but this deposit was stronger than the ice. The rare quartzite only exists in two other places—upstate New York and Switzerland—and attracts geologists to Baraboo from across the globe.

Information: Baraboo Chamber of Commerce | 600 W. Chestnut St., 53913-0442 | 800/227–2266 | www.baraboo.com.

Attractions

Al Ringling Theater. Evening movies are shown in this ornate theater built in 1915. The beautiful venue has high arched ceilings with gold-leaf accents and tall, dramatic red curtains in front of the stage and in doorways. | 136 4th Ave. | 608/356–8864 | Tours $3, students $2 | Daily 11 AM.

Circus World Museum. This huge museum chronicles the history of the circus in America with a collection of antique circus wagons, memorabilia, and miniature circuses. In summer there are live performances on the grounds. | 550 Water St. | 608/356–8341 | www.baraboo.com/cwm/circus.htm | $13.95 | May–Aug., daily 9–6; Sept.–Oct., Mon.–Sat. 9–5, Sun. 11–5; Nov.–Apr., Mon.–Sat. 10–4, Sun. 11–4.

Devil's Head Lodge Ski Area and Golf Resort. Fifteen miles southeast of Baraboo, this 250-acre ski and snowboarding area has 31 trails and a vertical drop of 500 ft. In summer it becomes a golf resort with an 18-hole golf course, mountain-bike trails, hiking trails, indoor and outdoor pools, tennis, a weight room, two restaurants, a bar, and a lounge. | S6330 Bluff Rd., Merrimac | 608/493–2251.

Devil's Lake State Park. You can camp, swim, rock climb, hike, fish, windsurf, enjoy a naturalist program, or, in winter, cross-country ski at this 8,000-acre park that includes a 360-acre spring-fed lake surrounded by 500-ft bluffs. | S5975 Park Rd. | 608/356–6618 | www.dnr.state.wi.us | $7 nonresidents, $5 residents | Daily.

Ho-Chunk Casino and Bingo. Try your luck at this large casino and bingo facility. | S3214A U.S. 12 | 800/746–2486 | Free | Daily, 24 hrs.

International Crane Foundation. This foundation is concerned with the study and preservation of cranes and the ecosystems on which they depend. The visitor center showcases the foundation's work and highlights the different crane species. Tours of the preserve are available by appointment or you can explore on your own. | E11376 Shady Lane Rd. | 608/356–9462 | www.baraboo.com/bus/icf/whowhat.htm | $7 | May–Oct., daily 9–5.

Mid-Continent Railway Museum. In North Freedom just 8 mi south of Baraboo, you can explore exhibits on railroad history, ride on an operating steam train, or dine in an old first-class car. Round-trip steam train rides depart at 10:30, 12:30, 2, and 3:30 | E8949 Walnut St. | 608/522–4261 | www.mcrwy.com | $9; special rates for children, senior citizens, and groups | Mid-May–Labor Day, daily; Sept.–Oct., weekends; trains depart 10:30, 12:30, 2, 3:30; closed Nov.–May.

Mirror Lake State Park. Partially surrounded by sandstone bluffs, this park, 3 mi south of the Dells, has excellent fishing, camping, swimming, and canoeing. It also has bike and cross-country ski trails. Within the park is the restored Set Peterson Cottage, designed in 1958 by Frank Lloyd Wright. Guided tours are offered, and the cottage is available for overnight rental. | E10320 Fern Dell Rd. | 608/254–2333 | www.dnr.state.wi.us | $7 nonresidents, $5 residents | Daily.

Sauk County Historical Museum. The Sauk County Historical Society runs this small museum displaying Native American and pioneering days artifacts as well as local textile products and geological findings. | 531 4th Ave. | 608/356–1001 | www.saukcounty.com | $4; special rates for children | Tues.–Sun. noon–5.

Time Travel Geologic Tour. You can get a detailed look at the fascinating geology of Devil's Lake on this fun and educational tour led by expert geologists. Groups choose the difficulty of their hike, but the higher you trek, the better the view. The 2½-hour tours leave from Three Little Devil's Scuba Shop at the north entrance to Devil's Lake State Park. | 608/356–8864 | www.naturesafari.com | $23; special rates for children | June–Aug., daily 10 AM and 1:30 PM; Apr., May, Sept., Oct., Sat. and Sun. 10 AM and 1:30 PM.

ON THE CALENDAR

JUNE: *Native American Artifact and Antique Show* This show held the last weekend in June at the Sauk county fairgrounds displays and sells antique Native American and Civil War–era artifacts such as guns, swords, knives, and decoys. | 800/277–2266.

Dining

Alpine Café. American/Casual. This cozy old café off the main square serves breakfast and lunch. Try the Alpine omelet with green peppers, onions, cheese, bacon, and French fries stuffed inside. | 117 4th St. | 608/356–4040 | $3–$5 | No credit cards | No dinner.

Log Cabin Family Restaurant. American. Home-cooked food is the rule in this replica of an old log cabin with many windows and views of surrounding businesses. Try the country-fried steak or the turkey dinner with potatoes. Pies are homemade and there is a special flavor every month. | 1215 8th St. | 608/356–8245 | $8–$13 | D, MC, V | Breakfast also available.

Little Village Café. Contemporary. This diner on the square has been here since the 1940s, and is a favorite spot for courthouse clientele. The menu changes frequently—specials can include Jamaican chicken burritos, sweet-potato pancakes, and Mediterranean Greek salad. Bar. | 146 4th Ave. | 608/356–2800 | $13–$19 | MC, V | Closed Sun., Mon.

Sand County Café. Contemporary. This café off the square in a house built in 1881 serves daily specials like shiitake mushroom and asiago fettuccine in addition to its menu of pork tenderloin, lasagna, salads, and quiches. Kids' menu. | 138 First St. | 608/356–5880 | $8–$16 | MC, V | Closed Sun., Mon.

Lodging

Best Western Baraboo Inn. This chain motel is 2 mi from town right on Highway 12, surrounded by fast-food and convenience stores. Some rooms have Jacuzzi tubs. Complimentary Continental breakfast. Cable TV. Pool. Hot tub. | 725 W. Pine St. (Hwy. 12) | 608/356–1100 | 60 rooms | $94–$114 | AE, D, DC, MC, V.

Frantiques Showplace. This 25-room Victorian mansion is filled with antiques. Suites have brass beds and feather quilts; one has a full kitchen and private entrance. The inn is located near a bike trail, a nature area, and a state park. Complimentary breakfast. No smoking. | 704 Ash St. | 608/356–5273 | 2 suites | $75–$77 | No credit cards.

Gollmar Guest House. This Victorian home was built between 1889 and 1894. Its past owners included a 19th-century mayor of Baraboo and Benjamin Gollmar, treasurer and part owner of Baraboo's Gollmar Brothers Circus from 1891 to 1916. The house has original frescoes, beveled glass, chandeliers, antiques, hardwood floors, beaded woodwork, a guest parlor, and an outdoor veranda-patio. Complimentary breakfast. One in-room hot tub. Library. No smoking. | 422 3rd St. | 608/356–9432 | fax 608/356–3847 | gollmar.bb@midplains.net | www.gollmar.com | 3 rooms | $80–$135 | MC, V.

Highlander Motel. This mom-and-pop, no-frills motel is on 10½ acres of densely wooded land on the edge of town. Cable TV. | S5230 Hwy. 12 | 608/356–4110 or 888/929–4410 | 10 rooms | $55–$85 | AE, D, DC, MC, V.

Pinehaven Bed and Breakfast. This rustic, chalet-style B&B is in the country near a small, spring-fed lake. Scenic bluffs and draft horses are on the property. Complimentary breakfast. In-room double hot tub (in cottage). No smoking. | E13083 Rte. 33 | 608/356–3489 | fax 608/356–0818 | www.dells.com/pinehaven | 4 rooms, 1 cottage | $79–$135 | MC, V.

Quality Inn. This motel is on Highway 12 at the outskirts of town. Retail outlets and fast-food restaurants line the road on either side of the motel. Restaurant, bar, room service. Refrigerators, in-room hot tubs in suites, cable TV. Pool. Hot tub. Gym. Video games. Laundry facilities. Business services. | 626 W. Pine St., Hwy. 12 | 608/356–6422 | fax 608/356–6422 | 84 rooms, 12 suites | $83–$163 | AE, D, DC, MC, V.

Spinning Wheel. This modern brick-and-wood motel is on the east side of town in a residential neighborhood not far from Highway 33. Cable TV. Some pets allowed (fee). | 809 8th St. | 608/356–3933 | 25 rooms | $63–$69 | AE, D, MC, V.

BAYFIELD

(Nearby towns also listed: Ashland, Hurley, Superior)

Residents of this picturesque town take pride in their Victorian mansions, many of which are restored and operating as inns or B&Bs. Bayfield is also the gateway to the Apostle Islands National Lakeshore, which has 22 coastal islands with lighthouses, sea caves, hiking trails, and blue-water sailing.

Information: **Bayfield Chamber of Commerce** | Box 138, 54814-0138 | 800/447–4094 | bayfield@win.bright.net | www.bayfield.org.

Attractions

★ **Apostle Islands National Lakeshore.** Twenty-one of the 22 Apostle Islands and 11 mi of mainland shoreline around the world's largest freshwater lake are preserved in this park which was established in 1970. You can hike, boat, fish, canoe, kayak, swim, or scuba dive. Lighthouse tours are available and there are backcountry campsites on 13 islands. In winter there's cross-country skiing. | Visitors center: 415 Washington Ave. | 715/779–3397 | Free; camping permits $15 for individual site | Daily.

You can cruise to many of the Apostle Islands and their lighthouses with the **Apostle Islands Cruise Service.** Cruises depart daily in season, which generally runs from mid-May to mid-October. | City Dock | 715/779–3925 or 800/323–7619 | $23.95; special rates for children | Mid-May–mid-Oct., daily 10, 10:30, 1:30, 2, 5:30.

The **Apostle Islands National Lakeshore Museum** in the restored Bayfield County Courthouse has exhibits and an audiovisual presentation on the history of the Apostle Islands. You can see a Fresnel lens from the Michigan Island Lighthouse. | 415 Washington Ave. | 715/779–3397 | Free | Memorial Day–Labor Day, daily 8–6; Labor Day–Oct., daily 8–5; Nov.–Memorial Day, weekdays 8–4:30.

Hokenson Brothers Fishery Museum. This museum showcases the tools and techniques once used at this former commercial fishery. Guided and self-guided tours are available at Little Sand Bay. | Little Sand Bay, off Rte. 13, north of Bayfield | 715/779–3397 | Free | Memorial Day–Labor Day, daily 9–5.

Madeline Island. This island is home to 2,418-acre Big Bay State Park with its picturesque sandstone bluffs, lake caves, 1½ mi of shoreline, and the Madeline Island Historical Museum. The park has campsites, a nature center, and hiking and cross-country ski trails. | 888/475–3386 | www.madelineisland.com | Free | Daily.

Madeline Island Ferry Line transports passengers and cars between Madeline Island and Bayfield. | Main St. | 715/747–2051 | $3.75; special rates for children; cars $8.50 | Apr.–Dec., daily.

Madeline Island Historical Museum is a State Historical Society site documenting 350 years of island history. | Cournal Woods Ave., La Pointe | 715/747–2801 or 715/747–2415 | $5.50 | July–Aug. daily 10–6.

Mt. Ashwabay Ski Area. This ski area 3 mi south of Bayfield has four downhill trails with a vertical drop of 317 ft, moguls on some hills, and cross-country skiing trails. All-day or half-day passes are offered and there is night skiing. | Rte. 1 | 715/779–3227 or 715/779–3335 | $12 day pass | Dec.–Mar., Wed. and weekends; Christmas week, daily.

Washburn Historical Museum and Cultural Center. This cultural center 12 mi south of Bayfield on Highway 13 has ongoing art and historical exhibits, workshops for adults and children, performing-arts programs, and more, all in a restored brownstone bank building listed on the National Register of Historic Places. | 1 E. Bayfield St., Washburn | 715/373–5591 | Donations accepted | Daily 10–4.

JUNE–JULY: *Sailboat Race Week.* Competing boats from across the United States and Canada leave from the Bayfield City Dock each morning during this race around the 22 Apostle Islands. Awards are presented at a banquet ceremony. | 800/447–4094.

JULY: *Bayfield Festival of Arts.* Artists from around the Midwest gather to show their watercolors, sculptures, jewelry, and textile arts downtown against the backdrop of the lake and the Apostle Islands in late month. There is also live music and a kids' corner. | 800/447–4094.

SEPT.: *Great Schooner Race.* This small schooner race which begins at the Bayfield City Dock is a fund-raising event for the historic Bayfield Pavilion building. | 800/447–4094.

OCT.: *Apple Festival.* This downtown event, held the first full weekend in October, was started 40 years ago by local orchards and includes arts, crafts, music, a carnival, apple sundaes, and other apple treats, along with 20 varieties of apples to sample and purchase. | 800/447–4094.

Dining

Egg Toss Café. Café. You can choose to sit at the counter, in the small dining room, or on the outdoor decks at this downtown breakfast joint known for its eggs Benedict and homemade waffles. | 41 Manypenny Ave. | 715/779–5181 | $5–$7 | MC, V | No dinner.

Maggie's Restaurant. American/Casual. Fake flamingos and flamingo memorabilia accent this local favorite, just off the main street downtown. It's known for great burgers, like the French burger with mushrooms, garlic, and blue cheese. The menu also includes homemade pizzas and local fish. | 257 Manypenny Ave. | 715/779–5641 | $5–$13 | D, MC, V.

Old Rittenhouse Inn. Contemporary. This restaurant's three dining rooms, housed in a late-19th-century Victorian, serve five-course prix fixe meals from a menu that changes daily. It's known for regional dishes such as apple glazed pork chops. Kids' menu. Sunday brunch. | 314 Rittenhouse Ave. (Rte. 13) | 715/779–5111 | $45 | MC, V | No lunch Nov.–Apr.

Pier Plaza 13. Seafood. Local trout and whitefish are the specialties here, though the menu also includes burgers. The dining room has pictures of lighthouses and boats on the walls and overlooks Lake Superior. Outdoor dining on a deck. | 15 Front St. | 715/779–3330 | $9–$12 | MC, V | Breakfast also available.

Lodging

Artesian House. This eclectic, contemporary B&B 3 mi south of Bayfield is set on 24 acres of meadows, wetlands, and walking trails. The Great Room has floor-to-ceiling windows with views of Lake Superior and Mt. Ashwabay. A golf course and ski resort are 5 mi away, and you can walk the 5 blocks to the boating marina. Complimentary breakfast. No smoking. | Rte. 1 | 715/779–3338 | fax 715/779–5350 | artesian@ranger.ncis.net | www.artesian-house.com | 4 rooms | $80–$120 | No credit cards.

Bayfield Inn. You'll be within easy walking distance of everything in town at this no-frills, downtown motel on the lake. Some rooms have water views. Restaurant. Cable TV. | 20 Rittenhouse Ave. | 715/779–3363 | 21 rooms | $85–$95 | D, MC, V.

Island View Place Bed and Breakfast. This B&B offers country charm on Lake Superior. Two suites are available, each with its own entrance and deck. Breakfast is served in your room. Complimentary breakfast. Kitchenettes, cable TV and in-room VCRs. Beach. Playground. No smoking. | Rte. 1 | 715/492–6585 | lorrie@ncis.net | www.island-view.com | 2 suites | $100–$120 | MC, V.

Old Rittenhouse Inn. Antiques fill the rooms in this complex of Victorians, one a painted lady. Restaurant (*see* Old Rittenhouse Inn, *above*), complimentary Continental breakfast. Some in-room hot tubs, no room phones, no TV. No smoking. | 301 Rittenhouse Ave. | 715/779–5111 | fax 715/779–5887 | www.rittenhouseinn.com | 21 rooms | $99–$240 | MC, V.

Seagull Bay Motel. Every room has a lake view in this simple motel on Lake Superior just a few blocks from downtown. The main building was built in 1990, but the cottage has been in this quiet, residential neighborhood since the 1940s. A walking or ski trail runs through the property and follows the shoreline. Some kitchenettes, cable TV. No smoking. | 325 S. 7th St. | 715/779–5558 | 24 rooms, 1 cottage | $50–$70 rooms, $70 cottage | D, MC, V.

Super 8. All rooms have indoor entrances, and some rooms have a view of the water at this standard chain hotel with a brick exterior. Bar, complimentary Continental breakfast. Cable TV. Hot tub, sauna. Video games. Business services. Some pet allowed (fee). | Harbor View Dr., Washburn | 715/373–5671 | fax 715/373–5674 | www.super8.com | 35 rooms | $79–$85 | AE, D, DC, MC, V.

Thimbleberry Inn. Five miles outside Bayfield on 40 wooded acres on Lake Superior, all the rooms in this contemporary house have modern, Scandinavian-style furniture, handmade quilts, large windows with beautiful water and forest views, and wood-burning fireplaces. Breakfast is preceded by coffee and fresh-baked muffins in your room. No in-room phones, no TV. Hiking. Cross-country skiing. | 105021 Pagent Rd. | 715/779–5757 | 3 rooms | $119–$139 | MC, V.

Winfield Inn. Set on 4½ acres overlooking Lake Superior, this inn has two separate buildings, a sundeck, and extensive gardens. No air-conditioning in some rooms, kitchenettes in apartments, cable TV. Pets allowed. | 225 E. Lyndee Ave. | 715/779–3252 | fax 715/779–5180 | www.winfieldinn.com | 25 rooms, 6 apartments | $59–$145 | AE, D, MC, V.

BEAVER DAM

MAP 11, C6

(Nearby towns also listed: Fond du Lac, Waupun)

Founded in 1841 by Thomas Mackie, Beaver Dam was incorporated as a city in 1856, the same year the railroad was built. The railroad linked Beaver Dam to the outside world, giving rise to manufacturing plants. Today Beaver Dam has small-town character, but also boasts a solid economic base of manufacturing, business, and industry. Beaver Dam Lake, on the western edge of the city, covers 6,600 acres, ideal for boating and fishing. A spring-fed swimming area is at the eastern edge of town.

Information: Beaver Dam Chamber of Commerce | 127 S. Spring St., 53916-2175 | 920/887–8879 | info@beaverdamchamber.com | www.beaverdamchamber.com.

Attractions

Beaver Dam Lake. This shallow 6,600-acre lake on the western edge of town is well stocked with fish. Boats are available to rent and a bait and tackle shop is nearby. | Rte. 33, west of town | 920/885–6766 | Free | Daily.

Dodge County Historical Museum. Located in the old Williams Free Library building, this museum offers a glimpse of pioneer life in southeastern Wisconsin. | 105 Park Ave. | 920/887–1266 | Free | Tues.–Sat. noon–4.

Wild Goose State Trail. You can bike, hike, or cross-country ski on this privately owned and maintained 34-mi trail running from Juneau to Fond du Lac. Group shuttle service is available. Southern trail entrance at parking lot on Highway 60, just east of Highway 23, about 12 mi southeast of town. | 920/386–3700 | Donations accepted | Daily.

ON THE CALENDAR

JUNE: *Swan City Car Show.* Between 400 and 500 antique and classic cars are on display every Father's Day at Sway City Park. The show includes DJ music and food. | 920/887–7111.

JULY: *Lake Days.* In the five days following the Fourth of July, myriad events take place, including: a beauty pageant, fishing and volleyball tournaments, live music, a Door County–style fish boil and beer tent in the evenings, a ski show, a karaoke contest, and demonstrations in angling and ambulances. Fireworks provide a grand finale on the final night. | 920/887–8879.

AUG.: *Dodge County Fair.* This mid-month county fair at the fairgrounds, 3 mi east of town, includes farm animals, rides, children's events, food, and entertainment. | 920/885–3586.

Dining

Bayside Supper Club. American. A large restaurant on Beaver Dam Lake known for prime rib, jumbo shrimp, homemade soups, and Friday-night seafood buffet. Salad bar. Kids' menu. Wine and beer. | W9231 Rte. G | 920/887–0505 | $8–$15 | MC, V | Closed Tues. No lunch.

China Palace. Chinese. Despite a 300-person seating capacity, the large communal tables in this popular restaurant, located in Beaver Dam Mall, are sometimes full and you might have to wait in line. Daily specials include standard fare such as chicken with garlic sauce. | 1645 N. Spring St. | 920/877–1155 | $7–$10 | AE, MC, V.

Chili John's Café. American. This all-American diner has been run by the same family since it opened in 1920 and claims to serve the best cheeseburgers and chile around. | 223 Front St. | 920/885–4414 | $3–$7 | No credit cards.

Lodging

Best Western Campus Inn. There's coffee in the lobby 24 hours a day at this chain hotel on a commercial strip on the outskirts of town where Highways 151 and 33 cross. Restaurant, bar. Cable TV. Pool. Hot tub. | 815 Park Ave. | 920/887–7171 | 94 rooms | $64–$74 | AE, D, DC, MC, V.

Grandview Motel. This no-frills, mom-and-pop roadside motel had a grand view when it was first built in the 1940s, but in the years since then a quiet, residential neighborhood has grown up around it. Cable TV. Some pets allowed. | 1510 N. Center St. | 920/885–9208 | fax 920/887–8706 | 22 rooms | $30–$40 | AE, D, MC, V.

Mayville Inn. This homey hotel 18 mi northeast of Beaver Dam is almost like a B&B with its relaxed atmosphere and individually decorated rooms. Bar, complimentary Continental breakfast. In-room data ports, some refrigerators, cable TV. Hot tub. Business services. | 701 S. Mountain Dr., Mayville | 920/387–1234 | fax 920/387–1234 | 29 rooms | $52–$85 | AE, D, MC, V.

BELOIT

MAP 11, D7

(Nearby towns also listed: Delavan, Janesville)

This city is on the Wisconsin–Illinois border and is home to the state's oldest college. Beloit has two historic districts, and its early history is steeped in the Yankee heritage of New England. Beloit's original settlers arrived in 1836 from Colebrook, New Hampshire, lured by the area's scenic river, fertile land, and temperate climate. Today Beloit is home to many large companies including Frito-Lay and Hormel, the producers of Spam.

Information: **Beloit Convention and Visitors Bureau** | 1003 Pleasant St., 53511-4449 | 800/423–5648 | info@visit beloit.com | www.visitbeloit.com.

Attractions

Angel Museum. Over 6,000 angels, including more than 600 black angels donated by Oprah Winfrey, are on display in this former Catholic church across from Beloit College, making this the world's largest angel collection. | 656 Pleasant St. | 608/362–9099 | www.angel-museum.org | $5; special rates for children and senior citizens | May–Sept., Mon.–Sat. 10–5, Sun. 1–4; Oct.–Apr., Tues.–Sat. 10–4; closed Jan., holidays.

Beckman Mill. This gristmill, 5 mi west of Beloit, was built in 1926 and is one of the last of its kind in the county. A guided tour will explain how the mill originally operated. | Junction Hwys. 81 and H | 800/423–5648 | Donations accepted | Tours Apr.–Oct., Sat. and Sun. 1–4.

Beloit College. This private liberal-arts school is Wisconsin's oldest college. Twelve hundred students attend classes on its 40-acre campus. The college is home to an art museum and an anthropology museum.

The sand-color, churchlike **Logan Museum of Anthropology** (608/363–2677 | Tues.–Sun. 11–4) was built in 1860 and became a museum for pre-Columbian ceramics, Native American artifacts, and paleolithic art in 1893. It's a working research institution, so you can see scholars cataloging artifacts inside an enormous glass cylinder. You can open storage drawers to explore artifacts for yourself.

The elegant, redbrick **Wright Museum of Art** (608/363–2677 | Tues.–Sun. 11–4) houses a permanent collection ranging from Asian decorative arts, to Egyptian and Mideastern objets d'art, to contemporary American and American Impressionist paintings. Temporary exhibits have included electronic and media arts, retrospectives on African-American artists, and displays on art conservation. | 700 College St. | 608/363–2000 | Free | Daily.

Hanchett-Bartlett Homestead. The grounds of this 1857 Victorian farmstead include the original stone barn and smokehouse, as well as a restored rural school and a picnic area. | 2149 St. Lawrence Ave. | 608/365–7835 | $2; special rates for children and senior citizens | June–Sept., Wed.–Sun. 1–4; also by appointment.

ON THE CALENDAR
JULY: *Riverfest.* This music festival held the week after the 4th of July in Riverside Park has more than 50 bands, as well as arts, crafts, food, a carnival, a lumberjack show, and helicopter and hot-air balloon rides. | 608/365–4838.

AUG.: *Celebrate Downtown Weekend.* Go-cart races, basketball tournaments, a sidewalk sale, and an evening street dance with a live band take over the downtown for a weekend early in the month. | 608/365–0150.

Dining
Butterfly Club. Contemporary. This elegant restaurant in a 1924 wood-frame building overlooks the countryside 2 mi outside of Beloit. Specialties include filet mignon and orange roughy parmesan, a cheese-topped broiled fish delicacy. Live music Wednesday, Friday, and Saturday. Kids' menu. | 5246 E. County Rte. X | 608/362–8577 | $7–$35 | AE, D, DC, MC, V | Closed Mon. No lunch Tues.–Sat.

Cindy's & Smitty's Hoot 'N Holler. American. This family-owned restaurant with booth seating is famous locally for its huge portions of traditional favorites like steaks and burgers. | 3464 S. Riverside Dr. | 608/365–3464 | $5–$8 | No credit cards.

Lottie B's Kitchen. Soul. Just a few blocks off Highway 75 serving southern favorites like corn bread, ribs, fried chicken, and, if you are lucky, sweet-potato cobbler. | 907 Bayliss Ave. | 608/364–0199 | $7–$10 | No credit cards.

Lodging
Comfort Inn. This two-story modern motel is right off Interstate 90 on a commercial strip. Complimentary Continental breakfast. Refrigerator in suites, cable TV, in-room VCRs available. Pool. Hot tub. Business services. Pets allowed. | 2786 Milwaukee Rd. | 608/362–2666 | fax 608/362–2666 | 56 rooms, 16 suites | $66–$75 | AE, D, DC, MC, V.

Driftwood Motel. This small, no-frills roadside motel is on the Rock River and some rooms have river views. The Beloit Mall is ½ mi away. Cable TV. | 1826 Riverside Dr. | 608/364–4081 | 12 rooms | $45–$50 | MC, V.

Fairfield Inn. You can get off Highway 81 and get right in the pool at this clean, convenient hotel. Complimentary Continental breakfast. Cable TV. Pool, hot tub. | 2784 Milwaukee Rd. | 608/365–2200 | 63 rooms | $59–$115 | AE, D, DC, MC, V.

Holiday Inn. This sprawling building in a residential neighborhood has three wings, a patio with furniture on the roof, a game room with a pool table, ping-pong, and foozball, as well as an indoor pool and gym. Restaurant, bar, room service. Cable TV. Pool. Hot tub. Gym. Business services. | 200 Dearborn, South Beloit | 815/389–3481 | fax 815/389–3481 | www.bassho-tels.com/holiday-inn | 172 rooms | $99–$109 | AE, D, DC, MC, V.

Holiday Inn Express. This hotel is on the outskirts of town. Complimentary breakfast. Cable TV. Pool. Gym. Business services. | 2790 Milwaukee Rd. | 608/365–6000 | fax 608/365–1974 | www.basshotels.com/hiexpress | 73 rooms | $71–$95 | AE, D, DC, MC, V.

BLACK RIVER FALLS

MAP 11, B5

(Nearby towns also listed: Eau Clair, Menomonie)

Rustic roads, rolling countryside, farms, and forests surround Black River Falls which is the seat of Jackson County. The area is known for deer hunting. Boating, fishing, and winter sports are also popular.

Information: **Black River Falls Chamber of Commerce** | 336 N. Water St., 54615 | 800/404–4008.

Attractions

Black River State Forest. Two forks of the Black River and 67,000 acres of pine and oak forest are encompassed in this park which lies 6 mi east of town and has canoeing, picnicking, swimming, hiking, horseback riding, cross-country skiing, and snowmobiling. | 910 Hwy. 54 | 715/284–1400 | www.dnr.state.wi.us/org/land/forestry/StateForests/index.htm | Free; $5 a day permits required for some recreational trails | Daily.

Thunderbird Museum and Shops. This complex 12 mi northeast of Black River Falls displays Native American art and artifacts, antique weapons, historical objects, and local minerals. | N9517 Thunderbird La., Hatfield | 715/333–5841 | $2.50; special rates for children and groups | Memorial Day–Labor Day, daily 9–5; May and Sept., Fri.–Sun. 9–5 or by appointment.

ON THE CALENDAR

MAY, SEPT.: *Winnebago Pow-Wow.* Native American tribes dance in traditional attire at this biannual event held on Memorial and Labor Day weekends at the Red Cloud Memorial Pow-Wow Grounds 3 mi northeast of town via Route 54. | 800/404–4008.

Lodging

Days Inn. This contemporary brick-and-stucco hotel in a wooded area has access to snowmobile trails directly from the grounds. Complimentary Continental breakfast. In-room data ports, cable TV, in-room VCRs available. Pool. Hot tub, sauna. Video games. Laundry facilities. Business services. Some pets allowed. | 919 Rte. 54 E | 715/284–4333 or 800/356–8018 | fax 715/284–9068 | 86 rooms | $55–$85 | AE, D, DC, MC, V.

Best Western Arrowhead Lodge. This three-story hotel has a Native American motif, with arrowhead effects on the walls outside and in. You can get to county snowmobile and the hotel's nature/fitness trails right from the grounds. Restaurant, bar (with entertainment Sat.). In-room data ports, cable TV, in-room VCRs available. Pool. Hot tub, sauna. Playground. Business services. Pets allowed. | 600 Oasis Rd. | 715/284–9471 or 800/284–9471 | fax 715/284–9664 | www.bestwestern.com | 144 rooms, 30 suites | $52–$190 | AE, D, DC, MC, V.

BOULDER JUNCTION

(Nearby towns also listed: Eagle River, Manitowish Waters, Sayner)

This secluded Northwoods vacation site is known as the Musky Capital of the World. With more than 190 lakes within 9 mi of town, there are unlimited opportunities for fishing, boating, canoeing, swimming, and waterskiing. Boulder Junction is surrounded by more than 200,000 acres of forest, and there are hundreds of miles of groomed trails for cross-country skiing and snowmobiling.

Information: Boulder Junction Chamber of Commerce | 5352 Park St., 54512-0286 | 800/466–8759 | boulderjct@boulderjct.org | www.boulderjct.org.

Attractions

Lumberjack Trail. This nature trail and many others like it of lengths from 1 to 10 mi, weave through the once-logged woods outside Boulder Junction. You can also choose to hike along several of the regional lakes. Pick up a trail map at the chamber of commerce. | 1 mi south of Boulder Junction | 800/466–8759 | Free | Daily.

ON THE CALENDAR

AUG.: *Musky Jamboree/Arts and Crafts Fair.* On the second sunday of August there are arts, crafts, a fun run, a flea market, entertainment, food, an antique car show, and a free musky tasting in Community Park, downtown. | 800/466–8759.
SEPT.: *World Championship Musky Classic.* Over 1,000 anglers take to the lakes for this fishing tournament which raises money for a scholarship fund. | 715/385–2400.

Dining

Guide's Inn. Continental. This downtown restaurant is located in a remodeled cedar-sided building with Northwoods decor and a wood-burning stove. Popular dishes on the large menu are the pan-fried walleye and the veal entrees. Kids' menu. | Hwy. M on the edge of town | 715/385–2233 | $14–$24 | MC, V | Closed Sun. No lunch.

Headwaters Restaurant and Tavern. American. There's a jukebox in the bar at this lively place across the river just outside of town. Menu items include ribs, pasta, burgers, and a few fish dishes. The two-for-one special Wednesday evening is popular with area senior citizens. | 5675 Hwy. M | 715/385–2601 | $8–$16 | MC, V | Closed Tues.

Lodging

Boulder Bear Motor Lodge. The wood-paneled cathedral ceiling, tall stone fireplace, and bearskins in the lobby accent this Northwoods lodge. There is hiking, biking, and snowmobile trail access on-site. Some rooms have whirlpool tubs and views of the woods. Complimentary Continental breakfast. Hot tub. Video games. | 5437 Park St. | 715/385–2662 | 20 rooms | $65–$75 | D, MC, V.

White Birch Village. This modern cottage complex is in Northern Highland State Forest 8 mi southeast of Boulder Junction. Each cottage has a fireplace and some have views of the lake. No air-conditioning, kitchenettes, TV in common room. Beach, dock, boating, fishing, bicycles. Playground. Laundry facilities. Business services. Pets allowed. | 8764 Rte. K | 715/385–2182 | fax 715/385–2537 | www.whitebirchvillage.com | 11 cottages | $600–$1,050 per week (7-day minimum stay) | No credit cards | Closed mid-Oct.–May.

Zastrow's Lynx Lake Lodge. This lodge in the woods on Lynx Lake 9 mi north of Boulder Junction has a knotty-pine interior. Two of the cottages have fireplaces. Weekly rates in season. Bar, dining room, complimentary breakfast and dinner in season. No air-conditioning, some kitchenettes, cable TV. Beach, boating, fishing, bicycles. Playground. Business services, airport shuttle. Pets allowed. | Rte. B, Presque Isle | 715/686–2249 or 800/882–5969 | fax

715/686–2257 | 11 cottages | $325 with 2 meals a day (7–day minimum stay) | D, MC, V | Closed Mar.–Apr. and late Oct.–late Dec.

BROOKFIELD

MAP 11, E6

(Nearby towns also listed: Milwaukee, Waukesha, Wauwatosa)

This growing residential Milwaukee suburb, minutes from the city via the I–94 expressway, is a perfect spot for golfers, with 30 courses within a 30-minute drive. Brookfield also has a large shopping center and a number of trendy strip malls.

Information: **Waukesha County Visitors Bureau** | 892 Main St., Pewaukee 53072-5812 | 800/366–1961 | www.visitwaukesha.org.

Attractions

Stonewood Village. Nine separate, Williamsburg-style buildings make up this quaint, upscale collection of antique, jewelry, and gift shops. | 17700 W. Capitol Dr. | 262/781–9703 | Mon.–Sat. 10–5, Sun. 11–3.

ON THE CALENDAR

JUNE: *Brookfield Art Festival.* This juried fine-arts show includes works from more than 100 artists from around the country, food stands, and live entertainment in Stonewood Village for a weekend at the end of the month. | 262/781–9703.

Dining

Fuddruckers Brookfield Restaurant. American. You serve and seat yourself at this place surrounded by strip malls and other businesses. Great burgers are the claim to fame here. | 16065 W. Bluemound Rd. | 262/784–3833 | $7–$10 | MC, V.

Maxim's. American. In a residential neighborhood next door to a Catholic church and school, this casual restaurant is popular with local families. Standards like burgers, fried chicken, and ribs share the menu with such Greek dishes as spanikopita and gyros. Breakfast is served all day. | 18025 W. Capitol Dr. | 262/783–4501 | $7–$19 | AE, D, MC, V.

Peach Garden. Chinese. Americanized Chinese standards are the fare at this strip-mall joint with a fountain and a fake peach tree in the dining room. The house special is shrimp, chicken, pork, and Chinese veggies with panfried noodles. Lunch buffet. | 2325 N. 124th St. | 262/797–8899 | $6–$10 | AE, D, MC, V.

Lodging

Courtyard by Marriott. This dependable, standard outlet of the chain with conference and meeting facilities is close to local corporate parks and caters to business travelers. Bar. Cable TV. Pool. Hot tub. Gym. Laundry facilities. Business services. | 16865 W. Bluemound Rd. | 262/821–1800 | 135 rooms, 9 suites | $79–$129 rooms, $129–$159 suites | AE, D, DC, MC, V.

Embassy Suites West. This all-suites hotel at the midpoint between a residential and an industrial area is built around a large, open atrium with a fountain and plants. Restaurant, bar, complimentary breakfast. In-room data ports, microwaves, refrigerators, cable TV. Pool. Hot tub. Gym. Business services, airport shuttle. | 1200 S. Moorland Rd. | 262/782–2900 | fax 262/796–9159 | 203 suites | $119–$169 | AE, D, DC, MC, V.

Fairfield Inn by Marriott. This white inn with blue trim is in a residential neighborhood near a busy intersection. Inside there's a small lobby with a TV room. Complimentary Continental breakfast. In-room data ports, cable TV. Pool. Business services. | 20150 W. Bluemound Rd. | 262/785–0500 | fax 262/785–1966 | 135 rooms | $69–$89 | AE, D, DC, MC, V.

Hampton Inn Brookfield. A modern hotel with pillars and a canopy at the entryway, the Hampton Inn is on a busy shopping street at the edge of a residential neighborhood. Complimentary Continental breakfast. Cable TV. Pool. Hot tub. Business services. | 575 N. Barker Rd. | 262/796–1500 | fax 262/796–0977 | www.hamptoninn.com | 120 rooms | $89–$99 | AE, D, DC, MC, V.

Motel 6. You can walk to movies, shopping, and restaurants from this two-story budget motel with a mansard roof, several gabled windows, and a bay window in front. Cable TV. Pool. | 20300 W. Bluemound Rd. | 262/786–7337 | 135 rooms, 9 suites | $47–$52 | AE, D, DC, MC, V.

Wyndham Garden. This colonial-style hotel, under 3 mi from downtown on a busy commercial road, is built around a landscaped courtyard. Restaurant, bar, picnic area. In-room data ports, cable TV, Pool. Hot tub. Gym. Video games. Business services, airport shuttle. | 18155 W. Bluemound Rd. | 262/792–1212 | fax 262/792–1201 | www.wyndham.com | 178 rooms | $110–$140 | AE, D, DC, MC, V.

BURLINGTON

(Nearby towns also listed: Delafield, East Troy)

This small town, which started as a farming community when it was founded in 1835, is filled with charm, and is not far from Geneva Lake, one of the deepest lakes in Wisconsin. Burlington is also home to the very unusual Spinning Top Exploratory Museum, which has a collection of 2,000 antique and modern tops, yo-yos, and gyroscopes. Other nearby small towns with attractions can easily be reached by car. Today Burlington's economy is based on manufacturing of all sorts, ranging from textiles to plastics.

Information:**Burlington Area Chamber of Commerce** | 112 E. Chestnut St., 53105-0156 | 262/763–6044 | bacc@mia.net | www.burlingtonareachamber.com.

Attractions

Brighton Dale Golf Club. This club 15 mi east of Burlington has two 18-hole courses as well as a nine-hole course. The Blue Spruce course is tough and has beautiful scenery and the White Birch course also has particularly challenging greens. | 830 248th Ave., Kansasville | 262/878–1440 | Apr.–Oct.

Burlington Historical Museum. Exhibits at this downtown museum document Burlington's history. | Jefferson St. and Perkins Blvd. | 262/767–2884 | Free | Sun. or by appointment.

1850 Log Cabin. This historic log cabin downtown in Wehmhoff Park is filled with authentic furnishings. Tours take you through the cabin, grounds, gardens, and shed, which contains original farm implements. The gardens reflect 1850s landscaping styles. | Wehmhoff Sq. | 262/767–2884 | Free | Mar.–Dec., Sun. 1–4 or by appointment.

Green Meadows Farm. You'll find a large petting zoo of farm animals, along with pony rides, tractor rides, and hayrides here, 10 mi northwest of Burlington. | 33603 High Dr. | 262/534–2891 | $9; special rates for children, senior citizens, and groups | Memorial Day–Labor Day, weekdays 10–12, Sat. 10–1.

Spinning Top Exploratory Museum. This exhibit of 2,000 items includes a variety of tops and 700 yo-yos. The museum also offers programs, videos, a live show, and experiments with tops. | 533 Milwaukee Ave. | 262/763–3946 | $6; no kids under 4 | By appointment only.

St. Francis Retreat Center. This 160-acre retreat near town has walking trails, stations of the cross in mosaic, a church, two chapels, beautiful gardens, and a grotto. Outdoor Sunday masses from Memorial Day through Labor Day. Reservations suggested. | 503 S. Browns Lake Rd. | 262/763–3600 | Rooms are $29–$50 | Daily.

Whitman School. This 1844 brick schoolhouse on the south end of town contains its original furnishings including desks, a teacher's table, and books. | Beloit and Sheldon Sts. | 262/767–2884 | Free | By appointment.

ON THE CALENDAR

MAY: *Chocolate City Festival.* This mid-month chocolate extravaganza held the weekend after Mother's Day on the Chocolate Fest Grounds includes a tent filled with chocolate foods for sale, as well as displays, a carnival, an art fair, live entertainment, a children's area, animal acts, and nonchocolate foods. | 262/763–6044.

JUNE–SEPT.: *Aquaducks Water Ski Show.* This Fischer Park water-ski show features athletes from four years old on up on Browns Lake every Saturday night in summer. | 262/763–6044.

JULY: *Chicken BBQ.* For nearly half a century town residents have made it a tradition to gather one weekend afternoon in mid-July in Echo Park to feast on butter-basted and broiled chicken while a community band plays. | 262/363–4899.

Dining

Cottonpicker Restaurant. American. Sit in the back and you will have a view of the pond behind this rural, woodsy restaurant 1 mi north of town. Queen Anne wing-back chairs are set prominently in the lobby. Prime rib, chicken, and seafood dishes fill the menu. Friday-night fish fry. Sunday brunch. | 210 S. Browns Lake Dr. | 262/534–5151 | $8–$12 | AE, MC, V.

Lodging

Americinn. Inside this modern, stone-front hotel in a quiet residential neighborhood you'll find a large stone fireplace, mounted animal heads, and a collection of ducks and plants. Complimentary Continental breakfast. Cable TV. Pool. Hot tub, sauna. | 205 S. Browns Lake Dr. | 262/534–2125 | fax 262/534–2125 | 50 rooms | $69–$140 | AE, D, DC, MC, V.

Hillcrest Inn and Carriage House. The view from the front porch of this 1908 Edwardian mansion includes beautifully landscaped flower gardens and a 7-mi panoramic view. The

© Corbis

KETTLE MORAINE

The Kettle Moraine area was carved out thousands of years ago when two giant glaciers collided and formed a geologic corridor.

In southeastern Wisconsin, the area stretches for 100 mi from north to south. The countryside is breathtaking, with an abundance of hills (called drumlins) and dense stands of trees. In between are hollows (the kettles) filled by marshes or clear lakes. Narrow ridges (known as eskers) slice through the landscape, and you'll find giant boulders (the moraines) that were deposited by the retreating glaciers.

The Kettle Moraine area is a popular place for hiking, biking, horseback riding, and cross-country skiing; it's also one of the best places to view spectacular Midwest fall colors either on foot or by car.

In southeastern Waukesha County, the small community of Eagle nestles against the eastern edge of Kettle Moraine State Forest. Eagle is an ideal base for hiking into the forest, where the glacial landscape is preserved in near pristine condition.

Towns listed: Burlington, Delavan, Elkhorn, Fort Atkinson, Lake Geneva.

rooms are furnished with antique hardwood beds and have a turn-of-the-20th-century flair with floral prints and lacy finishing touches. Carriage-house rooms have gas fireplaces. No TV in some rooms. No kids under 12. No smoking. | 540 Storle Ave. | 262/763–4706 | www.thehillcrestinn.com | 5 rooms, 1 suite | $90–$170 | MC, V.

CABLE

(Nearby town also listed: Hayward)

Originally a logging community, the Cable area now offers recreation and relaxation opportunities in all four seasons. The Chequamegon National Forest is the backdrop and economic lifeblood of the town and surrounding communities as the local economy is dependent on logging and tourism. The area is also home to many events including the American Birkebeiner XC-Ski Race and the Chequamegon Fat Tire Festival.

Information: **Cable Area Chamber of Commerce** | County Rd. M and 1st St, Box 217, 54821-0217 | 800/533–7454 | gocable@win.bright.net | www.cable4fun.com.

Attractions
Cable Area Natural History Museum. Environmental exhibits and interpretive programs, workshops, lectures, and field trips for adults and children illuminate Northern Wisconsin's natural history. | Rte. M and Randysek Rd. | 715/798–3820 or 715/798–3890 | Free | July–Aug., Tues.–Sat. 10–4, Sun. 10–2; Sept.–June, Tues.–Sat. 10–4.

Built in 1925, the historic **Forest Lodge Library** is attached to the Cable Area Natural History Museum. This full-service public library offers Internet access and includes a children's section as well as Wisconsin and Native American sections. There's a stone fireplace. Children's programs in summer. | Rte. M | 715/798–3189 | Free | Sept.–May, Tues. and Thurs. 10–5, Wed. 3–8, Sat. 10–1; June–Aug., Tues. and Thurs. 10–5, Sat. 10–4.

Drummond Museum and Library. Displays depict 100 years of the history of the logging town of Drummond, which lies 9 mi north of Cable and had one of the largest sawmills of its time. A large photo collection has scenes of virgin forests, logging camps, and mill operations. A wildlife collection features birds and animals indigenous to the area. | Superior and Owen Sts., Drummond | 715/739–6290 | Free | Tues.–Wed. 11–5, Thu. 11–7, Sat. 9–1.

Lakewoods Forest Ridges Golf Course. Lakewoods offers the best of Northwoods serenity and an 18-hole course designed by golf-architect Joel Goldstrand. The 6,066-yard course 8 mi from Cable has four tee positions and three water holes, and the property includes a pro-shop, teaching center, driving range, and practice putting area. | Hwy. M | 800/255–2561 | 18 holes, $45 | Apr.–Nov.

ON THE CALENDAR
FEB.: *American Birkebeiner.* More than 7,000 people from around the world participate in this 52K cross-country ski race on the last Saturday of the month. The race begins at the Cable Union airport in Cable and ends in downtown Hayward. There is a shorter event on the same day, a 26K race called the Kortelopet, which also starts at the Cable Union Airport and finishes at the Telemark Resort in Cable. | 800/533–7454 | www.birkie.com.
SEPT.: *Chequamegon Fat Tire Festival.* Thousands of riders apply to participate in this 30 mi off-road race each year and a lottery narrows participation to 1,700. Those who aren't chosen can compete in an essay contest for one of 50 special spots. This year's news is available in the 20-page festival newsletter, *Fat Tracks.* | 715/798–3594.

Dining

Corner Place. Eclectic. This small, cozy, downtown restaurant serves a wide range of food—everything from steaks to pizza to sandwiches. | Corner of Hwy. 63 and County Rd. M | 715/798–4900 | Reservations not accepted | $7–$16 | D, MC, V.

Lodging

Connors of Cable Bed and Breakfast. This 77-acre estate with spacious accommodations and attractive landscaping is in the heart of Chequamegon National Forest. Wildlife viewing and bike trails are on-site. Complimentary breakfast. No smoking. | RR 1 | 715/798–3661 or 800/848–3932 | fax 715/798–3663 | connorbb@win.bright.net | www.connorsbandb.com | 3 rooms, 1 cottage | $75–$105 | AE, MC, V.

Telemark Resort. The cathedral ceiling and ceiling-high windows of the lodge set the grand tone at this Northwoods resort 4 mi outside of town. Each year the resort hosts the last section of the Kortelopet ski race and every type of summer and winter outdoor sport is offered. You can rent all the equipment you need at the lodge and the 18-hole golf course is open to the public, not just guests. Restaurant. Cable TV. Indoor-outdoor pool. Hot tub, sauna. 18-hole golf course, tennis. Hiking, horseback riding, boating, fishing. Ice-skating, cross-country skiing, snowmobiling. | Junction Telemark Rd. and Hwy. M | 715/798–3999 or 877/798–4718 | 119 rooms, 6 suites, 58 condos | $95 rooms, $150–$275 suites, $150–$375 condos | AE, D, DC, MC, V.

CASSVILLE

MAP 11, B7

(Nearby towns also listed: Bagley, Prairie du Chien)

This town founded in 1831 with a single general store once made a bid to become Wisconsin's territorial capital. Riverside Park is the departure point for the Cassville car ferry, a great way to cross the Mississippi. Just north of town are Nelson Dewey State Park and Stonefield Village, which is the State Historical Society's museum of agricultural history and village life.

Information: **Department of Tourism** | Box 576, 53806-0576 | 608/725–5855 | cass-tour@pcii.net | www.cassville.org.

Attractions

Riverside Park. This park near the center of town is the departure point for the Cassville car ferry, which crosses the Mississippi River. | Between Crawford St. and Front St. | 608/725–5855 | Free | Daily.

Stonefield State Historic Site. This re-created 1890s rural village a mile north of Cassville is the State Historical Society's museum of agricultural history and village life. You can stroll through the town square or visit with costumed merchants and tradesmen in period shops. Historic farm implements are displayed in the museum, and a short walk across the road leads to the home of Wisconsin's first governor, Nelson Dewey, which has five original buildings and some authentic furnishings. | Rte. VV | 608/725–5210 | $7.50; special rates for children, senior citizens, and groups | Memorial Day weekend–June, daily 10–4; July, Aug., daily 10–5; Sept.–mid-Oct., daily 10–4.

ON THE CALENDAR

JAN.: *Bald Eagle Month.* Each Saturday of the month knowledgable volunteers guide eagle-viewing walks at Riverside Park and Nelson Dewey State Park, a speaker discusses various issues of birding in the Municipal Building, and there is a moonlight hike in the evening, weather permitting. | 608/725–5855.

Dining
Friedman's Supper Club. American. This local family favorite 12 mi south of town features prime-rib specials on Saturday. | 7540 Hwy. 133 | 608/763–2526 | $7–$20 | MC, V.

Lodging
Geiger House Bed & Breakfast. The owner, Sherry, greets you with a bowl of fruit on arrival at this 1855 Greek Revival house, one of the oldest homes in town, built by a German immigrant businessman whose family owned the house until 1969. Today, the rooms are named for him and members of the family. Two are country style in burgundy and navy with heavy oak beds and the third is in Victorian style with soft blues and yellows. Complimentary breakfast. TV in common area. No pets. No smoking. | 401 Denniston St. | 608/725–5411 or 800/725–5439 | 3 rooms | $65–$75 | AE, MC, V.

CEDARBURG

MAP 11, E6

(Nearby town also listed: West Bend)

Irish immigrants first settled this town in the early 1840s. Rural Cedarburg grew and prospered under the industry of the German families that followed. Today, the downtown has more than 100 businesses housed in registered historic buildings, and 100 more historic homes surround downtown.

Information: Cedarburg Chamber of Commerce | Washington Ave. and Spring St., Box 104, 53102 | 800/237–2874 | cedarbrg@execpc.com | www.cedarburg.org.

CEDARBURG

INTRO
ATTRACTIONS
DINING
LODGING

Attractions
Cedar Creek Settlement and Winery. This winery occupies the lower floors of a 130-year-old woolen-mill building in Cedarburg's historic section downtown. Wine tours and tastings are available. | N70 W6340 Bridge Rd. | 262/377–8020 or 800/827–8020 | $2 for tours; free tasting | Daily 10–5.

Cedarburg Cultural Center. Permanent and changing exhibits focus on the area's ethnic heritage. | W62 N546 Washington Ave. | 262/375–3676 | Donations accepted | Tues.-Sat 10–5, Sun. 1–5, Closed Mon.

Covered Bridge Park. Just 2½ mi north of town on Covered Bridge Road, this park features Wisconsin's last original covered bridge, which was built over Cedar Creek in 1846 and remained in service until 1962. Today the bridge is open to foot traffic and there's a picnic area next to the water. | Covered Bridge Rd. | 262/377–9620 | Free | Daily.

Historic Downtown Cedarburg. Designated a National Historic District, this area is filled with restored 1850s buildings now serving as cafés, taverns, and shops purveying gifts and antiques. | Along Washington Ave. | 262/377–9620 | Free | Daily.

Paul J. Yank's Brewery Works Fine Arts Complex. An 1843 brewery houses sculptor Paul J. Yank's working studio and the Ozaukee Art Center. Works of other artisans and craftspeople are exhibited as well. Exhibits change every six weeks. | W62 N718 Riveredge Dr. | 262/377–8230 | Donations accepted | Wed.–Sun. 1–4.

ON THE CALENDAR
FEB.: *Winter Festival.* This downtown festival held the first weekend of the month in the historic district includes a chile contest, a parade, snow golf, ice carving, sled-dog racing, and the Mill Pond Bed Race, in which costumed participants race over the ice carrying decorated beds. | 262/377–9620.

JUNE: *Stone and Century House Tour.* On this driving tour, held the first weekend in June, you visit houses that are more than 100 years old in Ozaukee and Washington counties. Many of the homes contain antiques, art, and collectibles. | 800/237–2874.

JULY: *Gathering on the Green.* This event in Mequon's Rotary Park, 10 mi south of Cedarburg, features dance and musical performances in the park. | 262/242–6187.

JULY–AUG.: *Ozaukee County Fair.* This traditional county fair held the first week of August at the county fairgrounds features livestock, a carnival, contests, exhibits, food, and music. | 262/377–9620.

SEPT.: *Wine and Harvest Festival.* This annual wine festival downtown attracts between 30,000 and 40,000 people and includes grape stomping, a grape-seed spitting contest, a farmers' market, a scarecrow contest, music, food samples, and craft shows. | 262/377–9620.

Dining

Barth's at the Bridge. American. Buffets draw crowds to this supper club on the Milwaukee River across from the Cedarburg Mill. Thursday is prime-rib buffet, Friday is seafood. Sunday brunch. | N58 W6194 Hwy. 57 | 262/377–0660 | $10–$13 | AE, MC, V | Closed Mon. No lunch Tues., Wed.

Boder's on the River. Contemporary. This large but cozy mid-19th-century rural inn is surrounded by gardens and trees. The lounge offers a view of the Milwaukee River. The main dining room is known for roast duck, sautéed fresh chicken livers, corn fritters, and homemade cherry and blueberry muffins. There is also a bar and grill called The Hunt Club. Kids' menu. Sunday brunch. | 11919 N. River Rd., Mequon | 262/242–0335 | $20–$26 | AE, D, DC, MC, V | Closed Mon.

Chip and Py's. Continental. About ½ mi southeast of Cedarburg, this bi-level restaurant has a large fireplace and a display of contemporary artwork. Try the veal piccata, lightly breaded sautéed veal cutlets topped with capers and a white wine and butter sauce. Live jazz on Friday, Saturday, and Wednesday evenings. | 1340 W. Town Square Rd., Mequon | 262/241–9589 | $20–$25 | AE, D, DC, MC, V | Closed Mon. No lunch Sun.

Kowloon. Chinese. A window table at this spacious restaurant on Cedarburg's main street gives a view of the town's historic buildings. The shrimp and beef stir-fries are popular. | W63 N145 Washington Ave. | 262/375–3030 | $7–$11 | AE, D, DC, MC, V | Closed Mon.

The Riversite. Contemporary. Perched on the side of the Milwaukee River 6 mi southeast of town this restaurant was built to look like a turn-of-the-20th-century mill. Inside, brass candelabras illuminate the dining room and choices include such dinners as broiled Chilean sea bass served with a mango and avocado salsa. | 11120 N. Cedarburg Rd., Mequon | 262/242–6050 | $25–$30 | AE, MC, V | Closed Sun.

Lodging

American Country Farm Bed and Breakfast. This 1844 stone cottage on the State and National Registers of Historic Places, is in the country outside historic Cedarburg, and surrounded by gardens. Inside are a wood-burning fireplace and antiques. Complimentary Continental breakfast. Cable TV. | 12112 N. Wauwatosa Rd., Mequon | 262/242–0194 | fax 262/242–9824 | 1 cottage | $85–$125 | MC, V.

Best Western Quiet House and Suites. A modern hotel in a rural setting 5 mi southeast of Cedarburg. The lobby has a large fireplace and a display of geese figurines. Complimentary Continental breakfast. In-room data ports, some in-room hot tubs, cable TV. Indoor-outdoor pool. Hot tub. Gym. Business services. Pets allowed (fee). | 10330 N. Port Washington Rd., Mequon | 262/241–3677 | fax 262/241–3707 | www.quiethouse.com | 55 rooms | $111–$190 | AE, D, DC, MC, V.

Breeze Inn to the Chalet. The four buildings of this motel, in a residential area 10 mi southeast of Cedarburg, were built to look like Swiss chalets with peaked roofs and wraparound porches. Restaurant, bar. Refrigerators, cable TV. Business services. Some pets allowed. | 10401 N. Port Washington Rd., Mequon | 262/241–4510 | fax 262/241–5542 | breeze-measap@worldnet.att.net | 41 rooms | $68–$175 | AE, D, DC, MC, V.

Country Inn and Suites. You can have a view of the woods if you ask for a room on the back of this quiet chain hotel 15 mi from Cedarburg. The property is at the junction of Highways 45 and 167 E, next to an upscale banquet hall. Complimentary breakfast. Some refrigerators, some microwaves, cable TV. Pool. Hot tub. | W. 188 N. 11020 Maple Rd., Germantown | 262/251–7700 | 3 rooms, 1 suite | $86–$90 rooms, $95–$140 suite | AE, D, DC, MC, V.

Stagecoach Inn Bed and Breakfast. This large stone building filled with antiques was a stagecoach stop before the Civil War and is now on the National Register of Historic Places. Two of the suites have fireplaces. Bar, complimentary Continental breakfast. In-room hot tubs in suites, cable TV in some rooms. Business services. No kids under 10. No smoking. | W61 N520 Washington Ave. | 262/375–0208 or 888/375–0208 | fax 262/375–6170 | info@stagecoach-inn-wi.com | www.stagecoach-inn-wi.com | 6 rooms, 6 suites | $80–$140 | AE, D, DC, MC, V.

Washington House. Period pieces fill this 1886 brick building in the center of Cedarburg's historic district. There are gardens behind the building and fireplaces in the common gathering room and in some guest rooms. Complimentary Continental breakfast. Some in-room hot tubs. Cable TV, in-room VCRs available. Sauna. Business services. | W62 N573 Washington Ave. | 262/375–3550 or 800/554–4717 | fax 262/375–9422 | www.washingtonhouseinn.com | 34 rooms | $78–$209 | AE, D, DC, MC, V.

CHIPPEWA FALLS

MAP 11, B4

(Nearby towns also listed: Eau Claire, Rice Lake)

Small-town life is preserved on Main Street, where architecturally significant buildings house a bustling business community. The city's oldest business is the Jacob Leinenkugel Brewing Company, owned and operated by the Leinenkugel family for five generations and still brewing strong. Settled in 1836 as primarily a lumber town, today Chippewa Falls is especially known for its pure water. Area attractions include the 300-acre Irvine Park, which houses the Chippewa Falls Zoo; several state parks are only a short drive away.

Information: **Chippewa Valley Convention and Visitors Bureau** | 3625 Gateway Dr., Suite F, Eau Claire 54701 | 715/831–2345 or 888/523–3866 | linda@eauclaire-info.com | www.chippewavalley.com.

Attractions

Brunet Island State Park. This 1,225-acre island park 22 mi north of Chippewa Falls on Route 64 is named for Jean Brunet, an early settler who ran a trading post here. Framed by the Chippewa and Fisher rivers, the park offers bays and lagoons perfect for swimming, canoeing, or fishing. There are also hiking and cross-country skiing trails and 69 campsites. | 23125 255th St., Cornell | 715/239–6888 | www.dnr.state.wi.us | $7 nonresidents, $5 residents | May–Oct., daily.

Chippewa Falls Zoo. This small zoo in Irvine Park exhibits many large animals. There's also a petting zoo for children. | 124 Bridgewater Ave. | 715/723–3890 | Free | Daily 7 (am)–dusk.

Cook-Rutledge Mansion. This restored 1873 home of one of the town's lumber barons features stained glass, crystal chandeliers, and intricately carved woodwork. | 505 W. Grand Ave. | 715/723–7181 | $3.50 | June–Aug., Thurs.–Sun. tours at 2, 3, or by appointment; Sept.–May by appointment.

Lake Wissota State Park. The 6,300-acre Lake Wissota, 6 mi east of town, was created in 1918 by the Minnesota-Wisconsin Light Power Company hydroelectric dam and is a good spot for boaters or anglers eager to catch walleye, muskie, or bass. On shore, there are hiking, mountain biking, and horseback-riding trails winding through prairie, woodland, and marsh. In winter, trails are maintained for cross-country skiing and snowmobiling. The park also has 81 campsites. | 18127 County Rd. O | 715/382-4574 | www.dnr.state.wi.us | $7 nonresidents, $5 residents | Daily; Apr.–Oct. for camping.

Leinenkugel Brewery. You can see how beer is made, from the fermentation tanks to the bottling plant to the warehouse. Free samples. Tour reservations recommended. | 1 Jefferson Ave. (Hwy. 124) | 888/534-6437 | Free | Mon.–Sat. 9:30–3, Sun. 11–3; closed Sun. Sept.–May.

ON THE CALENDAR
JULY: *Chippewa Valley Country Fest.* Camp on-site at the 320-acre festival grounds during this four-day country music extravaganza which features nationally known performers. | 800/326-3378.
JULY: *Northern Wisconsin State Fair.* Exhibits, livestock, crafts, 4-H displays, entertainment, food, carnival, vendors, and antiques at the Northern Wisconsin state fairgrounds Thursday–Sunday during the second weekend in July. | 888/523-3866.
AUG.: *Pure Water Days.* This event held on the third weekend of the month features food, entertainment, a craft show, a parade, artworks, children's games, sporting events, and a bike ride. | 888/523-3866.

Dining

Lindsay's on Grand. American. This casual family restaurant is in a large historic brick building downtown. Try the Montecristo sandwich—ham, turkey, and Swiss cheese, dipped in egg batter. Kids' menu. | 24 W. Grand Ave. | 715/723-4025 | Reservations not accepted | $5–$10 | No credit cards.

Olson's Ice Cream Parlor & Deli. Delicatessen. You can get sub sandwiches and hot sandwiches like grilled cheese on weekdays at this downtown spot with purple benches out front. Leave room for great ice cream. | 611 N. Bridge St. | 715/723-4331 | $3–$5 | No credit cards | No dinner.

Water's Edge Supper Club. Contemporary. You can eat outside on the deck or in the bar if you're feeling casual, or order steak or lobster in the linen-tablecloth dining room of this rural restaurant overlooking Lake Wissota, a beautiful 6-mi drive from town. Friday fish fry. Live music Sunday in summer on the deck. | 9504 Hwy. south | 715/723-0161 | $10–$20 | AE, D, DC, MC, V.

Lodging

Americinn. This hotel is in a residential neighborhood on the south side of town, 2 mi from downtown and the zoo. The cozy lobby has a sunroom and a brick fireplace. Complimentary Continental breakfast. In-room data ports, some microwaves, some refrigerators, cable TV. Pool. Hot tub. Business services. Pets allowed (deposit). | 11 W. South Ave. | 715/723-5711 | fax 715/723-5254 | 62 rooms | $65–$73 | AE, D, DC, MC, V.

Country Inn. This motor hotel on a commercial street has country charm both inside and out. The white façade is classically styled and punctuated with porches and benches— plaid couches accent the common spaces inside. Complimentary Continental breakfast. In-room data ports, some refrigerators, cable TV. Pool. Hot tub. Business services. | 1021 W. Park Ave. | 715/720-1414 | fax 715/720-1414 | 62 rooms | $70–$88 | AE, D, DC, MC, V.

Glen Loch. Rooms have outdoor entrances at this simple motel on 3½ acres in a commercial neighborhood at the north end of town. Picnic area. Cable TV. Pets allowed. | 1225 Jefferson Ave. | 715/723-9121 | 19 rooms | $26–$75 | AE, MC, V.

Indianhead Motel. On a bluff overlooking downtown, this dark brown, rustic building is independently owned. All rooms are at ground level. Some microwaves, some refrigerators, cable TV. Pets allowed. | 501 Summit Ave. | 715/723–9171 or 800/341–8000 | fax 715/723–6142 | dixie2@ecol.net | www.cvol.net/~dixie2 | 27 rooms | $55–$70 | AE, D, DC, MC, V.

McGilvray's Victorian Bed & Breakfast. The bedrooms of this neoclassical and Gregorian Revival 1893 downtown home with two-story white column portico has floral print accents and dark wood beds. No room phones, TV in common area. No pets. No kids under 12. No smoking. | 312 W. Columbia St. | 715/720–1600 or 888/324–1893 | 3 rooms | $69–$99 | No credit cards.

Park Inn International. This large dark-brown downtown hotel has a big-screen TV in a common area. Restaurant, bar, room service. Cable TV. Pool. Hot tub. Business services. Some pets allowed. | 1009 W. Park Ave. | 715/723–2281 or 800/446–9320 | fax 715/723–2283 | 67 rooms | $85–$120 | AE, D, DC, MC, V.

Pleasant View Inn Bed & Breakfast. You can choose from four themed guest rooms—either the Victorian, the Northwoods, the Secret Garden, or the Nautical room—in this home with a 60-ft deck on Lake Wissota 8 mi from downtown. All rooms have whirlpool tubs. Cable TV. No pets. No smoking. | 16649 96th Ave. | 715/387–4401 | 3 rooms | $99–$139 | AE, D, MC, V.

CRANDON

MAP 11, D3

(Nearby towns also listed: Antigo, Rhinelander)

Tiny Crandon lies in the heart of lumber country, not far from Rhinelander. Courthouse Square has 40 different species of trees from all over the world. If you would rather play bingo than study trees, make the short drive to the town of Mole Lake, where you can catch a game any day of the week.

Information: Crandon Area Chamber of Commerce | 201 S. Lake Ave., Box 88, 54520-0088 | 800/334–3387 | info@crandonwi.com | www.crandonwi.com.

Attractions

Camp Five Museum and *Lumberjack Special* Steam Train Tour. Take a ride on the *Lumberjack Special*, a 1916 steam train that travels from the historic Laona Depot to the Camp Five Museum complex. At the complex you can visit a logging museum with audiovisual displays and see an active blacksmith and harness shop, tour a turn-of-the-20th-century country store, visit an animal corral and a nature center, and take a surrey ride through the forest or a pontoon boat ride along the Rat River. The camp is 10 mi east of Crandon. | 5480 Connor Farm Rd., Laona | 715/674–3414 or 800/774–3414 | $14; special rates for children and groups | Mid-June–late Aug., Mon.–Sat. tours at 11, noon, 1, and 2.

ON THE CALENDAR

SEPT.: *Chevrolet World's Championship Off-Road Race.* Nineteen classes of dune buggies, pickup trucks, and cars compete at the Crandon Off-Road Raceway for the largest competitive purse in the Midwest. | 800/334–3387.

Dining

Copper Country Bar & Restaurant. Contemporary. Two miles from town, the buffet changes every day at this country restaurant with flowery curtains and wallpaper—sometimes it includes Mexican specialties, sometimes fish or prime rib. The bar is completely separate from the candlelit dining room. | 10139 Hwy. 8 W | 715/478–3270 | $8–$10 | AE, MC, V | Closed Tues.

Lodging

Four Seasons. This single-story, stone-sided motel near the center of town has rooms you can enter either from the outside or from a central hallway. Refrigerators, cable TV. Business services. | 304 W. Glen St. | 715/478–3377 or 888/816–6835 | fax 715/478–3785 | www.fourseasons-motel.com | 20 rooms | $38–$55 | AE, D, MC, V.

Lakeland Motel. This no-frills locally owned motel is downtown opposite a restaurant and down the street from a drugstore and flower shop. Cable TV. | 400 S. Lake Ave. | 715/478–2423 | 10 rooms | $44–$47 | D, MC, V.

DELAFIELD

MAP 11, D6

(Nearby towns also listed: Burlington, East Troy)

This pretty little town in the heart of Waukesha County's lake area is an antiques hunter's dream and offers plenty to do for those who love to fish, boat, and swim. The area is the eastern headquarters of the Glacial Drumlin State Trail, a 47-mi hiking/biking trail that runs between Waukesha and Cottage Grove. Delafield is also the home of the prestigious St. John's Military Academy, an Episcopal boy's prep school, with a beautiful campus of old stone buildings and a cozy chapel.

KODAK'S TIPS FOR PHOTOGRAPHING PEOPLE

Friends' Faces
- Pose subjects informally to keep the mood relaxed
- Try to work in shady areas to avoid squints
- Let kids pick their own poses

Strangers' Faces
- In crowds, work from a distance with a telephoto lens
- Try posing cooperative subjects
- Stick with gentle lighting—it's most flattering to faces

Group Portraits
- Keep the mood informal
- Use soft, diffuse lighting
- Try using a panoramic camera

People at Work
- Capture destination-specific occupations
- Use tools for props
- Avoid flash if possible

Sports
- Fill the frame with action
- Include identifying background
- Use fast shutter speeds to stop action

Silly Pictures
- Look for or create light-hearted situations
- Don't be inhibited
- Try a funny prop

Parades and Ceremonies
- Stake out a shooting spot early
- Show distinctive costumes
- Isolate crowd reactions
- Be flexible: content first, technique second

From *Kodak Guide to Shooting Great Travel Pictures* © 2000 by Fodor's Travel Publications

Information: **Delafield Chamber of Commerce** | Box 171, 53018-0171 | 262/646–8100 | delacham@delafieldchamber.org | www.delafieldchamber.org.

Attractions

Hawk's Inn. This 1847 Greek Revival stagecoach stop and inn is completely restored and filled with antiques, including original glassware and antique clothing. Guided tours available at no charge. | 426 Wells St. | 262/646–4794 | Free | May–Oct. Sat. 1–4.

St. John's Northwestern Military Academy. This boys' preparatory school which draws students from all corners of the globe has been operating on these 150 acres since 1884. The majestic stone campus buildings include three barracks, a chapel with stained glass, a dining hall, and an infirmary. | 1111 Genesee St. | 262/646–3311 | Free | Daily.

ON THE CALENDAR

JULY: *Delafield Days.* A weekend early in July is filled with antique shows, sports tournaments, an art show, and an evening street dance. | 262/646–8100.

Dining

Delafield Brewhaus. American. You have a view of the brass-accented steel fermenters and other brewery equipment from the dining room of this brewery and restaurant. On the menu: salads, burgers, pork chops, and steaks as well as specialty ales and beers. | 3832 Hillside Dr. | 262/646–7821 | $10–$20 | AE, D, MC, V.

Red Circle Inn. Contemporary. The Red Circle Inn opened as a stagecoach stop in 1848 and now claims to be the oldest restaurant in the state. The menu features steak, chicken, and seafood dishes as well as nightly specials. | N 44 W. 33013 Watertown Plank Rd. | 262/367–4883 | $20–$25 | AE, D, MC, V | Closed Sun., Mon. No lunch.

Lodging

Country Pride Inn. Across the street from the Smiley Barn, this hotel is in a commercial neighborhood in downtown Delafield. Some in-room hot tubs, cable TV. Pool. Hot tub, sauna. Business services. | 2412 Milwaukee St. | 262/646–3300 | fax 262/646–3491 | 56 rooms | $52–$62 | AE, D, DC, MC, V.

Quilted Decoy Bed & Breakfast. The warm and friendly innkeeper brings coffee and pastries to your room before the full breakfast in the dining room of this cozy, quiet house on 3 scenic acres of what was once farmland 3 mi from Pewaukee's downtown. One room has a whirlpool tub. Complimentary breakfast. Cable TV, phone in common area. | W. 281 N1265 Clover Leaf Court, Pewaukee | 262/547–1699 | 2 rooms | $85–$95 | MC, V.

DELAVAN

MAP 11, E7

(Nearby town also listed: Elkhorn)

Delavan was settled in 1836, but it was between 1847 and 1894 that the town exploded as hundreds of clowns, circus performers, and animals from some 26 circuses established their winter headquarters here. In the winter of 1870–71, the original P. T. Barnum circus was organized in Delavan. The circus organizations have all but vanished from the town though more than 150 members of the old Circus Colony are buried in Spring Grove and St. Andrew's cemeteries. Today, Delvan is home to more than 230 businesses including large companies like Sta-Rite Industries, Andes Candies, and the Outboard Marine Company. Agriculture also plays a strong roll in the local economy, especially dairy and beef cattle.

Information: **Delavan-Delavan Lake Area Chamber of Commerce** | 52 E. Walworth Ave., 53115 | 800/624–0052 | info@delavanwi.org | www.delavanwi.org.

DELAVAN

INTRO
ATTRACTIONS
DINING
LODGING

Attractions

Memorial Arboretum. This impressive collection of trees—some are memorialized and some species are labeled—overlooks Lake Comus. | N. Terrace St. | 262/728–5095 | Free.

ON THE CALENDAR

SEPT.: *Autumn Fest.* This fall festival, held on the last weekend of the month in Veterans Memorial Park, offers a carnival, a flea market, music, children's activities, arts, crafts, and food. | 262/728–5095.

Dining

Latimer House. Continental. This turn-of-the-20th-century home with a veranda and a cylindrical tower now houses a sophisticated restaurant serving such dishes as veal scallops with lemon, capers, and parsley and Sunday brunch with eggs sardo, poached eggs over crab meat and broccoli with hollandaise sauce. | 523 E. Walworth Ave. | 262/367–4883 | $9–$19 | MC, V | Closed Mon., Tues.

Millie's. German. This Pennsylvania-Dutch restaurant set on a 7-acre property 4 mi south of town was built in 1964 and modeled after an old farmhouse. The five dining rooms serve such favorites as chicken and dumplings and German apple pancakes filled with butter and cinnamon-spiced apples. | 2484 Rte. O | 262/728–2434 | Reservations not accepted | $7–$15 | No credit cards | Closed Mon. Mar.–June and Sept.–Dec.; closed weekdays Jan.–Feb.

Lodging

Allyn House Mansion Inn. This historic 10,000-sq-ft Queen Anne Eastlake mansion built in 1885 won the highest prize for historical home renovation from the National Trust in 1992. Five of the nine original fireplaces are in the guest rooms furnished in entirely Victorian-era antiques, including heavy four-poster beds in mahogany and walnut. Three rooms share a bath. Minimum two-night stay Saturdays May–October. Complimentary breakfast. No room phones, no TV. No kids under 12. No smoking. | 511 W. Walworth | 262/728–9090 | 8 rooms (3 with shared bath) | $100–$150 | MC, V.

Lake Lawn Resort. This 275-acre resort on Delavan Lake ¼ mi west of town opened in 1879. This country casual resort has a massive stone fireplace in the lobby, wood paneling in the rooms, and lake and golf-course views. Cable TV. Indoor-outdoor pool, lake. Spa. Golf. Boating. | 2400 E. Geneva Rd. | 800/338–5253 | 140 rooms, 140 suites | $169–$229 rooms, $259–$289 suites | AE, D, DC, MC, V.

DODGEVILLE

MAP 11, C6

(Nearby towns also listed: Madison, Spring Green)

In summer 1827, Henry Dodge, his family, and 40 miners set out for the Upper Mississippi lead-mine region from their home in Missouri, lured by tales of an abundance of lead deposits. The search brought Dodge to this area, where he negotiated a treaty with the local Native Americans. Dodge established himself in a small ravine now traversed by Fountain Street, and his party constructed a mining operation and built a fort for shelter. Over time, some residents also turned to farming and became merchants. Today Dodgeville remains an agricultural community, with new industries like retailer Land's End playing a larger part in the growing economy. Set in a region with a dramatic landscape of hills and valleys, Dodgeville is home to Wisconsin's second-largest state park, Governor Dodge State Park, a great spot for swimming, camping, boating, and hiking.

Information: **Dodgeville Revitalization Chamber, Tourist Information** | Box 141, 53533-01141 | 608/935–5993 | info@dodgeville.com | www.dodgeville.com.

Attractions

Governor Dodge State Park. Wisconsin's second-largest state park 3 mi north of town includes more than 5,000 acres with steep hills, stony bluffs, two man-made lakes, and a waterfall. You can camp, fish, swim, picnic, and use the trails for hiking, mountain biking, horseback riding, cross-country skiing, and snowmobiling. There's even an equestrian campground. | 4175 Rte. 23 | 608/935–2315 | www.dnr.state.wi.us | $7 nonresidents, $5 residents | Daily.

Military Ridge State Trail. You can ride or hike through the countryside on this 40-mi-long crushed-limestone trail which follows an old military road from 1855 and passes through Blue Mounds and Mt. Horeb on its way to Verona. Trail passes can by purchased from the Department of Natural Resources at the trail head. | 1500 N. John St. | 608/935–3368 | $3 trail pass required only for bicyclists 16 and older | Daily.

ON THE CALENDAR

JULY: *Farmers Appreciation Day.* This community festival held downtown in Harris Park on the second weekend in July offers a wide variety of events, including a parade, a craft show, a farm-toy show, a tractor pull, live music, and farm displays. | 608/935–9200.

Dining

Don Q Inn. American. The rustic main dining room in this refurbished 1914 barn is connected to the inn by a 300-ft underground tunnel. The dining room interior includes wood, brick, stained glass, and a large stone fireplace; the bar is made of old copper and bourbon barrels. On the menu are steaks, seafood, lobster, burgers, and fries. | 3656 U.S. Rte. 23 N | 608/935–2321 | $12–$36 | AE, D, MC, V | No lunch.

Lodging

Don Q Inn. The lobby of this offbeat motel 2 mi north of town has a large fireplace surrounded by old-style barbershop chairs. The 25 suites have themes—there's a cave, Cupid's corner (with a heart-shaped bed), jungle safari quarters, and others. Restaurant (see Don Q Inn), complimentary Continental breakfast. Some in-room hot tubs, cable TV. Indoor-outdoor pool. Hot tub. | 3656 Rte. 23 N | 608/935–2321 or 800/666–7848 | fax 608/935–2416 | www.fantasuite.com | 61 rooms | $80–$88 | AE, D, DC, MC, V.

House on the Rock Inn. The 40-ft submarine and the waterfall in the kids' pool at this cedarwood hotel with oversize rooms next to a supper club, echo the outrageous collections of its namesake museum, 7 mi north of the hotel. Bar, complimentary breakfast. Cable TV. Indoor-outdoor pool. Video games. | 3591 S. Hwy. 23 | 608/935–3711 | 114 rooms | $150–$200 | AE, D, MC, V.

New Concord Inn. This modern brick hotel with a white canopy at the entryway and hardwood floors and a fireplace in the lobby is less than 2 mi from downtown. Complimentary Continental breakfast. Some refrigerators, cable TV. Pool. Hot tub. Gym. Video games. | 3637 Rte. 23 N | 608/935–3770 or 800/348–9310 | fax 608/935–9605 | www.concordinn.com | 63 rooms | $89–$99 | AE, D, MC, V.

EAGLE RIVER

MAP 11, D2

(Nearby towns also listed: Boulder Junction, Manitowish Waters, Sayner)

Eagle River and the area that surrounds it is a classic Northwoods vacation spot. Located on the Chain of 28 Lakes, the largest chain of freshwater lakes in the world, Eagle River is famous for its clear, cool waters filled with game fish. Ice-cream parlors, candy stores, and souvenir shops line the town's main street. In winter, there is an abundance of cross-country skiing and snowmobiling.

Information: **Eagle River Chamber of Commerce, Information Center** | 116 S. Railroad St., Box 1917, 54521 | 800/359–6315 | info@eagleriver.org | www.eagleriver.org.

Attractions

International Snowmobile Racing Hall of Fame. This museum tracks the evolution of snow-mobiling with 25 vintage sleds, helmet exhibits, trophy displays, and videos of historic and contemporary races. | Hwy. 70 E, Box 720, St. Germain | 715/542–4488 | Donations accepted | Weekdays 8:30–4.

Trees For Tomorrow Natural Resources Education Center. Offers tours of the facility and of a demonstration forest and wildlife trail. | 519 Sheridan St. E | 715/479–6456 | Free | Daily, call for hrs.

ON THE CALENDAR

JAN.: *World Championship Snowmobile Derby.* The Derby Racetrack a mile north of town hosts a snowmobile competition, a motorcycle race on ice, fireworks, vendors, food, and entertainment the third week of the month. | 715/479–4424.
FEB.: *Klondike Days.* This late-month festival at the Derby Racetrack on U.S. 45 offers dog and horse pulls, a winter camp rendezvous, Native American exhibits and performances, arts, crafts, a chain-saw carving contests, and ice-sculpting contests. | 800/359–6315.
AUG.: *Paul Bunyan Fest.* Chain-saw sculpting demonstrations, beef sandwiches, and lots of fun downtown one afternoon early in the month. | 800/359–6315.
OCT.: *Cranberry Fest.* Cranberries for sale, family entertainment, arts, crafts, quilt and weaving demonstrations, a farmers' market, an antiques show, a bike tour, and a fun run/walk on the first full weekend of the month at the Vilas county fairgrounds. | 800/359–6315.

Dining

Bear's Den at Black Bear Lodge. Contemporary. Large windows face the woods and Little St. Germain Lake in this dining room with vinyl-covered bar stools, burgundy tablecloths, and scattered deer mounts. On the menu: Black Angus steak, pasta, ribs, and fish. Snow-mobiler's breakfast in winter. | 1279 Halberstadt Rd., St. Germain | 715/479–5778 | $9–$19 | D, MC, V | Closed Wed. No lunch.

Logging Camp Kitchen & Grill. Contemporary. Antique logging artifacts, quilts, and birch oil lamps set the scene in this turn-of-the-20th-century restaurant in the Pine Aire Resort, but the dinners are far more sophisticated than those served from logging camp kitchens of yore. Try the veal chardonnay with wild mushroom and barley risotto or pan-seared fresh local trout with wild rice lentil pilaf and toasted pine nuts. Everything is accompanied by fresh bread and grape-seed oil. | 4443 Chain O' Lakes Rd. | 715/479–8467 | $8–$22 | MC, V | Closed Wed. No lunch.

Smuggler's Lounge. American/Casual. The exceptional homemade Royal Bohemian horse-radish and Wisconsin ginseng sold at the gift shop is the draw at this sandwich spot down-town across from the information bureau. Special Smuggler's sandwiches are on Italian bread, with Italian seasonings, garlic, and butter. All-you-can-eat fish fry Friday. | 123 Rail-road St. | 715/479–3456 | $3–$7 | D, MC, V.

Lodging

Chanticleer Inn. This casual resort 3 mi east of Eagle River offers a lodge and freestand-ing villas set among pine, oak, and birch trees, on the shores of Voyager Lake, one of the Chain of 28 Lakes. There are 34 mi of cross-country ski trails on the property and a nine-hole golf course next door. Bar, dining room. 2 tennis courts (1 lighted). Beaches, boating, fishing. Cross-country skiing. Playground. Laundry facilities. Business services, airport shuttle. | 1458 E. Dollar Lake Rd. | 715/479–4486 or 800/752–9193 | fax 715/479–0004 | www.chanticleerinn.com | 76 rooms | $89–$370 | AE, D, MC, V.

Days Inn. This large colonial-style brick hotel is backed by trees with a field on one side; there are large windows in the lobby. Snowmobile trails lead directly to the hotel. Complimentary Continental breakfast. Some refrigerators, some in-room hot tubs, cable TV. Pool. Hot tub, sauna. Laundry facilities. Business services. Some pets allowed. | 844 Railroad St. N | 715/479–5151 or 800/356–8018 | fax 715/479–8259 | www.americanheritageinn.com | 93 rooms | $75–$84 | AE, D, DC, MC, V.

Eagle River Inn and Resort. At this two-story resort on Watermeet Lake a large wood carving of an eagle dominates the lobby. The modern rooms have lake views. Picnic area. Some in-room hot tubs, cable TV, in-room VCRs available. Pool. Hot tub. Miniature golf. Gym. Dock, boating. Playground. Business services. | 5260 Rte. 70 W | 715/479–2000 | fax 715/479–2000 | www.eriver-inn.com | 26 rooms, 10 suites | $59–$109 rooms, $99–$169 suites | D, DC, MC, V.

Gypsy Villa. This resort, 3 mi south of Eagle River, is spread over 2 mi and each villa has lots of space including 200 ft or more of private lake frontage, with a private swimming beach and pier. Most units are on Cranberry Island, in the middle of Cranberry Lake, one of the Chain of 28 Lakes. Maid service costs $20 a day. Picnic area. No air-conditioning in some rooms, kitchenettes, some in-room hot tubs, no room phones, cable TV in some rooms, in-room VCRs available. Wading pool. Hot tub. Tennis. Gym. Beach, dock, boating, fishing, bicycles. Playground. Laundry facilities. Business services. Pets allowed. | 950 Circle Dr. | 715/479–8644 or 800/232–9714 | fax 715/479–8780 | www.falmonoid.com/gypsy/gypsy.htm | 21 cottages, 6 apartment suites | $657–$1,957 for cottages (1-week minimum), $79–$99 for suites | AE, D, MC, V.

North Star Lodge and Resort. This rustic getaway in the woods along the lake shore trades in some modern amenities like TV and phones for quiet and solitude. No air-conditioning, no room phones, no TV. Beach. | 7919 Hwy. K, Star Lake | 715/479–4114 | 10 rooms, 17 cabins | $29–$35 rooms, $350–$1,350 cabins (per week) | No credit cards.

Whippoorwill Inn. Rooms have lake views through the trees at this hand-built secluded log cabin with three stone fireplaces nestled in the woods. Complimentary breakfast. No air-conditioning, no room phones, no TV. Pool. Hot tub. | 7919 Hwy. K, Star Lake | 715/542–3333 | 5 rooms | $125 | MC, V.

White Eagle Motel. This motel and its outdoor pool overlook the Eagle River, which flows into the Chain of 28 Lakes. There are woods with snowmobiling trails behind the building. Picnic area. No air-conditioning, cable TV. Pool. Hot tub, sauna. Driving range. Boating. Pets allowed. | 4948 Rte. 70 W | 715/479–4426 or 800/782–6488 | fax 715/479–3570 | www.whiteeaglemotel.com | 22 rooms | $60–$65 | D, MC, V.

EAST TROY

MAP 11, E7

(Nearby towns also listed: Burlington, Delafield)

Founded in 1835, East Troy originally had an economic base of agriculture and small business. Today the economy is also fueled by industry and education. There are several pretty, small lakes and a historic village square. East Troy's claim to fame is the East Troy Electric Railroad Museum. The town of Eagle is just a short drive away, at the eastern edge of the Kettle Moraine State Forest.

Information: East Troy Area Chamber of Commerce | 2905 Main St., Box 312, 53120-0312 | 262/642–3770 | easttroy@elknet.net | www.east-troy.wi.us.

Attractions

East Troy Electric Railroad Museum. This railroad museum has an extensive trolley collection and a historic train that offers lunch and dinner tours. An 11-mi round-trip leaves from a historic depot. | 2002 Church St. | 262/548–3837 | Admission varies per tour | Mid-May–late Oct; call for weekly schedule.

ON THE CALENDAR

SEPT.: *Bluegrass Festival.* More than a dozen bluegrass artists including a different top-name performer each year perform in the village square downtown on the second weekend of the month. Includes family events, contests, arts, crafts, displays, and food. | 262/642–3732.

Dining

Heaven City Restaurant. Contemporary. This restaurant 10 mi east of East Troy has six cozy candlelit dining rooms in a landmark building designed by one of Frank Lloyd Wright's students in 1917. A 50-year-old rubber tree dominates the atrium in the center of the restaurant. Try the smoked trout turnover, Kettle Moraine stuffed chicken, and Irish coffee soufflé. Tuesday is tapas night. Live music Tuesday and Thursday–Sunday. | S91 W27850 Rte. ES, Mukwonago | 262/363–5191 | Reservations essential | $15–$25 | AE, D, DC, MC, V | No lunch.

Lodging

Alpine Valley Resort. Tudor-style buildings give a European air to this ski and 27-hole golf resort set against the rolling hills of the Kettle Moraine. Restaurant, bar. Cable TV. 2 pools. Hot tub. Golf. Downhill skiing. Business services. | W. 2501 Hwy. D | 262/642–7374 | 124 rooms, 4 suites | $82–$200 | MC, V.

Kettle Moraine Inn. Built in 1830, this straightforward inn and tavern is one of the oldest buildings in the tiny town of Eagle, about 12 mi from East Troy, which has scarcely more than 1,000 residents. Restaurant, bar. Cable TV. | 201 Grove St., Eagle | 262/594–2121 | 4 rooms | $40–$60 | MC, V.

EAU CLAIRE

MAP 11, B4

(Nearby towns also listed: Black River Falls, Chippewa Falls, Menomonie)

Eau Claire (which is French for "clear water") became one of Wisconsin's busiest lumber towns after it was settled in 1844 at the junction of the Chippewa and Eau Claire rivers. Today you'll find extensive bike and walking trails along both streams. In winter, the town welcomes snowmobilers. The University of Wisconsin has an extension campus here, and the grounds are set between the rivers.

Information: **Eau Claire Chamber of Commerce** | 3625 Gateway Dr., Suite B, 54701 | 715/834–1204 | information@eauclairechamber.org | www.eauclairechamber.org.

Attractions

Chippewa Valley Museum. This museum in downtown Carson Park includes exhibits about the Ojibwa tribe, the area's first towns and industries, and early farm life. A turn-of-the-20th-century ice-cream parlor, a log house, a one-room school, and an 8-ft, 21-room dollhouse are on the premises. | 1204 Carson Park Dr. | 715/834–7871 | $3; special rates for children and groups | Memorial Day–Labor Day, daily 10–5; Labor Day–Memorial Day, Tues.–Sun. 1–4.

Dells Mills Museum. This National Historic Landmark, 20 mi southeast of Eau Claire on WI 12, was once a flour mill and is now a museum. Some 2,000 ft of belting and 175 pulleys move via water power. One-hour guided tours are available. | E18855 Rte. V | 715/286–2714 | $7 | May–late Oct., daily 10–5.

Paul Bunyan Logging Camp. This authentic reproduction of an 1890s logging camp is down-town in 134-acre Carson Park. | Carson Park Dr. | 715/835–6200 | www.paulbunyancamp.org | $3; special rates for children | Mid Apr.–Labor Day, daily 10–4:30; Labor Day–late Oct., Tues.–Sun. noon–4:30.

University of Wisconsin–Eau Claire. One of Wisconsin's most beautiful campuses, the university spans both banks of the Chippewa River in the heart of Eau Claire. Tours of the grounds are available. | 105 Garfield Ave. | 715/836–2637 | www.uwec.edu | Free | Daily; tours by reservation.

Foster Art Gallery. A wide variety of work by students and professional artists is displayed in the Fine Arts Building on the lower side of the campus across the river. | 105 Garfield Ave. | 715/836–3277 | www.uwec.edu | Free | Hrs. vary depending on exhibits.

James Newman Clark Bird Museum. Approximately 530 specimens and four dioramas depict native birds in their natural habitat in Phillips Hall. The museum surrounds the L. E. Phillips Planetarium. | 105 Garfield Ave. | 715/836–3523 | www.uwec.edu | Free | Weekdays 8–4:30.

L. E. Phillips Planetarium. This planetarium in the James Newman Clark Bird Museum in Phillips Hall seats 50 and is a focal point for classes in astronomy and the physical sciences, and for scheduled programs for school groups and the general public. | 105 Garfield Ave. | 715/836–3731 | www.uwec.edu | Fees for some programs | Hrs. vary, depending on programs.

ON THE CALENDAR

SEPT.: *International Fall Festival.* Live entertainment, crafts, cultural displays, ethnic foods, games, midway rides, a parade, and a juried crafts show downtown in mid-month. | 888/523–3866.

Dining

Camaraderie. American/Casual. Near the university campus, the restaurant is popular with students. It's dimly lit and accented with antiques; menu items include burgers and sandwiches. You can also sit in the outdoor beer garden. | 442 Water St. | 715/834–5411 | $5–$10 | MC, V.

Draganetti's Ristorante. Italian. This third-generation family-owned establishment began its tradition with a marriage between a Pole, Draganowski, and an Italian, Micaletti, in 1951. The northern and southern specialties include the 21-garlic-clove pasta with fresh spinach, mushrooms, and prosciutto over angel-hair pasta. Kids' menu. | Clairemont Ave. and Hwy. 53 | 715/834–9234 | $9–$17 | D, MC, V | Closed Sun., Mon. No lunch.

Fanny Hill Victorian Inn and Dinner Theatre. Continental. In summer you can eat outside on the deck of this restaurant in a Victorian inn. Try the Fire Roasted Prime-Rib Pork Chop crowned with a Papaya and Tomatillo Salsa accompanied by pan-seared southwestern spiced red potato tossed with andouille sausage, fresh sweet bell peppers and pearl onions. Dinner theater Thursday–Sunday (reservations essential). Sunday brunch. | 3919 Crescent Ave. | 715/836–8184 | $13–$30 | AE, D, DC, MC, V | Closed Mon., Tues.

Jericho's Lounge. Steak. This casual restaurant in the Best Western Midway is rumored to serve the best prime rib in town. There is live music Thursday and a comedy act Friday night. Sunday brunch. | 2851 Hendrickson Dr. | 715/834–9234 | $5–$15 | D, AE, MC, V | Breakfast also available; no lunch.

Norske Nook. American/Casual. The pies served here make the half-hour drive from Eau Claire well worth it. Traditional family fare such as burgers, chicken, and steak dishes are served in addition to *lefse* (a tortilla-like bread made from potatoes and flour) and other Norwegian specialties at the two locations, one across the street from the other, in downtown Osseo. | 207 and 13807 W. 7th St., Osseo | 715/597–3069 or 715/597–3688 | $5–$10 | D, MC, V | Breakfast also available.

Ridge Top at Mill Run. Contemporary. Part of the Mill Run Golf Club, this restaurant 7 mi from downtown is on a hill overlooking a golf course, with a view of the sunset. You can dine on bacon-wrapped beef tenderloin topped with caramelized onions and mushrooms or five-cheese tortellini in a honey-curry cream sauce with Spanish peanuts and dates. | 3905 Kane Rd. | 715/858–7967 | $9–$22 | AE, MC, V | Closed Sun., Mon., Tues.

Tokyo Japanese Restaurant. Japanese. Asian music in the air and Asian art on the walls set the stage for teppanyaki dining—in which Japanese chefs prepare your food on grills before your eyes—at this strip-mall restaurant. | 2426 London Rd. | 715/834–0313 | $11–$25 | AE, D, DC, MC, V | Closed Mon. No lunch Sat., Sun.

Lodging

Antlers. This brick motel is 8 mi from downtown, in a semi-commercial neighborhood just 1 mi from a local mall; there are frequent deer sightings on the edge of the woods in the backyard. Complimentary Continental Breakfast. Cable TV. Playground. | 2245 S. Hastings Way | 715/834–5313 or 800/423–4526 | fax 715/839–7582 | 33 rooms | $45–$75 | AE, D, MC, V.

Apple Tree Inn. This white colonial-style inn with rich oak woodwork throughout has four individually styled rooms, all with whirlpool tubs and fireplaces. You can choose to eat breakfast in your room, in the billiard room, or on the deck overlooking the backyard. Complimentary breakfast. In-room data ports, in-room VCRs. No pets. | 6700 Hwy. 53 S | 715/836–9599 | 4 rooms | $60–$119 | AE, D, MC, V.

The Atrium. This B&B with stained glass in some rooms is right on the edge of town, about 4 mi from downtown, but with trails winding through its 15 wooded acres, a small, secluded beach on Otter Creek, and a hammock in the wildflower garden, it feels more like a rural hideaway. There is a willow four-poster bed in one of the rooms. Complimentary breakfast. Cable TV. No pets. No kids under 12. No smoking. | 5572 Prill Rd. | 715/833–9045 or 888/773–0094 | 4 rooms | $85–$159 | MC, V.

Best Western Midway Hotel. This motel is 3 mi from downtown and just 1 mi from the University of Wisconsin in quiet, rolling countryside. Restaurant, bar (with entertainment), complimentary Continental breakfast, room service. In-room data ports, cable TV, in-room VCRs available. Pool. Hot tub, sauna. Video games. Business services, airport shuttle. | 2851 Hendrickson Dr. | 715/835–2242 | fax 715/835–1027 | www.bestwestern.com | 110 rooms | $79–$89 | AE, D, DC, MC, V.

Best Western White House. This modern, white brick motel less than 2 mi from downtown has a sunny pool area and a lobby with large windows and overstuffed chairs. Restaurant. In-room data ports, refrigerators, some in-room hot tubs, cable TV. Pool. Hot tub, sauna. Business services. | 1828 S. Hastings Way | 715/832–8356 | fax 715/836–9686 | www.bestwestern.com | 66 rooms | $63–$95 | AE, D, DC, MC, V.

Comfort Inn. This two-story brick motel is in a commercial area 10 mi from downtown. Complimentary Continental breakfast. In-room data ports, cable TV. Pool. Business services. Pets allowed. | 3117 Craig Rd. | 715/833–9798 | fax 715/833–9798 | 56 rooms | $54–$99 | AE, D, DC, MC, V.

Exel Inn. Three miles from downtown, this simple brick motel is surrounded by businesses. Complimentary Continental breakfast. 1 in-room hot tub, cable TV. Gym. Laundry facilities. Business services. Pets allowed. | 2305 Craig Rd. | 715/834–3193 | fax 715/839–9905 | 100 rooms | $47–$59 | AE, D, DC, MC, V.

Fanny Hill Victorian Inn and Dinner Theatre. This Victorian inn is on a hill overlooking the Chippewa River Valley, and is surrounded by an 8-acre garden. In addition to its 11 rooms, the inn has both a restaurant and a dinner theater that seats 275 for performances Thursday through Sunday evenings. Restaurant (see Fanny Hill Victorian Inn and Dinner Theatre, above), complimentary breakfast. Some in-room hot tubs, cable TV. Business services. | 3919 Crescent Ave. | 715/836–8184 or 800/292–8026 | fax 715/836–8180 | www.fanny-hill.com | 11 rooms | $89–$189 | AE, D, DC, MC, V.

Green Tree Inn and Suites. This mom-and-pop motel downtown has some permanent residents and many families return year after year. You can walk to the university, shopping, and dining. Complimentary Continental breakfast. Some kitchenettes, cable TV. Pets allowed. | 516 Galloway St. | 715/832–3411 | 20 rooms, 12 suites | $26–$40 | AE, D, DC, MC, V.

Hampton Inn. This large white stucco hotel in a commercial neighborhood 2 mi from downtown has landscaped gardens and a spacious lobby. In-room data ports, cable TV. Pool. Hot tub. Gym. Business services. | 2622 Craig Rd. | 715/833–0003 | fax 715/833–0915 | 106 rooms | $64–$99 | AE, D, DC, MC, V.

Maple Manor. This small, cozy brick motel is 3 mi north of Interstate 94 in a commercial area. Restaurant, bar, picnic area, complimentary breakfast. Some refrigerators, cable TV. Pets allowed. | 2507 S. Hastings Way | 715/834–2618 or 800/624–3763 | fax 715/834–1148 | www.mapleman@aol.com | 36 rooms | $35–$60 | AE, D, DC, MC, V.

Otter Creek Inn. Every room in this English Tudor–style home anchoring a wooded acre on the edge of town is furnished in Victorian style with floral prints, or deep blues or burgundy, and each has a whirlpool tub. There is a heated pool and gazebo tucked between the trees, as well. Complimentary breakfast. Cable TV. Pool. No pets. No kids under 12. No smoking. | 2536 Hwy. 12 | 715/832–2945 | 6 rooms | $79–$159 | AE, D. DC. MC, V.

Quality Inn. A large fireplace greets you in the lobby of this brick-accented hotel with two wings and a center courtyard with a pool. It is on a busy shopping strip. Restaurant, bar (with entertainment), complimentary breakfast, room service. In-room data ports, cable TV, in-room VCRs available. 2 pools. Hot tub, sauna. Business services. Pets allowed. | 809 W. Clairemont Ave. | 715/834–6611 | fax 715/834–6611 | www.qualityinn-eauclaire.com | 120 rooms | $59–$119 | AE, D, DC, MC, V.

Road Star Inn. This large white modern motor hotel within Eau Claire's city limits is part of a local chain. Complimentary Continental breakfast. Some refrigerators, cable TV. Some pets allowed. | 1151 W. MacArthur Ave. | 715/832–9731 or 800/445–4667 | fax 715/832–0690 | 62 rooms | $41–$47 | AE, D, DC, MC, V.

Ramada Inn and Conference Center. This large white, multilevel hotel 5 mi from downtown and 3 mi from a local mall is in a commercial area. Restaurant, bar, room service. In-room data ports, in-room hot tubs in suites, cable TV. Pool. Sauna. Business services, airport shuttle. | 1202 W. Clairemont Ave. | 715/834–3181 | fax 715/834–1630 | www.ramada-eauclaire.com | 198 rooms, 35 suites | $79–$179 | AE, D, DC, MC, V.

EGG HARBOR

MAP 11, F4

(Nearby towns also listed: Baileys Harbor, Ellison Bay, Ephraim)

This little Door County town never fails to delight. Its Main Street shops, galleries, and restaurants are in restored historic buildings, as well as newer ones that capture the village's Old Wisconsin charm. Just outside of town is the Birch Creek Music Center, a nationally acclaimed music academy with evening concerts in a barn. The Door County Stencil Company makes hand-stenciled clothing and sells it here in Main Street shops downtown, as well as throughout Door County.

Information: Door County Chamber of Commerce | 1015 Green Bay Rd., Box 406, Sturgeon Bay 54235-0406 | 800/527–3529 | door@mail.wiscnet.net | www.doorcountyvacations.com.

Attractions

Dovetail Gallery and Studio. This gallery features paintings, wood carving, pottery, stained glass, garden art, and art furniture. Elaborate flower gardens showcase copper garden-art sprinklers. | 7901 Rte. 42 | 920/868–3987 | Free | May–Feb., daily 10–6.

ON THE CALENDAR

MAY: *Festival of Blossoms.* A monthlong county-wide celebration of spring, featuring blossoming orchards, daffodils, and wildflowers. | 920/743–4456.

JUNE–AUG.: *Birch Creek Music Performance Center.* This renovated 100-year-old barn 3 mi east of town hosts approximately 30 summer concerts each year. | 920/868–3763.

Dining

Hof Restaurant. Contemporary. You'll have water views at this restaurant in the Alpine Resort where fresh whitefish and grilled steaks are the specialties. At breakfast try the Swiss toast—cream cheese–filled cinnamon bread with Door County cherries. | 7715 Alpine Rd. | 920/868–3000 | $7–$17 | AE, D, MC, V | Breakfast also available; closed for dinner weekdays Sept. 12–Oct.; closed end-Oct.–May; no lunch.

Landmark Restaurant. Contemporary. This modern restaurant in the Landmark Resort overlooks a golf course. On the menu: light fare, vegetarian dishes, and such specials as native whitefish or duck breast glazed with honey mustard and topped by a raspberry sauce. On Friday there are land and sea buffets and a perch fry, and on Saturday a prime-rib dinner. Sunday brunch. | 7643 Hillside Rd. | 920/868–3205 | $8–$19 | MC, V | No lunch Sun.

Shipwrecked Brewery Restaurant. Contemporary. The only microbrewery in Door County, this casual place in the center of town serves burgers, pastas, and steaks to accompany six house brews including a copper ale, a cherry wheat beer, and a porter. | 7791 Egg Harbor Rd. | 920/868–2767 | $12–$22 | AE, D, MC, V.

Trio Restaurant. Contemporary. You'll find Italian dishes such as smoked salmon and roasted red peppers with farfalle as well as classic French dishes like cassoulet and steak frites on the menu in this airy dining room with cathedral ceiling and exposed beams. | Hwy. 42 and County Hwy. E | 920/868–2090 | $10–$16 | AE, D, DC, MC, V | No lunch.

Village Café. Seafood. In the evening, this café on the northern edge of town serves only traditional fish boil. You sit outside in the garden and hear a Scandinavian tale from the fisherman who brought in the day's catch and after the pot has boiled over, dinner is served in the indoor dining room. At lunch homemade soups, burgers, and sandwiches are on offer. | 7928 Hwy. 42 | 920/868–3342 | $15 | D, MC, V | Breakfast also available; no dinner Mon., Wed., Sun.

Lodging

Alpine Resort. This resort sits on 300 acres on the Green Bay shore. Built in 1921, the lodge has original birch-bark wallpaper, as well as two large lobbies and screened porches. Restaurant, bar, picnic area. Kitchenettes (in cottages and homes), microwaves available, some refrigerators, no room phones. Pool. 27-hole golf course, putting green, tennis. Basketball, beach. Children's programs (ages 3–8), playground. Business services. Some pets allowed. | 7715 Alpine Rd. | 920/868–3000 | alpine@mail.wiscnet.net | www.alpineresort.com | 41 motel rooms, 5 suites, 20 cottages, 12 homes | $77–$101 rooms, $101 suites, $110–$162 cottages, $134–$288 homes | AE, D, MC, V | Closed late Oct.–mid-May.

Ashbrooke. This elegant white hotel with beautifully landscaped grounds is a five-minute drive from Peninsula State Park. The lobby has a fireplace, white wicker furniture, paintings, and lots of country charm. Complimentary Continental breakfast. Microwaves, refrigerators, some in-room hot tubs, cable TV. Pool. Hot tub, sauna. Gym. Business services. No kids under 14. No smoking. | 7942 Egg Harbor Rd. | 920/868–3113 | fax 920/868–2837 | www.ashbrooke.net | 36 rooms | $103–$177 | AE, MC, V.

Bay Point Inn. This two-story lodge sits high on a bluff overlooking Green Bay on the north edge of town. The small, cozy lobby has a stone fireplace. Picnic area, complimentary Continental breakfast. Kitchenettes, microwaves, in-room hot tubs, in-room TV, in-room VCRs and movies. Pool. Hot tub. Business services. | 7933 Rte. 42 | 800/707–6660 | fax 920/868–2876 | stay@baypointinn.com | www.baypointinn.com | 10 suites | $149–$189 | AE, D, DC, MC, V.

Egg Harbor Lodge. The two modern buildings of this downtown hotel on a bluff above the bay of Egg Harbor are connected by an open terrace with a fountain and seating area. Microwaves available, refrigerators, in-room hot tubs, cable TV. Pool. Hot tub. Putting green, tennis. No kids under 18. | 7965 Rte. 42 | 920/868–3115 | www.eggharborlodge.com | 24 rooms, 1 suite | $108–$149 rooms, $275 suite | AE, MC, V | Closed Nov.–Apr.

Landmark Resort. This stone and wood-sided resort on Green Bay about 2 mi from town has one-, two-, and three-bedroom modern condo units with blond cabinets in the full kitchens and your choice of a wooded or a water view. Cable TV. 4 pools. Hot tub, sauna. Tennis. Gym. | 7643 Hillside Rd. | 920/868–3205 | 294 suites | $174–$349 | D, MC, V.

Landmark Resort & Conference Center. Seventy miles north of Green Bay this luxurious four-building, 294 suite retreat nestled in the woods offers deluxe accommodations and plenty of recreational activities. Each of four buildings has the feel of a cozy lodge. Balconies with water or wooded views. Restaurant. Kitchenettes, some minibars, microwaves, refrigerators, cable TV. Indoor-outdoor pool. Hot tub, steam room. 27-hole golf course, tennis. Basketball, health club. Laundry facilities. | 7643 Hillside Rd. | 920/868–3205 or 800/273–7877 | fax 920/868–2569 | stay@thelandmarkresort.com | www.thelandmarkresort.com | 294 suites | $174–$324 | AE, DC, MC, V.

Landing. This inn has two rustic buildings surrounded by woods. The nautical prints on the walls of the lobby and in some rooms reflect the inn's name. Picnic area. Kitchenettes, microwaves, cable TV, in-room VCRs and movies. 2 pools. Hot tub. Tennis. Video games. Playground. Business services. | 7741 Egg Harbor Rd. | 920/868–3282 or 800/851–8919 | fax 920/868–2689 | landingresort@dcwis.com | www.thelandingresort.com | 60 condos | $119–$215 | D, MC, V.

Lull-Abi. This small modern motel on a wooded lot on the north end of town is built in the style of a Swiss chalet. Minibars in suites, microwaves, refrigerators. Hot tub. | 7928 Egg Harbor Rd. | 920/868–3135 | 23 rooms, 5 suites | $69–$95 rooms, $84–$95 suites | AE, D, MC, V | Closed Nov.–Apr.

Newport Resort. The large stone fireplace and forest-green sofas in the lobby and the vaulted, wood-paneled ceiling above the indoor pool lend a country-air to this large, cream-color hotel with a front veranda. Every suite has a kitchen, a fireplace, and a whirlpool. Complimentary Continental breakfast. Cable TV, in-room VCRs. Indoor-outdoor pool. Sauna. Gym. Playground. No pets. No smoking. | 7888 Church St. | 920/868–9900 | 59 suites | $120–$192 | D, MC, V.

Wildflower B&B. Surrounded by trees and wildflowers, this home, the town's only B&B, is a block from downtown or from the harbor. Each room has a private balcony and fireplace; one has a whirlpool. Complimentary breakfast. Microwave and refrigerator in common area, no room phones, cable TV. | 7821 Church St. | 920/868–9030 | 3 rooms | $120–$135 | D, MC, V.

ELKHART LAKE

MAP 11, E5

(Nearby towns also listed: Fond du Lac, Sheboygan)

Known for its good beaches, this resort community flanks the northern tip of the Kettle Moraine State Forest. It is also the home of Road America, an internationally famous motor-sports track that draws the world's top drivers for a series of prestigious races each summer. You can hunt, fish, boat, and camp in the area.

Information: Elkhart Lake Area Chamber of Commerce | Box 425, 53020-0425 | 920/876–2922 | elcoc@excel.net | www.elkhartlake.com.

Attractions

Broughton-Sheboygan County Marsh Park and Wildlife Area. This 13,000-acre area a mile northwest of town is open to hunting, fishing, and wildlife observation. A 30-acre developed park in the marsh has campgrounds, picnic areas, a restaurant, and canoe and boat rentals. | W7039 Rte. SR | 920/876–2535 | Free | Daily.

Elkhart Lake Depot Museum. This century-old railroad station, on the National Register of Historic Places, traces community history with original depot furnishings, photos, and memorabilia. | Rhine and Lake St. | 920/876–2922 | Donations accepted | Memorial Day–Labor Day, weekdays 10–6, Sat. 10–4:30.

Little Elkhart Lake. This 48-acre lake 2 mi south of town is 21 ft deep and surrounded by homes. There's a boat launch and small beach. | Rte. 67 | 920/876–2922 | Free | Daily.

Timm House. This Victorian painted lady 15 mi north of Elkhart Lake in New Holstein is furnished with original and period pieces and provides a glimpse of small-town life before the turn of the 20th century. | 1600 Wisconsin Ave., New Holstein | 920/898–5766 | $1 | Memorial Day–Labor Day, Sun. 1–4; rest of year by appointment.

Pioneer Corner Museum. This museum contains historic room displays, tools, toys, and a collection of more than 15,000 buttons. | 2103 Main St., New Holstein | $1 | Memorial Day–Labor Day, Sun. 1–4; rest of year by appointment.

Wade House & Wesley Jung Carriage Museum. Guides in 1850s attire give tours of the buildings included in this living-history museum in Greenbush. Wade House is a three-story 1850s Greek Revival stagecoach inn. The carriage museum has 100 horse-drawn vehicles and carriages and horse-drawn carriage rides are available. | W7747 Plank Rd., Greenbush | 920/526–3271 | www.shsw.wisc.edu | $7.75; special rates for children and senior citizens; carriage rides $1 | May–Oct., daily 9–5.

ON THE CALENDAR

JULY: *Texaco/Havoline 200 Champ Car Weekend.* Each year more than 100,000 spectators turn out to watch big names in open-wheel racing as they take part in a championship car shootout race at Road America, a 4-mi track, just south of town. | 920/892–4576.

AUG.: *Downtown Night.* Local restaurants serve food outside and there is live music on the square one evening in mid-month. | 920/876–2922.

Dining

Marsh Lodge. American. In a rustic log building in Broughton Sheboygan Marsh Park, this dining room is known for its home-cooked food, soup, and chile. | W7039 Rte. SR | 920/876–2535 | $5–$10 | No credit cards | Closed Mon.

Lodging

52 Stafford, An Irish Guest House. This late-19th-century building 6 mi from Elkhart Lake is on the National Register of Historic Places. All guest rooms have four-poster beds and common areas have stained-glass or leaded-glass windows, solid cherry woodwork, English wool carpeting, and brass chandeliers meant to recall small, personal Irish hostelries. Dining room, complimentary Continental breakfast, complimentary breakfast weekends. Some in-room hot tubs, cable TV. Business services. | 52 S. Stafford St., Plymouth | 920/893–0552 or 800/421–4667 | fax 920/893–1800 | www.classicinns.com | 19 rooms, 4 suites | $90–$140 | AE, D, DC, MC, V.

Osthoff Resort. This resort has 500 ft of sandy shoreline for swimming and boating. The impressive hotel has a stone fireplace and brass chandelier in the lobby and light, bright suites with large windows, kitchens, understated furnishings, and cream carpeting. Cable TV, in-room VCRs. Indoor-outdoor pool. Sauna. Tennis. Exercise equipment, volleyball, beach, boating, bicycles. | 101 Osthoff Ave. | 920/876–3366 or 800/876–3399 | 145 suites | $169–$399 | AE, D, DC, MC, V.

Victorian Village on Elkhart Lake. An authentic Victorian main building anchors this Victorian-style complex of nine buildings that offers a range of accommodations from suites to condos to town houses on the lakeshore. Restaurant, bar (with entertainment), dining room. In-room data ports, cable TV, in-room VCRs available. 2 pools. Miniature golf. Hiking, beach, dock, water sports, boating. Video games. Business services. | 279 S. Lake St. | 920/876–3323 | fax 920/876–3484 | www.vicvill.com | 70 rooms, 12 suites | $145–$325 | AE, D, MC, V.

ELKHORN

(Nearby town also listed: Delavan)

A neighboring community of Lake Geneva, Elkhorn is a good choice for a day trip. Elkhorn was settled in the early 1800s by three young land speculators who were looking for a site on which to found a village. Today Elkhorn's charming appearance and festive holiday spirit have caused it to be known as "Christmas Card Town," a reputation that has spread from coast to coast and is responsible for bringing in growing numbers of tourists each holiday season.

Information: Elkhorn Area Chamber of Commerce | Box 41, 53121-0041 | 262/723–5788 | elkchamber@elkhorn-wi.org | www.elkhorn-wi.org.

Attractions

Alpine Valley Ski Resort. This 90-acre ski resort just south of town near East Troy offers cross-country and downhill skiing and snowboarding. The vertical drop on the 12 downhill trails is 388 ft. | W2501 Rte. D | 262/642–7374 | Full day $23 weekdays, $29 weekends | Dec.–mid-Mar., daily.

Babe Mann Park. This 51-acre park surrounds Lake Elkhorn with sandy beaches great for picnics and swimming. Buy a parking permit at the police station at 404 North Washington Street. | 900 Proctor Dr. | 262/723–2219 | Season parking permit $25 | Daily.

Watson's Wild West Museum. Learn about western lore, pan for gold, and watch western movies at this museum at the north edge of town. You can also see a large collection of cowboy memorabilia, including saddles, harnesses, branding irons, western game mounts, a turn-of-the-20th-century general store, and an Old West dance hall saloon. Guided tours are available. | W4865 Potter Rd. | 262/723–7505 | $3.75; children $2.50 | June–Aug., Tues.–Sat. 10–5, Sun. 11–5; May and Sept.–Oct., Sat. 10–5, Sun. 11–5.

Webster House Museum. The restored home of Joseph Philbrick Webster, who wrote "In the Sweet Bye and Bye," includes the music room where Webster composed more than 1,000 hymns and ballads, and offers an exhibit of Civil War artifacts, a mounted game-bird collection, and a library for genealogical research. | 9 E. Rockwell St. | 262/723–4248 | $4; special rates for children, senior citizens, and groups | May–mid-Oct., Wed.–Sun. 1–5.

ON THE CALENDAR

AUG.: *Festival of Summer.* Downtown fills with a sidewalk sale, sweet corn and bratwurst stands, an arts-and-crafts fair, and, in the evenings, a street dance and beer tent the first weekend of the month. | 262/723–5788.
SEPT.: *Walworth County Fair.* This Labor Day weekend county fair is one of the largest in the Midwest and attracts thousands of people to the 90-acre fairgrounds. Attractions includes a carnival, a horse pull, tractor and truck pulls, horse shows, arts, crafts, food, harness racing, and entertainment. | 262/723–3228.

Dining

Sperino's Little Italy. Italian. There are wine bottles suspended from the ceiling and murals of Italian landscapes on the walls. The menu features Sicilian steak, pizzas, and tiramisu. | 720 N. Wisconsin St. | 262/723–2222 | $9–$18 | AE, D, DC, MC, V | Closed Mon. No lunch.

ELLISON BAY

MAP 11, F3

(Nearby towns also listed: Baileys Harbor, Egg Harbor, Ephraim)

This town on the Door County peninsula, founded in 1866, is home to bluffs, boats, and raw beauty. A nearby county park offers a breathtaking view of the water from the crest of a 200-ft-high escarpment, and quaint shops are filled with locally made pottery and other works of art. Activities include fishing and boating and some scuba diving.

Information: **Door County Chamber of Commerce** | 1015 Green Bay Rd., Sturgeon Bay 54235-0406 | 800/527–3529 | door@mail.wiscnet.net | www.doorcountyvacations.com.

Attractions

Death's Door Bluff. This bluff is at the very tip of the Door County peninsula, where numerous ships sank many years ago. | 800/527–3529 | Free | Daily.

Door County Maritime Museum. Commercial fishing, shipwrecks, and navigation are the focus of this museum 5 mi north of Ellison Bay. You'll see models, marine engines, photos, a 1917 Berylume pleasure craft, and a 1930s fishing tug. | 12724 Rte. 42, Gills Rock | 920/743–5958 | www.dcmm.org | $2; special rates for children | Daily 10–5.

Island Clipper/Viking Tour Train. You can take a 25-minute boat ride to Washington Island then ride the *Viking Tour Train,* a tram, for 90 minutes around the island. | 12731 Rte. 42, Gills Rock | 920/854–2972 | $14; special rates for children | Memorial Day–mid-Oct., daily 10–3.

Newport State Park. This 2,370-acre wild area with 11 mi of Lake Michigan shoreline is northeast of town, here you can hike, swim, fish, mountain bike, camp, cross-country ski, and snowshoe. | 475 Cty. Rte. NP | 920/854–2500 | www.dnr.state.wi.us | $7 nonresidents, $5 residents | Daily.

Washington Island Ferry Line. These ferries carry people, cars, and bikes to and from the island year-round in approximately 30 minutes. Washington Island's dock is full of shops in summer, and you can get a tour of the island here. On the mainland, catch the ferry at the Northport Pier at the end of Route 42. | 800/223–2094 or 920/847–2546 | fax 920/847–2807 | www.wisferry.com | $3.75 1-way; special rates for children; additional charges for cars, motorcycles, and bicycles | Daily.

ON THE CALENDAR

JUNE: *Old Ellison Bay Days.* This late-month community celebration downtown features food, a talent show, an ice-cream social, a soap-box derby, a parade, an art fair, and music. | 920/854–5786.

AUG.: *Perseid Meteor Shower.* You can watch a dazzling once-a-year meteor shower in mid-month—sometimes there are 50 meteors an hour—at Peninsula State Park, the darkest park on the peninsula. | 920/854–2500.

Dining

Grandma's Swedish. Scandinavian. This old inn with a water view 4 mi from Ellison Bay is known for its buffet and its fish boils, but there's also a small menu. Don't miss the pecan rolls baked on site. Salad bar. No smoking. | 1041 Rte. ZZ, Rowleys Bay | 920/854–2385 ext.

831 | Reservations not accepted for groups less than 10 | $14–$18 | D, MC, V | Closed Mon. and Thurs. Labor Day–Memorial Day.

Shoreline Restaurant. Continental. You can watch the sun set over the water from this restaurant in the Shoreline Resort. Nightly specials like crab-stuffed pasta shells are the stars of the menu. | 12747 Hwy. 42 | 920/854–2950 | $11–$16 | D, MC, V | Closed Nov.–Apr.

T Ashwell. Contemporary. A beach-stone fireplace dominates the dining room and there is a baby grand piano at the wine bar of this sophisticated spot where the menu changes frequently. Dishes have included sautéed duck layered with foie gras and a cherry and cranberry reduction. You can also choose to dine on the heated porch. Sunday brunch. | 11976 Mink River Rd. | 920/854–4306 | $17–$22 | AE, D, DC, MC, V | Closed Tues. No lunch.

Viking. American. Fish boils served at tables in a garden out back are the main attraction at this casual downtown restaurant. Kids' menu. Wine and beer. | 12029 Rte. 42 | 920/854–2998 | $9–$16 | AE, D, MC, V | Breakfast also available.

Lodging

Harbor House. This hotel's main building is a turn-of-the-20th-century mansion with a lake view, beach access, a charming porch with lattice work, and many period furnishings. A new Scandinavian Country wing overlooks the town's quaint fishing harbor and bluffs, and is perfect for sunset views. The Lighthouse Suite, in a newly constructed 35-ft lighthouse, is a two-room suite with a fireplace and a hot tub. Picnic area, complimentary Continental breakfast. Microwaves available, refrigerators, no room phones. Hot tub, sauna. Playground. Some pets allowed. No smoking. | 12666 Rte. 42 | 920/854–5196 | fax 920/854–9717 | www.door-county-inn.com | 7 rooms, 6 suites, 2 cottages | $60–$150 | AE, MC, V.

Hotel Disgarden Bed and Breakfast. This venerable hostelry established in 1902 has waterfront access and lots of country charm. Complimentary full breakfast. Some kitchenettes, refrigerators, in-room VCRs. Boating, bicycles. No smoking. | 12013 Rte. 42 | 920/854–9888 or 877/378–3218 | fax 920–854–5923 | hoteldisgarden@dcwis.com | www.dcwis.com/hoteldisgarden | 7 suites | $75–$120 | MC, V.

FISH BOILS AND FISH FRIES

No visit to Wisconsin would be complete without a Door County fish boil, or a Friday-night fish fry.

Fish boils came from Scandinavian settlers and lumberjacks who discovered this tasty way to enjoy local fish. Today, fish boils in the Door County Peninsula are as much fun to watch as they are to eat. The boils start with freshly caught whitefish steaks plunged into huge pots of salted water with onions and potatoes and boiled to perfection over an open fire. At completion, the chef completes the ritual with the "boil over," in which the flames are extinguished by overflowing water. Great fish boils can be found at many of the restaurants in the towns that dot the Door County Peninsula.

Friday-night fish fries are common at many Wisconsin restaurants. From small-town eateries to large big-city restaurants, servers shuttle huge trays of fish to hungry patrons. Some restaurants offer baked and broiled as well as fried fish, and choices may include perch, cod, northern, walleye, and catfish. Larger, more upscale establishments usually include fancy garnishes and side dishes with the fish while smaller establishments like corner taverns generally serve the fish with a dab of coleslaw.

© Corbis

Norrland Resort. You are free to take a canoe or rowboat out into the harbor to fish or just to putter around at this simply styled downtown resort on the water across the street from a supper club and a half block from the general store. The small beach has a fire pit and a shuffleboard. Cable TV. Beach, boating, fishing. | 12009 Hwy. 42 | 920/854–4875 | 6 rooms, 12 cottages | $65–$75 rooms, cottages $465–$825/week | MC, V.

Parkside Motel. This cream-color downtown motel across from the beach is separated from the road by a wide lawn sprinkled with trees. Simply furnished rooms have large windows with wooded views. Complimentary Continental breakfast. Microwaves, refrigerators, cable TV. | 11946 Hwy. 42 | 800/497–5221 | 15 rooms | $85 | D, MC, V.

Shoreline Resort. This white-frame waterfront motel, the northernmost resort on the Door County peninsula, is directly on Green Bay and has woods behind it. Tours to Washington Island depart next door. Picnic area. Microwaves, refrigerators. Dock. Business services. No smoking. | 12747 Rte. 42, Gills Rock | 920/854–2606 | fax 920/854–5971 | front@theshorelineresort.com | www.theshorelineresort.com | 16 rooms | $89–$104 | MC, V | Closed late Nov.–Apr.

Wagon Trail Resort, Restaurant, and Conference Center. This rustic resort with a large stone fireplace in the lodge is set on 100 wooded acres on the shore of Rowleys Bay. In winter cross-country ski trails cut through 30 acres of the resort's woods. There's also a game room with ping-pong and a pool table. Restaurant, picnic area. Kitchenettes (in suites, cottages, and homes), microwaves available, some refrigerators, in-room hot tubs. Pool. Hot tub, sauna. Tennis. Beach, boating, bicycles. Cross-country skiing. Children's programs (ages 2–9), playground. Laundry facilities. Business services. | 1041 Rte. ZZ | 920/854–2385 or 800/999–2466 | fax 920/854–5278 | frontdesk@wagontrail.com | www.wagontrail.com | 80 rooms in lodge, 8 suites, 10 cottages, 30 homes | $119–$335 | D, MC, V.

EPHRAIM

MAP 11, F3

(Nearby towns also listed: Baileys Harbor, Egg Harbor, Ellison Bay, Fish Creek)

Norwegian Moravian settlers founded the town in 1853 and named it Ephraim, after a biblical term that means "fruitful." Today's villagers have preserved a good deal of its history. Many buildings still reflect the hallmark Moravian tradition of elegantly simple architecture. Exhibits at a nearby barn museum give you a glimpse into the village's past. Villagers have also chosen to make their town dry, so if you stay here and want a drink with your dinner, you'll have to drive to nearby Ellison Bay, Sister Bay, or Fish Creek.

Information: Door County Chamber of Commerce | 1015 Green Bay Rd., Sturgeon Bay 54235-0406 | 800/527–3529 | door@mail.wiscnet.net | www.doorcountyvacations.com.

Attractions
City Farmer. This store has the area's most unusual fresh flowers, silk flowers, and antiques. | 10432 Rte. 42 | 920/854–7501 | Free | Daily.

ON THE CALENDAR
JUNE: *Fyr-Bal Fest.* This Scandinavian festival celebrates the beginning of summer with music, dance, crafts, food, a fish boil, beach bonfires, and a sailing regatta. | 920/854–4989.
JULY: *Children's Day.* The Ephraim Foundation sponsors this children's cultural event annually, with music making, art and crafts, cooking, and other forms of cultural expression organized around a different theme each year. | 920/854–9688.

Dining

Old Post Office Restaurant. American. Built at the turn of the 20th century as a post office, this home-style restaurant overlooks Eagle Harbor and many tables have views of the water. Barbecued ribs, chicken, and fish boil are on the dinner menu. Breakfast includes muffins, pancakes, and Belgian waffles all made with Door County cherries. Kids' menu. | 10040 Water St. | 920/854–4034 | $16 prix fixe | No credit cards | Closed Nov.–Apr. No lunch.

Second Story Restaurant. Contemporary. This casual harborside restaurant in the Ephraim Shores Motel has great water views. Chicken marsala, broiled whitefish, and other seafood dishes share the menu with sandwiches. | 10018 Hwy. 42 | 920/854–2371 | $8–$13 | MC, V | Breakfast also available.

Singing Bowl. American. This popular deli serves espresso drinks and smoothies, but is noted for healthful foods including many vegetarian specialties. Thai sesame noodles and pasta *della noce* (a bow-tie pasta with raisins, walnuts, and cheese) are just two. Lots of windows make this casual dining spot bright and cheery. Take Highway 42 to the north end of town. | 10450 Townline Rd., 54211 | 920/854–7376 | Reservations not accepted | $5–$10 | MC, V | Closed Tues. and Wed. Nov. 1–May 1.

Summer Kitchen Restaurant. Contemporary. This friendly local favorite on the north side of town is known for its homemade-soup bar, with selections that change daily, like French cabbage, tomato dill, and chicken dumpling. Beef tenderloin and pork chops are on the dinner menu. | 10425 Water St. | 920/854–2131 | $11–$15 | MC, V | Breakfast also available.

Wilsons Restaurant. American/Casual. Across the street from the water, you can sit outside at this ice-cream and burger joint with a red and white awning. It's famous for great milk shakes. | 9990 Water St. | 920/854–2041 | $4–$6 | MC, V.

Lodging

Bay Breeze Resort. The rooms in this sharp, white, two-story building overlooking Eagle Harbor have floral wallpaper borders, beds with simple light-wood headboards, whirlpool tubs, and water views. Air-conditioning, microwaves, refrigerators, cable TV. Pool. Hot tub. Beach. | 9844 Water St. | 920/854–9066 | 24 rooms | $104–$152 | D, MC, V.

Eagle Harbor Inn. The antiques-filled rooms and suites of this downtown hotel are spread across eight buildings on a 5-acre, parklike property a block from the beach. Picnic area, complimentary breakfast. In-room data ports, microwaves in suites, in-room hot tubs in suites, cable TV, in-room VCRs. Pool. Sauna. Gym. Playground. Business services. | 9914 Water St. | 920/854–2121 or 800/324–5427 | fax 920/854–2121 | nedd@eagleharbor.com | www.eagleharbor.com | 9 rooms, 32 suites | $175–$208 | D, MC, V.

Edgewater Inn. Built across from a beach on Green Bay in the early 1900s, this hotel has easy water access and water views from all rooms. Restaurant. Refrigerators, cable TV. Pool. | 10040 Rte. 42 | 920/854–2734 | fax 920/854–4127 | 26 rooms | $125–$245 | D, MC, V.

Ephraim Guest House. This stained-gray cedar inn with a small and simple lobby is a block from the bay on a little hillside with gardens in the rear. Some rooms have fireplaces and water views. Picnic area. Kitchenettes, some in-room hot tubs, cable TV, in-room VCRs. Laundry facilities. | 3042 Cedar St. | 920/854–2319 or 800/589–8423 | ephraimguesthouse@mail.doorcounty-wi.com | www.ephraimguesthouse.com | 16 suites | $150–$205 | AE, D, MC, V.

Ephraim Inn. This fine country home is just across the street from a beach. It has a large porch, a fireplace in the lobby, and some guest rooms with harbor views. Complimentary breakfast. Cable TV. No kids under 17. | 9994 Pioneer La. | 920/854–4515 or 800/622–2193 | fax 920/854–1859 | ephraiminn@aol.com | www.theephraiminn.com | 16 rooms | $95–$175 | AE, D, MC, V | Closed Mon.–Thurs. Nov.–Apr.

Ephraim Motel. This western-style wood motel on the outskirts of town has a large stone fireplace in the lobby, where breakfast is served. Complimentary Continental breakfast.

Microwaves, refrigerators, cable TV, in-room VCRs. Pool. | 10407 Rte. 42 N | 920/854–5959 or 800/451–5995 | frontdesk@ephraimmotel.com | www.ephraimmotel.com | 28 rooms | $70–$95 | MC, V | Closed Nov.–late Apr.

Ephraim Shores Motel and Restaurant. Beautiful sunsets are a daily treat at this downtown motel on Green Bay with a view of Eagle Harbor. You can walk the 100 yards through the peaceful garden to the beach. Some of the rooms have private decks and patios. Restaurant. Some microwaves, refrigerators, some in-room hot tubs, cable TV. Pool. Hot tub. Gym, beach, bicycles. Playground. Business services. No smoking. | 10018 Water St. | 920/854–2371 | fax 920/854–4926 | reservations@ephraimshores.com | www.ephraimshores.com | 46 rooms, 2 suites | $90–$210 | MC, V | Closed end Oct.–Apr.

Evergreen Beach. This quaint, old-fashioned turn-of-the-20th-century resort near the center of town has a private sand beach and a sundeck. All rooms face the water. Complimentary Continental breakfast. Microwaves, refrigerators, cable TV. Pool. Beach. Playground. Business services. No smoking. | Rte. 42 and German Rd. | 920/854–2831 or 800/420–8130 | fax 920/854–9222 | www.evergreenbeach.com | 30 rooms | $108–$122 | AE, D, MC, V | Closed end Oct.–mid-May.

French Country Inn. Built in 1911 as a summer home, this two-story, Prairie-style house is near the bay and the center of town. One of its common rooms has a wood-burning fireplace and outside the house is surrounded by an acre of gardens. Complimentary Continental breakfast. No air-conditioning, kitchenette in cottage. No kids under 13 in main building. No smoking. | 3052 Spruce La. | 920/854–4001 | fax 920/854–4001 | 7 rooms (5 with shared bath), 1 cottage | $65–$92 rooms, $530–$620 cottage (7–day minimum stay mid–June–late Aug.) | No credit cards.

Harbor View Resort. One and a half blocks uphill from downtown, the one- and two-bedroom suites overlook Eagle Harbor and have some of the most spectacular views in Door County. Cottages are in a wooded area. Weekly rentals only in summer. Kitchenettes, cable TV. | 9971 S. Dane St. | 920/854–2425 | 10 suites, 4 cottages | $1,000–$1,035 suites, $600–$815 cottages | D, MC, V.

High Point Inn. This impressive inn with bright red, gabled roof and tall windows houses one-, two-, and three-bedroom country-style condos with wing-back armchairs, oak cabinets, fireplaces, and whirlpool tubs. Microwaves, refrigerators, cable TV, in-room VCRs. Pool. Hot tub. Gym. Playground. Laundry facilities. Business services. No smoking. | 10386 Water St. | 800/595–6894 | 41 condos | $156–$248 | D, MC, V.

Hillside Hotel. This mid-19th-century downtown Victorian guest house is on the National Register of Historic Places and still has its original furnishings. A 100-ft veranda with rocking chairs gives a spectacular view of its private beach. Two cottages have hot tubs, fireplaces, kitchens, and front porches with old-fashioned swings. Complimentary breakfast. No air-conditioning in guest house, kitchenettes in cottages, no room phones, cable TV in common room. Business services. No smoking. | 9980 Rte. 42 | 920/854–2417 or 800/423–7023 | www.door-county-hotel.com | 11 rooms (4 with shared bath), 2 cottages | $94–$99 rooms, $175–$195 cottages | D, MC, V.

Lodgings at Pioneer Lane. Three themed rooms, each with a fireplace, whirlpool tub, and water view, capture the air of a Northwoods cabin, a cozy cottage, and a Swedish summer villa in this downtown home. Refrigerators, cable TV. | 9998 Pioneer La. | 920/854–7656, or 800/588–3565 | 3 rooms | $125–$175 | MC, V.

Pine Grove Motel. This downtown motel has angled balconies that provide water views. There's a game room with a pool table and darts. Refrigerators, some in-room hot tubs, cable TV. Pool. Hot tub. Gym. Laundry facilities. Business services. | 10080 Water St. | 920/854–2321 or 800/292–9494 | fax 920/854–2511 | 42 rooms | $85–$103 | D, MC, V | Closed Nov.–Apr.

Somerset Inn and Suites. This colonial-style building in a secluded wooded area has a white picket fence and flowers in front and a large stone fireplace is in the lobby. Ephraim Beach is 1 and ½ mi away. Picnic area. Microwaves, refrigerators, some in-room hot tubs, cable

TV. Two pools. Hot tubs. No smoking. | 10401 N. Water St. | 920/854–1819 or 800/809–1819 | fax 920/854–9087 | somersetinn@mail.doorcounty-wi.com | www.doorcountylodging.com/somerset.html | 20 rooms, 18 suites | $69–$99 rooms, $129–$139 suites | D, MC, V.

Trollhaugen Lodge. Each room in this charming European-style guest house is uniquely decorated; most have lovely views of the forest. Picnic area, complimentary Continental breakfast. Some microwaves, refrigerators, cable TV, in-room VCRs available. Outdoor hot tub. | 10176 Rte. 42 | 920/854–2713 or 800/854–4118 | trollhaugen@dcwis.com. | www.trollhaugenlodge.com | 8 rooms, 1 cabin, 1 lodge with 5 B&B rooms (showers only) | $49–$125 rooms, $149 log cabin | D, MC, V | Closed Nov.–mid-Apr.

Village Green Lodge. Afternoon tea is served at this homey motel with plaid sofas, wood paneling, and pine furniture in the rooms, and a stone fireplace and lanterns in the lobby. Complimentary breakfast. Refrigerators, cable TV. Pool. No smoking. | Box 21 Cedar St. | 920/854–2515 | 15 rooms, 2 suites | $97 rooms, $155 suites | D, MC, V.

FISH CREEK

MAP 11, F3

(Nearby towns also listed: Baileys Harbor, Egg Harbor, Ephraim)

Fish Creek's harbor is one of Door County's most popular jumping-off points for those traveling up and down the bay side of the peninsula by water. Within Fish Creek is the entrance to Peninsula State Park, where there are great views and the opportunity to hike, bike, camp, or just relax on the beach. Fish Creek is also the heart of the county's artistic life; here you'll find Peninsula Players (the country's oldest professional summer theater), as well as a music festival and a folklore theater. There are lots of quaint shops, galleries, and restaurants on the main street.

Information: **Fish Creek Civic Association** | Box 74, 54212-0074 | 800/577–1880 | www.doorcounty-wi.com/fishcreek.html.

Attractions

Edgewood Orchard Galleries. This restored stone fruit barn has been displaying the work of county artists in all mediums since 1969. | 4140 Peninsula Players Rd. | 920/868–3579 | Free | Mid-May–Oct., daily 10–5.

Peninsula State Park. This 3,762-acre peninsula on Green Bay waters has an 18-hole championship golf course, hiking, bicycle trails, camping, groomed ski trails, snowmobiling, sledding, swimming, boat rentals, a boat ramp, an observation tower, a summer theater, and fishing. See the 125-year-old Eagle Bluff lighthouse and enjoy more than 6 mi of shoreline. | 9462 Shore Rd. | 920/868–3258 | www.dnr.state.wi.us | $7 nonresidents, $5 residents | Daily 6 AM–11 PM.

ON THE CALENDAR

JUNE–SEPT.: *American Folklore Theatre.* Four original musical comedies are presented in the Peninsula State Park Amphitheater. | 920/868–9999.
JUNE–OCT.: *Peninsula Players.* America's oldest professional resident summer theater group offers performances in an outdoor pavilion 3 mi south of town. | 920/868–3287.
AUG.: *Peninsula Music Festival.* Musicians from orchestras from across the country come together for three weeks and 10 concerts of great classical works, such as the Tchaikovsky symphonies. | Door County Community Auditorium | 920/854–4060.

Dining

Bayside Tavern. American/Casual. By day, this spot serves basic pub food like burgers and soups; by night it's a hopping club showcasing local bands of all kinds. | 4160 Main St. | 920/868–3441 | $5–$10 | AE, MC, V.

C and C Supper Club. Continental. This downtown restaurant with two large dining rooms, a fireplace, and linen tablecloths is known for baby-back ribs and broiled local whitefish served with veggies and potatoes. There's a Monday-night taco special and brunch on weekends from Memorial Day to Labor Day. Salad bar. Entertainment Wednesday–Saturday Memorial Day–Labor Day. Kids' menu. Sunday brunch. | Corner of Spruce and Main Sts. | 920/868–3412 | $12–$17 | D, DC, MC, V | No lunch.

Carlos' Banditos. Eclectic. Mexico meets Italy in this casual spot. The menu offers tacos, lasagna, and fajitas, and margaritas come by the liter. Don't miss the whitefish burritos. Kids' menu. | 3931 Rte. 42 | 920/868–2255 | $10–$15 | AE, D, DC, MC, V.

Cookery. American. This family-style restaurant on Fish Creek's main street is surrounded by quaint shops. Large bay windows provide a view of the beach. Try the whitefish chowder, homemade jams, jellies, applesauce, and fruit pies. Kids' menu. Wine and beer. No smoking. | 920/868–3634 | Reservations not accepted | $10–$12 | MC, V | Closed weekdays Nov.–Apr.

Kortes' English Inn. Continental. This inn on a wooded property a mile north of town has lots of charm, with its beamed ceilings and walls full of work by local artists. The inn is noted for its Friday seafood buffet, its specialty coffees, and an extensive dessert list. Kids' menu. | 3713 Rte. 42 | 920/868–3076 | $16–$26 | DC, MC, V | Closed Nov.–Apr. No lunch.

Pelletier's Restaurant. American. This white-sided house with a large patio downtown is famous for its fish boil. Soups and sandwiches are served at lunch and the homemade waffles are great for breakfast. | Founder's Sq. | 920/868–3313 | $12 | No credit cards | Closed Nov.–Apr.

Summertime. Contemporary. This Prairie-style building looks almost Asian with its curved roofs. Inside, things are casual by day, and more dressed up after dark. The menu offers South African BBQ ribs, prime rib, pasta, and fresh fish. Open-air dining overlooking the water. | 1 N. Spruce St. | 920/868–3738 | fax 920/868–2683 | $15–$30 | AE, MC, V.

White Gull Inn. Contemporary. The antiques-filled dining room at this downtown inn built in 1896 is elegant yet cozy. You can order the Door County fish boil or sample the raspberry chicken almondine, almond-encrusted chicken breast drizzled with raspberry sauce. Kids' menu. Wine and beer. | 4225 Main St. | 920/868–3517 | fax 920/868–2367 | $19–$24 | AE, D, DC, MC, V.

Lodging

Applecreek Resort. This stone- and white-sided 1990s building is only a block from Peninsula State Park. Rooms range from very simple to more generously appointed semi-suites. Some kitchenettes, cable TV. Pool. Hot tub. | Hwy. 42 and County F | 920/868–3525 | 35 rooms, 1 guest house | $69–$139 rooms, $225 guest house | D, MC, V.

Beowulf Lodge. Surrounded by woods, this hotel lies in the heart of Door County. Nearby are bike, ski and snowmobile rentals and access to biking, cross-country skiing and snowmobiling trails. Picnic area. Many kitchenettes, cable TV, in-room VCRs available. Pool. Hot tub. Tennis. Laundry facilities. Business services. | 3775 Rte. 42 | 920/868–2046 or 800/433–7592 | fax 920/868–2381 | beowulflodge@mail.doorcounty-wi.com | www.beowulflodge.com | 51 rooms, 9 suites | $120–$135 | D, MC, V.

By-the-Bay. This downtown hotel is just across the street from a public beach. Cable TV. No smoking. | 4123 Rte. 42 | 920/868–3456 | bythebay@dcwis.com | 15 rooms, 1 suite | $92–$125 | D, MC, V | Closed Nov.–Apr.

Cedar Court Inn. One of Door County's oldest resorts, this charmer has several porches, landscaped grounds, and a white picket fence. Inside, it looks like an elegant farm home. Picnic area. Kitchenettes in cottages, microwaves available, refrigerators, some in-room hot tubs, cable TV, in-room VCRs available. Pool. Business services. No smoking. | 9429 Cedar St. | 920/868–3361 | fax 920/868–2541 | cedarct@dcwis.com | www.cedarcourt.com | 14 rooms, 9 cottages | $79–$158 rooms, $138–$250 cottages | MC, V.

Fish Creek Motel. A wide lawn and a few trees surround this downtown motel which is just across from the harbor. Rooms have either wooded or water views, and you can borrow bicycles for free. Cable TV. | 9479 Spruce St. | 920/868–3448 | 30 rooms | $78–$88 | MC, V.

Harbor Guest House. Originally the guest quarters for a large estate, this old-fashioned homey stone inn is on Fish Creek Harbor with a view of Green Bay. Boat slips are available. Kitchenettes, microwaves, cable TV. No smoking. | 9484 Spruce St. | 920/868–2284 | fax 920/868–1535 | www.harborguesthouse.com | 6 suites | $165–$225 (3–night minimum stay) | AE, MC, V.

Hilltop Inn. Mauve and deep-blue furnishings, fireplaces, and whirlpool tubs in all suites make this hotel on a hill on the north end of town especially cozy. Cable TV, in-room VCRs. Pool. Hot tub. Laundry facilities. | 3908 Hwy. F | 920/868–3448 | 19 suites | $179–$189 | D, MC, V.

Homestead. A stone fireplace sets the tone in the lobby of this modern hotel next to Peninsula State Park. Complimentary Continental breakfast. In-room data ports, microwaves in suites, refrigerators, cable TV, in-room VCRs and movies available. Pool. Hot tub, sauna. Gym. Business services. | 4006 Main St. | 920/868–3748 or 800/686–6621 | fax 920/868–2874 | www.homesteadsuites.com | 12 rooms, 37 suites | $129–$184 | D, MC, V.

Juniper Inn. This updated Gothic-style Victorian with a fireplace in the dining room is set back from the road on a high ridge with a view of cedar and tamarack forest. A golf course and Peninsula State Park are ¾ mi away. Dining room, complimentary Continental breakfast. Some in-room hot tubs, in-room VCRs. No smoking. | N9432 Maple Grove Rd. | 920/839–2629 or 800/218–6960 | fax 920/839–2095 | juniperinn@itol.com | www.juniperinn.com | 4 rooms | $75–$180 | MC, V.

Main Street Motel. This mom-and-pop motel is downtown between the famous fish boils, White Gull Inn and Pelletier's. There are three themed rooms—the birdhouse, the teddy bear, and the lighthouse room. Cable TV. | 4209 Main St. | 920/868–2201 | 29 rooms | $81–$92 | D, MC, V.

Settlement Courtyard Inn. This white stucco-and-stone hotel with country-French interior design sits on 240 acres of wooded property with hiking and cross-country skiing trails 1 mi south of Fish Creek. Complimentary Continental breakfast. Kitchenettes, some microwaves, cable TV, in-room VCRs available. Hiking. Cross-country skiing. Business services. | 9126 Rte. 42 | 920/868–3524 | fax 920/868–3048 | settlementinn@dcwis.com | www.dcty.com/settlement | 32 rooms | $64–$106 | AE, D, MC, V.

Thorp House Inn, Cottages, and Beach House. A turn-of-the-20th-century Victorian home with a library and many antiques is the center of this complex which overlooks the harbor from atop a hill. Picnic area. Complimentary Continental breakfast for rooms. No air-conditioning in cottages, kitchenettes (in suites and cottages), microwaves available, some in-room hot tubs, cable TV, in-room VCRs. Bicycles. No kids in main building. No smoking in main building. | 4135 Bluff Rd. | 920/868–2444 | fax 920/868–9833 | www.thorphouse-inn.com | 6 rooms, 3 suites, 6 cottages | $95–$185 rooms, $165–$185 suites, $95–$145 cottages | No credit cards.

Whistling Swan Inn. Built in 1887, this is the oldest Door County inn on the National and State Register of Historic Places. Rooms are filled with antiques and the large porch has a great view of the village of Fish Creek. Complimentary breakfast. Cable TV. Business services. No smoking. | 4192 Main St. | 920/868–3442 | fax 920/868–1703 | www.whistlingswan.com | 5 rooms, 2 suites | $104–$147 | AE, D, MC, V.

White Gull Inn. There are antiques throughout this 1896 village inn and all rooms have Victorian wallpaper and pencil-poster canopy beds. Cottages have fireplaces, porches, and painted iron beds or sleigh beds. Restaurant (*see* White Gull Inn). Cable TV, in-room VCRs and movies in cottages. Business services, airport shuttle. No kids in main lodge. | 4225 Main St. | 920/868–3517 | fax 920/868–2367 | innkeeper@whitegullinn.com | www.whitegullinn.com | 13 rooms, 4 cottages | $107–$250 rooms, $217–$265 cottages | AE, D, DC, MC, V.

FOND DU LAC

MAP 11, E5

(Nearby towns also listed: Oshkosh, Sheboygan)

Settled in 1835, Fond du Lac, which is French for "bottom of the lake," is a fairly large city located at the base of Lake Winnebago. Attractions are plentiful and diverse, such as a historic lighthouse and an antique carousel in 400-acre Lakeside Park, and a collection of German wood carvings in a downtown cathedral. Fond du Lac is a good starting point for day trips to a wide variety of nearby towns and attractions. Manufacturing forms much of the city's current economic base including the production of marine motors, machine tools, and food products.

Information: **Fond du Lac Convention and Visitors Bureau** | 19 W. Scott St., 54935-2342 | 800/937–9123 | visit@fdl.com | www.fdl.com.

Attractions

1856 Historic Octagon House. Furnished with period pieces, this restored 12-room, Civil War–era private home on the State Register of Historic Places was originally built as a fort and later used as part of the Underground Railroad. The house contains nine passageways, a secret room, and an underground tunnel, and is rumored to be haunted. | 276 Linden St. | 920/922–1608 | $8; special rates for children | Memorial Day–Labor Day, Mon., Wed., Fri. 1–4; rest of year by appointment only.

Galloway House and Village. The 30-room Galloway House, a stately Victorian, is the centerpiece of a village of 23 turn-of-the-20th-century buildings, including the Blakely Museum, the Adams House Resource Center, a photographer's shop, a country store, and other buildings depicting life in early times. Guided tours are available. | 336 Old Pioneer Rd. | 920/922–3690 | $6.50; special rates for children | Memorial Day–Labor Day, daily 10–5.

Kettle Moraine State Forest, Northern Unit. The imprint of the immense ice sheet that covered the upper Midwest some 20,000 years ago can be seen all around this forest. Two fingerlike lobes of the glaciers met here, along a northeast–to–southwest line. At their junction, billions of tons of sand, gravel, and rock were deposited as the ice slowly melted away 10,000 years ago. The glaciers' massive size and impact is seen from the dimension of the kames, the ridges or mounds of stratified drift deposited by the glaciers. Within the forest the largest kames rise more than 350 ft above the surrounding land. The forest's 28,000-acre Northern Unit has picnic and recreation areas, campgrounds, fishing, boating, and trails to hike, cross-county ski, and snowmobile. | N1765 Rte. G | 262/626–2116 | www.dnr.state.wi.us | $7 nonresidents, $5 residents; permits required for some recreational trails | Daily.

Films and exhibits at the **Henry Reuss Ice Age Visitor Center** 20 mi south of Fond du Lac and 15 mi north of West Bend explain how the glacier shaped this part of the state thousands of years ago. The veranda gives a view of the glacial landscape. | U.S. 45 | 920/533–8322 | Free | Weekdays 8:30–4, weekends 9:30–5.

Lake Winnebago. This is the largest inland lake in Wisconsin and the third-largest inland lake in the nation. Boat launches. | Access from U.S. 41, U.S. 151, Rte. 75, U.S. 45, and Rte. 23 | 800/937–9123 | Free | Daily.

Lakeside Park. This park on Lake Winnebago has a lighthouse, a minitrain, bumper boats, canoe rentals, a playground, and a white-tail deer exhibit. | Main St. | 920/929–2950 | www.fdl.com | Free | Daily; lighthouse mid-Apr.–mid-Oct.

Lamara Springs Llama Farm. Walk through llama pastures to see the animals close up and learn all about them and their many uses at this farm 6 mi south of Fond du Lac. Guided tours available. | W6158 Church Rd. | 920/923–0581 | $3; special rates for children | By appointment.

Ledge View Nature Center. Here, 25 mi north of Fond du Lac in Chilton, you'll find more than 100 acres, three natural solution caves open to the public, cave tours led by naturalists, maple-syrup making in season, a 60-ft observation tower, live animals, dioramas, and, in winter, groomed cross-country ski trails and snowshoes for rent. | W2348 Short Rd., Chilton | 920/849–7094 | Free; tours of cave $3; Spelunking $5; charges for some programs | Daily.

St. Paul's Cathedral. Contains a collection of nearly 40 German wood carvings, as well as carvings, murals, and stained glass by American artists. | 51 W. Division St. | 920/921–3363 | Free; guided tours $2 | Daily.

Silver Wheel Manor. Once a private home, this museum contains numerous antiques, including 2,000 dolls, model trains, and vintage costumes. | N6221 Rte. K | 920/922–1608 | $8; special rates for children | Mon., Wed., Fri.–Sat. by appointment.

ON THE CALENDAR

JUNE: *Walleye Weekend Festival and Mercury Marine National Walleye Tournament.* The world's largest fish fry takes place in Lakeside Park on the second full weekend of the month, along with outdoor music, a variety of family entertainment, tournaments, and more foods. | 800/937–9123.

Dining

Pier 15. American. You can grill your own steak on the open grill in the dining room of this downtown restaurant. There is also a variety of seafood dishes to accompany the 13 boats in the building, some over 70 years old, many suspended from the ceiling. | 15 W. Division St. | 920/921–2200 | $8–$21 | AE, D, MC, V | No lunch Sat., Sun.

Salty's Seafood and Spirits. Seafood. Mounted fish on the walls, fishnets filled with crabs and starfish, and large fish tanks set the tone at this restaurant on one of Fond du Lac's main streets. Try the deep-fried breaded haddock served with sautéed vegetables. Salad bar. | 503 N. Park Ave. | 920/922–9940 | Reservations not accepted | $13–$26 | AE, D, MC, V.

Schreiner's. American. Home-style cooking is the order of the day in this large restaurant that's been in business since 1938. Try the New England clam chowder—it has been a favorite here for 50 years and locals often buy it frozen to take home. The favorite treat at the bakery is a pecan roll. Kids' menu. | 168 N. Pioneer Rd. | 920/922–0590 | Reservations not accepted | $8–$13 | AE, D, MC, V.

Lodging

Days Inn. This simple, two-story motel 3 mi from downtown in a commercial area has a TV room in addition to its lobby. Complimentary Continental breakfast. In-room data ports, cable TV. Video games. Business services. Pets allowed. | 107 N. Pioneer Rd. | 920/923–6790 | fax 920/923–6790 | 59 rooms | $52–$75 | AE, D, DC, MC, V.

Dixon House. You can stroll on well-maintained trails through 80 acres of grounds or down to the river on this old farm. The century-old farmhouse has Victorian-style cozy rooms. Complimentary breakfast. Cable TV. Laundry facilities. No smoking. | W7190 Forest Ave. | 920/923–3340 | 2 rooms | $59–$75 | No credit cards.

Holiday Inn. This homey, antiques-decorated motel is 3 mi from downtown and just across the street from a golf course. There's live entertainment in the bar on weekends. Restaurant, bar, room service. In-room data ports, microwaves available, cable TV, in-room VCRs available. Pool. Hot tub. Putting green. Gym. Laundry facilities. Airport shuttle. Pets allowed. | 625 W. Rolling Meadows Dr. | 920/923–1440 | fax 920/923–1366 | www.holiday-inn.com | 139 rooms | $99–$170 | AE, D, DC, MC, V.

Northway. This standard highway motel with at-door parking is 1 mi from downtown right across from the airport. Restaurant, picnic area, complimentary Continental breakfast. Microwaves available, refrigerators, cable TV. | 301 S. Pioneer Rd. | 920/921–7975 | fax 920/921–7983 | 19 rooms | $55–$110 | AE, D, MC, V.

Stretch, Eat & Sleep Motel. The name says it all at this basic drive-to-your-door motel at the 24-hour truck-stop restaurant just off Highway 41 a mile from a mall. Restaurant. Cable TV. Pets allowed. | Pioneer Rd. | 920/923–3131 | 35 rooms | $26–$59 | D, MC, V.

FONTANA

MAP 11, E7

(Nearby town also listed: Lake Geneva)

The village of Fontana is a mecca for fishermen and water-sports lovers. Located on the west end of spring-fed Lake Geneva, this vacation spot is famous for its sandy swimming beach and striking locale. Beautiful Victorian homes can be seen around the lake.

Information: Geneva Lake West Chamber of Commerce | 125 Kenosha St., Box 118, 53125 | 262/275–5102 | www.glwchamber.org.

Attractions

Fontana Fen. You'll find one of the rarest wetlands, the fen, a prairie with peaty, alkaline soil which supports only a few species of grasses and other prairie plants, on this 10-acre conservation area with interpretive trails on Highway 67 between Fontana and Walworth. | Hwy. 67 between Fontana and Walworth | 262/248–3358 | Free | Daily.

ON THE CALENDAR
SEPT.: *Lake Geneva International Distance Triathlon.* This international Olympic triathlon includes a 9- to 10-mi swim, a 25-mi bike race, and a 10K run. | 800/345–1020 or 262/248–4323.

Dining
Chuck's Lakeshore Restaurant. American. The 7-mi view of Lake Geneva draws crowds to this casual second-story restaurant above a bar. The menu is small but varied, and includes steaks, seafood, pasta, sandwiches, and salads. Kids' menu. | 352 Lake St. | 262/275–3211 | $8–$20 | AE, D, MC, V | No lunch weekdays.

Lodging
The Abbey. The main building of this elegant lakeside hostelry is in a large A-frame wood structure surrounded by a wooded landscape. The beach is a 1 and ½ block walk from the hotel, which has lake views from many rooms. Bar, 4 dining rooms, room service. In-room data ports, cable TV, in-room VCRs. Five pools. Barbershop, beauty salon, hot tub, massage, spa. Tennis. Gym, water sports, boating, bicycles. Children's programs (weekends, ages 4–12). Business services. | 269 Fontana Blvd. | 262/275–6811 or 800/558–2405 | fax 262/275–3264 | 334 rooms, 19 condos | $165–$195 rooms, $475 condos | AE, D, DC, MC, V.

Fontana Village Inn. Only 2½ blocks from the public beach on Lake Geneva, this two-story roadside motel is on the town's main drag. Complimentary Continental breakfast on weekends. Cable TV. | 100 Dewey Ave. | 262/275–6700 | 140 rooms, 140 suites | $95–$125 | AE, MC, V.

FORT ATKINSON

(Nearby towns also listed: Janesville, Watertown)

This city was founded in 1832 when its namesake, General Henry Atkinson, built a stockade here. Today you can visit a replica at the edge of town, as well as a museum and dairy shrine located in the 1869 mansion of former Governor W. D. Hoard, the father of dairy farming in the state. Today Fort Atkinson is best known as the home of the Fireside Dinner Theatre, which offers musical performances by its professional theater company.

Information: Fort Atkinson Area Chamber of Commerce | 244 N. Main St., 53538-1828 | 888/733–3678 | fortcham@idcnet.com | www.fortchamber.com.

Attractions

Hoard Historical Museum. This Civil War–era house was home to Frank Hoard, the son of former Wisconsin Governor W. D. Hoard, known as the father of the state's dairy farming industry. Historical exhibits document the Black Hawk War of 1832, as well as the Civil War era, and other topics. | 407 Merchants Ave. | 920/563–7769 | www.hoardmuseum.org | Free | Memorial Day–Labor Day, Tues.–Sat. 9:30–4:30, Sun. 11–3; Labor Day–Memorial Day, Tues.–Sat. 9:30–3:30. Within the Hoard Historical Museum is the **National Dairy Shrine** museum, which chronicles the history of dairy farming in America through exhibits and a multimedia presentation. | 920/563–7769 | Free | Memorial Day–Labor Day, Tues.–Sat. 9:30–4:30, Sun. 11–3; Labor Day–Memorial Day, Tues.–Sat. 9:30–3:30. Also on the grounds is the **Dwight Foster House,** the 1841 home of an early pioneer and founder of Fort Atkinson. | 920/563–7769 | Free | Memorial Day–Labor Day, Tues.–Sat. 9:30–4:30, Sun. 11–3; Labor Day–Memorial Day, Tues.–Sat. 9:30–3:30.

I Love Funky's. This entertaining downtown store on the Rock River, where you can sit outside on the deck and sip a soda or a glass of wine from the bar, has two floors filled with carefully selected upscale upholstered furniture, jewelry, art, and antiques from all over the world. There is also a restaurant. | 90 S. Main St. | 920/568–0441 | Mon.-Wed. 10–6, Thur.-Fri. 10–8, Sat. 10–5, Sun. 11–4.

Panther Intaglio. This intaglio, a negative mound formed by scooping out the earth to leave an indented impression of an animal, is the only complete surviving intaglio in North America. It is in the shape of a panther. Look for the historical marker sign west of town. | 1236 Riverside Dr. | 920/563–3210 | Free | Daily.

ON THE CALENDAR

MAY: *Buckskinner Rendezvous.* This authentic reenactment encampment at the stockade in Rock River Park on Memorial Day weekend recalls the history of Old Fort Koshkonong. The focus is on fur traders and Native Americans, and features include authentic trade goods, food, and costuming. | 920/563–3210.

Dining

Chadwick's Manor. American. There are linen tablecloths in this supper-club dining room popular with local families where you can order steak or seafood. | 1655 Hwy. 12 | 920/968–1610 | $10–$14 | MC, V | Closed Sun.

Fireside Dinner Theatre. Contemporary. This sprawling restaurant built in 1964 includes a 435-seat theater-in-the-round. All meals have five courses, and the food is directly related to theater productions; if you are watching a German performance, German specialties will be on the menu. Steaks may be served on nonperformance days. | 1131 Janesville Ave. | 800/477–9505 | Reservations essential | $21–$29 | D, MC, V | Closed Mon., Tues., Fri., Sat.

Jimmy John's Gourmet Sandwiches. American/Casual. Don't let "gourmet" in the title and the Madison Ave. address throw you off, this place is simply a sub shop where you stand in line to choose your own toppings and seat yourself at booths. Try the cappicola ham, a special spicy Italian variety. | 108 Madison Ave. | 920/563–6400 | $3–$4 | No credit cards.

Lodging

Best Western Courtyard Inn. You can soak in a whirlpool tub after an evening at the Fireside Dinner Theater in one of the suites at this crisp white-and-red hotel next door to the theater. Complimentary Continental breakfast. In-room data ports, microwaves, refrigerators, cable TV. Pool. Hot tub. | 1225 Janesville Ave. | 920/563–6444 | fax 920/563–9510 | 58 rooms, 2 suites | $69–$110 | AE, D, DC, MC, V.

Cambridge House Bed and Breakfast. This turn-of-the-20th-century inn 10 mi northwest of Fort Atkinson is furnished with wing-back chairs, sleigh, canopy, and four-poster beds, and pedestal sinks. The original parquet floors, oak banisters, and stained-glass windows are still in place and there are period gardens with brick walkways and gazebos outside. Complimentary breakfast. In-room hot tubs, no TV. No smoking. | 123 E. Main St., Cambridge | 608/423–7008 or 888/859–8075 | cambridgehousebandb@juno.com | www.cambridge-house-inn.com | 4 rooms | $110 | MC, V.

Country Comforts Bed and Breakfast. This 100-year-old family farmhouse 10 mi west of Fort Atkinson has 4 acres of lawn and gardens, as well as spacious bedrooms. A sunburst-pattern leaded-glass window in the Rainbow Room, a sitting room where homemade cookies are served, creates rainbows when the sun shines. Complimentary breakfast. No smoking. | 2722 Highland Dr. | 608/423–3097 | info@country-comforts.com | www.country-comforts.com | 3 rooms, 1 suite | $75–$150 | AE, D, MC, V.

Mile–Away Motel. Near fast food and a gas station, this mom-and-pop budget-friendly motel is a mile from downtown. Cable TV. | 1225 Janesville Ave. | 920/563–6326 | 16 rooms | $38–$41 | D, MC, V.

Super 8. This small modern brick building with parking in front overlooks the Rock River. There's a walkway along the riverbank with patio and deck chairs. Bar, complimentary Continental breakfast. Cable TV. | 225 S. Water St. East | 920/563–8444 | fax 920/563–8444 | www.super8.com | 40 rooms | $50–$90 | AE, D, DC, MC, V.

FOUNTAIN CITY

MAP 11, B5

(Nearby towns also listed: Hudson, La Crosse)

This pretty town has many fine antiques shops and a community swimming pool open to visitors. Sandstone river bluffs make this area striking, as does 550-ft-high Eagle Bluff, the highest point on the Upper Mississippi River. An unusual attraction found here is Rock in the House, where in 1995 a 55-ton boulder fell from the bluffs and smashed into a house below, narrowly missing a resident. The owners turned their misfortune into a tourist attraction. There is also an auto and toy museum, a historical society museum, a state park, and a llama farm.

Information: Wisconsin Department of Tourism | Box 7976, Madison 53707-7976 | 800/372–2737 | tourinfo@tourism.state.wi.us | www.tourism.state.wi.us/.

Attractions

Merrick State Park. The marshy Mississippi backwaters in this haven for fishermen 2 mi north of town are home to herons, egrets, muskrats, and otters. Riverside camping, picnicking, hiking, swimming, and bird-watching are popular. | S2965 Rte. 35 | 608/687–4936 or 888/947–2757 | www.dnr.state.wi.us | $7 nonresidents, $5 residents; additional camping fees | Daily.

ON THE CALENDAR
SEPT.: *Old Time Farm Festival*. This Labor Day weekend family festival on privately owned farmland about 5 mi from town includes hay rides, breakfast, an ice-cream social, games, contests, soap making, and a display of old farm machinery including an old-time windmill. | 608/687–8436.

Dining
Hillside Fish House. Seafood. Lobster and frog legs share the menu with fish, shrimp, and a few beef dishes at this place with linen tablecloths and oldies radio music in the background 4 mi south of town on Highway 35. | Hwy. 35 | 608/687–6141 | $9–$25 | MC, V | No lunch.

Lodging
Fountain Motel. This simple, friendly family-run roadside motel on Highway 35 across from the river and a café is the only hotel in town. Refrigerators, cable TV. | 810 S. Main St. | 608/687–3111 | 13 rooms | $40–$80 | D, MC, V.

GALESVILLE

MAP 11, B5

(Nearby towns also listed: Fountain City, La Crosse)

This small Trempealeau County town is situated in a crook of bluffs overlooking Lake Marinuka. Here you will find many striking old Victorian homes with gingerbread trim and a number of Queen Anne mansions. The town square, as well as some streets in the town, are on the National Register of Historic Places.

Information: **Trempealeau County Clerk's Office** | 36245 Main St., Whitehall 54773-0067 | 715/538–2311 ext. 201 or 800/927–5339.

Attractions
Perrot State Park. Named after French explorer Nicholas Perrot, who wintered here in 1685–86, this state park at the junction of the Mississippi and Trempealeau rivers 12 mi northwest of Galesville has soaring 500-ft bluffs with a view of the Mississippi River valley. There are campgrounds, riverside picnic areas, a nature center, a boat launch, a canoe trail, 15 mi of hiking trails, and 9 mi of cross-country ski trails. Just off shore, completely surrounded by water, 384-ft Trempealeau Mountain has been a navigational landmark for more than three centuries. Native Americans considered the mountain sacred. Burial and ceremonial mounds can be found in the park. | Rte. 1, Trempealeau | 608/534–6409 | www.dnr.state.wi.us | $7 nonresidents, $5 residents | Daily.

Trempealeau National Wildlife Refuge. Over 5,000 acres of this 5,700-acre park 10 mi west of town off Highway 54 are wetlands. You can follow the 5-mi wildlife drive, or hike or bike as far as you like, or walk less than a mile on nature and prairie view trails. | W. Prairie Rd., Trempealeau | 608/539–2311 | Free | Daily dawn–dusk.

ON THE CALENDAR
OCT.: *Apple Affair*. This fall harvest festival centered in Galesville Town Square downtown is held on the first Saturday of the month in one of Wisconsin's prime apple-growing areas and features exhibits and craft displays, music, an omelet breakfast, a bratwurst lunch, bike tours for all ages, and a 10-ft apple pie. | 608/534–6780.

Dining

Arctic Springs Supper Club. American/Casual. One mile northwest of Galesville, this is cozy and scenic dining in a rustic oak and rock-walled building. Enjoy the house special prime rib or a seafood entrée while taking in the view of spring-fed Lake Marinuka. | County Rd. T, 54630 | 608/582-2672 | $8-$22 | D, MC, V | Closed Mon.

Lodging

Clark House Bed & Breakfast. A veranda surrounds this three-story home in the Ridge Avenue Historic District. The high ceilings, French library doors, hardwood floors, and glazed fireplace harken back to a leisurely era. Complimentary breakfast. Air-conditioning, no room phones, no TV. No smoking. | 20314 W. Ridge Ave. | 608/582-4190 | 3 rooms | $50-$60 | MC, V.

Sonic. Rooms in the two buildings of this brick motel less than 1 mi from Galesville center have outside entrances. The motel is right next to a bar and there is a deck looking out on nearby farms. Some kitchenettes, cable TV. | W21278 Rte. 54 | 608/582-2281 | 24 rooms, 2 kitchenettes | $42-$60 | MC, V.

GLENDALE

MAP 11, E6

(Nearby town also listed: Milwaukee)

This Milwaukee suburb's first settlers, mostly German Lutherans, purchased land here in the 1830s for $1.25 an acre. One of the area's better-known settlements, the Community of Good Hope, was built around 1834 at the present intersection of West Good Hope Road and North Green Bay Avenue. It was there that Jefferson Davis, soon-to-be president of the Confederacy, camped with his crew during a road-surveying project for the government. Glendale is home to three lovely parks and today has a large manufacturing base, as well as a variety of retailers and health-care facilities.

Information: Greater Milwaukee Convention and Visitors Bureau | 510 W. Kilbourn Ave., Milwaukee 53203-1402 | 414/273-7222 | www.officialmilwaukee.com.

Attractions

Sprecher Brewing Company. You can see the brewery itself, the cellar with Bavarian murals and historical artifacts, and sit in the indoor beer garden with an oompah band at this place known for its microbrews and gourmet sodas—the root beer is amazing. Tours are free and reservations are required. | 701 W. Glendale Ave. | 414/964-2739 | Free | Tours Sept.–May, Fri. 4, Sat. 1, 2, 3; June–Aug., Mon.–Thurs. at 4, Fri. 4, Sat. 1, 2, 3.

ON THE CALENDAR

JUNE–AUG.: *Music in the Glen.* A local nonprofit group hosts eight free outdoor concerts in Kletzsch Park and the Glen across from city hall throughout the summer. Music groups vary and include jazz, classical, swing, and barbershop quartets. | 414/352-6062.

Dining

Broadway Baby. American. This restaurant has an exposed brick and dimly lit lounge and dinner theater. You can dine on duck with cranberry sauce and wild rice or steak before the show or during the performance which is often a revived Broadway blockbuster. | 5132 W. Mill Rd. | 414/358-2020 | $18-$33 | D, MC, V | No show Mon., Tues., Thurs.

Zappas Contemporary Mediterranean Dining. Contemporary. This spacious restaurant is accented with Mediterranean colors, linen tablecloths, large floral arrangements, and vintage European advertisement art on the walls. The food is influenced by all the countries surrounding the Mediterranean. Try the pork tenderloin served with a chèvre and leek tart and bathed in Maille mustard reduction sauce, or the grilled shrimp wrapped in pancetta and basil leaves. Homemade sauces and desserts. | 400 W. Silver Spring Dr. | 414/906–9501 | $15–$28 | AE, DC, MC, V | Closed Mon.

Lodging

Baymont Inn Northeast. The Continental breakfast is delivered to your door in this chain hotel near shopping and fast food 7 mi from downtown. Complimentary Continental breakfast. Microwaves, refrigerators, cable TV. | 5110 N. Port Washington Rd. | 414/964–8484 | 107 rooms | $69–$89 | AE, D, MC, V.

Exel Inn–Northeast. This modern hotel off Interstate 43 is 5 mi from downtown Milwaukee on a street lined with hotels and fast food restaurants. There's a game room with ping-pong and air hockey. Complimentary Continental breakfast. In-room data ports, some microwaves, some in-room hot tubs, cable TV. Laundry facilities. Business services, free parking. Some pets allowed. | 5485 N. Port Washington Rd. | 414/961–7272 | fax 414/961–1721 | www.exelinns.com | 125 rooms | $65–$75 | AE, D, DC, MC, V.

Woodfield Suites. This modern brick building off Interstate 43 offers complimentary cocktails every evening. Complimentary Continental breakfast. In-room data ports, refrigerators, cable TV, in-room VCRs available. Two pools. Hot tub. Gym. Video games. Laundry service. Business services, free parking. | 5423 N. Port Washington Rd. | 414/962–6767 or 800/338–0008 | fax 414/962–8811 | 109 rooms | $115–$165 | AE, D, DC, MC, V.

GREEN BAY

MAP 11, E4

(Nearby towns also listed: Algoma, Appleton, Sturgeon Bay)

Wisconsin's second-oldest community, Green Bay was originally settled by the French as a fur-trading center. Jean Nicolet arrived in 1634, but Green Bay didn't grow into a permanent settlement until the mid-1700s. Today the town is most famous as the home of the professional football team, the Green Bay Packers. Packers history and memorabilia can be viewed at the Green Bay Packer Hall of Fame and Lambeau Field. But as a big city it has plenty of other attractions as well. The town's economic base consists of the paper, manufacturing, and medical industries.

Information: Green Bay Visitor and Convention Bureau | 1901 S. Oneida St., Box 10596, 54307-0596 | 888/867–3342 | tourism@dct.com | www.greenbay.org.

Attractions

Arvid E. Miller Memorial Library Museum. This museum 50 mi west of Green Bay on the Stockbridge Munsee Indian Reservation displays historical documents, a pre-European collection of Native American baskets, and beadwork. An exhibition of local Native American history represents the remnants of three tribes originally from the Hudson and Connecticut river valleys of New York and New England. | N8510 Moh Hecon Nuck Rd., Bowler | 715/793–4270 | Donations accepted | Weekdays 8–4:30.

Brown County Golf Course. A beautiful and challenging 18-hole course 7 mi west of Green Bay. | 897 Riverdale Dr., Oneida | 920/497–1731 | $32.50 for 18 holes; $18.25 for 9 holes | Early Apr.–mid-Nov.

Green Bay Packer Hall of Fame. Displays honor the football greats of the "Green and Gold." Tours of Lambeau Field, the site of the Packers' home games, are available. | 855 Lombardi Ave. | 920/499–4281 | $7.50; special rates for children and senior citizens; tours $7.50 | Daily 9–6; Lambeau Field tours mid-June–Labor Day; no tours on weekends of Packer home games.

Green Bay Packers. Wisconsin's NFL Packers are three-time Super Bowl champions. Home games are played at Lambeau Field. | 1265 Lombardi Ave. | 920/496–5700.

Hazelwood Historic Home Museum. Judge Martin, a major in the Civil War and president of Wisconsin's Second Constitutional Convention, built this Greek Revival in 1837. | 1008 S. Monroe Ave. | 920/437–1840 | $3; special rates for children and groups; additional fees for events | Memorial Day–Labor Day, Mon. and Wed.–Fri. 10–2, weekends 1–4; Labor Day–Memorial Day, group tours by appointment.

Heritage Hill State Park. A 48-acre complex of furnished historic buildings grouped into four areas: Belgian Farm (1905), Small Town (1871), Fort Howard (1836), and La Baye (1762). Costumed interpreters are stationed in each historic building. There are holiday programs in December. | 2640 S. Webster Ave. | 920/448–5150 | www.netnet.net/heritagehill | $6; special rates for children and senior citizens | Memorial Day–Labor Day, Tues.–Sat. 10–4:30, Sun. noon–4:30.

National Railroad Museum. One of the largest rail museums in America with more than 70 railroad cars and locomotives. Exhibits include General Dwight D. Eisenhower's World War II staff car and a Union Pacific Big Boy—the world's largest steam locomotive. The reception center has a library and multimedia presentation. You can take 20-minute train rides along a 1-mi track on the grounds. | 2285 S. Broadway | 920/437–7623 | $6; special rates for children, senior citizens, and families | May–mid-Oct., daily 9–5; mid-Oct.–Apr., call for hrs; train rides May–Sept., daily at 10, 11:30, 1, 2:30, and 4.

Neville Public Museum. Changing history, art, and science exhibits fill two floors of galleries. A permanent exhibit, On the Edge of the Inland Sea, takes you through 12,000 years of history in northeast Wisconsin, from the Ice Age to the present. | 210 Museum Pl. | 920/448–4460 | $3; special rates for children | Tues.–Sat. 10–4, Sun. noon–4.

Oneida Nation Museum. The heritage of the "People of the Standing Stone," who came to Wisconsin in the 1820s, is illuminated in permanent and hands-on exhibits at this museum 10 mi southwest of town. | W892 Rte. EE | 920/869–2768 | $2; guided tours $3; special rates for children and senior citizens | Tues.–Fri. 9–5.

Oneida Bingo and Casino. This elegant Native American gaming facility has a spacious 850-seat Bingo Hall with a smoke-free area, 60 blackjack tables and more than 2,500 reel slot and video machines. Table limits are from three dollars to two hundred dollars, and

© Artville

HARD-CORE PACKER FANS

Stop in any Wisconsin city—from large to small—and you're likely to see a sea of green and gold. Not green summer grass, and gold fall leaves, however, but Green Bay Packer green and gold. Football reigns supreme in Wisconsin all year long, but during the football season, Wisconsinites live and breathe the game.

Fans turn out in droves to Packer games, whether they're held in Green Bay at Lambeau Field or out of state. Many fans wear green-and-gold clothing with Packer logos, or some simply paint their skin in team colors. It's not unusual to see a line of men with their shirts off and their bodies a bright green. Often each man paints one letter on his chest; together, the letters might spell out "Pack," "Packer," or the name of a favorite player. This practice is the norm on pleasant fall days, as well as when the temperature plummets. Packer fans also wear cheesehead hats and other cheesehead paraphernalia, as well as hats that look like bratwurst (a favorite tailgating food).

In Wisconsin (a.k.a. "Packerland") loyal fans always love their home team—whether they win or lose.

everything in between. There are several restaurants and snack bars but no alcohol is allowed or served. Located across from Austin Straubel International Airport on Highway 172 just off of U.S. Highways 43 and 41. Free valet, parking, and shuttle bus service. | 2020/2100 Airport Drive | 800/238–4263; 920/497–8118 (Bingo); 920/494–4500 (Casino) | www.oneidabingoandcasino.net | free.

University of Wisconsin–Green Bay. Tours are available of this attractive campus 4 mi northeast of town. | 2420 Nicolet Dr. | 920/465–2000 | www.uwgb.edu | Tours free | Daily.

Performances at the **Weidner Center for the Performing Arts** include Broadway shows, community performances, symphonies, operas, and family shows. The center is recognized for outstanding acoustics in its main hall. Back-stage tours are available. | 920/465–2726 or 800/328–8587 | Tours free; performances fees vary | Tours daily with advance reservations.

ON THE CALENDAR

JUNE–AUG.: *Waterboard Warriors.* This water-ski show at the Brown county fairgrounds on the Fox River features barefoot skiing, a four-tier human pyramid, and jumps every Tuesday and Thursday evening. | 920/468–1987.

AUG.: *Folk Music Festival.* Local folk musicians gather to share their music with the community through concerts, workshops, dancing demonstrations, and instruction on the four outdoor stages of Heritage Hill State Park. | 920/448–5150 or 800/721–5150.

Dining

Backgammon Pub and Restaurant. American. The L-shape dining room wraps around the bar in this casual, kid-friendly joint on the Ramada Way strip with its many hotels. Big portions and reasonable prices make the grilled tenderloin that much more of a treat. Sunday brunch. | 2920 Ramada Way | 920/336–0335 | $6–$26 | D, MC, V.

Bistro John Paul. French. A romantic candlelit bistro with generously spaced tables perfect for private conversations. Try the sea scallops and be sure to look over the impressive wine list which won an award from *Wine Spectator* magazine. | 1244 Main St. | 920/432–2897 | $19–$22 | AE, D, DC, MC, V | No lunch.

Caffé Espresso. Mediterranean. A mural of medieval archers, musicians, and fencers runs along one wall of this café noted for its Italian espresso, salads, sandwiches, and chicken marsala. | 119 S. Washington St. | 920/432–9733 | $3–$15 | AE, D, MC, V | No lunch Sun.

Coconut Grille. Jamaican. This relative newcomer to the scene offers a change of pace from steak and potatoes. Dine in a bamboo hut and try one of the rasta pastas, rum-soaked lamb chops, coconut shrimp, or guava bar-b-q ribs (which are big enough to have appeared on Fred Flintstone's plate). There are also vegan selections. | 123 S. Washington St. | 920/431–9992 | $7–$20 | AE, D, DC, MC, V | Closed Sun., Mon.

Eve's Supper Club. American. On the top floor of a four-story building between Green Bay and DePere overlooking the Fox River, this supper club serves vegetarian dishes as well as steak, seafood, veal, and lamb. | 2020 Riverside Dr. (Rte. 57) | 920/435–1571 | $13–$50 | AE, D, DC, MC, V | Closed Sun. No lunch Sat.

Los Bandidos. Mexican. This family-run Mexican restaurant at the east end of Green Bay, 1 mi from downtown, offers homemade burritos, enchiladas, and fajitas. | 1258 Main St. | 920/432–9462 | $4–$13 | AE, D, DC, MC, V.

Union Hotel. American. You can expect upscale meat-and-potatoes dining at this brick turn-of-the-20th-century hotel and restaurant which has been in the same family for 83 years. | 200 N. Broadway | 920/336–6131 | $19–$22 | AE, D, MC, V | No lunch on weekends.

The Wellington. American. Love books? With walls lined with bookcases, this place feels like a Tudor-style English library. On the menu: beef Wellington and fresh seafood. Kids' menu. | 1060 Hansen Rd. | 920/499–2000 | $15–$25 | AE, DC, MC, V | Closed Sun. No lunch Sat.

Z Harvest Café. Contemporary. Large portraits of peppers, turnips, mushrooms, and other vegetables are painted on the walls of this rustic restaurant in the University Courtyard Shopping Center. Decorative cloths draped over hanging lights complete the artsy effect. Try the Smokey Z sandwich, made with smoked turkey, sauteed mushrooms, tomatoes and cheese. The potato-crusted roasted salmon is a popular dinner entree. | 2475 University Ave. | 920/468–1685 | $11–$19 | AE, D, MC, V | Closed Sun.

Lodging

Astor House. This 19th-century Victorian home in the Astor Historic Neighborhood is listed on the National Register of Historic Homes and is the only B&B in Green Bay. Complimentary Continental breakfast. In-room data ports, some in-room hot tubs, cable TV, in-room VCRs and movies. No smoking. | 637 S. Monroe Ave. | 920/432–3585 or 888/303–6370 | fax 920/436–3145 | astor@execpc.com | www.astorhouse.com | 5 rooms (4 with shower only) | $115–$152 | AE, D, MC, V.

Baymont Inn. This modern motel is in a commercial area a mile from the Bay Park Square Mall and 8 mi from downtown. Complimentary Continental breakfast. Microwaves available, cable TV, in-room VCRs and movies available. Business services. Some pets allowed. | 2840 S. Oneida St. | 920/494–7887 | fax 920/494–3370 | www.baymontinns.com | 78 rooms | $76–$82 | AE, D, DC, MC, V.

Best Western Midway Hotel. This large brick hotel 3 mi from downtown in a commercial area next to Lambeau Field, home to the Green Bay Packers, has two wings and a large center lobby with a seating area. Restaurant, bar, room service. In-room data ports, cable TV. Pool. Hot tub. Gym. Video games. Business services, airport shuttle, free parking. | 780 Packer Dr. | 920/499–3161 | fax 920/499–9401 | www.bestwestern.com | 145 rooms | $85–145 | AE, D, DC, MC, V.

Comfort Suites. Accommodations range from standard double suites to the presidential room at this all-suites hotel attached to the Rock Garden Supper Club in the northwest section of Green Bay, off Highway 41. Restaurant, complimentary Continental breakfast. In-room data ports, some minibars, microwaves, refrigerators, some in-room hot tubs, some in-room VCRs, cable TV. Pool. Hot tub. Exercise equipment. No pets. | 1951 Bond St. | 920/499–7449 | fax 920/499–0322 | 116 room | $89–$129 | AE, D, DC, MC, V.

Days Inn. This modern hotel is next to Port Plaza and right on the Fox River. Rooms have river views. Restaurant, bar. In-room data ports, microwaves available, cable TV. Pool. Business services, free parking. Pets allowed. | 406 N. Washington St. | 920/435–4484 | fax 920/435–3120 | 98 rooms | $70–$115 | AE, D, DC, MC, V.

Exel Inn. This brick motel is in a commercial area 1½ mi from Bay Park Square Mall and 7 mi from downtown. Complimentary Continental breakfast. In-room data ports, cable TV. Business services, free parking. Some pets allowed. | 2870 Ramada Way | 920/499–3599 | fax 920/498–4055 | 105 rooms | $49–$85 | AE, D, DC, MC, V.

Fairfield Inn by Marriott. This colonial-style hotel is three blocks from Bay Park Square Mall and 8 mi from downtown. Complimentary Continental breakfast. Microwaves available, cable TV. Pool. Hot tub. Business services, free parking. | 2850 S. Oneida St. | 920/497–1010 | fax 920/497–3098 | 63 rooms | $81–$100 | AE, D, DC, MC, V.

Green Bay Comfort Inn. A two-story hotel, just 10 minutes south of the airport, located in an industrial area and within walking distance to many restaurants. Free shuttle to the Oneida Casino. Complimentary Continental breakfast. In-room data ports, some refrigerators, cable TV. Pool. No pets. | 2841 Ramada Way | 920/498–2060 | fax 920/498–2060 | greenbayci@thar-aldson.com | www.comfortinn.com | 48 rooms, 12 suites | $57–$125 | AE, DC, MC, V.

Hampton Inn. This standard chain hotel is on the southwest side of Green Bay, 3 mi north of Lambeau Field on a commercial strip with a number of other hotels. Restaurant, complimentary Continental breakfast. In-room data ports, cable TV. Pool. Hot tub. Exercise equipment. | 2840 Ramada Way | 920/498–9200 | fax 920/498–3376 | www.hamptoninns.com | 115 rooms | $61–$115 | AE, D, DC, MC, V.

Hilton Garden Inn Green Bay. Geared toward the business traveler, these clean, efficient accommodations, cookie cutter in design, are typical of a chain hotel. Each of the rooms in this five-story building has two phone lines. Off Highway 41, two blocks east of Lambeau Field. Complimentary Continental breakfast. In-room data ports, microwaves, refrigerators, cable TV. Pool. Hot tub. No pets. | 1015 Lombardi Ave. | 920/405–0400 | fax 920/405–0512 | www.hilton.com | 125 rooms | $99–$189 | AE, D, DC, MC, V.

Holiday Inn–Airport. This standard hotel 2 mi from the Packer's Lambeau Field, 3 mi from the airport, and 7 mi from downtown, has a small lobby with a large-screen TV and a game room with ping-pong and a pool table as well as video games. Restaurant, complimentary breakfast, room service. Some refrigerators, cable TV. Pool. Hot tub. Video games. Business services, airport shuttle, free parking. | 2580 S. Ashland Ave. | 920/499–5121 | fax 920/499–6777 | 146 rooms | $65–$110 | AE, D, DC, MC, V.

Holiday Inn–City Centre. This seven-story hotel with a cement façade is on the banks of the Fox River, near the center of downtown. The lobby and rooms have a nautical motif and the hotel has a marina on the river. Restaurant, bar (with entertainment weekends), room service. Cable TV. Pool. Hot tub, sauna. Laundry facilities. Business services, free parking. Some pets allowed. | 200 Main St. | 920/437–5900 | fax 920/437–1199 | 146 rooms | $109–$129 | AE, D, DC, MC, V.

James Street Inn. This mid-19th-century feed mill has been renovated to look like a small country inn. It retains its original brickwork and sits between two parks in the historic downtown district of DePere 5 mi south of Green Bay. The lobby has an antique gas fireplace, bookshelves, an entertainment center, and a seating area. Complimentary wine, cheese, and appetizers are served in the parlor every evening. Complimentary Continental breakfast. Some microwaves, some in-room hot tubs, cable TV, in-room VCRs, and movies. Business services, free parking. | 201 James St., DePere | 920/337–0111 or 800/897–8483 | fax 920/337–6135 | jamesst@netnet.net | www.jamesstreetinn.com | 30 rooms | $69–$159 | AE, D, DC, MC, V.

Radisson Inn. This large, modern hotel is attached to the Oneida Bingo and Casino and is across the street from Austin Straubel Field airport. Restaurant, bar (with entertainment), room service. In-room data ports, refrigerators, some in-room hot tubs, cable TV. Pool. Hot tub. Gym. Business services, airport shuttle, free parking. | 2040 Airport Dr. | 920/494–7300 | fax 920/494–9599 | www.radisson.com | 301 rooms | $89–$139 | AE, D, DC, MC, V.

Ramada Inn. This modern hotel 5 mi from downtown in a commercial neighborhood has a large lobby with plants and crystal chandeliers. Restaurant, bar, room service. Cable TV. Pool. Hot tub, sauna. Putting green. Gym. Business services, airport shuttle, free parking. | 2750 Ramada Way | 920/499–0631 | fax 920/499–5476 | www.ramada.com | 156 rooms | $73–$99 | AE, D, DC, MC, V.

Regency Suites. This large downtown hotel caters to business travelers and offers double, executive, and king-size suites. An L-shaped skywalk connects the suites with the Port Plaza Mall, which is directly across the street. Restaurant, bar, complimentary breakfast. In-room data ports, microwaves, refrigerators, cable TV. Pool. Hot tub, sauna. Exercise equipment. Airport shuttle. | 333 Main St. | 920/432–4555 or 800/236–3330 | fax 920/432–0700 | www.regencygb.com | 241 suites | $130–$140 | AE, D, DC, MC, V.

Road Star Inn. This small, homey motel 2½ mi from downtown in a commercial neighborhood is part of a local chain. Complimentary Continental breakfast. Some refrigerators, cable TV. Free Parking. Pets allowed. | 1941 True La. | 920/497–2666 or 800/445–4667 | fax 920/497–4754 | 63 rooms | $45–$51 | AE, D, DC, MC, V.

Sky-Lit Motel. This small motel 3 mi from downtown on the edge of a residential neighborhood has front parking and outside entrances to rooms. Picnic area. Some kitchenettes, microwaves and refrigerators available, cable TV. Laundry facilities. Free parking. Some pets allowed. | 2120 S. Ashland Ave. | 920/494–5641 | fax 920/494–4032 | 24 rooms | $35–$60 | D, MC, V.

Super 8. This modern motel is 3 mi from the Packer's Lambeau Field and the airport and 6 mi from downtown. The lobby has a homey feel and there's parking for semi trucks out back. Complimentary Continental breakfast. Microwaves available, cable TV, in-room VCRs available. Hot tub, sauna. Laundry facilities. Business services, free parking. Pets allowed. | 2868 S. Oneida St. | 920/494–2042 | fax 920/494–6959 | www.super8.com | 84 rooms | $67–$73 | AE, D, DC, MC, V.

GREEN LAKE

MAP 11, D5

(Nearby towns also listed: Fond du Lac, Oshkosh)

This vacation community is the county seat and well known for its hospitality and golf courses. Right outside town is a 1,000-acre recreation area with camping, swimming, boat rentals, and golfing. From the business district you can take a cruise aboard a 60-ft passenger catamaran cruiser to see the state's deepest natural inland lake, Green Lake, where there is also good trout fishing, swimming, sailing, and ice boating.

Information: **Green Lake Area Chamber of Commerce** | 550 Mill St., 54941 | 800/253–7354 | info@greenlakecc.com | www.greenlakecc.com.

Attractions

Green Lake Conference Center. At this 1,000-acre complex on Green Lake, 5 mi north of town, you can camp, hike trails, hang out on the beach, or golf at the nationally known golf course of Lawsonia. Vintage homes and four hotels on the grounds have rooms available to rent. | W2511 Rte. 23 | 920/294–3323 | $7.50 per car (4–5 people) for walking, hiking; fees for camping and golf | Daily 24 hours.

Heidel House Cruises. Hour-long morning cruises are offered on the *Escapade.* Champagne breakfast cruises and dinner cruises are also available. Weekend cruises are offered Labor Day through October. | 643 Illinois Ave. | 920/294–3344 or 800/444–2812 | $9.95–$24.95 | Apr.–Labor Day, daily 9:30–3:30; Labor Day–Oct., weekends 9:30–3:30.

Ripon College. Founded in 1851, this small, liberal-arts college 4 mi north of Green Lake is on a shady, 250-acre campus. Many of the campus's 29 buildings are on the National Register of Historic Places. | 300 Campus Dr., Ripon | 920/748–8115 | www.ripon.edu | Free | Daily.

ON THE CALENDAR
DEC.: *International Christmas.* See Santa and enjoy crafts, music, refreshments, cookie decorating, and horse-and-wagon rides downtown on the first Saturday in December. | 800/253–7354.

Dining

Alfred's Supper Club. American. Housed in an 1870s Victorian, this restaurant serves beef, cut on the premises. Salad bar and kids' menu. | 506 Hill St. | 920/294–3631 | $9–$20 | D, MC, V | Closed Mon. Apr.–Oct. No lunch.

Boathouse Lounge & Eatery. American/Casual. This is the more casual of the two restaurants on the grounds of the Heidel House, just two blocks south of the main drag in Green Lake. Here you can enjoy light fare either indoors or out. Nightly entertainment Wednesday–Saturday by the in-house cover band. | 643 Illinois Ave. | 920/294–3344 and 800/444–2812 | $6–$15 | AE, D, MC, V.

Carvers on the Lake. Continental. This old-English-style restaurant overlooking Green Lake was built as a summer home in the early 1920s, then turned into a restaurant and B&B. There's an outdoor patio for cocktails, antiques throughout the dining room, and a Great Room bar with a vaulted ceiling and fireplace. Known for seafood, regional dishes, pasta, and rack of lamb. | N5529 Rte. A | 920/294–6931 | $17–$27 | MC, V | Closed Sun.–Mon. No lunch.

Heidel House's Grey Rock Mansion. Contemporary. There are stunning views of Green Lake from this 1940s mansion-turned-restaurant. The menu offerings change periodically to take advantage of seasonal produce, but you might be lucky enough to find fantastic seafood options like cedar-grilled walleye and sea bass drenched in buttery dill sauce. The kitchen also produces excellent steaks and chicken dishes, as well as pastries, tarts, and mousses for dessert. | 643 Illinois Ave. | 920/294–6299 | $17–$25 | AE, D, MC, V | No lunch.

Norton's Marine Dining Room. American. This log-frame building with a view of Green Lake caters to boaters. The large dining room has a fine view of the lake. Recommended dishes include Canadian walleye pike, lobster tail, and crab legs. | 380 S. Lawson Dr. | 920/294–6577 | $11–$49 | AE, MC, V.

Lodging

Bay View Motel & Resort. The rooms are fairly standard here but the location—on the edge of Green Lake's water front—is a draw. There's a private boat launch, fishing, and pontoon boats to rent, and you'll be within walking distance of downtown. Some kitchenettes, some microwaves, some refrigerators, cable TV. Dock, boating, fishing. No pets. | 439 Lake St. | 920/294–6504 | fax 920/294–0888 | bayview@vbe.com | www.wisvacations.com/bayviewmotel | 16 rooms, one 2-bedroom suite | $84–$92 | MC, V.

Carvers on the Lake. This 1920s lakeside inn 1 mi from town is filled with antiques and looks like an English country home. Most rooms have a lake view. Restaurant (*see* Carvers on the Lake, *above*), bar, picnic area, complimentary Continental breakfast, room service. Some microwaves, in-room hot tubs, cable TV, some room phones. No smoking. | N5529 Rte. A | 920/294–6931 | www.carversonthelake.com | 9 rooms (2 with shower only) | $75–$175 | MC, V.

Heidel House Resort and Conference Center. Set on a 20-acre Green Lake estate next to a golf course and 2 mi southeast of town, this multi-building resort was established in the 1940s and has grown over the years. Gardens surround stucco and colonial-style buildings and inside you'll find fireplaces warming both the library and the lobby. Restaurant, bar, dining room, picnic area, complimentary Continental breakfast, room service. Some microwaves, some refrigerators, some in-room hot tubs, cable TV. 2 pools, 2 hot tubs. Tennis. Exercise equipment. Beach, dock, fishing. Library. Kids' programs (ages 4–12). Business services. | 643 Illinois Ave. | 920/294–3344 or 800/444–2812 | fax 920/294–6128 | www.heidelhouse.com | 200 rooms | $199–$500 | AE, D, MC, V.

McConnell Inn Bed & Breakfast. This turn-of-the-20th-century Victorian is in a residential neighborhood south of Green Lake proper just a few blocks' walk from the beach, parks, and boating docks. Enjoy a family-style breakfast with goodies baked fresh by innkeeper and pastry chef Mary-Jo. Complimentary breakfast. Some refrigerators, some in-room hot tubs, no TV in some rooms. Library. No kids under 15. No smoking. | 497 S. Lawson | 920/294–6430 | www.mcconnellinn.com | 5 rooms | $60–$165; 2–night minimum weekend stay | MC, V.

Oakwood Lodge. This lodge set on a wooded hill overlooking the 7-mi length of Green Lake was built in 1867 as the largest guest house on the grounds of the Oakwood Resort, America's first summer resort west of Niagara Falls. Inside you'll find a stone fireplace, antiques, and a piano. There's also a stately balcony and an enclosed porch for breakfast. Complimentary breakfast. No air-conditioning, microwaves available, some in-room hot tubs, cable TV in common area, VCR available, no room phones. Dock, boating. No smoking. | 365 Lake St. | 920/294–6580 or 800/498–8087 | 12 rooms | $90–$125 | MC, V.

HALES CORNERS

MAP 11, E6

(Nearby towns also listed: Milwaukee, Waukesha, Wauwatosa)

A striking 50-acre formal botanical garden attracts visitors to Hales Corners, which is located just minutes from downtown Milwaukee.

Information: Greater Milwaukee Convention and Visitors Bureau | 510 W. Kilbourn Ave., Milwaukee 53203-1402 | 414/273–7222 | www.milwaukee.org/visit.htm.

Attractions

Whitnall Park. Whitnall houses the Boerner Botanical Gardens and Arboretum, which includes 40 acres of perennial, annual, and rock gardens; wildflowers; and crab-apple trees. An exhibit room holds a small art exhibit. | 5879 S. 92nd St., at Whitnall Park Dr. | 414/425–1130 | Free; $3.50 parking | Daily.

ON THE CALENDAR

JUNE: *Boerner in Bloom.* This nine-day floral celebration in the Boerner Botanical Gardens, a 40-acre English-style garden in Whitnall Park, includes garden walks, workshops, lectures, demonstrations, food, and music, planned to coincide with the blossoming of 50,000 roses. | 414/529–1870.

Dining

Ann's Italian Restaurant. Italian/American. This small, quaint restaurant in a former bungalow has lace curtains, small, intimate wooden tables, and a menu of hearty southern Italian fare like Sicilian steak. | 5969 S. 108th Pl. | 414/425–5040 | Reservations essential | $9–$16 | MC, V | No lunch.

Clifford's Supper Club. American. This casual, modern supper club has a menu of seafood, steaks, chicken, and pork chops and a Friday-night fish fry. Kids' menu. | 10418 W. Forest Home Ave. | 414/425–6226 | $9–$40 | AE, DC, MC, V | No lunch Sat., Sun.

Lodging

Embassy Motel. This no-frills, family-run motel is 7 mi east of Hales Corners in Franklin and just 300 ft off Highway 421. There are several restaurants within a mile of the motel. Some refrigerators. Pool. No pets. | 8253 S. 27th St., Franklin | 414/761–1234 | 38 rooms | $45–$65 | AE, D, DC, MC, V.

HAYWARD

MAP 11, B2

(Nearby town also listed: Cable)

Settled in 1881, this former logging town in the Northwoods is the starting point for the famed annual American Birkebeiner cross-country ski race, which finishes 47 kilometers north in Cable, on the edge of the Chequamegon National Forest. In summer, fishing and swimming in the nearby lakes are the main draws. Tourism and small business fuel the local economy.

Information: Hayward Area Chamber of Commerce | Box 726, 54843 | 800/724–2992 | www.haywardlakes.com.

Attractions

National Fresh Water Fishing Hall of Fame. Contains mounts and photos of record-size fish, historic rods and reels, antique outboard motors, and fishing memorabilia. You can stand in the jaws of a four-story-high muskellunge. | Hall of Fame Dr. | 715/634–4440 | $5 | Mid-Apr.–Nov 1., Daily 10–4:30.

JUNE: *Musky Festival.* For over 50 years the town of Hayward has been celebrating the 1949, 67½-pound catch landed by Cal Johnson. Held the third weekend in June, rain or shine, with fishing contests, parades, amusement rides, and food vendors. | 715/634–8662.
JULY: *Lumberjack World Championship.* The last weekend in July brings this nationally televised lumberjack championship with chain-saw carving, displays, tree climbing, and log rolling to the Lumberjack Bowl in downtown. | 800/724–2992.

Dining

Herman's Landing. American. The menu here aims to please the outdoorsman—you can start your day with Texas-style French toast or lumberjack pancakes and later enjoy burgers and Danish bay back pork ribs featuring Joe's rib sauce. | 8255 N. County Rd. CC | 715/462–3626 | $8–$11 | MC, V | Breakfast also available.

Karibalis. American. Housed in a historic 1910 brick building, this restaurant is a simple place with large windows and a fireplace. It's known for char-broiled steaks, burgers, and Canadian walleye pike. There's also open-air dining in a patio garden. Salad bar and kids' menu. | 212 Main St. | 715/634–2462 | $7–$20 | AE, D, MC, V.

Moose Café. American/Casual. Sit at the horseshoe-shape counter, at a table, or reserve the banquet room for the whole family. Breakfast starts early and is served all day—try the stuffed hash browns. | 106 N. Dakota Ave. | 715/634–8449 | $2–$6 | MC, V.

Lodging

Americinn. This brick motel is on the edge of town. The large lobby has a fireplace and there's a game room with a pool table. Picnic area, complimentary Continental breakfast. Microwaves, refrigerators, some in-room hot tubs, cable TV, in-room VCRs available. Pool. Hot tub, sauna. Business services. Some pets allowed (fee). | 15601 U.S. 63 N | 715/634–2700 or 800/634–3444 | fax 715/634–3958 | 42 rooms | $81–$96 | AE, D, DC, MC, V.

Best Western Northern Pine. Seven acres of wooded property surround this rustic, chalet-style motel in the countryside about a mile south of Hayward proper. Rooms have views of a pond and garden and there's a game room with a pool table. Picnic area, complimentary Continental breakfast. Microwaves available, some refrigerators, some in-room hot tubs, cable TV. Pool. Hot tub, sauna. Playground. Business services. | 9966 N. Rte. 27 | 715/634–4959 or 800/777–7996 | fax 715/634–8999 | www.bestwestern.com | 39 rooms | $59–$79 | AE, D, DC, MC, V.

Cedar Inn. A stone fireplace will greet you in the lobby of this small independently owned motel. The landscaped property is in a quiet neighborhood on the northern edge of town. Complimentary Continental breakfast. In-room data ports, microwaves available, refrigerators, cable TV. Hot tub, sauna. Business services. | 15659 Rte. 77 | 715/634–5332 or 800/776–2478 | fax 715/634–1343 | 23 rooms | $75–$140 | AE, D, MC, V.

Country Inn and Suites. This large hotel, 1 mi outside downtown Hayward in a suburban residential area, sports a Northwoods motif—with rustic furniture, deer antlers, and fish paintings on the walls, and a fireplace in the lobby. Restaurant, bar, complimentary Continental breakfast, room service. In-room data ports, microwaves, refrigerators, some in-room hot tubs, cable TV. Pool. Hot tub. Video games. Business services. Some pets allowed. | 10290 Rte. 27 S | 715/634–4100 | fax 715/634–2403 | 58 rooms, 8 suites | $73–$83 rooms, $113–$123 suites | AE, D, DC, MC, V.

Herman's Landing. These carpeted cabins in the heart of the Chippewa flowage, 20 mi southeast of Hayward, have ceiling fans and rent by the week in summer. The owners also run a bait shop and offer guided fishing trips. Restaurant. No air-conditioning, kitchenettes, refrigerators, no room phones, no TV. Lake. Boating, fishing. No pets. No smoking. | 8255 N. County Rd. CC | 715/462–3626 | hermans@win.bright.net | www.hermanslanding.com | 8 cabins | $1,200–$1,500 per week | MC, V.

Lumberman's Mansion Inn. This 1887 Victorian home directly across from Shue's Pond has gingerbread mill work, an oak staircase, maple floors, white-pine pocket doors, downstairs and upstairs parlors, and a carriage stoop. In good weather breakfast is served on the porch. Complimentary breakfast. In-room hot tubs, cable TV, in-room VCRs. Library. No pets. No smoking. | 15844 E. 4th St. | 715/634–3012 | fax 715/634–5724 | mansion@win.bright.net | www.haywardlakes.com/mansion | 5 rooms, 2 suites | $75–$95 | MC, V.

Mustard Seed Inn. This small inn has evocatively named rooms such as the Hunt Suite, the Cranberry and Cream Room, and the Garden Room. You can also opt for the guest cottage, equipped so you are completely self-sufficient. Either way you're just a block and a half away from antiquing, adventure outfitters, bike rentals, or a stroll around Shue's Pond. Complimentary breakfast. Some kitchenettes, some microwaves, some refrigerators, some in-room hot tubs, some in-room VCRs, TV in common area. Library. No pets. No smoking. | 10605 California Ave. | 715/634–2908 | 5 rooms, 1 cottage | $75–$105 | MC, V.

Northwoods Motel. This cozy ranch-style motel is surrounded by woods 2 mi north of downtown. Rooms are large and one has a full kitchen. Cable TV. Pets allowed. | 9854 N. Rte. 27 | 715/634–8088 or 800/232–9202 | 9 rooms | $46–$75 | AE, D, DC, MC, V.

Ross' Teal Lake Lodge. Accommodations range from cozy honeymoon log cabins to deluxe four-bedroom family homes at this lake resort on quiet Teal Lake (no motorboats), 7½ mi east of Hayward. The dining room in the lodge is open for breakfast and dinner. Restaurant. Kitchenettes, refrigerators, some in-room VCRs, no phones. Lake. Golf course, tennis. Hiking, boating, fishing. No pets. No smoking. | 12425 Ross Rd. | 715/462–3631 | rossteal@win.bright.net | www.rossteal.com | 8 guest homes | $300–$500 | MC, V | Closed Nov.–Apr.

Spider Lake Lodge Bed & Breakfast. The cozy rooms at this rustic, 1923 log-cabin lodge on the shores of Big Spider Lake, 18 mi northeast of Hayward, still have many of the lodge's original furnishings as well as hardwood floors and log walls. Some rooms have water views and everyone can enjoy the view from the screened-in porch. Complimentary breakfast. No room phones, no TV. Lake. Hiking. Beach, water sports, boating, fishing. Library. | 10472 W. Murphy Blvd. | 715/462–3793 and 800/OLD–WISC | fax 715/462–3793 | www.haywardlakes.com/slbb.htm | 7 rooms | $80–$110 | MC, V.

HOLCOMBE

MAP 11, B3

(Nearby towns also listed: Chippewa Falls, Eau Claire, Ladysmith)

If you want to see nature at its finest, tiny Holcombe, once a logging town, has lots to offer. The area's vast network of waterways is a paradise for swimmers, anglers, and boat-owners, while the town's parks and public recreation areas support a wide variety of outdoor activities including hiking, birding, camping, rock climbing, and mountain biking.

Information: **Chippewa Valley Convention and Visitors Bureau** | 3625 Gateway Dr., Suite F, Eau Claire, 53701 | 888/523–3866 | www.eauclaireinfo.com.

Attractions

Cobban Bridge. This one-lane metal bridge stretches across the Chippewa River, and is the oldest of its kind in Wisconsin. It is still being used, and gives spectacular views of the river. To reach the bridge, which is about 10 mi from Holcomb, head south from Cornell on Highway 178, then follow the historical markers. | Hwy. 178 | 888/523–3866 | Free | Daily.

Cornell Pulpwood Stacker. This huge, 175-ft steel structure in downtown Cornell's Mill Yard Park is the largest standing pulpwood stacker in the world. It was once used to stack huge piles of pulpwood during the area's logging days. It's right downtown, dominating the entire area, and can't possibly be missed. | 888/813–9706 | Free | Daily.

Old Abe Historical Marker. A scenic ride south along Highway 178 takes you past several historical markers. One of the most popular pays tribute to "Old Abe," the war eagle who fought with Wisconsin's 12th regiment in the Civil War. Abe was trained to act as a diversion to harry Confederate troops and go for their eyes while the Union soldiers advanced. Abe would lead the soldiers into battle, screaming and swooping at enemy troops. | Hwy. 178 | 715/723–0331 | Free | Daily.

Wooden Indian. A wooden Indian, carved in 1876 by a local logger who wanted the Indian to watch over the dam and protect loggers, still stands guard right in downtown today at Holcombe Village Hall. | 715/723–0331 | Free | Daily.

Chippewa Moraine. 4,000 acres of state park area sprawl over a swath of land carved out by retreating glaciers over 10,000 years ago. The area has deep kettle lakes, dramatic rocky outcroppings, and grassy fields dotted with wildflowers. A total of 23 mi of hiking trails criss-cross the park, but most are remote and not for the unexperienced explorer. | 1.9 mi east of the junction of Hwy. 40 and Rte. M in New Auburn | 715/967–2800 | Free | Daily, dawn to dusk.

Dining

Big Swede's. American. The Philly cheese-steak sandwich is a specialty at this casual, rustic restaurant north of Holcombe on Lake Holcombe, popular with locals and lake visitors alike. | 29840 Hwy. 27 | 715/595–4284 | $4–$8 | No credit cards | No lunch Mon.–Sat.

Pine Drive Resort Restaurant. American. Pizza, prime rib, Friday-night fish frys, and views of the Holcombe flowage are the draws at this Pine Drive Resort restaurant just off Highway M. Sunday brunch. | 27339 250th St. | 715/595–4201 | $5–$20 | AE, D, MC, V | Closed Tues. No lunch weekdays.

Smokin' Joe's Southern Grille & Bar. American. Cajun/Creole dishes share the limelight with American standards at this casual Paradise Shores Resort restaurant on Lake Holcombe about 1½ mi west of town, where most tables have a great view of the Holcombe flowage. Sunday brunch. | W26364 County M | 715/595–4701 | $5–$26 | AE, D, MC, V.

Lodging

Flater's Flambeau Point Resort. This small resort is in a rural area just northwest of Holcombe where the Chippewa and Flambeau rivers meet. All the two- or three-bedroom, brown wood cabins have water views. Bar. Boating. Playground. | N270 County E | 715/595–4771 | 5 rooms | $75 per night/$300 a week | MC, V.

Larry's South Shore Resort. This lakeside resort 2 mi west of Holcomb has 8 private cottages with lakeshore access, and is popular among vacationing families and fishermen. The one- and two-bedroom cabins are rented on a weekly basis from Memorial Day to Labor Day. Bar. Lake. Beach, boating. Playground. | 26064 County Hwy. M | 715/595–6260 | 11 rooms | $550–$650 a week | No credit cards | Closed Dec.–end Mar.

Paradise Shores Resort Hotel & Conference Center. This elegant modern resort is surrounded by 4,000 acres of water and woodland on the shore of Lake Holcomb. A large patio and paved lakeside walking paths enable you to appreciate the area's natural splendor from a distance, or you can jump right into the lake from the resort's private frontage. The main resort building is constructed partly from rustic logs, but the interior is refined, with carpeted floors, massive plate-glass windows looking out onto the lake, and plenty of comfortable lounge furniture for relaxing. Restaurant. Some kitchenettes, some refrigerators, some in-room hot tubs, cable TV. Pool, lake. Hot tub, sauna. Gym, hiking, water sports, boating, fishing, bicycles. Cross-country skiing, snowmobiling. Laundry services. Business services. | W26364 County M | 800/657–4512 | fax 715/595–6476 | info@paradiseshores.com | www.paradiseshores.com | 1 cottage, 1 apartment, 10 suites, 31 standard rooms | $80–$90 | AE, D, MC, V.

HUDSON

(Nearby town also listed: Fountain City)

At Hudson, the St. Croix River broadens and its waters serve as a sparkling backdrop to a lovely town. Hudson is a center for recreation, with boating, fishing, swimming, and parks. Hudson's historic residential district is home to the aptly named Octagon House, an 1855 eight-sided Victorian home that now serves as a museum. Hudson also has direct access to Minneapolis/St. Paul across the river. Many Hudsonites head over the bridge for the nightlife and cultural opportunities of the larger metropolitan area.

Information: Hudson Area Chamber of Commerce and Tourism Bureau | 502 2nd St., 54016 | 800/657–6775 | info@hudsonwi.org/explore.

Attractions

Marcus Sears Bell Farmstead. This 1884 Italianate farmhouse, 18 mi northeast of Hudson, forms the centerpiece of the New Richmond Heritage Center. The farmstead includes a barn with granary, a general store, a blacksmith shop, and a one-room schoolhouse. | 1100 Heritage Dr., New Richmond | 715/246–3276 or 888/320–3276 | fax 715/246–7215 | www.pressenter.com/~nrpsinc | $4 | Memorial Day–Labor Day, daily 10–4; Labor Day–Memorial Day, weekdays 10–4.

New Richmond Golf Club. Opened in 1923, this 18-hole course is challenging and surrounded by natural beauty. A dress code is enforced; no spikes allowed. | 1226 180th Ave., New Richmond | $33 for 18 holes | 715/246–6724 | Mid-Apr.–mid-Oct.

Octagon House. Built in 1855, this house is rich in local history and Americana. Furnishings include a grand piano famous for its two accidental dunkings in the St. Croix River when it fell off boats while being transported. | 1004 3rd St. | 715/386–2654 | $2 | May–Oct., Tues.–Sat. 10–11:30 and 2–4:30, Sun. 2–4.

Phipps Center for the Arts. Professional theatrical productions and cultural exhibits are year-round attractions here. Tours are available. | 109 Locust St. | 715/386–2305 | Admission varies | Daily.

St. Croix Meadows Greyhound Park. Matinee and evening greyhound and horse racing is offered in this world-class facility. | Rte. F | 715/386–6800 | $1 | Call for hrs.

Willow River State Park. Includes a nature center, a trout stream, a sandy beach, a campground, two dams, two lakes, and prairie remnants, all just 10 mi northwest of Hudson. | 1034 Rte. A, Somerset | 715/386–5931 | www.dnr.state.wi.us | $5–$7 | Daily.

ON THE CALENDAR
NOV.: *Christmas Tour of Homes and Craft Sale.* Privately owned homes throughout Hudson, including the Octagon House, are decorated for the holidays on the weekend before Thanksgiving. | 800/657–6775.

Dining
Chadwick's Seafood. Seafood. There's no river view here but the 150 gallon fish tank dividing the two dining rooms sets a nautical tone. The menu, which changes daily, includes select meats and wild game in addition to fish. | 708 6th St., N. Hudson | 715/381–8414 | $10–$20 | AE, D, MC, V | Closed Sun. No lunch Sat.

Mama Maria's. Italian. Just off the main drag in North Hudson, about five minutes from Hudson proper, Mama Maria's is famed for its generous portions of champagne chicken, cannelloni, and lasagna but also offers steak and seafood. There's outdoor seating on a cobblestone patio, or you can stay inside where murals of vineyards adorn the walls. Kids' menu. | 800 6th St., N. Hudson | 715/386–7949 | $9–$20 | AE, MC, V | Closed Mon. No lunch Sun.

Riverside. American. Enjoy a rib-eye with the works—veggie, potato, and salad—inside or out on the patio at this steak-and-seafood establishment. As the name suggests, it's right on the water. | 1st St. | 715/386–5504 | $8–$27 | AE, D, MC, V.

Lodging

Baker Brewster Victorian Inn. This antiques-filled 1882 Victorian is on a quiet tree-lined street six blocks east of the riverfront. Guests return for what has been deemed the "lick your plate" four-course breakfast. Evening treats include wine and Wisconsin cheese. Complimentary breakfast. Some in-room data ports, in-room hot tubs. | 904 Vine St. | 715/381–2895 or 877/381–2895 | dream@bakerbrewster.com | www.bakerbrewster.com | 6 rooms | $89–$159 | AE, D, MC, V.

Best Western Hudson House Inn. This large colonial-style motel is in a commercial area 2 mi from the center of town. Restaurant, bar (with entertainment), complimentary Continental breakfast, room service. In-room data ports, cable TV. Pool. Beauty salon, hot tub, sauna. Gym. Business services. Some pets allowed. | 1616 Crest View Dr. | 715/386–2394 | fax 715/386–3167 | www.bestwestern.com | 102 rooms | $72–$81 | AE, D, DC, MC, V.

Comfort Inn. This standard motel is in a commercial area 1½ mi from downtown. Complimentary Continental breakfast. Cable TV, in-room VCRs available. Pool. Hot tub. Laundry service. Business services. | 811 Dominion Dr. | 715/386–6355 | fax 715/386–9778 | www.choicehotels.com | 60 rooms | $53–$105 | AE, D, DC, MC, V.

Jefferson-Day House. This pre-Victorian home, with original Italianate Antebellum arch, is the oldest B&B in Hudson and sits on Historic 3rd Street. Inside you'll find molded plaster ceilings, antique queen-size beds, fireplaces, and a sterling-silver service for the four-course breakfast. Outside, wander through the perennial garden and courtyard or relax on the porch or in the gazebo. Complimentary breakfast. In-room data ports, some minibars, in-room hot tubs, no room phones, no TV. Laundry service. | 1109 3rd St. | 715/386–7111 | www.jeffersondayhouse.com | 4 rooms, one 3-bedroom suite | $129–$189 | D, MC, V.

Knollwood House Bed-and-Breakfast. This elegant 1886 brick farmhouse with a solarium is on 80 beautifully landscaped acres about 12 mi south of Hudson. There are trails for hiking or cross-country skiing on the property and a riding stable nearby. Complimentary breakfast. Pool. Hot tub, sauna. Putting green. Hiking. Cross-country skiing. | N8257 950th St. River Falls | 715/425–1040 or 800/435–0628 | www.innsofthevalley.com | 3 rooms (2 with shared bath), 1 suite | $100–$200 | No credit cards.

Phipps Inn. This grand late-19th-century home is on the National Register of Historic Places. Many of the rooms have whirlpool tubs and feather mattresses on canopied beds. Downtown Hudson is within easy walking distance of the Inn's quiet residential neighborhood, and all the attractions of the Minneapolis/St. Paul area are about 20 mi away. Dining room, complimentary breakfast. In-room hot tubs, no room phones. Bicycles. No smoking. | 1005 3rd St. | 715/386–0800 | www.phippsinn.com | 6 suites | $149–$189 | MC, V.

HURLEY

MAP 11, C2

(Nearby towns also listed: Ashland, Bayfield)

Founded in 1885 and located on the border with Michigan's upper peninsula, the city of Hurley made a name for itself as a wild and wooly outpost during the region's iron-mining days in the late 1800s. Today Hurley is best known for its waterfalls on the nearby Montreal River, and for great snowmobiling in winter. Considered the seat of Iron County, Hurley has a 19th-century courthouse that is listed on the National Register of Historic Places. The building has been turned into a museum devoted to the area's mining, logging, and farming heritage.

Information: Hurley Area Chamber of Commerce | 316 Silver St., 54534 | 715/561–4334 | www.hurleywi.com.

Attractions

Iron County Historical Museum. Housed in a former county courthouse, this museum displays mining, logging, and farming memorabilia. The building, with a tall tower and clock faces on all four sides, was originally a town hall and is on the National Register of Historic Places. The clockworks, installed in 1893, are still in operation. | 303 Iron St. | 715/561–2244 | Free | Mon., Wed., Fri.–Sat. 10–2.

Superior Falls. At the mouth of the Montreal River and Lake Superior, just ½ mi over the Michigan border, a bench-lined trail leads to a grand waterfall cascading down 90 ft. | Hwy. 122 | 715/561–4334 | Free | Daily dawn to dusk.

Whitecap Mountain Ski Area. Eight miles west of Hurley you will find more than 1 square mi of downhill skiing on 36 runs with a 450-ft vertical drop, some illuminated for night skiing. Cross-country trails are nearby. | County E, just south of the intersection of Rtes. 2 and 51 on Weber Lake | 715/561–2227 | www.skiwhitecap.com | $35 day pass | Nov.–Mar., daily; night skiing Tues. and Fri.–Sat.

ON THE CALENDAR

JULY–AUG.: *Iron County Heritage Festival.* For two weeks each summer Hurley takes time to honor it history with a parade, tours of old mining homes, a living-history walking tour of the Tavern District, golf tournaments, pancake breakfasts, and high-school reunions. Most events take place on or around Silver Street. | 715/561–4334.

AUG.: *Paavo Nurmi Marathon.* Wisconsin's oldest marathon starts in the dense northern woods 13 mi west of Hurley on the second Saturday of the month. Marathon-related goings-on include a spaghetti feed, opening ceremonies, and a post-race party and awards. | 715/561–4334.

DEC.: *Red Light Snowmobile Rally.* This downtown Hurley rally kicks off the snowmobile season on the second weekend of the month with events including a poker run, a radar run, a scavenger hunt, and a dance. | 715/561–4334.

Dining

Pasta Connection. Italian. Authentic cuisine and wood-fired pizzas are served on white tablecloths amid Italian-style murals of pastoral Mediterranean scenes. | 208 Silver St. | 715/561–4652 | $7–$15 | AE, D, MC, V | No lunch.

Lodging

Anton-Walsh House. This B&B is just one block off the main street of Hurley's small residential community and is an example of Foursquare Craftsman architecture. Rooms have names and themes and the hallways sport historic photos of Hurley during its founding days. Weekly deals are available between July and November. Complimentary breakfast. No room phones, TV in common area. Library. | 202 Copper St. | 715/561–2065 | fax 715/561–9977 | info@anton-walsh.com | www.anton-walsh.com | 3 rooms | $89–$99 | No credit cards.

JANESVILLE

(Nearby towns also listed: Beloit, Delavan)

The Rock River runs through downtown Janesville, a city that was founded in 1836 and now claims 10 historic districts; nearly 20% of all Wisconsin buildings on the National Register of Historic Places are here.

Information: **Janesville Area Convention and Visitors Bureau** | 51 S. Jackson St., 53545 | 800/487–2757 | www.janesvillecvb.com.

Attractions

Gray Brewing Company. The brewing tradition began for the Gray family in 1856 but from 1912 until 1994 beer brewing was suspended and only soft drinks were produced. Today, Gray sodas include root beer, cream soda, orange, and strawberry. Popular beers are the Honey Ale, Pale Ale, and Gray's Original Lager. | 2424 Court St. | 608/752–3552 | www.gray-brewing.com | $2 | Tours available the 1st and 3rd Sat. of each month at 1:30. Private group tours by arrangement.

Lincoln-Tallman Restorations. This complex downtown in the Look West Historic District includes the 26-room, Italianate William Tallman House, which hosted a visit from Abraham Lincoln in 1859. The original family furniture is here, including the bed in which Lincoln slept. | 440 N. Jackson St. | 608/752–4519 | $8 | Memorial Day–Labor Day, daily 9–4; Oct.–May, weekends 9–4.

Milton House Museum. This 20-room stagecoach inn, dating from 1844 and now listed on the National Register of Historic Places, was once a station on the Underground Railroad. A tunnel connects the inn to an 1837 log cabin. Other buildings in the complex, which is 8 mi northeast of Janesville, include a buggy shed and a country store. Tours are available. | 18 S. Janesville St., Milton | 608/868–7772 | www.miltonhouse.org | $5 | May, weekends 10–5; Memorial Day–Labor Day, daily 10–5; Oct. by appointment.

Riverside Park. This parks offers biking and walking paths, boat-launch facilities, and a wading pool along the banks of the Rock River. Next door is an 18-hole golf course. | N. Washington St. | 800/487–2757 | Free | Daily dawn to dusk.

Rotary Gardens. There are nine individual gardens, a wildlife sanctuary, and a visitor center. The gardens provide access to the National Ice Age Trail, now about a 400 mi-trail traversing through many parks across the state, it will be a 1,000-mi recreational trail when completed. You can bike, hike, and rollerblade on this portion of the trail. | 1455 Palmer Dr. | 608/752–3885 | Free | Daily dawn to dusk.

ON THE CALENDAR

MAY–SEPT.: *Water-ski show.* A national championship level water-ski team puts on a 1½-hour show every Wednesday evening in Traxler Park. | 800/487–2757.
JULY: *Rock County 4-H Fair.* This end-of-the-month event at the Rock County 4-H Fairgrounds on the east side of town includes a carnival, 4-H displays, food, entertainment, arts, crafts, and youth exhibits. | 608/755–1470.

Dining

Happy Joe's Pizza and Ice Cream Parlor. American. This small, family-style restaurant serves pizza, pasta, garlic bread, bread sticks, and ice cream. There's also a video-game room. | 2307 Milton Ave. | 608/756–4191 | $4–$10 | D, MC, V.

Lodging

Best Western Janesville Motor Lodge. A fireplace will greet you in the lobby of this motel on a commercial strip right off Interstate 90 at exit 171 East. Restaurant, bar, complimentary Continental breakfast, room service. Cable TV. Pool. Hot tub. Gym. Business services, airport shuttle. Pets allowed. | 3900 Milton Ave. | 608/756–4511 or 800/334–4271 | fax 608/756–0025 | www.bestwestern.com | 105 rooms | $59–$89 | AE, D, DC, MC, V.

Ramada Inn. This large, Y-shaped hotel is approximately 5 mi from downtown on a suburban commerical strip, surrounded by other similar lodgings and popular chain restaurants. The lobby has a seating area and a curving stairway to a balcony and four suites. Restaurant, bar, complimentary Continental breakfast, room service. In-room hot tub in 1 suite, cable TV. Pool. Hot tub. Putting green. Gym. Business services. | 3431 Milton Ave. | 608/756–2341 | fax 608/756–4183 | 185 rooms, 4 suites | $75–$210 | AE, D, DC, MC, V.

KENOSHA

MAP 11, E7

(Nearby town also listed: Racine)

Deep-water fishing, historic sites, and two big factory-outlet shopping malls are among the distractions in Kenosha, on Lake Michigan, just north of the Illinois border. Along the scenic waterfront are beaches, parks, marinas, and a nature preserve. To get a sense of the historic character of this community founded in 1835, take a walking or trolley tour of Kenosha's historic districts.

Information: **Kenosha Area Convention and Visitors Bureau** | 812 56th St., 53140 | 800/654–7309 | www.kenoshacvb.com.

Attractions

Bong State Recreation Area. This area offers camping, hiking, fishing, picnicking, cross-country skiing, snowmobiling, hang gliding, horseback riding, and year-round interpretive programs. It also includes a beach, a sled-dog training area, and an ultralight and hot-air balloon area. The area is 8 mi east of Burlington and 10 mi west of Kenosha, near the town of Union Grove. | 26313 Burlington Rd., Kansasville | 262/878–5600 | www.dnr.state.wi.us/org/land/parks/ | $7 | Daily.

Carthage College. Founded as a Lutheran institution in Illinois in 1847, the college was moved to 84 acres in Kenosha, along the Lake Michigan shore, in 1962. Campus tours are available. | 2001 Alford Park Dr. | 262/551–8500 | www.carthage.edu | Free | Tours weekdays, call for hrs.

Johnson Art Center. Carthage College's art center is home to hundreds of pieces of Civil War memorabilia. | 2001 Alford Park Dr. | 262/551–8500 | www.carthage.edu | Free | By appointment.

Kemper Center. This former Episcopal all-girls boarding school now includes the Anderson Arts Center, a regional modern-art gallery, and Kemper Pier, specially built for anglers with disabilities. Building tours are available by appointment. | 6501 3rd Ave. | 262/657–6005 | fax 262/657–6005 | www.kempercenter.com | Free | Daily.

Kenosha County Historical Society Museum. Local historical displays are on view in a turn-of-the-century mansion in Kenosha's historic district, downtown by Lake Michigan. | 220 51st Pl. | 262/654–5770 | $2 | Tues.–Fri. 10–4:30, weekends noon–4:30.

Kenosha Public Museum. Wildlife displays, Native American artifacts, and an ivory collection are on view downtown in the Civic Center. | 5608 10th Ave. | 262/653–4140 | Free | Daily 10–5.

Lakeshore Trolley. Take a 50-minute narrated ride through Kenosha's three National Register Historic Districts and along Lake Michigan. Hourly pickups at 7th Avenue and 58th Street. | Lakeshore Business District Office | 262/654–6344 or 800/411–4969 | $2; kids under 3 free | Memorial Day–Labor Day, Tues.–Fri. 11-4, weekends noon–6.

Prime Outlets at Kenosha. Seventy discount outlet stores are gathered under one roof. | I–94 and Hwy. 165 (Ext. 347) | 262/857–2101 | Free | Daily.

Southport Marina. This marina has 216 slips, a 2-mi walkway, and a playground. Parks and beaches are nearby. | 97 57th St. | 262/657–5565 | Free | Mid-Apr.–Nov., Tues.–Sat. 9–5, Sun. 9 AM–10 PM, closed Mon.; Dec.–mid-Apr., daily 9–4.

University of Wisconsin–Parkside. Chiwaukee Prairie is just one of the natural areas on the grounds of this 400-acre wooded campus, home to nearly 5,000 students. Tours are available by appointment. | 900 Wood Rd. | 262/595–2345 | Free | Daily.

ON THE CALENDAR

JUNE–AUG.: *Aquanuts Water Ski Show*. For nearly 20 years audiences have been thrilled by the crazy antics of this free water acrobatics event held at the Twin Lakes on Wednesday and Saturday evenings at 6 from Memorial Day through Labor Day. | 262/877–9655.

JUNE–AUG.: *Bristol Renaissance Fair*. This re-creation of a 16th-century English country fair and marketplace, 6 mi southwest of town in nearby Bristol, is where you can see costumed performers, actors, minstrels, dancers, artisans, crafts, and food. Open weekends from late June. | 847/395–777 | $16.50.

Dining

Brewmaster's Pub, Ltd. American/Casual. This comfortable family restaurant with seven taps sampling different microbrews is famed for its hearty sandwiches, including the Pub Club. | 4017 80th St. | 262/694–9050 | $6–$18 | AE, D, MC.

The Hobnob. Contemporary. Large windows provide a great view of Lake Michigan, and the ceilings are hand-painted to look like the inside of a tent. Specialties include veal scaloppine marsala and whitefish served on a plank with mixed greens. | 227 S. Sheridan Rd. | 262/552–8008 | $15–$25 | D, MC, V | No lunch.

House of Gerhard. German. A beer-stein collection and German memorabilia such as flags and vintage photos get you in the mood for the Wienerschnitzel and beef rouladen— braised beef rolls filled with mustard, bacon-crumbles, and pickles, and sprinkled with black pepper. For dessert try an airy meringue shell filled with ice cream, strawberries, and whipped cream. Kids' menu. | 3927 75th St. | 262/694–5212 | $10–$30 | AE, D, MC, V | Closed Sun. No lunch Sat.

Mangia Trattoria. Italian. You can dine inside or outside underneath umbrellas in the brick-walled garden outside, serenaded by a fountain. Pizzas are make in a wood-burning oven, the seafood is fresh, and the tiramisu is a specialty. | 5717 Sheridan Rd. | 262/652–4285 | $20–$30 | AE, D, DC, MC, V | No lunch Fri.–Sun.

Ray Radigan's. American. This former roadhouse is in a rural setting, 8 mi south of Kenosha. On the menu is fresh seafood and steak. | 11712 S. Sheraton Rd., Pleasant Prairie | 262/694–0455 | $16–$35 | AE, D, DC, MC, V | Closed Mon.

Lodging

Baymont Inn. This hotel is 4 mi from downtown, across from an outlet mall at the junction of Interstate 94 and Rte. 50. Complimentary Continental breakfast. In-room data ports, cable TV. Business services. Pets allowed. | 7540 118th Ave. | 262/857–7911 | fax 262/857–2370 | www.baymontinn.com | 95 rooms | $64–$84 | AE, D, DC, MC, V.

Holiday Inn Express. Rooms in this large, white stucco hotel downtown have views of Lake Michigan. A two-night minimum may be required on weekends. Cable TV. Pool. Hot tub. Business services. | 5125 6th Ave. | 262/658–3281 | fax 262/658–3420 | www.basshotels.com/hiexpress | 111 rooms | $85–$95 | AE, D, DC, MC, V.

Knights Inn. This standard motel is in a commercial area 5 mi from downtown. Several outlet stores are within walking distance. Some kitchenettes. Pets allowed. | 7221 122nd Ave. | 262/857–2622 | fax 262/857–2375 | 113 rooms | $58–$76 | AE, D, DC, MC, V.

Riley's Lily Lake Resort. Twenty minutes west of Kenosha, off highway 50, this small, laid-back beach motel has boat rentals, picnic tables, and a lakefront beach. Relax on the dock and watch the motorboats on Lily Lake. Complimentary Continental breakfast. Some refrigerators, cable TV. Lake. Beach, dock, water sports, boating. | 7910 328th Ave., Burlington | 262/537–2848 | 4 rooms, 2 suites | $65–$73 | AE, MC, V.

Southport B&B. This white colonial house is just two blocks from Lake Michigan and seven blocks north of downtown. It has a small porch and rooms are simple, comfortable, and wheelchair accessible. Complimentary Continental breakfast. Microwaves, refrigerators, in-room hot tubs, cable TV. Pets allowed. No smoking. | 4405 7th Ave. | 262/652–1951 | 2 rooms | $55–$60 | AE, D, DC, MC, V.

LAC DU FLAMBEAU

MAP 11, C2

(Nearby town also listed: Manitowish Waters, Park Falls)

When French fur traders saw members of the Chippewa, or Ojibwe, tribe spear-fishing at night by the light of torches, they were so struck by the image that they named the lake and the entire area after the practice. Today Lac du Flambeau ("Lake of the Torch") sits at the center of the Lac du Flambeau Indian Reservation. The region is imbued with Ojibway heritage and known for great fishing in the many area lakes. An impressive series of attractions showcase tribal culture.

Information: **Lac du Flambeau Chamber of Commerce** | Box 158, 54538-0158 | 715/588–3346.

Attractions

Chequamegon National Forest. In this 850,000-acre forest you will find the Penokee Overlook, which provides a scenic view from an observation platform built atop a high bluff. | 1170 4th St. south, Park Falls | 715/762–2461 | Free; permits required for some recreational trails | Daily.

George W. Brown Jr. Ojibwe Museum and Cultural Center. This downtown museum houses one of the finest collections of Native American artifacts in the north, including Ojibway arts and crafts, traditional clothing, and an authentic 24-ft dugout canoe that is more than 100 years old. Includes videos and dioramas depicting the four seasons of Ojibway life as it has been lived in the area for centuries. Programs, classes, and guided tours are available. | 603 Peace Pipe Rd. | 715/588–3333 | $2 | Call for hours.

Lac du Flambeau Tribal Hatchery. Owned and operated by the Lac du Flambeau Band of Lake Superior Chippewas, this hatchery raises brook, brown, and rainbow trout as well as walleye and muskellunge. Call in advance to schedule a tour. | 2500 Hwy. 47 north | 715/588–9613 | Free | Memorial Day–Labor Day, weekdays 8–5, closed weekends.

Wa-Swa-Goning Ojibwe Village. Exhibits at this outdoor museum surrounded by 20 acres of unspoiled woodland on the banks of Moving Cloud Lake include traditional lodges, birch-bark canoes, a maple-sugar camp, and artifacts. | Rtes. 47 and H | 715/588–3560 | $7 | Memorial Day–Labor Day, daily dawn to dusk.

Lake of the Torches Casino. 5,600 square feet of gambling, dancing, and dining await at this massive complex owned and operated by the Lac du Flambeau Band of Lake Superior Chippewa. You can try your hand on several hundred slot machines, video poker games, blackjack tables, and bingo tournaments. The casino is open 24 hours a day, and a complimentary hot buffet and drinks are free. | 510 Old Abe Rd. | 715/588–7070 or 800/25–TORCH | www.180025torch.com.

ON THE CALENDAR

JULY, AUG.: *Native American Artists' Show.* On two summer weekends, one in July and one in August, the Van Guthrie Library Mall hosts an outdoor showcase of Native American artists' work. July's show is coordinated with the Bear River Powwow. Call the Lac du Flambeau Chippewa Museum & Cultural Center for exact dates. | 622 Peacepipe Rd. | 715/588–3333.

JULY–AUG.: *Powwows.* Tuesday evenings bring Native American powwows with commentary in the Indian Bowl downtown, fronting Long Interlaken Lake. You are welcome to participate in dances. | 715/588–3346.

SEPT.: *Colorama.* This town-wide celebration of autumn and harvest time on the third weekend of the month includes Native American arts and crafts, food, entertainment, and decoy carving. | 715/588–3346.

Dining

Fence Lake Lodge. American. This log-cabin lodge is actually two restaurants overlooking Fence Lake, 5 mi from Lac du Flambeau. The fancier of the two serves smoked chicken, duck, and beef Wellington for dinner only. The casual restaurant serves soup, sandwiches, chile, and pizza. | 12919 Frying Pan Camp La. | 715/588–3255 | $14–$25 | AE, D, MC, V.

Jacobi's. Contemporary. You can check out the bar, circa 1904, or enjoy a stroll through the garden of this Victorian house south of Lac du Flambeau in Hazelhurst if you have a wait for a table in one of the two intimate dining rooms here. The house special is garlic-stuffed tenderloin with cognac mustard sauce and you'll be offered complimentary appetizers with entrées. | 9820 Cedar Falls Rd., Hazelhurst | 715/356–5591 | $14–$32 | MC, V | Closed Mon.; May–June also closed Tues.; Oct.–Apr. closed Sun.–Wed.

Lodging

Dillman's Bay. This resort on a 15-acre peninsula in White Sand Lake has striking views and offers lakeside cottages or motel accommodations. From mid-May to mid-October two or three different workshops in areas ranging from painting and wood carving to personal growth or corporate training are offered each week. No air-conditioning, some kitchenettes, TV in common area, no TV in some rooms. Tennis. Hiking, beaches, dock, water sports, boating, fishing, bicycles. Playground. Pets allowed. | 3285 Sand Lake Lodge La. | 715/588–3143 | fax 715/588–3110 | www.dillmans.com | 17 rooms, 18 cottages | $89–$150 | MC, V | Closed Nov.–Apr.

Thomsen's Thunderbird Hill Resort. This popular three-cottage cluster (two three-bedroom and one one-bedroom cottages) on Interlaken Lake—part of the Flambeau chain—is just 1 mi south of Lac du Flambeau. The bring-the-whole-family cottages are rented weekly—call for reservations early in the season as many guests are return visitors. No air-conditioning, kitchenettes, microwaves, refrigerators, cable TV. Lake. Beach, water sports, boating, fishing. No pets. | 2181 Hwy. D | 715/588–7284 summer, 920/775–4612 winter | 4 cottages | $465–$1,090 per week | No credit cards.

Ty-Back. Innkeepers Jane and Kermit Bekkum like to share the beauty of the 80 wooded acres surrounding their rough-cedar home, which is 4 mi north of Lac du Flambeau. Relax and take in lake views of Lake Bobidosh from the front deck or head down to the lake itself. Complimentary breakfast. No air-conditioning, no room phones, TV in common area. Lake. Hiking, beach, water sports, boating. Cross-country skiing. No smoking. | 3104 Simpson La., 54538 | 715/588–7851 | tybach1@networth.net | 2 rooms | $65–$75 | No credit cards.

LA CROSSE

(Nearby town also listed: Fountain City)

This city spreads from the edge of the Mississippi River to the base of steep bluffs. Permanent settlement of the area began in 1841 when Nathan Myrick first built a cabin on Barrons Island and began trading with the Winnebago tribe. Many industries, including logging, brewing, and agriculture, prospered here in the early years of settlement. The city's main street ends at Grandad Bluff city park, which rises 570 ft above the city. Head to the summit for a great view of Wisconsin, Minnesota, and Iowa, and you can see classic paddle-wheelers steaming down the Mississippi.

Information: La Crosse Area Convention and Visitors Bureau | 410 Veterans Memorial Dr., Riverside Park, 54601 | 800/658–9424 | www.wi.centuryinter.net/lacvb.

Attractions

Goose Island County Park. Located on an island in the Mississippi River, between La Crosse and the nearby town of Stoddard, this 1,000-acre park has more than 400 campsites, a swimming beach, boat-launch ramps, picnic facilities, and 6 mi of hiking/cross-country ski trails. | W6488 County Rd. GI | 608/785–9770 park, 608/788–7018 campground | Free; fees for camping | Daily; campgrounds mid-Apr.–Oct.

Grandad Bluff. More than 570 ft above the Mississippi River, this city park provides great views of the city and surrounding states. | Main St. | 608/789–7533 | Free | Daily.

Hixon House. This 15-room home looks exactly as it did in 1859, the year it was built and furnished. Includes historically accurate 19th-century gardens. | 429 N. 7th St. | 608/782–1980 | $4 | Memorial Day–Labor Day, daily 1–5; rest of year by appointment.

La Crosse Queen. This paddle-wheeler takes you on meal cruises and river excursions out of a dock in Riverside Park. | Riverside Park | 608/784–2893 | $10–$34 | Memorial Day–Oct., daily.

Mt. La Crosse Ski Area. Ten miles south of town, this mountain offers downhill and night skiing, intermediate cross-country trails, and snowboarding. It has 18 slopes and a 516-ft vertical drop. The longest run is 5,300 ft. The area has some very steep ski runs. | Old Town Rd. | 608/788–0044 or 800/426–3665 | www.mtlacrosse.com | $11–$32 | Dec.–mid-Mar., daily.

Pump House Regional Center for the Arts. You can catch local arts activities and performances downtown, just two blocks from Riverside Park. | 119 King St. | 608/785–1434 | Gallery free; performance prices vary | Tues.–Sat.

Riverside Amusement Park. Includes miniature golf, go-carts, batting cages, and kiddie carts, but no rides. | 1304 Interchange Pl. | 608/781–7529 | All activities $1–$5; special rates for kids | Memorial Day–Labor Day, Sun.–Thurs. 11–11, Fri.–Sat. 11 AM–midnight.

Riverside Park. This is a great place to view boat traffic on the Mississippi River. You can also board the *Julia Belle Swain*, a paddle-wheel steamer. The park is home to the La Crosse Convention and Visitors Bureau, which houses the Riverside Museum, featuring archaeological and local history displays concentrating on the river's importance to the growth and development of the area. | State St. | 608/783–6403 | Free | Daily.

The *Julia Belle Swain* is a floating palace with all the amenities of old-time riverboats. Weekend brunch, lunch, and dinner cruises are offered, along with two-day excursions to Prairie du Chien. All cruises include live music. Reservations required. | Riverside Park, on State St. | 608/784–4882 or 800/815–1005 | $22–$44 | June–Oct., daily.

Swarthout Museum. Changing local history exhibits go from prehistoric times to the 21st century. | 112 S. 9th St. | 608/782–1980 | Free | Tues.–Fri. 10–5, weekends 1–5, closed Mon.

Trempealeau Lakes. This scenic chain of seven small spring-fed lakes is popular for fishing. Some lakes are accessible to people in wheelchairs. | off Rte. 35, about 18 mi northwest of La Crosse | 608/534–6780 | Free | Daily.

ON THE CALENDAR
JULY: *Riverfest.* This five-day festival celebrated around July 4th weekend features fireworks, entertainment, food, and craft shows along the river at Riverside Park. | 800/658–9424.

JULY: *La Crosse Interstate Fair.* NASCAR racing, a midway, 4-H events, livestock, entertainment, and arts and crafts are on view at the West Salem Fairgrounds, 11 mi east of town in nearby West Salem, in mid-month. | 800/658–9424.

AUG.: *Great River Jazz Fest.* A weekend-long international jazz festival on the Oktoberfest Grounds. | 608/791–1190.

OCT.: *Oktoberfest.* The bulk of the Midwest's largest Oktoberfest celebration takes place in downtown La Crosse, with a parade, entertainment, food, and bands from Germany on the first weekend in October. Other events are held at the Northside Fairgrounds complex. | 800/658–9424.

Dining
Alpine Inn. American. At the entrance to Grandad Bluff, this steak-and-sandwich-grab-a-brewski, party-down tavern serves predominately Wisconsin brewed beers, and is complete with outdoor beer garden/deck and volleyball. | W5717 Bliss Rd. | 608/784–8470 | $3–$7 | No credit cards.

Buzzard Billy's Flying Carp Café. Cajun/Creole. There's usually jazz or blues wailing from the speakers at this family spot. Try the seafood eggplant *pirogues,* wedges of hollowed-out eggplant filled with seafood, sauteed mushrooms, and green onions, then drizzled with a cheese/cream sauce; or consider the cajun-blackened walleye, catfish, or whitefish, sprinkled with zesty spices and sided with spicy rice and zucchini slices. | 222 Pearl St. | 608/796–2277 | $5–$14 | AE, D, DC, MC, V.

Fayze's. American. Brick walls adorned with La Crosse memorabilia set the familial tone of this restaurant/bakery famous for sandwiches served on a homemade, fluffy, Lebanese Talame roll. | 135 S. 4th St. | 608/784–9548 | $3–$13 | D, DC, MC, V | Breakfast also available.

Freighthouse. American. This late-19th-century former train station, now on the National Register of Historic Places, offers fine dining in a casual atmosphere. The Chicago, Milwaukee, and St. Paul Railroad cars are still on view outside the restaurant. Fresh seafood, prime rib, and steaks are a specialty. Open-air dining overlooks the Mississippi River. | 107 Vine St. | 608/784–6211 | Reservations not accepted | $13–$20 | AE, D, DC, MC, V | No lunch.

Piggy's. American. Downtown on the riverfront, this is a cozy place with its dark wood-paneled walls and antiques. As the name implies, this is a place for meat: hickory-smoked barbecued ribs, pork chops, and smoked prime rib. Salad bar. Kids' menu. | 328 S. Front St. | 608/784–4877 | $16–$40 | AE, D, DC, MC, V | No lunch Sun.

Traditions. Contemporary. A former bank, this intimate, brick-walled spot 6 mi north of La Crosse is marked by chef/owner Mary Cody's use of seasonal ingredients and regional specialties in dishes like pan-seared walleye and beer-cheese soup. | 201 Main St., Onalaska | 608/783–0200 | $17–$24 | AE, D, DC, MC, V | No lunch.

Lodging
Best Western Midway. This chain hotel is on the Black River, 3 mi from downtown and ½ mi from Riverside Amusement Park. Restaurant, bar. Complimentary Continental breakfast. In-room data ports, cable TV, in-room VCRs. Pool. Hot tub. Gym. Dock. Business services. | 1835 Rose St. | 608/781–7000 | fax 608/781–3195 | www.bestwestern.com | 121 rooms | $85–$129 | AE, D, DC, MC, V.

Days Inn. Most rooms in this chain motel on French Island have wonderful views of the Mississippi River. The hotel is just 1 mi from downtown and 2 mi from Riverside Amusement Park. Restaurant, bar, complimentary Continental breakfast. Cable TV. Pool. Hot tub, sauna. Video games. Business services. | 101 Sky Harbor Dr. | 608/783–1000 | fax 608/783–2948 | 148 rooms | $59–$79 | AE, D, DC, MC, V.

Exel Inn. This modest, one-story motel is two blocks from Riverside Amusement Park and 5 mi from downtown. Cable TV. Laundry facilities. | 2150 Rose St. | 608/781–0400 | fax 608/781–1216 | 102 rooms | $40–$70 | AE, D, DC, MC, V.

Four Gables Bed & Breakfast. This brick, 1906 Queen Anne Victorian home aims to be a romantic, peaceful getaway ¼ mi out of town. Complimentary breakfast. No air-conditioning, no room phones, TV in common area. Library. No pets. No kids. No smoking. | W. 5648 Hwy. 14-61 | 608/788–7958 | fax 608/788–7958 | 3 rooms | $75–$90 | No credit cards.

Guest House Motel. A standard brick, 1960s-era motel in downtown La Crosse. Restaurant. Cable TV. Pool. No pets. | 810 S. 4th St. | 608/784–8840 or 800/274–6873 | fax 608/782–5598 | robin@centuryinter.net | www.visitor-guide.com/guesthouse | 39 rooms | $48–$68 | AE, D, MC, V.

Hampton Inn. This cheery, pale-yellow motel is one of several just a few blocks from Riverside Amusement Park and 5 mi from downtown. Complimentary Continental breakfast. Cable TV. Pool. Hot tub. Gym. | 2110 Rose St. | 608/781–5100 or 800/426–7866 | fax 608/781–3574 | 101 rooms | $69–$109 | AE, D, DC, MC, V.

Martindale House Bed-and-Breakfast. This bright yellow 1850s Italianate home, now on the National Historic Register, is just six blocks east of downtown La Crosse. Complimentary breakfast. Some kitchenettes, some in-room hot tubs, no room phones. No pets. No kids. No smoking. | 237 S. 10th St. | 608/782–4224 | www.lacrosse-wisconsin.com | 4 rooms | $74–$155 | MC, V | Closed Nov. 2–end Mar.

Night Saver Inn. Another motel on Rose Street, not far from Riverside Amusement Park and about 5 mi from downtown. Complimentary Continental breakfast. In-room data ports, cable TV, in-room VCRs available. Hot tub. Gym. Business services. | 1906 Rose St. | 608/781–0200 or 800/658–9497 | fax 608/781–0200 | www.visitor-guide.com/nightsaver | 73 rooms | $54–$62 | AE, D, DC, MC, V.

Radisson. Many rooms in this eight-story hotel have views of the Mississippi River. The large lobby has marble floors; paintings depict the riverfront during the 1900s. Restaurant, bar (with entertainment), complimentary Continental breakfast. Cable TV. Pool. Hot tub. Gym. Business services, airport shuttle. Pets allowed. | 200 Harborview Plaza | 608/784–6680 or 800/333–3333 | fax 608/784–6694 | www.radisson.com | 170 rooms | $109–$169 | AE, D, DC, MC, V.

Road Star Inn. Part of a local chain, this motel is in a commercial area 2½ mi from downtown and right off Interstate 90. Complimentary Continental breakfast. Some in-room data ports, some microwaves, refrigerators, cable TV. Business services. | 2622 Rose St. | 608/781–3070 or 800/445–4667 | fax 608/781–5114 | 110 rooms | $42–$57 | AE, D, DC, MC, V.

Super 8. This motel, one of several on commercial Rose Street, has a large lobby with leather furniture, a wood fireplace, and a seating area and a breakfast room with a TV. Complimentary Continental breakfast. Some in-room hot tubs, cable TV. Pool. Hot tub. Laundry facilities. | 1625 Rose St. | 608/781–8880 | fax 608/781–4366 | www.super8.com | 82 rooms | $69–$159 | AE, D, DC, MC, V.

LADYSMITH

MAP 11, B3

(Nearby town also listed: Rice Lake)

Located in rustic Rusk County, sights include the 27-mi Blue Hills section of the Ice Age Trail, the Chippewa, Flambeau, Thornapple and Jump rivers, and crystal-clear waters filled with trout. You can canoe and fish throughout the area. Tourism, farming, and industry support the economy.

Information: **Ladysmith Tourism Information** | 205 W. 9th St., 54848 | 715/532–2642.

Attractions

Flambeau River State Forest. This preserve, 13 mi northeast of Ladysmith, was established in 1930; the original 3,600 acres has grown to 90,000. Northern hardwood species such as sugar maple, red maple, yellow birch, and white ash dominate the landscape, and the fall foliage is spectacular. Forty miles of the Flambeau River flow through the forest to make canoeing one of the most popular activities. | Rte. M, north off Hwy 8 E | 715/332–5271 | Free; permits required for some recreational trails | Daily.

ON THE CALENDAR

MAY–OCT.: *Van Wey's Flea Market and Auctions.* About 1,500 visitors come to this summer event each year, 4 mi west on Highway 8 between Ladysmith and nearby Bruce. There are some 150 booths with antiques, collectibles, clothing, farm equipment, autos, campers, trucks, and trailers. | 715/532–6044 | wwww.fleamarketguide.com.
JULY: *Northland Mardi Gras.* A nighttime Venetian boat parade on the river Flambeau, a street parade, crafts, tournaments, sporting events, food, entertainment, and a carnival in Memorial Park take place on the second weekend of the month. | 715/532–2642.
AUG.: *Rusk County Fair.* 4-H events, a mud-truck run, truck and tractor pulls, a demolition derby, horse shows, food, and entertainment are found at the Rusk County fairgrounds Thursday–Sunday of the second weekend of the month. | 715/532–2642.

Dining

Back Door Café. American. Built around 1919, this country-style restaurant has pressed-tin ceilings and old-fashioned signs on the walls. Check out the lumberjack pancakes—nearly a foot long—if you're hungry enough. The Friday-night fish fry draws a crowd. | 102 W. 2nd St. N | 715/532–3029 | $5–$7 | No credit cards.

Lodging

Americinn. This standard motel is set in a rural area just south of the intersection of Highways 8 and 27, about a mile from downtown Ladysmith. The grounds are landscaped with flower beds. Top-notch fishing is nearby. Pool. | 800 W. College Ave. | 715/532–6650 or 800/634–3444 | fax 715/532–6987 | www.americinn.com | 37 rooms | $70–$80 | AE, D, MC, V.

Best Western El Rancho. This hotel is on 20 acres of woods and fields just about a mile outside of town and in winter there are groomed trails for cross-country skiing. Some rooms have outside entrances, others are off interior hallways. Restaurant, bar. Cable TV. Cross-country skiing. Business services. Pets allowed. | 8500 W. Flambeau Ave. | 715/532–6666 | fax 715/532–7551 | www.bestwestern.com | 27 rooms | $63–$70 | AE, D, DC, MC, V.

LAKE GENEVA

MAP 11, E7

(Nearby town also listed: Delavan)

Great shops, restaurants, candy stores, and striking Lake Geneva greet you as you enter this popular resort community, settled in 1840. Wealthy Chicago families discovered the area just after the Civil War and began building summer homes here. Today the elegant, often historic estates still surround the scenic lake, although most are on private roads and can only be viewed from the water aboard small cruise boats; you can also see some homes by walking a footpath that skirts the water's edge. This four-season resort area has golf courses and Big Foot Beach State Park, where you can camp, hike, and swim on Geneva Lake.

Information: **Lake Geneva Convention and Visitors Bureau.** | 201 Wrigley Dr., 53147 | 800/345–1020 | www.lakegenevawi.com.

Attractions

Big Foot Beach State Park. Named for Chief Big Foot of the Potowatomi tribe, this state park is within the Lake Geneva city limits and offers camping, hiking, shaded picnic areas, and a sand beach with 1,900 ft of lake frontage. | 1452 Rte. H | 262/248–2528 | www.dnr.state.wi.us | $7 nonresidents, $5 residents | 3rd Mon. in May–Nov. 1.

Geneva Lake. This 5,000-acre lake offers a wide variety of water activities and spectacular shorelines. This area was the site of President Calvin Coolidge's summer White House. | 201 Wrigley Dr. | 800/345–1020 | Free | Daily.

Geneva Lake Cruise Line. Narrated boat tours of historic Geneva Lake offering brunch, lunch, and dinner and Dixieland cruises leave from the Riviera Docks. The boats are also used for one of the most unusual—and daring—mail-delivery services in the nation: carriers leap between docks and moving boats to speed the mail to its rightful recipient. | 812 Wrigley Dr. | 262/248–6206 or 800/558–5911 | $11–$45 | May–Oct., daily.

Geneva Lake Shore Path. One of the most popular tourist attractions in this area is a 20.6-mi path that winds around the lake. You can see mansions from the path, which can be accessed through any public park on the lake. A map, called "Walk, Talk & Gawk" gives directions and points of interest. Shorter walks are also mapped out, including an easy 2-mi route. Maps are available free at the Lake Geneva Convention & Visitors Bureau at 201 Wrigley Drive | Geneva Lake | 800/345–1020 | Free | Daily.

Wilmot Mt. Downhill skiing and snowboarding, with 25 runs, and a vertical drop of 230 ft can be found 20 mi from Lake Geneva, on the Iowa-Wiscosin border. The longest run is 2,500 ft. | 11931 Fox River Rd., Wilmot | 262/862–2301 | $16.50–28.50 | Late-Nov.–Mar., daily.

ON THE CALENDAR

FEB.: *Winterfest.* On the first weekend of the month downtown fills with food stands, entertainment, a winter carnival, a lighted torch parade, fireworks, and kids' activities, not to mention the U.S. National Snow Sculpting Competition. | 800/345–1020.

AUG.: *Venetian Festival.* A carnival, entertainment, food, a lighted boat parade, and fireworks light up Flatiron Park on the third weekend of the month. | 800/345–1020.

DEC.: *Christmas in the Country.* Christmas decorations, horse-drawn carriage rides, downhill and cross-country skiing, food, and entertainment are on tap Christmas week at the Grand Geneva Resort. | 800/558–3417 | www.grandgeneva.com.

Dining

Popeye's on Lake Geneva. American. This sprawling, lake-view restaurant deck is filled with old ship parts, large maps, and tables topped with treasure maps. The bar is made out of a boat. Try the fried cod with potato pancakes and applesauce, or the homemade broccoli-cheddar soup. | 811 Wrigley Dr. | 262/248–4381 | $12–$17 | D, MC, V.

Red Geranium. American. Crisp-white walls painted with cheery red geraniums and punctuated with big windows make the dining room here seem particularly spacious and comfortable. The menu features such creatively prepared classics as hickory-smoked boneless porkchops sided with roasted red potatoes, and fresh, barely blackened whitefish crusted with savory herbs. Open-air dining on patio and in courtyard gazebo. Kids' menu. Parking. | Main St. | 262/248–3637 | $17–$30 | AE, D, MC, V.

Ristorante Brissago. Italian. Located in the Grand Geneva Resort, this third-story restaurant has white linen tablecloths and views of wooded hills, the 18th hole of the resort's golf course, and the lake. Specialties include stuffed shrimp and orzo, and filet mignon. | Hwy. 50 and Hwy. 21 | 262/248–8811 | $11–$28 | AE, D, MC, V | Closed Mon. No lunch.

St. Moritz. Continental. This restaurant in an elaborate late-19th-century Victorian has five lake-view dining rooms, including a glassed-in veranda. The menu offers veal, fresh fish, and lamb. | 327 Wrigley Dr. | 262/248–6680 | $18–$30 | AE, D, MC, V | Closed Mon. No lunch.

Temple Garden. Chinese. This restaurant looks like a Tibetan temple inside with its elaborate Buddhist shrine and large portrait of the Dalai Lama. Try the scallion pancakes and dumplings. | 724 W. Main St. | 262/249–9188 | $7–$12 | D, MC, V | No lunch Sun., Mon.

Lodging

Ambassador. This single-story hotel is on 10 landscaped and wooded acres. Its spacious lobby has a large brick fireplace and a stained-glass window. Next door there's a miniature golf course. Complimentary Continental breakfast. Some refrigerators, some in-room hot tubs, cable TV. Pool. Hot tub, sauna. Tennis. Business services. No smoking. | 415 Wells St. | 262/248–3452 | fax 262/248–0605 | 18 rooms | $69–$89 | AE, D, MC, V.

Budget Host Diplomat. The light-beige brick building has an unassuming lobby space with a couple of comfortable lounge chairs and free coffee. Guest rooms are what you'd expect from a mid-range chain motel, with faux-wood panelling and soothing watercolor prints on the walls. The surrounding area has plenty of popular restaurants to choose from, and Geneva Lake is less than 5 mi away. Picnic area. Cable TV, in-room VCRs available. Pool. Business services. | 1060 Wells St. | 262/248–1809 | fax 262/248–2455 | 23 rooms | $42–$111 | AE, D, MC, V.

French Country Inn. Part of this old-world charmer on the shores of Lake Como (less than a mile from Geneva Lake), was built in Denmark for Chicago's Columbian Exposition in 1893; you can still see the original furnishings and cherry wood throughout the main building. All rooms have lake views. Golf is nearby. Restaurant, complimentary breakfast. Cable TV. Pool. Beach. Business services. | 4190 West End Rd. | 262/245–5220 | fax 262/245–9060 | www.frenchcountryinn.com | 32 rooms | $125–$260 | MC, V.

General Boyd's Bed & Breakfast. Originally homesteaded in 1839 by General John W. Boyd of the 3rd Wisconsin Territorial Militia, this B&B sits on 6 acres of rolling hills. Classic timber-pegged barns, 20 varieties of trees, and perennial and wildflower gardens accent the property, which is dominated by native white-oak trees. There is a spacious living room with a large fieldstone fireplace, a dining room, and a library. Complimentary breakfast. No room phones, no TV. | W2915 County Trunk BB | 262/248–3543 | www.generalboydsbb.com | 4 rooms | $95–$135 | AE, D, MC, V.

Grand Geneva Resort and Spa. This elegant Prairie-style resort on 1,300 rolling acres includes two PGA golf courses, riding stables, and a private lake. 3 restaurants (*see* Ristorante Brissago, bar (with entertainment). In-room data ports, cable TV, in-room VCRs and movies. Three pools. Hot tub, spa. Driving range, golf courses, putting green, tennis. Gym, boating, bicycles. Cross-country skiing, downhill skiing. Kids' programs (ages 6 weeks–14), playground. Business services, airport shuttle, free parking. | 7036 Grand Geneva Way | 262/248–8811 or 800/558–3417 | fax 262/248–3192 | www.grandgeneva.com | 318 rooms, 37 suites | $229–$259 rooms, $249–$409 suites | AE, D, DC, MC, V.

Interlaken Resort and Country Spa. This hostelry 4 mi west of Lake Geneva is a modern building backed by acres of unspoiled woodland and has a fantastic view of Lake Como from almost every room. Restaurant, bar (with entertainment), room service. Cable TV, in-room VCRs and movies. 3 pools, wading pool. Barbershop, beauty salon, hot tub. Tennis. Exercise equipment. Water sports, boating, ice-skating. Cross-country skiing, snowmobiling. Video games. Kids' programs (ages 5–13). Business services, free parking. | W4240 Rte. 50 | 262/248–9121 or 800/225–5558 | fax 262/245–5016 | www.interlakenresort.net | 144 rooms, 64 villas | $145–$165 rooms, $222–$292 villas | AE, D, DC, MC, V.

Oaks Inn. This Italianate antebellum inn downtown is filled with three centuries of antique furniture and paintings; there are 18th-century Chinese Chippendale dining room chairs on the breakfast porch. Complimentary Continental breakfast. Cable TV, in-room VCRs, no room phones. | 421 Baker St. | 262/248–9711 | fax 262/249–8529 | www.oaksinn.com | 6 rooms, 1 suite | $100–$200 | MC, V.

Pederson Victorian Bed & Breakfast. This 1880 Victorian has gingerbread trim and is landscaped with wildflowers. You can take curl up on one of the porches or in the comfortable parlor and read from the books available. Beds are made with line-dried linens. there is a cat in residence. Complimentary breakfast. No room phones, no TV. | 1782 Hwy. 120 N | 262/893–1054 or 888/764–9653 | hanahawk@genevaonline.com | 4 rooms | $85–$120 | MC, V.

Roses Bed-and-Breakfast. This secluded colonial, a block from Lake Geneva, has a casual, English-country look. The main level has a wraparound porch, large windows, and an outdoor deck. Complimentary breakfast. Cable TV. Some pets allowed. No smoking. | 429 S. Lake Shore Dr. | 262/248–4344 or 888/767–3262 | fax 262/248–5766 | www.rosesbnb.com | 5 rooms | $110–$155 | D, MC, V.

T. C. Smith Historic Inn Bed & Breakfast. A National Historic Landmark, this 1845 Victorian mansion gives a view of the lake but is also close to downtown. It's furnished with period antiques, museum-worthy paintings, and oriental carpets. Outside is a water garden, a goldfish pond, and a gazebo. Complimentary breakfast. Cable TV. Beach, bicycles. | 865 Main St. | 262/248–1097 or 800/423–0233 | fax 262/248–1672 | www.tcsmithinn.com | 8 rooms | $125–$365 | AE, D, MC, V.

LAND O' LAKES

MAP 11, D2

(Nearby towns also listed: Eagle River, Sayner)

This small village on the Wisconsin–Michigan border is close to the Nicolet National Forest. In both the south and the west part of town there are 37 medium-to-large-sized and more than 100 small-to-tiny crystal-clear lakes with miles of scenic shoreline, flanked by 21,000 acres of virgin timber. Fishing, both in summer and winter, is a favored sport here.

Information: **Land O' Lakes Chamber of Commerce** | Rte. B and U.S. 45 | 800/236–3432 or 715/547–3432.

Attractions

Sylvania Wilderness Area. Just about every sport available is offered in these 21,000 acres of virgin timber and dozens of crystal-clear lakes: camping, hiking, swimming, hiking, cross-country skiing, snowmobiling, hunting, fishing, trapping, and canoeing. | Entry station on Thousand Island Lake Rd. | 800/236–3432 | Free with vehicle pass (obtained at the entry station, or by mail in advance). Fees vary for camping | Daily.

ON THE CALENDAR

JULY: *Art Impressions Show.* Downtown, on the fourth Saturday of the month, local and national artists show and sell their work outdoors in front of Town Hall, with folk music accompaniment. | 715/547–3432.

Dining

Bear Trap. American. You can choose from specialties such as grilled scallops, steaks and chops, while old-time tunes filter in from the lounge. There's a rustic Northwoods feel here with antiques from Wisconsin's logging days. | 4703 Hwy. B | 715/547–3422 | Reservations not accepted | $7–$33 | AE, MC, V | Closed Sun., Mon. No lunch.

Lodging

Gateway Lodge. Constructed by Northwoods craftsmen almost a century ago on the boundary line that separates Wisconsin and Michigan, this landmark resort is built entirely of hand-hewn logs. The inviting lobby has a large, hand-built fireplace that you can gather around. Rustic suites and studios have kitchenettes and are decorated with natural wood. Cable TV. | 4103 County Hwy. B | 715/547–3321 or 800/848–8058 | fax 715/547–3325 | www.gateway-lodge.com | 72 rooms | $50–$70 | AE, D, DC, MC, V.

Sunrise Lodge. This resort on Lac Vieux Desert just north of Land O' Lakes has modern cottages of varying size spread along the lakefront and interspersed with fragrant evergreen trees. The resort offers swimming and fishing in the warmer months, and snowmobiling, cross-country skiing, and ice-fishing when things get chilly. The main building houses a restaurant, recreation room with board games, a pool table, and books. Restaurant, picnic area. No air-conditioning in some rooms, kitchenettes, refrigerators, TV in common area. Miniature golf, tennis. Beach, boating, fishing, bicycles. Cross-country skiing. Kids' programs (ages 3–16), playground. Business services, airport shuttle. Pets allowed. | 5894 W. Shore Dr. | 715/547–3684 or 800/221–9689 | fax 715/547–6110 | www.sunriselodge.com | 21 cottages | $90–$300 | AP | D, MC, V.

LITTLE CHUTE

MAP 11, E5

(Nearby town also listed: Appleton)

LITTLE CHUTE

INTRO
ATTRACTIONS
DINING
LODGING

Quaint Little Chute is on the Fox River, surrounded by wooded areas with trails for hiking and cross-country skiing. The village, which is made up of residential areas, small businesses, and industry, has five parks and a wide variety of recreational facilities, including two soccer fields and two ice-skating rinks.

Information: Fox Cities Convention and Visitors Bureau | 3433 W. College Ave., Appleton 54914 | 800/236–6673 | tourism@foxcities.org | www.foxcities.org.

Attractions

Doyle Park. The big heated pool and 201-foot spiral water slide are the main draws to this diminutive park in the hot summer months, but there's also a basketball court, picnic facilities, and lots of beautiful old trees to stroll among. | 100 Van Buren St. | 920/788–7380 | Park is free, pool is $1 | Pool closed Sept.–May.

Heesakker Park. Right on the Fox River, this park has wooded hiking and walking trails, cross-country skiing routes, soccer fields, and two separate ice-skating rinks. | 1509 Lincoln Ave. | 920/788–7380 | Free | Daily, dawn to dusk.

ON THE CALENDAR

SEPT.: *Kermis Dutch Festival.* "Kermis" is a Dutch word meaning "after mass," and this celebration was so named because of its religious origins. Today, the Kermis festival celebrates Little Chute's Dutch heritage with a Dutch costume contest, a fish boil, a basketball tournament, parades, raffles, and a fireworks display. | 920/788–7380.

JUNE: *Great Wisconsin Cheese Festival.* A weekend of fun in downtown Doyle Park, early in the month, includes a parade, a cheese-curd-eating contest, cheese carving, cheese tasting, a cheesecake contest, and midway rides. | 800/236–6673.

MADISON

(Nearby towns also listed: Dodgeville, Spring Green)

Big-city culture mixes with small-town charm in Wisconsin's capital. It was founded in 1829, when James Duane Doty, a territorial judge and land speculator, traveled through the isthmus and liked it so much he bought 1,200 acres for $1,500 and plotted a town grid. In 1836 he persuaded the territorial legislature to designate his paper city as the site of the new capital.

The city center is dominated by the State Capitol. On Wednesday and Saturday mornings, from early spring to late fall, the surrounding square becomes an open-air market as area farmers sell their diverse foods, such as 20 varieties of bean sprouts and freshly made summer sausage. Students from the University of Wisconsin can often be found in great numbers shopping or browsing on busy State Street which extends westward from the corner of Capitol Square. The small boutiques of this pedestrian zone alternate between vintage clothing, New-Age gifts, music stores, and coffee shops. There area has a number of Frank Lloyd Wright buildings, though some are private homes and not open to the public. The university, state government, and manufacturing provide much of Madison's economic base.

Information: Greater Madison Convention and Visitors Bureau | 615 E. Washington Ave. | 800/373–6376 | www.visitmadison.com.

NEIGHBORHOODS

Mansion Hill Historic District. This area, settled by the city's upper class in the mid-19th century, is filled with ornate older homes. It sits on a wooded hill along the shores of Lake Mendota, north of the state capitol, between Gorham, Gilman, Henry, and Butler streets.

Third Lake Ridge Historic District. This neighborhood was built by a diverse group of residents, including the wealthy and not-so-wealthy in many architectural styles. Some of the area's buildings are on the National Register of Historic Places, or are designated as Madison Landmarks. The area is on a glacial plain on the north shore of Lake Monona and runs between Spaight and Rutledge streets along the lakeside to Williamson Street, and between South Blount and South Few streets. Small Orton Park is here.

TRANSPORTATION INFORMATION

Airports: Dane County Regional Airport is served by domestic carriers. | 400 International La. | 608/246–3380.

Bus lines: Greyhound | 2 S. Bedford St. | 800/231–2222.

Intra-city Transit: Madison Metro is the local bus system. | 608/266–4466.

Attractions

ART AND ARCHITECTURE

Monona Terrace Community and Convention Center. This 250,00-square-ft structure on the shore of Lake Monona, near the State Capitol, is Madison's newest downtown showpiece. Designed by Frank Lloyd Wright in 1938, and finally completed in 1997, the center has a rooftop garden, a café, a sports hall of fame, and a memorial to singer Otis Redding, who died in a plane crash nearby. | 1 John Nolen Dr. | 608/261–4000 | Free | Daily.

State Capitol. Designed in the style of the Capitol building in Washington, D.C., the State Capitol is downtown on the highest point of land on the isthmus. The building dominates the skyline for miles and is flooded with light at night. Public tours are conducted daily. | Capitol Sq. | 608/266–0382 | Free | Daily.

BEACHES, PARKS, AND NATURAL SIGHTS

Lake Kegonsa State Park. This park on the northeast corner of Lake Kegonsa, 20 mi south of Madison, offers sailing, boating, swimming, fishing, and waterskiing, as well as family camping, hiking, summer interpretive programs, and cross-country skiing. | 2405 Door Creek Rd., Stoughton | 608/873–9695 | www.dnr.state.wi.us | Daily; campground May–Oct.

Olbrich Botanical Gardens. Olbrich's 14 acres on the north side of Lake Monona include rose, herb, rock, and perennial gardens. A 50-ft-high pyramidal glass conservatory houses tropical plants and flowers. | 3330 Atwood Ave. | 608/246–4551 | www.olbrich.org | Free; conservatory $1 | Daily 8–8.

CULTURE, EDUCATION, AND HISTORY

Edgewood College. Located on the shores of Lake Wingra west of downtown, this liberal-arts college founded in 1927 has some 2,000 students. The grounds also contain the Edgewood Campus Grade School and the Edgewood High School. Tours of the campus are available. | 1000 Edgewood College Dr. | 608/257–4861 | www.edgewood.edu | Free | Daily.

Sonderegger Science Center. This new $10-million facility near the center of the campus is considered a national model for science education from kindergarten through college. An ever-changing variety of displays, educational outreach programs, interactive exhibits, and on-site kids' programs make the Center more than just another museum. | 855 Woodrow St. | 608/257–4861 | www.edgewood.edu | Free | Daily.

Marshall Hall. This former carriage house dates back to the Civil War. The building has been a dorm since 1927. | 855 Woodrow St. | 608/257–4861 | www.edgewood.edu | Free | Daily.

Native American Bird Effigy Mounds at Edgewood College. The college's grounds contain dozens of Native American bird effigy mounds, including an eagle mound that measures 100-ft tall and 200-ft wide. The eagle mound is in a courtyard in front of the Oscar Rennebohm Library. Other mounds are in the center of campus. | 855 Woodrow St. | 608/257–4861 | www.edgewood.edu | Free | Daily.

University of Wisconsin–Madison. Considered one of the most beautiful campuses in the country, this university on Lake Mendota less than a mile west of the State Capitol is world famous for excellence in academics and sports. Well over 30,000 undergraduate and graduate students call the UW home, and follow courses of study in academic schools of nursing, journalism, business, law, and biochemistry. A wide variety of tours are available, but they must be booked in advance. | 500 Lincoln Dr. | 608/265–9500 | Campus tours free; other tours vary in admission | Daily.

Built in 1917, the double-deck **Camp Randall Stadium and Fieldhouse** is home to the Badgers, the University of Wisconsin's football team. The site ranks among the nation's largest school-owned stadiums. It includes a study area for student-athletes, training and weight rooms, and a display of football memorabilia. Tours by appointment. | 1440 Monroe St. | 608/262–7425 | Free | Tours Tues. and Thurs. at 10, Wed. at 1.

The University of Wisconsin's 85-ft, 56-bell **Carillon Tower** overlooking Lake Mendota was a gift of the classes of 1917–1926. A concert is held in front of the tower every Sunday afternoon in warmer months. | 1160 Observatory Dr. | 608/265–9500 | Free | Daily.

The **Elvehjem Museum of Art,** a fine study resource for University of Wisconsin students, contains a permanent collection of fine art, ranging from Renaissance oil paintings to modernist sculpture. Chamber-music concerts are given on Sundays. | 800 University Ave. | 608/263–2246 | Free | Tues.–Fri. 9–5, weekends 11–5. Closed Mon.

Memorial Library is the University of Wisconsin's main library. Built in 1950, it houses 5.4 million volumes, including the university research library, a rare-book collection, and university archives. | 728 State St. | 608/262–3193 | Free | Daily.

Scenic **Observatory and Willow Drives** cover about 3 mi and allow you to see two different areas of the University of Wisconsin campus. Observatory Drive starts at Park Street, near the entrance to Memorial Union, and gives a spectacular view of the lake and the campus grounds. Willow Drive, which features beautiful weeping willow trees, starts at the west end of Observatory Drive and takes you down roads along the lower level of the campus, by the lake. | 716 Langdon St. | Free | Daily.

Constructed in 1878, the historic **Washburn Observatory** was the first major private gift to the University of Wisconsin. | 1401 Observatory Dr. | 608/265–9500 | Free | Tours by appointment only.

MUSEUMS

Madison Art Center. This cultural center in a restored movie theater downtown in the Civic Center mounts more than a dozen exhibitions each year. | 211 State St. | 608/257–0158 | Free | Tues.–Thurs. 11–5, Fri. 11–9, Sat. 10–9, Sun. 1–5.

State Historical Museum. Wisconsin history is the focus of permanent and changing exhibits ranging from prehistoric Native American culture to contemporary social issues. The museum is on Capitol Square, right downtown. | 30 N. Carroll St. | 608/264–6555 | Free | Tues.–Sat. 10–5, Sun. noon–5.

Wisconsin Veterans Museum. Dioramas depicting important military battles and exhibits from the Civil War to the present honor all state veterans. Full-size aircraft, scale models of 19th- and 20th-century ships, and military artifacts are also on display. The submarine periscope protruding through a gallery roof provides a novel view of downtown on Capitol Square. | 30 W. Mifflin St. | 608/267–1799 | Free | Oct.–Mar., Mon.–Sat. 9–4:30; Apr.–Sept., Mon.–Sat. 9–4:30, Sun. noon–4.

RELIGION AND SPIRITUALITY

First Unitarian Society Meeting House. Built in 1950, this church just west of the University of Wisconsin–Madison campus was designed by Wisconsin native Frank Lloyd Wright. | 900 University Bay Dr. | 608/233–9774 | Free | By appointment.

SHOPPING

Dane County Farmers' Market. Vendors sell a wide variety of cheese, fish, meat, and baked goods twice a week at Capitol Square and on Capitol Street, just to the east. | Capitol Sq., 200 Martin Luther King Jr. Blvd. (Wed); on Capitol St. (Sat.) | 920/563–5037 | Free | 9–5.

SIGHTSEEING TOURS/TOUR COMPANIES

Betty Lou Cruises. A 51-ft, 49-passenger motor yacht leaves from the Mariner's Inn Restaurant for lunch, dinner, moonlight, and fall foliage-appreciation cruises on Lake Mendota. Reservations required. | 5360 Westport Rd. | 608/246–3136 | $25–$45 | Tours by appointment only.

OTHER POINTS OF INTEREST

Henry Vilas Zoo. Hundreds of birds and animals from all over the world are on display here in reproduction habitats. Most of the zoo's denizens are for observing only, but there is a small petting zoo with smaller, more kid-friendly critters like baby goats and sheep. If you're fond of scaly creatures, pay a visit to the herpetarium, which is home to dozens of reptiles. The zoo is southwest of the University of Wisconsin–Madison campus, in Vilas Park on Lake Wingra. | 702 S. Randall Ave. | 608/266–4732 | Free | Daily 10–4.

U.S.D.A. Forest Products Laboratory. Tours of the research facility at the western edge of the University of Wisconsin–Madison campus are available. You can see what wood pulp gets used for and how paper products are made environmentally friendly. Suggested for kids 12 and up. | 1 Gifford Pinchot Dr. | 608/231–9200 | Free | Mon.–Thurs. 2 PM for tours (no groups larger than 8).

ON THE CALENDAR

FEB.: *Garden Expo.* More than 150 garden-related exhibits, educational seminars, a garden display, and garden products are for sale at the Alliance Energy Center on the third weekend of the month. | 800/373–6376.

JULY: *Art Fair on the Square.* Some 100,000 people come to this juried show on the second weekend of the month to view works by local and national artists at this Capitol Square annual. There's also ongoing entertainment. | 800/373–6376.
JULY: *Dane County Fair.* A carnival, food, entertainment, arts, crafts, and a livestock competition take place at the Alliance Energy Center in mid-month. | 800/373–6376.
SEPT.: *Taste of Madison.* Local restaurants sell their specialties in outdoor stands in Capitol Square on the first weekend of the month. | 800/373–6376.

WALKING TOUR
Capitol Square area (approximately 2½ hours)
Start your tour at Madison's showcase convention center, **Monona Terrace,** located along John Nolen Drive, overlooking Lake Monona. Walk away from the lake head along Martin Luther King, Jr. Street to the **State Capitol.** If you happen to be in the square on a Wednesday or Saturday between May and October, you can visit the **Dane County Farmers' Market,** where vendors sell a wide variety of farm-related goods. The **State Historical Museum** and the **Wisconsin Veterans Museum** are also located in the square and are worth a visit. The Historical Museum has four floors of permanent and changing exhibits on many aspects of the state's history. Still heading away from the lake, walk down State Street, which starts between the Historical Museum and the Veterans Museum. On State Street you'll see lots of college students sipping flavored coffees, browsing in bookstores, chatting over lunch, or shopping in funky stores. Continue walking along State Street for about six blocks to Lake Street, then turn right and go one block to Langdon Street. There you'll see the **Memorial Library,** part of the University of Wisconsin–Madison system. Continue along Langdon for another block to Park Street, then turn left. When you reach the corner of Park Street and University Avenue, you'll see the **Elvehjem Museum of Art,** also part of the UW–Madison system. Continue along University Avenue for about five blocks until Babcock Drive intersects. Turn right onto Babcock and walk four blocks to Observatory Drive to see **Washburn Observatory.** Head about two blocks farther down Observatory Drive (going west) and you can view the **University of Wisconsin–Madison** on your left. Return to Babcock Street and cross over University Avenue. Turn right on Randall, heading away from Lake Mendota and toward Lake Wingra. Walk about three blocks to the **Camp Randall Stadium and Fieldhouse,** then continue another seven blocks to the **Henry Vilas Zoo,** which has lots of animals, a picnic/playground area, and a swimming beach. You could also end your walking tour with a visit to the **Edgewood College** campus, near Edgewood Drive. To get to the college, head west on the city side (not the lake side) of Vilas Park Drive, a curving main street that circles the zoo. Vilas Park Drive will intersect with Edgewood Drive after just a few blocks. Both the zoo and the Edgewood campus are located along the shores of Lake Wingra and offer striking views. Return from the zoo by walking along Vilas Park Drive, on the non–lake side of the road, heading toward Lake Monona. Turn right onto Drake Street, and walk about five blocks to Park Street, and turn left. Walk one block along Park and it will turn into Washington Avenue (also called U.S. 151). Continue along Washington for about 10 blocks until you reach Capitol Square. From the square, return to **Monona Terrace** via a short walk down Martin Luther King, Jr. Street.

MADISON

INTRO
ATTRACTIONS
DINING
LODGING

Dining

INEXPENSIVE
Bluephies. Contemporary. This hip little joint is in a red brick strip mall near the Edgewood campus. Dinner entrees to consider include a grilled Portobello mushroom sandwich, topped with sauteed onions and melted mozzarella, served on an organic wheat bun and sided with sun-dried tomatoes, artichoke hearts, and black olives, or possibly the cornmeal-crusted catfish or jerk chicken gorgonzola. | 2701 Monroe St. | 608/231–3663 | $8–$16 | AE, D, DC, MC, V.

China House. Chinese. This Szechuan and Hunan restaurant is a local favorite and also serves dim sum. | 1256 S. Park St. | 608/257–1079 | $7–$12 | AE, MC, V.

Damon's "the Place for Ribs." American. Large platters of ribs and four big-screen TVs featuring sporting events vie for the "most popular" title at this casual restaurant. You can eat at a large bar or nearby tables. | 8150 Excelsior Dr. | 608/836–6466 | $5–$15 | AE, D, DC, MC, V.

Ella's Deli. Kosher. Mechanical toys move across the ceiling, a bear drinks water, and kids and adults alike can take a spin on the outdoor carousel. Sandwiches and sundaes are popular; but don't attempt to tackle Ella's famous ice-cream-and-hot-fudge-over-grilled-poundcake sundae without some help. Full dinners are also available. | 2902 E. Washington Ave. | 608/241–5291 | Reservations not accepted | $6–$10 | MC, V.

Radical Rye. American/Deli. You can fill out your own order slip for huge sandwiches loaded with fresh-sliced deli meats and vegetables, then smothered with toppings of your choosing. There's also always vegetarian chili and a soup of the day. Big windows looking out onto State Street are great for people-watching. | 231 State St. | 608/256–1200 | $6–$8 | AE, MC, V.

Wild Iris Café. Eclectic. This intimate little café with wood floors has great breakfasts. Lunch and dinner menus feature contemporary sandwiches, some Southwestern-inspired specials, and other unusual dishes like pasta jambalaya and a delicate, lemon-infused angel-hair pasta dusted with Parmesan cheese. | 1125 Regent St. | 608/257–4747 | $7–$15 | MC, V.

© Artville

CHEESEHEADS AND PROUD OF IT

Just as the green and gold Green Bay Packers uniform is standard attire for the team's players at a football game, a cheesehead is standard attire for Packer fans and those who want to boast of being from Wisconsin. These hats, made in the shape of a wedge of cheese, originated when an out-of-stater tried to insult Wisconsinite Chris Becker by calling him a cheesehead. Becker took some foam, cut it into the shape of a hunk of Swiss cheese, burned holes into it, colored it yellow, and plopped it on his head. The hat was an instant success. Locals picked up on the idea and Becker went into business by creating the firm Foamation Inc., located in the Milwaukee suburb of St. Francis.

Today you can find cheesehead earrings, pins, ties, baseball hats, soap on a rope, and Christmas ornaments; there is also a cheesehead cowboy hat, a cheesehead football autographed by Packer Reggie White, and even a cheesehead firefighter helmet made for Wisconsin's professional firefighters for fund-raising purposes.

Becker says cheesehead hats have become synonymous with Wisconsin, and are being purchased worldwide. Cheesehead hat owners include comedian Tim Allen and entertainer Reba McEntire. Becker says Jay Leno received one from the late comedian Chris Farley (a Madison native), and that a cheesehead hat is said to have saved the life of a man who is now one of his employees. When the small plane the man was in plummeted toward the ground, the man put the foam hat in front of him to cushion his landing. According to representatives of the FAA, doing so saved his life.

MODERATE

Come Back In. American. This downtown restaurant is cozy, casual, and eclectic with its displays of memorabilia, old photographs of patrons and Madison history, and antique tin signage and bric-a-brac here and there. Known for giant sandwiches and blackened prime rib. | 568 E. Wilson St. | 608/255–4674 | $10–$15 | MC, V | No lunch.

Essen Haus. German. This downtown restaurant with old-world charm displays some 3,000 beer steins and serves hearty fare like Wienerschnitzel and sauerbraten. Live music nightly. | 514 E. Wilson St. | 608/255–4674 | $10–$20 | MC, V | Closed Mon. No lunch.

Nau-Ti-Gal. American. In summer, at this nautically themed restaurant in an old tavern, you can dine 30 ft from the Yahara River, which feeds into the northern tip of Lake Mendota. Seating outdoors is on the expansive wrap-around deck, and indoors at cozy tables just big enough for small groups of friends. Fresh fish is on the menu every day, but you can also feast on Key West chicken stuffed with seafood, or even a shark steak. Sunday brunch. | 5360 Westport Rd. | 608/244–4464 | $12–$20 | MC, V | Closed Super Bowl Sun. and Mon. and Nov.–Feb.

Quivey's Grove. American. Antiques fill this restaurant in an 1855 mansion and its stables 15 mi from Madison. One of the two dining rooms is formal, with white tablecloths, the other is casual and rustic. Duck, lamb, and quail are all top-notch. Kids' menu. Parking. | 6261 Nesbitt Rd., Fitchburg | 608/273–4900 | $12–$26 | AE, D, MC, V.

EXPENSIVE

Admiralty. French Continental. This elegant restaurant downtown in the Edgewater Hotel, with a view of Lake Mendota, serves one of the best Sunday brunches in Madison. Known for fresh fish. Open-air dining is on a secluded patio. Entertainment Friday and Saturday April–October. Sunday brunch. | 666 Wisconsin Ave. | 608/256–9071 | $25–$50 | AE, DC, MC, V.

Coachman's Inn. American. The fireplace warms the bar of this antiques-filled dining room, and there's an excellent brunch on Sundays. The menu includes hearty pub sandwiches, homemade soups and stews, and some pasta dishes. Salad bar. Sunday brunch. | 984 Rte. A, Edgerton | 608/884–8484 | $20–$30 | AE, D, MC, V | Closed Labor Day–Memorial Day.

Granita. Italian. Located in a historic building dating from 1913, this place is like an old-style Sicilian home with its pictures from Italy and its Italian memorabilia. For dinner, you can choose from a variety of classic Northern Italian dishes like pasta primavera and chicken marsala. | 111 S. Hamilton Ave. | 608/251–9500 | $14–$38 | AE, DC, MC, V | Closed Sun. No lunch.

L'Étoile. French. In this Capitol Square restaurant hung with French impressionist paintings, the menu changes seasonally, and the chef uses primarily local ingredients. Try the mushroom and hickory-nut strudel (the nuts are indigenous to the area, the mushrooms are in season, and the strudel is served with vegetables from local farmers' markets). | 25 N. Pinckney St. | 608/251–0500 | $20–$30 | D, DC, MC, V | Closed Sun. No lunch.

Mariner's Inn. Seafood. A seafaring motif prevails at this dressy—yet not stuffy—establishment overlooking Lake Mendota, with lots of glossy, high-polish wood everywhere and large windows. The menu has some steak and pasta selections, but the main focus here is on the fish and seafood, which come fresh from the nearby lakes daily. Try the pan-seared walleye, or perhaps a salmon steak. Early-bird suppers, excluding Saturday. | 5339 Lighthouse Bay Dr. | 608/246–3120 | Reservations essential for 5 or more | $15–$25 | MC, V | No lunch.

Lodging

INEXPENSIVE

Capitol Motel. Built in the 1960s, this simple motel is family owned and operated. Cable TV. | 881 W. Beltline Hwy. | 608/271–3100 | fax 608/271–3695 | 30 rooms | $35–$55 | MC, V.

Econo Lodge. This basic motel has two separate light-colored brick buildings, and a large lobby with a TV. Complimentary Continental breakfast. Microwave available, cable TV. Business services. | 4726 E. Washington Ave. | 608/241–4171 | fax 608/241–1715 | 97 rooms | $54–$69 | AE, D, DC, MC, V.

Exel Inn. This colonial-style motel on the east side of Madison has a small, standard lobby. Guest rooms are equipped with faux-walnut wood-veneer furniture, and there are unobtrusive watercolor prints on the walls. Complimentary Continental breakfast. In-room data ports, microwaves available, some refrigerators. Exercise equipment. Laundry facilities. Business services. Some pets allowed. | 4202 E. Towne Blvd. | 608/241–3861 | fax 608/241–9752 | 102 rooms | $42–$75 | AE, D, DC, MC, V.

Madison Hostel. This hostel, in a once-private, now-overhauled 3-story house, is within 5 blocks of the university campus, State Street, and the Capitol. It's popular among backpackers, international tourists, and the youngish, adventuresome set. There are shared as well as private rooms, and all guests share bath facilities. Guests have access to the kitchen and laundry facilities. TV in common area. | 141 S. Butler St. | 608/441–0144 | madisonhostel@yahoo.com | www.sit.wisc.edu/~hostel | 9 rooms | $15–$36 | MC, V.

Select Inn. This motel has a large modern lobby with a cozy fireplace. Complimentary Continental breakfast. Some minibars, some refrigerators, cable TV. Hot tub. Business services. Pets allowed (deposit). | 4845 Hayes Rd. | 608/249–1815 or 800/641–1000 | fax 608/249–1815 | www.selectinn.com | 97 rooms | $39–$89 | AE, D, DC, MC, V.

MODERATE

Best Western West Towne Suites. This modest motel has an unexpectedly elaborate lobby with vaulted ceilings, artwork, large plants, and a crystal chandelier. Complimentary breakfast. In-room data ports, microwaves available, refrigerators, cable TV. Exercise equipment. Laundry facilities. Business services. Pets allowed. | 650 Grand Canyon Dr. | 608/833–4200 | fax 608/833–5614 | www.bestwestern.com | 101 suites | $62–$105 | AE, D, DC, MC, V.

Fairfield Inn by Marriott. You access rooms on the first and second floors of this large, modern motel via outside doors; rooms on the third floor open to interior hallways. The lobby has a TV. Complimentary Continental breakfast. Cable TV. Pool. Business services. | 4765 Hayes Rd. | 608/249–5300 | fax 608/240–9335 | www.fairfieldinn.com | 134 rooms | $69–$89 | AE, D, DC, MC, V.

Hampton Inn–East. This large, four-story modern hotel has a homey lobby filled with plants and artwork, and you can help yourself to complimentary fruit and fresh-brewed coffee. Complimentary Continental breakfast. Microwaves available, cable TV. Pool. Hot tub. Exercise equipment. Business services. | 4820 Hayes Rd. | 608/244–9400 | fax 608/244–7177 | www.hampton-inn.com | 116 rooms | $69–$109 | AE, D, DC, MC, V.

Ivy Inn. A fireplace dominates the lobby of this colonial-style, red brick hotel in central Madison, and the University of Wisconsin campus is directly across the street. Restaurant, bar. Cable TV. Business services, free parking. Pets allowed. | 2355 University Ave. | 608/233–9717 | fax 608/233–2660 | 57 rooms | $60–$90 | AE, DC, MC, V.

Madison Inn. This modern, six-story hotel is close to the university and downtown area. Complimentary Continental breakfast. Cable TV. | 601 Langdon St. | 608/257–4391 | fax 608/257–2832 | 75 rooms | $80–$90 | AE, D, DC, MC, V.

EXPENSIVE

Baymont Inn and Suites. This two-story modern inn has a cozy lobby with a seating area. A big-screen TV is in the lounge. Bar, complimentary Continental breakfast. Refrigerator in suites, cable TV. Pool. Hot tub. Exercise equipment. Laundry facilities. Business services, airport shuttle, free parking. Some pets allowed. | 8102 Excelsior Dr. | 608/831–7711 | fax 608/831–1942 | www.baymontinn.com | 129 rooms, 14 suites | $92–$104 rooms, $104–$125 suites | AE, D, DC, MC, V.

Best Western Inn on the Park. A large, modern 9-story, brick-and-glass-skinned hotel on Capitol Square has views of the Capitol, Lake Mendota, and Lake Monona from the rooms. Two restaurants, two bars. In-room data ports, cable TV. Pool. Hot tub. Exercise equipment. Business services, airport shuttle, free parking. | 22 S. Carroll St. | 608/257–8811 | fax 608/257–5995 | www.bestwestern.com | 213 rooms | $109–$124 | AE, D, DC, MC, V.

Collins House. A lumber baron's former home that's now on the National Register of Historic Places, this cozy, Prairie School-style inn overlooks Lake Mendota six blocks east of the Capitol. Complimentary breakfast. Microwaves, some in-room hot tubs. TV, VCR (with movies) in common area. No smoking. | 704 E. Gorham St. | 608/255–4230 | fax 608/255–0830 | www.collinshouse.com | 5 rooms | $95–$160 | D, MC, V.

East Towne Suites. This all-suites hotel has a spacious lobby decorated in maroon and hunter green and is accented in light brick. It offers executive boardrooms, meeting rooms, and conference rooms. Complimentary Continental breakfast. Refrigerators, cable TV. Pool. Hot tub. Exercise equipment. | 4801 Anamark Dr. | 608/224–2020 or 800/950–1919 | fax 608/244–3434 | 123 rooms | $70–$105 | AE, D, DC, MC, V.

The Edgewater. This 9-story, blond-brick hotel was built in 1949 right downtown on the edge of Lake Monona. Most rooms have a view of the lake, and some have a view of the Capitol. Crystal chandeliers, and polished oak embellish the lobby. State Street's shops and restaurants are only 4 blocks away, and you can relax on the hotel's private pier in fine weather. Restaurant, bar, room service. Some microwaves, cable TV. Massage. Business services, airport shuttle. Some pets allowed. | 666 Wisconsin Ave. | 608/256–9071 or 800/922–5512 | fax 608/256–0910 | www.gowisconsin.com/edgewater | 116 rooms | $98–$295 | AE, DC, MC, V.

Holiday Inn. This modern motel is on the east side of Madison. There's a fireplace in the large plant-filled lobby. Restaurant, bar. Cable TV. Pool. Hot tub. Business services, airport shuttle, free parking. | 3841 E. Washington Ave. | 608/244–2481 | fax 608/244–0383 | www.basshotels.com/holiday-inn | 197 rooms | $99–$158 | AE, D, DC, MC, V.

Howard Johnson Plaza Hotel. This concrete, somewhat bunker-like hotel is on the edge of the University of Wisconsin campus. There's a carport and two parking lots, and a homey and spacious lobby with small trees. Restaurant, bar, room service. Some refrigerators, cable TV. Pool. Hot tub. Health club. Business services, airport shuttle, free parking. | 525 W. Johnson St. | 608/251–5511 | fax 608/251–4824 | www.hjplazamadison.com | 163 rooms | $92–$160 | AE, D, DC, MC, V.

Sheraton. This eight-story hotel with a marble and plant-filled lobby is across the street from the Alliance Energy Center. 2 restaurants, bar. In-room data ports, cable TV. Pool. Hot tub, sauna. Exercise equipment. Business services, airport shuttle. | 706 John Nolen Dr. | 608/251–2300 or 800/325–3535 | fax 608/251–1189 | www.sheraton.com | 237 rooms | $99–$145 | AE, D, DC, MC, V.

Woodfield Suites. This modern, 4-story redbrick hotel is about 10 mi from the downtown area and the university campus, in a largely commercial suburban division surrounded by popular chain restaurants and mini-malls. Complimentary cocktails are served every evening. Kids can have fun with the indoor play equipment and pinball machines. Four restaurants are located within 1 mi. Complimentary Continental breakfast. In-room data ports, refrigerators, cable TV, in-room VCRs available. 2 pools. Hot tub. Gym. Video games. Laundry service. Business services, airport shuttle, free parking. Pets allowed. | 5217 Terrace Dr. | 608/245–0123 or 800/338–0008 | fax 608/245–1644 | www.woodfieldsuites.com | 120 rooms | $99–$145 | AE, D, DC, MC, V.

VERY EXPENSIVE

Annie's Bed-and-Breakfast. This quiet, pastoral Craftsman-style B & B a block from Lake Mendota has just one room, a suite that takes up an entire floor and includes a master bedroom, a small bedroom, 1½ baths, and a library with a fireplace. A double hot tub in the bathroom is surrounded by plants and mirrors; there's even a sound system. The grounds overlook Warner Park—a beautifully landscaped area with gardens, a gazebo, and a lily pond. There's a two-night minimum stay. Dining room, picnic area, complimentary breakfast. In-room data ports, microwave available, refrigerator, in-room hot tub, in-room VCR (and movies). Business services. No kids under 10. | 2117 Sheridan Dr. | 608/244–2224 | fax 608/244–2224 | www.bbinternet.com/annies | 1 suite | $179–$189 | AE, MC, V.

Cameo Rose Bed & Breakfast. This huge Victorian has 8,000 square ft of living space, a wraparound porch, and sits on 120 acres of rolling hills. The building is furnished with antiques as well as plush reproductions. There's a double hot tub in one bedroom and a fireplace in another. Made-from-scratch breakfasts are served on antique china and crystal. Complimentary breakfast. TV in common area. Hiking. | 1090 Severson Rd. | 608/424–6340 | www.cameorose.com | 5 rooms | $110–$150 | MC, V.

Comfort Suites. This six-story all-suites hotel is near a large shopping mall and a handful of restaurants. Complimentary breakfast. Microwaves, refrigerators, cable TV. Pool. Hot tub. Exercise equipment. | 1253 John Q. Hammons Dr. | 608/836–3033 or 800/221–2222 | fax 608/836–0949 | www.choicehotels.com | 162 rooms | $115–$140 | AE, D, MC, V.

Livingston Inn. This 5,000-square-ft Gothic Revival Bed-and-Breakfast, built in 1857, is across from Lake Mendota. It is furnished with antiques and beautifully landscaped gardens surround the home. A complimentary full breakfast is offered on weekends, an expanded Continental breakfast during the week. Wine and appetizers are also served daily. Complimentary breakfast. Cable TV. No smoking. | 752 E. Gorham St. | 608/257–1200 | fax 608/257–1145 | www.thelivingston.com | 4 rooms | $150–$290 | AE, MC, V.

Madison Concourse Hotel and Governor's Club. This 13-story light-brick hotel just north of Capitol Square is filled with large windows and an elegant lobby with marble and plants. The Governor's Club is located on the top three floors of the hotel and offers the best views, as well as appetizers, and cocktails. 2 restaurants, bar (with entertainment), complimentary Continental breakfast (for Governor's Club). Some microwaves, some in-room hot tubs, cable TV. Pool. Barbershop, beauty salon, hot tub. Exercise equipment. Business services, airport shuttle. | 1 W. Dayton St. | 608/257–6000 or 800/356–8293 | fax 608/257–5280 | www.concoursehotel.com | 357 rooms | $109–$179 | AE, D, DC, MC, V.

Mansion Hill Inn. This 1858 Italianate mansion four blocks from the Capitol has a four-story spiral staircase and individually decorated rooms, among them the Turkish Nook (with a sultan's bed and steam shower) and the Oriental Suite (with a separate sitting room, a skylight, and double whirlpool). Complimentary Continental breakfast. In-room data ports, minibars, some in-room hot tubs, cable TV, in-room VCRs available. Business services. No kids under 12. No smoking. | 424 N. Pinckney St. | 608/255–3999 or 800/798–9070 | fax 608/255–2217 | www.mansionhillinn.com | 11 rooms | $120–$340 | AE, MC, V.

Residence Inn by Marriott. This inn is made up of 10 simply styled brick buildings that look like condos with a gatehouse in the center. All rooms are suites, with private entries. The gatehouse has a fireplace, TV, and a dining area. Restaurant, picnic area, complimentary Continental breakfast. Kitchenettes, microwaves, cable TV, in-room VCRs. Pool. Hot tub. Exercise equipment. Laundry facilities. Free parking. Some pets allowed. | 501 D'Onofrio Dr. | 608/833–8333 | fax 608/833–2693 | www.residenceinn.com | 80 suites | $120–$150 | AE, D, DC, MC, V.

MANITOWISH WATERS

MAP 11, C2

(Nearby towns also listed: Boulder Junction, Eagle River, Lac du Flambeau, Sayner)

The Lake Superior Chippewa Native Americans were the first people to have an impact on this area when they established a camp on the east shore of Manitowish Lake. The

Chippewa made sugar, fished, raised corn, and picked berries. Today cranberry farming is one of the town's largest businesses. Hiking, nature trails, cross-country skiing, snowshoeing, wildlife watching, and interpretive programs are found at North Lakeland Discovery Center. You can canoe the many lakes and streams which weave throughout this forested county town.

Information: **Manitowish Waters Chamber of Commerce** | Box 251 54545-0251 | 715/543–8488 | www.manitowishwaters.org.

Attractions

Diamond J. Stable. Trail rides, pony rides, and lessons are offered here; all rides are guided. | Hwy. 51 north | 715/543–8333 | $18 | Memorial Day–Labor Day, daily 9–4.

North Lakeland Discovery Center. The 66 acres encompassed by this nonprofit conservation center include woodlands, lakes, a cranberry bog, hiking, biking, and skiing trails, and 11 rustic bunkhouses in the woods for warm-weather camping. The Center also maintains several hundred yards of private beach, a sauna house, an amphitheater, campfire ring, and a large do-it-yourself kitchen for group functions, all available to the public for nominal fees or free-will donations. The Center hosts dozens of events throughout the year, including a summer triathlon and interactive programs and lectures involving everything from how to wax your skis properly to a crash-course in dog-sledding. | 215 W. County Rte. West | 888/626–9877 | Free | Daily 8–5; trails and grounds open 24 hours.

ON THE CALENDAR

JULY: *4th of July Celebration.* Fireworks, a crafts and flea market, food (including hundreds of juicy, fresh-grilled bratwurst), entertainment, bake sale, airplane rides, an aquatic ski show, and, of course, a parade, all make for an old-fashioned 4th along Rest Lake. | 888/626–9877.
JULY–AUG.: *Skiing Skeeters.* This water-ski show in Rest Lake Park runs on Wednesday and Saturday evenings and features a variety of shows with a large number of nonprofessional performers. | 888/626–9877 | Admission varies per event.

Dining

Blue Bayou Inn. Cajun. Fine dining in the Northwoods overlooking Lake Manitowish, just north of Spider Lake Bridge. The Bayou is known for both American and Cajun foods. | 288 S. Hwy. 51 | 715/543–2537 or 800/533–9671 | $15–$28 | D, MC, V | Closed Nov.–Apr. and Sun. except holiday weekends.

Lodging

Great Northern Motel. Mounted animals and animal heads are everywhere at this motel on San Domingo Lake 3 mi northwest of Manitowish Waters. Restaurant, bar, complimentary Continental breakfast. No air-conditioning, cable TV. Pool. Hot tub, sauna. Beach. Video games. Business services. Pets allowed. | 5720 N. U.S. 51, Mercer | 715/476–2440 | fax 715/476–2205 | www.mercerwi.com | 80 rooms | $59–$69 | D, MC, V.

Voss' Birchwood Lodge. This rustic lodge, dating from 1910, has rooms and cottages overlooking the Manitowish Waters Chain of Lakes. There's a spacious fireside lounge and a restaurant with a view of the lake. The one- to three-bedroom cottages have an Early American decor and all have fireplaces; they are available by the week only. No TV in some rooms. Hiking, beach, boating, fishing. | 715/543–8441 (in season) or 715/543–8443 (off season) | 6 rooms in lodge, 20 cottages | $85 lodge, $850–$975 per week cottages | No credit cards | Closed Oct.–May.

MANITOWISH
WATERS

INTRO
ATTRACTIONS
DINING
LODGING

MANITOWOC

MAP 11, E5

(Nearby towns also listed: Sheboygan, Two Rivers)

Wisconsin's self-styled Maritime Capital occupies some prime real estate on the shores of Lake Michigan. Manitowoc was settled in 1836. Long a shipbuilding center, it is now home to the largest maritime museum on the Great Lakes. A classic candy store with antique soda fountain and the Pinecrest Historical Village are downtown, and a living-history museum with more than 20 historic buildings is nearby.

Information: **Manitowoc Visitors Convention Bureau** | Box 966, 54421-0966 | 800/627–4896 | manitowocvcb@lakefield.net | www.manitowoc.org.

Attractions

Hidden Valley Ski Area. This ski area has 7 trails and slopes, some lighted for night skiing, and a vertical drop of just a little over 200 ft. It's 13 mi northwest of Manitowoc. | 7711 E. Hidden Valley Rd. | 920/863–2713 | Lift tickets $23 | Mon.–Sat. 9–8.

Lincoln Park Zoo. Home to arctic fox, timber wolves, fallow deer, and wild sheep from Africa. | 1200 N. 8th St. | 920/683–4685 | Donations accepted | Daily 8–5.

Pinecrest Historical Village. This 60-acre outdoor museum with more than 20 authentically restored buildings from the Manitowoc County area, circa 1900, includes a gallery of changing exhibits, a nature trail, and a gift shop. | 924 Pinecrest La. | 920/684–5110 | $5 | May–June, daily 9–4; July–Labor Day, daily 9–5; Labor Day–Oct. 21, daily 10–4; first weekend in Dec. 10–4.

Rahr-West Art Museum. Housed in a Victorian mansion, this museum holds permanent collections of Chinese ivory carvings, international dolls, porcelains, 19th-century art and furniture, and American art. | 610 N. 8th St., at Park St. | 920/683–4501 | Donations accepted | Mon., Tues., Thurs., Fri. 10–4; Wed. 10–8; weekends 11–4.

S.S. *Badger*, Manitowoc is the embarkation point of the 410-ft *Badger*, the last remaining steam-powered passenger-and-car ferry sailing on the Great Lakes between Manitowoc and Ludington, Michigan. Trips take four hours; ferries carry up to 620 passengers and 130 autos. | Lake View Dr. | 920/684–0888 or 800/841–4243 | $38 1-way; $46 for cars | Departure times vary throughout the year; call for specific times.

Wisconsin Maritime Museum. Among the 21,000 square ft of displays at this museum, the largest maritime museum on the Great Lakes, is a large three-dimensional facade that re-creates Manitowoc's waterfront during the 19th century. | 75 Maritime Dr. | 920/684–0218 | $3.95; special rates for senior citizens, kids, and groups | Memorial Day–Labor Day, daily 9–6; Labor Day–Memorial Day, Mon.–Sat. 9–5, Sun. 11–5.

The World War II submarine **U.S.S. *Cobia*,** a National Historic Landmark, is moored in the Manitowoc River next to the Wisconsin Maritime Museum. Guided tours are available; the last starts an hour before closing. | 75 Maritime Dr. | 414/684–0218 | $5.95 (includes admission to the Wisconsin Maritime Museum).

Zunker's Antique Car Museum. A collection of more than 40 cars, an antique gas station, automobile memorabilia, and antique motorbikes and cycles take you back through more than 70 years of automobile history. | 3722 MacArthur Dr. | 920/684–4005 | $3; special rates for kids | May–Sept., daily; Oct.–Apr., by appointment.

ON THE CALENDAR

DEC.: *Christmas at Pinecrest*. Pinecrest Historical Village celebrates Christmas the first weekend in December with traditional ethnic holiday customs, horse-drawn sleigh rides, music, decorated trees, hot cider, and homemade cookies. | 800/627–4896 or 920/684–4445.

Dining

Beerntsen's Confectionary. American. Established as a drugstore in 1932, this charming sweet shop has preserved all the original woodwork, mirrors, and fixtures. You can get a light lunch here of the soup-and-sandwich variety, or peruse the vast selection of old-fashioned penny candies, hand-dipped chocolates, and seasonal novelty treats. There's also an ice cream parlor and malt shop inside. | 108 N. 8th. St. | 920/684–9616 | $4–$6 | No credit cards.

Luigi's. Italian. Hot-pink tablecloths, brass chandeliers, and lots of colorful framed prints and posters on the walls make this casual restaurant popular with dining couples or families with kids. The menu is rife with Italian favorites, including a particularly rich fettuccine alfredo and Sicilian pizza on handmade crust. The restaurant even grows their own herbs and vegetables to ensure freshness. | 6124 Hwy. 151 | 920/684–4200 | $5–$13 | MC, V | Closed Mon.

Lodging

Holiday Inn. This is a large, redbrick building with a plant-filled atrium behind the lobby. Restaurant, bar (with entertainment), picnic area, room service. Microwaves, some refrigerators, cable TV, in-room VCRs. Pool. Hot tub. Gym. Video games. Business services, free parking. | 4601 Calumet Ave. | 920/682–6000 | fax 920/682–6140 | www.basshotels.com/holiday-inn | 203 rooms | $101–$140 | AE, D, DC, MC, V.

Inn on Maritime Bay. This modern, redbrick building on Lake Michigan has an atrium lobby with lofty, vaulted ceilings, partial glass walls, and a panoramic view of Lake Michigan. Most guest rooms also have views of the water, and Manitowoc's famous Maritime Museum is only a few blocks away. Several restaurants and lounges are also in the immediate vicinity. Restaurant, bar, room service. In-room data ports, microwaves available, refrigerators, cable TV. Pool. Hot tub, sauna. Business services, airport shuttle, free parking. Some pets allowed. | 101 Maritime Dr. | 920/682–7000 or 800/654–5353 | fax 920/682–7013 | 107 rooms | $75–$185 | AE, D, DC, MC, V.

West Port Bed-and-Breakfast. This Italianate brick mansion dating from 1879 has large windows and fireplaces, a large parlor with a gas fireplace, and a wide stairway leading to a spacious front porch. The dining room still has its original parquet floor. Dining room, complimentary breakfast. Refrigerators, in-room hot tubs, cable TV. No smoking. | 635 N. 8th St. | 920/686–0465 or 888/686–0465 | www.innsite.com/inns/A002857.html | 3 rooms | $90–$115 | MC, V.

MARINETTE

MAP 11, E4

(Nearby towns also listed: Menominee, Oconto, Peshtigo)

Settled in 1795, Marinette is the seat of the county of the same name. The town lies at the mouth of the Menominee River where the river spills into Green Bay, right at the border between Wisconsin and Michigan's Upper Peninsula. The surrounding countryside is crisscrossed with miles of fast-flowing streams and rivers. Nine waterfalls, white-water rafting, and canoeing are only a short drive away. The town itself is home to the Marinette County Historical Museum.

Information: Marinette Area Chamber of Commerce | Box 512, 54143-0512 | 800/236–6681 | www.cybrzn.com/chamber.

Attractions

City Park. Hiking and summer camping near downtown plus a picnic area, a playground, a shelter, and grills. Public baseball diamonds are nearby. | Carney Ave. near downtown | 715/732–5222 or 800/236–6681 | Free | Daily; camping Apr.–Sept.

Marinette County Historical Museum. This museum on Stephenson Island details the area's rich lumbering and maritime history with a giant diorama of a logging camp, a century-old log cabin, displays of Native American artifacts, and several scale models of the Great Lakes schooners—called lumberhookers—that transported milled lumber to Milwaukee and Chicago. | On Stephenson Island | 715/732–0831 | Donations accepted | Memorial Day weekend–late Sept., daily 10–4:30; rest of year tours by reservation only.

ON THE CALENDAR
JUNE–AUG.: *Theatre on the Bay.* Area groups and professionals from throughout the state perform three different plays every summer on weekends at the University of Wisconsin Center–Marinette County. | 715/735–4300 or 715/735–4313.

Dining
Tradewinds Bar and Restaurant. American. Two dining rooms decked out with northwoods knotty-pine panelling and low, amber light provide a cozy backdrop against which to savor barbecued ribs, fresh perch, prime rib, chicken, shrimp, lobster, pasta, and hearty sandwiches. | W1820 U.S. 41 | 715/735–3104 | $8–$10 | No credit cards.

Lodging
Best Western–Riverfront Inn. In this six-story, modern building with a large lobby, half the rooms face the city, half face the Menomonee River. Restaurant, bar, room service. Cable TV. Pool. Business services, free parking. | 1821 Riverside Ave. | 715/732–0111 | fax 715/732–0800 | www.bestwestern.com | 118 rooms, 3 suites | $69–$75 | AE, D, DC, MC, V.

Lauerman Guest House. This Victorian-era home overlooks the Menominee River and is decked out in period furnishings. Complimentary breakfast. Some in-room hot tubs. | 1975 Riverside Ave. | 715/732–7800 | 7 rooms | $55–$75 | AE, D, MC, V.

Super 8. A small lobby with a TV and seating area greet you as you enter this modest chain property, which is on the outskirts of town. Complimentary Continental breakfast. Cable TV. Hot tub, sauna. Business services. Some pets allowed. | 1508 Marinette Ave. | 715/735–7887 | fax 715/735–7455 | www.super8.com | 68 rooms | $38–$51 | AE, D, DC, MC, V.

MARSHFIELD

MAP 11, C4

(Nearby towns also listed: Stevens Point, Wisconsin Rapids)

Relaxed, friendly Marshfield is home to botanical gardens, a park, and Wisconsin's fourth-largest zoo, which has more than 200 animals and birds. Settled in 1872, as a railroad community it was named after John J. Marsh, one of the original settlers. Today it is a haven for those interested in water sports, and its streams are filled with walleye and bass.

Information: **Marshfield Visitors and Promotion Bureau** | Box 868, 54449-0868 | 800/422–4541 | macmacci@wctc.net | www.marshfieldchamber.com.

Attractions
Upham Mansion. Built in 1880, this restored downtown home of former Wisconsin Governor William Henry Upham contains elegant Victorian furnishings. The mansion's Heritage Rose Garden has more than 30 varieties. | 212 W. 3rd St. | 715/387–3322 or 800/422–4541 | Donations accepted | Wed. and Sun. 1:30–4; rose garden June–Sept. (same hours).

Wildwood Park and Zoo. This 60-acre zoo established in 1924, is Wisconsin's fourth largest. There's a large aviary and more than 200 animals, such as snow monkeys, grizzly bears, and buffaloes. | Roddis Ave. just off 17th St. | 715/384–4642 or 800/422–4541 | Free | Early

May–mid-Sept., daily 8–7:30; mid-Sept.–mid-Oct., weekdays 8–6, weekends noon–6; mid-Oct.–early May, weekdays 8–3, closed weekends.

ON THE CALENDAR

JUNE: *Dairyfest.* To celebrate Wisconsin's well-earned reputation as the nation's dairy capital, Marshfield hosts a parade, an old-fashioned picnic, an antique car show, a magic show, crafts, entertainment, and fireworks citywide on the first weekend after Memorial Day. | 800/422–4541.

SEPT.: *Central Wisconsin State Fair.* Over 250 arts-and-crafts booths, a beer garden, a baking contest, a food center, and live entertainment are held in Wildwood Park at the south end of town on the third weekend of the month. | 800/422–4541.

SEPT.: *Fall Fest.* Over 250 arts-and-crafts booths, antiques, Amish specialties, entertainment, and a bake-off in downtown Wildwood Park in mid-month. | 800/422–4541.

Dining

Melody Gardens Ice Cream Parlor. American. This old-fashioned, family-style restaurant downtown offers booths and tables for dining. Complete dinners are available as well as soups, salads, and sandwiches. All the ice cream is homemade, and the parlor has some antique woodwork and fixtures. | 1200 S. Oak Ave. | 715/384–3326 | $6–$10 | No credit cards.

Lodging

Comfort Inn Marshfield. This chain hotel adjacent to Northway Mall is in a commercial district just ¾ mi north of downtown and 1½ mi east of McMillian Wildlife Refuge, a state wildlife park. It is also only four blocks away from one of the leading medical centers of the country, St. Joseph's Hospital/Marshfield Clinic. The hotel offers video and VCR rentals on site. Guest rooms have modern wooden furnishings and green carpeting. Complimentary Continental breakfast, air conditioning, in-room data ports, some microwaves, some refrigerators, some in-room hot tubs, cable TV, room phones, TV in common area. Indoor pool, gym. No pets. | 114 E. Upham St. | 715/387–8691 | fax 715/387–3001 | www.comfortinn.com | 36 rooms, 10 suites | $65–$74, $90 suites | AE, D, DC, MC, V.

Amerihost Inn Marshfield. This hotel in a commercial district is 5 miles north of downtown shopping, Wildwood Park and the Marshfield Public Zoo. Rooms and suites are done in burgundy and navy; suites have separate sitting areas and two have balconies overlooking the pool. Complimentary Continental breakfast, air conditioning, in-room data ports, in-room safes, some microwaves, some refrigerators, cable TV, room phones, TV in common area. Indoor pool, sauna, gym. No pets allowed. | 2107 N. Central Ave. | 715/384–5240 or 800/434–5800 | www.amerihostinn.com | 52 rooms, 8 suites | $65, $90 suites | AE, D, DC, MC, V.

MAUSTON

(Nearby towns also listed: Baraboo, Tomah, Wisconsin Dells)

Mauston was settled in 1840. Five state parks, a railroad museum, and a museum dedicated to artist Norman Rockwell are nearby. Mauston is also close to Wisconsin Dells, where there are several water theme parks and other attractions.

Information: Mauston Area Chamber of Commerce | Box 171, 53948-0171 | 608/847–4142.

Attractions

Buckhorn State Park. This state park fills a 2,500-acre peninsula in Castle Rock Lake, which is actually a wide point in the Wisconsin River, 12 mi northeast of Mauston. You'll find a full range of water-related activities, including an interpretive canoe trail in the backwaters. | W8450 Buckhorn Park Ave., Necedah | 608/565–2789 | www.dnr.state.wi.us | $7 non-residents, $5 residents | Apr.–Oct., daily.

JULY: *Freedom Fest.* This Riverside Park festival on the second weekend of the month includes a carnival, kids' activities, live bands, food, and a parade. | 608/847–4142.

Dining

Tom's Diner. American. An old-school diner with booths and a sandwich counter, Tom's is a little piece of Americana. You can eat a complete lunch for about $5—and that includes coffee and a slice of homemade pie. The menu features burgers and fries, but there are also hearty classics like hot-beef sandwiches, potatoes and gravy, and ham 'n' eggs. | 403 State Rd. 82 | 608/847–4001 | $3–$5 | No credit cards.

Dry Gulch Saloon and Eatery. American. As the name might suggest, this casual, family-friendly restaurant has a Western-themed interior. Rough wood planking and the odd serape give the place a high-desert attitude. The menu is well-stocked with crowd-pleasing classics like quesadillas, burgers, hot wings, and tacos. | 112 E. State St. | 608/847–4777 | $6–$10 | D, MC, V.

Lodging

Travelodge. This three-story motel has a small, cozy lobby with a fireplace. Guest rooms are outfitted with the usual modular wood-veneer furnishings common to mid-range chain lodgings. In summer months, the motel is often booked by vacationers in the area to visit the nearby Wisconsin Dells. Bar. Some in-room hot tubs, cable TV. Pool. Hot tub. | 1700 E. Bridge St., New Lisbon | 608/562–5141 | fax 608/562–6205 | 61 rooms | $65–$80 | AE, D, DC, MC, V.

Walsh's K and K. You don't need directions to find this motel about 5 mi northeast of Mauston—just look for a really big rock. Castle Rock, a local tourist attraction covering about 3 acres of land and said to be one of the most photographed rocks in the United States, casts its long shadow into the motel's backyard. Castle Rock Lake is 15 minutes away by car. The hotel, which has no stairs, is just a few blocks from I-90/94. Microwaves, refrigerators, cable TV. Laundry facilities. Business services. | 219 U.S. 12 and Rte. 16, Camp Douglas | 608/427–3100 | fax 608/427–3824 | 14 rooms | $44–$50 | AE, D, DC, MC, V.

Woodside Ranch Resort. This ranch-style resort on 1,400 acres is on the side of a hill with woods behind it. The land in front runs directly downhill to the Lemonweir River. Many accommodations are log cabins, and there is a petting zoo on-site. There is a social director on the property who coordinates group activities and social opportunities for guests to get to know each other and take full advantage of the resort's facilities. Bar (with entertainment), dining room, picnic area. No room phones, TV in common area. Pool, wading pool. Sauna. Tennis. Hiking, horseback riding. Boating, fishing. Sleigh rides. Video games. Kids' programs (ages infant–12), playground. Laundry facilities. Pets allowed. | W. 4015 Rte. 82 | 608/847–4275 or 800/626–4275 | www.woodsideranch.com | 14 rooms, 23 cabins | $275 (2-night minimum stay) | D, MC, V.

MAYVILLE

MAP 11, E6

(Nearby town also listed: Beaver Dam, Waupun, West Bend)

Settled in 1845, the city's downtown business district was added to the National Register of Historic Places in 1995. You'll find plaques with historic information on many of Main Street's older buildings. The town's wildlife refuge is an excellent location for viewing birds during migratory seasons. Mayville is on the Rock River in northeast Dodge County, a 45-minute drive from Milwaukee.

Information: **Main Street Mayville, Inc.** | 52 N. Main St., 53050 | 920/387–1167 | mainstreetmayville@powerweb.com | www.powerweb.net/mainstmayville/.

Attractions

Historic Main Street. A walk along Mayville's Main Street will take you past no less than 40 buildings listed on the National Register of Historic Places, each with a plaque. A map with information on the sites is available through Mainstreet Mayville, Inc. | Main St. | 920/387–1167 | fax 920/387–7167 | Free | Daily.

Horicon National Wildlife Refuge. Half of this 32,000-acre refuge is marshland where hundreds of thousands of Canada geese and other waterfowl, and hundreds of other species of birds rest and feed during their annual migrations. A boardwalk over the marsh enables you to get closer to the birds. Thirty-four miles of trails are open year-round for hiking, biking, snowshoeing, and wildlife observation. You can also fish here. Boat tours of the marsh are available. | W4279 Headquarters Rd. | 920/387–3658 or 800/937–9123 | Free | Weekdays 7:30–4.

Mayville Historical Society. In 1968 the historical society restored the former John Hollenstein Wagon & Carriage Factory and the adjoining Hollenstein Home and turned them into a museum. The former factory now contains artifacts, pictures, and manuscripts documenting Mayville's history. The downstairs rooms of the former home have antique furnishings and pictures while the upstairs rooms have special exhibits, including vintage clothing and historic infants' and kids' paraphernalia. | Corner of Bridge and German Sts. | 920/387–4326 | Donations accepted | May–Oct., 2nd and 4th Sun. each month, 1:30–4:30; guided tours by appointment.

Mayville White Limestone School Museum. This historic building, listed on the National Register of Historic Places since 1976, was used as a public school from 1857 to 1981. Today it features a display called "classrooms of the past," a wild-game display, a gallery of more than 1,000 photos that chronicle nature and rural Wisconsin, and a baseball hall of fame room. | Corner of N. Main St. & Buchanan St. | 920/387–3474 | Donations welcomed | 1st and 3rd Sun. of each month, 1:30–4:30; or by appointment.

ON THE CALENDAR

OCT.: *Audubon Days 2000.* The first weekend in October brings three days of family fun celebrating the return of migrating Canada geese to the Horicon Marsh. Events in Fireman's Park on the east side of Rock River include a parade, a bicycle tour, a run/walk, a rubber duck race, music, entertainment, a flea market, displays of wildlife art, and kids' activities. | 800/256–7670.

Dining

Audubon Inn Restaurant American. Specialties such as orange roughy, Chicken Kathleen (a feta cheese and kalamata olive–topped chicken dish), and beef tenderloin are served on white cloth-covered tables near an old-fashioned bar in the historic Audubon Inn. | 45 N. Main St. | 920/387–5858 | $14–$22 | AE, D, MC, V | No lunch, no dinner Sun.; breakfast for inn guests only.

Back Street Café. American. This casual, cheery, family-style downtown restaurant is popular with locals. The menu offers a variety of Mexican dishes, including a Mexican breakfast omelet, in addition to standard American fare. | 11 N. School St. | 920/387–7164 | $3–$7 | No credit cards | Breakfast also available; no dinner Sat., Sun.

Tony's Pizza & Italian Restaurant. Italian. Pizza is the specialty at this downtown eatery. Have a look up at this historic building's high tin ceilings from the 1890s while you wait for such house specialties as the 30-inch-long "football pizza" or chicken parmigiana, which is a boneless, skinless breast of chicken very lightly breaded and topped with a tangy tomato sauce and lots of melted mozzarella cheese. | 40 S. Main St. | 920/387–9900 | $5–$7 | D, MC, V | Closed Mon. No lunch Sat.–Thurs.

Lodging

Audubon Inn. This blond-brick Victorian home is within 3 mi of the Horicon Marsh and has been designated a National Historic Landmark. It has elaborate oak carving, stained-

MAYVILLE

INTRO
ATTRACTIONS
DINING
LODGING

glass windows, and an etched skylight depicting the annual migration of Canada geese through the marsh. Restaurant, complimentary Continental breakfast. In-room hot tubs, cable TV. Business services. | 45 N. Main St. | 920/387–5858 or 800/421–4667 | fax 920/387–2847 | www.classicinns.com | 17 rooms | $109–$119 | AE, D, DC, MC, V.

Coopers Hillcrest Motel. This mom-and-pop motel is in a rural area about 8 mi from the center of Mayville and 4 mi from Horicon Marsh. It's often booked with nature enthusiasts in town to see the Canada geese migration between September and November. Microwaves, refrigerators. | W1124 Hwy. 33 | 920/387–2125 | 24 rooms | $21–$30 | No credit cards.

Iron Ridge Motel. This brick downtown hotel, built in the mid-1980s, is right in the heart of town. Pool. Hot tub. | 121 Alrosa La. | 920/387–4090 | 19 rooms | $49–$55 | AE, MC, V.

MENASHA

MAP 11, E5

(Nearby towns also listed: Appleton, Neenah)

Settled in 1843, Menasha sits across from its twin city of Neenah at the top of Lake Winnebago, where the Fox River flows from the lake. Gracious homes built by turn-of-the-20th-century paper barons are scattered throughout these twin cities. Water power afforded by the Fox River helped establish Menasha as an industrial center in the mid to late 19th century. Its industrial heritage carries through to today, with the paper industry providing the economic underpinning of the city and the area.

Information: Fox Cities Convention and Visitors Bureau | 3433 W. College Ave., Appleton 54914 | 800/236–6673 | tourism@foxcities.org | www.foxcities.org.

Attractions
High Cliff State Park. Glaciers formed the area where this park stands on high limestone bluffs overlooking Lake Winnebago 9 mi east of town. There's camping, boating, horseback riding, cross-country skiing, hiking, and snowmobiling, as well as a marina and an observation tower. | N7475 High Cliff Rd. | 920/989–1106 | www.dnr.state.wi.us | $7 nonresidents, $5 residents | Daily.

Part of High Cliff State Park, the **High Cliff General Store Museum** displays antiques relevant to the park's history. A nature center is behind the museum. | N7526 Lower Cliff Rd. | 920/989–1106 | Free | Memorial Day–Labor Day, weekends 9–4.

Smith Park. This 24-acre park near downtown offers swings, slides, and other playground equipment, as well as tennis, picnic areas, softball, cross-country skiing, and a boat launch. | Keyes St. | 920/751–5106 | Free | Daily.

ON THE CALENDAR
SEPT.: *Seafood Fest and Lobster Bash.* The third weekend of the month brings seafood galore—1½-pound lobsters and grilled salmon steaks—as well as live bands to Jefferson Park on U.S. 41. | 800/236–6673.

Dining
Trim B's. American. This downtown restaurant with yellow awnings and flags on the roof is a favorite in the Fox Cities for its fresh seafood platters and its many-windowed dining room. | Walnut and Lawrence Sts. | 920/734–9204 | $10–$25 | AE, DC, MC, V | No lunch weekends.

Lodging
Amerihost Inn Kimberly. This hotel in a commercial area 1 mi north of downtown Kimberly is 10 mi north of Menasha. Suites have separate sitting areas, and all rooms are in

burgundy and navy. Complimentary Continental breakfast, air conditioning, in-room data ports, in-room safes, some microwaves, some refrigerators, cable TV, room phones, TV in common area. Indoor pool, hot tub, sauna. No pets. | 761 Truman St., Kimberly | 920/788–4400 or 800/434–5800 | fax 920/788–4466 | www.amerihostinn.com | 52 rooms, 8 suites | $75, $125 suites | AE, D, DC, MC, V.

MENOMONEE FALLS

MAP 11, E6

(Nearby town also listed: Milwaukee)

Located in Waukesha County, Menomonee Falls is home to Old Falls Village, a re-creation of the original Menomonee Falls settlement in the mid-1880s, with several original historic buildings that have been moved to the site. A former railroad spur that has been converted to a 10½-mi nature trail is open for bicycling, walking, hiking, snowmobiling, and cross-country skiing. The trail starts downtown and runs along the scenic Menomonee River.

Information: Waukesha Area Convention and Visitors Bureau | 223 Wisconsin Ave., Waukesha 53186-4926 | 800/366–8474 | visit@wauknet.com | www.wauknet.com/visit.

Attractions

Holy Hill National Shrine of Mary, Help of Christians. This religious site just outside of Menomonee Falls is one of the most picturesque in the Midwest. Around 1855, a resident of the town of Erin erected a huge wooden cross on the hill. A French hermit who worshiped at the cross experienced a miraculous cure, beginning a wave of pilgrimages to Holy Hill, a custom that continues today. The original wooden cross may still be viewed in the vestibule of the lower church. This site also provides a breathtaking view of the surrounding countryside. | 1525 Carmel Rd., Hubertus | 262/628–1838 | Free | Daily; group tours by appointment.

Little Switzerland Ski Area. Fifteen slopes and trails, some lighted for night skiing, are not far from Menomonee Falls. It's 20 mi north via U.S. 41, on Route AA. | 105 Rte. AA, Slinger | 262/644–5020 or 800/358–7669 | Lift tickets $22 | Nov.–Mar., daily; limited hours Dec. 24–25.

Old Falls Village. This re-creation of the original mid-1880s Menomonee Falls settlement just outside of the modern-day incarnation includes several historic buildings that have been moved to the site. | N96 W15191 County Line Rd. | 262/255–8346 | $3 | May–Sept., Sun. 1–4; also by appointment.

ON THE CALENDAR

SEPT.: *Falls Fall Fair.* More than 110 exhibitors show and sell crafts and fine arts in the Associated Bank parking lot on Main Street on the third Sunday of the month. | 262/251–8797.

Dining

De Marinis Menomonee Falls. Italian. This spacious, casual restaurant with booths has a menu of pizzas, steaks, and large Italian sandwiches. Vegetable pizza is a specialty. | N88 W15229 Main St. | 262/253–1568 | $7–$15 | AE, D, MC, V | No lunch on weekends.

Fox and Hounds. American. The building that houses this English pub-like eatery dates from 1843. It's in a wooded rural area on the outskirts of downtown. | 1298 Freiss Lake Rd., Hubertus | 262/628–1111 | $21–$30 | AE, D, DC, MC, V | Closed Sun. No lunch.

Jerry's Old Town Inn. Cajun. More than 500 pig decorations fill this casual restaurant just outside downtown Menomonee Falls; there are even sculpted pigs in the parking lot. Predictably, the menu is packed with porcine offerings, ranging from pork ribs to pork chops to pork loin; you'll also find steak and Cajun specialties. Kids' menu. | N116 W15841 Main St., Germantown | 262/251–4455 | $14–$20 | AE, MC, V | No lunch.

Lohmann's Steak House. American. In Germantown across the street from Menomonee Falls, this spacious, semi-dressy restaurant hosts a very popular Friday-night fish fry with the freshest of lake perch and cod. Prime rib, steak, barbecued ribs, and duck are also on the menu. Kids' menu. | W183 N9609 Appleton Ave., Germantown | 262/251–8430 | $12–$20 | AE, D, DC, MC, V | Closed Sun.

Lodging

Super 8. This is a modern stucco motel, surrounded by parking, in a rural area. Complimentary Continental breakfast. Cable TV. Pool. Hot tub. Laundry facilities. Business services. Pets allowed (deposit). | N96 W17490 County Line Rd., Gemantown | 262/255–0880 | fax 262/255–7741 | www.super8.com | 100 rooms | $49–$69 | AE, D, DC, MC, V.

MENOMONIE

MAP 11, A4

(Nearby towns also listed: Black River Falls, Eau Claire)

Settled in 1859 and located on the Red Cedar River, Menomonie is a former lumber town now dominated by antiques shops and tourists. Restored historic buildings fill the downtown area, including the famous Mabel Tainter Memorial Theater. Menomonie is the gateway to Red Cedar State Trail, a 14-mi hiking and biking route.

Information: **Chippewa Valley Convention and Visitors Bureau** | 3625 Gateway Dr., Suite F, Eau Claire 54701 | 888/523–3866 | www.chippewavalley.net.

Attractions

Caddie Woodlawn County Park. Named for the famous kids' book *Caddie Woodlawn*, the park contains the family home of the book's real-life heroine, Caroline Woodhouse, as well as picnic facilities. It's about 9 mi south of Menomonie, in downtown Downsville. | 715/235–2070 | $3 | Daily.

Empire in Pine Museum. Operated by the Dunn County Historical Society, this museum about 4 mi south of Menomonie displays logging artifacts from the 1870s and recounts the history of Knapp, Stout & Company, the world's largest pine milling operation in its day. The complex also includes a blacksmith shop, a cook's shanty, a bunkhouse, and the restored Louisville Post Office, which originally served the local village of Louisville from 1865 to 1900. | Main St., Downsville | 715/664–8690 | $2 | May–mid-Oct., Tues.–Sun. 1–5, closed Mon.; also by appointment.

Mabel Tainter Memorial. This building on the National Register of Historic Places was constructed in 1889 to honor the memory of Andrew and Bertha Tainter's daughter, who died at the age of 19. Now restored to its original opulence, the Tainter Theater presents musical and theatrical performances periodically throughout the year and maintains a reading room and exhibit gallery. Tours are offered daily. | 205 Main St. | 715/235–9726 or 800/236–7675 | $4 | Mon.–Sat. 10–5, Sun. 1–5.

Russell J. Rassbach Heritage Museum. This museum in Wakanda Park documents the history of Dunn County. Displays highlight technological innovations, archaeological finds, Civil War history, and more. Authentic Victorian rooms and ever-changing exhibits and displays offer insight into the Victorian lifestyle. | 1820 Wakanda Dr. in Wakanda Park, off I–94 | 715/232–8685 | $4 | Wed.–Sun. 10–6.

Wilson Place Museum. This downtown home contains the furnishings of three generations of the lumber-baron family that founded the Knapp-Stout Lumber Company, formerly the largest white-pine lumbering company in the world. The museum also features exhibits about the city of Menomonie and the University of Wisconsin–Stout. | 10 Wilson Circle | 715/235–2283 | $4.50 | Memorial Day–Labor Day, daily 1–5; Mid-Nov.–Dec. 31, daily 1–8. All other times by appointment only.

ON THE CALENDAR

JAN.: *Winter Fest.* On the second, third, and fourth weekends of the month, Carson Park on U.S. 12 is given over to car races on ice, a snow-sculpted kids' slide, a candlelit cross-country ski race, kids' games, and sleigh rides. | 888/523–3866.

NOV.–JAN.: *Victorian Christmas.* Tours of decorated homes and historic attractions throughout the Chippewa Valley area, as well as live entertainment from Thanksgiving through New Year's. | 888/523–3866.

Dining

Culver's. American. One of several Culver's restaurants to be found in this part of Wisconsin, this super-casual, family-friendly spot serves Culver's famous "butter burgers"—hand-patted quarter-pound beef patties on toasted, buttered buns with pickle, onion, lettuce, and tomato—as well as rich, homemade frozen custard. You can eat in, take out, or drive through. | 1330 Stout Rd. | 715/233–0330 | $3–$5 | MC, V.

Old 400 Depot Café. American. Made-from-scratch pies of every description, hearty meat and vegetable sandwiches, and fresh soups-of-the-day are served in this casual restaurant housed in an old train station. | 2616 Hills Ct. | 715/235–1993 | $8–$12 | D,MC,V.

Jake's Supper Club. American. The big draw at this laid-back spot about 5 mi north of Menomonie is the prime rib, which is thick, juicy, and sided with new potatoes. Pre-dinner, you can enjoy the atmosphere in Jake's Polynesian-themed tiki bar, or look out over the waters of Lake Tainter from the deck out back. | E 5690 Rte. D | 715/235–2465 | $8–$15 | D, MC, V.

Mardi Gras Café. Cajun. You can get nearly anything served blackened here—chicken, fish, or steak, all served with spicy extras like red beans and dirty rice. If you prefer, the menu also features more familiar items like pizzas, pub sandwiches, and hot wings. The adjacent lounge has a full bar. | 1919 Stout Rd. | 715/232–6418 | $7–$12 | D, MC, V.

Lodging

Best Western Holiday Manor Motor Lodge. This Holiday Inn has six wings surrounding a courtyard with trees and grass. The large lobby is cozy and country-rustic. Bar, complimentary Continental breakfast. Cable TV. Pool. Hot tub. Gym. Business services, free parking. | 1815 N. Broadway | 715/235–9651 | fax 715/235–6568 | www.bestwestern.com | 138 rooms | $63–$79 | AE, D, DC, MC, V.

Bolo Country Inn. This inn and its restaurant have a black-labrador dog theme, right down to the artwork on the walls and the black lab-emblazoned carpeting. The inn is in a mostly rural area just outside of town. Restaurant, bar, picnic area, complimentary Continental breakfast. Cable TV. Pets allowed. | 207 Pine Ave. | 715/235–5596 | fax 715/235–5596 | 25 rooms | $49–$79 | AE, DC, MC, V.

MIDDLETON

MAP 11, D6

(Nearby town also listed: Madison)

Called "The Good Neighbor City" this friendly community in south-central Wisconsin has thriving businesses and good schools. This area was once a popular campsite for the Algonquin Indians who were known as "mound builders" and their mark can still be seen on the land today. Middleton was first settled by the English but German immigrants followed and a German-language supplement appeared in the local paper for many years. Middleton is on the western shore of Lake Mendota, and is about 5 mi from Madison. Many of Middleton's residents work in the capital or for the nearby University of Wisconsin.

Information: **Middleton Tourism Commission** | 7426 Hubbard Ave., 53562 | 800/688–5694 | pbaker@ci.middleton.wi.us | www/visitmiddleton.com.

Attractions

Capital Brewery. This traditional Wisconsin brewery offers tours on Friday and Saturday in summer and on Saturday the rest of the year. | 7734 Terrace Ave. | 608/836–7100 | Free | June–Aug., Fri. and Sat. at 1 and 3:30; Sept.–May, Sat. at 1 and 2:30.

Middleton Area Historical Society. Exhibits and artifacts on Middleton history. | 7410 Hubbard Ave. | 608/836–7614 | Free | Mid-Apr.–mid-Oct., Tues. and Sat. 1–4; tours by appointment.

Walter R. Bauman Outdoor Aquatic Center. A maximum of 724 people can cavort in the 345,580 gallons of water here at any one time. If you decide to take the plunge, you'll find two 134-ft-run water slides, interactive water play equipment, a sand playground, and two sand volleyball courts. | 2400 Park Lawn Pl. | 608/836–3450 | $3–$4; $2–$3 for age 3 to 17; 2 and under free | Weekdays 11:30–8; weekends 11–8; closed Sept.–May.

ON THE CALENDAR
JUNE: *Festival of Forks.* The first weekend in June brings this family event with lots of food and music plus plenty of games and entertainment for kids to Terrace Avenue downtown. | 800/688–5694.

Dining

Fitzgerald's of Middleton. American. Steaks, seafood, prime rib, pasta, barbecued ribs, and chicken served in a casual but elegant atmosphere with white linen, candles, lots of flowers, and ceiling fans. Sunday brunch. | 3112 W. Beltline Hwy. | 608/831–7107 | Reservations not accepted Fri. | $12–$30 | AE, D, MC, V | No dinner Sun.

Louisanne's. Cajun/Creole. Live piano music, stone walls, and low curved ceilings set this restaurant apart. Specialties include Lemon Pesto Shrimp and Lobster, Tenderloin Cordon Bleu, and Chicken Louisanne—a chicken dish with sautéed spinach and a Creole mustard sauce. | 7464 Hubbard Ave. (Beltline Hwy., Exit 251) | 608/831–1929 | Reservations essential | $12–$30 | AE, D, MC, V | Closed Sun. No lunch.

Stamm House. American. This restaurant is housed in a former stagecoach station built in 1847. There is a full-service bar and lounge downstairs, and a cozy, pub-like dining area upstairs. Specialties include the fish fry, a homemade chicken-and-dumpling dinner, steaks, and prime rib. | 6625 Century Ave. (Hwy. M) | 608/831–5835 | $8–$17 | MC, V.

Lodging

Fairfield Inn. A chain motel built in 1996 on the outskirts of town close to the Madison border. Complimentary Continental breakfast. In-room data ports. Pool. Hot tub. | 8212 Greenway Blvd. | 608/831–1400 | fax 608/831–1435 | jdirksen@ncghotels.com | www.ncghotels.com | 104 rooms | $69–$89 | AE, D, DC, MC, V.

Marriott Madison West. This modern conference center and hotel is set in a bustling part of town just 15 mi from the heart of Madison. It has a large lobby with an atrium and waterfall. Restaurant, bar. Pool. | 1313 John Q. Hammons Dr. | 608/831–2000 | fax 608/831–2040 | www.marriott.com | 292 rooms | $95–$144 | AE, DC, C, MC, V.

Trotta's Colonial Motel. This family-owned and -operated 1960s motel has three buildings right on the Beltline Highway. Some rooms have direct access to the pool. Cable TV. Pool. Hot tub. | 3001 W. Beltline Hwy. | 608/836–1131 | 31 rooms | $47–$57 | AE, D, MC, V.

MILWAUKEE

(Nearby towns also listed: Brookfield, Glendale, Hales Corners, Waukesha, Wauwatosa)

On the shores of Lake Michigan, Milwaukee, Wisconsin's largest city, has a small-town spirit because it is more a collection of neighborhoods than a sprawling urban metropolis. First settled by Potowatomi and later by French fur traders in the 18th century, the city boomed with the arrival of German brewers whose presence is still felt. The city is filled with museums, art centers, and an abundance of ethnic restaurants including German, Serbian, and Irish. The Milwaukee Zoo is ranked among the best in the country. Modern steel and glass high-rises share downtown space with historic 19th-century buildings. The city is Wisconsin's primary commercial and manufacturing center and also has an international seaport.

Information: Greater Milwaukee Convention and Visitors Bureau | 510 W. Kilbourn Ave., 53203-1402 | 800/554–1448 | www.officialmilwaukee.org.

NEIGHBORHOODS

Brewers Hill. This area of beautifully refurbished homes and commercial buildings dating from the 19th century is near downtown Milwaukee. Not many years ago, most of these buildings were derelict, but a group of enthusiastic home owners—who bought them sometimes for just a few thousand dollars—changed all that. The neighborhood's boundaries are Lloyd and Vine streets, Hubbard and Palmer streets, and 2nd Street.

Concordia. The Concordia neighborhood was once home to the well-appointed mansions and grand houses of the city's upper crust. Although the area fell into disrepair for a time, today most of these striking buildings, in many different styles, have been refurbished and beautifully landscaped. In 1985 Concordia was listed on the National Register of Historic Places. Boundaries are North 27th Street, North 35th Street, Highland Boulevard, and West Wisconsin Avenue.

Third Ward. This neighborhood, listed on the National Register of Historic Places, is close to the Milwaukee River and is made up of a mix of large, often historic buildings (from former warehouses to furniture stores). Many have been restored and now house upscale shops, restaurants, and condos. Old-fashioned street lamps illuminate the area, and a small park and a pedestrian mall along Broadway Street strike a verdant note. The area is roughly bounded by Broadway, Water, and Erie streets, and St. Paul Avenue.

TRANSPORTATION INFORMATION

Airports: General Mitchell International Airport Six miles south of downtown via Interstate 94: served by domestic and international carriers. | 5300 S. Howell Ave. | 414/747–5300.

Amtrak: | 433 W. St. Paul Ave. | 800/872–7245.

Bus Lines: Milwaukee County Transit System Operates buses to and from the airport and throughout Milwaukee County. | 414/344–6711.

Greyhound: | 606 N. 7th St. | 800/231–2222.

Attractions

ART AND ARCHITECTURE

★ **Captain Frederick Pabst Mansion.** Completed in 1892 for beer baron Captain Frederick Pabst, this 37-room Flemish Renaissance–style mansion is a treasured Milwaukee landmark. The exterior is tan pressed-brick with carved-stone and terra-cotta ornamentation, and the interior is filled with woodwork, ironwork, marble, tile, stained glass, and period furnishings. There's a special holiday display around Christmastime. | 2000 W. Wisconsin Ave. | 414/931–0808 | $7; special rates for senior citizens and kids | Mon.–Sat. 10–3:30, Sun. noon–3:30.

City Hall. A 393-ft clock tower tops this German Renaissance, Romanesque, and Flemish-style building dating from 1895. | 200 E. Wells St. | 414/286–3200 | Free | Weekdays 8–4:45.

Grain Exchange. This spectacular 10,000-square-ft Victorian Renaissance building downtown is now a commercial venue, but you can look into some of its main rooms when special events are not being held. | 225 E. Michigan St. | 414/276–7840 | Free | Weekdays 9–5.

Jeremiah Curtin House. This limestone cottage southwest of downtown was the boyhood home of Jeremiah Curtin, a linguist and diplomat. Built in 1846, it is an excellent example of Irish cottage architecture. | S. 84th St. and W. Grange Ave., Greendale | 414/273–8288 | Donations accepted | July–Aug., call for hours.

Kilbourntown House. Built in 1844 and restored in 1938, this home on the National Register of Historic Places displays 19th-century furnishings and decorative arts. It's in Estabrook Park, between Hampton Avenue and Capitol Drive. | 4400 W. Estabrook Dr. | 414/273–8288 | Donations accepted | Late June–Labor Day, weekdays by appointment.

Pabst Theater. Built in 1895 and remodeled in 1976, this refurbished Victorian theater downtown is on the National Register of Historic Places and presents top music and theatrical entertainment. Of special note is its giant Austrian-crystal chandelier. | 144 E. Wells St. | 414/286–3663 | Free | Sat. 11:30 AM for public tours; private tours by appointment.

BEACHES, PARKS, AND NATURAL SIGHTS

Bradford Beach. This long strip of beach along Lake Michigan gets busy in summer, with sunbathers, joggers, swimmers, in-line skaters, skateboarders, and bicyclists. Food booths and vendors are near the center of the strip, within walking distance from any part of the beach. | 2400 N. Lincoln Memorial Dr. | 414/645–4095 | Free | Daily.

Cathedral Square. This parklike square just a few blocks from the lakefront and within walking distance of downtown was built on the site of Milwaukee's first courthouse. Across the street is beautiful St. John's Cathedral, the first Roman Catholic cathedral in Wisconsin. | E. Kilbourn Ave. and Jefferson St. | 414/273–7222 | Free | Daily.

Havenwoods State Forest. This state forest on the northwest side of Milwaukee has an environmental awareness center and nature trails. | 6141 N. Hopkins | 414/527–0232 | www.dnr.state.wi.us/org/land/parks/ | Free | Daily.

★ **Mitchell Park Horticultural Conservatory.** Known to residents as "The Domes," this conservatory has three 85-ft glass domes featuring tropical, arid, and seasonal plant displays. It's south of downtown. | 524 S. Layton Blvd., at W. Pierce St. | 414/649–9800 | $4; special rates for senior citizens and kids | Daily 9–5.

Père Marquette Park. This small but pretty park is along the banks of the Milwaukee River. | Old World 3rd St. and W. Kilbourn Ave. | 414/273–7222 | Free | Daily.

Schlitz Audubon Center. This 225-acre lakeshore nature preserve north of town contains woodlands, meadows, bluffs, and fields, as well as an interpretative center with literature and visitor information about the Center and surrounding area. | 1111 E. Brown Deer Rd. | 414/352–2880 | $4 for trails; special rates for kids | Tues.–Sun. 9–5.

Timber Wolf Farm and Preservation Society. You can learn about the endangered Eastern timber wolf at this preserve and educational center, which conducts outreach and educational programs related to the preservation of the species as well as providing a home for a pack of 16 full-blooded timber wolves. | 6669 S. 76th St., Greendale | 414/425–8264 | $1 | Weekends 10–3.

Historic Turner Hall. This cream city brick structure downtown, across from Bradley Center, was built between 1832 and 1833 to house the Milwaukee Turners, a local gymnastics club. Today Turner gymnasts still practice in the building's gymnasium, and the structure has been designated a National Historic Landmark. In addition to the gym, it houses a restaurant with hand-painted murals, photos of Turner gymnasts, original hardwood floors, and stained-glass windows. The building's top-floor ballroom was Milwaukee's showplace in the 1800s and is said to have inspired the famous waltz "After the Ball," by Charles K. Harris. Artifacts and information about the Turners' local and national influence are on display. Call in advance to schedule a tour. | 1034 N. 4th St. | 414/272–1733 | Free | Weekdays 9–5, weekends by appointment.

Marcus Center for the Performing Arts. Home to the Milwaukee Symphony Orchestra, Milwaukee Ballet Company, Florentine Opera of Milwaukee, and First Stage Milwaukee Theater for Children downtown. | 929 N. Water St. | 414/273–7206 | Box office daily.

The **First Stage Milwaukee Theater for Children** performs plays developed from kids' literature. | 929 N. Water St. | 414/273–7206 | $7.25–$14.75 | Sept.–June.

The **Florentine Opera of Milwaukee** stages four operas each season at the Pabst Theater and the Marcus Center for the Performing Arts. | 734 N. Water St., Suite 1315 | 414/291–5700 or 800/32–opera | www.florentineopera.org | $20–$90 | Sept.–June.

The repertoire of the world-class **Milwaukee Ballet Company** includes classic to contemporary ballets. *The Nutcracker* is a regular holiday visitor. Performances are at the Marcus Center for the Performing Arts. | 504 W. National Ave. | 414/643–7677 | Admission price varies | Sept.–May.

The **Milwaukee Symphony Orchestra** performs more than 100 concerts of classical and popular music every year in Milwaukee and throughout the state. | 330 E. Kilbourn Ave. | 800/291–7605 | www.milwaukeesymphony.org | $15–$75 | Sept.–June.

Marquette University. Founded in 1881, Marquette University provides a Jesuit-based urban education for more than 10,000 students per year. The school's 51 campus buildings are scattered over 80 acres just west of downtown Milwaukee. Students here work toward Associate's, Bachelor's, Master's, and Doctoral degrees, as well as credentials in dentistry and law. Marquette is also the home of Jesu Church, a Milwaukee landmark. Campus tours are available. | 1442 W. Wisconsin Ave. | 414/288–7250 | www.marquette.edu | Free | Mon.–Sat. tours available by reservation.

Marquette Hall's 48-bell carillon is near the center of the Marquette University campus.

Patrick and Beatrice Haggerty Museum of Art. Just west of downtown, this museum houses Marquette University's collection of more than 10,000 works of art. Exhibits vary from Renaissance and Baroque pieces to modern paintings, sculptures, prints, photography, and decorative arts. | 530 N. 13th St. | 414/288–1669 | www.marquette.edu/haggerty | Free | Mon.–Wed. and Fri.–Sat. 10–4:30, Thurs. 10–8, Sun. noon–5.

In 1964 the small, stone, 15th-century **St. Joan of Arc Chapel** was brought to Milwaukee in pieces from its original site near Lyons, France. One stone, which is discernibly colder than the others, was reputedly kissed by Joan before she was sent to her death. | 1442 W. Wisconsin Ave. | 414/288–7150 | Free | Daily dawn to dusk.

Milwaukee Maritime Center. See ships being built and learn the history of the Great Lakes' trade routes. The center is just a few blocks from downtown. | 500 N. Harbor Dr. | 414/276–7700 | www.wis-schooner.org | Donations accepted | Mon.–Sat. 10–3, Sun. noon–3.

Old World 3rd Street. This charming street starts downtown and runs north. The most interesting section is around Juneau and State streets, where you'll find old-fashioned street lights, as well as a wide selection of ethnic restaurants and specialty food stores. A park edges the river where Old World 3rd Street and State Street meet. | 414/273–7222 | Free | Daily.

University of Wisconsin–Milwaukee. Founded in 1956, this urban teaching and research university is in a quiet residential neighborhood in Milwaukee's upper east side, just blocks from Lake Michigan. The campus itself occupies 19 grassy acres, and some 23,000 graduate and undergraduate students work their way through more than two dozen degree programs. Three campus art venues display avant-garde exhibits by regional, national, and international artists. | 3253 N. Downer Ave. | 414/229–1122 | Free | Daily.

The **Golda Meir Library,** on the University of Wisconsin–Milwaukee campus, is used by the entire Milwaukee community. It houses the American Geographical Society Collection, which includes maps, globes, atlases, charts, books, and journals. | 2311 E. Hartford Ave. | 414/229–6202 | www.uwm.edu | Free | Call for hours.

The University of Wisconsin–Milwaukee's **Manfred P. Olson Planetarium** was built in 1966 and named for a professor of physics. Programs are offered throughout the year. No kids under 6. | 1900 E. Kenwood Blvd. | 414/229–4961 | www.uwm.edu | $1 | Call for show/exhibit times.

War Memorial Center. Built to honor Milwaukee's war veterans, this modern building overlooks Lake Michigan and is home to the Milwaukee Art Museum. Sculptures on grounds. | 750 N. Lincoln Memorial Dr. | 414/273–5533 | Free; art museum $5 | Daily 8–8.

MUSEUMS

America's Black Holocaust Museum. This downtown museum traces the history of slavery in the Americas and illustrates the toils and struggles of African Americans since its abolition. Exhibits change regularly and include artwork, photography, lecture series, educational programs, and literary showcases. | 2233 N. 4th St. | 414/264–2500 | $5; special rates for kids and groups | Mon.–Sat. 9–6.

Betty Brinn Children's Museum. A hands-on museum just east of downtown for kids of all ages features ever-changing exhibits designed to include kids in the learning process by encouraging them to touch, explore, and question. Past exhibits have included walk-throughs of a giant human ear, a miniature interactive town square, and programs on language and communication. | 929 E. Wisconsin Ave. | 414/291–0888 | $4 | Mon.–Sat. 9–5, Sun. noon–5; Sept.–May, closed Mon.

Charles Allis Art Museum. This museum is in an elegant Tudor-style home built in 1911 for the first president of the Allis-Chalmers Manufacturing Company. The museum has stained-glass windows and a collection of paintings and objets d'art from around the world, including works by major 19th- and 20th-century French and American painters. | 1801 N. Prospect Ave. | 414/278–8295 | $3; kids free | Wed.–Sun. 1–5.

Milwaukee County Historical Center. This museum in a former bank building at Pere Marquette Park displays early firefighting equipment, military artifacts, toys, and women's fashions, and includes a research library with naturalization records and genealogical resources. | 910 N. Old World 3rd St. | 414/273–8288 | Donations accepted | Weekdays 9:30–5, Sat. 10–5, Sun. 1–5.

The **Milwaukee Art Museum,** within the War Memorial Center, maintains a collection of American, European, modern, and contemporary art by such artists as Georgia O'Keeffe, Pablo Picasso, Marc Chagall, and Andy Warhol, and hosts a number of traveling exhibits as well. The Haitian collection is one of the best outside of Haiti. | 750 N. Lincoln Memorial Dr. | 414/224–3200 | $5; special rates for senior citizens, kids, and groups | Tues.–Wed. and Fri.–Sat. 10–5, Thurs. noon–9, Sun. noon–5.

★ **Milwaukee Public Museum.** Known for its collection of more than 6 million specimens and artifacts, this downtown museum has many stunning exhibits, including the walk-through "Streets of Old Milwaukee," which depicts the city in the 1890s; the two-story "Rain Forest"; and the "Third Planet," which contains full-size dinosaurs and a cavern you can enter to learn about the earth's surface. | 800 W. Wells St. | 414/278–2700 | www.mpm.edu | $6.50; special rates for senior citizens, kids, and groups; free for kids under 4; free for Milwaukee County residents on Mon. | Daily 9–5.

Discovery World (James Lovell Museum of Science, Economics, and Technology), an educational science center within the Milwaukee Public Museum complex, contains more than 150 interactive exhibits on magnets, motors, electricity, health, and computers. Attractions include the "Great Electric Show" and the "Light Wave–Laser Beam Show." | 815 N. James Lovell St. | 414/765–0777 | $5.50; special rates for senior citizens and kids | Daily 9–5.

The **Humphrey IMAX Dome Theater,** part of the Milwaukee Public Museum, screens educational films in the round, projected onto an eight-story-high screen. | 414/319–4629 | www.humphreyimax.com | $6.50 | Sun.–Wed. 10:30–4:30, Thurs.–Sat. 10:30–8:30.

Villa Terrace Decorative Arts Museum. This Italianate villa, originally a private home, overlooks Lake Michigan and is now a museum dedicated to the decorative arts. Beautiful gardens surround the museum, which is on Milwaukee's east side. | 2220 N. Terrace Ave. | 414/271–3656 | $3; kids free | Wed.–Sun. 1–5.

Wisconsin Black Historical Society Museum. This museum in central Milwaukee has a 15-panel mural tracing African-Americans from Egypt to Milwaukee, an exhibit on African-American labor in Wisconsin, and photos and artifacts depicting the African-American heritage. | 2620 W. Center St. | 414/372–7677 | $5; special rates for senior citizens, kids, and groups | By reservation only.

RELIGION AND SPIRITUALITY

Cathedral of St. John the Evangelist. This large, ornate cathedral on the lower east side of central Milwaukee was once the seat of the Archdiocese of Milwaukee. | 802 N. Jackson St. | 414/276–9814 | Free | Daily.

Notre Dame Convent. Modeled after a Bavarian castle, this 1862 building has a beautiful bell tower. The convent still fulfills its original purpose as home to the School Sisters of Notre Dame. Approximately 2,000 nuns are buried in a cemetery on the 90-acre grounds. | Watertown Plank Rd., Elm Grove | 262/782–1450 | Free | Daily.

Old St. Mary's Church. Built in 1846 and listed on the National Register of Historic Places, this striking cream city brick church downtown is the oldest Catholic church in Milwaukee. King Ludwig of Bavaria donated the painting of the Annunciation that hangs above the altar. | 836 N. Broadway St. | 414/271–6180 | Free | Daily.

St. Josaphat Basilica. Built by immigrant parishioners and local craftsmen at the turn of the 20th century, this striking basilica south of downtown is a superb example of Renaissance Revival architecture. Limestone from a Chicago post office was used on the facade, and the church's copper dome was modeled after the one atop St. Peter's in Rome. Inside are art-glass windows from Austria, hand-painted murals, and a remarkable collection of relics. | 601 W. Lincoln Ave. | 414/645–5623 | $3 | Daily; Sun. morning tours by appointment.

St. Stephen Catholic Church. The collection of wood carvings here is world-famous. The church is a few blocks southwest of downtown. | 5880 S. Howell Ave. | 414/483–2685 | Donations accepted | Daily; tours by appointment.

SPORTS AND RECREATION

Milwaukee Admirals. This local hockey team plays at Bradley Center, just north of downtown. | 1001 N. 4th St. | 414/227–0550 | $10–$20 | Early Oct.–mid-Apr.

Milwaukee Brewers. Major League Baseball's Brewers came to Milwaukee in 1970. Home games are at Miller Park. | 414/933–9000 or 414/345–3000 | $10–$30 | Apr.–early Oct.

Milwaukee Bucks. This NBA team plays at Bradley Center. | 1001 N. 4th St. | 414/227–0500 | $7–$70 | Nov.–Apr.

Pettit National Ice Center. The largest ice center in the country is also an Olympic training complex, with an Olympic-size skating rink, two hockey rinks, and plenty of space for jogging. You can watch local Olympic speed skaters practice, or take a turn on the ice yourself. | 500 S. 84th St. | 414/266–0100 | $5 | Daily 9–5.

SIGHTSEEING TOURS/TOUR COMPANIES

Edelweiss Cruise Dining. Enjoy a sightseeing, luncheon, champagne, cocktail, moonlight, or dinner cruise on Lake Michigan, in a European-style, flat-bottomed canal boat. It boards downtown. Reservations required. | 1110 Old World 3rd St. | 414/272–3625 | Admission varies per cruise/event | Oct.–Apr.; call for schedule.

Iroquois Boat Line Tours. Take a 90-minute tour down the Milwaukee River, starting in downtown on the west bank of the river and terminating at Lake Michigan. The tours highlight local history. Boats are double-decker, with canopied tops and below-deck window viewing. Board at the Clybourn Street Bridge. | 414/384–8606 | Daily cruises $8.50 | Late June–Labor Day; call for schedule.

OTHER POINTS OF INTEREST

Miller Brewing Co. Beer tasting, a gift shop, and guided tours are available at the brewery, about 2 mi west of downtown. | 4251 W. State St. | 414/931–2337 | Free | Tours by prior arrangement only; call for tour days and hours.

Milwaukee County Zoo. The Milwaukee County Zoo is one of the finest zoos in the nation, housing more than 3,000 wild animals and birds, including some endangered species. The zoo's attractions include educational programs, a petting zoo, narrated tram tours, and miniature-train rides. | 10001 W. Bluemound Rd. | 414/771–3040 or 414/771–5500 | $6.50; special rates for senior citizens, kids, and Wisconsin residents | Daily 9–6.

Milwaukee Journal Sentinel. In 1995 the *Milwaukee Journal* and the *Milwaukee Sentinel* merged to form the *Milwaukee Journal Sentinel*, Milwaukee's largest newspaper. Tours allow you to see old and new presses, as well as the paper's large newsroom. | 333 W. State St., at 4th St. | 414/224–2419 | www.jsonline.com | Free | Groups by appointment.

Port of Milwaukee. Originally serving the Milwaukee River and Great Lakes, this area became an international port with the opening of the enlarged St. Lawrence Seaway in 1959. During a self-guided tour, you can see equipment being made to handle the heavy cargo that passes through the port. | 2323 S. Lincoln Memorial Dr. | 414/286–3511 | Free | Daily.

© Artville

CUSTARD—THAT DAIRY TREAT

Wisconsin does its dairy history proud with a grand version of frozen custard, a thick and creamy, ice-cream-like dessert made with egg yolks. Frozen-custard stands can be found throughout the state, especially in Milwaukee. The stands range from little mom-and-pops to large local chains. Most stands have billboards highlighting the flavor of the day along with a list of other available flavors. In general, the warmer the day, the longer the line is likely to be, but this rich and creamy treat is well worth any wait.

ON THE CALENDAR

JUNE: *CajunFest.* There's a gumbo and jambalaya cook-off, a crawfish-eating contest, music, and entertainment at State Fair Park. | 414/476–7303 | www.cajunfest.org.

JUNE: *RiverSplash!* Every summer, crowds throng to Pere Marquette Park to enjoy towering fountains in the Milwaukee River illuminated at night, fireworks on a river barge, music, entertainment, and food. | 414/297–9855.

JUNE–JULY: *Summerfest.* The self-styled "World's Largest Music Festival" is held on its own grounds in Henry Maier Festival Park. It showcases more than 2,500 national, regional, and local acts, and also includes a sports area, a carnival, a kids' play area, face painting, arts, ethnic foods, and vendors. Traditionally the event begins on the last Thursday in June and runs through July 4. | 414/273–2680 or 800/837–3378.

JUNE: *Polish Fest.* Polish music, food, dancing, and a cultural village in Henry Maier Festival Park. Held on the third weekend of the month. | 414/529–2140.

JULY: *Bastille Days.* French food, a faux Eiffel Tower, French music, and a 5K run called "Storm the Bastille." Held in Cathedral Square and surrounding streets, just east of the downtown area, on the second weekend of the month. | 414/271–1416.

JULY: *Great Circus Parade.* This parade of vintage circus wagons, horses, clowns, elephants, and marching bands winds through downtown Milwaukee. | 608/356–8341.

JULY: *Festa Italiana.* Italian food, music, entertainment, and fireworks. Held in Henry Maier Festival Park on the third weekend of the month. | 414/223–2180.

JULY: *German Fest.* German music, dancing, and food, plus fireworks and a parade. Held in Henry Maier Festival Park on the last weekend of the month. | 414/464–9444.

AUG.: *African World Festival.* Gospel music, food, a kids' area, an African village, and cultural events. Held in Henry Maier Festival Park on the first weekend of the month. | 414/372–4567.

AUG.: *Irish Fest.* Irish food, music, and dancing. Held in Henry Maier Festival Park on the third weekend of the month. | 414/476–3378.

AUG.: *Mexican Fiesta.* Mexican food, music, and dancing, plus fireworks and a run. Held in Henry Maier Festival Park on the last weekend of the month. | 414/383–7066.

AUG.: *Wisconsin State Fair.* This large fair includes a carnival, live entertainment, food booths, arts, crafts, farm animals, kids' activities, and body-building and weight-lifting competitions. The fair is held mid-month in West Allis. | 414/266–7000.

NOV.: *Holiday Folk Fair.* Peruse authentic crafts from around the world and learn to say "hello" in dozens of languages. Booths at the fair are run by citizens from countries all over the world, and they'll stamp your faux passport at each booth you visit. Munch your way around the globe by sampling the delicious homemade specialties at numerous food stands. The event is held in State River Park on the weekend before Thanksgiving. | 414/225–6225.

WALKING TOUR

Downtown Milwaukee and Beyond (approximately 2½ hours)

Start this tour with a visit to the **Milwaukee Art Museum,** on Lincoln Memorial Drive along Milwaukee's lakefront. After you tour the museum, be sure to check out the pieces of artwork on the grounds as well. From the front of the museum walk straight ahead, away from the lake heading west. Walk to the first light, turn left, and walk one block to Wisconsin Avenue and the **Betty Brinn Children's Museum,** a great hands-on museum for kids of all ages. Continue West along Wisconsin Avenue to Jefferson Street, turn right on Jefferson, and walk two blocks to reach charming **Cathedral Square,** a great place to people-watch, have a snack, or just relax. Return to Jefferson Street and head back toward Wisconsin Avenue. Two blocks before Wisconsin Avenue, you'll see Wells Street. Turn right onto Wells Street and walk about three blocks to **Milwaukee City Hall,** which has interesting architectural elements both inside and out. Continue along Wells Street in the same direction, and you'll pass the **Pabst Theater,** where musical and artistic performances are held regularly. Continue along Wells Street for about two blocks, passing over the Milwaukee River, until you reach **Old World 3rd Street.** Turn right, walk about a block, and you'll see pretty streets with old-fashioned light fixtures, cobblestone walkways, unique shops, and great ethnic restaurants. Have lunch at a local eatery, or grab a snack at one of the specialty food stores in the area. You can also spend some time in **Pere Marquette Park,** which is next to the **Milwaukee County Historical Center.** Both the park and the historical society are on the Milwaukee River. Backtrack to Wells Street, turn right onto Wells, and walk about four blocks to James Lovell Street, formerly known as 7th Street. There you'll find the **Milwaukee Public Museum, Discovery World (the James Lovell Museum of Science, Economics, and Technology),** and the **Humphrey IMAX Dome Theater.** If you have the time, take a stroll through the museum's "Streets of Old Milwaukee" exhibit to see what this large city looked like in the 1890s, see some of the more than 140 interactive exhibits at Discovery World, or watch a film in the round at the IMAX. Return to James Lovell Street, turn right (south), and walk one block to Wisconsin Avenue. Turn right on Wisconsin Avenue and take a leisurely stroll to 20th Street, where the **Captain Frederick Pabst Mansion** is. You can tour this Flemish Renaissance–style mansion completed in 1892 to see how the homes and gardens of old Milwaukee once looked. Return to the **Milwaukee Art Museum** by walking toward the lake along Wisconsin Avenue. On the way, you'll pass the Grand Avenue Retail Center, which has lots of great shops.

Dining

INEXPENSIVE

Club Tres Hermanos. Mexican. This large, basic restaurant south of downtown has Mexican decorations and music, and serves chips, salsa, seafood soup, and classic favorites like chimichangas and tacos. Kids' menu. No smoking | 1332 W. Lincoln Ave. | 414/384–9050 | $8–$15 | AE, MC, V.

Elsa's on the Park. American. Stop at this casual spot across from Cathedral Square for a hamburger or a pork-chop sandwich. | 833 N. Jefferson St. | 414/765–0615 | $5–$10 | AE, MC, V | No lunch weekends.

Watts Tea Shop. English. This shop above George Watts and Sons, Milwaukee's premier purveyor of silver, china, and crystal, serves breakfast and lunch in addition to tea. Try the sunshine cake. | 761 N. Jefferson St. | 414/291–5120 | $6–$10 | AE, D, MC, V | Closed Sun. No dinner.

MODERATE

Balistreri's Bluemound Inn. Italian. Try the veal Balistreri, veal topped with eggplant and spinach; the pollo carciofi, chicken served on pasta with artichoke hearts and spinach; or whitefish Frangelico at this casual restaurant on the west side of Milwaukee. | 6501 W. Bluemound Rd. | 414/258–9881 | $10–$49 | AE, D, DC, MC, V | No lunch weekends.

Bavarian Inn. German. This chalet on 14 acres of grounds displays soccer memorabilia and handmade chandeliers. You'll find a wild-game platter and grilled kangaroo on the menu, along with the predictable sauerbraten and schnitzels. Live music Friday. Kids' menu. Sunday brunch. | 700 W. Lexington Blvd. | 414/964–0300 | $13–$18 | AE, D, DC, MC, V | Closed Mon. No lunch Fri., Sat.

Coquette Café. French. This country-French café is in Milwaukee's Third Ward, just south of downtown. The beer is specially brewed to complement the menu, which is filled with dishes like roasted mussels, thin-crust Niçoise and Alsatian pizzas, vegetable sandwiches, and grilled skirt steak. No smoking | 316 N. Milwaukee St. | 414/291–2655 | $16–$27 | MC, V | Closed Sun. No lunch Sat.

County Clare. Irish. This restaurant looks like a traditional Irish pub, with deep-green walls, a long, ornate bar, and Gaelic sayings on the walls. The menu includes such dishes as corned beef and cabbage, hearty pub sandwiches, and homemade soups-of-the-day. Traditional Irish music on Sundays. | 1234 N. Astor St. | 414/272–5273 | $10–$25 | AE, D, DC, MC, V.

De Marinis. Italian. This bustling restaurant is in a residential area across the Hoan Bridge, minutes from downtown Milwaukee. It's cozy and casual, and serves pizza and pasta. The tomato sauce is homemade. | 1211 E. Conway St., Bay View | 414/481–2348 | $15–$25 | D, MC, V | No lunch.

Dos Bandidos. Mexican. Jumbo margaritas in a variety of flavors are a specialty at this cozy neighborhood cantina. The bar is hopping, and the restaurant serves fajitas and vegetable crisps. Parking. Open-air dining on secluded patio. | 5932 N. Green Bay Ave. | 414/228–1911 | Reservations not accepted | $7–$20 | AE, D, MC, V | No lunch Sun.

Eagan's. American. Impressionist paintings hang on the walls of this chic downtown restaurant. The large bar pours 450 kinds of liquor, and the kitchen serves delicacies such as oysters Rockefeller and lobster. Enjoy open-air dining on the patio overlooking popular Water Street. Sunday brunch. | 1030 N. Water St. | 414/271–6900 | Reservations not accepted | $7–$25 | AE, D, DC, MC, V.

Giovanni's. Italian. Giovanni's is a bright restaurant with a busy bar on a quiet corner in a largely residential district. The menu is varied, with lots of chicken and pasta options, but the real standouts are the veal dishes, like veal marsala (tender medallions sauteed in olive oil with mushrooms and wine sauce) or veal cotoletta (a choice cut lightly breaded and sauteed in olive oil, then dusted with Italian seasonings). | 1683 N. Van Buren St. | 414/291–5600 | $17–$27 | AE, D, DC, MC, V | No lunch weekends.

Historic Turner Restaurant. American. The spacious, high-ceilinged dining area of this gymnastics center has original wood floors, high-backed booths, and an old-style bar accented with brass. The walls are filled with photos of local gymnasts and gymnastics memorabilia. The menu includes pasta dishes, a fish fry, oversize sandwiches, and jumbo nacho platters, as well as homemade soups. | 1034 N. 4th St. | 414/276–4844 | $10–$16 | AE, DC, MC, V.

Izumi's. Japanese. This small, cozy restaurant on the east side of town has a sushi bar and a menu of traditional Japanese fare, such as udon and sukiyaki. Wine, beer, and sake only. | 2178 N. Prospect Ave. | 414/271–5278 | $8–$21 | AE, DC, MC, V | No lunch weekends.

Jack Pandl's Whitefish Bay Inn. American. This quaint and cozy restaurant in a residential area near the lake serves whitefish, German pancakes, and specialty desserts. Kids' menu. Parking. | 1319 E. Henry Clay St., Whitefish Bay | 414/964–3800 | $15–$25 | AE, D, DC, MC, V.

John Ernst. German. Opened in 1938, this downtown brick establishment is Milwaukee's oldest restaurant, and it's filled with German-style knick-knacks and antiques, along with lots of dark wood paneling and intimate booths. The menu includes sauerbraten and Wienerschnitzel, along with more Continental offerings like roast duck and prime rib. Entertainment. Kids' menu. Sunday brunch. | 600 E. Ogden Ave. | 414/273–1878 | $16–$20 | AE, D, DC, MC, V | Closed Mon.

Judy's Kitchen. American. This informal restaurant has a large fireplace and a kitchen counter where you can watch the chef at work. The menu is seasonal and might include bass sautéed with lemon butter, or pork tenderloin. You can eat outside on the front porch. Judy's is in a suburb, about 12 mi from downtown. No smoking | 600 W. Brown Deer Rd., Bayside | 414/352–9998 | $18–$25 | AE, MC, V | Closed Sun. No lunch Sat.

King and I. Thai. Thai paintings and wood carvings set the scene for this restaurant's delicious pad Thai and volcano chicken. Large windows overlook the Milwaukee River. | 823 N. 2nd St. | 414/276–4181 | $10–$20 | AE, D, DC, MC, V | No lunch weekends.

Mimma's Café. Italian. This café is east of downtown in a clapboard building dating from 1890; inside are columns, and walls sponge-painted in subtle hues. The kitchen prepares recipes from northern Italy to Sicily, including some 50 different pasta dishes. | 1307 E. Brady St. | 414/271–7337 | $12–$25 | AE, D, DC, MC, V | No lunch.

Old Town Serbian Gourmet House. Eastern European. This large, candlelit restaurant south of downtown is full of old-world charm, with linen tablecloths and cityscapes on the walls. The menu lists Serbian specialties—such as *sarma* (stuffed sauerkraut rolls) and beef *burek* (spiced meat wrapped with grape leaves)—as well as American, French, and other ethnic dishes. Kids' menu. Ethnic strolling music on weekends. | 522 W. Lincoln Ave. | 414/672-0206 | $12–$18 | AE, D, DC, MC, V | Closed Mon. No lunch weekends.

Pandl's in Bayside. American. This restaurant 10 mi north of downtown is set back from the road near an Audubon center, and is surrounded by trees. Floor-to-ceiling windows in back give you a view of passing deer, raccoon, and birds. The dining room is done in hunter green, accented with antiques and dried floral arrangements. Salad bar. Kids' menu. Sunday brunch. | 8825 N. Lake Dr., Bayside | 414/352-7300 | $15–$25 | AE, D, DC, MC, V.

Pleasant Valley Inn. Contemporary. The building that houses this restaurant was originally a tavern in the middle of a privately owned park. Today, the Inn is surrounded by a quiet, mostly residential neighborhood. On the menu: Continental offerings, like roast duck and prime rib, but also some more creative dishes like stuffed whitefish, which consists of two large fish filets wrapped around a filling of artichoke, spinach, and melted Parmesan cheese. Kids' menu. | 9801 W. Dakota St., West Allis | 414/321-4321 | $16–$26 | AE, D, DC, MC, V | Closed Mon. No lunch.

Safe House. American. Bar stools at this downtown restaurant with an espionage theme move up and down at the whim of the bartender. The place is known for its sandwiches and specialty drinks. There's a DJ on Friday and Saturday evenings, a magician Sunday–Wednesday evenings, and comedy acts Thursday evenings. Kids are welcome. | 779 N. Front St. | 414/271-2007 | $10–$16 | AE, MC, V | No lunch Sun.

Saz's State House. American. This turn-of-the-20th-century brick roadhouse west of downtown is known as a fun nightspot with great food. It's almost always crowded, with a diverse group of customers enjoying ribs and filet mignon in the beer garden. Sunday brunch. | 5539 W. State St. | 414/453-2410 | $10–$25 | AE, D, MC, V.

Singha Thai. Thai. This large informal restaurant with Thai decorations and white linen tablecloths serves pad thai, tom yum soup, and other traditional fare. | 2237 S. 108th St., West Allis | 414/541-1234 | $8–$18 | MC, V | No lunch Sun.

Star of Burleigh. Greek. This casual, family-style corner restaurant is almost always filled with regular neighborhood customers. It has booths, plus an old-style counter, and serves Greek country salads, feta cheese omelets, gyros, stir-fry dishes, and roasted chicken. It's on Milwaukee's northwest side, a 15-minute drive from downtown. | 8401 W. Burleigh St. | 414/442-5340 | $10–$15 | MC, V.

Three Brothers. Eastern European. This small, candlelit Serbian restaurant occupies an 1897 cream city brick building that is on both the national and state registers of historic places. A Schlitz globe tops the building, which was originally a Schlitz Brewing Company distribution point and tavern. There are fresh flowers on the tables and in the large windows, and original paintings by Serbian and Yugoslav artists hang on the walls. The menu lists beef burek, roast leg of lamb, and suckling pig. | 2414 S. St. Clair St., Bay View | 414/481-7530 | $11–$16 | No credit cards | Closed Mon. No lunch.

West Bank Café. Vietnamese. This downtown restaurant has linen tablecloths, plants, and large windows. Try the catfish in a clay pot or the chicken lemongrass. No smoking | 732 E. Burleigh St. | 414/562-5555 | $10–$20 | AE, MC, V | No lunch.

Yen Ching. Chinese. In the large dining area north of downtown the ceiling is painted gold and the bar and trim are made of natural redwood. Representative menu items include long-standing favorites like lemon chicken, mu-shu pork, and a particularly spicy rendition of Mongolian beef. | 7630 W. Good Hope Rd. | 414/353-6677 | $15–$25 | AE, D, DC, MC, V | No lunch Sat.

EXPENSIVE

Bartolotta's Lake Park Bistro. French. This bistro in a 1903 building has a view of Lake Michigan, 20-ft ceilings, and cypress pine hardwood floors covered with oriental rugs. The menu includes roast monkfish and Wisconsin trout, and the sauces are rich and buttery. Kids' menu. Sunday brunch. | 3133 E. Newberry Blvd. | 414/962–6300 | $25–$35 | AE, D, DC, MC, V | No lunch Sat.

Boulevard Inn. American. This elegant restaurant in Cudahy Tower, downtown, has a fine lake view and warm red walls, accented by white tablecloths and fresh flowers. Some dishes, such as the Caesar salad, are prepared tableside. You can also order fresh fish or the veal medallions sautéed with asparagus and crab meat. German dishes such as Wiener-schnitzel are also served. Open-air dining on terrace. Pianist. Kids' menu. Sunday brunch. | 925 E. Wells St. | 414/765–1166 | $18–$32 | AE, D, DC, MC, V.

Elm Grove Inn. Continental. This light gray barn of a building dating from 1855 is 20 mi from Milwaukee. You can sit in a high-backed mahogany booth near the fireplace as you eat fresh fish, veal, or beef. | 13275 Watertown Plank Rd., Elm Grove | 414/782–7090 | $20–$30 | AE, D, MC, V | Closed Sun. No lunch Sat.

Karl Ratzsch's. German. This downtown eatery is a city institution. The paneling has a true vintage patina, and murals on the walls depict Austrian fables. Menu items include planked whitefish, roast goose shank, duck, aged prime steak, sauerbraten, chicken, and veal schnitzel. Pianist Friday and Saturday evenings. Kids' menu. | 320 E. Mason St. | 414/276–2720 | $20–$32 | AE, D, DC, MC, V | Closed Sun. No lunch.

Mader's. German. Hummel figurines, beer steins, and German paintings fill this down-town establishment, which serves sauerbraten and roast pork shank. Sunday Viennese brunch. Kids' menu. | 1037 N. Old World 3rd St. | 414/271–3377 | $20–$30 | AE, D, DC, MC, V.

Maniaci's Café Siciliano. Continental. Brick columns, tile floors, and a Sicilian courtyard set the scene in this intimate restaurant about 3 mi from downtown. Sicilian cuisine is the specialty, with dishes such as penne with shrimp and scallops and stuffed veal chops. | 6904 N. Santa Monica Blvd., Fox Point | 414/352–5757 | $20–$35 | AE, MC, V | Closed week of July 4 and Sun. No lunch.

Polaris. American. At this elegant, candlelit revolving restaurant—on the 22nd floor of the Hyatt Regency hotel—you can see all of Milwaukee while dining. Select from prime rib au jus, filet mignon, Wienerschnitzel, fettuccine with shrimp and spinach, or roast chicken. Sunday brunch. | 333 W. Kilbourn Ave. | 414/276–1234 | $24–$30 | AE, D, DC, MC, V | No lunch Sat.

Porterhouse Restaurant. American. This large modern restaurant south of downtown serves charbroiled steak, ribs, seafood, veal, stuffed orange roughy, and poultry. Kids' menu. Parking. | 800 W. Layton Ave. | 414/744–1750 | $17–$50 | AE, D, DC, MC, V | Closed Mon. No lunch Sun.

Red Rock Café. American. This casual restaurant north of downtown serves a menu of fish, tenderloin, chicken, and vegetarian pasta dishes. Kids' menu. Sunday brunch. No smoking | 4022 N. Oakland Ave. | 414/962–4545 | $16–$26 | MC, V.

Steven Wade's Café. Contemporary. This restaurant 15 minutes from downtown serves fresh fish, and the menu includes items such as tortellini with bay scallops and crab meat. There's a fireplace, and the walls are hung with original paintings. | 17001 Greenfield Ave., New Berlin | 414/784–0774 | $21–$37 | AE, D, DC, MC, V | Closed Sun. No lunch Mon., Sat.

Weissgerber's Third Street Pier. Continental. This elegant downtown dining room in a six-story riverfront plaza has a view of the Milwaukee River, lots of shiny brass and fresh flow-ers, and a menu of steak and fresh fish. Desserts such as cherries jubilee and bananas Foster are prepared tableside. Lunch, dinner, and cocktail cruises on Lake Michigan are available. Open-air dining is available on a patio overlooking the river. Jazz trio Friday nights, pianist Thursday-Saturday. Kids' menu. | 1110 N. Old World 3rd St. | 414/272–0330 | $20–$35 | AE, D, DC, MC, V | No lunch.

MILWAUKEE

INTRO
ATTRACTIONS
DINING
LODGING

VERY EXPENSIVE

English Room. Continental. Theodore Roosevelt and Enrico Caruso, among others, have eaten in this richly furnished Pfister Hotel centenarian. The walls are hung with opulent artwork, and the menu features well-heeled standbys like roast duck, lamb, and a very satisfying prime rib. | 424 E. Wisconsin Ave. | 414/390–3832 | $30–$40 | AE, D, DC, MC, V | No lunch.

Grenadier's. Continental. Elegantly set tables grace this downtown restaurant. Try the Dover sole sautéed with lemon capers or the seared fresh tuna on ocean salad with seaweed. Pianist nightly. | 747 N. Broadway Ave., at Mason St. | 414/276–0747 | Jacket required | $30–$40 | AE, D, DC, MC, V | Closed Sun. No lunch Sat.

Harold's. Contemporary. Harold's is a romantic restaurant in the Grand Milwaukee Hotel. Enjoy your meal under soft lighting, while seated in a velvet-upholstered booth, separated from other diners by etched-glass panels. Menu selections range from adventuresome— like roasted duck breast stuffed with duck pate and sided with wild game stuffing of elk, antelope, and yams—to more familiar staples like filet mignon, which in this case is doused with melted bleu cheese and sided with chopped mushrooms. | 4747 S. Howell Ave. | 414/481–8000 | $30–$40 | AE, D, DC, MC, V | Closed Sun. No lunch Sat.

★ **Sanford.** Contemporary. Chef Sanford D'Amato has won nationwide fame for the cuisine of his elegant downtown restaurant. The four-star establishment resides in what used to be a grocery store, accented everywhere with fresh-cut floral arrangements and lots of local art. The menu changes regularly to take advantage of seasonal produce, but some more ambitious offerings have included wood-grilled elk loin and a different weeknight ethnic feast every month. No smoking | 1547 N. Jackson St. | 414/276–9608 | $38–$50 | AE, D, DC, MC, V | Closed Sun. No lunch.

Lodging

INEXPENSIVE

Exel Inn–South. This motel is just a five-minute drive from the airport, right off Interstate 94 at the College Avenue Exit (Number 319). Complimentary Continental breakfast. In-room data ports, some microwaves, cable TV. Laundry facilities. Business services, free parking. Some pets allowed. | 1201 W. College Ave. | 414/764–1776 | fax 414/762–8009 | www.exelinns.com | 110 rooms | $47–$69 | AE, D, DC, MC, V.

Golden Key Motel. This cozy, two-story motel is convenient to Wisconsin State Fair Park, restaurants, and shopping. Refrigerators, cable TV. Pool. | 3600 S. 108th St., Greenfield | 414/543–5300 | 23 rooms | $45–$75 | AE, D, MC, V.

Red Barn Hostel. This hostel, 13 mi southwest of downtown, is alongside Long Leaf Trail, a 76-mi biking and hiking trail. The hostel is in the lower level of a hand-hewn barn, which dates from 1923. There are separate sleeping areas for men and women as well as one room that can accommodate a family. A botanical garden and 18-hole golf course adjoins the property. The hostel is open May to October; it has no heat. Kitchen. No TV. | 6750 Loomis Rd., Greendale | 414/529–3299 | 20 rooms | $12–$16 | No credit cards | Closed Nov.–Apr.

Western Inn and Suites. This modern brick building is 5 mi from town. The small lobby has a seating area and plants. Restaurant, bar, picnic area, room service. Cable TV. Pool. Hot tub. Exercise equipment. Playground. Laundry facilities. Business services, free parking. | 201 N. Mayfair Rd. | 414/771–4400 | fax 414/771–4517 | 230 rooms | $43–$70 | AE, D, DC, MC, V.

Whitnall View Motel. Two buildings—one old and one new—make up this small hotel about 3 mi from Milwaukee's downtown area. Refrigerators, cable TV. | 6991 S. 108th St., Franklin | 414/425–4370 | 19 rooms | $50 | MC, V.

MODERATE

Acanthus Inn Bed & Breakfast. Built in the Queen-Anne style for a local family at the turn of the century, the inn has retained all the charm and elegance of the period. Located in the Concordia neighborhood, it is surrounded by other large, elegant old homes. The Acanthus has its original woodwork and light fixtures, pocket doors, fireplaces and even a built-in china cabinet with carved cherubs and shells in the dining room. Some rooms share a bath. Complimentary breakfast. TV in common area. | 3009 W. Highland Blvd. | 414/342–9788 | walterb@uwm.edu | 6 rooms, 4 with shared bath | $85–$135 | AE, MC, V.

Baymont Inn and Suites. This three-story white brick building off U.S. 45 at exit 46 is near a shopping center and several restaurants. Complimentary Continental breakfast. In-room data ports, some microwaves, cable TV. Business services, free parking. Some pets allowed. | 5442 N. Lovers Lane Rd. (Rte. 100) | 414/535–1300 | fax 414/535–1724 | www.baymontinns.com | 140 rooms | $77–$87 | AE, D, DC, MC, V.

Crane House B&B. Lush perennial gardens surround this 1895 Victorian home, painted in shades of purple, green, blue, and yellow. Each of the four rooms has a theme, such as the "Beach Room" and the "Radio Room." An elaborate three-course breakfast might include almond-crusted sweet rolls, the Crane's special bacon buns, or mushroom-asparagus quiche. Complimentary guest pickup from airport, or bus or train station. Complimentary breakfast. TV in common area. | 346 E. Wilson St., Bay View | 414/483–1512 | info@cranehouse.com | www.cranehouse.com | 4 rooms | $70–$90 | D, MC, V.

Days Inn. This standard chain hotel is conveniently located in the West Allis business district, close to Wisconsin State Fair Park. Restaurant, bar, complimentary Continental breakfast. Cable TV. | 1673 S. 108th St., West Allis | 414/771–3399 | fax 414/771–0557 | 86 rooms | $60–$80 | AE, D, MC, V.

Hampton Inn–Northwest. This chain hotel 10 mi northwest of Milwaukee has a large lobby with seating, plants, and a TV. Complimentary Continental breakfast. In-room data ports, some microwaves, cable TV. Pool. Hot tub. Exercise equipment. Business services, free parking. | 5601 N. Lovers Lane Rd. | 414/466–8881 | fax 414/466–3840 | www.hampton/inn.com | 108 rooms | $79–$99 | AE, D, DC, MC, V.

Hospitality Inn. This inn is a modern five-story building just a five-minute drive from the airport. The large, elegant lobby has pillars and adjoins a café with a fireplace. Restaurant, complimentary Continental breakfast, room service. Some refrigerators, some in-room hot tubs, cable TV. 2 pools. Hot tub. Exercise equipment. Airport shuttle, free parking. | 4400 S. 27th St. | 414/282–8800 or 800/825–8466 | fax 414/282–7713 | hotel@hospitalityinn.com | www.hospitalityinn.com | 167 rooms, 81 suites | $68–$100 | AE, D, DC, MC, V.

Red Roof Inn. This standard chain motel has outdoor entries, and is about 2 mi from downtown. Cable TV. Business services, free parking. Pets allowed. | 6360 S. 13th St., Oak Creek | 414/764–3500 | fax 414/764–5138 | 108 rooms | $59–$79 | AE, D, DC, MC, V.

EXPENSIVE

Astor Hotel. Antiques fill this eight-story hotel near Lake Michigan. The building is on the National Register of Historic Places. Guest rooms, though not as opulent as the grand lobby, are nevertheless large and outfitted with antique-reproduction cherrywood furniture and some impressive views of downtown Milwaukee. Restaurant, complimentary breakfast. Some kitchenettes, cable TV. Free parking. | 924 E. Juneau Ave. | 414/271–4220 or 800/558–0200 | fax 414/271–6370 | 97 rooms, 30 suites | $87–$97 rooms, $123–$143 suites.

Brumder Mansion Bed-and-Breakfast. This striking B&B dates from 1910. The furnishings are antique and the woodwork original. The lower level has a professional theater and master acting studio, and the surrounding neighborhood is a historical district with many similar old homes and buildings. Downtown Milwaukee is less than a mile away. Complimentary wine, soda, and snacks are served every evening. Complimentary breakfast. Some in-room hot tubs, no TV in some rooms, in-room VCRs and movies. No smoking. | 3046 W. Wisconsin Ave. | 414/342–9767 | fax 414/342–4772 | brumder@execpc.com | www.brumdermansion.com | 3 rooms (with shared bath), 2 suites | $85–$170 | AE, D, DC, MC, V.

MILWAUKEE

INTRO
ATTRACTIONS
DINING
LODGING

Clarion Hotel and Conference Center. This modern three-story chain motel is across the street from the airport. Restaurant, bar, complimentary Continental breakfast, room service. Pool. Exercise equipment. Laundry facilities. Business services, airport shuttle, free parking. | 5311 S. Howell Ave. | 414/481–2400 | fax 414/481–4471 | 180 rooms | $99–$129 | AE, D, DC, MC, V.

County Clare. The guest rooms and pub at this inn are within walking distance of Lake Michigan and downtown, and reflect the look of Ireland, from the architecture to the stained-glass windows and wood-burning fireplace. Rooms have queen-size four-poster beds. Restaurant (See County Clare). In-room data ports, in-room hot tubs, cable TV. Business services, free parking. | 1234 N. Astor St. | 888/942–5273 | fax 414/290–6300 | www.classicinns.com | 30 rooms | $70–$130 | AE, D, DC, MC, V.

Four Points Sheraton. This six-story hotel 1 mi north of the airport has antique reproduction wood furniture and lots of tasteful multimedia art on the guest room walls. 2 restaurants, bar. In-room data ports, some refrigerators, cable TV. 2 pools. Exercise equipment. Video games. Business services, airport shuttle, free parking. | 4747 S. Howell Ave. | 414/481–8000 or 800/558–3862 | fax 414/481–8065 | 510 rooms | $100–$140 | AE, D, DC, MC, V.

Hilton Inn Milwaukee River. This modern five-story gray brick hotel is in a rural area off U.S. 43. The lobby has a fireplace, seating, plants, and a view of the Milwaukee River. Restaurant, bar. In-room data ports, some refrigerators, cable TV. Pool. Exercise equipment. Business services, free parking. | 4700 N. Port Washington Rd. | 414/962–6040 | fax 414/962–6166 | 163 rooms | $82–$128 | AE, D, DC, MC, V.

Hotel Wisconsin. Built in 1913, this 11-story downtown hotel is the second oldest in Milwaukee. The interior includes oak paneling, stained glass, fancy glasswork bearing a badger emblem, and a grandfather clock that is original to the hotel. Restaurant. Some microwaves, some refrigerators, cable TV. Video games. Laundry facilities. Business services, free parking. Pets allowed. | 720 N. Old World 3rd St. | 414/271–4900 | fax 414/271–9998 | 234 rooms | $69–$149 | AE, D, DC, MC, V.

Manchester Suites–Airport. This brown brick building was built in 1988. The lobby has a sitting area, and there's front and rear parking. Complimentary breakfast. In-room data ports, microwaves, refrigerators, cable TV. Business services, airport shuttle, free parking. | 200 W. Grange Ave. | 414/744–3600 or 800/723–8280 | fax 414/744–4188 | 100 suites | $64–$89 | AE, D, DC, MC, V.

Manchester Suites–Northwest. All rooms in this modern building are suites. The large lobby is filled with paintings and plants. Complimentary breakfast. In-room data ports, microwaves, refrigerators, cable TV. Exercise equipment. Business services, free parking. | 11777 W. Silver Spring Dr. | 414/462–3500 or 800/723–8280 | fax 414/462–8166 | www.manchestersuites.com | 123 suites | $95–$105 | AE, D, DC, MC, V.

Manderlay Bed-and-Breakfast. This cream city brick Queen Anne–style B&B in the Concordia Historic District was built in 1886 as a private home for coal merchant David W. Howie and is now on the National Register of Historic Places. The B&B is filled with antiques and Persian carpets, stained-glass windows, elaborate woodwork, and an eclectic collection of art and decorative objects. Two rooms have fireplaces. Lovely gardens surround the house. Dining room, complimentary breakfast. Some in-room hot tubs, in-room VCRs (and movies), no TV in some rooms. | 3026 W. Wells St. | 414/931–7597 | 4 rooms | $89–$129 | No credit cards.

VERY EXPENSIVE

Hilton Milwaukee City Center. This brick hotel next to the city's convention center was built in 1929, and its lobby is as elegant as ever. The hotel is linked to the convention center via a glass-enclosed walkway. Restaurant, bar, room service. In-room data ports, cable TV. Barbershop, beauty salon. Exercise equipment. Business services, free parking. | 509 W. Wisconsin Ave. | 414/271–7250 | fax 414/271–1039 | 500 rooms | $149–$169 | AE, D, DC, MC, V.

Holiday Inn Milwaukee City Centre. Within blocks of all the restaurants, shopping, and sightseeing opportunities in downtown Milwaukee, this upscale hotel has a modern, glass-enclosed lobby and spare-but-comfortable guest rooms. Restaurant, bar, room service. In-room data ports, some microwaves, cable TV. Pool. Business services, parking (fee). | 611 W. Wisconsin Ave. | 414/273–2950 | fax 414/273–7662 | www.travelbase.com/destinations/milwaukee/holiday-inn | 245 rooms | $134–$180 | AE, D, DC, MC, V.

Hotel Metro. This Art Deco all-suite hotel is in the heart of Milwaukee's business and entertainment district. Some suites have whirlpools and fireplaces. There's an outdoor café as well as a ballroom for receptions. Restaurant. Some in-room hot tubs, cable TV. Business services. | 411 E. Mason St. | 414/272–1937 | fax 414/223–1158 | www.hotelmetro.com | 65 rooms | $150–$250 | AE, D, DC, MC, V.

Hyatt Regency. This 22-story white building downtown has an atrium and a revolving rooftop restaurant. A skywalk takes you from the hotel directly to the Grand Avenue Shopping Center. Restaurants (*see* Polaris), bar. Some microwaves, cable TV, some in-room VCRs and movies. Exercise equipment. Business services, free parking. | 333 W. Kilbourn Ave. | 414/276–1234 | fax 414/276–6338 | www.hyatt.com | 484 rooms | $155–$195 | AE, D, DC, MC, V.

Park East. This 5-story modern redbrick-and-glass building sprawling on the edge of downtown has an elegant, large lobby. You can grab the hotel's complimentary downtown shuttle to get where you want to go without all the hassle of parking. Restaurant, bar, complimentary Continental breakfast. In-room data ports, some microwaves, some refrigerators, some in-room hot tubs, cable TV, in-room VCRs. Gym. Business services. | 916 E. State St. | 414/276–8800 or 800/328–7275 | fax 414/765–1919 | info@parkeasthotel.com | www.parkeasthotel.com | 159 rooms | $108–$179 | AE, D, DC, MC, V.

★ **Pfister Hotel.** This luxury hotel built in 1893, one of America's first all-electric hotels, is home to the largest collection of 19th- and 20th-century Victorian art on display at any hotel in the world—more than 80 pieces. The spacious and elegant lobby has few peers; its highlights include old-world murals on curved ceilings; decorative, gold-embossed plasterwork; artwork; marble; and massive chandeliers. William McKinley, Harry S. Truman, Neil Diamond, Aretha Franklin, Barry Manilow, Paul McCartney, Elvis Presley, Johnny Cash, Bill Cosby, Mikhail Baryshnikov, Leonard Bernstein, and Luciano Pavarotti have all stayed here. Some rooms are in a 23-story tower added in 1966. Three restaurants (*see* English Room,

CHICKEN DANCE A.K.A DANCE LITTLE BIRD

From small and informal Wisconsin weddings and parties to posh events, both the young and the old enthusiastically hop onto the dance floor, flap their arms, and shake their bottoms to the beat of the Chicken Dance. When the tune plays, couples rush to the center of the dance floor and face each other. To the beat of the music, they open and close their hands like a bird's bill, flap their arms like wings, wiggle their tails like a bird, and clap four times.

This choreographed dance trend began when a Milwaukee bandleader named Bob Kames heard a tune called "The Chicken Dance" in Germany more than a quarter of a century ago. Although he liked the song—and the gestures that went along with it—he thought the music was a bit too slow, and the timing of the gestures were off. Kames therefore made some changes and released the tune as "Dance Little Bird" in 1982, creating an instant hit. Although Kames gave the song a new name, Wisconsinites still refer to it as "The Chicken Dance."

At weddings in Wisconsin, "The Chicken Dance" is probably the most frequently played song—after the grand march.

© Artville

above), bar (with entertainment), room service. In-room data ports, cable TV, some in-room VCRs. Pool. Beauty salon. Business services, free parking. | 424 E. Wisconsin Ave. | 414/273–8222 or 800/558–8222 | fax 414/273–5025 | info@thepfisterhotel.com | www.pfister-hotel.com | 307 rooms, 68 suites | $174–$262 rooms, $224–$314 suites | AE, D, DC, MC, V.

Ramada Inn Downtown. This brick chain hotel is one block from the city's Wisconsin Center convention center. Room service. Cable TV, some in-room VCRs and movies. Pool. Exercise equipment. Business services, parking (fee). | 633 W. Michigan St. | 414/272–8410 | fax 414/272–4651 | www.execpc.com/~ramadadt | 155 rooms | $108–$118 | AE, D, DC, MC, V.

Wyndham Milwaukee Center. This modern, elegant hotel in the Flemish Renaissance style overlooks the Milwaukee River. The large lobby has marble, ornate woodwork, a fountain, and large floral arrangements. The hotel is downtown, just a few blocks from the theater district. Restaurant, bar (with entertainment), room service. Cable TV, in-room VCRs available. Hot tub. Exercise equipment. Business services, free parking. | 139 E. Kilbourn Ave. | 414/276–8686 | fax 414/276–8007 | 221 rooms, 77 suites | $159–$256 | AE, D, DC, MC, V.

MINERAL POINT

MAP 11, C6

(Nearby towns also listed: Monroe, Platteville)

Walk down the main street in Mineral Point and you might think you're in a Cornish village. Although originally settled in 1827 by people from New England and the South, miners from Cornwall, England, soon followed in the 1830s, and they constructed stone buildings like those of their homeland. Some of these houses have been restored and are part of the city's historic district. Mineral Point has great shopping with art and crafts galleries, and antiques and specialty shops.

Information: Mineral Point Chamber/Main Street Program | 225 High St., 53565-1209 | 888/764–6894 | www.mineralpoint.com/index.htm.

Attractions

Historic District. The first district in Wisconsin to be listed on the National Register of Historic Places, this area covers the entire city and includes more than 500 structures in various architectural styles, both residential and commercial buildings. Driving and walking tours are available through the visitors center in the heart of downtown. | Chamber/Main St., 225 High St.; visitors center on U.S. 151 | 608/987–3201 or 888/764–6894 | $3 for maps | Chamber/Main St., weekdays 8:30–5; visitors center May–Sept., daily 10–4.

Pendarvis State Historical Site. At this state historic site, costumed interpreters tell tales of life on Shake Rag Street as they lead you through six restored 19th-century cottages and row houses. The street's name refers to the custom of women shaking dish rags from doorways, signaling the men in the mines across the valley that the noon meal was ready. | 114 Shake Rag St. | 608/987–2122 | $7; special rates for senior citizens, kids, and groups | May–Oct., daily 9–4.

ON THE CALENDAR

SEPT.: *Cornish Festival and Taste of Mineral Point.* Sample a variety of foods from local restaurants including the area's famous spicy, nut-and-raisin filled Cornish pastries called figgy hobbin. Bus tours of the Mineral Point Historic District and Cornish and Celtic entertainment are also part of the festivities. This downtown festival is held the last weekend of the month. | 888/764–6894.

Dining

Red Rooster Café. American. Decorated with a rooster motif, this breakfast-only café is known for its pastries, bread pudding, and figgy hobbin—a Cornish pastry with walnuts, raisins, brown sugar, and cinnamon served with hot caramel and whipped cream. Sandwiches and homemade pies are also popular. | 158 High St. | 608/987–9936 | $5–$7 | No credit cards.

Lodging

Brewery Creek Inn. This bed-and-breakfast in a century-old stone warehouse also includes a restaurant and brewery. Some rooms have hot tubs and fireplaces. Restaurant, complimentary breakfast. | 23 Commerce St. | 608/987–3298 | fax 608–987–4388 | www.brewerycreek.com | 5 rooms | $129–$165 | AE, D, MC, V.

Redwood. This small motel just outside of town offers you a quiet, pastoral setting amidst pastureland and an adjacent mini-golf course. Guest rooms are somewhat sparsely decorated and hung with original paintings and photographs. Cable TV. Miniature golf. Business services, airport shuttle. | 625 Dodge St. | 608/987–2317 or 800/321–1958 | fax 608/987–2317 | 28 rooms | $47–$52 | D, MC, V.

MINOCQUA

MAP 11, C3

(Nearby towns also listed: Eagle River, Woodruff)

The greater Minocqua area is part of the Lakeland Area of Vilas and Oneida counties, so named for the more than 200 lakes, streams, and ponds found here. There's great fishing, boating, and waterskiing, as well as an extensive network of trails for hiking, biking, cross-country skiing, and snowmobiling.

Information: Minocqua–Arbor Vitae–Woodruff Area Chamber of Commerce | Box 1006, 54548-1006 | 800/446–6784 | mavwacc@minocqua.org | www.minocqua.org.

Attractions

Circle M Corral Family Fun Park. Includes a water slide, bumper boats, go-carts, a train ride, miniature golf, pony rides, batting cages. | 10295 Rte. 70 W | 715/356–4441 | www.circlemcorral.com | Day passes $21.95 | Mid-May–early Oct., 10–6.

Jim Peck's Wildwood. At this wildlife park you can pet a porcupine, hug a llama, feed tame deer, and see a bear and hundreds of other animals in a natural setting. | 10094 Rte. 70 | 715/356–5588 | $7; special rates for kids | May–mid-Oct., daily.

Minocqua Winter Park. This park for cross-country skiers 3 mi outside of town contains 75 km of cross-country trails, 65 km for skating and striding, and 10 km for striding only. | 12375 Scotchman Lake Rd. | 715/356–3309 | $7–$19; special rates for kids and families | Dec.–Mar., Mon.–Wed. and Thurs.–Sun. 9–5. Closed Weds.

Wilderness Cruise. Sightseeing, luncheon, and dinner cruises on the Willow Reservoir about 4 mi south of Minocqua in nearby Hazelhurst. | 4973 Willow Dam Rd., Hazelhurst | 715/453–3310 or 800/472–1516 | $9.50–$28.95; special rates for kids | Mid-May–mid-Oct., daily.

ON THE CALENDAR

MAY–OCT.: *Northern Lights Playhouse.* This professional theater company in Hazelhurst, 10 mi from Minocqua, performs musicals, comedies, and kids' theater as part of its rotating repertoire. | 715/356–7173.

Dining

Norwood Pines. American. This Northwoods-style building, surrounded by 100-year-old pine trees, has two fireplaces and a screened-in porch for summer dining. Regional favorites on the menu include fresher-than-fresh whitefish filets, lightly battered, deep-fried perch, and walleye. Pianist, sing-along Friday night. Kids' menu. | 10171 Rte. 70 W | 715/356–3666 | $14–$20 | AE, D, DC, MC, V | Closed Sun. No lunch.

Paul Bunyan's Northwoods Cook Shanty. American. One mile north of downtown, this restaurant is molded after hundred-year-old logging shanties. To re-create the look, Wisconsin woodsmen hand cut northern Wisconsin white and Norway pine and fit them together. All meals are served "family-style" in large bowls and platters, and seconds—or thirds—are encouraged. Dinner menus vary from night to night, but count on hearty servings of favorites like ribs, boiled or fried fish, corn-on-the cob, and lots of mashed potatoes with gravy. Kids are charged per year of age. All food is made from scratch. Kids' menu. | 8653 U.S. 51 N | 715/356–6270 | $10–$11 | D, MC, V | Closed mid-Oct.–early May.

Red Steer. American. This restaurant in a rural area half a mile south of town offers steaks, seafood, lobster, and chicken in a dining room with a huge stone fireplace. Kids' menu. | 8230 U.S. 51 S | 715/356–6332 | $10–$19 | AE, D, DC, MC, V | No lunch.

Thirsty Whale. American. This building, right on the shore of Lake Minocqua, has had many lives: it was a livery for transport from the city of Minocqua, a boathouse, a popular nightspot, and now it's a casual restaurant. Lunch and early dinners are served on an open deck over the water or inside a covered deck. Specialties are mushroom Swiss burgers, spicy Cajun chicken, and deep-fried cheese curds. | 623 Park Ave. | 715/356–7108 | $6–$12 | No credit cards | Closed Nov.–Dec. and Apr.–mid-May.

Lodging

Americinn of Minocqua. This downtown hotel is set on a snowmobile, hiking, and biking trail. A public park with a beach and boat landing is across the street. Cable TV. Pool. Hot tub, sauna. | 700 Hwy. 51 N, 54548 | 715/356–3730 or 800/634–3444 | fax 715/356–6958 | www.americinn.com | 66 rooms | $95–$110 | AE, D, MC, V.

Aqua Aire. Within walking distance of downtown, this simple motel on Lake Minocqua overlooks the beach and the tennis and volleyball courts at Lake Minocqua Park. Picnic area. Refrigerators, cable TV. Docks. Business services. Some pets allowed. | 806 U.S. 51 N | 715/356–3433 | fax 715/356–3433 | 10 rooms (shower only) | $59–$79 | MC, V.

Best Western Lakeview Motor Lodge. Some rooms have lake views in this chalet-style motel on Lake Minocqua. The motel maintains a stretch of private beach for sunbathing and swimming, as well as a lakeside boardwalk and several piers for docking boats and fishing. Downtown Minocqua is only a half-block away, with plenty of shopping and dining opportunities. Picnic area, complimentary Continental breakfast. Some in-room hot tubs, cable TV. Dock. Business services. Pets allowed. | 311 E. Park Ave. | 715/356–5208 | fax 715/356–1412 | www.bestwestern.com | 41 rooms | $86–$116 | AE, D, DC, MC, V.

Minocqua Comfort Inn. This standard inn, in the heart of the city, is backed by a thick stand of trees. Complimentary Continental breakfast. Cable TV. Pool. | 8729 U.S. 51 N | 715/358–2588 | fax 715/356–1402 | www.choicehotels.com | 51 rooms | $75–$135 | AE, D, DC, MC, V.

New Concord Inn. This downtown colonial-style hotel has an elegant lobby with a fireplace. Bar, complimentary Continental breakfast. Some refrigerators, some in-room hot tubs, cable TV, in-room VCRs available. Pool. Hot tub. Video games. Business services. | 320 Front St. | 715/356–1800 | fax 715/356–6955 | 53 rooms | $88–$93 | AE, D, DC, MC, V.

Wild Goose Resort. The cabins at this resort on Round Lake in the Chequamegon National Forest 20 mi west of Minocqua have knotty-pine interiors and screened-in porches that face the lake. Each cabin has one or two bedrooms. Bar, picnic area. No room phones. Lake. Beach, dock, boating. | N15061 Thorofare Rd. | 715/762–3566 or 800/884–6673 | 6 cabins | $420 per week per cabin (7-day minimum stay) | No credit cards.

MONROE

(Nearby towns also listed: Madison, New Glarus, Platteville)

A lead-mining boom in the 1820s brought a stream of miners to this area. Today Monroe's economic base is industry and dairy farming. The county seat of Green County, Monroe is known as the Swiss Cheese Capital of the World. Cheese—especially Swiss cheese—is known as Green County Gold, and area factories produce more than 55 million pounds of it each year. A Romanesque courthouse building which has a 120-ft clock tower dominates downtown.

Information: Monroe Area Chamber of Commerce | 1505 9th St., 53566-1425 | 608/325–7648 | www.monroechamber.org.

Attractions

Alp and Dell Cheesery, Deli and Country Café. Here you can watch how cheese is made, buy food for a picnic, or grab a bite at the café. | 657 2nd St. | 608/328–3355 | Free | Mon.–Sat. 9–5, Sun. 10–4.

Franklin Cheese Co-Op, Gobeli Cheesemakers Inc. Discover how Farmers, Muenster, and other local cheeses are made at this factory. | W7256 Franklin Rd. | 608/325–3725 | Free | Mon., Tues., Thurs.–Sat. tours from 9 to 11 AM.

Yellowstone Lake State Park. At this 875-acre state park about 30 mi west of Monroe you can fish, boat, swim from a beach and camp at wooded sites along the bluffs. | 7896 Lake Rd., Blanchardville | 608/523–4427 | www.dnr.state.wi.us | $7 nonresidents, $5 residents | Daily.

ON THE CALENDAR

JULY: *Green County Fair.* This popular event attracts thousands to the Green County fairgrounds each summer. See nationally acclaimed country-western musicians, rodeos, quarter-horse racing, demolition derby, and harness races. There are also carnival rides, cheese tasting, livestock, and crafts. | 608/325–7648.

JULY: *Balloon Rally.* See how balloons are prepared for flight at this hot-air-balloon rally, held at the Green County fairgrounds mid-month. The preparations begin in the early morning, around 6, or in the early evening, around 6:30. | 608/325–7648.

Dining

Peppercorn Café. American. Fine dining in a casual atmosphere can be found at this restaurant on the north side of town. Steaks, seafood, and pasta dishes are all good. | 180 18th Ave. N | 608/329–2233 | $9–$17 | AE, MC, V | Closed Sun., Mon.

Lodging

Chenoweth House Bed & Breakfast. This San Francisco–style Queen Anne was built in 1887 and is listed on the National Register of Historic Places. Some original features are gas and electric light fixtures and stained- and beveled-glass windows. Complimentary breakfast. TV in common area. | 2004 10th St. | 608/325–5064 | fax 608/325–5068 | innkeeper@chenoweth-house.com | www.chenowethhouse.com | 4 rooms | $85–$99 | D, MC, V.

Knights Inn. This basic brick motel 1 mi from downtown Monroe has a large lobby with a TV and a lounge area. In-room data ports, in-room safes, cable TV. Business services. | 250 N. 18th Ave. | 608/325–4138 or 800/325–1178 | fax 608/325–1282 | www.knightsinn.com | 64 rooms, 48 suites | $30–$150 | AE, D, MC, V.

MOUNT HOREB

(Nearby towns also listed: Madison, Spring Green)

Mount Horeb wears its Norwegian heritage on its sleeve, especially on Main Street. The street is decorated with life-size, carved wooden trolls, which are classic creatures of Norwegian folklore. The downtown area is filled with specialty shops, antiques stores, artists' studios, and the world-famous Mount Horeb Mustard Museum, which has thousands of different mustards.

Information: **Mount Horeb Area Chamber of Commerce** | Box 84, 53572-0084 | 888/765–5929 | www.danenet.wicip.org/mthoreb/.

Attractions

Blue Mound State Park. This 1,153-acre state park 5 mi west of Mt. Horeb is built atop mounds that have been a southwestern Wisconsin landmark since pioneer days. View the surrounding countryside from the observation towers, and hike or ski the nature trails. There are also scenic picnic areas, and a large swimming pool. | 4350 Mounds Park Rd., Blue Mounds | 608/437–5711 | www.dnr.state.wi.us | $7 nonresidents, $5 residents | Daily.

Cave of the Mounds. Four miles west of town, this registered National Natural Landmark known for the variety, color, and delicacy of its formations is one of the most significant caves in the upper Midwest. Grounds include gardens, picnic areas, a visitors center, and a nature trail. The cave temperature is 50°F year-round. | Brigham Farm, Blue Mounds | 608/437–3038 | www.caveofthemounds.com. | $10; special rates for senior citizens, kids, and groups | Mid-Mar.–mid-Nov., daily 9–5; mid-Nov.–mid-Mar., weekends 9–5, closed weekdays.

Little Norway. This farmstead was built by Norwegian settlers in 1856; today costumed guides lead you through authentically furnished log buildings and a wooden church built for Chicago's 1893 Columbian Exposition. The church's many treasures include an original manuscript written in 1873 by Norwegian composer Edvard Grieg. | 3576 Rte. JG N, Blue Mounds | 608/437–8211 | www.littlenorway.com | $8; special rates for senior citizens, kids, and groups | May–June and Sept.–Oct., daily 9–5; July–Aug., daily 9–7.

Mount Horeb Area Museum. For a full history of Mount Horeb, this museum has it all: local artifacts, school, church, and regional government records, photographs, textiles, and plot maps from 1860 to the present. | 100 S. 2nd St. | 608/325–7648 | www.trollway.com | Free | Fri.–Sun. 10–4.

Mount Horeb Mustard Museum. This tiny museum houses a collection of more than 3,400 different kinds of mustards. You can sample various mustards, chutneys, hot sauces, salsas, jams, curds, vinegars, marinades, and so on. Discover new ways to use mustard in cooking, and go home with a whimsical "Poupon-U" collegiate T-shirt. | 109 E. Main | 608/437–3986 or 800/438–6878 | www.mustardmuseum.com | Free | Daily 10–5.

ON THE CALENDAR

OCT.: *Fall Festival.* This downtown event includes a craft show, a quilt display, ethnic music, food booths, horse-and-buggy rides, and historical exhibits. | 888/765–5929 | www.trollway.com.

Dining

David W. Heiney's Dining and Spirits. Contemporary. There's lots of atmosphere at this downtown restaurant in nearby Black Earth. Dishes ranging from prime cut beef to seafood are served in a converted 1888 home that's on the National Register of Historic Places. | 1221 Mills St., Black Earth | 608/767–2501 | $11–$29 | AE, MC, V | Closed Sun.–Tues. No lunch.

Lodging
Karakahl Country Inn. The exterior of this inn resembles a Viking ship and the Nordic theme continues inside with high ceilings, skylights and lots of wood. The overall look is modern, however, from the modular guest room furnishings to the glass-walled pool area and state-of-the-art fitness center. Restaurant, bar. Cable TV. Pool. Sauna. | 1405 Business 18, 151 E | 608/437-5545 | fax 608/437-5908 | 75 rooms | $60-$120 | AE, D, DC, MC, V.

NEENAH

(Nearby towns also listed: Appleton, Menasha, Shawano)

Founded in 1843, Neenah sits across from its twin city of Menasha at the top of Lake Winnebago, where the Fox River flows out from the lake. Water power generated from Fox River channels gave rise to the birth of these twin cities. The area has turn-of-the-20th-century homes built by paper-mill barons. Today, Neenah and Menasha are among the nation's leading suppliers of paper products. Publishing, printing, and associated paper industries dominate the local economy.

Although the cities are casually regarded as one, their governments are separate. Today Neenah is ranked the third best market for business development among all small metropolitan areas in the nation, based on a survey of entrepreneurs starting or growing a business.

Information: Fox Cities Convention and Visitors Bureau | 3433 W. College Ave., Appleton 54914 | 800/236-6673 | tourism@foxcities.org | www.foxcities.org.

Attractions
Bergstrom-Mahler Museum. Houses one of the world's largest and finest collections of glass paperweights, and an important collection of Germanic glass that spans four centuries. | 165 N. Park Ave. | 920/751-4658 | Donations accepted | Tues., Wed., Fri. 10-4:30; Thurs. 10-8; weekends 1-4:30.

Doty Cabin. This structure in Doty Park is a replica of the home of James Duane Doty, Wisconsin's second territorial governor. The cabin, which is on the National Register of Historic Places, exhibits Native American items and local artifacts dating from the 19th century. In the park are flower beds and footbridges leading to an island in the Fox River. | 700 Lincoln St. | 920/751-4614 | Donations accepted | June-Aug., daily noon-4; late May and early Sept., weekends noon-4.

Neenah Lighthouse. You can fish from the deck of this lighthouse, built in 1945. | Lakeshore Ave., Kimberly Point Park | 920/751-4614 | Free | Daily.

ON THE CALENDAR
SEPT.: *Jazzfest.* This Labor Day weekend jazz festival on Lake Winnebago in Shattuck Park showcases regional and national jazz artists on two stages. | 800/236-6673 or 920/722-1920.

Dining
Bradke's Restaurant. American. Look for the big EAT sign if you're driving on Highway 41 near Neenah. Favorites at this mom-and-pop diner are roast beef, meat loaf, ribs, mashed potatoes, and some 21 kinds of homemade pie. The Friday-night fish fry is also a draw. Breakfast starts at 5 AM. | 1022 Main St. | 920/722-3706 | $4-$6 | MC, V | Closed Sun. No dinner Sat.

Lodging

Norm's Motel. This small hostelry in the heart of town is attached to the owner's house. | 1403 Green Valley Rd. | 920/725–6984 | 11 rooms | $30–$60 | No credit cards.

Park Plaza Valley Inn. This comfortable downtown hotel has a rustic-lodge look with an antler chandelier and reproductions of Remington statues in the lobby. Some rooms have Lake Winnebago views; within walking distance are numerous restaurants and shops as well as a park and the Fox River. Two restaurants, bar. Some microwaves, some refrigerators, in-room data ports, cable TV, in-room VCRs available. Pool. Hot tub. Gym. Business services, airport shuttle. | 123 E. Wisconsin Ave. | 920/725–8441 or 800/725–6348 | fax 920/725–4387 | 107 rooms | $75–$105 | AE, D, DC, MC, V.

Parkway. This hotel's two red-and-white buildings are 2 mi southwest of downtown on a commercial strip that's also home to a bowling alley and several fast-food restaurants. Picnic area, complimentary Continental breakfast. Cable TV. Pool. Playground. Some pets allowed. | 1181 Gillingham Rd. | 920/725–3244 | 19 rooms (8 with showers only) | $35–$90 | AE, D, MC, V.

NEW GLARUS

(Nearby towns also listed: Mineral Point, Monroe)

Swiss immigrants settled this pretty little village in 1845, and the community has nurtured Swiss customs, crafts, and cuisine. Locals observe Swiss traditions throughout the year and enjoy sharing them with visitors. Today the village is known as Wisconsin's "Little Switzerland." There are many chalet-style homes throughout town with old German proverbs in German script painted just underneath the roof ledges. Take a peak in the Bank of New Glarus in summer, and you will notice that all the women tellers are wearing traditional dirndls—ornately embroidered Alpine dresses with laced bodices.

Information: **Tourism and Chamber of Commerce** | Box 713, 53574-0713 | 800/527–6838 | www.newglarus-wi.com.

Attractions

Chalet of the Golden Fleece. This Swiss chalet of a museum downtown houses a collection of wood carvings, jewelry, china, and other items. | 618 2nd St., at 7th Ave. | 608/527–2614 | $3; special rates for senior citizens and kids | May–Nov. 1, daily 10–4:30; bus tours by reservation in Apr.

New Glarus Woods State Park. Camping, hiking trails, picnic and playground areas on 450 acres 1½ mi south of New Glarus. | Rte. 69 just south of town | 608/527–2335 | www.dnr.state.wi.us | $7 nonresidents, $5 residents | Apr.–Oct., daily.

Sugar River State Trail. This 23-mi trail for hiking, bicycling, snowmobiling, and cross-country skiing was built on an abandoned railroad bed. The trail has level grade, wooden trestles across streams, and passes through a covered bridge. Bicycles may be rented at trail headquarters. Next to the trail head is the Whistle Stop Ice Cream Shop, a popular stop for a sweet treat. | 418 Railroad St. | 608/527–2334 | Free | Daily.

Swissland Miniature Golf. Play 18 holes of landscaped, fully animated miniature golf. | 7600 Hwy. 69 S | 608/527–5605 | $5.50 | Memorial Day–Aug., daily; Sept.–Oct., weekends.

Swiss Historical Village Museum. Twelve original and replica buildings showcase Swiss pioneer life on the west edge of town. Also worth checking out is the historical cemetery adjacent to the museum complex. | 612 7th Ave. | 608/527–2317 | $6; special rates for kids | May–Oct., daily 9–4:30.

MAY: *Community Festival.* This traditional Memorial Day weekend celebration at Village Park has family activities such as tug-of-war, clowns, juggling, games, music, and food. | 800/527–6838 or 608/527–2095.

JUNE: *Heidi Festival.* A performance of the play *Heidi*, authentic Swiss entertainment (like yodeling and Alpine-horn playing), a crafts fair, an art fair, a flea market, a street dance—all downtown at New Glarus High School Auditorium on the third weekend of the month. | 800/527–6838 | $7.

AUG.: *Swiss Volksfest.* This celebration of Swiss Independence Day, the first Sunday of the month features yodeling, flag throwing, Alpine-horn blowing, and demonstrations of *Thalerschwingen* (a traditional way to make music with a coin in a bowl) in the Wilhelm Tell Shooting Park a mile north of town. | 800/527–6838.

SEPT.: *Wilhelm Tell Festival.* This Labor Day weekend celebration centers around performances (in both English and German) of the pageant *Wilhelm Tell* in the wooded amphitheater on the Wilhelm Tell Grounds. Other events, some of which take place in the New Glarus High School Auditorium or the Village Park, include an Alpine fest, an art fair, a craft fair, a book sale, street dancing, and a fashion show of Swiss costumes. | 800/527–6838.

Dining

Puempels Olde Tavern. American. This 100-year-old restaurant and bar is known for good soups and sandwiches. Locals as well as visitors congregate here. | No. 6 on 6th Ave. | 608/527–2045 | $2–$5 | No credit cards.

Lodging

Chalet Landhaus. These two enormous Swiss-style chalets have huge pine beams, riotous flowerboxes, whitewashed walls, and acres of hardwood inside. Downtown New Glarus is only a couple of blocks away. Restaurant. Some in-room hot tubs, cable TV. Business services. Pets allowed. | 801 Hwy. 69 | 608/527–5234 | fax 608/527–2365 | landhaus@madison.tds.net | www.chaletlandhaus.com | 67 rooms, 6 suites | $76–$145 | AE, D, MC, V.

Jeanne Marie's Bed & Breakfast. Three rooms are available in this 1910 redbrick house, furnished in country antiques. There's a large backyard with a flower garden. A full breakfast is served on weekends; expanded continental on weekdays. Complimentary breakfast. No room phones, TV in common area. | 318 10th Ave. | 608/527–5059 | 3 rooms | $50–$70 | MC, V.

Swiss-Aire. Red and white flowers bloom in window boxes and in jumbo whiskey barrels outside this basic motel on Highway 69. A bike trail crosses the property. Picnic area, complimentary Continental breakfast. Cable TV. Pool. Pets allowed. | 1200 Hwy. 69 | 608/527–2138 or 800/798–4391 | swissaire@mail.tdsnet.com | 26 rooms | $51–$65 | D, MC, V.

OCONOMOWOC

MAP 11, D6

(Nearby towns also listed: Brookfield, Milwaukee, Waukesha)

Known as the Newport of the West for its many palatial lakeside homes, Oconomowoc is 10 mi from downtown Milwaukee by expressway. The Potowatomi tribe laid the foundation to what they called "Coo-no-mo-wauk," which means "where the waters meet." In 1837, the first white man, Charles Sheldon, built a cabin in the area. Today Oconomowoc is made up of many beautiful old homes and thriving industries, thanks in part to the influx of wealthy Milwaukeeans looking to build homes and businesses away from the bustle of the big city.

Information: **Oconomowoc Convention and Visitors Bureau** | Box 27, 53066-0027 | 800/524–3744 | www.oconomowoc.com.

Attractions

Highlands Ski Hill. Six different runs, and a snowboard park 3 mi outside of town. Interstate 94 to Route 67. | Rte. 67 | 262/567–2577 | Lift tickets $14 | Nov.–Mar., daily.

Honey Acres and Honey of a Museum. This site all about bees and honey includes a slide show on beekeeping, displays about beekeeping around the world, information on pollination and beeswax, a live bee tree, and honey tastings. It's 12 mi north of Oconomowoc. | N1557 Rte. 67, Ashippun | 920/474–4411 | Free | May–Oct., weekdays 9–3:30, weekends noon–4.

Oconomowoc Historical Society Museum. Step back in time and trace the early history of the city. January to April the museum is open by appointment only. | 103 S. Jefferson St., 53066 | 262/569–0740 | Free | May–Dec., Fri.–Sun. 1–5 or by appointment; Jan.–Apr., by appointment only.

ON THE CALENDAR

AUG.: *Festival Week/Festival of the Arts.* This 10-day mid-month festival features a lighted boat parade, fireworks, band concerts, food tasting, a street dance on the downtown boardwalk, and a juried art fair with artists from around the country. | 800/524–3744.

Dining

Golden Mast Inn. German. German and American standards such as Wiener schnitzel and prime rib share space on the menu at this restaurant 5 mi northeast of Oconomowoc. Open-air dining in a beer garden. Kids' menu. Sunday brunch. | W349 N. 5293 Lacy La., Okauchee | 262/567–7047 | $20–$30 | AE, D, MC, V | Closed Oct.–Apr., Mon. No lunch Mon.–Sat.

Red Circle Inn. Contemporary. Just outside Oconomowoc in the village of Nashotah you'll find the Red Circle Inn, which is one of Wisconsin's oldest restaurants. The chefs prepare some creative interpretations of old stand-bys, like poached salmon with tangy mustard sauce and a wide array of pates served with toast points for appetizers. There's also a popular fish-fry on Friday nights. | 33013 Watertown Plank Rd., Nashotah | 262/367–4883 | $18–$25 | AE, D, MC, V | Closed Sun. No lunch Mon.

Stone Bank Pub & Eatery. English. This British-style restaurant and pub has a wide variety of foods, including such traditional dishes as beef Wellington and Scotch eggs. There are 18 foreign and domestic brews on tap. Live music on selected nights. | N67 W3395 County Trunk K | 262/966–1975 | $11–$18 | AE, D, MC, V | Closed Mon. No lunch Tues.–Fri.

Lodging

Inn at Pine Terrace. This elegant Victorian mansion half a mile north of town in Waukesha County's Lake District was inspired by Austrian castle architecture. You'll find period furnishings, hand-printed reproduction wallpaper, high ceilings, and elaborate carved doors and trim. Complimentary Continental breakfast. Cable TV. Pool. | 361 Lisbon Rd. | 262/567–7463 | 13 rooms | $65–$145 | AE, D, DC, MC, V.

Lake Country Inn. This nicely landscaped colonial-style inn is off a network of major highways and thoroughfares. There's a comfortable plant-filled lobby and lounge with a TV and fireplace. Complimentary Continental breakfast. Cable TV. | 1367 W. Wisconsin Ave. | 262/569–9600 | fax 262/569–9666 | 35 rooms | $68–$80 | AE, D, MC, V.

Olympia Resort and Spa. This resort at the south end of Oconomowoc where the town gives way to the woods has an 18-hole golf course, and is a short drive from Highlands Ski Hill. The lobby has a huge stone fireplace with seating around it, marble tables, desks, and a baby grand piano. 2 bars, dining room, room service. Refrigerators, cable TV. 2 pools. Barbershop, beauty salon, hot tub, spa. Driving range, 18-hole golf course, tennis. Gym. Video games. Business services. | 1350 Royale Mile Rd. | 262/567–0311 or 800/558–9573 | fax 262/567–5934 | denise@olympia.execpc.com | www.olympiaresort.com | 256 rooms, 15 suites | $99–$119 | AE, D, DC, MC, V.

OCONTO

(Nearby towns also listed: Green Bay, Marinette, Menomonie, Peshtigo)

Oconto, the Oconto County seat, is the site of Copper Culture Mound Park, where you can see artifacts from the 5,000-year-old Native American civilization that created the parks' mounds at a museum in town. Self-guided tours through the Historic Main Street District take you a step back in time to the area's logging heyday. The waters of Green Bay are less than 2 mi away from the town square, making Oconto popular among anglers and water-sports enthusiasts.

Attractions

Beyer Home Museum. Exhibits from the area's logging industry as well as Native American Indian artifacts are displayed in a restored mansion. Guided tours are available. | 917 Park Ave. | 920/834-2255 | $3 | June–Labor Day, daily 9–4.

Copper Culture Mound Park. Located just west of Oconto, this state park is open for picnicking. The adjacent museum has artifacts from the Copper Culture Indians, who were among Wisconsin's earliest inhabitants. An advanced civilization, they mined copper locally, produced tools and ornaments, and traded with other Native American cultures as far away as New Mexico. | On Mill St., near junction of West and Mott Sts. | 920/834-2255 | Free | Park daily; museum June–Aug., weekends 12–4.

ON THE CALENDAR

JUNE: *Old Copper Festival.* The second weekend of June brings a lumberjack championship, a 1950s street dance, a truck pull, an antique and collector car show, a parade, fireworks, historic Main Street tours and wagon rides, a kids' fishing tournament, pony rides, and more. | 888/626-6862.

Dining

Wayne's Family Restaurant. American. While American cuisine predominates, Italian and Mexican dishes are popular as well. If you're an early-bird, breakfast is served from 5 AM. | 805 Brazeau Ave. | 920/834-4262 | $6–$10 | D, MC, V | Breakfast also available.

Lodging

Ramada Limited. There are river views from one side of this standard two-story hotel. Complimentary Continental breakfast. Cable TV. Pool. Hot tub. | 600 Brazeau Ave. | 920/834-5559 | fax 920/834-5619 | 47 rooms | $70–$90 | AE, D, DC, MC, V.

OSHKOSH

(Nearby towns also listed: Fond du Lac, Sheboygan)

Settled in 1836, this homey small town on the western shore of Lake Winnebago is a favorite among aviation buffs. One of the world's largest flying events, the EAA AirVenture Oshkosh, is held here each year, attracting more than 12,000 airplanes and 800,000 spectators from all over the world. In addition, Oshkosh has well-preserved historic buildings and a state university. There are also world-class museums in restored mansions, performing arts, boat excursions, and specialty shops. This is also home of the Oshkosh B'Gosh Overall company.

Information: Oshkosh Convention and Visitors Bureau | 2 N. Main St., 54901-4897 | 800/876-5250 | www.ci.oshkosh.wi.us.com.

OSHKOSH

INTRO
ATTRACTIONS
DINING
LODGING

Attractions

EAA Air Adventure Museum. Original airplanes and extensive exhibits tell the history of aviation. You can even take a flight aboard an antique airplane at EAA's Pioneer Airport, which is just behind the museum. Each summer the airport hosts the EAA AirVenture Oshkosh. | Wittman Regional Airport, 3000 Poberezny Rd. | 920/426–4818 | $8; special rates for senior citizens, kids, and families | Mon.–Sat. 8:30–5 (8–8 during EAA AirVenture Oshkosh).

Fox River Brewing Co. This microbrewery has observation windows so you can watch the brew being made. Tours are available; call for appointment. | 1501 Arboretum Dr. | 920/232–2337 | Free | Call for appointment.

Grand Opera House. This working theater built in 1883 reflects the architecture and opulence of the Victorian era. Tours are available. Seasonal performances can include anything from rock concerts to ballet to community theater. | 100 High Ave. | 920/424–2355 | www.grandoperahouse.org | $2; special rates for kids.

Menomonie Park Zoo. Many species of native and exotic animals on Lake Winnebago. Kids can enjoy miniature train rides, bumper boats, and canoes. | Hazel and Merritt Sts. | 920/236–5080 | Free | Mid-May–mid-Sept., daily 9–7:30.

Oshkosh Public Museum. Changing exhibits focus on regional history, natural history, and decorative arts. On permanent display is the famous 1895 Apostles Clock constructed by German immigrant Mathias Kitz. Every hour miniature apostles come out and bow to Jesus. | 1331 Algoma Blvd. | 920/424–4731 | www.publicmuseum.oshkosh.net | Free | Tues.–Sat. 9–5, Sun. 1–5.

Paine Art Center and Arboretum. Period rooms and galleries used for changing exhibitions of both local and regional art fill this Tudor-style mansion built in 1927. There are botanical gardens on the grounds. | 1410 Algoma Blvd. | 920/235–6903 | $5; special rates for senior citizens, kids, and groups | www.publicmuseum.oshkosh.net | Tues.–Sun. 11–4.

Pioneer Princess. This 49-passenger boat is the only excursion boat on Lake Winnebago. Public cruises run 1½ to 2 hours and themes are sightseeing, cocktail, dinner, moonlight, and an ice-cream social. Private charters also available. | 1000 Pioneer Dr. | 920/233–1980 or 800/683–1980 | $10.95–$29.95 | Memorial Day–Labor Day.

University of Wisconsin–Oshkosh. An art gallery, a theater, and the school's large sports center are open to the public for viewing. Tours of the 165-acre campus are available. | 800 Algoma Blvd. | 920/424–0202 | www.uwosh.edu | Free | Campus tours weekdays; Sat. by appointment.

ON THE CALENDAR

FEB.: *Echoes of the Past Trade Fair.* This showcase for historic reenactors held in the Expo Building at Winnebago County fairgrounds the last full weekend of the month features merchants and craftsmen selling goods for reenactors interested in the period from 1700 to 1860, as well as demonstrations and fashion shows. | 920/233–5332.

JULY–AUG.: *EAA AirVenture Oshkosh.* More than 800,000 people and 12,000 airplanes come to Whittman Regional Airport over seven days for the world's largest sport aviation event beginning on the last weekend in July. | 800/236–4800.

Dining

Fin 'n' Feather Showboats. American. This restaurant on the Wolf River 13 mi northwest of Oshkosh in Winneconne is designed to look like an old riverboat. It's full of nautical memorabilia and has a menu with lots of fish dishes as well as steak and pasta, but it never leaves the dock. To cruise while you dine you can board the owners' real ship, the *Showboat II.* Salad bar. Buffet Sunday brunch. | 22 W. Main St., Winneconne | 920/582–4305 | $8–$25 | AE, MC, V.

Fratello's. Italian. This two-tiered restaurant overlooks the Fox River. Specialties are pizza and pasta. | 1501 Arboretum Dr. | 920/232–2337 | $11–$20 | AE, MC, V.

Robbins. Continental. Candles on the tables and a glowing fireplace set the mood at this special-occasion restaurant, the menu includes shrimp and tenderloin. Kids' menu. | 1810 Omro Rd. | 920/235–2840 | $9–$24 | AE, MC, V.

Wisconsin Farms. American. This relaxed, very casual family restaurant on the outskirts of downtown looks like a barn on the outside. Inside, crafts and knickknacks cover the walls. Standard fare includes prime rib, roasted chicken, spaghetti, and pork chops. The cinnamon rolls are a special treat. Kids' menu. | 2450 S. Washburn St. | 920/233–7555 | www.foodspot.com/wifarmrest/~.html | $6–$12 | D, MC, V.

Lodging

Americinn. At the west side of town, this standard hotel is just across the street from an airport—hence the airplane motif. Suites are also available. Complimentary Continental breakfast. Cable TV. Pool. Hot tub, sauna. | 1495 W. South Park Ave. | 920/232–0300 or 800/634–3444 | www.americinn.com | 90 rooms | $65–$125 | AE, D, MC, V.

Baymont Inn. This standard inn is on the northwestern side of town. Complimentary Continental breakfast. Cable TV. | 1950 Omro Rd. | 920/233–4190 or 800/428–3438 | fax 920/233–8197 | www.baymontinn.com | 98 rooms | $59–$89 | AE, D, DC, MC, V.

Fairfield Inn by Marriott. This downtown hotel is within easy walking distance of several restaurants and stores as well as Oshkosh's medical center. The lobby has a seating area and there's an adjacent breakfast room. Complimentary Continental breakfast. Some microwaves, some refrigerators, in-room data ports, cable TV. Pool. Hot tub. Video games. Business services. | 1800 S. Koeller Rd. | 920/233–8504 | fax 920/233–8504 | 57 rooms, 10 suites | $58–$78 | AE, D, DC, MC, V.

Howard Johnson. This standard motel occupies a spot on a strip of similar establishments and popular chain restaurants close to Whittman Regional Airport. Parking is sheltered by a carport. Bar. Cable TV. Pool. Hot tub. Business services. Some pets allowed. | 1919 Omro Rd. | 920/233–1200 | fax 920/233–1135 | 100 rooms | $70–$75 | AE, D, DC, MC, V.

Park Plaza Hotel. The restaurant and lounge at this downtown hotel overlook the Fox River. The lobby has a glass atrium with tropical plants and several seating areas. Some rooms have water views, as well. Restaurant, bar. In-room data ports, microwaves available, some refrigerators, cable TV, in-room VCRs available. Pool. Hot tub. Gym. Business services, airport shuttle. Some pets allowed. | 1 N. Main St. | 920/231–5000 | fax 920/231–8383 | relax@parkinn.com | www.parkinn.com | 179 rooms | $79–$135. | AE, D, DC, MC, V.

Pioneer Inn. This sprawling resort and marina occupies a private island in Lake Winnebago. All rooms have balconies overlooking the lake. The resort maintains a vast stretch of private beach for swimming, sunning, and fishing, as well as a fleet of bicycles and watercraft for guests to use. The resort is a popular spot for corporate retreats and wedding parties. 2 restaurants, bar. In-room data ports, some microwaves, some in-room hot tubs, cable TV, in-room VCRs available. 2 pools, wading pool. Hot tub. Basketball, gym, volleyball, beach, boating, bicycles. Business services, airport shuttle. | 1000 Pioneer Dr. | 920/233–1980 or 800/683–1980 | fax 920/426–2115 | www.pioneerresort.com | 192 rooms | $119–$139 | AE, D, DC, MC, V.

Ramada Inn. This chain hotel is on a commercial strip within walking distance of dining and shopping, and less than a mile from downtown. The atrium lobby has a fountain and tropical plants as well as a fireplace and a seating area. Restaurant, room service. Microwave available, cable TV. Pool. Hot tub. Gym. Laundry facilities. Business services, airport shuttle. | 500 S. Koeller St. | 920/233–1511 | fax 920/233–1909 | 132 rooms | $60–$90 | AE, D, DC, MC, V.

PARK FALLS

MAP 11, C2

(Nearby towns also listed: Lac du Flambeau, Woodruff)

Before European settlers came to this area, it was the land of the Ojibwe. Government surveyors mapped the country in 1865 when hunters, trappers, and traders walked the woods. In 1876 Frenchmen settled the first homesteads along the North Fork of the Flambeau River at what became known as Muskellunge Falls. The Wisconsin Central Railway opened rail service between Milwaukee and Ashland in the summer of 1877, the same year the first school was established in a small log hut on the south side of town. Today Park Falls is the largest city in Price County and has the most extensively managed ruffed grouse habitat in the world, consisting of many miles of mowed and covered roads and numerous wildlife openings also benefiting deer, bear, rabbits, and songbirds. The National Forest here has many lakes and streams; you'll also find all kinds of trees like aspen, maple, pine, and balsam. Popular activities include canoeing, hiking, camping, and cross-country skiing.

Information: Park Falls Area Chamber of Commerce | 400 4th Ave. S, Suite 8, 54552-1121 | 800/762–2709 | www.parkfalls.com.

Attractions

Chequamegon National Forest. This 860,000-acre preserve contains a number of lakes idea for fishing and canoeing. The nearest local landmark is the Penokee Overlook, which provides a great view from an observation platform built atop a high bluff. There's also camping, varying distances of hiking trails, as well as cross-country sking, horseback riding, and snowmobiling. | 1170 4th Ave. South | 715/762–2461 | Fees for camping and some other activities | Memorial Day–Sept., daily; Oct.–Memorial Day, weekdays.

Flambeau Paper Co. Office Building. This operating paper mill located downtown is on the National Register of Historic Places. This was the area's first paper mill and helped establish the town. | 200 N. 1st Ave. | 800/762–2709 | Free | Daily 9–6.

Old Abe–Veteran's Memorial. Old Abe, a Civil War–era eagle, was a mascot for the troops of the 8th Wisconsin infantry. He was born in 1861 atop a huge white pine tree growing along the banks of the North Fork above Park Falls. A statue of Old Abe in City Hall Park honors all Park Falls' veterans. | Rte. 13 | 800/762–2709 | Free | Daily.

Old Town Hall Museum. Four miles south of town on Highway 13 in Fifield, you'll find this museum, run by the Price County Historical Society. It's in an 1894 building and on the National Register of Historic Places. There are exhibits on logging and local history. | 7213 Pine St., Fifield | 715/762–4571 | $5; special rates for families | Memorial Day–Labor Day, Fri. and Sun. 1–5.

Park Theater. This downtown movie theater containing an old-fashioned big screen has been restored to its original Art Deco splendor. | 199 N. 2nd Ave. | 715/762–2293 | Free | Daily tours by appointment.

Post Office Lumberjack Mural. The foyer of this downtown post office displays a mural by Madison artist James Watrous depicting the area's logging era. U.S. 13 to downtown. | 109 N. 1st St. | 800/762–2709 | Free | Mon.–Sat. 9–4:30.

Round Lake Logging Dam. In the late 1800s this dam 20 mi east of Park Falls was one of approximately 100 dams that kept the pines moving to sawmills in the Chippewa River Valley. This dam was placed on the National Register of Historic Places in 1981, and it was restored in 1995. Visit and learn how it operated and the part it played in the 19th-century logging industry. | U.S. Forest Rd. 144, off of Rte. 70 | 800/762–2709 | Free | Daily.

Smith Rapids Covered Bridge. Built in 1991, this bridge next to the Chequamegon National Forest's Smith Rapids Campgrounds is 14 mi east of Park Falls, near Fifield. It is the only glue-laminated Town lattice-covered bridge in Wisconsin. The pattern was patented in the 1920s by its designer, Ithiel Town. The bridge passes over the south fork of the Flambeau River, a popular destination for canoeists. | U.S. Forest Rd. 148 | 800/762–2709 | Free | Daily.

Timm's Hill County Park. Twenty-five miles south of Park Falls, at 1,951½ ft above sea level, Timm's Hill is the highest geographical point in Wisconsin and its accompanying park is bordered by spring-fed Timm's Lake to the north and Bass Lake to the south—both more than 30 ft deep. The park has an observation tower, walking and cross-country ski trails, a picnic shelter, a playground, and a monument to early settlers. There is snowmobiling adjacent to the park, which connects to the Ice Age Trail system. From town of Spirit, turn south on Route C and go 1 mi. | Rte. C, Normal Building, Phillips | 800/762–2709 | Free | Daily.

Tuscobia-Park Falls State Trail. This 73-mi trail, which includes a portion of the Ice Age Trail, is used for biking, hiking, and motorized sports. This trail was originally built as a railroad line from Tuscobia to Park Falls. | Rte. E or Rte. 70 | 800/762–2709 | Free | Daily.

Wisconsin Concrete Park. Nineteen miles south of Park Falls in Phillips, this park is a tribute to the late Fred Smith who, at age 65 began construction of a "concrete park" on about 3½ acres within his homestead. A self-taught artist, Smith created concrete monuments of famous fictional and historical figures including Paul Bunyan, Kit Carson, Abraham Lincoln, Sacajawea, Ben Hur and some 200 others using wooden armatures covered with layers of hand-mixed cement. The figures are decorated with shards of broken glass and found objects. Before his death, the park was in his backyard. His home is now a gift shop and there is a nature trail on the site. | 126 Cherry St., Phillips | 715/339–6475 or 715/339–4100 | Donations accepted | Daily.

ON THE CALENDAR
AUG.: *Flambeau Rama.* Bed races, frog jumping, a classic auto show, arts, crafts, live entertainment, food, and a parade on the first weekend in August. | 800/762–2709.
AUG.: *Butternut Lake Muskie Tournament.* This is a popular annual fishing tournament that's fun for participants and spectators alike. Entry fee is $250 per person; up to 60 boats can participate. | 800/762–2709.

Dining
Annie's. American. This bar and grill does a thriving take-out business. You can sit at the bar and order taco pizzas, fried cheese curds, chicken strips, and a wide variety of sandwiches. | 177 4th Ave. S | 715/762–4109 | $4–$17 | No credit cards.

Coffee Shop Too. American. This casual spot in the Park Mall has a full menu and daily specials and is noted for homemade pies. Specialties include beef stroganoff, pork and dumplings, and Friday-night fish fries. Breakfast is served all day. | 177 Division St. | 715/762–1668 | $2–$7 | MC, V | Closed weekends. No dinner.

Flambeau Lanes Restaurant. American. This bar and lounge in the Northway Motor Lodge attracts regulars for its simple fare; the specialty here is homemade pizza. | 1127 S. 4th Ave. | 715/762–3237 or 800/844–7144 | $2–$12 | AE, D, DC, MC, V.

Frontier Inn. American. This rustic family-run restaurant is in a rural, wooded area about 10 mi northeast of Park Falls. It's known for hearty breakfasts, specialty sandwiches, fish fry, and homemade pizzas. There's an antiques shop and a bait shop on the property. | 1391 N. Hwy. 182, Springstead | 715/583–4400 | Reservations not accepted | $5–$15 | MC, V | Closed Mon.

Hicks' Landing. American. Noted for lobster, choice steaks, home-baked bread, and relish trays, this restaurant has been in business since 1951, just 5 mi south of Park Falls. | Trail No. 121 N12855 Hicks Rd., Fifield | 715/762–5008 | $7–$25 | MC, V | Closed Mon. except holidays. No lunch Mon.–Sat.

Liebelt's Supper Club. American. This modern downtown supper club serves up barbecued ribs, prime rib, charbroiled shrimp, and New York strip steak. Salad bar. | 344 Division St. | 715/762–3481 | $8–$10 | AE, MC, V.

Ruffed Grouse Inn. German. In addition to German specialties, such as schnitzel and sauerbraten, the family-style restaurant is noted for its "Bloomin' Onion" (a whole onion sliced into a flower shape, lightly battered, and deep-fried), pizzas, steaks, liver and onions, and chicken. | 915 N. 4th. St. | 715/762–2222 | $4–$16 | AE, D, MC, V | Closed Sun. No lunch.

Lodging

The Birches. Rustic housekeeping cottages surround a large main lodge and newly built motel rooms with kitchenettes located on Boot Lake, about 10 mi northeast of Park Falls. Cottages are rented by the week only. Hiking, boating, fishing. Cross-country skiing, snowmobiling. | HCR 2, Springstead | 888/308–5421 | 20 cottages | $57 motel units, $315 cottages | MC, V | Cottages closed mid. Oct–mid May.

Boyd's Mason Lake Resort. This century-old resort 5 mi south of Park Falls consists of cabins with access to four private lakes on a 2,600-acre private estate. The lakes are professionally managed for muskies, walleyes, and bass. There's a three- to five-night minimum stay, depending upon the time of year. TV in common area. Hiking, beach, boating, fishing, bicycles. Pets allowed. | Box 57, Fifield | 715/762–3469 | 18 cabins | $80 | May–mid-Oct. | AP | No credit cards.

Buckhorn Retreat. The former 1920s Buckhorn Tavern is now a vacation cottage on 30 acres in the heart of Chequamegon National Forest 11 mi east of Park Falls. There's plenty of country charm and a sprinkling of antiques throughout. The Great Room has a gas fireplace and the kitchen is fully equipped. Kitchenette, cable TV, no phone. Hiking, fishing, biking. Cross-country skiing, snowmobiling. Laundry service. Some pets allowed. No smoking. | 344 Division St., Eisenstein | 715/762–2086 (days) or 715/762–3132 (evenings) | fax 715/762–4544 | www.parkfalls.com/buckhornretreat | 1 cottage | $85–$115 (2–night minimum stay) | D, MC, V.

Cedar Lodge. This small resort has two cottages and a cedar-log lodge on the Turtle Flambeau Flowage 21 mi east of Park Falls. Cottage rental includes use of the lodge's rowboats. The lodge also maintains a dock for fishing and a section of private sand beach. Restaurant, bar. Boating, fishing. Snowmobiling. Video games. | 964 Hiawatha Rd., Butternut | 715/476–2511 | fax 715/476–2511 | 7 lodge rooms, 2 cottages | $40 rooms, $450–$475 cottages (7–night minimum stay, 4–6 people) | No credit cards.

Cry of the Loon Resort. The two- and three-bedroom cabins at this small resort 18 mi northeast of Park Falls all face the sandy shoreline of the Turtle Flambeau Flowage and have knotty-pine interiors and gas-log fireplaces. Picnic area. Kitchenettes. Lake. Boating, fishing. Some pets allowed (fee). | 6505 O'Meara Rd., Butternut | 715/476–2502 | 4 cabins | $500 (7–night minimum stay in summer) | MC, V.

Donner's Bay Resort. You can stay in modern wooden cabins with enclosed porches nestled on the Turtle Flambeau Flowage 23 mi north of Park Falls. Bar, picnic area. No TV in some cabins. Hiking, beach, boating, fishing. Snowmobiling. Video games. Playground. | 974 Hiawatha Rd., Butternut | 715/476–2555 | 6 cabins | $300–$425 (7–day minimum stay) | No credit cards.

Double E Resort. A 14-ft boat is supplied with each cabin at this family resort backed by white birch trees near the Chequamegon National Forest and 3 mi from Turtle Flambeau Flowage fishing area. Kitchenettes. Beach, boating. Some pets allowed. | 1610 N. Double EE Rd. | 715/583–4477 | www.lodging.org | 4 cabins | $385–$395 (7–day minimum stay) | D | Closed Nov.–Apr.

Flambeau Resort. Rustic but modern wood cabins built in the 1940s are nestled amid birch and pine trees in the Chequamegon National Forest within 200 ft of the south fork of the Flambeau River. Each rental comes with a boat. Golfing is nearby. Restaurant, bar. Hiking, boating, fishing, bicycles. Snowmobiling. Video games. Playground. Pets allowed. | N15355 East Rd. | 715/762–2178 or 715/762–4757 | 7 cabins | $150 (2–night minimum stay) | MC, V.

Idle Hour Resort. Secluded among the pines and hardwood trees in the heart of Chequamegon National Forest, this family-style resort on Pike Lake was built in the mid 1900s and is 20 mi east of Park Falls on Highway 70. From mid-June to mid-August, only weekly stays are available. Kids' area. Some microwaves, no phones, no TV. Fishing. Cross-country skiing, snowmobiling. | N14516 Shady Knoll Rd., Pike Lake | 715/762–3872 | fax 715/762–3842 | idlehour@ballcom.com | 14 cottages | $55–$70 | No credit cards.

Moose Jaw Resort. Twenty miles east of Park Falls, on Round Lake (part of the Pike-Round Chain of Lakes), in the heart of the Chequamegon National Forest. The main lodge was built in 1887, at the height of northern Wisconsin's logging days. Today the resort is updated and has modern amenities. A big-screen TV is in the dining room. Cabins, some log, have screened porches, and a boat or canoe is included with each rental. Restaurant, bar, picnic area. Kitchenettes. Basketball, volleyball, beach, boating, fishing. Snowmobiling. Playground. Pets allowed. | N15098 Shady Knoll Rd. | 715/762–3028 | 7 cabins | $300–$525 (7–day minimum stay) | MC, V.

Northway Motor Lodge. This modern motel in Park Falls is connected to a recreation center, where there are 12 cross-country ski trails, lakes for fishing, and hunting grounds. A snowmobile and ATV trail passes through the property, and you can rent snowmobiles and snowmobile gear nearby. Offers RV and trailer parking. Complimentary Continental breakfast. Cable TV. Pool. Hot tub, sauna. Gym, racquetball, volleyball. Video games. | 1127 S. 4th Ave. | 715/762–2406 or 800/844–7144 | fax 715/762–2162 | 32 rooms | $59–$69 | AE, D, DC, MC, V.

Oxbo Resort on the Flambeau. Sixteen miles east of Park Falls, this rustic wood lodge built in 1922 is in the heart of the Flambeau River State Forest. Cabins are scattered along the river and hidden among the trees. There are campgrounds and a trailer area on the grounds. Restaurant, bar. Kitchenettes, no room phones, no TV. Hiking, boating, bicycles. Snowmobiling. | At the junction of Rte. 1 and Rte. 70, Oxbo | 715/762–4786 | 3 cabins | $45–$65 | MC, V | Closed Apr.

Pike Lake Inn Bed & Breakfast. This two-story log inn is in the middle of the Chequamegon National Forest. Rooms are paneled with knotty pine. There is excellent fishing on the nearby chain of four lakes. if you bring your snowmobile, you can use the Price County snowmobile trails outside your door. Complimentary breakfast. TV in common area. | W883 Hwy. 70 | 715/762–3990 | 4 rooms | $45–$60 | No credit cards.

Redemption Ranch Guest House. This restored farmhouse on a working horse ranch is available for weekend or weekly rentals. Rooms are done in pickled pine; the modern bathrooms maintain an antique look. Snowmobiling, hiking, golfing, and fishing are close by. Complimentary breakfast. Boating. | N15696 County Rd. B | 715/762–4891 | 1 guest house, accommodates up to 8 people | $85 per day for up to 4 adults. Weekly rentals for 4 adults start at $500 | MC, V.

Ron's Northern Pines Resort. These rustic cabins with screened porches are 3½ mi northwest of Park Falls on the south end of 1,006-acre Butternut Lake, which is noted for its musky fishing; walleye, crappie, perch, and other fish are also abundant. ATV trails and a casino are nearby. Restaurant, bar, picnic area. Kitchenettes. Beach, docks, boating, fishing. Snowmobiling. Playground. | N16243 Lakeshore Dr., Butternut | 715/762–3001 or 800/762–3001 | 9 cabins | $48–$71 | No credit cards.

PESHTIGO

MAP 11, E4

(Nearby towns also listed: Marinette, Oconto)

One of the worst fires in American history took place here in 1871 and destroyed what had been the logging boomtown of Peshtigo. Some 1,000 people were killed, and hundreds of thousands of acres of forest were decimated. When residents rebuilt the

PESHTIGO

INTRO
ATTRACTIONS
DINING
LODGING

town, they preserved their history in the Peshtigo Fire Museum. Surrounding Marinette County, crisscrossed by streams and rivers, there are many waterfalls that are good for white-water rafting and canoeing.

Information: Peshtigo Chamber of Commerce | Box 36, 54157-0036 | 715/582–0327 | www.peshtigochamber.com.

Attractions

Badger Park. This 60-acre park on the Peshtigo River has camping, water sports, a large playground, trails, and a beach. | N. Emery Ave.; U.S. 41 | 715/582–4321 or 715/582–3041 | Free | Daily.

Cramer's Vernon Hills Golf Club. An 18-hole course with a driving range rents carts and clubs, and also has a popular bar and grill. | W4244 Hwy. 41 | 715/582–9200 | $18 weekdays, $20 weekends | Apr.–Oct.

Peshtigo Fire Museum. Many historians consider the 1871 Peshtigo fire far worse than the Great Chicago Fire on the same day—and call it the single worst fire disaster in American history. It destroyed the logging boomtown as well as hundreds of thousands of forest acreage, and claimed more than 1,000 lives. The museum closes on October 8, the anniversary of the fire, and reopens in late May. | 400 Oconto Ave. | 715/582–3244 | Donations accepted | Late May–early Oct., Daily 9–5.

ON THE CALENDAR
SEPT.: *Peshtigo Historical Day.* A parade, a run/walk, old-time displays, food, and entertainment on the third Saturday of the month in Badger Park. | 715/582–0327.

Dining
Cramer's Vernon Hills Bar & Grill. American. Casual dining overlooking an 18-hole golf course. Favorites are taco salads, chicken sandwiches, and Friday-night fish fry. There are picnic benches for outside dining. | W4244 Hwy. 41 | 715/582–9200 | $3–$6 | MC, V | Closed Jan., Feb.

Lodging
Drees Motel. This owner-operated motel has standard rooms at a good price. Cable TV. | 790 French St. | 715/582–4559 or 800/245–0402 | 16 rooms | $38–$45 | MC, V.

PLATTEVILLE

MAP 11, C7

(Nearby towns also listed: Mineral Point, Monroe)

The area around pretty Platteville was one of the first to be settled by Europeans drawn here by rich lead deposits. Platteville's pair of mining museums recall the town's early-19th-century origins through a pair of mining museums. The University of Wisconsin–Platteville campus is the site of the Chicago Bears' summer training camp and an annual Shakespeare festival.

Information: Platteville Chamber of Commerce | Box 16, 53818-0016 | 608/348–8888 | chamber@platteville.com | www.platteville.com.

Attractions
Mitchell-Rountree Stone Cottage. This historic building was built in 1837 of locally quarried limestone and is the oldest stone homestead in Platteville. Considered to be a masterpiece of joiner's art, it contains the original Rountree furnishings. The cottage is open by appointment only. | W. Madison St. & Hwy. 81 | 608/723–2287 | Free.

Rollo Jamison Museum. This museum is named for the local collector who gathered this eclectic variety of arrowheads, art, appliances, tools, games, and antiques and collectibles dating from the early 1900s. The Mining Museum is also located here. | 405 E. Main St. | 608/348–3301 | $6; special rates for kids and groups | May–Oct., daily 9–5; Nov.–Apr., weekdays 9–5; group tours by reservation.

Exhibits at the **Mining Museum** on the grounds of the Rollo Jamison Museum explore the region's history of zinc and lead mining. While you're above ground, you can ride the mine train, authentic ore cars are pulled by a restored mine locomotive. You then descend 90 steps into the Bevins Lead Mine to see the miners' underground world. Take Route 81 or U.S. 151. | 405 E. Main St. | 608/348–3301 | Free with Rollo Jamison Museum admission | May–Oct., daily 9–5; Nov.–Apr., weekdays 9–5; group tours by reservation.

University of Wisconsin–Platteville. The Platteville Normal School and the Wisconsin Mining School merged in 1959 and joined the University of Wisconsin family in 1979; there are 5,000 students. The Chicago Bears hold their summer training camp on the 75-acre campus 15 mi east of the Mississippi River; a Shakespeare festival is also held here each year. | 1 University Plaza | 608/342–1125 | www.uwplatt.edu | Free | Daily.

ON THE CALENDAR
JULY–AUG.: *Chicago Bears Summer Training Camp.* Watch these NFL bruins as they undergo their summer training at the University of Wisconsin–Platteville from late July to mid-August. | 608/348–8888.
JULY–AUG.: *Wisconsin Shakespeare Festival.* This Shakespeare festival draws approximately 6,000 people for the 30 performances in a rotating repertoire from the first weekend in July to the first weekend in August on the University of Wisconsin–Platteville campus. | 608/342–1298.

Dining
Mc Dermotts. American/Casual. W. C. Fields memorabilia fills this casual restaurant. The menu mixes Italian and Mexican dishes with steak, sandwiches, burgers, and seafood. Kids' menu. | 300 McGregor Plaza | 608/348–7700 | $6–$12 | D, MC, V.

Ogden's Arthur Tavern & Restaurant. American. This bustling restaurant and bar was a blacksmith shop in the 1920s and '30s. Locals gather here for Friday night seafood specials including fish fries, clam strips, catfish, and scallops. Breakfast is served all day. | 9396 State Rd. 80, Arthur | 608/348–7788 | $7–$19 | No credit cards | Closed Mon.

Timbers. Continental. Steak and seafood anchor the menu at this elegant restaurant housed in a Frank Lloyd Wright–style wooden building in the residential part of town. There's live music every night as well as a collection of instruments, including accordions, drums, chimes, and banjos, on the walls. Pianist weekends, organist nightly. Kids' menu. Sunday brunch. | 670 Ellen St. | 608/348–2406 | $10–$25 | AE, D, DC, MC, V.

Lodging
Best Western Welcome Inn. This motel in a two-story, white-and-gray brick colonial-style building is 15 mi outside of downtown Platteville. There are two entryways and a porch with pillars. Complimentary Continental breakfast. Cable TV. Laundry facilities. | 420 W. Maple, Lancaster | 608/723–4162 | fax 608/723–4843 | www.bestwestern.com | 22 rooms | $56–$69 | AE, D, DC, MC, V.

Governor Dodge Motor Inn. White pillars and a canopy accent the front of this motel five blocks from the University of Wisconsin–Platteville. Restaurant. Cable TV, in-room VCRs available. Pool. Hot tub. Gym. Business services. Some pets allowed. | U.S. 151 W | 608/348–2301 | fax 608/348–8579 | 74 rooms | $65–$77 | AE, D, DC, MC, V.

Gribble House Bed & Breakfast. This Victorian Italianate home, built in 1872, is painted four shades of green. There are 8-ft-high arched windows, antiques, and a fireplace. VCRs and movies are available for in-room viewing. Complimentary breakfast. | 260 W. Cedar St. | 608/348–7282 | 3 rooms | $50–$75 | MC, V.

Super 8. This two-story white brick building overlooking the Platte River is nearly the length of a football field. Many guest rooms have views of the river flowing by. Complimentary Continental breakfast. Some refrigerators, cable TV. Hot tub, sauna. Laundry facilities. Business services. Pets allowed (fee). | 100 Rte. 80/81 south | 608/348–8800 | fax 608/348–7233 | www.super8.com | 73 rooms | $58–$75 | AE, D, DC, MC, V.

Walnut Ridge Bed & Breakfast. This rustic-modern log guest house was hand-hewn by the owner with historic accuracy, he even used original tools. On the property is the owner's own 1800s log cabin. Guests are treated to a complimentary bottle of wine. Complimentary breakfast. No in-room TV. Hot tub. | 2238 Hwy. A | 608/348–9359 | fax 608/348–3898 | www.walnutridgewi.com | 1 guest cabin | $140 | MC, V.

Wisconsin House. This redbrick inn was built during the lead-mining boom in 1846 and has served as a stagecoach station, a private home, and an apartment building. It was resurrected once again in 1985 as a bed and breakfast, and today houses dozens of antiques and bits of area history. The inn is in the little town of Hazel Green, about 15 mi southeast of Platteville. Many parts of the building are original, and two of the three floors have large porches with wicker furniture. They serve a complimentary dinner on Saturday. Complimentary breakfast. Cable TV in common area, VCR available, no room phones. No smoking. | 2105 Main St., Hazel Green | 608/854–2233 | wishouse@mhtc.net | www.wisconsinhouse.com | 8 rooms (2 with shared bath), 2 suites | $55–$115 | AE, D, MC, V.

PORTAGE

(Nearby towns also listed: Baraboo, Wisconsin Dells)

Pretty and quiet, Portage is conveniently located near Wisconsin Dells. Settled in 1835, it has many historic homes and buildings, including part of an original fort built in 1828. The area also has the home of 1921 Pulitzer Prize winner Zona Gale. It's 14 mi northeast of Baraboo, on a heavily wooded bend of the Wisconsin River. The town's wealth of natural beauty and proximity to lakes, rivers, and woodlands make it a destination for outdoor sports enthusiasts and nature lovers.

Information: **Portage Area Chamber of Commerce** | 391 W. Wisconsin St., 53901-2137 | 800/474–2525 | www.portagewi.com.

Attractions

Cascade Mt. Ski Area. This ski area with 27 trails—the longest a mile long—and a 460-ft vertical drop has day and night skiing and snowboarding. It's 3 mi west of Portage. | Rte. 33 | 608/742–5588 or 800/992–2754 | www.cascademountain.com | Daily lift ticket $38–$46 | Sat. before Thanksgiving–late Mar.

Fort Winnebago Surgeons' Quarters. Fort Winnebago, 2 mi east of Portage, was built in 1826 as living quarters for army surgeons. The log house is the only remaining building of the original fort. Inside are original furnishings. | W8687 Rte. 33 E | 608/742–2949 | $3.50 | Mid-May–mid-Oct., daily 10–4.

Historic Indian Agency House. Two-hundred-year-old elm trees stand in front of this restored 1932 wood home which was built for agent John Kinzie and his wife, Juliette Magill Kinzie, who wrote *Wau-bun*, a classic account of life on the Wisconsin frontier. Inside are five bedrooms, five fireplaces, and period furniture. The exterior has original siding. Hour-long tours are available. | Agency House Rd. | 608/742–6362 | $3.50 | Mid-May–mid-Oct., daily 10–4.

Myrtle Lintner Spear Museum. There are exhibits of Columbia County farm and home-life from the early 1900s in this small museum about 6 mi due east of Portage. The museum is also open by appointment. | 112 N. Main St., Pardeeville | 608/429–3121 | $3 | Mid-June–Sept., Tues.–Sat. 10–4.

Silver Lake. This 75-acre spring-fed lake, on the west side of town, is 42 ft deep and has a boat landing, a sandy bottom, public swimming, and great fishing. | Silver Lake Dr. | 608/742–2176 or 608/742–2178 | Free | Daily.

Zona Gale House. Zona Gale, a native of Portage, won a Pulitzer Prize in 1921 for her stage comedy *Miss Lulu Bett*. She is remembered as a talented playwright and author, as well as an active suffragette. This Georgian Revival home has classic 1800s details throughout. | 506 W. Edgewater St. | 608/742–7744 | $2; special rates for kids and groups | Tours daily by appointment.

ON THE CALENDAR
AUG.: *Taste of Portage.* There's free entertainment, kids' games, a crafts fair, and a farmers' market at this food fair in Market Square on the last Saturday in August. | 800/474–2525.

Dining
Cimarolis. American. A seafood buffet is the popular choice at this busy restaurant located 7 mi outside of town. Steaks are also served here. | W11793 State Rd. 127 | 608/742–2238 | $10–$15 | MC, V | No lunch.

Lodging
Breese Waye Bed & Breakfast. In the center of town, this Victorian Italianate home was built in 1880 by Llewelyn Breese, the first secretary of state of Wisconsin. There are fireplaces, two parlors, and fine details like crown molding, pocket doors, and parquet floors. Complimentary breakfast. TV in common area. | 816 MacFarlane Rd. | 608/742–5281 | www.breesewaye.com | 4 rooms | $70–$80 | No credit cards.

Ridge Motor Inn. On the north side of town, this brick motel with a large, modern lobby is walking distance to strip malls and restaurants. Restaurant, bar, room service. Some kitchenettes, cable TV, in-room VCRs and movies. Pool. Hot tub, massage. Gym, volleyball. Video games. Laundry facilities. Business services. Pets allowed. | 2900 New Pinery Rd. | 608/742–5306 | fax 608/742–5306 | 113 rooms, 9 suites | $49–$99 | AE, D, DC, MC, V.

Riverbend Inn. Forty acres of fields and trees, bordered by the Baraboo River, surround this comfortable 1905 Victorian farmhouse with a large, screened front porch; inside are original wood accents, parquet floors, and large windows. Complimentary full breakfast. Some in-room hot tubs. No smoking. | W10928 Rte. 33 | 608/742–3627 or 800/820–8264 | www.insight.com | 4 rooms | $65–$105 | MC, V.

PORT WASHINGTON

MAP 11, E6

(Nearby towns also listed: Cedarburg, Milwaukee, Sheboygan, West Bend)

Port Washington, settled in 1835, is an attractive city right on Lake Michigan that claims the first man-made harbor dug in North America. Because of the town's prime lakefront location, it's a popular destination among anglers and water sports enthusiasts. Thousands of Milwaukeeans make the short drive north in the summer to escape the city heat and crowds.

Information: Port Washington Tourism Council | Box 153, 53074-0153 | 262/284–0900 | www.discoverusa.com/wi/ptwash.

Attractions

Eghart House. Leopold Eghart, a local probate judge, lived in this Victorian cottage, built in 1872. Some of the period furnishings are original to the home. | 316 Grand Ave. | 262/284–2897 | $1 | Memorial Day–Labor Day, Sun. 1–4.

Light Station Museum. This 1860 lighthouse set on a hill north of downtown provides information on Port Washington's local and maritime history. | 311 E. Johnson St. | 262/284–0900 | Donations accepted | Memorial Day–Labor Day, Sun. 1–4.

Pioneer Village. The village, 10 mi northwest of Port Washington, has a collection of 20 log, stone, and frame buildings from the mid- to late 19th century. | 4880 Rte. I, Saukville | 262/284–0900 | $4 | Memorial Day–Labor Day, Wed. and weekends; Labor Day–2nd Sun. in Oct., weekends; call for hours.

ON THE CALENDAR

JULY: *Port Fish Day.* The world's largest one-day outdoor fish fry takes place downtown on the lakefront on the third Saturday in July. | 800/719–4881.

Dining

Another Thyme. American. Gourmet health food is served in this former hardware store. A natural-food store is adjacent to the restaurant. Popular items include vegetarian dishes, soups, salads, salmon, and healthful cookies and brownies. | 308 N. Franklin St. | 262/284–5754 | $4–$7 | D, MC, V | Closed Sun. No dinner.

Newport Shores. American. This casual restaurant overlooks Lake Michigan and has a 97-ft-long, horseshoe-shape bar. You'll find steak, sandwiches, fish, and prime rib on the menu. Leave room for the chocolate silk pie or the blueberry sour-cream pie. Sunday brunch. | 407 E. Jackson St. | 262/284–6838 | $7–$21 | AE, D, DC, MC, V | Closed Mon. No lunch Tues.–Thurs.

Smith Brothers Fish Shanty. Seafood. The menu here features fish, burgers, sandwiches, and beers brewed on the premises. Large windows provide a good view of the Port Washington marina and Lake Michigan. Open-air dining on deck. Kids' menu. | 100 N. Franklin St. | 262/284–5592 | $13–$55 | D, DC, MC, V.

Lodging

Best Western Harborside Motor Inn. Located downtown, this is a standard brick hotel. Bar. Some in-room hot tubs, cable TV. Pool. Hot tub, sauna. Dock. Video games. Business services, free parking. Pets allowed. | 135 E. Grand Ave. | 262/284–9461 | fax 262/284–3169 | www.bestwestern.com | 96 rooms | $99–$119 | AE, D, DC, MC, V.

Grand Inn Bed & Breakfast. This three-story 1907 Victorian painted lady is in the heart of town. The home is furnished with many antiques. A TV and VCR are in the lounge. Complimentary full breakfast. | 832 W. Grand Ave. | 262/284–6719 | 2 rooms | $120–$125 | MC, V.

Port Washington Inn Bed & Breakfast. When this house was built in 1903 the chandeliers were equipped to operate with electricity or gas. The house retains its stained-glass and leaded-glass windows and hardwood floors, and each room is decorated with antiques. Four blocks from Lake Michigan, the inn is on one of the highest points in town and the suite has a view of the lighthouse and harbor. Complimentary breakfast. Cable TV, some in-room phones. No pets. No kids under 12. No smoking. | 308 W. Washington St. | 262/284–5583 or 877/794–1903 | 3 rooms, 1 suite | $100–$125 rooms, $145 suite | AE, MC, V.

West Bend Inn. This 1970s gray brick motel 17 mi west of Port Washington has fantasy suites with themed decor like Arabian nights, caves, and castles. Other rooms are more pedestrian, with modular furniture and unassuming art prints on the walls. Bar, complimentary Continental breakfast. In-room VCRs, Indoor-outdoor pool. Hot tub, sauna. Video games. Business services, free parking. | 2520 W. Washington St., West Bend | 262/338–0636 or 800/727–9727 | fax 262/338–4290 | wbinn@hnet.net | www.fantasuite.com | 61 rooms, 26 suites | $62–$199 | AE, D, DC, MC, V.

PRAIRIE DU CHIEN

(Nearby towns also listed: Bagley, Cassville)

Settled by the French in 1736, Prairie du Chien is one of the state's prettiest river towns. Located at the confluence of the Wisconsin and Mississippi rivers, the area was first populated by Native Americans and followed by French explorers and fur traders. Villa Louis, a Victorian country estate, and other historical sites preserve the history of the town.

Information: Prairie du Chien Chamber of Commerce and Tourism Council | Box 326, 53821-0326 | 800/732–1673 | www.prairieduchien.org.

Attractions

Kickapoo Indian Caverns. These caverns 15 mi southeast of town are the largest subterranean caves in the state and once sheltered local Native Americans. They were rediscovered by lead miners in the 1800s. | W. 200 Rhein Hollow Rd., Wauzeka | 608/875–7723 | $8 | Mid-May–Oct., daily.

La Riviere Park. This park southeast of town has nature trails, rare native prairie plants, rustic camping, and an equestrian campground. | Vineyard Coulee Rd. | 608/326–2241 (Wisconsin Information Center) | Free | Daily.

EAGLES, EGRETS, AND TUNDRA SWANS

Wisconsin's diverse geography makes the state a natural destination for bird-watchers. The state attracts North America's largest population of wintering eagles with the heaviest concentrations along the Mississippi and Wisconsin rivers. Some other particularly fine spots to view birds are the Chequamegon National Forest, the Horicon Marsh, and the Nicolet National Forest.

More than 225 species—including migrating tundra swans—have been sighted at the 885-acre Chequamegon National Forest in the northwestern part of the state.

The 32,000-acre Horicon Marsh northeast of Beaver Dam is known worldwide for its spring and fall migrations and boasts sightings of 268 species. Fall is the best time to view Canada geese. Earlier in the season, from May through July, pontoon-boat tours of the marsh give you a spectacular view of heron and egret rookeries. The area is also the largest nesting site east of the Mississippi River for redhead ducks.

The Nicolet National Forest, which has its headquarters in Rhinelander, covers 661,000 acres in northeastern Wisconsin. Rare species seen in the forest include the boreal chickadee, gray jay, northern tree-toed woodpecker, and spruce groups. The many lakes in the area draw bald eagles, common loons, and ospreys.

Information on scheduled birding trips around the state can be obtained by contacting the Wisconsin Society for Ornithology at 920/294–3021. Information on sightings throughout the state is available by calling the Birding Hot Line at 414/352–3857.

© Corbis

Nelson Dewey State Park. This 750-acre park has wooded family campsites with showers, scenic picnic areas, and views of the Mississippi River from soaring bluffs, where in winter you can often see bald eagles. | 12190 Rte. VV | 608/725–5374 | www.dnr.state.wi.us | $7 nonresidents, $5 residents | Daily.

Prairie du Chien Museum at Fort Crawford. This museum on the southern end of town at Route 35 and U.S. 18 focuses on medical history from the 1800s to the present. Relics of 19th-century medicine in Wisconsin include displays of Native American herbal remedies, an old-fashioned drugstore, a dentist's office, and a doctor's office. | 717 S. Beaumont Rd. (Rte. 35 and U.S. 18) | 608/326–6960 | $4; special rates for senior citizens, kids, and groups | May–Oct., daily 10–5.

Villa Louis. This Victorian estate on the west side of town was built on the banks of the Mississippi by fur trader Hercules Dousman. Today it houses a collection of china, glass, artwork, books, and silver used by the Dousman family from 1843 to 1913. Exhibits in the former carriage house depict Prairie du Chien's early history. Exhibits in the old Astor Fur Warehouse, on the villa grounds, explore the early fur trade. | 521 Villa Louis Rd., off U.S. 18 | 608/326–2721 | $8; special rates for senior citizens, kids, and groups | May–Oct., daily 9–5:30.

Wyalusing State Park. In this 2,700-acre park 12 mi southeast of Prairie du Chien are hiking trails, scenic campgrounds, and picnic areas. Watch for wild turkeys, turkey vultures, eagles, and deer. Ancient Native American mounds line Sentinel Ridge trail, which provides beautiful views of the Mississippi River valley. At Point Lookout, you can observe the confluence of the Mississippi and Wisconsin rivers 300 ft below. | 13342 Rte. C, Wyalusing | 608/996–2261 | www.dnr.state.wi.us | $7 nonresidents, $5 residents | Daily.

ON THE CALENDAR

SEPT.: *Villa Louis Carriage Classic.* More than 90 horse-drawn vehicles compete in area shows, as well as on cross-country and obstacle courses on the second weekend in September. The classic also includes the largest pleasure-driving event in the Midwest. | 608/326–8555.

Dining

Barn Restaurant. American. This restaurant was once a barn and still looks like one: it's weatherbeaten on the outside and you can see the roof on the inside. But that doesn't stop the crowds from coming to the Friday-night seafood buffet or the Sunday champagne brunch. Those are the only two days the Barn is open for business. | French Town Rd. | 608/326–4941 | $6–$10 | MC, V | Closed Mon.–Thurs. and Sat. No dinner Sun.

Coaches Family Restaurant. American. A family dining spot with booths and tables, a fireplace, and country decor. Chicken and homemade pizzas are popular items. Breakfast is served from 5 AM. | 634 S. Marquette Rd. | 608/326–8115 | $5–$8 | AE, D, DC, MC, V.

Huckleberry's Restaurant. American. A variety of perpetual favorites like whitefish and walleye filets and chicken-fried steak are served here, and there are also regularly changing specials. Friday night there is a seafood and chicken buffet; Sunday a buffet brunch. Breakfast served daily. | 1916 S. Marquette Rd. | 608/326–8584 | $5–$10 | MC, V.

Spring Lake Inn. American. The paneled walls of this Northwoods family-style restaurant, in a small 1950s brick roadhouse, display beer steins, deer and bear heads, and fish. On the menu are steaks, seafood, half-pound burgers, deep-fried cod, Mississippi catfish, and prime rib. | 608/326–6907 | Reservations not accepted | $6–$14 | No credit cards.

Lodging

Best Western–Quiet House and Suites. Light gray-blue siding and stone masonry cover this two-story motel. Inside, a country Victorian motif prevails—you'll find Amish pieces and refurbished antiques including an old dry sink. Many rooms have a theme—there's a Mississippi riverboat room, a dairy state/barn room, and an Art Deco room. In-room data ports, kitchenettes (in suites), some in-room hot tubs, cable TV. Pool. Hot tub. Gym. Business services. Pets allowed. | Rtes. 18 and 355 | 608/326–4777 | fax 608/326–4787 | www.best-western.com | 42 rooms, 2 suites | $93–$111 | AE, D, DC, MC, V.

Brisbois Motor Inn. A large canopy of trees and pretty flowers front this 1950s motel with outside entrances. Cable TV. Pool. Playground. Airport shuttle. | 533 N. Marquette Rd. | 608/326–8404 or 800/356–5850 | fax 608/326–8404 | 46 rooms | $59–$84 | AE, D, DC, MC, V.

Holiday Motel. This bluish-gray motel in a long building dating from 1954 has outside room entrances and a small lobby. Cable TV. Business services. Some pets allowed. | 1010 S. Marquette Rd. | 608/326–2448 or 800/962–3883 | fax 608/326–2413 | 18 rooms | $55–$75 | AE, D, MC, V.

La Maison Ravoux. This pre-1830s French Canadian home has been completely restored and includes original wood floors, painted woodwork, and early American and French-Canadian antiques. The two-story house has a shared living room, dining room, and a guest sitting room with exposed beams that is furnished with items from the French fur-trade era. There's a good collection of books on the early history of Wisconsin, the Mississippi River, and the fur-trading industry. Complimentary breakfast. TV in common area. | 316 N. Beaumont Rd. | 608/326–0458 | fax 608/326–8225 | www.bestinns.com | 3 rooms (2 with shared bath) | $55–$65 | MC, V.

Newmann House Bed-and-Breakfast. This Victorian-style home is downtown near shops and the Mississippi River. It has an elegant wrap-around porch and inside, the parlor and dining room are furnished with antiques. Dining room, complimentary breakfast. Cable TV. No smoking. | 121 N. Michigan St. | 608/326–8104 or 888/340–9971 | lneumann@mhtc.net | 5 rooms | $75–$85 | No credit cards.

Prairie Motel. Three separate brick and stucco buildings make up this single-story motel on the south end of town. A miniature golf course is about 2 blocks away; a bowling alley and a movie theater are also nearby. Picnic area. Some refrigerators, cable TV. Pool. Playground. Pets allowed. | 1616 S. Marquette Rd. | 608/326–6461 or 800/526–3776 | 32 rooms | $65–$75 | D, MC, V.

Preacher's Inn. Built in 1996 in the Victorian shingle style, this two-story inn even has a tower and turret. It is filled with antiques, has hardwood floors and crown molding and sits on 20 acres in the scenic Kickapoo valley area 11 mi northeast of the heart of town. One room has a private bath and attached library. Complimentary breakfast. TV in common area. | 34909 Winegar La. | 608/875–6108 | reservations@thepreachersinn.com | www.thepreachersinn.com | 3 rooms (2 with shared bath) | $70–$90 | MC, V.

PRAIRIE DU SAC

INTRO
ATTRACTIONS
DINING
LODGING

PRAIRIE DU SAC

MAP 11, C6

(Nearby towns also listed: Baraboo, Reedsburg, Sauk City)

Prairie du Sac is the sister village to Sauk City, Wisconsin's oldest incorporated village; it is also the home of the Wollersheim Winery, the state's oldest winery, and the site of the prestigious cow-chip throwing contest. The village is set amid rolling meadows, dramatic bluffs, serene forests, and cool lakes and streams. Canoeing is a popular activity; in winter, eagles nest here and sightings are common.

Information: Sauk Prairie Area Chamber of Commerce | 207 Water St., Suite D, Sauk City 53583 | 800/683–2453 | www.saukprairie.com.

Attractions

Tripp Memorial Museum. There is a large display of mounted animals and historic exhibits on the Prairie Du Sac and Sauk City areas. | 565 Water St. | 800/683–2453 | Free | Usually open weekends, call for hours.

Wollersheim Winery. This winery is tucked into the southern slope of Sugarloaf Bluff, which overlooks the Wisconsin River. Founded in the mid-1800s Wollersheim Winery's vineyard is one of the oldest in America. There are guided tours of the vineyard and wine cellars, with tastings at the end of the tour. | 7876 Rte. 188 | 608/643–6515 or 800/847–9463 | $3.50; special rates for kids | Daily 10–5.

ON THE CALENDAR

SEPT.: *Wisconsin State Cow Chip Throw.* This family event in Marion Park features cow-chip tosses for fun and prizes, chip chucking for kids, a beer garden, a kids' parade, live music, breakfast, and an arts-and-crafts fair. | 800/683–2453.

OCT.: *Harvest Festival.* The first full weekend in October brings a grape stomp, grape-spitting and cork-tossing contests to the Wollersheim Winery. There's also a food tent, a wine garden, and winery tours. | 800/847–9463.

Dining

Sauk Prairie Eagle Inn. American. This small brick café is at the edge of town where highways 78, 60, 188, and 12 intersect. Specials include roast pork, Polish sausage, and goulash. Breakfast served daily. | 644 Water St. | 608/643–4516 | $5–$12 | No credit cards.

Lodging

Prairie Garden Bed-and-Breakfast. This wood-and-brick farmhouse is set high on a hill and is shaded by lovely mature trees. Inside are cathedral ceilings and a stone fireplace. This B&B is a block from Lake Wisconsin and less than a mile and a half from downtown Prairie du Sac. Complimentary full breakfast. Cable TV. Some pets allowed. No smoking. | W13172 Rte. 188, Lodi | 608/592–5187 or 800/380–8427 | fax 608/592–5853 | prairiegarden@bigfoot.com | www.prairiegarden.com | 4 rooms | $55–$115 | MC, V.

Skyview Motel. This simple hotel along Highway 12 offers good value. Cable TV. | S9645 U.S. Hwy. 12, 53578 | 608/643–4344 | 19 rooms | $35–$65 | MC, V.

Victorian Treasure Inn. There are actually two large wood-frame Victorian homes making up this peaceful B&B, separated by a grassy expanse of well-tended lawn just a few blocks from historic downtown Lodi and 12 mi east of Prairie du Sac. Spacious verandas

© Artville

COW-CHIP THROWING COMPETITIONS

Wisconsinites love sports, especially ones that involve throwing things. Popular team events are football, baseball, basketball, and—of course—cow-chip throwing.

Although still a fairly new sport, cow-chip throwing contests are growing in popularity in Wisconsin as fast as you can flip a chip. The big event of the year—the Wisconsin State Cow-Chip Throw and Art Fair—is held each Labor Day weekend in Prairie du Sac. Residents of this town—which is, of course, surrounded by farmland—call the event one of the state's oldest traditions. Promoters say that each year championship chip flippers compete for the coveted prize of a trip to Beaver, Oklahoma, to attend the national championship, an event that draws people from all over the world. The cow-chip throw includes a corporate cow-chip challenge and chip chucking for kids. Anyone at least 16 years of age can compete, but they must follow the rules, such as: chips must be at least 6 inches in diameter; contestants must select chips from the wagon load provided by the Official Meadow Muffin Committee. Rules state: "To alter or shape in any way chips selected from the wagon subjects the contestant to a 25-ft penalty. When throwing, gloves will not be allowed. To get a better hold, you may lick your fingers before you throw."

wrap around the fronts of both 1890s homes, and guest rooms are decorated with a tasteful combination of antiques and modern reproductions. Complimentary breakfast. In-room hot tubs. No kids. No smoking. | 115 Prairie St., Lodi | 608/592–5199 or 800/859–5199 | fax 608/592–7147 | innkeeper@victoriantreasure.com | www.victoriantreasure.com | 7 suites | $115–$185 | D, MC, V.

RACINE

(Nearby town also listed: Kenosha)

Say "Racine" in Wisconsin, and locals automatically think of *kringle,* a delicious Danish pastry made in the shape of a giant letter *O.* Kringles come with a variety of tasty fillings and can be found in bakeries all over town. Kringles aren't Racine's only claim to fame, however; the city is on Lake Michigan and has a quaint marina with shops and restaurants, and several historic and architectural sites, such as a lighthouse built in 1880 and the S. C. Johnson Wax corporate headquarters designed by Wisconsin native Frank Lloyd Wright. Racine was founded in 1834.

Information: Racine County Convention and Visitors Bureau | 345 Main St., 53403 | 800/ 272–2463 | www.racine.org.

Attractions

Charles A. Wustum Museum of Fine Arts. An 1856 Italianate mansion houses permanent and changing art exhibits. It's on the northwest side of Racine in a suburban neighborhood five minutes from downtown. | 2519 Northwestern Ave. | 262/636–9177 | Free | Mon. and Thurs. 11–9; Tues., Wed., Fri., Sat. 11–5; Sun. 1–5; closed between exhibits.

Golden Rondelle Theater. Brought to Racine at the close of the 1964 World's Fair, the theater has a space-age design that works well with adjacent buildings in the the corporate headquarters complex, which was designed by Frank Lloyd Wright. The theater has an extensive film program. Tours of the S. C. Johnson Wax headquarters begin here. | S. C. Johnson Wax Guest Relations Center, 1525 Howe St., at 14th and Franklin Sts. | 262/260–2154 | Free | Films Fri. 9:15, 10, 11, 1:15, 2, 3; tours Fri. 9:15, 11, 1:15, 3. Reservations required.

Lakeview Stables. You can horseback ride or take hand-led pony rides through wooded areas, past a pond and a lake and over hills. | 4218 Seven Mile Rd. | 262/639–6141 | $5–15 trail rides | May–mid-Nov.

Racine County Historical Museum. This museum housed in the former Carnegie Public Library has extensive archives. | 701 S. Main St. | 262/636–3926 | Free | Museum: Tues.–Fri. 9–5, weekends 1–5. Archives: Tues. and Sat. 1–4.

Racine Zoological Gardens. The 32-acre zoo on the shore of Lake Michigan has dozens of exotic species ranging from brightly colored flamingoes to endangered animals like the snow leopard, orangutan, and white rhino. | 2131 N. Main St. (Rte. 20) | 262/636–9189 | Free | Memorial Day–Labor Day daily 9–8; winter hours 9–4.

Wind Point Lighthouse. Built in 1880, this 112-ft lighthouse is believed to be the oldest and tallest lighthouse still in use on the Great Lakes. | 345 Main St. | 262/634–3293 | Free | Daily.

ON THE CALENDAR

JULY: *Salmon-A-Rama.* One of the world's largest freshwater fishing events takes place on the second and third weekends in July and includes food and entertainment. | 800/ 272–2463.

Dining

Blue Diamond Family Restaurant. American. Chicken stir-fry is the most popular item at this restaurant, but an extensive menu offers a wide variety of other dishes ranging from burgers to steaks. There's also a Friday-night fish fry. Breakfast served daily. | 3925 Durand Ave. | 262/554–8555 | $6–$9 | D, DC, MC, V.

Great Wall. Pan-Asian. Lanterns and Chinese art decorate this large restaurant on the south side of town. On the menu are such standards as sesame chicken and Happy Family, and a dish with chicken, beef, shrimp, and scallops. | 6025 Washington Ave. | 262/886–9700 | $15–$20 | AE, D, MC, V | Closed Mon. No lunch.

Hob Nob. American. This candlelit restaurant on Lake Michigan has an intimate dining room, as well as larger dining areas, all with water views. Dishes range from steaks and pork chops to lobster and fish. | 277 S. Sheridan Rd. | 262/552–8008 | $18–$25 | AE, DC, MC, V | No lunch.

Lodging

Christmas House Bed & Breakfast. This huge—nearly 10,000-square-ft—Classic Revival mansion was built in 1893. Much of the interior is original, from the woodwork, crown molding, and coffered cherry-wood ceiling in the library, and the stained-glass windows made in England. Rooms can be rented individually or the entire house can be booked for special events. Common areas include a front parlor, library, dining room, and living room. Some rooms have whirlpools, one has a fireplace. Complimentary breakfast. Microwaves, refrigerators, cable TV. | 116 10th St. | 262/633–0014 | fax 262/–633–9876 | 5 rooms | $75–$225 | AE, MC, V.

Days Inn. This two-story motel is on the Root River, in a quiet wooded area on the northeast side of town. There's a fireplace in the lobby. Restaurant, bar, picnic area, room service. In-room data ports, in-room hot tubs (in suites), cable TV. Pool. Laundry facilities. Business services, free parking. Pets allowed. | 3700 Northwestern Ave. | 262/637–9311 | fax 262/637–4575 | 109 rooms, 3 suites | $49–$69 | AE, D, DC, MC, V.

Knights Inn. In all four single-story buildings here, you can park in front of your room and enter directly from the parking lot. The motel, built in the late 1980s, is in a commercial area with restaurants and two shopping malls nearby. Complimentary Continental breakfast. Cable TV, in-room VCRs and movies available. Pets allowed. | 1149 Oakes Rd. | 262/886–6667 or 800/843–5644 | fax 262/886–6667, ext. 136 | 107 rooms | $45–$57 | AE, D, DC, MC, V.

REEDSBURG

MAP 11, C6

(Nearby towns also listed: Baraboo, Prairie du Sac)

Established in 1850 and named after D. C. Reed, who established the sawmill that enabled settlers to have cut lumber with which to build permanent homes in the area. Today, Reedsburg is a world leader in butter production. The town is also home to a Norman Rockwell museum which contains some 4,000 pieces of the artist's work—one of the largest collections in the world. Reedsburg is at the southern end of the 22-mi 400 State Trail, a popular biking/hiking path that parallels the Baraboo River on a resurfaced former railroad bed.

Information: **Reedsburg Area Chamber of Commerce** | Box 142, 53959-0142 | 800/844–3507 | www.reedsburg.com.

Attractions

Carr Valley Cheese Factory. Head 12 mi west of Reedsburg past rolling hills and corn fields to this factory where you can learn how cheese is made. | S3797 Rte. G, La Valle | 608/986–2781 | Free | Mon.–Sat. 8–4.

400 State Trail. This 22-mi former railroad bed along the Baraboo River is popular for biking and hiking. In Elroy, it connects with the Elroy–Sparta Trail, creating an additional 100 mi of trail. You can get state bike passes (required) at the Reedsburg train depot where the trail can also be accessed. Hiking is free. | 240 Railroad St. | 800/844–3507 | $3 daily bike pass | Daily.

Museum of Norman Rockwell Art. This museum's more than 4,000-piece collection of works by the famous *Saturday Evening Post* artist is one of the world's largest. A video on Rockwell's life is shown hourly. | 227 S. Park St. (Rte. 33) | 608/524–2123 or 800/844–3507 | $5; special rates for senior citizens, kids, and groups | Mid-May–late Oct., Mon.–Sat. 9–5, Sun. 10–5; call for hrs. rest of year.

Park Lane Model Railroad Museum. This model train museum displays more than 3,000 models of trains, farm tractors, fire trucks, and cars. | S2083 Herig Rd. | 608/254–8050 | $2.50 | By appointment only.

Pioneer Log Village and Museum. Three miles east of Reedsburg and operated by the Reedsburg Historical Society, this 11-building complex is comprised of a school, a church, a blacksmith shop, and a country store dating from 1850. It's 3 mi east of Reedsburg via Route 33. | Rtes. 23 and 33 | 800/844–3507 | Donations accepted | Memorial Day–late Sept., weekends 1–4.

ON THE CALENDAR

JUNE: *Butter Festival.* This celebration has nothing to do with butter, but there's oodles of entertainment. You'll find a carnival, a parade, a tractor pull, a demolition derby, mud races, food, entertainment, arts, and crafts at Nishan Park on Route H on the 6 days leading up to Father's Day. | 800/844–3507.

Dining

Ende House Brewery Restaurant. American. Prime rib and blackened steaks are the most popular items in this Victorian painted lady. You can watch beer being brewed while you dine. | 1020 E. Main St. | 608/524–8600 | $9–$22 | MC, V | Closed Mon. in Oct.–Apr. No lunch weekends.

Lodging

Lavina Inn Bed & Breakfast. This colonial Queen Anne was built at the turn of the 20th century and has original chandeliers and hardwood floors. There is a wraparound porch where breakfast is served. The inn is across from City Park and close to Spring Green attractions. Complimentary breakfast. No TV. | 325 3rd St. | 608/524–6706 | www.lavina.com | 3 rooms | $80–$85 | MC, V.

RHINELANDER

MAP 11, D3

(Nearby towns also listed: Antigo, Crandon)

If it's Northwoods beauty you're seeking, check out Rhinelander. With more than 230 lakes within a 12-mi radius, water routes established the city as a logging center in 1880. Today local waterways help support the town's main industry, paper making. Recreational opportunities abound. Outside the chamber of commerce, there's a 10-ft replica of the town mascot, the Hodag, a fabled green beast with horns.

Information: **Rhinelander Area Chamber of Commerce** | Box 795, 54501-0795 | 800/236–4386 | info@ci.rhinelander.wi.us | www.ci.rhinelander.wi.us.

Attractions

Consolidated Papers Forest Tour. This 16-mi self-guided auto tour east of Rhinelander educates visitors about forestry. In winter you can use the road as a ski trail. It's ¼ mi west of U.S. 45 and 8. | 1825 Hwy. 7 E, Monico | 715/422–3789 | Free | Daily.

Northwood Golf Course. This beautiful 18-hole course opened in 1989 has tight, narrow fairways. | 6301 U.S. 8 W | 715/282–6565 | Late Mar.–late Oct.

Pioneer Park. Home to the Logging Museum Complex which has exhibits on how loggers plied their trade, and also includes the Civilian Conservation Corps Museum, the restored Soo Line Depot, and an old schoolhouse. | On Business Hwy. 8 and Rte. 47 | 715/369–5004 or 800/236–4386 | Donations accepted | Mid-May–Labor Day, daily 10–5.

Rhinelander Historical Society Museum. This Colonial Revival home and former boardinghouse was built in 1898. There is an extensive collection of writings and artifacts showcasing community history. Check out the replica of a World War I soldier's bedroom. | 9 S. Pelham St., 54501 | 715/282–6120 | Free | Jun.–Aug., Mon.–Fri. 9–5; Sept.–May, Tues. 10–4.

ON THE CALENDAR

JULY: *Hodag Country Festival.* This outdoor country-music festival celebrating the fabled green beast is held on the second weekend in July. | 800/762–3803.
OCT.: *Oktoberfest.* German food, music, and beer downtown on the second weekend in October. | 800/236–4386.

Dining

Fireside Supper Club. American. Steak, barbecued ribs, and seafood attract regulars to this busy supper club overlooking Town Line Lake. | 6012 Hwy. K | 715/369–4717 | Reservations not accepted Fri. | $7–$23 | AE, D, DC, MC, V | Closed Sun. No lunch.

Fleur's South 17 Supper Club. American. Steaks, seafood, chops, ribs, and pasta draw crowds to this restaurant overlooking Lake Julia. | 3220 Boyce Dr. | 715/369–1743 | Reservations not accepted Fri. | $7–$29 | No credit cards | No lunch.

Rhinelander Café. American. Diving helmets, antique ship parts, ropes, brass wheels from ships, and cocktail tables made of ship hatch doors set a nautical tone, but the most popular dishes here are prime rib and steak covered with peppers and onions. Kids' menu. | 33 N. Brown St. | 715/362–2918 | $9–$26 | D, DC, MC, V.

Tula's. American. This casual, family-style restaurant in the Oneida Mall offers an all-you-can-eat fish fry on Wednesday and Friday, as well as all-you-can-eat chicken dinner with fried or baked chicken on Sunday. The menu includes pasta favorites such as lasagna and spaghetti. Open-air dining on a patio with views of the Wisconsin River. Kids' menu. Sunday brunch. | 232 S. Courtney Dr. | 715/369–5248 | $10–$15 | D, MC, V.

Lodging

Americinn. Flower beds and a putting green front this motel. A deer-antler chandelier hangs in the colonial-style lobby. Complimentary Continental breakfast. Some refrigerators, cable TV, in-room VCRs available. Pool. Hot tub, sauna. Laundry facilities. Business services. Pets allowed. | 648 W. Kemp St. | 715/369–9600 | fax 715/369–9613 | 52 rooms (3 with shower only), 10 suites | $70 | AE, D, DC, MC, V.

Best Western Claridge. This two-story brick motel in close to the courthouse and downtown shopping. Out front is a trout pond, inside a fireplace adorns the lobby. Restaurant, bar, room service, cable TV. Pool. Hot tub. Gym. Laundry facilities, laundry service. Business services, airport shuttle. Pets allowed. | 70 N. Stevens St. | 715/362–7100 | fax 715/362–3883 | www.claridge-bestwestern.com | 81 rooms, 4 suites | $66 | AE, D, DC, MC, V.

Breezy Point Resort. Located on Lake Thompson, this resort has one- to three-bedroom cottages dating from 1918, still with the original log construction exterior. It's an ideal family spot, with a swing set, basketball hoops, volleyball, badminton, and horseshoes. At the start and end of the season two-night minimum stays are available; the rest of the year weekly rentals only. Beach, boating. | 3510 Cedar La. | 715/369–0550 | 7 cottages | $60–$100 per night, $350–$550 per week | No credit cards | Closed Oct.–May.

Duck's Haven Resort. This resort has three two-bedroom cottages and a duplex that was a former boathouse, situated along 80-acre Long Lake, 15 mi from Rhinelander. Each cottage has access to its own boat. Beach, dock, boating, fishing. | 7553 Rustic La. | 715/272–1718 | 4 cottages | $50–$55 per night, $300–$325 per week | No credit cards | Closed Dec.–Apr.

Holiday Acres. One thousand acres surround this rustic two-story wood-and-brick lodge and its cottages on Lake Thompson just 4 mi east of Rhinelander. Some cottages are more modern than others; all come with their own parking and boat, and some have screened-in porches. There are cross-country ski trails on the property. Bar, dining room, picnic area, room service. Kitchenettes in cottages, cable TV, in-room VCRs and movies available. Pool. Tennis. Beach, water sports, boating, bicycles. Cross-country skiing, snowmobiling. Playground. Business services, airport shuttle. Pets allowed. | 4060 S. Shore Dr. | 715/369–1500 or 800/261–1500 | fax 715/369–3665 | hacres@newnorth.net | www.holidayacres.com | 28 lodge rooms, 28 cottages | $94 | AE, D, DC, MC, V.

Holiday Inn. This member of the chain is four blocks from downtown in a commercial area. The comfortable lobby has a fireplace, rustic furniture, and a brass chandelier. Restaurant, bar, room service. Cable TV, in-room VCRs and movies available. Pool. Hot tub. Gym. Video games. Laundry facilities. Business services, airport shuttle. | 668 W. Kemp St. | 715/369–3600 | fax 715/369–3600 ext. 276 | www.basshotels.com/holiday-inn | 102 rooms | $66 | AE, D, DC, MC, V.

Kafka's Resort. Beautifully landscaped grounds surround these modern brick-and-aluminum-sided cottages, which cover 15 acres. Some cottages have oak floors, cedar closets, porches, and large picture windows overlooking Lake George. All come with a boat. No maid service. Bar, picnic area. No air-conditioning, kitchenettes, cable TV. Beach, boating, fishing. Snowmobiling. Playground. Airport shuttle. | 4281 W. Lake George Rd. | 715/369–2929 or 800/426–6674 | www.kafkas-resort.com | 10 cottages | $550 (7–day minimum stay) | No credit cards.

RICE LAKE

MAP 11, B3

(Nearby towns also listed: Chippewa Falls, Eau Claire, Ladysmith, Spooner)

Founded as a logging camp in the 1850s, Rice Lake thrives today with recreational activities from fishing and hiking to golfing and gaming. Tourism has supplanted logging as the area's number-one industry, and visitors come by the thousands to appreciate Rice Lake's largely unspoiled lakeshores and woodlands. The area is criss-crossed with snowmobile and cross-country ski trails, and on cold winter nights, the northern lights can often be seen playing across the star-strewn sky.

Information: Rice Lake Area Chamber of Commerce and Tourism Barron County | 37 S. Main St., 54868-2226 | 800/523–6318 | www.chamber.rice-lake.wi.us.

Attractions

Bruce Museum. This museum and genealogical research center is in the Old Bruce Newsletter Building, headquarters of Bruce's first newspaper. You can see the burn holes from the hot lead of the presses on the museum's hardwood floors. The museum changes its exhibit yearly. It is also open by appointment. | 155 River Ave. East, Bruce | 715/868–5475 | Free | Memorial Day—Labor Day, Mon.–Wed., Fri. 10–4.

Red Barn Summer Theater. There are evening performances of plays and musicals. | 2247 22nd St. | 800/523–6318 | $9–$10 | June–Aug.

Pioneer Village Museum. 28 historic buildings from around Barron county have been moved to the grounds of this museum complex; they include a steepled church, an old train depot, and a sod farmstead home. You can arrange for a guided tour, or explore the buildings on your own. The museum is just 6 mi south of Rice Lake in nearby Cameron. | 1870 13½ St., Cameron | 715/458–2841 | Adults $2, kids $1 | Thurs.–Sun. 1–5; Closed Labor Day–May 31.

Rice Lake Speedway. Stock and late-model racecars roar around the ⅓ mi clay track here. The raceway was built in 1952 and has been a local entertainment focal point ever since. | 2002 22½ Ave. | 715/736–1163 | Admission varies per event | Closed Sept.–Apr.

ON THE CALENDAR
JUNE: *Aquafest.* Ten days of softball and golf tournaments, a parade, bands, food, and arts-and-crafts shows all lead up to Father's Day. | 800/523–6318.
JULY: *County Fair.* There's the usual carnival, along with a demolition derby, harness racing, truck pulls, tractor pulls, 4-H shows, and animals galore at the Barron County fairgrounds in late July. | 800/523–6318.

Dining
Kid's Korner Pizza. Italian. Pizzas, salads, and subs (both hot and cold) all come in exceptionally large portions here. A favorite is "pizza fries"—a pizza crust topped with garlic butter and cheese, cut in strips, and served with tomato sauce. | 322 N. Main St. | 715/234–6531 | $2–$20 | No credit cards | Closed Sun.

Lehman's Supper Club. American. Steaks, prime rib, seafood, homemade soups, and popovers are served on linen-topped and candlelit tables. | 2911 S. Main St. | 715/234–2428 | $10–$25 | AE, D, DC, MC, V | Closed Mon.

Lodging
Americinn. A two-story country-style motel with fabulous Norwegian rosemaling trim, and a fireplace in the large lobby. Complimentary Continental breakfast. In-room data ports, some refrigerators, in-room hot tubs in suites, cable TV. Pool. Hot tub. Business services. | 2906 Pioneer Ave. S | 715/234–9060 or 800/634–3444 (reservations) | fax 715/234–9060 | 36 rooms, 7 suites | $65–$71 | AE, D, DC, MC, V.

Canoe Bay Inn and Cottages. Located on 200 forested acres with two small lakes, this Prairie-style lodging complex is 18 mi southeast of Rice Lake. Every room has a fireplace and a private deck. Restaurant, picnic area, complimentary breakfast, room service. Microwaves available, refrigerators, in-room hot-tubs, in-room VCRs and movies, no room phones. Spa. Dock, boating. Business services. No kids. No smoking. | Rte. 1, Chetek | 715/924–4594 or 800/568–1995 | fax 715/924–2078 | mail@canoebay.com | www.canoebay.com | 5 rooms, 10 cottages, 1 lodge | rooms $270–$285, $310–$420 cottages, $700 lodge | D, MC, V.

Currier's Lakeview. This chalet-style motel is on a wooded 4-acre peninsula on Rice Lake, next to a 10-acre park. Each room is different, and all have themed decor such as fishing, logging, and hummingbird haven. Picnic area, complimentary Continental breakfast. Some kitchenettes, refrigerators, cable TV. Beach, dock, boating. Snowmobiling. Airport shuttle. Pets allowed. | 2010 E. Sawyer St. | 715/234–7474 or 800/433–5253 | www.wisconsintourism.com | 19 rooms | $53–$104 | AE, D, MC, V.

Evergreen. This one-story wood motel dating from the 1900s has a small, cozy lobby with a gas fireplace. It's 1 mi from the Indianhead Speedway. Complimentary Continental breakfast. Cable TV. Business services. | 1801 W. Knapp St. | 715/234–1088 | fax 715/234–1088 | 20 rooms, 1 suite | $55–$66 | AE, D, MC, V.

Hemlock Lake Resort. Small, simple cabins are surrounded by trees and a 400-acre lake with four islands. Hemlock Lake is part of a chain that includes Red Cedar, Hemlock, and Balsam lakes. Cabins accommodate up to eight people. Nearby is golfing, hiking, and bicycling. Kitchenettes, refrigerators, TV in common area. Hiking, beach, dock, water sports, boating, fishing. | 28th St., off Hwy. 48 | 715/234–8232 | 6 rooms | $70 per night, $325 per week | No credit cards | Closed Oct.–Apr.

Red Cedar Springs Resort. Eight two- and three-bedroom cottages make up this cozy resort on Lake Chetac, about 20 mi north of Rice Lake on County Road M. Four cottages overlook the lake; two are tucked away in the woods; and two others are between the woods and the water. The lake is stocked with pan fish, walleye, and northern pike. There's a large play area for small kids, as well as volleyball, basketball, and horseshoes. Weekly rentals only. Kitchenettes, refrigerators, TV in common area. Hiking, beach, dock, boating. | 2985 E. Shore Dr., Birchwood | 715/354–7854 or 800/236–7854 | www.wisvacations.com/red-cedarspringsresort | 8 rooms | $460–$580 per week | No credit cards.

Super 8. There's a breakfast nook and a fireplace in the rustic lobby of this simple chain motel about 14 mi south of Rice Lake. Complimentary breakfast. In-room data ports, cable TV. Pool. Hot tub. Business services. | 115 2nd St., Chetek | 715/924–4888 | fax 715/924–2538 | www.super8.com | 40 rooms | $49–$72 | AE, D, DC, MC, V.

SO FRESH THEY SQUEAK

No trip to "America's Dairyland" would be complete without a visit to a cheese factory. And no visit to a cheese factory would be complete without sampling some of the state's famous cheese curds. Sure you can find cheese curds in the refrigerated dairy sections of food stores across the state, but they are not nearly as delicious as fresh cheese curds bought directly from a cheese factory.

Cheese curds are small, oblong pieces of cheese taken out of the production process before being pressed into blocks or wedges, then aged. They can be made from different kinds of cheese, and may be bright to dull orange or off-white in color, but most commonly they are Cheddar.

Fresh cheese curds are so popular and customer demand can be so high that many factories schedule specific days for making the curds. When visiting a cheese factory, be sure to take a tour if available, then ask how fresh their cheese curds are. If they are truly fresh, they will be warm, have just a hint of salt, and will squeak when you sink your teeth into them. If they are less fresh, not only will they not squeak, but they may taste a bit too salty, and will be drier than their fresh counterparts.

Fresh or refrigerated, cheese curds usually come in bags, and the pieces are generally pressed together. The best way to eat them is to just pry the pieces apart with your fingers—and enjoy!

© Corbis

RICHLAND CENTER

MAP 11, C6

(Nearby towns also listed: La Crosse, Sparta)

Settled in 1849, this pretty town sits in a countryside crisscrossed with rivers and narrow valleys, and punctuated with steep, wooded hills. Architect Frank Lloyd Wright was born here in 1867 and one of his buildings remains. A scenic drive 45 mi to the northwest leads to the Lower Coulee Region, one of the more preserved areas of the state, where the Mississippi River traverses prairies, meadows, pine forests, and rolling hills, ending at Coon Valley.

Information: **Richland (County) Area Chamber/Main Street Partnership** | Box 128, 53581-0128 | 800/422–1318 | rcedc@mwt.net.

Attractions

A. D. German Warehouse. This massive redbrick-and-concrete warehouse was designed for a local commodities wholesaler by Frank Lloyd Wright in 1917. It is one of Wright's few public buildings, and the only example from that decade in which he employed sculptural ornamentation. Wright called this building his Mayan temple. | 300 S. Church St. | 608/647–2808 or 800/422–1318 | $5 | May–Oct., by appointment only.

Eagle Cave Natural Park. This 150-acre privately owned park has the state's largest onyx cave, as well as picnic areas, an outdoor campground, and a small lake for swimming and fishing. Guided tours are offered in summer, and kids' groups camp in the cave in winter. It's 14 mi southwest of Richland Center. | 16320 Cavern Ln., Blue River | 608/537–2988 | Tours $5; special rates for kids | Memorial Day–Labor Day, Tues.–Sun. 10–5; winter camping in cave mid-Sept.–mid-May for kids' groups only.

ON THE CALENDAR

JUNE: *June Dairy Day/Farm Dairy Breakfast.* This dairy breakfast featuring pancakes, sausage, and all sorts of dairy treats including yogurt, milk, cheeses, and cheese curds, is held at a different Richland Center area dairy farm each year on the second Saturday in June. | 800/422–1318.

JUNE: *Wisconsin High School State Rodeo Finals.* Over 7,000 spectators enjoy 13 different rodeo events with contestants from much of the Midwest as well as Canada at this Richland County fairgrounds competition on the third weekend in June. | 800/422–1318.

OCT.: *Centerfest.* The first weekend in October brings open houses at area apple orchards, historic reenactments, an antique classic car show, a bike tour, a chile cook-off, and sidewalk sales. | 800/422–1318.

Dining

Peaches Restaurant. American. A Friday-night seafood buffet and a Saturday-night prime rib and seafood buffet make this rural area restaurant a popular spot. | 28295 E. U.S. Hwy. 14 | 608/647–8886 | $5–$16 | MC, V | Closed Mon. No dinner Sun.

Lodging

Lamb's Inn Bed & Breakfast. This restored farmhouse from the late 1800s sits on 180 acres in Little Willow valley. There is also a modern two-bedroom loft cottage on the property available for rent. Discover country living here with a fresh spring, wandering cats, dogs, and goats, and an old-fashioned rope swing. There's a full kitchen in the cottage. Complimentary breakfast. No room phones, no TV. | 23761 Misslich Dr. | 608/585–4301 | fax 608/585–2242 | www.lambs-inn.com | 4 rooms, 1 cottage | $85–$150 | D, MC, V.

ST. CROIX FALLS

(Nearby town also listed: Hudson)

St. Croix Falls was first established as a logging and milling town in the 1840s. Expansion followed the construction of a dam and powerhouse; today businesses line downtown streets. Wisconsin's first state park, Interstate Park, is at the edge of the town, which is also the headquarters of the St. Croix National Scenic Riverway.

Information: **Polk County Information Center** | 710 Rte. 35 South, 54024 | 800/222–7655 | polkcountyinfo@win.bright.net | www.polkcountytourism.com.

Attractions

Crex Meadows Wildlife Area. Wildlife fills this 30,000-acre prairie and marshland, preserved by the Wisconsin department of natural resources. Rare prairie plants provide habitat for 246 species of native and migrating birds such as sandhill cranes, trumpeter swans, and herons which nest here. Maps outlining self-guided auto tours are available at the interpretive center, which is 25 mi north of St. Croix and 1 mi north of Grantsburg. | DNR Ranger Station in Grantsburg | 715/463–2899 | Free | Daily 24 hrs.

Gandy Dancer State Bicycle Trail. This 47-mi state bike trail runs from St. Croix Falls to Danbury. You can access the trail and get a biking pass (required) at the Polk County Information Center, at the southern end of the trail. In winter, the trail is ideal for snowmobiling. | 710 Hwy. 35 S | 715/483–1410 or 800/222–7655 | Free for hiking, $3 for bike pass | Daily.

Governor Knowles State Forest. This 55-mi-long, 2-mi-wide, 32,500-acre forest is a buffer zone for the St. Croix National Scenic Riverway. Adjacent to the state forest are more than 100,000 acres of county forests and two large wildlife areas: Fish Lake Wildlife Area and Crex Meadow Wildlife Area. Governor Knowles State Forest, named for a conservation-minded governor, is good for canoeing on the St. Croix River. There are about 20 access points along the river; the headquarters is in Grantsburg, 25 mi north of St. Croix Falls. | Rte. 70 | 715/463–2898 | www.dnr.state.wi.us/org/land/forestry/StateForests/index.htm | Free; permits required for some recreational trails | Daily.

Interstate State Park. Created in 1900, this 1,400-acre park in St. Croix Falls was Wisconsin's first state park. Visit the Dalles of the St. Croix River, a deep gorge carved by the St. Croix River, and hike the Pothole Trail to see unusual holes drilled in rocks by glacial waters. The park's Ice Age Interpretive Center displays photographs, murals, a film, and other information about Ice Age glaciers at Lake O' the Dalles in the park. You'll also find riverside picnic areas, a family campground, a beach with swimming, and a bathhouse. It's two blocks south of U.S. 8 on Route 35, at the south edge of town. | Rte. 35 | 715/483–3747 | www.dnr.state.wi.us | $7 nonresidents, $5 residents | Daily.

St. Croix National Scenic Riverway. This federal preserve encompasses 250 mi of the St. Croix and Namekagon rivers. The visitor center, at the north end of town, has exhibits about logging and early settlers. Canoe rentals are available and the staff can help plan canoe trips on the riverway which range in difficulty from beginner to moderate. | Massachusetts and Hamilton Sts. | 715/483–3284 | Free; fees for canoe rentals only | Memorial Day–Labor Day, daily.

Trollhaugen Ski Resort. In operation since 1950, this 100-acre ski area 3 mi south of St. Croix Falls has a vertical drop of 260 ft and 22 runs, all covered by snowmaking machines and illuminated for night skiing. Cross-country skiing is also available. It's 3 mi south on Route 35 to Dresser, then 1 mi east on Route F. | 2232 100th Ave., Dresser | 715/755–2955 or 800/826–7166 | www.trollhaugen.com | $16–$29 (includes special rates for senior citizens, kids, and groups) | Nov.–Mar.

ON THE CALENDAR

FEB.: *Candlelight Ski.* Cross-country ski, hike, or snowshoe by candlelight, then warm up with a fire and hot beverage at the end of the trail in Interstate Park on the second Saturday in February. | 800/222–7655 or 715/483–3747.

Dining

Wayne's Restaurant. American. This restaurant offers family-style dining and is known for homemade soups, barbecued ribs, and pies; strawberry pie is the house specialty. Counter seating available. Open 24 hours. | 1961 U.S. Hwy. 8 | 715/483–3121 | $3–$10 | AE, D, MC, V.

Lodging

Dalles House Motel. This two-story motel at the edge of town is next to Interstate State Park. Restaurants and a nightclub are nearby. In-room data ports, some in-room hot tubs, cable TV. Pool. Sauna. Laundry facilities. Business services. | 726 Vincent St. S | 715/483–3206 or 800/341–8000 (reservations) | fax 715/483–3207 | 50 rooms | $43–$85 | AE, D, DC, MC, V.

Wissahickon Farms Country Inn. This inn looks like a rustic frontier store. Accommodations consist of a living room, kitchen, and bedroom and can fit up to four people. The inn is about a mile east from the center of town. Complimentary breakfast. In-room VCR. | 2263 Maple Dr. | 715/483–3986 | 1 room | $125 | MC, V.

ST. GERMAIN

MAP 11, D3

(Nearby towns also listed: Eagle River, Woodruff)

St. Germain was named after a French soldier in the late 1600s who married an Ojibwe woman and settled with the tribe. This town is home to the Snowmobile Racing Hall of Fame, and there is also an expansive network of cross-country skiing trails in the surrounding Nicolet National Forest and American Legion State Forest. A short drive to the south is Three Lakes, where you can take a winery tour and visit a local history museum.

Information: **St. Germain Chamber of Commerce** | Box 155, 54558-0155 | 800/727–7203 | chamber@st-germain.com | www.st-germain.com.

Attractions

International Snowmobile Racing Hall of Fame. There's a complete display of historic race sleds, including some world-championship sleds. Clothing, photos, and films illustrate races from the 1960s to today. Gift shop. | 6035 Hwy. 70 E | 715/542–4463 | Free | Mon.–Fri. 8:30–4:30, weekends by appointment.

ON THE CALENDAR

SEPT.: *Fall Fest.* A scarecrow contest, hayrides, a farmers' market, an arts-and-crafts show, food, and entertainment in Community Park on the third Saturday in September. | 800/727–7203.

Dining

Clearview Supper Club. American. Dine on ribs, prime rib, roast duck, or steaks at this log-cabin supper club that sits alongside a snowmobile trail. | 8599 Big St. Germain Dr. | 715/542–3474 | Reservations not accepted | $9–$19 | D, MC, V | Closed Tues. No lunch.

Spang's. Italian. You'll be seated on polished oak church pews and offered such favorites as pizza and fettuccine alfredo at this restaurant between St. Germain and nearby Eagle River. You can also eat in an enclosed gazebo garden room. Kids' menu. | 6229 Rte. 70 E | 715/479–9400 | Reservations not accepted | $8–$16 | AE, D, DC, MC, V | No lunch.

Lodging

Esch's Serenity Bay. Log cabins, each with a waterfront view and a boat line the shores of Little St. Germain Lake, 2 mi east of town. Grounds are attractive, with many plants, and, during the summer, they hang baskets of flowers from the cabin doors. No maid service—there is an additional charge of $3 per bed for linens if you do not bring your own. Picnic area. No air-conditioning, kitchenettes, in-room data ports, cable TV. Tennis. Beach, dock, water sports, boating. Playground. Business services. | 1276 Halberstadt Rd. | 715/479–8866 | eschsbay@aol.com | www.serenitybay.com | 9 cottages | $950–$1,250 (7–day minimum stay) | MC, V | Closed Nov.–Mar.

Krings' Retreat. This five-bedroom frame home on Dam Lake can accommodate up to 12 people. There are two sets of living quarters, separated by a great room. Enjoy the lake from a deck or relax by the fireplace. Some per-night rentals available; call for details. In-room VCR. Beach, boating, fishing. | 5100 Cooper La. | 715/542–3300 | www.nobody@kringsretreat.com | 5 rooms | $500–$1,200 | No credit cards.

St. Germain Bed-and-Breakfast. Some 19,000 acres of the Veteran's National Forest surround this three-story rustic 1970s wooden home surrounding by pine trees. A large family room serves as a common area with a TV, VCR, refrigerator, microwave, and fireplace. It's halfway between Eagle River and Minocqua. Complimentary full breakfast. Pool. Hot tub. Tennis. Snowmobiling. | 6255 Rte. 70 E | 715/479–8007 or 888/479–8007 | fax 715/479–8007 | jjoseph@newnorth.net | 4 rooms | $80–$85 | MC, V.

SAUK CITY

MAP 11, C6

(Nearby towns also listed: Baraboo, Madison, Prairie du Sac)

Sauk City is Wisconsin's oldest incorporated village (it was incorporated in 1854). With its sister village, Prairie du Sac, it lies in the heart of some of the most striking countryside in the upper Midwest. Rolling hills, pastoral meadows, dramatic bluffs, forests, lakes, and streams make it a popular spot year-round.

Information: Sauk Prairie Area Chamber of Commerce | 207 Water St., Suite D, 53583 | 608/643–4168 or 800/68–EAGLE | speagle@bankpds.com | www.saukprairie.com.

Attractions

Blackhawk River Runs. You can rent canoes (and arrange for shuttle service) here for do-it-yourself canoe trips on the Wisconsin River. Put-ins along the river allow for trips ranging from 9 to 90 mi and take one to five days. The company has a shuttle service for longer trips. | On Hwy. Y about 3 mi south of Sauk City in Mezomanie | 608/643–6724 | $32 per day; prices vary for overnight trips | May 15–Sept. 30, daily.

Pharmacy Museum. This historic building, dating from the 1890s, was moved to its present location in the year 2000. You can see what a Reconstruction Era post-and-beam, false-front pharmacy looked like, as well as seeing other historic items related to Sauk City. | 616 Water St. | 800/68–EAGLE | Free | Memorial Day–Labor Day, weekends 12–4 or by appointment; Labor Day–Memorial Day, by appointment only.

St. Norberts Catholic Church. The oldest Catholic church in Wisconsin, St. Norberts is on a hill about 1 mi outside Sauk City and has great views of the surrounding countryside. | 8944 Hwy. Y, Roxbury | 608/643–6611 | Free | Daily.

ON THE CALENDAR

OCT.: *Walden West Fest.* This literary festival held in Free Thinkers Park, at Polk and Jefferson streets on the second Sunday in October celebrates the life of local author August Derleth who wrote about 150 books and is said to be the state's most prolific author. Events include tours of sites related to Derleth's life, speakers, and literary information. | 800/68–EAGLE.

Dining

Dorf Haus. German. The motto here is why rock and roll when you can polka? The area's largest restaurant, this German-American supper club is filled with antiques, stained glass, and paintings of famous German castles and kings. Specialties include German dishes, fish fry, and seafood. Kids' menu, banquet facilities, entertainment, outdoor dining, dinner theater. Sunday brunch. Bavarian smorgasbord dinners on first and third Monday from June to October. The restaurant is 2 mi southeast of Sauk City. | 8931 Hwy. Y, Roxbury | 608/643–3980 | $5–$17 | D, MC, V | Closed Mon. and Tues. No lunch.

Gathering Restaurant. American. You can sit at the counter or at one of the booths or tables of this family-owned restaurant that offers homemade bread, such standards as roast beef and roast pork, and breakfast at any time of the day. It's 1 mi from the heart of town. Dinner ends early, at 5, except on Friday when the restaurant stays open until 8. | E11394 Hwy. 12 | 608/643–3473 | $4–$8 | AE, D, MC, V.

Green Acres Restaurant. American. This restaurant at the edge of town near the Wisconsin River was once a dance hall but now looks more like a stately old home. Specialties are prime rib, ribs, and steaks. | 7438 Hwy. 78 | 608/643–5159 | $10–$15 | AE, D, DC, MC, V | No lunch.

Lodging

Cedarberry Inn Motel. This locally owned motel is 1 mi west of downtown in a commercial area on Hwy. 12, within ½ mi of several restaurants and shops. Some in-room hot tubs, cable TV. Pool. Hot tub. Business services. Game room. | 855 Phillips Blvd. (on Hwy. 12) | 608/643–6625 or 800/342–6625 | fax 608/643–6459 | www.baraboonow.com/cedarberry/ | 38 rooms, 6 suites | $53–$80 | AE, D, DC, MC, V.

Highlander Motel. This small motel with 11 acres of nicely landscaped grounds, lots of flowers, and a friendly staff is in a rural area 10 mi north of town and 1½ mi from Devil's Lake State Park. Picnic area. Cable TV. | S5230 Hwy. 12, Baraboo | 608/356–4410 or 888/929–4410 | www.baraboonow.com/highlander/ | 10 rooms | $55–$65 | AE, D, DC, MC, V.

Skyview Motel. This 1970s brick motel 2 mi north of town is surrounded by trees and has walking paths and a kids' play area on its 6-acre property. Some in-room hot tubs, cable TV. | S65 9645 Hwy. 12, Prarie du Sac | 608/643–4344 | 18 rooms, 1 suite | $35–$65 | AE, D, MC, V.

SAYNER

MAP 11, D2

(Nearby towns also listed: Boulder Junction, Eagle River, Manitowish Waters)

Located in Vilas County, where lakes outnumber towns, Sayner is a perfect place for water sports and bonding with nature. The area that surrounds Sayner has more than 1,300 lakes, 73 rivers and streams, and a half-million acres of forestland. A historical museum with Native American artifacts, logging memorabilia, and the world's first snowmobile is located in town.

Information: Sayner-Star Lake Chamber of Commerce | Box 191, 54560-0191 | 888/722–3789.

Attractions

Vilas County Historical Museum. There are more than 48,000 items here, including the first snowmobile ever built. There is a fishing guides exhibit from 1890 to 1960, a vintage boat display, and antique musical instruments. | 217 Main St. | 715/542–3388 or 888/722–3789 | $2 | Mid-May–Sept., daily 10–4.

SEPT.: *Colorama Brunch and Craft Show.* Local artists and craftspeople show and sell their work in the downtown Sayner Community Building on the last Sunday in September. | 888/722–3789.

Dining

Sayner Pub. American. A large selection of sandwiches and pizza are served in this family-style restaurant and bar. The Friday-night fish fry keeps the staff hopping. When the Green Bay Packers play, the three TVs at the bar are the main attraction. | 310 Main St. | 715/542–3647 | $3–$11 | MC, V | Breakfast served on weekends only.

Lodging

Froelich's Sayner Lodge. For rustic comfort and tranquility, stay at this 1920 lakeside lodge. The main house has cathedral ceilings with floor-to-celing windows. The cottages have lake views and most also have a screened-in porch. Bar. No air-conditioning, no room phones. Pool. Tennis. Hiking, boating, fishing. Playground. Pets allowed. | 3221 Plum Lake Dr. | 715/542–3261 or 800/553–9695 | www.saynerlodge.com | 11 lodge rooms, 20 cottages | $65–$190 | MC, V | Closed Nov.–May.

Plum Gate Resort. Choose from six renovated cottages with one to three bedrooms, most with views of Plum Lake. Some cottages with fireplaces can be used year-round. The resort is within walking distance of restaurants, library, the city park, and tennis and basketball courts. Full kitchens, TV. Beach, boating, fishing, bicycles. Pets allowed. | 3047 Plum Lake Dr. | 715/542–2224 | fax 715/542–3722 | www.innline.com | 6 cottages | $50–$85 per night, $315–$675 per week | No credit cards.

SHAWANO

MAP 11, E4

(Nearby towns also listed: Appleton, Menasha, Neenah)

The center of a lively recreational area that includes Shawano Lake, the Wolf River, and over eight city parks, in Shawano you can fish, swim, hike, bicycle, horseback ride, and go white-water rafting. The town was settled in 1843, and its history is documented at the Heritage Park Museum, a series of historic buildings that border the Wolf River channel. Gaming operations in nearby Keshena, which became popular with tourists in the 1980s, have led to capital improvements and increased employment in the area.

Information: Shawano Area Chamber of Commerce | Box 38, 54166-0038 | 800/235-8528 | tmac@shawano.com | www.shawano.com.

Attractions

Heritage Park Museum. Set in a park alongside the Wolf River channel, the six historic buildings that make up this museum complex include exhibits on the immigrants, loggers and farmers that settled the area in the 19th century. Guided tours go through a one-room school house, a stone building with historic hardware and logging equipment, and a pioneer log cabin. | 524 N. Franklin St. | 715/524–2139 | $2 suggested donation | Jun.–Sept., Wed., Sat., and Sun. 1:30–4:30.

Menomonee Casino and Hotel. Las Vegas–style gambling about 7 mi north of Shawano. Route H to HH. | Rte. 47, Keshena | 800/343–7778 | Free | Daily 24 hrs.

Menomonee Logging Camp Museum. The more than 20,000 artifacts in the seven log buildings of this museum date from Wisconsin's logging days. | Rte. 47 and Rte. VV | 715/799–3757 | $3; special rates for senior citizens and kids | May–mid-Oct., Tues.–Sat. 9–3:15.

Shawano Lake. On 6,063 acres, this 42-ft-deep lake hosts boats, marinas, and beaches; the property includes food facilities, a park, a roller rink, and a campground. | 800/235–8528 | Free | Daily.

Wolf River Beach. This small beach with a kids' swimming area is behind the town hospital. | 5th St. and Riverside Dr. N, just outside town | 800/235–8528 | Free | June–mid-Aug., daily.

ON THE CALENDAR
SEPT.: *Shawano County Fair.* 4-H entries, carnival rides, livestock judging, a horse show, music, and food stands at the fairgrounds during the first week in September. | 800/235–8528.

Dining
Anello's Torch Light. Italian. Servers dress in sequined vests in colors that change with the season at this casual spot with dishes like *polo bianco* (sautéed chicken breast baked with prosciutto, mushrooms, and cheeses over pasta), veal Parmesan, crab, steak, and manicotti. Salad bar. | 1276 E. Green Bay St. | 715/526–5680 | $10–$30 | AE, D, MC, V | No lunch.

North Shore Club. American. The menu includes steaks, seafood, duck, pork chops, barbecued ribs, homemade soups, and salads. There is also a full seafood menu that incudes blue gill, walleye, perch, haddock, scallops, and shrimp. The restaurant is 3 mi northwest of town, across the road from Shawano Lake. | W6014 Lake Dr., Wescott | 715/526–2280 | $7–$16 | MC, V | Closed Mon.; closed Thurs. Apr.–Nov. No lunch.

Lodging
Americinn. On the east side of town, this standard motel is one long building with a glass-enclosed pool in front. The lobby has a fireplace and a breakfast nook. Complimentary Continental breakfast. In-room data ports, refrigerator in suites, cable TV, in-room VCRs available. Pool. Hot tub, sauna. Business services. | 1330 E. Green Bay St. | 715/524–5111 | fax 715/526–3626 | 47 rooms | $69–$75 | AE, D, DC, MC, V.

Best Western Village Haus Motor Lodge. Near the airport on the east side of town, this wood-and-brick lodge has a courtyard and domed pool area. There's complimentary cheese in the small, simple lobby every afternoon. There's a movie theater and strip-mall approximately 5 blocks away. Restaurant, bar. Cable TV. Pool. Hot tub. Beach. Cross-country skiing. Video games. Business services. | 201 Airport Rd. | 715/526–9595 or 800/553–4479 | fax 715/526–9826 | villhaus@frontiernet.net | www.bestwestern.com/villagehaus | 89 rooms, 3 suites | $65–$70 | AE, D, DC, MC, V.

Five Keys Bed & Breakfast. This restored Queen Anne Victorian has maple, oak, and birchwood throughout, as well as the original oak dining-room hutch. There's a large front porch from which perennial gardens can be enjoyed. The B&B is in the center of town near restaurants. Complimentary breakfast. TV in common area. | 103 S. Franklin St. | 715/526–5567 | fivekeys@frontiernet.net | 5 rooms (2 with shared bath) | $60–$80 | No credit cards.

SHEBOYGAN

MAP 11, E5

(Nearby towns also listed: Manitowoc, Two Rivers)

The western edge of lake Michigan is the focal point of this attractive shoreline city settled in 1818. Today, Sheboygan's lakefront has a new marina flanked by striking beaches. A boardwalk along the Sheboygan River is lined with galleries, shops, and restaurants. The downtown area, called the Harbor Centre district, underwent major renovations during the 1990s, and now boasts numerous boutiques, restaurants, galleries, and several newly restored historic buildings. One of the city's leading families are the Kohlers of plumbing-fixture fame.

Information: **Sheboygan (County) Convention and Visitors Bureau** | 712 Riverfront Dr., Suite 101, 53081-4665 | 800/457–9497 | sccc@tcbi.com | www.sheboygan.com.

Attractions

John Michael Kohler Arts Center. This former family mansion, built in 1882 in the Italian Villa style, plays a key role in the rejuvenated downtown scene, serving as a visual- and performing-arts complex devoted to contemporary American art. A wing added in 1999 added six new gallery spaces. Plays and musical events are staged here along with an annual outdoor festival. | 608 New York Ave. (Rte. 23) | 920/458–6144 | Free | Mon., Wed., Fri. 10–5; Tues., Thurs. 10–8; weekends 10–4.

Kohler-Andrae State Park. Just south of town is this 1,000-acre park on a mile-long stretch of Lake Michigan beach backdropped by sand dunes. You can beachcomb, swim, camp, and hike four trails which range from 1 to 2½ mi. The Sanderling Nature Center has nature exhibits and interpretive programs. Interstate 43, Exit 120, on Lake Michigan. | 1520 Old Park Rd. | 920/451–4080 | www.dnr.state.wi.us | $7 nonresidents, $5 residents | Daily.

Lakeland College. Founded by German immigrants in 1862 and run as a religious institution, it became a liberal-arts school in 1956 and was renamed Lakeland College. Some 850 students attend school at this 700-acre campus, which includes a fine-arts gallery, a nature area, and a museum. The campus is 7 mi west of Sheboygan. Take Interstate 43 to Route 42, north to Route A. | W3718 South Dr., County M, Plymouth | 920/565–2111 | www.lakeland.edu | Free | Daily.

Old Plank Road Trail. This 17-mi county recreation trail is half paved and half turfed and runs from Sheboygan to Greenbush, passing Kohler, Sheboygan Falls, and Plymouth. Great for roller blading, horseback riding, hiking, biking, and snowmobiling. | 3000 Erie Ave. | 920/457–9495 or 800/457–9497 | Free | Daily.

Sheboygan County Historical Museum. Exhibits in this museum complex on the western edge of town showcase Sheboygan County history. You can visit the 1852 Judge David Taylor home, an 1864 log house, an 1867 cheese factory, and an 1890s barn. Tours are available. | 3110 Erie Ave. | 920/458–1103 | $3 | Apr.–Oct., Tues.–Sat. 10–5, Sun. 1–5; Nov.–Mar., Tues.–Sat. 10–5, Sun. 1–5.

Waelderhaus. The daughter of the Kohler Company founder built this house in 1931 in memory of her father. It is a replica of the 1850 Kohler home in Vorarlberg, Austria. Tours are available. Waelderhaus is 3 mi west of Sheboygan. | W. Riverside Dr., Kohler | 920/452–4079 | Free | Daily tours at 2, 3, and 4.

SHEBOYGAN

INTRO
ATTRACTIONS
DINING
LODGING

ON THE CALENDAR
JAN.: *Polar Bear Swim.* On January 1 about 400 people, some wearing costumes, dip into chilly Lake Michigan at Northside Beach and swim among chunks of ice no matter how low the temperature drops. You are welcome to join them. | 800/457–9497.
JULY: *Great Cardboard Boat Regatta.* People-powered cardboard boats race along the riverfront off Rotary Park, at Pennsylvania and Broughton Drives, every July 4. The Titanic Award—for the most dramatic sinking—is among the awards offered. | 800/457–9497.
JULY: *Holland Festival.* The last Friday and Saturday in July bring a parade, a play, a raffle, a craft fair, Dutch dancing, and food stands to Memorial Park on Van Altana Ave. | 800/457–9497.
JULY: *Outdoor Arts Festival.* Approximately 130 artists display their work at this juried art fair on the grounds of the John Michael Kohler Arts Center at New York Avenue and 6th Street on the third weekend in July. | 800/457–9497.

Dining

City Streets Riverside. American. This former warehouse in a small shopping district overlooking Sheboygan's historic Fish Shanty Village dates from 1895 and now offers steaks, fresh pastas, seafood, prime rib, and crab legs. | 712 Riverfront Dr. | 920/457–9050 | $15–$20 | AE, DC, MC, V | Closed Sun. No lunch Sat.

Dragonwyck. Chinese. There are daily lunch and dinner buffets at this bright restaurant decorated with pictures and artwork of China. Select from 50 items on the menu. | 1213 Superior Ave. | 920/452–5010 | $6–$15 | MC, V.

Faye's Too Italian House. Italian. Specialties here are thin-crust pizzas, lasagna, spaghetti, ravioli, and Italian sandwiches. | 820 Madison Ave. | 920/565–2138 | $7–$10 | No credit cards | No lunch.

The Immigrant. Continental. There are six small dining rooms, each named and decorated in honor of a different European country in this upscale restaurant 5 mi west of Sheboygan. Whether you are seated in the English, the French, or the German room, you will be offered such dishes as rack of lamb, braised rabbit leg, and seared yellowfin tuna. Entertainment Friday and Saturday. | American Club, 444 Highland Dr., Kohler | 920/457–8000 | Jacket required | $30–$40 | AE, D, DC, MC, V | Closed Sun., Mon. No lunch.

Richard's. American. Linen tablecloths and fresh flowers add polish to this 1840s former stagecoach inn 5 mi west of Sheboygan in the small town of Sheboygan Falls. The kitchen turns out such dishes as prime rib, pasta primavera, and crab legs, as well as good oysters Rockefeller. | 501 Monroe St., Sheboygan Falls | 920/467–6401 | $10–$35 | MC, V | Closed Mon. No lunch weekends.

Lodging

American Club. Built in 1918 to house immigrant workers at the Kohler factory, this red brick Tudor-style residence reopened as a luxury resort in 1981. Elegance emanates from the grand lobby and comfortable sitting areas, complete with plush furniture, handcrafted woodwork, and chandeliers. Rooms are filled with luxurious 18th century-style furniture, and feature state-of-the-art bathrooms with whirlpool tubs. The adjacent carriage house, also built in 1918, boasts newly remodeled rooms and the recently opened Kohler Water Spa. The resort, about 5 mi west of Sheboygan in Kohler, is set on 500 acres of rolling hills and meadows, some of which is meticulously landscaped, and part of which acts as a wildlife preserve. 3 restaurants, bar (with entertainment), room service. In-room data ports, minibars, some refrigerators, in-room hot tubs, cable TV, in-room VCRs and movies available. Pool. Hot tub, spa. Golf courses, tennis. Gym. Bicycles, hiking, horseback riding. Shops. Business services. | Highland Dr., Kohler | 920/457–8000 or 800/344–2838 | fax 920/457–0299 | www.americanclub.com | Main house: 223 rooms, 13 suites. Carriage house: 43 rooms, 9 suites | $250–$480 rooms, $555–$950 suites | AE, D, DC, MC, V.

Baymont Inn. Just west of town, this standard brick hotel is painted white with green shutters and is near restaurants and shopping malls. Complimentary Continental breakfast. Cable TV. Business services. Some pets allowed. | 2932 Kohler Memorial Dr. | 920/457–2321 | fax 920/457–0827 | www.baymontinn.com | 96 rooms | $70–$100 | AE, D, DC, MC, V.

Best Value Inn This quiet motel in a rural area 6 mi south of town has two sections with either outside or inside entrances to rooms. Each room is decorated differently; one is furnished with antiques. Picnic area, complimentary Continental breakfast. Some microwaves, refrigerators, cable TV. Business services. Some pets allowed. | 3900 Motel Rd. | 920/458–8338 or 800/341–8000 | fax 920/459–7470 | www.imalodging.com | 32 rooms | $47–$64 | AE, D, DC, MC, V.

Comfort Inn. This modern, two-story hotel is in a rural area on the outskirts of town, but just 1 mi north of the city. Complimentary Continental breakfast. Cable TV. Pool. Hot tub. | 4332 N. 40th St. | 920/457–7724 or 800/228–5150 | fax 920/457–2597 | www.choicehotels.com | 59 rooms | $95–$105 | AE, D, DC, MC, V.

English Manor Bed & Breakfast. This 1908 four-story English Tudor is listed on the state's Register of Historic Places. Guest rooms all have private baths and sitting areas, and each has different amenities, such as hot tubs and fireplaces. There are the original bathroom fixtures, oak built-ins, beamed ceilings, hardwood floors, and even a billiards room and a pub in the lower level. Afternoon tea and wine and cheese are served daily. Complimentary breakfast. Cable TV. Exercise equipment. | 6332 Michigan Ave. | 920/208–1952 or 877/481–0941 | fax 920/208–3792 | englman@excel.net | www.english-manor.com | 5 rooms | $85–$125 | MC, V.

Gramma Lori's Bed-and-Breakfast. This antiques-furnished 1875 farmhouse outside town still has its original woodwork and hardwood floors. Antiques are for sale in three vast barns. Complimentary breakfast. 1 in-room hot tub, cable TV in common area, in-room VCRs. No smoking. | W1681 Garton Rd. | 920/565–3853 | fax 920/565–4352 | grammalori@tcbi.com | wwwgrammalori.com | 3 rooms | $80–$150 | D, MC, V.

Inn on Woodlake. Built in 1994, this Northside inn has turrets and looks over an 11-acre spring-fed lake with a private beach and a pretty shopping complex. A circular drive leads you to the front entrance. Mission-style furniture fills the lobby, which is dominated by a large fireplace. The inn is 5 mi west of town. Complimentary Continental breakfast. Some refrigerators, cable TV, in-room VCRs (movies available). Pool. | 705 Woodlake Rd., Kohler | 920/452–7800 or 800/919–3600 | fax 920/452–6288 | www.innonwoodlake.com | 121 rooms | $175–$300 | AE, D, DC, MC, V.

Lake View Mansion bed-and-breakfast. Listed on the state's Register of Historic Places, this 1912 redbrick Georgian mansion overlooks Lake Michigan. There are 11 fireplaces, built-in buffets, bookcases, hand-carved woodwork, and hardwood floors. You can roam the entire first floor of this 10,000-square-ft house, which includes a library, large foyer, living room, dining room, and sunroom. Complimentary beverages are available all day. Complimentary breakfast. One in-room hot tub, no room phones, cable TV. | 303 St. Clair Ave. | 920/457–5253 | www.lakeviewmansion.com | 4 rooms | $125–$200 | AE, D, MC, V.

Rochester Inn. Rooms in this former general store and post office, built in 1848, have hot tubs as well as four-poster beds and Queen Anne furniture. The inn is 5 mi west of town. Complimentary breakfast. Microwaves available, in-room hot tubs, cable TV, in-room VCRs. Cross-country skiing. No smoking. | 504 Water St., Sheboygan Falls | 920/467–3123 or 800/421–4667 | rochesterinn@excel.net | www.rochesterinn.com | 1 room, 5 suites | $100–$150 | AE, MC, V.

Yankee Hill Inn bed-and-breakfast. Two separate houses make up this B&B on a hill overlooking downtown: the Gothic Italianate Henry H. Huson House, built in 1870, and the Gilbert L. Huson House, a Queen Anne–style home, built in 1891. Both are filled with antiques, and the Henry H. Huson House is listed on the National Register of Historic Places. The inn is 12 mi west of Sheboygan on Highway 23. Picnic area, complimentary breakfast. No air-conditioning in most rooms, microwaves available, many in-room hot tubs, cable TV in common area, VCR available. Business services. No smoking. | 315 and 405 Collins St., Plymouth | 920/892–2222 | fax 920/892–6228 | yankee@excel.net | www.yankeehillinn.com | 12 rooms (3 with shower only) | $76–$104 | D, MC, V.

SISTER BAY

MAP 11, F3

(Nearby towns also listed: Ellison Bay, Ephraim, Fish Creek)

Door County's largest community north of Sturgeon Bay, Sister Bay was settled in 1857 by Norwegian immigrants. Originally two communities (Big Sister Bay and Little Sister Bay), the Village of Sister Bay was formally created in 1912. In the early days, the town's economy was built on the lumber-shipping business. Today it thrives on tourism, as

Sister Bay is known for its excellent shopping, great restaurants, and the striking Green Bay shoreline. There is a fine sand beach downtown, and a well-developed waterfront park system where there are weekly outdoor concerts in summer.

Information: **Sister Bay Advancement Association** | Box 351, 54234-0351 | 920/854–2812 | www.sisterbaytourism.com.

Attractions

Anderson House Museum. When Alex and Emma Anderson moved from Marinette to Sister Bay in 1865, they moved this house with them—across the ice and a mile uphill. The renovated farmhouse has two stories on one side, one story on the other and it's furnished with period pieces. You'll find the house off of Rte. 57 on the south end of town. | Rte. 57 at Country La. and Fieldcrest Rd. | 920/854–9242 | elindem@dcwis.com | Free | Mid-May–mid Oct., weekends and holidays 11–3.

ON THE CALENDAR

OCT.: *Sister Bay Fall Festival.* This oldest continuing fall festival in Door County, held on the third weekend of the month, features a parade, a ping-pong ball drop, food, entertainment, arts, crafts, and fireworks. | 920/854–2812.

Dining

Al Johnson's Swedish Restaurant and Butik. Scandinavian. Servers dress in traditional Swedish garb here and, in summer, goats clip the grass that carpets the roof. From the windows in the expansive dining room, you can see the harbor and main street. The kitchen is known for its limpa bread, pickled herring, and fruit soups. Kids' menu. | 702-710 N. Bay Shore Dr. | 920/854–2626 | $14–$18 | AE, D, MC, V.

Anne's Corner Café & Catering. American. This deli and café is small, but it does a big business with sandwiches and salads. Popular items are curried-chicken salad; the Islander Sandwich, with turkey, lingonberries and cheddar cheese; and the Peninsula Sandwich made with roast beef, cucumbers, onions, and cream-cheese-and-chives dressing. Outside dining only during summer. | 326 Country Walk La. | 920/854–5061 | Closed Labor Day–Memorial Day. No dinner weekdays | $3–$8 | D, MC, V.

Mission Grille. American. This restaurant, in a former Catholic church, has stained-glass windows, and pews for seating. Specialties include black Angus steak, lamb, duck, pasta, and fresh seafood. | At intersection of Hwys. 42 & 57 | 920/854–9070 | fax 920/854–5566 | $11–$23 | AE, D, MC, V | Closed Sun.–Wed. and Nov.–Mar. No lunch Thurs.–Fri., Sat.

Shoreline Restaurant. Seafood. This restaurant overlooks the western shores of Green Bay. The seafood includes local whitefish, salmon, shrimp, and Chilean sea bass and is often made with ethnic ingredients. The porch, with just six tables, offers more intimate dining. | 12747 State Rd. 42 | 920/854–2950 | Reservations not accepted | $11–$18 | D, MC, V | Closed Nov.–end Apr.

Sister Bay Café. Scandinavian. Locals congregate at this small, bright, and cheery restaurant on Sister Bay's main street. Scandinavian memorabilia accent the room and window seats have a great view of passersby. Try Norwegian farmer's stew and *risegrot*—a hot, creamy, rice pudding–like dish that is a breakfast favorite. | 611 Bay Shore Dr. | 920/854–2429 | $9–$20 | DC, MC, V | Closed Jan.–Mar. and some weekends rest of year.

Lodging

Bluffside Motel. This peaceful motel, a cluster of interconnected simple buildings, is close to downtown, below a bluff, trees, and wildflowers. Picnic tables. Microwaves available, refrigerators, cable TV. | 403 Bluffside La. | 920/854–2530 | bluffside@ricknet.net | 16 rooms, 1 suite | $65–$71 | MC, V | Closed Nov.–Apr.

Century Farm Motel. Located on a country farm just 2 mi south of the heart of Sister Bay, this motel is actually four separate cottages. Refrigerators. Pets allowed. | 10068 Hwy. 57 | 920/854–4069 | 4 cottages | $45–$60 | No credit cards | Closed mid-Oct.–mid-May.

Coachlite Inn and Suites. One long balcony wraps around this simple, modern building dating from 1982. Picnic area. Microwaves, some in-room hot tubs, cable TV. | 830 S. Bay Shore Dr. | 920/854–9462, 920/854–5503, or 800/745–5031 | fax 920/854–9011 | 22 rooms, 2 suites | $69–$119 | MC, V.

Country House Resort. Fountains surrounded by flowers front this rustic resort with 16 wooded, nicely landscaped acres on the Green Bay shoreline. Picnic area, complimentary Continental breakfast. Some microwaves, refrigerators, some in-room hot tubs, cable TV. Pool. Hot tub. Tennis. Dock, boating, bicycles. No kids under 13. Business services. | 715 N. Highland Rd. | 920/854–4551 or 800/424–0041 | fax 920/854–9809 | countryhouse@mail.door-county-wi.com | www.country-house.com | 46 rooms | $103–$258 | AE, D, MC, V.

Edge of Town. Two buildings make up this quiet and homey motel at the north edge of town. Behind the building is a waterfall and lawn furniture with umbrellas for summer-time relaxing. Microwaves, refrigerators, cable TV, no room phones. Some pets allowed. | 11092 Rte. 42 | 920/854–2012 | 9 rooms | $67 | D, MC, V.

Helm's Four Seasons. Flowers surround this Germanic motel in Sister Bay, right on the Green Bay waterfront. Most rooms are on the ground floor; many have parking in front. Com-plimentary Continental breakfast. Kitchenettes in apartments, refrigerators, cable TV. Pool. Hot tub. Dock. Snowmobiling. Laundry facilities. | 414 Mill Rd. | 920/854–2356 | fax 920/854–1836 | frontdesk@helmsfourseasons.com | www.helmsfourseasons.com | 41 rooms, 9 apartments | $99–$108, $129–$205 apartments | MC, V.

Hotel Du Nord. This concrete block complex built in 1982 sprawls along Green Bay and is backed by a thick woods. Restaurant, bar. Some refrigerators, some in-room hot tubs, cable TV. Pool. Hot tub. Beach, dock. Laundry facilities. Business services, airport shuttle. | 11000 N. Bayshore Rd. (Rte. 42) | 920/854–4221 or 800/582–6667 | fax 920/854–2710 | hotel-dunord@doorcounty-wi.com | www.hoteldunord.com | 37 rooms | $120–$185 | AE, D, MC, V.

Inn at Little Sister Hill. Quaint yet modern, this cedar-sided country inn is south of town in a quiet location surrounded by trees. There's a pool and a swing made for two out front. Picnic area. Kitchenettes, microwaves, refrigerators, cable TV, in-room VCRs and movies. Pool. Playground. Laundry facilities. | 2715 Little Sister Hill Rd. | 920/854–2328 or 800/768–6317 | fax 920/854–2696 | theinn@dcwis.com | www.doorcounty-wi.com/PHP/theinn/index.html | 26 suites | $149 | D, MC, V | Closed Nov.–Apr.

Liberty Park Lodge & Shore Cottages. This lodge dates from 1898 and the windows, trim, and fireplace are all original. Some lodge rooms have hot tubs and fireplaces. Most of the cottages have waterfront views; a few are nestled in the woods. All cottages have refrig-erators. Continental breakfast. Beach, dock, boating, fishing. | Hwy. 42 north | 920/854–2025 | 14 rooms in lodge, 12 cottages | $90–$140 | MC, V | Closed Nov.–Apr.

Little Sister Resort. This resort has rustic cedar chalets, cottages, and homes in the woods on Little Sister Bay. Weekly rentals only from July to August; two-day rates any other time. Picnic area. Cable TV. Tennis. Hiking, beach, boating, bicycles. Playground. Laundry facili-ties. | 360 Little Sister Rd. | 920/854–4013 | fax 920/854–5076 | lsroffice@littlesisterre-sort.com | www.littlesisterresort.com | 8 cottages, 6 chalets, 5 cabins, 2 homes | $63–$150 cottages, $65–$150 chalets, $65–$150 cabins, $100–$200 homes. Rates are per person | MC, V | Closed Nov.–Apr.

Nordic Lodge. In a quiet, wooded setting opposite a golf course between Ephraim and Sis-ter Bay, this lodge is on 5 landscaped acres; many porches have views of the countryside. Picnic area, complimentary Continental breakfast. Microwaves available, cable TV. Pool. Hot tub. No smoking. | 2721 Hwy. 42 | 920/854–5432 | fax 920/854–5974 | nordiclodge@dcwis.com | www.thenordiclodge.com | 33 rooms | $79–$92 | D, MC, V | Closed Nov.–Apr.

Open Hearth Lodge. This is a modern lodge on 6½ acres of manicured lawn. The sunken lobby has love seats and easy chairs facing a large stone fireplace. Microwaves available, refrigerators, cable TV. Pool. Hot tub. Playground. | 1109 S. Bay Shore Dr. | 920/854–4890 | openhearth@mail.doorcounty-wi.com | www.dcwis.com/openhearth | 32 rooms | $89–$119 | AE, D, MC, V.

Scandia Cottages. On the north end of Sister Bay, these secluded wood cottages are decorated in a country style with handmade quilts; cottages are on 2 acres, and lovely perennial gardens are in between them. Picnic area. Kitchenettes, cable TV, no room phones. No smoking. | 11062 Beach Rd. | 920/854–2447 | www.scandiacottages.com | 7 cottages | $65–$80 | MC, V.

Sweetbriar Bed & Breakfast. This Cape Cod–style country retreat has both antique and modern furnishings. Guest rooms are all suites; most have fireplaces and whirlpool tubs. Complimentary breakfast. No room phones, no TVs. No smoking. | 102 Orchard Dr. | 920/854–7504 | fax 920/854–9885 | www.sweetbriar-bb.com | 6 rooms | $129–$175 | D, MC, V.

SPARTA

MAP 11, B5

(Nearby towns also listed: La Crosse, Richland Center, Tomah)

Settled in 1849, this town calls itself the Bicycling Capital of America, because of its proximity to nationally known bike trails—among them the Elroy–Sparta State Trail, the first rails-to-trails bicycle route in the country. The "world's largest bike," an old-fashioned high wheeler made of fiberglass, is displayed at the south end of town. Downtown Sparta also has a lovely historic district and makes a good home base for day trips to nearby attractions.

Information: Sparta Convention and Visitor's Bureau | 123 N. Water St., 54656-2576 | 800/354-2453. | bikeme@centurytel.net | www.spartawisconsin.com.

Attractions

Elroy–Sparta State Trail. Sparta is the western terminus of this state trail which includes tunnels built in 1873 by the Chicago and North Western Railroad. The 32-mi trail passes through Norwalk, Wilton, and Kendall to Elroy. At Kendall, 26 mi southeast of town, the main bike-trail headquarters is in a restored railroad depot. | Kendall Depot, White St. (Rte. 71), Kendall | 608/463–7109 | $3 for biking on trails | May–Oct., Sun.–Fri. 8–7, Sat. 8–8 for biking; call for winter snowboarding hrs.

Kendall Depot. The main headquarters of the Elroy–Sparta State Trail is in a restored wood building from the 1900s which is on the State Register of Historic Places. Run cooperatively by the villages along the trail, the Kendall Depot provides information on services and activities in the areas. Historic railroad photos and artifacts are also on exhibit. Get your trail pass at the depot, which also has an electric vehicle available at no charge to people with special needs who wish to ride the trail. | Free | May, daily 9–5; June–Aug., daily 7–7; Sept., Oct., daily 9–5.

ON THE CALENDAR
AUG.: *Blaze Daze and Monroe County Century Challenge.* This early-August family festival in Memorial Park includes a 45-mi bike race, a bike tour, a bike rodeo, a bike swap meet, trick bike riding, food, and live entertainment. | 800/354–2453.

Dining
Eastern Chinese Restaurant. Chinese. Traditional as well as more Americanized Chinese fare is served in this homey restaurant that is decorated like a pagoda. Spicy chicken dishes are a specialty. | 110 S. Water St. | 608/269–6868 | $5–$15 | No credit cards.

Foxhole Pub. American. Popular items here include hamburger baskets, steaks, and seafood. Lots of dark wood, booths, and a big oval bar give the pub a casual feel. | Hwy. 21 east | 608/269–6271 | $7–$16 | D, MC, V | Closed Sun. No lunch Sat.

Lodging

Best Nights Inn. This inn, in a residential area near the center of town, consists of four single-story buildings. Refrigerators, cable TV. Pets allowed. | 303 W. Wisconsin St. | 608/269–3066 | fax 608/269–3175 | www.Bestnightsinn.bizonhe.net | 28 rooms | $32–$82 | AE, D, DC, MC, V.

Country Inn. With its big first-floor porch, this wood motel looks like a very large country house. The country-style lobby has a green-tile gas fireplace, hardwood floors, country wreaths, and stenciling. Bar, complimentary Continental breakfast. Some refrigerators, cable TV. Pool. Hot tub. Laundry facilities. Business services. Pets allowed. | 737 Avon Rd. | 608/269–3110 or 800/456–4000 | fax 608/269–6726 | 61 rooms | $79–$81 | AE, D, DC, MC, V.

Downtown Motel. The rooms of this single-story, brick-front building were updated in 1999. The bike trail is adjacent to this downtown motel. Restaurant. Cable TV. | 509 S. Water St. | 608/269–3138 | 17 rooms | $50 | MC, V.

Heritage Motel. This L-shape wood-sided motel with parking in front is on the west side of town; restaurants are nearby. Cable TV. Pool. Hot tub. Pets allowed. | 704 W. Wisconsin St. | 608/269–6991 or 800/658–9484 | 22 rooms | $40–$42 | AE, D, MC, V.

Justin Trails. On 200 acres, this country-style antiques-filled wood farmhouse is bright yellow with white trim and green shutters. One of the cottages is a wood-frame former granary refurbished with modern amenities. The other two cottages are newly built, natural log homes with exposed log interior walls. Complimentary full breakfast. Some in-room hot tubs, no TV in some rooms. Hiking. Cross-country skiing. | 7452 Kathryn Ave. | 608/269–4522 or 800/488–4521 | fax 608/269–3280 | justntrailsbb@centuryinter.net | www.justin-trails.com | 3 rooms, 1 suite, 3 cabins | $85–$155 rooms, $145–$155 suite, $175–$200 cabins | AE, D, MC, V.

Spartan Motel. This family-owned and -operated motel is located on the west side of town. There's a decent play area for kids. Picnic area. Cable TV. | 1900 W. Wisconsin St. | 608/269–2770 | 8 rooms | $36–$38 | AE, D, MC, V.

Strawberry Lace Inn Bed & Breakfast. This Italianate Victorian home has 12-ft ceilings, a curved staircase, and two covered four-season porches, one with a fireplace and one filled with cozy wicker furniture. Four-course gourmet breakfasts are a house specialty, and are served on china and crystal. Rooms are filled with antiques, and one has a hot tub, wet bar, and television. Complimentary breakfast. In-room data ports, no in-room phones. TV in common area. No smoking. | 603 N. Water St. | 608/269–7878 | strawberry@centuryinter.net | www.spartan.org/sbl | 5 rooms | $90–$145 | MC, V.

Sunset Motel & Mobile Home Court. Family owned and operated, this maroon-and-white motel has been in business since 1961. Cable TV, refrigerators. | 1009 W. Wisconsin St. | 608/269–9932 | 9 rooms | $35–$60 | MC, V.

Waarvik's Century Farm B&B. About 40 mi west of Sparta, you can stay at Grandma's, in the 1885 wood farmhouse with guest rooms, or in the Pioneer's Cabin, a 1860 hand-hewn white-oak log-cabin cottage, once used as a granary; a 90-gallon livestock tank serves as your bathtub and flour sacks curtain the windows. Set on 110 wooded acres, close to three bike trails, berry picking, and hiking trails. Complimentary full breakfast. Kitchenette in log cabin, TV available. No smoking. | N4621 Rte. H, Elroy | 608/462–5521 or 888/462–8595 | 4 rooms, 1 log-cabin cottage | $50 rooms, $125 cabin | No credit cards | Closed Nov.–Apr.

SPOONER

MAP 11, A3

(Nearby town also listed: Rice Lake)

Settled in 1883, this town is in the Northwoods in Washburn County, surrounded by some 900 lakes and miles of scenic rivers and acres of forestland. Riding stables, historical museums, golf courses, antiques shops, and a wildlife sanctuary are just some of the attractions here. You can also ride in refurbished railway cars dating from 1910 to 1930, see a railroad museum, and visit a fish hatchery.

Information: **Spooner Area Chamber of Commerce** | 122 N. River St., 54801-0406 | 800/367-3306 | washburncotour@centurytel.net | www.washburncounty.com.

Attractions

Forts Folle Avoine Historical Park. This park, whose name means "crazy oats" in French, includes two reconstructed fur-trading posts from 1802, a full Woodlands Native American village, and some Ojibwe buildings and artifacts. In the visitor center is a reconstructed 5,000-square-ft log cabin, moved from the Boundary Waters Canoe Area in Minnesota, and you can see films about the area and learn the history of fur-trading villages. A museum and a gift shop are also on-site. Sunday brunch until Labor Day. Operated by the Burnette County Historical Society, it's between Danbury and Webster, 40 mi northwest of Spooner. | 8500 Rte. U, Danbury | 715/866-8890 or 800/788-3164 | $5; special rates for kids and families | Memorial Day–Labor Day, Wed.–Sun. 9–5.

Governor Tommy Thompson's Fish Hatchery. The world's largest fish hatchery was named in 1999 for Wisconsin's governor. The fish are raised here and then released into area lakes. | 951 W. Maple St. | Free | Weekdays 8–4; tours available mid-Apr.–mid-Oct. at 10 and 2 | 715/635-4147 or 800/367-3306.

Museum of Wood Carving. Life-size wood carvings of the Last Supper and other biblical scenes in downtown Shell Lake, about 6½ mi south of Spooner. | U.S. 63, downtown Shell Lake | 715/468-7100 | $4; special rates for kids | May–Oct., daily 9–6.

Railroad Memories Museum. Nine large rooms in this museum in the former Chicago and North Western Railway depot are filled with historic railroad artifacts, railroad videos, photos, equipment, and a model display. | 400 Front St. (Rte. 70) | 715/635-3325 or 715/635-2752 | $3; special rates for kids | Memorial Day–Labor Day, daily 10–5; also by appointment.

Trego Town Park. This 4½-acre park on the Namekagon River in Trego about 7 mi north of Spooner has 50 campsites and a picnic area. You can also swim in the river. | U.S. 53, Trego | 715/635-9931 or 715/635-6075 | Free; campgrounds $12–$15 | Daily.

ON THE CALENDAR

JUNE: *Badger Wheels Car Show.* Displays of antique and classic cars, military vehicles, cycles, antique tractors, as well as swap meets and crafts demonstrations at the Washburn County fairgrounds on the second Sunday in June. | 715/635-3740.
JULY: *Heart of the North Rodeo.* This professional rodeo includes a parade, a fun run, a barbecue, a cowboy church service, and live music at the Washburn County fairgrounds early in the month. | 800/367-3306.

Dining

Nick's Family Restaurant. American. Burgers, broasted chicken (marinated chicken that is deep fried under pressure), and pizza burgers (seasoned pork and beef patties with pizza toppings) are popular here. Breakfast served from 5 AM. | 122 Vine St. | 715/635-3129 | $6–$9 | MC, V.

Lodging

Country House Lodging and RV Park. In a quiet residential area south of town, this traditional 1958 motel on 3 acres has an RV park behind it and is alongside a walking trail through the woods. There's also an indoor golf simulator. Bar. Cable TV, in-room VCRs available. Pool. Hot tub. Business services. | 717 S. River St. | 715/635–8721 | bjcrites@spacestar.net | www.spoonerwisconsin.com/motel.htm | 22 rooms | $53–$95 | AE, D, MC, V.

Green Acres. This motel is in a quiet area at the south edge of town set back from the highway on 5 landscaped acres dotted with mature trees and flower beds. All rooms get bright morning sunshine. Picnic areas. Microwaves available, cable TV. Playground. Business services. Some pets allowed (fee). | N. 4809 U.S. 63 south | 715/635–2177 | 21 rooms | $49–$89 | AE, D, MC, V.

Green Valley Inn Bed & Breakfast. This hand-hewn log home has a loft overlooking the living room, and a stone fireplace. It accommodates up to five people. There are comfy stuffed sofas and chairs and a piano. Outside is a large porch with swings and more oversized chairs. Complimentary breakfast. No pets. No smoking. | N4781 Julie Ann Dr. | 715/635–7300 | 1 room | $65 | No credit cards | Closed mid-Oct.–Apr.

SPRING GREEN

MAP 11, C6

(Nearby towns also listed: Dodgeville, Madison, Mount Horeb)

The fame of this small town on the Wisconsin River is far greater than its size might warrant. That's because the celebrated architect Frank Lloyd Wright built his home, Taliesin, just outside Spring Green. Spring Green has attracted a large community of artisans, as well as a nationally recognized classical theater company. Just south of town is House on the Rock, a former artist's retreat built atop a 60-ft chimney of rock; over time it has grown into a huge complex of buildings housing a museum of oddities and collectibles. The area consists of scenic rolling hills and large tracts of farmland.

Information: Spring Green Chamber of Commerce | Box 3, 53588-0003 | 608/588–2054 | www.springgreen.com.

Attractions

American Players Theatre. Classical theater is performed in this 1,133-seat outdoor natural amphitheater 3 mi south of downtown. | 5950 Golf Course Rd. | 608/588–7401 | June–early Oct., Tues.–Thurs. 7:30, Fri., Sat. 8, Sat. 3, Sun. 6.

Avoca Prairie. Wisconsin's pre-settlement prairie once covered 2 million acres. Today a little more than 2,000 scattered acres survive, including this 970-acre wet-mesic (moderately wet) prairie, the largest tall-grass prairie east of the Mississippi. The prairie borders the Wisconsin River, and is included as a part of the Lower Wisconsin Riverway. To get here from Spring Green, head 7 mi west on Highway 14 to Lone Rock, and then another 5 mi west on Highway 133, to the prairie's edge. | 5 mi west of Lone Rock, off Hwy. 133 | 608/588–2054 or 800/588–2042 | Free | Daily.

Frank Lloyd Wright Visitor Center. The center offers four different tours of famed Wisconsin native architect Frank Lloyd Wright's home and grounds. You'll also find a restaurant and changing exhibits. | 5607 Rte. C | 608/588–7900 | Admission varies per site and tour | May–Oct., daily 8:30–5:30; reservations required for some tours.

House on the Rock. This artist's retreat atop a 60-ft chimney of rock 9 mi south of Spring Green is an architectural wonder, with massive fireplaces inside the building and pools of running water on the premises. Displays include a circus building, a doll building, the world's largest carousel, a mill house, and the Music of Yesterday which has four rooms with music machines that play tunes like "Dance of the Sugar Plum Fairies." There's also a Heritage of the Sea building which has a giant sea creature fighting an octopus. Self-guided tours takes four–five hours. The museum is approximately 7 mi south of town. | 5754 Rte. 23, Wyoming | 608/935–3639 | $19.50; special rates for kids and for groups with advance reservations | Daily 9–7; last ticket sold at 6 PM.

Taliesin. Famed architect Frank Lloyd Wright lived in this home on the banks of the Wisconsin River for the last 50 years of his life. The house still has original furniture, art collections, gardens, courtyards, and the tea circle, a dining area. Guided tours are available; strolling the grounds unguided is not allowed. | 5607 County Hwy. C | 608/588–7900 | fax 608/588–7514 | www.taliesinPreservation.org | Admission varies per tour; no kids under 13 for some tours; reservations required for some tours | May–Oct., daily 8:30–5:30.

Frank Lloyd Wright designed the **Hillside Studio and Theatre** in 1902 as a boarding school for his aunts to run, which they did for 15 years. In the 1930s it became the summer quarters for students at the Frank Lloyd Wright School of Architecture. The interior can be toured. Route 23 to Route T. | 5607 County Hwy. C | 608/588–7900 | fax 608/588–7514 | www.taliesinPreservation.org | Admission varies per tour; no kids under 13 for some tours; reservations required for some tours | May–Oct., daily 8:30–5:30.

Tower Hill State Park. This 78-acre park 3 mi south of town is named for the shot tower and melting house that were located here in the 1850s and produced lead shot used in shotguns. Shot was made by dropping molten lead from the tower into the water far below. The park also includes picnic areas and camping, you can hike to the tower and melting house. | 5808 Rte. C, Arena | 608/588–2116 | www.dnr.state.wi.us | $7 nonresidents, $5 residents | Mid-Apr.–Oct.

Dining

Post House. American. You'll find home-style cooking here in one of oldest operating restaurants in the state—the original restaurant was established in 1857. Turkey, leg of lamb, prime rib, and roast duck are the top-selling items in this casual spot. | 127 W. Jefferson St. | 608/588–2595 | Reservations not accepted Fri. | $10–$17 | MC, V | Closed Mon. from Nov.–May. No lunch.

Lodging

Hill Street Bed & Breakfast. This Queen Anne Victorian is in a residential area just a few blocks from downtown. Standout features include oak woodwork, crown molding, a large staircase at the entryway, two living rooms, and a front porch with swings. Cats on premises. Complimentary breakfast. TV in common area. | 353 W. Hill St. | 608/588–7751 | www.hillstreetbb.com | 7 rooms (2 with shared bath) | $70–$85 | MC, V.

Prairie House. Built in 1983 in Frank Lloyd Wright Prairie style, this motel has modern, spacious rooms. On the pretty landscaped grounds are a water fountain, and hardwood trees and evergreens. Some refrigerators, cable TV. Hot tub. Exercise room. | E4884 U.S. 14 | 608/588–2088 | www.execpc.com/~phouse | 51 rooms | $68–$85 | AE, D, MC, V.

Round Barn Lodge. This hostelry started life as a dairy barn in 1914 and housed some two dozen cattle until 1949 when it was converted first into a truck stop and then into a full-service restaurant and bar; you can still see the original rafters 50 ft up. Guest rooms have cathedral ceilings. Restaurant, bar. Cable TV. 2 pools. Hot tub, sauna. Game room. | Hwy. 14 | 608/588–2568 | fax 608/588–2100 | roundbrn@mhtc.net | www.roundbarn.com | 44 rooms | $80–$110 | AE, D, MC, V.

STEVENS POINT

MAP 11, C4

(Nearby towns also listed: Marshfield, Wausau, Wisconsin Rapids)

Settled in 1838, this city sits in the heart of the Wisconsin River valley where you'll find industry, higher education, historic sites, and natural beauty. Insurance is the city's largest industry, but brewing holds a special place. The Steven's Point Brewery was founded in 1857 and remained family owned until recently.

Information: **Stevens Point Area Convention and Visitors Bureau** | 340 Division St. North, 54481 | 800/236–4636 | www.spacvb.com.

Attractions

Central Wisconsin Children's Museum. Hands-on activities for kids and their families include arts and crafts, books, and storytelling. | Center Point Mall, off Main St., on 3rd Court. | 715/344–2003 | $1 | Thurs.–Sat. 9:30–4.

George W. Mead Wildlife Area. This 28,000-acre wildlife reserve 30 mi northwest of Stevens Point, near the village of Milladore, spans through Portage, Wood, and Marathon counties. You can sightsee, hike, fish, hunt, and pick berries. | 715/457–6771 | Free | Daily.

Stevens Point Brewery. Founded in 1857, this is one of the nation's few remaining successful hometown breweries. | 2617 Water St. at Beer St. | 715/344–9310 | $2 | Weekdays 8–5, Sat. 10–3:30, Sun. 11–4; Sept.–May closed Sun.

University of Wisconsin–Stevens Point. This member of the University of Wisconsin system began in 1894 as Stevens Point Normal School. The campus hosts some 9,000 students and includes a nature reserve with a visitor center, an art center, a natural history museum, and a planetarium. | 2100 Main St. (U.S. 10) | 715/346–4242 or 715/346–0123 | www.uwsp.edu | Free | Daily.

STEVENS POINT

INTRO
ATTRACTIONS
DINING
LODGING

ON THE CALENDAR
FEB.: *Let's Talk Fishing Seminar/Sport Show.* Prominent state and national fishing guides conduct seminars and there are more than 75 displays of outdoor sports–related equipment at the Holiday Inn on the north end of town. | 715/344–2879.

Dining

Aldo's Italian Restaurant. Italian. Locals come to this redbrick building for homemade pizzas and chicken dinners—and then knock down some pins in the connected bowling alley. | 2300 Strongs Ave. | 715/341–9494 | $3–$10 | No credit cards.

Arbuckles Eatery. American. Popular items here are pizzas, pastas, and salads. | 1320 Strongs Ave. | 715/341–2444 | $4–$14 | MC, V | Closed Sun.

Pagliacci Taverna. Italian. Pastas, pizzas, sandwiches, giant salads, and unusual appetizers are on the menu at this spot on the north side of town. There's a subdued Italian motif and, as in the dining room of The Restaurant, which is right next door, lots of oak and stained glass. Open-air dining with a garden view is shared with The Restaurant. | 1800 N. Point Dr. | 715/346–6010 | $15–$20 | AE, MC, V | Closed Sun. No lunch Fri. and Sat.

The Restaurant. American. The menu changes quarterly but usually features steaks, venison, and chicken dishes at this upscale restaurant with oak tables and stained-glass windows. Open-air dining with a garden view. | 1800 N. Point Dr. | 715/346–6010 | $15–$25 | AE, MC, V | Closed Sun. No lunch.

Lodging

Baymont Inn. This modern building on the east side of town is near a mall, the university, the municipal airport, and golf. Complimentary Continental breakfast. In-room data ports, cable TV. Pool. Laundry facilities. Business services. Pets allowed. | 4917 Main St. | 715/344–1900 | fax 715/344–1254 | 74 rooms | $44–$79 | AE, D, DC, MC, V.

Best Western Royale Inn & Conference Center. This three-story wood-and-brick inn at the center of town offers comfortable rooms and suites. Restaurant, bar, complimentary Continental breakfast. Cable TV. Pool. Hot tub, sauna. | 5110 Main St. | 715/341–5110 or 877/811–0217 | fax 715/341–5007 | 120 rooms | $59–$90 | AE, D, DC, MC, V.

Comfort Suites. This three-story cream-color brick building is in a commercial area on the northern outskirts of town. Complimentary Continental breakfast. Some in-room data ports, refrigerators, some in-room hot tubs, cable TV. Pool. Hot tub. Exercise room. Laundry facilities. Business services, free parking. | 300 N. Division St. | 715/341–6000 | fax 715/341–8908 | 105 suites | $79–$139 | AE, D, DC, MC, V.

Dreams of Yesteryear Bed & Breakfast. This Queen Anne Victorian is listed on both the State and National Register of Historic Places. The interior woodwork is all golden oak, and there are leaded-glass windows and maple hardwood floors. A golden oak staircase runs to the third floor where there are rooms in what was once a ballroom. English gardens surround the house, which is on a large city lot in a residential area. There is a playhouse on the property that is original to the house. Complimentary breakfast. No TV in some rooms, TV in common area. | 1100 Brawley St. | 715/341–4525 | fax 715/341–4248 | www.dreamsofyesteryear.com | 6 rooms (2 with shared bath) | $60–$140 | AE, D, MC, V.

Holiday Inn. On the north side of town, this six-story hotel is centered around a glass-enclosed holidome filled with trees and plants. A six-story tower is at one side of the lobby. Restaurant, bar (with entertainment), room service. In-room data ports, cable TV, in-room VCRs and movies. Pool. Hot tub. Exercise room. Laundry facilities. Business services, airport shuttle, free parking. Pets allowed. | 1501 N. Point Dr. | 715/341–1340 | fax 715/341–9446 | www.basshotels.com/holiday-inn | 295 rooms | $109–$168 | AE, D, DC, MC, V.

Maple's Motel Too. This cheery yellow brick motel has standard rooms as well as larger ones with kitchenettes. Comforters, pillows, and stuffed chairs give this motel a comfortable, homey ambience. Some kitchenettes, in-room VCRs. | 3416 Church St. | 715/344–4857 | 12 rooms | $30–$37 | AE, D, DC, MC, V.

Point Motel. This modern stone structure built in 1970 is on a city lot, with parking, trees, bushes, and flower beds in front. Complimentary Continental breakfast. Cable TV, in-room VCRs available. Pets allowed (fee). | 209 Division St. | 715/344–8312 | 44 rooms | $36–$50 | AE, D, DC, MC, V.

A Victorian Swan on Water. This 1889 Victorian home, downtown near the Wisconsin River, has ornate crown moldings, unusual wood floors and woodwork, fireplaces, and many antiques inside. Outside, an attractively landscaped yard has a small waterfall and lots of flowers. Complimentary full breakfast. In-room hot tub (in suite), TV in common area. No smoking. | 1716 Water St. | 715/345–0595 or 800/454–9886 | fax 715/345–0569 | victorian@g2a.net | www.bbinternet.com/victorian-swan | 3 rooms, 1 suite | $60–$130 | AE, D, MC, V.

STURGEON BAY

MAP 11, F4

(Nearby towns also listed: Algoma, Baileys Harbor, Green Bay)

Often called "Wisconsin's Friendliest Small Town," Sturgeon Bay is the county seat and the only city on the Door County peninsula. It was settled in 1835, and its economy was originally based on the lumber industry; that changed, however, when the canal linking Green Bay and Lake Michigan opened to shipping in 1882. Today Sturgeon Bay has a quaint downtown area with unique shops, galleries, restaurants, and B&Bs. The waterfront was reconstructed in 1995 adding a new marina, museum, restaurants, and condos.

Information: **Sturgeon Bay Community Development Corporation** | 23 N. 5th Ave., 54235-0212 | 920/743–3924 | vacation@sturgeonbay.net | www.sturgeonbay.net.

Attractions

Door County Historical Museum. Portrays all aspects of Door County history. Highlights include a fire station that has replicas of trucks that kids can climb on, and a wildlife exhibit. | 18 N. 4th St. | 920/743–5809 | Free | May–Oct., daily 10–4:30; Nov.–Apr. by appointment.

Miller Art Museum Gallery. In the same building as the Door County Library, this art museum has changing exhibits as well as a permanent collection of the works of 20th-century Wisconsin artists. | 107 S. 4th St. | 920/743–6578 | Free | Mon.–Thurs. 10–5 and 7PM–9PM, Fri.–Sat. 10–5.

ON THE CALENDAR

MAY: *Shipyards Tour.* The Door County Maritime Museum sponsors a walking tour of downtown shipyards the second Saturday in May. | 920/743–6246.

AUG.: *Classic Wooden Boat Show and Festival.* You can spend a day on the waterfront viewing old, restored, or recently crafted boats at this event, held the first full weekend in August at the Door County Maritime Museum. | 920/743–5958.

Dining

Bayou On Third. Cajun/Creole. Gumbo and seafood dishes range from mild to extra spicy. There is also an extensive wine list and beer menu. Diners can enjoy recordings of Cajun music as well as jazz and blues. | 50 S. 3rd Ave. | 920/743–3033 | $10–$16 | AE, D, MC, V | Closed Sun.–Wed. Nov.–Apr. No lunch.

Dal Santo's Restaurant. Italian. The most popular dishes in this former train station are pasta in spicy sauces. Train memorabilia predominates here. | 341 ½ N. 3rd St. | 920/743–6100 | $5–$15 | AE, D, MC, V.

Grey Stone Castle. American. Popular items are burgers, steaks, lobster, shrimp, perch, bluegill, and chicken. But the best-selling item is the prime-rib sandwich. The menu is identical for lunch and dinner. | 8 N. Madison Ave. | 920/743–9923 | $6–$10 | AE, D, MC, V.

Inn at Cedar Crossing. Contemporary. Hormone-free steaks, ostrich, and quail are served in an 1884 storefront on a shop-filled street in the historic district. The dining areas are cozy and there's a small antique bar. | 336 Louisiana St. | 920/743–4249 | $22–$35 | D, MC, V.

Mill Supper Club. American. Built in 1930 as a bar, this supper club 3 mi north of Sturgeon Bay serves chicken dinners family style—with large platters of chicken and heaping bowls full of mashed potatoes and other side dishes so you can help yourself. You can also order prime rib or seafood. Kids' menu. | 4128 Hwys. 42/57 | 920/743–5044 | Reservations not accepted | $15–$20 | AE, D, MC, V | Closed Mon. No lunch.

Perry's Cherry Diner. Greek. This 1950s-style diner is known for gyros, moussaka, Greek salads, spanikopita, and old-fashioned malts and was voted restaurant of the year in Wisconsin by Wisconsin Trails Magazine, and by the Wisconsin Red Cherry Growers Association. | 230 Michigan St. | 920/743–9910 | Reservations not accepted | $5–$12 | No credit cards.

Pudgy Seagull Restaurant. American. This restaurant occupies a modern building in Sturgeon Bay's historic district. The wood-paneled dining room is decorated with paintings of the town's history and is known for seafood and roasted chicken. | 113 N. 3rd Ave. | 920/743–5000 | Reservations not accepted | $10–$15 | MC, V.

Lodging

Barbican Olde English Guest House. These are three restored late 19th-century houses, filled with antiques, in the historic waterfront district, one block from the bay or downtown. Gardens are beautifully landscaped with arbors, a fishpond, and a bridge, with wicker furniture on the porches, hanging flower baskets, and some private terraces. Complimentary Continental breakfast, room service. Some microwaves, refrigerators, in-room hot tubs, cable TV, in-room VCRs, no room phones. | 132 N. 2nd Ave. | 920/743–4854 or 877/427–8491 (toll free) | www.barbicanbandb.com | 18 suites in 3 buildings | $115–$220 | MC, V.

Bay Shore Inn. Three separate buildings make up this 1890 gray cedar inn with beautiful English gardens planted in the 1920s. Guest rooms face the water in two of the buildings. All accommodations are full suites. Picnic area. Kitchenettes, microwaves, in-room hot tubs, cable TV, in-room VCRs. 2 pools. Hot tub. Tennis. Beach, boating, bicycles. Exercise room. Game room. Playground. Laundry facilities. Business services. | 4205 Bay Shore Dr. | 920/743–4551 or 800/556–4551 | fax 920/743–3299 | bayshoreinn@itol.com | www.foremostresorts.com/bayshore | 31 suites | $174–$279 | AE, D, MC, V.

Best Western Maritime Inn. This rustic, cedar-sided inn has a maritime theme with a ship's wheel, ship wallpaper, and nautical photos in the lobby. Complimentary Continental breakfast. Microwaves available, some refrigerators, cable TV. Pool. Hot tub. Video games. Business services. | 1001 N. 14th Ave. | 920/743–7231 | fax 920/743–9341 | www.bestwestern.com | 91 rooms | $91–$130 | AE, D, DC, MC, V.

Lodging

Bridgeport Resorts. This contemporary all-suites hotel is in the heart of the city, near shopping and restaurants. Complimentary Continental breakfast. Some refrigerators, in-room hot tubs, cable TV, in-room VCRs. 2 pools. Hot tub, sauna. Gym. Video games. Playground. | 50 W. Larch St. | 920/746–9919 or 800/671–9190 | fax 920/746–9918 | www.bridgeportresort.net | 72 rooms | $135–$270 | AE, D, MC, V.

Chadwick. This 1895 inn has original woodwork, antique glassware throughout, and an 1823 Chickering piano. Complimentary Continental breakfast. In-room hot tubs, cable TV, no room phones. Airport shuttle. | 25 N. 8th Ave. | 920/743–2771 | fax 920/743–4386 | nrbrey@itol.com | 3 suites | $110–$125 | MC, V.

Chal-A Motel. This brick-and-stone motel 2 mi north of downtown has a museum featuring collections of cars, toys, and 2,000 Barbie dolls. You'll pay $2.50 to see them, even if you're a guest. You can cross-country ski on the 100 acres surrounding the motel. Cross-country skiing. | 3910 Hwys. 42/57 | 920/743–6788 | 20 rooms | $39–$59 | MC, V.

Chanticleer Guest House. Sheep graze on this B&B's 30 acres of flower gardens, creeks, fishponds, and streams. The guest house and guest barn, each housing four suites, retain their original exposed beams, wood floors, fireplaces, and high-back beds; there are even

© Artville

FROM DRUMLINS TO ESKERS: WISCONSIN'S ICE AGE TRAIL

Drumlins, moraines, kames, kettles, and eskers were created by glaciers as they pushed their way across the Wisconsin landscape. At their peak 15,000 years ago, glaciers covered two-thirds of the state. When the ice withdrew 5,000 years later the imprints it left behind made this land among the best examples of glacial geology in America. Many sites shaped by glaciers are now linked by the Wisconsin Ice Age Trail which winds through 31 counties. Ultimately, the trail will be 1,000 mi long; 600 mi of the trail have been completed. The Ice Age Trail starts near Sturgeon Bay, in Door County, and makes its way through the state to the St. Croix area in Polk County. The trail is designed for walking, hiking, snowshoeing, and cross-country skiing, and is maintained by volunteers from the Ice Age Park and Trail Foundation in partnership with the National Park Service and the Wisconsin Department of Natural Resources. Take a half-hour walk or a five-day trek through spruce bogs, marshes, remnant prairies, and streams and keep a look out for wild turkeys, Canada geese, sandhill cranes, and red and gray foxes as they are commonly seen.

You can find maps of the trail, schedules of organized hikes, and learn more about the glacial history of Wisconsin at the Ice Age Park and Trail Foundation's website at www.iceagetrail.org.

rafters and hay pulleys in the guest barn. Cross-country skiing on-site. Picnic area, complimentary Continental breakfast. Microwaves, refrigerators, in-room hot tubs, in-room VCRs. Pool. Sauna. Hiking. No kids. | 4072 Cherry Rd. (County Hwy. HH) | 920/746–0334 | fax 920/746–1368 | chanticleer@itol.com | www.chanticleerguesthouse.com | 8 suites, 2 cabins | $120–$190 | D, MC, V.

Cherry Hills Lodge and Golf Resort. Golf art decorates this lodge on the challenging 18-hole Cherry Hills Golf Course. Rooms have decks with views of the links and the Door County countryside. Bar, dining room, picnic area. Refrigerators, cable TV. Pool. Hot tub. 18-hole golf course. Cross-country skiing. Business services. | 5905 Dunn Rd. | 920/743–4222 or 800/545–2307 | fax 920/743–4222 | cherryhl@mail.wiscnet.net | www.golfdoorcounty.com | 31 rooms | $112 | AE, D, DC, MC, V.

Cliff Dwellers. This lodge-and-cottage complex nestles between cliffs and the shore about 5 mi from downtown. Lodge rooms have large porches with flower boxes; cottages range from rustic brown to cheery white buildings accented with flowers. Complimentary breakfast. Kitchenettes in cottages, cable TV. Pool. Hot tub, sauna. Tennis. Boating, bicycles. | 3540 N. Duluth Ave. | 920/743–4260 | cliffdwellers@dcwis.com | 16 lodge rooms, 13 cottages | $95–$105 rooms, $105–$175 cottages | AE, D, MC, V | Closed Nov.–Apr.

Colonial Gardens Bed & Breakfast. This 1877 colonial has great views of Sturgeon Bay. All rooms are suites and have fireplaces, double whirlpool tubs, and private entrances with porches. Breakfast is delivered right to your room. Complimentary breakfast. Refrigerators, in-room VCRs. | 344 N. 3rd Ave. | 920/746–9192 | fax 920/746–9193 | www.colgardensbb.com | 5 suites | $120–$175 | D, MC, V.

Connie's Cabins. Set on Clark's Lake, this resort has a small beach and is in a heavily wooded area at the end of a dead-end road. Log cabins come in one or two bedrooms and are available by the week only. Beach, water sports, boating. | 5541 Clark's Lake Rd. | 920/823–2222 | 3 rooms | $700–$900 per week | No credit cards.

Holiday Motel. Built in the 1950s, this white motel with red awnings in the downtown historic district has flowers out front in summer. Complimentary Continental breakfast. Microwaves available, refrigerators, cable TV, VCR and movies available in common area. Business services. Some pets allowed. | 29 N. 2nd Ave. | 920/743–5571 | 18 rooms | $50–$69 | AE, D, DC, MC, V.

Inn at Cedar Crossing. This antiques-filled late-19th-century brick inn is on a quaint, historic downtown street. The common areas are elegant yet cozy. Restaurant (*see* Inn at Cedar Crossing), complimentary Continental breakfast. Some in-room hot tubs, cable TV, in-room VCRs and movies. Business services, airport shuttle. No smoking. | 336 Louisiana St. | 920/743–4200 | fax 920/743–4422 | innkeeper@innatcedarcrossing.com | www.innatcedar-crossing.com | 9 rooms | $99–$169 | AE, D, MC, V.

Leathem Smith Lodge. This 1921 brick motel at the eastern edge of town, about 1/4 mi from the historic district, opened as a small inn and has expanded and remodeled several times. Some microwaves, some refrigerators, cable TV, in-room VCRs and movies available. Pool. 9-hole golf course, putting green, tennis. Playground. Business services. | 1640 Memorial Dr. | 920/743–5555 or 888/366–7947 | fax 920/743–5355 | thelodge@itol.com | www.leath-emsmithlodge.com | 63 rooms, 16 suites | $89–$192 | AE, MC, V.

Scofield House. This restored 1902 painted lady was the residence of one of Sturgeon Bay's first mayors and is filled with antiques, stained glass, and ornate ceilings, heavily ornamented original woodwork and parquet floors. Complimentary full breakfast. Many in-room hot tubs, cable TV, in-room VCRs and movies, no room phones. Business services. No kids. No smoking. | 908 Michigan St. | 920/743–7727 or 888/463–0204 | fax 920/743–7727 | scofhse@mail.wiscnet.net | www.scofieldhouse.com | 6 rooms | $98–$202 | No credit cards.

White Birch Inn. This antiques-filled inn is a homey place with its knotty-pine trim and hardwood floors in a residential neighborhood 1/2 mi south of downtown. Restaurant, picnic area, complimentary Continental breakfast, room service. Airport shuttle. | 1009 S.

Oxford Ave. | 920/743–3295 | fax 920/743–6587 | www.whitebirchinn.com | 16 rooms, 6 suites | $49–$140 | MC, V.

White Lace Inn. Four late-19th-century wood homes connected by gardens make up this inn in the downtown historic district. Each building is a different pastel color, pink, green, powder blue, or yellow; a white-pillared portico fronts the main structure. Rooms are elegant, with antiques, canopy beds, and some fireplaces. Complimentary full breakfast. Microwaves available, no smoking, some in-room hot tubs, in-room VCRs available, no TV in some rooms. No kids. | 16 N. 5th Ave. | 920/743–1105 | fax 920/743–8180 | romance@whitelaceinn.com | www.whitelaceinn.com | 18 rooms | $139–$229 | AE, D, MC, V.

SUPERIOR

MAP 11, A1

(Nearby towns also listed: Ashland, Bayfield, Hurley)

French explorers first came to this area in the mid-1600s and established a trading post, but this Douglas County city didn't grow dramatically until after Lake Superior was opened to ocean traffic in the 1850s. When a railroad came to the area, it expanded once again as immigrants came to work in mines and on docks.

Superior is at the far western end of Lake Superior. It has a deep-water harbor that is an international inland ocean port linked to the Atlantic Ocean by the St. Lawrence Seaway. It has a lighthouse, fine sand beaches, and a 4-mi-long sand bar in the harbor from which you can watch birds. Just to the south there are 431 lakes and the state's tallest waterfall, 165-ft-high Big Manitou Falls in Pattison State Park.

Information: **Superior Douglas County Chamber of Commerce Convention and Visitors Bureau** | 205 Belknap St., 54880 | 800/942–5313 | superior@visitsuperior.com | www.superiorwi.net.

Attractions

Amnicon Falls State Park. You can picnic beside a sparkling waterfall in this state park, which has many cataracts and four waterfalls—three of them nearly 30 ft tall. There are picnic facilities, campsites, nature trails, and a covered bridge that leads to an island. West on Route 13 to Route U. | Rte. U | 715/398–3000 in summer; 715/399–3111 in winter | www.dnr.state.wi.us | $7 nonresidents, $5 residents | Late Apr.–early Oct.

Barker's Island. This man-made island accessible by bridge from the east side of town has the S.S. *Meteor* Maritime Museum, excursions to the Duluth–Superior harbor, and a small park with swimming in Lake Superior. | 715/394–5712 | Free | Mid-May–mid-Oct., daily 10–5. **Duluth–Superior Vista Fleet excursions** include lunch and dinner cruises, as well as narrated two-hour Duluth–Superior harbor tours. Cruises sail back and forth between Duluth and the Superior side of Barker's Island. | Barker's Island Dock | 715/394–6846 or 218/722–6218 | Standard tour $9.25; special rates for kids | Mid-May–mid-Oct.

After you cross the bridge from the mainland, you'll find the **S.S. *Meteor* Museum,** the country's last whaleback lakes freighter, so named because the hull is shaped like a whale. The vessel was built in Superior in 1896. Nearby, a seaman's memorial pays tribute to the 29 men who died in the famous wreck of the *Edmund Fitzgerald*. | Barker's Island | 715/392–5742 | $5; special rates for senior citizens, kids, and families | Memorial Day–mid-Oct., Mon-Sat. 10–5, Sun. 11–5 (tours).

Brule River Canoe Rental. You can explore the wet and wild Brule River by canoe or kayak. Trips are geared for beginners as well as experienced canoeists and run from 4 to 16 mi long. Shuttle service is available. Fees vary depending upon number of boats and trip selected. Call for information. It's north on Highway 2 in Brule, 30 mi east of Superior. | Box 145, Brule 54820 | 715/372–4983 or 800/942–5313 | fax 715/372–5038 | Generally Apr.–Oct., depending on weather. Call for exact dates.

Brule River State Forest. With its many distinct habitats, this 41,000-acre forest, 30 mi east of Superior, in Brule, is home to many birds and mammals including deer, ruffed grouse, geese, bald eagles, osprey, timber wolves, bobcats, otters, bears and songbirds. | 6250 S. Ranger Rd., Brule | 715/372–4866 | www.dnr.state.wi.us/org/land/forestry/StateForests/index.htm | Free; permits required for cross-country ski trails | Daily.

Fairlawn Mansion and Museum. A restored 42-room Victorian wood mansion overlooking Barker's Island houses exhibits on local and Native American history. | 906 E. 2nd St. | 715/394–5712 | $7 | Daily 9–5.

Nemadji Golf Course The 18-hole East/West Course, opened in 1981, is noted for its excellent greens and friendly staff. | 5 N. 58th St. E | 715/394–0266 | Mid-Apr.–Oct.

Old Fire House and Police Museum. This museum in a 1898 former fire station on the east end of town displays vintage police and fire-engine memorabilia, including old fire engines, handcuffs, and police firearms. | 402 23rd Ave. E | 715/398–7558 | $5 | May– Sept., daily 10–5.

Pattison State Park. This 1,376-acre state park 12 mi south of Superior is home to the 165-ft Big Manitou Falls, Wisconsin's highest waterfall, as well as 30-ft Little Manitou Falls and a deep gorge between dark basalt cliffs which was carved by the Black River. The park has camping, hiking, swimming, snowmobiling, and cross-country skiing. | 6294 S. Rte. 35 | 715/399–3111 | www.dnr.state.wi.us | $7 nonresidents, $5 residents | Daily.

Superior Municipal Forest. This 4,500-acre municipal forest in the western part of town is the second-largest forest within the city limits, and has cross-country skiing and hiking on 28 mi of trails; there's also an archery range. | N. 28th St. and Wyoming Dr. | 715/394–0270 | Free | Daily.

ON THE CALENDAR

JULY: *Head-of-the-Lakes Fair.* The last weekend of the month brings country-and-western and rock music, a demolition derby and stock car racing, rides, and arts-and-crafts displays to the fairgrounds. | 715/394–7848.
JULY: *Woodies on the Water.* More than 50 wooden boats that were built or restored by their owners are on display at Barker's Island Marina. They include canoes, sailboats, kayaks, and powerboats. | 218/834–5958 or 800/942–5313 | www.visitsuperior.com.
SEPT.: *Murphy Oil USA Spirit of the Lake Fall Fest Parade.* A celebration of autumn along Ogden Avenue and Belknap Street with city-wide yard sales and a parade that includes floats, antique cars, horses, bagpipers, a band, and costumed dogs. | 715/394–7716 or 800/942–5313 | www.visitsuperior.com.

Dining

Kastern's Choo-Choo Bar & Grill. American. This restaurant is in two train cars and a caboose that were taken off the tracks in 1932. You can dine in one of the original dining booths from a parlor car. The same menu is used for lunch and dinner, but there are always daily specials. Popular items are burgers, chicken, bratwurst patties, and cheese balls. | 5002 E. 3rd St. | 715/398–3788 | $4–$6 | MC, V.

Godfather's Pizza. Italian. Pizza is the mainstay at this restaurant, but appetizers and desserts are also on the menu. An all-you-can-eat pizza lunch and dinner buffet includes the salad bar. There's also an area where kids can play while parents relax after a meal. | 2802 Banks Ave. | 715/392–4753 | $5–$19 | No credit cards | No dinner Wed.–Sat.

Shack Smokehouse and Grille. Contemporary. This supper club in the north part of town is casual by day and elegantly candlelit at night. The main claim to fame here is the barbecue with smoked hickory wood and is similar to Kansas City BBQ; also popular are local lake trout, walleye, and prime rib. On Friday, there's a fish fry. | 3301 Belknap St. | 715/392–9836 | $9–$20 | D, DC, MC, V.

Lodging

Androy Hotel. This seven-story brick hotel, built in 1925, is the tallest building in the city. There are also long-term apartment rentals here. Bar. Cable TV. Laundry facilities. | 1213 Tower Ave. | 715/394–7731 | fax 715/394–9826 | 80 rooms | $36–$53 | AE, MC, V.

Barker's Island Inn. In this modern inn set among the marina, restaurants, and small shops, rooms overlook the marina or Superior Harbor. Restaurant, bar, room service. Cable TV. Pool. Hot tub, sauna. 2 tennis courts. Game room, video games. Laundry facilities. Business services. | 300 Marina Dr. | 715/392–7152 or 800/344–7515 | fax 715/392–1180 | www.visitduluth.com/barkers | 112 rooms | $52–$181 | AE, D, DC, MC, V.

Best Western Bay Walk Inn. This colonial-style building is in a residential area about ½ mi from Lake Superior. Brick pillars support an entry portico, and a fireplace and sofas make the lobby comfortable. Complimentary Continental breakfast. Some refrigerators, cable TV, in-room VCRs and movies available. Pool. Hot tub, sauna. Video games. Laundry facilities. Business services. Some pets allowed. | 1405 Susquehanna | 715/392–7600 | fax 715/392–7680 | 50 rooms | $55–$81 | AE, D, DC, MC, V.

Best Western Bridgeview Motor Inn. This brownstone building dating from 1966 is at the foot of a bridge as you enter the north side of town. There is a restaurant next door. Complimentary Continental breakfast. Some microwaves, some refrigerators, cable TV. Pool. Hot tub, sauna. Laundry facilities. Business services. Pets allowed. | 415 Hammond Ave. | 715/392–8174 | fax 715/392–8487 | 96 rooms | $60–$100 | AE, D, DC, MC, V.

Prime Rate Hotel. This L-shape building is on the waterfront and near the S.S. *Meteor* Museum. Cable TV. Pool. Hot tub, sauna. Laundry facilities. Business services. | 110 Harbor View Pkwy. | 715/392–4783 | fax 715/392–4787 | 110 rooms | $89–$99 | AE, D, DC, MC, V.

Super 8. This wood rectangular building is near restaurants and a truck stop in a suburban area. RVs are welcome to park here. Snowmobiling on-site behind the hotel. Complimentary Continental breakfast. Cable TV. Business services. | 4901 E. 2nd St. | 715/398–7686 | fax 715/398–7339 | www.super8.com | 40 rooms | $63–$72 | AE, D, DC, MC, V.

Superior Inn. This large, two-story inn is near downtown. Complimentary Continental breakfast. Cable TV. Pool. Hot tub, sauna. | 525 Hammond Ave. | 715/394–7706 or 800/777–8599 | fax 715/394–7708 | www.superiorinn.com | 69 rooms, 1 suite | $69–$135 | AE, D, MC, V.

THREE LAKES

MAP 11, D3

(Nearby towns also listed: Boulder Junction, Eagle River)

This town is on the western edge of Nicolet National Forest and is ideal for a Northwoods vacation. There are some 28 lakes in the area where you can water-ski, fish, and boat. In winter, Three Lakes is a snowmobilers' playground. Indoor amusements include browsing the town museum and touring the winery for a taste of the local cranberry wine.

Information: Three Lakes Information Bureau, Inc. | Box 268, 54562-0268 | 800/972–6103 | www.threelakes.com.

Attractions

Nicolet National Forest, Eagle River Ranger District. This 661,000-acre forest is 7 mi east of Eagle River, which is 10 mi north of Three Lakes. There are numerous trails for hiking, cross-country skiing, horseback riding, and snowmobiling. Biking, fishing, hunting, and camping, and scenic drives are also popular. Highways 32, 55, and 70 all pass through the forest, and offer several access points along the way. | 4364 Wall St., Eagle River | 715/479–2827 | Free | Daily.

Three Lakes Historical Museum. This museum showcases Three Lakes' history in a turn-of-the-20th-century home surrounded by perennial flower gardens. You can learn about the town's lumber history and local cranberry production. | 1798 Huron St. | 715/546–2295 | Free | June–Sept., Tues.–Sat. 11–3; Oct.–May, by appointment only.

Three Lakes Winery. On the west side of town, this winery in a 1972 railway depot is known for its cranberry wine and other cranberry and fruit products. Tours and tastings are available. | 6971 Gogebic St. | 715/546–3080 | Free | Mon.–Sat. 9–5, Sun. 10–4:30; guided tours late May–mid-Aug.; self-guided tours rest of year.

ON THE CALENDAR
SEPT.: *Nicolet Wheel-a-Way.* This 30-mi bike tour through Nicolet National Forest is held on the first Saturday of the month. | 800/972–6103.

Dining
Cindy's Country Café. American. A potbellied stove and a collection of vintage soda and beer bottles are strewn about this café. Only breakfast and lunch are served—the omelets, Belgian waffles, and sandwich specials stand out. Regular customers have white mugs with their names on them hanging on the wall. | 1672 Superior St. | 715/546–3733 | $5–$10 | MC, V | No dinner.

Lodging
Oneida Village Inn. This modern two-story building in downtown Three Lakes has a cathedral ceiling in the dining room where dinner and Sunday brunch are served. The game room has air hockey and pool tables. Restaurant, bar. Cable TV. Video games. Business services. Pets allowed. | 1785 Superior St. | 715/546–3373 or 800/374–7443 | fax 715/546–8060 | ovi@newnorth.net | www.wisvacations.com | 47 rooms | $49–$80 | AE, D, DC, MC, V.

Whispering Pines Resort. Six small, rustic cottages line the water of this resort on Round Lake, which is part of the Three Lakes Eagle River chain of 28 lakes. One- to three-bedroom cottages have screened-in porches. Weekly rentals only. Boating, fishing. | 8029 Burchmore Rd. | 715/546–2124 | whsprngpns@newnorth.net | 6 cottages | $365–$500 | No credit cards | Closed Oct.–May.

YOUR FIRST-AID TRAVEL KIT

- ❑ Allergy medication
- ❑ Antacid tablets
- ❑ Antibacterial soap
- ❑ Antiseptic cream
- ❑ Aspirin or acetaminophen
- ❑ Assorted adhesive bandages
- ❑ Athletic or elastic bandages for sprains
- ❑ Bug repellent
- ❑ Face cloth

- ❑ First-aid book
- ❑ Gauze pads and tape
- ❑ Needle and tweezers for splinters or removing ticks
- ❑ Petroleum jelly
- ❑ Prescription drugs
- ❑ Suntan lotion with an SPF rating of at least 15
- ❑ Thermometer

*Excerpted from *Fodor's: How to Pack: Experts Share Their Secrets*
© 1997, by Fodor's Travel Publications

TOMAH

(Nearby town also listed: Sparta)

Tomah, named after a celebrated Menomonee chief, straddles one of Wisconsin's busiest intersections, Interstates 90 and 94. Often called the Gateway to Cranberry Country, it is one of the nation's top cranberry producers, a number of cranberry bogs are on the north side of town. There's also a quaint little red schoolhouse in the town park.

Information:**Tomah Chamber of Commerce/Convention and Visitors Bureau** | Box 625, 54660-0625 | 800/948–6624 | tchamber@mwt.net. | www.tomahchamber.com.

Attractions

Cranberry Expo Ltd. This museum tells the history of the area's cranberry industry through a guided tour and video. Cranberry products are available to sample and buy. | 28388 County Trunk EW, Warrens | 608/378–4878 | $5 | Apr.–Sept. 10–4.

Little Red Schoolhouse. This one-room school built in 1864, in use until the mid 1960s, stands in Gillett Park on the southern end of town. | 1300 S. Superior Ave. | 608/372–2166 or 608/374–7420 | Free | Memorial Day–Labor Day, daily 1–5.

Mill Bluff State Park. This 1,400-acre park just east of town is famous for its 100-ft sandstone bluffs. You can climb stone steps built by the Civilian Conservation Corps to the top of Mill Bluff and check out the dramatic view from the observation deck. A rustic campground with 12 sights, a beach, and a pond for swimming are on-site. | 15919 Funnel Rd. | 608/427–6692 | www.dnr.state.wi.us | $7 nonresidents, $5 residents | Memorial Day–mid Oct., daily.

Necedah National Wildlife Refuge. This 45,000-acre federal reserve 20 mi west of Tomah is a good place to see deer, turkey, cranes, and timber wolves. There's hiking and cross-country skiing on 3½ acres of trails, a road that goes through the refuge, and an observation tower that looks out over a pond. Hunting and fishing are permitted in some areas. | W7996 20th St., Necedah | 608/565–2551 | Free | Daily, daylight hrs. only.

Wildcat Mountain State Park. These 3,470 acres of steep hills and deep, narrow valleys are 30 mi south of Tomah. An overlook gives you a view of the Kickapoo River valley and the town of Ontario, 3 mi away. There are also three picnic areas and 4 mi of hiking trails. | State Hwy. 33 E, Ontario | 608/337–4775 | www.dnr.state.wi.us | $7 nonresidents, $5 residents | Daily.

Wisconsin National Guard Memorial Library and Museum. Housed in an 1890s log building in Camp Douglas 12 mi east of Tomah, this museum chronicles the history of the Wisconsin National Guard beginning with its establishment after the Civil War. Army and air guard units, veterans' personal histories, and rare volumes documenting the guards' exploits through two world wars tell the story. Self-guided tours take you through the post where there are displays and a gun range. You can also see vintage aircraft, and visit a target area. | 101 Independence Dr., Camp Douglas | 608/427–1280 | Free | Wed.–Sat. 9–4, Sun. 10–2.

ON THE CALENDAR

SEPT.: *Cranberry Festival.* Cranberry-bog tours, cranberry foods, a farmers' market, a flea market, antiques, a parade, and music on the last full weekend of the month. | 800/948–6624 or 608/378–4200.

Dining

Badger Restaurant. American. Fried chicken is a specialty here, also on the menu are pasta dishes, roast beef, and turkey. Breakfast served daily. | 1210 Superior Ave. | 608/372–9552 | $6–$12 | MC, V.

Burnstad's European Café. Russian. You'll find dishes such as noodle soup, chicken spaetzle soup, and charbroiled steak as well as homemade desserts at this casual café with a gazebo and fountains out back. | 701 E. Clifton | 608/372–3277 | $8–$15 | AE, D, DC, MC, V | Breakfast also available.

Carlton Restaurant & Lounge. American. Steaks, seafood, and lobster are specialties here, as well as a salad bar with 20-plus items. Save room for homemade desserts such as turtle cheesecake and Mississippi mud pie. | 309 Superior Ave. | 608/372–4136 | $11–$20 | MC, V | Closed Sun.–Tues. No lunch.

Smitty's Overtime Inn. American. Popular dishes are New York strip steak, crab legs, and the Friday-night fish fry. Mexican food is also on the menu with enchiladas and burritos the top sellers. Breakfast served daily. | 8293 State Hwy. 173 | 608/372–5499 | $3–$16 | No credit cards.

Lodging

Budget Host Daybreak. This rustic cedar hotel is made up of three separate buildings. Rooms are individually decorated to pay tribute to famous Wisconsinites, such as Frank Lloyd Wright and Laura Ingalls Wilder. Inside you'll find their photos and objects common to their personalities. The hotel is next to snowmobile trails and a municipal park. Microwaves and refrigerators available, cable TV. Business services. Small pets allowed. | 215 E. Clifton St. | 608/372–5946 | fax 608/372–5947 | 32 rooms | $63–$73 | AE, D, MC, V.

Comfort Inn. On the north side of town, this two-story brick motel is just off the highway near a truck stop and other hotels and businesses. Complimentary Continental breakfast. Refrigerators in suites, cable TV. Pool. Hot tub. Business services. Pets allowed. | 305 Wittig Rd. | 608/372–6600 | fax 608/372–6600 | 44 rooms, 8 suites | $53–$80 | AE, D, DC, MC, V.

Cranberry Suites. A convenience store is the entrance to this contemporary all-suite hotel. Microwaves, refrigerators, some in-room hot tubs, in-room VCRs. | 319 Wittig Rd. | 608/374–2801 or 800/243–9874 | fax 608/374–2805 | 33 rooms | $75–$99 | AE, D, DC, MC, V.

Holiday Inn. This simple two-story building with a small lobby and a canopy at the front entrance is on the north part of town and has a lake in back and woods with trails for hiking or cross-country skiing. Restaurant, bar, room service. In-room data ports, some refrigerators, cable TV. Pool. Hot tub, sauna. Cross-country skiing. Game room, video games. Laundry facilities. Business services. | Rte. 21 and I–94 | 608/372–3211 | fax 608/372–3243 | www.basshotels.com/holiday-inn | 100 rooms | $80 | AE, D, DC, MC, V.

Lark Inn. At this inn on 4 acres on the north side of town you can stay in historic 1920s log cabins with cathedral ceilings, or in the main building. Restaurant, picnic area, room service. Some kitchenettes, microwaves, refrigerators, cable TV, in-room VCRs and movies available. Laundry facilities. Pets allowed. | 229 N. Superior Ave. | 608/372–5981 or 800/447–5275 | fax 608/372–3009 | www.larkininn.com | 25 rooms, 5 cabins | $69–$81 | AE, D, DC, MC, V.

Pleasant Acres. This one-story 1950s motel is painted a soothing sky blue and is accented with white. On the north end of town in a commercial district, the inn is within 1 mi of several restaurants, and across the street from a shopping center. Cable TV, some microwaves, some refrigerators. | 1305 N. Superior Ave. | 608/372–9343 | 14 rooms | $48–$62 | AE, D, MC, V.

Red Gables Motel. This family-owned and -operated motel is 1 mi from town. The owners live on-site. Cable TV, microwaves. | 1001 N. Superior Ave. | 608/372–6868 | 12 rooms | $40 | AE, D, MC, V.

Super 8. This T-shape building, on the east side of town, has parking spaces for large trucks. Complimentary Continental breakfast. Some refrigerators, cable TV. Laundry facilities. Business services. Pets allowed (deposit). | 1008 E. McCoy Blvd. | 608/372–3901 | fax 608/372–5792 | www.super8.com | 65 rooms | $57–$67 | AE, D, DC, MC, V.

TWO RIVERS

(Nearby towns also listed: Manitowoc, Sheboygan)

Still active as a deep-water sportfishing port, Two Rivers has a population of 13,500 and an important claim to fame: back in 1881 the ice-cream sundae is said to have been created here. There are sweeping sand beaches along the city's Lake Michigan shoreline. Small industry is the town's primary economic base.

Information: **Two Rivers Information Center c/o Historical Society** | 1622 Jefferson St., 54241 | 920/793–2490.

Attractions

Point Beach Energy Center. Head 9 mi north of Two Rivers and explore the world of energy and electricity via audiovisual displays and computer games; there's also a nature trail. | 6600 Nuclear Dr., Two Creeks | 920/755–4334 | Free | Daily 9–4:30.

Point Beach State Forest. This 2,900-acre preserve has campsites and 11 mi of trails through the pines for hiking, mountain biking, and cross-country skiing; there's also a beach on Lake Michigan. | 9400 County Hwy. O | 920/794–7480 | www.dnr.state.wi.us/org/land/forestry/StateForests/index.htm | 7$ nonresidents, $5 residents; permits required for some recreational trails | Daily.

Rogers Street Fishing Village Museum. This re-created French Canadian fishing village on the National Register of Historic Places preserves Two Rivers' maritime history. The museum displays a 1936 commercial fishing tug and a large collection of artifacts retrieved from shipwrecks; the museum also runs tours of Two Rivers' 1883 North Pier Lighthouse. | 2116 Jackson St.; Rte. 42 | 920/793–5905 | $2; special rates for kids | May–Oct., daily 10–4; Nov.–Apr., by appointment.

Two Rivers History Museum. This museum is housed in a former nunnery dating from 1902. Some items from area churches are on display. There is also an exhibit on the ethnic diversity of Two Rivers. | 1810 Jefferson St. | 920/793–1103 | Free; fees for tour groups (fees vary) | Daily 10–4.

ON THE CALENDAR

SEPT.: *Ethnic Festival.* The area's largest ethnic festival celebrates local cultural diversity with the music, food, and dance of more than 50 nations in Central Park mid-month. | 920/793–2490.

Dining

Machut's Supper Club. American. This family-style restaurant seats 225. Broasted chicken, barbecued ribs, and steak are popular. The restaurant is just 1 mi north of downtown, but feels like it's in the countryside. Brunch is served on Sundays. | 3911 Lincoln Ave. | 920/793–9432 | $4–$17 | AE, D, MC, V | Closed Mon.–Tues. No lunch.

Lodging

Village Inn and Suites. This contemporary inn is across from Lake Michigan and popular with families. It has a snack bar and game area. Some suites have hot tubs. Bar, complimentary Continental breakfast. Pool. Video games. | 3310 Memorial Dr. | 920/794–8818 or 800/551–4795 | 28 rooms, 8 suites | $65–$150 | AE, D, MC, V.

WASHINGTON ISLAND

(Nearby towns also listed: Ellison Bay, Sister Bay)

Settled in 1869, this Door County area was originally named Colonel John Miller Island in 1815, after the leader of the first white men to set foot on the island; in 1816, the name was changed to honor a schooner called the George Washington. Many original settlers were from Iceland, and today the island is the oldest Icelandic community in the United States. With 14,000 acres, it is the largest of Door County's islands, and it is great for bicycling, boating, golf, leisurely drives, gallery-going, and shopping. Don't leave without sampling some of the famous Door County cherries; the county is one of the largest cherry producing areas in the country, and the local berries are diligently used in baked goods and pies. From the northeast corner of the island, Rock Island State Park is just a short ferry ride away.

Information: Washington Island Chamber of Commerce | Rte. 1, Box 222, 54246-9768 | 920/847–2179 | www.washingtonislandwi.org.

Attractions

Cherry Train Tours. The 90-minute Washington Island tours via an open-air tram make stops at many of the island's museums and historic sites, at an arts and nature center, at scenic spots along the shoreline, and at a local ostrich farm. You'll also pass by a few private cherry orchards on the island. Take the Washington Island Ferry Line (at Northport Pier) to the island to catch the tour; the bright red trams pick passengers up at the ferry dock on Washington Island. | Washington Island ferry boat dock | 920/847–2039 | $6 | Memorial Day–Labor Day, daily 10:15, 11:45, 1:45, and 3:15; mid-May–Memorial Day and Labor Day–late Oct., daily 11 and 1.

Jacobson Museum. This small museum is dedicated to Jens Jacobson, a renowned woodworker who immigrated from Denmark in 1881. The museum features pieces he built on a foot-powered scroll saw. There are also Native American artifacts and Icelandic, Norwegian, and Danish memorabilia. | Little Lake Rd. 54246 | 920/847–2213 | $1 | Mid-May–mid-Oct. 9–4:30.

Rock Island State Park. This 905-acre island was once the private estate of millionaire inventor Chester Thordarson, who built several stone buildings on Washington Island between 1918–1929. Exhibits in the castlelike boathouse and Viking Hall explore the island's history and natural surroundings. You can hike on 10 mi of trails through deciduous hardwood forests, and backpacking is permitted. | Take Rock Island Ferry from Washington Island north ferry boat dock | Summer: 920/847–2235; winter: 920/847–3156 | www.dnr.state.wi.us | $7 nonresidents, $5 residents | Daily.

Washington Island Farm Museum. On this 3-acre complex there are five original farm buildings dating back to the late 1800s, including a log cabin and a barn. On display is a collection of field machinery, hand tools, photos, and homemaking artifacts. | Jackson Harbor Rd. | 920/847–2156 | Donations accepted | Memorial Day–mid-Oct., daily 10–5 (grounds and buildings); no building tours rest of year.

ON THE CALENDAR

AUG.: *Scandinavian Dance Festival.* Dance, food, desserts, demonstrations, and a tour of a Norwegian church take over the town on the first full weekend of the month. | 920/847–2179.

Dining

Findlay's Holiday Inn. Scandinavian. This small restaurant with harbor views is attached to a Holiday Inn and like the hotel is decorated with Norwegian wood carvings and old

Norwegian plates. Breads, jams, and soups are all homemade and perch and whitefish anchor the menu; on Friday night there's a perch dinner. Cherry pie made from Door County cherries is a specialty. Salad bar. Wine, beer. No smoking. | 1 Main Rd. | 920/847–2526 | $5–$12 | MC, V | Closed Nov.–Apr.

Ship's Wheel Restaurant. American. This octagonal-shape restaurant is just beyond Washington Island ferry dock overlooking Lake Michigan. The walleye fry and prime rib are the top-selling items. Breakfast served daily. | Lobdel Point Rd. | 920/847–2640 | $6–$15 | MC, V.

Lodging
Findlay's Holiday Inn and Viking Village. This two-story cedar building faces Lake Michigan. Windows have lattice trim, and there's a library and fireplace in the lobby; a grass roof covers the exterior entryway. Norwegian rosemaling (folk art that depicts roses and other flowers), carvings, and paintings from local artists fill the interior. Wildflower gardens edge the lake side of the building. Restaurant (*see* Findlay's Holiday Inn). No air-conditioning in some rooms. Beach. Business services. | Detroit Harbor Rd. | 920/847–2526 or 800/522–5469 | fax 920/847–2752 | vacation@holidayinn.net | www.holidayinn.net | 16 rooms | $100–$125 | MC, V.

Gibson's West Harbor Resort. This 7-acre resort overlooks both the Green Bay waters and the West Harbor. The first level of this 1879 clapboard house is occupied by the owners, but upstairs there are nine guest rooms that share two bathrooms. Guests have access to the kitchen and dining room. There are also housekeeping cottages with kitchenettes and two to three bedrooms that are available for daily or weekly rental. TV and VCR in common area. Video games. Beach, water sports, boating, fishing. | Rte. 1 | 920/847–2225 | 9 rooms (with shared bath), 6 cottages | $28–$40 rooms; $60–$65 per night cottages, $300–$325 per week | No credit cards | Cottages closed Nov.–Apr.; rooms open year-round.

WATERTOWN

MAP 11, D6

(Nearby towns also listed: Fort Atkinson, Janesville)

This Dodge County town, settled in 1836, is near Horicon Marsh and surrounded by spectacular scenery. Places of interest include the five-story, 57-room, pre–Civil War Octagon House, which is completely furnished, and an 1850s lumberyard that has been transformed into 12 specialty shops.

Information: Watertown Area Chamber of Commerce | 519 E. Main St., 53094-3873 | www.watertownchamber.com | 920/261–6320.

Attractions
The Market Specialty Shopping Mall. This 1850s post-and-beam lumberyard was restored and redesigned in the 1990s, and is now home to 12 antiques, artisan, and specialty shops. Much of the original structure remains, and cobblestone walkways inside the mall are made from paving bricks from the streets of old Milwaukee. A 50-dealer antiques shop occupies the entire second floor; much of the lower level is taken up by artists selling blacksmith work, metal sculpture, jewelery, and stained glass and fiber arts. The Upper Krust Pie Shop and Restaurant, also in the mall, bakes over 100 kinds of pies, and is a local favorite. | 210 S. Water St. | 920/262–2348 | Free | Mon.–Thurs. 10–6, Fri. 10–8, Sat. 10–5, Sun. 11–4.

Octagon House. Perhaps the largest pre–Civil War home in Wisconsin, this 1856 brick structure has five floors, a spiral staircase, and some 57 rooms. | 919 Charles St. | 920/261–2796 | $4.50 | May–Memorial Day and after Labor Day–late Oct., daily 11–3; Memorial Day–Labor Day, daily 10–4.

On the grounds of the Octagon House and included in the tour is **America's First Kindergarten,** a restored school where the nation's first kindergarten was held in 1856.

Watertown Aquatic Center. Water slides and a swimming pool are the main attractions here. | 1009 Perry St. | 920/262–8085 | $3; season passes available | Jun.–Aug.; weekdays 11–8, Sat. 11–7, Sun. 1–7.

ON THE CALENDAR

APR.: *Fair Day.* A popular event since the 1800s, this farmer's market kicks off in April, then continues to run all year on the second Tuesday of each month. Produce, baked goods, and crafts are for sale. | 920/261–6320.

AUG.: *Riverfest.* The first full weekend of the month brings a water show, log-rolling competitions, a craft fair, a midway, entertainment, food booths, and bands to Riverside Park on the north side of the city. | 920/261–6320.

Dining

Froggys. American. Specialties at this sports bar are the Friday-night fish fry, steaks, and sandwiches. A DJ provides music some nights. | 301 E. Main St. | 920/206–0918 | $5–$7 | AE, D, MC, V | Closed Mon. No dinner weekends.

Lodging

Karlshuegel Bed & Breakfast. This stucco inn, on 7 landscaped acres 1 mi north of downtown, was built in 1917. Inside are vaulted ceilings and large, bright rooms. One of the rooms can accommodate up to four people and has a private bath; others share a bath. Kids are welcomed here. Complimentary breakfast. Cable TV. | 749 N. Church St. | 920/261–3980 | 4 rooms (3 with shared bath) | $60–$85 | No credit cards.

WAUKESHA

MAP 11, E6

(Nearby towns also listed: Brookfield, Milwaukee)

Just 15 mi west of Milwaukee, Waukesha is rural community with real small-town charm. It was settled in 1834. Diversions include shopping malls, museums, and Kettle Moraine State Forest which has prime hiking, mountain biking, and cross-country ski trails.

Information: **Waukesha Area Convention and Visitors Bureau** | 2240 N. Grandview Blvd., 53188-4926 | 800/366–8474 | visit@wauknet.com | www.visitwaukesha.org.

Attractions

Hartford Heritage Auto Museum. This museum 35 mi southeast of Waukesha has the largest collection of antique cars and trucks in the state, including the rare Kissel which was built in Hartford from 1906 to 1931. | 147 N. Rural St., Hartford | 262/673–7999 | $6 | May–Sept., Mon.–Sat. 10–5, Sun. noon–5; Oct.–Apr. Wed.–Sat. 10–5, Sun. noon–5.

Kettle Moraine State Forest, Southern Unit. The immense ice sheet that covered the upper Midwest some 20,000 years ago left its imprint all around this forest. The southern section has 21,000 acres of glacial hills and is known for its extensive 60 mi of trail, part of which lie within the Ice Age Trail system. The forest is 2 mi west of Eagle, which is 13 mi west of Waukesha, and you can hike, bike, swim, and cross-country ski. | S. 91 W. 39091 Hwy. 59, Eagle | 262/594–6200 or 888/947–2757 | www.dnr.state.wi.us/org/land/forestry/State-Forests/index.htm | Free; permits required for some recreational trails | Daily.

Naga-Waukee Golf Course. Ten mi west of town, this 18-hole public course opened in 1966. | 1897 Maple Ave., Pewaukee | 262/367–2153 | Apr.–Oct.

Old World Wisconsin. This state historic society museum 17 mi southwest of Waukesha is made up of more than 50 authentic farmhouses, barns, and village shops of Wisconsin's pioneer immigrants. Originally scattered throughout the state, these buildings were

WAUKESHA

INTRO
ATTRACTIONS
DINING
LODGING

moved here and reassembled on this site. The buildings are grouped into an 1870s crossroads village and various ethnic farmsteads. Costumed interpreters demonstrate pioneer folkways. | S103 W37890 Rte. 67, Eagle | 262/594–6304 | $11 | May–Oct., daily 10–5.

Retzer Nature Center. Part of the Waukesha County park system, this nature center 3 mi west of downtown has a visitor center, live animals, a touch-and-discover area for small kids, and 5 mi of hiking trails. | W284 S1530 Rd. DT | 262/896–8007 | www.retzernc@execpc.com | Free | Daily 8–10.

Waukesha County Museum. Formerly the courthouse, this museum is listed on the National Register of Historic Places and chronicles Native American, pioneer, and military history; there's also a historic toy display and a re-created fur-trading post. A new Civil War exhibit features life-sized dioramas of a soldier camp and of the underground railroad. | 101 W. Main St. | 262/521–2859 | Free | Tues.–Sat. 9–4:30, Sun. noon–4.

ON THE CALENDAR
JULY: *Riverfest.* A family event in Frame Park with carnival rides; bike, pontoon, and paddleboat rides; a marketplace with food; gifts and toys; plus magicians and music. | 800/366–8474.
JULY–AUG.: *Waukesha County Fair.* This fair at the Waukesha County Exposition Center, held the seven weekends leading up to Labor Day, features food, entertainment, arts, crafts, kids' areas, animals, tractor and truck pulls, a carnival, and a demolition derby. | 262/544–5922.

Dining
Bits of Britain. English. The lace-covered tables of this downtown tea shop are housed in what was once a hotel owned by one of Milwaukee's first beer brewers. The menu offers 100 kinds of tea and such English favorites as mulligatawny, an Indian-inspired chicken-and-lamb soup flavored with curry, and Victoria sponge, a yellow cake with lemon curd or jam and whipped cream. | 294 W. Main St. | 262/896–7772 | $5–$12 | AE, D, MC, V | No dinner.

Mama Mia's in Downtown Waukesha. Italian. Pizza, lasagna, and Italian salads are the specialties at this cozy restaurant decorated with wine jugs. Keep your napkin handy: the garlic bread drips with butter. | 800 Clinton St. | 262/547–6503 | $8–$13 | AE, D, MC, V | No lunch weekends.

Seven Seas. American. Large picture windows are great for viewing sunsets over Lake Nagawicka at this restaurant 10 mi west of Waukesha. The menu offers pasta, perch, cod, and prime rib, and every Friday there's a fish fry. Open-air dining on a covered terrace close to the lake. Kids' menu. Sunday brunch. | 1807 Nagawicka Rd., Hartland | 262/367–3903 | $20–$40 | AE, D, MC, V | Closed Tues. Oct.—Apr. No lunch Mon.–Sat.

Waukesha Depot Restaurant. American. This restaurant is in a residential part of town in Waukesha's now-retired 1881 train depot. Steaks and ribs are on the menu and there's a fish fry every Friday. Sunday brunch. | 319 Williams St. | 262/549–2242 | $15–$25 | AE, MC, V | No lunch Sat.

Weissgerber's Gasthaus Inn. American. Beer steins and German crests adorn the walls of this local favorite serving stick-to-your-ribs fare such as pork shank, steaks, broiled salmon, and blackened shrimp. There's a beer garden surrounded by trees out back. | 2720 N. Grandview Blvd. | 262/544–4460 | $20–$30 | AE, MC, V | No lunch weekends.

Lodging
Country Inn Hotel & Conference Center. Located in the Kettle Moraine countryside, this modern hotel sits on 40 sprawling acres. It has a pavilion, an outdoor theater for entertainment, a gazebo and landscaped gardens. Rooms and common areas are elegant, with marble floors, plush furnishings, and artwork. 2 restaurants, bar, complimentary Continental breakfast, room service. Refrigerators, cable TV. Pool. Tennis. Gym. Business services. | 2810

Golf Rd. | 262/547–0201 or 800/247–6640 | www.countryinnhotel.com | 158 rooms, 142 suites | $99–$229 | AE, D, MC, V.

Select Inn of Waukesha. This chalet-style motel on the south side of town has themed suites including the Gallery Room which has an art gallery, and the Tackle Box Room complete with a canoe and fishing rods. Complimentary Continental breakfast. Refrigerators (in some suites). Business services. Pets allowed (deposit). | 2510 Plaza Ct. | 262/786–6015 or 800/ 641–1000 | fax 262/786–5784 | 91 rooms, 9 suites | $56–$70 | AE, D, DC, MC, V.

WAUPACA

(Nearby towns also listed: Appleton, Oshkosh, Wautoma)

This charming town is near the Chain of Lakes, a string of 22 interconnected lakes, and the winding Crystal River which is reputed to be excellent for trout fishing. The town is a good base for all kinds of water-sports vacations, including canoeing, fishing, and swimming. Nearby Hartman Creek State Park has four lakes with lovely areas for picnicking. Tourism and manufacturing form the economic base of this small town.

Information: Waupaca Area Chamber of Commerce | 221 S. Main St., 54981 | 888/417– 4040 | discoverwaupaca@waupacaareachamber.com | www.waupacaareacham-ber.com.

Attractions

Clear Water Harbor Cruises. Two excursion boats tour the Chain of Lakes from Clear Water Harbor 4 mi west of Waupaca. Available cruises include: champagne brunch, cocktails, and a church-service cruise; each lasts about an hour. | N. 2757 County Hwy. QQ | 715/258–2866 | Free | May–late Sept., daily 10–2.

Covered Bridge. Three miles south of town, this bridge built in 1970 spans the Crystal River behind the Red Mill Colonial Shop, an antiques store. | N. 2190 County Hwy. KN | 715/258– 7385 | Free | Mon.–Sat. 9–5, Sun. 1–5.

Ding's Dock. Canoe or tube down the Crystal River from Ding's Dock. Rentals and tour pack-ages are available. | N2498 W. Columbia Lake Dr. | 888/417–4040 | May–early Sept.

Hartman Creek State Park. This woodsy, 1,300-acre state park 6 mi west of downtown Wau-paca has hiking and cross-country ski trails, a sandy beach perfect for swimming, and wooded campsites. In summer there are evening nature programs. | N2480 Hartman Creek Rd. | 715/258–2372 | www.dnr.state.wi.us | $7 nonresidents, $5 residents | Daily 6 AM–11 PM.

South Park. This former Native American campground is now a city park with picnic shel-ters, playground, bathhouse, a sandy beach with swimming in Shadow Lake, and a fish-ing pier where you might catch northern pike or perhaps some bass. | S. Main St. | 715/258– 7343 | Free | Daily.

Hutchinson House Museum. This 1854 Victorian home was the first frame house in the city. It was moved from its original site on Franklin Street to South Park, and it still con-tains original period furnishings. Docents lead tours. | S. Main St. | 715/258–5958 | $1.50 | Memorial Day–Labor Day, Fri.–Sun., 1–4:30.

ON THE CALENDAR

APR.: *Waupaca Fine Art Show.* This professionally juried art show at the Hendrickson Center features local and Midwest artists working in a variety of media. | 888/417–4040.
JUNE: *Strawberry Fest.* This family festival celebrates spring on the third Saturday of the month with arts, crafts, kids' activities, and foods made with strawberries. | 888/417–4040.

SEPT.: *Fall-O-Rama*. Arts, crafts, food, and entertainment are part of the autumn celebration at this family event in South Park on the third Saturday of the month. | 888/417–4040.

Dining

Crystal Lounge. American. The Crystal Burger, a half-pound burger topped with bacon, cheese, tomato and lettuce, is the biggest draw, but locals also come for beer-battered perch and cod, chile, and daily soup specials. | 1332 Churchill St. | 715/258–8594 | $5–$9 | No credit cards | Closed Sun.

Lodging

Windmill Manor Bed & Breakfast. This 1890s white farmhouse was updated inside for guests, but looks much as it did near the turn of the 20th century on the outside. A four-story lighthouse—once part of the farm—is just next door. You can laze on the patio or on the 75-ft-long porch with swings, or take a ride on a bicycle built for two. One room is actually a three-room suite. Complimentary breakfast. In-room hot tubs, cable TV. | N2919 County Rd. QQ | 715/256–1770 | fax 715/258–6554 | www.windmill-manor.com | 4 rooms, 1 suite | $85–$115 rooms, $135 suite | AE, MC, V.

WAUPUN

(Nearby towns also listed: Beaver Dam, Fond du Lac)

This Dodge County town was founded in 1839. The surrounding countryside is criss-crossed by forested trails and the area is known as the wild goose center of Wisconsin because hundreds of thousands of geese migrate through here. Diversions include antiques shops, outdoor sculptures, and a Christmas store filled with an impressive collection of Italian glass ornaments, open all year.

Information: Waupun Chamber of Commerce | 121 E. Main St., 53963 | 920/324–3491 | www.waupunchamber.com.

Attractions

City of Sculpture. City of Sculpture, Waupun's unofficial epithet, refers to the eight life-size bronze sculptures scattered throughout town that were created between 1929 and 1939 by Clarence Shaler, Laredo Taft, and James Earl Frasier. All of the statues depict historical figures or events, the most famous one being Frasier's "End of the Trail," which captures the plight of the Native American with the image of a lone warrior slumped on a horse. Most of the statues are made by Shaler, and express heroic, idyllic, and religous portrayals of pioneer life. The visitor center can supply brochures showing their locations. | Visitor center: 121 E. Main St., Suite A | 920/324–3491 | Free | Daily.

Kristmas Kringle Shoppe. This two-story store looks like a Bavarian chalet and contains the largest collection of Italian glass Christmas ornaments in the United States. The inside is laid out like an old European street, with lighted trees and street lamps. There are more than 70 themed Christmas trees on display, along with hundreds of collectibles, animated figures, and imported ornaments. | 1330 S. Main St. | 800/721–2525 | www.kristmaskringle.com | Free | Mon., Tues., Thurs. 9–6; Wed., Fri. 9–8; Sat. 9–6; Sun. 10–5.

ON THE CALENDAR

SEPT.: *Volksfest*. German music and dancing, food, beverages, and crafts at the Senior Center and in the City Auditorium on the weekend after Labor Day. | 920/324–3491 or 920/324–3220.

Dining

House of Hunan. Chinese. This small Main Street restaurant takes its name from China's Hunan province which like neighboring Szechuan is noted for its liberal use of hot chile pepper. If you like spicy food, try the General Tso's chicken. | 300 E. Main St. | 920/324–8992 | $7–$10 | MC, V | Closed Mon.

Lodging

Americinn Motels. This modern two-story hotel has standard rooms plus five suites and is close to area restaurants. Complimentary Continental breakfast. Some in-room hot tubs, cable TV. Pool. Hot tub, sauna. | 5 Gateway Dr. | 920/324–2500 or 800/634–3444 | 33 rooms, 5 suites | $60–$110 | AE, D, DC, MC, V.

Inn Town Motel. This country-blue hostelry with white trim and flower beds in front is in a quiet residential area near downtown. Waterfowl decoys decorate the office. Rooms have outdoor access. Microwaves available, refrigerators, cable TV. | 27 S. State St. | 920/324–4211 or 800/433–6231 | fax 920/324–6921 | djjago@powerweb.net | 16 rooms | $43–$50 | AE, D, MC, V.

WAUSAU

MAP 11, D4

(Nearby towns also listed: Marshfield, Stevens Point, Wisconsin Rapids)

Since the mid 1800s, this community of 39,000 on the Wisconsin River has evolved from a lumbering town to a thriving city with a diverse commercial and industrial base. There is a 10-block historic district of original 1800s homes surrounded by huge trees and manicured lawns. Marathon County is the world's leading producer of ginseng, and Wausau is a center for the buying and selling of the herb. Just south of town is Rib Mountain, one of the oldest geologic formations on earth.

Information: Wausau/Central Wisconsin Convention and Visitors Bureau | 10204 Park Plaza, Suite B 20, Mosinee 54455 | 888/948–4748 | www.wausaucvb.org.

Attractions

Grand Theater. This Greek Revival theater opened in 1929 and was restored in 1987. It has classic examples of colonnades, gold leaf, marble statues, and the original limestone facade. Today it hosts live theater, touring Broadway shows, symphony concerts, and performances by local artists and community theaters; ticket prices vary by performance. A slide show and free tour of the building is available by appointment. | 415 4th St. 54403 | 715/842–0988 or 888/239–0421 | Free.

Leigh Yawkey Woodson Art Museum. Housed in an elegant 1929 mansion, this art museum displays collections of Royal Worcester porcelain and 19th- and 20th-century glass. "Birds in Art," an internationally known annual exhibition, runs for about 10 weeks beginning the weekend after Labor Day. | 700 N. 12th St., at Franklin St. | 715/845–7010 | Free | Tues.–Fri. 9–4, weekends noon–5.

Marathon County Historical Museum. Located downtown, this former home of wealthy lumberman Cyrus Yawkey was built in 1901 and has restored Victorian rooms, a model railroad display, and a one-room schoolhouse on-site. | 403 McIndoe St. | 715/848–6143 | Donations accepted | Tues.–Thurs. 9–4:30, weekends 1–4:30.

Rib Mountain State Park. Rib Mountain is one of the oldest geologic formations on earth. At 1,940 ft, it is the third-highest point in Wisconsin. Check out the view of the Wisconsin River valley from the observation tower. Campsites, picnic areas, and 7 mi of hiking and cross-country ski trails are in the park. It's 2 mi west of downtown Wausau, off North Mountain Rd. | 4200 Park Rd., Rib Mountain | 715/842–2522 | www1.reserveamerica.com/usa/wi/ribm/ | $7 nonresidents, $5 residents | Daily; camping mid-Apr.–mid-Oct.

Granite Peak Ski Area. At this 100-acre ski area, 21 runs are laid out down 624-ft vertical drops. The main lodge is a rustic, split-stone chalet. | 3605 N. Mountain Rd. (U.S. 51/Rte. 39) | 715/845–2846 | Daily lift tickets $32 | Mid-Dec.–mid-Mar.

ON THE CALENDAR
AUG.: *Big Bull Falls Blues Festival.* This outdoor musical event features nationally known blues performers in Fern Island Park the last weekend in August. | 888/948–4748.
AUG.: *Wisconsin Valley Fair.* Marathon Park hosts entertainment, food stands, rides, and exhibitions for six days in early August. | 888/948–4748.
SEPT.: *Wausau Festival of Arts.* More than 100 juried artists present their work all along Third Street for this festival that takes place the weekend after Labor Day. Other art-related events are also held throughout town in conjunction with this festival. | 715/842–1676 or 888/948–4748.

Dining
Austin's Restaurant and Lounge. American. This large restaurant specializes in steak, chicken, and fish. Homemade desserts change weekly. | 201 N. 17th Ave. | 715/842–1394 | $5–$16 | AE, D, DC, MC, V | No dinner Sun.

Carmelo's. Italian. This small restaurant has a view of the Rib Mountain Ski Area. There's panfried haddock at the Friday-night fish fry. Any other day, sample the shrimp scampi, fettuccine Alfredo, or the tenderloin. | 3605 N. Mountain Rd. | 715/845–5570 | $10–$20 | AE, D, MC, V | No lunch.

Michael's. Continental. This wooden A-frame restaurant in the Rib Mountain section of Wausau has a casual atmosphere. Mirrors hang on the walls; clown fish and five different varieties of angelfish swim around in large aquariums in the dining area and lounge. You can start dinner with the shrimp chartreuse, served with cream sauce and flambéed in golden liquor, and follow with the roast Wisconsin duckling with wild rice and a dark cherry sauce. The veal maison with scallops, shrimp, and lobster is also a good bet. Kids' menu. | 2901 Rib Mountain Dr. | 715/842–9856 | $15–$20 | AE, D, DC, MC, V | Closed Sun. No lunch.

Wagon Wheel. American. This rustic restaurant in a 1946 wood-and-brick ranch-style building has been in operation for more than 50 years, and has two fireplaces, hardwood floors, candlelight, and linen tablecloths. All beef is dry-aged and charcoal-broiled. Also on the menu: barbecued ribs, seafood, and wild-rice soup. | 3901 N. 6th St. | 715/675–2263 | $20–$35 | AE, D, MC, V | Closed Sun. No lunch.

Wausau Mine Co. American/Casual. Italian- and Mexican-inspired dishes such as chicken Alfredo, pizza, burritos, and taco salads share space on the menu with steaks, burgers, and sandwiches at this casual spot. Old mining equipment on the walls recall Upper Peninsula history. Kids' menu. | 3904 W. Stewart Ave. | 715/845–7304 | Reservations not accepted Fri., Sat. | $12–$25 | D, DC, MC, V.

Lodging
Baymont Inn. Two miles from downtown, on the western edge of Wausau, this inn has a country decor, with quilts in the rooms. There's a landscaped lawn and the lobby has a breakfast area. Several restaurants are within 5 blocks of the inn. *USA Today* newspaper is complimentary. Complimentary Continental breakfast. In-room data ports, cable TV. Pool. Business services. Pets allowed. | 1910 Stewart Ave. | 715/842–0421 | fax 715/845–5096 | www.baymontinn.com | 95 rooms | $62–$65 | AE, D, DC, MC, V.

Best Western Midway Hotel. This standard motel 5 mi south of town, in Rib Mountain, has a small, contemporary lobby with a polished-rock floor and leather furniture. Shuttles run to the Rib Mountain Ski Area. Restaurant, bar, picnic area, room service. In-room data ports, cable TV. Pool. Hot tub, sauna. Playground. Business services, airport shuttle. Pets allowed (fee). | 2901 Martin Ave., Rib Mountain | 715/842–1616 | fax 715/845–3726 | 99 rooms | $80–$95 | AE, D, DC, MC, V.

Exel Inn. This brick motel is near the center of town near Highway 51 and has a view of Rib Mountain. Complimentary Continental breakfast. Cable TV. Video games. Laundry facilities. Business services. Pets allowed. | 116 S. 17th Ave. | 715/842–0641 | fax 715/848–1356 | 122 rooms | $48–$52 | AE, D, DC, MC, V.

Ponderosa Motel. This simple motel has just eight rooms and is good value for the money. Cable TV. | 2101 Grand Ave. | 715/842–3388 | 8 rooms | $32 | D, MC, V.

Rib Mountain Inn. This chalet-style inn is at the base of Rib Mountain, just a 15-minute walk from skiing. Picnic areas, complimentary Continental breakfast. Refrigerators, some in-room hot tubs, cable TV, in-room VCRs and movies. Hot tub, sauna. Driving range. Business services. Pets allowed. | 2900 Rib Mountain Way | 715/848–2802 | fax 715/848–1908 | 16 rooms, 4 villas, 4 apartments | $78–$114 rooms, $148–$219 villas, $250–$308 apartments | AE, D, DC, MC, V.

Rosenberry Inn bed-and-breakfast. This 1908 home was built in the Prairie School style of architecture. All rooms have private baths. One is a suite with a sitting room, another has a wood-burning fireplace. Complimentary breakfast. No TV in some rooms. | 511 Franklin St. | 715/842–5733 | fax 715/843–5659 | www.rosenberryinn.com | 5 rooms, 3 suites | $70–$100 rooms, $80–$160 suites | MC, V.

Super 8. This standard motel on the west side of town is near the business district and within walking distance of restaurants. Complimentary Continental breakfast. Cable TV. Pool. Hot tub. Business services. Pets allowed. | 2006 Stewart Ave. | 715/848–2888 | fax 715/842–9578 | www.super8.com | 88 rooms | $69 | AE, D, DC, MC, V.

Westwood Conference Center. This conference center is centrally located to restaurants and shopping. Bar, complimentary Continental breakfast. Cable TV. Gym. Business services. | 1800 W. Bridge St. | 715/847–9200 or 800/468–8470 | fax 715/847–8848 | 72 rooms | $60–$83 | AE, D, DC, MC, V.

WAUTOMA

MAP 11, D5

(Nearby towns also listed: Green Lake, Waupaca)

Much of the land around this popular resort and recreation area is devoted to Christmas-tree farming. Each year, one of the area's largest tree farms ships 750,000 trees to dealers throughout the country. Because of its relative proximity to the larger cities of Chicago, Milwaukee, and Madison, and because of the many surrounding lakes and forests, tourism is the primary industry here. The historic Main Street shopping district boasts small boutiques, specialty shops and local restaurants and bakeries.

Information: **Wautoma Area Chamber of Commerce** | 210 E. Main St. 54982 | 920/787–3488 or 877/928–8662 | www.1wautoma.com.

Attractions

Nordic Mountain Ski Area. Eight miles north of town on 420-acre Mt. Morris county park, this ski area has 13 runs and 6 mi of trails down 265 vertical ft. | Hwy. W, Wild Rose | 920/787–3324 or 800/253–7266 | www.nordicmountain.com/ | Daily lift ticket $20 | Dec.–early Mar.

Waushara County Historical Museum. This museum is located in an old jail. The back is where the cells were—and still are; the front is where the sheriff and his family lived. Today the family quarters are filled with period pieces. There's a chart that was used to measure height, and a fingerprinting area for the prisoners. | 221 S. Saint Marie St. | 920/787–7584 | Donations | June–Aug., Wed. and Sat., 1–4.

Wild Rose Pioneer Museum. Most buildings in this pioneer village are original to the site, including an 1873 house built by the first town marshall, Elijah Stewart. The cluster of buildings also includes a barn and a country store dating from the 1870s, a school that's circa 1894, a bank/post office from the early 1900s, and replicas of a smokehouse, a blacksmith shop, a carriage house, and a weaving room. The complex is in the center of Wild Rose, 8 mi north of Wautoma on Route 22 (Main Street). | Main St., Wild Rose | 920/622–3364 | $1; special rates for kids | Mid-June–Labor Day, Wed. and Sat. 1–3.

ON THE CALENDAR
FEB.: *Winterfest.* Sumo wrestling, broom ball, coed snow volleyball, a cribbage tournament, a snowmobile jumping event, a pancake breakfast, a casino night, bowling, and a DJ and karaoke come to the Waushara County fairgrounds and other venues throughout town early in the month. | 920/787–3976.

Dining
Peck's Plantation Restaurant. American. Top items at this restaurant include prime rib, spaghetti, and huge salads. | W7612 State Rds. 21 and 73 | 920/787–3301 | $8–$15 | AE, MC, V.

Lodging
Silercryst Motel. This two-story vine-covered motel overlooks Silver Lake. Restaurant. Cable TV. Beach, boating, dock, fishing. Video games. | W7015 Hwy. 21 E | 920/787–3367 | fax 920/787–1537 | www.silvercryst.com | 22 rooms | $65–$75 | D, MC, V.

WAUWATOSA

MAP 11, E6

(Nearby towns also listed: Brookfield, Glendale, Milwaukee, Waukesha)

Just minutes from downtown Milwaukee (adjacent to the Milwaukee County Zoo), Wauwatosa, settled in 1835, was first called Hart's Mills, after Charles Hart, who established a gristmill on the Menomonee River. It grew rapidly from 1836 to the early 1900s and many of the buildings from that era are preserved. Today Wauwatosa's economic base is industry and small business.

Information: Wauwatosa Area Chamber of Commerce | 909 N. Mayfair Rd., Suite 201, 53226-2640 | 414/453–2330.

Attractions
Annunciation Greek Orthodox Church. Famed Wisconsin architect Frank Lloyd Wright called this church on the northwest side of Milwaukee (his last major building), his "little jewel." The blue-domed Byzantine-style church opened in 1961 and is a major drawn in this town. | 9400 W. Congress St. | 414/461–9400 | $2 | Tues. and Fri. by prearranged group tour.

Harley-Davidson Inc. Take a one-hour tour of the home of the Harley. Kids over 12 only. | 11700 W. Capitol Dr., northwest of downtown area | 414/535–3666 | Free | Call for tour schedule.

Lowell Damon House. This pine–and–black wood colonial was built in 1847 and decorated with mid-19th-century furniture and art; it is Wauwatosa's oldest home. | 2107 Wauwatosa Ave. | 414/273–8288 or 414/771–1265 | Donations accepted | Sun. and Wed. by reservation.

SEPT.: *Tosafest.* Entertainment on three stages, food, drink, soccer, tennis, a twilight fun run, and a kids' area take over downtown the weekend after Labor-Day. | 414/453–2330.

Dining

Chancery Restaurant. American. This downtown restaurant has several dining rooms with leaded-glass windows, high-back wood booths, and old photos on the walls. The menu changes frequently, but the burgers and sandwiches are always huge. | 7613 W. State St. | 414/453–2300 | Reservations not accepted Fri. | $20–$30 | D, MC, V.

Edwardo's Natural Pizza Restaurant. Pizza. This busy restaurant not far from the Milwaukee County Zoo has spacious booths in two dining rooms, and a menu that stars bruschetta and deep-dish stuffed pizzas. | 10845 Bluemound Rd. | 414/771–7770 | $15–$20 | AE, D, DC, MC, V.

Jake's. American. Heaping plates of ultrathin French-fried onion rings draw locals to this small, cozy restaurant with barn-wood walls and stained glass accents. Try the clam chowder, escargots, or one of the excellent steak dishes; the Bailey's chocolate-chip cheesecake, made on the premises, is also a crowd-pleaser. Kids' menu. | 6030 W. North Ave. | 414/771–0550 | $11–$24 | AE, DC, MC, V | No lunch.

Ristorante Bartolotta. Italian. This small, intimate northern Italian trattoria in an old Pabst tavern dating from the late 1800s looks as if it was transported from Italy with its wood-burning stove and wooden bar. Cream city brick inside and out, and family photos from the "old country" cover the walls. Fish, meats, and pizzas are cooked in a wood-burning oven, and all pasta is homemade; try the sautéed veal chop with marsala cream sauce. Open-air dining is street-side, and looks out over the historic downtown area. Entertainment Monday–Wednesday. No smoking. | 7616 W. State St. | 414/771–7910 | $25–$30 | AE, D, DC, MC, V | No lunch weekends.

Lodging

Best Western Midway Hotel. This standard hotel is across the street from the zoo and near large shopping centers. Restaurant, bar, room service. In-room data ports, some refrigerators, cable TV. Pool. Hot tub. Exercise room. Laundry facilities. Business services, airport shuttle, free parking. | 251 N. Mayfair Rd. | 414/774–3600 | fax 414/774–5015 | 116 rooms | $97–$130 | AE, D, DC, MC, V.

Days Inn. This three-story inn is along a busy highway and close to shopping. Restaurant, bar, complimentary Continental breakfast. Cable TV. Pool. | 11811 W. Bluemound Rd. | 414/771–4500 | fax 414/771–4501 | 125 rooms | $60–$80 | AE, D, DC, MC, V.

Exel Inn–West. This simple modern hotel is across the street from the zoo and 2 mi from large shopping malls. Complimentary Continental breakfast. Cable TV. Business services. Some pets allowed. | 115 N. Mayfair Rd. (U.S. 100) | 414/257–0140 | fax 414/475–7875 | 123 rooms | $56–$80 | AE, D, DC, MC, V.

Forty Winks Inn. This Frank Lloyd Wright Prairie design in stone and glass was actually designed by his protégé Russell Barr Williamson, and is 2 mi north of the Mayfair Shopping Center and the Brookfield Square Mall. Some refrigerators, cable TV. | 11017 W. Bluemound Rd. | 414/774–2800 or 800/946–5746 | fax 414/774–9134 | 31 rooms (12 with shower only) | $74–$86 | AE, D, MC, V.

Holiday Inn Express. Ten miles northwest of town, this modern brick motel with a fireplace in its large lobby is attractively landscaped with trees, shrubs, and flower beds. Complimentary Continental breakfast. Some refrigerators, cable TV. Business services. | 11111 W. North Ave. | 414/778–0333 | fax 414/778–0331 | www.basshotels.com/hiexpress | 122 rooms | $84–$119 | AE, D, DC, MC, V.

Radisson. The elegant lobby has a marble floor covered with a custom-made rug designed in a colorful pattern; paintings of famous Milwaukee sights and instruments represent-

WAUWATOSA

INTRO
ATTRACTIONS
DINING
LODGING

ing the Milwaukee symphony fill the lobby. The zoo and restaurants are nearby. Restaurant, bar, room service. In-room data ports, cable TV. Pool. Sauna. Business services, airport shuttle. | 2303 N. Mayfair Rd. (Rte. 100) | 414/257–3400 | fax 414/257–0900 | 151 rooms | $139–$179 | AE, D, DC, MC, V.

WEST BEND

(Nearby town also listed: Cedarburg)

This small town on the banks of the Milwaukee River was settled in 1845. Today the vintage 1800s buildings have been refurbished and are used as museums and restaurants. This quiet community is home to about 28,000 people, and the West Bend appliance company is located here. Nearby are factory-outlet malls and the Kettle Moraine State Forest is just to the north.

Information: **West Bend Area Chamber of Commerce** | Box 522, 53095-0522 | 888/338–8666 | info@wbchamber.org | www.wbchamber.org.

Attractions

Lizard Mound County Park. Listed on the National Register of Historic Places, this 32-acre park contains unusual earthen effigy mounds built between 1,000 BC and AD 500. There's a picnic area and a self-guided nature trail. | Rte. A | 262/338–2666 | Free | Daily.

Washington County Historical Society Museum. Farm equipment, photos, and town documents make up the collection in this downtown historical society museum which in 1886 was the county jail and county courthouse. Check out the cell block and the former sheriff's quarters. | 320 S. 5th Ave. | 262/335–4678 | Free | Wed.–Fri. 10–4, Sun. 1–4.

West Bend Art Museum. This downtown museum, in a 1930s redbrick colonial, contains a century's worth of Wisconsin art; the collection dates back to 1850. | 300 S. 6th Ave. | 262/334–9638 | Free | Wed.–Sat. 10–4:30, Sun. 1–4:30.

ON THE CALENDAR

AUG.: *Germanfest.* This festival, held the last full weekend before Labor Day, features German music and dance, German food, a special "fest" beer, a farmers' market, a pancake breakfast, and an art fair. | 262/338–3909.

Dining

George Webb Restaurant. American. Regulars flock to this restaurant for chile, soups, and burgers—24 hours a day. | 852 Main St. | 262/338–1518 | $3–$8 | MC, V.

Lodging

Welcome Home Bed & Breakfast. This contemporary home is surrounded by mature woods and prairies and has lots of windows and screened-in porches. Baths are across the halls from the rooms, are wheelchair accessible, and have hot tubs. Guests have access to the kitchen. Complimentary Continental breakfast. Cable TV. | 4260 W. Hawthorne Dr. | 262/675–2525 | fax 262/675–0817 | www.hnet.net/~welcomehome | 2 rooms | $50 | No credit cards.

West Bend Inn. This gray brick inn on the west side of town was built in the 1970s. The suites have themes like Ceasar's Court, Tree House, Jungle Safari, and Pearl Under the Sea. Bar, complimentary Continental breakfast. In-room VCRs and movies available. Indoor-outdoor pool. Hot tub, sauna. Game room. Business services. | 2520 W. Washington St. | 262/338–0636 or 800/727–9727 | fax 262/338–4290 | wbinn@hnet.net | www.fantasuite.com | 61 rooms, 26 suites | $62–$79 | AE, D, DC, MC, V.

WISCONSIN DELLS

(Nearby towns also listed: Baraboo, Portage)

Settled in 1856, this town along the Wisconsin River is now one giant water attraction and one of the state's most popular family vacation destinations. Informally known as "The Dells," the natural beauty of the bluffs and deep river gorges is contrasted by the more commercial attractions and amusements, which melt into the twin city of Lake Delton, 2 mi south of downtown Wisconsin Dells. You'll find the largest water parks in the United States, championship golf courses, casino gambling, water-ski shows and—most popular of all—the famous *Wisconsin Ducks*, a World War II–era amphibious landing craft that drives from the street right into the river. To experience the undeveloped side of the Dells, visit nearby Rock Arbor and Mirror Lake state parks.

Information: Wisconsin Dells Visitor and Convention Bureau | 701 Superior St., 53965-0390 | 800/223–3557 | www.wisdells.com.

Attractions

Beaver Springs Fishing Park and Riding Stables. All species of trout, ranging in length from 6 to 40 inches, fill the six ponds at this public facility on the north side of town. Also on the site are a 50,000-gallon aquarium and riding stables offering 30- to 45-minute rides. Fishing is available. | 600 Trout Rd. | 608/254–2735 | Fishing fees vary; stables $16.98; aquarium $5.50 | Daily; call for hours.

Christmas Mountain Village. Ice rinks, hiking trails, a swimming pool, 27 holes of golf, and 1,000 acres for both downhill and cross-country skiing. Although primarily a golf resort, one cross-country ski trail with a vertical drop of 320 ft is open during the winter. The village is 4 mi west of town. | S944 Christmas Mountain Rd. | 608/254–3971 | Admission to village free; lift tickets $27; golf prices vary | Daily; Dec.–Apr. 9–10, May–Oct. 7–11.

Dells Boat Tours. Excursion cruises take you through the bluffs of the Upper and Lower Dells. | 11 Broadway, in heart of Wisconsin Dells | 608/254–8555 | www.dells.com/boattour.html | $15.75 for Upper Dells tour; $11.50 for Lower Dells tour; $20 for both tours; special rates for kids | Call for hrs.

Dells Ducks. A one-hour amphibious tour down the Wisconsin River. | 1550 Wisconsin Dells Pkwy. | 608/254–6080 | $15; special rates for kids | June–Aug., daily 9–7; Apr., May, Sept., Oct., daily 10–5.

Familyland—The Family Water Park. This 3-acre water park includes water slides, a wave pool, and a kids' area. Inside there's a kiddie play area, hot tubs, and water basketball. | 1701 Wisconsin Dells Pkwy. (U.S. 12) | 608/254–7766 | www.wisdellstreasureisland.com | $17.95–$22.95 | Call for hrs.

H. H. Bennett Studio and History Center. This museum is dedicated to the works of noted nature photographer H. H. Bennett, the man who helped make the Wisconsin Dells famous. Items in what was Bennett's original studio (built in 1875) include his photographs, cameras, and other memorabilia. | 215 Broadway | 608/253–3523 | $5.75 | Jan.–Apr. and Oct., weekends 10–5; May–mid-Jun. and mid-Aug.–Sept., daily 10–5; mid-June–mid-Aug., daily 10–8. Closed Nov.–Dec.

HoChunk Bingo and Casino. Blackjack, slots, and bingo are among the games at this casino 7 mi south of Wisconsin Dells. | S3214 U.S. Hwy. 12, Baraboo | 800/746–2486 | Free | Daily 24 hrs.

Lost Canyon Tours. Half-hour horse-and-carriage rides through cliff-walled gorges depart every 10 to 15 minutes from the south shore of Lake Delton, a mile from Wisconsin Dells.

| 720 Canyon Rd., Lake Delton | 608/254–8757 | $5.50 | Early May–mid-Oct., daily 8:30–8; last tour leaves at 7.

Mirror Lake State Park. You'll find camping, swimming, canoeing, and hiking on 20 mi of trails. This 2,050-acre park is near Rocky Arbor State Park, just 4 mi southwest of Wisconsin Dells. | E10320 Fern Dell Rd., Baraboo | 608/254–2333 | www.dnr.state.wi.us | $7 nonresidents, $5 residents | Daily.

Noah's Ark Water Park. With 70 acres of water slides and rides, restaurants, snack stands, stores, miniature golf, and more, this is America's largest water park. It's about 1 mi from Wisconsin Dells | 1410 Wisconsin Dells Pkwy., Lake Delton | 608/254–6351 | www.noahsarkwaterpark.com | $24.99 | Mid-May–Labor Day, daily 9–8; June hours vary.

Original Wisconsin Ducks. Tours of scenic wilderness trails around and in the Lower Dells and Lake Delton via amphibious World War II landing craft. It's 5 mi from Wisconsin Dells. | 1890 Wisconsin Dells Pkwy., Lake Delton | 608/254–8751 | www.wisdells.com/ducks | $14.50 | Apr.–May, daily 9–4; Memorial Day–Labor Day, daily 8–7; Labor Day–mid-Nov., daily 9–4; hours may vary in spring and fall.

Ripleys Believe It or Not! Museum. In downtown Wisconsin Dells, you can witness the strange, the unbelievable, the bizarre, and the downright loony. | 115 Broadway | 608/253–7556 | www.conceptattractions.com | $7.95; special rates for kids | Memorial Day weekend–Labor Day, daily 9 AM–midnight; Labor Day–mid-Oct., daily 10–10; Apr.–Memorial Day, daily 10–6.

Riverside and Great Northern Railway. Take a half-hour ride through the woods on a 15-inch gauge steam-powered railroad. Departs every 45 minutes from the northeast part of town. | N115 Hwy. N | 608/254–6367 | $6 | Memorial Day–Labor Day, daily 10–5:30; Labor Day–Oct. and April–Memorial Day, weekends 10–4; Nov.–Dec., weekends 10–2.

Riverview Park and Waterworld. This downtown water park has water slides, roller coasters, Ferris wheels, bumper cars, go-carts, and carousels. | 700 U.S. 12 | 608/254–2608 | www.riverviewpark.com | $15.99 | May and Sept., daily 10–5; Jun.–Aug., daily 10–11.

Rocky Arbor State Park. Camping and hiking at this 232-acre preserve is among spectacular sandstone cliffs. It's 1½ mi north of Wisconsin Dells. | E10320 Fern Dell Rd., Baraboo | 608/254–8001 (in summer), 608/254–2333 (in winter) | www.dnr.state.wi.us | $7 nonresidents, $5 residents | Memorial Day–Labor Day; Sun.–Thurs. 8 AM –11, Fri.–Sat. 8 AM–midnight.

Tommy Bartlett's Robot World and Exploratory. One hundred interactive exhibits as well as an original Russian MIR space station. It's 3 mi. south of Wisconsin Dells on U.S. 12. | 560 Wisconsin Dells Pkwy., Lake Delton | 608/254–2525 | www.tommybartlett.com | $8.75; special rates for kids | Daily 9–9.

Tommy Bartlett's Thrill Show. Professional water-skiers and daredevil entertainers from around the world perform in this two-hour show, which also features dance troops, juggling acts, and singers. It's 3 mi south of Wisconsin Dells. | 560 Wisconsin Dells Pkwy., Lake Delton | 608/254–2525 | www.tommybartlett.com | $11.13–$17.70; special rates for kids | Memorial Day weekend–Labor Day, daily 1, 4:30, and 8:30.

Wisconsin Deer Park. Deer are raised at this park/petting zoo in the center of town. | 583 U.S. 12 | 608/253–2041 | $5.75; special rates for kids | May–mid-Oct., daily 9–8.

ON THE CALENDAR

JAN.: *Flake Out Festival*. Join the locals in this two-day annual event that includes Wisconsin's only officially recognized snow sculpting competition—the icy statuettes are elaborate pieces of art. Other events include a snowman building competition, ice carving, ice skating, horse-drawn sleigh rides, food, entertainment, fireworks and other participatory family activities. | 800/223–3557.

Dining

Bean & Berry Bistro. American. Vegetarian dishes are a specialty here. Save room for the homemade desserts. Breakfast is served daily. | 1009 Stand Rock Rd. | 608/253–9394 | $4–$7 | No credit cards.

Black Bart's Stagecoach Buffet. American. This all-buffet restaurant specializes in barbecued ribs and seafood. The buffet table stretches out 40 ft. Breakfast is served daily. | 420 State Hwy. 13 | 608/253–2278 | $10–$15 | AE, D, MC, V.

Cheese Factory Restaurant. Vegetarian. Basic Mexican dishes such as burritos and chimichangas, plus pizzas and a variety of international dishes like chicken tofu Kiev and Chinese stir-fry, are on the menu at this rustic place with high, beamed ceilings and shiny black-and-white tile floors just 2 mi southwest of downtown Wisconsin Dells in Lake Delton. The edible flowers used to garnish many dishes are grown in the restaurant's own gardens. Live entertainment on Sat. evenings. Kids' menu. | 521 Wisconsin Dells Pkwy. S, Lake Delton | 608/253–6065 | $17–$25 | AE, MC, V | Closed Tues. Memorial Day–Labor Day. No dinner Sun. Labor Day–Memorial Day.

The Del-Bar. American. Designed in the Frank Lloyd Wright Prairie style, this large restaurant in the center of Lake Delton, 1 mi south of Wisconsin Dells, has fireplaces, lots of stained glass, and several dining areas. Offerings include pan-fried native walleye, prime aged steaks, and the wonderful 10-ounce filet Jim with a madeira demiglace. Kids' menu. | 800 Wisconsin Dells Pkwy., Lake Delton | 608/253–1861 | www.dells.com/delbar/index.htm | $20–$30 | AE, D, DC, MC, V | No lunch.

Fischer's. American. Linens, candles, and flowers on the glass-topped tables add elegance to this casual eatery, housed in a wood-and-stone building on Lake Delton's main strip. Try the excellent prime rib, slow roasted for an entire day, or the salmon filet with dill sauce. The restaurant is 3 mi south of downtown Wisconsin Dells. Kids' menu. | 441 Wisconsin Dells Pkwy. S, Lake Delton | 608/253–7531 | $15–$20 | D, MC, V | No lunch.

Ishnala Supper Club. American. This rustic log lodge overlooking the lake in Mirror Lake State Park, 2 mi south of Wisconsin Dells, was a trading post in the 1800s; an addition was later designed by one of Frank Lloyd Wright's apprentices and added to the original building. You can have drinks and appetizers on the decks outside. Inside beamed ceilings and Native American rugs set the mood and a live Norway pine tree is rooted in the ground and grows through the roof. On the menu: barbecued ribs, aged meats, prime rib, roast Wisconsin duckling, and fish dishes such as Atlantic salmon and orange roughy. Kids' menu. | S2011 Ishnala Rd., Lake Delton | 608/423–4122 | Reservations not accepted | AE, MC, DC, V | No lunch.

Mexicali Rose at the Lighthouse. Mexican. Favorite dishes include fajitas, chile rellenos, and a dish called Drunken Shrimp (shrimp cooked in Mexican beer and covered with a mild sherried cheese sauce). The restaurant overlooks the Wisconsin River, near the dock at the Lower Dells. | 195 State Rd. 13 | 608/254–6081 | $9–$12 | AE, D, DC, MC, V.

Paul Bunyan's Northwoods Cook Shanty. American. Replicating an 1890s logging-camp cook shanty and built of hand-hewn northern Wisconsin white and Norway pine, this restaurant boasts a large menu with such standards as steaks and burgers. Kids are charged on a sliding scale according to their age. Kids' menu. | 411 Rte. 13 | 608/254–8717 | $12 | D, MC, V | Closed mid-Oct.–Apr.

Secret Garden Café. Vegetarian. This bright and cheery café in a Victorian B&B in downtown Wisconsin Dells offers such meatless fare as a Portobello mushroom sandwich and Thai stir-fry and coffees from a cappuccino bar. Edible flowers used as garnish are grown in the B&B's gardens. Open-air dining on a wood deck under oak trees. Kids' menu. | 910 River Rd. | 608/254–4214 | $7–$14 | AE, MC, V | Closed Tues. last week June–Labor Day. No dinner Sun. rest of year.

Wally's House of Embers. American. This restaurant 2 mi south of downtown Wisconsin Dells is warm and inviting with its antiques, three fireplaces, and stained-glass hanging lamps. The veranda is tropical with its bright papier maché birds and posters of palm trees. Try the smoked ribs, coconut shrimp, or herb-rubbed beef filet with béarnaise sauce. Open-air dining on an enclosed gazebo filled with plants and flowers. Kids' menu. | 935 Wisconsin Dells Pkwy., Lake Delton | 608/253–6411 | $15–$20 | AE, MC, V | No lunch.

Wintergreen Grill. American. This casual, family-style restaurant ½ mi south of Wisconsin Dells has a fireplace in the lounge area. Menu includes barbecue ribs, pizza, and seafood such as walleye pike. Buffet breakfast Sunday. Kids' menu. Wine and beer. | 60 A Gasser Rd., Lake Delton | 608/254–7686 | $12–$22 | AE, D, DC, MC, V.

Lodging

Alakai Hotel & Suites. Built in 1999 this large hotel has a brick exterior and is modern in style. Inside there is a Hawaiian theme, with palm plants and Hawaiian flowers in the common areas, and Hawaiian print bedspreads and white wicker furniture in the rooms. A indoor water play area with two slides, a geyser, and a wading pool is popular with kids. Microwaves, refrigerators, some in-room hot tubs, cable TV. 3 pools, wading pool. Hot tub, sauna. Video games. | 1030 Wisconsin Dells Pkwy. S | 608/253–3803 or 800/593–9392 | fax 608/254–4679 | www.alakaihotel.com | 100 rooms | $110–$210 | AE, D, MC, V.

American World. This motel consists of three modern, all-brick buildings on 11 acres next to an amusement park in the center of town. RV parking is available. Restaurant, picnic area. Microwaves available, some refrigerators, some in-room hot tubs, cable TV. 6 pools. 2 hot tubs, saunas. Tennis. Laundry facilities. Business services. | 400 Wisconsin Dells Pkwy. | 608/253–4451 or 800/433–3557 | fax 608/254–4770 | david@americanworld.com | www.americanworld.com | 117 rooms in 3 buildings | $89–$129 | AE, D, DC, MC, V.

Best Western Ambassador Inn. This simple brown wood L-shaped hotel has a large fish tank in the lobby and is just outside downtown. Picnic area. Minibar in suites, microwaves available, refrigerators, cable TV, in-room VCRs and movies available. 2 pools, wading pool. Hot tub, sauna. Game room, video games. Laundry facilities. Business services. | 610 Frontage Rd. S | 608/254–4477 | fax 608/253–6662 | www.dells.com/bestwest.html | 181 rooms, 27 suites | $118–$128 | AE, D, DC, MC, V.

Black Hawk. This wood motel has large picture windows and you can park in front of your unit. It's downtown, within walking distance of restaurants. Kitchenettes (in cottages), microwaves and refrigerators available, some in-room hot tubs, cable TV, in-room VCRs and movies available. Indoor-outdoor pool, wading pool. 2 hot tubs, 2 saunas. Game room. Playground. Laundry facilities. | 720 Race St. | 608/254–7770 | fax 608/253–7333 | www.dells.com/blackhwk.html | 75 rooms, 9 cottages | $55–$110 rooms, $65–$170 cottages. | AE, D, DC, MC, V | Closed Nov–Mar.

Great Wolf Lodge. The lobby at this large log lodge, in the midst of a water-park resort, has a vaulted ceiling and a three-story stone fireplace. In every room there are handcrafted furnishings and a large-screen TV. On-site there are more than 70,000 square ft of indoor and outdoor water-park attractions, including 13 water slides (two of which are four-story outdoor slides). The lodge/waterpark is 7 mi north of downtown Wisconsin Dells, in a commercial district right off Interstate 90/94. Restaurant. Microwaves, refrigerators, cable TV. Pool. Gym. Game room. | 1400 Great Wolf Dr., Lake Dalton | 608/253–2222 or 800/559–9653 | fax 608/253–2224 | blackwlf@dellsnet.com | www.greatwolflodge.com | 300 rooms | $199–$339 | AE, D, DC, MC, V.

Buckley House Bed & Breakfast. This renovated farmhouse was built in 1914 and sits on 6 acres with a pond, rolling hills, and flower gardens. There's a wraparound front porch, and a deck from which to admire the view. The inn is 12 mi northeast of Wisconsin Dells. Complimentary breakfast. No TV. No smoking. | 3765 County Rd. P, Oxford | 608/586–5752 or 888/689–4875 | www.thebuckleyhouse.com | 3 rooms | $90–$150 | D, MC, V.

Calico House B&B. This simply styled home is filled with country furniture. Rooms have handmade quilts, queen-size beds, and share a bathroom. There is an inviting front porch with a swing and chairs for relaxing. Complimentary Continental breakfast. TV and VCR in common area. No smoking. | 240 S. Burrit Ave. | 608/254–2400 | 3 rooms (all with shared bath) | $50 | No credit cards.

Camelot Hotel and Suites. Turrets hug this castle-style hotel, and a two-story waterfall cascades into a swimming pool below. It's 5 mi from downtown. Microwaves, refrigerators, in-room hot tubs in some suites, cable TV. Hot tub. Video games. | 1033 Wisconsin Dells Pkwy. S | 608/253–3000 | fax 608/253–3001 | www.dellshotels.com | 113 rooms, 13 suites | $145–$150 rooms, $195 suites | AE, D, MC, V.

Caribbean Club Resort. Gardens, palm trees, and waterfalls surround this resort on Lake Delton. The pool has a waterfall and a 6-ft-high slide. It's on the edge of Lake Delton, 2 mi southwest of Wisconsin Dells on a strip with other resorts. Kitchenettes, in-room hot tubs. 2 pools. Hot tub, sauna. Beach, dock, boating. | 1093 Canyon Rd., Lake Delton | 608/254–4777 or 800/800–6981 | fax 608/253–4197 | 67 suites | $165–$255 | AE, D, MC, V.

Carousel Inn and Suites. This bright and cheerful water park–inn looks like candyland with the water park fronting the hotel. The whole place is casual and rustic, with bright pink and green colors. It's in the center of town surrounding by restaurants and hotels. Picnic area. Refrigerators, some in-room hot tubs, cable TV. Pool. Hot tub. Game room. Playground. Business services. | 1031 Wisconsin Dells Pkwy. | 608/254–6554 or 800/648–4765 | fax 608/254–6554 | www.wintergreen.com/carousel | 102 rooms (16 with shower only) | $149–$179 | AE, D, MC, V | Closed late Sept.–mid-May.

Chula Vista Theme Resort. This stone-and-wood southwestern-theme resort is 30 ft above the Wisconsin River, on a cliff in the Upper Dells. Family water activities are a major focus; there's a 60,000-square-ft indoor water park, a sand lot for volleyball, and a Jacuzzi big enough for 50 people. Adjacent is an 18-hole golf course. It's 2½ mi north of downtown businesses. Bar, 3 dining rooms, room service. Microwaves, some in-room hot tubs, cable TV. 5 pools, wading pool. Hot tub. Miniature golf, tennis. Exercise room, hiking. Business services. | 4031 N. River Rd. | 608/254–8366 or 800/388–4782 | fax 608/254–7653 | chula@dell-snet.com | www.wisdells.com/chulavista | 302 rooms | $159–$459 | AE, D, DC, MC, V.

Cliffside Resort and Suites. This modern three-story resort is on Lake Delton, about 2 mi west of Wisconsin Dells. You can lounge on decks or the boat dock and see the Tommy Bartlett water show held across the lake. Most of the rooms have private decks with lake views. Some in-room hot tubs, cable TV. Pool. Sauna. Beach, dock, boating, fishing. Laundry facilities. | 351 Canyon Rd., Lake Delton | 608/254–8521 or 800/695–3481 | fax 608/254–8521 | www.dells.com/clifside.html | 55 rooms | $105–$120 | AE, D, DC, MC, V.

Comfort Inn. This yellow-and-green wood-frame building is near downtown and several restaurants are within walking distance. Complimentary Continental breakfast. Microwaves, refrigerators, cable TV. Pool. Hot tub. Video games. Business services. | 703 Frontage Rd. N | 608/253–3711 | fax 608/254–2164 | 75 rooms | $99–$125 | AE, D, DC, MC, V.

Days Inn. This is a standard brick hotel in downtown Wisconsin Dells. Microwaves available, cable TV. Indoor-outdoor pool. Hot tub, sauna. Business services. | 944 U.S. 12 | 608/254–6444 | fax 608/254–6444 | www.dells.com/daysinn.html | 100 rooms | $129–$149 | AE, D, DC, MC, V.

Diamond Hotel. This modern hotel is in the center of the strip between Noah's Ark and the Original Wisconsin Ducks. An outdoor pool has a waterfall and two slides. There's also a casino shuttle and a game room. Picnic area. Microwaves, refrigerators, some in-room hot tubs (in suites), cable TV. 4 pools. Sauna. Basketball, volleyball. Video games. Playground. | 1630 Wisconsin Dells Pkwy. | 608/253–6500 or 800/353–1630 | fax 608/253–7354 | www.dellshotels.com | 80 rooms | $115–$120 | AE, D, DC, MC, V.

Grand Marquis Resort Hotel and Suites. This ultramodern hotel has an emphasis on water fun—there is a Dinosaur slide, a three-shoot water slide, and a turtle pool. Located in the southern part of Lake Delton, the hotel is 4 mi south of downtown Wisconsin Dells. Picnic area. Microwaves, refrigerators, some in-room hot tubs in suites, cable TV. 3 pools. 3 hot tubs, sauna. Playground. | 840 Wisconsin Dells Pkwy. S, Lake Delton | 608/254–4843 or 800/447–2636 | 79 rooms | $118–$128 | AE, D, MC, V.

Hawk's View Bed & Breakfast. This contemporary inn looks like a Swiss chalet. Rooms have fireplaces. There is a two-story cottage with a private deck available. Complimentary breakfast. Microwaves, refrigerators, in-room VCRs (and movies). Hot tubs. | E11344 Pocahontas Circle | 608/254–2979 | fax 608/254–2979 | snggls@jvlnet.com | www.hawks-view.com | 3 rooms, 1 cottage | $99–$169 | MC, V.

Antiqua Bay Waterpark Resort. This brick-and-stucco building in downtown Wisconsin Dells has a large dome housing a kids' pool, a lap pool, and fountains. It's 3 mi from Noah's Ark Water Park. Restaurant, bar, room service. Microwaves available, cable TV. 5 pools. 2 hot tubs, sauna. Game room. Kids' program (ages 2–12). Laundry facilities. Business services. | 655 Frontage Rd. | 608/254–8306 | fax 608/253–2829 | info@antiquabay.com | www.antiquabay.com | 228 rooms | $129–$134 | AE, D, DC, MC, V.

Hotel Atlantis. With its water falls, water slides, and plunge pool, this hotel looks more like a theme park than a hotel. Some rooms have balconies overlooking Noah's Ark Water Park. The game room is especially large and has pool tables and air hockey. It's on the south side of town. Restaurant, bar, picnic area. Microwaves, refrigerators, some in-room hot tubs, cable TV. 4 pools. 3 hot tubs, sauna. Game room. Playground. | 1570 Wisconsin Dells Pkwy. | 608/253–6606 or 800/800–6179 | www.theatlantishotel.com | 72 rooms | $140–$150 | MC, V.

International Motel. This modern motel is made up of three Miami-stone buildings. Picnic area. Refrigerators available, cable TV. Pool, wading pool. Playground. Some pets allowed. | 1311 E. Broadway | 608/254–2431 | www.dells.com/international/index.html | 45 rooms | $50–$80 | AE, D, DC, MC, V | Closed early Nov.–Apr.

Luna Inn and Suites. This modern, U-shape two-story building has a small lobby with a seating area. It's downtown, across from Noah's Ark Water Park. Picnic area. Some microwaves, some refrigerators, some in-room hot tubs in suites, cable TV. 2 pools. Hot tub. Game room, video games. | 1111 Wisconsin Dells Pkwy. | 608/253–2661 or 800/999–5862 | fax 608/253–2661 | www.dells.com/luna.html | 70 rooms, 46 suites | $45–$95 | AE, D, MC, V | Closed Nov.–Mar.

Mayflower I. Rooms in this simple wood-and-brick motel have either outside or inside entrances. Noah's Ark Water Park and a restaurant are next door. Picnic area. Microwaves, refrigerators, some in-room hot tubs, cable TV. 4 pools, wading pool. Hot tub, sauna. Game room, video games. Playground. Laundry facilities. Business services. | 910 Wisconsin Dells Pkwy. | 608/253–6471 or 800/345–7407 | fax 608/253–7617 | mayflowr@midplains.net | www.dells.com/mayflower | 72 rooms | $78–$98 | AE, D, DC, MC, V.

Mayflower II. Two of these three modern buildings are connected, and one houses only suites. Rooms are entered from either the outside or inside. Picnic area. Microwaves, refrigerators, some in-room hot tubs, cable TV. 2 pools, wading pool. Hot tub, sauna. Playground. Laundry facilities. Business services. | 930 Wisconsin Dells Pkwy. | 608/254–7878 or 800/253–7666 | fax 608/254–6264 | 80 rooms | $98–$108 | AE, D, DC, MC, V.

Meadowbrook Resort. This resort is located on 12 acres in a wooded, secluded area with a pond that empties into the Wisconsin River. All buildings are log, and many rooms are rustic with wooden walls and fireplaces. Nightly campfires. Picnic area. Kitchenettes in cabins, microwaves, refrigerators, in-room hot tubs (in some cabins), cable TV, no room phones. Pool. Fishing. Playground. | 1533 River Rd. | 608/253–3201 | 6 rooms, 26 cabins | $119–$129 | AE, D, MC, V | Closed Oct.–Apr.

Monaco Motel Resort and Suites. This cheerful white motel with light green and red accents has nicely landscaped grounds and a kiddie pool. Next to Noah's Ark Water Park. Picnic area. Microwaves, cable TV. 2 pools. Sauna. Playground. Laundry service. | 1310 Wisconsin Dells Pkwy. | 608/254–7550 or 800/892–6542 | 70 rooms | $95–$105 | AE, D, MC, V.

Paradise. This modern building sits on 12 acres of hills and woods in the center of Wisconsin Dells. Refrigerators, some in-room hot tubs, cable TV. Pool, wading pool. Hot tub. Playground. | 1700 Wisconsin Dells Pkwy. | 608/254–7333 | fax 608/253–2350 | 47 rooms | $75–$135 | AE, D, MC, V.

River Inn. This five-story white building is just two blocks from downtown; restaurants and stores are nearby. Restaurant, bar, room service. Some microwaves, refrigerators, cable TV. 2 pools. Hot tub. Exercise room. Playground. Business services. | 1015 River Rd. | 608/253–1231 or 800/659–5395 | fax 608/253–6145 | sikik@jvlnt.com | www.dells.com/riverinn.html | 54 rooms | $84–$129 | AE, D, DC, MC, V.

Riviera Motel. Park at your door at this brick motel in the heart of town, between Noah's Arch Water Park and Tommy Bartlett's water show. Some rooms have fireplaces. Picnic area. Some microwaves, some in-room hot tubs, cable TV. 2 pools. Hot tub, sauna. Business services. | 811 Wisconsin Dells Pkwy. | 608/253–1051 or 800/800–7109 | fax 608/253–9038 | www.rivierasuites.com | 49 rooms | $99–$125 | D, MC, V.

Sunset Bay Resort. This wood resort is on 5 forested acres overlooking Lake Delton 2 mi south of downtown. Playgrounds and picnic areas are between the four buildings. Picnic areas, complimentary Continental breakfast. Some microwaves, cable TV. 2 pools, wading pool. Hot tub. Exercise room, beach. Video games. Playground. Business services. | 921 Canyon Rd., Lake Delton | 608/254–8406 or 800/435–6515 | fax 608/253–2062 | sunsetbay@dellsnet.com | www.sunsetbayresort.com | 30 rooms, 36 suites, 6 cottages | $118–$130 rooms, $115–$225 suites, $95–$225 cottages | D, MC, V.

Wintergreen Resort and Conference Center. This luxury resort was built in the early 1990s in Victorian style. Chandeliers illuminate the large lobby. The pool has water slides, fountains, and a special water-park area for kids. The resort is near Mirror Lake State Park in the center of Lake Delton. Restaurant, picnic area, room service. Microwaves, refrigerators, some in-room hot tubs, cable TV. 15 pools. Hot tub, sauna. Gym. Game room. Laundry facilities. Business services. | 60 Gasser Rd., Lake Delton | 608/254–6554 or 800/648–4765 | fax 608/253–6235 | winterg@tcs.itis.com | www.wintergreen-resort.com | 111 rooms | $124–$159 | AE, D, MC, V.

WISCONSIN RAPIDS

MAP 11, D5

(Nearby towns also listed: Marshfield, Stevens Point, Wausau)

In 1831, settlers in Wisconsin Rapids harnessed the river to power a sawmill. A few years later they built a pulp mill. Since then, Wisconsin Rapids and its southern neighbors Port Edwards and Nekoosa have been a center for the paper production. The cranberry industry also plays a dominant role in this town.

Information: Wisconsin Rapids Area Chamber of Commerce | 1120 Lincoln St., 54494 | 800/554–4484 | chamber@wctc.net | www.wisconsinrapidsarea.com.

Attractions

Alexander House. This house, along the Wisconsin River, has art exhibits and archives from the area. It's 4 mi south of Wisconsin Dells. | 1131 Wisconsin River Dr., Port Edwards 54469 | 715/887–3442 | Free | Sun., Tues., Thurs. 1–4.

Consolidated Papers, Inc. See how paper is made as you tour this factory. In Biron, 3 mi from the factory, you can also take a 1½-mi self-guided walking tour through the woods to learn about forest management. Pick up a self-guided tour booklet at the visitor center. | Jackson St. and 4th Ave. | 715/422–3789 | Free | Plant tour Wed., Thurs., Sat. 10 AM.

Rudolph Grotto Gardens and Wonder Cave. Walk through these gardens to explore a cave and see religious statues, including a memorial to the Blessed Virgin. It's 8 mi north of Wisconsin Rapids. | 6957 Grotto Ave., Rudolph | 715/435–3120 | Gardens and grounds free; cave $2.50; special rates for kids | Cave and gift shop Memorial Day–Labor Day, daily 10–5; after Labor Day by appointment. Grounds open daily.

South Wood County Historical Corporation Museum. This museum in the center of town documents the history of the region's cranberry industry and contains replicas of a general store, a doctor's office, and other exhibits illustrating life in Wood County in the 1800s. | 540 3rd St. S | 715/423–1580 | Donations accepted | May–Oct., Sun.–Thurs. 1–4; small group and school tours by appointment.

ON THE CALENDAR
JUNE: *Grand River Fest.* This mid-June event offers food, entertainment, arts, crafts, kids' activities, and a parade. | 800/554–4484.
AUG.: *Annual Wisconsin Rapids Car Show.* The highlights of this ongoing event held the first weekend in August are a swap meet, and a car corral where show cars are offered for sale, and a parade of some 700 cars through town. | 715/325–3002.

Dining
All-American Bistro. American. Specialties in this centrally located restaurant are prime rib and standard Italian fare. | 1630 8th St. S | 715/423–8030 | $9–$22 | AE, MC, V.

Lodging
Cozy Inn & RV Park. This mom-and-pop motel has standard motel units plus full hookups for 16 RVs. Campers have access to showers and laundry facilities. A lake is just 1 mi away. Restaurant, bar. | 2710 Plover Rd. | 715/423–1220 | 12 rooms | $30–$45 | MC, V.

WOODRUFF

MAP 11, C2

(Nearby towns also listed: Eagle River, Minocqua)

Considered part of greater Minocqua, this former logging town has a wealth of water sports. There are 3,200 lakes, streams, and ponds in the area, as well as world-class fishing, boating, and waterskiing. Today about 95% of the land known as the town of Woodruff is owned by federal, state, and county governments and is not available for private sale, so this enviable recreational environment is protected for future generations. It's no wonder that tourism is the economic base for Woodruff and the surrounding Lakeland cities.

Information: **Minocqua–Arbor Vitae–Woodruff Area Chamber of Commerce** | Box 1006, 54548-1006 | 800/446–6784 | mavwacc@minocqua.org | www.minocqua.org.

Attractions
Northern Highland–American Legion State Forest. This is the most-visited state property in Wisconsin, as well as the largest, with 222,000 acres of forest and lakes. There are hundreds of miles of trails for hiking and cross-country skiing as well as camping and fishing year-round. The forest was established in 1925 to protect the stream flow at the headwaters of the Wisconsin, Flambeau, and Manitowish rivers. | 4125 County Hwy. M; Boulder Park

| 715/385–2704 | www.dnr.state.wi.us/org/land/forestry/StateForests/index.htm | $7 non-residents, $5 residents; permits required for some recreational trails | Daily.

Woodruff State Fish Hatchery. Established in 1900, this is one of the largest cool-water hatcheries in the world, producing large muskellunge fingerlings, northern pike, and walleye. The hatchery has a show pond with various native Wisconsin fish species; mounted Wisconsin game fish are also on display. | 8770 Rte. J | 715/385–9215 | Free | Memorial Day–Labor Day, weekdays 11 and 2 (tours).

ON THE CALENDAR
AUG.: *People's Choice Art Show.* An arts-and-crafts show held on the second full weekend in August at the senior Community Center. | 715/356–4317.

Dining
Stingray's Bar & Grill. American. The menu features homemade soups, sandwiches, and the king-size filet mignon. There are 15 TVs to view while dining. The restaurant is ½ mi north of Woodruff. | 134 Hwy. 51 N., Arbor Vitae | 715/356–3097 | $6–$14 | AE, MC, V.

Lodging
Northwoods Nod-A-Way Bed & Breakfast. This bed-and-breakfast is surrounded by forests, pastures, and trails where horses and dogs roam. Complimentary breakfast. Hiking. Library. | 10530 Townline Rd. | 715/356–7700 | 3 rooms (2 with shared bath) | $70–$85 | No credit cards.

Index

Notes

Notes

TALK TO US
Fill out this quick survey and receive a free *Fodor's How to Pack* (while supplies last)

1 Which Road Guide did you purchase?
(Check all that apply.)
- ❏ AL/AR/LA/MS/TN
- ❏ AZ/CO/NM
- ❏ CA
- ❏ CT/MA/RI
- ❏ DE/DC/MD/PA/VA
- ❏ FL
- ❏ GA/NC/SC
- ❏ ID/MT/NV/UT/WY
- ❏ IL/IA/MO/WI
- ❏ IN/KY/MI/OH/WV
- ❏ KS/OK/TX
- ❏ ME/NH/VT
- ❏ MN/NE/ND/SD
- ❏ NJ/NY
- ❏ OR/WA

2 How did you learn about the Road Guides?
- ❏ TV ad
- ❏ Radio ad
- ❏ Newspaper or magazine ad
- ❏ Newspaper or magazine article
- ❏ TV or radio feature
- ❏ Bookstore display/clerk recommendation
- ❏ Recommended by family/friend
- ❏ Other:_____

3 Did you use other guides for your trip?
- ❏ AAA
- ❏ Compass American Guide
- ❏ Fodor's
- ❏ Frommer's
- ❏ Insiders' Guide
- ❏ Mobil
- ❏ Moon Handbook
- ❏ Other:_____

4 Did you use any of the following for planning?
- ❏ Tourism offices ❏ Internet ❏ Travel agent

5 Did you buy a Road Guide for (check one):
- ❏ Leisure trip
- ❏ Business trip
- ❏ Mix of business and leisure

6 Where did you buy your Road Guide?
- ❏ Bookstore
- ❏ Other store
- ❏ On-line
- ❏ Borrowed from a friend
- ❏ Borrowed from a library
- ❏ Other:_____

7 Why did you buy a Road Guide? (Check all that apply.)
- ❏ Number of cities/towns listed
- ❏ Comprehensive coverage
- ❏ Number of lodgings ❏ Driving tours
- ❏ Number of restaurants ❏ Maps
- ❏ Number of attractions ❏ Fodor's brand name
- ❏ Other:_____

8 Did you use this guide primarily:
- ❏ For pretrip planning   ❏ While traveling
- ❏ For planning and while traveling

9 What was the duration of your trip?
- ❏ 2-3 days   ❏ 11 or more days
- ❏ 4-6 days   ❏ Taking more than 1 trip
- ❏ 7-10 days

10 Did you use the guide to select
- ❏ Hotels   ❏ Restaurants

11 Did you stay primarily in a
- ❏ Hotel   ❏ Hostel
- ❏ Motel   ❏ Campground
- ❏ Resort   ❏ Dude ranch
- ❏ Bed-and-breakfast ❏ With family or friends
- ❏ RV/camper   ❏ Other:_____

12 What sights and activities did you most enjoy?
- ❏ Historical sights   ❏ Shopping
- ❏ Sports   ❏ Theaters
- ❏ National parks   ❏ Museums
- ❏ State parks   ❏ Major cities
- ❏ Attractions off the beaten path

13 How much did you spend per adult for this trip?
- ❏ Less than $500   ❏ $751-$1,000
- ❏ $501-$750   ❏ More than $1,000

14 How many traveled in your party?
___ Adults   ___ Children   ___ Pets

15 Did you
- ❏ Fly to destination   ❏ Rent a van or RV
- ❏ Drive your own vehicle ❏ Take a train
- ❏ Rent a car   ❏ Take a bus

16 How many miles did you travel round-trip?
- ❏ Less than 100   ❏ 501-750
- ❏ 101-300   ❏ 751-1,000
- ❏ 301-500   ❏ More than 1,000

17 What items did you take on your vacation?
- ❏ Traveler's checks   ❏ Digital camera
- ❏ Credit card   ❏ Cell phone
- ❏ Gasoline card   ❏ Computer
- ❏ Phone card   ❏ PDA
- ❏ Camera   ❏ Other

18 Would you use Fodor's Road Guides again?
- ❏ Yes   ❏ No

19 How would you like to see Road Guides changed?
- ❏ More ❏ Less Dining
- ❏ More ❏ Less Lodging
- ❏ More ❏ Less Sports
- ❏ More ❏ Less Activities
- ❏ More ❏ Less Attractions
- ❏ More ❏ Less Shopping
- ❏ More ❏ Less Driving tours
- ❏ More ❏ Less Maps
- ❏ More ❏ Less Historical information
- ❏ Other:_____

20 Tell us about yourself.

❏ Male   ❏ Female

Age:
- ❏ 18-24   ❏ 35-44   ❏ 55-64
- ❏ 25-34   ❏ 45-54   ❏ Over 65

Income:
- ❏ Less than $25,000   ❏ $50,001-$75,000
- ❏ $25,001-$50,000   ❏ More than $75,000

Name:_____   E-mail:_____

Address:_____ City:_____ State:_____ Zip:_____

Fodor's Travel Publications
Attn: Road Guide Survey
280 Park Avenue
New York, NY 10017

The information herein will be treated in confidence. Names and addresses will not be released to mailing-list houses or other organizations.

Atlas

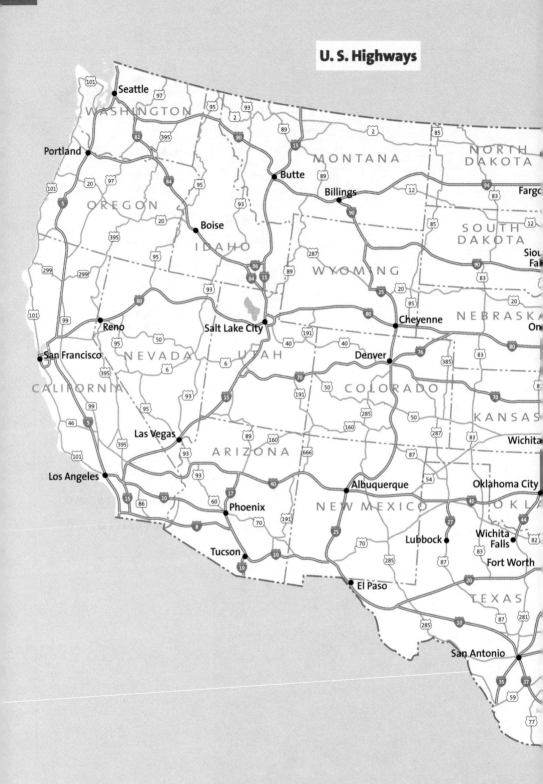

U. S. Highways

Copyright ©2001 by Maps.com and Fodors LLC

2

Distances and Driving Times

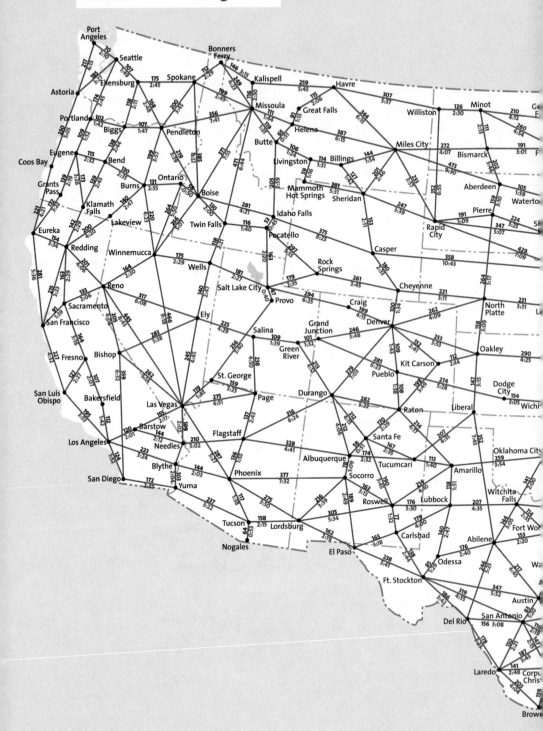

Copyright ©2001 by Maps.com and Fodors LLC

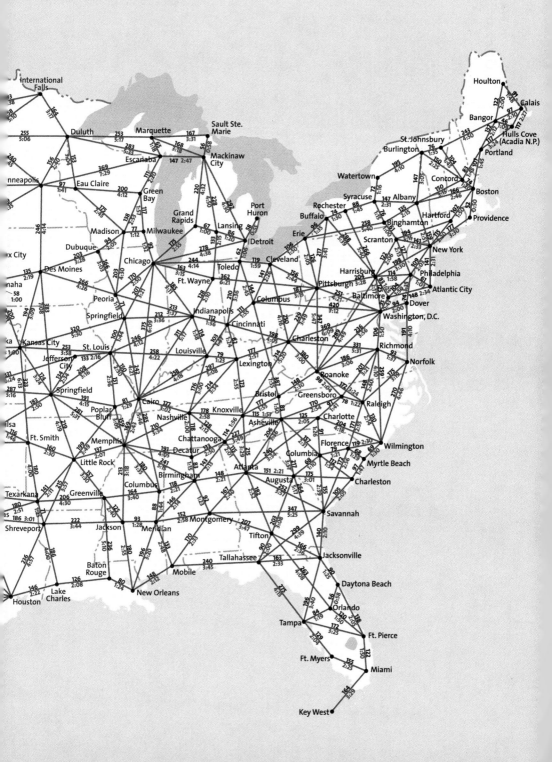

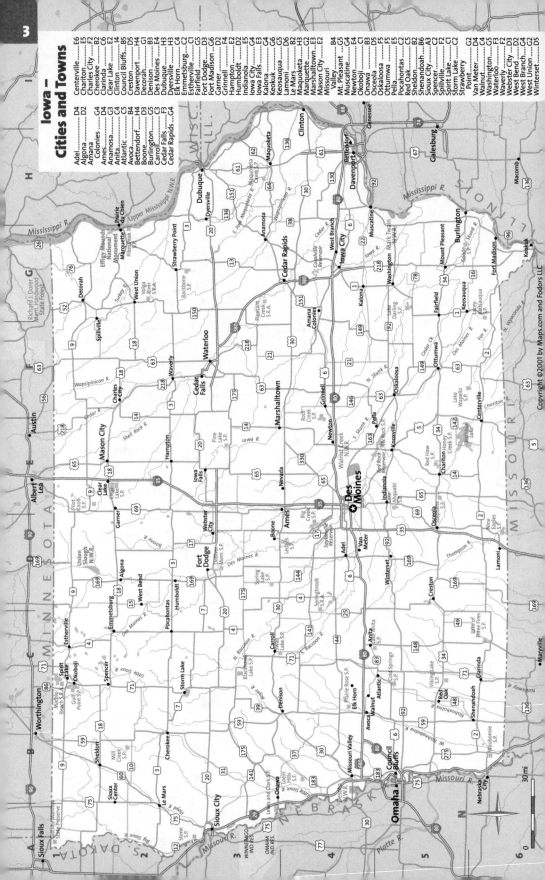

Iowa –
Cities and Towns

Copyright ©2001 by Maps.com and Fodors LLC

3

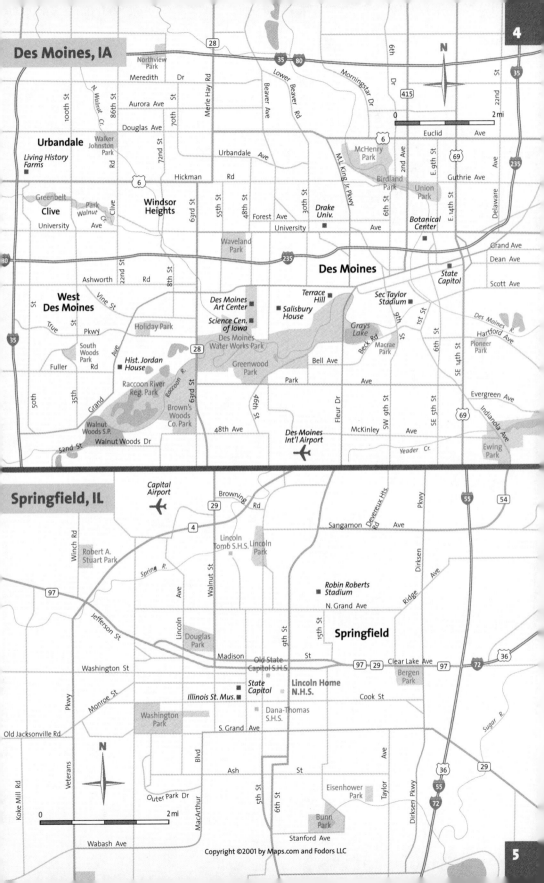

SEE MAP 8

Lake Michigan

WISCONSIN

INDIANA

IOWA

Copyright ©2001 by Maps.com and Fodors LLC

Downtown Chicago, IL

Goose Island

Seward Park

Crosby St
Kingsbury St
Larabee St
Hudson Ave
Sedgwick St
Orleans St
Hill St
Wendell St
Oak St
Walton St
Locust St
Chestnut St
Institute Pl

Oak St

Maple St
Cedar St
Bellevue Pl

Oak St

Washington Square
Delaware St

La Salle St
Clark St
State St

Rush St

Chestnut
Pearson St

Chicago Ave

Walton Pl
Delaware Pl

Museum of Contemporary Art

Lakeshore

Oak Street Beach

Outer Harbor

Halsted St

Kingsbury St

Superior St
Huron St
Erie St

Franklin St
Wells St
Dearborn St
State St
Wabash Ave
Rush St

Michigan Ave

Superior St
Huron St
Erie St

Northwestern University

St Clair St

Fairbanks Ct

McClurg Ct

Lake Shore Dr

Olive Park

Navy Pier Park

River North

Erie St

Ohio St

Ontario St

Ohio St

Near North

Ohio St

Navy Pier

Chicago Children's Museum

Navy Pier

Grand Ave

Grand Ave

Illinois St

Illinois St

Streeter Dr

Hubbard St
Kinzie St

N. Milwaukee Ave
Desplaines St
Jefferson St
Clinton St
Canal St

Hubbard St
Kinzie St

Water St

North Pier Fest. Market

River Esplanade Park

90
94

Chicago R.

Wacker Dr

N. Water St

Centennial Fountain & Arc

S. Water St

Field Blvd

Randolph St

Wells St
La Salle St
Franklin St

Lake St

Randolph St

N. Green St
Halsted St
Clinton St

Washington Blvd

Madison St
Monroe St
Adams St
Jackson Blvd

Washington Blvd

The Loop

Clark St
Dearborn St
State St
Wabash Ave
Garland Ct

Michigan Ave

Chicago Cultural Center

Monroe Dr

Grant Park

Chicago Harbor

Lake Michigan

J.F.K. EXPY

Sears Tower

De Paul Univ.

Jackson Dr

Lincoln Statue

41

Van Buren St

Van Buren St

EISENHOWER EXPY
290

Congress Pkwy

Buckingham Fountain

Harrison St

Desplaines St

Harrison St

Mus. of Contemporary Photography

Grant Park

Polk St

Wells St
La Salle St

8th St

9th St

Balbo Dr

Columbus Dr

Taylor St

State St
Wabash Ave

Printer's Row

Shedd Aquarium

Adler Planetarium & Astronomy Mus.

Roosevelt Rd

Plymouth Ct

13th St

Field Museum

Solidarity Dr

Northerly Island

W. Maxwell St

Jefferson St
Clinton St
Canal St

14th St

Clark St

15th St

16th St

Michigan Ave

McFetridge Dr

Northerly Island Park

W. 14th St

14th Pl

15th Pl

Newbury Ave
Halsted St
Union St

17th St

Soldier Field

12th St. Beach

W. 16th St

18th St

18th St

Waldron Dr

Burnham Park Harbor

DAN RYAN EXPY

Jefferson St
Clinton St
S. Normal Ave

Stewart Ave

South Branch Chicago R.

Wentworth Ave
La Salle St

19th St

Wabash Ave

Cullerton Ave

Prairie Ave

18th Dr

41

Merrill C. Meigs Field

W. 18th St

W. 19th St

S. Peoria St
S. Canalport Ave

Grove St

Archer Ave

State St

Indiana Ave

Calumet Ave

Burnham Park

90
94

Cermak Rd

Lumber

Princeton

22nd Pl
Alexander

Grove Ave

Archer Av

Federal St

Cermak Rd

Cottage Grove Ave

McCormick Place

Chinatown

23rd St

23rd St

State St

23rd St

N

0   0.5 mi

Copyright ©2001 by Maps.com and Fodors LLC

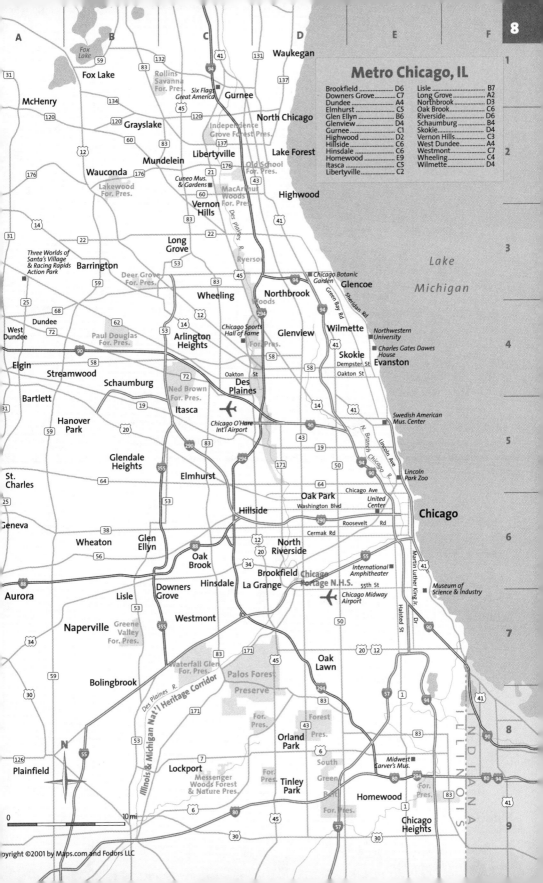

Metro Chicago, IL

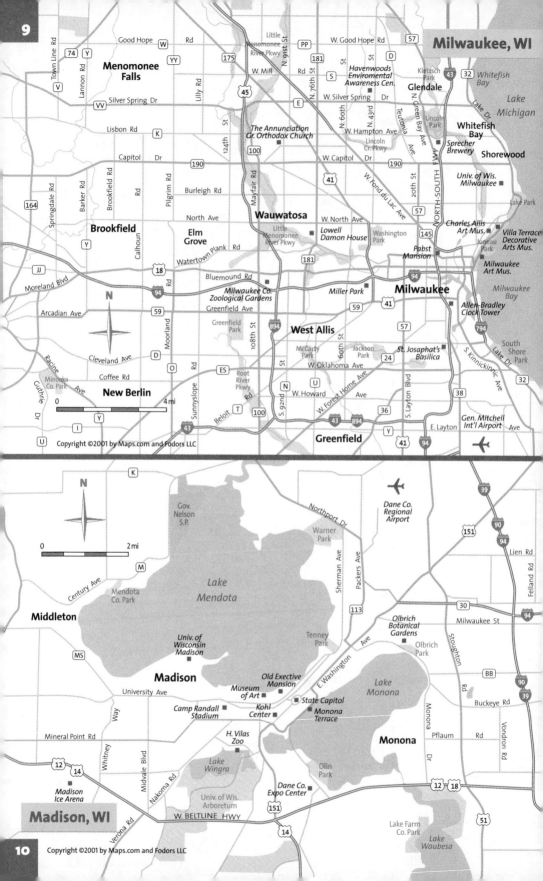

Milwaukee, WI

Good Hope Rd
W
74
Y
YY
175
PP
181
W. Good Hope Rd
57
Town Line Rd
Lannon Rd
V
Menomonee Falls
Little Menomonee River Pkwy
N 91st St
St
St
D
Kletzsch Park
43
32
Whitefish Bay
Lake Michigan
W. Mill
Rd
S
Havenwoods Enviromental Awareness Cen.
Glendale
Lilly Rd
VV
Silver Spring Dr
45
E
W. Silver Spring
Dr
N. 60th
W. 43rd St
N. 76th St
Lincoln Park
Sprecher Brewery
Whitefish Bay
Lisbon Rd
K
The Annunciation Gr. Orthodox Church
W. Hampton Ave
Teutonia Ave
N. Green Bay Ave
Shorewood
Capitol
Dr
124th
100
W. Capitol
Dr
Lincoln Cr. Pkwy
190
20th St
Lincoln Park
Charles Allis Art Mus.
Univ. of Wis. Milwaukee
Villa Terrace Decorative Arts Mus.
Springdale Rd
164
Barker Rd
Brookfield Rd
Pilgrim Rd
Mayfair Rd
Burleigh Rd
190
41
W. Fond du Lac Ave
57
Lake Park
Brookfield
Calhoun
Y
North Ave
Elm Grove
Little Menomonee River Pkwy
Wauwatosa
W. North Ave
Lowell Damon House
Washington Park
145
Pabst Mansion
Juneau Park
Milwaukee Art Mus.
JJ
18
Watertown Plank Rd
181
94
Milwaukee
Milwaukee Bay
Moreland Blvd
94
Bluemound Rd
N
Milwaukee Co. Zoological Gardens
Miller Park
59
41
Allen-Bradley Clock Tower
794
Arcadian Ave
59
Greenfield Ave
Greenfield Park
West Allis
57
South Shore Park
Moorland Rd
D
Cleveland Ave
O
108th St
McCarty Park
Jackson Park
24
St. Josaphat's Basilica
S. Kinnickinnic Ave
32
Coffee Rd
New Berlin
ES
Root River Pkwy
60th St
N
U
W. Oklahoma Ave
S. Layton Blvd
Lake Dr
0   4 mi
Sunnyslope Rd
S. 92nd St
Beloit Rd
T
100
N
U
W. Howard
Ave
W. Forest Home Ave
36
38
I
Y
43
Coffee Rd
Gen. Mitchell Int'l Airport
Ave
U
Greenfield
41
94
894
E. Layton

Copyright ©2001 by Maps.com and Fodors LLC

K
N
39
Gov. Nelson S.P.
Northport Dr
Dane Co. Regional Airport
151
90
94
Lien Rd
0   2 mi
M
Warner Park
Sherman Ave
Packers Ave
Felland Rd
Century Ave
Lake Mendota
30
Milwaukee St
94
Middleton
Mendota Co. Park
113
Olbrich Botanical Gardens
Stoughton Rd
MS
Univ. of Wisconsin Madison
Tenney Park
E. Washington Ave
Olbrich Park
BB
90
39
Madison
University Ave
Old Executive Mansion
Museum of Art
State Capitol
Lake Monona
Monona Dr
Buckeye Rd
Way
Camp Randall Stadium
Kohl Center
Monona Terrace
Whitney
Midvale Blvd
Mineral Point Rd
H. Vilas Zoo
Monona
Pflaum
Rd
Vondron Rd
12
14
Lake Wingra
Olin Park
12
18
Madison Ice Arena
Nakoma Rd
Univ. of Wis. Arboretum
Dane Co. Expo Center
151
14
Verona Rd
W. BELTLINE HWY
Lake Farm Co. Park
51
Lake Waubesa

Madison, WI

Copyright ©2001 by Maps.com and Fodors LLC

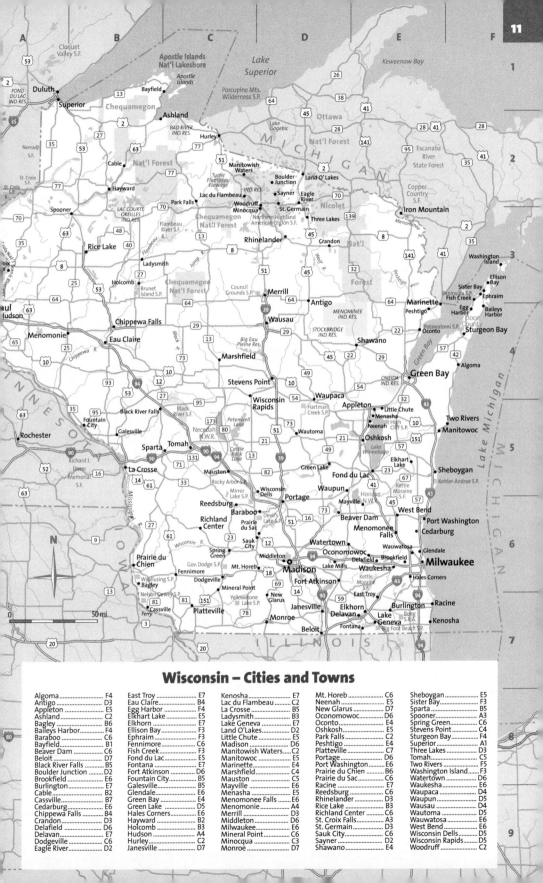

Wisconsin – Cities and Towns

Missouri – Cities and Towns

Copyright ©2001 by Maps.com and Fodors LLC

Wyandotte
County Park

635
Missouri R.
35
210

Leavenworth Ave
5

Parallel   Pkwy

59th St
55th St

169
29

**Kansas
City**

9

State   Ave
24   40

7th St
18th St

69
5

Kansas
City
Downtown
Airport

71

Front St
Gardner Ave

River Front Rd

Missouri R.

Kentucky   Rd

KANSAS   TPK

40

70

169

Kessler
Park

435

Kentucky
Rd

River Rd

Liberty Rd

Harry S.
Truman
Lib. &
Mus.

Salisbury
Rd

Kansas   Ave

Kansas Ave

32

670

Independence Ave

24

12

Sterling Ave

Harry S.
Truman
N.H.S.

Truman Rd

32

Metropolitan   Ave

169

118th St

Truman Rd

23rd   St

23rd St

River Rd

Kansas R.

Kaw Dr

635

Gibbs   Rd

Shawnee Dr

69

Southwest   Blvd

Rainbow Blvd

**Kansas
City**

Crysler Ave

78

Independence

Holliday Dr

Oak Grove
Rd

Roeland
Park

Southwest   Blvd

56

Southwest Trfwy

Van Brunt Blvd

Kauffman
Stadium

40

35th   Ave

291

*Quivira
Lake*

Shawnee

Johnson Dr

69   **Mission**

169

Univ. of
MO-K.C.

39th St

Jackson
Ave

31st St

Arrowhead
Stadium

70

39th   St

47th   St

40

Shawnee
Dr

Mission Pkwy

12

67th St

Johnson   Dr

Merriam

Roe   Ave

Mission Rd

63rd St

Prospect Ave

Swope Pkwy

Blue Ridge Cutoff

Raytown Rd

Little Blue
Trace
County
Park

Velie

Noland Rd

V

*Lakewood
Lakes*

Midland

67th St

75th St

Lamar Ave

**Prairie
Village**

83rd St

Nieman Rd

Wornall   Rd

Ward   Pkwy

Blue Pkwy

63rd   St

Blue Ridgeblvd

Raytown Rd

Raytown

Lees Summit Rd

47

*Lake
Shawnee
Mission
Park*

Lackman Rd

Pflumm Rd

Quivira Rd

Santa Fe
Trail Dr

87th St

169

75th   St

Gregory Blvd

85th   St

Troost Ave

Swope
Park

79th   St

350

Gregory
Blvd

435

95th St

Holmes Rd

71

*Unity
Lakes*

Leinwebe
Rd

Lenexa

56

103rd St

Roe Ave

435

Hillcrest

Bannister   Rd

Blue Ridge Blvd

Noland Rd

N

111th   St

College   Blvd

50   169

50

470

50

107th St

0   5 mi

Copyright ©2001 by Maps.com and Fodors LLC

Willard Rd

160

■ Dickerson Park Zoo

44

Springfield-Branson
Regional Airport

Kearney St

Grant Ave

National Ave

Doling
Park

LOOP
44

Air &
Military
■ Museum

West Bypass

Division St

Division St

44

LOOP
44

Chestnut   Expy

BUS
65

College St

St. Louis St

H

Discovery
Center   ■

Wilsons R.

Grand St

160

13

Springfield

Southwest
Missouri
■ State Univ.

Campbell Ave

Kimbrough Ave

Grand St

Sunshine St

D

N

Greene
Park

■ Japanese
Stroll Garden

Seminole St

Glenstone Ave

13

0   2 mi
FF

Battlefield Rd

Battlefield Rd

Copyright ©2001 by Maps.com and Fodors LLC